ANNUAIRE EUROPÉEN

EUROPEAN YEARBOOK

ANNUAIRE EUROPÉEN

VOL. VIII

EUROPEAN YEARBOOK

PUBLIÉ SOUS LES AUSPICES DU
CONSEIL DE L'EUROPE

PUBLISHED UNDER THE AUSPICES OF
THE COUNCIL OF EUROPE

SPRINGER-SCIENCE+BUSINESS MEDIA, B.V.
1961

L'Annuaire européen vise à encourager l'étude méthodique des organisations européennes et de leurs activités. Il est publié sous la responsabilité d'un Comité de rédaction, organe officieux et apolitique auquel il n'appartient pas d'exprimer une opinion sur un aspect quelconque des affaires internationales.

The aim of the European Yearbook is to promote the scientific study of European organisations and their work. It is published under the responsibility of an Editorial Committee, which is an unofficial and non-political body precluded from expressing an opinion on any aspect of international affairs.

DOI 10.1007/978-94-015-2886-3

Originally published by Martinus Nijhoff, The Hague, Netherlands 1961

MyCopy version of the original edition 1961

www.springer.com/mycopy

Pour toutes communications,
relatives à la rédaction de cet Annuaire,
écrire à l'adresse suivante:
Editorial communications should be addressed to:

The Joint Editors
European Yearbook
The Council of Europe
Strasbourg

TABLE DES MATIÈRES

ARTICLES

SECTION DOCUMENTAIRE

TABLE OF CONTENTS

ARTICLES

DOCUMENTARY SECTION

CHAPITRE V. CONSEIL DE L'EUROPE

SECTION BIBLIOGRAPHIQUE

ARTICLES

ATLANTIC UNITY VERSUS EUROPEAN DIVISION

by

MICHAEL A. HEILPERIN [1]

Editors' Note

The Editors of this Yearbook seek to offer to readers something more than static reports on the various European organisations. In the present volume, planned in 1960 and produced in 1961, the principal focus of general interest was bound to be the halting progress towards European economic integration. It is to this subject, then, that the first two of our articles in Volume VIII are devoted. We thought it would be interesting to have, on the one hand, the angle of vision of a distinguished American scholar and writer on political and economic affairs and, on the other hand, the point of view of someone representing the 'neutral' Members of E.F.T.A. It is perhaps all the more striking that the diagnosis of the patient's condition is virtually identical.

No apology is needed for the duplication of material: where our readers may justly have cause for complaint is in the fact that these two articles written in the late spring of 1961 are likely to be somewhat out of date when Volume VIII is actually issued (early in 1962). But this cannot be helped: the time-lag required for the printing process is necessarily a minimum of six months for a volume of some 700 pages such as the European Yearbook.

The year 1960 will remain in the economic history annals of the Western world as the year in which the European Free Trade Association (E.F.T.A.) became a reality and O.E.E.C. came to an end, to be superseded by the newly-formed Organisation for Economic Co-operation and Development (O.E.C.D.). It was in the realm of Western economic co-operation a key year and, if all goes well, it may prove to have been – to use Sir Winston CHURCHILL's famous phrase – another "hinge of fate". For, even before the divisions in Western Europe were healed, even before the Six and the Seven got together to make Eighteen, the goal of economic co-operation of a highly integrated kind crossed the Atlantic: the United States and Canada which were only associate Members of the O.E.E.C. will be *full Members* of the O.E.C.D. and the latter will be, therefore, an organisation of "Atlantic" scope.

The idea of convening *outside the O.E.E.C.* a conference of the 18 Governments represented in O.E.E.C. plus the Governments of the United States and Canada and a representation

[1] The author of this article, after occupying a number of academic posts, now holds a Chair of international economic relations at the Institut de Hautes Études Internationales, Geneva. He has been for many years Western Europe correspondent for *Time* and *Fortune Inc.* and is an Associate Editor of *Fortune* since 1959.

of the E.E.C. Commission was discussed and adopted at the time of the Western "Summit" Conference in Paris in December 1959; and the conference duly met in January 1960. The *Convention* establishing the O.E.C.D. was signed on December 14th, 1960; ratifications followed in 1961, starting with that of the United States in March, and the new agency will have taken over from the old before 1961 is over. (But all through 1960 the O.E.E.C. could only mark time).

In regard to two other developments seeds may well have been sown in 1960 which may not blossom up till 1962: Britain's attitude towards "joining the Common Market" and Frances' attitude towards the United Kingdom as a European Power. More will be said on these matters below. What must be stressed from the outset, however, is that the success of the Atlantic economic venture depends upon the realisation of economic integration of O.E.E.C. – Europe; and the former having been decided upon, great pressures will be brought to bear for the achievement of the latter. For Atlantic unity sought by the O.E.C.D. cannot be achieved so long as there is division in Western Europe. If the O.E.C.D. is to be more than a hope, more than an empty frame, the division of Europe into the "Six" and the "Seven" (not forgetting the "five others": Greece, Turkey, Spain, Ireland and Iceland, some of whom are Members of N.A.T.O.) must be ended at an early date. As will be shown, this is an essentially political problem; it calls for political decisions at the highest level, and the quest for greater Atlantic unity and cohesion may well catalyse such political decision-making.

It seems essential to emphasize here the longer-run perspectives in order to assess as best we can the nature of the turning that the West took in 1960. European economic co-operation in the O.E.E.C. setting broke down when, in November 1958, the negotiations for an O.E.E.C.-wide Free Trade Area were called off. Faced with the imminent danger of declining co-operation, even of disintegration, the Western world sought a way out through "Atlanticizing" the O.E.E.C. This is the road we are on now: and our progress along that road will depend on the achievement of several interwoven objectives: European economic integration leading to a close approximation to Atlantic free trade; monetary reform in an Atlantic setting; the development of a common constructive policy towards under-developed countries, both as regards assistance to growth and as regards trade liberalisation. The O.E.C.D. Convention of December 14th, 1960, is provided with a mandate to accomplish all of this: and there is every possibility of moving ahead fast in 1961, 1962 and the years to follow, given the political will to act.

THE EUROPEAN FREE TRADE ASSOCIATION

Set up by the Stockholm Treaty of November 20th, 1959, the E.F.T.A. groups together the United Kingdom, Denmark, Norway, Sweden, Switzerland, Portugal and Austria. These are the six economically advanced countries of Western Europe not in the Common Market, together with Portugal which, though not economically advanced, is a hard-currency country asking for no special treatment. Although the E.F.T.A. is an essentially commercial arrangement, along the lines of the "free trade area" concepts, (*i.e.* free trade for goods of "area origin" and no common outside tariff), the first year of its operations has revealed a strong *political* determination on the part of all the Governments concerned to make a success of it. Severally and jointly, the Governments of E.F.T.A. have taken great pains to make it clear that their ultimate objective is a single free-trading European market. The E.F.TA. is not regarded by its Members as an end in itself: this is a consequence of its commercial and non-political character. The Common Market organisation, on the other hand, being a part of a wider political design of its Member countries, is "an end in itself" – as is, indeed any customs union. Nonetheless, in the course of the 1957–58 negotiations carried out at the O.E.E.C. by the "MAUDLING Committee", there was to be observed wide support *within* the Common Market for the establishment of an O.E.E.C.-wide free trade area. The E.F.T.A. is what was susceptible of speedy achievement once the wider plan had to be given up – for the time being at least. The elements in the Common Market which recalled, was among the main objectives of the Marshall Plan, inherited by the O.E.E.C.). It is *technically impossible* to construct a bridge to span a customs union and a free trade area: these are arrangements based on totally different concepts. The two most immediately obvious solutions would be: *a*) to bring the E.F.T.A. Members into an enlarged Common Market; *b*) to bring the Common Market *as a unit* into E.F.T.A. as its eighth Member. But such simple solutions rarely appeal to the political mind. Accordingly, more complex formulae have been proposed; the most widely and seriously discussed among these has been produced by Professor Alfred MUELLER-ARMACK, Secretary of State in the German Ministry of Economic Affairs. It combines features of a customs union with those of a free trade area and with some inbetween positions: the plan is of great ingenuity and of considerable complexity – and it may be, for these reasons, a good starting-point for future negotiations. The goal is, of course, to achieve, in one way or another, an integrated single market in Western Europe, based on free trade, free capital movements and free migration. Does this require as many institutional arrangements as are foreseen in the Rome Treaty – or can it be done with as few such arrangements as E.F.T.A. is endowed with? The solution lies probably inbetween these two extremes, all the more so, should the Six wish to preserve their separate identity within the framework of a "single market".

There is little doubt among leading European experts, such as Baron SNOY ET D'OPPUERS of Belgium, that *technically* some form of merger between the two groups is possible. What is needed, however, and appears to be lacking for the time being, is the *political will* to bring the two groups together. In this context, the two most often heard questions are these. Does Britain want to join the Common Market? Does France want the United Kingdom to become intimately associated with an integrated Europe?

BRITAIN AND THE COMMON MARKET

There has been, since 1957, an extraordinary evolution in British thinking, official and otherwise, about economic association with Europe. The *White Paper* of February 1957 envisaged a "European industrial free trade area", excluding agriculture and accepting no institutional arrangements. By the end of 1960, the notion was well established that the British Government might be willing to enter into an all-European customs union (*cf.* initially the statement by Mr. HEATH at the Council of W.E.U. February 1961). This is a long road travelled at a fast pace, and the point reached is very promising for the future. Britain's joining the European Free Trade Association was an important step, tying the U.K. economically to an important group of Continental countries. And the search for an arrangement between the E.F.T.A. and the Common Market led inevitably in the direction of an *examen de conscience* concerning the feasibility for Britain of joining a wide customs union.

The House of Commons debate of July 25th, 1960, marked an important landmark along Britain's road to Europe. The motion introduced by Mr. Selwyn LLOYD, then Foreign Secretary, read: "That this House recognizes the need for political and economic unity in Europe, and would welcome the conclusion of suitable arrangements to that end, satisfactory to all the Governments concerned". Although this looks innocuous enough at first glance, the words "and political" cannot fail to catch one's eye. They are the "operative words" of the motion, and Mr. Selwyn LLOYD's speech was a lengthy elaboration of the theme. "If Britain were to be regarded as outside Europe we could not fulfil our complete rôle in the world", he emphasised, and he added: "Nor do I believe that Europe would be complete without us". After a debate that went on for four-and-a-half hours, the motion was carried by the unanimity of Conservative and Labour votes with four Liberal votes cast against it. This vote, with its bipartisan character, can be regarded as a turning-point in Britain's relations with Continental Europe, involving as it does parliamentary recognition of the need for political as well as economic ties. Once this principle is acquired, the rest should be negotiable – assuming, of course, that Continental Europe wants close political and economic ties with Britain. And this centres primarily around Franco-British relations.

If the Liberal members voted "No" to the above-quoted motion, it was presumably because the motion did not go far enough. Throughout 1960, the Liberal press (*The Economist, The Observer, The Manchester Guardian*) campaigned in favour of Britain's joining the Common Market outright. And, in the first months of 1961, this campaign continued, not (one gathers) without encouragement from the American Government. Yet is the problem as simple as all that? The Rome Treaty is a highly negotiated and very detailed document. The "SPAAK Report" of April 1956 which served as a basis for these negotiations was in itself a long-negotiated document. All the parties to the Rome Treaty took care to safeguard their special interests and to provide for their particular problems. Such a treaty cannot be simply signed – as it stands – by another country. Some matters, such as the level of the common tariff, voting power, *etc.* must by the nature of the document be revised with each new accession. This is why Article 237 of the Rome Treaty provides that any applicant for membership in the E.E.C. would have to conclude with the Member States an agreement setting out "the conditions of admission and the adjustments to this Treaty necessitated thereby"; this agreement would have to be ratified by all the contracting States. But every new prospective Member of the E.E.C. would have its own special interests to take account of and its own special problems to be recognised – just as was the case with the initial Six. This is, doubtless, what Mr. MACMILLAN had in mind when answering a question in the House of Commons on April 25th, 1961: "We must not over-simplify this problem by talking about joining the Common Market, like joining a club, paying the subscription, and assuming that is all there is to it. It is a difficult, complicated matter. We have great interests to consider in honour and duty – our obligations to the Commonwealth which date from longstanding arrangements, our obligations to our own agriculture, and, of course, to our partners in E.F.T.A.".

As regards the metaphor of joining a club, it is well to bear in mind that an applicant to club membership *can* be blackballed! It is an open question at this time just how eager the Common Market is to enlarge its membership. The real danger is, of course, not "blackballing" but protracted, endless and fruitless negotiations. Of this Mr. MACMILLAN is very well aware; on the above-cited occasion, he also remarked: "I should be very unhappy if formal negotiations were started which led to no result. That would have a very bad effect in Europe as a whole". Hence the basic need for what may appear as an impossible *tour de force:* decide upon the outcome of negotiations before they start! Yet the paradox disappears if we realize that what is intended is a two-level operation: the *political* "agreement to agree"; and the *technical* negotiation over particular problems. There was such a political will to agree prior to the start of the Val Duchesse negotiations which led to the Rome Treaty. And a similar determination to agree would have to come into existence prior to any future negotiation to establish a "single market" in Western Europe. The protagonists for the creation of this political will are the U.K. and France.

The United Kingdom would no doubt be willing to enter into a joint integration scheme with the Six *provided that:* 1. the Commonwealth relations are safeguarded; 2. British agriculture continues to be protected and 3. Britain's E.F.T.A. partners are enabled to join in the new arrangements. A word of comment on each of these points.

The maintenance of British ties with the Commonwealth is as important to the rest of the Atlantic world as it is to the United Kingdom. For the Commonwealth is one of the best links between the West and great parts of the "under-developed world" of Asia and Africa. The same holds for the French *Communauté*. It should not tax too heavily the ingenuity of statesmen to find a formula which would include under the same set of rules the Commonwealth and the "Overseas Countries and Territories" to which Part IV of the Rome Treaty relates. It has been suggested that the O.E.C.D. might be very helpful in elaborating such common rules.

The problem of British agriculture is also one that should be susceptible of a satisfactory and rational solution, acceptable to all. The fact is that agricultural protectionism is, for good or for evil, a common feature of all the Western countries. Since every one goes about it in different ways, there is a difficult socio-political job of harmonisation to be done. Even the Six have not agreed as yet on a common agricultural policy – which shows how difficult the problem is. It may become more difficult by increasing the number of countries involved, each with its historic patterns and habits: maybe a "common agricultural policy" is a snare and a delusion in the first place? If it is, free trade in everything else can be promoted, anyway. If it is not, then the greater difficulty resulting from a larger group of countries will be eventually surmounted in the end. So long as every country wants to protect its agriculture and give its farmers a standard of living in excess of what the market economy would provide, divergences as to method are not fundamental enough to prevent the formation of a wide European "single market".

As regards, finally, the E.F.T.A., it is clear that the British Government does not intend to break it up in favour of associating itself with the Common Market. Any acceptable solution must therefore be such as to bring in the E.F.T.A. group as a whole. Anything else would be highly prejudicial to European unity and to Atlantic co-operation. If Britain were to "join the Common Market" and let E.F.T.A. go by the board, the result would be not only economic but also political disintegration in Western Europe – and a most serious crisis for N.A.T.O. It is very fortunate, in the wider perspective as well as in the narrower, that the British Government is so plainly on record as to its determination *not* to abandon the E.F.T.A.

FRANCE AND BRITAIN

On May 31st, 1960, General de GAULLE delivered a most important television broadcast on European affairs. In this address, the President of the French Republic listed geographic barriers which once used to set Europeans against one-another, but are no longer obstacles to European unity. Among these barriers, such as the Rhine, the Alps, the Pyrenees, *etc.* de GAULLE also included the English Channel. This marked a significant change from views expressed in Volume III of his

War Memoirs (published in October 1959), in which a united Europe is referred to as the "third planetary Power", the other two being: the Anglo-Saxon world and the Soviet camp. If the Western frontier of Europe ran through the English Channel in the *War Memoirs*, it was thus placed *west of the British Isles* in the address of May 31st, 1960. Although this change of emphasis is considered as real and important by some people who should be in a position to know, there has been, so far, no action to follow up these words.

These words, however, were gladly heard in London. In the House of Commons, on June 23rd, 1960, Mr. Peter THORNEYCROFT asked Mr. (now Lord) HEATHCOAT-AMORY, then Chancellor of the Exchequer, whether his "attention has been called to the far-sighted broadcast by President de GAULLE to the French people?" [1] This was the Chancellor's reply: "I have read President de GAULLE's statement with very great interest. I am quite sure that the United Kingdom and our partners in the European Free Trade Association will be very glad to enter into negotiations with the Members of the European Economic Community on the basis of that statement". This is a weighty pronouncement. The doors to a negotiation appear to be open ... but so far nothing has happened. It is to be hoped that General de GAULLE will follow up his above-cited statement by a real initiative.

O.E.C.D.: BORN IN DEADLOCK

The story of O.E.C.D. belongs to the year 1961 and thereafter; the *Convention* of December 14th, 1960 – like the original O.E.E.C. Convention – is a frame which needs filling. But there is no doubt that the new agency will be handicapped as long as the "split" in Western Europe persists. Unlike the O.E.E.C., the new agency will be "outward-looking". The prime task of O.E.E.C. was to further the reconstruction of Europe with the help of the MARSHALL Plan. After 1950 it aimed at the elimination of discriminations and quotas in intra-European trade. It pro-

---

[1] The relevant passages will be found in an *Appendix* at the end of this article.

moted a great many other ventures in the realm of intra-European economic co-operation. The O.E.C.D. can continue all this as far as needed; but its aim is also to extend coordination to the Atlantic group as a whole, including the United States and Canada; and to develop combined policies towards under-developed countries. If all goes well with it, the O.E.C.D. can become a true *Western pole of economic attraction* for the under-developed countries of the other continents. This can be done through development assistance on a widening and deepening scale; but to be successful it must be also done through trade. And this is where the dangers of being born in deadlock are clearly visible. For only an economically united West can practise liberal trade policies towards under-developed countries. Only if and when free trade has been established – fully or to a large extent – among all the Western countries, can they jointly undertake a liberal trade policy towards the rest of the world.

LOOKING AHEAD

Nothing will do short of a real comprehensive "Grand Design" for the West, *i.e.* for the O.E.C.D. membership. The "Grand Design" has a trade aspect and a monetary aspect. The latter – which it would exceed the scope of this article to dwell upon at any length – involves a monetary reform, or a set of reforms, which would make the currencies of the Western nations stable and secure. In view of the trade deadlock it would be wise for the O.E.C.D. to look swiftly and deeply into the monetary problem; and a good start appears to have been made in that direction in the spring of 1961.

On the trade side, once the deadlock has been broken (presumably – some day – in top-level Franco-British conversations from which *the determination to agree* will emerge), the first step would be the establishment of a wide, free-trading European market, possibly an all-European customs union (which would not prevent the Six from keeping a political identity if they so desire). Under the voting procedures of the O.E.C.D., the European Members could agree on such a scheme without the United States and Canada being either obliged to follow or able to interfere. Indeed, if the "single market" is in accordance with the rules of the G.A.T.T., the United States Government would assuredly not interfere. But the result of such an agreement among European Members of the O.E.C.D. would be to produce a challenge to which North America could only offer one response: an offer to bargain downwards trade barriers existing on both sides of the Atlantic. The opening of Europe to American goods and of America to European goods, with remaining tariffs being rare and low – such might well be the Atlantic trade situation in several years' time. Such a near-free trade across the Atlantic and full free trade within Western Europe would create – especially when firmly based on solid currencies – the "pole of economic attraction" which has been mentioned before. The spread of freer trade could then proceed through the instrumentalities of the G.A.T.T. – indeed then only would this useful institution come into its own at last.

ANNEXE

Extrait de l'allocution radiodiffusée et télévisée du Président de Gaulle du 31 mai 1960

... Notre alliance est apparue comme une réalité vivante. Pour qu'elle le soit plus encore, la France doit y avoir son rôle à elle et sa personnalité.

... Mais si l'alliance atlantique est actuellement nécessaire à la sécurité de la France et des autres peuples libres de notre ancien continent, il s'agit pour eux, à l'abri de ce bouclier, de s'organiser en vue de la puissance et du développement communs. Leurs épreuves leur ont fait voir combien ils avaient payé cher leurs divisions et leurs conflits. Ni le Rhin, ni les Pays-Bas, ni les Alpes, ni les Pyrénées, ni la Manche, ni la Méditerrannée pour lesquels ils se sont si longuement et terriblement battus ne les dressent plus les uns contre les autres. Entre eux les haines n'ont plus cours. Au contraire, la nostalgie qu'inspire à chacun d'eux son abaissement relatif par rapport aux nouveaux grands empires les réunit dans le sentiment qu'ensemble ils retrouveraient cette grandeur dont les siècles leur ont donné le génie et l'habitude. A quoi s'ajoute le fait qu'ils constituent un tout incomparable tandis que, précisément, notre époque, qui abolit les distances et les obstacles, réclame de grands ensembles.

Contribuer à bâtir l'Europe occidentale en un groupement politique, économique, culturel et humain, organisé pour l'action, le progrès, la défense, c'est à quoi la France veut s'appliquer. Déjà l'Allemagne Fédérale, l'Italie, la Hollande, la Belgique et le Luxembourg coopèrent avec elle directement dans plusieurs domaines. En particulier, le Marché Commun des Six entrera le 31 décembre dans sa réalisation pratique. Sans doute, les participants ne veulent-ils pas que cette institution puisse blesser les autres pays d'Europe et l'on doit compter qu'un accommodement sera trouvé entre les intérêts. Sans doute aussi faut-il que les nations qui s'associent ne cessent pas d'être elles-mêmes et que la voie suivie soit celle d'une coopération organisée des états, en attendant d'en venir peut-être à une imposante confédération. Mais la France, pour ce qui la concerne, a reconnu la nécessité de cette Europe d'Occident qui fut jadis le rêve des sages et l'ambition des puissants et qui apparaît aujourd'hui comme la condition indispensable de l'équilibre du monde.

Or, en définitive et comme toujours, ce n'est que dans l'équilibre que l'univers trouvera la paix. Sur notre ancien continent, l'organisation d'un groupement occidental, tout au moins équivalent à celui qui existe à l'Est, pourra permettre un jour, sans risque pour l'indépendance et la liberté de chacun et compte tenu de l'évolution vraisemblable des régimes, d'établir l'entente européenne entre l'Atlantique et l'Oural. Alors l'Europe tout entière, cessant d'être coupée en deux par des ambitions et des idéologies qui deviendraient périmées, redeviendrait le foyer capital de la civilisation.

RÉSUMÉ DE L'ARTICLE DU PROFESSEUR HEILPERIN

L'année 1960 sera marquée dans les annales de l'histoire économique du monde occidental par la réalisation de l'Association Européenne de Libre-Échange et par le remplacement de l'O.E.C.E. par l'O.C.D.E. Cette année pourrait bien être, selon le fameux mot de Sir Winston CHURCHILL, ,,un tournant du destin'' (*a hinge of fate*). Les efforts toujours en cours en vue d'une intégration européenne plus étroite ont été, en effet, devancés par une coopération économique véritablement atlantique, puisque les États-Unis et le Canada sont devenus membres de plein droit de l'O.C.D.E.

Ces événements se préparaient en 1959 par les négociations dont le but était d'établir l'A.E.L.E. et par le ,,sommet'' occidental qui a eu lieu à Paris en décembre, où une Conférence était prévue, en dehors de l'O.E.C.E., réunissant les dix-huit gouvernements membres de celle-ci ainsi que ceux des États-Unis et du Canada, ainsi que des représentants de la Commission de la Communauté Économique Européenne. Cette Conférence aboutit à la signature de la Convention de l'O.C.D.E. en décembre 1960.

Il convient de faire ressortir deux autres développements mis en branle en 1960, mais qui ne pourraient probablement se réaliser qu'en 1962: le ralliement éventuel de la Grande-Bretagne au Marché Commun et la prise de position de la France vis-à-vis du Royaume-Uni en tant que puissance européenne (*voir ci-dessous*). Il est évident que le succès de l'opération économique atlantique dépend essentiellement de la réalisation de l'intégration économique de 'l'Europe de l'O.E.C.E.' et par conséquent des pressions seront sans doute exercées d'au-delà de l'Atlantique pour achever cette intégration. Grâce à la création de l'O.C.D.E., les pays des Six et des Sept seraient en mesure de sortir de l'impasse où ils se trouvaient tout au long de 1960. Or, il est indispensable que les divisions européennes – en groupes de six, de sept (et n'oublions pas les cinq autres pays, la Grèce, la Turquie, l'Espagne, l'Irlande, l'Islande, dont plusieurs sont membres de l'O.T.A.N.) – soient prochainement effacées. Ce qui implique des décisions politiques; et de telles décisions pourraient être catalysées par les efforts vers une union atlantique plus poussée.

Les mesures prises par l'Occident dans le courant de 1960–1961, doivent être jugées dans des perspectives à long terme. Voici en quoi elles ont consisté.

1. Les risques de désintégration éventuelle de la coopération économique européenne entraînés par l'échec des négociations pour une zone de libre-échange ont contraint l'Occident à rechercher une solution par „l'atlantisation" de l'O.E.C.E.

2. L'exécution de ce plan est fonction de l'accomplissement de plusieurs objectifs interdépendants: un système de libre-échange qui serait, dans la mesure du possible, à l'échelle atlantique, complétant ainsi une intégration économique européenne; une réforme monétaire dans un cadre atlantique; une politique commune vis-à-vis des pays sous-développés qui se concrétiserait par une aide au développement de ces pays, ainsi que par une libéralisation des échanges.

L'ASSOCIATION EUROPÉENNE DE LIBRE-ÉCHANGE

Cette Association mise sur pied par le Traité de Stockholm du 20 novembre 1959 groupe les six pays économiquement avancés de l'Europe occidentale non membres du Marché Commun: le Royaume-Uni, le Danemark, la Norvège, la Suède, la Suisse et l'Autriche, avec l'addition du Portugal en tant que pays de monnaie forte. Malgré les bases purement commerciales de l'A.E.L.E. (établie d'après les principes d'une zone de libre-échange) une volonté politique croissante s'y est manifestée pendant ses deux ans d'existence. Les Gouvernements de l'A.E.L.E. se sont clairement exprimés en faveur d'une expansion vers un marché européen unique de caractère libéral qui grouperait les Six, les Sept et quelques-uns des cinq autres. A l'inverse du Marché Commun qui par ses aspects politiques est une „fin en soi" (comme toute union douanière, d'ailleurs) l'A.E.L.E., grâce à son caractère commercial et non politique, n'est pas pour ses membres une „fin en soi". Cependant, pendant les réunions de la Commission Maudling de 1957 et 1958, les représentants des Six s'étaient montrés prêts à appuyer l'établissement d'une zone de libre-échange pour tous les pays de l'O.E.C.E. Une fois ces plans échoués, seule l'A.E.L.E. semblait offrir des possibilités de progrès rapides; et son objectif final de réunir les deux groupes continua à trouver l'appui de certains éléments du Marché Commun restés fidèles à leurs idées.

Le seul exemple de mésentente entre les deux groupes – ce fut un incident de courte durée et sans suites – démontre pertinemment les implications politiques de la scission dans l'économie européenne. Les auteurs du Traité de Stockholm s'étaient efforcés de synchroniser les délais prévus avec ceux du Traité de Rome. La Communauté, fondée deux ans avant l'A.E.L.E., avait décrété une période transitoire de douze ans. L'A.E.L.E., rejetant une proposition pour une période transitoire de cinq ans, a adopté un délai de dix ans pour faciliter l'engrènement des deux systèmes. Une proposition d'accélération, soutenue par le Gouvernement français et la Commission de la C.E.E. à Bruxelles, en elle-même louable dans une période d'expansion économique en Europe, était sévèrement jugée par l'A.E.L.E. puisqu'elle compromettait la synchronisation des systèmes. En fait, des divergences surgissaient au sein du Marché Commun (les Pays-Bas et l'Allemagne s'opposaient à la hausse des droits de douane pour certains produits où leurs tarifs nationaux se trouvaient en-dessous du tarif commun de la Communauté) et, après quelques mois de négociations, les pays du Marché Commun se sont mis d'accord pour une accélération, mais d'une année seulement – pas de quoi s'énerver! L'A.E.L.E. a ensuite rétabli la situation par une accélération analogue.

Deux points à noter à cet égard. Premièrement la synchronisation n'est pas un problème de premier plan dans le cadre de l'intégration éventuelle des Six et des Sept: les experts seront toujours capables de fixer des délais pour une libération des échanges avant telle ou telle date convenue. Deuxièmement, et ceci est beaucoup plus important, il y a lieu en tout cas de poursuivre l'accélération, c'est-à-dire que la période transitoire des deux Traités, de Rome et de Stockholm, devrait être réduite dans la mesure du possible, car c'est dans une ère de prospérité que les tendances vers le libre-échange sont encouragées, et une récession – même si celle-ci est peu probable en Europe à présent – pourrait les freiner dangereusement. Les deux groupes feront bien de s'armer en vue d'une telle contingence, et on peut attendre d'autres accélérations en 1961–1962.

RAPPORTS ENTRE LES SIX ET LES SEPT

La grande question européenne de portée internationale est celle des Six et des Sept: quels seront les effets à longue échéance, en termes de distortion aux courants des échanges et de l'orientation des investissements, intérieurs et extérieurs, de l'existence de deux groupes de libre-échange? Ce fait aura – il l'a déjà pour quelques pays – des conséquences plus ou moins défavorables, même si, selon les prévisions existantes pour la période de transition, ces conséquences ne se révèlent qu'après quelques années. Si le schisme ne devait pas persister, à quoi bon bâtir un „pont" entre Six et Sept? On doit admettre que la volonté de trouver une solution au problème existe chez tous les Sept et chez quelques-uns des Six, sinon en France ou au sein de la Commission de la C.E.E.

Le mot courant d'un „pont" ne décrit pas avec exactitude, du reste, les caractéristiques essentielles d'une intégration économique en Europe occidentale, puisque les conceptions d'une union douanière et d'une zone de libre-échange sont techniquement incompatibles. Deux solutions possibles existent:

a) introduire les membres de l'A.E.L.E. dans un Marché Commun élargi;
b) embaucher ce Marché Commun comme une seule unité en tant que 8ème membre de l'A.E.L.E.

De telles solutions paraissent trop simplistes aux esprits politiques; de là les plans plus compliqués, par exemple, celui du Professeur A. MUELLER-ARMACK, Secrétaire d'État au Ministère des Affaires économiques de la République Fédérale d'Allemagne, qui réunit avec maîtrise des aspects d'une union douanière et ceux d'une zone de libre-échange et qui pourrait donc servir de base de discussion.

Les organismes institutionnels nécessaires pour réaliser le but d'un marché unique, fondé sur les principes de libre-échange, et d'un mouvement libre des capitaux et de la main d'oeuvre, ne seront probablement ni si nombreux que ceux prévus dans le Traité de Rome, ni si exigus que ceux de l'A.E.L.E. Une solution intermédiaire aiderait les Six à garder leur identité séparée dans le cadre d'un „marché unique". Et une fusion éventuelle est, selon les experts européens, *techniquement* réalisable. Ce n'est que la *volonté politique* qui manque, et sous ce rapport les deux questions surmentionnées restent à résoudre: la Grande-Bretagne désire-t-elle devenir membre du Marché Commun et la France envisage-t-elle une association étroite du Royaume-Uni à une Europe intégrée?

GRANDE-BRETAGNE ET MARCHÉ COMMUN

L'opinion en Grande-Bretagne sur cette question a beaucoup évolué depuis 1959, quand le Gouvernement, dans un „*White Paper*", a exclu l'agriculture d'une zone industrielle de libre-échange et rejeté tout organisme institutionnel. En 1960, le Gouvernement a envisagé de participer à une union douanière pan-européenne. Son adhésion à l'A.E.L.E. menait inévitablement vers un examen de conscience dans ce but. La motion défendue par Mr. Selwyn LLOYD, alors Secrétaire d'État des Affaires étrangères, à la Chambre des Communes en juillet 1960 comportait la phrase importante de „l'unité *politique* et économique en Europe" et cette motion capitale a réuni les votes unanimes des conservateurs et des travaillistes (avec 4 abstentions libérales). La voie est donc ouverte à la négociation, si l'Europe continentale désire des liens avec la Grande-Bretagne, et cela dépend des rapports franco-britannique. D'ailleurs les abstentions libérales s'expliquent par le désir, exprimé par toute la presse anglaise libérale, que la Grande-Bretagne devienne membre de plein droit du Marché Commun, et, depuis le début de 1961, la campagne se propage (encouragée, dit-on, par le Gouvernement américain). Est-ce si simple? Aucun pays ne peut se rallier au Traité de Rome tout entier comme ça; le Traité même prévoit la nécessité d'une négociation entre tout nouveau candidat et les pays membres (par exemple au sujet du niveau du tarif commun, de la puissance de vote, *etc.*, et un accord éventuel devrait être ratifié par chacune des Parties Contractantes. Mr. MACMILLAN démontrait les difficultés impliquées pour l'Angleterre quand il parlait, à la Chambre des Communes, des obligations vis-à-vis du Commonwealth, à l'égard de l'agriculture nationale et vis-à-vis des partenaires de l'A.E.L.E. D'autre part, si on parle de devenir membre d'un ,,club'' on doit se rappeler qu'un candidat peut être rejeté! Même si le Marché Commun ne ,,rejette'' pas la candidature de la Grande-Bretagne, des négociations prolongées et infructueuses porteraient grand tort à l'idée européenne. L'essentiel est en effet dans cette affaire de décider le résultat voulu, l'aboutissement avant de négocier! Le paradoxe se résoud si on accepte que la première opération soit *politique*, par exemple ,,un accord pour tomber d'accord'' et la deuxième soit de négocier les *techniques* nécessaires. Cette méthode d'aborder le problème a pleinement réussi dans les négociations qui ont mené au Traité de Rome et elle doit être appliquée à toute négociation tendant vers un ,,marché unique'' en Europe occidentale. Les responsabilités incombent dans ce cas à la France et au Royaume-Uni.

En somme dès le printemps de 1961, le Royaume-Uni semblait prêt à coopérer à un plan commun d'intégration avec les Six, sous réserve de trois conditions:

1. la sauvegarde de ses rapports avec le Commonwealth;
2. la prolongation du système de protection de l'agriculture britannique, et;
3. la possibilité d'adhésion offerte à ses partenaires de l'A.E.L.E.

1. Puisque le Commonwealth (et également la Communauté française) sert de lien indispensable entre l'Occident et une grande partie des territoires sous-développés de l'Asie et de l'Afrique, on peut espérer, dans l'intérêt du monde occidental tout entier, l'acceptation d'une formule pour soumettre à un règlement identique le Commonwealth et les ,,pays et les territoires d'Outre-Mer'' cités dans la IVème Partie du Traité de Rome.

2. La protection de l'agriculture est pratiquée par tous les pays occidentaux, à vrai dire de façons différentes et donc difficiles à harmoniser. Les Six eux-mêmes n'ont pas résolu le problème. Est-il à prévoir qu'il se compliquerait davantage quand les pays participants seront plus nombreux? Ou, après tout, ,,une politique commune pour l'agriculture'' n'est-elle qu'une pure illusion? Dans ce cas, rien n'empêche pour tout autre

produit l'application d'un système de libre-échange. Dans le cas contraire, on résoudra à la longue le problème de l'extension vers d'autres pays.

3. Finalement, il est évident que le Gouvernement britannique n'a nullement l'intention d'abandonner ses partenaires de l'A.E.L.E. à leur sort, en faveur du Marché Commun. La solution définitive doit permettre à l'A.E.L.E. de s'y associer comme un seul groupe. Si les intentions britanniques étaient autres, l'intégration économique et politique de l'Europe encourrait des dangers graves – et l'O.T.A.N. également.

LA FRANCE ET LA GRANDE-BRETAGNE

Dans un important discours télévisé, le 31 mai 1960, le général de GAULLE énuméra les barrières géographiques qui ne sont plus des obstacles à l'unité européenne, telles que le Rhin, les Alpes, *etc.*, et il a cité aussi la Manche. Il est à noter que, par contre, dans ses *Mémoires de Guerre*, Volume III, il avait désigné comme troisième „puissance planétaire'' une Europe unifiée, à côté du monde Anglo-Saxon et du camp soviétique. Donc, à son avis, la frontière occidentale de l'Europe se serait déplacée à l'ouest des îles britanniques. Est-ce là une façon d'ouvrir la porte à l'entrée de la Grande-Bretagne en Europe ? On peut le croire – avec beaucoup de gens bien informés – mais jusqu'ici, les actions n'ont pas succédé aux paroles. Par une réponse donnée à la Chambre des Communes, le Chancelier de l'Échiquier a montré qu'il considérait ces propos comme une invitation à la négociation et qu'il était prêt, au nom du Royaume-Uni, et au nom de ses partenaires de l'A.E.L.E., à accepter. Ne peut-on espérer des initiatives concrètes de la part du général de GAULLE ?

O.C.D.E. : NÉE D'UNE IMPASSE

La Convention du 14 décembre 1960 qui instaura l'O.C.D.E. est, comme celle de l'O.E.C.E., un cadre qui attend d'être complété – et ceci s'avérera difficile dans les conditions de scission de l'Europe occidentale. L'O.C.D.E. continuera à exercer les fonctions ultra-européennes de l'O.E.C.E., mais elle vise aussi plus loin, à une coordination atlantique, et à une politique commune vis-à-vis des pays sous-développés. Si elle réussit cette derniere tâche, elle agira comme un véritable pôle d'attraction économique pour ces pays. Son succès dépend surtout des échanges, et les dangers de l'impasse en Europe au moment de sa création sont évidents : aucune politique libérale vis-à-vis des autres pays du monde n'est réalisable tant qu'elle n'a pas établi une politique homogène de libre-échange au service des pays de l'Occident.

L'AVENIR

Ce qu'il faut donc, c'est un „Grand Dessein'' pour les pays membres de l'O.C.D.E., dont les deux aspects seront les échanges et les monnaies. Pour ce dernier, des réformes en vue de stabiliser les monnaies de l'Ouest devraient être mises sur pied d'urgence par l'O.C.D.E.

Dans le cas des échanges, une fois l'impasse franchie, un marché européen extensif de libre-échange peut s'établir, éventuellement une union douanière pan-européenne. Les États-Unis et le Canada ne seraient pas obligés de suivre les membres européens – ni d'intervenir. La seule réponse possible des États-Unis serait d'accepter le défi et de se mettre à négocier l'abaissement des barrières douanières des deux côtés de l'Atlantique. Ainsi se créera un système approximatif de libre-échange atlantique et de libre-échange complet en Europe occidentale – ce qui constituerait le pôle d'attraction économique mentionné ci-dessus. Ce système doit s'élargir par la suite sous les auspices du G.A.T.T. – qui enfin jouerait pleinement son rôle.

ECONOMIC RELATIONS IN EUROPE: THE PATTERN

by

GUNNAR HECKSCHER [1]

The beginning of the nineteen sixties has been a very eventful period with regard to economic developments in Europe. On the whole, all European countries have been favoured by trade trends, and no new difficulties have arisen. At the same time, the organisational pattern of European economic affairs has tended to become tolerably clear. The O.E.E.C. has gone, succeeded by the O.E.C.D. For once, there were no major difficulties on the part of Congress in ratifying an international agreement drawing the United States into closer relationships with Europe. It is true that we know as yet very little about how the new Organisation is going to develop. One cannot help having certain reservations: there will be, no doubt, wider, but perhaps less intensive, co-operation, and some of the apparently lasting achievements of the O.E.E.C. are liable to get lost in the process. Nor does one yet quite know where the emphasis will lie in the work of the new Organisation. But, on the other hand, the transition period has proved less difficult than was expected, and the new officials of O.E.C.D., led by their Secretary-General, are apparently quite determined not to let any chances of Western economic co-operation go by default.

As for the European Economic Community, developments have proved increasingly satisfactory. Ties between the Member countries have been strengthening, the industrial customs union is being strengthened, and the problem of Greece has been solved by a treaty which opens up great possibilities for the future relationship of the E.E.C. with other less-developed areas as well.

---

[1] The author is Professor of Political Science at the University of Stockholm. As a member of Parliament (Conservative) he has played a conspicuous part in the economic debates of the Consultative Assembly at Strasbourg. He is Chairman of the Assembly's Economic Committee.

The E.F.T.A. agreement has duly come into force and is working very smoothly. Contrary to some expectations the device of a free trade area is proving technically capable of easy realisation; and, moreover, the peculiar geographical structure of the new organisation appears to create less difficulty than was expected in some circles. Like the E.E.C., E.F.T.A is attempting to accelerate the process of securing internal free trade, and it seems likely that this tendency will become more accentuated in the future.

During the G.A.T.T. session in the spring of 1961, the position both of the E.E.C. – and particularly the common tariff – and of E.F.T.A. were, of course, under consideration. G.A.T.T. Members outside the two groups manifested certain misgivings, and, when this article is being written, it seems unlikely that either of the groupings will be explicitly approved by G.A.T.T. Nor, on the other hand, will they be condemned. The attitude of G.A.T.T. Members to the new organisations is perhaps best characterised as a tacit waiver: things are allowed to go on, as they are going, but with the reservation that they are not entirely in accordance with the intentions and wishes of other G.A.T.T. Members. One reason for this attitude is doubtless the fact that the G.A.T.T. tariff negotiations as a whole are proving extremely difficult and will probably have to go on over a very long period of time. The Contracting Parties are, in point of fact, getting so familiar with the machinery that each of them is able to use it to put pressure on the others in favour of its own interests, and hard bargains are being driven. This should not cause undue concern, nor should it obscure the fact that there is still a general tendency towards liberalisation of trade.

Thus, the picture seems almost uniformly bright. There is a boom in Europe today, and no immediate indication of further depressions or recessions can be seen. This, however, should not make us forget that a great number of latent problems still remain and they may come to the surface as soon as there is any deterioration of the general economic atmosphere.

In the first place, the boom is, as usual, being reflected in inflationary tendencies. These appear conspicuously in the monetary field, and it is presumably partly because of them that movements of "hot money" in Europe are constantly causing difficulties both to the Central Banks and to Governments. Basically, however, the main problem is one of cost inflation. Wage costs are today virtually everywhere in Europe the main factor in costs of production, and organised employees are insistent in trying to get the best possible immediate bargain at any given moment. Especially since no danger of depression appears, this is apt to lead to a rise in the costs of production which may be going on at a greater speed than the rise in productivity, thus causing disturbances on the several national markets as well as in the exchange of goods. Such disturbances are the more likely since economic growth remains very uneven, both over the whole post-war period and from year to year. It may be surmised that the pressure for higher wages is in fact particularly dangerous in those countries where economic growth is still going on at a slower pace.

The economic split of free Europe is showing its consequences in the fact that both the E.E.C. and E.F.T.A. are increasing trade between their Members at an appreciably higher pace than the pace of development of European or world trade in general. Even if tariff differences are not yet sufficiently important to divert the flow of commerce into new channels, the very expectations on the part of the business community concerning future trade relationships are apparently quite important in this respect. Consequently, if developments are allowed to continue along the present lines the result may well be that diversion of commerce becomes greater than what is warranted by the actual importance of the trade split.

Even the E.E.C. has not yet managed to find a solution to the problem of a common agricultural policy. On the whole, the basic reason for this is probably the same as the reason for the difficulties in developing an agricultural policy for Europe as a whole, namely that the immediate national objective of each Member State still seems to be to maintain or even increase its agricultural production, finding new markets for it; while there are many indications that what Europe actually needs is stabilisation of agricultural production at the present level or even a reduction in the output. Since agriculture is traditionally non-competitive, for *political* reasons the latter objective is exceedingly difficult to achieve. Incidentally, the situation in the United States in this respect is exactly the same.

Another consequence of the trade split between the Six and the Seven is that European countries belonging to neither group are apt to be forgotten in the process of evolution, the only exception being the E.E.C. Treaty of Association with Greece. Moreover, these difficulties are closely related to the agricultural problem, since European countries outside the two groups are on the whole those which are particularly dependent on finding markets for agricultural and other primary products. So far, co-operation between E.E.C. and E.F.T.A. has not even reached the point where they could agree on dividing the responsibilities for their weaker European brethren. By the same token, Europe is as yet frankly not doing nearly enough to shoulder its responsibilities with regard to under-developed countries and areas in other parts of the world, and the somewhat sentimental discussion which is being carried on in a number of European countries (as well as in the United States) with regard to these countries as yet shows little consciousness that what the under-developed countries need is trade rather than aid. Nor, of course, is Europe showing much willingness to condition its own production of agriculture and other primary products to the need for more exchange with under-developed areas.

The United States balance-of-payments difficulties still loom surprisingly large in the European picture. After all, they are on the whole caused less by the unwillingness of Europe to accept American goods than by entirely different causes. But, insofar as they express the change in trade relationships, the reason, of course, is that cost inflation has gone even further in the United States than in Europe – in short that American goods are in many cases "pricing themselves out of Europe". Both the EISENHOWER and the KENNEDY Administrations, apparently, were unwilling to look these realities squarely in the face, and the result was a negative attitude towards the "discrimination" against American goods unavoidably accompanying any European economic integration.

The new Administration in Washington, however, has patently been seeking to get around this difficulty by insisting that the United States was willing to "pay a price" for *political* unity in Europe – that is to say that they would not have any major objection to discrimination if it were part of a settlement strengthening the political cohesion of the Six and bringing other European nations, notably the British, into line. To what extent the price to be paid is really of any major importance seems doubtful, but there can be no doubt that the argument came to exercise considerable influence over the views of the public on both sides of the Atlantic.

It is not surprising in these circumstances that all sorts of rumours were abroad concerning what might next happen in European economic relationships. On the one hand, it was being suggested in some circles – without the slightest foundation in fact – that E.F.T.A. had been a dismal failure and that the free trade area approach was proving just as impossible as M. MONNET and others have always said it would be. On the other hand, there were something like bi-monthly rumours to the effect that "Britain is about to join the Common Market". These rumours were then developed, on the one hand, so as to indicate that the other E.F.T.A. countries were about to be jilted, and, on the other hand, in appeals to the very genuine European feeling which is growing up in Great Britain today. For obvious reasons, the spreaders of these rumours, naturally, have taken great care not to be too specific and they are content to bypass the very real difficulties which any entry of Great Britain into the Common Market is bound to entail.

It should not be assumed that these rumours were just the result of artificial attempts to change the situation. On the contrary, they were spreading and becoming important precisely because of the widespread and fundamental concern virtually everywhere in Europe over the existing trade split. The problem of European economic integration is not coming any nearer a solution acceptable to all, and it is characteristic that the so-called Committee of the Twenty-One, headed by the Dutch

Foreign Minister, Mr. LUNS, does not seem to have achieved much – except loads of statistics. But this situation is not acceptable to the public in any European country, and so there has been increasing pressure on Governments everywhere to break the deadlock and bring about some kind of a solution – some people would say, any solution.

If we could turn the clock back to the discussions in the MAUDLING Committee in the autumn of 1958, or even to the days of the Messina Conference, it seems obvious that not only the British but also the Scandinavians would be far less uncompromising than they were in those days. Prevaling opinion in Great Britain today seems to feel that it was a mistake on the part of the British Government not to have participated directly in the establishment of the Common Market. The Scandinavian and Swiss Governments would probably today accept a degree of harmonisation in a European Economic Association which they held to be out of the question in the course of the MAUDLING negotiations. And, finally, the German and Benelux Governments would wish nothing more than to mediate between the French, on the one hand, and the E.F.T.A. Governments, on the other, in order to establish some kind of European economic association. At present, however, this is not, apparently, much of a help. The British Government has been taking up an entirely pragmatic attitude, seeking all sorts of solutions and excluding no possibilities. The French Government and the Commission of the Common Market remain Cartesian in their attitudes; no half-measures are acceptable. There is also mutual disagreement on the relative importance of the economic and "political" aspects of the problem, a fact which is causing particular difficulties in the case of the Austrian, the Swedish, the Swiss and, of course, the Finnish Governments, all of which are exceedingly sensitive to any suggestion of political impulsion in their attitude of aloofness to power-politics.

There is thus no lack of plans for a solution of Europe's split. Some people think that the thing to do is to enlarge the Common Market by the inclusion of Great Britain and other E.F.T.A. countries not bound to the policy of neutrality or non-alliance.

The difficulty of this solution lies, among other things, in the fact that the Common Market embodies an exceedingly nice balance of interests. Any modification in the present system, for instance by negotiating a new common tariff, would upset the balance and is consequently on the face of it not acceptable to all the present Members, and least of all to the French. On the other hand, a Common Market comprising, in addition to its present Members, Great Britain and a couple of other E.F.T.A. countries would, in fact, be very different from the existing one and would therefore require a new balance, in many respects different from the existing one. It is an over-simplification to speak simply about "joining" the existing European Economic Community, since enlargement itself of that organisation would transform it into something very different from the present.

Next, the adhesion of the United Kingdom to the E.E.C. is, as has been frequently pointed out, conditioned by her obligations both to the Commonwealth and to E.F.T.A. Regardless of any moral considerations no Western European Power could today bear the onus of repudiating existing commitments – this would damage their negotiating position for any new arrangement to be made to such an extent as to be virtually impossible. The problem of Commonwealth relations should not be overestimated, but it is undoubtedly real and will become particularly apparent as soon as the Common Market starts dealing seriously with problems of agriculture. Incidentally, attempts at strengthening and further integrating E.F.T.A. are also coming up against the same difficulty. It seems unavoidable that E.F.T.A. also must develop an agricultural policy, but any such policy must take due account of the interests of Commonwealth countries outside Europe, as well as of Ireland and the under-developed areas.

The other approach is to form a European economic association, comprising both E.E.C., E.F.T.A. and European nations outside both groups. In most European countries, public opinion seems to be in favour of this solution rather than of any other. The Consultative Assembly of the Council of Europe has developed the possibilities of such an economic association in a number of Recommendations and Reports which have received wide-au service de leurs propres intérêts. Ceci ne doit pas, pourtant, nous préoccuper excessivement et ne change rien au fait qu'il y a encore de par le monde une tendance générale vers la libéralisation du commerce.

Cependant, ce tableau plutôt rassurant de perspectives favorables pour l'Europe, sans indication de dépression ou de récession, ne doit pas nous cacher qu'il subsiste un grand nombre de problèmes, lesquels monteront à la surface sans aucun doute dès que la conjoncture générale se gâtera. Le premier de ces problèmes est celui des tendances inflationnistes dans le domaine monétaire. C'est un problème qui est, comme d'habitude, créé par le *boom* actuel, d'où les embarras d'argent spéculatif auxquels sont acculés les banques centrales et les gouvernements. Mais le problème fondamental est toujours celui de l'inflation des charges. Les salaires, facteur principal, disons-le, des dépenses de productivité, se trouvent continuellement sous la pression des salariés organisés, de sorte que des hausses de salaire entraînent nécessairement une hausse des frais de production qui est susceptible de dépasser toute augmentation de productivité. D'autre part les perturbations occasionnées autant sur les marchés nationaux que dans les échanges ont tendance à se renforcer dans les pays où le développement économique est encore retardataire.

L'effet de la scission économique en Europe se manifeste dans le fait que l'expansion des échanges à l'intérieur de la C.E.E. et de l'A.E.L.E. se développe à un rythme supérieur à celui du commerce européen ou mondial, d'autant plus que, même si les disparités des tarifs douaniers ne sont pas encore suffisamment importants pour faire dévier le commerce dans de nouvelles directions, les opinions des gens d'affaire sur le développement probable des échanges pourraient encourager une déviation substantielle qui ne serait pas justifiée par l'importance actuelle de la division de l'Europe libre.

Il faut bien avouer que la Communauté des Six n'a pas encore su trouver une solution pour ses problèmes de politique agricole commune; car, à l'instar de l'Europe dans son ensemble (et, soit dit en passant, des États-Unis), chaque État s'efforce de maintenir, voire d'augmenter, sa production agricole et cherche de nouveaux débouchés, tandis que ce dont a besoin l'Europe, c'est d'une stabilisation de la production agricole. Or, pour des raisons *politiques*, une telle stabilisation s'avère toujours difficile, l'agriculture étant, par tradition, non concurrentielle.

Les pays qui n'appartiennent ni au groupe des Six ni à celui des Sept risquent, bien entendu, d'être pris de court dans l'évolution de ces courants commerciaux sauf la Grèce, grâce à son traité d'association avec la C.E.E. – et il faut se rappeler que les embarras de ces pays sont étroitement liés avec le problème agricole, puisque leur vie même dépend de leur pouvoir d'écouler leurs produits agricoles ou leurs matières premières.

Les deux groupements de l'Europe libre d'aujourd'hui ne se sont pas encore mis d'accord même sur le partage des responsabilités vis-à-vis de ces pays faibles de l'Europe, et, de plus, ils sont loin d'apporter des bienfaits adéquats aux pays et régions sous-développés dans d'autres parties du monde. L'attitude plutôt sentimentale de certains pays européens (et des États-Unis) ne tient pas suffisamment compte du fait que ces pays ont besoin surtout d'échanges et non de secours. L'Europe n'a certes pas manifesté le désir d'ajuster le cadre de sa production agricole ou de matières premières à ce besoin d'augmenter les échanges avec les pays sous-développés.

Les difficultés actuelles qu'éprouvent les États-Unis pour leur balance de paiements ont encore des répercussions pour l'Europe, quoique la raison principale de ce déséquilibre ne soit aucunement un refus de la part de l'Europe d'accepter des produits américains. Le motif primordial, en ce qui concerne les échanges, c'est que l'inflation des prix a atteint de telles proportions aux États Unis que les prix de leurs produits ne sont plus à l'échelle européenne. Constatons que le Gouvernement de KENNEDY, comme celui d'EISENHOWER, s'oppose en principe à toute discrimination contre les produits américains telle que celle que l'intégration économique européenne est susceptible d'entraîner. Mais la nouvelle Administration à Washington cherche à trouver une solution à ce problème en acceptant une certaine discrimination comme contrepartie d'une éventuelle union *politique* de l'Europe, à condition que cette acceptation renforce spécifiquement la cohésion des Six et assure l'adhésion à l'organisation communautaire d'autres pays, notamment du Royaume-Uni. L'importance d'un tel marchandage est, à vrai dire, douteuse, mais l'argument paraît exercer de l'influence sur l'opinion des deux côtés de l'Atlantique.

Il n'est pas étonnant que des rumeurs de tout genre circulent sur l'avenir des rapports économiques européens. D'une part les gens affirment – sans aucune justification – que l'A.E.L.E. a échoué, comme M. MONNET et d'autres personnalités l'avaient toujours prévu. Ou bien d'autres répandent volontiers le bruit que le Royaume-Uni va „rallier le Marché Commun" – avec l'arrière-pensée qu'il finira de la sorte par laisser tomber les autres pays de l'A.E.L.E.: une telle affirmation, du reste, est susceptible en tout cas de contribuer à l'essor de l'esprit européen en Grande-Bertagne.

De telles assertions ne sont pas que des tentatives artificielles de modifier la situation telle qu'elle se présente aujourd'hui; elles découlent d'une sérieuse préoccupation à l'égard de la scission en Europe. En vérité, nous sommes encore loin d'une solution acceptable: le Comité des 21, par exemple, présidé par le Ministre des Affaires étrangères des Pays-Bas, M. LUNS, n'a abouti qu'à des tas de statistiques.

Toutefois, la pression de l'opinion publique persiste, convaincue qu'il faudra sortir de l'impasse, n'importe comment, entend-on dire.

Ce qui est certain, c'est que depuis les débats à la „Comité MAUDLING" de 1958, disons plutôt depuis la Conférence de Messine, les Britanniques et les Scandinaves en sont venus à prendre une position moins intransigeante: en Angleterre aujourd'hui la majorité des gens considèrent que le Royaume-Uni a eu tort de ne pas participer directement à l'instauration du Marché Commun. Les Gouvernements scandinaves et la Suisse accepteraient à l'heure qu'il est certaines mesures d'harmonisation qui étaient alors hors de question pour eux. Les Gouvernements de la République Fédérale et des pays du Benelux ne demandent pas mieux que d'agir en médiateurs entre les Français d'une part et les Gouvernements de l'A.E.L.E. d'autre part, pour aboutir à telle ou telle association économique européenne. Ce qui, cependant, n'avance pas beaucoup les choses pour les Britanniques. Ceux-ci continuent à se conduire en pragmatistes, tandis que la France et la Commission de la C.E.E. restent obstinément cartésiennes: pas de demi-mesures. Enfin le désaccord sur l'importance des aspects économiques ou politiques du problème persiste: toute impulsion politique crée des difficultés, surtout pour les gouvernements qui se tiennent à distance de tout ce qui s'appelle politique de puissance – les Autrichiens, les Suédois, les Suisses et, bien entendu, les Finlandais.

Parmi les plans de redressement, il y a certes, en premier lieu, l'élargissement du Marché Commun de façon à y faire entrer la Grande Bretagne et d'autres pays de l'A.E.L.E. qui ne sont pas liés par une politique de neutralité ou de non-alliance. Mais il faut bien se dire que toute modification des dispositions du Traité de Rome, comme par exemple la renégociation du tarif douanier commun, aurait comme conséquence un bouleversement de l'équilibre délicatement établi des intérêts des six pays signataires du Marché Commun, bouleversement qui léserait avant tout la France. D'autre part, dire que la Grande Bretagne va „rallier" le Marché Commun équivaut à une simplification excessive du problème, car, précisément, l'extension du Marché Commun à d'autres États, et notamment au Royaume-Uni, le transformerait de bout en bout.

L'adhésion du Royaume-Uni est conditionnée, de toute façon, par ses obligations vis-à-vis du Commonwealth et vis-à-vis des nations membres de l'A.E.L.E. Il va sans dire qu'aucun pays de l'Europe occidentale ne saurait mettre en péril sa réputation de négociateur – ne parlons pas de considérations morales – en méconnaissant ses obligations existantes.

Dans les discussions qui ont eu lieu jusqu'ici, le problème du Commonwealth a été quelque peu surfait, mais il deviendrait infailliblement une réalité substantielle si le Marché Commun en venait sérieusement aux prises avec les problèmes de l'agriculture. (Soit dit en passant, l'A.E.L.E. doit faire face au problème identique, et la politique qu'elle développera par la suite devra nécessairement tenir compte du facteur Commonwealth, ainsi que de l'Irlande et des régions sous-développées).

L'autre moyen de reconstruire l'unité économique de l'Europe libre – et c'est celui préconisé par la majorité des personnes – consiste à mettre sur pied une association économique européenne qui comprendrait la C.E.E., l'A.E.L.E. et les pays n'appartenant à aucun de ces deux groupes. L'Assemblée Consultative du Conseil de l'Europe s'est vue accorder un notable soutien parlementaire pour ses rapports et recommandations tendant vers cette solution. Le projet d'E.L.E.C. et le projet dit de MÜLLER-ARMACK abondent dans ce sens – et ils considèrent comme chose acquise que les membres de la Communauté donnent toujours une préférence à la solution d'une union douanière qualifiée plutôt que d'accepter un rabâchage du projet originel d'une zone de libre-échange. Du point de vue rationnel, c'est assurément vrai, mais il faut bien avouer que, dans les circonstances actuelles, la différence entre la C.E.E. et une union douanière européenne paraît être plutôt idéologique, sinon structurelle, et non pas économique. Avec un tel projet, chaque pays encourrait le grand risque de perdre son identité dans une organisation plus étendue.

Le fait est que l'Accord du G.A.T.T. vise à empêcher précisément le genre d'arrangement préférentiel qui serait l'étoffe de toute solution transactionnelle. Ce paradoxe sauterait aux yeux si, par exemple, la proposition était adoptée que les membres non britanniques du G.A.T.T. offrent aux pays du Commonwealth, de façon unilatérale, sur leurs marchés les mêmes préférences dont ils bénéficient en Grande-Bretagne. Une telle proposition est à tel point à l'encontre des principes du G.A.T.T. que même une „suspension tacite de jugement" ne serait plus de mise.

Voilà. C'est dire que les difficultés fondamentales sont majeures. S'il y avait une volonté politique de trouver une solution aux problèmes, sans doute les moyens ne feraient pas défaut. Pourquoi cette volonté politique n'existe-t-elle pas? Est-ce parce que des tendances isolationnistes subsistent encore en Europe, ou est-ce parce qu'on continue à n'envisager que des solutions purement économiques? Ou bien est-ce que la politique de puissance reste la principale préoccupation des grandes nations européennes, comme, du reste, des États-Unis?

Le général de GAULLE n'est peut-être pas le seul à estimer que les problèmes des échanges et des relations économiques, – „le commissariat", c'est le terme qu'il emploie – doivent se placer à l'arrière, et non pas – jamais – à l'avant de l'armée.

L'ASSOCIATION DES PAYS D'OUTRE-MER AU MARCHÉ COMMUN

par

ROBERT LEMAIGNEN [1]

Publié l'année dernière par M. Ernest MILCENT, l'actuel correspondant du journal *Le Monde* à Dakar, un petit livre subtil porte un titre bien révélateur: *L'Afrique entre en scène.*

De ce point de vue, le prochain voyage annoncé par M. KROUTCHEV en Afrique – notamment en Guinée – n'est pas seulement un indice, mais une consécration. On a dit que, dans une large mesure, le XIXe siècle avait été celui de l'explosion des nationalismes européens. On dira peut-être qu'après l'atome, le XXe aura été celui de l'explosion des nationalismes dans les pays sous-développés, d'abord en Orient (première moitié du siècle), puis en Afrique (seconde moitié).

Afrique du Nord, Ghana, Nigeria, Egypte, Kenya, Guinée, Togo et Cameroun, Congo belge, Nyassaland, Tanganyika, Somalies, et aujourd'hui la Rhodésie et l'Afrique du Sud – les explosions du nationalisme africain sont devenues comme le fait de chaque jour. L'Afrique est aujourd'hui pour le monde, et pour l'Est comme pour l'Ouest, *un enjeu politique.*

Dans cette compétition, quelle est la position de l'Europe, en particulier de cette Europe des Six qui, au troisième rang mondial en puissance économique, est au premier rang peut-être par sa culture, sa civilisation, sa „charge d'histoire"? De cette Europe qui entretient avec l'Afrique des liens traditionnels de culture, de langue, d'échanges économiques? De cette Europe qui aborde l'Afrique aujourd'hui sous une forme nouvelle et communautaire, par *l'association des pays d'outre-mer* au Marché Commun, laquelle peut sans doute être considérée comme la première approche *globale* des problèmes du sous-développement parce qu'elle traite aussi bien des institutions que des échanges, des investissements et de l'assistance technique.

[1] Monsieur Robert LEMAIGNEN est membre de la Commission de la Communauté Économique Européenne.

Il faut bien dire cependant que, dans les quatre directions principales que je viens d'indiquer, le Traité de Rome ne pouvait prétendre tout régler et tout prévoir. Ses auteurs ne pouvaient penser, en 1957, qu'il était sérieusement possible de figer le sort et les conditions de 25 pays d'outre-mer associés groupant 55 millions d'hommes – pour la plupart en Afrique – dont l'évolution politique s'est déroulée, depuis cette date, selon un rythme foudroyant. En fait, l'une des caractéristiques du Traité de Rome, et l'un de ses principaux avantages dans les dispositions qui intéressent l'outre-mer, est sa grande souplesse qui permet, avec un minimum d'imagination et beaucoup de bonne volonté, les adaptations nécessaires à cette évolution. C'est ce que je voudrais montrer ici, en reprenant successivement les quatre grands domaines de notre action.

L'ÉVOLUTION POLITIQUE – L'ADAPTATION INSTITUTIONNELLE

Le premier problème posé aux responsables de la Communauté Économique Européenne, et peut-être le plus redoutable, naquit d'une constatation peu encourageante: à peine mis en application, le Traité de Rome se trouvait politiquement dépassé outre-mer.

Décidée à une époque où, dans l'outre-mer français, la loi-cadre de 1956 n'accordait encore qu'une semi-autonomie de droit interne, l'association de ces pays au Marché Commun apparaissait une nouvelle fois comme un statut „octroyé", décidé par leur métropole sans consultation des principaux bénéficiaires. L'Afrique, avec la passion de l'égalité qui la caractérise, devait supporter d'autant plus mal une telle situation que son accession à la souveraineté internationale allait se faire, sans coup férir, en deux ou trois années. On dénonçait de toutes parts les survivances du vieux statut colonial, l'insuffisante africanisation des cadres de l'exécutif du Marché Commun, l'absence quasi totale de représentation des pays associés dans les institutions de la Communauté. Le danger était grand de voir dans cette association comme un enfant mort-né.

Que fallait-il faire, en particulier, pour ces pays associés qui accédaient à l'indépendance jour après jour et qui venaient interroger la Communauté Européenne pour lui demander, avec une confiance touchante qu'il importait de ne pas décevoir, selon quelles modalités, et sur la base de quels textes il leur était possible de continuer leur association? Convenait-il de répondre que, le passage à la souveraineté internationale constituant une transformation radicale des conditions antérieures, les anciens associés devaient être désormais considérés comme des pays tiers, en dehors de tout lien d'association avec la Communauté, d'où la nécessité d'entreprendre de longues et laborieuses négociations diplomatiques, sur la base de l'article 238 du Traité? Convenait-il, au contraire, d'affirmer que l'indépendance ne signifiait pas nécessairement rupture des relations d'association existantes, dès lors que ces relations auraient été *librement* confirmées par des pays associés devenus des États souverains?

Les deux thèses étaient, sur le plan juridique, défendables mais ce sont, en définitive, des considérations d'opportunité qui ont fait pencher la balance en faveur de la seconde, parce qu'elle permet d'obtenir des résultats plus immédiats, en évitant les complications d'une négociation lourde dans chaque cas particulier alors que, de toute façon, une négociation générale doit intervenir pour le renouvellement de la Convention d'application de l'association dont l'effet se terminera le 31 décembre 1962. On oublie trop souvent, en effet, que si les négociateurs du Traité de Rome ont effectivement „octroyé" l'association aux pays d'outre-mer, ils ne l'ont fait que suivant des modalités dont la durée était dès le départ limitée à 5 ans. Ils prévoyaient donc en 1957 – et la sagesse de cette prévision est aujourd'hui évidente – que sur le continent africain en pleine mue il était prudent de ne réglementer qu'à court terme, en laissant à des négociations ultérieures entre parties également souveraines le soin d'arrêter d'autres dispositions.

En attendant cette négociation, le Conseil de Ministres de la Communauté Économique Européenne, suivant les recommandations qui lui avaient été faites par la Commission exécutive, a proposé une solution au problème du Togo devenu indépendant dans un sens pragmatique qui pouvait faire jurisprudence pour tous les pays associés accédant à la souveraineté internationale: dans le cas où un tel pays exprime librement le désir de poursuivre son association à la C.E.E., suivant la 4e partie du Traité de Rome et les modalités de la Convention d'application, il est possible de lui donner satisfaction jusqu'au moment où cette Convention sera révisée pour faire place, le 1er janvier 1963, à une nouvelle convention. Jusqu'à cette date, il a donc été admis que les relations d'association étaient maintenues selon un régime de fait; l'accession à l'indépendance n'a pu les rompre dès lors que les Parties étaient d'accord pour les poursuivre; il ne s'agit plus que de les aménager à titre provisoire, par des arrangements dont la discussion a été proposée au Togo et qui porteront sur les modalités de la représentation directe de cette République auprès de la Communauté Économique Européenne dans la mesure où le Gouvernement de Lome ne désirera pas se faire représenter par les autorités françaises. Il est donc fort vraisemblable qu'avant quelques mois, la Communauté pourra accueillir à Bruxelles, si le Gouvernement local le demande, un chargé d'affaires togolais qui sera associé, d'une manière ou d'une autre, aux travaux intéressant le Togo de certains organes de la C.E.E., et que des solutions analogues seront adoptées pour les autres pays associés qui, en accédant à la souveraineté internationale, auront confirmé leur désir de continuer leur association au Marché Commun, comme ils l'ont fait presque tous jusqu'alors.

Cette importante décision montre que la C.E.E. se considère comme ayant, vis-à-vis de ses associés d'outre-mer, des responsabilités qui ne s'éteignent pas, bien au contraire, avec leur passage à l'indépendance et qu'elle sait imaginer, sans juridisme excessif, des solutions souples qui permettent d'adapter l'association à l'évolution politique, en donnant aux associés l'occasion de faire entendre leur voix à Bruxelles. C'était là l'essentiel car il était essentiel, dans des pays où priment actuellement les considérations politiques, de régler tout d'abord ce problème politique. Il n'en demeure pas moins que l'indépendance, même si elle apparaît quelquefois dans l'opinion africaine comme une espèce de solution magique, n'a pas du même coup réglé les problèmes économiques qui demeurent, et en premier lieu celui de l'expansion des échanges.

L'EXPANSION DES ÉCHANGES COMMERCIAUX

C'est un des buts du Traité de Rome, en ce qui concerne l'outremer, que de développer les échanges entre les pays membres européens et les pays associés en supprimant progressivement, par le désarmement douanier et contingentaire, toutes les discriminations commerciales entre les Six sur les marchés d'outremer; en ouvrant les marchés européens aux produits tropicaux des pays associés qui bénéficieront, sur ces marchés, d'une certaine protection assurée par le tarif extérieur commun; enfin, en favorisant les échanges interafricains puisque ces derniers devront bénéficier, selon les termes mêmes du Traité, du régime de libération des échanges qui intervient entre l'Europe et l'Afrique. Notons en passant que cette dernière mesure, dont l'importance n'avait peut-être pas été entièrement aperçue au moment de la négociation du Traité de Rome, va dans le même sens que les tentatives de regroupement qui se multiplient en Afrique, dans le but de créer de véritables „espaces économiques", au point qu'on parle aujourd'hui couramment d'un „marché commun africain".

Théoriquement, les pays d'outre-mer associés ne peuvent perdre à ces dispositions. Cela est vrai de leurs importations car la multiplication de leurs fournisseurs, et de leurs sources d'approvisionnement, est de nature à exercer, sur le niveau des prix locaux, une pression salutaire qui seule peut permettre une large concurrence. Cela est vrai aussi de leurs exportations car, le problème du placement des matières premières d'origine tropicale étant essentiel pour ces pays, il est évident qu'un libre accès à un marché en expansion de 160 millions de consommateurs constitue *a priori* un élément favorable.

Dans les faits, comment se sont traduites ces dispositions commerciales du Traité et de la Convention d'application? Sans doute, on ne pouvait pas s'attendre, pour la première année de désarmement douanier et contingentaire, à des modifications substantielles dans la structure des courants commerciaux. Cependant, l'analyse des statistiques du commerce extérieur des États membres avec l'Afrique pour l'année 1959, permet déjà quelques constatations intéressantes.

Cette analyse fait justice, tout d'abord, des critiques souvent désagréables qui ont été adressées, dans certaines organisations internationales, à la C.E.E. qu'on accusait bien vite de créer, par la préférence accordée aux pays d'outre-mer associés, de véritables détournements de trafic au détriment des pays tiers non associés. Or il est significatif d'observer que, par rapport à 1958, les échanges des Six pays membres de la C.E.E. se sont nettement accrus en 1959 avec les pays africains non associés: ils ont augmenté en valeur de 10% avec l'Ethiopie, de 23% avec la Nigeria, de 25% avec le Ghana, de 33% avec la Fédération des Rhodésies et du Nyassaland, de 51% avec le Soudan et de 52% avec le Libéria.

Un examen superficiel pourrait faire croire, ensuite, que cette progression du commerce avec les pays tiers s'est faite précisément au détriment des pays associés africains, dont les échanges avec la Communauté Économique Européenne ont régressé de 184 millions de $, soit de 11 à 12%. Or, il n'en est rien, car ces chiffres sont exprimés dans l'unité monétaire européenne (qui a la même valeur que le dollar des É.U.) et la cause essentielle du recul des échanges C.E.E. - pays associés est le recul des échanges entre la France et les pays d'outre-mer de sa zone: ces échanges ont diminué de 215 millions de $ et de 20%, soit à peu près le taux de la dévaluation du franc intervenue le 1er janvier 1959.

Au contraire, il est intéressant de noter qu'en ce qui concerne l'écoulement des produits des pays associés – question qui tient particulièrement au coeur de ceux-ci – l'Allemagne a accru ses importations de 17%, l'Italie de 33%, les Pays-Bas de 9% et l'Union Économique Belgo-Luxembourgeoise de 19%. Si l'on raisonnait uniquement dans une perspective française, on pourrait dire sans se tromper que les partenaires européens de la France dans le Marché Commun ont bien „rempli leur contrat".

Si l'intégration des échanges Europe-Afrique est donc, sans rigidité, sur une voie qui n'est pas mauvaise, on peut par contre se demander si les moyens prévus par le Traité pour assurer la promotion de ces échanges sont bien suffisants. De ce point de vue, il apparaît qu'à l'extrême fragilité de l'économie des pays d'outre-mer deux remèdes supplémentaires peuvent et doivent être apportés: l'industrialisation d'une part, et la régularisation des revenus des producteurs ruraux, d'autre part.

L'industrialisation va dans ce sens à coup sûr; elle contribue à amortir les fluctuations des cours des matières premières, parce que les produits semi-finis ou finis, qui se stockent plus aisément, sont beaucoup moins sensibles aux fluctuations conjoncturelles. A cet égard, des craintes ont pu naître, dans les pays associés, d'une stérilisation de l'effort engagé depuis une dizaine d'années pour industrialiser les pays d'outre-mer. On a pu redouter que, le Traité de Rome étant un instrument de libre-échange, le circuit classique de l'échange des matières premières contre les produits finis ne reprenne sa vigueur, sous la forme d'un nouveau Pacte Colonial à Six, corollaire historique du libéralisme.

Rien ne serait plus inexact et l'on ne dira jamais assez que ce Traité libre échangiste a prévu une exception importante au libre-échange: dans le but précisément de protéger les jeunes industries d'outre-mer contre les effets d'une concurrence qui serait selon toute probabilité mortelle. Il faut rappeler, en effet, que l'article 133 a déclaré expressément que les pays d'outre-mer associés „peuvent percevoir des droits de douane qui répondent aux nécessités de leur développement et aux besoins de leur industrialisation ou qui, de caractère fiscal, ont pour but d'alimenter leur budget". La seule exigence imposée par le Traité est que ces droits de douane soient appliqués, sans discrimination, aux importations des six États membres.

La régularisation des revenus des producteurs ruraux vient aujourd'hui à la mode, après avoir été longtemps contestée par les économistes. Je voudrais m'y arrêter car ce problème me paraît, à vrai dire, fondamental.

Au cours des cinquante dernières années, les dix-huit principales productions de base qui couvrent environ 90% des productions des pays tropicaux, ont connu des fluctuations annuelles moyennes de 14% dans les prix, de 19% en volume et de 23% en recettes d'exportation. Cela veut dire que, chaque année, les producteurs ont vu le prix qu'ils recevaient pour la récolte de leurs champs varier de 19% en moyenne – et cette moyenne ne traduit pas psychologiquement la gravité du phénomène.

Car rien ne décourage plus les producteurs que les sautes désordonnées des cours sur lesquelles ils n'ont aucune prise. Et rien n'est plus décevant, ni plus stérile, qu'une action de vulgarisation entreprise en période de cours favorables, alors que la dépression se manifeste au moment où l'on va toucher le but, avec cette conséquence grave d'une porte de confiance du paysan dans les conseils qui lui avaient été donnés et qu'il avait suivis.

Pour prendre un exemple particulièrement frappant, que s'est-il passé concrètement en 1958? Au cours de cette année, la baisse du prix des matières premières produites par les pays tropicaux ayant été en moyenne voisine de 20% et les ventes de ces produits étant de l'ordre de 25 milliards de dollars, c'est donc une perte de 5 milliards de dollars que les pays pauvres ont subie, pour une large part au bénéfice des pays riches.

Or, selon les évaluations de M. Paul HOFFMAN, Président-Directeur du Fonds Spécial des Nations-Unies, le total mondial de l'aide gouvernementale et privée aux pays en voie de développement n'a pas excédé 4 milliards de dollars pour l'année 1957/58. A quoi sert d'investir si l'effet pratique des investissements doit être annulé par l'instabilité des cours des produits de base?

Il est donc plus que jamais urgent d'apporter des éléments de solution à ce grave problème, ce qui peut être fait sur deux plans différents: sur un plan mondial tout d'abord, car l'état de certains marchés (comme celui du café, où deux années de consommation sont stockées) est arrivé à un point tel qu'à ce niveau seules des mesures d'envergure peuvent présenter une certaine efficacité; mais aussi, pour beaucoup d'autres produits, sur un plan simplement régional par un „coup d'épaule" donné à des organismes régulateurs qui ont fait leurs preuves, du type des marketing-boards britanniques ou des caisses de stabilisation des pays d'outre-mer français. Sur ce plan, la Commission de la C.E.E. a déjà présenté certaines suggestions qui font l'objet d'études et de discussions au niveau des experts nationaux des six pays membres. Le fait que la Communauté Économique Européenne soit actuellement le principal importateur mondial de matières premières (avec le 1/3 environ du commerce des produits de base) justifie largement qu'elle prenne ici quelques initiatives dont l'effet serait particulièrement sensible sur le marché, étant donnée la position qu'elle y occupe.

La solution de ce difficile problème est de nature à constituer l'un des leviers essentiels du développement. Sans elle, ainsi qu'on l'a vu, sont illusoires les investissements, qui constituent le second des leviers de ce développement, à propos duquel la C.E.E. apporte des éléments très positifs.

LES INVESTISSEMENTS DE CAPITAUX

Le Traité de Rome a fixé comme objectif principal à l'association des pays d'outre-mer de „favoriser les intérêts et la prospérité des habitants de ces pays de manière à les conduire au développement économique, social et culturel qu'ils attendent". Parmi les moyens employés pour atteindre cet objectif, le plus concret peut-être – et en tout cas le mieux connu aujourd'hui des bénéficiaires – est représenté par les contributions de la Communauté Économique Européenne, en tant que telle, aux investissements que demande le développement de ces pays.

Ces contributions sont assurées par le Fonds Européen de Développement, organe communautaire géré par les institutions de la Communauté dont l'action est complémentaire de celle des États membres. Ce Fonds est doté, pour les 5 années de la période 1958/1962 de plus de 580 millions de dollars, soit environ 2,9 milliards de nouveaux francs. Le caractère progressif du volume des crédits annuellement disponibles doit être souligné et, en particulier, le fait que le montant de la dernière annuité (1962) s'élève à environ 234 millions de dollars, soit près de 1,2 milliard de nouveaux francs.

Les deux principaux contributeurs, en valeur absolue, sont l'Allemagne et la France qui verseront chacune, au total, 200 millions de dollars. Puis viennent la Belgique et les Pays-Bas (chacun 70 millions), l'Italie (40 millions) et le Luxembourg (un peu plus de 1 million).

Du point de vue des pays bénéficiaires, ce sont de très loin les pays d'outre-mer entretenant avec la France des relations particulières qui se sont taillé la part du lion: avec 88% du total des crédits disponibles, ils recevront globalement 511 millions de dollars, soit près de 2,6 milliards de nouveaux francs. On a tenu compte, pour cette répartition, aussi bien de l'effort bilatéral français qui était et demeure considérable, que de l'importance des concessions faites par la France en ouvrant à la concurrence commerciale de ses partenaires les marchés d'outre-mer qu'elle s'était jusqu'alors réservée.

Les interventions du Fonds ne peuvent être appliquées qu'à des projets présentés par les gouvernements des pays bénéficiaires car – c'est une règle d'or de la C.E.E. dans son action outre-mer – ces gouvernements demeurent pleinement maîtres de la conception de leur propre développement. Ces interventions, sous cette condition de base, peuvent concerner le financement, exclusivement sous forme de dotations non remboursables:

- ,,de certaines institutions sociales, notamment d'hôpitaux, d'établissements d'enseignement ou de recherche technique, d'institutions d'orientation ou de promotion des activités professionnelles des populations;
- ,,d'investissements économiques d'intérêt général directement liés à l'exécution d'un programme comportant des projets de développement productifs et concrets''.

Entre ces deux grands secteurs – définis par la Convention d'application elle-même – la répartition des interventions est fixée chaque année par le Conseil de Ministres; elle est actuellement de 70% pour le secteur économique et de 30% pour le secteur social.

Enfin, du point de vue de l'exécution, les projets approuvés sont réalisés par des adjudications ouvertes aux entreprises des six pays membres ainsi que des pays associés; le contrôle est assuré sur place par des ,,contrôleurs techniques'' nommés par la Commission.

Telle est la procédure. Il importe de savoir où en sont les réalisations concrètes. De ce point de vue, il est incontestable que l'action du Fonds Européen de Développement a débuté fort lentement. En fait, l'année 1958 ne pouvait voir autre chose que la mise en place des institutions de la Communauté elle-même, la mise au point et l'approbation des règlements du Fonds, le recrutement des spécialistes nécessaires, bref le rôdage d'une machine dont les rouages sont constitués par des pièces détachées de six pays différents, les hommes ayant des traditions, des habitudes de pensée extrêmement diverses.

Il n'est donc pas étonnant que la première année (1958) n'ait pu voir de financements importants. La première convention avec un pays d'outre-mer associé (le Ruanda-Urundi) n'a d'ailleurs été signée que le 7 avril 1959 et c'est véritablement l'année 1959 qui peut être considérée comme la première année d'activité réelle du Fonds: 69 projets y furent approuvés pour un montant global de l'ordre de 50 millions de dollars.

Par la suite, le rythme d'approbation des projets d'investissements a été sensiblement accéléré et l'année 1960 apparaît, elle, comme une année d'activité normale. Au 30 juin 1960, en effet, le volume des projets engagés a déjà doublé par rapport à la fin de 1959: 105 projets ont été approuvés pour un montant global, en autorisations d'engagement, de près de 99 millions de dollars. On prévoit qu'à la fin de 1960, et depuis l'origine de ses interventions, le Fonds aura engagé plus de 160 millions de dollars pour 180 projets. La machine est maintenant sur les rails.

Il n'est pas sans intérêt de déterminer, en élargissant quelque peu ce débat, la place que représente cet effort de la Communauté Économique Européenne dans l'effort que déploie l'ensemble du monde libre pour l'aide financière à l'ensemble des pays en voie de développement.

Selon les calculs de M. Paul Hoffman, Président-Directeur du Fonds Spécial des Nations-Unies, l'aide financière du monde libre pour l'année 1957/58 s'est élevée à 2,4 milliards de dollars pour l'aide gouvernementale (dont 86% par la voie bilatérale et 14% par la voie multilatérale), auxquels il faut ajouter 1,6 milliard de dollars représentant les flux de capitaux privés à destination des pays en voie de développement. Globalement, l'aide financière du monde libre est donc de l'ordre de 4 milliards de dollars par an, chiffre qui ne semble pas avoir été sensiblement modifié en 1960.

Les principaux contributeurs sont l'O.N.U. et la B.I.R.D. (350 millions de dollars par an), les États-Unis (1.500), la Grande-Bretagne (600) et la France (1.200 millions de dollars, soit 6 milliards de nouveaux francs). Par rapport au revenu national, il est connu que c'est la France qui supporte la charge la plus élevée: les 1.200 millions de dollars qu'elle consacre annuellement à l'aide aux pays en voie de développement représentent plus de 2% du revenu national français.

Selon M. Hoffman, les 4 milliards de dollars annuels ainsi attribués par le monde libre ne dépassent pas encore 3,2 dollars *per capita* puisqu'ils se répartissent – très inégalement d'ailleurs – entre 1.250.000.000 d'hommes. Considérée par rapport à cette masse humaine, l'aide publique additionnelle apportée par le Fonds de Développement de la C.E.E. (en moyenne 116 millions de dollars par an) ne représenterait donc, théoriquement, qu'une infime augmentation de l'effort du monde libre: moins de 10 cents *per capita*.

En fait, cette aide additionnelle s'applique spécifiquement à 55 millions d'hommes vivant dans les pays d'outre-mer associés à la C.E.E. Elle représente donc pour eux un effort supplémentaire public de 2,1 dollars *per capita*, qui viennent s'ajouter aux efforts bilatéraux des six pays membres dont l'aide communautaire européenne est, par définition, complémentaire, ainsi qu'aux investissements de capitaux privés qui ne peuvent manquer de suivre les capitaux publics. Si l'on veut donner un exemple plus précis, il convient de comparer l'aide publique de la C.E.E. aux pays d'outre-mer entretenant avec la France des relations particulières (100 millions de dollars par an en moyenne), avec l'aide publique bilatérale que la France accorde à ces mêmes pays (200 millions de dollars par an en moyenne). La France n'ayant pas, bien au contraire, diminué son effort propre, on voit que l'intervention de la C.E.E. se traduit en définitive, pour les pays d'outre-mer associés de la zone franc, par un accroissement net de leurs investissements publics qui s'élève à 50%. Une telle contribution est considérable.

L'ASSISTANCE TECHNIQUE AUX PAYS EN VOIE DE DÉVELOPPEMENT

L'assistance, ou mieux la coopération technique puisque cette appellation tend aujourd'hui à se substituer à l'ancienne, aurait pu être examinée avant les investissements puisque les organisations internationales considèrent généralement la coopération technique comme une activité de „pré-investissement", qui prépare la voie à l'aide financière et conditionne le plus souvent son efficacité. En fait la coopération technique, recouvrant toutes les formes d'aide qui se traduisent par une communication du savoir, est aussi bien nécessaire avant que pendant les investissements.

Ce qu'il faut retenir, en effet, c'est l'énormité des besoins en cadres et techniciens qui se manifestent d'une façon criante dans le tiers monde, et surtout la marge qui existe encore entre les besoins non satisfaits et les moyens actuellement mis à la disposition des pays en voie de développement, quelle que soit l'importance de ces moyens.

La multiplicité des organismes – multilatéraux, régionaux, bilatéraux, privés – qui s'intéressent à la coopération technique est telle qu'une vue d'ensemble des résultats est aujourd'hui une entreprise délicate. La Commission de la C.E.E., qui désirait y voir clair avant de déterminer une politique d'ensemble à l'égard des pays en voie de développement, a fait établir une telle synthèse qui, à ma connaissance, n'avait jamais été faite auparavant.

Il ressort de cette étude que l'ordre de grandeur actuel des réalisations de coopération technique financées par des fonds d'origine publique, dans le monde entier, s'élève à 500 millions de dollars par an, soit un peu plus de 1/5 de l'aide publique totale à l'ensemble des pays sous-développés du monde. Cette aide technique, dont les six pays membres de la C.E.E. financent à eux seuls près de la moitié notamment par la voie bilatérale, représente une contribution déjà importante à la satisfaction des besoins en techniciens et en moyens de formation professionnelle: on peut estimer, en effet, que la totalisation des disponibilités actuelles dans le monde aboutit, chaque année, à mettre à la disposition des pays sous-développés 25.000 bourses pour des étudiants et stagiaires, et 52.000 experts, cadres et techniciens importés de l'extérieur.

Or, aussi impressionnants qu'ils paraissent, ces chiffres sont tragiquement insuffisants. M. Paul HOFFMAN évalue à 1 million de personnes le nombre des experts, cadres et techniciens qualifiés qui seraient selon lui nécessaires pour engager un développement d'envergure des 100 pays sous-développés qui groupent 1.250 millions d'hommes. Au regard de ces besoins, les quelques 25.000 boursiers et 52.000 experts de la coopération technique ne peuvent évidemment combler que les lacunes les plus criantes.

La Communauté Économique Européenne veut donc, là encore, prendre sa part du fardeau. Déjà, sur les ressources de son budget ou sur celles de son Fonds de Développement, elle déploie une certaine activité de coopération technique au bénéfice des pays d'outre-mer qui lui sont associés. Elle accueille dans ses services de jeunes fonctionnaires africains et malgaches qui, d'une part peuvent compléter leur formation professionnelle avec une ouverture sur les problèmes européens, et d'autre part ne manquent pas d'apporter aux services de Bruxelles leur expérience irremplaçable d'hommes africains. Elle finance des études de planification, des recherches portant sur l'évaluation des ressources naturelles (minières et agricoles, en particulier), des études démographiques, des institutions de formation technique ou professionnelle.

Surtout, elle est soucieuse de mieux utiliser un potentiel technique qui existe actuellement dans les six pays membres, sous la forme d'Instituts de Recherches tout à fait remarquables, spécialisés depuis longtemps dans les problèmes tropicaux et qui ne sont pas employés à plein. Une première mesure d'urgence vient d'être décidée: un programme spécial de 100 bourses, financées par le budget de la Commission, sera mis en application dès la prochaine rentrée scolaire, pour assurer la formation spécialisée, d'un niveau post-universitaire et dans les Instituts des six pays membres, de ressortissants des pays d'outre-mer associés.

La Commission est désireuse, enfin, d'élargir son action de coopération technique en dépassant le cadre des pays associés, afin d'apporter une contribution propre au vaste effort de coordination de l'aide aux pays en voie de développement auquel on assiste actuellement sur le plan occidental, avec la création du *Development Assistance Group* qui a déjà tenu deux réunions à Washington et à Bonn et qui en tiendra une troisième en septembre 1961, à Washington précisément sur un ordre du jour qui fait une large place à la coopération technique. La Commission de la C.E.E. a donc soumis à la discussion des experts nationaux des six pays membres un plan d'ensemble pour une action d'envergure dans ce domaine essentiel. Ce plan repose sur deux propositions concrètes:

a) Création d'un Institut Européen de Développement, géré paritairement par les pays donateurs et les pays bénéficiaires, qui se consacrerait, au profit de l'ensemble des pays en voie de développement, à une double tâche de coopération technique: d'une part formation professionnelle et recherche; d'autre part envoi sur le terrain, à la demande des pays sous-développés, d'équipes opérationnelles et polyvalentes d'experts de coopération technique pour des missions concrètes, notamment dans le domaine de l'évaluation des ressources naturelles et de la planification. Cet Institut, qui permettrait de mettre en oeuvre un effort additionnel et communautaire de coopération technique, travaillerait en étroite liaison avec une série d'instituts, centres de recherches et de formation qu'il agréerait comme ses correspondants dans les pays participants comme dans les pays en voie de développement eux-mêmes.

b) Organisation, également sur une base paritaire avec les pays bénéficiaires, d'un Plan Régional de Coopération Technique pour l'ensemble du continent africain. Ce Plan Régional, inspiré de la technique du Plan de Colombo pour l'Asie du Sud et du Sud-Est, s'efforcerait de réaliser, sans bureaucratie excessive, la coordination des politiques bilatérales de coopération. Il est important de remarquer que, dans la conception de la Commission, ce Plan serait largement ouvert, aussi bien du côté des bénéficiaires puisqu'il pourrait s'adresser aux pays africains non associés qui exprimeraient le désir d'y participer, que du côté des donateurs puisqu'il ferait appel à d'autres pays européens que les Six, exerçant des responsabilités en Afrique, et enfin aux États-Unis qui apportent déjà, en Asie, un appui substantiel au Plan de Colombo.

LE MAÎTRE-MOT: COOPÉRATION

La conception même du Plan dont je viens de définir les grandes lignes me permettra de conclure. On ne saurait trop insister, en effet, sur l'idée qui est à la base de nos initiatives à l'égard des pays en voie de développement. Cette idée est celle d'une gestion paritaire, sur un pied d'égalité entre pays contributeurs et pays bénéficiaires, parce qu'aujourd'hui le maître-mot d'une politique dans le tiers-monde, c'est la coopération.

Faute d'avoir compris une telle nécessité, faute d'avoir compris que les pays en voie de développement ont non seulement une dignité, mais encore une richesse d'expérience à apporter, que de plans techniquement impeccables, et d'ailleurs animés des meilleures intentions, ont rencontré soit l'indifférence, soit la suspicion, soit la franche hostilité, et en définitive l'échec pur et simple!

Il en est ainsi en particulier, des relations entre l'Europe et l'Afrique, qu'elles se situent dans le cadre de l'association à la Communauté des Six ou dans un cadre plus large. Car, comme l'écrivait Gabriel d'ARBOUSSIER, l'ancien Président du Grand Conseil de Dakar, dont les paroles doivent être méditées par les Européens comme par les Africains:

,,L'Europe a besoin aujourd'hui de trois éléments: l'espace, l'énergie et les matières premières. L'Afrique attend les hommes, les techniciens et les capitaux. C'est dans *un échange de dons* que se trouve l'intérêt mutuel des deux continents et l'approfondissement de leur destinée".

SUMMARY

There are many indications that, if the 19th century was the period of the "explosion" of European nationalism, the 20th century is signalised by the explosion of nationalism in the under-developed countries – in the East in the first half of the century, in Africa in the second. Note, for example, the title of M. Ernest MILCENT's little book, "Africa makes its bow ("*L'Afrique entre en scène*"); note, also, Mr. KHRUSHCHEV's proposed visit to Africa, notably to Guinea.

The daily growing list of countries where nationalism has "broken out" makes Africa, both for the East and for the West, *one of the stakes in world politics*. Where does Europe stand in this competitive situation, especially the Europe of the Six, as the third power in terms of world economic strength, but perhaps the first by reason of its culture, its civilisation and its "weight" in world history? Its traditional links with Africa – of culture, language, economic exchanges – are changing into a new "Community" form of *association of the overseas countries with the Common Market*. Here is surely the first *global* approach to problems of under-development, since it includes institutions as well as trade, investments and technical assistance.

It was out of the question that the Treaty of Rome of 1957, should have settled matters for all time in all these respects, for 25 associated overseas countries, grouping 55 million people, mostly in Africa. Fortunately its authors endowed the Treaty with the necessary flexibility to enable it to adapt itself to this lightning evolution.

POLITICAL EVOLUTION – THE ADAPTATION OF INSTITUTIONS

The first, and perhaps the most thorny, problem facing the European Economic Community was the fact that from the start the Treaty of Rome was indeed politically overtaken by events overseas. In French overseas territories, where only semi-autonomy was accorded by the "framework" law of 1956, membership of the Common Market seemed indeed to have been thrust on them from above, and this was the more incompatible with their natural passion for equality in that they were to achieve sovereignty on the international plane within two or three years. The manifold accusations of outmoded colonial status, of inadequate African recruitment to the executive of the Common Market, of almost complete lack of representation of the associated countries in the Community institutions, threatened to make this association a dead letter.

What, then, could be done to answer the questions put by these countries, with a touching confidence, as to how they could associate themselves with the European Community? Was the answer, now that they had achieved sovereignty on the international plane, to be that they were to rate as third countries, with no particular links with the Community, and thus be forced to embark on laborious diplomatic negotiations under Article 238 of the Treaty? Or was it to be that existing ties should continue, once they had been *freely* confirmed by the associated countries when they became sovereign States?

Both these theses were justifiable in legal terms, but the second offered the opportunity of more immediate results, by avoiding complicated negotiations in each separate case. In any case the Implementing Convention relating to the Association, although it may have "granted" association to overseas countries, did so, by wise foresight in view of the general ferment in Africa, for only five years, and so a general negotiation must in any case be undertaken in 1962.

The Council of Ministers of the European Economic Community proposed a solution for Togoland, when it became independent, which may serve as a precedent for other countries achieving sovereignty. On this view, such a country can choose freely to continue its association with the E.E.C. until the new convention comes into force on 1st January, 1963. As in the case of Togoland, provisional arrangements would be made for direct representation of the country concerned to the E.E.C. insofar as it does not wish to be represented by the French authorities. Almost all the countries attaining independence have expressed the wish to continue this association, and can, therefore, be represented in Brussels by a *chargé d'affaires* accredited to those organs of the E.E.C. which are of interest to them. This important decision demonstrates that the E.E.C., far from regarding its responsibilities as ceasing when one of the associated countries achieves independence, has the imagination to suggest solutions in line with political developments – a basic necessity in countries where politics are the primary consideration. Independence, which sometimes seems in African minds to be the open sesame to all problems, does not automatically settle economic problems, above all the expansion of trade.

THE EXPANSION OF TRADE

One of the fundamental aims of the Treaty of Rome is to develop trade between the European Member countries and the associated countries by the progressive abolition of all trade discrimination between the Six in overseas markets: by opening European markets to tropical products from associated countries which would be protected to a certain extent by the external common tariff, and by encouraging trade within Africa, which by the terms of the Treaty will benefit by the system of trade liberalisation between Europe and Africa. This measure has taken on more importance than its authors foresaw, as more and more attempts are made to re-group territories into real "economic areas", so much so that the term, "an African Common Market", is now common parlance.

In theory the associated overseas countries cannot lose by these arrangements: in regard to imports by the pressure exercised by broad competition on local prices; in regard to exports, since access to an expanding market of 160 million consumers will help to solve the basic problem of outlets for their raw materials.

How have these commercial provisions of the Treaty and of the Implementing Convention worked out in practice? In the first year of customs and quota disarmament big changes in the pattern of trade could not be expected, but statistics provide some interesting facts. An analysis of these statistics gives the lie to the accusation made by some international organisations that the E.E.C. was, through the preference granted to associated overseas countries, distorting trade to the detriment of non-associated third countries. The fact is that, in comparison with 1958, trade between the Members of the E.E.C. and non-associated African countries has shown a marked increase in 1959. (Increases of 10% with Abyssinia, 23% with Nigeria, *etc.*).

It might appear at first glance that this increase had been made at the expense of the associated African countries, whose trade with the E.E.C. has fallen by 184 million dollars, *i.e.* by 11 to 12%. This is, however, not the case, for these figures are expressed in the European Monetary Unit (of the same value as the U.S. dollar), and the basic cause of this reduction is the decline in trade between France and the overseas countries of the franc area. (A decline of 215 million dollars, or 20% – roughly the rate of the devaluation of the franc on 1st January, 1959).

From the opposite angle it is interesting to note that in connection with the marketing of products from the associated countries – one of their main preoccupations – imports to Germany increased by 17%, to Italy by 33%, to the Netherlands by 9%, and to the B.L.E.U. by 19%. Looked at from the French angle, it can be said that France's European partners have indeed "fulfilled their contract".

Even though trade integration as between Europe and Africa may seem to be getting along relatively unhampered, it is a question whether the Treaty is adequately equipped to encourage the development of trade.

Two remedies to counter the extreme economic fragility of overseas countries seem desirable: industrialisation, and the stabilisation of incomes of rural producers.

Industrialisation is an obvious help in softening the impact of price-fluctuations of raw materials, which are much more susceptible than semi-finished or finished products. The overseas countries, indeed, feared that the efforts towards industrialisation of the last ten years might be brought to nought, because the Treaty of Rome, an instrument of free trade, might revive the old cycle of raw materials being exchanged against finished products a kind of latter-day six-Power "Colonial Pact". It cannot be over-emphasised that the Rome Treaty, even though it is essentially an instrument of free trade, made one all-important exception, precisely aimed at protection of nascent overseas industries against what might probably be fatal competition. Indeed, Article 133 expressly permitted customs duties necessary to development and industrialisation, or of a fiscal nature to contribute to their budgets. The Treaty insists only that these customs duties shall apply to the imports of all six Member States.

The stabilisation of incomes of rural producers, a tenet whose effectiveness has long been disputed by economists, appears to be of fundamental importance. The eighteen chief basic products from tropical countries – about 90% of their production – over the last fifty years have experienced average annual fluctuations of 14% in prices, 19% in volume and 23% in export income. This represents a variation of 19% on the average for crop-prices – but the psychological effect is even graver. Producers feel helpless to control these ups and downs; if a depression sets in just as they hope to reap the benefits of improved methods urged on them, they lose confidence. 1958 affords a striking example. Prices for raw materials in these countries fell then by about 20%, making a loss to the poorer countries – mostly to the advantage of the rich – of 5,000 million dollars on sales amounting to about 25,000 million dollars. According to Mr. Paul HOFFMAN, Managing Director of the United Nations Special Fund, the total world aid, governmental and private, to the development countries did not exceed 4,000 million dollars for 1957–8. What good does such an investment do when it is cancelled out by instability of prices?

There are two possible approaches to this problem: at the world level, first, for markets, *e.g.* coffee, where sweeping reform is needed; and at the regional level for a number of other products, by giving a helping hand to established regulatory agencies, *e.g.* the British Marketing Boards, the Stabilisation Funds for the French Overseas Territories. The E.E.C. Commission has set its national experts to work on such plans, and it is in a particularly strong position since the E.E.C. is the leading world importer of raw materials (with about one-third of the trade in basic products). This is the first problem to be solved, for the second, fillip to trade investments cannot play its part until it is.

CAPITAL INVESTMENTS

The most material help that can be offered to the overseas countries to encourage their prosperity – the main aim of the association laid down in the Treaty of Rome, and the one most obvious to the recipient – is in the form of sums for investment contributed by the E.E.C. These are made available by the European Development Fund, which is managed by the Institutions of the Community and whose action is supplementary to that of Member States. For 1958–62 the Fund is endowed with more than 580 million dollars, and the progressive character of the volume of credits is noteworthy, as is the fact that the latest annual amount (for 1962) comes to about 234 million dollars. The main contributors are the Federal Republic of Germany and France (200 million dollars each) followed by Belgium and the Netherlands (70 millions), Italy (40 millions) and Luxembourg (just over 1 million).

Among the countries benefiting, the lion's share is obtained by those States linked with France, with 88% of the total available credits (511 million dollars in all). This takes into account France's considerable bilateral efforts, past and present, and the fact that she has opened to her partners the markets previously reserved to herself.

The Fund can act only on projects submitted by the Governments of the countries benefiting – for the golden rule of the E.E.C. is that they remain masters of the shaping of their development. Subject to this proviso, the Fund can back, exclusively by non-repayable grants, the financing of certain social institutions, *e.g.* hospitals, vocational training institutions, and of general economic investments involving productive and development projects. The Council of Ministers decides each year on the allocations to these sectors – at present 70% to the economic, and 30% to the social.

To realise these projects, tenders are invited from enterprises in the six Member countries and in the associated countries. Supervision on the spot is the responsibility of "technical controllers" appointed by the Commission.

To turn from procedure to practice, it must be admitted that the European Development Fund got off to a very slow start. In 1958 it was not possible to do more than run-in a machine made up of parts from six different countries, where different traditions and habits of mind prevail. The first year, therefore, saw no important financial operation. The first really active year was 1959, when 69 projects were approved for a total expenditure of some 50 million dollars. But 1960 looks like being what can be considered a normal year, with an accelerated rate of approved projects double that at the end of 1959 – 105 projects approved, involving nearly 99 million dollars. The totals will be, at the end of 1960, 180 projects and 160 million dollars.

How does this effort of the E.E.C. fit into the world picture? According to Mr. HOFFMAN's figures, financial aid from the free world to under-developed countries amounts to 4,000 million dollars a year (in 1957/8 divided between 2,400 millons of governmental aid and 1,600 millions private capital), a figure that is likely to remain constant in 1960. The chief contributors are the U.N. and I.B.R.D. (350 million dollars annually) the U.S.A. (1,500); Great Britain (600); France (1,200, *i.e.* 6,000 million new francs). France bears the heaviest burden, as its contribution represents more than 2% of the national revenue.

According to Mr. HOFFMAN, this expenditure amounts only to an allocation of 3.2 dollars a head, since it is shared out – very unequally – among 1,250,000,000 people. In relation to this mass of humanity, the effort of the E.E.C. adds only 10 cents a head to this effort. But E.E.C.'s contribution is directed to the overseas countries associated with it, and for them it adds 2.1 dollars a head to bilateral contributions of the six countries and to private investment. For example, the public aid given by the E.E.C. to countries associated with France amounts to an average of 100 million dollars annually. As France gives to those countries 200 million dollars yearly, E.E.C.'s contribution makes a notable increase of 50%.

TECHNICAL ASSISTANCE TO COUNTRIES IN COURSE OF DEVELOPMENT

Technical assistance or, to use the modern term, co-operation is both a necessary preliminary to investment and its effective use, and an accompaniment to it, in the form of communication of knowledge. One must remember the crying need in the uncommitted world for supervisory personnel and technicians, and, above all, the gap between the unsatisfied needs and the available means to meet them in under-developed countries. The Commission of the E.E.C. tackled a delicate problem, never before embarked on, the author thinks, when it drew up a comprehensive table of all the agencies – multilateral, regional, bilateral, private – engaged in technical co-operation, in order to get a clear picture before making its own plans. The Commission found that funds from public sources in the world as a whole amount to 500 million dollars yearly, or a little over one-fifth of total public aid to under-developed countries. Of this the E.E.C. countries alone contribute nearly half, mostly by bilateral agreement – an important contribution to the demand for technicians and occupational training media. Nevertheless, how tragically inadequate these figures are can be seen from Mr. HOFFMAN's estimates that 1 million experts, technicians and supervisors are needed in the 100 backward countries with a population of 1,250 million people.

To take its share of this burden, the E.E.C. has drawn on its own budget and on its Development Fund, to give technical co-operation to countries associated with it, in the form of recruitment of young African and Malagasy civil servants to its service, financing of planning studies, research particularly for the evaluation of mineral and agricultural natural resources, *etc.* The Commission also seeks to use more effectively the existing remarkable research institutes on tropical problems, and as a first step it has financed 100 scholarships for nationals of the overseas countries to take post-graduate specialist training in those institutes, during the next university year.

The Commission wishes also to contribute, outside the countries associated with the E.E.C., to the vast effort being made by the West in the "Development Assistance Group". This plan is based on two concrete proposals: *a*) the creation of a European Development Institute, managed on an equal footing by the giving and receiving countries, on the double task of technical co-operation involving occupational training and research, on the one hand, and the dispatch of field-teams of experts, especially for the evaluation of natural resources and planning, on the other. This Institute will co-operate closely with existing organs, which will act for it in the participating and development countries; *b*) the organisation of a Regional Technical Co-operation Plan for the African continent as a whole, modelled partly on the Colombo Plan, to co-ordinate bilateral co-operation policies. It should be noted that the Commission intends this scheme to be open to non-associated African countries – and also to European countries outside the Six, as well as to the United States.

THE KEY-WORD: CO-OPERATION

In conclusion the author emphasises the underlying principle of the Plan – the sharing of management on an equal footing between the countries contributing and those benefiting. Without this spirit of co-operation, which recognises the natural dignity no less than the rich experience of the countries in process of development, the best-laid schemes will come to nought. This is especially true of relations between Europe and Africa, whether under the aegis of the Six or in a larger setting. The words of Gabriel d'ARBOUSSIER, one-time President of the Grand Council of Dakar, should be meditated by both Europeans and Africans, when he wrote: "Europe today has need of three elements; space, energy and raw materials. Africa is waiting for men, technicians and capital. The mutual interest of the two continents and the working out of their destiny are thus to be found in an *exchange of gifts*".

FINLAND AND THE ECONOMIC INTEGRATION OF EUROPE

by

REINO ROSSI [1]

Prior to the First World War, the greater part of Finland's foreign trade was with Russia. The achievement of independence and severance from Russia at the end of the War also involved a radical change in the conditions of foreign trade. For a number of reasons, relations with the Soviet Union cooled appreciably. Nor did the economic conditions in the Soviet Union appear to offer a basis for maintenance of the former trade relations with Finland. Thus Finland's growing export industry, at that time represented principally by the timber and paper industry, was obliged to find new markets in the West. Furthermore the major share of imports came from Western sources of supply.

After the Second World War the picture again changed considerably. The loss of the War entailed delivery by Finland of war indemnities to the Soviet Union in the form of goods, mostly comprising products of the shipbuilding and engineering industries. In addition to the war indemnities, commercial trade with the Soviet Union also developed rapidly from the start; since completion of the indemnity deliveries, the Soviet Union has continued to purchase similar products from Finland. Apart from the Soviet Union, Finland has good and active trade relations with all the other countries of the Eastern *bloc*.

Although Finland's position in regard to commercial policy is thus at present in better accord with the policy of neutrality which the country has endeavoured to pursue during the whole period of independence, the greater part of her foreign trade is still carried on with the Western world. At its highest, the share of the Eastern *bloc* in foreign trade was in the region of about 30 per cent, and, as things are, it amounts to about one-fifth only. It is therefore natural that the efforts to attain economic integration in Western Europe have *ab initio* aroused great interest in Finland.

---

[1] The author is a member of the Board of Management of the Bank of Finland.

The creation of the European Economic Community, important though it is as a marketing area for articles of the Finnish forest industry, did not in itself signify a direct threat to Finnish export competition. This is, above all, due to the fact that the principal countries competing with Finland in the export of forest products are outside this area, so that Finland was not placed in an unfavourable position in relation to them. When the efforts to establish a wider free trade area failed towards the end of 1958, and the countries outside the Six began to plan their own free trade association, the situation from Finland's standpoint became more dangerous and of more immediate concern. So it was that in connection with the Saltsjöbaden negotiations in the summer 1959, the Finnish Government announced officially that Finland was interested in establishing collaboration with the European Free Trade Association in the making. The need for collaboration became even more acute when the other Scandinavian countries, with whom the establishment of a Nordic Customs Union had been under discussion for two or three years, now announced that, in view of the altered circumstances, they were no longer interested in this project. Thus the only possibility that existed for Finland to safeguard her commercial interests in Western Europe was that of endeavouring to join E.F.T.A. Finland's position of neutrality meant that adherence to the European Economic Community was as impossible for her as it was, for instance, for Sweden or Austria.

The actual negotiations with E.F.T.A. began in January 1960. In trying to establish the scope and the basic aims of the negotiations, the Finnish Government devoted its primary attention to three points. First, the establishment of relations in one form or another to E.F.T.A. must not lead to the creation of any supra-national body that would restrict Finland's right of self-determination. Secondly, Finland had to aim at an agreement such as would take sufficient heed of the special economic circumstances of the country and would ensure a sufficiently long period of adaptation, particularly for some branches of the home market industry. Thirdly, the agreement should be of a nature such as to enable Finland to fulfil and to honour all previously concluded commercial treaties.

The negotiations carried on with the representatives of the E.F.T.A. countries in the winter and spring of 1960 resulted at the end of May in a draft agreement, signed in Lisbon, which essentially fulfilled the first two basic requirements referred to. The E.F.T.A. countries showed very great understanding in regard to the difficulties of adaptation of the Finnish home market industry. This showed itself chiefly in the fact that for some sensitive branches of production, such as the textile, leathers and footwear industries, agreement was reached on a slower time-table for the first years than that of E.F.T.A. for reduction of the rates of duty; after the basic reduction of 20 per cent, the subsequent reduction of duty of similar dimensions would not be introduced until the beginning of 1965. It was stipulated, however, that all duties should be abolished by 1970.

Another concession made by the E.F.T.A. countries, and one of at least equal material importance, was that Finland was to be entitled to maintain the quantitative import restriction in regard to some articles of fundamental importance in her trade with the Soviet Union. In the main, these comprise solid and liquid fuels and artificial fertilizers. Other articles that play a very important part in trade with the Soviet Union, such as grain, fodder, cotton and sugar, are already, in accordance with the Stockholm Convention, among the agricultural products beyond the scope of the actual E.F.T.A. Agreement. Altogether, Finland buys these articles from the Soviet Union to the extent of about four-fifths of the total value of their imports, while their share of Finnish imports from the Soviet Union represents about two-thirds. These imports are principally paid for by such products of the engineering and shipbuilding industries as were included in the deliveries of the war indemnities, and which have since become an essential part of normal trade. If Finland had to transfer purchases of the above-mentioned goods to the West, she would obviously be unable to maintain her imports at the present level without becoming involved in grave difficulties in respect of her balance of payments.

As the third concession of importance to Finland's internal economic policy, it should be mentioned that Finland obtained the right of applying measures of control to some fish and marine fats in order to protect the production of her own live-stock economy.

Apart from these principal material concessions, and some other minor stipulations, Finland undertook by the terms of the agreement fully to observe the provisions of the Stockholm Convention. In this way, a material basis was found for an association between Finland and E.F.T.A. According to the Lisbon draft agreement, Finland would have become an associate Member of E.F.T.A., and would have had a seat and vote in the E.F.T.A. Council.

However, the Lisbon draft agreement, although it constituted an important step, did not in itself represent a settlement of the E.F.T.A. question for Finland. There still remained the third of the basic aims mentioned above, that of making the new agreement harmonise with Finland's earlier commercial responsibilities. This meant, above all, that Finland had to come to an understanding with the Soviet Union – satisfactory to the E.F.T.A. countries and, within a wider framework, all the G.A.T.T. countries – as regards the question of the most-favoured-nation clause contained in the trade pact concluded with the Soviet Union in 1947. It was evident that the settlement of this point would prove to be a difficult and delicate task, especially as many E.F.T.A. countries that had the same kind of most-favoured-nation clause in their trade agreements with the Soviet Union had not recognised its validity in regard to the free trade association.

Finland has never questioned the validity of the most-favoured-nation clause contained in her trade agreement with the Soviet Union. Nevertheless, she desired to confer with the Soviet Union concerning a new customs treaty on a new basis which, while guaranteeing the commercial benefits of the Soviet Union in the Finnish market, could be compatible with the E.F.T.A. and G.A.T.T. principles. Negotiations on this question were started in September 1960, and were concluded by an agreement on customs matters signed in Moscow on 24th November. The preamble to the agreement states that, in view of the countries being neighbours, of the treaty of friendship and mutual assistance concluded between them and of other commercial treaties, the parties to the agreements consider it right to conclude an agreement according to which the Soviet Union *de facto* obtains the same customs benefits as those which Finland may in one form or another in its association with E.F.T.A. be prepared to concede to these countries.

Quantitatively, these concessions in customs duty are of no great current significance in trade between Finland and the Soviet Union, as the share of the products subject to the E.F.T.A. customs scheme amounts to only about 6 per cent of the total trade. The Soviet Union, however, devoted more attention to the question of principle, as well as to the possibility that finished industrial goods might in course of time play a larger part in trade.

It was very understandable that the extension of this E.F.T.A. concession to embrace the Soviet Union evoked some anxiety and doubt among the E.F.T.A. countries. They consequently considered it appropriate to alter the institutional system of the Lisbon draft agreement. According to the agreement, eventually signed on 27th March, 1961, Finland forms a special free trade association, as an eighth country with the seven E.F.T.A. countries, and is thus not herself a Member of E.F.T.A. This new body, the E.F.T.A.-Finland Association, has its own Joint Council in which each is represented. The material stipulations of the Lisbon draft agreement are included unchanged in this final agreement. At the time of writing, the agreement has been submitted to the Parliaments of the different countries for ratification, and it is expected to come into force on 1st July, 1961. Finland will then effect a reduction of 30 per cent in the E.F.T.A. rates of duty on all commodities except those for which a system of delayed reduction of duty has been approved. The original reduction on these will be only 20 per cent.

From Finland's point of view, the result may be considered satisfactory. It should be regarded as the basic consideration for the future commercial policy, and internal economic expansion, that the competitive ability of Finnish products in the markets of Western Europe is not restricted by customs duty discrimination. Otherwise, Finland would not be able to diversify her exports and increase her production on a broader basis. Bearing in mind the present intermediate stage of the efforts to achieve commercial integration in Western Europe, the solution now reached can, obviously, not be regarded as final from Finland's standpoint. As regards Finland's basic aims to maintain a commercial policy directed impartially to West and East it is, of course, self-evident that the process of development will be followed closely and with interest. Finland hopes that in possibly altered circumstances she may find a solution which will satisfy her basic aims set for the commercial policy of the country.

SUMMARY

Jusqu'à la fin de la Première Guerre mondiale, quand la Finlande obtint son indépendance de la Russie, la plus grande partie de son commerce extérieur se faisait avec la Russie. Par la suite, ses rapports de plus en plus tendus avec la Russie l'ont poussée à chercher à l'Ouest des débouchés pour ses exportations en pleine croissance, notamment pour les produits des industries du bois et du papier; la plupart de ses importations venaient également de l'Ouest.

La Deuxième Guerre mondiale a entraîné un revirement radical. La Finlande a dû payer à l'Union soviétique des indemnités de guerre sous forme de marchandises, surtout de produits des industries de la construction maritime et des industries mécaniques. Les échanges commerciaux avec la Russie se développaient dès le début, et une fois terminées les livraisons suivant le programme des indemnités de guerre, l'U.R.S.S. a continué d'acheter des produits de ces mêmes catégories. La Finlande a su établir de bonnes relations commerciales avec tous les autres pays du bloc communiste. Mais, en dépit de sa politique de neutralité – neutralité qui fut son objectif constant depuis l'acquisition de son indépendance – la majorité de ses échanges se fait toujours avec les pays de l'Ouest. En effet ses échanges avec le bloc de l'Est ne constituent qu'un cinquième de la totalité de son commerce extérieur. Les efforts en vue de réaliser l'intégration économique en Europe occidentale ont donc toujours été pour elle d'un intérêt capital.

La création de la Communauté Économique Européenne, à vrai dire, ne portait pas préjudice à la Finlande en tant qu'exportateur, puisque ses principales exportations, produits de l'industrie forestière, concurrenciaient surtout celles des pays non membres de la Communauté. Mais à la suite de l'échec, en 1958, du projet de construction d'une zone de libre-échange plus vaste, et comme conséquence, de l'établissement par les pays non membres des Six de leur propre association européenne de libre-échange, la situation de la Finlande se trouva plus gravement atteinte. De sorte que le Gouvernement finlandais, dans le courant de l'été de 1959, proclama par la voie officielle qu'il serait dans son intérêt de collaborer étroitement à l'élaboration des plans en vue d'une Association Européenne de Libre-Échange. Cette nécessité apparut encore plus pressante lors de l'abandon par les autres pays scandinaves, en raison de l'évolution de la situation, de leur projet, déjà depuis longtemps en discussion, de former une union douanière nordique. Essayer de rallier l'A.E.L.E. restait pour la Finlande le seul moyen de sauvegarder ses intérêts commerciaux en Europe occidentale. Comme, par exemple, dans les cas de la Suède et de la Suisse, sa politique de neutralité l'empêchait, bien entendu, de devenir membre de la Communauté Économique Européenne.

Les pourparlers avec l'A.E.L.E. ont débuté en janvier 1960. Dans le but de bien définir et délimiter la portée et les buts des négociations, la Finlande donna la priorité à trois points spécifiques. En premier lieu, elle déclara que l'établissement de relations avec l'A.E.L.E., quelque forme qu'elles revêtissent, ne devrait pas entraîner la création d'un organisme supranational qui imposerait des restrictions à l'autonomie du pays. Deuxièmement, l'accord éventuel devrait tenir compte des circonstances économiques particulières à la Finlande et devrait lui accorder, par exemple, des délais assez longs pour que l'economie du pays pût s'adapter à de nouvelles exigences. Troisièmement, les termes de l'accord devraient lui permettre de continuer à remplir ses obligations dans les traités commerciaux existants.

Les négociations ont abouti à un projet d'accord, signé à Lisbonne, qui remplissait les deux premières conditions. Les pays de l'A.E.L.E. s'étaient montrés compréhensifs à l'égard des difficultés d'adaptation du marché intérieur de la Finlande. Ils ont accordé, par exemple, pour les secteurs sensibles, tels que les textiles, les cuirs et les chaussures, des délais pour la réduction des tarifs douaniers plus prolongés que ceux accordés entre eux par les pays de l'Association; il a été stipulé, cependant, que tous les droits de douane seraient supprimés avant le début de 1970. Par une autre concession de grande importance pour la Finlande – et grâce à laquelle son commerce avec l'Union soviétique était bel et bien sauvegardé – on lui permettait de maintenir des restrictions quantitatives d'importation pour certains produits tels que les carburants solides et liquides et les engrais artificiels. D'autres denrées intéressant les échanges avec l'U.R.S.S. (céréales, coton, fourrage, sucre, *etc.*) font partie des produits agricoles exclus d'office de l'accord A.E.L.E., sous les termes de la Convention de Stockholm. Ces importations se paient par les produits des industries mécaniques et de construction maritime mentionnés ci-dessus. Si la Finlande était obligée de s'adresser aux pays de l'Ouest pour l'achat de ces importations, elle ne serait pas en mesure d'en maintenir le niveau actuel sans être acculée à des embarras sérieux pour sa balance des paiements.

Une troisième concession majeure a permis à la Finlande de faire appliquer des mesures de contrôle en ce qui concerne quelques matières grasses d'origine marine afin de protéger son élevage de bétail.

A part ces concessions et un certain nombre de dispositions de moindre importance, la Finlande s'est engagée par les termes du projet d'accord à accepter intégralement la Convention de Stockholm, et une base matérielle aurait donc été fournie pour une association entre la Finlande et l'A.E.L.E. d'après laquelle elle deviendrait un membre associé nanti du droit de vote et d'un siège au Conseil de l'A.E.L.E.

Mais l'adhésion de la Finlande à l'A.E.L.E. ne s'est pas réglée de la sorte, car il restait toujours la troisième condition: celle d'assurer l'harmonisation du nouvel accord avec les engagements commerciaux existants. Il s'agissait avant tout de parachever un accord avec l'Union soviétique – susceptible de satisfaire ét les pays de l'A.E.L.E. ét ceux du G.A.T·T. – sur la clause de la nation la plus favorisée, laquelle avait été insérée dans le pacte sur les échanges signé avec l'Union soviétique en 1947. Une solution à ce problème s'avérait d'autant plus difficile que bien des pays de l'A.E.L.E. n'avaient pas reconnu la validité, quant à l'Association Européenne de Libre-Échange, d'une clause semblable dans leurs accords avec l'U.R.S.S.

Constatons que la Finlande n'avait jamais mis en doute la validité de cette clause de son accord avec l'U.R.S.S. Mais elle a tenu à conférer avec l'Union soviétique en vue d'un nouveau traité douanier. Et en effet les négociations, entameés en septembre 1960, ont abouti à un accord douanier signé à Moscou le 24 novembre 1960.

Cet Accord garantit à l'U.R.S.S. une situation privilégiée sur le marché finlandais en lui accordant *de facto* les mêmes avantages douaniers que ceux que pourrait accorder la Finlande, par suite de son association avec l'A.E.L.E., aux pays de celle-ci. Ces concessions de tarif douanier ont pour le moment peu d'importance quantitative, mais l'Union soviétique a tenu à insister sur le principe – et a prévu en plus l'extension du privilège aux marché des produits finis.

Les pays de l'A.E.L.E. ont été naturellement quelque peu préoccupés par l'extension de cette facilité à l'U.R.S.S. et ils ont décidé en conséquence de modifier le système institutionnel du projet d'accord de Lisbonne. Par un arrangement, signé le 27 mars 1961, une association spéciale de libre-échange a été instituée entre la Finlande, en tant que huitième pays, et les Sept de l'A.E.L.E. La Finlande n'est pas pour autant membre de l'A.E.L.E., et cette nouvelle association a son propre Conseil commun. D'autre part, les dispositions du projet d'accord de Lisbonne restent entières dans cet accord définitif.

Au moment où cet article est rédigé, l'accord définitif a été soumis pour ratification aux parlements des pays intéressés: on attend son entrée en vigueur dès le 1er juillet 1961. A partir de cette date la Finlande réduira ses droits de douane de 30% conformément à la réduction effectuée par les Sept sauf, bien entendu, pour les produits auxquels sont accordés des delais spéciaux, produits pour lesquels l'abaissement initial ne sera que de 20%.

Pour la Finlande, l'aboutissement des pourparlers est donc nettement satisfaisant. En variant les produits exportés, elle a assuré l'expansion de son commerce d'exportation ainsi que le développement de sa production pour le marché intérieur, et elle ne verra ses produits défavorisés, sur les marchés de l'Europe occidentale, par aucune discrimination douanière.

Le processus d'intégration économique de l'Europe n'a, du reste, atteint qu'un stade intérimaire, pour la Finlande comme pour les autres pays, et l'évolution future du commerce va retenir l'attention toute particulière de la Finlande, en tant que client impartial de l'Est et de l'Ouest. Elle espère, dans des circonstances qui auront peut-être quelque peu évolué, atteindre les buts essentiels de sa politique commerciale, complexe, mais dont la tendance reste la même.

EUROPE AND THE UNITED NATIONS

by

ULRICH SCHEUNER [1]

I. EUROPE'S SITUATION IN A CHANGING WORLD

Since the foundation of the League of Nations 40 years ago, there have been fundamental changes in the international community. In the year 1920, in spite of the effects of the First World War, the political centre of the world was to all appearances still in Europe. It would have appeared strange, indeed, to have the headquarters of the organisation outside the old Continent. The European States made up about half the original Members of the League, and, above all, the whole activity of the League was determined and influenced by the European legal tradition. The ideas of President WILSON had made a decisive contribution both as to the structure and the functions of the League, and, though indeed the United States remained aloof from Geneva, we should remember that the statesmen and diplomats of the Latin American States all along made valuable contributions to its work. And these men, after all, by their education, belonged to the selfsame tradition of international law, as it had developed in modern European history. The importance given to European legal systems was expressed in the fact that, out of eleven judges of the Permanent Court of Justice, seven always were members of the European nations.[2] It would be easy to amplify these observations by references to the composition of the Secretariat, the appointment of first an Englishman and, secondly, a Frenchman as Secretary-General, the choice of places of meeting and the difficulties of making the influence of the League equally effective outside Europe. That does not mean that League diplomacy ignored the problems of other continents, the League made its attempt to mediate in

---

[1] Dr. SCHEUNER is Professor of International Law and Public Law in the University of Bonn.

[2] *cf.* the first and the last list of the Judges of the Court. *Publications of the Court.* Series E. No. 1. Report 1922–25, p. 9 and No. 16 Report 1939–45, p. 24.

the Manchurian conflict and in the Chaco war between Bolivia and Paraguay and it committed itself to the attempt to restrain Italy through sanctions from her purpose in Ethiopia. But the fact that the United States was absent, to begin with, and later the departure of Japan, represented a definite obstacle to the efficiency of the League in other parts of the world.

To sum up, the League of Nations, in its various manifestations and in its activities, showed a certain concentration on the European tradition and the European scene.

Anyone who looks at the situation in this second half of the 20th century is confronted by a very different picture. After two world wars, the position of Europe has been decisively impaired. And the root cause is not so much the economic consequences of the War, though they were indeed a big factor in Europe's weakness at the time when the United Nations came into being. The fact is that the relative position of the European States in the world has substantially changed. For this there are three primary reasons. First of all, the deep-seated conflict of political systems in Europe itself, the rift between the democratic Governments of the West and the Communist *régimes* of East Europe. This divergence originated, it is true, in 1917, through the October Revolution in Russia, but the Soviet Union, nevertheless, became a Member of the League in 1933, and played a somewhat discreet rôle there. Another factor belonging to that earlier period was, of course, the repudiation by Germany and Italy of the traditional principles of European law and of their specific obligations in the Covenant, which not simply weakened the League, but also affected the position of Europe as a whole.

As things are today, Europe in the United Nations speaks with two quite different voices. One group is formed by the Communist *bloc* (nine States); the U.S.S.R., Albania, Bulgaria, Rumania, Hungary, Czechoslovakia, Poland and the two constituent States of the Soviet Union – the Bielo-Russian S.S.R. and the Ukrainian S.S.R. This group manifests a very definite unity of views and behaviour. The other eighteen European Members (and they include Turkey and Cyprus) present a much less unitary picture. But these countries are the ones which uphold the European tradition and of whom people think when they are talking of Europe in the more restricted sense. The contrast of the two political systems in Europe is so immense that there is simply no community of view or behaviour between them. Indeed, the non-Communist States of Europe appear, rather, to be more closely allied to the United States and other countries which have inherited the European tradition in other parts of the world.

The second reason for the metamorphosis is the passing of military leadership to the United States and the U.S.S.R. Western Europe, even though it includes two atomic Powers, is no longer independent in its policies. True it is involved in the conflict of the two world Powers, but it represents only one element in their struggle over the balance of power. Great Britain and France do still take part in the deliberations and decisions of those who determine international policy, but the real contest is that between the two major Powers enveloping Western Europe from East and West. And European States can have no hope of catching up with the technical superiority and the strategical primacy of these two world Powers.

The third major change consists in the disappearance of European supremacy in large parts of Asia and Africa. After the First World War the responsibilities of the European Powers over large areas of the world reached their peak, through the extension of European influence to the Near East. Since the end of World War Two the European position in those areas has precipitously declined. A growing number of independent States have come into being in Asia and Africa, and this has modified the political balance in the world fundamentally. Europe is now just another continent, and the importance of the States outside Europe – economic and political – is constantly increasing.

In a fast-changing world, however, Europe still has it within her power – even without the Soviet Union – to make an important contribution to man's destiny. Europe's economic potentialities, now completely restored and indeed extended, could, if united in a single whole, match those of either of the two world Powers. Europe still holds sway in terms of civilisation and science over the whole world. And indeed this influence o

Western civilisation is perhaps increasing. The peoples of Asia and Africa are the more open to it in the very process whereby they are intent on securing their independence. It is probable that we are only at the threshhold of a vast process of Westernisation of the world. Though the political supremacy of the European States is fast vanishing, there remains, then, the sway of Western civilisation and the Western way of life. This is true indeed, paradoxically, even where the Soviet Union has a predominant influence. For its advisers and engineers are by way of introducing the peoples of other continents to those tools of modern technical civilisation which have been made by the West and which are "in our days" spreading all over the world.

For the first time in history the world constitutes in political and economic respects a real unity in which changes in one part of the world have their repercussions in all countries, and in which political events in far distant lands have their influence on high policy. The United Nations came into being at a time when the emancipation of the Asian-African continent did not form anything like such a clear picture as it does today. When the United Nations was founded the horizon was occupied by the whole world, with the result that the United Nations, to a degree to which the League of Nations could never aspire to attain, has acquired the character of a universal community of States. Such a thing was not possible without substantial changes in its construction.

What all this means is that Europe within the United Nations structure could, from the outset, only play a much more modest rôle than it did in the League of Nations. The facts are there to show that, in terms of externals of membership and voting power, the European position has been substantially restricted. The real importance of Europe, however, cannot be measured in this way. It is something which goes beyond percentage figures and statistics. Europe is still one of the central points of international policy and – perhaps even more – a decisive field for economic exchanges and cultural interpenetration. The connections with other parts of the world – formerly partaking of the nature of hegemony – have been very much loosened.

But the ties have not been sundered completely, and in the world of today they are being revived in a different form through economic aid, through association and through cultural relations.

II. NUMBERS AND VOTES

In the discussions about the shape of things to come, from the point of view of international organisation, which took place during the War, Sir Winston CHURCHILL, already in 1943, developed the notion of a Council of Europe. Regional arrangements were at that time visualised for other areas too; *e.g.* Eastern-Asia or the Arab countries.[1]

When the plans for the United Nations took concrete form these ideas faded into the background. The American statesmen, concerned to contrive a universal organisation, and only ready to admit a kind of regional collaboration, such as obtained in the Organisation of American States, were not interested in regional *blocs*. They were afraid that the consequence would be isolationist tendencies, the formation of *blocs* within the framework of the United Nations and, consequently, dangers for the one-world conception which was in their minds. And the Soviet Union, similarly, resisted such plans, in which the Russians scented, as in the CHURCHILL-Danube Federation Plan, a direct opposition to their purpose of expansion. That is why regional arrangements obtained only a somewhat modest place in Articles 52–53 of the Charter. And the European organisations which developed not long after the War, from the Council of Europe to O.E.E.C., came into being outside the framework of the United Nations.

Both in the way in which the League of Nations was built up and in the construction of the United Nations, the European tradition of the "Concert of Europe" played a certain rôle. Thus in each of the two organisations a permanent seat in the Council was assigned to the Great Powers, and thereby the task was bestowed on them to take the most important decisions, to give leadership. This idea had the full support of the Soviet Union.

---

[1] G. L. GOODWIN – *Britain and the United Nations*. 1957.

At the Tripartite Conference Dinner given on February 4th, 1945, at the Livadia in Yalta, Marshal STALIN spoke out plainly in favour of this position of the three Great Powers, and against any idea of equality with smaller States.[1]

It was in accordance with this idea that we have the arrangements for the distribution of seats in the Security Council and the attribution of all important decisions to the Council. This constitutional framework of the international organisation has, of course, always worked out in Europe's favour. In the period between the two world wars the rôle of leading Powers was almost entirely confined to European States, since, as I have said, the United States were not present in Geneva and Japan resigned from the League on March 27th, 1933. As things are today, three out of the five permanent seats are held by European Powers. And this gives the European States substantial weight in regard to the ever-present problem of the representation of China, especially inasmuch as they, and not only Russia, have in practice made full use of the right of veto. In the original conception of the United Nations, the Assembly, with its equality of votes for all States, the "town meeting", as it were, of the international community, lagged far behind the Security Council in importance. But, as we know, as a result of the "Cold War", the decision-making power of the Council has been more and more impaired; after the campaign in Korea, under the influence of American diplomacy, the rôle of the General Assembly became much more important, and the equaliterian principle produced a shift of the balance of forces in the United Nations. Instead of a Directory of the principal Powers which should make all major decisions, in many cases the Assembly has taken charge; and in the Assembly the Great Powers have been compelled to try to win over the small countries to support their policies – or at least to collect together the necessary one-third of the votes required to prevent a Recommendation going through. The change in the relevant importance of the United Nations organs, that is to say, has at the same time enhanced the importance of the smaller States. Since the big wave of December 14th, 1955, whereby sixteen States came into the

[1] *Foreign Relations of the United States* – the Conferences of Malta and Yalta (Department of State Publication 6199), p. 589.

United Nations simultaneously, the increase of membership has worked exclusively to the benefit of Asian and African States.

It has often been remarked that the distribution of votes in the General Assembly – particularly since the importance of the Assembly has increased – is disproportionate to the real responsibility of the States. Consequently, the problem of weighted voting has been studied in various quarters, and practical proposals have indeed been put forward to bring voting more into line with the basic factors of power and importance (population, military and economic strength, financial contribution to the United Nations, *etc.*).[1] It is in fact not likely that reform proposals of this kind will be translated into reality. The present position for the ninety-nine Members shows the following breakdown: Asia 21; Africa 26; America 22; Australia 2; Europe (including Turkey) 28.

Nevertheless, any such geographical analysis does not give a true picture of the real grouping of States. The European votes are divided between the Communist *bloc* (nine votes); the Members of N.A.T.O. (twelve votes) and seven non-committed States (Finland, Sweden, Yugoslavia, Ireland, Iceland, Spain and Cyprus). Now, if you take as your basis the antagonism of the two political systems, this means that over and against the nine votes of the Communist alliance there is a group of 21 countries which can be rated as representatives of the Western tradition in the world, and which do not take up a markedly neutral position (Latin-America apart). The result is then that neither the United States nor the Soviet Union can muster the necessary voting power without attracting into their orbit the countries from Latin America, Asia or Africa. Western influence, actually, can now no longer be sure of obtaining the necessary one-third voting power in the General Assembly which is required to stop a Resolution being adopted.

A variety of conclusions can be drawn from this state of affairs. Among many people, and notably for public opinion in

---

[1] *cf.* C. L. Patijn. A Formula for Weighted Voting. *Symbolae Verzijl*, p. 255; F. D. Wilcox and C. M. Marcy *Proposals for Changes in the United Nations.* The Brookings Institution, 1955. p. 344.

the larger European countries, this lack of proportion between representation and real importance is regarded as a matter for criticism, and such people, in view of the inclination of many States to make their voting in the Assembly dependent on anti-colonial emotions, or topical considerations of policy, fear that this must represent a permanent handicap for the Western countries.[1]

Experience does not, in fact, confirm such forebodings – though it is perfectly true that the diplomacy of the two world Powers is bound increasingly to come into line with at least a section of the "free" State-groupings. It has been demonstrated that the new States of Asia and Africa, unmindful of the decisions of Bandung, have only rarely voted together.[2] The Congo crisis of 1960–61, for example, clearly shows that there is likely to be differential voting among such States for a long time to come.

On the other side it can be maintained that the fact that these Great Powers have to consider this problem of securing a majority in the General Assembly may well be a factor for peace. It does indeed compel the two world Powers to behave more responsibly. What is more, the situation in the Assembly in most recent times has patently been an inducement for the Great Powers, the Soviet Union included, to seek once again to secure decisions in the Security Council. In that Council, as a rule, there are five European countries out of the eleven members. And when you look at other United Nations bodies of less importance, the participation of European States (the Soviet Union included), is fairly substantial. Among eighteen members of the Economic and Social Council, Europe has eight, among the fifteen judges of the International Court of Justice, normally, there are six from Europe.[3]

A relatively larger proportion of persons from the European States will be found in the composition of the staff of the United Nations. The recruitment of that staff is undertaken – subject

[1] L. C. Green. The Double Standard of the United Nations – *Yearbook of World Affairs*, 1957. p. 104.

[2] See H. Kunzmann. Die Bandungstaaten in der Vollversammlung der Vereinten Nationen – *Europa-Archiv*, 1956. p. 761.

[3] These facts are cited in the work by G. L. Goodwin mentioned above.

to wide-ranging geographical considerations – more or less according to their amount of financial contribution to the United Nations: the United States contribute something like 33%, Western Europe something like 20% and the Soviet Union with its satellites also something like 20%. Though indeed there is not such a large proportion of European personnel *vis-à-vis* the others as was the case in the League of Nations staff,[1] it is a fact that the European countries are tolerably well represented. An attempt to lay down a minimum quota of officials for the Secretariat in relation to each of the Member States has not been successful.[2]

III. THE TRADITION OF INTERNATIONAL LAW

Leaving aside statistical data, a more important element is the considerable influences which stem from the European tradition in international law. The bases of modern international law are European. In this respect, admittedly, there are, at the present time, certain difficulties. The jurists of the Soviet Union no longer maintain the view that international law might constitute only, at best a slender bridge between the world of the *bourgeois* countries and the new Socialism. But they are inclined to raise objections against many elements of traditional international law – as they are to champion new principles from their particular point of view. Above all, they see future developments in quite a different light. Whereas our Western ideas are by way of whittling away the concept of sovereignty, and laying emphasis on the duties of States towards the community of nations, Soviet doctrine abides by the idea of absolute sovereignty. Then, the Communists give the idea of intervention a special interpretation such as to admit of support for all "wars of liberation" from outside. That their ideas about the protection of foreign property diverge from those of the Western countries need not be stressed here. The points of difference are all the

[1] In 1930, out of 109 senior posts in the League of Nations Secretariat (apart from offices outside Geneva and correspondents in other countries) 16 only were occupied by non-Europeans (in the Administrative Service the figures were 113 out of 322), *cf.* LN – *Official Journal*, 1930. p. 1248.

[2] The principles were laid down in Resolution 1097 (XI). The proposal by Bulgaria mentioned in the text, was negatived by the XIIth Assembly – 14th December, 1957.

more far-reaching in that numerous features of the Soviet conception – for instance the attitude towards the nationalisation of foreign investments – have attracted careful attention in newly-fledged States. In any discussion about principles it is one of the most important tasks of European legal science to defend the idea of the unity of international law, above all political differences, and to demonstrate to the new nations that these traditional principles do not simply serve the interests of certain States, but are the fruit of long experience and are likewise conducive to the welfare of all nations.[1]

In this connection the activities of the United Nations for human rights have no little importance. The European States have taken a lively share in the work of the United Nations Commission on Human Rights. The debates about human rights and, still more about their enforcement, show the very real difficulties confronting the international community, in view of the differences in social and political views and conditions in different parts of the world. Here, of course, the European States have set an example through their conclusion of the European Convention on Human Rights of 4th November, 1950; they have shown that an agreement about human rights limited to the most essential freedoms but with those freedoms secured by international institutions (Commission and Court) can represent a substantial advance towards the safeguarding of fundamental rights.

IV. REGIONALISM

The recognition that the cleavage of States in the post-war period would make it impossible to realise the security system prefigured in the United Nations Charter was a potent incentive for regional security undertakings in all parts of the world. Under the aegis of Article 51 of the Charter, which permits agreements for collective self-defence, a number of regional alliances for defence purposes were formed among the European States. So it was that in this part of the world the North Atlantic

---

[1] *Cf.* W. FRIEDMANN, *Some Impacts of Social Organisation on International Law;* D. SCHINDLER, Völkerrecht und Zivilisation. *Schweizer Jahrbuch für internationales Recht*, 1958; E. L. BINDSCHEDLER, *Jahrbuch für internationales Recht*, 1959.

Treaty Organisation (1949) and the Warsaw Pact group came to confront each other. Other European groupings came into being without any connection with the United Nations (Article 52), limited to the States of Western Europe. It may, perhaps, be observed in this connection that those concerned more particularly with economic and financial co-operation, specifically O.E.E.C. (now O.E.C.D.) and the European Payments Union (now European Monetary Agreement), are closely bound up with agencies of the United Nations. And among these bodies there is one European economic organisation which embraces the Western States and the countries of the Communist *bloc*, the Economic Commission for Europe. This United Nations body does a useful job with its statistical surveys and annual reports – but, because of the East-West cleavage, necessarily remains outside active participation in European economic developments.

The actual importance of European regionalism should indeed not be overrated. Precisely because of the close ties which have hitherto linked European States with areas outside Europe, the trend is continually for European States to assume international obligations that go beyond Europe. The most patent example of this, of course, is the Commonwealth, whose membership extends over the whole world and for whom political and economic ties – however loose they may be – are an inducement for nations of every continent to come together in a community of interests. It should be said here perhaps that in the United Nations the Commonwealth States as such do not form a coherent *bloc* – but they do manifest agreement on quite a number of questions. Then, too, the European Economic Community, through the association with it of African territories, reaches beyond the narrower European domain. European regionalism – though indeed it may have led to more tightly-knit inner groupings – in most of the forms in which it presents itself (*e.g.* the cleavage between the E.E.C. and E.F.T.A.) does not exclude the maintenance and development of Europe's links with areas outside Europe.

V. EUROPE AND EXTRA-EUROPEAN TERRITORIES

While purely European affairs have, then, come to occupy only a relatively minor place in the United Nations' activities, the relations of European States with territories outside the European continent have not seldom kept the United Nations' organs busy. The reason for this, of course, lies in the ever-increasing momentum of the movement away from the European States' colonial hegemony. The beginnings of this process of development go back to the time of the League of Nations and the Mandates System. Apart from the case of Iraq, which claimed and secured its independence in 1931, and Syria and Lebanon which were on the verge of getting theirs in 1939, the principle of independence from colonial rule (autonomy) had then no substantial effects. During the Second World War, however, there were sundry proclamations indicating the readiness of Great Britain, the Netherlands and France, to grant, after the War, a large measure of autonomy to their overseas possessions. Developments have in fact gone far beyond the original intentions. In 1947 Great Britain decided to concede the independence to India, Pakistan and Burma – and since then has allowed other countries in uninterrupted succession to gain full sovereignty (the latest example being Sierra Leone, in 1961). The United Nations, it may be said, by its intervention in the conflict between the Netherlands and Indonesia made a decisive contribution to the achievement by the latter of her independence. There was in fact in the Charter no clear lead given on this question of decolonialisation: the arrangements for the trusteeship system suggested that the architects of the United Nations, like most of the States concerned, were reckoning on a fairly long period of transition. And the result has been that the United Nations has tended to treat questions of emancipation from colonial rule case by case. The General Assembly has, in accordance with the usual practice, refused to accept the objection of a State on the ground of domestic jurisdiction (Article 2 para. 7) and has indeed continually assumed the prerogative of taking the matter on to the plane of a discussion of human rights, sometimes proceeding to recommendations. Among the European States it has been France, of course, which has been the principal accused – first on account of Tunis and Morocco (1953–54), subsequently over Algeria. These colonial problems have indeed had no little importance for a small group of European States and at times have caused something like a rift between these European elements and the United Nations as such.

This state of affairs came to light most clearly when the United Nations intervened in the Congo question in 1960. The three Resolutions of the Security Council of 14th July, 22nd July, and 9th August, 1960, and the Resolution adopted by the Emergency General Assembly on 20th September, 1960, called upon Belgium to withdraw her troops from the whole area of the Congo, though in the event the dispatch of a United Nations force into the Congo failed to achieve the desired object of restoring the unity of the territory and preventing the outbreak of local conflicts. This action by the United Nations, which, of course, had the support of numerous Asiatic and African States, produced some criticism from Belgium. Supported at first by the Soviet Union, it came to be challenged later on by the Russians. With the sole exception of France, which maintained her reservations, the attitude of the United Nations on this question obtained the approval of all the European States (outside the Communist *bloc*).

To the extent that European States are the administrators of trust territories, one may say that there has been, on the whole, good measure of co-operation with the Trustee Council. Many of these areas, either on account of economic weaknesses, or geographical remoteness (the South Sea territories) are, in fact, not yet ripe for independence, so that this relationship may yet endure for quite a time.

In its arrangements for technical assistance for under-developed countries, the United Nations, supported by experts from a number of European States, has been able to play an important rôle. But the U.N. as such has not succeeded, so far, in securing a central position in the matter of the granting of economic and financial aid.

VI. PUBLIC OPINION

If the number of the original Members of the United Nations which were European States was definitely restricted, this has been subsequently remedied, especially through the admission of the "package deal" group of States on 14th December, 1955. Even countries like Spain, against which in the early years after the War the United Nations, under Soviet leadership, had taken action, with the recommendation that diplomatic relations should remain severed, was then taken in as a Member. The same is true of former enemy States. Only Switzerland has remained aloof from the United Nations because, as a neutral State, she was not prepared to undertake any obligations to take part in any sanctions. The acceptance of Austria (1955) has indeed shown that the United Nations is ready to take account of the special situation of a State that is neutral – though in this particular instance no specific declaration was made.

Among the countries in Europe which do not belong to the United Nations is Germany. Germany's membership is excluded as is that of certain countries in Asia – Korea and Vietnam – by the fact of the country being partitioned, with the political problems which are involved. But the Federal Republic of Germany, and Switzerland too, does belong to United Nations Specialised Agencies. And she maintains diplomatic representation by an office in New York. Following the practice of the League of Nations the United Nations does not include among its Members tiny European States like Liechtenstein, Monaco, Andorra, San Marino or the Vatican City – though some of these belong to the Specialised Agencies.

When one tries to weigh up the relative importance of the various European States in the United Nations, one is struck at once by the fact that, much more than in the League of Nations, countries with neutralist tendencies or such as formerly took only a minor part in international politics, have come to take on much more importance in the United Nations. The fact is that, in the world of today, within the various policy conflicts such "neutral" States not seldom have a special responsibility. One thinks of the fact that the two first Secretaries-General came from "neutral" countries, Norway and Sweden. And the same phenomenon was illustrated when the United Nations Emergency Force was set up in 1956 (in connection with the Suez conflict) as also when the International Force was instituted for the Congo in 1960: in neither case were any contingents forthcoming from the Great Powers.

In the actual European disputes of the periods since 1945 the United Nations has played no more than a minor rôle, though no doubt its existence has brought about a certain *détente* in the struggle between the West and the Communist *bloc*. To effect a *rapprochement* between the two groups was not within the capacity of the organisation. Its attempt to offer mediation in the question of Berlin's status in 1951 came to nothing. The countries of the East invoked Article 53 of the Charter against any such intervention and refused to co-operate. Then the dispute about Cyprus came to an end through the Treaty of 19th February, 1959, without any mediation on the part of the United Nations. Equally fruitless was the effort to enforce the Human Rights provisions in the peace treaties with Bulgaria, Rumania and Hungary. Appeal was made to the International Court of Justice, but this only led to a recognition that, without the required co-operation of the countries concerned, there was no way of securing respect for such provisions. Whether the United Nations is likely to be called in again in the question of the Italian peace treaty in relation to the autonomy of the Alto Adige and the Trento cannot at present be forecast. One can say that in a number of minor disputes – for example, the shooting down of an American aircraft in 1953 – the United Nations has contrived to exercise a moderating influence.

Public opinion in Europe did not, it must be said, welcome the United Nations with the same substantial hopes as was the case when the League of Nations came into being. Consequently, there has not been so much disappointment. From the outset this international organisation has been soberly and realistically regarded. There was never any idea that it would collect together into its hands all the threads of international policy, and so it has been regarded as quite natural that to a very large extent major policy events should take place outside the organisation on East River. This is particularly the case for the closer ties formed in Europe itself, for security questions and for relations with Asiatic and African States. But, on the other hand, co-operation inside the United Nations is everywhere regarded as important. The delegations from the European countries in New York are always led by well-known political personalities, and meetings of the Council and of the General Assembly are treated with due solemnity. For a whole series of important questions, *e.g.* in the questions of disarmament, international finance, technical aid for the under-developed countries, the United Nations plays a preponderant part. Europe co-operates fully, too, in the Specialised Agencies, several of which have their headquarters in European cities.

To sum up, the responsibility of the United Nations for the safeguarding of peace, its efforts for disarmament, above all in regard to the atomic weapon, find a powerful echo in European opinion. If the United Nations appears today, when its seat is in the United States, a world organisation somewhat more remote from Europe, nevertheless, just as the rôle of the European States in the organisation is one far exceeding their numbers of voting power, so it has an assured place, one may say, in contemporary European politics. The United Nations constitutes an instrument of international diplomacy without which the visible conflicts in Europe would doubtless become more dangerous. That is why it is regarded in Europe as a guarantee of peace, nay, indeed, a necessity in the "one world" of our times.

RÉSUMÉ

1. LA POSITION DE L'EUROPE DANS UN MONDE EN ÉVOLUTION

Depuis la création de la Société des Nations, il y a 40 ans, des changements fondamentaux se sont produits dans la communauté internationale. En 1920, malgré les conséquences de la Première Guerre mondiale, le choix de l'Europe – qui, selon toute apparence, demeurait le centre politique du monde – s'imposait comme siège de la Société des Nations. Près de la moitié des membres originaires de la S.D.N. étaient des États européens et, surtout, les activités de l'Organisation étaient régies par la tradition juridique européenne. Bien que les États-Unis fussent demeurés à l'écart de l'institution de Genève, la structure et les attributions de celle-ci s'inspiraient des idées du Président WILSON et l'action utile des hommes d'État et des diplomates d'Amérique latine s'inscrivait – en raison de leur formation – dans la tradition même du droit international européen. L'importance de cette tradition était illustrée de diverses manières: par la composition de la Cour Permanente de Justice où, sur onze juges, sept ont toujours été des ressortissants d'États européens; par la composition du Secrétariat; par le choix du Secrétaire Général (dont le premier fut un Anglais et le deuxième un Français); par le choix des lieux de réunions et notamment par les difficultés rencontrées pour étendre l'influence de la S.D.N. hors d'Europe. En fait, la S.D.N. n'a pas ignoré les problèmes des autres continents, comme en témoignent ses efforts pour s'entremettre dans le conflit de la Mandchourie et dans la guerre du Chaco, et pour appliquer des sanctions contre l'Italie de déjouer ses projets éthiopiens. Mais, hors d'Europe, son action fût gêné par l'absence des États-Unis, et plus tard par le retrait du Japon.

Il semble donc que les activités de la Société des Nations se soient, dans une certaine mesure, centrées sur la tradition et sur la scène européennes.

Dans la seconde moitié du vingtième siècle, la situation est toute différente. Après deux guerres mondiales, l'Europe s'est trouvée affaiblie de façon décisive, non seulement sur le plan économique, mais plus encore par le fait que la position des États européens dans le monde a subi d'importantes modifications.

La première raison de ce changement a été le conflit des systèmes politiques dans l'Europe elle-même, conflit remontant, il est vrai, à la Révolution russe d'octobre 1917; l'Union soviétique devint cependant membre de la S.D.N. en 1933. La S.D.N. et l'Europe elle-même se trouvèrent également affaiblies par le fait que l'Allemagne et l'Italie rejetèrent les principes juridiques européens et répudièrent les obligations qui leur incombaient en vertu du Pacte.

Il en résulte qu'à l'heure actuelle, l'Europe s'exprime, aux Nations Unies, par deux voix différentes: d'une part celle des neuf États du bloc communiste qui manifestent une nette unité de vues et d'attitude; d'autre part celle des dix-huit autres pays européens (parmi lesquels la Turquie et Chypre) qui forment un groupe beaucoup moins homogène, mais qui maintiennent ce que l'on considère comme la véritable tradition européenne, bien qu'ils paraissent aujourd'hui plus étroitement alliés aux États-Unis et à d'autres pays plus éloignés, héritiers de cette tradition. Entre ces deux systèmes, il n'existe pas de communauté de vues ou d'attitude.

La deuxième raison de ce changement, c'est la suprématie militaire des États-Unis et de l'U.R.S.S. L'Europe occidentale ne peut jouer qu'un rôle mineur dans la lutte fondamentale entre les deux puissances qui l'encadrent à l'Est et à l'Ouest, et elle ne peut espérer les rattraper sur les plans technique et stratégique.

La troisième raison c'est que la suprématie européenne, qui avait atteint son apogée après la Première Guerre mondiale, a disparu dans une grande partie de l'Asie et de l'Afrique. Depuis la fin de la Deuxième Guerre mondiale, ce déclin s'est précipité. Un grand nombre d'États indépendants se sont créés dans ces régions et l'importance croissante prise, sur les plans économique et politique, par des États situés hors d'Europe, a fondamentalement modifié le tableau politique.

Toutefois, même sans l'Union soviétique, l'Europe pourrait jouer un rôle important dans le destin de l'humanité et, pourrait, si elle était unie, rivaliser sur le plan économique avec l'une ou l'autre des deux puissances mondiales. Du point de vue de la civilisation et de la science, son influence s'exerce encore dans le monde entier et même s'accroît au fur et à mesure que les pays d'Asie et d'Afrique qui luttent pour leur indépendance y deviennent plus accessibles. Aussi paradoxal que cela paraisse, il en est ainsi même dans les pays où prédomine l'influence soviétique, car la civilisation technique qui leur vient de la Russie tire son origine de l'Europe occidentale.

Pour la première fois dans l'histoire, le monde se trouve unifié par le fait que les événements d'ordre économique et politique qui se produisent dans une partie du monde se répercutent dans toute son étendue. Au moment où les Nations Unies ont été fondées, l'émancipation de l'Asie et de l'Afrique était loin d'offrir une image aussi claire qu'aujourd'hui. L'Organisation a revêtu – ce qui n'a jamais été le cas pour la S.D.N. –, le caractère d'une communauté universelle, de sorte que l'on pourrait forcément s'attendre à ce que des changements substantiels se produiraient dans sa structure. Ainsi le rôle de l'Europe devait, dès le début, être plus modeste qu'au temps de la S.D.N. tant en ce qui concerne le nombre de pays membres et que le nombre des voix. Mais son influence ne réside pas seulement dans ces éléments apparents. L'Europe demeure l'un des centres de la politique internationale et un terrain d'élection pour les échanges économiques et culturels. Ses liens avec le reste du monde se sont relâchés mais sans jamais se briser, et ils sont en train de renaître sous une forme différente par l'aide économique, par l'association et par les relations culturelles.

II. PAYS MEMBRES ET NOMBRE DE VOIX

Lors des discussions qui eurent lieu pendant la Guerre, à propos de la structure d'une organisation internationale, Sir Winston CHURCHILL suggéra, dès 1943, la création d'un Conseil de l'Europe et d'autres accords régionaux furent également envisagés, par exemple pour l'Asie de l'Est et les pays arabes. Ces projets passèrent à l'arrière plan lorsque les Nations Unies commencèrent à prendre corps en tant qu'organisation mondiale n'admettant, sous l'influence américaine, qu'une collaboration régionale mais non des blocs régionaux susceptibles de mettre en péril le conception américaine selon laquelle le monde est ,,un''.

Les Russes, eux aussi, combattirent ces plans régionaux – par exemple, le Plan de Fédération du Danube de CHURCHILL – qui gênaient leurs projets expansionnistes. Les accords régionaux n'occupèrent donc qu'une place réduite – à l'article 52 de la Charte – et les organisations européennes d'après-guerre (Conseil de l'Europe, O.E.C.E. *etc*...) furent créées en dehors des Nations Unies.

Mais, comme à la S.D.N., la notion de „Concert européen" joua un rôle. Dans les deux organisations, un siège permanent au Conseil fut attribué aux trois Grandes Puissances, leur confiant ainsi le *leadership*, principe qui fut pleinement admis par la Russie, à la Conférence de Yalta. Le système du Conseil de Sécurité joue en faveur de l'Europe (comme, par exemple, à propos de la Chine), étant donné que trois des cinq sièges permanents sont détenus par des États européens qui, tout comme l'Union soviétique, exercent leur droit de veto. Dans la conception originale, l'Assemblée, où chaque État membre dispose d'une voix, était appeleé à jouer un rôle moins important que celui du Conseil de Sécurité. Mais les pouvoirs de décision du Conseil ont été dans une large mesure, paralysés par la Guerre froide. Après la campagne de Corée, l'Assemblée Générale a, sous l'influence américaine, pris une importance accrue – et l'équilibre des forces s'est déplacé du fait que les grandes puissances ont dû se concilier les bonnes grâces des petits pays pour obtenir le tiers des voix nécessaire au rejet d'une recommandation. L'importance croissante des petits pays, surtout depuis que seize États sont devenus en même temps membres de l'Organisation, le 14 décember 1955, a joué exclusivement en faveur des pays d'Asie et d'Afrique.

Un système de voteponderé a été envisagé étant donné que la répartition des voix est manifestement hors de proportion avec l'importance des États membres (appréciée selon des critères tels que la population, la puissance militaire et économique, la contribution financière à l'O.N.U.), mais il est peu probable que ce projet de réforme soit mis en oeuvre.

Pour les 99 États membres, la répartition actuelle des voix est la suivante: Asie 21; Afrique 26; Amérique 22; Australie 2; Europe (y compris la Turquie) 28. Mais ces chiffres ne reflètent pas exactement la façon dont les pays sont groupés. Les voix européennes se répartissent entre le bloc communiste (9 voix), les membres de l'O.T.A.N. (12) et 7 États non-engagés (Finlande, Suède, Yougoslavie, Irlande, Islande, Espagne et Chypre). Si l'on prend comme base les deux systèmes politiques opposés, on trouve en face des 9 voix du bloc communiste, un groupe de 21 pays représentant la tradition occidentale et qui ne sont pas nettement neutralistes (sauf les pays de l'Amérique latine). Ainsi, ni les États Unis, ni l'Union soviétique ne peuvent réunir le nombre décisif de voix sans l'appui des pays d'Amérique latine, d'Asie ou d'Afrique; et les nations de tradition occidentale ne peuvent pas non plus être sûres de recueillir le tiers des voix nécessaire pour empêcher l'adoption d'une résolution.

Dans les grands pays européens, nombreux sont ceux qui craignent que cette disproportion entre la représentation des États et leur importance réelle ne constitue un *handicap* permanent pour les nations occidentales, étant donné que dans leur vote, nombre d'États se laissent guider par des sentiments anti-colonialistes ou par des considérations politiques d'actualité; mais en fait, ces craintes ne se trouvent pas confirmées. Les nouveaux États d'Asie et d'Afrique ont rarement voté dans le même sens, comme on a pu le constater à propos de la crise du Congo.

En revanche, on peut prétendre que la nécessité où se trouvent les grandes puissances de chercher à obtenir une majorité est un facteur de paix et les encourage à agir avec plus de discernement. En outre, toutes ces puissances, y compris l'Union soviétique, ont été de nouveau ces temps derniers, incitées à s'efforcer d'obtenir des décisions au sein du Conseil de Sécurité dont cinq des onze membres sont des pays européens. D'autres organes moins importants des Nations Unies comportent un nombre substantiel de pays européens parmi lesquels l'Union soviétique.

Le personnel des Nations Unies comprend un pourcentage relativement plus élevé d'agents européens. En principe, le recrutement s'effectue en tenant compte du montant des contributions financières (sous réserve de considérations d'ordre géographique), dont le pourcentage est approximativement le suivant: États-Unis 33%; Europe occidentale 20%; Union soviétique et ses satellites 20%.

III. LA TRADITION DU DROIT INTERNATIONAL

Abstraction faite des statistiques, un facteur plus important est l'influence de la tradition européenne dont est issu l'ensemble du droit international moderne. Il est vrai qu'il existe actuellement certaines difficultés dues au fait que les juristes soviétiques sont portés à critiquer de nombreux aspects de ce droit international traditionnel, ou à défendre des principes nouveaux conformes à leur intérêt. Surtout, ils envisagent l'évolution à venir sous un jour entièrement différent. Les idées occidentales tendent à amenuiser le concept de souveraineté et à mettre l'accent sur les devoirs des États à l'égard de la communauté des nations. La doctrine soviétique, elle, s'en tient au concept de souveraineté absolue. En outre, elle interprête la notion d'intervention de telle manière que toutes les „guerres de libération" puissent être appuyées du dehors. La position soviétique à l'égard de la protection des biens étrangers est connue, et la différence de conception est d'autant plus grosse de conséquences que les États ayant récemment accédé à l'indépendance étudient les méthodes soviétiques, par exemple en ce qui concerne la nationalisation des investissements étrangers. La science juridique européenne doit donc défendre le principe de l'unité du droit international par delà toutes les divergences d'ordre politique et convaincre les nouveaux États que ces principes traditionnels ne sont pas de simples expédients, mais sont le fruit d'une longue expérience et contribuent au bien-être de tous les peuples.

A cet égard, les travaux de la Commission des Droits de l'Homme des Nations Unies, auxquels les États européens ont pris une part active, revêtent une grande importance. Les discussions, notamment celles concernant la mise en application des droits de l'homme, font apparaître les difficultés découlant des différences de conceptions et de conditions sociales et politiques à travers le monde. Les États européens ont donné l'exemple en signant, le 4 novembre 1950, la Convention des Droits de l'Homme, qui ne vise que les droits fondamentaux mais qui garantit ces droits par le moyen d'institutions internationales (Commission et Cour).

IV. RÉGIONALISME

Les alliances régionales furent encouragées dès le début, lorsqu'il apparut clairement que, dans le monde divisé de l'après-guerre, le système de sécurité préfiguré dans la Charte, ne pourrait être mis sur pied, et un certain nombre de ces alliances se constituèrent entre États européens, dans le cadre de l'article 52 de la Charte. C'est ainsi que l'Organisation du Traité de l'Atlantique Nord (1949) et le Pacte de Varsovie furent créés concurremment. Les États de l'Europe occidentale instituèrent d'autres organisations sans liens avec les Nations Unies. Celles qui s'occupent de la coopération économique et financière, notamment l'O.E.C.E. – aujourd'hui l'O.C.D.E. – travaillent en coopération étroite avec les organismes des Nations Unies. L'un de ces organismes, la Commission économique pour l'Europe, réunit les États occidentaux et les pays du bloc communiste.

L'importance du régionalisme européen ne doit pas être surestimée, car les liens étroits qui unissent l'Europe au reste du monde la poussent à assumer des obligations internationales, dépassant ses propres frontières. A cet égard, l'exemple le plus frappant est celui du Commonwealth. Mais il convient de noter que celui-ci ne forme pas un bloc cohérent aux Nations Unies, bien que les États qui le composent manifestent leur unité de vues sur de nombreux problèmes. La Communauté économique européenne à laquelle sont associés des territoires africains, dépasse, elle aussi, les frontières de l'Europe. Ainsi, le régionalisme européen n'exclut pas le maintien et le développement de liens avec des pays situés hors d'Europe.

V. L'EUROPE ET LES TERRITOIRES EXTRA-EUROPÉENS

Bien que les affaires purement européennes occupent une place relativement réduite dans les activités des Nations-Unies, l'évolution rapide de la décolonisation a posé à l'Organisation de nombreux problèmes. Le début de cette évolution remonte, il est vrai, à l'époque de la Société des Nations et du régime des Mandats. Le principe de l'autonomie n'avait alors reçu que de rares applications. (L'Irak est devenu indépendant en 1931; la Syrie et le Liban étaient sur le point de le devenir en 1939). Mais au cours de la Deuxième Guerre mondiale, la Grande-Bretagne, les Pays-Bas et la France annoncèrent leur intention d'accorder, après la fin des hostilités, une large autonomie à leurs possessions d'outre-mer. Ces intentions furent, en fait, dépassées par les événements. En 1947, la Grande-Bretagne accorda l'indépendance à l'Inde, au Pakistan et à la Birmanie, puis à une série d'autres territoires (le dernier en date étant la Sierra Leone, devenue indépendante en 1961). Les Nations Unies, par leur intervention dans le conflit entre les Pays-Bas et l'Indonésie, contribuèrent de façon décisive à l'accession de ce territoire à l'indépendance. La plupart des États intéressés ayant manifestement compté que le processus de la colonisation s'étendrait sur une assez longue période, la Charte ne contenait pas de directive précise en la matière, de sorte que les Nations Unies ont été amenées à s'occuper de chaque cas au fur et à mesure qu'il se présentait. L'Assemblée Générale, d'ailleurs, a refusé d'admettre l'objection d'un État, fondée sur le principe de la compétence nationale, et a fréquemment porté le débat sur le plan des droits de l'homme en ayant parfois recours à des recommandations. Parmi les États européens, c'est la France qui a été la principale accusée, d'abord à propos de la Tunisie et du Maroc (1953–54) puis de l'Algérie. L'importance que ces problèmes revêtent, pour un petit nombre de pays européens, a même failli parfois créer une scission entre eux et les Nations Unies.

A cet égard, l'exemple le plus frappant a été celui de la crise congolaise en 1960. Plusieurs résolutions ont invité la Belgique à retirer ses forces armées du Congo, et, finalement un contingent des Nations Unies a été envoyé dans le pays. Cette action des Nations Unies qui avait, bien entendu, recueilli l'appui de nombreux États d'Afrique et d'Asie fut cependant fortement critiquée par la Belgique. L'Union soviétique soutint d'abord la politique suivie, puis s'y opposa, mais à l'exception du bloc soviétique et de la France qui maintint ses réserves, les pays européens approuvèrent l'attitude des Nations Unies.

Les États européens ayant des territoires sous tutelle ont, dans l'ensemble, coopéré de façon satisfaisante avec le Conseil de Tutelle et ce régime devra peut-être subsister encore longtemps dans les régions économiquement peu développées ou lointaines.

Avec le concours d'experts de certains États européens, les Nations Unies ont fourni une importante aide technique aux pays sous-développés, mais l'Organisation n'est pas parvenue à centraliser en elle-même l'octroi de l'aide économique et financière.

VI. L'OPINION PUBLIQUE

Si, à l'origine, le nombre d'États européens, membres des Nations Unies, était nettement limité, la position de l'Europe au sein de l'organisation, s'est renforcée par la suite, notamment depuis l'admission „en bloc" d'un groupe d'États, le 14 décembre 1955. Même l'Espagne (avec laquelle les relations diplomatiques sont demeurées rompues après la Guerre, sur la recommandation des Nations Unies), d'anciens États ennemis, et des pays neutres tels que l'Autriche, ont obtenu leur admission.

L'Allemagne est l'un des États européens qui ne sont pas admis aux Nations Unies en raison des problèmes posés par le partage du territoire et cette considération s'applique également à la Corée et au Vietnam. Toutefois, l'Allemagne (et la Suisse) font partie des institutions spécialisées, de même que les très petits pays européens (tels que le Liechtenstein) qui ne peuvent être membres des Nations Unies.

Il convient de noter que, par comparaison avec l'influence qu'ils exerçaient à la S.D.N., les pays de tendance neutraliste ou ceux qui ne jouaient qu'un rôle mineur sur la scène internationale ont acquis une place beaucoup plus importante aux Nations Unies où ils assument assez souvent des responsabilités particulières. C'est ainsi que le premier Secrétaire Général était norvégien et que le Secrétaire Général actuel est suédois, et la Suède et la Norvège, pays „neutralistes", ont fourni des contingents aux forces des Nations Unies, mises sur pied lors de la crise de Suez, puis de celle du Congo, en 1960, alors que les grandes puissances n'en ont fourni aucun.

Dans les différends spécifiquement européens, les Nations Unies n'ont joué qu'un rôle mineur, bien qu'elles aient, par leur existence même, amené une certaine détente entre le bloc occidental et le bloc communiste. Les Nations Unies n'ont pas été en mesure d'opérer un rapprochement entre ces deux groupements (comme en témoigne l'échec de sa tentative de médiation à propos de Berlin en 1951); elles n'ont pas non plus contribué au règlement du conflict de Chypre, ni à assurer le respect des dispositions relatives aux droits de l'homme, contenues dans les Traîtés de paix avec la Bulgarie, la Roumanie et la Hongrie. La Cour internationale de Justice a dû se borner à reconnaître que la coopération des pays intéressés était nécessaire pour assurer le respect de ces droits.

Il est impossible de préciser si les Nations Unies seront de nouveau appelées à intervenir à proppos du problème de l'autonomie du Haut Adige et de Trente. On peut dire que dans un certain nombre de conflits d'ordre mineur, elles ont exercé une influence modératrice.

L'opinion publique a été d'autant moins déçue par les Nations Unies qu'elle n'avait pas placé dans cette Organisation d'aussi grands espoirs que dans la S.D.N. lors de sa création. Il a été admis, dès le début, que l'Organisation ne pourrait réunir entre ses mains tous les fils conducteurs de la politique internationale et que nombre d'initiatives devraient être prises en dehors d'elle; tel a été le cas notamment en Europe, dans le domaine de la défense et des relations avec les États d'Asie et d'Afrique – mais en revanche, l'importance de la coopération au sein des Nations Unies est reconnue partout.

Les délégations européennes sont conduites par d'éminentes personnalites, et les réunions du Conseil et de l'Assemblée revêtent le caractère de solennités. Dans maints domaines importants – désarmement, finance internationale, assistance technique aux pays sous-développés – les Nations Unies jouent un rôle prépondérant. L'Europe coopère pleinement aux travaux des institutions spécialisées dont plusieurs ont leur siège dans des villes européennes.

En résumé, les efforts des Nations Unies en ce qui concerne la sauvegarde de la paix, le désarmement et surtout le contrôle des armes atomiques, trouvent un puissant écho dans l'opinion européenne. L'Organisation peut paraître éloignée de l'Europe, mais le rôle des États européens dépasse de loin le nombre de voix dont ils disposent aux Nations Unies et celles-ci se sont acquis une place dans la politique contemporaine de l'Europe. Sans cette Organisation, les conflits qui divisent l'Europe pourraient bien devenir plus dangereux, et c'est pourquoi les pays européens voient en elle une garantie de paix, voire une nécessité dans le monde d'aujourd'hui qui est „un".

LE FONDS DE RÉÉTABLISSEMENT DU CONSEIL DE L'EUROPE

par

PIERRE SCHNEITER

La nécessité d'une aide mutuelle entre les peuples a été une des grandes leçons de la dernière Guerre.

L'Amérique a donné, par le Plan MARSHALL, le premier exemple d'une coopération compréhensive et secourable.

Avec le Fonds Monétaire, la Banque Mondiale, le Conseil Économique et Social, le Haut Commissariat pour les Réfugiés et de nombreux organismes spécialisés (F.A.O., Santé, *etc.*) les Nations Unies ont progressivement mis en place les grandes institutions d'assistance technique qui s'efforcent de promouvoir, à l'échelon planétaire et dans les domaines les plus variés, la solidarité des pays les plus riches avec les plus pauvres, de ceux qui ont atteint le plus haut degré d'évolution et d'expansion avec ceux qui sont encore en voie de développement.

Un semblable arsenal d'institutions devrait être unique pour assurer la coexistence pacifique entre toutes les nations du monde et aurait dû rendre inutile la création de nouveaux organismes à l'échelon régional.

Mais on sait, hélas, que des incidences politiques ont rompu l'unanimité de 1945 et amené quelques perturbations dans la réalisation du magnifique programme de la Charte des Nations Unies.

Un cas précis est celui des réfugiés.

En 1949, le recensement de ces victimes du conflit, qui avaient trouvé asile dans les pays de l'Europe occidentale, donnait le chiffre de 12 millions d'individus, dont plus de 9 millions d'Allemands expulsés ou réfugiés.

Cette pression démographique brutale s'exercant sur des pays en partie détruits et désorganisés, s'ajoutant pour certains au chômage et à l'accumulation d'un excédent naturel de popu-

[1] M. P. SCHNEITER est Représentant Spécial pour les réfugiés nationaux et les excédents de population, du Conseil de l'Europe.

lation que l'arrêt des courants migratoires n'avait pas permis de résorber, aurait dû justifier la prise en charge immédiate de ce grave et douloureux problème par les Nations Unies.

En fait, 2 millions environ d'étrangers seulement purent bénéficier de l'appui de l'Organisation Internationale pour les Réfugiés (O.I.R.) car toutes les tentatives se heurtèrent à la thèse de certains États membres de l'ON.U. selon laquelle la qualification de réfugié doit être limitée à „toute personne qui se trouve hors du pays dont elle a la nationalité ou, si elle n'a pas de nationalité, hors du pays où elle avait sa résidence habituelle".

Cette définition enlevait aux 9 millions d'Allemands la qualité de réfugiés parce qu'ils n'avaient pas accepté de vivre sous le régime politique imposé aux Provinces allemandes de l'Est, à la Pologne et à la Tchécoslovaquie.

Bien plus leur repatriement immédiat, prélude aux châtiments réservés aux traîtres, était réclamé comme constituant un „devoir international".

Ainsi s'établissait, pour des motifs purement politiques, une distinction fondamentale entre réfugiés internationaux relevant de la protection des Nations Unies et réfugiés nationaux abandonnés à leur sort.

Il appartenait au Conseil de l'Europe de reconnaître et de combler cette lacune et telles furent, en effet, les conclusions d'un Comité d'Experts réunis en 1951 et dont les travaux devaient aboutir en 1953 à suggérer au Comité des Ministres l'institution d'une délégation permanente des 15 Gouvernements pour toutes les questions de l'espèce, sous l'étiquette „Représentant Spécial pour les Réfugiés Nationaux et Excédents de Population".

Appelé, en décembre 1953, à l'honneur d'assumer cette mission, je considérais que si l'inhumaine sévérité de la définition de réfugié adoptée par les Nations Unies empêchait ainsi la grande organisation internationale de s'intéresser directement au sort de quelques 10 millions d'autres expulsés, évadés, déracinés et sans foyer – ce chiffre devait d'ailleurs s'accroître d'année en année démontrant la permanence du problème – il appartenait aux 15 pays Européens réunis dans le Conseil de l'Europe, d'assimiler leur sort à celui des excédents naturels de population et, par conséquent, de rechercher les moyens des 3 solutions possibles, savoir:

- fournir sur le territoire national un foyer et un emploi
- encourager les migrations entre États Européens en vue de tendre à un équilibre démographique plus rationnel
- faciliter l'émigration outre-mer dans la mesure où celle-ci s'avérait encore nécessaire.

Le programme soumis en mai et décembre 1954 au Comité des Ministres comportait une action concertée à mener dans les domaines politiques et financiers avec la définition suivante:

> „L'avenir de l'Europe dépend de la solution que les Européens donneront au problème démographique. Ils doivent avant tout s'efforcer d'atteindre un meilleur équilibre des populations en Europe et chercher d'un commun accord, avec les autres peuples, des débouchés hors d'Europe pour les excédents encore inabsorbés. Une fraternité européenne doit s'établir; les plus riches, les mieux nantis, doivent aider les plus pauvres".

Sur la base de ces principes il était proposé aux Gouvernements des pays membres d'accepter les engagements suivants:

I. *Dans le domaine politique*

a) Exploiter au maximum les possibilités d'absorption existant en Europe même pour l'excédent de population, en:

(*i*) encourageant par des efforts communs et par une coordination de toute l'aide internationale possible les mesures d'intégration sur place prises dans les pays affectés par le problème;

(*ii*) appliquant une politique d'immigration plus libérale, notamment par la conclusion d'accords spéciaux avec les pays surpeuplés portant sur l'installation sur leur sol des travailleurs, des agriculteurs et des artisans provenant de ces pays;

b) Élaborer par étapes une politique d'émigration européenne commune en passant par les stages suivants: information mutuelle, consultation régulière sur la conclusion d'accords bilatéraux avec les pays d'outre-mer, adoption d'un accord-type sur l'émigration, établissement des contingents d'émigration par pays surpeuplés européens;

c) Prendre des mesures en vue d'assurer la formation professionnelle des migrants européens qui ne peuvent pas en recevoir une dans leur pays de résidence;

d) Mener une action d'information publique en Europe et Outre-Mer pour rallier le concours de l'opinion publique aux mesures envisagées ci-dessus;

e) Charger un organe coordinateur européen d'une mission de coordination et d'impulsion politique en vue de mettre en oeuvre les engagements pris ci-dessus. Cet organe coordinateur devrait être appuyé par un Comité de hauts fonctionnaires spécialisés en la matière, auquel pourraient être représentés aussi bien les pays membres du Conseil de l'Europe que les européens membres du C.I.M.E. non membres du Conseil de l'Europe, ainsi que le Haut Commissaire des Nations Unies pour les Réfugiés et les organisations internationales intéressées.

II. *Dans le domaine financier*

a) Constituer un Fonds européen destiné à financer par des prêts remboursables l'installation des réfugiés nationaux et des excédents de population;

b) Contribuer, par des sommes remboursables, à ce Fonds dont la gestion serait confiée à un organisme bancaire international déjà existant;

c) Charger l'organe coordinateur européen d'affecter, sous le contrôle du Comité des hauts fonctionnaires ci-dessus mentionné, les sommes mises à la disposition de ce Fonds aux différents bénéficiaires.

Constamment soutenu par des Recommandations pressantes de l'Assemblée Consultative, toujours approuvé sur le plan politique et administratif, ce programme devait se heurter, en ce qui concerne l'action financière, à certaines réticences du Comité des Ministres

Si les 15 pays du Conseil de l'Europe restaient unanimes à reconnaître que le problème des réfugiés et des excédents de population intéressait leur nations respectives dans la mesure où elle est préjudiciable à la prospérité et à la stabilité de la communauté européenne toute entière, certains d'entre eux estimaient toutefois qu'à cet égard la responsabilité première des solutions à promouvoir pesait d'abord sur les Gouvernements des pays affectés.

D'autres pouvaient faire valablement état de leur situation financière intérieure et des efforts qu'ils s'étaient déjà imposés, soit pour résoudre sur le plan national les difficultés que la présence des réfugiés avait fait surgir, soit pour participer à l'effort entrepris sur le plan international par les Nations Unies.

Ce défaut d'unanimité dans l'aspect financier de l'action entreprise en faveur des réfugiés et des excédents de population retarda la création du Fonds jusqu'à la réunion du Comité des Ministres du 13 décembre 1955, où furent envisagées et admises la possibilité et l'application en la matière de la procédure d'un accord partiel.

A sa session suivante, le 16 avril 1956, le Comité des Ministres approuva par sa Résolution 9 les Statuts définitifs du Fonds, et 8 pays faisaient connaître leur adhésion immédiate, à savoir la Belgique, la France, la Grèce, la République Fédérale d'Allemagne, l'Islande, le Luxembourg, l'Italie et la Turquie.

Aux termes du Rapport qui a servi de base à sa création, le Fonds devait être alimenté par des contributions gouvernementales recouvrables destinées à l'attribution de prêts remboursables à long terme.

Au capital de départ fixé à 10 millions de dollars pour l'ensemble des 15 pays du Conseil de l'Europe, réduit à moins de 7 millions de dollars par l'adhésion, jusqu'à ce jour de 8 seulement d'entre eux, le Fonds ne pouvait avoir d'autres ambitions que de constituer un établissement-pilote, une sorte de banc d'essais pour d'ultérieures réalisations communes plus larges en faveur des excédents de population.

Cependant, il convenait malgré la modicité de ses moyens de lui conférer le caractère d'un Établissement de crédit constitué entre Gouvernements par une souscription en capital de fondation et de le soumettre au respect des usages de la technique bancaire classique.

En vérité par les fins qu'il poursuit, le Fonds n'est pas une banque commerciale ordinaire, ni une organisation de bienfaisance.

Son action s'ajoute aux efforts des Gouvernements nationaux

qui tentent de sortir les réfugiés et les excédents de population de leur état de non intégration économique.

Il est donc une organisation de large solidarité humaine sur base bancaire tendant à mobiliser le capital là où il est disponible afin de l'acheminer vers les lieux où il est encore insuffisant.

Ses Statuts, qui ont été approuvés par le Comité des Ministres par sa Résolution (56) 9 du 16 avril 1956, ne sont pas différents, dans les principes de tous ceux des organismes similaires publics ou privés.

Comme eux, ils comprennent:

- la définition des objectifs et la nature des opérations,
- les conditions d'adhésion, de retrait et de liquidation,
- les modalités d'administration, de direction et de contrôle (Comité de Direction, Conseil d'Administration, Gouverneur, Comité de Surveillance)

Toutefois, deux caractéristiques lui confèrent une physionomie particulière:

1. La situation *sui generis* qui „rattache le Fonds au Conseil de l'Europe et le soumet comme tel à sa haute autorité" (article 1er) bien qu'un Accord Additionnel aux Privilèges et Immunités du Conseil de l'Europe ait été conclu le 31 mars 1959 pour conférer au Fonds la pleine personnalité juridique et lui consentir certains privilèges et avantages fiscaux.

2. Les droits reconnus au Comité de Direction – qui constitue en fait l'assemblée générale des membres – d'interpréter ou de modifier en cas de besoin les Statuts sans toutefois changer les objectifs (articles IX et XV).

En acceptant par une Résolution particulière (56) 10, de renoncer à l'immunité de juridiction dans chaque cas où une action en justice serait intentée pour l'exécution d'un contrat, le Comité des Ministres a permis au Fonds de se prévaloir de tous les avantages, privilèges et immunités accordés au Conseil de l'Europe et de bénéficier de ses services et de son organisation matérielle.

Ces témoignages de confiance imposaient aux dirigeants du Fonds d'y répondre par une série de mesures strictes garantissant qu'aucun abus ne serait fait de ces facilités.

C'est à ce titre qu'au cours de ce premier exercice une réglementation précise a été établie par le Comité de Direction et le Conseil d'Administration, pour que la doctrine financière du Fonds et l'attribution des prêts soient entourées de toutes les garanties désirables et marquent sans équivoque la limite des risques encourus.

Cette réglementation fixe la procédure intérieure des organes du Fonds, celle de la transmission et de l'étude des projets qui doivent, sous peine de non-recevabilité, être présentés par l'intermédiaire des gouvernements membres au Secrétariat Général du Conseil de l'Europe, les conditions d'établissement et de signature des contrats de prêts, l'unité de compte dans laquelle ils sont consentis (dollars U.S.A.) et la définition préalable, dans un Règlement des prêts – inspiré de celui de la Banque Internationale – des droits et obligations contractuels et des emprunteurs.

Une difficulté s'est élevée, à cet égard, sur la rigueur de l'article VI des Statuts imposant aux gouvernements membres d'assortir les projets présentés par eux d'une „garantie" particulière.

S'agissait-il d'une garantie d'État, impliquant nécessairement une approbation parlementaire, pouvant aboutir, par suite, à une quasi-paralysie du système?

Le droit de modification et d'interprétation des Statuts a permis au Comité de Direction d'interpréter libéralement le texte en décidant que les prêts pouvaient être octroyés, lorsqu'ils étaient assortis de garanties matérielles jugées suffisantes par le Conseil d'Administration, mais que l'engagement gouvernemental devait subsister dans tous les cas quant à la couverture des risques de change et de transférabilité.

Diverses autres décisions ont fixé les priorités d'emploi des moyens du Fonds, limité sa structure administrative au strict minimum, établi le budget de gestion, les règles de comptabilité administrative, les conditions de recrutement de personnel *etc.*

Le capital, appelé par quarts successifs, a été définitivement versé à la fin de 1960.

Mais le problème fondamental demeurait celui des réalisations.

Comment, avec un capital de départ relativement minime, satisfaire aux demandes susceptibles d'être présentées autrement que par la recherche des techniques usuelles du refinancement ?

Sur les suggestions de la Banque des Règlements Internationaux qui a accepté de conseiller le Fonds sur le choix des procédures les plus efficaces pour remplir ses objectifs, les souscriptions des États membres, centralisées et converties en monnaies librement convertibles par cette grande institution financière, ont été employées à la constitution d'un portefeuille d'obligations des États membres, ou garanties par eux, afin de servir de couverture et de gage complémentaires aux opérations d'émission du Fonds.

Ainsi préparé à affronter le marché privé des capitaux, le Fonds a pu réussir dès son second exercice social une première émission pilote de 2 millions de dollars U.S. grâce au concours qu'il a trouvé auprès d'un Syndicat de Banquiers européens conduit par une importante Banque de Bruxelles.

Le succès de cette première tentative qui devait être suivi, en avril 1959, d'une réussite plus importante encore puisque l'emprunt émis à cette date s'est élevé à 10 millions de dollars est dû au caractère original de la structure de son endettement.

Le Fonds a, en effet, constitué au profit des souscripteurs de ces obligations un gage collectif et non discriminatoire, géré par un *trustee* et représenté, partie par les effets ou *promissory-notes* remis par tous nos emprunteurs, partie par des titres de notre propre portefeuille.

La valeur nominale des effets ou *promissory-notes* étant égale au chiffre de l'émission, le Fonds a consenti, à titre de sûreté complémentaire, un gage collatéral en titres égal à 25% du montant des obligations.

Par cette procédure, le souscripteur de l'émission possède trois étages de garanties, à savoir:

- à titre primaire, celle du Fonds lui-même
- à titre secondaire, celle des débiteurs du Fonds et dans l'hypothèse d'un défaut de ces derniers, à concurrence d'un pourcentage très élevé du quart, les obligations d'État déposées en gage collatéral.

Le dessaisissement au profit d'un trustee indépendant des deux garanties secondaires ajoute encore un élément de sécurité supplémentaire.

Cette formule n'est pas inédite en elle-même. Mais l'accueil et la diversité des souscripteurs de nos obligations ont prouvé qu'elle est applicable à un échelon international et pour un ensemble de débiteurs d'origine et de situations variées.

Ainsi l'expérience démontre que la mobilisation à long terme de l'épargne peut être progressivement obtenue, pour la réalisation de programmes économiques et sociaux intéressant à la fois plusieurs pays, sans immobilisations initiales trop onéreuses pouvant impliquer la prédominance des uns et la dépendance des autres et perdre, de ce fait, son caractère de solidarité désintéressée.

De plus, l'estimation globale du gage permet d'harmoniser la rigueur des règles du crédit bancaire, en ce qui concerne notamment les taux d'intérêts, et de réaliser une coopération égalitaire, qui correspond à l'esprit d'union étroite entre nations européennes auquel le Statut du Conseil de l'Europe se réfère.

Un témoignage valable de l'appréciation obtenue par le système institué a été fourni par l'autorisation accordée aux Compagnies d'Assurances allemandes – importants souscripteurs de notre deuxième émission – d'admettre nos obligations en fonds de couverture.

On sait que, dans les différents pays, des dispositions strictes réglementent l'emploi des ressources des Compagnies d'Assurances ou Entreprises de Crédit différé autres que leurs ressources propres, c'est-à-dire, en fait, les primes versées par leur clientèle.

L'indépendance de jugement dont bénéficient et font preuve les Offices qui ont mission de surveiller et d'agréer les placements des Compagnies d'Assurances et les garanties dont ils s'entourent, permettent d'affirmer que, dans la pratique, l'admission d'un emprunt en fonds de couverture est un indice de la qualité de cet emprunt.

Ainsi, sans toucher à ses ressources propres autrement que pour constituer le gage collatéral de ses émissions, le Fonds s'est procuré 12 millions de dollars qui ont été affectés à des prêts en faveur des 4 pays reconnus prioritaires savoir: l'Allemagne, la Grèce, l'Italie et la Turquie.

A la fin de 1960, le Fonds avait accordé:

– A la République Fédérale d'Allemagne – 5 prêts en $ ou en DM pour un total équivalent à $3.190.000 essentiellement destinés à la construction de logements pour les réfugiés nationaux.

- Au Royaume de Grèce – 2 prêts en dollars d'un montant de $1.561.500 pour la plus grande partie destinés à contribuer à la mise en valeur de l'Epire.
- A la République Italienne – 3 prêts en dollars pour un montant de $5.195.000 destinés à la création d'importants centres de formation professionnelle.
- A la République Turque – 2 prêts d'un montant de $1.872.000 également destinés à la création de centres de formation professionnelle et réétablissement de réfugiés nationaux.
- En outre, 11 petits prêts d'un montant total de $280.000 ont été accordés à des Sociétés Immobilières, dites „Coopératives de Castors" destinés au logement familial d'ouvriers italiens travaillant en France.

Dans le cas de la Grèce et de la Turquie l'emprunteur est le Gouvernement lui-même. Dans le cas de l'Allemagne et de l'Italie les emprunteurs sont d'importants organismes para-administratifs (I.R.I., D.E.P.F.A., *etc.*).

Pour des objectifs similaires et pour les mêmes emprunteurs le Fonds vient de réaliser, au début de 1961, une troisième émission de 10 millions de dollars actuellement en cours de répartition entre les quatre pays intéressés, ce qui portera au cours de l'année le montant des prêts à une somme dépassant 22 millions de dollars.

Cette masse de prêts représente plus de trois fois le montant du capital souscrit par les États membres étant rappelé que ce capital, augmenté des réserves que le Fonds a pu constituer pendant ses quatre premiers exercices, soit au total environ $7.350.000, se trouve lui-même intégralement constitué par le portefeuille du Fonds en obligations émises par les États membres.

Telles sont les réalisations du Fonds de Réétablissement du Conseil de l'Europe à ce jour.

Certes elles n'ont satisfait qu'une très faible partie des besoins reconnus en faveur des réfugiés nationaux et des excédents de population.

La situation démographique de l'Europe et la permanence, 15 ans après la fin de la Guerre, d'un problème de réfugiés nationaux [1] nécessiteraient des moyens bien plus importants.

Mais il n'en demeure pas moins que les résultats obtenus par le Fonds de Rééstablissement constituent un témoignage concret de solidarité européenne dans le domaine capital de l'action sociale.

A cet égard la voie ouverte au Fonds et pour laquelle il souhaite vivement recueillir l'adhésion d'autres États n'est pas concurrente de celle des autres organismes financiers internationaux dont l'objectif est plus spécialement économique.

On peut même soutenir qu'elle est complémentaire dans la mesure où il ne suffit pas d'aider les pays en voie de développement ou ceux qui sont encore affectés par des problèmes de réfugiés ou d'excédents de population en construisant des usines ou en développant d'autres investissements productifs.

Pour servir ces investissements, utiliser ces usines il faut une main-d'oeuvre qualifiée par une formation professionnelle adéquate et il faut que ces ouvriers bénéficient d'une habitation décente pour eux-mêmes et leur famille.

C'est à ces objectifs précis et essentiellement humains que s'est attaché le Fonds de Rééstablissement du Conseil de l'Europe.

SUMMARY

The last War demonstrated the necessity for mutual aid among nations, and in the MARSHALL Plan America set an example of intelligent and fruitful co-operation. Alongside the Monetary Fund, the World Bank, the Economic and Social Council, the High Commissioner for Refugees and many other specialised organisations (Food, Health, *etc.*), the United Nations has continued to build up institutions of technical assistance, to associate, on a word-wide scale and in many domains, poor with rich countries, highly-developed with under-developed. To ensure world-wide peaceful co-existence such a battery of institutions should be unique, and they should have obviated the need for regional organisations.

But alas, the high hopes of 1945 and of the Charter have been thwarted in many fields, specifically in the case of refugees.

In 1949 a census of those war-victims who had sought refuge in Western Europe came to 12 million people, of whom 9 million were German expellees or refugees. The United Nations might well have been justified in taking on this grave problem of demographic pressure on countries

[1] Pendant les dimanche et lundi de Pâques 1961, 6.000 Allemands ont sollicité refuge en Allemagne occidentale.

suffering from war damage and disorganisation, and in certain cases from under-employment and the cumulative effect of a population denied emigration. But, in fact, only about 2 million could benefit under the terms of the International Refugee Organisation (I.R.O.), as these were interpreted by some Member States of the U.N. to apply only to those who were living outside the country of which they were nationals – or, if they were stateless, outside the country where they had their habitual residence. Thus the 9 million Germans who had rejected the political *régime* imposed on the East German provinces, Poland and Czechoslovakia were not covered by this definition of a refugee. On top of that, repatriation of these unfortunates was being demanded, as a prelude to their punishment as "traitors".

So, for purely political reasons, a distinction was made between *international* refugees, who came under the protection of the United Nations, and *national* refugees, abandoned to their fate.

The Council of Europe set about filling this gap, and a Committee of Experts, meeting from 1951 to 1953, recommended to the Committee of Ministers the creation of a permanent delegation of the 15 Governments in the person of a "Special Representative for National Refugees and Over-population". The author had the honour of being nominated to this post, and, in view of the inhuman definition which hampered the United Nations, he considered that the countries of the Council of Europe should link the destinies of the 10 million excluded from U.N. jurisdiction to the natural surplus of population, and attempt to implement three possible solutions: to settle these people in a home or an employment on their national territory; to encourage intra-European migration; to increase the volume of overseas migration where necessary. A programme submitted in May and December 1954 suggested concerted action in the political and financial fields in order to achieve a better distribution of population and to seek openings outside Europe. As the report said, "The concept of European brotherhood must prevail".

On the basis of these principles the following commitments were suggested to Member Governments:

I. *In the political field*

a) to exploit to the full Europe's own powers of absorption by:
- (*i*) encouraging the local settlement of surplus population within the countries affected by the problem;
- (*ii*) applying a more liberal immigration policy, especially by agreements with over-populated countries that could absorb workers, agricultural labourers and craftsmen;

b) to prepare a common European immigration policy by the following stages: mutual exchange of information, regular consultation on making bilateral agreements with overseas countries; adoption of a model agreement on emigration and establishment of emigration quotas by over-populated European countries;

c) to provide vocational training for those who cannot acquire it in the country of their residence;

d) to conduct a public information campaign in Europe and overseas to gain public support for the above measures;

e) to appoint a European co-ordinating body to achieve these ends by general and political co-ordination. This body should be assisted by a Committee of senior officials experienced in these problems, on which should be represented Council of Europe Member countries, European countries Members of I.C.E.M. though not of the Council, as well as the United Nations High Commissioner for Refugees and other international Organisations concerned.

II. *In the financial field*

a) to set up a European Fund for financing by means of loans the settlement of national refugees and surplus population;

b) to contribute reimbursable payments to the Fund, whose operation should be entrusted to an existing international banking organisation;

c) to instruct the European co-ordinating institution, under the supervision of the Committee mentioned above, to allocate among the various beneficiaries the sums available.

The programme had the support of Recommendations of the Consultative Assembly and was approved politically and administratively, but the Committee of Ministers was reluctant to take the necessary financial action. Although all the countries of the Council of Europe recognised that the situation concerned each and all of them insofar as it was prejudicial to the whole European community, some regarded the problem as primarily the responsibility of the Governments in the countries immediately effected. Others could justifiably plead their internal financial situation or the help they had already accorded. These differences delayed agreement on the creation of the Fund, until, eventually, in December 1955 the Committee of Ministers accepted that the way to proceed was by means of a partial agreement. Thus the Fund was set up in April 1956, and eight countries immediately sponsored it, *i.e.* Belgium, France, Germany, Greece, Iceland, Italy, Luxembourg and Turkey.

By the terms of the original report, Governments were to contribute recoverable sums to finance long-term reimbursable loans. The 10 million dollars at first decided upon were reduced to 7 millions by the adherence of only 8 out of the 15 Member countries, and this meant that the Fund could act only as a kind of testing-ground for future schemes. Nevertheless, it had to be properly constituted as an intergovernmental Credit Establishment and to conform to current banking practice. By reason of its aims it is more than a mere commercial bank or a charity organisation, and it attempts to supplement national efforts for refugees by directing the capital raised where it is needed.

Its statutory provisions, approved by the Committee of Ministers in April 1956, are on the same lines as those of similar private or public organisations and include a definition of aims, a description of the nature of its operations, conditions of membership, withdrawal and liquidation, as well as methods of administration, direction and control. Two characteristics give it, however, a special status:

1. the legal situation by which the Fund is attached (Article 1) to the Council of Europe and administered under its supreme authority, and
2. the rights conferred upon the Governing Body to interpret or amend the Articles, where necessary, without, however, making any change in their stated aims. (Articles IX and XV).

By agreeing to waive immunity from jurisdiction in cases arising out of the execution of contracts the Committee of Ministers has enabled the Fund to avail itself of all the privileges and services of the Council of Europe. The managers of the Fund had to guard against abuse of these facilities by laying down strict measures of guarantee for its financial policy, and the allocation of loans while clearly delimiting the risks incurred. These regulations determine the internal procedure of the organs of the Fund, the transmission and study of projects, and conditions governing establishment and signature of loan contracts, the accounting unit (U.S. dollars) and prior definition of borrowers' rights and obligations.

A difficulty arose over the interpretation of Article VI, which laid down that projects submitted by Member Governments should be accompanied by a special "guarantee". If this implied a State guarantee requiring Parliamentary approval, there was a risk of semi-paralysis of the system, but the right of the Governing Body to amend and interpret the Articles of Agreement made a more liberal interpretation possible. Thus material guarantees judged adequate by the Administrative Council were accepted, but for coverage of exchange and transferability risks Government commitments had to be maintained. Various other decisions covered priorities accorded to the Fund's resources, limitation of its administrative structure to the minimum, recruitment, *etc.*

The capital called up in successive quarters was definitely completed by the end of 1960.

The basic problem was *how* to achieve the objectives. How was it possible, with a relatively insignificant initial capital, to satisfy the likely demands, except by recourse to the usual methods of re-financing? The Bank for International Settlements, which has acted as a counsellor to the Fund, undertook to centralise Member States' subscriptions and convert them into convertible currencies, which would be invested and serve as cover or additional security for loans made by the Fund.

Thanks to the co-operation of a European banking syndicate, led by a big Brussels bank, the Fund was enabled to make a first model issue of 2 million U.S. dollars, and this success was followed in April 1959 by a loan issue of up to 10 million U.S. dollars. This was made possible by the unusual character of the system by which the Fund covered subscribers by a collective and non-discriminatory guarantee. This is re-inforced by a collateral guarantee in bonds valued at 25% of the sum of obligations.

Thus the guarantees given to the subscribers are three-fold: first, by the Fund itself, secondly, by the debtors to the Fund, and, if they default, by Government bonds deposited as a collateral guarantee. The structure is further reinforced by the placing of the security in the hands of an independent trustee. This is no new formula, but in practice it has proved applicable on an international scale and for a whole range of debtors of different kinds.

Experience has, therefore, shown that long-term loans can be raised to back economic and social programmes for several countries without involving some of them in initial immobilisation of capital, which might have endangered the basic principle of disinterested solidarity. The spirit of close and equal European co-operation, embodied in the Council of Europe, is also encouraged by the world-wide character of the guarantee system. The validity of the system is further demonstrated by the authorisation given to German insurance companies to recognise the Fund's bonds as cover.

Thus, without using its own resources, except for setting up the collateral guarantee for its issues, the Fund has acquired 12 million dollars, which have been loaned to the four countries with prior claims: Germany, Greece, Italy and Turkey. (*For details see pages 99-100*).

Early in 1961 the Fund made a third issue to those countries of 10 million dollars, so that for the whole year loans will come to more than 22 million dollars.

This amounts to more than three times the capital subscribed by Member States, which, increased by the reserves amassed by the Fund in its first four annual operations is entirely made up by the investments of the Fund in bonds issued by Member States.

The Fund's achievements have met only a small part of the needs of national refugees and over-population, which need much more expenditure, but they do give an example of European solidarity in the all-important social field. The Fund would welcome the support of more States; it is, after all, in no way in competition with organisations working more especially in the economic field. It is indeed complementary to their work, since their plans for building factories or other productive forms of investment to help under-developed countries or those with a refugee or over-population problem demand trained workers, and those workers need decent homes for themselves and their families.

These specific and essentially human objectives are the principles governing the Resettlement Fund of the Council of Europe.

THE INTERNATIONAL TRIBUNAL IN SAARLAND

by

E. F. W. Besly [1]

The International Tribunal, or, to give it just once its rather cumbersome but proper title, the Tribunal of International Composition in the Saar, was an institution of very limited jurisdiction and very limited duration. It was created by the Council of the Western European Union to cope in a judicial manner with some of the problems which arose in Saarland as a direct consequence of the Plebiscite of 23rd October, 1955, in which the voters had decided by a majority of 67.7 per cent to 32.3 per cent against the adoption of the European Statute and in favour of reincorporation in the Federal Republic of Germany.

The intention of this article is to give some account of the workings and experience of this International Tribunal – from the point of view of the judges to whom fell the very interesting task of exercising its functions. For this purpose it is unnecessary to delve very deeply into the fascinating studies either of its historical origin or of its constitutional standing. At the same time, however, the picture which it is hoped to present of the Tribunal in action would be very incomplete without at least a background on these two matters, and this consideration must be the excuse for summarising the events which led up to the decision to create the Tribunal which was made in November 1955 and the legislative and other measures which were taken to carry that decision into effect.

Historically it is necessary to look back to the end of hostilities in 1945 when Saarland was occupied by United States forces. For the next two years it was incorporated in the French Zone of Occupation but in 1947 it became an autonomous State, in economic union with France. The complete autonomy of Saarland during the period between 1947 and the Plebiscite of 1955 is seen from the fact that it had normal diplomatic relations with a number of foreign nations and established in Paris in particular a diplomatic mission, receiving a French Ambassador in Saar-

[1] The author was President of the Tribunal of International Composition in the Saar, set up by the Council of W.E.U. in November 1955.

brücken in return. In October 1954 an agreement on the future political status of the Saar was signed by France and the Federal Republic of Germany which came to be generally known as the European Statute. The essence of the regime which was to be established under this agreement was that the Saar was to have complete internal autonomy but that the economic and customs union with France was to be maintained and a European Commissioner was to act on behalf of the Saar in foreign relations. The agreement was not, however, to be put into force until it had been approved by a referendum, in which, generally speaking, all the inhabitants of the Saar were entitled to take part. The period between the publication of the text of the proposed Statute and the referendum, which took place actually on 23rd October, 1955, was, naturally, one of great political activity in the course of which feelings ran very high between those in favour of the proposed regime and those who were bitterly opposed to any suggestion of a severance of the Saar from the Fatherland of Germany.

It was to meet this situation, and also the even more dangerous situation which had to be contemplated when the result of the voting was known, that the Council of the Western European Union appointed as early as May 1955 a special Commission known as the Referendum Commission to proceed to Saarbrücken and remain there until after the Referendum had taken place. It was hoped that the presence of this Commission would guarantee the free exercise of voting rights and ensure the respect of the terms of the Resolution of the Council of 11th May, 1955, that no person was to suffer any prejudice by reason of the attitude which he adopted during the three months preceding the referendum and during the referendum itself. From all accounts the Commission carried out its difficult task with remarkable success, but when the referendum was completed on the 23rd October and the result of the voting was made known it became clear that there was still a very real danger of civil disturbances. Strikes were threatened and the adherents of the defeated parties, which had supported the proposed European Statute and the HOFFMANN Government, feared reprisals and victimisation at the hands of the parties of the *Heimatbund* which must inevitably come into power in the elections which would follow the resignation of their leader. Moreover, with the referendum duly completed the mandate of the Commission itself would come to an end and its restraining influence would cease.

Fortunately, all this was clear both to the Council of the Western European Union and to the Governments of France and of the Federal German Republic who were watching events closely, and it was decided to take immediate steps to prolong the life of the Referendum Commission and to entrust it with the task of seeing that no person should at any time suffer prejudice by reason of his previous political attitude, either before or during the recent elections, and of making recommendations to the Council as to the best means of carrying this principle into effect. The caretaker Government presided over by M. Heinrich WELSCH fully shared in the desire to prevent any further deterioration in the politital situation, and with the approval of Parliament he promised to collaborate. No time was lost. On the 28th November the Council of the Western European Union passed a Resolution deciding to set up in the Saar a Tribunal of International Composition, as an important contribution to the maintenance of democratic liberties there, and to recommend to the Saar Government to take the necessary measures, before the date fixed for the elections (18th December), to have the text of the instrument creating this Tribunal incorporated in the legislation of Saarland as approved by the Council. The text was duly prepared by the Council and submitted to the Government, which approved it and placed it before Parliament. The necessary legislation was passed without delay. The text of the Statute was published in the *Official Gazette* on 15th December, 1955.

Having had no part in the drafting of the Statute of the Tribunal, but having worked under it for three and a half years, I think I should be allowed to say that it seems to be a model document of its kind, short, clear and comprehensive. The jurisdiction of the Tribunal is set out in Article 1 and naturally corresponds with its *raison d'être*, namely to hear and decide all claims based on a prejudice suffered after the 23rd October, 1955, by any person resident in the Saar or having had the right to vote in the Referendum of 23rd October, 1955, or by any group of persons or any organisation other than Government organisations situated in the Saar, by reason of the political attitude adopted by them since the 8th May, 1945, or during the period of preparation for the Parliamentary elections of the 18th December, 1955, or during these elections. Within this very limited field the competence of the Tribunal was stated to be exclusive of any other Court. Although the occasions when there might have been a conflict on the ground of competence between the Tribunal and the normal Judicature were few, it was useful to have this position laid down from the outset. Very useful, too, was the provision that the Tribunal had the power to order any measure of reparation appropriate to the case, including annulment of measures taken or orders issued, although it left to them a rather heavy responsibility in deciding how far such drastic remedies might be appropriate in any case. But most helpful of all were the short but precious words "*Il juge en équité*" I will not anticipate at this stage what I shall have to say later about the importance of this provision in enabling the Tribunal to decide some of the more difficult cases which came before it, except to say that it was never lost sight of in our deliberations.

Having thus defined its jurisdiction the Statute went on to lay the foundation-stones of the Tribunal itself. It was to be instituted not later than the 1st January, 1956, for a period of three years and to be composed of five judges. The judges were to be chosen from the Member States of Western European Union other than France and Germany and not more than one from each. Each such State was to submit to the Council of the Western European Union three candidates from which the Council would choose one after consulting the Government of the Saar. When the Tribunal had thus been completed it was to elect its own President and Vice-President for one year, with right to re-election.

Having regard to the certainty that each of the five judges would necessarily be drawn from and accustomed to a quite different judicial system, the framers of the Statute most wisely went on to lay down in outline the basic rules which were to govern the Tribunal in the execution of its judicial functions. Thus it was provided that all claims were to be addressed to the President and must be made within three months from the date of the act or omission which gave rise to the prejudice. As for prejudices caused before the date of the installation of the Tribunal, the latest time for presenting the claim was to be three months after that date. The Rules of Internal Organisation and the Rules of Procedure were to be fixed by the Tribunal itself after consultation with the Saar Government with the approval of the Council of the Union. They were to follow as far as possible those generally adopted in the Saar. The parties were to be allowed to be represented by their lawyers at all stages. The procedure was to be that normally adopted in many European countries whereby one of the judges is appointed in each instance to make an individual study of the pleadings and the case generally and to prepare a Report to be communicated to the other judges and deposited at the Tribunal for the inspection of the parties before the trial of the case. In the course of these preliminary stages which might or might not include the examination of witnesses it was to be the duty of the reporting Judge to attempt a settlement between the parties. The tribunal was expressly given the right to decide the question of its own competence and no provision was made for any appeal from its decisions. The Government of the Saar was obliged to execute its judgments.

Having thus conceived in outline the scope, structure and powers of the Tribunal, the Council completed its work by providing for the personnel other, of course, than the judges. There was to be a Registrar, a subject of one of the Member States of the Western European Union other than France or Germany, who would be appointed by the Council after consultation with the Government of the Saar. The Registrar was to share with the judges a very generous measure of diplomatic privilege on Saar territory. As for the rest of the staff for the working of the Tribunal the President was to prepare a *cadre* and submit it to the Council for approval. When it was approved the President was to make the necessary appointments to each post and fix the salaries after consultation with the Saar Government. As was only to be expected all the expenses of the Tribunal were to be supported by the Saar Government which also undertook to give its entire support to the Tribunal in the execution of its mission.

How faithfully the Saar Government honoured this undertaking will I hope become apparent in the course of this article. In fact it is in great part to record this debt of gratitude that this article has been written. The Tribunal was naturally always conscious that its functions and indeed its very presence could not but be regarded by the large majority of the people and by the Government as an imposition, and a rather expensive imposition. Nevertheless, full collaboration was always forthcoming from all Departments of the Government when need arose, and the most pleasant relations were enjoyed with the members of the Civil Service and of the Bar with whom the Tribunal came in contact.

The actual date of the formation of the Tribunal must be regarded as the 22nd February, 1956 – the date on which the nomination of the five judicial members and the Registrar were approved by the Council. The persons nominated as judges were the following: – from Belgium Mr Raymond BAEYENS, assistant Auditor-General of the Council of State: from Italy Mr. Italo TELCHINI, member of the *Avvocature dello Stato* of Trente; from Luxembourg Dr. Charles HEURTZ, a high official who had held many Government posts both legal and diplomatic; from the Netherlands Mr J. H. MARINUS, a judge in the High Court of Justice at the Hague, and from the United Kingdom Mr. E. F. W. BESLY, at that time practising in London after being Legal Counsellor to the British Embassy in Cairo for ten years and Judge of the British Consular Court in Egypt. The post of Registrar was filled by the appointment of Mr. E. Van CUTSEM, a Belgian lawyer then holding an important post in the Belgian Military administration at Cologne. In accordance with the Statute the first act of the Tribunal was to elect its president and vice-president for one year, and the result was that the writer, whose age no doubt lent him a certain respect, was chosen to be President and Mr. MARINUS was chosen as Vice-President. These posts were open to re-election each year but the members most loyally maintained their original choices in office throughout the life of the Tribunal. The writer was always conscious of the honour thus done to him by his colleagues, more particularly because in some ways he was the least well equipped for the work. It is always a little difficult for a lawyer who has been brought up and who has practised under the Anglo-Saxon system of non-codified law and the judicial procedure of the English Courts to adapt himself completely to the Continental codes and procedure. In this case there was the additional handicap that, whereas the other four judges and the Registrar were all conversant with the German language, the writer was not. It is, of course, a usual experience in Courts of international composition that a great deal of work falls on the interpreter, because to insist on all the members being experts in several languages would be to restrict most unwisely the possibility of having the best jurists. In the case of the Tribunal the presence of a qualified interpreter at all the audiences did adequately surmount this difficulty, but the necessity of carrying on all the deliberations in and having all the documents translated into French, which was the highest common factor linguistically of the members, must have added considerably to the strain put on the other judges and on the Secretariat.

The first meeting of the members of the Tribunal was fixed for March 13th at Saarbrücken. After mutual identification, slightly reminiscent of the traditional meeting of the explorers STANLEY and LIVINGSTONE in Central Africa, the members set about creating the necessary machinery without delay. The first essential was a building where the Secretariat could work and receive the public and where the sittings of the Tribunal could be held. Examination of the building at 11 *Am Staden*, which had been used by the Referendum Commission, and which was a good-sized house in a quiet road bordering on the river, showed that two rooms on the ground floor could be turned into quite an adequate Court Room, which could be reached by the judges, if somewhat deviously through the kitchen and scullery, without having to pass through the audience, and that the remainder of the building would provide excellent accommodation for the Registrar and his staff and rooms for the judges to work in. The President approached Dr. NEY, then Prime Minister, to ask for these premises to be allocated to the Tribunal, and the request was readily granted. Having thus established a headquarters the Tribunal proceeded to consider the question of staff. This involved in practice a decision on how the work of the Tribunal was to be planned, for the purpose of performing its task in the most practical and economical manner. It was decided that there should be established a Secretariat which would always be open to applicants, and that for this purpose the Registrar must reside in Saarbrücken throughout the life of the Tribunal. As for the judges it was understood that their attendances at Saarbrücken were to be intermittent as the necessity for their presence arose. It seemed best to plan for four sessions to be held in the course of each year at approximately equal intervals, thus allowing the process of exchange of written pleadings to be carried on between the sessions until an adequate number of cases were ready for hearing. By fixing the date of the next sessions before the departure of the members of the Court in each case it was found possible, with the competent control of the Registrar, to keep up a regular flow of cases ready for hearing, and so ensure that the time of the judges was not wasted. The system was in fact very like that of the Courts of Assize in England. It did, of course, involve the setting up of a Secretariat under the control of a resident Registrar, which would be adequate to deal with the written pleadings of the parties and the quite voluminous correspondence in both French and German. As some of the complaints were expected to be directed against the administrative authorities, and some complainants might be afraid that by submitting a claim they would be endangering their position, it was considered necessary to ask for the appointment at a correspondingly high salary of a secretary for the Registrar who should be a first-class linguist, at least in French and German, and not a citizen of or resident in the Saar. This, too, had to be the subject of a special request by the President to Dr. NEY and was readily granted, although it is not without interest to add that during the last two years of the Tribunal the foreign secretary was replaced by a Saar resident – with no perceptible repercussions.

Thirdly, after providing for its premises and its Secretariat the Tribunal at its first meeting in March 1956 had to consider its Rules of Internal Organisation and Rules of Procedure, which under Article 7 of its Statute it was instructed to draft for the approval of the Council after reference to the Saar Government, bearing in mind the relevent legislation in the Saar. For a number of reasons it was clear that the Rules should, with certain modifications to meet the special requirements of the Court, be based as closely as possible on the Rules applied in France and Germany and, of course, the Saar. The English system, where different, was obviously not appropriate. For this reason it was decided to appoint a drafting committee consisting of the Vice-President and the Italian and Belgian judges, and to call on the Belgian judge to prepare the preliminary drafts for the Committee to consider and bring up to the Tribunal for discussion and decision at the next sessions, which were fixed for April. Considering that the writer had no share in the hard work of elaborating in accordance with the provisions of the Statute, the drafts of the two Instruments, which with very slight changes were adopted by the Tribunal, found acceptable to the Saar Government and approved by the Council, it is not out of place for me to claim that its work was well and quickly done.

The Rules of Internal Organisation (*Règlement Intérieur*) gave formal confirmation of its judicial hierarchy amongst the members of the Tribunal, and their relations with the Registrar, and prescribed their particular functions. It also provided that the Registry was to be established in the Tribunal building and was to be open on all working days, and that the Registrar was to reside in Saarbrücken, as had been decided. In these Rules it was also provided that there were to be at least four ordinary sessions of the Tribunal each year.

The Rules of Procedure were, of course, of the greatest importance for the smooth working of the Tribunal and as in the event they worked very satisfactorily they deserve a closer study. The first essential was to decide on the language to be used, and it was decided to make both German and French the official languages of the Tribunal. All claims, pleadings and other documents emanating from the parties could be in either of these languages, but all judgments orders and other acts of the Tribunal had to be in both. Further all pleadings, depositions or other documents which were submitted in French had to be translated into German, unless both the parties agreed to renounce this right.

The procedure laid down was intended to provide the simplest method by which, with the assistance of the Registrar and his Secretariat, the claimant could put his case clearly before the Tribunal as rapidly as possible, even if he decided not to avail himself of the right to be represented by a lawyer. In practice it was found that claimants usually did obtain legal assistance, and, naturally, the Tribunal was greatly assisted by the lawyers who appeared before them. It was, however, quite possible for claimants to prepare their own case for hearing by following out the Rules. The claim had to be made in writing and signed by the claimant or his legal representative. It had to include the name and address of the claimant and of the person against whom it was made, and to state the object of the claim, and to give a summary of the facts and considerations on which it was based. On receipt of the claim it was provided that the Registrar would peruse it and if, as was often the case where no legal representative was engaged, it did not conform to the minimum requirements of the Tribunal, he would advise the claimant how to complete or amend it within fourteen days. This done and the claim entered in the Register, the Registrar sent a copy to the other side, which then had four weeks in which to prepare its defence and submit it to the Registrar. In anticipation of the probability, which was fully justified, that many of the claims would be made against the Government or other public authorities, it was thought necessary to provide that in all such cases the official dossier of the claimant and documents relating to the claim should be submitted to the Tribunal. This provision was one of the few to which exception was at first taken by the Saar Government, but it was eventually accepted – with the very proper exception of documents the production of which before a Saarbrücken Court would be refused.

The Registrar sent to the claimant a copy of the Defence and a notice of the deposit at the Tribunal of the dossier and other documents, which he had a right to peruse there. After the receipt of his copy of the Defence the claimant had fourteen days in which to deliver a Reply by way of further pleadings if he so desired, and if he did so the Defendant had a similar period in which to deliver a Rejoinder. In order that no party should be put out of Court by failure to keep to these time limits in their pleadings the President was given the power to extend them in his discretion. This power was frequently exercised in suitable cases and was not abused.

As soon as a claim had been entered by the Registrar the President nominated one of the Judges to examine it and eventually to prepare the Report. In order to avoid unnecessary waste of time and money by all concerned it was provided that in cases in which on the face of the claim the Tribunal was manifestly incompetent this judge should suspend the ordinary procedure, and submit an immediate report to the Tribunal, which would deliver a judgment of incompetence at the next audience without being obliged to hear the parties. This provision, which proved most valuable in practice, was intended to meet such cases as where the claimant complained of injustices real or imaginary suffered under the HITLER regime, or after the War under the HOFFMANN administration, or generally under the mistaken impression that the Tribunal was there to right all wrongs. There were quite a number of such claims, occasionally absurd and always rather pathetic.

On the occasion of the first call by the President on the Prime Minister, Dr. NEY had urged him most strongly that the Tribunal should do all in its power to reach settlements by agreement rather than let the claims go through to judgment. Having regard to the whole purpose behind the Tribunal this was clearly of very great importance, and it was, therefore, provided in the Rules that as soon as the pleadings were completed the judge should summon the two parties to meet before him at the Tribunal with a view to reaching a conciliation. If this failed the judge completed his preparation of his report, availing himself of the right to call and examine witnesses on oath, including expert witnesses, and to correspond directly with any administrative or judicial authority, and to call for any document subject only to the exception noted above. When his report was completed he deposited it with the Registrar who notifed the parties, who were entitled to see it at the Registry.

The cause was now ready for trial and the President fixed the date and time for the hearing. The hearings were open to the public, with the right reserved for the Tribunal to order a hearing *in camera* if essential in the interest of public order or of the parties. It never was. The proceedings at the hearing were controlled by the President. Each party was entitled to address the Tribunal in person or through his legal representative in turn, and frequently at the invitation of the Court the claimant was allowed to reply to the arguments of the Defence. With the consent of the Tribunal too fresh evidence could be introduced at the hearing, and if still further evidence appeared to be available but not ready for production the President, by exercising his right to decide when the hearing was to be closed, could adjourn it until such evidence could be produced.

The decisions of the Tribunal were to be made by a majority of the judges present at the hearing, the President having the casting vote in the case of an equal division. It was provided that the judgment must give the reasons for the decision, and that it must be pronounced in German and French in open Court and signed by all the members of the Tribunal who had rendered it, and by the Registrar. Thus there was no possibility of a minority judgment, and the judgment was the judgment of the whole Tribunal. There was no appeal but provision was made for the rectification of errors in the text of the Judgment and for determination by the Tribunal itself of any misunderstanding arising from divergence in meaning between the German and French texts.

In addition to this normal and inevitably rather slow procedure it was considered necessary to provide a special and very rapid means by which urgent measures could be taken by the Tribunal to preserve the *status quo* pending the final decision on the claim where serious and irreparable prejudice might otherwise have been caused to the claimant. This took the form of an interlocutory application to the President setting out the circumstances justifying the urgent measure demanded. Notice was to be given to the other party which had the right to submit written observations, after which the President if satisfied that the application was well founded could order any measures necessary to maintain the *status quo* until the final decision of the claim.

The texts of the Rules of Court and Rules of Procedure were duly agreed with the Saar Government and approved by the Council and published in the *Official Gazette* of 27th June, 1956, the date which was also fixed as the date from which the three months was to run within which claims referring to prejudices suffered before the institution of the Tribunal were to be submitted. The work of the Tribunal then began. Claims began to pour in in a steady flow which continued over the next three years without ever becoming a spate. The first sessions of the Tribunal were held in July 1956, in the course of which the Prime Minister invited the members to a well attended reception to meet the leading members of the Government, the Parliament, and the Judiciary, at which he made a well-chosen speech of welcome in which he once more reminded them of his hope that they would use every effort to reach conciliation. Before the work of the Tribunal was terminated in September 1959 there were to be 13 more sessions at intervals of approximately three months. The total of final judgments pronounced were seventy-two. In twenty of these the claimant was completely successful. In three he was partly successful. In seventeen his claim was rejected under the simplified procedure referred to above which was applied in cases of manifest incompetence and in sixteen after a full hearing. In the remaining sixteen cases the claimant withdrew his claim after reaching a satisfactory settlement and this was recorded by the Tribunal. Copies of all judgments in addition to being delivered to all the parties were sent to Geneva to be preserved in the Library of the United Nations.

The claims themselves were very much what must have been expected. In almost every case they were made by supporters or adherents of the defeated HOFFMANN regime. In fact of the complaints within the competence of the Tribunal the only exception was a claim for wrongful dismissal by a former employee of the French Embassy whose dismissal was on the facts admitted amply justified – no matter what his political colour had been. The grounds of the complaints fell for the most part into one of the following three categories:

a) dismissal from Government employment or deprivation of legal rights to pension and other due emoluments;

b) unfair treatment of Government or municipal officials or persons employed by semi-public bodies such as State Broadcasting;

c) unfair and discrimatory treatment in municipal organisations.

Cases under category *a*) were perhaps the simplest to deal with. They mostly concerned persons who had been taking a conspicuous part in public life under the previous administration, and where it could be shown that they had been dismissed not strictly in accordance with the existing regulations it was difficult to refute the claim that there was a political motive. Thus amongst the first claims to be dealt with were those submitted by Mr. HOFFMANN himself, his Minister of the Interior Mr. HECTOR, and the Chief of Police. In the case of the first two the Tribunal awarded some appropriate adjustments of the scale of pensions and reimbursements which had been offered, and in the case of the third a sum by way of compensation for loss of office, not being satisfied that the allegations of misfeasance were well founded. These three cases, naturally, received a certain amount of publicity and some of the details of the claims came in for hostile criticism and ridicule, directed really more against the claimants than the Tribunal. But on the whole this class of case did not raise any serious difficulty. In the case of the two Ministers where a pecuniary adjustment was awarded by the Tribunal, this was what had been asked for. In the third case reinstatement was asked for but was refused by the Tribunal. Judging, as it was required to do, in equity the Tribunal decided from the beginning that it would not use the power of reinstatement in cases where for any reason it would be unrealistic and would not work, and to order the new Administration to reinstate as head of the Police Force an officer who under the old regime had rightly or wrongly been regarded by themselves as their enemy would not have been in the interest of public security, or of the claimant himself. The same principle was applied in other similar cases but in others again reinstatement or at least appointment to a post of comparable status was found to be possible and was ordered.

The most numerous class of claims came under category *b*) above. It was only to be expected that with the coming into office of a new Government, intensely devoted to their Fatherland of Germany and resentful no doubt of the regime which had existed in the Saar since the War, the position of prominent supporters of the defeated Government, particularly those in the public service, should have been felt to be insecure. Such persons were quick to notice any treatment which they received from their seniors in the official hierarchy, and to regard any change in their post or their status as a measure of retaliation against them personally. In a number of cases this was found to be the case, but the Tribunal had to be on its guard against generalisation in claims of this nature. It was not always easy to distinguish between a genuine case of unfair treatment and the mere termination of exceptional and sometimes even irregular advantages enjoyed under the late regime. One frequent cause of complaint was a posting, sometimes even in a slightly higher grade, away from the capital, whereby the complainant lost the exceptional allowance of about 8000 francs a month which went with a post in Saarbrücken. Naturally it was not reasonable to act on the proposition that all supporters of the past regime should serve permanently in the capital, and it was not always easy to be sure whether the posting complained of was discriminatory or merely in the interest of the service. More serious cases were those in which an official was transferred from one Ministry to another where he felt himself less at home or less likely to achieve a successful career. In all such cases the Tribunal had first to decide whether in strict law or in strict compliance with the Rules of the service the transfer was regular. If it was, it was difficult to hold that it was a prejudice due to his political attitude *etc.*, because it was not *prima facie* a prejudice at all. On the other hand, it was always possible to come to the conclusion that even within the ambit of the Rules there had been an exercise of discretionary power based on a motive which brought the matter into the competence of the Tribunal. It was in deciding questions of this nature that perhaps most of all the application of the rule of Equity was necessary. There were several cases where the Tribunal was satisfied that the claimant had been the subject of administrative measures which were prejudices within the meaning of the Statute, but which were nevertheless not such as to justify the Tribunal in annulling the measure. Sometimes, quite clearly, the post from which the claimant had been moved was one in which he could not possibly have been maintained under the new regime – just because of his previous political colour and associations. In some such cases it was decided to award a reasonable money compensation. In doing this the Tribunal considered that it was giving a fair interpretation to the Statute by which it was bound. The exact meaning of Equity in this context is not easy to define. The interpretation given by the Tribunal after much consideration was that where strictly legal considerations led to doubtful or unfair conclusions they should be amplified or even tempered by common sense.

A rather interesting problem was set to the Tribunal by the provisions of the Franco-German Treaty which came into force in January 1957. Under this instrument France formally accepted the application to the Saar of the fundamental law of the Federal German Republic, and it was agreed that no person should suffer any prejudice by reason of his previous attitude over the Saar question. Under Section *3*) of Annexe I of this Treaty it was provided that all permanent officials of Government or other public administrations, and certain other categories on limited engagements, should have a special right to retire with a pension or indemnity if they expressed the desire to do so for disinterested motives arising from their attitude to the Saar question. The intention was to compensate those who had reason to fear that they had so far compromised themselves by their previous political activities that they could not hope to obtain advancement under the new regime. In quite a number of cases this special right was exercised and the official obtained his pension or indemnity. There was, however, the obvious possibility of abuse by persons claiming to be in danger as adherants of the HOFFMANN party for the purpose of drawing these benefits, and transferring immediately to another employment, perhaps with better pay and prospects. Thus the Tribunal found itself in the rather anomalous position of being asked to regard the refusal of a public administration to recognise the claim of an official to have been a supporter of the policy of a European Statute as a prejudice caused to him because he had supported that policy. Here again the broad principles of Equity had to be called in and if it was found that the career of the official was really threatened for this reason competence was accepted and a remedy found.

The third category *c*) included some difficult and rather complicated cases, involving allegations of malpractice by persons who held important offices in municipal and local government offices. The fact that the duration of the mandates of persons elected to such office did not coincide with those of Parliament meant that supporters of the old regime frequently remained in office, and in many cases were not prepared to retire. This led to great tension in such administrations and in some cases to nearly complete suspension of their very important activities. In one case almost all the members of a Council refused to serve under the elected mayor, and in several very serious and voluminous accusations of malpractices were levied against the holders of municipal office. The Tribunal was faced with the necessity of examining all such charges sometimes over a long period to decide how far, if at all, they were well-founded, and whether in sum they amounted to conduct which would justify dismissal. Only if no adequate grounds could be found to justify the treatment complained of by the claimant could it be regarded as a prejudice within the competence of the Tribunal. These cases exemplified very well a point that was inherent in all cases, that the competence of the Tribunal could really only be decided when the Tribunal was in a position to decide the case. In the early days the Defendants were inclined to challenge the competence of the Tribunal as a preliminary issue, but experience showed that under the Statute the question of competence, otherwise than that dependant on the status of the parties or the date of the matter complained of, could not be usefully divorced from the substance of the claim.

Little publicity was given to the judgments of the Tribunal in the Saar Press. During the first few months there were a few rather hostile and ill-natured articles, in certain newspapers known to be of extremist tendencies, in which some of the details of the early decisions were shorn from their context and held up to ridicule, or the regretted ignorance of the President of the German language was suggested as an indication of his general incompetence; but these attacks were very occasional and were discontinued as the Tribunal began to make real headway with its work. After about a year the President was invited to give a Press conference but rather regretfully had to decline because of the possibility of misunderstandings. I did, however, offer to answer in writing any questions they cared to submit, and they accepted the offer and made perfectly fair use of the material I was able to give. One of the questions was the very pertinent one whether we thought the Tribunal was doing any good. At that stage I was only able to say that time alone would show, but that if we did succeed in doing so we would be extremely satisfied.

By the beginning of 1959 the flow of new cases was slowing down and the Tribunal had to consider how its work could properly be brought to an end. Having regard to the very considerable interval usually experienced between the filing of the claim and the final judgment, and to the great variation in the length of such intervals, it was clear that the only practical method was to fix a date after which no further claim would be accepted. By agreement with the Government of the Saar and the Council this date was fixed at the end of June 1959 and notice to this effect was published in the *Official Gazette*. This done it was a simple matter to fix the last sessions in September which would continue until all the outstanding cases had been dealt with.

When one looks back now at the work of the Tribunal it is more possible to take stock of its value and thus take up the earlier challenge of the journalists. I think the Tribunal succeeded in establishing confidence amongst potential claimants so they were not afraid to submit their complaints. This was a very essential condition for the work of the Tribunal. It was easy to forget, amid the bright and prosperous activity of the busy town, how recently for some of the inhabitants there had been a life of oppression and fear, and it came quite as a shock to the Tribunal in one of the hearings when an elderly and rather frail-looking claimant was asked how he had spent six years of his life which seemed to be missing from his *dossier*, to hear him reply that he had spent them in Dachau. In most cases, perhaps more particularly where Government Departments were concerned, the defendants adopted a reasonable attitude and either offered an acceptable settlement or, more often, accepted with a good grace to carry out the award of the Tribunal. It seems possible even that the judgment of the Tribunal may have enabled them in some cases to treat the claimant in a manner which they would have liked to do, but which public opinion would not otherwise have tolerated. Perhaps, too, it is not unreasonable to claim that the powers given to the Tribunal and the knowledge that they would be exercised in suitable cases may have had the effect of preventing injustices which might otherwise have occurred, more especially in the early days of the new administration when feeling ran high particularly in the Press. It is not for the Tribunal, perhaps least of all for the President, to claim that its mission was successful. I would like to think that it did succeed in righting the wrongs suffered by a few persons who would otherwise have been without redress, and that it contributed to some extent in helping the population of the Saar to adjust their political differences in the common interest of all. Be this as it may, when the judges dispersed for the last time to their various countries after the final session at the end of September 1959 they had added one small stone to the mosaic of European history.

RÉSUMÉ

Le Tribunal de composition internationale de la Sarre a été créé par le Conseil de l'Union de l'Europe Occidentale pour apporter une solution à quelques-uns des problèmes résultant du référendum du 23 octobre 1955; on sait que par ce référendum les votants s'étaient prononcés par 67.7% des voix contre 32,3% pour la réintégration de la Sarre dans la République Fédérale d'Allemagne et avaient ainsi rejeté le Statut dit européen.

Avant de décrire le fonctionnement de ce Tribunal et de dresser le bilan de son activité, l'auteur qui y a siégé en qualité de président, dressera un tableau rapide de son origine historique et de sa constitution.

En 1945, à la fin de la Guerre, la Sarre a été occupée par l'armée américaine, puis elle a été incorporée pendant deux ans dans la zone d'occupation française. En 1947, elle est devenue un État autonome, lié à la France par une union économique. A partir de cette date jusqu'en 1955, elle a entretenu ses propres relations diplomatiques. En octobre 1954, la France et la République Fédérale d'Allemagne ont signé le „Statut européen", aux termes duquel la Sarre devait conserver intégralement son autonomie interne et maintenir son union économique et douanière avec la France; un haut-commissaire européen devait la représenter dans le domaine des relations étrangères, mais il avait été stipulé que ce régime n'entrerait en vigueur qu'à la suite d'un référendum auquel participeraient tous les habitants de la Sarre.

L'intervalle qui s'est écoulé entre la publication de ce document et le référendum du 23 octobre 1955 a été marqué dans la Sarre par une grande tension politique et l'on se rendit compte que cette tension risquait de s'aggraver après la publication des résultats du référendum. Pour faire face à cette première difficulté, le Conseil de l'Union de l'Europe Occidentale nomma, en mai 1955, une Commission de Référendum, qui fut chargée de se rendre à Sarrebruck et d'y demeurer jusqu'après le référendum. Cette Commission réussit à atteindre le but qu'elle s'était fixé, c'est-à-dire à assurer le libre exercice des droits de vote, et à empêcher – comme le stipulait une résolution du Conseil – quiconque de subir un préjudice en raison de l'attitude qu'il avait adoptée pendant le trimestre ayant précédé le référendum, ou pendant le référendum lui-même.

Cependant, le Conseil de l'U.E.O. et les Gouvernements français et allemand s'avisèrent que la suppression de la Commission risquerait de conduire à une situation dangereuse au moment de la proclamation des résultats du référendum. Il y avait lieu, en effet, de craindre des désordres – grèves ou représailles possibles contre les partisans du Gouvernement HOFFMANN – lorsque les partis du *Heimatbund* prendraient le pouvoir, ce qui ne faisait pas de doute. C'est pourquoi le mandat de la Commission fut prolongé afin de lui permettre de présenter au Conseil des recommandations destinées à éviter des représailles, solution à laquelle se rallia le Gouvernement prévoyant de M. Heinrich WELSCH.

Le 28 novembre 1955, le Conseil de l'U.E.O. adopta une résolution relative à la création en Sarre d'un Tribunal de composition internationale chargé de contribuer à la sauvegarde des libertés démocratiques et de recommander au Gouvernement sarrois les mesures nécessaires à adopter, avant les élections du 18 décembre, pour incorporer le texte de cet instrument dans la législation sarroise. Ce projet fut mené à bonne fin et le texte du Statut du Tribunal fut publié dans la *Gazette officielle* du 15 décembre 1955.

L'auteur considère ce document, ou trois ans et demi durant il a puisé ses directives, comme un modèle dans son genre. L'article premier stipule que le Tribunal connaît, à l'exclusion de toute autre juridiction, de tous les cas où des personnes physiques résidant en Sarre ou y ayant le droit de vote, ou des organisations non-gouvernementales prétendent avoir subi des préjudices en raison d'attitudes politiques adoptées depuis le 8 mai 1945, ou pendant la période pré-électorale ou pendant les élections. Cette clause s'est révélée utile dans les quelques cas où un conflit de compétence aurait pu surgir entre ce Tribunal et les tribunaux sarrois. Il en a été de même pour la clause conférant au Tribunal la lourde responsabilité d'ordonner des réparations. Mais, ainsi qu'il sera démontré plus loin, la disposition la plus utile et celle que les juges ont eu constamment présente à l'esprit est la clause suivante: il [le Tribunal] juge „en équité".

Après avoir défini la compétence du Tribunal, le Statut stipule que le Tribunal doit etre institué au plus tard le 1er janvier 1956 pour une durée de trois ans et qu'il se compose de cinq juges. Ces juges sont désignés parmi les ressortissants des États membres de l'U.E.O. autres que la France et l'Allemagne; le Tribunal ne peut comprendre plus d'un ressortissant d'un même État membre et le Conseil choisit les juges, après avis du Gouvernement sarrois, parmi les troits candidats présentés par chaque État membre. Le Tribunal élit lui-même son Président et son Vice-Président pour une durée d'un an. Ceux-ci sont rééligibles.

Étant donné que les juges appartenaient à des États membres dont les systèmes judiciaires diffèrent profondément, les règles organiques du Tribunal ont été judicieusement définies. C'est ainsi que les requêtes devaient être adressées au Président et introduites dans un délai de trois mois à compter de la date où s'était produit le préjudice subi ou, lorsque celui-ci avait été causé avant l'institution du Tribunal, dans un délai de trois mois à compter de la date de cette institution. Le Règlement intérieur et le Règlement de procédure devaient tenir compte, dans la mesure du possible, des dispositions en vigueur en Sarre. Les parties pouvaient se faire représenter par leurs conseillers juridiques. La procédure adoptée était la procédure normalement en vigueur en Europe, selon laquelle un des juges prépare, pour chaque affaire, un rapport à l'intention des autres juges, et le dépose au Tribunal afin que les parties puissent le consulter; une procédure de conciliation est également prévue. La décision du Tribunal est sans appel et le Gouvernement sarrois est tenu de se rallier à ses jugements.

Le Conseil a complété ces dispositions par diverses mesures relatives aux autres membres de son personnel. Il a institué une charge de greffier, dont le titulaire jouit, sur le territoire de la Sarre, de privilèges diplomatiques aussi étendus que les juges; il a d'autre part institué un cadre dont la composition doit être soumise pour approbation au Président du Conseil. Celui-ci procède aux nominations au sein de ce cadre et fixe les traitements qui, de même que tous les autres frais afférents au fonctionnement du Tribunal, sont à la charge du Gouvernement sarrois.

Nous tenons, dans cet article, à rendre hommage au Gouvernement sarrois ainsi qu'à l'administration et au barreau qui ont collaboré de bonne grâce avec une institution que beaucoup considéraient comme une lourde charge.

Le Tribunal a été effectivement constitué le 22 février 1956, date à laquelle le Conseil a approuvé la nomination des cinq juges et du greffier. L'auteur du présent article en était le Président et M. J. H. MARINUS (Pays-Bas), le Vice-Président. Le Président et le Vice-Président ont été réélus chaque année, en dépit du manque de familiarité de l'auteur avec les méthodes judiciaires du Continent et de la langue allemande.

(Les noms des autres juges, etc. figurent à la page. 111).

Le Tribunal s'est réuni pour la première fois à Sarrebruck le 13 mars et il s'est installé dans les locaux situés au No. 11, *Am Staden*. Il fut décidé que le greffier résiderait à Sarrebruck afin que le public puisse toujours avoir accès au Secrétariat. Les juges devaient se rendre à Sarrebruck lorsque besoin en serait. Il était prévu quatre sessions annuelles dont la date devait chaque fois être fixée lors de la session précédente, de manière à assurer la mise en état régulière des causes grâce à l'échange, entre les sessions, de conclusions écrites sur les cas à soumettre aux juges. On avait également jugé nécessaire d'adjoindre au greffier un secrétaire très qualifié, bon linguiste; on s'attendait en effet à voir déposer contre les autorités administratives de nombreuses plaintes et il fallait rassurer les demandeurs quant aux conséquences qui pourraient en résulter sur leur situation. Le poste, dont la création fut approuvée sans difficulté par le Dr NEY, nouveau Premier Ministre, fut d'abord confié à un non-Sarrois, puis pendant les deux dernières années, à un Sarrois – sans que l'on ait constaté de différence sensible. Il fut décidé que les Règlements du Tribunal se fonderaient autant que possible, sur les règlements en vigueur en France, en Allemagne et bien entendu en Sarre; le Comité de Rédaction chargé de les établir s'acquitta promptement et efficacement de ce travail.

Le Règlement Intérieur contient les dispositions relatives aux locaux, au greffier et aux sessions dont il a été question plus haut.

Le Règlement de Procédure mérite une étude plus attentive, car il a pour objet d'assurer le bon fonctionnement du Tribunal.

Les langues officielles prévues sont l'allemand et le français. La plupart des requérants sont assistés par un conseiller juridique, mais le Règlement prévoit que le requérant peut préparer lui-même son dossier avec l'aide du greffier, afin de le rendre conforme aux conditions requises par le Tribunal. Après enregistrement de la demande, expédition de l'acte est délivrée à la partie adverse qui dispose de quatre semaines pour préparer et soumettre sa défense. Comme, à ce qu'on prévoyait, de nombreuses plaintes ont été déposées contre le gouvernement ou d'autres autorités publiques, le Règlement stipule que le dossier officiel du requérant et les documents concernant la demande doivent être soumis au Tribunal – une des rares clauses auxquelles le Gouvernement sarrois s'était d'abord opposé, mais qu'il accepta finalement.

Le requérant reçoit ensuite une copie du mémoire en défense ainsi que l'avis de dépôt du dossier et des documents annexes au Tribunal; il peut en prendre connaissance. Il dispose de deux semaines pour faire parvenir une réplique et la partie adverse dispose à son tour de deux semaines pour présenter une duplique. Il est loisible au Président de proroger ces délais, et tel a été souvent le cas.

Le juge désigné par le Président pour examiner les recours enregistrés par le greffier peut, s'il estime que le Tribunal est manifestement incompétent, déposer immédiatement un rapport au Tribunal, qui peut se déclarer incompétent à la prochaine audience. Cette disposition s'est révélée très utile dans de nombreux cas, parfois absurdes et toujours pitoyables, où le requérant se plaignait de mauvais traitements, réels ou imaginaires, subis sous les régimes d'HITLER ou d'HOFFMANN ou croyait à tort que le Tribunal était là pour redresser tous les torts.

Le Dr NEY, Premier Ministre, avait demandé personnellement au Président que le Tribunal ait l'obligation de faire comparaître les parties en conciliation; c'est pourquoi le Règlement stipule que les juges et les deux parties se réunissent en vue d'une tentative de conciliation. Si celle-ci échoue, le juge rapporteur établit un rapport qu'il dépose auprès du greffier. Celui-ci en avise les parties qui peuvent le consulter.

La procédure se poursuit alors et le Président fixe la date et l'heure de l'audience à laquelle l'affaire sera appelée. Celle-ci est publique; le Tribunal n'a jamais exercé son droit de prononcer le huis clos dans l'intérêt public ou dans l'intérêt des parties. De nouveaux témoignages peuvent être admis au cours de l'audience; le Président peut également ordonner le renvoi de celle-ci en attendant de nouvelles dépositions.

Les décisions du Tribunal sont prises à la majorité des juges présents, la voix du Président étant, si besoin est, prépondérante. Le jugement doit être motivé et prononcé en allemand et en français en audience publique; il est signé par tous les membres du Tribunal qui l'ont rendu et par le greffier. Il n'y a donc pas de jugement rendu à la minorité. Il n'est pas possible d'en appeler du jugement, mais le Tribunal peut rectifier des erreurs d'écriture ou des divergences entre les textes français et allemand.

Parallèlement à cette procédure normale et inévitablement lente, le Tribunal avait la possibilité de prendre des mesures conservatoires pour garantir le *statu quo* et pour protéger le requérant contre un préjudice grave dans l'attente d'une décision. Le Président statuait en référé lorsqu'une demande motivée à cet effet avait été déposée et que des observations écrites avaient été présentées par la partie adverse.

Les textes du Règlement Intérieur et du Règlement de Procédure ont été publiés dans la Gazette officielle du 27 juin 1956; le Tribunal est entré en fonction et il a été saisi régulièrement de diverses affaires pendant les trois années suivantes. Entre le mois de juillet 1956 et le mois de septembre 1959, date à laquelle le Tribunal a cessé de fonctionner, quatorze sessions ont eu lieu. Soixante-douze jugements définitifs ont été prononcés. Dans vingt cas les requérants ont obtenu entière satisfaction et dans trois cas leur demande a été reconnue partiellement fondée. Dans dix-sept cas les demandes ont été rejetées pour incompétence manifeste, après une procédure simplifiée et dans seize cas elles ont été rejetées après mise en oeuvre de la procédure intégrale. Dans les seize autres cas, les requérants ont retiré leurs demandes après la conclusion d'un règlement transactionnel satisfaisant dont le Tribunal a dressé procès-verbal. Les copies des jugements prononcés étaient communiquées à toutes les parties intéressées; elles sont conservées à la Bibliothèque des Nations Unies à Genève.

Ainsi qu'il était à prévoir, les demandes relevant de la compétence du Tribunal avaient été introduites – à une exception près – par des partisans ou des adhérents du régime HOFFMANN renversé. Les plaintes reçues portaient sur trois catégories de faits: *a*) destitution de fonctionnaires d'État ou perte des droits légaux à la retraite ou à d'autres émoluments dûs; *b*) traitement injuste infligé soit à des fonctionnaires de l'État, soit à des agents municipaux, soit enfin à des personnes employées dans des organismes semi-publics tels que la Radio-diffusion d'État; *c*) traitement injuste et discriminatoire dans des organisations municipales. Les cas de la catégorie *a*) concernaient surtout des personnes qui avaient été en vue dans les administrations précédentes et il était difficile de réfuter la thèse selon laquelle un motif politique était à l'origine de leur renvoi. Les cas les plus notoires furent ceux de M. HOFFMANN lui-même, de son Ministre de l'Intérieur et du Chef de la Police. Le règlement de ces cas ne présentait, en général, pas de difficultés; dans celui des deux ministres et dans d'autres, il fut procédé à des compensations. Souvent la réintégration – qui avait été demandée dans le cas du Chef de la Police, par exemple, – n'était pas dans l'intérêt public ou dans celui du requérant lui-même. Jugeant en équité, le Tribunal ne réintégra pas le Chef de la Police dans ses fonctions. Dans certains cas, cependant il ordonna la réintégration ou la nomination à un poste similaire.

La plupart des demandes relevaient de la catégorie *b*). Comme il était normal après un changement de régime, les partisans notoires de l'ancien régime ne se sentaient pas en sécurité et étaient sensibles à tout acte pouvant être interprété comme une mesure de représailles de la part du nouveau Gouvernement dévoué corps et âme au *Vaterland* et plein de ressentiment à l'égard de l'ancien régime. Il était souvent difficile de faire la distinction entre un traitement injuste et la fin d'une situation exceptionnelle – ou même irrégulière – dont le requérant avait bénéficié sous l'ancien régime. De nombreuses requêtes invoquaient l'affectation à un poste hors de la capitale et la perte de l'indemnité mensuelle de 8.000 frs, mais les partisans de l'ancien régime ne pouvaient s'attendre à rester tous dans la capitale; le motif de la nouvelle affectation pouvait être aussi bien une mesure discriminatoire qu'un déplacement normal. Le Tribunal devait d'abord décider si la nouvelle affectation était légale et conforme aux usages en vigueur dans l'administration, mais même lorsque cela semblait être le cas, le requérant pouvait avoir subi un préjudice au sens de la loi. Il ne pouvait manifestement être réintégré dans son poste, puisque son passé politique était la vraie raison de son déplacement, mais le Tribunal pouvait ordonner le paiement d'une compensation en espèces. C'est là que la notion d'équité jouait un rôle particulièrement utile. L'interprétation la plus proche de cette expression particulièrement imprécise qu'ait pu donner le Tribunal, était que dans les cas où le droit strictement dit aboutit à des conclusions douteuses ou injustes, celles-ci doivent être complétées ou même tempérées par le bon sens.

Une disposition du traité franco-allemand de janvier 1957, soulevait un problème intéressant; cette disposition prévoyait que les fonctionnaires permanents du gouvernement ou d'autres administrations publiques ainsi que certains autres fonctionnaires étaient fondés à faire valoir leurs droits à la retraite, s'ils estimaient ne plus pouvoir espérer d'avancement en raison de leurs activités politiques sous le régime précédent. Cette clause n'a pas été sans donner de bons résultats dans beaucoup de cas, mais elle prêtait également à des abus de la part de personnes qui, prétendant être en danger pour avoir soutenu le régime HOFFMANN, cherchaient à obtenir le versement d'indemnités de manière à prendre, ensuite, un autre emploi si possible mieux rémunéré. Le Tribunal se trouvait ainsi dans une situation tout à fait anormale: on lui demandait de considérer le refus d'une administration publique de reconnaître qu'un fonctionnaire avait été partisan de la politique du Statut européen comme un préjudice subi par ce fonctionnaire pour avoir appuyé ladite politique. Là encore, le Tribunal a appliqué le principe d'équité au sens large du terme et si la carrière d'un fonctionnaire était menacée, il se déclarait compétent et trouvait une solution.

Dans la catégorie *c*) il y eu quelques cas difficiles où étaient invoquées, notamment, des fautes professionnelles de la part d'employés d'administrations municipales ou locales. Étant donné que la durée des mandats de ces personnes ne coïncidait pas avec celle des membres du Parlement, les partisans de l'ancien régime étaient souvent restés en fonction, ce qui provoquait une grande tension dans ces administrations, et même parfois, l'interruption complète de leurs importantes activités. Ces accusations, parfois très étoffées, conduisaient le Tribunal à entreprendre des enquêtes remontant très loin et ce n'est que lorsqu'il était impossible de trouver une raison valable, justifiant le traitement dont le requérant se plaignait, que, le cas pouvait être considéré comme relevant de sa compétence. Ces exemples illustrent un point commun à tous les autres cas, à savoir que la question de la compétence – autre que celle qui résultait de la situation des parties ou de la date de l'acte incriminé – ne pouvait être dissociée utilement du fond même de la plainte. Pendant les premiers temps de l'existence du Tribunal, les défendeurs avaient tendance à contester d'abord la compétence du Tribunal, mais par la suite on admit que celle-ci ne pouvait être dissociée du fond même de la plainte.

A l'origine, la presse sarroise publia, dans les journaux de tendances extrémistes, des articles assez hostiles au Tribunal; tantôt ceux-ci relevaient quelques détails des décisions pour les ridiculiser, tantôt ils mettaient l'accent sur l'incompétence du Président en raison notamment de son ignorance de la langue allemande. Mais ces attaques devaient cesser au fur et à mesure que progressaient les activités du Tribunal. Un an après son institution, le Président dut décliner avec regret, en raison des malentendus possibles, une invitation à tenir une conférence de presse, mais il proposa de répondre à des questions écrites et ses réponses furent commentées équitablement par la presse.

Au début de 1959, les cas nouveaux devinrent moins fréquents et le Tribunal dut envisager de se dissoudre. Il fallut fixer une date limite pour le dépôt des demandes; avec l'accord du Gouvernement sarrois et du Conseil, il fut décidé de fixer celle-ci à fin juin 1959, de manière à pouvoir tenir une dernière session en septembre.

Une des questions posées par les journalistes au Président était la suivante: „Les juges estiment-ils que le Tribunal fait oeuvre utile"? Le président répondit que seul l'avenir le montrerait. On peut, désormais, formuler une opinion à titre rétrospectif. Le président estime que le Tribunal a réussi à inspirer confiance au public, si bien que les requérants n'éprouvaient aucune crainte à introduire leurs demandes. C'était là, un fait très important, car on avait tendance à oublier, dans l'atmosphère active et prospère qui règnait à Sarrebruck, que certains plaignants avaient souffert de l'oppression dans le passé – tel ce vieillard auquel on demanda de rendre compte de ses activités pendant une période de six ans passée sous silence dans son dossier et qui répondit qu'il les avait passés à Dachau. Dans l'ensemble, les défendeurs proposaient un règlement raisonnable ou exécutaient de bonne grâce les décisions du Tribunal; dans quelques cas, celles-ci leur ont même offert l'occasion de traiter certains requérants comme ils l'auraient désiré, sans oser le faire de leur propre initiative par crainte de l'opinion publique.

Par sa seule existence, le Tribunal a probablement aussi prévenu certaines injustices, surtout au début de la nouvelle administration. Il n'est pas exagéré de prétendre que le Tribunal a rendu justice à certaines personnes qui auraient fait l'objet d'un traitement inéquitable et qu'il a aidé la population sarroise à régler ses divergences politiques dans l'intérêt commun de tous. Lorsque les juges se dispersèrent en septembre 1959, ils avaient apporté une petite pierre à la mosaïque de l'histoire européenne.

BENELUX

par

C. D. A. van Lynden [1]

La création du Benelux, première expérience d'intégration et de coopération économique européenne, remonte à plus de seize ans. Le présent article expose les réalisations effectuées au cours de cette période et les objectifs qui restent encore à atteindre. Après un bref aperçu historique, seront examinés successivement: l'Union douanière (1948); la Pré-union (1949); la politique commerciale commune (1953); la libre circulation des personnes (1960) et le Traité instituant l'Union économique (1960).

APERÇU HISTORIQUE

Depuis 1581, et de longs siècles durant, la Belgique, les Pays-Bas et le Luxembourg connurent des destins différents.

Les Pays-Bas, qui avaient préservé leur indépendance, et la Belgique, qui subissait la loi de princes étrangers, furent réunis en un Royaume des Pays-Bas par le Congrès de Vienne de 1815. Cette Union, à caractère politique et économique, naquit de soucis exclusivement politiques. Elle ne fut guère heureuse et entraîna, en 1830, la déclaration d'indépendance de la Belgique, après laquelle chaque pays a suivi sa voie propre. Les relations commerciales entre la Belgique et les Pays-Bas détérioraient toutefois à tel point qu'une guerre tarifaire s'est même déclenchée et ce n'est qu'en 1849 que l'on mit fin à cette situation. Une détente se manifesta en 1863; la Belgique et les Pays-Bas signèrent un traité de commerce, supprimant le péage sur l'Escaut. Ils essayèrent même, entre 1879 et 1890, de conclure une Union douanière; leurs efforts, pourtant, n'aboutirent à aucun résultat.

Le Luxembourg faisait, avant 1581, partie des Pays-Bas. Ce pays a suivi ensuite des destins similaires à ceux des territoires belges. En 1815, le Luxembourg devint un Grand-Duché, le Roi des Pays-Bas étant, jusqu'en 1890, en même temps Grand-Duc de Luxembourg.

---

[1] Le Dr. C. D. A. baron van Lynden est depuis plusieurs années Secrétaire Général de l'Union Économique Benelux.

Ce n'est qu'en 1921 qu'une première manifestation concrète d'intégration économique, préfiguration du futur Benelux, se fait jour. La Belgique et le Luxembourg signèrent le Traité d'Union économique Belgo-Luxembourgeoise (U.E.B.L.), liant les deux États pour cinquante ans, sans possibilité de dénonciation unilatérale. A cette époque, les circonstances étaient particulièrement favorables à la conclusion d'un tel Traité. En effet, s'il existait, en 1921, des droits d'entrée, fixés par des traités de commerce prévoyant souvent une clause de la nation la plus favorisée, il n'était pas question, à cette époque-là, de contingents, licences ou taxes de transmission *etc.* Ce n'est que bien plus tard que les législations économiques, monétaires, sociales et fiscales ont pris l'ampleur que nous connaissons aujourd'hui. Le Traité d'Union économique Belgo-Luxembourgeoise s'est appuyé, en fait sur le principe du *Zollverein* qui avait lié autrefois le Luxembourg à la Confédération germanique.

En 1930, les petits pays d'Europe occidentale et les États scandinaves tentèrent de s'associer économiquement, par l'adhésion à la Convention d'Oslo. Essai stérile, tout comme la Convention d'Ouchy, qui envisageait une réduction progressive de 10% annuellement pendant cinq ans, des droits d'entrée respectifs. La Convention d'Ouchy fut un échec parce que ni la Grande Bretagne, ni les États-Unis d'Amérique n'entendaient renoncer à la clause inconditionnelle de la nation la plus favorisée reprise dans leurs accords bilatéraux. Bien que cette clause se retrouve dans l'Accord Général sur les Tarifs et le Commerce (le G.A.T.T.) conclu en 1948, ce dernier autorise dans son article XXIV une exception en faveur des unions douanières et économiques.

En 1933, un accord commercial fut signé entre les Pays-Bas et l'Union Économique Belgo-Luxembourgeoise. Il se heurta, au cours des années précédant la Seconde Guerre mondiale, à des difficultés répétées: dévaliation du franc belge, suivie de celle du florin néerlandais.

La Seconde Guerre mondiale réunit à Londres les trois Gouvernements en exil. Résolus à assurer le relèvement économique de leurs pays dès la fin des hostilités, les dirigeants belges, néerlandais et luxembourgeois conclurent, en 1943, un Accord Monétaire suivi, le 5 septembre 1944, de la Convention douanière Néerlando-Belgo-Luxembourgeoise.

Le 3 février 1958 enfin, la cérémonie de signature du Traité instituant l'Union économique Benelux se déroula dans le décor prestigieux de la salle des Chevaliers à La Haye. Par ce Traité, entré en vigueur le 1er novembre 1960, les trois pays du Benelux se donnent pour objectif:

1. de créer un territoire économique dans lequel aucune entrave ne s'oppose à la libre circulation des personnes, des biens, des capitaux et des services;
2. d'instaurer, dans les trois pays, une politique économique, financière et sociale coordonnée;
3. de mettre sur pied une politique commerciale et de paiements commune à l'égard des pays tiers.

L'UNION DOUANIÈRE

Le climat économique défavorable né de la Guerre, que subissaient les trois pays, les accords commerciaux bilatéraux en vigueur avec d'autres pays ainsi que les difficultés techniques relatives à l'établissement d'un nouveau tarif commun de droits d'entrée ont retardé la mise en vigueur de la Convention douanière signée en 1944. Toutefois, après que le Protocole du 14 mars 1947 eût précisé la portée de la Convention en instituant entre autres le Secrétariat Général et en fixant l'Union économique comme objectif final, les barrières douanières furent levées le 1er janvier 1948. Ce jour-là, tous les droits d'entrée furent abolis d'un coup entre les trois pays du Benelux.

Le tarif extérieur commun des droits d'entrée, mis en place le 1er janvier 1948, comporte des droits *ad valorem* correspondant, en général, à peu près à la moyenne arithmétique des droits spécifiques belgo-luxembourgeois et des droits *ad valorem* néerlandais d'avant-guerre. Comme, en raison de leur structure économique, les pays de Benelux sont évidemment axés sur le commerce international et qu'ils importent et exportent par conséquent un pourcentage élevé de leur production nationale, le tarif Benelux est relativement bas et la protection des industries nationales par la voie des droits de douane est plutôt exceptionnelle: les recettes en droits de douane, dans l'ensemble du territoire Benelux, ne représentent que 5% de la valeur des importations. Pour les pays tiers, ce tarif commun des droits d'entrée a fait du Benelux une entité, qui s'est manifestée surtout au cours des négociations tarifaires successives qui, entamées en 1948, ont mené à l'Accord général sur les Tarifs et le Commerce (G.A.T.T.).

Et pourtant, à cette époque, le Benelux n'était guère un marché commun. En effet, la situation financière – surtout celle des Pays-Bas – exigeait des mesures de restrictions des importations. Les Pays-Bas déjà traditionnellement débiteurs structurels de l'U.E.B.L. avant la Seconde Guerre mondiale, étaient gravement atteints par cette guerre dans leur capacité d'exportation et ce n'est que grâce aux larges crédits que l'U.E.B.L. accorda aux Pays-Bas, immédiatement après la Seconde Guerre mondiale, que le commerce intra-Benelux a pu se développer. Cette solution présentait cependant des difficultés qui ont pris fin en 1950 grâce à l'aide MARSHALL qui assurait le financement des déficits commerciaux intra-européens via les droits dits „de tirage" et, ensuite, d'une manière plus permanente, grâce à l'entrée en vigueur de l'Union Européenne de Paiements. Ce n'est qu'à ce moment que les conditions nécessaires étaient remplies pour la conclusion de l'Accord de Pré-Union.

LA PRÉ-UNION

L'Accord de Pré-Union, entré en vigueur avec effet rétroactif au 1er juillet 1949, visait: „la libération progressive du trafic des marchandises entre les territoires des partenaires, la coordination systématique de la politique commerciale et monétaire des partenaires à l'égard des pays tiers et la préparation d'un régime contractuel unique à l'égard de ces derniers".

La liberté des échanges commerciaux intra-Benelux ne pouvait toutefois pas s'appliquer immédiatement à tous les produits agricoles et alimentaires. Le Protocole agricole, signé en 1950, instaura, pour le commerce de ces produits, un système de prix minima et de prélèvements lié à un régime de préférence. Le produit de ces prélèvements est réparti, par moitié, entre l'U.E.B.L. et les Pays-Bas.

Au cours de la période de 1952–1953, les Gouvernements se

sont spécialement intéressés aux difficultés constatées dans certains secteurs industriels où s'imposait une procédure particulière permettant de résoudre les disparités dans les conditions de concurrence. La Déclaration gouvernementale de Knokke (14 octobre 1952) créa des comités spéciaux où siégèrent des délégués des secteurs privés intéressés. Ces comités ont proposé le Protocole du 24 juillet 1953, prévoyant la coordination des politiques économiques et sociales. Le Protocole permit de résoudre les difficultés par des contacts directs entre les milieux professionnels intéressés des Pays-Bas et de l'U.E.B.L. Pas une seule fois, il ne fallut recourir au fonds de réadaptation Benelux créé au moment de la signature du Protocole

LA POLITIQUE COMMERCIALE COMMUNE

Depuis l'instauration du tarif extérieur des pays du Benelux au 1er janvier 1948, aucun secteur n'a accompli autant de progrès spectaculaires dans la voie de l'Union économique totale que celui de la politique commerciale extérieure. Cela n'a rien de surprenant: en effet, le marché commun, qui constitue l'un des buts de l'Union économique et dont le principe est le libre-échange des produits entre les pays membres, ne doit pas seulement s'étendre aux produits nationaux et aux marchandises nationalisées, mais aussi aux marchandises importées de pays tiers.

Toutefois, les marchandises importées ne peuvent circuler librement dans tout le territoire du Benelux qu'à condition que les pays partenaires appliquent le même régime à l'importation de produits provenant d'autres pays. Il est évident que la pratique de régimes d'importation différents, conjuguée à la liberté d'échange à l'intérieur du Benelux, attirerait vers le pays partenaire, qui adopte une politique plus sévère, un indésirable courant de marchandises importées via le territoire du partenaire moins restrictif.

Inversement, la libre circulation de produits nationaux est condition préalable à l'instauration d'une politique commerciale commune car, aussi longtemps que certains produits d'origine nationale ne peuvent pas circuler librement dans les pays partenaires, il va de soi que la libre circulation demeure exclue pour les produits similaires importés. Aussi, les milieux responsables de la politique commerciale extérieure ont-ils toujours insisté sur l'urgence de libérer dans le Benelux le trafic des produits nationaux. En effet, ces milieux se sentaient attirés non seulement par la création du marché commun des Trois, mais aussi par les avantages qu'ils escomptaient d'une attitude commune des pays partenaires du Benelux, dans le domaine de la politique commerciale, lors des négociations menées aussi bien avec chacun des pays tiers que dans le cadre des organisations internationales s'occupant de politique commerciale notamment: G.A.T.T., O.E.C.E., organisations et groupes d'études internationaux pour les matières premières.

Ces préoccupations, complexes et souvent interférentes, ont trouvé leur expression dans le Protocole relatif à la politique commerciale, conclu le 9 décembre 1953, à Luxembourg, entre les pays du Benelux et entré en vigueur le 18 août 1956, après sa ratification par les Parlements des trois pays.

Comment le Benelux a-t-il exécuté ce Protocole?

Avant tout, les listes des produits dont l'importation est libérée par les pays du Benelux ont été fusionnées. C'est-à-dire que l'on a groupé en une seule liste commune de libre importation les produits pour lesquels les pays du Benelux pratiquaient, chacun pour son territoire, une politique de libre importation, soit à l'égard des pays de l'O.E.C.E., soit à l'égard de la zone dollar ou encore à l'égard des pays membres du G.A.T.T.

Par cette fusion, l'un des pays du Benelux ne pouvait donc plus revenir sur la liberté accordée à l'importation, sans que les autres partenaires ne lui emboîtent le pas et ne marquent leur accord. De plus, les marchandises importées sous ce régime furent libérées dans les échanges commerciaux intra-Benelux. A l'égard de l'O.E.C.E., cette réalisation se concrétisa par la liste de libération Benelux présentée à Paris. Une liste identique fut établie pour la zone dollar et les pays membres du G.A.T.T. Le Benelux libéra, dans son territoire, la circulation des marchandises importées de ces pays.

Mais il n'était possible de réaliser le libre trafic intra-Benelux qu'après avoir instauré également un régime d'importation commun pour les produits, provenant de pays tiers, dont la libre importation n'était pas autorisée soit par l'un des partenaires, soit par les deux, et auxquels s'appliquaient des restrictions quantitatives.

Pour une partie de ces produits, la libération intra-Benelux fut réalisée moyennant la conclusion des accords commerciaux Benelux avec certains pays tiers dans lesquels des contingents à l'importation et à l'exportation, valant pour l'ensemble du territoire du Benelux, furent établis.

Pour une autre partie de ces produits, l'entité Benelux a fixé des contingents autonomes à l'importation, valables pour tous les pays tiers. Ce sont les contingents „globaux". Étant donné que la libre concurrence permet à tous les pays tiers de prendre part à ces contingents, ce système est considéré, à juste titre, comme un pas dans la voie vers la libération. Il convenait, pour fixer la hauteur des contingents, de respecter rigoureusement les engagements souscrits par les pays du Benelux dans le cadre du G.A.T.T., engagements selon lesquels les restrictions appliquées par une union économique ne peuvent dépasser le total des restrictions appliquées, avant sa constitution, par chacun des pays adhérents. Cette condition ne suscite pas de difficultés dans le cadre de la politique libérale à l'importation et à l'exportation des pays du Benelux.

Finalement, pour un nombre restreint de produits, il s'est révélé impossible de libérer, dès à présent, les échanges commerciaux intra-Benelux. Il s'agit, en l'occurrence, principalement de certains produits agricoles. A ce sujet, les Ministres du Benelux ont décidé, le 3 mai 1955, une harmonisation des politiques agricoles des trois pays qui permettrait de réaliser le libre échange intra-Benelux de ces produits dans un délai de 7 ans. Cet ensemble de dispositions figure actuellement dans le Traité d'Union économique.

L'ensemble du secteur non libéré dans le trafic intra-Benelux n'atteint pas 3% du commerce entre les pays partenaires. Néanmoins, des efforts s'imposent encore pour intégrer, à la première occasion propice, ces produits dans le marché commun des Trois et dans la politique commerciale commune. C'est précisément à l'occasion des négociations, menées par le Benlux avec les pays tiers, en vue de conclure des accords commerciaux, que l'on constate la lacune que constitue, dans la position du Benelux, la nécessité de présenter encore des contingents séparés.

Des exceptions à la politique commerciale commune subsistent non seulement à l'importation mais aussi à l'exportation. Il se présente, en effet, que le pays exportateur, en l'occurrence l'U.E.B.L. ou les Pays-Bas, gère des contingents à l'exportation en lieu et place et, dans la plupart des cas, à la demande du pays tiers importateur. En l'occurrence, il s'agit également surtout de produits agricoles. En pareil cas, il n'est pas encore possible de fixer des contingents communs à l'exportation pour les produits en cause, tant que l'on n'a pas assuré une gestion Benelux à l'exportation. Avant d'en arriver là, il faudra harmoniser certaines réglementations. Or, celles-ci sont très souvent compliquées et fort étroitement subordonnées aux différences qui se manifestent dans l'organisation interne du marché de ces produits dans chacun des pays. La coordination de ces réglementations est une tâche particulièrement ardue.

Les pays du Benelux ont toujours insisté, au cours de leurs négociations avec les pays tiers, sur le fait que, dans leur politique commerciale commune, ils s'attachent au progrès constant du trafic commercial et qu'ils ont la conviction que la liberté des échanges commerciaux avec les pays tiers, tout comme la liberté que ces pays accordent aux échanges avec les pays du Benelux, contribue le plus efficacement à la réalisation de cette politique.

La majeure partie du commerce Benelux s'effectue sous un régime commun à l'importation et à l'exportation. Ce régime tout entier figure dans le Traité instituant l'Union économique. Les statistiques, reprises ci-après, (*voir p. 145*) révèlent clairement que, de 1950 à 1960, non seulement les échanges commerciaux entre les partenaires ont augmenté dans de notables proportions (de 150%), mais que le commerce avec les pays tiers, lui aussi, a progressé notablement. Ce dernier présente, en effet, une augmentation plus sensible (128%) que le commerce mondial qui, au cours de cette période, s'est accru de 100%.

LIBRE CIRCULATION DE PERSONNES

Une Convention abolissant le contrôle des documents de voyage aux frontières intérieures du Benelux est entrée en vigueur le 1.7.1960.

Aux termes de cette Convention, les trois pays agissent de

commun accord en matière d'octroi de visas et de contrôle aux frontières extérieures du Benelux et le visa accordé à un étranger est valable, en règle générale, pour l'ensemble du territoire Benelux.

Le marché commun du travail Benelux concrétisé officiellement par l'entrée en vigueur, le 1er novembre 1960, du Traité de Travail mérite également de retenir l'attention.

Le régime institué par ce Traité de Travail est celui de la libre circulation: les nationaux des trois pays peuvent circuler librement sur le territoire du Benelux, offrir ou prendre, sur un pied d'égalité, tout travail auprès d'un employeur privé sans qu'ils soient obligés d'en demander au préalable l'autorisation.

Cela signifie que le permis de travail est supprimé pour les ressortissants belges, néerlandais et luxembourgeois, sur le territoire de Benelux.

Le Traité comporte également des dispositions positives instaurant entre les services de l'emploi des trois pays une étroite coopération administrative, de manière à favoriser une certaine mobilité de la main-d'oeuvre.

TRAITÉ INSTITUANT L'UNION ÉCONOMIQUE BENELUX

Ce qui précède démontre clairement que la création et le parachèvement du Benelux ont été entrepris par des pionniers, qui n'avaient ni précédent, ni modèle auquel se référer. Pas à pas, ils ont dû explorer le terrain afin de découvrir les domaines où la coopération et la coordination des politiques s'imposaient avant de conclure un Traité d'Union économique qui, après 14 années de travail ardu, est enfin entré en vigueur le 1er novembre 1960. Aussi, ce Traité est-il avant tout la synthèse des arrangements conclus au cours des années en différentes matières. En cent articles exactement, le Traité d'Union fixe le but de l'Union économique, organise ses institutions et trace le chemin qui conduira à cette Union.

Une Convention transitoire énumère les exceptions actuelles aux principes du marché commun et détermine, pour la plupart d'entre elles, le délai dans lequel elles prendront fin.

Les secteurs qui, à l'heure actuelle, ne sont pas encore entièrement intégrés dans l'Union économique, sont les suivants:

1. *Établissement*

La faculté du Comité de Ministres de consentir à des mesures discriminatoires sera supprimée avant le 1er novembre 1965, les législations en matière d'établissement devant être harmonisées pour cette date. La pêche, par les ressortissants d'un des pays partenaires, dans les eaux territoriales d'un autre pays partenaire, sera libre, après cette même date.

2. *Adjudications par les pouvoirs publics*

Avant le 1er novembre 1963, la clause de sauvegarde en matière d'adjudications publiques sera levée. De plus, à partir de cette date, l'application du principe de non-discrimination en matière d'adjudications s'étendra à tous les pouvoirs publics, y compris les pouvoirs sur les opérations, sur lesquelles l'État n'exerce pas une action réelle.

3. *Libre circulation des travailleurs salariés*

Avant le 1er novembre 1965, la clause de sauvegarde en matière de mise au travail de travailleurs dans le cadre du Benelux sera supprimée. Avant cette date, la libération de la circulation des travailleurs, se trouvant dans les liens d'un contrat d'engagement maritime, sera également effectuée, complétant ainsi l'achèvement du Benelux pour les salariés.

4. *Échanges commerciaux intra-Benelux*

Avant le 1er novembre 1965, les dispositions législatives ou réglementaires, constituant des entraves indues à la libre circulation, devront être coordonnées de manière telle que ces entraves soient levées.

A cette même date, les restrictions aux échanges commerciaux qui s'appliquaient encore au moment de l'entrée en vigueur du Traité d'Union devront être éliminées.

5. *Produits agricoles*

Avant le 1er novembre 1965, l'harmonisation des politiques agricoles devra être réalisée en vue de la suppression de l'application des régimes spéciaux pour les échanges de produits agricoles figurant aux listes A, B et C annexées au Traité d'Union afin que ces produits puissent circuler librement dans le commerce intra-Benelux.

6. *Transports*

Avant le 1er novembre 1963, les transports par route de marchandises seront libres. De même, le régime spécial concernant le transport de sable et de gravier des Pays-Bas vers la Belgique sera-t-il supprimé à cette date.

7. *Problèmes dans le domaine fiscal*

Tel qu'il est exposé ci-dessus, le tarif douanier commun Benelux est entré en vigueur le 1er janvier 1948. Toutefois, à l'égard des autres impôts indirects tels que les droits d'accise et la taxe de transmission, les progrès furent moins marqués. Une convention portant instauration de droits d'accise communs a été conclue en 1950, qui, sauf sur quelques points d'importance secondaire, n'a pas encore pu être mise en application.

La solution définitive n'a pas encore été trouvée en matière de taxe de transmission, pour laquelle le Traité ne prescrit pas d'unification mais une certaine harmonisation. Il convient de remarquer que la Convention transitoire ne pose pas de délai fixe pour l'entrée en vigueur des règles en matière d'impôts indirects prévues par le Traité. A l'égard des impôts directs, les pays du Benelux doivent s'efforcer de réduire graduellement les différences susceptibles de fausser les conditions de concurrence.

Le Traité d'Union économique instaure un certain nombre d'organismes, il en confirme les diverses procédures suivies jusqu'à présent ainsi que les résultats déjà acquis.

Le Traité maintient l'organisation des institutions de l'Union, telles qu'elles se sont développées et qu'elles ont fonctionné, à la satisfaction générale, au cours de la période de 1948–1960.

Contrairement à la C.E.C.A., à la C.E.E. et à l'Euratom, le Benelux n'a pas de Haute Autorité ou de Commission qui, indépendamment des Gouvernements nationaux, a sa propre compétence. L'intégration Benelux s'est complètement réalisée par la voie des négociations directes entre les Gouvernements. L'expérience a démontré que cette forme de collaboration a assuré le progrès constant de l'intégration économique des trois pays. Le Secrétariat Général, point central de coordination, est actuellement le seul organisme commun des trois pays.

Les dispositions de ce Traité, entré en vigueur le 1er novembre 1960, permettront d'éliminer les dernières entraves à caractère non économique (critères de qualité, *etc.*).

Le Traité prévoit également la coordination des politiqies économiques, financières et sociales des trois pays. La mise au point d'une des bases de cette coordination, notamment l'unification des structures des budgets des trois États et leur comparaison, a été réalisée.

C'est ainsi que le Traité jette les bases pour la création d'un seul marché homogène et dynamique des trois pays tout en incitant ces derniers à rester le catalyseur pour la création d'un marché européen plus vaste, comparable à celui des États-Unis d'Amérique.

INFLUENCE DE BENELUX SUR LE DÉVELOPPEMENT FUTUR DE L'EUROPE

L'oeuvre expérimentale accomplie par les pays du Benelux a incontestablement servi d'exemple et de stimulant au développement de l'intégration économique dans un cadre plus large.

Il convient de souligner, à ce sujet, qu'après la faillite de la Communauté Européenne de Défense, ce sont les Ministres des Affaires étrangères des pays du Benelux qui, à Messine, ont relancé les négociations pour une Union économique entre le Benelux, la France, l'Allemagne et l'Italie, négociations qui, en fin de compte, ont abouti aux Traités de Rome. On peut donc affirmer, ainsi que l'a dit dernièrement le baron SNOY ET D'OPPUERS, que „le Benelux est le laboratoire de l'intégration européenne".

En effet, l'expérience Benelux a convaincu les Gouvernements des trois pays de la nécessité de considérer celle-ci comme une étape vers un marché européen plus large et plus complet. Les États de Benelux n'ont pas non plus considéré le Marché Commun des Six comme une finalité en soi: de là, la position en flèche qu'ils n'ont cessé de prendre pour la réalisation d'une association entre le Marché Commun et les autres pays membres de l'O.E.C.E. D'ailleurs, les données géographiques de base de l'économie européenne des Six l'orientent vers l'extérieur. Une politique d'autarchie est, pour le marché commun, contradictoire à ses intérêts fondamentaux. Dès lors, il est évident que les partenaires de Benelux n'auront de cesse que lorsqu'ils auront fait partager aux autres pays du Marché Commun leur conviction pour élargir le marché constitué entre eux et l'étendre à l'ensemble de l'Europe libre.

Ceci coïncide d'ailleurs avec les intérêts traditionnels des pays du delta des grands fleuves européens. Situés au centre géographique de la zone la plus industrialisée d'Europe, disposant d'un *Hinterland* naturel aisément accessible aux moyens de transport les plus modernes, ayant des siècles d'expérience du négoce maritime, il est tout à fait naturel que les pays du Benelux perçoivent avec acuité particulière les possibilités prodigieuses de mise en valeur de l'écononie européenne dans un contexte européen élargi et par une politique ouverte sur le monde.

Cette vocation à l'expansion et à l'élargissement des échanges constitue sans doute le rôle providentiel qui s'impose aux pays du Benelux vis-à-vis de l'Europe. Leur participation aux cultures latine, germanique et anglo-saxonne, leur don de compénétration des races, leur permettent de voir plus facilement que d'autres les points communs d'intérêt et les pôles de cristallisation sur lesquels doit être axée la grande économie européenne. Ils ont un rôle de catalyseurs qui doit être systématiquement mis en oeuvre et servir à la construction des données économiques indispensables pour assurer, pendant des siècles, le rayonnement de la civilisation chrétienne qui est la caractéristique fondamentale de l'Europe.

DÉVELOPPEMENT DU COMMERCE DES PAYS DU BENELUX ET DU COMMERCE MONDIAL (EN MILLIONS DE $ U.S.A.)

	Commerce Benelux		Commerce mondial
	avec des pays tiers	entre pays partenaires	
1950	5.917	574	56.776
1951	8.177	745	76.737
1952	7.811	706	73.870
1953	7.706	742	74.853
1954	8.456	826	77.535
1955	9.597	956	84.171
1956	10.790	1.032	93.602
1957	11.389	1.227	100.489
1958	10.767	1.190	95.659
1959	11.780	1.270	101.100
1960	13.400	1.420	(110.000)

Source: Commerce Benelux: ***Bulletins de Statistique Benelux.***
Commerce mondial: ***Bulletins statistiques de l'O.E.C.E.***

COMMERCE INTRA-BENELUX

COMMERCE INTRA-BENELUX						
Période	Importations U.E.B.L. en provenance des Pays-Bas		% des imp. totales de l'U.E.B.L.	Importations aux Pays-Bas en provenance de l'U.E.B.L.		% des imp. totales des Pays-Bas
	x mln FB	x mln fl		x mln FB	x mln fl	
1948	7.189	435	8,3	12.099	732	14,7
1953	16.619	1.263	13,8	20.475	1.556	17,2
1954	17.068	1.297	13,5	-24.222	1.841	17,0
1955	18.811	1.430	13,3	29.011	2.205	18,1
1956	21.363	1.624	13,1	35.265	2.680	18,9
1957	24.302	1.847	14,2	37.047	2.816	18,1
1958	24.581	1.868	15,7	32.355	2.459	17,9
1959	27.171	2.065	15,9	36.145	2.747	18.5
1960	29.400	2.232	14,9	41.500	3.155	18,4

SUMMARY

It is more than sixteen years since the creation of Benelux, the first experiment in European integration and economic co-operation. This article describes its progress and achievements during that period, and the goals not yet reached. After a brief historical survey, the following phases are examined: the Customs Union (1948); the Pre-Union (1949); the common commercial policy (1953); the free circulation of persons (1960), and the Treaty setting up the Economic Union (1960).

HISTORICAL SURVEY

Since 1581 the destinies of Belgium, the Netherlands and Luxembourg have followed different paths.

By the Congress of Vienna in 1815 the Netherlands and Belgium for purely political reasons were united as a Kingdom of the Netherlands, but the union broke down in 1830, after which date each country went its separate way. Commercial relations reached their nadir in a tariff war that continued till 1848. In 1863 a commercial treaty improved relations, and between 1879 and 1890 efforts – unsuccessful, however – were made to create a Customs Union.

Luxembourg before 1581 was part of the Netherlands, and thereafter had a history similar to that of Belgium. In 1815 it became a Grand-Duchy, and up to 1890 the King of the Netherlands was also Grand-Duke of Luxembourg.

The first concrete instance of economic integration fore-shadowing Benelux was the Belgo-Luxembourg Treaty of Economic Union in 1921, based on the *Zollverein* principle. Circumstances were then propitious for such a union, since, apart from entry dues often involving a most-favoured-nation clause, legislation in these matters – economic, monetary, social and fiscal – was a much simpler affair than it is today.

The Oslo Convention of 1930 and the Ouchy Convention were attempts to unite economically the small Western European countries and the Scandinavian States, both of which failed to achieve their object. The Ouchy Convention failed because neither Great Britain nor the United States of America would renounce the unconditional most-favoured-nation clause included in their bilateral agreements. This clause does, indeed, appear in G.A.T.T. (1948), but Article XXIV makes an exception in favour of customs and economic (free trade) unions.

A commercial agreement made in 1933 between the Netherlands and the Belgo-Luxembourg Union ran into difficulties before the First Wold War, with the devaluation of the Belgian franc and then of the Netherlands florin.

The three Governments-in-Exile in London during the Second World War concluded a Monetary Agreement in 1943, and the Netherlands-

Belgo-Luxembourg Customs Convention in 1944, to aid the economic recovery of their countries after the War. And, finally, on 3rd February, 1958, the Treaty creating the Benelux Economic Union was signed at The Hague and became law in 1960.

The aims of this Treaty were:

1. to create an economic territory in which persons, goods, capital and services could circulate freely;
2. to co-ordinate the economic, financial and social policies of the three countries;
3. to initiate a common commercial and payments policy in relation to third countries.

THE CUSTOMS UNION

The actual entry into operation of the Customs Convention, signed in 1944, was delayed by various factors: post-war economic conditions, existing bilateral agreements, technical difficulties in setting up a new common tariff or régime of entry dues, *etc.* On 1st January, 1948, however, all entry dues between the three countries were abolished at one fell swoop.

The common external tariff, in operation from the same date, lays down *ad valorem* duties corresponding, more or less, to the arithmetical average of specific Belgo-Luxembourg dues and those in force in the Netherlands before the War. As the Benelux Countries' economies are rooted in international trade, the Benelux tariff is relatively low, and national industries have customs protection only in exceptional cases. (Revenue from customs dues represents only 5% of the value of imports.) The common tariff towards third countries made a single unit of Benelux, as was shown during the negotiations leading to G.A.T.T.

Benelux, however, at that stage was hardly a common market, for the financial position, especially in the Netherlands, imposed the need for import restrictions. The Netherlands had to receive large credits from the Belgo-Luxembourg Economic Union (B.L.E.U.) to build up its export trade after the Second World War, before intra-Benelux trade could develop. The difficulties still encountered were overcome in 1950 thanks to MARSHALL Aid. Only then were the necessary conditions for the Pre-Union Agreement fulfilled.

THE PRE-UNION

The Pre-Union Agreement, which became law in 1949, with retroactive effect, aimed at progressive liberation of exchange of goods between the Member countries, systematic co-ordination of their commercial and monetary policies in relation to third countries and the preparation of a single contractual régime towards them.

All agricultural and food products could not be included at once in the free intra-Benelux market, and an Agricultural Protocol, in 1950, established a system of minimum prices and levies linked to a preference system, the money raised by these levies to be apportioned equally between the B.L.E.U. and the Netherlands.

In 1952–3 special measures had to be taken by the Governments to overcome disparities in conditions of competition in some industrial sector, and the Governmental Declaration of Knokke set up special committees on which were represented the private sectors concerned. The Protocol they drew up aimed at co-ordination of economic and social policies by direct contact between Dutch and B.L.E.U. professional circles, without it ever being necessary to have recourse to the Benelux readaptation fund created by the Protocol.

THE COMMON COMMERCIAL POLICY

It is not surprising that, since the installation of the external tariff of Benelux countries on 1st January, 1948, the most spectacular advances towards total economic union have been achieved in the field of external commercial policy. For the Common Market aimed at including not only national and nationalised goods but those imported from third countries. The free circulation of such imported goods demands equivalent import regulations among all the partners, however, so as not to favour a country applying stricter rules and attracting goods *via* one less restrictive.

From the opposite angle, free circulation of national products is a basic condition in setting up a common commercial policy, since restrictions in this field involve necessarily restrictions on similar imported products. The organisers of the scheme realised that the free exchange of national goods among Benelux countries would entail advantages not only within the Three, but also in their commercial dealings with third countries, and with international bodies, such as G.A.T.T. and O.E.E.C., and international bodies or study groups dealing with raw materials.

A Protocol on commercial policy, taking into account these ideas, was concluded between the Benelux countries on 9th December, 1953, and came into force after ratification by the Parliaments of the three countries, on 18th August, 1956.

This has been achieved by the creation of a single list of goods up to then freely imported by each country separately, to be freely imported by all Benelux countries, whether from O.E.E.C. countries, the dollar zone, or G.A.T.T. countries. These imported goods were also freed on the intra-Benelux market, so that their circulation throughout Benelux was free.

A necessary preliminary to free intra-Benelux trade was a common import system for goods from third countries, where one or two of the countries applied restrictive practices. For some of these, goods agreements were made with third countries on import and export quotas, applicable to the whole Benelux area. For others, Benelux fixed autonomous import quotas, known as "global" quotas, which mark an advance towards liberation. In fixing these quotas Benelux commitments within G.A.T.T. were fully respected, and the liberal import and export policy advocated by Benelux has met with no difficulties in this field.

Finally, for a small number of goods it has proved impossible so far to set up a free Benelux market. The Benelux Ministers decided, on 3rd May, 1955, to harmonise their agricultural policies in order to achieve free trade in these products within seven years. The Treaty of Economic Union included provisions to this effect.

The net result is that to day only 3% of the trade between the Benelux partners remains outside the system of free exchange of goods, and this gap, which became evident during negotiations on commercial agreements with third countries, must be filled at the first favourable occasion.

Anomalies in the common commercial policy exist for exports as well as for imports, for the B.L.E.U. or the Netherlands apply certain export quotas at the request of third countries, especially for agricultural products. Common export quotas call for a common Benelux direction in this field – a difficult task considering the differences existing between the organisation of these markets in the three countries.

The Benelux countries have always upheld, in their dealings with third countries, the importance of a consistent development of trade, based on the freedom accorded to and by those countries.

The success of this common system, in imports and exports, which is embodied in the Treaty setting up the Economic Union, is demonstrated by statistics (*see Table, p. 145*), for between 1950 and 1960 trade between the partners of Benelux rose by 150%, and with third countries by 128%, in comparison with world trade which increased only by 100%.

FREE CIRCULATION OF PERSONS

On 1st January, 1960, the examination of travel permits at frontiers inside Benelux was abolished by a Convention, under which the three countries take joint action on the issue of visas and control of frontiers outside Benelux. Generally speaking, a foreign visa is valid for the whole Benelux territory.

The Treaty on Manpower, of 1st November, 1960, sets up officially the common market in manpower, it institutes the free circulation of nationals of the three countries on Benelux territory, and the right to offer or accept private employment without reference to any authority. Thus the requirement of a work permit is abolished within Benelux. Close administrative co-operation between labour exchanges is instituted to make labour more mobile.

THE TREATY SETTING UP THE BENELUX ECONOMIC UNION

All that has gone before emphasises the pioneer character of the work done in order to find ways and means of co-ordinating economic policies, and this work was crowned, after 14 years, by the achievement of a Treaty of Economic Union, which came into force on 1st November, 1960, and which is a synthesis of all preceding arrangements. A transitional

SECTION DOCUMENTAIRE

DOCUMENTARY SECTION

MEMBRES DES ORGANISATIONS EUROPÉENNES PRINCIPALES

31 décembre 1960

	Rhine Commission [1]	Benelux	Western European Union	O.E.E.C. [2]	Council of Europe	Coal and Steel Community	Euratom	E.E.C.	Nordic Council [3]	Conference of Ministers of Transport [4]	Organisation for Nuclear Research C.E.R.N.	Civil Aviation Conference [5]	European Conference of Postal and Tele-communications Administrations	European Free Trade Association
Austria				×	×					×		×	×	×
Belgium	×	×	×	×	×	×	×	×		×	×	×	×	
Denmark				×	×				×	×	×	×	×	×
Finland									×				×	
France	×		×	×	×	×	×	×		×	×	×	×	
German F.R.	×		×	×	×	×	×	×		×	×	×	×	
Greece				×	×					×	×	×	×	
Iceland				×	×				×			×	×	
Ireland				×	×							×	×	
Italy			×	×	×	×	×	×		×	×	×	×	
Luxembourg		×	×	×	×	×	×	×		×		×	×	
Netherlands	×	×	×	×	×	×	×	×		×	×	×	×	
Norway				×	×				×	×	×	×	×	×
Portugal				×						×		×	×	×
Spain				×						×		×	×	
Sweden				×	×				×	×	×	×	×	×
Switzerland	×			×						×	×	×	×	×
Turkey				×	×					×		×	×	
United Kingdom	×		×	×	×					×	×	×	×	×
Yugoslavia											×			

[1] Les États-Unis d'Amérique sont également membres de la Commission centrale pour la navigation du Rhin.
[2] Le Canada et les États-Unis d'Amérique étaient des membres associés. A partir de 1955 la Yougoslavie avait le statut d'observateur. Cette organisation s'est convertie maintenant en l'O.C.D.E.
[3] La Finlande est devenue membre du Conseil nordique en 1956.
[4] Les États-Unis d'Amérique sont représentés dans des sessions de la conférence par un observateur.
[5] La Yougoslavie est représentée par un observateur.

MEMBERS OF THE PRINCIPAL EUROPEAN ORGANISATIONS

31st December, 1960

	Rhine Commission [1]	Benelux	Western European Union	O.E.E.C.[2]	Council of Europe	Coal and Steel Community	Euratom	E.E.C.	Nordic Council [3]	Conference of Ministers of Transport [4]	Organisation for Nuclear Research C.E.R.N.	Civil Aviation Conference [5]	European Conference of Postal and Tele-communications Administrations	European Free Trade Association
Austria				■	■					■		■	■	■
Belgium	■	■	■	■	■	■	■	■		■	■	■	■	
Denmark				■	■				■	■	■	■	■	■
Finland									■				■	
France	■		■	■	■	■	■	■		■	■	■	■	
German F.R.	■		■	■	■	■	■	■		■	■	■	■	
Greece				■	■					■	■	■	■	
Iceland				■	■				■			■	■	
Ireland				■	■							■	■	
Italy			■	■	■	■	■	■		■	■	■	■	
Luxembourg		■	■	■	■	■	■	■		■		■	■	
Netherlands	■	■	■	■	■	■	■	■		■	■	■	■	
Norway				■	■				■	■	■	■	■	■
Portugal				■						■		■	■	■
Spain				■						■		■	■	
Sweden				■	■				■	■	■	■	■	■
Switzerland	■			■						■	■	■	■	■
Turkey				■	■					■		■	■	
United Kingdom	■		■	■	■					■	■	■	■	■
Yugoslavia											■			

[1] The U.S.A. are also a Member of the Rhine Commission.
[2] Canada and the U.S.A. were Associate Members. From 1955 onwards Yugoslavia had the status of an observer. This organisation has now been converted into O.E.C.D.
[3] Finland acceded to the Nordic Council in 1956.
[4] The U.S.A. are represented at meetings of the Conference by an observer.
[1] Yugoslavia is represented by an observer.

CHAPITRE I

COMMISSION CENTRALE POUR LA NAVIGATION DU RHIN

A. COMPTE RENDU DE L'ACTIVITÉ DE LA COMMISSION CENTRALE EN 1960

1. COMPOSITION ET PERSONNEL DE LA COMMISSION CENTRALE

Au cours de l'année 1960, M. KIEWIET DE JONGE de la Délégation des Pays-Bas a donné sa démission pour raisons de santé, tandis que de nouveaux membres, MM. OYEVAAR, KLEINJAN, VONK et RIPHAGEN ont été désignés par leur Gouvernement pour former cette délégation.

En conséquence, la composition de la Commission Centrale était la suivante à la fin de l'année 1960:

Président:	M. Adrien THIERRY;
Allemagne:	
Commissaires:	MM. SEIERMANN, KREUTZWALD, SCHNEIDER, AHLERS,
Commissaires-suppléants:	Mlle. VON KOEPPEN, M. BORMANN;
Belgique:	
Commissaires:	MM. COENE, FRANCOIS,
Commissaire-suppléant:	M. DEVADDER;
États-Unis:	
Commissaire:	Mme. HARVEY;
France:	
Commissaires:	MM. GROS, LAVAL, GRAFF, BONET-MAURY;
Grande-Bretagne:	
Commissaire:	M. WALTER,
Commissaire-suppléant:	M. CLARKE;
Pays-Bas:	
Commissaires:	MM. SCHAEPMAN, OYEVAAR, KLEINJAN,
Commissaire-titulaire:	M. VONK,
Commissaire-suppléant:	M. RIPHAGEN;
Suisse:	
Commissaires:	MM. SCHALLER, TURRETTINI,
Commissaires-suppléants:	MM. OESTERHAUS, MANGOLD.

CHAPTER I

CENTRAL COMMISSION FOR THE NAVIGATION OF THE RHINE

A. PROGRESS REPORT OF THE CENTRAL COMMISSION FOR 1960

1. COMPOSITION AND STAFF OF THE CENTRAL COMMISSION

During 1960, Mr. KIEWIET DE JONGE of the Netherlands' delegation retired for health reasons and new members, MM. OYEVAAR, KLEINJAN, VONK and RIPHAGEN, were appointed by their Government to that delegation.

The composition of the Central Commission was therefore as follows at the end of 1960:

President:	M. Adrien THIERRY;
Germany:	
Commissioners:	MM. SEIERMANN, KREUTZWALD, SCHNEIDER, AHLERS,
Deputy Commissioners:	Mlle. VON KOEPPEN, M. BORMANN;
Belgium:	
Commissioners:	MM. COENE, FRANCOIS,
Deputy Commissioner:	M. DEVADDER;
United States:	
Commissioner:	Mrs. HARVEY;
France:	
Commissioners:	MM. GROS, LAVAL, GRAFF, BONET-MAURY;
Great Britain:	
Commissioner:	M. WALTER,
Deputy Commissioner:	M. CLARKE;
Netherlands:	
Commissioners:	MM. SCHAEPMAN, OYEVAAR, KLEINJAN,
Titular Commissioner:	M. VONK,
Deputy Commissioner:	M. RIPHAGEN;
Switzerland:	
Commissioners:	MM. SCHALLER, TURRETTINI,
Deputy-Commissioners:	MM. OESTERHAUS, MANGOLD.

2. ACTIVITÉS DE LA COMMISSION CENTRALE

Sessions plénières et réunions de Comités tenues au cours de l'année.

La Commission Centrale a tenu deux sessions ordinaires du 4 au 6 mai et du 26 au 28 octobre à Strasbourg. Elle a, en outre, tenu une courte session extraordinaire, à Paris, le 6 juillet.

Les Comités se sont réunis comme suit:

le Comité technique permanent, deux fois, sous la présidence de M. OESTERHAUS, le 3 mai à Strasbourg, et sous la présidence de M. KLEINJAN, le 25 octobre à Strasbourg;

le Comité du règlement de police, six fois, sous la présidence de M. FRANCOIS, les 12 et 13 janvier à Strasbourg, du 5 au 7 avril à Bruxelles, le 2 mai, les 21 et 22 juin, du 5 au 7 octobre et le 24 octobre à Strasbourg;

le Comité du règlement de visite, cinq fois, sous la présidence de Mme. HARVEY, les 12 et 13 janvier à Strasbourg, sous la présidence de M. MANGOLD, les 5 et 6 avril à Bruxelles, le 2 mai, le 20 juin et le 24 octobre à Strasbourg;

le Comité de révision du règlement de visite, trois fois, sous la présidence de M. SCHNEIDER, le 25 mai à Fribourg en Breisgau, les 6 et 7 juillet et les 12, 13 et 14 octobre à Strasbourg;

les Comités du règlement de visite et du règlement de police ensemble, sous la présidence de Mme. HARVEY et de M. FRANCOIS, le 13 janvier à Strasbourg;

le Comité des questions sociales, de travail et de formation professionnelle, sous la présidence de M. COENE, cinq fois, le 14 janvier à Strasbourg, le 8 avril à Bruxelles, le 3 mai à Strasbourg, le 2 juin à Paris et le 25 octobre à Strasbourg;

les Comités réunis du règlement de police, du règlement de visite, des questions sociales et de formation professionnelle, sous la présidence de M. COENE, deux fois, les 21 et 22 juin, les 4 et 5 octobre à Strasbourg;

le Comité restreint des essais de poussage, sous la présidence de M. VERHEY, sept fois, les 26 et 27 janvier à Mannheim, les 1er et 2 avril à St. Goar, les 9 et 10 juin à Duisbourg, le 23 juin à Strasbourg, le 3 août à Paris, le 5 octobre à Strasbourg, les 13 et 14 décembre à Strasbourg;

le Comité des douanes, sous la présidence de M. SCHNEIDER, deux fois, le 3 mai et le 25 octobre à Strasbourg;

le Comité des règlements du transport des matières dangereuses, deux fois, sous la présidence de M. SCHNEIDER, le 3 mai et sous la présidence de M. CLARKE le 25 octobre;

le Comité du Groupe d'experts „gaz liquéfiés", sous la présidence de M. VERHEY, les 29 et 30 novembre à Strasbourg;

le Comité de droit fluvial, sous la présidence de M. TURRETTINI, le 29 août à Genève;

le Comité économique, sous la présidence de M. THIERRY, le 2 juin à Paris;

la Chambre des rapporteurs, sous la présidence de M. BONET-MAURY, le 13 avril et sous la présidence de M. THIERRY, le 27 octobre, à Strasbourg.

Régime conventionnel

Le régime conventionnel, c'est-à-dire la Convention révisée pour la navigation du Rhin de 1868, dite „Acte de Mannheim", les clauses relatives à la navigation du Rhin du Traité de Versailles et les autres accords subséquents n'ont pas subi de modifications au cours de l'année.

2. ACTIVITIES OF THE CENTRAL COMMISSION

Plenary Sessions and Committee meetings during the year.

The Central Commission held two ordinary Sessions, 4th–6th May, and 26th–28th October, in Strasbourg. It also held a short extraordinary Session at Paris on 6th July.

The committees met as follows:

The Technical Standing Committee, twice: under the Chairmanship of Mr. OESTERHAUS, on 3rd May at Strasbourg, and under the Chairmanship of Mr. KLEINJAN, on 25th October at Strasbourg.

The Police Control Committee, six times: under the Chairmanship of Mr. FRANCOIS, on 12th and 13th January at Strasbourg, on 5th to 7th April at Brussels, on 2nd May, 21st and 22nd June, 5th to 7th October and 24th October at Strasbourg.

The Inspection Control Committee, five times: under the Chairmanship of Mrs. HARVEY on 12th and 13th January at Strasbourg, under the Chairmanship of Mr. MANGOLD, on 5th and 6th April at Brussels, 2nd May, 20th June and 24th October at Strasbourg.

The Committee for Revision of Inspection Control, three times: under the Chairmanship of Mr. SCHNEIDER, on 25th May at Freiburg-in-Breisgau, on 6th and 7th July and 12th–14th October at Strasbourg.

The Police Control Committee and Inspection Control Committee together, under the Chairmanship of Mrs. HARVEY and Mr. FRANCOIS on 13th January at Strasbourg.

The Committee on Social Questions, Labour and Training, under the Chairmanship of Mr. COENE, five times: on 14th January at Strasbourg, 8th April at Brussels, 3rd May at Strasbourg, 2nd June at Paris and 25th October at Strasbourg.

The Combined Committees of Police Control, Inspection Control, Social Questions and Training, under the Chairmanship of Mr. COENE, twice: on 21st and 22nd June, and on 4th and 5th October at Strasbourg;

The Restricted Committee on Pushing Trials, under the Chairmanship of Mr. VERHEY, seven times: on 26th and 27th January at Mannheim and on 1st and 2nd April at St. Goar, on 9th and 10th June at Duisbourg, on 23rd June at Strasbourg, on 3rd August at Paris, on 5th October and on 13th and 14th December at Strasbourg.

The Customs Committee, under the Chairmanship of Mr. SCHNEIDER, twice: on 3rd May and on 25th October at Strasbourg.

The Committee on Regulation of the Transport of Dangerous Materials, twice: under the Chairmanship of Mr. SCHNEIDER, on 3rd May and under the Chairmanship of Mr. CLARKE, on 25th October.

The Committee of Experts on Liquefied Gases, under the Chairmanship of Mr. VERHEY, on 29th and 30th November at Strasbourg.

The Committee on River Law, under the Chairmanship of Mr. TURRETTINI, on 29th August at Geneva.

The Economic Committee, under the Chairmanship of Mr. THIERRY, on 2nd June at Paris.

The Chamber of Rapporteurs, under the Chairmanship of Mr. BONET-MAURY, on 13th April and under the Chairmanship of Mr. THIERRY on 27th October at Strasbourg.

Treaty provisions

No change has been made this year in the treaty provisions, that is to say the revised Convention for the Navigation of the Rhine of 1868, known as "The Mannheim Act", the clauses of the Treaty of Versailles regarding Rhine navigation, and the other later agreements.

B. SECRÉTARIAT

Le Secrétariat était, à la même époque, composé comme suit:

Secrétaire Général:	M. H. WALTHER (Suisse),
Ingénieur en Chef:	M. J. H. VERHEY (Pays-Bas),
Secrétaire Général adjoint:	M. P. BERRYER (Belgique).

En Suisse et en France, les inspecteurs de la navigation étaient:

pour le secteur suisse:	M. JOST, Ingénieur cantonal à Bâle;
pour le secteur I.A.:	
de la frontière suisse à l'embouchure de la Lauter:	M. DELMAS, Ingénieur des Ponts et Chaussées à Strasbourg.

B. LIST OF OFFICERS

Secretary-General:	M. H. WALTHER (Switzerland),
Chief Engineer:	M. J. H. VERHEY (Netherlands),
Deputy Secretary-General:	M. P. BERRYER (Belgium)

In Switzerland and in France, navigation inspectors were:

for the Swiss sector:	M. JOST, District Engineer in Basle;
for the I.A. sector:	
for the Swiss frontier at the mouth of the Lauter:	M. DELMAS, Engineer for Bridges and Roadways at Strasbourg.

CHAPITRE II

UNION ÉCONOMIQUE BENELUX

A. CHRONOLOGIE

1960

1 janvier: En exécution des dispositions du Traité de la C.E.E. y relatives, la valeur totale des contingents Benelux et des contingents globaux, a été majorée de 20% au regard de 1959.
Prorogation jusqu'au 31 décembre 1960 de l'Accord commercial conclu entre les pays du Benelux et la Pologne.
Prorogation jusqu'au 31 décembre 1960 de l'Accord commercial conclu entre les pays du Benelux et la Hongrie.
Entrée en vigueur de l'Accord commercial Benelux avec la Bulgarie.

1 février: Suppression de la carte de travailleur frontalier entre les Pays-Bas et la Belgique.
1–4 février: Pourparlers en Commission mixte Benelux-France, à Bruxelles.
9–20 février: Pourparlers en Commission mixte entre les pays du Benelux et la Pologne.
10 février: Publication de l'Arrêté 1960 en matière de Tarifs (nouveau Tarif Benelux des droits d'entrée à partir du 1er mars).
16 février: Signature, par les pays du Benelux, du régime des échanges en matière de commerce et de paiement pour 1960, conclu entre la Finlande et la plupart des pays de l'O.E.C.E. dont les pays du Benelux.
20 février: Conférence intergouvernementale Benelux à Bruxelles, qui approuve entre autres un régime d'échanges commerciaux en produits agricoles non libéres.
26–27 février: Réunion du Conseil Interparlementaire de Benelux: discussion du troisième Rapport commun des Gouvernements et de la Convention relative à la coopération en matière de réglementation des importations, des exportations et du transit.
1 mars: Entrée en vigueur du nouveau Tarif Benelux de droits d'entrée (Arrêté 1960 en matière de Tarifs).
9 mars: Signature de l'Accord commercial Benelux-Grèce.
15–16 mars: Examen et adoption par la Deuxième Chambre néerlandaise du projet de loi approuvant le Traité d'Union Économique Benelux.

1 avril: Entrée en vigueur de l'Accord des paiements Benelux-Bulgarie, signé le 19 mars.
11 avril: Réunion du Comité Benelux de Ministres. Il y est convenu entre autres d'abolir le contrôle des passeports aux frontières intérieures à partir du 1er juillet et de mener une politique commune en matière de visas. L'unanimité a également été acquise sur la liberté mutuelle d'établissement et de séjour des personnes.
13 avril: Paraphe, à Madrid, de l'Accord commercial Benelux-Espagne, pour la période du 15 avril 1960 au 15 avril 1961.
9 mai: Réunion du Conseil Interparlementaire de Benelux: discussion de la Convention concernant le transfert du contrôle des personnes et de la Convention concernant la liberté du choix de domicile.
12 mai: La Chambre des Représentants de Belgique approuve le Traité d'Union Économique Benelux.
28 mai: Entrée en vigueur de la convention de la nation la plus favorisée Benelux-Honduras.

CHAPTER II

BENELUX ECONOMIC UNION

A. CHRONOLOGY

1960

1 January: In accordance with the relevant provisions of the E.E.C. Treaty, the total value of Benelux quotas and global quotas was increased by 20% as compared with 1959.
Extension of the Trade Agreement between the countries of Benelux and Poland: to be valid until 31st December, 1960.
Extension of the Trade Agreement between the countries of Benelux and Hungary: to be valid until 31st December, 1960.
Entry into force of the Trade Agreement between Benelux and Bulgaria.

1 February: Suppression of frontier worker's card between the Netherlands and Belgium.

1–4 February: Discussions in Joint Committee between Benelux countries and France at Brussels.

9–20 February: Discussions in Joint Committee between Benelux countries and Poland.

10 February: Publication of 1960 Regulation relating to Tariffs (new Benelux Tariff on rights of entry to be valid from 1st March).

16 February: Signature by the Benelux countries of Trade and Payments Agreement for 1960 concluded between Finland and most of the O.E.E.C. countries, including the countries of Benelux.

20 February: Benelux Intergovernmental Conference at Brussels approves *inter alia* a Trade Agreement on non-liberated agricultural products.

26–27 February: Meeting of the Benelux Interparliamentary Council: discussion of the third Joint Governmental Report and of a Convention relating to co-operation in regard to the regulation of imports, exports and goods in transit.

1 March: Entry into force of the new Benelux Tariff on rights of entry (Tariff Regulation 1960).

9 March: Signature of the Trade Agreement between Benelux and Greece.

15–16 March: Consideration and adoption of the Bill ratifying the Benelux Treaty of Economic Union by the Netherlands Second Chamber.

1 April: Entry into force of the Payments Agreement between Benelux and Bulgaria, signed on 19th March.

11 April: Meeting of the Benelux Committee of Ministers. It is agreed *inter alia* to abolish passport control within the Benelux area from 1st July and to pursue a common policy as regards visas. Unanimity is also reached concerning the free right of establishment and residence of persons.

13 April: Trade Agreement between Benelux and Spain initialled at Madrid: to be valid from 15th April, 1960 to 15th April, 1961.

9 May: Meeting of the Benelux Interparliamentary Council: discussion on the Convention relating to the transfer of control of persons, and on the Convention relating to the free choice of domicile.

12 May: Benelux Treaty of Economic Union ratified by the Belgian Chamber of Representatives.

28 May: Entry into force of the most-favoured-nation Convention between Benelux and Honduras.

Considérant qu'en vertu de l'article 56 dudit Traité, ils doivent également examiner dans quelle mesure le traitement des ressortissants d'une Partie Contractante sur le territoire d'une autre Partie Contractante doit faire l'objet d'une réglementation plus précise en ce qui concerne la protection légale et judiciaire de leur personne, de leurs droits et de leurs intérêts,

Sont convenus des dispositions suivantes:

Article 1

Les ressortissants de chacune des Parties Contractantes peuvent entrer sur le territoire des autres Parties Contractantes à la seule condition d'être en possession d'un document d'identité.

La nature de ce document est déterminée par le Comité de Ministres institué par l'article 15 du Traité d'Union.

Article 2

Les ressortissants de chacune des Parties Contractantes sont autorisés à s'établir sur le territoire des autres Parties Contractantes, s'ils jouissent de moyens d'existence suffisants et s'ils sont de bonne vie et moeurs.

Article 3

Les ressortissants de l'une des Parties Contractantes qui séjournent ou s'établissent sur le territoire d'une autre Partie Contractante ne sont tenus de se conformer aux dispositions légales et réglementaires en vigueur sur ce territoire concernant le contrôle des étrangers, que dans la mesure où elles visent l'inscription dans les registres communaux, la prorogation, le renouvellement, le remplacement, le port et la présentation des titres de séjour ainsi que les formalités requises en cas de changement de résidence ou de départ du pays.

Article 4

Sans préjudice des dispositions de l'article 5, les ressortissants de l'une des Parties Contractantes qui séjournent ou qui ont été autorisés à s'établir sur le territoire d'une autre Partie Contractante, ne peuvent faire l'objet d'une mesure d'éloignement que s'ils constituent un danger pour l'ordre public ou la sécurité nationale.

Pour l'application de cet article, le seul fait d'être dépourvu de moyens d'existence n'est pas considéré comme un danger pour l'ordre public.

Article 5

Les ressortissants de l'une des Parties Contractantes établis depuis trois ans sur le territoire d'une autre Partie Contractante ne peuvent faire l'objet d'une mesure d'éloignement que s'ils constituent un danger pour la sécurité nationale ou si, ayant été l'objet d'une condamnation définitive pour un crime ou délit particulièrement grave, ils constituent une menace pour la communauté de ce pays.

Article 6

Dans les cas prévus aux articles 4 et 5, les ressortissants de l'une des Parties Contractantes qui séjournent ou qui ont été autorisés à s'établir sur le territoire d'une autre Partie Contractante peuvent, au lieu d'être éloignés du territoire, être contraints à quitter des lieux ou régions déterminés et à en demeurer éloignés ou à résider en un lieu déterminé sans préjudice des voies de recours qui pourraient être prévues par la législation du pays de résidence.

Whereas by virtue of Article 56 of the said Treaty, they must also examine in what measure the treatment of nationals of one Contracting Party in the territory of another Contracting Party shall be the subject of more detailed regulations with regard to the legal and judicial protection of their person, rights and interests,

Have agreed as follows:

Article 1

Nationals of each of the Contracting Parties may enter the territory of the other Contracting Party on the sole condition of being in possession of a valid identity document. The nature of such document shall be determined by the Committee of Ministers set up by Article 15 of the Union Treaty.

Article 2

Nationals of each of the Contracting Parties shall have the right to establish themselves in the territory of the other Contracting Parties provided they have adequate means of subsistence and are of good character.

Article 3

Nationals of one Contracting Party residing or establishing themselves in the territory of another Contracting Party shall be required to conform only to such laws and regulations governing the control of foreigners in that territory as concern registration with the municipal authorities, the extension, renewal, replacement, holding and presentation of residence permits and the formalities required in the case of a change of residence or on leaving the country.

Article 4

Without prejudice to the provisions of Article 5, nationals of one of the Contracting Parties who reside or who have been authorised to establish themselves in the territory of another Contracting Party may be expelled only if they endanger public order or national security. For the purposes of this Article, the sole fact of being without means of subsistence shall not be considered as an offence against public order.

Article 5

Nationals of one Contracting Party who have been established for three years in the territory of another Contracting Party may be expelled only if they endanger national security or if, as a result of having been convicted of a particularly serious offence, they represent a danger to society in that country.

Article 6

In the cases provided for in Articles 4 and 5, nationals of one Contracting Party who reside or who have been authorised to establish themselves in the territory of another Contracting Party may, instead of being expelled from the territory, be required to leave particular places or regions and to keep away therefrom or to reside in a specific place without prejudice to any legal remedy which may be prescribed by the law of the country of residence.

Article 7

Les ressortissants de l'une des Parties Contractantes autorisés à s'établir sur le territoire d'une autre Partie Contractante ne peuvent faire l'objet d'une mesure d'éloignement qu'après avis donné au Ministre de la Justice du pays de résidence par une autorité compétente de ce pays, devant laquelle les intéressés peuvent faire valoir leurs moyens de défense et se faire représenter ou assister par un avocat de leur choix.

Au surplus, notification de la mesure d'éloignement est adressée directement et préalablement à son exécution aux services compétents de la Partie Contractante dont l'intéressé est ressortissant.

La notification indique les motifs de la mesure d'éloignement.

Article 8

Conformément à l'article 31 du Traité d'Union, il est institué une Commission pour la libre Circulation et l'Établissement des Personnes

Sans préjudice des dispositions de l'article 30 du Traité d'Union, cette Commission a pour mission de suivre l'application de la présente Convention.

Elle a également pour tâche de faire toutes propositions au Comité de Ministres tendant à améliorer les modalités d'application de la Convention et, pour autant que de besoin, à en reviser ou à en compléter les dispositions.

Article 9

Nonobstant les dispositions de l'article 2 § 2 *g*) du Traité d'Union, chacune des Parties Contractantes peut imposer les restrictions qu'elle juge utiles en ce qui concerne l'aliénation – même par parts de propriété –, la mise en location ou toute autre forme de cession de jouissance de navires et bateaux nationaux, ainsi que l'acquisition de bateaux par ses ressortissants et de navires destinés à battre pavillon national.

L'article 2 § 2 *g*) du Traité d'Union ne préjuge pas la réglementation relative à la réquisition et à l'expropriation de navires, bateaux et aéronefs, ainsi que de leurs cargaisons.

Article 10

Sont abrogés à dater du jour de l'entrée en vigueur de la présente Convention les dispositions de la Convention d'Établissement et de Travail entre la Belgique et les Pays-Bas, conclue à Genève, le 20 février 1933, ainsi que les dispositions de la Convention d'Établissement et de Travail entre les Pays-Bas et le Luxembourg, conclue à La Haye, le 1er avril 1933, qui ne sont pas abrogées par le Traité instituant l'Union Économique Benelux, signé le 3 février 1958, ou par le Traité de Travail entre la Belgique, le Luxembourg et les Pays-Bas, signé le 7 juin 1956.

Article 11

La présente Convention sera ratifiée et les instruments de ratification seront déposés auprès du Secrétariat Général de l'Union Économique Benelux.

Elle entrera en vigueur le premier jour du deuxième mois qui suivra le dépôt du troisième instrument de ratification et restera en vigueur, aussi longtemps que le Traité instituant l'Union Économique Benelux.

Article 7

Nationals of one Contracting Party who are authorised to establish themselves in the territory of another Contracting Party may be expelled only after notification to the Minister of Justice of the country of residence by a competent authority of that country before whom the persons concerned shall have the right to be represented or assisted by a counsel of their choosing.

The deportation order shall be notified directly and before execution to the competent authorities of the Contracting Party of which the person concerned is a national. Notice of deportation shall state the reasons therefor.

Article 8

In pursuance of Article 31 of the Union Treaty, a Committee on the Free Movement and Establishment of Persons shall be set up.

Without prejudice to the provisions of Article 30 of the Union Treaty, the Committee's task shall be to keep track of the execution of this Convention.

The Committee shall also submit to the Committee of Ministers proposals designed to improve the practical implementation of the Convention and, if necessary, to amend or supplement its provisions.

Article 9

Notwithstanding the provisions of Article 2, paragraph 2 *g*) of the Union Treaty, any of the Contracting Parties may impose such restrictions as it deems necessary on the transfer – even by way of shares in the property –, on the leasing or on any other form of surrender of possession of nationally owned ships and boats, and on the purchase by its nationals of boats or ships intended to fly the national flag. Article 2, paragraph 2 *g*) of the Union Treaty shall be without prejudice to any regulations concerning the requisitioning and expropriation of ships, boats and aircraft and their cargo.

Article 10

From the date of the entry into force of the present Convention the following shall be abrogated: those provisions of the Convention on Establishment and Labour between Belgium and the Netherlands, concluded at Geneva on 20th February, 1933, and of the Convention on Establishment and Labour between the Netherlands and Luxembourg, concluded at The Hague on 1st April, 1933, that have not been rescinded by the Treaty instituting the Benelux Economic Union, signed on 3rd February, 1958, or by the Labour Treaty between Belgium, Luxembourg and the Netherlands, signed on 7th June, 1956.

Article 11

The present Convention shall be ratified and the instruments of ratification deposited with the Secretariat-General of the Benelux Economic Union.

The Convention shall enter into force on the first day of the second month following the deposit of the third instrument of ratification and shall remain in force as long as the Treaty instituting the Benelux Economic Union.

En foi de quoi les Plénipotentiaires dûment autorisés ont signé la présente Convention.

Fait à ....,
le ....
en triple exemplaire, en langues française et néerlandaise, les deux textes faisant également foi.

Pour

Pour

Pour

Paraphé à Bruxelles, le 11 avril 1960.

2. CONVENTION ENTRE LE ROYAUME DE BELGIQUE, LE GRAND-DUCHÉ DE LUXEMBOURG ET LE ROYAUME DES PAYS-BAS CONCERNANT LE TRANSFERT DU CONTRÔLE DES PERSONNES VERS LES FRONTIÈRES EXTÉRIEURES DU TERRITOIRE DU BENELUX

Sa Majesté le Roi des Belges,
Son Altesse Royale la Grande-Duchesse de Luxembourg,
Sa Majesté la Reine des Pays-Bas,

Désireux de resserrer davantage les liens qui existent déjà entre Leurs Pays, notamment en vertu du Traité instituant l'Union Économique Benelux, signé à La Haye le 3 février 1958;

Considérant qu'il convient de supprimer le contrôle des personnes aux frontières intérieures dans le territoire du Benelux, de faciliter la circulation des étrangers à l'intérieur de ce territoire et d'adopter une politique commune concernant le franchissement des frontières extérieures;

Ont décidé de conclure une convention à cet effet et ont désigné comme Plénipotentiaires:

Sa Majesté le Roi des Belges:
Son Excellence Monsieur P. Wigny, Ministre des Affaires étrangères;
Son Altesse Royale la Grande-Duchesse de Luxembourg:
Son Excellence Monsieur E. Schaus, Ministre des Affaires étrangères;
Sa Majesté la Reine des Pays-Bas:
Son Excellence Monsieur J. M. A. H. Luns, Ministre des Affaires étrangères;

Lesquels, après avoir communiqué leurs pleins pouvoirs trouvés en bonne et due forme, sont convenus des dispositions suivantes:

Article 1

Aux termes de la présente Convention, il faut entendre:

1. par „territoire du Benelux": l'ensemble des territoires, en Europe, du Royaume de Belgique, du Grand-Duché de Luxembourg et du Royaume des Pays-Bas;
2. par „État tiers": tout État autre qu'un État du Benelux;
3. par „étranger": toute personne qui n'est pas un ressortissant de l'un des États du Benelux;
4. par „frontières extérieures":

a) la frontière entre le territoire du Benelux et le territoire d'un État tiers ou la haute mer;

b) tout aéroport ou tout port de mer situé dans le territoire du Benelux par lesquels s'effectue un mouvement de personnes en provenance ou à destination d'un État tiers;

In witness whereof the Plenipotentiaries duly authorised thereto have signed this Convention.

Done at ....
this ....
in three copies, in French and Dutch, both texts being equally authentic.

For

For

For

Initialled at Brussels on 11th April, 1960.

2. CONVENTION BETWEEN THE KINGDOM OF BELGIUM, THE GRAND DUCHY OF LUXEMBOURG AND THE KINGDOM OF THE NETHERLANDS CONCERNING THE TRANSFER OF ENTRY AND EXIT CONTROLS TO THE EXTERNAL FRONTIERS OF THE BENELUX TERRITORY

His Majesty the King of the Belgians,
Her Royal Highness the Grand-Duchess of Luxembourg,
Her Majesty the Queen of the Netherlands,
Desirous of tightening the bonds which already exist between Their Countries, in particular by virtue of the Treaty instituting the Benelux Economic Union, signed at The Hague on 3rd February, 1958;
Considering that entry and exit controls at the internal frontiers of the Benelux territory should be abolished, that the movement of foreigners in this territory should be facilitated and that a common policy concerning the crossing of the external frontiers should be adopted;
Have decided to conclude a convention to this end and have appointed as Plenipotentiaries:
His Majesty the King of the Belgians;
His Excellency Mr. P. WIGNY, Minister for Foreign Affairs;
Her Royal Highness the Grand Duchess of Luxembourg:
His Excellency Mr. E. SCHAUS, Minister for Foreign Affairs;
Her Majesty the Queen of the Netherlands:
His Excellency Mr. J. M. A. H. LUNS, Minister for Foreign Affairs;
Who, having exhibited their powers, found in good and due form, have agreed as follows:

Article 1

For the purposes of this Convention:
1. the expression "Benelux territory" means the whole of the territory, in Europe, of the Kingdom of Belgium, of the Grand-Duchy of Luxembourg and of the Kingdom of the Netherlands;
2. the expression "third State" means any State other than a Benelux State;
3. the term "foreigner" means any person who is not a national of one of the Benelux States;
4. the expression "external frontiers" means:
a) the frontier between the Benelux territory and the territory of a third State or the high seas;
b) any air-port or sea-port situated in the Benelux territory at which movements of persons to or from third States take place;

5. par „frontières intérieures": les frontières entre les territoires des États du Benelux;
6. par „Groupe de travail": un Groupe de travail ministériel institué conformément à l'article 21 du Traité instituant l'Union Économique Benelux;
7. par „Commission spéciale": une Commission spéciale instituée conformément à l'article 31 du même Traité.

Article 2

Dès l'entrée en vigueur de la présente Convention, chacune des Hautes Parties Contractantes supprime le contrôle des personnes aux frontières intérieures et exerce à ses frontières extérieures un contrôle valable pour le territoire du Benelux.

Article 3

Les Hautes Parties Contractantes s'engagent à adopter une politique commune tant sur le plan intérieur qu'à l'égard des États tiers en ce qui concerne l'application de la présente Convention. A cette fin, Elles se prêtent mutuellement assistance.

Article 4

Il est institué un visa valable pour le territoire du Benelux. Le visa est délivré de commun accord sur base d'instructions établies par le Groupe de travail.

Dans des cas à déterminer par le Groupe de travail, ou à défaut d'un commun accord dans des cas exceptionnels, la validité territoriale du visa peut être limitée.

Article 5

Les étrangers en possession des documents requis et disposant de moyens de subsistance suffisants ou de la possibilité de les acquérir par un travail légalement autorisé, peuvent entrer dans le territoire du Benelux, à moins qu'ils ne soient signalés comme indésirables dans ce territoire ou considérés comme pouvant compromettre la tranquillité publique, l'ordre public ou la sécurité nationale.

Article 6

Le Groupe de travail arrête les règles essentielles selon lesquelles s'exerce le contrôle des personnes aux frontières extérieures.

Article 7

Les étrangers qui entrent dans un des pays du Benelux sont tenus de déclarer leur arrivée aux autorités compétentes de ce pays. Le Groupe de travail fixe, suivant les catégories d'étrangers, les délais et conditions dans lesquels cette déclaration doit être faite.

Il peut dispenser certaines catégories d'étrangers de l'obligation de déclaration.

Article 8

Les étrangers entrés régulièrement dans le territoire du Benelux peuvent en respectant l'obligation prévue à l'article 7 et pour autant qu'ils continuent à remplir les conditions prévues à l'article 5, circuler dans chacun des pays du Benelux pendant une durée à déterminer par le Groupe de travail.

5. the expression "internal frontiers" means the frontiers between the territories of the Benelux States;

6. the expression "Working Party" means a ministerial Working Party set up in accordance with Article 21 of the Treaty instituting the Benelux Economic Union;

7. the expression "Special Committee" means a Special Committee set up in accordance with Article 31 of the same Treaty.

Article 2

From the moment of the entry into force of the present Convention each of the High Contracting Parties shall abolish entry and exit controls at the internal frontiers and shall effect at the external frontiers a control which is valid for the whole Benelux territory.

Article 3

In implementing the present Convention, the High Contracting Parties undertake to adopt a common policy both on the internal plane and *vis-à-vis* third States. To this end They shall render each other assistance.

Article 4

A visa shall be instituted for the Benelux territory. The visa shall be granted by common agreement on the basis of rules established by the Working Party.

In cases to be specified by the Working Party, or failing common agreement in exceptional cases, the territorial validity of the visa may be restricted.

Article 5

Foreigners in possession of the necessary documents and of adequate means of subsistence, or capable of acquiring such means through legally authorised work, may enter the Benelux territory unless they have been found undesirable in that territory or are considered as likely to disturb the peace, offend against public order or endanger national security.

Article 6

The Working Party shall lay down the basic rules governing entry and exit controls at the external frontiers.

Article 7

Foreigners entering a Benelux country shall declare their arrival to the competent authorities of that country. The time-limits and other conditions for making such declarations shall be prescribed by the Working Party in respect of each category of foreigners.

The Working Party may exempt certain categories of foreigners from the obligation to declare their arrival.

Article 8

Foreigners having lawfully entered the Benelux territory may, provided they comply with the obligation laid down in Article 7 and in so far as they continue to fulfil the conditions laid down in Article 5, travel in each of the Benelux countries during a period to be fixed by the Working Party.

Sans préjudice de l'application de l'article 7, les étrangers porteurs d'un titre de séjour délivré dans un des pays du Benelux peuvent également circuler dans les deux autres pays du Benelux sous le seul couvert de ce document, pourvu qu'ils remplissent les autres conditions prévues à l'article 5. Le Groupe de travail détermine les titres de séjour admis et fixe la durée pendant laquelle les étrangers porteurs de ces titres sont autorisés à circuler dans les deux autres pays du Benelux.

Article 9

Chacune des Hautes Parties Contractantes s'engage à réadmettre dans les cas et les conditions à déterminer par le Groupe de travail les étrangers qui, venant de son territoire, sont entrés dans le territoire d'une autre Partie Contractante et y sont indésirables.

Article 10

Un étranger indésirable dans un des pays du Benelux peut, sur demande motivée adressée par le Ministre de la Justice de ce pays aux Ministres de la Justice des deux autres pays, être considéré comme indésirable dans le territoire du Benelux pour autant que la mesure dont il fait l'objet ait été prise:

a) à la suite d'une condamnation encourue par cet étranger pour un crime ou pour un délit pouvant donner lieu à extradition;

b) pour le motif que la présence de cet étranger constitue un danger pour l'ordre public ou la sécurité nationale.

Il est donné suite à cette demande à moins que des raisons spéciales ne s'y opposent.

Article 11

Les Hautes Parties Contractantes s'engagent à harmoniser leurs lois et règlements relatifs à la répression des infractions aux dispositions concernant l'entrée et la circulation des étrangers.

L'entrée et la circulation irrégulières d'un étranger dans un pays du Benelux sont, sans préjudice de l'application des dispositions pénales, prévues dans ce pays, considérées comme un motif d'éloignement de l'étranger par les autorités de tous les pays du Benelux. L'infraction à un arrêté d'éloignement, étendu au territoire du Benelux conformément à l'article 10 de la présente Convention, est considérée comme une infraction aux dispositions légales ou réglementaires correspondantes du pays où l'infraction a été constatée.

Les autorités compétentes de chacun des pays se communiquent tous renseignements utiles concernant des infractions commises ou des faits qui tendent à faire croire qu'une infraction est ou sera commise en matière d'entrée, de circulation et de séjour des étrangers. Elles se communiquent en outre les renseignements concernant les faits qui peuvent donner lieu à l'application d'une sanction administrative contre un étranger.

Les renseignements obtenus en vertu de l'alinéa 3 ne peuvent être utilisés qu'en vue de l'application des lois et règlements relatifs à l'entrée, à la circulation et au séjour des étrangers, sauf en cas d'accord des autorités qui ont fourni ces renseignements.

Article 12

Chacune des Hautes Parties Contractantes se réserve le droit de réinstaurer temporairement, en tout ou en partie, le contrôle des personnes aux frontières intérieures pour des raisons découlant de l'ordre public ou de la sécurité nationale.

Without prejudice to the provisions of Article 7, foreigners holding a residence permit issued in one of the Benelux countries may also travel in the two other Benelux countries on the strength of such permit alone, provided that they fulfil the other conditions laid down in Article 5. The Working Party shall determine what residence permits shall be admissible and shall fix the period during which foreigners holding these permits shall be authorised to travel in the two other Benelux countries.

Article 9

Each of the High Contracting Parties undertakes to readmit in cases and under conditions to be determined by the Working Party foreigners who from its territory have entered the territory of another Contracting Party and are considered undesirable there.

Article 10

Any foreigner considered undesirable in one of the Benelux countries may, in response to a substantiated request made to this effect by the Minister of Justice of that country to the Ministers of Justice of the two other countries, be considered as undesirable throughout the Benelux territory if he has been subjected to a penalty:

a) as a result of his having been convicted of a crime or extraditable offence;

b) on the grounds that his presence endangers public order or national security.

Failing special reasons to the contrary, such request shall be complied with.

Article 11

The High Contracting Parties undertake to harmonise their laws and regulations relating to the punishment of infringements of the provisions concerning the entry and movement of foreigners.

Any foreigner who unlawfully enters one of the Benelux countries and travels therein shall, without prejudice to the penal laws of that country, be liable to expulsion by the authorities of all the Benelux countries. Disregard of an expulsion order applicable to the whole Benelux territory in accordance with Article 10 of the present Convention, shall be considered as a violation of the corresponding legal provisions or regulations of the country where it occurs.

The competent authorities of each country shall furnish one another with all necessary information concerning offences committed or evidence leading to the belief that an offence has been or will be committed in the matter of the entry, movement or sojourn of foreigners. They shall, in addition, communicate to each other any facts which may result in the application of an administrative penalty to a foreigner.

Information obtained by virtue of paragraph 3 may only be used for the purpose of enforcing the laws and regulations relating to the entry, movement and sojourn of foreigners, except with the agreement of the authorities which have supplied the information.

Article 12

Each of the High Contracting Parties reserves the right temporarily to re-establish, in whole or in part, entry and exit controls at the internal frontiers for reasons of public order or national security.

Le Groupe de travail fixe les modalités d'exécution de cette faculté.

Le Comité de Ministres fait, dans le plus bref délai, rapport au Conseil Interparlementaire Consultatif tant sur les mesures prises que sur les raisons qui les ont justifiées.

Article 13

Le Groupe de travail veille à l'application de la présente Convention et à la réalisation des objectifs fixés par celle-ci et prend les décisions nécessaires à cet effet. Les décisions sont prises à l'unanimité.

Article 14

Chacune des Hautes Parties Contractantes s'engage à prendre les mesures nécessaires en vue de la mise en concordance de sa réglementation avec les décisions prises par le Groupe de travail.

Article 15

La Commission spéciale a pour mission:

1. d'élaborer les règles communes relatives à l'exécution de la présente Convention;
2. de faire au Groupe de travail toutes propositions tendant à améliorer les modalités d'application de la présente Convention et, pour autant que de besoin, tendant à en reviser ou compléter les dispositions;
3. de faire au Groupe de Travail toutes propositions quant à l'opportunité d'entamer avec des États tiers des négociations en vue de conclure des conventions sur les matières faisant l'objet de la présente Convention;
4. d'exécuter les décisions du Groupe de travail ou d'en promouvoir l'exécution et de suivre l'exécution, par les administrations nationales, des décisions prises.

La Commission spéciale s'adresse directement au Groupe de travail, seul compétent pour lui donner des directives.

La Commission spéciale arrête son règlement d'ordre intérieur et le soumet à l'approbation du Groupe de travail.

Article 16

Les différends qui pourraient s'élever entre les Hautes Parties Contractantes en ce qui concerne l'interprétation de la présente Convention, sont soumis au Collège arbitral institué par le Traité d'Union Économique Benelux.

Article 17

La présente Convention sera ratifiée et les instruments de ratification seront déposés auprès du Gouvernement belge qui les transmettra au Secrétariat Général de l'Union Économique Benelux dès l'entrée en vigueur de la présente Convention.

Article 18

La présente Convention entrera en vigueur le lendemain du jour du dépôt du troisième instrument de ratification et restera en vigueur aussi longtemps que le Traité instituant l'Union Économique Benelux.

En foi de quoi, les Plénipotentiaires ont signé la présente Convention et l'ont revêtue de leur sceau.

The Working Party shall determine the manner in which this option may be exercised.

The Committee of Ministers shall, in the shortest possible time, report to the Consultative Interparliamentary Council on the measures taken and the reasons underlying them.

Article 13

The Working Party shall ensure the implementation of this Convention and the achievement of its objectives, and shall adopt the necessary resolutions to this end. Such resolutions shall be unanimous.

Article 14

Each of the High Contracting Parties undertakes to introduce the necessary measures with a view to bringing its regulations into conformity with the resolutions of the Working Party.

Article 15

The Special Committee shall:

1. establish common rules for the implementation of this Convenion;
2. submit proposals to the Working Party designed to improve the practical implementation of this Convention and, if necessary, to amend or supplement its provisions;
3. submit to the Working Party proposals on the advisability of entering into negotiation with third States with a view to concluding conventions on the matters forming the subject of this Convention;
4. implement the resolutions of the Working Party or promote their implementation, and keep track of their execution by national administrations.

The Special Committee will report directly to the Working Party which alone is competent to issue it with instructions.

The Special Committee shall draw up its own rules of procedure and shall submit them for approval to the Working Party.

Article 16

Disputes which may arise between the High Contracting Parties concerning the interpretation of this Convention shall be submitted to the College of Arbitrators instituted by the Treaty of the Benelux Economic Union.

Article 17

This Convention shall be ratified and the instruments of ratification shall be deposited with the Belgian Government, which will transmit them to the Secretariat-General of the Benelux Economic Union as soon as the Convention enters into force.

Article 18

This Convention shall enter into force on the day following the date of deposit of the third instrument of ratification and shall remain in force as long as the Treaty instituting the Benelux Economic Union.

In witness whereof, the Plenipotentiaries have signed this Convention and have affixed their seal thereto.

Fait à Bruxelles, le 11 avril 1960, en trois exemplaires, en langues française et néerlandaise, les deux textes faisant également foi.

Pour le Royaume de Belgique:

P. WIGNY

Pour le Grand-Duché de Luxembourg:

E. SCHAUS

Pour le Royaume des Pays-Bas:

J. M. A. H. LUNS

3. DÉCISION DU COMITÉ DE MINISTRES DE L'UNION ÉCONOMIQUE BENELUX INSTITUANT UNE COMMISSION POUR LA LIBRE CIRCULATION ET L'ÉTABLISSEMENT DES PERSONNES

Le Comité de Ministres de l'Union Économique Benelux,
Vu l'article 31 du Traité d'Union,
Vu l'article 8 de la Convention portant exécution des articles 55 et 56 du Traité d'Union, signée à Bruxelles, le 19 septembre 1960.
A pris la présente décision:

Article 1

1. En vue de l'application de la Convention portant exécution des articles 55 et 56 du Traité d'Union, signée à Bruxelles, le 19 septembre 1960 et conformément à l'article 31 de ce Traité, il est institué une Commission pour la Libre Circulation et l'Établissement des Personnes dont les attributions sont fixées par ladite Convention.
2. La Commission prévue à l'alinéa 1er du présent article est composée de fonctionnaires des Ministères intéressés à désigner par les Ministres des Affaires étrangères et de la Justice de chacun des trois Gouvernements.

Article 2

La présente décision entre en vigueur en même temps que la Convention portant exécution des articles 55 et 56 du Traité d'Union.

Fait à Bruxelles, le 3 novembre 1960.

Le Président du Comité de Ministres,

P. WIGNY (s.)

4. DÉCISION DU COMITÉ DE MINISTRES DE L'UNION ÉCONOMIQUE BENELUX INSTITUANT UN GROUPE DE TRAVAIL ET UNE COMMISSION SPÉCIALE EN VUE DE L'EXÉCUTION DE LA CONVENTION CONCERNANT LE TRANSFERT DU CONTRÔLE DES PERSONNES VERS LES FRONTIÈRES EXTÉRIEURES DU BENELUX, SIGNÉE À BRUXELLES LE 11 AVRIL 1960

Le Comité de Ministres de l'Union Économique Benelux,
Vu la Convention concernant le transfert du contrôle des personnes vers les frontières extérieures du Benelux, signée à Bruxelles, le 11 avril 1960,

Done at Brussels, this 11th day of April, 1960, in three copies, in the French and Dutch languages, both texts being equally authoritative.

For the Kingdom of Belgium:

P. WIGNY

For the Grand Duchy of Luxembourg:

E. SCHAUS

For the Kingdom of the Netherlands:

J. M. A. H. LUNS

3. RESOLUTION OF THE COMMITTEE OF MINISTERS OF THE BENELUX ECONOMIC UNION INSTITUTING A COMMITTEE ON THE FREE MOVEMENT AND ESTABLISHMENT OF PERSONS

The Committee of Ministers of the Benelux Economic Union,

Having regard to Article 31 of the Union Treaty,

Having regard to Article 8 of the Convention, signed in Brussels on 19th September, 1960, implementing Articles 55 and 56 of the Union Treaty,

Have resolved as follows:

Article 1

1. For the purpose of giving effect to the Convention signed in Brussels on 19th September, 1960, implementing Articles 55 and 56 of the Union Treaty, and in pursuance of Article 31 of the said Treaty, a Committee on the Free Movement and Establishment of Persons is hereby instituted whose powers are laid down in the said Convention.

2. The Committee provided for in paragraph 1 of this Article shall be composed of officials of the competent Ministries, who shall be appointed by the Ministers for Foreign Affairs and the Ministers of Justice of each of the three Governments.

Article 2

This resolution shall take effect at the same time as the Convention implementing Articles 55 and 56 of the Union Treaty.

Done at Brussels, this 3rd day of November, 1960.

(signed) P. WIGNY

Chairman of the Committee of Ministers.

4. RESOLUTION OF THE COMMITTEE OF MINISTERS OF THE BENELUX ECONOMIC UNION INSTITUTING A WORKING PARTY AND A SPECIAL COMMITTEE WITH A VIEW TO IMPLEMENTING THE CONVENTION TRANSFERRING ENTRY AND EXIT CONTROLS TO THE EXTERNAL FRONTIERS OF BENELUX, SIGNED AT BRUSSELS ON 11TH APRIL, 1960

The Committee of Ministers of the Benelux Economic Union,

Having regard to the Convention on the Transfer of Entry and Exit Controls to the External Frontiers of Benelux, signed at Brussels on 11th April, 1960.

Vu le Protocole relatif à l'exécution de ladite Convention, signée à Bruxelles, le 20 juin 1960,

Vu les articles 21 et 31 du Traité d'Union,

A pris la présente décision:

Article 1

1. En vue de l'exécution de la Convention concernant le transfert du contrôle des personnes vers les frontières extérieures du Benelux, signée à Bruxelles le 11 avril 1960, et en application de l'article 21 du Traité d'Union, il est institué un Groupe de travail dont les attributions sont celles fixées par ladite Convention.

2. Le Groupe de travail prévu à l'alinéa 1 du présent article est composé des Ministres des Affaires étrangères et de la Justice de chacun des trois Gouvernements.

3. Chaque délégation peut inviter d'autres membres de son Gouvernement à prendre part à une réunion déterminée du Groupe de travail, chaque fois qu'elle l'estime opportun.

Article 2

1. En vue de l'exécution de la Convention citée à l'article 1er de la présente décision, et en application de l'article 31 du Traité d'Union, il est institué une Commission spéciale pour la circulation des personnes dont la mission est fixée dans ladite Convention.

2. La Commission spéciale prévue à l'alinéa 1er du présent article est composée de fonctionnaires des Ministères intéressés à désigner par les Ministères des Affaires étrangères et de la Justice, de chacun des trois Gouvernements.

Article 3

1. Chaque Gouvernement désigne comme délégués un chef de délégation et quatre membres au maximum pour le représenter au sein de la Commission spéciale.

2. Chaque délégué peut être représenté par un suppléant.

3. Chaque délégation peut se faire assister d'experts. Les experts non-fonctionnaires ne peuvent être convoqués à une réunion que moyennant l'accord de la Commission spéciale; ils sont tenus de garder le secret sur les points indiqués par la Commission spéciale.

Article 4

La Commission spéciale fait annuellement rapport au Groupe de travail.

Article 5

Les décisions prises par le Groupe de travail constitué par le Protocole du 20 juin 1960 sont considérées comme étant prises par le Groupe de travail institué par la présente décision.

Article 6

La présente décision entre en vigueur le jour de sa signature.

Fait à Bruxelles, le 3 novembre 1960.

Le Président du Comité de Ministres,

P. WIGNY (s.)

Having regard to the Protocol regarding the execution of the same Convention, signed at Brussels on 20th June, 1960.

Having regard to Articles 21 and 31 of the Union Treaty,

Have resolved as follows:

Article 1

1. With a view to giving effect to the Convention on the Transfer of Entry and Exit Controls to the External Frontiers of Benelux, signed at Brussels on 11th April, 1960, and in pursuance of Article 21 of the Union Treaty, a Working Party shall be set up whose powers are laid down in the said Convention.

2. The Working Party provided for in paragraph 1 of this Article shall be composed of the Ministers for Foreign Affairs and of the Ministers of Justice of each of the three Governments.

3. Each delegation may invite other members of its Government to take part in a meeting of the Working Party whenever it deems advisable.

Article 2

1. With a view to giving effect to the Convention referred to in Article 1 of this decision and in pursuance of Article 31 of the Union Treaty, a Special Committee on the movement of persons shall be instituted whose function is defined in the said Convention.

2. The Special Committee provided for in paragraph 1 of this Article shall be composed of officials of the competent Ministries, who shall be appointed by the Ministers for Foreign Affairs and the Ministers of Justice of each of the three Governments.

Article 3

1. Each Government shall appoint one head of delegation and not more than four members to represent it on the Special Committee.

2. Each delegate may be represented by an alternate.

3. Each delegation may be assisted by experts. Experts who are not civil servants may take part in a meeting only with the agreement of the Special Committee; they shall maintain secrecy in regard to such matters as the Special Committee may indicate.

Article 4

The Special Committee shall report annually to the Working Party.

Article 5

The decisions taken by the Working Party set up by the Protocol of 20th June, 1960, shall be considered as having been taken by the Working Party instituted by this Resolution.

Article 6

This Resolution shall take effect on the day of its signature.

Done at Brussels, this 3rd day of November, 1960.

(signed) P. WIGNY

Chairman of the Committee of Ministers.

C. PUBLICATIONS

(texte unique pour les deux langues)

Bulletin Benelux. Le Traité instituant l'Union Économique Benelux entrant en vigueur le 1er novembre 1960, il a été décidé de publier un Bulletin Benelux qui paraîtra six fois par an. Quatre numéros sortiront de presse au cours de l'année 1960. Ce Bulletin reprendra des communications et textes officiels ainsi que des articles relatifs à l'Union Économique Benelux.

Analyse des Budgets Belge, Néerlandais et Luxembourgeois, 1957–1959. Le présent rapport de la Commission pour l'Étude de la Comparaison des Budgets des Institutions Publiques et Parastatales, analyse, à l'instar de ceux des années antérieures, les dépenses et recettes d'État des trois pays.

La structure des dépenses de l'État, réparties selon les catégories économiques importantes telles que les investissements, la consommation, les transferts, est analysée dans la première partie de ce document; la seconde traite de la destination des dépenses suivant les principaux objets d'intervention de l'État.

L'analyse des dépenses de l'État s'intéresse tout spécialement à la politique fiscale des pays du Benelux. Les divergences dans la charge fiscale globale et sa répartition entre les impôts sur le revenu et les impôts majorant les prix, y sont tout particulièrement commentées.

L'annexe statistique comporte des tableaux détaillés dans lesquels les dépenses budgétaires pour les années 1957–1959 sont rangées selon les catégories économiques et fonctionnelles principales.

Benelux: Classification fonctionnelle uniforme des dépenses publiques. Cette étude contient la classification uniforme des dépenses publiques selon des critères fonctionnels, appliquée dans le budget des pays de Benelux.

Benelux 1948–1958. Aperçu statistique de dix années de coopération. En collaboration avec le Secrétariat Général, la Commission de Coordination des Statistiques a composé un ouvrage détaillé qui fournit un aperçu comparatif des statistiques de base des trois pays, pour autant que celles-ci intéressent le Benelux. Le volume a trait aux dix années qui se sont écoulées depuis l'entrée en vigueur de l'Union Douanière jusqu'à la signature de l'Union Économique.

Chacun des 19 chapitres est précédé d'une introduction qui commente les statistiques. En outre, cet ouvrage est illustré de plusieurs graphiques ainsi que de cartogrammes et de quelques cartes, tandis qu'une table des matières fascilite la recherche des renseignements désirés.

Bulletin trimestriel de statistique. En collaboration avec l'Institut National de Statistique de Belgique, le Bureau Central de Statistique des Pays-Bas, le Ministère des Affaires économiques et l'Office de la Statistique Générale du Luxembourg, le Secrétariat Général édite quatre fois par an, un „Bulletin Trimestriel de Statistique Benelux".

Cette publication fournit les statistiques les plus courantes, pour les trois pays du Benelux.

Dans ce Bulletin Trimestriel, les statistiques de base, publiées pour les trois pays dans l'Aperçu statistique „Benelux 1948–1958", sont mises à jour.

Le „Bulletin Trimestriel de Statistique Benelux" contient donc les chiffres les plus récents, disponibles en matière d'emploi et chômage,

(Lire la suite en p. 187)

(suite de p. 186)

agriculture et pêche, production industrielle, commerce extérieur et intra-Benelux, transport et communications, finances, prix et salaires.

Statistiques de la population. Cette publication commente en détail les statistiques de la population disponibles dans les pays de Benelux et analyse leur comparabilité.

Textes de base de l'Union Économique Benelux. Il est apparu que les services publics comme les milieux privés éprouvaient le besoin de disposer d'un recueil qui reprend d'une manière très claire et très pratique tous les principaux textes fondamentaux qui seront d'application dès l'entrée en vigueur de l'Union Économique, ainsi que d'un système permettant l'insertion rapide et dans l'ordre des modifications apportées à ces conventions ainsi que des textes des nouvelles conventions Benelux qui seront conclues dans l'avenir.

C'est pourquoi le Secrétariat Général publie un volume à feuillets mobiles (format 22 × 18 cm) pourvu d'une reliure en plastic à anneaux qui reprend les textes néerlandais et français de tous les importants accords Benelux, classés systématiquement.

Politique des salaires 1958–1959. Un nouvel aperçu, portant sur la politique des salaires suivie par les trois pays en 1958 et en 1959, sera publié dans le courant du mois d'août 1960.

Cette publication constitue le second supplément à la brochure „La politique des salaires", parue le 31 décembre 1956; le premier supplément date du mois de mars 1958.

L'Industrie du papier dans les pays de Benelux. Cette publication présente de données comparables relatives à la production, la consommation, le personnel, les investissements, *etc.* dans l'industrie du papier des pays de Benelux.

D. ORGANIGRAMME

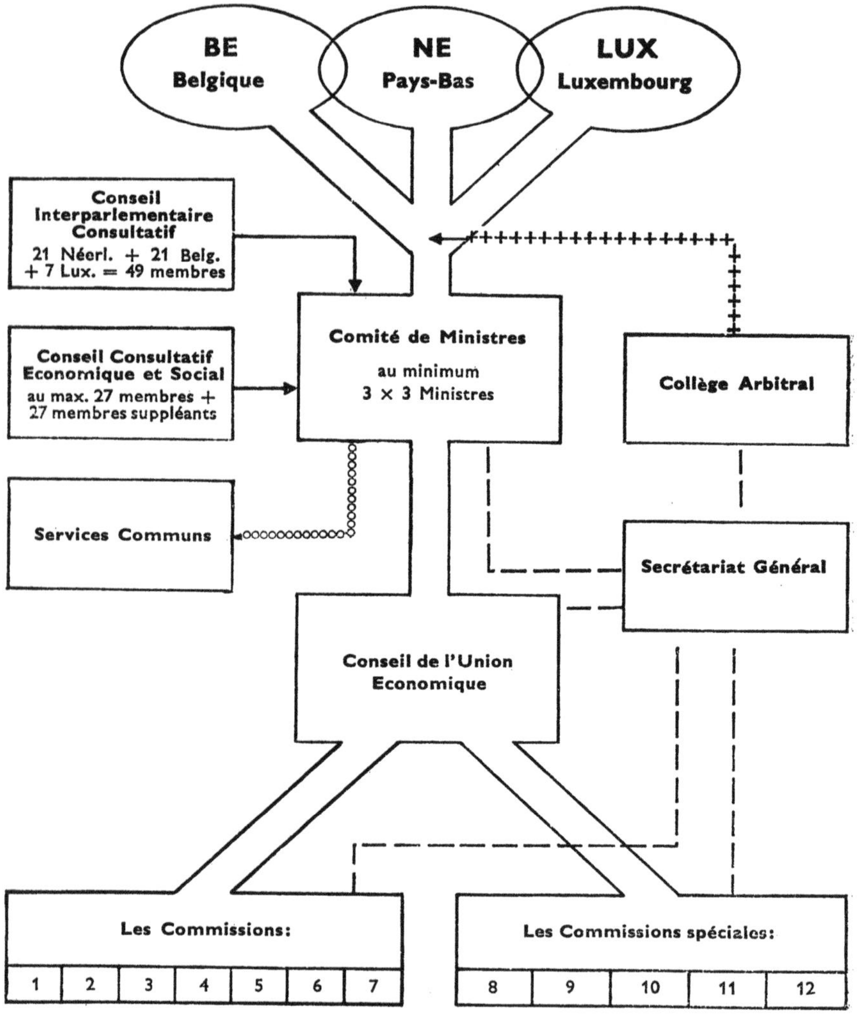

1 relations économiques avec l'étranger
2 problèmes monétaires et financiers
3 industrie et commerce
4 agriculture, ravitaillement et pêche
5 problèmes douaniers et fiscaux
6 communications
7 problèmes sociaux
8 coordination des statistiques
9 comparaison des budgets publics
10 adjudications
11 santé publique
12 classes moyennes

——— = avis
+ + + + = arbitrage de litiges
oooo = institution de services-Benelux
— — = travaux de secrétariat et de greffe

D. ORGANISATION CHART

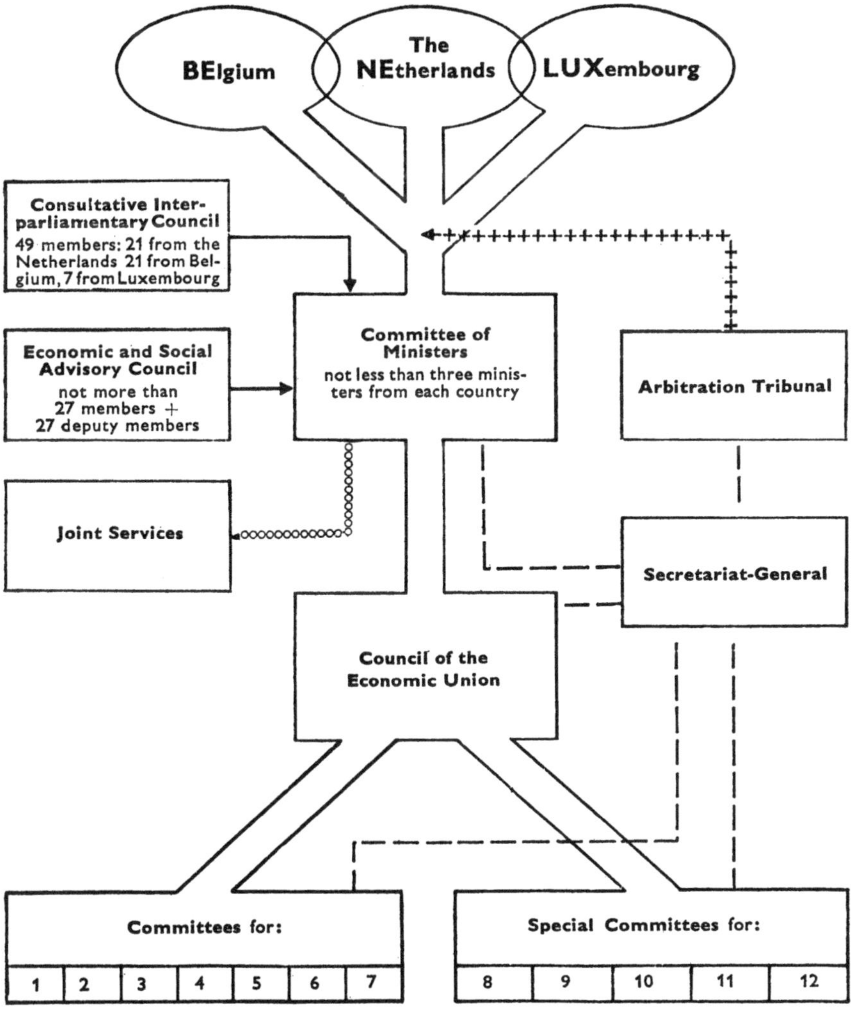

1 foreign economic relations;
2 monetary and financial problems;
3 industry and commerce;
4 agriculture, food supplies and fisheries;
5 customs and taxation;
6 transport;
7 social problems;

8 co-ordination of statistics;
9 comparison of the government budgets;
10 public tenders;
11 public health;
12 independent retail trade and handicrafts.

——— = advice
+ + + + = settlement of disputes

oooo = setting-up of Benelux services
—— = secretariat and registry activities

CHAPITRE III

UNION DE L'EUROPE OCCIDENTALE

A. CHRONOLOGIE DES PRINCIPAUX ÉVÉNEMENTS DE 1960

Du 1er janvier au 31 décembre 1960, le Conseil de l'U.E.O. s'est réuni 28 fois, dont 3 à l'échelon ministériel.

4 février: Le Conseil se réunit à Londres, à l'échelon ministériel, sous la présidence de Monsieur E. Schaus, Ministre des Affaires étrangères du Luxembourg et Président en exercice du Conseil. Au cours de la réunion, le Conseil manifeste l'intention de développer les consultations politiques dans le cadre de l'U.E.O., sans préjudice des consultations qui ont lieu au sein de l'O.T.A.N. Le Président de l'Assemblée de l'U.E.O., Monsieur V. Badini Confalonieri, assiste à une partie de la session.

31 mai–3 juin: L'Assemblée de l'U.E.O. tient à Paris sa sixième session ordinaire (première partie). M. Badini Confalonieri est réélu Président par acclamation. Monsieur van Houten, Secrétaire d'État aux Affaires étrangères des Pays-Bas et Président du Conseil par intérim, présente le cinquième Rapport annuel du Conseil à l'Assemblée. L'Assemblée entend notamment: Monsieur Jules Moch, délégué de la France au Comité du Désarmement des Dix, Monsieur F.-J. Strauss, Ministre de la Défense de la République Fédérale d'Allemagne et Monsieur John Profumo, Ministre d'État aux Affaires étrangères du Royaume-Uni. Les Généraux Valluy et Challe, du S.H.A.P.E., sont également présents. Dans l'une de ses recommandations, l'Assemblée demande aux Gouvernements des sept États membres d'examiner la possibilité d'une adhésion du Royaume-Uni comme plein Membre à la Communauté Européenne de l'Énergie Atomique.

16 juin: Le Conseil des Ministres se réunit à La Haye, sous la présidence de Monsieur J. M. A. H. Luns, Ministre des Affaires étrangères des Pays-Bas et Président en exercice du Conseil. Conformément à la décision prise lors de leur réunion précédente (*voir ci-dessus*), les ministres poursuivent leurs consultations politiques.

13 septembre: Entrée en vigueur, après ratification par les sept États membres, du Protocole relatif à l'adhésion de la République Fédérale d'Allemagne et de l'Italie aux Conventions concernant les Travailleurs frontaliers et les Stagiaires, signé à Paris le 10 décembre 1956 (voir *Annuaire européen*, Vol. IV p. 284).

24 octobre: La huitième réunion commune du Conseil et de la Commission des Questions de Défense et des Armements de l'Assemblée a lieu à Bruxelles, sous la présidence de Monsieur Pierre Wigny, Ministre des Affaires étrangères de Belgique et Président en exercice du Conseil. La délégation parlementaire est conduite par Monsieur F. Mulley (Royaume-Uni), Vice-Président de la Commission. Les échanges de vues portent sur de nombreuses questions relatives à la défense.

25 octobre: La deuxième réunion commune du Conseil et de la Commission des Affaires générales de l'Assemblée a lieu à Bruxelles, sous la présidence de Monsieur P. Wigny. La Commission est conduite par son Président, Monsieur Peter Kirk (Royaume-Uni). Les échanges de vues portent notamment sur les relations entre le Royaume-Uni et les Six.

CHAPTER III

WESTERN EUROPEAN UNION

A. CHRONOLOGY OF PRINCIPAL EVENTS IN 1960

During the period January–December 1960
the Council of W.E.U. held 28 meetings,
including 3 at Ministerial level.

4 February: The Council met at Ministerial level in London under the chairmanship of Monsieur E. SCHAUS, Luxembourg Foreign Minister and Chairman in Office of the Council. In the course of the meeting the Ministers stated their intention to develop political consultations within W.E.U., without prejudice to consultations in N.A.T.O. The President of the W.E.U. Assembly, Signor V. BADINI CONFALONIERI, attended part of the session.

31 May–3 June: The Assembly of W.E.U. met in Paris for the first part of the sixth Ordinary Session. Signor BADINI CONFALONIERI was re-elected President by acclamation. The fifth Annual Report of the Council was presented by Mr. van HOUTEN, Secretary of State for Foreign Affairs of the Netherlands and Acting Chairman of the Council. The Assembly was addressed by M. Jules MOCH, French delegate to the Ten-Power Disarmament Committee, Mr. F.-J. STRAUSS, Minister of Defence of the Federal Republic of Germany, and Mr. John PROFUMO, Minister of State for Foreign Affairs of the United Kingdom. Generals VALLUY and CHALLE, of S.H.A.P.E., were also present. One of the recommendations adopted proposed that the Governments of the seven Member States of W.E.U. should examine together the possibility of the United Kingdom acceding to Euratom as a full Member.

16 June: The Council met at Ministerial level in The Hague under the chairmanship of Mr. J. M. A. H. LUNS, Netherlands Foreign Minister and Chairman in Office of the Council. In line with their decision at the previous meeting (*see above*), the Ministers continued their policy of political consultation.

13 September: The Protocol concerning the adherence of the Federal Republic of Germany and Italy to the Conventions on Frontier Workers and Student Employees, signed in Paris on 10th December, 1956 (see *European Yearbook* Vol. IV, p. 285) entered into force on completion of the ratification formalities by the seven Member States.

24 October: The eighth joint meeting between the Council and the Assembly Committee on Defence Questions and Armaments took place in Brussels under the chairmanship of Monsieur Pierre WIGNY, Belgian Foreign Minister and Chairman in Office of the Council. The Assembly Committee was led by the Vice-Chairman, Mr. F. MULLEY (United Kingdom). A wide range of questions on defence subjects was discussed.

25 October: The second joint meeting between the Council and the General Affairs Committee of the Assembly was held in Brussels under the chairmanship of Monsieur P. WIGNY. The Committee was headed by its chairman, Mr. Peter KIRK (United Kingdom). The subject of the United Kingdom's relations with the Six was included in the discussion.

17 novembre: Le Conseil des Ministres se réunit à Bruxelles sous la présidence de Monsieur Pierre WIGNY, Président en exercice. Il reçoit à cette occasion plusieurs membres de la Commission des Affaires générales de l'Assemblée, réunie à Bruxelles à cette même date.

29 novembre–2 décembre: L'Assemblée de l'U.E.O. tient à Paris sa sixième session ordinaire (deuxième partie). Le Conseil y est représenté par son Président en exercice, Monsieur Pierre WIGNY, qui prononce une allocution. L'Assemblée entend également: Monsieur DEBRÉ, Premier Ministre français; le Général NORSTAD, Commandant suprême des forces alliées en Europe, et Monsieur MESSMER, Ministre des Armées du Gouvernement de la République française. L'une des recommandations adoptées par l'Assemblée porte sur l'accession du Royaume-Uni aux Communautés des Six.

Modifications intervenues en cours d'année
dans le représentation au Conseil
(niveau des ambassadeurs)

22 juillet: Sir Evelyn SHUCKBURGH succède à Sir Anthony RUMBOLD comme délégué du Royaume-Uni.

23 novembre: Monsieur René van MEERBEKE, ambassadeur de Belgique à Londres, prend congé de ses collègues au moment de quitter ses fonctions.

B. ACTIVITÉS

1. AGENCE POUR LE CONTRÔLE DES ARMEMENTS

1. En 1960, l'Agence a continué à exercer sa tâche conformément aux dispositions du Protocole no. IV des Accords de Paris et aux directives arrêtées par le Conseil de l'U.E.O. Cette tâche est double: elle doit d'une part vérifier que les niveaux de certaines armes mentionnées dans les Accords précités ne dépassent pas dans les États membres les niveaux déterminés conformément aux dispositions du Traité (contrôle quantitatif) et, d'autre part, s'assurer que les engagements pris par la République Fédérale d'Allemagne de ne pas fabriquer certains types d'armements sont respectés (contrôle de non-fabrication).

2. Bien que d'importantes mesures doivent encore être prises sur le plan juridique en vue de permettre un contrôle complet, les activités de l'Agence ont été fort importantes en 1960, notamment grâce à la collaboration des autorités compétentes des États intéressés.

a) Dans le domaine du contrôle quantitatif, l'Agence a vérifié les niveaux appropriés des armements soumis à contrôle sur le continent européen en exploitant notamment les données statistiques et budgétaires fournies par les États membres en réponse à son questionnaire annuel; elle a également procédé à une étude complémentaire des budgets nationaux publiés. Ce dépouillement a été facilité par l'assistance reçue de l'O.T.A.N. en ce qui concerne le secteur couvert par l'alliance atlantique, tandis que les Gouvernements des États-Unis et du Canada ont communiqué des renseignements détaillés sur l'aide extérieure.

En outre, l'Agence a inspecté des dépôts militaires placés sous commandement national ou sous commandement O.T.A.N., en ce dernier cas en coopération avec le S.H.A.P.E. Elle a ainsi pu vérifier effectivement sur place les renseignements fournis en réponse à son questionnaire; les résultats ont été extrêmement satisfaisants.

L'Agence a aussi procédé à des contrôles quantitatifs sur place dans de nombreuses usines de fabrication d'armes et de matériel; ici également,

17 November: The Council met at Ministerial level in Brussels under the chairmanship of Monsieur Pierre WIGNY, Chairman in Office. Members of the General Affairs Committee of the Assembly, who were meeting in Brussels at the same time, were received by the Council.

29 November–2 December: The Assembly of W.E.U. met in Paris for the second part of the sixth Ordinary Session. The Council were represented by their Chairman in Office, Monsieur Pierre WIGNY, who addressed the Assembly. Guest speakers included Monsieur DEBRÉ, Prime Minister of France, General NORSTAD, Supreme Allied Commander Europe, and Monsieur MESSMER, Minister of the Armed Forces of France. The accession of the United Kingdom to the Communities of the Six formed the subject of one of the recommendations.

During 1960 the following change took place in the Council at ambassadorial level:

22 July: Sir Evelyn SHUCKBURGH became United Kingdom delegate in place of Sir Anthony RUMBOLD.
23 November: The Belgian Ambassador, Monsieur René van MEERBEKE, took leave of his colleagues on retirement from his post in London.

B. ACTIVITIES

1. ARMAMENTS CONTROL AGENCY

1. The Agency continued to carry out its activities throughout 1960 in accordance with the provisions of Protocol No. IV of the Paris Agreements and the directives issued by the Council of W.E.U. Its duties are twofold, firstly, to check that the stocks of certain armaments listed in the Agreements, subject to control in each Member country, do not exceed the levels laid down as appropriate in accordance with the Treaty (quantitative control); secondly, to satisfy itself that the undertakings given by the Federal Republic of Germany not to manufacture certain types of armaments are being observed (non-production control).

2. In spite of the fact that essential legal procedure has yet to be completed before controls can become entirely effective, the Agency registered considerable achievements in 1960, thanks in great part to the co-operation afforded by competent authorities in all the countries concerned.

a) In the field of quantitative controls, the appropriate levels of weapons subject to inspection on the mainland of Europe were verified on the basis of statistical and budgetary data supplied by Member States in reply to the annual questionnaire; an additional study was made of the relevant sections of published national budgets. The processing of material was facilitated by assistance from N.A.T.O. with regard to the sector covered by the Atlantic Alliance, while the United States and Canadian Governments furnished detailed information on external aid.

The Agency also visited military depots under both national and N.A.T.O. command, the latter inspections being carried out in co-operation with S.H.A.P.E. It was thus able to make an effective field check of the information provided in answer to its questionnaire; the results were found to be highly satisfactory.

Further quantitative controls were carried out in a number of factories manufacturing arms and equipment; stocks held and quantities being les stocks détenus et les quantités produites ont été comparés aux informations fournies en réponse au questionnaire. La Convention du 14 décembre 1957 portant garantie d'ordre juridictionnel pour la sauvegarde des droits privés n'étant pas encore entrée en vigueur, ces mesures de contrôle ont revêtu la forme d'exercices.

b) Dans le cadre du contrôle de non-fabrication, on citera notamment la visite de plusieurs fabriques de produits chimiques ainsi que d'autres usines d'armements. L'Agence a pu constater une fois de plus que les engagements de non-fabrication pris en vertu des Accords de Paris étaient respectés.

3. L'étude et la mise au point des méthodes de contrôle des armes nouvelles (engins guidés, par exemple) ont fait d'importants progrès au cours de l'année 1960. Les principes fondamentaux qui régissent ce contrôle sont semblables à ceux appliqués dans le cas des armes classiques, mais la grande diversité des engins et leurs conditions particulières de stockage exigent que chaque type soit examiné séparément. Les inspections ont permis d'acquérir une expérience utile en vue de l'amélioration des techniques de contrôle et leur adaptation au progrès scientifique.

En outre, l'Agence a recueilli systématiquement un ensemble important de données fort utile pour la préparation des contrôles des produits chimiques soumis à son contrôle. D'autre part, la liste des armes chimiques à contrôler a été complétée par l'adjonction d'un nouveau groupe comprenant des substances de très haute toxicité.

En ce qui concerne les armes biologiques, l'Agence a effectué un travail considérable en 1960 en matière de documentation scientifique et de recherche sur la possibilité de cultures en quantité massive de microorganismes pathogènes capables de constituer des armes biologiques.

2. COMITÉ PERMANENT DES ARMEMENTS

Pendant l'année 1960, les activités du Comité Permanent des Armements relatives à la définition et à l'étude des matériels nouveaux ont été influencées par l'introduction des nouvelles procédures de l'O.T.A.N. et par l'incidence qu'elles ont eu sur la politique d'armement de certains gouvernements.

Toutefois, le Groupe *ad hoc*, qui est composé de représentants du War Office et des Chefs d'État-Major des Forces Terrestres des six pays du Continent, ainsi que ses sous-groupes spécialisés, ont poursuivi avec succès leur tâche consistant à définir en commun les caractéristiques militaires des diverses armes de l'avenir. Cinq accords de ce genre ont été ratifiés en 1960 contre deux en 1959. Ces accords se rapportaient à un système d'armes guidés tactiques sol-sol à courte portée, un système d'armes sol-air pour l'intervention à basse altitude, à une arme autodéfense sol-air, aux matériels de détection des mines et de déminage. En outre, le sous-groupe approprié a réalisé de nouveaux progrès dans la définition des caractéristiques d'une famille d'armes antichars; ces armes ont donné lieu à des démonstrations aussi bien en France qu'au Royaume-Uni pendant l'année 1960. Des études très détaillées sur les mérites comparés des différents types de munitions antichars ont également été effectuées par le même sous-groupe.

Le Comité Permanent des Armements n'a pas eu à traiter en 1960 des besoins concernant les matériels des forces navales ou aériennes, qui sont étudiés à l'O.T.A.N.; toutefois, des membres du Secrétariat du Comité Permanent des Armements assistent, en qualité d'observateurs, aux réunions du Comité Directeur Naval de l'O.T.A.N. qui a eu pour origine des travaux du C.P.A.

Le Comité Permanent des Armements a été tenu informé de manière détaillée des sujets qui sont examinés dans le cadre des arrangements biproduced were checked against the replies to the questionnaire. Since the Convention of 14th December, 1957, providing a legal guarantee to safeguard private rights is not yet in force, these control measures took the form of "exercises".

b) "Non-production" controls included visits to several chemical factories as well as to other types of arms factory. The Agency was once more able to report that the undertakings made in the Paris Agreements not to manufacture certain armaments were being observed.

3. The study and development of control methods for new weapons (*e.g.* guided missiles) progressed favourable during 1960. The basic principles followed are similar to those applied in the case of conventional arms, but the great diversity of new missiles being produced and their special conditions of storage require that each type be considered as a separate case. Inspections have yielded useful experience with regard to the improvement of control technique and its adaptability to scientific progress.

The Agency was also able to assemble a great deal of information of considerable value for the planning of controls in relation to those chemical products which come under its supervision. Furthermore, the list of controllable chemical weapons was extended to include a new group of highly toxic substances.

As regards biological weapons, the Agency carried out a considerable amount of work in 1960 on scientific documentation and research into the possibility of the mass cultivation of pathogenic micro-organisms which could be used in biological warfare; the work is being systematically continued.

2. STANDING ARMAMENTS COMMITTEE

The activities of the Standing Armaments Committee during 1960 in the definition and development of new equipment were affected by the introduction of new procedures in N.A.T.O. and their influence on the armaments policy of certain Governments.

Nevertheless, the *Ad Hoc* Group, composed of representatives of the British War Office and the Army Chiefs of Staff of the six continental countries, and its specialised sub-groups, continued successfully with their task of drawing up agreed military characteristics of a variety of future weapons. While, during 1959, two such agreements were ratified, five were ratified in the course of 1960. These covered a short-range tactical surface-to-surface guided weapons system; a low altitude surface-to-air system; a self-defence surface-to-air weapon; mine detection equipment and mine-clearance equipment. In addition, progress was made by the appropriate Sub-Group in defining the characteristics of a family of anti-tank weapons, which were the subject of demonstrations both in France and the United Kingdom during 1960. Very detailed studies of the comparative merits of differing types of anti-tank ammunition have also been conducted by this Sub-Group.

The Committee was not concerned in 1960 with naval or air force requirements, since these are handled within N.A.T.O.; however, members of the Secretariat of the Standing Armaments Committee continued to attend as observers meetings of the N.A.T.O. Naval Steering Group, which had its origins in the S.A.C.

The Standing Armaments Committee was informed in detail of the subject matter being discussed within the context of the bi- and trilateral et trilatéraux établis au cours des dernières années entre des pays membres de l'U.E.O. Ces arrangements sont destinés à promouvoir l'échange des renseignements qui présentent essentiellement un caractère scientifique et technique, en vue de déterminer les possibilités d'action commune. Les déclarations faites par les pays qui participent à ces échanges de vues bi- et trilatéraux ont montré qu'une large gamme de sujets intéressant les forces terrestres navales et aériennes sont en cours d'examen, fournissant ainsi l'occasion, dans le cas où les pays le désireraient, d'élargir le champ de la coopération en matière d'études et de recherches.

Dans ses relations avec les autres organismes, le Comité Permanent des Armements a pris soin d'éviter les doubles emplois avec les travaux de l'O.T.A.N. en ce qui concerne la coordination des politiques d'armement.

3. ACTIVITÉS SOCIALES ET CULTURELLES

1. *Rationalisation des institutions européennes*

Au début de 1959, Monsieur Wigny, Ministre des Affaires étrangères de Belgique, avait présenté au Comité des Ministres du Conseil de l'Europe un mémorandum sur la rationalisation des institutions européennes autres que celles des Six. Un comité spécial, chargé d'étudier ce mémorandum et de formuler des recommandations sur les mesures d'application pratique à prendre, a proposé le transfert au Conseil de l'Europe de l'exercice des activités sociales et culturelles de l'Union de l'Europe occidentale. En avril 1959, cette proposition fut adoptée en principe par les Ministres des Affaires étrangères des pays intéressés; il a été convenu que les modalités d'application de cette décision seraient mises au point par les organes ministériels des deux organisations.

Le Conseil de l'U.E.O. tenait particulièrement à assurer que les activités visées seraient poursuivies sous l'égide du Conseil de l'Europe avec la même efficacité que par le passé.

2. *Procédure de transfert au Conseil de l'Europe des activités sociales et culturelles de l'U.E.O.*

Voici la procédure de transfert convenue entre les deux organisations:

a) Le transfert sera effectué de manière à poursuivre l'exercice des activités visées dans le cadre du Conseil de l'Europe dans des conditions aussi efficaces qu'à l'U.E.O.; il ne modifie pas la portée du Traité de Bruxelles révisé.

b) L'objectif précité sera réalisé par la procédure des Accords partiels, déjà en vigueur au Conseil de l'Europe. A cet effet, le Comité des Ministres du Conseil de l'Europe autorisera les États membres de l'U.E.O. à continuer entre eux dans le cadre du Conseil de l'Europe, dans la mesure où ils l'estiment nécessaire, les activités qui ont fait l'objet du transfert.

c) Les méthodes de travail suivies dans le passé à l'U.E.O. continueront à être appliquées dans le cadre de l'Accord partiel précité.

d) Toute activité entrant dans le cadre d'un Accord partiel pourra, le cas échéant, être étendue à d'autres États membres du Conseil de l'Europe. Les comités constitués dans le cadre d'un Accord partiel feront des rapports sur leurs activités au Comité des Ministres du Conseil de l'Europe et celui-ci, siégeant dans sa composition réduite aux représentants des États membres participant à l'Accord partiel, décidera de la suite à donner à ces rapports.

Un chapitre sur les activités en question sera inclus dans le rapport statutaire du Comité des Ministres à l'Assemblée Consultative.

3. *Application de la procédure de transfert*

Les Secrétaires Généraux chargés des mesures d'exécution relatives au transfert sont convenus de transférer séparément chacun des principaux arrangements which have been established in recent years between Member countries of W.E.U. These are intended to promote the exchange of information, primarily of a scientific and technical nature, with a view to singling out possibilities for joint action. The statements made by the countries participating in the bi- and trilateral discussions showed that a wide range of subjects, affecting army, navy and air force, is under review, and should provide the opportunity, should countries so desire, for extending the field of co-operation in research and development.

As regards its relationship with other agencies, the Standing Armaments Committee has been careful to avoid duplication of effort with N.A.T.O. in the co-ordination of armaments policies.

3. SOCIAL AND CULTURAL ACTIVITIES

1. *Rationalisation of European Institutions*

Early in 1959 M. WIGNY, Belgian Minister for Foreign Affairs, had submitted to the Committee of Ministers of the Council of Europe a memorandum on the rationalisation of European institutions other than those of the Six. A Special Committee, set up to study this memorandum and to make recommendations on the practical steps that might be taken towards such rationalisation, proposed that exercise of the social and cultural activities of Western European Union should be transferred to the Council of Europe. In April 1959 this proposal was adopted in principle by the Ministers for Foreign Affairs of the countries concerned and it was agreed that detailed arrangements for implementing the decision should be worked out by the ministerial organs of the two Organisations.

The W.E.U. Council were particularly anxious to ensure that the activities of their social and cultural committees would be continued under the aegis of the Council of Europe with the same effectiveness as in the past.

2. *Procedure for transfer of W.E.U. social and cultural activities to the Council of Europe*

The following procedure was agreed between the two Organisations.

a) The transfer would be carried out in such a way as to ensure that the activities in question could be pursued as effectively in the Council of Europe as hitherto in W.E.U.; it does not affect the scope of the Revised Brussels Treaty.

b) This would be achieved by the procedure of Partial Agreements already in operation in the Council of Europe. To this end, the Committee of Ministers of the Council of Europe would authorise the Member States of W.E.U. to continue to the extent which they considered necessary within the Council of Europe the activities included in the transfer.

c) The working methods hitherto employed by W.E.U. would be maintained under this Partial Agreement.

d) Any activity covered by a Partial Agreement could, as required, be extended to other Member States of the Council of Europe. Committees set up under a Partial Agreement would report on their activities to the Committee of Ministers of the Council of Europe, which, at meetings limited to representatives of Member States party to the Partial Agreement, would decide what action to take on such reports.

A chapter on the activities in question would be incorporated in the report which the Committee of Ministers is required to submit to the Consultative Assembly.

3. *Implementation of the transfer procedure*

The Secretaries-General, who were responsible for implementing the transfer, agreed that each main social and cultural committee should be comités sociaux et culturels, compte tenu de l'état des travaux. Le transfert commençait le 15 avril, pour s'achever le 27 mai 1960.

L'une des tâches principales incombant à chacun des comités avant le transfert fut d'établir la liste des activités dont ils recommandaient la continuation dans le cadre du Conseil de l'Europe. Les listes adoptées par le Comité social, le Comité de Santé publique, le Comité pour la Réadaptation et le Réemploi des Invalides et le Comité culturel, ont été approuvées par le Conseil de l'U.E.O. et par le Comité des Ministres du Conseil de l'Europe.

4. COMITÉ DE L'ADMINISTRATION PUBLIQUE

1. *Rencontre de fonctionnaires*

La onzième rencontre de fonctionnaires organisée par le Comité de l'Administration publique a eu lieu en Belgique du 17 mai au 3 juin 1960. Elle avait pour thème général: ,,La coopération des services publics entre eux et avec l'initiative privée'', thème étudié dans le cadre de trois domaines concrets de l'administration: la sécurité routière; la construction de logements; la production, le transport et la distribution de l'énergie électrique. Un grand nombre de fonctionnaires des sept pays membres y a pris part. L'étude a été menée suivant la méthode éprouvée mise au point par le Comité au cours des dix dernières années: d'abord une brève période d'information commune aux trois groupes de travail, ensuite une période de visites et de voyages, au cours de laquelle chaque groupe a poursuivi séparément l'étude de son sujet particulier, et, enfin, une dernière période réunissant l'ensemble des participants pour la discussion et l'adoption des rapports. Il leur a ainsi été donné d'enrichir leur expérience administrative grâce aux contacts établis avec des fonctionnaires ayant un sens de l'administration différent du leur, et de découvrir ou d'approfondir un système politico-administratif très original.

2. *Visites d'étude*

Au cours de l'année, le nombre des visites d'étude s'est maintenu à son niveau précédent et l'on peut affirmer que la valeur de l'expérience ainsi acquise par les bénéficiaires et l'intérêt de tels échanges dans la perspective d'une meilleure compréhension mutuelle sur le plan des méthodes et des pratiques administratives est de plus en plus reconnue.

Si l'organisation même des visites d'étude incombe aux pays intéressés, le Comité s'emploie à en perfectionner la formule, de façon à les rendre aussi fructueuse que possible. C'est ainsi qu'il a choisi des thèmes généraux relatifs à des problèmes fondamentaux de l'administration publique, destinés à servir de toile de fond aux études dont il s'agit.

Durant la période 1952–1959, 266 fonctionnaires ont bénéficié, sous l'une ou l'autre forme, de cette activité du Comité, les administrations les plus souvent visitées étant dans l'ordre, celle du Royaume-Uni, de la France, des Pays-Bas, de la République Fédérale d'Allemagne, de la Belgique et de l'Italie; depuis 1958 le nombre de visites d'étude a connu une augmentation de plus de 80%.

Dans un domaine voisin, le Comité de l'Administration publique a entrepris la réalisation de ,,stages à l'étranger''. Cette initiative tend à faire accomplir à de jeunes fonctionnaires un séjour d'un mois dans une administration étrangère, comme fonctionnaires de cette administration, dans le service correspondant à celui auquel ils sont affectés dans leur pays. L'objectif à atteindre à long terme serait de voir un tel stage reconnu comme une étape indispensable de la formation des futurs hauts fonctionnaires.

3. *Études administratives*

En matière d'études administratives, le Comité a terminé au cours de handed over individually with due regard to their working time-table. The transfer began on 15th April and was finally completed on 27th May, 1960.

One of the main tasks of each of the committees, while still remaining organs of W.E.U., was to propose a list of activities which in their view should be pursued in the Council of Europe. The lists adopted by the Social Committee, the Public Health Committee, the Committee on the Rehabilitation of the Disabled and the Cultural Committee were accepted by both the Council of W.E.U. and the Committee of Ministers of the Council of Europe.

4. PUBLIC ADMINISTRATION COMMITTEE

1. *Course for Government Officials*

The eleventh Course for Government Officials organised by the Public Administration Committee took place in Belgium from 17th May to 3rd June, 1960. The general theme, "Co-operation between public authorities and between those authorities and private organisations", was considered in relation to three sectors of administration: road safety, construction of living accommodation, and the production, transmission and distribution of electric power. A considerable number of officials from the seven Member countries took part. The course was organised on the lines devised and perfected by the Committee over the previous ten years; it consisted of a short initial briefing period combining all three working groups, followed by a period for visits and travel during which each group devoted intensive study to its particular subject, and a final period in which all took part in the discussion and adoption of the reports. Their administrative experience had been enriched by the contacts made with officials having a very different background and tradition of government, and they were able to explore or to improve their knowledge of a highly distinctive politico-administrative system.

2. *Study visits*

During the past year, the number of study visits has remained at its previous level and there is growing recognition of the value of the experience gained by officials taking part and of the contribution made by such exchanges to a better mutual understanding of administrative methods and practice.

While the actual organisation of study visits is the responsibility of the countries concerned, the Committee direct their efforts to improving the formula in order that the best results may be obtained. Thus, they select certain main themes relating to basic problems of public administration, for use as guidance in such studies.

Between 1952 and 1959, 266 officials took advantage in one form or another of the facilities offered by the Committee; the highest number of visits were to government departments in the United Kingdom, followed by France, the Netherlands, Germany, Belgium and Italy. The number has increased by over 80% since 1958.

Along similar lines, the Public Administration Committee have now introduced a scheme for "training periods abroad". The intention is that young officials should be seconded for a month to a foreign government department, in branches corresponding to their own at home. The ultimate aim would be the recognition of such secondment as an essential stage in the training of future senior officials.

3. *Administrative studies*

As regards administrative studies, the year 1960 saw the Committee l'année son étude comparative sur la formation et le perfectionnement des fonctionnaires supérieurs dans les sept pays membres; un rapport d'ensemble a été établi sur la base des réponses à un questionnaire. Le Comité continue ses travaux sur un aspect particulier de ce sujet, à savoir les méthodes en usage en matière de formation.

Le Comité a entrepris en outre une étude comparative concernant *L'organisation politique, administrative et judiciaire des États de l'Europe occidentale*, destinée à combler une lacune en cette matière, et qui devrait de ce fait rendre de grands services dans les milieux notamment de l'administration et de l'université.

C. PRINCIPAUX FONCTIONNAIRES

au 31 décembre 1960

Secrétaire Général: M. L. GOFFIN
Secrétaire Général délégué: Dr. H. BOEX
Secrétaire Général adjoint: Mr. P. B. FRASER
Conseiller juridique: M. S. FREY

Adresse: 9 Grosvenor Place, London S.W. 1.
Téléphone: Belgravia 5351
Télégramme: Euruni, Knights, London

Secrétaire Général adjoint et Chef du Secrétariat international du Comité Permanent des Armements: Général Pierre BRISAC

Directeur de l'Agence pour le Contrôle des Armements: Amiral E. FERRERI

Directeur adjoint: Lt. Gen. G. C. BUURMAN VAN VREEDEN

Chef de la Division Information et Études: M. COIGNARD

Chef de la Division Inspections et Contrôles: Air Vice-Marshal PIDCOCK

Chef de la Division Administration et Affaires juridiques: Dr. H. J. OSTHUS

Adresse: 30 Rue La Pérouse, Paris XVIème
Téléphone: Carnot 08.00

Greffier de l'Assemblée de l'U.E.O.: M. F. HUMBLET

Adresse: 36 Rue La Pérouse, Paris XVIème
Téléphone: Carnot 08.00
Télégramme: Uneurop – Paris.

complete their enquiry into the training of senior civil servants and refresher courses in the seven Member countries, and a collective report was drawn up on the basis of replies to a questionnaire. One aspect of this subject is still under consideration, namely, training methods in present use.

The Committee have undertaken a comparative study entitled *The political, administrative and judicial structure of the States of Western Europe;* this work should meet a real need and is likely to prove particularly useful in government and university circles.

C. PRINCIPAL OFFICIALS

as at 31 December, 1960

Secretary-General: M. L. GOFFIN
Deputy Secretary-General: Dr. H. BOEX
Assistant Secretary-General: Mr. P. B. FRASER
Legal Counsellor: M. S. FREY

Address: 9 Grosvenor Place, London, S.W. 1.
Telephone: Belgravia 5351
Telegrams: Euruni, Knights, London

Assistant Secretary-General and Head of the International Secretariat of the Standing Armaments Committee: General Pierre BRISAC
Director of the Agency for the Control of Armaments: Admiral E. FERRERI
Deputy Director: Lt. Gen. G. C. BUURMAN VAN VREEDEN
Head of Information and Research Division: M. COIGNARD
Head of Inspection and Control Division: Air Vice-Marshal PIDCOCK
Head of Administrative and Legal Division: Dr. H. J. OSTHUS

Address: 30 Rue La Pérouse, Paris XVIe.
Telephone: Carnot 08.00

Clerk of the W.E.U. Assembly: M. F. HUMBLET

Address: 36 Rue La Pérouse, Paris XVIe.
Telephone: Carnot 08.00
Telegrams: Uneurop – Paris.

CHAPITRE IV

ORGANISATION EUROPÉENNE DE COOPÉRATION ÉCONOMIQUE

A. CHRONOLOGIE

1960

12 février: L'O.E.C.E. accorde à l'Espagne un crédit de vingt cinq millions de dollars fournis par le Fonds Européen.

20 février: L'O.E.C.E. accorde à l'Islande un crédit de douze millions de dollars fournis par le Fonds Européen.

10 mars: L'Agence Européenne pour l'Énergie Nucléaire de l'O.E.C.E. (E.N.E.A.) publie son deuxième rapport au Conseil de l'Europe.

26 avril: L'O.E.C.E. publie son onzième rapport économique annuel: *L'Europe et l'Économie mondiale.*

11 mai Sir Robert HANKEY succède à Sir Hugh ELLIS-REES en qualité de Chef de la Délégation permanente du Royaume-Uni auprès de l'O.E.C.E.

7 juillet: S.A.R. le Prince ALBERT DE LIÈGE inaugure, à Mol, l'ouverture des travaux de construction de l'usine de traitement des combustibles nucléaires de l'O.E.C.E.

20 juillet: Le Conseil de l'O.E.C.E. recommande la signature de la Convention, sur la responsabilité civile dans le domaine de l'Énergie Nucléaire.

22 juillet: L'O.E.C.E. met à la disposition de l'Islande une nouvelle tranche de crédits de cinq millions de dollars fournis par le Fonds Européen.

28 juillet: Le Royaune-Uni est réélu à la présidence du Conseil de l'O.E.C.E. pour l'année 1960–1961. Mr. Thorkil KRISTENSEN est nommé Secrétaire Général de l'O.E.C.E. à partir du 1er septembre et Secrétaire Général désigné de l'O.C.D.E. Il assurera la présidence des réunions du Comité Préparatoire de l'O.C.D.E.

29 juillet: Signature de la Convention internationale de l'E.N.E.A. sur la Responsabilité civile dans le domaine de l'Énergie Nucléaire.

3 août: Prolongation du projet O.E.C.E. de réacteur de Halden. Première séance du Tribunal de Sécurité Nucléaire créé par l'O.E.C.E.

30 septembre: Accord de la collaboration entre l'E.N.E.A. et l'Agence Internationale de l'Énergie Atomique.

5 octobre: Le réacteur à eau lourde bouillante de Halden entre en ébullition.

29 novembre: La Suède libère ses importations d'électricité en provenance des autres pays de l'O.E.C.E.

B. TEXTES FONDAMENTAUX

1. *AGENCE EUROPÉENNE POUR L'ÉNERGIE NUCLÉAIRE*

a) CONVENTION SUR LA RESPONSABILITÉ CIVILE DANS LE DOMAINE DE L'ÉNERGIE NUCLÉAIRE

LES GOUVERNEMENTS de la République Fédérale d'Allemagne, de la République d'Autriche, du Royaume de Belgique, du Royaume de Danemark, de l'Espagne, de la République Française, du Royaume de Grèce, de la République Italienne, du Grand-Duché de Luxembourg, du Royau-

CHAPTER IV

ORGANISATION FOR EUROPEAN ECONOMIC CO-OPERATION

A. CHRONOLOGY

1960

12 February: O.E.E.C. grants Spain a credit of twenty-five million dollars from the European Fund.
20 February: O.E.E.C. grants Iceland a credit of twelve million dollars from the European Fund.
10 March: O.E.E.C. European Nuclear Energy Agency (E.N.E.A.) publishes its Second Report to the Council of Europe.
26 April: O.E.E.C. publishes its Eleventh Annual Report *Europe and the World Economy.*
11 May: Sir Robert HANKEY succeeds Sir Hugh ELLIS-REES as Head of the United Kingdom Delegation to O.E.E.C.

7 July: H.R.H. Prince ALBERT OF LIÈGE inaugurates work on O.E.E.C. nuclear fuel processing plant at Mol.

20 July: O.E.E.C. Council recommends signature of nuclear liability Convention.

22 July: O.E.E.C. grants Iceland a further credit of five million dollars from the European Fund.

28 July: The United Kingdom is re-elected to the Chairmanship of the Council for 1960–1961. Mr. Thorkil KRISTENSEN (Denmark) is appointed Secretary-General as from 1st September, and Secretary-General designate of O.E.C.D. He will preside over meetings of the O.E.C.D. Preparatory Committee.
29 July: Signature of the E.N.E.A. international Convention on Third Party Liability in the field of Nuclear Energy.
3 August: Prolongation of the O.E.E.C. Halden reactor project. First meeting of the Nuclear Safety Tribunal.
30 September: Collaboration Agreement between E.N.E.A. and the International Atomic Energy Agency.
5 October: Halden boiling heavy water reactor achieves boiling.

29 November: Sweden frees power exchange with other O.E.E.C. countries.

B. BASIC TEXTS

1. EUROPEAN NUCLEAR ENERGY AGENCY

a) CONVENTION ON THIRD PARTY LIABILITY IN THE FIELD OF NUCLEAR ENERGY

THE GOVERNMENTS of the Federal Republic of Germany, the Republic of Austria, the Kingdom of Belgium, the Kingdom of Denmark, Spain, the French Republic, the Kingdom of Greece, the Italian Republic, the Grand Duchy of Luxembourg, the Kingdom of Norway, the Kingdom of me de Norvège, du Royaume des Pays-Bas, de la République Portugaise, du Royaume-Uni de Grande-Bretagne et d'Irlande du Nord, du Royaume de Suède, de la Confédération Suisse et de la République Turque;

CONSIDÉRANT que l'Agence Européenne pour l'Énergie Nucléaire, créée dans le cadre de l'Organisation Européenne de Coopération Économique (appelée ci-après l',,Organisation''), est chargée de promouvoir l'élaboration et l'harmonisation des législations intéressant l'énergie nucléaire dans les pays participants, en ce qui concerne notamment le régime de la responsabilité civile et de l'assurance des risques atomiques;

DÉSIREUX d'assurer une réparation adéquate et équitable aux personnes victimes de dommages causés par des accidents nucléaires, tout en prenant les mesures nécessaires pour éviter d'entraver le développement de la production et des utilisations de l'énergie nucléaire à des fins pacifiques;

CONVAINCUS de la nécessité d'unifier les règles fondamentales applicables dans les différents pays à la responsabilité découlant de ces dommages, tout en laissant à ces pays la possibilité de prendre, sur le plan national, les mesures complémentaires qu'ils estimeraient nécessaires et éventuellement d'étendre les dispositions de la présente Convention aux dommages résultant d'autres accidents nucléaires que ceux qu'elle couvre;

SONT CONVENUS de ce qui suit:

Article 1

a) Au sens de la présente Convention:

(*i*) ,,Un accident nucléaire'' signifie tout fait ou succession de faits de même origine ayant causé des dommages, dès lors que ce fait ou ces faits ou certains des dommages causés proviennent ou résultent des propriétés radioactives, ou à la fois des propriétés radioactives et des propriétés toxiques, explosives ou autres propriétés dangereuses des combustibles nucléaires ou produits ou déchets radioactifs.

(*ii*) ,,Installation nucléaire'' signifie les réacteurs à l'exception de ceux qui font partie d'un moyen de transport; les usines de préparation ou de fabrication de substances nucléaires; les usines de séparation des isotopes de combustibles nucléaires; les usines de traitement de combustibles nucléaires irradiés; les installations de stockage de substances nucléaires à l'exclusion du stockage de ces substances en cours de transport, ainsi que toute autre installation dans laquelle des combustibles nucléaires ou des produits ou des déchets radioactifs sont détenus et qui serait désignée par le Comité de Direction de l'Agence Européenne pour l'Énergie Nucléaire (appelé ci-après le ,,Comité de Direction'').

(*iii*) ,,Combustibles nucléaires'' signifie les matières fissiles comprenant l'uranium sous forme de métal, d'alliage ou de composé chimique (y compris l'uranium naturel), le plutonium sous forme de métal, d'alliage ou de composé chimique et toute autre matière fissile qui serait désignée par le Comité de Direction.

(*iv*) ,,Produits ou déchets radioactifs'' signifie les matières radioactives produites ou rendues radioactives par exposition aux radiations résultant des opérations de production ou d'utilisation de combustibles nucléaires, à l'exclusion d'une part, des combustibles nucléaires et, d'autre part, des radioisotopes qui, hors d'une installation nucléaire, sont utilisés ou destinés à être utilisés à des fins industrielles, commerciales, agricoles, médicales ou scientifiques.

(*v*) ,,Substances nucléaires'' signifie les combustibles nucléaires (à l'exclusion de l'uranium naturel et de l'uranium appauvri) et les produits ou déchets radioactifs.

(*vi*) ,,Exploitant'' d'une installation nucléaire signifie la personne déthe Netherlands, the Portuguese Republic, the United Kingdom of Great Britain and Northern Ireland, the Kingdom of Sweden, the Swiss Confederation and the Turkish Republic;

CONSIDERING that the European Nuclear Energy Agency, established within the framework of the Organisation for European Economic Co-operation (hereinafter referred to as the "Organisation"), is charged with encouraging the elaboration and harmonization of legislation relating to nuclear energy in participating countries, in particular with regard to third party liability and insurance against atomic risks;

DESIROUS of ensuring adequate and equitable compensation for persons who suffer damage caused by nuclear incidents whilst taking the necessary steps to ensure that the development of the production and uses of nuclear energy for peaceful purposes is not thereby hindered;

CONVINCED of the need for unifying the basic rules applying in the various countries to the liability incurred for such damage, whilst leaving these countries free to take, on a national basis, any additional measures which they deem appropriate, including the application of the provisions of this Convention to damage caused by nuclear incidents not covered therein;

HAVE AGREED as follows:

Article 1

a) For the purposes of this Convention:

(*i*) "A nuclear incident" means any occurrence or succession of occurrences having the same origin which causes damage, provided that such occurrence or succession of occurrences, or any of the damage caused, arises out of or results from the radioactive properties, or a combination of radioactive properties with toxic, explosive, or other hazardous properties of nuclear fuel or radioactive products or waste or with any of them.

(*ii*) "Nuclear installation" means reactors other than those comprised in any means of transport; factories for the manufacture or processing of nuclear substances; factories for the separation of isotopes of nuclear fuel; factories for the reprocessing of irradiated nuclear fuel; facilities for the storage of nuclear substances other than storage incidental to the carriage of such substances; and such other installations in which there are nuclear fuel or radioactive products or waste as the Steering Committee of the European Nuclear Energy Agency (hereinafter referred to as the "Steering Committee") shall from time to time determine.

(*iii*) "Nuclear fuel" means fissionable material in the form of uranium metal, alloy, or chemical compound (including natural uranium), plutonium metal, alloy, or chemical compound, and such other fissionable material as the Steering Committee shall from time to time determine.

(*iv*) "Radioactive products or waste" means any radioactive material produced in or made radioactive by exposure to the radiation incidental to the process of producing or utilizing nuclear fuel, but does not include 1. nuclear fuel, or 2. radioisotopes outside a nuclear installation which are used or intended to be used for any industrial, commercial, agricultural, medical or scientific purpose.

(*v*) "Nuclear substances" means nuclear fuel (other than natural uranium and other than depleted uranium) and radioactive products or waste.

(*vi*) "Operator" in relation to a nuclear installation means the person signée ou reconnue par l'autorité publique compétente comme l'exploitant de cette installation nucléaire.

b) Le Comité de Direction pourra décider qu'une catégorie d'installations nucléaires, de combustibles nucléaires ou de substances nucléaires sera, en raison des risques réduits qu'elle comporte, exclue du champ d'application de la présente Convention.

Article 2

La présente Convention ne s'applique ni aux accidents nucléaires survenus sur le territoire d'États non-contractants, ni aux dommages subis sur ces territoires, sauf si la législation nationale en dispose autrement, sans préjudice toutefois des droits de recours prévus à l'Article 6 *d*).

Article 3

L'exploitant d'une installation nucléaire est responsable conformément à la présente Convention:

a) de tout dommage aux personnes; et

b) de tout dommage aux biens, à l'exclusion

(*i*) des biens qui sont détenus par lui, sous sa garde ou sous son contrôle au site de l'installation et en rapport avec l'exploitation de celle-ci, et

(*ii*) dans le cas prévu à l'Article 4, du moyen de transport sur lequel les substances nucléaires en cause se trouvent au moment de l'accident nucléaire,

s'il est établi que ce dommage (appelé ci-après le „dommage") est causé par un accident nucléaire mettant en jeu soit des combustibles nucléaires, produits ou déchets radioactifs détenus dans cette installation, soit des substances nucléaires provenant de cette installation, sous réserve des dispositions de l'Article 4.

Article 4

Dans le cas de transport de substances nucléaires, y compris le stockage en cours de transport, et sans préjudice de l'Article 2:

a) L'exploitant d'une installation nucléaire est responsable de tout dommage, conformément à la présente Convention, s'il est établi qu'il est causé par un accident nucléaire survenu hors de cette installation et mettant en jeu des substances nucléaires transportées en provenance de cette installation, à condition que l'accident survienne.

(*i*) avant que les substances nucléaires aient été prises en charge par un autre exploitant d'une installation nucléaire située sur le territoire d'une Partie Contractante; ou

(*ii*) si le destinataire du transport est situé sur le territoire d'un État non-contractant, avant qu'elles aient été déchargées du moyen de transport par lequel elles sont parvenues sur le territoire de cet État.

b) L'exploitant visé au paragraphe *a*) (*i*) du présent Article est, dès le moment de la prise en charge des substances nucléaires, l'exploitant responsable conformément à la présente Convention, de tout dommage causé par un accident nucléaire ultérieur mettant en jeu lesdites substances nucléaires.

c) Dans le cas où des substances nucléaires sont expédiées d'un lieu situé hors des territoires des Parties Contractantes à destination d'une installation nucléaire située sur ces territoires avec l'accord de l'exploitant de cette installation, celui-ci est responsable, conformément à la présente Convention, de tout dommage causé par un accident nucléaire survenu après que les substances nucléaires en cause ont été chargées sur le moyen de transport par lequel elles sont expédiées du territoire de l'État non-contractant.

designated or recognised by the competent public authority as the operator of that installation.

b) The Steering Committee may, if in its view the small extent of the risks involved so warrants, exclude any nuclear installation, nuclear fuel, or nuclear substances from the application of this Convention.

Article 2

This Convention does not apply to nuclear incidents occurring in the territory of non-Contracting States or to damage suffered in such territory, unless national legislation otherwise provides and except in regard to rights of recourse referred to in Article 6 *d*).

Article 3

The operator, of a nuclear installation shall be liable, in accordance with this Convention, for:

a) damage to or loss of life of any person; and

b) damage to or loss of any property other than

(*i*) property held by the operator or in his custody or under his control in connection with, and at the site of, such installation, and

(*ii*) in the cases within Article 4, the means of transport upon which the nuclear substances involved were at the time of the nuclear incident,

upon proof that such damage or loss (hereinafter referred to as "damage") was caused by a nuclear incident involving either nuclear fuel or radioactive products or waste in, or nuclear substances coming from such installation, except as otherwise provided for in Article 4.

Article 4

In the case of carriage of nuclear substances, including storage incidental thereto, without prejudice to Article 2:

a) The operator of a nuclear installation shall be liable, in accordance with this Convention, for damage upon proof that it was caused by a nuclear incident outside that installation and involving nuclear substances in the course of carriage therefrom, only if the incident occurs

(*i*) before the nuclear substances involved have been taken in charge by another operator of a nuclear installation situated in the terrority of a Contracting Party; or

(*ii*) before the nuclear substances involved have been unloaded from the means of transport by which they have arrived in the territory of a non-Contracting State, if they are consigned to a person within the territory of that State.

b) The operator referred to in paragraph *a*) (*i*) of this Article shall, from his taking charge of the nuclear substances, be the operator liable in accordance with this Convention for damage caused by a nuclear incident occurring thereafter and involving the nuclear substances.

c) Where nuclear substances are sent from outside the territory of the Contracting Parties to a nuclear installation situated in such territory, with the approval of the operator of that installation, he shall be liable, in accordance with this Convention, for damage caused by a nuclear incident occurring after the nuclear substances involved have been loaded on the means of transport by which they are to be carried from the territory of the non-Contracting State.

d) L'exploitant responsable conformément à la présente Convention doit remettre au transporteur un certificat délivré par ou pour le compte de l'assureur ou de toute autre personne ayant accordé une garantie financière conformément à l'Article 10. Le certificat doit énoncer le nom et l'adresse de cet exploitant ainsi que le montant, le type et la durée de la garantie. Les faits énoncés dans le certificat ne peuvent être contestés par la personne par laquelle ou pour le compte de laquelle il a été délivré. Le certificat doit également désigner les substances nucléaires et l'itinéraire couverts par la garantie et comporter une déclaration de l'autorité publique compétente que la personne visée est un exploitant au sens de la présente Convention.

e) La législation d'une Partie Contractante peut prévoir qu'à des conditions qu'elle détermine, un transporteur peut être substitué, en ce qui concerne la responsabilité prévue par la présente Convention, à un exploitant d'une installation nucléaire située sur le territoire de ladite Partie Contractante, par décision de l'autorité publique compétente, à la demande du transporteur et avec l'accord de l'exploitant, si les conditions requises à l'Article 10 *a*) sont remplies. Dans ce cas, le transporteur est considéré, aux fins de la présente Convention, pour les accidents nucléaires survenus en cours de transport de substances nucléaires, comme exploitant d'une installation nucléaire située sur le territoire de ladite Partie Contractante.

Article 5

a) Si les combustibles nucléaires, produits ou déchets radioactifs mis en jeu dans un accident nucléaire ont été détenus successivement dans plusieurs installations nucléaires et sont détenus dans une installation nucléaire au moment où le dommage est causé, aucun exploitant d'une installation dans laquelle ils ont été détenus antérieurement n'est responsable du dommage. Si les combustibles nucléaires, produits ou déchets radioactifs mis en jeu dans un accident nucléaire ont été détenus dans plusieurs installations nucléaires et ne sont pas détenus dans une installation nucléaire au moment où le dommage est causé, aucune personne autre que l'exploitant de la dernière installation nucléaire dans laquelle ils ont été détenus avant que le dommage ait été causé ou que l'exploitant qui les a pris en charge ultérieurement, n'est responsable du dommage.

b) Si le dommage implique la responsabilité de plusieurs exploitants conformément à la présente Convention, leur responsabilité est solidaire et cumulative; toutefois, lorsqu'une telle responsabilité résulte du dommage causé par un accident nucléaire mettant en jeu des substances nucléaires en cours de transport, le montant total maximum de la responsabilité desdits exploitants est égal au montant le plus élevé fixé pour un des exploitants conformément à l'Article 7. En aucun cas, la responsabilité d'un exploitant résultant d'un accident nucléaire ne peut dépasser le montant fixé, en ce qui le concerne, à l'Article 7.

Article 6

a) Le droit à réparation pour un dommage causé par un accident nucléaire ne peut être exercé que contre un exploitant responsable de ce dommage conformément à la présente Convention; il peut également être exercé contre l'assureur ou contre toute autre personne ayant accordé une garantie financière à l'exploitant conformément à l'Article 10, si un droit d'action directe contre l'assureur ou toute personne ayant accordé une garantie financière est prévu par le droit national.

b) Aucune autre personne n'est tenue de réparer un dommage causé par un accident nucléaire; toutefois, cette disposition ne peut affecter *d*) The operator liable in accordance with this Convention shall provide the carrier with a certificate issued by or on behalf of the insurer or other financial guarantor furnishing the security required pursuant to Article 10. The certificate shall state the name and address of that operator and the amount, type and duration of the security, and these statements may not be disputed by the person by whom or on whose behalf the certificate was issued. The certificate shall also indicate the nuclear substances and the carriage in respect of which the security applies and shall include a statement by the competent public authority that the person named is an operator within the meaning of this Convention.

e) A Contracting Party may provide by legislation that, under such terms as may be contained therein and upon fulfilment of the requirements of Article 10 *a*), a carrier may, at his request and with the consent of an operator of a nuclear installation situated in its territory, by decision of the competent public authority, be liable in accordance with this Convention in place of that operator. In such case for all the purposes of this Convention the carrier shall be considered, in respect of nuclear incidents occurring in the course of carriage of nuclear substances, as an operator of a nuclear installation on the territory of the Contracting Party whose legislation so provides.

Article 5

a) If the nuclear fuel or radioactive products or waste involved in a nuclear incident have been in more than one nuclear installation and are in a nuclear installation at the time damage is caused, no operator of any nuclear installation in which they have previously been shall be liable for the damage. If the nuclear fuel or radioactive products or waste involved in a nuclear incident have been in more than one nuclear installation and are not in a nuclear installation at the time damage is caused, no person other than the operator of the last nuclear installation in which they were before the damage was caused or an operator who has subsequently taken them in charge shall be liable for the damage.

b) If damage gives rise to liability of more than one operator in accordance with this Convention, the liability of those operators shall be joint and several: provided that where such liability arises as a result of damage caused by a nuclear incident involving nuclear substances in the course of carriage, the maximum total amount for which such operators shall be liable shall be the highest amount established with respect to any of them pursuant to Article 7 and provided that in no case shall any one operator be required, in respect of a nuclear incident, to pay more than the amount established with respect to him pursuant to Article 7.

Article 6

a) The right to compensation for damage caused by a nuclear incident may be exercised only against an operator liable for the damage in accordance with this Convention, or, if a direct right of action against the insurer or other financial guarantor furnishing the security required pursuant to Article 10 is given by national law, against the insurer or other financial guarantor.

b) No other person shall be liable for damage caused by a nuclear incident, but this provision shall not affect the application of any inter-l'application des accords internationaux dans le domaine des transports qui sont en vigueur ou ouverts à la signature, à la ratification ou à l'adhésion, à la date de la présente Convention.

c) Toute personne qui est responsable d'un dommage causé par un accident nucléaire en vertu d'un accord international visé au paragraphe *b*) du présent Article ou en vertu de la législation d'un État non-contractant a un droit de recours contre l'exploitant responsable de ce dommage conformément à la présente Convention dans la limite fixée conformément à l'Article 7.

d) Dans le cas d'un accident nucléaire survenu sur le territoire d'un État non-contractant ou d'un dommage subi sur ce territoire, toute personne ayant son lieu principal d'exploitation sur le territoire d'une Partie Contractante, ou ses préposés, ont un droit de recours contre l'exploitant qui serait responsable en l'absence de l'Article 2, pour toute réparation à laquelle ils seraient tenus par suite de cet accident ou de ce dommage, dans la limite fixée conformément à l'Article 7.

e) Le Conseil de l'Organisation peut décider que les transporteurs ayant leur lieu principal d'exploitation sur le territoire d'un État non-contractant peuvent bénéficier des dispositions du paragraphe *d*) du présent Article. En prenant cette décision, le Conseil doit tenir compte des dispositions générales relatives à la responsabilité civile dans le domaine de l'énergie nucléaire en vigueur dans cet État non-contractant ainsi que de la mesure dans laquelle les ressortissants d'une Partie Contractante, et les personnes ayant leur lieu principal d'exploitation sur le territoire d'une Partie Contractante, peuvent bénéficier de ces dispositions.

f) L'exploitant n'a un droit de recours que

(*i*) si le dommage résulte d'un acte ou d'une omission procédant de l'intention de causer un dommage, contre la personne physique auteur de l'acte ou de l'omission intentionnelle;

(*ii*) si et dans la mesure où le recours est prévu expressément par contrat;

(*iii*) si et dans la mesure où sa responsabilité se trouve engagée en vertu de l'Article 7 *e*) par un accident nucléaire, au cours d'un transit effectué sans son consentement, pour un montant excédant celui qui est fixé en ce qui le concerne, conformément à l'Article 7 *b*), contre le transporteur ayant effectué le transit, sauf si ce transit a pour objet de sauver ou de tenter de sauver des vies ou des biens ou est provoqué par des circonstances indépendantes de la volonté du transporteur.

g) Pour autant que l'exploitant ait un droit de recours contre une personne en vertu du paragraphe *f*) du présent Article, ladite personne ne peut avoir un droit de recours contre l'exploitant en vertu des paragraphes *c*) et *d*) du présent Article.

h) Si la réparation du dommage met en jeu un régime national d'assurance médicale, de sécurité sociale ou de réparation des accidents du travail et maladies professionnelles, les droits des bénéficiaires de ce régime et les recours éventuels pouvant être exercés contre l'exploitant sont réglés par la loi de la Partie Contractante ayant établi ce régime.

Article 7

a) Le total des indemnités payables pour un dommage causé par un accident nucléaire ne peut dépasser le montant maximum de la responsabilité, fixé conformément au présent Article.

b) Le montant maximum de la responsabilité de l'exploitant pour les dommages causés par un accident nucléaire est fixé à 15.000.000 d'unités de compte de l'Accord Monétaire Européen, telles qu'elles sont définies à la date de la présente Convention (appelées ci-après „unités de compte").

national agreement in the field of transport in force or open for signature, ratification or accession at the date of this Convention.

c) Any person who is liable for damage caused by a nuclear incident under any international agreement referred to in paragraph *b*) of this Article or under any legislation of a non-Contracting State shall have a right of recourse, within the limitation of the amount of liability established pursuant to Article 7, against the operator liable for that damage in accordance with this Convention.

d) Where a nuclear incident occurs in the territory of a non-Contracting State or damage is suffered in such territory, any person who has his principal place of business in the territory of a Contracting Party or who is the servant of such a person shall have a right of recourse for any sums which he is liable to pay in respect of such incident or damage, within the limitation of liability established pursuant to Article 7, against the operator, who, but for the provisions of Article 2, would have been liable.

e) The Council of the Organisation may decide that carriers whose principal place of business is in the territory of a non-Contracting State should benefit from the provisions of paragraph *d*) of this Article. In taking its decision, the Council shall give due consideration to the general provisions on third party liability in the field of nuclear energy in such non-Contracting State and the extent to which these provisions are available to the benefit of nationals of, and persons whose principal place of business is in the territory of, the Contracting Parties.

f) The operator shall have a right of recourse only

(*i*) if the damage caused by a nuclear incident results from an act or omission done with intent to cause damage, against the individual acting or omitting to act with such intent;

(*ii*) if and to the extent that it is so provided expressly by contract;

(*iii*) if and to the extent that he is liable pursuant to Article 7 *e*) for an amount over and above that established with respect to him pursuant to Article 7 *b*), in respect of a nuclear incident occurring in the course of transit of nuclear substances carried out without his consent, against the carrier of the nuclear substances, except where such transit is for the purpose of saving or attempting to save life or property or is caused by circumstances beyond the control of such carrier.

g) If the operator has a right of recourse to any extent pursuant to paragraph *f*) of this Article against any person, that person shall not, to that extent, have a right of recourse against the operator under paragraphs *c*) and *d*) of this Article.

h) Where provisions of national health insurance, social security, workmen's compensation or occupational disease compensation systems include compensation for damage caused by a nuclear incident, rights of beneficiaries of such systems and rights of recourse by virtue of such systems shall be determined by the law of the Contracting Party having established such systems.

Article 7

a) The aggregate of compensation required to be paid in respect of damage caused by a nuclear incident shall not exceed the maximum liability established in accordance with this Article.

b) The maximum liability of the operator in respect of damage caused by a nuclear incident shall be 15,000,000 European Monetary Agreement units of account as defined at the date of this Convention (hereinafter referred to as "units of account"): provided that any Contracting Party,

Toutefois, un autre montant plus ou moins élevé peut être fixé par la législation d'une Partie Contractante, compte tenu de la possibilité pour l'exploitant d'obtenir l'assurance ou une autre garantie financière requise à l'Article 10, sans toutefois que le montant ainsi fixé puisse être inférieur à 5.000.000 d'unités de compte. Les montants prévus au présent paragraphe peuvent être convertis en monnaie nationale en chiffres ronds.

c) L'exception résultant de l'alinéa *b*) (*ii*) de l'Article 3 peut être écartée par la législation d'une Partie Contractante, à condition qu'en aucun cas l'inclusion des dommages au moyen de transport n'ait pour effet de réduire la responsabilité de l'exploitant pour les autres dommages à un montant inférieur à 5.000.000 d'unités de compte.

d) Le montant fixé en vertu du paragraphe *b*) du présent Article pour la responsabilité des exploitants d'installations nucléaires situées sur le territoire d'une Partie Contractante ainsi que les dispositions de la législation d'une Partie Contractante prise en vertu du paragraphe *c*) du présent Article, s'appliquent à la responsabilité desdits exploitants quel que soit le lieu de l'accident nucléaire.

e) Une Partie Contractante peut subordonner le transit de substances nucléaires à travers son territoire, à la condition que le montant maximum de la responsabilité de l'exploitant étranger en cause soit augmenté, si elle estime que ledit montant ne couvre pas d'une manière adéquate les risques d'un accident nucléaire au cours de ce transit. Toutefois, le montant maximum ainsi augmenté ne peut excéder le montant maximum de la responsabilité des exploitants d'installations nucléaires situées sur le territoire de cette Partie Contractante.

f) Les dispositions du paragraphe *e*) du présent Article ne s'appliquent pas

(*i*) au transport par mer lorsqu'il y a, en vertu du droit international, un droit de refuge dans les ports de ladite Partie Contractante, par suite d'un danger imminent, ou un droit de passage inoffensif à travers son territoire;

(*ii*) au transport par air lorsqu'il y a, en vertu d'un accord ou du droit international, un droit de survol du territoire ou d'atterrissage sur le territoire de ladite Partie Contractante.

g) Les intérêts et dépens liquidés par le Tribunal saisi d'une action en réparation en vertu de la présente Convention ne sont pas considérés comme des indemnités au sens de la présente Convention et sont dus par l'exploitant en sus du montant des réparations qui peuvent être dues en vertu du présent Article.

Article 8

a) Les actions en réparation, en vertu de la présente Convention, doivent être intentées sous peine de déchéance, dans le délai de dix ans à compter de l'accident nucléaire. Dans le cas de dommage causé par un accident nucléaire mettant en jeu des combustibles nucléaires, produits ou déchets radioactifs qui étaient au moment de l'accident volés, perdus ou abandonnés et n'avaient pas été récupérés, le délai de déchéance de dix ans part du moment du vol, de la perte ou de l'abandon. Toutefois, la législation nationale peut fixer un délai de déchéance ou de prescription de deux ans au moins, soit à compter du moment où le lésé a eu connaissance du dommage et de l'exploitant responsable, soit à compter du moment où il a dû raisonnablement en avoir connaissance, sans que le délai de dix ans puisse être dépassé, si ce n'est conformément au paragraphe *c*) du présent Article.

b) Dans les cas prévus à l'Article 13 *d*) (*i*) 2), ou (*ii*), il n'y a pas d'échéance de l'action en réparation si, dans le délai prévu au paragraphe *a*) du présent Article,

(*i*) une action a été intentée, avant que le Tribunal visé à l'Article 17 taking into account the possibilities for the operator of obtaining the insurance or other financial security required pursuant to Article 10, may establish by legislation a greater or less amount, but in no event less than 5,000,000 units of account. The sums mentioned above may be converted into national currency in round figures.

c) Any Contracting Party may by legislation provide that the exception in Article 3 *b*) (*ii*) shall not apply: provided that, in no case, shall the inclusion of damage to the means of transport result in reducing the liability of the operator in respect of other damage to an amount less than 5,000,000 units of account.

d) The amount of the liability of operators of nuclear installations in the territory of a Contracting Party established in accordance with paragraph *b*) of this Article as well as the provisions of any legislation of a Contracting Party pursuant to paragraph *c*) of this Article shall apply to the liability of such operators wherever the nuclear incident occurs.

e) A Contracting Party may subject the transit of nuclear substances through its territory to the condition that the maximum amount of liability of the foreign operator concerned be increased, if it considers that such amount does not adequately cover the risks of a nuclear incident in the course of the transit: provided that the maximum amount thus increased shall not exceed the maximum amount of liability of operators of nuclear installations situated in its territory.

f) The provisions of paragraph *e*) of this Article shall not apply

(*i*) to carriage by sea where, under international law, there is a right of entry in cases of urgent distress into the ports of such Contracting Party or a right of innocent passage through its territory; or

(*ii*) to carriage by air where, by agreement or under international law, there is a right to fly over or land on the territory of such Contracting Party.

g) Any interest and costs awarded by a court in actions for compensation under this Convention shall not be considered to be compensation for the purposes of this Convention and shall be payable by the operator in addition to any sum for which he is liable in accordance with this Article.

Article 8

a) The right of compensation under this Convention shall be extinguished if an action is not brought within ten years from the date of the nuclear incident. In the case of damage caused by a nuclear incident involving nuclear fuel or radioactive products or waste which, at the time of the incident have been stolen, lost, or abandoned and have not yet been recovered, the period for the extinction of the right shall be ten years from the date of the theft, loss, or abandonment. National legislation may, however, establish a period of not less than two years for the extinction of the right or as a period of limitation either from the date at which the person suffering damage has knowledge or from the date at which he ought reasonably to have known of both the damage and the operator liable: provided that the period of ten years shall not be exceeded except in accordance with paragraph *c*) of this Article.

b) Where the provisions of Article 13 *d*) (*i*) 2, or (*ii*) are applicable, the right of compensation shall not, however, be extinguished if, within the time provided for in paragraph *a*) of this Article,

(*i*) prior to the determination by the Tribunal referred to in Article 17, n'ait pris une décision, devant l'un des tribunaux entre lesquels ledit Tribunal peut choisir; si le Tribunal désigne comme tribunal compétent, un autre tribunal que celui devant lequel l'action a déjà été intentée, il peut fixer un délai dans lequel l'action doit être intentée devant le tribunal compétent ainsi désigné;

(*ii*) une demande a été introduite auprès d'une Partie Contractante en vue de la désignation du tribunal compétent par le Tribunal conformément à l'Article 13 *d*) (*i*) 2) ou (*ii*), à condition qu'une action soit intentée après cette désignation dans le délai qui serait fixé par ledit Tribunal.

c) La législation nationale peut fixer un délai de déchéance supérieur à dix ans, si elle prévoit des mesures pour couvrir la responsabilité de l'exploitant à l'égard des actions en réparation introduites après l'expiration du délai de dix ans.

d) Sauf disposition contraire du droit national, une personne ayant subi un dommage causé par un accident nucléaire qui a intenté une action en réparation dans le délai prévu au présent Article peut présenter une demande complémentaire en cas d'aggravation du dommage après l'expiration de ce délai, tant qu'un jugement définitif n'est pas intervenu.

Article 9

Sauf disposition contraire de la législation nationale, l'exploitant n'est pas responsable des dommages causés par un accident nucléaire si cet accident est dû à des actes d'un conflit armé, d'une invasion, d'une guerre civile, d'une insurrection ou à des cataclysmes naturels de caractère exceptionnel.

Article 10

a) Tout exploitant devra être tenu, pour faire face à la responsabilité prévue par la présente Convention, d'avoir et de maintenir, à concurrence du montant fixé conformément à l'Article 7, une assurance ou une autre garantie financière correspondant au type et aux conditions déterminés par l'autorité publique compétente.

b) L'assureur ou toute autre personne ayant accordé une garantie financière ne peut suspendre l'assurance ou la garantie financière prévue au paragraphe *a*) du présent Article, ou y mettre fin sans un préavis de deux mois au moins donné par écrit à l'autorité publique compétente, ou, dans la mesure où ladite assurance ou autre garantie financière concerne un transport de substances nucléaires, pendant la durée de ce transport.

c) Les sommes provenant de l'assurance, de la réassurance ou d'une autre garantie financière ne peuvent servir qu'à la réparation des dommages causés par un accident nucléaire.

Article 11

La nature, la forme et l'étendue de la réparation, ainsi que la répartition équitable des indemnités sont régies, dans les limites prévues par la présente Convention, par le droit national

Article 12

Les indemnités payables conformément à la présente Convention, les primes d'assurance et de réassurance ainsi que les sommes provenant de l'assurance, de la réassurance ou d'une autre garantie financière en vertu de l'Article 10 et les intérêts et dépens visés à l'Article 7 *g*), sont librement transférables entre les zones monétaires des Parties Contractantes.

an action has been brought before any of the courts from which the Tribunal can choose; if the Tribunal determines that the competent court is a court other than that before which such action has already been brought, it may fix a date by which such action has to be brought before the competent court so determined; or

(*ii*) a request has been made to a Contracting Party to initiate a determination by the Tribunal of the competent court pursuant to Article 13 *d*) (*i*) 2, or (*ii*) and an action is brought subsequent to such determination within such time as may be fixed by the Tribunal.

c) National legislation may establish a period longer than ten years if measures have been taken to cover the liability of the operator in respect of any actions for compensation begun after the expiry of the period of ten years.

d) Unless national law provides to the contrary, any person suffering damage caused by a nuclear incident who has brought an action for compensation within the period provided for in this Article may amend his claim in respect of any aggravation of the damage after the expiry of such period provided that final judgment has not been entered by the competent court.

Article 9

Except in so far as national legislation may provide to the contrary, the operator shall not be liable for damage caused by a nuclear incident due to an act of armed conflict, invasion, civil war, insurrection, or a grave natural disaster of an exceptional character.

Article 10

a) To cover the liability under this Convention, the operator shall be required to have and maintain insurance or other financial security of the amount established pursuant to Article 7 and of such type and terms as the competent public authority shall specify.

b) No insurer or other financial guarantor shall suspend or cancel the insurance or other financial security provided for in paragraph *a*) of this Article without giving notice in writing of at least two months to the competent public authority or in so far as such insurance or other financial security relates to the carriage of nuclear substances, during the period of the carriage in question.

c) The sums provided as insurance, reinsurance, or other financial security may be drawn upon only for compensation for damage caused by a nuclear incident.

Article 11

The nature, form and extent of the compensation, within the limits of this Convention, as well as the equitable distribution thereof, shall be governed by national law.

Article 12

Compensation payable under this Convention, insurance and reinsurance premiums, sums provided as insurance, reinsurance, or other financial security required pursuant to Article 10, and interest and costs referred to in Article 7 *g*), shall be freely transferable between the monetary areas of the Contracting Parties.

Article 13

a) Les tribunaux compétents en vertu de la législation d'une Partie Contractante sur le territoire de laquelle est située l'installation nucléaire dont l'exploitant est responsable, sont seuls compétents pour statuer sur les actions introduites en vertu des Articles 3, 6 *a*), 6 *c*) et 6 *d*).

b) Dans le cas d'un accident nucléaire survenu en cours de transport, les tribunaux compétents en vertu de la législation de la Partie Contractante sur le territoire de laquelle se trouvaient lors de l'accident les substances nucléaires mises en jeu, sont seuls compétents, sous réserve des dispositions du paragraphe *c*) du présent Article.

c) Si un accident est survenu hors des territoires des Parties Contractantes en cours de transport ou si le lieu où se trouvaient, lors de l'accident, les substances nucléaires mises en jeu, ne peut être déterminé, ou si les substances nucléaires mises en jeu se trouvaient, lors de l'accident, sur un territoire relevant de plus d'une Partie Contractante, les tribunaux compétents en vertu de la législation de la Partie Contractante sur le territoire de laquelle est située l'installation nucléaire dont l'exploitant est responsable sont seuls compétents.

d) Si, en vertu des paragraphes *a*) ou *c*) du présent Article, les tribunaux de plusieurs Parties Contractantes sont compétents, la compétence est attribuée,

(*i*) dans le cas d'un accident nucléaire survenant au cours d'un transport de substances nucléaires.

1. aux tribunaux compétents, en vertu de la législation locale, au lieu du territoire de la Partie Contractante où est immatriculé le moyen de transport sur lequel les substances nucléaires en cause se trouvaient au moment de l'accident nucléaire à condition que ces tribunaux soient compétents en vertu du paragraphe *c*) du présent Article; ou

2. à défaut d'un tel tribunal, à celui qui est désigné à la demande d'une Partie Contractante intéressée, par le Tribunal visé à l'Article 17, parmi les tribunaux compétents en vertu du paragraphe *c*) du présent Article, comme étant le plus directement lié à l'affaire;

(*ii*) dans tout autre cas, aux tribunaux compétents en vertu de la législation de la Partie Contractante désignée par ledit Tribunal, à la demande d'une Partie Contractante intéressée, comme étant le plus directement liés à l'affaire.

e) Lorsque les jugements prononcés contradictoirement ou par défaut par le tribunal compétent en vertu des dispositions du présent Article sont exécutoires d'après les lois appliquées par ce tribunal, ils deviennent exécutoires sur le territoire de toute autre Partie Contractante dès l'accomplissement des formalités prescrites par la Partie Contractante intéressée. Aucun nouvel examen du fond de l'affaire n'est admis. Cette disposition ne s'applique pas aux jugements qui ne sont exécutoires que provisoirement.

f) Si une action en réparation est intentée contre une Partie Contractante en tant qu'exploitant responsable en vertu de la présente Convention, ladite Partie Contractante ne peut invoquer son immunité de juridiction devant le tribunal compétent en vertu du présent Article.

Article 14

a) La présente Convention doit être appliquée sans aucune discrimination fondée sur la nationalité, le domicile ou la résidence.

b) Le ,,droit national'' et la ,,législation nationale'' signifient le droit ou la législation nationale du tribunal compétent en vertu de la présente Convention pour statuer sur les actions résultant d'un accident nucléaire; le droit ou la législation nationale est applicable pour toutes les questions de fond et de procédure qui ne sont pas réglées spécialement par la présente Convention.

Article 13

a) Jurisdiction over actions under Article 3, 6 *a*), 6 *c*) and 6 *d*) shall lie only with the courts competent in accordance with the legislation of the Contracting Party in whose territory the nuclear installation of the operator liable is situated.

b) In the case of a nuclear incident occurring in the course of carriage, jurisdiction shall, except as otherwise provided in paragraph *c*) of this Article, lie only with the courts competent in accordance with the legislation of the Contracting Party in whose territory the nuclear substances involved were at the time of the nuclear incident.

c) If a nuclear incident occurs outside the territory of the Contracting Parties in the course of carriage, or if the place where the nuclear substances involved were at the time of the nuclear incident cannot be determined, or if the nuclear substances involved were in territory under the jurisdiction of more than one Contracting Party at the time of the nuclear incident, jurisdiction shall lie only with the courts competent in accordance with the legislation of the Contracting Party in whose territory the nuclear installation of the operator liable is situated.

d) Where jurisdiction would lie with the courts of more than one Contracting Party by virtue of paragraphs *a*) or *c*) of this Article, jurisdiction shall lie,

(*i*) in the case of a nuclear incident occurring in the course of carriage of nuclear substances,

1. with the courts competent in accordance with the legislation of the Contracting Party at the place in its territory where the means of transport upon which the nuclear substances involved were at the time of the nuclear incident is registered, provided that they are competent under paragraph *c*) of this Article; or

2. if there is no such court, with that one of the courts which is competent under paragraph *c*) of this Article, determined, at the request of a Contracting Party concerned, by the Tribunal referred to in Article 17 as being the most closely related to the case in question;

(*ii*) in any other case, with the courts competent in accordance with the legislation of the Contracting Party determined, at the request of a Contracting Party concerned, by the said Tribunal as being the most closely related to the case in question.

e) Judgments entered by the competent court under this Article after trial, or by default, shall, when they have become enforceable under the law applied by that court, become enforceable in the territory of any of the other Contracting Parties as soon as the formalities required by the Contracting Party concerned have been complied with. The merits of the case shall not be the subject of further proceedings. The foregoing provisions shall not apply to interim judgments.

f) If an action is brought against a Contracting Party as an operator liable under this Convention, such Contracting Party may not invoke any jurisdictional immunities before the court competent in accordance with this Article.

Article 14

a) This Convention shall be applied without any discrimination based upon nationality, domicile, or residence.

b) "National law" and "national legislation" mean the national law or the national legislation of the court having jurisdiction under this Convention over claims arising out of a nuclear incident, and that law or legislation shall apply to all matters both substantive and procedural not specifically governed by this Convention.

c) Le droit et la législation nationale doivent être appliqués sans aucune discrimination fondée sur la nationalité, le domicile ou la résidence.

Article 15

a) Il appartient à chaque Partie Contractante de prendre les mesures qu'elle estime nécessaires en vue d'accroître l'importance de la réparation prévue par la présente Convention.

b) Pour la part des dommages dont la réparation proviendrait d'une intervention financière mettant en jeu des fonds publics et qui excéderait le montant minimum de 5.000.000 d'unités de compte prévu à l'Article 7, l'application de ces mesures, quelle que soit leur forme, pourrait être soumise à des conditions particulières dérogeant aux dispositions de la présente Convention.

Article 16

Les dispositions prises par le Comité de Direction en vertu de l'Article 1 *a*) (*ii*), 1 *a*) (*iii*) et 1 *b*), sont adoptées par accord mutuel des membres représentant les Parties Contractantes.

Article 17

Tout différend entre deux ou plusieurs Parties Contractantes relatif à l'interprétation ou à l'application de la présente Convention sera examiné par le Comité de Direction et à défaut de solution amiable soumis, à la demande d'une Partie Contractante intéressée, au Tribunal créé par la Convention en date du 20 décembre 1957 sur l'Établissement d'un Contrôle de Sécurité dans le Domaine de l'Énergie Nucléaire.

Article 18

a) Des réserves portant sur une ou plusieurs dispositions de la présente Convention peuvent être formulées à tout moment avant la ratification ou l'adhésion à la présente Convention, ou avant la notification faite en vertu de l'Article 23 en ce qui concerne le ou les territoires visés par cette notification; ces réserves ne sont recevables que si leurs termes ont été expressément acceptés par les Signataires.

b) Toutefois, l'acceptation d'un Signataire n'est pas requise, si celui-ci n'a pas lui-même ratifié la Convention dans un délai de douze mois à partir de la date où la notification de la réserve lui a été communiquée par le Secrétaire Général de l'Organisation, conformément à l'Article 24.

c) Toute réserve acceptée conformément au présent Article peut être retirée à tout moment par notification adressée au Secrétaire Général de l'Organisation.

Article 19

a) La présente Convention sera ratifiée. Les instruments de ratification seront déposés auprès du Sécrétaire Général de l'Organisation.

b) La présente Convention entrera en vigueur dès que cinq au moins des Signataires auront déposé leur instrument de ratification. Pour tout Signataire qui la ratifiera ultérieurement, la présente Convention entrera en vigueur dès qu'il aura déposé son instrument de ratification.

Article 20

Les modifications à la présente Convention seront adoptées par accord mutuel de toutes les Parties Contractantes. Elles entreront en vigueur lorsqu'elles auront été ratifiées ou confirmées par les deux tiers des Parties *c*) That law and legislation shall be applied without any discrimination based upon nationality, domicile, or residence.

Article 15

a) Any Contracting Party may take such measures as it deems necessary to provide for an increase in the amount of compensation specified in this Convention.

b) In so far as compensation for damage involves public funds and is in excess of the 5,000,000 units of account referred to in Article 7, any such measure in whatever form may be applied under conditions which may derogate from the provisions of this Convention.

Article 16

Decisions taken by the Steering Committee under Article 1 *a*) (*ii*), 1 *a*) (*iii*) and 1 *b*) shall be adopted by mutual agreement of the members representing the Contracting Parties.

Article 17

Any dispute arising between two or more Contracting Parties concerning the interpretation or application of this Convention shall be examined by the Steering Committee and in the absence of friendly settlement shall, upon the request of a Contracting Party concerned, be submitted to the Tribunal established by the Convention of 20th December, 1957, on the Establishment of a Security Control in the Field of Nuclear Energy.

Article 18

a) Reservations to one or more of the provisions of this Convention may be made at any time prior to ratification of or accession to this Convention or prior to the time of notification under Article 23 in respect of any territory or territories mentioned in the notification, and shall be admissible only if the terms of these reservations have been expressly accepted by the Signatories.

b) Such acceptance shall not be required from a Signatory which has not itself ratified this Convention within a period of twelve months after the date of notification to it of such reservation by the Secretary-General of the Organisation in accordance with Article 24.

c) Any reservation admitted in accordance with this Article may be withdrawn at any time by notification addressed to the Secretary-General of the Organisation.

Article 19

a) This Convention shall be ratified. Instruments of ratification shall be deposited with the Secretary-General of the Organisation.

b) This Convention shall come into force upon the deposit of instruments of ratification by not less than five of the Signatories. For each Signatory ratifying thereafter, this Convention shall come into force upon the deposit of its instrument of ratification.

Article 20

Amendments to this Convention shall be adopted by mutual agreement of all the Contracting Parties. They shall come into force when ratified or confirmed by two-thirds of the Contracting Parties. For each

Contractantes. Pour toutes Parties Contractantes qui les ratifieront ou confirmeront ultérieurement, les modifications entreront en vigueur à la date de cette ratification ou confirmation.

Article 21

a) Tout Gouvernement d'un pays membre ou associé de l'Organisation, non Signataire de la présente Convention, pourra y adhérer par notification adressée au Secrétaire Général de l'Organisation.

b) Tout Gouvernement d'un autre pays non Signataire de la présente Convention pourra y adhérer par notification adressée au Secrétaire Général de l'Organisation et avec l'accord unanime des Parties Contractantes. L'adhésion prendra effet à la date de cet accord.

Article 22

a) La présente Convention est conclue pour une durée de dix ans à compter de la date de son entrée en vigueur. Toute Partie Contractante pourra mettre fin en ce qui la concerne à l'application de la présente Convention au terme de ce délai en donnant un préavis d'un an à cet effet au Secrétaire Général de l'Organisation.

b) La présente Convention restera par la suite en vigueur pour une période de cinq ans, vis-à-vis des Parties Contractantes qui n'auront pas mis fin à son application conformément au paragraphe *a*) du présent Article et ultérieurement, par périodes successives de cinq ans, vis-à-vis des Parties Contractantes qui n'y auront pas mis fin au terme de l'une de ces périodes, en donnant un préavis d'un an à cet effet au Secrétaire Général de l'Organisation.

c) Une conférence sera convoquée par le Secrétaire Général de l'Organisation pour examiner la révision de la présente Convention, au terme de la période de cinq ans qui suivra la date de son entrée en vigueur ou, à tout autre moment, à la demande d'une Partie Contractante, dans un délai de six mois à compter de cette demande.

Article 23

a) La présente Convention s'applique aux territoires métropolitains des Parties Contractantes.

b) Tout Signataire ou Partie Contractante peut, au moment de la signature ou de la ratification de la présente Convention ou de son adhésion à la présente Convention, ou ultérieurement à tout moment, indiquer par notification adressée au Secrétaire Général de l'Organisation que la présente Convention s'applique à ceux de ses territoires, y compris les territoires pour lesquels la Partie Contractante est responsable dans les relations internationales, auxquels elle n'est pas applicable en vertu du paragraphe *a*) du présent Article et qui sont désignés dans la notification. Une telle notification peut, en ce qui concerne tout territoire qui y est désigné, être retirée en donnant un préavis d'un an à cet effet au Secrétaire Général de l'Organisation.

c) Les territoires d'une Partie Contractante, y compris ceux pour lesquels elle est responsable dans les relations internationales, auxquels la présente Convention ne s'applique pas, sont considérés aux fins de ladite Convention comme territoires d'un État non-contractant.

Article 24

Le Secrétaire Général de l'Organisation donnera communication à tous les Signataires et Gouvernements ayant adhéré à la Convention de la réception des instruments de ratification, d'adhésion et de retrait, ains

Contracting Party ratifying or confirming thereafter, they shall come into force at the date of such ratification or confirmation.

Article 21

a) The Government of any Member or Associate country of the Organisation which is not a Signatory to this Convention may accede thereto by notification addressed to the Secretary-General of the Organisation.

b) The Government of any other country which is not a Signatory to this Convention may accede thereto by notification addressed to the Secretary-General of the Organisation and with the unanimous assent of the Contracting Parties. Such accession shall take effect from the date of such assent.

Article 22

a) This Convention shall remain in effect for a period of ten years as from the date of its coming into force. Any Contracting Party may, by giving twelve months' notice to the Secretary-General of the Organisation, terminate the application of this Convention to itself at the end of the period of ten years.

b) This Convention shall, after the period of ten years, remain in force for a period of five years for such Contracting Parties as have not terminated its application in accordance with paragraph *a*) of this Article, and thereafter for successive periods of five years for such Contracting Parties as have not terminated its application at the end of one of such periods of five years by giving twelve months' notice to that effect to the Secretary-General of the Organisation.

c) A conference shall be convened by the Secretary-General of the Organisation in order to consider revisions to this Convention after a period of five years as from the date of its coming into force or, at any other time, at the request of a Contracting Party, within six months from the date of such request.

Article 23

a) This Convention shall apply to the metropolitan territories of the Contracting Parties.

b) Any Signatory or Contracting Party may, at the time of signature or ratification of or accession to this Convention or at any later time, notify the Secretary-General of the Organisation that this Convention shall apply to those of its territories, including the territories for whose international relations it is responsible, to which this Convention is not applicable in accordance with paragraph *a*) of this Article and which are mentioned in the notification. Any such notification may in respect of any territory or territories mentioned therein be withdrawn by giving twelve months' notice to that effect to the Secretary-General of the Organisation.

c) Any territories of a Contracting Party, including the territories for whose international relations it is responsible, to which this Convention does not apply shall be regarded for the purposes of this Convention as being a territory of a non-Contracting State.

Article 24

The Secretary-General of the Organisation shall give notice to all Signatories and acceding Governments of the receipt of any instrument of ratification, accession, withdrawal, notification under Article 23, and que des notifications faites en vertu de l'Article 23 et des décisions prises par le Comité de Direction en vertu de l'Article 1 *a*) (*ii*), 1 *a*) (*iii*) et 1 *b*). Il leur notifiera également la date de l'entrée en vigueur de la présente Convention, le texte des modifications adoptées et la date de l'entrée en vigueur desdites modifications, ainsi que les réserves faites conformément à l'Article 18.

ANNEXE I

Les réserves suivantes ont été acceptées à la date de la signature de la présente Convention.

1. *Article 6 a):*

Réserve du Gouvernement de la République Fédérale d'Allemagne, du Gouvernement de la République d'Autriche et du Gouvernement du Royaume de Grèce.

Réserve du droit de laisser subsister, par une disposition de la législation nationale, la responsabilité d'une personne autre que l'exploitant, à condition que cette personne soit entièrement couverte, même en cas d'action mal fondée, par une assurance ou une autre garantie financière obtenue par l'exploitant.

2. *Article 6 b)* et *c):*

Réserve du Gouvernement de la République d'Autriche, du Gouvernement du Royaume de Grèce, du Gouvernement du Royaume de Norvège et du Gouvernement du Royaume de Suède.

Réserve du droit de considérer leurs lois nationales comportant des dispositions équivalentes à celles des accords internationaux visés à l'Article 6 *b*) comme des accords internationaux aux fins de l'Article 6 *b*) et *c*).

3. *Article 7:*

Réserve du Gouvernement du Royaume-Uni de Grande-Bretagne et d'Irlande du Nord.

Réserve du droit d'appliquer, en ce qui concerne les exploitants des installations nucléaires situées sur le territoire du Royaume-Uni autres que les Départements Gouvernementaux et l'Atomic Energy Authority, les paragraphes *a*), *b*) et *c*) de l'Article 7

(*i*) comme si les paragraphes *a*) et *b*) de l'Article 7 prévoyaient qu'un montant de 14.000.000 d'unités de compte doit être disponible pour l'indemnisation des dommages dont un exploitant est responsable aux termes de la Convention et qui seraient causés par des accidents nucléaires survenant au cours de la période pendant laquelle l'exploitant est tenu d'avoir et de maintenir une assurance ou autre garantie financière pour son installation conformément au droit du Royaume-Uni;

(*ii*) comme si le paragraphe *c*) de l'Article 7 disposait qu'en ce qui concerne les dommages visés au paragraphe (*i*) ci-dessus, un montant de 5.000.000 d'unités de compte doit être disponible pour l'indemnisation des dommages autres que ceux causés au moyen de transport; et

(*iii*) comme si les paragraphes *a*) et *b*) de l'Article 7 prévoyaient que tout versement dépassant ledit montant de 14.000.000 d'unités de compte sera, sans préjudice de l'application de l'Article 15 *b*), subordonné à l'adoption par le Parlement de dispositions permettant d'allouer des fonds supplémentaires.

decisions of the Steering Committee under Article 1 *a*) (*ii*), 1 *a*) (*iii*) and 1 *b*). He shall also notify them of the date on which this Convention comes into force, the text of any amendment thereto and of the date on which such amendment comes into force, and any reservation made in accordance with Article 18.

ANNEX I

The following reservations were accepted at the time of signature of this Convention:

1. *Article 6 a):*

Reservation by the Government of the Federal Republic of Germany, the Government of the Republic of Austria and the Government of the Kingdom of Greece

Reservation of the right to provide, by national law, that persons other than the operator may continue to be liable in addition to the operator on condition that these persons are fully covered in respect of their liability, including defence against unjustified actions, by insurance or other financial security obtained by the operator.

2. *Article 6 b)* and *c):*

Reservation by the Government of the Republic of Austria, the Government of the Kingdom of Greece, the Government of the Kingdom of Norway and the Government of the Kingdom of Sweden

Reservation of the right to consider their national legislation which includes provisions equivalent to those included in the international agreements referred to in Article 6 *b*) as being international agreements within the meaning of Article 6 *b*) and *c*).

3. *Article 7:*

Reservation by the Government of the United Kingdom of Great Britain and Northern Ireland

Reservation of the right, in respect of operators of nuclear installations situated in the territory of the United Kingdom other than Government Departments and the Atomic Energy Authority, that Article 7 *a*), *b*) and *c*) shall be applied

(*i*) as if Article 7 *a*) and *b*) provided that, in respect of damage for which such an operator is liable under this Convention and which is caused by nuclear incidents occurring within the period for which the insurance or other financial security relating to his installation is required by the law of the United Kingdom to be maintained, an amount of 14,000,000 units of account shall be available for all compensation;

(*ii*) as if the proviso to Article 7 *c*) provided that in respect of such damage as is mentioned in paragraph (*i*) above 5,000,000 units of account shall be available for compensation in respect of damage other than damage to the means of transport; and

(*iii*) as if Article 7 *a*) and *b*) provided that any payment in excess of the said amount of 14,000,000 units of account shall, without prejudice to the application of Article 15 *b*), be conditional upon Parliamentary approval of the arrangements whereby further funds are to be provided.

4. *Article 19:*

Réserve du Gouvernement de la République Fédérale d'Allemagne, du Gouvernement de la République d'Autriche, et du Gouvernement du Royaume de Grèce.

Réserve du droit de considérer la ratification de la présente Convention comme entraînant l'obligation conformément au droit international de prendre dans l'ordre interne des dispositions relatives à la responsabilité civile dans le domaine de l'énergie nucléaire conformes aux dispositions de la présente Convention.

ANNEXE II

Cette Convention ne peut être interprêtée comme privant une Partie Contractante sur le territoire de laquelle des dommages auront été causés par un accident nucléaire survenu sur le territoire d'une autre Partie Contractante, des recours qui pourraient lui être ouverts en application du droit international.

En foi de quoi les Plénipotentiaires soussignés, dûment habilités, ont apposé leurs signatures au bas de la présente Convention.

Fait à Paris, le 29 juillet 1960, en français, en anglais, en allemand, en espagnol, en italien et en néerlandais, en un seul exemplaire qui restera déposé auprès du Secrétaire Général de l'Organisation Européenne de Coopération Économique qui en communiquera une copie certifiée conforme à tous les Signataires.

EXPOSÉ DES MOTIFS

1. La production et l'utilisation de l'énergie atomique comportent des risques sans comparaison avec ceux dont le monde a l'expérience. On ne peut se faire une idée exacte des possibilités d'accidents et de leurs conséquences, en raison de la sécurité particulière de fonctionnement qui a caractérisé jusqu'à présent les installations atomiques. Malgré ce résultat remarquable, on peut penser qu'à mesure que cette nouvelle source d'énergie sera plus largement utilisée, les accidents seront plus fréquents. Les experts sont, pour la plupart, enclins à estimer que la probabilité d'une catastrophe due à l'énergie nucléaire est extrêmement faible, mais, si minime que soit le risque, un accident reste possible, qui pourrait causer des dommages considérables, tant aux personnes qui en seraient victimes qu'aux entreprises exploitant une installation nucléaire ou dont l'activité est liée à cette installation.

2. Plusieurs raisons imposent un régime spécial de responsabilité civile. D'abord suivant le droit en vigueur, les exploitants d'installations nucléaires seraient soumis à une responsabilité illimitée, alors qu'ils ne peuvent manifestement obtenir une garantie financière illimitée. Ensuite, il n'est pas moins essentiel que tous ceux qui sont associés à l'exploitation d'installations nucléaires soient protégés. Ceux qui fournissent des services, des matériaux ou de l'équipement à l'occasion de la mise au point, de la construction, de la modification, de l'entretien, de la réparation ou de l'exploitation d'une installation nucléaire, ne doivent pas être soumis à une responsabilité illimitée, comme cela résulterait des règles et usages juridiques en vigueur. Les charges financières très lourdes que pourrait entraîner cette responsabilité illimitée risqueraient de compromettre sérieusement le développement de l'industrie nucléaire.

3. Le régime spécial de la responsabilité civile devrait, autant que possible, reposer sur des principes uniformes pour tous les pays d'Europe occidentale. Les effets et les répercussions d'un accident nucléaire ne

4. *Article 19:*

Reservation by the Government of the Federal Republic of Germany, the Government of the Republic of Austria, and the Government of the Kingdom of Greece

Reservation of the right to consider ratification of this Convention as constituting an obligation under international law to enact national legislation on third party liability in the field of nuclear energy in accordance with the provisions of this Convention.

ANNEX II

This Convention shall not be interpreted as depriving a Contracting Party, on whose territory damage was caused by a nuclear incident occurring on the territory of another Contracting Party, of any recourse which might be available to it under international law.

IN WITNESS WHEREOF, the undersigned Plenipotentiaries, duly empowered, have signed this Convention.

DONE in Paris, this twenty-ninth day of July Nineteen Hundred and Sixty, in the English, French, German, Spanish, Italian and Dutch languages in a single copy which shall remain deposited with the Secretary-General of the Organisation for European Economic Co-operatoin by whom certified copies will be communicated to all Signatories.

EXPLANATORY MEMORANDUM

1. The production and use of atomic energy involves hazards unlike those with which the world has long been familiar. Knowledge of possible accidents and their consequences is limited by the remarkable safety record which has hitherto governed atomic energy activities. Despite this excellent safety record, it is only reasonable to expect that as the new source of energy becomes more widely used accidents will happen more frequently. Most experts incline to the view that the probability of a catastrophic nuclear incident is extremely low, but however slight the probability, the possibility remains, and enormous losses could fall both upon the public exposed to injury and upon the undertakings operating or associated with the operation of a nuclear installation.

2. A special régime for third party liability is indispensable. Firstly, the potential risks, under existing legal rules, would expose operators of nuclear installations to unlimited liability. It would clearly not be possible to obtain unlimited financial protection. Secondly, it is vitally important that all those who are associated with the operation of nuclear installations should be likewise protected. Those who supply services, materials or equipment, in connection with the planning, construction, modification, maintenance, repair or operation of a nuclear installation, should not be exposed to unlimited liability which could result if existing legal principles and practices were to apply. The heavy financial burden which could result from unlimited liability could thus seriously endanger the development of the nuclear industry.

3. The elaboration of a special régime for third party liability should as far as possible provide a uniform system for all Western European countries. The effects and repercussions of a nuclear incident will not stop

s'arrêteront pas aux frontières politiques ou géographiques et il est vivement souhaitable que les personnes soient protégées aussi bien d'un côté de la frontière que de l'autre.

4. En outre, l'ampleur que peut prendre un accident nucléaire impose une coopération internationale entre les pools nationaux d'assurances. Seul un regroupement efficace des ressources du marché européen des assurances, notamment par la co-assurance et la réassurance, permettra la constitution d'une garantie financière suffisante pour faire face aux demandes de réparation qui pourraient être présentées. L'établissement de règles uniformes de responsabilité civile dans toute l'Europe est essentiel pour que cette collaboration se réalise.

5. D'ailleurs, cette réglementation uniforme viendra compléter les mesures en cours d'élaboration dans les domaines connexes et importants de la santé et de la sécurité publiques et de la prévention des accidents. Cet ensemble de mesures permettra de créer les conditions juridiques et sociales nécessaires pour que l'industrie nucléaire parvienne rapidement à son plein épanouissement.

Enfin, un accord international peut faciliter la solution des problèmes de responsabilité civile qui se posent sur le plan national.

6. Le problème de la responsabilité civile consiste essentiellement à savoir à qui, dans quelle mesure et à quelles conditions incombe la responsabilité juridique envers les personnes qui peuvent avoir subi des dommages causés par des accidents nucléaires. Il faut déterminer, pour un accident nucléaire donné, la part de responsabilité à la charge de l'exploitant ou des personnes associées à l'exploitation de l'installation, celle que doivent supporter les victimes du dommage et enfin la mesure dans laquelle l'État doit participer à la réparation de ceux-ci. La solution de ce problème suppose une conciliation des divers intérêts en cause.

D'une part, le public doit être sûr de trouver une protection adéquate contre des dangers inconnus, ceci pour des raisons à la fois juridiques et psychologiques et, d'autre part, le développement de l'industrie nucléaire ne doit pas être compromis par une responsabilité trop lourde qui serait insupportable en cas d'accident catastrophique et ne pourrait être couverte par l'assurance.

Cette conciliation des divers intérêts en cause s'avère difficile, étant donné surtout la multiplicité et la variété des règles et principes juridiques qu'il y a lieu de modifier ou d'écarter.

Champ d'Application de la Convention

7. La Convention institue un régime d'exception et son objet se limite aux risques de caractère exceptionnel, auxquels ne peuvent s'appliquer les règles et usages du droit commun. Chaque fois que des risques, même liés à des activités nucléaires, peuvent être normalement soumis au droit en vigueur, ils sont laissés en dehors du domaine de la Convention.

La Convention ne s'applique ni aux accidents nucléaires survenus sur le territoire d'États non contractants, ni aux dommages subis sur ces territoires, sauf disposition contraire de la législation d'une Partie Contractante [articles 2 et 23 *a*)] et sous réserve du cas particulier des transporteurs, qui peuvent avoir un recours contre les exploitants, alors même que ceux-ci ne sont pas responsables d'après la Convention (*voir* paragraphe 36). Il est entendu que les territoires au sens de la Convention incluent les eaux territoriales.

8. Le régime spécial de la Convention ne s'applique qu'aux accidents nucléaires survenant dans certaines installations nucléaires ou en liaison avec celles-ci, ou pendant le transport des substances nucléaires définies par la Convention. Les États ont cependant la faculté d'appliquer les dispositions de la Convention aux dommages résultant d'accidents nucléaires non couverts par la Convention.

at political or geographical frontiers and it is highly desirable that persons on one side of a frontier should be no less well protected than persons on the other side.

4. Furthermore, the possible magnitude of a nuclear incident requires international collaboration between national insurance pools. Only an effective marshalling of the resources of the European insurance market by co-insurance and reinsurance will enable sufficient financial security to be made available to meet possible compensation claims. The establishment of uniform third party liability regulations throughout Europe is a vital factor if this collaboration is to be achieved.

5. Such uniform regulations will, moreover, supplement the measures under elaboration in the related and important fields of public health and safety and the prevention of accidents. All these measures together will provide the legal and social conditions necessary for the rapid and full development of the nuclear industry.

Lastly, an internationally agreed system may facilitate the solution to third party liability problems on a national basis.

6. The core of the third party liability problem is upon whom and in what proportions and conditions should fall the risk of legal liability to persons who may suffer damage caused by nuclear incidents. How much of this risk should be borne by the operator or those associated with the operation of the installation in a particular nuclear incident, how much by the individuals who have suffered the damage, and finally to what extent should States make available public funds for compensation. The solution to the problem involves devising means of harmonizing the separate sets of interests.

On the one hand, the public exposed must be ensured of adequate protection in the face of unknown dangers, both for legal and for psychological reasons, and, on the other hand, the growth of the nuclear industry should not be hindered by a burden of liability which would be intolerable in the case of an incident assuming catastrophic proportions and which could not be covered by conventional insurance.

A balance of these interests involved is not easy to attain, especially in view of the multiplicity and variety of legal rules and traditions which may have to be modified or laid aside.

Scope of Application of the Convention

7. The Convention provides an exceptional régime and its scope is limited to risks of an exceptional character for which common law rules and practice are not suitable. Whenever risks, even those associated with nuclear activities, can properly be dealt with through existing legal processes, they are left outside the scope of the Convention.

The Convention does not apply to nuclear incidents occurring in the territory of non-Contracting States or to damage suffered in such territory, unless the national legislation of a Contracting Party otherwise provides [Articles 2 and 23 *a*)], and with one small exception which grants certain carriers a right of recourse aginst operators even though operators are not liable under the Convention (*see* paragraph 36). The term "territory" as used in the Convention is understood to include territorial seas.

8. The special régime of the Convention applies only to nuclear incidents occurring at or in connection with certain nuclear installations, or in the course of transport of nuclear substances as defined. States remain free, however, to apply the provisions of the Convention to damage caused by nuclear incidents not covered by the Convention.

L'accident nucléaire est défini comme un fait ou succession de faits de même origine ayant causé des dommages, à condition que le fait ou les faits dommageables ou certains des dommages causés soient dus à la radioactivité ou à la fois à la radioactivité et à des propriétés toxiques, explosives ou autres propriétés dangereuses de combustibles nucléaires, produits ou déchets radioactifs. Ainsi, une émission incontrôlée de radiations s'étendant sur une certaine période de temps est considérée comme un seul accident nucléaire, si elle a pour cause un phénomène unique, alors même qu'il y aurait eu une interruption dans l'émission de radioactivité. Il résulte de cette définition de l'accident nucléaire que, lorsque le fait dommageable et le dommage sont dus l'un et l'autre à la radioactivité, il y a lieu à réparation. Inversement, si le fait dommageable et le dommage sont de nature classique, il n'y a pas lieu à réparation au titre de la Convention. Une demande en réparation peut cependant être introduite en vertu de la Convention, si un accident dû à la radioactivité est la cause d'un dommage de nature classique à des personnes ou à des biens, ou si un accident de nature classique provoque à des personnes ou à des biens un dommage dû à des radiations ionisantes.

9. Les installations nucléaires sont les réacteurs autres que ceux faisant partie d'un moyen de transport (*voir* paragraphe 11), les usines de préparation et de fabrication de substances nucléaires, les usines de séparation des isotopes de combustibles nucléaires, les usines de traitement de combustibles irradiés et les installations de stockage des substances nucléaires. En cas de stockage de substances nucléaires en cours de transport, les installations utilisées pour ce stockage sont exclues du champ d'application de la Convention. Les combustibles nucléaires sont les matières fissiles, c'est-à-dire l'uranium, y compris l'uranium naturel, sous toutes ses formes et le plutonium sous toutes ses formes. Les substances nucléaires sont les combustibles nucléaires (à l'exclusion de l'uranium naturel et de l'uranium appauvri) et les produits ou déchets radioactifs. On entend par uranium appauvri l'uranium contenant l'isotope U 235 dans une proportion inférieure à celle de l'uranium naturel.

Certaines opérations, comme l'extraction, le broyage et la concentration physique des minerais d'uranium ne comportent pas une radioactivité intense et les risques résultant de ces opérations affectent plutôt les personnes directement en cause que le public en général. C'est pourquoi ces activités n'entrent pas dans le cadre du régime d'exception de la Convention. Les usines de préparation ou de fabrication d'uranium naturel ou appauvri, les installations de stockage d'uranium naturel ou appauvri, ainsi que le transport d'uranium naturel ou appauvri, sont également exclus de la Convention, car la radioactivité reste faible et il n'y a pas de risque de criticalité.

En outre, les installations où se trouvent de faibles quantités de matières fissiles, comme les laboratoires de recherches, sont hors du cadre de la Convention, Il en est de même des accélérateurs de particules. Enfin, lorsque des matières, comme des sels d'uranium, sont utilisées accessoirement pour diverses activités industrielles qui ne sont pas liées à l'industrie nucléaire, cet emploi ne fait pas tomber l'usine en cause sous le coup de la Convention.

10. De même, les risques résultant de l'utilisation industrielle, commerciale, agricole, médicale ou scientifique des radioisotopes sont hors du cadre de la Convention, lorsque les radioisotopes sont effectivement utilisées. Ces risques n'ont pas un caractère exceptionnel et leur couverture fait déjà l'objet, depuis plusieurs années, d'opérations courantes des compagnies d'assurances. Malgré l'extension rapide de l'usage des radioisotopes dans de nombreux domaines, qui obligeront à des précautions sérieuses et continues pour la protection de la santé, il n'y a guère de possibilité de catastrophe; aucun problème particulier de responsabilité civile ne se pose donc et le régime juridique existant peut être maintenu.

A nuclear incident is defined as any occurrence or succession of occurrences having the same origin which causes damage, provided that the occurrence or succession of occurrences, or any of the damage caused, are due to radioactivity or a combination of radioactivity with toxic, explosive or other hazardous properties of nuclear fuel or radioactive products or waste. Thus, for example, an uncontrolled release of radiation extending over a certain period of time is considered to be a nuclear incident if its origin lies in one single phenomenon even though there has been an interruption in the emission of radioactivity. With this definition of "nuclear incident" it is clear that where both the occurrence and the damage are due to radioactivity, compensation may be claimed. Similarly, where the occurrence and the damage are conventional, there will be no claim. Compensation may, however, be claimed under the Convention either where an occurrence due to radioactivity causes conventional damage or injury or where an occurrence of conventional origin causes radiation damage or injury.

9. Nuclear installations are defined as reactors other than those comprised in any means of transport (*see* paragraph 11), factories for the manufacture or processing of nuclear substances, factories for the separation of isotopes of nuclear fuel, factories for the reprocessing of irradiated nuclear fuel, and facilities for the storage of nuclear substances. Where the storage of nuclear substances is incidental to their carriage, the facilities for such storage are excluded from the scope of the Convention. Nuclear fuel is defined as fissionable material, *i.e.* uranium, including natural uranium in all its forms, and plutonium in all its forms. Nuclear substances are defined as nuclear fuel other than natural uranium and depleted uranium and radioactive products or waste. Depleted uranium means uranium which contains a smaller proportion of the isotope U 235 than is contained in natural uranium.

Some activities, as for example, mining, milling and the physical concentration of uranium ores, do not involve high levels of radioactivity and such hazard as there is concerns persons immediately involved in those activities rather than the public at large. Hence, these activities do not fall within the scope of the exceptional régime of the Convention. Factories for the manufacture or processing of natural or depleted uranium, facilities for the storage of natural or depleted uranium, and the transport of natural or depleted uranium, since the level of radioactivity is low and there are no criticality risks, are also excluded.

Installations where small amounts of fissionable materials are to be found, such as research laboratories, are likewise outside the Convention. Particle accelerators, too, are excluded. Finally, where materials, such as uranium salts, are used incidentally in various industrial activities not related to the nuclear industry, such usage does not bring the plant concerned within the scope of the Convention.

10. Similarly, risks which arise in respect of radioisotopes used for any industrial, commercial, agricultural, medical or scientific purpose are excluded from the scope of the Convention, once the radioisotopes are applied for these purposes. Such risks are not of an exceptional nature and, indeed, have been covered by the insurance industry in the ordinary course of business for some years. Despite the rapidly increasing use of radioisotopes in many fields, which will require continual and careful observance of health protection precautions, there is little possibility of catastrophe. Hence no special third party liability problems are posed and the matter is left to existing legal régimes.

Toutefois, si un accident mettant en jeu des radioisotopes se produit dans une installation nucléaire et que les dommages proviennent des propriétés particulières de ces matières, on considère qu'il s'agit d'un accident nucléaire couvert par la Convention. Bien que quelques cas limites puissent se présenter, cette solution permet de déterminer, de façon générale, le moment où les radioisotopes sortent du champ d'application de la Convention.

11. Pour des raisons diverses, la propulsion nucléaire n'est pas couverte par la Convention. Seuls, les réacteurs qui ne font pas partie d'un moyen de transport quelconque entrent dans le champ d'application de la Convention; les réacteurs faisant partie d'un moyen de transport et utilisés ou destinés à être utilisés pour la propulsion de ce moyen de transport sont donc exclus. L'expérience des sous-marins atomiques rapproche le jour où des navires marchands seront propulsés par l'énergie nucléaire et il est encourageant de constater que les assureurs maritimes paraissent devoir être en mesure d'offrir une couverture satisfaisante aux armateurs de navires marchands à propulsion nucléaire lorsque ceux-ci seront prêts à entrer en service, mais l'exploitation commerciale de ces navires est encore assez lointaine.

On discute souvent de la propulsion nucléaire des avions, mais l'utilisation commerciale de ce moyen de transport est plus éloignée encore. En raison des problèmes particuliers qui se posent dans ce domaine, il ne semble pas opportun pour l'instant d'étendre à la propulsion nucléaire les dispositions de la Convention.

12. Il en va de même pour la fusion nucléaire; celle-ci est peut-être à la veille de prendre un essor tel que son importance économique sera considérable dans quelques décennies. Mais, tant que ses possibilités d'application ne seront pas mieux connues, il ne semble ni possible ni nécessaire de couvrir la fusion nucléaire.

13. Afin de prévoir les transformations à venir et les activités nouvelles pouvant comporter des risques exceptionnels, il est stipulé que le Comité de Direction de l'Énergie Nucléaire, organe directeur de l'Agence Européenne pour l'Énergie Nucléaire de l'O.E.C.E. (E.N.E.A.), peut étendre le champ d'application de la Convention à d'autres installations nucléaires [article 1 *a*) (*ii*)]. En outre, le Comité de Direction peut inclure de nouvelles matières dans la définition des combustibles nucléaires [article 1 *a*) (*iii*)]. Il peut également décider que des installations nucléaires ou des combustibles ou substances nucléaires actuellement inclus cesseront, en raison des risques réduits qu'ils comportent, d'être couverts par la Convention [article 1 *b*)]. Les décisions du Comité de Direction relatives à ces questions sont prises, conformément aux Statuts de l'E.N.E. A., par accord mutuel des membres du Comité de Direction représentant les Parties Contractantes [article 16].

Nature de la Responsabilité

14. En Europe occidentale, à quelques exceptions près, la tradition législative ou jurisprudentielle veut que l'exercice d'une activité dangereuse entraîne une présomption de responsabilité pour le risque créé. En raison des risques particuliers résultant des activités qui entrent dans le cadre de la Convention et de la difficulté de faire la preuve d'une faute étant donné la nouveauté des techniques de l'énergie atomique, cette présomption a été admise pour la responsabilité nucléaire. C'est-à-dire que la responsabilité est en principe objective et résulte du risque, indépendamment de toute faute [articles 3 et 4]; ceci ne signifie pas, toutefois, que le seul fait d'entreprendre une activité nucléaire ou de transporter un combustible nucléaire ou des produits ou déchets radioactifs doive être considéré comme entraînant en soi-même une présomption de faute; mais, lorsqu'un accident se produit, la responsabilité de l'exploitant de l'installation nucléaire en cause est objective.

If, however, an incident occurs involving radioisotopes which are in a nuclear installation and causes damage arising out of or resulting from the special properties of these materials as defined, the nuclear incident is covered by the Convention. Whilst there may be some borderline cases, this solution indicates in a general way the moment in time when radioisotopes fall outside the Convention.

11. For different reasons, nuclear propulsion is excluded from the scope of the Convention. Only reactors other than those comprised in any means of transport are covered; *i.e.* reactors which are used, or incorporated for use, in a means of transport for the purpose of propelling it, are excluded. The feasibility of merchant ship propulsion has clearly been brought nearer by the success of the atomic-powered submarines, and it is encouraging to note that it is possible that the marine insurance market will be in a position to offer a satisfactory cover to commercial owners of nuclear-propelled ships when they are ready to take the water, but commercial exploitation is still some way off.

The possibility of nuclear-propelled aircraft is frequently discussed but commercial development is even further away. In view of the special problems which are posed in this field, it is not felt appropriate at present for nuclear propulsion to be covered by the Convention.

12. The same position is true with regard to nuclear fusion, which may be on the threshold of a development which will render it of great economic importance in a few decades. But until the nature of the development is clearer it does not seem possible or necessary to take nuclear fusion into consideration.

13. So as to take account of future developments as well as new activities which may involve risks of an exceptional kind, it is provided that the Steering Committee for Nuclear Energy, the governing body of O.E.E.C.'s European Nuclear Energy Agency (E.N.E.A.), may extend the scope of the Convention to other nuclear installations [Article 1 *a*) (*ii*)]. The Steering Committee may furthermore include new materials in the definition of nuclear fuel [Article 1 *a*) (*iii*)]. It may also decide that a nuclear installation or nuclear fuel or nuclear substances at present included may, by reason of the small risks involved, cease to be covered by the Convention [Article 1*b*)]. Decisions of the Steering Committee in all these matters are taken, in accordance with the Statute of E.N.E.A., by mutual agreement of the members of the Steering Committee representing Contracting Parties [Article 16].

Nature of Liability

14. In Western Europe, with but few exceptions, there is a long-established tradition of legislative action or judicial interpretation that a presumption of liability for hazards created arises when a person engages in a dangerous activity. Because of the special dangers involved in the activities within the scope of the Convention and the difficulty of establishing negligence in view of the new techniques of atomic energy, this presumption has been adopted for nuclear liability. Absolute liability is therefore the rule; liability results from the risk irrespective of fault [Articles 3 and 4]. This does not, however, mean that merely to engage in a nuclear activity or to transport nuclear substances is to be considered in itself as a presumption of fault; but where an incident occurs, the liability of the operator of the nuclear installation concerned is absolute.

PERSONNE RESPONSABLE – INSTALLATIONS

15. Toute la responsabilité est concentrée sur une personne, à savoir l'exploitant de l'installation nucléaire où l'accident nucléaire se produit. D'après la Convention, l'exploitant – et l'exploitant seul – est responsable des accidents survenant dans l'installation, à l'exclusion de toute autre personne. Bien entendu, la Convention ne vise que la responsabilité civile. L'exploitant d'une installation nucléaire y est défini comme étant la personne désignée ou reconnue comme tel par l'autorité publique compétente en ce qui concerne l'installation nucléaire en cause [article 1 *a*) (*vi*)]. Dans les cas où il existe un système de licence ou d'autorisation, l'exploitant est le bénéficiaire de la licence ou de l'autorisation. Dans tous les autres cas, c'est la personne qui, par décision de l'autorité publique compétente, est tenue, en vertu de la Convention, d'avoir la couverture financière nécessaire pour faire face au risque de responsabilité civile. Ainsi, au cours des opérations d'essai, lorsque le fournisseur, pendant une période d'expérimentation initiale, exploite un réacteur avant qu'il soit remis à celui à qui il est destiné, le responsable est la personne désignée pour ces essais par l'autorité compétente. Quand une action est introduite, le tribunal saisi est tenu de considérer comme exploitant la personne considérée comme tel par l'autorité publique compétente du pays où est située l'installation en cause.

Deux motifs principaux ont conduit à concentrer toute la responsabilité sur l'exploitant, ce qui constitue une restriction des droits reconnus à la victime par le droit commun de la responsabilité. D'abord, il est souhaitable d'éviter les difficultés et délais qui résulteraient dans chaque cas de la possibilité d'actions en responsabilité multiples. Ensuite, il serait nécessaire, pour couvrir tous ceux qui pourraient être associés à l'exploitation d'une installation nucléaire en plus de l'exploitant, de contracter des assurances spéciales très onéreuses et dont il n'est pas même sûr qu'elles pourraient être obtenues.

16. Aucune autre personne n'est tenue de réparer les dommages causés par un accident nucléaire survenant dans une installation nucléaire ou imputable à une installation [article 6 *b*)]. Cette règle n'affecte pas les principes du droit international public concernant la responsabilité éventuelle des États entre eux en cas de faute. Lorsque l'exploitant est éxonéré en vertu de l'article 9, on revient au droit commun et les responsables peuvent, par conséquent, être poursuivis comme auteurs du dommage.

17. Le principe suivant lequel la responsabilité doit être concentrée sur l'exploitant implique essentiellement qu'aucune action ne peut être intentée contre une autre personne et notamment contre une personne ayant fourni des services, des matériaux ou de l'équipement à l'occasion de la mise au point, de la construction, de la modification, de l'entretien, de la réparation ou de l'exploitation de l'installation nucléaire.

D'après le droit commun, au contraire, si un accident provenait d'un défaut des plans ou des matériaux fournis, la victime aurait une action contre le fournisseur, notamment en invoquant ce qu'on appelle le „vice de la chose" (*products liability*).

18. L'exploitant pourrait en outre avoir un droit de recours en raison des indemnités qu'il aurait payées à des victimes. La notion de responsabilité unique a donc pour corollaire l'exclusion de tout recours de l'exploitant (ou de l'assureur, ou de toute autre personne ayant accordé une garantie financière et subrogée aux droits de l'exploitant) contre les fournisseurs, en raison des sommes qu'il aurait versées à titre de réparation.

19. Il y a, toutefois, trois exceptions à cette règle. D'abord, si le dommage causé par un accident nucléaire résulte d'un acte ou d'une omission faite avec l'intention de causer un dommage, le droit de recours de l'ex-

Person Liable–Installations

15. All liability is channelled onto one person, namely the operator of the nuclear installation where the nuclear incident occurs. Under the Convention, the operator – and only the operator – is liable for nuclear incidents at installations and no other person is liable. The Convention deals, of course, only with civil liability. The operator of a nuclear installation is defined as the person designated or recognized as the operator of that nuclear installation by the competent public authority [Article 1*a*) (*vi*)]. Where there is a system of licensing or authorization, the operator will be the licensee or person duly authorized. In all other cases he will be the person required by the competent public authority, in accordance with the provisions of the Convention, to have the necessary financial protection to meet third party liability risks. Thus, during test operation when a reactor, for the initial trial period, is normally operated by the supplier before being handed over to the person for whom the reactor was supplied, the person liable will be appropriately designated by the competent public authority. Where an action is brought, the court concerned will be bound to consider the operator as the person considered as the operator by the competent public authority of the country where the operator's installation is situated.

Two primary factors have motivated in favour of this channelling of all liability onto the operator which involves a limitation of the rights of an injured person under the law of torts to sue the person causing the damage. Firstly, it is desirable to avoid difficult and lengthy questions of complicated legal cross-actions to establish in individual cases who is legally liable. Secondly, special insurance would otherwise be needed to cover the liability of all those who might be associated with the operation of a nuclear installation as well as the liability of the operator, which would be very expensive and which it is not certain would be available.

16. No other person is liable for compensation for damage caused by a nuclear incident at or in connection with a nuclear installation [Article 6 *b*)]. This rule is not intended to affect the rules of public international law with regard to any possible responsibility of States towards each other in the event of tortious acts. Where the operator is exonerated in pursuance of Article 9, common law applies and those responsible may therefore be sued as ordinary tortfeasors.

17. It is essential to the notion of channelling liability onto the operator that no actions may lie against any other person and in particular, for example, any person who has supplied any services, materials or equipment in connection with the planning, construction, modification, maintenance, repair or operation of a nuclear installation.

In the ordinary course of law, on the contrary, should an incident arise due to a defect in design or in material supplied, a person suffering damage may well have a right of action against the supplier, for example, on the basis of the so-called products liability.

18. Furthermore, the operator might well have a recourse for indemnity in respect of any compensation which he has to pay for damage to third parties. A corollary to the notion of channelling is therefore that possible recourse actions by the operator (or the insurer or other financial guarantor to whom the operator's right of recourse may have been transferred) against suppliers in respect of any sums which the operator has paid as compensation are barred.

19. There are, however, three exceptions to this rule. Firstly, where the damage caused by a nuclear incident results from an act or omission done with the intention of causing damage, the operator's normal right

ploitant contre l'auteur de l'acte ou de l'omission est expressément retenu [article 6 *f*) (*i*)]. Mais ce droit de recours ne peut être exercé que contre la personne physique qui agit ou omet d'agir dans l'intention de causer un dommage. Il n'y a pas de recours contre l'employeur de cette personne et le principe *respondeat superior* est écarté. La mise en cause de l'employeur en raison d'actes ou d'omissions intentionnels d'individus a été exclue car elle irait à l'encontre du but de la Convention. Selon celle-ci, les exploitants d'installations nucléaires ne peuvent jamais être tenus à réparation au-delà du maximum fixé en vertu de l'article 7, même si le dommage a été causé intentionnellement. Cette responsabilité maximum doit être couverte par une assurance ou une autre garantie financière. Si un recours était ouvert pour un montant illimité contre les sociétés qui fournissent des matériaux aux exploitants en raison des actes ou omissions de leurs préposés, il serait impossible de trouver l'assurance ou la garantie financière nécessaires et ceci créerait pour les fournisseurs un risque sérieux, de nature à entraver le développement de l'industrie nucléaire.

En second lieu, le droit de recours peut être exercé dans les cas et dans la mesure où il résulte expressément de stipulations contractuelles [article 6 *f*) (*ii*)]. Le droit de recours peut évidemment être exercé par l'assureur ou un autre garant agissant en vertu d'une subrogation.

La troisième exception vise le cas où une Partie Contractante subordonne, conformément à l'article 7 *e*), le transit de substances nucléaires à travers son territoire à la condition que le montant maximum de la responsabilité de l'exploitant étranger en cause soit augmenté et porté au montant maximum de la responsabilité des exploitants d'installations nucléaires situées sur son territoire. Dans ce cas, l'exploitant en cause a un recours contre le transporteur si le transit a été effectué sans son consentement, et si sa responsabilité se trouve engagée pour un montant excédant celui qui est fixé en ce qui le concerne conformément à l'article 7 *b*), sauf si le transit a pour objet de sauver ou de tenter de sauver des vies ou des biens ou est provoqué par des circonstances indépendantes de la volonté du transporteur [article 6 *f*) (*iii*)]. Cette disposition vise aussi à décourager le transit non autorisé.

Les dispositions de l'article 6 *f*) concernant les recours de l'exploitant ne visent pas son droit d'action contre le co-auteurs d'un dommage au cas où plus d'un exploitant est responsable.

20. Si un dommage implique la responsabilité de plusieurs exploitants, ceux-ci sont responsables solidairement, c'est-à-dire que chacun des exploitants peut faire l'objet d'une action en réparation pour le total du dommage. Le montant des indemnités payables est, par conséquent, égal à la somme des montants maximums de la responsabilité de chacun des exploitants en cause. Toutefois, cette règle ne s'applique pas aux accidents nucléaires mettant en jeu des substances nucléaires en cours de transport; dans ce cas, le montant total des indemnités payables est égal au montant le plus élevé de la responsabilité fixé pour l'un des exploitants en cause. En aucun cas, que l'accident nucléaire se soit produit dans une installation, soit imputable à une installation, ou soit survenu en cours de transport, la responsabilité de l'exploitant ne peut être mise en jeu au delà du montant maximum fixé, en ce qui le concerne pour un accident nucléaire, conformément à l'article 7 [article 5 *b*)]. C'est le droit commun du partage de la responsabilité entre des personnes solidairement responsables, qui règle les recours des différents exploitants entre eux en raison des indemnités payées aux tiers.

21. Dans l'hypothèse d'un accident nucléaire provoqué par des matières volées, perdues ou abandonnées, la responsabilité incombe à l'exploitant de l'installation d'où les matières provenaient immédiatement avant l'accident [article 3].

of recourse against the individual who so acts or omits to act is specifically retained [Article 6 *f*) (*i*)]. The right of recourse is limited to a right against the individual physical person who acts or omits to act with intent to cause damage. There is no right of recourse against the employer of such a person and the principle of *respondeat superior* is thus excluded. Imputation to the employer of acts or omissions of individuals done with intent to cause damage has been barred, for it would be contrary to the purpose of the Convention. Under the Convention, operators of nuclear installations can never be held to any civil liability beyond the maximum laid down pursuant to Article 7 even if the damage was caused by them with intent to cause damage. For this maximum liability, insurance or other financial security will be available. If undertakings supplying operators were to be held liable for acts or omissions of their employees by way of actions in recourse for an unlimited amount, it would be impossible for them to obtain the necessary insurance or other financial security. This would involve serious consequences for suppliers and impede the development of the nuclear industry.

Secondly, rights of recourse may be exercised where and to the extent that they are expressly provided for in contractual arrangements [Article 6 *f*) (*ii*)]. These rights of recourse may, of course, be exercised by the insurer or other financial guarantor by way of subrogation.

Thirdly, where a Contracting Party, pursuant to Article 7 *e*), subjects the transit of nuclear substances through its territory to the condition that the maximum amount of liability of the foreign operator concerned is increased up to the limit fixed for operators of nuclear installations in its territory and a transit is carried out without his consent, the operator concerned has a right of recourse against the carrier in question to the extent that he is liable in excess of the amount fixed for him pursuant to Article 7 *b*), except where the transit is for the purpose of saving or attempting to save life or property or is caused by circumstances beyond the control of the carrier [Article 6 *f*) (*iii*)]. This provision is an additional discouragement to unauthorized transits.

The provisions of Article 6 *f*) relating to the operator's right of recourse do not include his rights to recover from joint tortfeasors in the case where more than one operator is liable.

20. Where the damage gives rise to the liability of more than one operator, the liability of the different operators involved is joint and several and any of them may therefore be sued for the whole amount of the damage. The total amount of compensation available is therefore the aggregate of the sums of each of the operators concerned. This rule, however, does not apply to a nuclear incident involving nuclear substances in the course of carriage; here the total amount of compensation is the highest amount established with respect to any of them. In any event, whether the nuclear incident occurs at or in connection with an installation or in the course of transport, no operator is liable to pay more than the maximum amount established for him in respect of a nuclear incident in accordance with Article 7 [Article 5 *b*)]. The ordinary operation of common law as regards contributions between persons jointly and severally liable will regulate the recovery of sums paid as compensation to third parties as between the different operators involved.

21. In the event of a nuclear incident involving materials which have been stolen, lost or abandoned, liability is imposed on the operator from whose nuclear installations the materials came immediately before such an event [Article 3].

PERSONNE RESPONSABLE – TRANSPORT

22. Lorsqu'un accident nucléaire survient au cours d'un transport de substances nucléaires, le responsable ne peut être que le transporteur ou l'exploitant de l'installation nucléaire pour laquelle les matières sont transportées. Le choix de la personne responsable n'affecte aucunement les conventions qu'elle a pu passer et, inversement, ces conventions ne peuvent avoir d'effet à l'égard des tiers.

Il semblerait normal qu'en cours de transport la responsabilité incombe au transporteur et c'est la solution du droit commun. Toutefois, dans le cas de matières radioactives, des considérations particulières interviennent. Le transporteur ne sera généralement pas en état de vérifier les précautions prises par l'expéditeur des matières quant à leur emballage et à l'étanchéité des récipients. En outre, si le transporteur est responsable, il doit s'assurer pour une responsabilité qui peut être élevée et ceci a pour effet d'augmenter le coût du transport pour l'exploitant. L'assurance-transport ne couvre normalement que la valeur des marchandises transportées, c'est-à-dire leur perte ou leur destruction, et ne s'étend pas aux dommages que ces marchandises pourraient causer à des tiers.

23. Si l'on retient la responsabilité de l'exploitant, il y a lieu de préciser quel est l'exploitant responsable: est-ce celui qui expédie les substances nucléaires ou celui qui les reçoit? En principe, la responsabilité doit incomber à l'exploitant qui expédie les matières, puisqu'il a la charge d'emballer ces matières et de les mettre dans des récipients, conformément aux règles de sécurité et de protection de la santé applicables aux transports [article 4 *a*)].

24. La responsabilité de l'exploitant expéditeur prend fin lorsque les matières ont été prises en charge par un autre exploitant d'une installation nucléaire située sur le territoire d'une Partie Contractante [article 4 *a*) (*i*)]. Ainsi, du point de vue de la victime, il appartient à l'expéditeur de fournir la preuve qu'un autre exploitant a pris en charge les substances nucléaires. En principe, le moment précis de la prise en charge est déterminé, en cas de litige, par le tribunal compétent (*voir cependant* paragraphe 31).

25. Toutefois, si le lieu de destination des matières est sur le territoire d'un État non-contractant, la situation est différente, car la Convention ne peut rendre responsables des personnes qui ne relèvent pas de la juridiction des Parties Contractantes. La responsabilité de l'exploitant expéditeur subsiste alors, jusqu'à ce que les matières aient été déchargées du moyen de transport qui les a amenées sur le territoire de l'État non-contractant [article 4 *a*) (*ii*)].

26. Dans le cas inverse, si des matières sont transportées du territoire d'un État non-contractant à celui d'une Partie Contractante, c'est-à-dire lorsque l'expéditeur ne se trouve pas sur le territoire d'une Partie Contractante, la règle est différente, car il est essentiel pour les victimes qu'il y ait toujours un responsable sur le territoire des Parties Contractantes. Dans ce cas, la responsabilité incombe à l'exploitant auquel les matières sont destinées et avec l'accord duquel elles ont été expédiées [article 4 *c*)].

27. Ici encore, il est nécessaire de préciser exactement le moment où commence la responsabilité de l'exploitant installé sur le territoire d'une Partie Contractante, auquel les matières sont destinées et avec l'accord duquel elles ont été expédiées. Cette responsabilité commence lorsque les matières ont été chargées sur le territoire de l'État non-contractant d'où elles sont expédiées à bord du moyen de transport qui les a amenées. Dans ce cas, le principe général posé par l'article 2 reste valable et l'exploitant ne sera pas responsable des accidents nucléaires survenus ou des dommages causés sur le territoire d'États non-contractants.

28. Ainsi qu'il a été indiqué (*voir* paragraphe 7), l'exploitant n'est responsable en vertu de la Convention, sauf si la législation nationale

PERSON LIABLE – TRANSPORT

22. When nuclear incidents occur in the course of transport of nuclear substances, the choice of the person liable must fall either upon the carrier or upon the operator of the nuclear installation in connection with which the materials are carried. The choice will not affect any contractual arrangements which may be made by the person liable and, in turn, such arrangements will not, of course, have any effect upon third persons.

It would seem normal, in the case of transport, for the carrier to be the person liable and this is the present situation at common law. However, in the case of radioactive materials, very special considerations are involved. The carrier will generally not be in a position to verify the precautions in packing and containment taken by the person sending the materials. Moreover, if the carrier is to be liable he will have to obtain the necessary insurance coverage in respect of potentially high liability, and this would result in increased transport charges for the operator. Transport insurance ordinarily covers only the value of the goods transported, *i.e.*, their loss or destruction, and does not extend to damage which such goods may cause to third persons.

23. If liability is to be imposed on the operator, the operator in question must be defined: is it to be the operator who sends nuclear substances or who receives them? In principle, liability is imposed on the operator sending the materials since he will be responsible for the packing and containment and for ensuring that these comply with the health and safety regulations laid down for transport [Article 4 *a*)].

24. The liability of the sending operator ends when the materials have been taken in charge by another operator of a nuclear installation situated in the territory of a Contracting Party [Article 4 *a*) (*i*)]. Thus, from the point of view of the person suffering damage, the burden of proof will be on the sending operator to show that some other operator has taken charge of the nuclear substances. The precise moment of the taking in charge will normally be determined by the competent tribunal in the event of actions (but *see also* paragraph 31).

25. If however, the materials are consigned to a destination in a non-Contracting State, different rules apply, for the Convention clearly cannot impose liability upon persons not subject to the jurisdiction of the Contracting Parties. The liability of the sending operator comes to an end when the materials have been unloaded from the means of carriage by which they have arrived in the territory of the non-Contracting State [Article 4 *a*) (*ii*)].

26. In the converse situation, where materials are being carried from a non-Contracting State to a Contracting Party, *i.e.*, where there is no sender in the territory of the Contracting Parties, another rule applies. It is vital for victims that there should always be somebody liable within the territory of the Contracting Parties: liability in this case is imposed upon the operator for whom the materials are destined and with whose approval they have been sent [Article 4 *c*)].

27. Here again, it is necessary to define exactly the point when the liability of the operator in the territory of a Contracting Party for whom the materials are destined, and with whose approval they have been sent, begins. This operator's liability will begin when the materials have been loaded on the means of transport by which they are to be carried from the territory of the non-Contracting State from which they are sent. In this case also the general principle of Article 2 applies and the operator will not be liable for nuclear incidents occurring in or damage suffered in the territory of non-Contracting States.

28. As has already been pointed out (*see* paragraph 7), the operator will not be liable under the Convention, unless national legislation other-

dispose autrement, ni des accidents nucléaires survenus sur le territoire d'un État non-contractant ni des dommages subis sur ces territoires, bien qu'il puisse faire l'objet d'un recours des transporteurs (*voir* paragraphe 36).

29. Le principe général de la responsabilité exclusive de l'exploitant comporte une exception. Une Partie Contractante peut prévoir, par une disposition législative, si les conditions de l'article 10 *a*) relatives à la garantie financière sont remplies, la possibilité de substituer le transporteur à l'exploitant d'une installation nucléaire située sur son territoire. Cette substitution se fait par décision de l'autorité publique compétente, dans les conditions prévues par la loi. Elle ne peut être décidée qu'à la demande du transporteur et avec l'accord de l'exploitant de l'installation nucléaire située sur le territoire de la Partie Contractante en question. Une fois la décision prise, le transporteur est responsable à la place de l'exploitant conformément à la Convention. Le transporteur est considéré, aux fins de la Convention, pour les accidents nucléaires survenus au cours du transport des substances nucléaires, comme l'exploitant d'une installation nucléaire située sur le territoire de la Partie Contractante dont la législation a permis la substitution [article 4 *e*)].

Dans le cas où le transporteur, pour un transport de substances nucléaires expédiées par plusieurs exploitants ou destinées à plusieurs exploitants, assume la responsabilité aux lieu et place des exploitants en cause, il est considéré comme représentant à lui seul chacun des exploitants et les règles relatives au cas où plusieurs exploitants sont responsables, s'appliquent comme s'il n'y avait pas eu substitution.

30. Pour faciliter le transport des matières radioactives, en particulier en cas de transit par un certain nombre de pays, il est prévu que pour chaque transport l'exploitant responsable en vertu de la Convention doit fournir au transporteur un certificat délivré par l'assureur ou le garant prévu à l'article 10, ou en son nom. Ce certificat doit énoncer le nom et l'adresse de l'exploitant responsable et donner des précisions sur la garantie financière. Ces indications ne peuvent être ultérieurement contestées par la personne par laquelle ou pour laquelle le certificat a été délivré. Le certificat doit également désigner les substances nucléaires et l'itinéraire couverts par la garantie et comporter une déclaration par l'autorité publique compétente que la personne visée est un exploitant au sens de la Convention [article 4 *d*)].

31. Une Partie Contractante peut, en cas de transport de substances nucléaires expédiées de l'étranger à destination d'une installation située sur son territoire, exiger que l'exploitant de l'installation prenne en charge ces substances à leur entrée sur son territoire. De même, au cas où des substances nucléaires sont expédiées à l'étranger, par l'exploitant d'une installation nucléaire située sur son territoire, une Partie Contractante peut exiger que ces substances restent sous la responsabilité de l'exploitant jusqu'à la sortie de son territoire.

32. Le fait, pour un transporteur, de posséder un certificat ne lui donne aucun droit de pénétrer sur le territoire d'une Partie Contractante. En outre, une Partie Contractante peut subordonner le transit de substances nucléaires à travers son territoire à la condition que le montant maximum de la responsabilité de l'exploitant étranger en cause soit augmenté si elle estime, compte tenu du danger que présente le transport des substances nucléaires dans le cas particulier, que ce montant ne couvre pas d'une manière adéquate les risques d'un accident nucléaire au cours du transit. Toutefois, le montant maximum ainsi majoré ne peut excéder le montant maximum de la responsabilité des exploitants d'installations nucléaires situées sur le territoire de cette Partie Contractante [article 7 *e*)].

wise provides, for nuclear incidents occurring in or damage suffered in the territory of a non-Contracting State, though there may be recourse against him by carriers (*see* paragraph 36).

29. There is one exception to the basic principle that only the operator is liable under the Convention. A Contracting Party may, by legislation, on condition that the requirements of Article 10 *a*) with regard to financial security are fulfilled, provide that a carrier be liable under the Convention in substitution for an operator of a nuclear installation in its territory. Such substitution will be in accordance with the terms laid down in the legislation and by decision of the competent public authority. Moreover, the substitution must be requested by the carrier and have the consent of the operator of the nuclear installation situated in the territory of the Contracting Party in question. Once the decision has been taken, the carrier will be liable in accordance with the Convention in place of that operator. For all the purposes of the Convention, the carrier is then considered, in respect of nuclear incidents occurring in the course of carriage of nuclear substances, as an operator of a nuclear installation in the territory of the Contracting Party whose legislation has provided for the substitution [Article 4 *e*)].

Where, in respect of the carriage of nuclear substances coming from or destined for different operators, the carrier has assumed, by substitution, the liability of each of the operators concerned, such carrier is considered as if he were each of the different operators concerned and the rules relating to liability of more than one operator will apply in the same way as if there had been no substitution.

30. In order to facilitate the transport of radioactive materials, especially in the event of transit through a number of countries, it is provided that in respect of each carriage the operator liable in accordance with the Convention must provide the carrier with a certificate issued by or on behalf of the insurer or other person providing the financial security required pursuant to Article 10. This certificate must contain the name and address of the operator liable and the details of the financial security. This information may not be subsequently contested by the person by whom or on whose behalf the certificate was issued. The certificate must also include an indication of the nuclear substances involved and the carriage in respect of which the security applies, as well as a statement by the competent public authority that the person named is an operator within the meaning of the Convention [Article 4 *d*)].

31. For transport of nuclear substances to or from installations situated in its territory, a Contracting Party may require the operators of the installations for whom the substances are carried from abroad to take the substances in charge the moment the substances reach its territory. Similarly, in the case of nuclear substances sent by operators of nuclear installations in its territory to a foreign destination, a Contracting Party may require that the nuclear substances shall remain in the charge of such operators until they have left its territory.

32. The possession of a certificate by a carrier does not imply any right to enter the territory of a Contracting Party. Moreover, a Contracting Party may subject the transit of nuclear substances through its territory to the condition that the maximum amount of liability of the foreign operator concerned is increased if it considers, taking account of the special dangers of the nuclear substances in the particular transit in question, that such amount does not adequately cover the risks. But the maximum amount thus increased cannot exceed the maximum amount of liability of operators of nuclear installations situated in its territory [Article 7 *e*)].

Il a été reconnu, d'autre part, que le droit international accorde un droit de refuge dans les ports en cas de danger imminent et un droit de passage inoffensif à travers les eaux territoriales et qu'il peut y avoir, en vertu d'un accord ou du droit international, un droit de survol ou d'atterissage sur le territoire des États. Par suite, les dispositions de l'article 7 *e*) ne s'appliquent pas au transit par mer ou par air dans ces deux cas [article 7 *f*)].

33. Si un transport, ce qui pourrait être le cas normal, comporte des matières radioactives expédiées par plusieurs exploitants différents, ceux-ci sont solidairement responsables à concurrence du montant le plus élevé fixé pour l'un d'entre eux conformément à l'article 7. Comme il a été précisé (*voir* paragraphe 20), il n'y a pas cumul des montants dans le cas d'un accident nucléaire survenant en cours de transport.

34. Il a paru opportun d'éviter toute possibilité de conflit avec les accords internationaux en matière de transport qui sont en vigueur ou ouverts à la signature, à la ratification ou à l'adhésion à la date de la Convention, étant donné notamment que des pays non européens sont parties à ces accords. On entend par „accords internationaux en matière de transport" les accords internationaux visant la responsabilité civile pour les dommages causés par un moyen de transport, les accords internationaux relatifs à la collision de moyens de transport ainsi que les accords internationaux sur les connaissements. Pour écarter toute possibilité de conflit, il est prévu que la Convention n'affecte pas l'application de ces accords [article 6 *b*)].

35. Ainsi, une personne qui subit sur le territoire d'une Partie Contractante un dommage causé par un accident nucléaire au cours d'un transport peut avoir deux actions: l'une contre l'exploitant responsable aux termes de la Convention et l'autre contre le transporteur, en vertu des accords internationaux en matière de transport.

Lorsque l'exploitant responsable est en même temps transporteur, par exemple s'il transporte des substances nucléaires sur un moyen de transport lui appartenant, ces deux actions ne peuvent être introduites que contre une seule personne. Dans ce cas, l'exploitant ne peut tirer avantage des dispositions des accords internationaux en matière de transport pour réduire ou modifier sa responsabilité telle qu'elle résulte de la présente Convention.

36. Une personne dont la responsabilité est mise en cause en vertu d'un tel accord international ou de la loi d'un État non-contractant a un recours contre l'exploitant responsable, dans la limite du montant de la responsabilité fixé conformément à l'article 7 [article 6 *c*)]. Toutefois, dans le cas d'un accident nucléaire survenu ou d'un dommage subi sur le territoire d'un État non-contractant, ce recours ne peut être exercé que par une personne ayant son lieu principal d'exploitation sur le territoire d'une Partie Contractante, ou par les préposés de cette personne [article 6 *d*)]. Cette disposition, qui ouvre un recours contre l'exploitant dans un cas où, suivant la Convention, il n'est pas responsable envers les victimes, c'est-à-dire dans les États non-contractants, constitue la seule dérogation au principe général de l'article 2; mais cette exception ne joue qu'à concurrence de la limite de responsabilité fixée pour l'exploitant en cause conformément à l'article 7 de la Convention. Une personne qui a un recours contre l'exploitant ne peut l'exercer que dans la mesure où l'exploitant n'a pas lui-même de recours contre elle [article 6 *g*)].

37. Une disposition spéciale permet au Conseil de l'O.E.C.E. de décider que les transporteurs ayant leur lieu principal d'exploitation sur le territoire d'un État non-contractant peuvent également avoir un recours contre l'exploitant dans les mêmes conditions que les personnes ayant leur lieu principal d'exploitation sur le territoire d'une Partie Contractante. En prenant cette décision, le Conseil doit tenir compte des dispo-

It was recognized, however, that a right of entry in case of urgent distress into the ports of States and a right of innocent passage through territorial seas is granted under international law and that by agreement or under international law there may be a right to fly over or land on the territory of States; hence the provisions of Article 7 *e*) do not apply to a transit by sea or by air in these cases [Article 7 *f*)].

33. Where, and this may well be a normal case, the carriage involves materials sent by a number of different operators, the maximum total amount for which such operators are jointly and severally liable is the highest amount established with respect to any of them pursuant to Article 7. As has already been stated (*see* paragraph 20), there is no accumulation of amounts for a nuclear incident in the course of transport.

34. It has been thought advisable not to interfere with existing international agreements in the field of transport in force or open for signature, ratification or accession at the date of the Convention, especially since countries outside Europe are parties to them. International agreements in the field of transport are understood to mean international agreements dealing with third party liability for damage involving a means of transport, international agreements dealing with collisions involving a means of transport and international agreements dealing with bills of lading. To avoid the possibility of conflicting provisions, it is laid down that the Convention does not affect the application of such agreements [Article 6*b*)].

35. Hence, a person suffering damage caused by a nuclear incident occurring in the course of transport may have two rights of action: one against the operator liable under the Convention and another against the carrier liable under existing international agreements in the field of transport.

Where the operator liable is at the same time the carrier, for example, where he transports nuclear substances on his own means of transport, these two possible actions may be brought against one person. In this case, however, the operator cannot take advantage of the provisions of international agreements in the field of transport to reduce or alter his liability under the Convention.

36. A person so liable under any international agreement or under any legislation of a non-Contracting State has a right of recourse against the operator liable under the Convention within the limitation of the amount of liability established pursuant to Article 7 [Article 6 *c*)]. If a nuclear incident occurs in the territory of a non-Contracting State or damage is suffered in such territory, a right of recourse is also available to a person who has his principal place of business in the territory of a Contracting Party or who is the servant of such a person [Article 6 *d*)]. This rule, which provides a recourse against the operator in circumstances where he is not liable under the Convention to persons suffering damage, *i.e.* in non-Contracting States, is the only derogation from the general principle of Article 2 but, of course, is only available within the limit laid down for the operator in question pursuant to Article 7 of the Convention. Any person who has a right of recourse against the operator can only exercise this right of recourse to the extent that the operator does not have a right of recourse against him [Article 6 *g*)].

37. A special provision enables the O.E.E.C. Council to decide that carriers whose principal place of business is in the territory of a non-Contracting State may also enjoy rights of recourse against the operator to the same extent as persons having their principal place of business in the territory of a Contracting Party. In making its decision, the Council has to give due consideration to the general provisions on third party

sitions générales sur la responsabilité civile dans le domaine de l'énergie nucléaire en vigueur dans cet État non-contractant et de la mesure dans laquelle les ressortissants d'une Partie Contractante ou les personnes ayant leur lieu principal d'exploitation sur le territoire d'une Partie Contractante bénéficient de ces dispositions [article 6 *e*)].

Toutes les règles relatives au transport s'appliquent aux divers moyens de transport.

Actions

38. Les actions en réparation pour dommages causés par des accidents nucléaires survenus dans une installation nucléaire, liés à son exploitation ou survenus en cours de transport, ne peuvent en principe être introduites, selon la Convention, que contre l'exploitant. Toutefois, l'action contre l'assureur ou contre un autre garant, aux lieu et place de l'exploitant ou en même temps que contre l'exploitant, subsiste si la législation du tribunal compétent permet l'action directe dans ce cas [article 6 *a*)].

Dommages ouvrant Droit à Réparation

39. La Convention ne contient pas de disposition définissant en détail les dommages matériels ou corporels qui ouvrent droit à réparation. Il est nécessaire seulement qu'il s'agisse d'un dommage à des personnes ou à des biens et qu'un lien de causalité existe entre ce dommage et l'accident nucléaire. Étant donné la diversité des règles législatives ou jurisprudentielles relatives à la responsabilité dans les pays européens, on a laissé au tribunal compétent le soin de décider, suivant la loi nationale applicable, ce qui doit être considéré comme dommage aux personnes ou aux biens et de déterminer dans quelle mesure une indemnité peut être accordée, par exemple dans le cas d'un dommage purement moral ou d'un dommage subi par une personne à charge ou une autre personne qui se trouve privée de son droit à une pension alimentaire [article 3].

40. La Convention, toutefois, prévoit deux exceptions en ce qui concerne les dommages aux biens. En premier lieu, aucune réparation n'est due lorsque le dommage est causé à des biens détenus par l'exploitant, sous sa garde ou sous son contrôle, en rapport avec l'installation et à son site. Les dommages aux biens qui sont l'objet de contrats passés par l'assuré ne sont pas normalement couverts par l'assurance responsabilité civile. Il semble toutefois que les assureurs puissent déroger à la pratique normale et couvrir des biens détenus par l'exploitant au site de l'installation, s'ils sont sans rapport avec son exploitation.

En second lieu, aucune réparation n'est due, en principe, pour les dommages causés au moyen de transport sur lequel les substances nucléaires en jeu se trouvent au moment d'un accident nucléaire survenu en cours de transport hors d'une installation nucléaire. L'expression moyen de transport ne couvre pas les bâtiments ou installations fixes tels que ponts, tunnels, câbles électriques ou voies de chemin de fer.

Une Partie Contractante peut toutefois, par une disposition législative, inclure le dommage causé au moyen de transport, à condition qu'en aucun cas cette inclusion n'ait pour effet de réduire la responsabilité de l'exploitant pour les autres dommages à un montant inférieur à 5.000.000 d'unités de compte de l'Accord Monétaire Européen [article 7 *c*)]. Si cette inclusion est prévue, 5.000.000 d'unités de compte sont en principe réservés aux autres dommages; mais, si le total des indemnités dues pour ces dommages est inférieur à ce chiffre, la part non utilisée de ce montant peut servir au besoin à la réparation des dommages causés au moyen de transport. Si, par contre, les indemnités dues pour les autres dommages dépassent 5.000.000 d'unités de compte, la répartition du montant total liability in the field of nuclear energy in such non-Contracting State and the extent to which these provisions are available to the benefit of nationals of, and persons whose principal place of business is in, the territory of the Contracting Parties [Article 6 *e*)].

All these rules relating to transport apply to all the different means of transport.

Actions

38. Although actions for compensation under the Convention, whether arising out of nuclear incidents occurring at or in connection with nuclear installations or in the course of transport, can in principle only be brought against the operator, the right to bring actions against the insurer or other person providing the financial security, either as an alternative to the operator or in addition to him, is maintained where the national law of the court having jurisdiction grants a right of direct action in such a case [Article 6 *a*)].

Damage giving Right to Compensation

39. The Convention contains no detailed provisions determining the kind of damage or injury which will be compensated, but it is provided merely that damage must be to persons or property and related causally to a nuclear incident. What should be considered as damage to persons or property and the extent to which compensation will be recoverable, for example, for purely moral damages or by dependents and others who suffer a loss of right to support, in view of the very wide divergence of legal principles and jurisprudence in the law of torts in European countries, is left to be decided by the competent court in accordance with the national law applicable [Article 3].

40. There are, however, two limitations in respect of property. Firstly, there is no right of compensation under the Convention for damage to on-site property which is held by the operator or in his custody or under his control in connection with his installation. Normally, damage to property in regard to which a person has a contractual relationship is not covered by third party insurance. It seems likely that insurers may make an exception to their normal practice and provide insurance where the property is held at the site of a nuclear installation but has no connection with its operation.

Secondly, there is in principle no right of compensation for damage to the means of transport upon which the nuclear substances involved were at the time of a nuclear incident occurring in the course of carriage and outside a nuclear installation. Means of transport do not include fixed buildings or installations such as bridges, tunnels, electric cables or railway lines.

A Contracting Party may, however, by legislation provide for the inclusion of damage to the means of transport on condition that such inclusion does not reduce the liability of the operator in respect of other damage to less than 5,000,000 European Monetary Agreement units of account [Article 7 *c*)]. Where such inclusion is provided for, 5,000,000 u/a are thus in principle earmarked for other damage, but if such other damage is less than this amount, the part of the amount not used is available, if necessary, for compensation for damage to the means of transport. On the other hand, if other damage is more than 5,000,000 u/a there will be proportional distribution of the total amount available to cover all the damage including damage to the means of transport. This disponible se fait proportionnellement pour tous les dommages, y compris les dommages causés au moyen de transport, de telle sorte que les indemnités payées pour les autres dommages peuvent dépasser le montant de 5.000.000 d'unités de compte mais ne peuvent être inférieures à ce montant.

Si les biens appartiennent à l'exploitant lui-même, aucune action en réparation ne saurait en tout cas être admise, nul ne pouvant agir contre lui-même.

41. Si un droit à réparation résulte de stipulations contractuelles, il n'est pas effecté par la Convention.

Accidents du Travail et Maladies Professionnelles

42. Les dispositions de l'article 3 s'appliquent à toute victime d'un dommage causé par un accident nucléaire, qu'il s'agisse d'un tiers se trouvant à l'intérieur ou à l'extérieur de l'installation ou d'un préposé de l'exploitant de cette installation. Dans la plupart des pays, les préposés victimes d'un dommage bénéficient aussi à ce titre des prestations prévues par le régime national d'assurances médicales, de sécurité sociale ou de réparation des accidents du travail et maladies professionnelles. Il a été admis qu'en principe les préposés, qu'ils travaillent dans l'installation ou dans d'autres établissements, devraient conserver le bénéfice de ces prestations, mais cette question est laissée à la loi établissant ce régime, à laquelle il appartient aussi de décider si les préposés peuvent prétendre en outre à une réparation en vertu de la Convention. Cette loi déterminera également si les organismes responsables de l'application du régime national peuvent se retourner contre l'exploitant pour obtenir le remboursement des sommes qu'ils ont versées, étant entendu qu'en tout cas l'exploitant ne peut être tenu de payer au delà du montant maximum de sa responsabilité [article 6 *h*)].

Limitation du Montant de la Responsabilité

43. A défaut d'une limitation de la responsabilité de l'exploitant, les risques pourraient, dans les circonstances les plus défavorables, entraîner une responsabilité dépassant ce dont on a jusqu'à présent l'expérience. Même avec une limitation, il ne sera pas toujours facile aux exploitants de trouver la couverture financière nécessaire pour faire face à ces risques.

Le montant maximum de la responsabilité pour un même accident nucléaire, qu'il se produise dans une installation nucléaire, en rapport avec cette installation ou au cours d'un transport de substances nucléaires, a été fixé à 15.000.000 d'unités de compte A.M.E. Une Partie Contractante peut, toutefois, compte tenu de la possibilité pour l'exploitant d'obtenir l'assurance ou une autre garantie financière requise à l'article 10, prévoir dans sa loi un montant plus ou moins élevé que 15.000.000 d'unités de compte; ce montant ne peut toutefois être inférieur à 5.000.000 d'unités de compte. Comme l'unité de compte de l'Accord Monétaire Européen du 5 août 1955 peut être modifiée par les Parties à cet Accord, la Convention précise qu'il s'agit de l'unité de compte définie à la date de sa signature [article 7 *a*) et *b*)].

44. A défaut de disposition spéciale sur le montant maximum de la responsabilité pour les accidents nucléaires en cours de transport, un exploitant pourrait être responsable pour des montants différents selon les pays traversés. Pour éviter cette situation, il est prévu que le montant maximum est celui qui est fixé pour les installations nucléaires par la loi nationale de l'exploitant responsable [article 7 *b*)].

might involve paying compensation of more than 5,000,000 u/a for other damage but cannot result in reducing the amount of compensation for such other damage below 5,000,000 u/a.

Where property belongs to the operator himself, no action for compensation would lie in any event since a person cannot sue himself.

41. Where a right to compensation for damage exists by virtue of contractual arrangements, such right remains unaffected by the Convention.

INDUSTRIAL ACCIDENTS AND OCCUPATIONAL DISEASES

42. Any person who suffers damage caused by a nuclear incident, whether he is a third party inside or outside the installation or an employee of the operator of the installation in question, is covered by Article 3. In most countries, employees who suffer damage may also be entitled in respect of such damage to compensation under national health insurance, social security, workmen's compensation or occupational disease compensation systems. In principle it is felt that benefits under such systems should be retained for employees whether of the installation in question or employed in other establishments, but it is left to the law establishing such systems to decide this as well as whether employees should also be entitled to compensation under the Convention. This law will also decide whether the bodies responsible for such systems can turn to the operator to recover for payments made, it being understood that in any event the operator cannot be obliged to pay more than the maximum liability laid down [Article 6 *h*)].

LIMITATION OF LIABILITY IN AMOUNT

43. In the absence of a limitation of liability, the risks could in the worst possible circumstances involve financial liabilities greater than any hitherto encountered. Even with a limitation, it will not always be easy for operators to find the necessary financial security to meet the risks.

The maximum liability in respect of any single nuclear incident, whether occurring at or in connection with a nuclear installation or in the course of carriage of nuclear substances, has been fixed at 15,000,000 u/a. A Contracting Party may, however, taking into account the possibilities for the operator of obtaining the insurance or other financial security required pursuant to Article 10, establish by special legislation a greater or lesser amount than 15,000,000 u/a but in no event less than 5.000,000 u/a. Since the units of account of the European Monetary Agreement of 5th August, 1955, may be altered by the Parties to that Agreement, it is provided that the units of account referred to should be as valued at the date of the Convention [Article 7 *a*) and *b*)].

44. If no special rule were envisaged with respect to maximum liability for nuclear incidents occurring in the course of transport, an operator might be liable for varying amounts depending on the countries crossed in the course of the voyage. To avoid this it is provided that the maximum liability will, in the same way as for nuclear incidents occurring at or in connection with nuclear installations, be determined by the national legislation of the operator liable [Article 7*b*)].

45. La possibilité d'écarter la limitation de responsabilité en cas de faute de l'exploitant ou de ses préposés a été envisagée, mais il est à craindre qu'à défaut d'expérience de l'exploitation des installations nucléaires, la notion de négligence ou de faute grave ne soit très difficile à définir et que l'on ait tendance à lui donner une trop large portée. En outre, une responsabilité illimitée pourrait bien provoquer la ruine de l'exploitant, sans procurer pour autant le moyen de réparer les dommages causés.

46. Le montant maximum de la responsabilité, fixé par l'article 7, ne comprend ni les intérêts, ni les dépens liquidés par le tribunal saisi d'une action en réparation. Ces intérêts et dépens sont dus par l'exploitant en sus du montant des indemnités qu'il est tenu de payer en vertu de l'article 7 [article 7 *g*)].

LIMITATION DE LA RESPONSABILITÉ DANS LE TEMPS

47. Les dommages corporels causés par une contamination radioactive peuvent ne se manifester qu'un certain temps après l'exposition aux radiations. Le délai dans lequel les actions peuvent être introduites est donc d'une grande importance. Il sera sans doute difficile pour les exploitants et les personnes leur ayant accordé une garantie financière de maintenir pendant une longue période les réserves nécessaires pour faire face, au titre des polices en cours ou expirées, à une responsabilité qui peut être élevée mais dont le montant est indéterminé. D'autre part, il serait déraisonnable de ne prévoir aucune possibilité d'indemnisation des victimes chez lesquelles le dommage ne se manifesterait que tardivement.

La situation est encore compliquée par la difficulté de prouver si un dommage différé a été réellement causé ou non par l'accident nucléaire. Il faut donc trouver un compromis entre les intérêts des victimes et ceux des exploitants.

Un délai de dix ans est prévu à compter de l'accident nucléaire, à l'expiration duquel le droit à réparation est éteint si aucune action n'a été introduite devant le tribunal compétent [article 8 *a*)]. Les règles relatives à la détermination du tribunal compétent figurent dans l'article 13 (*voir* paragraphes 54–56). Si plusieurs tribunaux peuvent être compétents, la compétence est déterminée par le Tribunal de Contrôle de Sécurité de l'O.E.C.E. [article 13 *d*) (*i*) 2 et (*ii*)]. Dans ces cas, une victime ne peut pas intenter une action avant que le Tribunal n'ait fixé la compétence. Pour faire face à cette situation, il est prévu qu'il n'y a pas déchéance de l'action en réparation si une action a été intentée dans le délai fixé, avant que le Tribunal de Contrôle de Sécurité n'ait pris une décision, devant l'un des tribunaux entre lesquels ce Tribunal peut choisir, ou si une demande a été introduite auprès d'une Partie Contractante en vue de la désignation du tribunal compétent par le Tribunal de Contrôle de Sécurité conformément l'article 13 *d*) (*i*) 2, ou (*ii*), à condition qu'une action soit intentée après cette désignation dans le délai qui serait le cas échéant fixé par ce Tribunal [article 8 *b*)].

Si des combustibles ou des substances nucléaires ont été volés, perdus ou abandonnés – par exemple en cas d'abandon de substances radioactives lors d'un accident en mer – le délai de dix ans pour introduire l'action part de la date à laquelle les matières ont été volées, perdues ou abandonnées [article 8 *a*)].

Toutefois, les États peuvent fixer un délai plus court, de deux ans au moins, à compter du moment où le lésé a eu ou aurait dû normalement avoir connaissance du dommage et de l'exploitant responsable, sans que le délai de dix ans puisse être dépassé [article 8 *a*)]. Ce délai plus court peut être un délai ordinaire de prescription susceptible d'être suspendu ou même interrompu, lorsque la loi l'admet, par une simple demande extra-judiciaire, mais la suspension ou l'interruption ne peut avoir pour

45. The possibility of removing the limit in the case of fault on the part of the operator or his employees was considered, but it was feared that in the absence of experience in operating nuclear installations, the notion of fault or gross negligence would be very difficult to define and would tend to be given a wide interpretation. Moreover, unlimited liability could easily lead to the ruin of the operator without affording any substantial contribution to compensation for the damage caused.

46. The amount fixed for the maximum liability in accordance with Article 7 does not include interest and costs awarded by a court in actions for compensation. Such interest and costs are payable by the operator in addition to any sum for which he is liable under Article 7 [Article 7 *g*)].

LIMITATION OF LIABILITY IN TIME

47. Bodily injury caused by radioactive contamination may not become manifest for some time after the exposure to radiation has actually occurred. The legal period during which an action may be brought is therefore a matter of great importance. Operators and their financial guarantors will naturally be concerned if they have to maintain, over long periods of time, reserves against outstanding or expired policies for possibly large but unascertainable amounts of liability. On the other hand, it is unreasonable for victims whose damage manifests itself late to find no provision has been made for compensation to them.

A further complication is the difficulty of proof involved in establishing or denying that delayed damage was, in fact, caused by the nuclear incident. A compromise has necessarily been arrived at between the interests of those suffering damage and the interests of operators.

A period of ten years running from the date of the nuclear incident is provided, after which a right to compensation is extinguished if no action has been brought before a competent court [Article 8 *a*)]. The rules governing the choice of the competent court are laid down in Article 13 (*see* paragraphs 54–56) and where more than one court might be competent, the competent court is left to be determined by the O.E.E.C. Security Control Tribunal [Article 13 *d*) (*i*) 2 and (*ii*)]. In these cases a victim cannot bring his action until the Tribunal has made its determination. In order to deal with this situation, it is provided that the right to compensation shall not be extinguished if, within the time provided for, prior to the determination by the Tribunal, an action has been brought before any of the courts from which the Tribunal can choose or a request has been made to a Contracting Party to institute a determination pursuant to Article 13 *d*) (*i*) 2, or (*ii*) by the Tribunal and an action is brought subsequent to such determination within the time, if any, fixed by the Tribunal [Article 8 *b*)].

Where nuclear fuel or nuclear substances have been stolen, lost or abandoned – *e.g.* in the case of the jettisoning of a cargo after a nuclear incident in the course of transport – it is provided that the period for bringing actions is ten years from the date of the theft, loss or abandonment [Article 8*a*)].

States may, however, establish a shorter period of not less than two years running from the time when the damage and the operator liable have become known to the victim or ought reasonably to have become known, provided that the ten-year period is not exceeded [Article 8 *a*)]. This shorter period may constitute a conventional period of prescription which may be suspended or interrupted even, where this is recognized, by a mere extra-judiciary demand, provided always that such suspension effet de prolonger le délai au delà de la période de dix ans à compter de l'accident nucléaire. Un État a la possibilité de considérer au contraire le délai plus court comme un délai de déchéance qui éteint le droit à réparation.

Dans deux cas seulement, des actions peuvent être intentées hors du délai de dix ans. Un État peut laisser subsister le droit à réparation au-delà de ce délai, à condition qu'il s'engage à indemniser l'exploitant en cas de réclamation présentée hors du délai de dix ans [article 8 *c*)]. En outre, en cas d'aggravation des dommages au titre desquels une action en réparation a été intentée dans les délais, une demande complémentaire peut être présentée au delà des délais, à condition que le tribunal compétent n'ait pas encore rendu de jugement définitif [article 8 *d*)].

Exonérations

48. La responsabilité objective de l'exploitant n'est pas sujette aux cas d'exonération classiques tels que la faute de la victime, la force majeure, le cas fortuit ou la faute d'un tiers, qu'il s'agisse d'événements normalement prévisibles et évitables ou non. Si des précautions peuvent être prises, l'exploitant de l'installation nucléaire est à même de les prendre, tandis que les victimes éventuelles n'ont aucune possibilité de se protéger.

Les seuls cas d'exonération prévus concernent les dommages causés par un accident nucléaire dû à certains troubles de caractère international comme les actes d'un conflit armé ou d'une invasion, de caractère politique comme la guerre civile ou l'insurrection, enfin à des cataclysmes naturels de caractère exceptionnel, c'est-à-dire catastrophiques et totalement imprévisibles; tous ces événements en effet mettent en jeu la responsabilité de la nation dans son ensemble. Aucun autre cas d'exonération n'est prévu, mais un État peut, par une loi nationale, réduire davantage les cas d'exonération [article 9].

Lorsque l'accident ou le dommage est causé en totalité ou en partie par la victime, il appartient au tribunal compétent de décider, selon la législation nationale applicable, dans quelle mesure il sera tenu compte de cette faute pour la fixation de l'indemnité.

Ainsi qu'il a été indiqué (*voir* paragraphe 16), en cas d'exonération de l'exploitant, le droit commun s'applique et les responsables peuvent être poursuivis comme auteurs du dommage.

Couverture de la Responsabilité

49. Pour faire face à sa responsabilité envers les victimes, l'exploitant est tenu de disposer d'une garantie financière à concurrence du montant maximum fixé conformément à l'article 7 de la Convention [article 10 *a*)]. Cette garantie financière peut prendre la forme d'une caution financière, d'avoirs liquides, plutôt sans doute d'une assurance. La combinaison d'une assurance, d'une autre garantie financière et d'une garantie de l'État est également acceptable. Un exploitant peut changer son assurance ou autre garantie, à condition de ne pas tomber au-dessous du montant maximum.

Bien que l'exploitant soit tenu de disposer d'une garantie financière pour chaque accident nucléaire, il semble que l'assurance ne pourra être obtenue que par installation ou pour une certaine période plutôt que par accident. Aucune disposition de la Convention n'empêche de le faire à condition que des mesures soient prises, si le montant maximum de l'assurance se trouve réduit ou épuisé à la suite d'un premier accident nucléaire, pour que l'exploitant dispose d'une garantie financière égale au montant maximum en cas d'accidents ultérieurs.

Il incombe à l'autorité publique compétente de fixer le type et les or interruption does not have the effect of prolonging the period beyond ten years from the date of the nuclear incident. On the other hand, the shorter period may be an absolute period after which no right to compensation exists.

Nonetheless, proceedings may be brought after the ten-year period in two exceptional cases: a State may provide that rights to compensation may continue to exist after the expiry of the ten-year period if it undertakes to cover the liability of the operator over and above the ten-year period [Article 8 *c*)]; secondly, a person who suffers an aggravation of the damage for which he has already brought an action for compensation within the time limit laid down, may amend his claim after the expiry of the time limit provided that no final judgment has yet been entered by the competent court [Article 8 *d*)].

EXONERATIONS

48. The absolute liability of the operator is not subject to the classic exonerations for tortious acts, *force majeure*, Acts of God or intervening acts of third persons, whether or not such acts were reasonably foreseeable and avoidable. In so far as any precautions can be taken, those in charge of a nuclear installation are in a position to take them, whereas potential victims have no way of protecting themselves.

The only exonerations lie in the case of damage caused by a nuclear incident directly due to certain disturbances of an international character such as acts of armed conflict and invasion, of a political nature such as civil war and insurrection, or grave natural disasters of an exceptional character, which are catastrophic and completely unforeseeable, on the grounds that all such matters are the responsibility of the nation as a whole. No other exonerations are permitted. It is provided, however, that a State may, by national law, even further restrict the exonerations [Article 9].

Where the incident or damage is caused wholly or partly by the person suffering damage, it will be for the competent court, in accordance with national law, to decide the effect of such negligence upon the claim for compensation.

As has been pointed out (*see* paragraph 16), where the operator is exonerated, common law applies and those responsible may therefore be sued as ordinary tortfeasors.

SECURITY FOR LIABILITY

49. To meet liability towards victims, it is provided that the operator shall be required to have and maintain financial security up to the maximum amount established pursuant to Article 7 of the Convention [Article 10 *a*)]. Financial security may be in the form of conventional financial guarantees or ordinary liquid assets, though more probably, insurance coverage. A combination of insurance, other financial security and State guarantee may be accepted. An operator may change the insurance or other financial security, provided that the maximum amount is maintained.

Although the operator will thus be required to have financial security available for each nuclear incident, in practice insurance coverage will, it seems, only be available per installation for a fixed period of time rather than in respect of a single incident. There is nothing in the Convention which prevents this, provided that the maximum amount available is not reduced or exhausted as a result of a first incident without appropriate measures being taken to ensure that financial security up to the maximum amount is available for subsequent incidents.

It is for the competent public authority to determine the type and conditions de l'assurance ou des autres garanties financières que l'exploitant est tenu d'avoir. Ceci n'implique pas la création d'une autorité de contrôle en matière d'assurance dans les pays où il n'en existe pas actuellement, mais seulement le contrôle nécessaire pour garantir l'exécution des dispositions de la Convention. L'autorité publique compétente devra notamment veiller à ce que les polices d'assurances soient satisfaisantes, c'est-à-dire qu'elles ne contiennent pas de clauses qui les rendent inopérantes, par exemple que l'assureur ou garant ne puisse opposer de moyens de défense, comme le non-paiement des primes, contre les personnes qui demanderaient réparation.

Quelles que soient les conditions fixées par l'autorité publique compétente, des circonstances défavorables peuvent se présenter, comme la faillite du garant, ou, si l'assurance a été obtenue par installation pour une période déterminée, l'impossibilité pratique de rétablir, après un premier accident, la garantie financière à concurrence du montant total de la responsabilité. Il a été admis que ces circonstances n'écartent pas l'obligation de l'exploitant résultant de l'article 10, pas plus que celle de l'État, qui est tenu de faire en sorte que l'exploitant dispose toujours d'une garantie financière égale à sa responsabilité maximum. Les Parties Contractantes pourraient donc être amenées à intervenir dans ces cas pour éviter que leur responsabilité internationale ne puisse être mise en jeu.

Il appartient de même à l'autorité publique compétente de décider, dans le cas d'une personne exploitant au même site plusieurs réacteurs ou autres installations nucléaires au sens de la Convention, si elle est tenue de disposer d'une assurance ou autre garantie financière pour chacune des installations nucléaires ou pour l'ensemble des installations situées au même site.

Le principe fondamental est qu'une garantie financière doit exister à concurrence du montant prévu à l'article 7 pour chaque accident nucléaire, quel que soit le système adopté par l'autorité publique compétente pour l'autorisation ou l'assurance des installations nucléaires.

Les exploitants de toutes les installations nucléaires définies dans la Convention sont tenus de disposer de cette garantie financière, qu'il s'agisse de petits réacteurs de recherches ou de centrales nucléaires à l'échelle industrielle. Ceci peut sembler entraîner une lourde charge pour une université ou un institut de recherches par exemple; mais les primes qui seront fixées pour les différentes installations nucléaires, compte tenu notamment de la puissance, de l'utilisation et de l'emplacement, seront, pour l'exploitant, d'un montant très variable selon le type d'installation. Dans ces conditions, la fixation d'un montant uniforme pour la responsabilité de l'exploitant ne paraît pas devoir entraîner, pour les institutions d'enseignement ou de recherches, une charge sensiblement plus lourde que si la couverture exigée était réduite en ce qui les concerne.

Les relations entre l'exploitant et l'assureur ou autre garant financier, par exemple en ce qui concerne les droits de recours que ceux-ci peuvent avoir contre l'exploitant, sont laissées à législation de chaque État.

50. Pour éviter dans la mesure du possible que la couverture ne soit à aucun moment inférieure au montant maximum fixé, il est prévu que la garantie financière ne peut être suspendue ou éteinte pendant la période pour laquelle la police est conclue, sans un préavis d'au moins deux mois donné à l'autorité publique compétente. Celle-ci a, bien entendu, la faculté d'exiger un préavis plus long. Lorsque la garantie couvre la responsabilité de l'exploitant pour des accidents nucléaires en cours de transport, l'autorité publique compétente doit s'assurer que cette garantie est accordée pour toute la période pendant laquelle la responsabilité de l'exploitant peut être mise en jeu du fait d'un transport et en particulier qu'elle ne peut être ni suspendue, ni éteinte avant que le transport ait été achevé [article 10 *b*)].

terms of the insurance or other financial security which the operator will be required to hold. The type and terms envisaged do not imply the establishment of a supervisory authority in the field of insurance in those countries where control by such an authority over insurance activities does not at present exist, but only the control necessary to ensure compliance with the Convention. Thus the competent public authority must ensure that insurance policies are satisfactory in that they do not contain clauses which might render them ineffective, for example, that the insurer or other financial guarantor cannot put up any defences such as non-payment of premiums against persons seeking compensation.

Whatever conditions are laid down by the competent public authority, something untoward could happen, such as where the financial guarantor is bankrupt, or where insurance is per installation for a fixed period and after a first incident it is impossible to reinstate the financial security up to the maximum liability of the operator. It was recognized that these circumstances could not set aside the obligation of the operator under Article 10 or that of the State which is required to ensure that the operator always holds financial security up to his maximum liability. The Contracting Parties may therefore be led to intervene in such a situation to avoid their international responsibilities being involved.

The competent public authority has also to decide whether, where the operator operates a number of reactors or other nuclear installations within the meaning of the Convention at the same site, it is necessary for him to have and maintain insurance or other financial security for each of the nuclear installations or for the site as a whole.

The guiding principle is that financial security must be available in the amount provided for pursuant to Article 7 for each nuclear incident, whatever system is adopted by the competent public authority in regard to licensing and insurance of nuclear installations.

Operators of all the nuclear installations covered by the Convention are required to hold the financial protection whether the installations are small research reactors or fully-fledged nuclear power stations. This may seem to weigh heavily, for example, on a university or research institute. But the premiums for different types of nuclear installations, by taking account of factors such as power, use and location, will mean costs to the operator which vary considerably according to the type of installation. This being so, the fixing of a uniform amount for the operator's liability should not, in principle, involve a heavier burden for educational or research institutions than if the security required for them were to be reduced.

The relations between the operator and the insurer or other financial guarantor, for example, with regard to rights of recourse against the operator by these persons, are left to be settled by each State.

50. To ensure as far as possible that there will never be a period in which less than the full amount fixed is available, it has been necessary to provide that the financial security can only be suspended or cancelled, *i.e.*, brought to an end before the expiry of the period provided for in the policy, after a period of at least two months' notice has been given to the competent public authority. The competent public authority may, of course, fix a longer period of notice. Where the financial security is provided in respect of the operator's liability for nuclear incidents occurring in the course of transport, the competent public authority must be satisfied that the financial security is provided for the duration of the liability of the operator in respect of any carriage, and, in particular, that it cannot be suspended or cancelled before a transport has been completed [Article 10 *b*)].

51. Les sommes provenant de la garantie financière ne peuvent servir qu'à la réparation des dommages causés par un accident nucléaire; il n'est pas nécessaire de les mettre à part, mais elles ne peuvent servir au règlement d'autres créances [article 10 *c*)].

NATURE, FORME ET ÉTENDUE DES INDEMNITÉS

52. Les demandes en réparation présentées à la suite d'un accident nucléaire peuvent différer beaucoup par leur nature, leur montant et leur date; il peut être nécessaire d'assurer une répartition équitable du montant disponible pour la réparation, si ce montant est dépassé ou susceptible de l'être. Il incombe au tribunal compétent de décider, conformément à la législation nationale, de la nature, de la forme et de l'étendue de la réparation dans les limites prévues par la Convention et d'assurer une répartition équitable des indemnités [article 11]. Ainsi, l'octroi de pensions et leur montant, ou les effets de la faute de la victime sur le montant de la réparation auxquels il a déjà été fait allusion, seront réglés par le droit national.

Il appartient à chaque État de décider si les mesures nécessaires pour assurer une répartition équitable doivent être prises d'avance ou lorsque des demandes sont introduites. Ces mesures peuvent comprendre une limitation par victime ou des limites distinctes pour les dommages aux personnes et les dommages aux biens.

TRANSFERT DES INDEMNITÉS

53. Pour donner effet aux dispositions de la Convention, en ce qui concerne notamment l'unité de juridiction pour toutes les actions résultant d'un même accident nucléaire et l'exécution sur le territoire de toutes les Parties Contractantes des jugements rendus, il est indispensable d'écarter tout obstacle résultant par exemple du contrôle des changes ou d'autres réglementations financières. En vertu du Code de la Libération de l'O.E.C.E., les primes d'assurances relatives aux risques nucléaires ne sont transférables que si ces risques ne peuvent pas être couverts dans le pays où ils existent. Les primes de réassurances, de même que les indemnités, dépens et intérêts, sont librement transférables. Les garanties financières autres que les assurances, qui peuvent être accordées pour satisfaire aux conditions de l'article 10 de la Convention, ne sont pas prévues.

Dans ces conditions, pour assurer une libération complète et pour permettre en outre à des pays qui ne sont pas parties au Code de la Libération de l'O.E.C.E. d'adhérer plus facilement à la Convention, il est prévu que les primes d'assurance et de réassurance, les sommes qui doivent être payées au titre de l'assurance ou d'une autre garantie financière, ainsi que les sommes dues à titre d'indemnités, intérêts et dépens, seront librement transférables entre les zones monétaires des Parties Contractantes [article 12]. Cette liberté de transferts en matière d'assurances n'a toutefois pas pour objet de porter atteinte aux réglementations nationales relatives aux assurances, par exemple à celles qui concernent la constitution des réserves techniques.

COMPÉTENCE ET EXÉCUTION DES JUGEMENTS

54. Bien des raisons conduisent à admettre la compétence d'un seul tribunal pour connaître de toutes les actions dirigées contre un exploitant à la suite d'un même accident nucléaire, y compris des actions directes contre les assureurs ou autres garants et les actions tendant à faire constater un droit à réparation. Il est essentiel qu'il y ait un mécanisme juridique unique, pour garantir que la limite maximum de la responsabilité ne sera pas dépassée. De plus, si des tribunaux de plusieurs pays pouvaient être saisis et statuer sur des litiges relatifs à un même accident,

51. All sums provided as financial security can only be drawn upon to pay compensation for damage caused by a nuclear incident; they need not be segregated but cannot be used to meet any other claims [Article 10 *c*)].

NATURE, FORM AND EXTENT OF COMPENSATION

52. Claims for compensation following a nuclear incident may differ greatly in nature, amounts and time, and measures may be necessary to ensure an equitable distribution of the amount of compensation available if this amount is or may be exceeded. It will be for the competent court, in accordance with national law, to decide the nature, form and extent of the compensation, within the limits of the Convention, as well as equitable distribution [Article 11]. Thus, the granting of annuities and their amounts and, as has already been noted, the effect on his claim to compensation of contributory negligence on the part of a person suffering damage, will be decided by national law.

It is for each State to decide whether measures for equitable distribution should be taken in advance or at the time when actions are brought. Measures may involve providing a limit per person suffering damage or limits for damage to persons and damage to property.

TRANSFER OF COMPENSATION

53. If the system envisaged under the Convention – in particular the recognition of a single competent forum to deal with all actions arising out of the same nuclear incident and the enforceability of its judgments in all Contracting Parties – is to be effective, it is necessary to ensure that there are no impediments, for example, by way of exchange control or other financial regulations. Under the O.E.E.C. Code of Liberalisation, insurance premiums in respect of nuclear risks are only transferable if the risks cannot be covered in the country where they exist. Reinsurance premiums as well as compensation, costs and interest, are freely transferable. Financial guarantees other than insurance which may be provided to comply with Article 10 of the Convention are not covered.

In order, therefore, to ensure a comprehensive liberalisation and in addition to facilitate the accession to the Convention of countries which are not parties to the O.E.E.C. Code of Liberalisation, it is laid down that insurance and reinsurance premiums, sums which have to be paid out as insurance or reinsurance, or other financial security, as well as sums due as compensation and interest and costs, shall be freely transferable between monetary areas of the Contracting Parties [Article 12]. This freedom to transfer in regard to insurance is not intended, however, to affect national regulations governing insurance activities such as, for example, the establishment of technical reserves.

JURISDICTION AND ENFORCEMENT OF JUDGMENTS

54. There are many factors motivating in favour of a single competent forum to deal with all actions against the operator – including direct actions against insurers or other guarantors and actions to establish rights to claim compensation – arising out of the same nuclear incident. Most important is the need for a single legal mechanism to ensure that the limitation on liability is not exceeded. Moreover, if suits arising out of the same incident were to be tried and judgments rendered in the

la répartition équitable des indemnités pourrait poser des problèmes insolubles.

Il est prévu que l'instance compétente est le tribunal compétent en vertu de la législation du pays dans lequel se trouve l'installation où s'est produit l'accident nucléaire [article 13 *a*)].

55. Les accidents nucléaires survenant en cours de transport appellent des dispositions spéciales. La juridiction compétente est, dans ce cas, celle du lieu où se trouvaient les substances nucléaires au moment de l'accident [article 13 *b*)]. Si le lieu de l'accident ne peut être déterminé, par exemple, en cas de contamination radioactive continue au cours d'un transport, il est prévu, afin de maintenir l'unité de juridiction pour un même accident, que le tribunal compétent est celui du pays où est située l'installation dont l'exploitant est responsable [article 13 *c*)]. La même règle s'applique dans le cas où l'accident survient au cours d'un transport, en dehors du territoire des Parties Contractantes [article 13 *c*)]. Il est vrai que le recours à la juridiction de l'exploitant peut présenter, en raison de l'éloignement, certains inconvénients pratiques pour les victimes, mais il n'a pas été possible de trouver une autre solution leur permettant d'agir devant leurs tribunaux nationaux tout en maintenant l'unité de juridiction.

56. S'il résulte des dispositions relatives à la compétence que les tribunaux de plusieurs Parties Contractantes peuvent être saisis, des dispositions spéciales sont nécessaires, afin de maintenir l'unité de juridiction.

Il est prévu qu'en cas d'accident nucléaire en cours de transport, la compétence appartient au tribunal du lieu d'immatriculation du moyen de transport, à condition que ce lieu se trouve sur le territoire d'une Partie Contractante [article 13 *d*) (*i*) 1].

Si le moyen de transport n'est pas immatriculé, si son lieu d'immatriculation ne peut être déterminé ou s'il se trouve hors du territoire d'une Partie Contractante, la compétence est attribuée au tribunal désigné parmi les tribunaux compétents, sur demande d'une Partie Contractante intéressée, par le Tribunal international créé par la Convention de l'O.E.C.E. sur le Contrôle de Sécurité en date du 20 décembre 1957, comme étant le plus directement lié à la cause [article 13 *d*) (*i*) 2)].

Dans tous les autres cas, si la responsabilité d'exploitants ressortissants de plusieurs Parties Contractantes se trouve engagée, la compétence est attribuée, de la même manière, au tribunal désigné par le Tribunal international de Contrôle de Sécurité [article 13 *d*) (*ii*)].

57. Le tribunal compétent en vertu de la Convention connaît de toutes les actions qui peuvent être dirigées contre un exploitant, soit directement par une victime [article 3], soit par suite du recours d'une personne responsable en vertu des dispositions relatives aux transports ou en vertu de la législation d'un État non-contractant [article 6 *c*) et *d*)]. Le tribunal compétent pour connaître du recours d'un exploitant fondé sur l'article 6 *f*) ou du recours en règlement de responsabilité intenté par un exploitant contre d'autres exploitants en cas de responsabilité solidaire, n'est pas fixé par la Convention et il est déterminé par la législation nationale.

58. Le principe de l'unité de juridiction a pour conséquence que les jugements définitifs rendus par le tribunal doivent être exécutoires dans les autres pays sans nouvel examen du fond. C'est pourquoi l'exequatur des jugements définitifs doit être accordé par toute autre Partie Contractante dès lors que les formalités nécessaires ont été accomplies [article 13 *e*)].

Les jugements définitifs exécutoires en vertu de l'article 13 *e*) ne comprennent pas les jugements rendus contre une personne autre que l'exploitant, qui serait responsable en vertu de l'article 6 *b*), les jugements rendus sur un recours de l'exploitant en vertu de l'article 6 *f*), sur un courts of several different countries, the problem of assuring equitable distribution of compensation might be insoluble.

The choice of the forum falls most obviously upon the court competent in accordance with the national legislation of the Contracting Party in whose territory the installation giving rise to the nuclear incident is situated [Article 13 *a*)].

55. Nuclear incidents occurring in the course of transport entail special arrangements. The competent jurisdiction is that of the place where the nuclear substances were at the time of the incident [Article 13 *b*)]. If the place of the incident cannot be determined, for example, in the case of an incident due to continuous radioactive contamination in the course of transport, in order to secure a single jurisdiction for the same incident the competent court is that of the place where the installation of the operator liable is situated [Article 13 *c*)]. Where the nuclear incident occurs outside the territories of the Contracting Parties in the course of carriage, the same rule applies [Article 13 *c*)]. Whilst there might be some practical disadvantages for the victims in recourse to the jurisdiction of the operator as a result of the distance involved, it has not been possible to find another solution which would enable the victims to refer to their national courts and which would at the same time secure unity of jurisdiction.

56. If the provisions relating to jurisdiction result in the courts of more than one Contracting Party being competent, special rules have been included to secure unity of jurisdiction.

It is provided that for nuclear transport incidents, jurisdiction will lie with the court competent at the place where the means of transport used is registered, provided that this is in the territory of a Contracting Party [Article 13 *d*) (*i*) 1].

If there is no such registration or the place of registration is not clear or the means of transport is registered outside the territories of the Contracting Parties, jurisdiction will lie with one of the courts which would have been competent, determined, at the request of a Contracting Party concerned, by the International Tribunal established under the O.E.E.C. Security Control Convention of 20th December, 1957, as being the most closely related to the case in question [Article 13 *d*) (*i*) 2].

In any other case involving operators from different Contracting Parties, the competent court is determined by the above-mentioned Tribunal in the same way [Article 13 *d*) (*ii*)].

57. The competent court in all cases is intended to deal with all actions which might be brought against an operator, either directly by persons suffering damage [under Article 3] or in recourse by other persons who might be liable under international agreements in the field of transport or under the legislation of a non-Contracting State [Article 6 *c*) and *d*)]. The forum for actions in recourse by an operator under Article 6 *f*) or for actions for contribution by an operator against other operators in the case of joint and several liability is not fixed in the Convention and will be decided by national law.

58. The concept of a single forum carries with it the need to ensure that final judgments rendered in that forum can be enforceable in the other countries without re-examination of the merits. Hence such final judgments will be enforceable in any of the other Contracting Parties as soon as the formalities required have been complied with Article 13 *e*)].

Final judgments enforceable under Article 13 *e*) do not include judgments rendered against persons other than the operator liable under Article 6 *b*), judgments rendered in actions in recourse by the operator under Article 6 *f*), actions in recourse against the operator under Article recours contre l'exploitant prévu par l'article 6 *b*) ou *c*) ou sur un recours en règlement de responsabilité entre personnes solidairement responsables.

59. Dans le cas où une Partie Contractante est exploitant d'une installation nucléaire couverte par la Convention, il est prévu qu'elle ne peut invoquer l'immunité de juridiction dont elle pourrait jouir au lieu où l'action en réparation est introduite en vertu de la Convention [article 13 *f*)].

Droit Applicable

60. Le tribunal compétent doit appliquer les dispositions de la Convention sans aucune discrimination fondée sur la nationalité, le domicile ou la résidence [article 14 *a*)] et, pour toute question de fond ou de procédure qu'elle ne règle pas, son droit et sa législation nationale, y compris les règles du droit international privé, qui ne sont pas affectées par la Convention, sauf dans les deux cas mentionnés ci-dessous. Le droit et la législation nationale doivent également s'appliquer sans aucune discrimination fondée sur la nationalité, le domicile ou la résidence [article 14 *c*)].

Il y a deux exceptions à la règle selon laquelle la loi applicable par le tribunal compétent est la *lex fori*. Si l'installation de l'exploitant responsable n'est pas située sur le territoire de la Partie Contractante dont la loi détermine le tribunal compétent, le montant de responsabilité de l'exploitant en cause n'est pas fixé par la *lex fori* mais par la loi de la Partie Contractante sur le territoire de laquelle l'installation est située; c'est cette loi qui règle également le point de savoir si cette responsabilité inclut ou non le dommage causé au moyen de transport.

Intervention de l'État

61. La limitation de la responsabilité implique nécessairement la possibilité d'une indemnisation réduite des dommages subis; en cas d'accident catastrophique, il pourrait arriver que le montant disponible pour l'indemnisation ne suffise pas pour faire face à toutes les demandes. Pour des raisons sociales et psychologiques, il semble difficile d'accepter cette conséquence sans reconnaître que l'intervention de l'État peut être nécessaire.

62. Par ailleurs, il a été admis qu'outre les dispositions qui peuvent être nécessaires pour assurer que les conditions fixées à l'article 10 en ce qui concerne la garantie financière sont remplies (*voir* paragraphe 49), une Partie Contractante peut prendre les mesures qu'elle estime nécessaires en vue d'accroître, dans le cadre de la responsabilité civile de l'exploitant ou en dehors, l'importance de la réparation prévue par la Convention [article 15 *a*)]. Si une Partie Contractante prend des mesures en vue d'une réparation au-delà du montant de 5.000.000 d'unités de compte, et pour autant que cette réparation mette en jeu des fonds publics, l'application des mesures prises dans le cadre de la responsabilité civile de l'exploitant ou en dehors peut être soumise à des conditions particulières dérogeant aux dispositions de la Convention; entre autres, ces mesures ne doivent pas nécessairement s'appliquer sans discrimination à toutes les victimes [article 15 [*b*)]. Ainsi la Convention ne règle pas les moyens et méthodes d'effectuer l'intervention de l'État et l'attribution à des victimes étrangères du bénéfice d'une indemnisation complémentaire des dommages dépassant 5.000.000 d'unités de compte au moyen de fonds publics, doit être réglée en dehors de la Convention.

Les rapports entre l'État et les exploitants, en ce qui concerne les recours de l'État contre les exploitants, sont laissés à chaque État.

6 *b*) and *c*), or actions for contribution between persons jointly and severally liable.

59. Where a Contracting Party is the operator of a nuclear installation under the Convention, it is provided that such Party may not invoke any jurisdictional immunities which it might have where it is sued for compensation under the Convention [Article 13 *f*)].

Law Applicable

60. The competent court must apply the provisions of the Convention without any discrimination based upon nationality, domicile or residence [Article 14 *a*)] and for all matters, both substantive and procedural, not governed by these provisions, the national law or legislation, including rules of private international law, which are not affected by the Convention except for the two cases mentioned below. Such national law or legislation must also be applied without any discrimination based upon nationality, domicile or residence [Article 14 *c*)].

There are two exceptions to the rules that the law to be applied by the competent court is the *lex fori*. Where the installation of the operator liable is not situated in the territory of the Contracting Party in accordance with whose legislation the court is competent, the court will determine the maximum liability of such operator not on the basis of the *lex fori* but on the basis of the law of the Contracting Party in whose territory the installation is situated; it will also determine whether or not his liability includes damage to the means of transport on this same basis.

Additional Compensation

61. The establishment of a limited liability necessarily involves a possible reduction in compensation for damage suffered, and in the event of a catastrophe it may well be that the limited amount of compensation available is inadequate to meet all the claims. For social and psychological reasons it seems difficult to accept this consequence without recognizing that the intervention of the State may be necessary.

62. Furthermore, it is recognized that in addition to any intervention which may be necessary to ensure that the requirements of Article 10 with regard to financial security are fulfilled (*see* paragraph 49), a Contracting Party may take such measures as it deems necessary to provide for an increase in the amount of compensation specified in the Convention [Article 15 *a*)] whether within the third party liability of the operator or outside such liability. Where a Contracting Party takes measures to provide for compensation above 5,000,000 u/a in so far as it is to be paid out of public funds, such measures, whether within the third party liability of the operator or outside such liability, may be applied under special conditions which derogate from the provisions of the Convention and in particular need not be applied without discrimination to all victims [Article 15 *b*)]. Hence, the Convention does not regulate the methods and means of application of State intervention and the availability of additional compensation above 5,000,000 u/a out of public funds for foreign victims is left to be dealt with outside the Convention.

The relations between the State and operators in so far as actions by the State against its operators are concerned, are left to be settled by each State.

CLAUSES FINALES

63. Les clauses finales de la Convention contiennent des dispositions concernant les différends [article 17], les réserves [article 18], la ratification [article 19], les modifications [article 20], l'adhésion [article 21], la durée, la révision et le retrait [article 22], la notification de l'application de la Convention aux territoires dont une Partie Contractante assure les relations internationales [article 23] et la communication aux Signataires de la réception des divers instruments déposés en exécution des clauses finales [article 24]. En cas de différends relatifs à l'interprétation de la Convention, il est prévu que ces différends seront examinés par le Comité de Direction de l'E.N.E.A. et qu'à défaut de solution amiable ils seront, à la demande d'une Partie Contractante intéressée, soumis au Tribunal international créé par la Convention de l'O.E.C.E. sur le Contrôle de Sécurité en date du 20 décembre 1957. Le Tribunal agira conformément aux dispositions régissant son organisation et son fonctionnement, qui figurent dans le Protocole annexé à la Convention sur le Contrôle de Sécurité.

2. *ORGANISATION DE COOPÉRATION ET DE DÉVELOPPEMENT ÉCONOMIQUES*

a) CONVENTION RELATIVE A L'ORGANISATION DE COOPÉRATION ET DE DÉVELOPPEMENT ÉCONOMIQUES

LES GOUVERNEMENTS de la République Fédérale d'Allemagne, de la République d'Autriche, du Royaume de Belgique, du Canada, du Royaume de Danemark, de l'Espagne, des États-Unis d'Amérique, de la République Française, du Royaune de Grèce, de l'Irlande, de la République d'Islande, de la République Italienne, du Grand-Duché de Luxembourg, du Royaume de Norvège, du Royaume des Pays-Bas, de la République Portugaise, du Royaume-Uni de Grande-Bretagne et d'Irlande du Nord, du Royaume de Suède, de la Confédération Suisse et de la République de Turquie;

CONSIDÉRANT que la puissance et la prospérité de l'économie sont essentielles pour atteindre les buts des Nations Unies, sauvegarder les libertés individuelles et accroître le bien-être général;

ESTIMANT qu'ils peuvent progresser très efficacement dans cette voie en renforçant la tradition de coopération qui s'est développée entre eux;

RECONNAISSANT que le redressement et le progrès économiques de l'Europe, auxquels leur collaboration au sein de l'Organisation Européenne de Coopération Économique a apporté une contribution très importante, ont ouvert de nouvelles perspectives permettant de renforcer cette tradition et de l'appliquer à des tâches nouvelles et à des objectifs plus larges;

CONVAINCUS qu'une coopération plus large constituera une contribution essentielle à des relations pacifiques et harmonieuses entre les peuples;

RECONNAISSANT que leurs économies dépendent de plus en plus les unes des autres;

DÉTERMINÉS, grâce à des consultations mutuelles et à la coopération, à développer au maximum et à utiliser plus efficacement leurs capacités et leurs possibilités pour réaliser la plus forte expansion possible de leur économie et améliorer le bien-être économique et social de leurs peuples;

ESTIMANT que les nations plus avancées dans le domaine économique devraient coopérer pour aider au mieux de leurs facultés les pays en voie de développement économique;

FINAL CLAUSES

63. The final clauses of the Convention deal with disputes [Article 17], reservations [Article 18], ratification [Article 19], amendments [Article 20], accession [Article 21], duration, revision and withdrawal [Article 22], notification of the application of the Convention to territories for whose international relations the Contracting Party is responsible [Article 23], and notice to the Signatories of receipt of the various instruments deposited pursuant to the final clauses [Article 24]. In the case of disputes as to the interpretation of the Convention, it is provided that these shall be examined by the Steering Committee of E.N.E.A. and in the absence of friendly settlement shall, upon the request of a Contracting Party concerned be submitted to the International Tribunal set up by the O.E.E.C. Security Control Convention of 20th December, 1957. The Tribunal will act in accordance with the rules governing its organisation and functioning, which are set out in the Protocol annexed to the Security Control Convention.

2. *ORGANISATION FOR ECONOMIC CO-OPERATION AND DEVELOPMENT*

a) CONVENTION ON THE ORGANISATION FOR ECONOMIC CO-OPERATION AND DEVELOPMENT

THE GOVERNMENTS of the Republic of Austria, the Kingdom of Belgium, Canada, the Kingdom of Denmark, the French Republic, the Federal Republic of Germany, the Kingdom of Greece, the Republic of Iceland, Ireland, the Italian Republic, the Grand Duchy of Luxembourg, the Kingdom of the Netherlands, the Kingdom of Norway, the Portuguese Republic, Spain, the Kingdom of Sweden, the Swiss Confederation, the Turkish Republic, the United Kingdom of Great Britain and Northern Ireland, and the United States of America;

CONSIDERING that economic strength and prosperity are essential for the attainment of the purposes of the United Nations, the preservation of individual liberty and the increase of general well-being;

BELIEVING that they can further these aims most effectively by strengthening the tradition of co-operation which has evolved among them;

RECOGNISING that the economic recovery and progress of Europe to which their participation in the Organisation for European Economic Co-operation has made a major contribution, have opened new perspectives for strengthening that tradition and applying it to new tasks and broader objectives;

CONVINCED that broader co-operation will make a vital contribution to peaceful and harmonious relations among the peoples of the world;

RECOGNISING the increasing interdependence of their economies;

DETERMINED by consultation and co-operation to use more effectively their capacities and potentialities so as to promote the highest sustainable growth of their economies and improve the economic and social well-being of their peoples;

BELIEVING that the economically more advanced nations should co-operate in assisting to the best of their ability the countries in process of economic development;

Reconnaissant que la poursuite de l'expansion du commerce mondial constitue l'un des facteurs les plus importants propres à favoriser l'essor des économies des divers pays et à améliorer les rapports économiques internationaux;

Déterminés à réaliser ces desseins d'une façon compatible avec les obligations découlant de leur participation à d'autres organisations, institutions ou accords internationaux;

Sont convenus des dispositions suivantes pour la reconstitution de l'Organisation Européenne de Coopération Économique en Organisation de Coopération et de Développement Économiques:

Article 1

L'Organisation de Coopération et de Développement Économiques (appelée ci-dessous l',,Organisation") a pour objectif de promouvoir des politiques visant:

a) à réaliser la plus forte expansion possible de l'économie et de l'emploi et une progression du niveau de vie dans les pays membres, tout en maintenant la stabilité financière, et à contribuer ainsi au développement de l'économie mondiale;

b) à contribuer à une saine expansion économique dans les pays membres, ainsi que non membres, en voie de développement économique;

c) à contribuer à l'expansion du commerce mondial sur une base multilatérale et non discriminatoire conformément aux obligations internationales.

Article 2

En vue d'atteindre ces objectifs, les Membres conviennent, tant individuellement que conjointement:

a) d'assurer l'utilisation efficace de leurs ressources économiques;

b) dans le domaine scientifique et technologique, d'assurer le développement de leurs ressources, d'encourager la recherche et de favoriser la formation professionnelle.;

c) de suivre des politiques conçues pour assurer la croissance économique et la stabilité financière interne et externe, et d'éviter que ne se développent des situations qui pourraient mettre en danger leur économie ou celle d'autres pays;

d) de poursuivre leurs efforts en vue de réduire ou de supprimer les obstacles aux échanges de biens et de services, ainsi qu'aux paiements courants, et de maintenir et étendre la libération des mouvements de capitaux;

e) de contribuer au développement économique des pays membres et non-membres en voie de développement économique par des moyens appropriés et, en particulier, par l'apport à ces pays de capitaux, en tenant en outre compte de l'importance que présentent pour leur économie la fourniture d'assistance technique et l'élargissement des débouchés offerts à leurs produits d'exportation.

Article 3

En vue d'atteindre les objectifs fixés à l'Article 1 et de remplir les engagements énumérés à l'Article 2, les Membres conviennent:

a) de se tenir mutuellement informés et de fournir à l'Organisation les renseignements nécessaires à l'accomplissement de ses tâches;

b) de se consulter d'une manière continue, d'effectuer des études et de participer à des projets acceptés d'un commun accord;

c) de coopérer étroitement, s'il y a lieu par une action coordonnée.

RECOGNISING that the further expansion of world trade is one of the most important factors favouring the economic development of countries and the improvement of international economic relations; and

DETERMINED to pursue these purposes in a manner consistent with their obligations in other international organisations or institutions in which they participate or under agreements to which they are a party;

HAVE THEREFORE AGREED on the following provisions for the reconstitution of the Organisation for European Economic Co-operation as the Organisation for Economic Co-operation and Development:

Article 1

The aims of the Organisation for Economic Co-operation and Development (hereinafter called the "Organisation") shall be to promote policies designed:

a) to achieve the highest sustainable economic growth and employment and a rising standard of living in Member countries, while maintaining financial stability, and thus to contribute to the development of the world economy;

b) to contribute to sound economic expansion in Member as well as non-member countries in the process of economic development; and

c) to contribute to the expansion of world trade on a multilateral, non-discriminatory basis in accordance with international obligations.

Article 2

In the pursuit of these aims, the Members agree that they will, both individually and jointly:

a) promote the efficient use of their economic resources;

b) in the scientific and technological field, promote the development of their resources, encourage research and promote vocational training;

c) pursue policies designed to achieve economic growth and internal and external financial stability and to avoid developments which might endanger their economies or those of other countries;

d) pursue their efforts to reduce or abolish obstacles to the exchange of goods and services and current payments and maintain and extend the liberalisation of capital movements; and

e) contribute to the economic development of both Member and non-member countries in the process of economic development by appropriate means and, in particular, by the flow of capital to those countries, having regard to the importance to their economies of receiving technical assistance and of securing expanding export markets.

Article 3

With a view to achieving the aims set out in Article 1 and to fulfilling the undertakings contained in Article 2, the Members agree that they will:

a) keep each other informed and furnish the Organisation with the information necessary for the accomplishment of its tasks;

b) consult together on a continuing basis, carry out studies and participate in agreed projects; and

c) co-operate closely and where appropriate take co-ordinated action.

Article 4

Sont Membres de l'Organisation les Parties Contractantes à la présente Convention.

Article 5

En vue d'atteindre ses objectifs, l'Organisation peut:

a) prendre des décisions qui, sauf disposition différente, lient tous les Membres;

b) faire des recommandations aux Membres;

c) conclure des accords avec ses Membres, des États non-membres et des organisations internationales.

Article 6

1. A moins que l'Organisation n'en décide autrement à l'unanimité pour des cas spéciaux, les décisions sont prises et les recommandations sont faites par accord mutuel de tous les Membres.
2. Chaque Membre dispose d'une voix. Si un Membre s'abstient de voter une décision ou une recommandation, une telle abstention ne fait pas obstacle à cette décision ou recommandation, qui est applicable aux autres Membres mais pas au Membre qui s'abstient.
3. Aucune décision ne peut lier un Membre aussi longtemps qu'il ne s'est pas conformé aux prescriptions de sa procédure constitutionnelle. Les autres Membres peuvent convenir que cette décision s'appliquera provisoirement entre eux.

Article 7

Un Conseil, composé de tous les Membres, est l'organe duquel émanent tous les actes de l'Organisation. Le Conseil peut se réunir en sessions de ministres ou de représentants permanents.

Article 8

Le Conseil désigne, chaque année, un Président qui préside les sessions ministérielles, et deux Vice-Présidents. Le Président peut être désigné pour une année supplémentaire consécutive à son premier mandat.

Article 9

Le Conseil peut créer un Comité Exécutif et tout organe subsidiaire nécessaire pour atteindre les objectifs de l'Organisation.

Article 10

1. Un Secrétaire Général responsable devant le Conseil est nommé par celui-ci pour une période de cinq ans. Il est assisté d'un ou plusieurs Secrétaires Généraux suppléants ou Secrétaires Généraux adjoints nommés par le Conseil, sur la proposition du Secrétaire Général.
2. Le Secrétaire Général préside le Conseil aux sessions de représentants permanents. Il prête son concours au Conseil sous toute forme nécessaire et peut soumettre des propositions au Conseil ou à tout autre organe de l'Organisation.

Article 11

1. Le Secrétaire Général nomme le personnel utile au fonctionnement

Article 4

The Contracting Parties to this Convention shall be Members of the Organisation.

Article 5

In order to achieve its aims, the Organisation may:

a) take decisions which, except as otherwise provided, shall be binding on all the Members;

b) make recommendations to Members; and

c) enter into agreements with Members, non-member States and international organisations.

Article 6

1. Unless the Organisation otherwise agrees unanimously for special cases, decisions shall be taken and recommendations shall be made by mutual agreement of all the Members.
2. Each Member shall have one vote. If a Member abstains from voting on a decision or recommendation, such abstention shall not invalidate the decision or recommendation, which shall be applicable to the other Members but not to the abstaining Member.
3. No decision shall be binding on any Member until it has complied with the requirements of its own constitutional procedures. The other Members may agree that such a decision shall apply provisionally to them.

Article 7

A Council composed of all the Members shall be the body from which all acts of the Organisation derive. The Council may meet in sessions of Ministers or of Permanent Representatives.

Article 8

The Council shall designate each year a Chairman, who shall preside at its ministerial sessions, and two Vice-Chairmen. The Chairman may be designated to serve one additional consecutive term.

Article 9

The Council may establish an Executive Committee and such subsidiary bodies as may be required for the achievement of the aims of the Organisation.

Article 10

1. A Secretary-General responsible to the Council shall be appointed by the Council for a term of five years. He shall be assisted by one or more Deputy Secretaries-General or Assistant Secretaries-General appointed by the Council on the recommendation of the Secretary-General.
2. The Secretary-General shall serve as Chairman of the Council meeting at sessions of Permanent Representatives. He shall assist the Council in all appropriate ways and may submit proposals to the Council or to any other body of the Organisation.

Article 11

1. The Secretary-General shall appoint such staff as the Organisation

de l'Organisation conformément aux plans d'organisation approuvés par le Conseil. Le statut du personnel est soumis à l'approbation du Conseil.

2. Étant donné le caractère international de l'Organisation, le Secrétaire Général, les Secrétaires Généraux suppléants ou adjoints et le personnel ne solliciteront ni recevront de directives d'aucun des Membres de l'Organisation, ni d'aucun Gouvernement ou autorité extérieurs à l'Organisation.

Article 12

Dans les conditions qu'il appartient au Conseil de déterminer, l'Organisation peut:

a) exprimer des voeux à des États non membres et des organisations;

b) établir et entretenir des relations avec des États non membres et des organisations;

c) inviter des Gouvernements non membres et des organisations à participer à des activités de l'Organisation.

Article 13

La représentation dans l'Organisation des Communautés Européennes instituées par les Traités de Paris et de Rome en date des 18 avril 1951 et 25 mars 1957 est définie dans un Protocole Additionnel no. 1 à la présente Convention.

Article 14

1. La présente Convention sera ratifiée ou acceptée par les signataires conformément à leurs règles constitutionnelles respectives.

2. Les instruments de ratification ou d'acceptation seront déposés auprès du Gouvernement de la République Française, désigné comme Gouvernement dépositaire.

3. La présente Convention entrera en vigueur:

a) soit avant le 30 septembre 1961, dès que les instruments de ratification ou d'acceptation auront été déposés par tous les signataires;

b) soit le 30 septembre 1961, si à cette date quinze signataires au moins ont déposé ces instruments, et à l'égard de ces signataires, ainsi qu'à l'égard de tout autre signataire dès le dépôt de son instrument de ratification ou d'acceptation;

c) soit après le 30 septembre 1961, mais au plus tard deux ans après la signature de la présente Convention, dès que ces instruments auront été déposés par quinze signataires, et à l'égard de ces signataires, ainsi qu'à l'égard de tout autre signataire dès le dépôt de son instrument de ratification ou d'acceptation.

4. Les signataires n'ayant pas déposé leur instrument de ratification ou d'acceptation lors de l'entrée en vigueur de la Convention pourront participer aux activités de l'Organisation dans les conditions qui seront fixées par accord entre l'Organisation et lesdits signataires.

Article 15

La reconstitution de l'Organisation Européenne de Coopération Économique prendra effet lors de l'entrée en vigueur de la Convention, et ses objectifs, organes, pouvoirs et nom seront dès lors ceux qui sont prévus dans la Convention. La personnalité juridique que possède l'Organisation Européenne de Coopération Économique se continuera dans l'Organisation, mais les décisions, recommandations et résolutions de l'Organisation Européenne de Coopération Économique requièrent l'approbation du Conseil pour être applicables après l'entrée en vigueur de la présente Convention.

require in accordance with plans of organisation approved by the Council. Staff regulations shall be subject to approval by the Council.

2. Having regard to the international character of the Organisation the Secretary-General, the Deputy or Assistant Secretaries-General and the staff shall neither seek nor receive instructions from any of the Members or from any Government or authority external to the Organisation.

Article 12

Upon such terms and conditions as the Council may determine, the Organisation may:

a) address communications to non-member States or organisations;

b) establish and maintain relations with non-member States or organisations: and

c) invite non-member Governments or organisations to participate in activities of the Organisation.

Article 13

Representation in the Organisation of the European Communities established by the Treaties of Paris and Rome of 18th April, 1951, and 25th March, 1957, shall be as defined in Supplementary Protocol No. 1 to this Convention.

Article 14

1. This Convention shall be ratified or accepted by the Signatories in accordance with their respective constitutional requirements.

2. Instruments of ratification or acceptance shall be deposited with the Government of the French Republic, hereby designated as depositary Government.

3. This Convention shall come into force:

a) before 30th September, 1961, upon the deposit of instruments of ratification or acceptance by all the Signatories; or

b) on 30th September, 1961, if by that date fifteen Signatories or more have deposited such instruments as regards those Signatories; and thereafter as regards any other Signatory upon the deposit of its instrument of ratification or acceptance;

c) after 30th September, 1961, but not later than two years from the signature of this Convention, upon the deposit of such instruments by fifteen Signatories, as regards those Signatories; and thereafter as regards any other Signatory upon the deposit of its instrument of ratification or acceptance.

4. Any Signatory which has not deposited its instrument of ratification or acceptance when the Convention comes into force may take part in the activities of the Organisation upon conditions to be determined by agreement between the Organisation and such Signatory.

Article 15

When this Convention comes into force the reconstitution of the Organisation for European Economic Co-operation shall take effect, and its aims, organs, powers and name shall thereupon be as provided herein. The legal personality possessed by the Organisation for European Economic Co-operation shall continue in the Organisation, but decisions, recommendations and resolutions of the Organisation for European Economic Co-operation shall require approval of the Council to be effective after the coming into force of this Convention.

Article 16

Le Conseil peut décider d'inviter tout Gouvernement prêt à assumer les obligations de membre, à adhérer à la présente Convention. Cette décision doit être prise à l'unanimité; toutefois, le Conseil peut admettre à l'unanimité, dans un cas particulier, la possibilité d'abstention, étant entendu que, nonobstant les dispositions de l'Article 6, la décision s'applique alors à tous les Membres. L'adhésion prend effet lors du dépôt de l'instrument d'adhésion auprès du Gouvernement dépositaire.

Article 17

Toute Partie Contractante pourra mettre fin, en ce qui la concerne, à l'application de la présente Convention, en donnant un préavis d'un an à cet effet au Gouvernement dépositaire.

Article 18

Le siège de l'Organisation est à Paris, sauf si le Conseil en décide autrement.

Article 19

La capacité juridique de l'Organisation et les privilèges, exemptions et immunités de l'Organisation, de ses fonctionnaires et des représentants de ses Membres auprès d'elle, sont définis dans le Protocole Additionnel no. 2 à la présente Convention.

Article 20

1. Chaque année, conformément à un Règlement financier adopté par le Conseil, le Secrétaire Général soumet à l'approbation du Conseil un budget annuel, des comptes et tout budget annexe demandé par le Conseil.
2. Les dépenses générales de l'Organisation, approuvées par le Conseil, sont réparties conformément à un barème qui sera arrêté par le Conseil. Les autres dépenses sont financées sur la base fixée par le Conseil.

Article 21

Dès la réception des instruments de ratification, d'acceptation, d'adhésion ou de préavis de retrait, le Gouvernement dépositaire en donnera communication à toutes les Parties Contractantes et au Secrétaire Général de l'Organisation.

En foi de quoi, les Plénipotentiaires soussignés, dûment habilités, ont apposé leurs signatures au bas de la présente Convention.

Fait à Paris, le quatorze décembre mil neuf cent soixante, en français et en anglais, les deux textes faisant également foi, en un seul exemplaire qui sera déposé auprès du Gouvernement dépositaire, qui en communiquera une copie certifiée conforme à tous les signataires.

PROTOCOLE ADDITIONNEL No. 1 A LA CONVENTION RELATIVE A L'ORGANISATION DE COOPÉRATION ET DE DÉVELOPPEMENT ÉCONOMIQUES

Les signataires de la Convention relative à l'Organisation de Coopération et de Développement Économiques;

Article 16

The Council may decide to invite any Government prepared to assume the obligations of membership to accede to this Convention. Such decision shall be unanimous, provided that for any particular case the Council may unanimously decide to permit abstention, in which case, notwithstanding the provisions of Article 6, the decision shall be applicable to all the Members. Accession shall take effect upon the deposit of an instrument of accession with the depositary Government.

Article 17

Any Contracting Party may terminate the application of this Convention to itself by giving twelve months' notice to that effect to the depositary Government.

Article 18

The Headquarters of the Organisation shall be in Paris, unless the Council agrees otherwise.

Article 19

The legal capacity of the Organisation and the privileges, exemptions, and immunities of the Organisation, its officials and representatives to it of the Members shall be as provided in Supplementary Protocol No. 2 to this Convention.

Article 20

1. Each year, in accordance with Financial Regulations adopted by the Council, the Secretary-General shall present to the Council for approval an annual budget, accounts, and such subsidiary budgets as the Council shall request.

2. General expenses of the Organisation, as agreed by the Council, shall be apportioned in accordance with a scale to be decided upon by the Council. Other expenditure shall be financed on such basis as the Council may decide.

Article 21

Upon the receipt of any instrument of ratification, acceptance or accession, or of any notice of termination, the depositary Government shall give notice thereof to all the Contracting Parties and to the Secretary-General of the Organisation.

In witness whereof, the undersigned Plenipotentiaries, duly empowered, have appended their signatures to this Convention.

Done in Paris, this fourteenth day of December, Nineteen Hundred and Sixty, in the English and French languages, both texts being equally authentic, in a single copy which shall be deposited with the depositary Government, by whom certified copies will be communicated to all the Signatories.

SUPPLEMENTARY PROTOCOL No. 1 TO THE CONVENTION ON THE ORGANISATION FOR ECONOMIC CO-OPERATION AND DEVELOPMENT

The signatories of the Convention on the Organisation for Economic Co-operation and Development;

SONT CONVENUS de ce qui suit:

1. La représentation dans l'Organisation de Coopération et de Développement Économiques, des Communautés Européennes instituées par les Traités de Paris et de Rome, en date des 18 avril 1951 et 25 mars 1957, sera réglée conformément aux dispositions institutionnelles de ces Traités.

2. Les Commissions de la Communauté Économique Européenne et de la Communauté Européenne de l'Énergie Atomique ainsi que la Haute Autorité de la Communauté Européenne du Charbon et de l'Acier participeront aux travaux de cette Organisation.

EN FOI DE QUOI, les Plénipotentiaires soussignés, dûment habilités, ont apposé leurs signatures au bas du présent Protocole.

FAIT à Paris, le quatorze décembre mil neuf cent soixante, en français et en anglais, les deux textes faisant également foi, en un seul exemplaire qui sera déposé auprès du Gouvernement de la République Française, qui en communiquera une copie certifiée conforme à tous les signataires.

PROTOCOLE ADDITIONNEL No. 2 A LA CONVENTION RELATIVE A L'ORGANISATION DE COOPÉRATION ET DE DÉVELOPPEMENT ÉCONOMIQUES

LES SIGNATAIRES de la Convention relative à l'Organisation de Coopération et de Développement Économiques (appelée ci-dessous l',,Organisation");

SONT CONVENUS de ce qui suit:

L'Organisation jouit de la capacité juridique et l'Organisation, ses fonctionnaires et les représentants de ses Membres auprès d'elle jouissent des privilèges, exemptions et immunités suivants:

a) sur le territoire des Parties Contractantes à la Convention de Coopération Économique Européenne du 16 avril 1948, de la capacité juridique, des privilèges, exemptions et immunités prévus dans le Protocole Additionnel no. 1 à cette Convention;

b) au Canada, de la capacité juridique, des privilèges, exemptions et immunités prévus dans tout accord ou arrangement sur la capacité juridique, les privilèges, exemptions et immunités qui interviendra entre le Gouvernement du Canada et l'Organisation;

c) aux États-Unis, de la capacité juridique, des privilèges, exemptions et immunités prévus dans l'*Executive Order* no. 10133 du 27 juin 1950, conformément aux dispositions de *International Organisations Immunities Act*; et

d) dans tout autre pays, de la capacité juridique, des privilèges, exemptions et immunités prévus dans tout accord ou arrangement sur la capacité juridique, les privilèges, exemptions et immunités qui interviendra entre le Gouvernement intéressé et l'Organisation.

EN FOI DE QUOI, les Plénipotentiaires soussignés, dûment habilités, ont apposé leurs signatures au bas du présent Protocole.

FAIT à Paris, le quatorze décembre mil neuf cent soixante, en français et en anglais, les deux textes faisant également foi, en un seul exemplaire, qui sera déposé auprès du Gouvernement de la République Française, qui en communiquera une copie certifiée conforme à tous les signataires.

HAVE AGREED as follows:

1. Representation in the Organisation for Economic Co-operation and Development of the European Communities established by the Treaties of Paris and Rome of 18th April, 1951, and 25th March, 1957, shall be determined in accordance with the institutional provisions of those Treaties.

2. The Commissions of the European Economic Community and of the European Atomic Energy Community as well as the High Authority of the European Coal and Steel Community shall take part in the work of that Organisation.

IN WITNESS WHEREOF, the undersigned Plenipotentiaries, duly empowered, have appended their signatures to this Protocol.

DONE in Paris, this fourteenth day of December, Nineteen Hundred and Sixty, in the English and French languages, both texts being equally authentic, in a single copy which shall be deposited with the Government of the French Republic, by whom certified copies will be communicated to all the Signatories.

SUPPLEMENTARY PROTOCOL No. 2 TO THE CONVENTION ON THE ORGANISATION FOR ECONOMIC CO-OPERATION AND DEVELOPMENT

THE SIGNATORIES of the Convention on the Organisation for Economic Co-operation and Development (hereinafter called the "Organisation");

HAVE AGREED as follows

The Organisation shall have legal capacity and the Organisation, its officials, and representatives to it of the Members shall be entitled to privileges, exemptions, and immunities as follows:

a) in the territory of the Contracting Parties to the Convention for European Economic Co-operation of 16th April, 1948, the legal capacity, privileges, exemptions, and immunities provided for in Supplementary Protocol No. 1 to that Convention;

b) in Canada, the legal capacity, privileges, exemptions, and immunities provided for in any agreement or arrangement on legal capacity, privileges, exemptions, and immunities entered into between the Government of Canada and the Organisation;

c) in the United States, the legal capacity, privileges, exemptions, and immunities under the International Organisations Immunities Act provided for in Executive Order No. 10133 of 27th June, 1950; and

d) elsewhere, the legal capacity, privileges, exemptions, and immunities provided for in any agreement or arrangement on legal capacity, privileges, exemptions, and immunities entered into between the Government concerned and the Organisation.

IN WITNESS WHEREOF, the undersigned Plenipotentiaries, duly empowered, have appended their signatures to this Protocol.

DONE in Paris, this fourteenth day of December, Nineteen Hundred and Sixty, in the English and French languages, both texts being equally authentic, in a single copy which shall be deposited with the Government of the French Republic, by whom certified copies will be communicated to all the Signatories.

PROTOCOLE RELATIF A LA REVISION DE LA CONVENTION DE COOPÉRATION ÉCONOMIQUE EUROPÉENNE DU 16 AVRIL 1948

Les Gouvernements de la République Fédérale d'Allemagne, de la République d'Autriche, du Royaume de Belgique, du Royaume de Danemark, de l'Espagne, de la République Française, du Royaume de Grèce, de l'Irlande, de la République d'Islande, de la République Italienne, du Grand-Duché de Luxembourg, du Royaume de Norvège, du Royaume des Pays-Bas, de la République Portugaise, du Royaume-Uni de Grande-Bretagne et d'Irlande du Nord, du Royaume de Suède, de la Confédération Suisse et de la République de Turquie, qui sont les Parties Contractantes à la Convention de Coopération Économique Européenne du 16 avril 1948 (appelée ci-dessous la „Convention") et les Membres de l'Organisation Européenne de Coopération Économique;

Désireux que les objectifs, organes et pouvoirs de cette Organisation soient à nouveau définis et que les Gouvernements du Canada et des États-Unis d'Amérique soient Membres de cette Organisation reconstituée;

Sont convenus de ce qui suit:

Article 1

La Convention est révisée; de ce fait, lui est substituée la Convention relative à l'Organisation de Coopération et de Développement Économiques qui doit être signée ce jour.

Article 2

1. Le présent Protocole entrera en vigueur dès l'entrée en vigueur de la Convention relative à l'Organisation de Coopération et de Développement Économiques.
2. La Convention cessera d'avoir effet à l'égard de tous les signataires du présent Protocole dès l'entrée en vigueur de la Convention relative à l'Organisation de Coopération et de Développement Économiques.

En foi de quoi, les Plénipotentiaires soussignés, dûment habilités, ont apposé leurs signatures au bas du présent Protocole.

Fait à Paris, le quatorze décembre mil neuf cent soixante, en français et en anglais, les deux textes faisant également foi, en un seul exemplaire qui sera déposé auprès du Gouvernement de la République Française, qui en communiquera une copie certifiée conforme à tous les signataires.

MÉMORANDUM D'ACCORD POUR L'APPLICATION DE L'ARTICLE 15 DE LA CONVENTION RELATIVE A L'ORGANISATION DE COOPÉRATION ET DE DÉVELOPPEMENT ÉCONOMIQUES

L'Article 15 de la Convention relative à l'Organisation de Coopération et de Développement Économiques (appelée ci-dessous la „Convention") prévoit que les décisions, recommandations et résolutions (appelées ci-dessous les „actes") de l'Organisation Européenne de Coopération Économique requièrent l'approbation du Conseil de l'Organisation de Coopération et de Développement Économiques (appelé ci-dessous le „Conseil") pour être applicables après l'entrée en vigueur de la Convention.

PROTOCOL ON THE REVISION OF THE CONVENTION FOR EUROPEAN ECONOMIC CO-OPERATION OF 16TH APRIL, 1948

THE GOVERNMENTS of the Republic of Austria, the Kingdom of Belgium, the Kingdom of Denmark, the French Republic, the Federal Republic of Germany, the Kingdom of Greece, the Republic of Iceland, Ireland, the Italian Republic, the Grand Duchy of Luxembourg, the Kingdom of the Netherlands, the Kingdom of Norway, the Portuguese Republic, Spain, the Kingdom of Sweden, the Swiss Confederation, the Turkish Republic, the United Kingdom of Great Britain and Northern Ireland being the Contracting Parties to the Convention for European Economic Co-operation of 16th April, 1948 (hereinafter called the "Convention") and the Members of the Organisation for European Economic Co-operation;

DESIROUS that the aims, organs, and powers of the Organisation be redefined and that the Governments of Canada and the United States of America be Members of that Organisation as re-constituted;

HAVE AGREED as follows:

Article 1

The Convention shall be revised and as a consequence thereof it shall be replaced by the Convention on the Organisation for Economic Co-operation and Development to be signed on today's date.

Article 2

1. This Protocol shall come into force when the Convention on the Organisation for Economic Co-operation and Development comes into force.
2. The Convention shall cease to have effect as regards any Signatory of this Protocol when the Convention on the Organisation for Economic Co-operation and Development comes into force.

IN WITNESS WHEREOF, the undersigned Plenipotentiaries, duly empowered, have appended their signatures to this Protocol.

DONE in Paris, this fourteenth day of December, Nineteen Hundred and Sixty, in the English and French languages, both texts being equally authentic, in a single copy which shall be deposited with the Government of the French Republic, by whom certified copies will be communicated to all the Signatories.

MEMORANDUM OF UNDERSTANDING ON THE APPLICATION OF ARTICLE 15 OF THE CONVENTION ON THE ORGANISATION FOR ECONOMIC CO-OPERATION AND DEVELOPMENT

Article 15 of the Convention on the Organisation for Economic Co-operation and Development (hereinafter called the "Convention") provides that decisions, recommendations and resolutions (hereinafter called "acts") of the Organisation for European Economic Co-operation shall require approval of the Council of the Organisation for Economic Co-operation and Development (hereinafter called the "Council") to be effective after the coming into force of the Convention.

En vertu d'une Résolution adoptée à la réunion ministérielle des 22–23 juillet 1960, un Comité Préparatoire a été créé et chargé de poursuivre l'examen des actes de l'Organisation Européenne de Coopération Économique, de déterminer les actes dont il convient de recommander l'approbation au Conseil et de proposer, le cas échéant, les modifications nécessaires en vue d'adapter ces actes aux fonctions de l'Organisation de Coopération et de Développement Économiques.

A cette réunion ministérielle, il a été convenu qu'il devrait y avoir le maximum de certitude au sujet de l'approbation par le Conseil des actes de l'Organisation Européenne de Coopération Économique, conformément aux recommandations du Comité Préparatoire; il a été également convenu que le Canada et les États-Unis, n'étant pas Membres de l'Organisation Européenne de Coopération Économique, devraient avoir une certaine latitude en ce qui concerne lesdites recommandations.

En conséquence, les signataires de la Convention sont convenus de ce qui suit:

1. Les représentants des signataires au Conseil voteront l'approbation des actes de l'Organisation Européenne de Coopération Économique conformément aux recommandations du Comité Préparatoire, sauf dispositions contraires ci-dessous.

2. Tout signataire qui n'est pas Membre de l'Organisation Européenne de Coopération Économique sera dégagé de l'engagement prévu au paragraphe 1, en ce qui concerne toute recommandation ou partie de recommandation du Comité Préparatoire spécifiée par notification au Comité Préparatoire dans les dix jours du dépôt de son instrument de ratification ou d'acceptation de la Convention.

3. Si un signataire donne notification conformément au paragraphe 2, tout autre signataire aura le droit de demander, dans les quatorze jours de cette notification, que le Comité Préparatoire réexamine la recommandation ou partie de recommandation en cause, s'il considère que cette notification change la situation au regard de ladite recommandation ou partie de recommandation dans un de ses aspects importants.

4. *a*) Si un signataire donne notification conformément au paragraphe 2 et qu'il n'y ait pas de demande en vertu du paragraphe 3 ou qu'à la suite d'une demande le réexamen par le Comité Préparatoire n'aboutit pas à une modification de la recommandation ou partie de recommandation en cause, le représentant au Conseil du signataire ayant donné notification s'abstiendra de voter sur l'acte ou la partie d'acte auquel elle se rapporte.

b) Si le réexamen par le Comité Préparatoire prévu au paragraphe 3 aboutit à une modification de la recommandation ou partie de recommandation en cause, le représentant au Conseil du signataire ayant donné notification pourra s'abstenir de voter sur l'acte ou la partie d'acte auquel elle se rapporte.

c) L'abstention d'un signataire conformément aux sous-paragraphes *a*) et *b*) du présent paragraphe, en ce qui concerne un acte ou une partie d'acte, ne fait pas obstacle à l'approbation de cet acte ou partie d'acte qui est applicable aux autres signataires mais pas au signataire qui s'abstient.

5. Les dispositions du présent Mémorandum concernant les mesures à prendre avant le vote au Conseil entreront en vigueur dès sa signature; les dispositions concernant le vote au Conseil entreront en vigueur pour chaque signataire lors de l'entrée en vigueur de la Convention à l'égard de ce signataire.

En foi de quoi, les soussignés ont apposé leurs signatures au bas du présent Mémorandum.

Fait à Paris, le quatorze décembre mil neuf cent soixante, en français

Pursuant to a Resolution adopted at the Ministerial Meeting of 22nd–23rd July, 1960, a Preparatory Committee has been established and instructed to carry further the review of the acts of the Organisation for European Economic Co-operation, to determine which acts should be recommended to the Council for approval, and to recommend, where necessary, the modifications required in order to adjust these acts to the functions of the Organisation for Economic Co-operation and Development.

At the said Ministerial Meeting it was agreed that there should be the maximum possible degree of certainty as regards approval by the Council of acts of the Organisation for European Economic Co-operation in accordance with the recommendations of the Preparatory Committee; it was also agreed that Canada and the United States, not being Members of the Organisation for European Economic Co-operation, should have a certain latitude with respect to the said recommendations.

Therefore the Signatories of the Convention have agreed as follows:

1. The representatives of the Signatories on the Council shall vote for approval of acts of the Organisation for European Economic Co-operation in accordance with the recommendations of the Preparatory Committee, except as otherwise provided hereinafter.

2. Any Signatory which has not been a Member of the Organisation for European Economic Co-operation shall be released from the commitment set out in paragraph 1 with respect to any recommendation or part thereof of the Preparatory Committee which it specifies in a notice to the Preparatory Committee no later than ten days after the deposit of its instrument of ratification or acceptance of the Convention.

3. If any Signatory gives notice pursuant to paragraph 2, any other Signatory, if in its view such notice changes the situation in regard to the recommendation or part thereof in question in an important respect, shall have the right to request, within fourteen days of such notice, that the Preparatory Committee reconsider such recommendation or part thereof.

4. *a*) If a Signatory gives notice pursuant to paragraph 2 and no request is made pursuant to paragraph 3, or, if such a request having been made, the reconsideration by the Preparatory Committee does not result in any modification of the recommendation or part thereof in question, the representative on the Council of the Signatory which has given notice shall abstain from voting on the act or part thereof to which the recommendation or part thereof in question pertains.

b) If the reconsideration by the Preparatory Committee provided for in paragraph 3 results in a modified recommendation or part thereof, the representative on the Council of the Signatory which has given notice may abstain from voting on the act or part thereof to which the modified recommendation or part thereof pertains.

c) Abstention by a Signatory pursuant to sub-paragraph *a*) or *b*) of this paragraph with respect to any act or part thereof shall not invalidate the approval of that act or part which shall be applicable to the other Signatories but not to the abstaining Signatory.

5. The provisions of this Memorandum relating to actions to be taken before the voting in the Council shall come into force upon its signature; the provisions relating to the voting in the Council shall come into force for each Signatory upon the coming into force of the Convention as regards that Signatory.

In witness whereof, the undersigned have appended their signatures to this Memorandum.

Done in Paris, this fourteenth day of December, Nineteen Hundred et en anglais, les deux textes faisant également foi, en un seul exemplaire qui sera déposé auprès du Gouvernement de la République Française, qui en communiquera une copie certifiée conforme à tous les signataires.

b) RAPPORT DU COMITÉ PRÉPARATOIRE

INTRODUCTION[1]

1. Le Comité Préparatoire, institué par la Résolution ministérielle du 23 juillet 1960, a siégé du 14 septembre au 23 nobembre 1960, sous la présidence de M. Thorkil KRISTENSEN, Secrétaire Général désigné de l'O.C.D.E. La principale tâche assignée au Comité était d'achever le projet de Convention, de définir la structure de l'Organisation rénovée et de déterminer ceux des Actes de l'O.E.C.E. dont il convient de recommander l'approbation au Conseil de l'O.C.D.E. Le Comité a accompli cette tâche et l'accord a été réalisé sur des recommandations couvrant l'ensemble de ces points.

2. L'Organisation rénovée, dont le Canada et les États-Unis seront Membres, portera le nom d'Organisation de Coopération et de Développement Économiques. Elle succédera à l'Organisation Européenne de Coopération Économique après ratification de la Convention. En vue d'assurer au mieux la transition, le Comité Préparatoire estime qu'il est essentiel que les travaux de l'O.E.C.E. au cours de la période de transition soient renforcés et orientés vers les buts indiqués dans la nouvelle Convention et le présent Rapport; en outre, le Canada et les États-Unis devraient être associés étroitement à ces travaux. En même temps, le Comité Préparatoire devrait être chargé d'élaborer des propositions complémentaires destinées à faciliter l'entrée en vigueur de l'O.C.D.E.

3. Nos pays ont atteint une phase nouvelle dans le développement de leurs économies. La restauration de l'économie de l'Europe, soutenue par l'aide des États-Unis et assurée grâce à la coopération au sein de l'O.E.C.E., a été réalisée avec succès; elle a permis le rétablissement de la convertibilité externe des monnaies de la plupart des pays européens. En même temps, une plus grande liberté des échanges et paiements, s'accompagnant de rapides progrès techniques, ont accru l'interdépendance des économies des différents pays. Une coopération internationale sur une base élargie est devenue de plus en plus nécessaire.

4. C'est pour tenir compte de cette situation et pour mieux satisfaire aux exigences présentes que la nouvelle Convention propose pour objectifs fondamentaux à la nouvelle Organisation:

a) réaliser la plus forte expansion possible de l'économie et de l'emploi et une progression du niveau de vie dans les pays Membres, tout en maintenant la stabilité financière, et contribuer ainsi au développement de l'économie mondiale;

b) contribuer à une saine expansion économique dans les pays Membres comme dans les pays non-membres en voie de développement économique; et

c) contribuer à l'expansion du commerce mondial sur une base multilatérale et non discriminatoire conformément aux obligations internationales.

5. En poursuivant l'ensemble de ses activités, l'Organisation devrait s'efforcer d'être un instrument efficace destiné non seulement à assurer l'équilibre et la prospérité économiques dans les pays Membres, mais aussi à améliorer directement ou indirectement la situation des pays en voie de développement; à ce dernier égard, nous croyons en effet que les pays Membres de l'Organisation ont des responsabilités particulières.

---

[1] Le Rapport du Comité Préparatoire et les recommandations qu'il contient ont été approuvés par les Ministres lors de la réunion du 13 décembre 1961 (*voir* Document no. 10, page 109).

and Sixty, in the English and French languages, both texts being equally authentic, in a single copy which shall be deposited with the Government of the French Republic, by whom certified copies will be communicated to all the Signatories.

b) REPORT OF THE PREPARATORY COMMITTEE

INTRODUCTION [1]

1. The Preparatory Committee constituted by the Ministerial Resolution of 23rd July, 1960, held sessions from 14th September to 23rd November, 1960, under the Chairmanship of Mr. Thorkil KRISTENSEN, Secretary-General Designate of the O.E.C.D. The main task of the Committee was to complete the Draft Convention, to define the structure of the reconstituted Organisation and to determine which Acts of the O.E.E.C. should be recommended to the Council of the O.E.C.D. for approval. The Committee have accomplished their task and reached agreement on recommendations covering these fields.

2. The reconstituted Organisation which will include Canada and the United States as Members, will be called the Organisation for Economic Co-operation and Development. It will succeed the O.E.E.C. after ratification of the Convention. In order to ensure a smooth transition, the Preparatory Committee think it important that the work of the O.E.E.C. in the interim should be strengthened and oriented towards the goals set forth in the new Convention and the present Report, and that Canada and the United States should be closely associated with this work. At the same time, the Preparatory Committee should be instructed to work out further proposals to facilitate the coming into being of the O.C.E.D.

3. We have now entered a new phase in the development of our economies. The reconstruction of the European economy, sustained by United States aid and furthered by co-operation within the O.E.E.C., has been successfully accomplished and has led to the achievement of external convertibility of most European currencies. At the same time, freer trade and payments combined with rapid technological progress have made the economies of individual countries increasingly interdependent. The need for international co-operation on a wider basis has become ever more compelling.

4. It is against this background and in order better to meet the needs of today that the new Convention sets out as the aims of the reconstituted Organisation:

a) to achieve the highest sustainable economic growth and employment and a rising standard of living in Member countries, while maintaining financial stability and thus to contribute to the development of the world economy;

b) to contribute to sound economic expansion in Member as well as non-member countries in the process of economic development; and

c) to contribute to the expansion of world trade on a multilateral, non-discriminatory basis in accordance with international obligations.

5. In all its activities the Organisation should aim at being an effective instrument not only for securing prosperous and balanced economies in Member countries, but also for improving directly and indirectly the situation of less-developed countries, in which respect we feel that the Members of the Organisation have a special responsibility.

---

[1] The Report of the Preparatory Committee and the recommendations contained therein were approved at the Ministerial Meeting on 13th December, 1960, (*see* Document No. 10, page 109).

Partie I

LA STRUCTURE DE L'O.C.D.E.

Introduction

6. La Résolution ministérielle du 23 juillet 1960 a chargé le Comité Préparatoire de „définir la structure de l'Organisation rénovée et d'établir le mandat des principaux organes nécessaires à l'accomplissement des tâches actuelles convenus pour l'Organisation rénovée".

7. Pour donner suite à ces instructions, le Comité Préparatoire soumet ci-dessous des recommandations relatives à la création, sous l'autorité du Conseil, des Comités de l'O.C.D.E. nécessaires à la réalisation des objectifs de l'Organisation et contenant la description des tâches qui incomberaient à ces Comités.

Le Comité Préparatoire inclut aussi, dans la présente Partie, des mandats pour les Comités qui ont la responsabilité principale de la mise en oeuvre des objectifs de l'Organisation, tels qu'ils sont énoncés à l'article premier de la Convention, à savoir l'expansion économique, l'aide aux pays en voie de développement économique et les échanges.

Le Comité Préparatoire n'a pas fait de recommandations concernant la création de chacun des Comités de l'Organisation. Le Comité Préparatoire pourrait recommander la création de Comités supplémentaires après la signature de la Convention. Dans ses Recommandations, le Comité Préparatoire a cherché à laisser au Conseil la plus grande latitude possible pour définir les mandats des Comités de l'O.C.D.E. et déterminer les rapports entre ces Comités. Le Conseil de l'O.C.D.E. sera évidemment habilité à modifier comme il lui semblera convenable la structure de l'Organisation; il pourra établir de nouveaux Comités, supprimer des Comités existants ou modifier leurs mandats.

8. Outre le mandat général relatif à la structure qui lui a été donné aux termes de la Résolution O.C.D.E.(60)14, le Comité Préparatoire a été spécialement chargé par les Ministres, aux termes du paragraphe 5 de la Résolution O.C.D.E.(60)13 sur l'aide aux pays en voie de développement, de faire des recommandations sur les modalités d'application de cette Résolution.

9. Étant donné la nouveauté et l'importance de cette tâche, le Comité Préparatoire a particulièrement recherché la souplesse dans la structure qu'il recommande en ce domaine. Il est d'avis que la plupart des instances de l'Organisation devraient s'occuper, et s'occuperont de plus en plus, de la mise en oeuvre de l'article 1 *b*) de la Convention. Lorsque le Secrétaire Général estime devoir obtenir l'avis de spécialistes, il peut les consulter individuellement ou créer des groupes d'experts. Pour des aspects particuliers de ces tâches, il y aura le Comité d'Aide au Développement dont la création a été décidée par la Résolution ministérielle mentionnée ci-dessus. Le Comité Préparatoire a aussi défini les fonctions du Comité d'Examen des Situations Économiques et des Problèmes de Développement, du Comité d'Assistance Technique, du Comité des Paiements et de certains autres Comités de façon à donner effet au paragraphe 4 de cette Résolution.

10. Les paragraphes ci-après traitent des Comités qui existeront ou dont le Comité Préparatoire recommande la création dès les débuts de l'Organisation.

Comité de Politique Économique

11. Le Comité Préparatoire recommande la création d'un Comité de Politique Économique qui sera le principal organe de l'Organisation

PART I

STRUCTURE OF THE O.E.C.D.

INTRODUCTION

6. The Ministerial Resolution of 23rd July, 1960, instructed the Preparatory Committee "to define the structure of the reconstituted Organisation and to draw up the terms of reference of the main organs necessary for the accomplishment of the tasks currently agreed for the reconstituted Organisation".

7. In fulfilment of this instruction the Preparatory Committee herewith submit recommendations concerning the establishment of the Committees of the O.E.C.D., under the Council, required to implement the aims of the Organisation, with descriptions of the tasks which these Committees would perform.

The Preparatory Committee also include in this Part mandates for those Committees which will have the broadest responsibilities for carrying out the aims of the Organisation as set forth in Article 1 of the Convention, namely economic growth, assistance to countries in the process of economic development and trade.

The Preparatory Committee have not made recommendations about the establishment of each and every Committee in the Organisation. The Preparatory Committee might recommend the establishment of additional Committees following the signature of the Convention. In their recommendations the Preparatory Committee have sought to reserve the greatest possible latitude to the Council to define the terms of reference of O.E.C.D. Committees and to determine the relationships among them. The Council of the O.E.C.D. will, of course, be competent to modify the structure of the Organisation in any way it deems appropriate, it will be able to establish new Committees, abolish existing ones or change their terms of reference.

8. In addition to the general mandate on structure set forth in Resolution O.E.C.D.(60)14, the Preparatory Committee received a specific instruction from the Ministers, in paragraph 5 of Resolution O.E.C.D.(60) 13 on Aid to Developing Countries, to make recommendations on how this Resolution should be implemented.

9. Because of the newness and importance of this task, the Preparatory Committee have especially sought flexibility in the structure they recommend in this field. They are of the opinion that most of the organs of the O.E.C.D. will and should be increasingly concerned with the implementation of Article 1 *b*) of the Convention. When the Secretary-General feels the need for specialist advice, he can consult individual experts or call together expert groups. For particular aspects of these tasks, there will be the Development Assistance Committee whose establishment was decided upon by the above-mentioned Ministerial Resolution. The Preparatory Committee have also described the functions of the Economic and Development Review Committee, the Technical Assistance Committee, the Payments Committee and of some other Committees in such a manner as to give effect to paragraph 4 of that Resolution.

10. The following paragraphs deal with the Committees which will exist or which the Preparatory Committee recommend should be established at the inception of the Organisation.

ECONOMIC POLICY COMMITTEE

11. The Preparatory Committee recommend the creation of an Economic Policy Committee to the main body of the Organisation in

en matière de politique économique. A ses sessions devraient participer des fonctionnaires de rang élevé ayant une part importante de responsabilités dans l'élaboration de la politique économique générale. Le Comité pourra faire au Conseil des propositions et des recommandations.

12. Il est en outre recommandé que le mandat du Comité de Politique Économique soit le suivant:

a) Le Comité de Politique Économique examinera la situation et les politiques économiques et financières des pays Membres, en vue d'atteindre les objectifs de la Convention.

b) Dans l'examen de la politique économique des pays Membres, le Comité accordera une attention particulière aux conséquences internationales de leurs politiques, en tenant compte de l'interdépendance croissante de leurs économies et en reconnaissant que les efforts de chacun d'eux seront influencés par les actions des autres, de façon à établir un climat de compréhension mutuelle favorable à un ajustement harmonieux des politiques.

Comité d'Examen des Situations Économiques et des Problèmes de Développement

13. Le Comité Préparatoire recommande la création d'un Comité d'Examen des Situations Économiques et des Problèmes de Développement qui assurera, entre autres tâches qui pourraient lui être confiées, l'examen annuel de la situation économique des pays Membres.

Ce Comité étudierait les programmes de développement des pays Membres en voie de développement économique et présenterait au Conseil des commentaires et des recommandations à ce sujet; il lui donnerait également des avis sur les autres problèmes de développement que ces pays Membres pourraient soumettre à l'Organisation, en vue d'aider le Conseil à assurer la bonne coordination des activités des autres Comités chargés d'exécuter les tâches, découlant du paragraphe 4 de la Résolution ministérielle en date du 23 juillet 1960 [O.C.D.E.(60)13]. Le Comité aurait le droit de demander au Secrétaire Général de convoquer des experts à titre individuel ou des groupes d'experts pour donner au Comité les avis qui pourraient sembler nécessaires dans des cas déterminés.

Comité d'Aide au Développement

14. Ainsi qu'il en est décidé dans la Résolution ministérielle en date du 23 juillet 1960 [O.C.D.E.(60)13], le Groupe d'Aide au Développement deviendra le Comité d'Aide au Développement lorsque l'O.C.D.E. entrera en activité; il aura le mandat suivant:

a) Le Comité poursuivra les consultations relatives aux méthodes à appliquer pour rendre disponibles les ressources nationales afin d'aider les pays et régions en voie de développement économique, et pour accroître et améliorer l'afflux de capitaux à long terme et les autres formes d'aide au développement en faveur de ces pays et régions.

b) Le Comité d'Aide au Développement aura les fonctions, les caractéristiques et la composition qu'aura le Groupe d'Aide au Développement lors des débuts de l'Organisation.

c) Le Comité choisira son Président, présentera périodiquement des rapports au Conseil et à ses propres Membres, recevra le concours du Secrétariat dans les conditions qui seront convenues avec le Secrétaire Général, sera habilité à formuler des recommandations concernant des questions de son ressort aux pays représentés au Comité et au Conseil, et invitera des représentants d'autres pays et d'organisations internationales à participer aux discussions concernant des questions particulières en tant que de besoin.

matters of economic policy. Its sessions should be attended by senior officials with a major responsibility in the formulation of general economic policies. The Committee may make proposals and recommendations to the Council.

12. It is further recommended that the mandate of the Economic Policy Committee should be as follows:

a) The Economic Policy Committee will keep under review the economic and financial situation and policies of Member countries with a view to attaining the objectives of the Convention.

b) In reviewing the economic policy of Member countries, the Committee will pay special attention to the international effects of national policies in the light of the increasing interdependence of their economies and of the recognition that efforts of individual countries will be influenced by the actions of others, with a view to establishing a climate of mutual understanding conducive to the harmonious adjustment of policies.

Economic and Development Review Committee

13. The Preparatory Committee recommend the establishment of an Economic and Development Review Committee which will, among other tasks assigned to it, be responsible for the annual examination of the economic situation of Member countries.

The Committee would study and make comments and recommendations to the Council on the development programmes of the Member countries in the process of economic development, and advise the Council on other development problems that such Member countries may submit to the Organisation, with a view to assisting the Council in ensuring that the responsibilities of the other committees charged with carrying out the tasks arising out of paragraph 4 of the Ministerial Resolution of 23rd July, 1960 [O.E.C.D.(60)13] are adequately co-ordinated. The Committee would have the right to request the Secretary-General to call upon individual experts or expert groups to advise the Committee as may seem necessary in any given case.

Development Assistance Committee

14. As decided by the Ministerial Resolution of 23rd July, 1960 [O.E.C.D.(60)13], the Development Assistance Group shall, upon the inception of the O.E.C.D., be constitued as the Development Assistance Committee, and given the following mandate:

a) The Committee will continue to consult on the methods for making national resources available for assisting countries and areas in the process of economic development and for expanding and improving the flow of long-term funds and other development assistance to them.

b) The Development Assistance Committee will acquire the functions, characteristics and membership possessed by the Development Assistance Group at the inception of the Organisation.

c) The Committee will select its Chairman, make periodic reports to the Council and its own Members, receive assistance from the Secretariat as agreed with the Secretary-General, have power to make recommendations on matters within its competence to countries on the Committee and to the Council, and invite representatives of other countries and international organisations to take part in particular discussions as necessary.

d) Le Comité d'Aide au Développement ne pourra agir au nom de l'Organisation qu'avec l'approbation du Conseil.

e) Dans le cas où les attributions du Comité d'Aide au Développement seraient étendues au delà de celles qui sont définies à l'alinéa *a*) ci-dessus, tout pays Membre non représenté au Comité d'Aide au Développement pourra saisir le Conseil de la question.

COMITÉ D'ASSISTANCE TECHNIQUE

15. Le Comité Préparatoire recommande la création d'un Comité d'Assistance Technique pour traiter des problèmes d'assistance technique conformément à l'article 2 *e*) de la Convention. Ce Comité, qui pourrait faire des recommandations au Conseil dans le cadre de son mandat, serait principalement chargé de l'élaboration et du contrôle des programmes d'assistance technique qui seraient organisés au bénéfice des pays Membres en voie de développement ou, dans des cas particuliers, des régions en voie de développement des pays Membres. Les programmes d'assistance technique envisagés seraient du type de ceux qui sont actuellement mis en oeuvre par l'O.E.C.E. pour des pays Membres.

COMITÉ DES ÉCHANGES

16. Ainsi qu'il a été décidé par la Résolution ministérielle en date du 23 juillet 1960 [O.C.D.E.(60)9 (Final)], il sera institué, lors de l'entrée en activité de l'O.C.D.E., un Comité des Échanges qui assumera notamment les fonctions suivantes:

a) Confrontation à intervalles réguliers ou à la demande d'un Membre des politiques commerciales générales et des pratiques en matière d'échanges, compte tenu de la nécessité de maintenir un système de commerce multilatéral permettant aux Membres d'échanger librement des biens et des services entre eux et avec les pays tiers, tout en maintenant un équilibre raisonnable des balances internationales de paiements;

b) Examen de problèmes spécifiques en matière d'échanges intéressant principalement les Membres et leurs territoires d'outre-mer;

c) Examen des problèmes à court et à long terme non encore réglés, entrant dans le mandat du Comité des Questions Commerciales, créé lors de la réunion des Ministres des vingt Membres et Membres Associés de l'Organisation Européenne de Coopération Économique et des Représentants des Communautés Européennes, tenue à Paris les 13 et 14 janvier 1960.[1]

Comme le précise la Résolution ministérielle susmentionnée, il est entendu que les dispositions relatives au Comité des Échanges énoncées plus haut permettraient à tout pays Membre d'obtenir que le Comité examine et discute rapidement les mesures prises par un autre Membre dans le domaine des échanges et qui porteraient préjudice à ses intérêts, en vue de supprimer ou d'atténuer le préjudice en question.

On trouvera exposés au chapitre 2 de la Partie II du présent rapport les méthodes et moyens par lesquels le Comité des Échanges exercera ses fonctions.

COMITÉ DES PAIEMENTS

17. Le Comité Préparatoire recommande la création d'un Comité des Paiements chargé de donner au Conseil des avis sur les activités de l'O.C.D.E. en matière de paiements, y compris les transactions invisibles, les mouvements de capitaux et les aspects des questions de financement

---

[1] Le Comité Préparatoire a proposé de remplacer par cet alinéa, l'alinéa *c*) du paragraphe 1 du document O.C.D.E.(60)9(Final).

d) The Development Assistance Committee may act on behalf of the Organisation only with the approval of the Council.

e) In case the responsibilities of the Development Assistance Committee were to be extended beyond those set forth under *a*), any Member country not represented in the Development Assistance Committee could bring the matter before the Council.

TECHNICAL ASSISTANCE COMMITTEE

15. The Preparatory Committee recommend the creation of a Technical Assistance Committee to deal with questions of technical assistance in accordance with Article 2 *e*) of the Convention. This Committee, which might make any recommendation to the Council within its mandate, would be mainly responsible for drawing up and supervising the programmes of technical assistance which would be arranged for the benefit of Member countries or, in special cases, areas of Member countries, in the process of development. The technical assistance programmes contemplated would be similar in type to those operated at present on behalf of Member countries by the O.E.E.C.

TRADE COMMITTEE

16. As decided by the Ministerial Resolution of 23rd July, 1960 [O.E.C.D.(60)9(Final)] there shall, upon the inception of the O.E.C.D., be constituted a Trade Committee which shall carry out, in particular, the following functions:

a) Confrontation of the general trade policies and practices at regular intervals or whenever requested by a Member having in mind the need for maintaining a system of multilateral trade which would enable Members to exchange goods and services freely with each other and with other countries under conditions of reasonable overall equilibrium in international balance of payments;

b) Examination of specific trade problems primarily of interest to Members and their overseas territories; and

c) Consideration of any short and long-term problems falling within the terms of reference of the Committee on Trade problems established at the Meeting of Ministers of the twenty Members and Associate Members of the Organisation for European Economic Co-operation and Representatives of the European Communities held at Paris on 13th–14th January, 1960, and which remain outstanding.[1]

As stated in the above-mentioned Ministerial Resolution, it is understood that the provisions relating to the Trade Committee set out above would enable any Member country to obtain prompt consideration and discussion by the Committee of trade measures by another Member which adversely affect its interests, with a view to removing or minimizing such adverse effects.

A description of the ways and means in accordance with which the Trade Committee shall exercise its functions is given in Part II, Chapter 2, of this Report.

PAYMENTS COMMITTEE

17. The Preparatory Committee recommend the creation of a Payment Committee to advise the Council on O.E.C.D. activities in the field of payments, including invisible transactions, capital movements and such aspects of long-term financing as may be assigned by the Council to the

[1] The Preparatory Committee have proposed this paragraph in place of paragraph 1 *c*) of O.E.C.D. (60)9(Final).

à long terme dont le Conseil saisirait le Comité. Ce Comité examinera les rapports du Comité des Transactions Invisibles et du Comité Directeur de l'Accord Monétaire Européen, et il adressera au Conseil ses commentaires sur ces rapports. Le Conseil de l'O.C.D.E. établira le mandat du Comité des Paiements et définira ses relations avec les autres instances de l'Organisation.

COMITÉ DIRECTEUR DE L'ACCORD MONÉTAIRE EUROPÉEN

18. Le Comité Directeur de l'Accord Monétaire Européen est maintenu avec la composition et le mandat définis dans l'Accord Monétaire Européen et dans les Directives pour l'application de cet Accord. Le Canada et les États-Unis n'ont pas l'intention d'adhérer à cet Accord.

COMITÉ DES TRANSACTIONS INVISIBLES

19. Le Comité Préparatoire recommande la création d'un Comité des Transactions Invisibles, dont la composition et le mandat seront définis dans le Code de la Libération des Opérations Invisibles Courantes et le Code de la Libération des Mouvements de Capitaux.

COMITÉ DES ASSURANCES

20. Le Comité Préparatoire recommande la création d'un Comité ou d'un Groupe des Assurances qui sera chargé de poursuivre les activités menées actuellement par l'O.E.C.E. dans ce domaine et d'assumer toute autre fonction que le Conseil pourrait décider de lui confier.

AGRICULTURE ET PÊCHERIES

21. Le Comité Préparatoire a convenu que les activités de l'Organisation en matière d'agriculture et de pêcheries devraient être renforcées et intégrées étroitement aux autres activités de l'Organisation orientées vers les objectifs de la Convention.

22. En ce qui concerne l'agriculture, le Comité Préparatoire recommande la création d'un Comité, responsable devant le Conseil, qui sera chargé d'examiner les problèmes et les politiques agricoles ayant une incidence sur les objectifs de la Convention, de donner des avis et de faire des recommandations à l'Organisation sur ces questions.

23. Le Comité devra se réunir au niveau des Ministres en vue d'examiner les problèmes primordiaux dans le domaine de l'agriculture, y compris ceux qui sont liés aux autres aspects des travaux de l'Organisation.

24. Des dispositions appropriées devront être prises en ce qui concerne les activités dans le secteur des pêcheries; un Comité spécial et distinct sera créé.

25. Le Comité Préparatoire a chargé son Président de consulter les Ministres responsables sur les moyens de donner effet à ces recommandations et de lui faire des propositions avant l'entrée en vigueur de la Convention.

26. Le Comité pourra être autorisé par le Conseil à assumer des tâches opérationnelles.

COMITÉ DU PERSONNEL SCIENTIFIQUE ET TECHNIQUE ET COMITÉ DE LA RECHERCHE SCIENTIFIQUE

27. Dans le domaine scientifique et technique, le Comité Préparatoire recommande que soient créés:

a) un Comité du Personnel Scientifique et Technique dont le mandat et le programme d'activité seraient analogues à ceux du Comité Direc-

Committee. This Committee will review the reports of the Committee for Invisible Transactions and of the Board of Management of the European Monetary Agreement and forward to the Council any comments on these reports. The terms of reference of the Payments Committee and its relationship to other bodies of the Organisation will be determined by the Council of the O.E.C.D.

Board of Management of the European Monetary Agreement

18. The Board of Management of the European Monetary Agreement will be retained with the composition and mandate defined in the European Monetary Agreement and in the Directives for the application of the Agreement. Canada and the United States do not intend to accede to this Agreement.

Committee for Invisible Transactions

19. The Preparatory Committee recommend the creation of a Committee for Invisible Transactions with the composition and mandate to be defined in the Code of Liberalisation of Current Invisible Operations and in the Code of Liberalisation of Capital Movements.

Insurance Committee

20. The Preparatory Committee recommend the creation of an Insurance Committee or Group to continue the activities of the type now undertaken by the O.E.E.C. and to deal with such other functions in this field as the Council may decide.

Agriculture and Fisheries

21. The Preparatory Committee agree that the activities of the Organisation concerning agriculture and fisheries should be strengthened and closely integrated with the Organisation's other activities in pursuit of the objectives of the Convention.

22. With regard to agriculture, the Preparatory Committee recommend the creation of a Committee responsible to the Council to consider, advise and make recommendations to the Organisation on agricultural problems and policies pertinent to the objectives of the Convention.

23. The Committee shall meet at Ministerial level in order to examine major problems in the agricultural sector, including those connected with other aspects of the Organisation's work.

24. With regard to activities in the fisheries sector, appropriate arrangements will have to be made by creating a special, separate, Committee.

25. The Preparatory Committee have requested their Chairman to consult the Ministers concerned on the way to give effect to these recommendations and to make proposals to the Committee before the coming into force of the Convention.

26. The Committee may be authorized by the Council to assume operational tasks.

Committee for Scientific and Technical Personnel and Committee for Scientific Research

27. In the field of science and technology, the Preparatory Committee recommend the creation of:

a) a Committee for Scientific and Technical Personnel which will have similar terms of reference and carry on a similar programme of teur de l'O.E.C.E. pour les Questions de Personnel Scientifique et Technique; et

b) un Comité de la Recherche Scientifique qui serait chargé des activités relatives à la recherche scientifique et d'autres activités scientifiques.

AGENCE EUROPÉENNE POUR L'ÉNERGIE NUCLÉAIRE

28. Le Comité Préparatoire recommande que l'Agence Européenne pour l'Énergie Nucléaire soit maintenue dans sa forme actuelle au sein de l'Organisation.

COMITÉS POUR L'ÉNERGIE ET L'INDUSTRIE

29. Le Comité Préparatoire recommande que soit maintenue une coopération entre les pays Membres dans le domaine de l'énergie et de l'industrie. A cette fin, le Secrétaire Général fera, si possible avant l'entrée en vigueur de la Convention et au plus tard un an après son entrée en vigueur, des propositions concernant la création, le rôle, la nature et la durée du mandat des Comités ou Groupes de l'Organisation dans ces domaines. Il consultera les Délégations, les Présidents des Comités existants et tous experts dont il désirerait recueillier l'avis.

30. Ses propositions devront tenir compte:

a) des objectifs de l'Organisation, de sa structure et des activités dont le Comité Préparatoire recommande la continuation;

b) de la nécessité de concentrer le plus possible les activités de l'Organisation pour renforcer son efficacité;

c) des vues des Gouvernements Membres en ce qui concerne les activités de l'Organisation, y compris l'intérêt que certains pays attachent au maintien de la collaboration qui s'est développée entre l'O.E.C.E. et les différents secteurs de l'industrie;

d) d'activités analogues poursuivies au sein d'autres Organisations internationales.

31. Lorsque les propositions du Secrétaire Général leur seront soumises, le Comité Préparatoire ou le Conseil de l'O.C.D.E. devront les considérer dans leur ensemble en vue de prendre une décision établissant une structure utile et cohérente, aux éléments de laquelle un nombre suffisant et représentatif de pays sont prêts à participer.

32. Le Comité Préparatoire recommande que la structure des Comités actuels soit maintenue jusqu'à ce qu'elle soit remplacée par la nouvelle mais pas au delà d'un an après la mise en vigueur de la Convention. Certains Comités pourraient être supprimés plus tôt si le Conseil en décidait ainsi.

COMITÉ DU TOURISME

33. Le Comité Préparatoire recommande que la coopération dans le domaine du tourisme soit continuée. A cet effet, la structure actuelle devrait être réexaminée et adaptée en fonction des besoins futurs.

COMITÉS DES TRANSPORTS MARITIMES

34. Le Comité Préparatoire recommande la création d'un Comité des Transports Maritimes chargé de tenir l'Organisation au courant des événements importants survenus dans le domaine des transports maritimes. Le Comité sera aussi chargé de tenir des consultations au sujet de la politique des Membres, et pourra présenter des recommandations au Conseil dans les cas où il jugera approprié de le faire. Les rapports et recommandations du Comité des Transports Maritimes

activities to that of the O.E.E.C. Governing Committee for Scientific and Technical Personnel and

b) a Committee for Scientific Research which would be responsible for activities concerning scientific research and other activities in the field of science.

EUROPEAN NUCLEAR ENERGY AGENCY

28. The Preparatory Committee recommend that the European Nuclear Energy Agency should be retained in its present form within the Organisation.

COMMITTEES FOR ENERGY AND INDUSTRY

29. The Preparatory Committee recommend that co-operation among Member countries in the fields of Energy and Industry be maintained. The Secretary-General will, if possible before the coming into force of the Convention and not later than one year after its coming into force, make proposals as to the creation, role, nature and length of the mandate of the committees or groups of the Organisation in these fields. He will consult Delegations, the Chairmen of existing committees and any experts whose opinion he desires.

30. His proposals should take into account:

a) the aims and structure of the Organisation and the activities which the Preparatory Committee recommend should be pursued;

b) the need for the greatest possible concentration of its activities, so as to increase its effectiveness;

c) the views of the Member Governments concerning the Organisation's activities in the fields of Energy and Industry, including the value attached by certain countries to maintaining the collaboration which has developed between O.E.E.C. and the various sectors of industry;

d) similar activities in other international organisations.

31. When the Secretary-General's proposals are submitted, the Preparatory Committee or the O.E.C.D. Council should consider them in their entirety, with a view to taking a decision establishing a useful and coherent structure in which a sufficient and representative number of countries are willing to participate.

32. The Preparatory Committee recommend that the existing committee structure should be retained until it is replaced by the new structure, but not for more than one year after the coming into force of the Convention. Individual committees might be abolished earlier if the Council so decided.

TOURISM COMMITTEE

33. The Preparatory Committee recommend that co-operation in the field of tourism should be continued. To this effect the present structure should be reviewed and adapted in the light of future requirements.

MARITIME TRANSPORT COMMITTEE

34. The Preparatory Committee recommend the creation of a Maritime Transport Committee which shall be responsible for keeping the Organisation informed of significant developments in the field of maritime transport. The Committee shall also be responsible for consultations concerning the policies of Members and may submit recommendations to the Council in cases where this appears appropriate. The reports and/or recommendations of the Maritime Transport Committee should

seront soumis, en tant que de besoin, aux instances compétentes de l'Organisation pour commentaires, avant leur présentation au Conseil.

COMITÉ DE LA MAIN-D'ŒUVRE

35. Le Comité Préparatoire recommande la création d'un Comité de la Main-d'Œuvre qui traitera des problèmes de main-d'œuvre liés à la réalisation des objectifs généraux de l'Organisation et des questions sociales qui sont étroitement liées aux problèmes de main-d'œuvre. Ce Comité poursuivra aussi les travaux de l'O.E.C.E. en ce qui concerne les mouvements de main-d'œuvre en Europe. Il pourra remplir, si le Conseil lui en donne mandat, certaines tâches opérationnellles.

COMITÉ FISCAL

36. Le Comité Préparatoire recommande la création d'un Comité Fiscal qui sera chargé de poursuivre les activités du type de celles menées actuellement par l'O.E.C.E. et d'assumer toute autre fonction dans ce domaine que le Conseil pourrait décider de lui confier.

GROUPE D'EXPERTS POUR LES PRATIQUES COMMERCIALES RESTRICTIVES

37. Le Comité Préparatoire recommande la création d'un Groupe d'experts en matière de pratiques commerciales restrictives, qui sera chargé de poursuivre les activités du type de celles menées actuellement par l'Agence Européenne de Productivité et d'assumer toute autre fonction dans ce domaine que le Conseil pourrait décider de lui confier.

ACTIVITÉS ACTUELLES DE L'AGENCE EUROPÉENNE DE PRODUCTIVITÉ

38. Le Comité Préparatoire recommande que la responsabilité des projets suivants de l'Agence Européenne de Productivité qui ne seraient pas achevés lors de l'entrée en vigueur de la nouvelle structure soit transférée comme suit:

a) Les projets actuels de l'Agence Européenne de Productivité conçus spécialement pour les pays Membres en voie de développement économique seraient transférés au Comité d'Assistance Technique. Ce Comité pourrait aussi servir de forum où s'institueraient comme auparavant les discussions et la coopération concernant le Programme de formation dans les pays tiers;

b) Les projets relevant actuellement de l'Agence Européenne de Productivité en matière de recherche appliquée seraient transférés au Comité de la Recherche Scientifique.

39. Le Comité Préparatoire recommande que lui soit confié le soin d'examiner, après la signature de la Convention, tous les autres programmes en cours de l'Agence Européenne de Productivité, en tenant compte des buts et des objectifs de l'Organisation, en vue de définir les domaines d'activité pour lesquels des programmes devraient être établis à l'avenir. Il sera entendu que ceux des programmes opérationnels qui pourraient être poursuivis entre un nombre restreint de pays seront financés par ces pays. Cet examen engloberait les dispositions relatives à l'organisation, au financement et à l'administration de ces activités. Enfin, le Comité Préparatoire reconnaît la nécessité d'arrangements appropriés pour assurer le contrôle administratif et financier des activités opérationnelles dans l'O.C.D.E. Il propose d'étudier ces questions au cours de la prochaine phase de ses travaux et d'examiner, à cette occasion, si un organe, autre que le Conseil, serait nécessaire pour coordonner toutes les activités mentionnées ci-dessus et la répartition des ressources entre elles.

40. Le Comité Préparatoire estime aussi que les organismes nationaux

where appropriate be submitted to the relevant bodies of the Organisation for comment prior to submission to the Council.

MANPOWER COMMITTEE

35. The Preparatory Committee recommend the creation of a Manpower Committee to deal with manpower questions connected with the general objectives of the Organisation and those social questions which are closely linked with manpower problems. This Committee would also continue the work of the O.E.E.C. in connection with manpower movements in Europe. The Committee could, if the Council so instructed it, carry out certain operational tasks.

FISCAL COMMITTEE

36. The Preparatory Committee recommend the creation of a Fiscal Committee to continue the activities of the type now undertaken by the O.E.E.C. and to deal with such other functions in this field as the Council may decide.

GROUP OF EXPERTS ON RESTRICTIVE BUSINESS PRACTICES

37. The Preparatory Committee recommend the creation of a Group of Experts on Restrictive Business Practices to continue the activities of the type now undertaken by the European Productivity Agency and to deal with such other functions in this field as the Council may decide.

PRESENT ACTIVITIES OF THE EUROPEAN PRODUCTIVITY AGENCY

38. The Preparatory Committee recommend that responsibility for the following European Productivity Agency projects not completed when the new structure comes into force should be transferred as follows:

a) Present European Productivity Agency projects especially designed for Member countries in the process of economic development should be transferred to the Technical Assistance Committee. This Committee would also provide a forum for discussion and co-operation, as hitherto, on the Third Country Training Programme;

b) Present European Productivity Agency applied research projects should be transferred to the Committee for Scientific Research.

39. The Preparatory Committee recommend that they should be instructed to review all other current European Productivity Agency programmes after the signature of the Convention, in the light of the aims and objectives of the Organisation, with a view to defining those fields of activity for which programmes should be established in the future. It will be understood that such operational programmes as may be continued among a limited number of countries will be financed by those countries. This review should embrace the organisational, financial and administrative arrangements for these activities. Finally, the Preparatory Committee recognise the need for adequate arrangements to ensure administrative and financial control of the operational activities of the O.E.C.D. They propose that they should consider these matters during the next phase of their work and in this connection examine whether any organ other than the Council is required to co-ordinate all the activities mentioned above and the allocation of resources among them.

40. The Preparatory Committee are also of the opinion that national

auxquels la possibilité a été donnée, dans le cadre de l'Agence Européenne de Productivité, d'échanger leurs expériences et leurs informations, pourraient se voir offrir la même possibilité dans le cadre de l'Organisation.

Partie II

EXAMEN DES ACTES DE L'O.E.C.E.

Introduction

41. La Résolution ministérielle du 23 juillet 1960 a chargé le Comité Préparatoire „de poursuivre l'examen des actes de l'Organisation Européenne de Coopération Économique; de déterminer les Actes dont il convient de recommander l'approbation au Conseil de l'Organisation rénovée; et de proposer, le cas échéant, les modifications nécessaires en vue d'adapter ces Actes aux fonctions de l'Organisation rénovée telles qu'elles sont actuellement convenues par les Gouvernements".

42. Les conclusions auxquelles le Comité Préparatoire a abouti à la suite de l'examen des Actes de l'O.E.C.E. peuvent se ramener aux quatre catégories suivantes:

43. *Première catégorie.* Dans le cas où le Comité Préparatoire a conclu au maintien d'un Acte de l'O.E.C.E. sans amendement de substance, il a formulé une recommandation à cet effet dans le présent rapport. En vertu du Mémorandum d'Accord pour l'application de l'article 15 de la Convention, cet Acte devra alors être approuvé par le Conseil de l'O.C.D.E., sauf s'il fait l'objet d'un réexamen conformément au Mémorandum d'Accord.

44. La plupart des Actes maintenus doivent faire l'objet d'amendements de pure forme en raison des références qu'ils contiennent aux organes de l'O.E.C.E. dont les compétences seront transférées aux organes correspondants de l'O.C.D.E. Parfois, des dispositions de ces Actes sont devenues caduques par l'effet de dispositions contraires d'Actes ultérieurs de l'O.E.C.E. maintenus eux aussi. Le Comité Préparatoire n'a pu procéder à la mise au point des textes et propose que ce travail soit effectué aussitôt que possible après la signature de la Convention.

45. Il a été admis que sauf mention contraire dans le présent rapport, le maintien d'un Acte laisse subsister les réserves ou interprétations dont cet Acte ou certaines de ses dispositions ont fait l'objet au cours de son examen, soit par le Conseil de l'O.E.C.E., soit par le Comité Préparatoire; dans ce dernier cas, ces réserves ou interprétations figurent dans le présent rapport.

46. Il peut résulter de l'objet même d'un Acte, d'une disposition qui y figure ou que le Comité Préparatoire propose d'y insérer que cet Acte ne s'appliquera pas aux Membres de l'O.C.D.E. qui n'étaient pas Membres de l'O.E.C.E. Le présent rapport indique les cas dans lesquels des Actes maintenus ne s'appliquent pas ou peuvent ne pas s'appliquer auxdits Membres. Cette indication a la portée d'une Recommandation au sens du paragraphe 1 du Mémorandum d'Accord pour l'application de l'article 15 et permet auxdits Membres de s'abstenir lors du vote au Conseil de l'O.C.D.E. sans avoir recours à la procédure du paragraphe 2 du Mémorandum d'Accord.

47. *Deuxième catégorie.* Dans certains cas, le Comité Préparatoire a conclu au maintien d'un Acte, tout en convenant de modifications de fond à lui apporter, et a formulé des recommandations à cet effet dans le présent rapport. En vertu du Mémorandum d'Accord pour l'application de l'article 15, l'Acte devra alors être approuvé par le Conseil de l'O.C.D.E., avec les amendements prévus par le Comité Préparatoire, sauf s'il fait l'objet d'un réexamen conformément au Mémorandum d'Accord.

bodies which were, within the European Productivity Agency, given facilities for exchanging their experience and information, could be given similar facilities in the Organisation.

Part II

REVIEW OF THE ACTS OF THE O.E.E.C.

Introduction

41. The Ministerial Resolution of 23rd July, 1960, instructed the Preparatory Committee "to carry further the review of the Acts of the Organisation for European Economic Co-operation; to determine which Acts should be recommended to the Council of the reconstituted Organisation for approval; and to propose, where necessary, the modifications required in order to adapt these Acts to the functions of the reconstituted Organisation as currently agreed by Governments".

42. The conclusions reached by the Preparatory Committee as a result of the review of the Acts of the O.E.E.C. may be classified in the four following categories:

43. *First category*. In cases where the Preparatory Committee concluded that an Act of the O.E.E.C. should be retained without modification of substance, they have made a recommendation to that effect in this Report. By virtue of the Memorandum of Understanding on the Application of Article 15 of the Convention, that Act must then be approved by the O.E.C.D. Council, unless it is reconsidered in accordance with that Memorandum.

44. Most of the Acts retained require purely formal amendments as they contain references to bodies of the O.E.E.C. the functions and powers of which will be transferred to corresponding bodies of the O.E.C.D. In some cases, certain provisions of Acts have become obsolete as a result of contrary provisions in subsequent Acts of the O.E.E.C. which are also retained. The Preparatory Committee have been unable to put the texts in appropriate form and propose that this task be carried out as soon as possible after the signature of the Convention.

45. It is recognised that in the absence of any indication to the contrary in this Report, a retained Act carries with it any reservations or interpretations concerning it or any of its provisions made in the course of its consideration by the O.E.E.C. Council, or made in the course of its consideration by the Preparatory Committee and noted in this Report.

46. It may result either from the subject matter of an Act, or from a provision contained in it or proposed to be inserted in it by the Preparatory Committee, that such Act will not apply to the Members of the O.E.C.D. not previously Members of the O.E.E.C. This Report indicates the instances in which retained Acts do not or may not apply to such Members. These indications are equivalent to recommendations within the meaning of paragraph 1 of the Memorandum of Understanding on the Application of Article 15. They will permit the new Members to abstain at the time of voting in the O.E.C.D. Council without having to invoke the procedure of paragraph 2 of that Memorandum.

47. *Second category*. In certain cases, the Preparatory Committee have concluded that an Act should be retained but have agreed upon modifications of substance to be made to it and have submitted recommendations to that effect in this report. By virtue of the Memorandum of Understanding on the Application of Article 15, such an Act must then be approved by the O.E.C.D. Council with the amendments specified by the Preparatory Committee, unless it is reconsidered pursuant to that Memorandum.

48. Parfois, le Comité Préparatoire n'a pas été en mesure d'arrêter le texte même des amendements à apporter à un Acte maintenu, mais s'est borné à convenir du sens général dans lequel cet Acte ou certaines de ses parties devraient être modifiés. Il appartiendra alors au Comité Préparatoire, après la signature de la Convention, sur la base des recommandations contenues à ce sujet dans le présent rapport, de formuler les amendements à apporter à cet Acte, pour permettre son approbation par le Conseil de l'O.C.D.E.

49. *Troisième catégorie.* Dans d'autres cas, le Comité Préparatoire n'a pas conclu au maintien d'un Acte mais a convenu que certaines activités, principes ou règles prévus par cet Acte devraient être maintenus ou faire l'objet d'un nouvel examen dans des conditions déterminées.

50. Les recommandations à cet effet, contenues dans le présent rapport, ne tombent pas sous le coup du Mémorandum d'Accord pour l'application de l'article 15, puisqu'elles ne portent pas sur le maintien d'un Acte de l'O.E.C.E. Or, des recommandations par elles-mêmes n'engagent pas en principe les Gouvernements ou Organisations auxquels elles s'adressent, qui doivent seulement les prendre en considération, mais conservent leur liberté d'appréciation sur la suite qu'il convient de leur donner.

51. C'est pourquoi il est apparu nécessaire qu'en approuvant le présent rapport la Réunion ministérielle accepte les recommandations qu'il contient. Cette acceptation confirmerait la détermination des Gouvernements que les travaux ultérieurs du Comité Préparatoire et de l'O.C.D.E. soient menés conformément à ces recommandations.

52. Le Comité Préparatoire a estimé que cette acceptation suffit pour assurer que ces recommandations soient mises en œuvre par le Conseil de l'O.C.D.E.

53. *Quatrième catégorie.* Dans le cas où le Comité Préparatoire n'a pas conclu au maintien d'un Acte et n'a pas fait de recommandation en ce qui le concerne dans son rapport, l'Acte deviendra caduc, en vertu de l'article 15 de la Convention, lors de l'entrée en vigueur de celle-ci.

Chapitre 1

Politiques Économiques Génerales

54. Le Comité Préparatoire recommande que l'Organisation poursuive les examens périodiques de l'évolution de la situation économique des pays Membres. Il estime que les examens annuels au sein de l'O.E.C.E. ont donné des résultats valables et qu'ils méritent d'être poursuivis, le Conseil de l'Organisation pouvant y apporter toutes les améliorations qu'il jugera utiles.

55. Le Comité Préparatoire recommande aussi que, conformément à l'obligation qui leur est faite de tenir l'Organisation informée, chaque pays Membre soumette à l'Organisation, à l'attention de ses organes compétents, des informations concernant les modifications de sa politique qu'il estimerait de nature à exercer une influence notable sur son économie.

56. Le Comité n'estime pas nécessaire de maintenir les Résolutions *C (56) 36 (Final)*, contenant des Directives pour les travaux de l'O.E.C.E., et *C (58) 213*, concernant la situation économique.

57. Cependant, le Comité estime utile de rappeler que certains principes énoncés dans les Actes ci-dessus restent valables. Ainsi les problèmes à long terme de l'expansion économique méritent une étude plus intensive et les Gouvernements doivent chercher à les résoudre individuellement et conjointement. Dans la recherche de mesures permettant de réaliser à la fois l'expansion et l'equilibre, les pays Membres doivent

48. In certain cases, the Preparatory Committee have not been able to specify the actual wording of the amendments to be made to an Act which has been retained, but have confined themselves to agreeing on the general sense in which the Act or part thereof should be amended. It will then be for the Preparatory Committee, after the signature of the Convention and on the basis of the recommendations on the subject contained in this Report, to formulate the amendments to be made to the Act so that it can be approved by the Council of the O.E.C.D.

49. *Third category.* In other cases, the Preparatory Committee have not concluded that Acts should be retained but have agreed that certain activities, principles or rules provided for in the Act should be retained or should be the subject of further consideration under specified conditions.

50. The recommendations to this effect contained in this Report do not come within the scope of the Memorandum of Understanding on the Application of Article 15 since they do not provide for the retention of Acts of the O.E.E.C. As a rule, recommendations by themselves are not binding on the Governments or organisations to which they are addressed, which are merely required to take them into consideration, but retain freedom of judgment as to the action to be taken upon them.

51. For this reason, it appears necessary that the Ministerial Meeting, in approving this Report, should accept the recommendations contained in it. This acceptance would confirm the determination of Governments that the subsequent work of the Preparatory Committee and the O.E.C.D. be carried on in accordance with those recommendations.

52. The Preparatory Committee consider that this acceptance is sufficient to assure that their recommendations will be carried out by the O.E.C.D. Council.

53. *Fourth category.* In cases where the Preparatory Committee have not concluded that an Act should be retained and have made no recommendations relating to the Act in its Report, the Act will lapse by virtue of Article 15 of the Convention as soon as the Convention comes into force.

Chapter 1

General Economic Policies

54. The Preparatory Committee recommend that the Organisation should continue the periodic review of economic developments in Member countries. They believe that the results of the existing O.E.E.C. annual review confrontation are worth while and that they deserve to be continued with any appropriate improvements to be decided by the Council of the Organisation.

55. The Preparatory Committee also recommend that, in line with the obligation to keep the Organisation informed, each Member country should submit to the Organisation, for the attention of the competent bodies of the latter, information with regard to changes in its policy which it considers have a significant impact on its economy.

56. The Committee do not think it necessary to retain *Resolution C (56)36(Final)* containing directives for the work of the O.E.E.C. or *Resolution C(58)213* concerning the economic situation.

57. The Committee nevertheless think it worth recalling that some of the principles set out in the Acts referred to above remain valid. Thus the problems involved in long-term economic expansion merit intensive study and Governments should try to deal with these problems individually and jointly. In their endeavours to achieve expansion and equilibrium by the most appropriate measures, Member countries should take into

prendre en considération les effets de leurs mesures sur les autres pays et les avantages qu'ils auront à poursuivre ces objectifs de concert.

Chapitre 2

Échanges

Introduction

58. Les travaux du Comité Préparatoire sur les questions commerciales ont été déterminés par le mandat particulier que comporte la Résolution relative aux échanges, O.C.D.E.(60)9 (Final), adoptée par les Ministres à la Réunion du 23 juillet 1960. Ce mandat comprend deux tâches:

- l'élaboration des méthodes et moyens par lesquels le Comité des Échanges de l'O.C.D.E. exercera les fonctions indiquées dans cette même Résolution;
- l'examen des Actes commerciaux de l'O.E.C.E. à l'exception des engagements du Code de la Libération en matière de libération des échanges.

Dans ses travaux, le Comité Préparatoire a tenu compte des objectifs généraux de l'Organisation dans le domaine commercial, tels qu'ils sont définis par les articles 1 *c*) et 2 *d*) du projet de Convention.

59. Le Comité Préparatoire a convenu que l'ensemble des conclusions qui figurent dans le présent chapitre, constitue une recommandation qu'il est proposé à la Réunion ministérielle d'accepter.

Méthodes et moyens

60. En vue de définir les méthodes et moyens par lesquels le Comité des Échanges exercera ses fonctions, le Comité Préparatoire a passé en revue les activités que ce Comité aura à entreprendre. Il s'est limité à esquisser les grandes lignes de ces activités, ce qui aura entre autres pour effet de laisser au Comité des Échanges une grande souplesse dans l'organisation de ses travaux.

Le Comité Préparatoire fait en outre des propositions sur la structure du Comité des Échanges. Les règles sur la nature et la fréquence des rapports du Comité des Échanges au Conseil ainsi que les dispositions détaillées de procédure concernant ce Comité seront à déterminer ultérieurement.

Aucune mention n'est faite ci-dessous de la fonction définie au paragraphe 1 *c*) de la Résolution O.C.D.E.(60)9 (Final) qui a trait aux problèmes entrant dans le mandat du Comité des Questions Commerciales. Le Comité Préparatoire estime que les méthodes et moyens nécessaires pour traiter ces problèmes importants devront être mis au point ultérieurement.

A. Activités du Comité des Échanges

Informations

61. Le projet de Convention dispose déjà à l'article 3 *a*) que les pays Membres se tiendront mutuellement informés et fourniront à l'Organisation les renseignements nécessaires à l'accomplissement de ses tâches. Le Comité Préparatoire estime que cette information devrait prendre la forme de notifications faites à l'Organisation et portées par celle-ci à la connaissance des pays Membres. Le Comité des Échanges aura à veiller à ce que l'information dans le domaine des échanges (application de restrictions quantitatives, *etc.*) soit assurée d'une manière adéquate

consideration the effects of their actions on others and the advantages of pursuing these objectives in concert.

Chapter 2

Trade

INTRODUCTION

58. The Preparatory Committee's work on trade questions has been determined by the special mandate embodied in the Resolution on trade O.E.C.D.(60)9(Final), adopted by the Ministers at the meeting of 23rd July, 1960. This mandate comprises two tasks:

- to work out ways and means in accordance with which the Trade Committee of the O.E.C.D. shall exercise its functions as set out in that Resolution;
- to study the Acts on trade in the O.E.E.C. other than the undertakings of the Code of Liberalisation with regard to liberalisation of trade.

In their work the Preparatory Committee bore in mind the general objectives of the Organisation in the field of trade as defined in Articles 1 *c*) and 2 *d*) of the Draft Convention.

59. The Preparatory Committee have agreed that all the conclusions set out in this chapter constitute a recommendation which the Ministerial Meeting is invited to accept.

WAYS AND MEANS

60. With a view to working out the ways and means by which the Trade Committee will function, the Preparatory Committee reviewed the activities which this Committee will be called upon to undertake. They have limited themselves to giving a broad outline of these activities; one effect of this will be to permit the Trade Committee a high degree of flexibility in arranging its work.

The Preparatory Committee also make certain proposals for the structure of the Trade Committee. The rules for the nature and frequency of the reports of the Trade Committee to the Council and the detailed rules of procedure concerning this Committee will have to be determined at a later date.

No reference is made in this chapter to the function defined in paragraph 1 *c*) of Resolution O.E.C.D.(60)9(Final), relating to the consideration of problems falling within the terms of reference of the Committee on Trade Problems. The Preparatory Committee consider that the necessary ways and means for dealing with these important problems will have to be worked out at a later stage.

A. Activities of the Trade Committee

Information

61. The draft Convention already provides, in Article 3 *a*), that Member countries will keep each other informed and will furnish the Organisation with the information necessary for the accomplishment of its tasks. The Preparatory Committee consider that this information should take the form of notifications made to the Organisation which would bring them to the knowledge of the Member countries. The Trade Committee will have to make certain that information in the field of trade (application of quantitative restrictions, *etc.*) is ensured and kept

et tenue à jour. De l'avis du Comité Préparatoire, il s'agit là d'une tâche essentielle qui est à la base de toutes les autres activités du Comité des Échanges.

Confrontations

62. Les confrontations à intervalles réguliers dans le domaine des échanges qui n'ont pas de précédent dans le cadre de l'O.E.C.E., constituent un élément essentiel des activités commerciales au sein de l'O.C.D.E. Au cours de ces confrontations, la politique commerciale générale de chaque pays Membre et ses pratiques en matière d'échanges seront examinées en portant une attention particulière aux aspects importants qui caractérisent cette politique et aux modifications appréciables intervenues dans son application, notamment en ce qui concerne l'incidence que cette politique peut avoir sur la situation économique d'autres pays. Le Comité Préparatoire estime qu'au départ le Comité des Échanges devrait procéder à une confrontation large et assez détaillée et acquérir ainsi les données et les connaissances de base qui l'aideraient à déterminer, en fonction des circonstances, le programme des confrontations ultérieures. (Au début, les confrontations à intervalles réguliers pourraient, par exemple, avoir lieu une fois par an; cette périodicité pourrait ensuite être modifiée à la lumière de l'expérience.) Du fait de l'interdépendance entre la politique commerciale et les politiques économiques et financières, il faudra tenir compte dans l'organisation des confrontations de la nécessité d'une coordination avec les travaux des autres instances de l'O.C.D.E. Il conviendrait de prendre en considération l'expérience acquise lors des confrontations des politiques économiques à l'O.E.C.E.

Pour assurer l'efficacité des confrontations, il est nécessaire que les questions sur lesquelles elles porteront soient choisies en fonction de leur intérêt pratique et de leur actualité et qu'elles soient clairement posées avant chaque confrontation.

Si les circonstances l'exigent, des confrontations *ad hoc* pourraient être organisées, par exemple au cas où un changement important serait intervenu dans la politique commerciale d'un pays Membre depuis la dernière confrontation régulière ou encore si, à la suite d'une modification substantielle dans sa situation, un pays Membre n'apportait pas à sa politique commerciale les changements appropriés.

Examens de problèmes commerciaux

63. Le Comité des Échanges sera amené à examiner les problèmes visés au paragraphe 1 *b*) de la Résolution O.C.D.E.(60)9 (Final); ces problèmes pourraient être soulevés par exemple à l'issue d'une confrontation. Il aura également à examiner les aspects commerciaux de questions plus générales traitées par d'autres organes de l'O.C.D.E.

64. Le Comité des Échanges exercera ses fonctions, dans la mesure où elles concernent des pays Membres en voie de développement économique, à la lumière des dispositions de l'article 2 *e*) du projet de Convention.

Cas particulier de pays Membres demandant ou ayant reçu un prêt sur le Fonds européen

65. Le Comité Préparatoire estime qu'il faudra adapter au cadre de l'O.C.D.E. les activités actuelles de l'O.E.C.E. en matière d'échanges dans le cas de prêts sur le Fonds européen, demandés ou reçus par des pays Membres, de façon à assurer la participation du Comité des Échanges aux travaux concernant l'octroi de ces prêts. Le Comité des Échanges devrait procéder à un examen détaillé et continu de la politique commer-

up to date. In the opinion of the Preparatory Committee, this is an essential task which underlies all other activities of the Trade Committee.

Confrontation

62. Confrontation at regular intervals in the field of trade, which is without precedent in the O.E.E.C., constitutes an essential feature of the trade activities of the O.E.C.D. In the course of these confrontations, the general trade policy of each Member country and its trade practices will be examined with special attention to the outstanding features of policy and any significant modification in its application, especially as to the incidence which such policy may have on the economic situation of other countries. The Preparatory Committee think that at the outset, the Trade Committee should carry out a wide-ranging and fairly detailed confrontation and thus acquire the background information and knowledge which would assist it to determine the programme of subsequent confrontations in the light of circumstances. (To begin with, regular confrontation could, for example, take place once a year; this timing might be altered later in the light of experience). Owing to the interdependence between trade policy and economic and financial policies, confrontation must be arranged with due consideration for the need to co-ordinate it with the work of the other O.E.C.D. bodies. Regard should be had to experience gained in the field of confrontation of economic policies in O.E.E.C.

If this confrontation is to be effective, the questions covered must be selected in the light of their practical interest and topical character and must be clearly formulated before each confrontation.

Should circumstances so require, *ad hoc* confrontations could be arranged, for example, in the event of a major modification in the trade policy of a Member country since the last regular confrontation or if, following a substantial change in its situation, a Member country did not make the appropriate changes in its trade policy.

Examination of trade problems

63. The Trade Committee will be called upon to examine the problems specified in paragraph 1 *b*) of the Resolution O.E.C.D.(60)9(Final); such problems may, for example, arise out of a confrontation. It will also have to consider the trade aspects of more general questions dealt with by other organs of the O.E.C.D.

64. The Trade Committee will carry out its functions, as they relate to Member countries in the process of economic development, in the light of the provisions of Article 2 *e*) of the draft Convention.

Special case of Member countries applying for or receiving loans from the European Fund

65. The Preparatory Committee consider that the present trade activities of the O.E.E.C. in the case of loans applied for or received by Member countries from the European Fund should be adapted to the framework of the O.E.C.D. with a view to ensuring the participation of the Trade Committee in the work concerning the granting of these loans. The Trade Committee should carry out a detailed and continuous examin-

ciale des pays en cause et formuler toutes recommandations appropriées, notamment sur la politique que ces pays devraient adopter en vue de maintenir ou d'accroître la libération des échanges, ou de la rétablir le plus rapidement possible. A ce sujet, il convient d'établir une liaison appropriée entre le Comité des Échanges et les organes de l'O.C.D.E. chargés des questions de paiements.

Utilisation et adaptation de différentes procédures

66. Le Comité Préparatoire estime qu'il convient de laisser au Comité des Échanges le soin d'élaborer par le détail ses propres procédures pour l'organisation adéquate de ses activités sous les différentes rubriques mentionnées ci-dessus.

Il serait conforme à l'esprit de la Résolution relative aux Échanges que ces procédures fussent arrêtées de telle sorte que toutes les fonctions du Comité des Échanges fussent remplies aussi efficacement et aussi rapidement que possible. En conséquence, le Comité Préparatoire considère comme souhaitable que le Comité des Échanges adapte ses procédures à la nature des problèmes qui relèvent de sa compétence afin d'éviter un formalisme excessif. Dans ce sens, et suivant les cas, les pays Membres qui désirent soulever un problème résultant de mesures prises en matière d'échanges par d'autres pays Membres pourraient demander une consultation selon une procédure souple.

Dans l'exercice de ses fonctions, le Comité des Échanges tiendra dûment compte du fait que les pays Membres doivent pouvoir obtenir que les problèmes commerciaux soient examinés et discutés rapidement, ainsi qu'il est prévu dans la Résolution.

B. Structure du Comité des Échanges

67. Le Comité Préparatoire estime que le Comité des Échanges devrait être un Comité plénier composé de fonctionnaires responsables de l'exécution de la politique commerciale de leurs Gouvernements. Ces fonctionnaires pourraient se faire représenter. Le Comité Préparatoire tient toutefois à souligner l'importance de la continuité dans la représentation au sein du Comité des Échanges.

Le Comité des Échanges devrait avoir la possibilité de confier des travaux à des organes subsidiaires dont il pourrait lui-même déterminer la composition. Ceci s'applique également à des travaux que le Comité aurait à effectuer conjointement avec d'autres Comités de l'O.C.D.E.

68. La représentation des Communautés Européennes est déjà prévue par la Convention (article 13 et Protocole Additionnel no. 1). La représentation du Secrétaire Général de l'Association Européenne de Libre-Échange est prévue par la Résolution O.C.D.E.(60)15 (Final). De plus, le Comité Préparatoire désire souligner l'importance de la liaison avec le G.A.T.T. et l'intérêt qu'il attache à la présence du Secrétaire Exécutif du G.A.T.T. ou de son représentant aux réunions du Comité des Échanges. Le Comité Préparatoire a convenu que les arrangements appropriés à cet effet devraient être décidés par le Conseil de l'O.C.D.E. qui examinerait en même temps la question d'une représentation réciproque.

Examen des Actes

69. En examinant les Actes commerciaux de l'O.E.C.E., le Comité Préparatoire entend que le passage de l'O.E.C.E. à l'O.C.D.E. ne peut pas être interprêté comme ouvrant la voie à un recul par rapport aux résultats déjà atteints dans le domaine de la libération, mais qu'au contraire, les Gouvernements des futurs pays Membres de l'O.C.D.E. ont

ation of the trade policy of the countries concerned and make any appropriate recommendations, especially as to the policy which those countries should follow in order to maintain or increase trade liberalisation, or restore it as rapidly as possible. In this connection, an appropriate liaison should be established between the Trade Committee and the organs of O.E.C.D. dealing with payment questions.

Use and adaptation of various procedures

66. The Preparatory Committee are of the opinion that the Trade Committee should be left to work out its own procedures in detail for the proper organisation of its activities under the various headings given above.

It would be in the spirit of the Resolution on Trade that these procedures be arranged so that all the functions of the Trade Committee will be carried out in the most efficient and expeditious manner possible. The Preparatory Committee consider therefore that it would be desirable for the Trade Committee to adapt its procedures to the nature of the problems for which it has a responsibility, with a view to avoiding unnecessary formalism. In this sense, and according to circumstances, any Member country wishing to raise a problem arising out of the trade measures taken by other Members may ask for a consultation under an informal procedure.

In carrying out its tasks, the Trade Committee shall have due regard to the fact that Member countries are to be able to obtain prompt consideration and discussion of commercial problems as provided for in the Resolution.

B. Structure of the Trade Committee

67. The Preparatory Committee think that the Trade Committee should be a plenary committee where senior officials responsible for the execution of the trade policy of their Governments represent the Member countries; these senior officials should be entitled to be represented by a deputy. The Preparatory Committee, however, wish to stress the importance of continuity in representation on the Trade Committee.

The Trade Committee should have power to delegate work to subsidiary bodies whose composition it would itself determine. This also applies to the work which the Committee would have to do jointly with other O.E.C.D. Committees.

68. The representation of the European Communities is already specified in the Convention (Article 13 and Supplementary Protocol No. 1). The representation of the Secretary-General of the European Free Trade Association is ensured by virtue of Resolution O.E.C.D.(60) 15(Final). The Preparatory Committee further desire to stress the importance of liaison with the G.A.T.T. and the interest it attaches to the attendance of the Executive Secretary of the G.A.T.T. or his representative at meetings of the Trade Committee. The Preparatory Committee agreed that appropriate arrangements to this end should be made by the O.E.C.D. Council which would consider the question of reciprocal representation at the same time.

CONSIDERATION OF THE ACTS

69. In considering the trade Acts of the O.E.E.C., the Preparatory Committee note that the transition from the O.E.E.C. to the O.E.C.D. will not be looked upon as opening the door to any withdrawal from the level of liberalisation already achieved but that, on the contrary, the Governments of the prospective Members of the O.E.C.D. have the

l'intention de poursuivre leurs efforts pour développer les échanges conformément à leurs engagements internationaux.

Conformément au mandat qui lui a été donné par la réunion ministérielle en juillet, le Comité Préparatoire a examiné les Actes commerciaux de l'O.E.C.E. Ces actes sont énumérés dans l'annexe I.

Eu égard aux considérations exposées ci-après, le Comité Préparatoire ne recommande pas le maintien de ces Actes dans l'O.C.D.E.

70. Le Comité Préparatoire recommande que le contenu des Actes marqués d'un astérisque soit examiné par l'O.C.D.E. dès sa constitution, en vue de déterminer dans quelle mesure et sous quelle forme le contenu de ces Actes devrait être repris dans l'O.C.D.E. pour réaliser efficacement les objectifs commerciaux acceptés. Il est aussi recommandé que l'O.C.D.E. s'inspire notamment des travaux accomplis par l'O.E.C.E. sur les points considérés, y compris en particulier ceux qui ont trait aux difficultés de balance de paiements, dans la mesure où ces travaux sont en rapport et compatibles avec ses fonctions, afin de tirer parti, dans l'élaboration de ses propres conclusions, de l'expérience antérieurement acquise; elle devrait être animée par l'esprit général de coopération, dont on a fait preuve à l'O.E.C.E., qui s'est révélé si utile lorsque des difficultés ont surgi dans le passé et qui caractérisera également l'Organisation rénovée.

71. En ce qui concerne le problème des pays Membres qui ne sont pas Parties Contractantes au G.A.T.T., le Comité Préparatoire a constaté que seule l'Islande n'adhère pas et n'a pas demandé son adhésion à l'Accord Général sur les Tarifs Douaniers et le Commerce. Pour ce pays, le Comité des Échanges devrait élaborer une solution adéquate.

Chapitre 3

L'Accord Monétaire Européen et les actes de l'O.E.C.E. relatifs à cet Accord

72. Les conclusions et recommandations formulées par le Comité Préparatoire dans le présent chapitre sont fondées sur celles du Comité Directeur de l'Accord Monétaire Européen.

73. Il est convenu que l'Accord Monétaire Européen et les Actes de l'O.E.C.E. y relatifs seront maintenus après la reconstitution de l'O.E.C.E. Le maintien de l'A.M.E. ne nécessite pas l'approbation du Conseil de l'O.C.D.E., car il s'agit d'un Accord multilatéral soumis à la ratification de chacun des signataires qui ne constitue pas, en soi, un „Acte de l'Organisation".

A. Amendements a apporter a l'Accord Monétaire Européen

74. Les dispositions actuelles de l'A.M.E. ne sont pas de nature à gêner son fonctionnement après la reconstitution de l'O.E.C.E. Il sera néanmoins nécessaire d'harmoniser d'une part la rédaction de certains articles et du préambule de l'A.M.E. et d'autre part le texte définitif de la Convention relative à l'O.C.D.E. ainsi que des décisions concernant la structure de cette Organisation.

Le Comité Préparatoire recommande que le Comité Directeur de l'A.M.E. soit invité à soumettre au Conseil avant le 30 septembre 1961 les amendements à apporter à l'A.M.E. en raison de la reconstitution de l'O.E.C.E., ainsi que les amendements que le Comité Directeur pourrait proposer à la suite de l'examen général du fonctionnement de l'Accord (qui est prévu à l'article 32 de l'A.M.E. et au paragraphe 29 *c*) des Directives pour l'application de l'Accord). Ces amendements revêtiront la forme d'une Décision du Conseil dans les cas où ils porteront sur des dispositions de l'A.M.E. mentionnées à l'article 26 dudit Accord; dans intention of pursuing their efforts to develop trade in accordance with their international obligations.

In accordance with the mandate given to them by the Ministerial Meeting in July, the Preparatory Committee have examined the trade Acts of O.E.E.C. These are listed in Annex 1.

Having in mind the considerations below, the Preparatory Committee are not recommending the retention of these Acts in O.E.C.D.

70. It is recommended by the Preparatory Committee that the content of the Acts identified by an asterisk should be examined in the O.E.C.D. upon its inception, with a view to determining to what extent and in what form the content of these Acts should be taken into account in the O.E.C.D. for the effective achievement of the agreed trade objectives. It is also recommended that the O.E.C.D. should, *inter alia*, look to the work done by the O.E.E.C. on the subject matters in question, including in particular those dealing with balance of payments difficulties, to the extent that this work is relevant to and consistent with its functions, in order to benefit for its own assessments from the experience previously gained; it should be guided by the common spirit of co-operation achieved in O.E.E.C. which proved so useful when difficulties arose in the past and which will equally characterise the reconstituted Organisation.

71. With regard to the problem of Member countries who are not contracting parties to the General Agreement on Tariffs and Trade, the Preparatory Committee note that Iceland is the only country which is not a contracting party and which has not applied to be a contracting party of the G.A.T.T. In the case of this country the Trade Committee should work out a suitable solution.

Chapter 3

The European Monetary Agreement and the related Acts of O.E.E.C.

72. The conclusions and recommendations in this chapter are based on those of the Board of Management of the European Monetary Agreement.

73. It is agreed that the European Monetary Agreement and the related Acts of the O.E.E.C. should be continued after the reconstitution of the O.E.E.C. The continuation of the E.M.A. does not require the approval of the O.E.C.D. Council, since the E.M.A. is a multilateral Agreement subject to ratification by each of its Signatories and, as such, is not an "Act of the Organisation".

A. Amendments to the European Monetary Agreement

74. The continued satisfactory operation of the E.M.A. after the reconstitution of the O.E.E.C. will not be hampered by its existing provisions. It will, however, be necessary to bring the drafting of certain Articles of the E.M.A. and of its Preamble into line with the final text of the O.E.C.D. Convention and of the Decisions on the structure of the O.E.C.D.

The Preparatory Committee recommend that the Board of Management of the E.M.A. should be instructed to submit, before 30th September, 1961, the amendments to the E.M.A. needed as a result of the reconstitution of the O.E.E.C., together with any amendments which the Board may propose in the light of its comprehensive review of the operation of the E.M.A. (provided for in Article 32 of the E.M.A. and paragraph 29 *c*) of the Directives for the Application of the E.M.A.). Such amendments will take the form of a Decision of the Council insofar as they relate to parts of the E.M.A. referred to in its Article 26; otherwise, les autres cas ils feront l'objet d'un Protocole Additionnel. Les amendements résultant de la reconstitution de l'O.E.C.E. devront prendre effet dès l'entrée en vigueur de la Convention relative à l'O.C.D.E.

75. Le Comité Préparatoire recommande que le Protocole Additionnel à l'A.M.E. mentionné au paragraphe précédent prévoie que les Parties Contractantes à l'A.M.E. qui n'auront pas encore ratifié ou accepté la Convention relative à l'O.C.D.E. lorsqu'elle entrera en vigueur pourront prendre part aux décisions du Conseil de l'O.C.D.E. nécessaires à l'exécution de l'Accord. Cette clause permettrait d'éviter que, la Convention de l'O.E.C.E. n'étant plus en vigueur, les „décisions du Conseil" au sens de l'article 18 de l'A.M.E. ne puissent être prises que par les Parties Contractantes qui auraient ratifié la Convention de l'O.C.D.E. conformément à l'article 14 (3) *b*) ou *c*).

76. Il est tenu compte dans les recommandations du Comité relatives aux fonctions du Comité des Échanges de l'O.C.D.E. (*voir* chapitre 2 cidessus, paragraphe 65) des liens importants établis au titre de l'A.M.E. et des Actes y relatifs entre l'application de l'A.M.E. et la politique commerciale des pays Membres.

77. Certaines Délégations ont proposé que, à l'occasion de la reconstitution de l'O.E.C.E. en O.C.D.E., la durée maximum de deux ans prévue pour les crédits consentis sur le Fonds Européen soit prolongée. Le Comité Directeur de l'A.M.E. estime que, en raison de son importance et de ses conséquences pour le fonctionnement de l'Accord, cette question devra être étudiée dans le cadre plus large de l'examen général de l'A.M.E. auquel il doit être procédé avant le 30 septembre 1961.

Le Comité Préparatoire recommande que le Comité Directeur de l'A.M.E. reçoive mandat pour examiner toutes les dispositions de l'Accord concernant l'octroi de crédits sur le Fonds Européen au cours de son examen général de l'Accord et de soumettre toutes propositions appropriées au Conseil avant le 30 septembre 1961. Le Comité Préparatoire note que le Comité Directeur a l'intention d'entendre les représentants des Délégations qui ont proposé l'extension du délai de deux ans afin de connaître parfaitement leur point de vue sur ce problème.

B. Approbation des Actes de l'O.E.C.E. se rapportant a l'A.M.E.

78. L'approbation du Conseil de l'O.C.D.E. n'est pas nécessaire pour trois catégories d'Actes de cette nature, à savoir: (*i*) ceux qui ont déjà produit tous leur effets; (*ii*) ceux qui portent amendement à l'A.M.E. ou aux Directives pour l'application de cet Accord (car ces amendements sont devenus partie intégrante de l'A.M.E.) et (*iii*) les Décisions du Comité Directeur de l'A.M.E. (La Décision no. 2 du Comité Directeur qui établit le Règlement intérieur de cet organe a été adoptée en vertu de l'article 19 (*i*) de l'A.M.E. et c'est pourquoi elle restera en vigueur lorsque la Convention de l'O.E.C.E. cessera d'être applicable. Les pouvoirs en vertu desquels le Comité Directeur a adopté ses autres décisions lui ont été délégués par le Conseil de l'O.E.C.E. dans les Actes dont l'approbation par le Conseil de l'O.C.D.E. est recommandée plus bas, Cette approbation impliquera le maintien en vigueur des décisions du Comité Directeur fondées sur les Actes ainsi approuvés).

79. Le Comité Préparatoire recommande que le Conseil de l'O.C.D.E. approuve les Actes de l'O.E.C.E. énumérés dans l'annexe II. Il conviendra d'apporter quelques modifications de pure forme à ces Actes pour tenir compte de la reconstitution de l'O.E.C.E.; ainsi, les références à l'O.E.C.E. ou aux instances de cette Organisation qui ne seraient pas maintenues ou changeraient de dénomination devront être supprimées ou modifiées. De tels amendements devront être examinés après que la

they will take the form of a Supplementary Protocol to the E.M.A. The amendments relating to the reconstitution of the O.E.E.C. should be given effect on the date of the coming into force of the O.E.C.D. Convention.

75. The Preparatory Committee recommend that the Supplementary Protocol to the E.M.A. referred to in the preceding paragraph, should provide that those Contracting Parties to the E.M.A. which have not yet ratified or accepted the O.E.C.D. Convention when it comes into force may take part in decisions of the O.E.C.D. Council required for the execution of the E.M.A. The purpose of this is to avoid a situation in which, the O.E.E.C. Convention having ceased to apply. "decisions of the Council", within the meaning of Article 18 of the E.M.A., could be taken only by those Contracting Parties which had ratified the O.E.C.D. Convention, under its Articles 14(3) *b*) or *c*).

76. The important links, established under the E.M.A. and the related Acts, between the application of the E.M.A. and the trade policy of Member countries, are taken into account in the Committee's recommendations concerning the tasks of the Trade Committee of the O.E.C.D. (*see* Chapter 2 paragraph 65 of this part of the Report).

77. Certain Delegations have proposed that, on the occasion of the reconstitution of the O.E.E.C. as the O.E.C.D., the two-year limit for the credits granted by the European Fund should be extended. The Board of Management of the E.M.A. considers that, in view of the importance of this question and the implications for the operation of the E.M.A., it requires examination in the wider context of the review of the E.M.A. as a whole, to be carried out before 30th September, 1961.

The Preparatory Committee recommend that the Board of Management of the E.M.A. should be instructed to examine all the provisions of the E.M.A. relating to the granting of credits by the European Fund in the course of the Board's comprehensive review of the E.M.A., and to submit appropriate proposals to the Council before 30th September, 1961. The Committee note that it is the Board's intention to hear representatives of the Delegations which have proposed an extension of the two-year period for the Fund's credits, in order to obtain full information concerning their views on this problem.

B. Approval of the Acts of the O.E.E.C. relating to the E.M.A.

78. Three categories of these Acts do not require approval by the Council of the O.E.C.D.: (*i*) those which have fulfilled their purpose; (*ii*) those which amend the E.M.A. or the Directives for the Application of the E.M.A. (these amendments having become an integral part of the E.M.A. or of the Directives); and (*iii*) the Decisions of the Board of Management of the E.M.A. (Decision No. 2 of the Board of Management laying down its Rules of Procedure was adopted by virtue of Article 19 (*i*) of the E.M.A. and, for that reason, will remain in force after the O.E.E.C. Convention ceases to apply. The powers under which the other Decisions of the Board were adopted, were delegated to the Board by the O.E.E.C. Council in Acts which are recommended below for approval by the O.E.C.D. Council. This approval will imply that the Decisions of the Board based on the Acts thus approved remain effective).

79. The Preparatory Committee recommend that the Acts of the O.E.E.C. set out in Annex II should be approved by the Council of the O.E.C.D. Some amendments to these Acts, of a purely formal nature, will be required as a result of the reconstitution of the O.E.E.C.; thus, references to the O.E.E.C. or to those of its organs which are not continued or which are given a new title should be deleted or amended. Such

Réunion ministérielle aura pris des décisions au sujet des organes subsidiaires de l'O.C.D.E.

Chapitre 4

Opérations invisibles courantes et Mouvements de capitaux

80. Le Comité Préparatoire a constaté que l'accord a pu se faire dans une large mesure sur cette question et que des progrès substantiels ont été accomplis dans l'adaptation et la révision des dispositions du Code de la Libération relatif aux opérations invisibles courantes et du Code des Mouvements de Capitaux. Il a été convenu, en principe, d'étendre sans discrimination les avantages de la libération à tous les Membres du Fonds Monétaire International.

Les deux Codes de la Libération

81. Le Comité Préparatoire a convenu que la Note 1 à la Liste des rubriques libérées, qui a trait aux obligations des Membres en matière de transports maritimes, serait maintenue sans modification dans le Code révisé des opérations invisibles courantes. La déclaration générale sur la politique de transports maritimes, contenue dans la seconde partie de la Note, ne s'appliquera pas aux États-Unis parce qu'elle est, dans une certaine mesure, incompatible avec la législation américaine actuelle; la position des États-Unis sera indiquée par une observation insérée à la suite de la Note. La position de la Turquie en ce qui concerne la Note 1 reste inchangée.[1]

82. Les Gouvernements du Canada et des États-Unis n'ont pas encore achevé leur examen des projets de Codes et ils ne seront probablement pas en mesure de faire connaître leur position à temps pour la Réunion ministérielle. Dans ces conditions, il n'y pas été possible de soumettre de nouveaux Codes, étant donné notamment que leur approbation est subordonnée à un accord concernant la rédaction d'une clause dérogatoire spéciale (sur le principe de laquelle l'accord a pu se faire), à la question de savoir si les dispositions relatives aux films devront être maintenues intégralement ou seulement en partie dans le Code des opérations invisibles courantes, et au maintien dans le Code des Mouvements de Capitaux d'une clause facultative visant à sauvegarder le degré de libération atteint.

83. N'étant donc pas à même de présenter des projets de Codes révisés, le Comité Préparatoire recommande:

a) que son mandat soit prorogé de façon à lui permettre d'adapter et de réviser les dispositions du Code de la Libération traitant des opérations invisibles courantes et le Code des Mouvements de Capitaux afin:

(*i*) de tenir compte des conditions nouvelles qui prévaudront après l'institution de l'O.C.D.E.;

(*ii*) d'étendre les avantages de la libération à tous les membres du Fonds Monétaire International sur une base non discriminatoire;

(*iii*) de permettre à tous les Membres de l'O.C.D.E. d'adhérer aux Codes;

b) que, pour assurer la continuité en attendant l'approbation des Codes révisés par le Conseil de l'O.C.D.E., les Actes suivants soient prorogés provisoirement entre les Membres de l'O.E.C.E.

- Code de la Libération, Titres II, III, V, VI, VII, Annexes B et C. Édition du Code de la Libération mise à jour au 1er juillet 1960;

---

[1] C/M(57)10, Point 79.

amendments should be considered after the Ministerial Meeting has decided on the subsidiary organs of the O.E.C.D.

Chapter 4

Current Invisible Operations and Capital Movements

80. The Preparatory Committee have noted that a large measure of agreement has been reached on this subject and that substantial progress has been made in the adaptation and revision of the provisions of the Code of Liberalisation dealing with current invisibles and of the Capital Movements Code. It is agreed in principle to extend the benefits of liberalisation to all members of the International Monetary Fund on a non-discriminatory basis.

The Two Codes of Liberalisation

81. The Preparatory Committee agreed that Note 1 to the List of liberalised items which deals with Members' obligations in connection with maritime transport would be retained unchanged in the revised Current Invisibles Code. The general statement on shipping policy in the second part of the Note will not apply to the United States because it is to some extent in conflict with existing United States legislation, and the United States position will be indicated by a remark following the Note. The position of Turkey concerning Note 1 remains unchanged.[1]

82. The Canadian and United States authorities have not yet completed their review of the draft Codes and will probably not be able to formulate their position in time for the Ministerial Meeting. In these circumstances it has not been possible to submit new Codes, since these are in particular subject to agreement on the drafting of a clause of special derogation (on the principle of which agreement has been reached) on the question whether the provisions regarding films should be retained fully or only in part in the Current Invisibles Code, and on the retention in the Capital Movements Code of a hortatory provision to safeguard existing liberalisation.

83. As they are thus unable to put forward drafts of the revised Codes the Preparatory Committee recommend:

a) the extension of their mandate to adapt and revise the provisions of the Code of Liberalisation dealing with current invisibles, and the Capital Movements Code in order to:

(*i*) take account of the new conditions prevailing after the O.E.C.D. is established;

(*ii*) extend the benefits of liberalisation to all members of the International Monetary Fund on a non-discriminatory basis; and

(*iii*) enable all Members of the O.E.C.D. to adhere to them:

b) that, in order to ensure continuity pending approval of the revised Codes by the Council of the O.E.C.D., the following Acts should be continued provisionally among Members of the O.E.E.C.:

- Code of Liberalisation, Parts II, III, V, VI, VII; Annexes B and C. Edition of the Code of Liberalisation brought up to date on 1st July, 1960.

[1] *Cf.* C/M(57)10, item 79.

- Code de la Libération des Mouvements de Capitaux. – Édition du Code de la Libération des Mouvements de Capitaux amendée et mise à jour en juin 1960;
- Décision du Conseil en date du 14 octobre 1960 portant amendement au Code de la Libération des Mouvements de Capitaux [C(60)194 (Final)];
- Section VI de la Recommandation du Conseil relative aux Échanges et aux Paiements, en date du 2 février 1960 [C(60)35], amendée comme suit:

  „Les avantages découlant de la libération des transactions invisibles courantes et des mouvements de capitaux, en application du Code de la Libération et du Code de la Libération des Mouvements de Capitaux, devraient être étendus sur une base non-discriminatoire à tous les membres du Fonds Monétaire International".

AUTRES ACTES

84. Le Comité Préparatoire recommande en outre que les Actes suivants de l'O.E.C.E. soient prorogés sans modification. Il serait entendu que le Secrétariat apporterait à ces textes, lors de leur édition, les amendements de forme rendus nécessaires par l'entrée en vigueur de la Convention sur l'O.C.D.E. et du Mémorandum d'Accord sur l'application de l'Article 15 de la Convention, ainsi que par la révision de la structure institutionnelle.

Actes traitant de la situation spéciale de la Grèce, de l'Islande, de l'Espagne et de la Turquie

- Résolution du Conseil en date du 30 juillet 1957 concernant le recours de l'Islande à l'article 20 *a*) du Code de la Libération [C/M(57)25, Point 246 *a*)].
- Décision du Conseil en date du 17 juin 1960 concernant l'application à l'Espagne des dispositions du Titre II du Code de la Libération. (Recours à l'article 20 *a*) dudit Code). [C(60)95 (Final)].
- Décision du Conseil en date du 4 décembre 1959 concernant l'application à la Grèce, à l'Islande, à l'Espagne et à la Turquie des dispositions du Code de la Libération des Mouvements de Capitaux [C(59) 79 (Final)].

Mandats du Comité des Transactions Invisibles concernant l'extension de la libération

- Résolution du Conseil chargeant le Comité des Transactions Invisibles d'étudier la possibilité d'éliminer, en matière de transports routiers, les restrictions sur les transports internationaux et les transports intérieurs liés au trafic international. [19 octobre 1956: C/M(56)37, Point 328 *d*), et 30 juillet 1958: C/M (58) 25, Partie I, Point 236].
- Résolution du Conseil chargeant le Comité des Transactions Invisibles de poursuivre ses travaux concernant les assurances, en s'attachant particulièrement aux points suivants:

  (*i*) les accords de validation en matière de sécurité sociale et d'assurance sociale;

  (*ii*) la libération des assurances couvertes par la rubrique chapitre III, A/3: „Toutes autres assurances";

  (*iii*) l'établissement de critères internationaux communs de solvabilité des assureurs;

  (*iv*) la création d'un bureau international qui jouerait le rôle de centre d'information ou délivrerait des certificats de solvabilité reconnus par tous les pays.

  [7 février 1958: C/M (58) 4, Point 34 *g*)].

- Code of Liberalisation of Capital Movements. Edition of the Code of Liberalisation of Capital Movements and amendments thereto brought up to date in June, 1960.
- Decision of the Council of 14th October, 1960, amending the Code of Liberalisation of Capital Movements. [C(60)194(Final)];

- Section VI of Recommendation of the Council on Trade and Payments of 2nd February, 1960, [C(60)35] amended as follows:

  "The benefits of liberalisation of current invisible transactions and capital movements deriving from the Code of Liberalisation and from the Code of Liberalisation of Capital Movements should be extended on a non-discriminatory basis to all members of the International Monetary Fund".

OTHER ACTS

84. The Preparatory Committee recommend furthermore that the following Acts of the O.E.E.C. should be continued unchanged. It would be understood that amendments of form necessitated as a result of the coming into force of the O.E.C.D. Convention and the Memorandum of Understanding on the Application of Article 15 of the Convention, as well as the revision of the institutional structure, would be made by the Secretariat as editing adaptations.

Acts dealing with the Special Position of Greece, Iceland, Spain and Turkey

- Resolution of the Council of 30th July, 1957, concerning the invocation by Iceland of Article 20 *a*) of the Code of Liberalisation (C/M(57)25 item 246 *a*)].
- Decision of the Council of 17th June, 1960, concerning the Application to Spain of Part II of the Code of Liberalisation, (Invocation of Article 20 *a*) of that Code). [C(60)95(Final)].
- Decision of the Council of 4th December, 1959, concerning the Application to Greece, Iceland, Spain and Turkey of the Provisions of the Code of Liberalisation of Capital Movements. [C(59)79(Final)].

Mandates of the Committee for Invisible Transactions concerning Further Liberalisation

- Resolution of the Council instructing the Committee for Invisible Transactions to study the possibility of removing, in the field of road transport, restrictions on international carriage and domestic carriage connected with international carriage. [19th October, 1956; C/M(56)37 item 328 *d*), and 30th July, 1958; C/M(58)25, Part I, item 236].
- Resolution of the Council instructing the Committee for Invisible Transactions to continue studies in the insurance field, especially with regard to:

(*i*) validation agreements in connection with social security and social insurance;

(*ii*) liberalisation of insurance falling under the item Chapter III, A/3, All other insurance;

(*iii*) the establishment of a common international standard of solvency for insurers;

(*iv*) the establishment of an international bureau to act as clearing house for information or to issue internationally acceptable certificates of solvency.

[17th February, 1958; C/M(58)4, item 34 *g*)].

85. Le Comité Préparatoire recommande enfin que l'Acte suivant soit prorogé sous réserve des amendements indiqués ci-après:

Acte traitant de la position spéciale de la Grèce

– Décision du Conseil en date du 21 mai 1954, abrogeant les articles 3*d*) et 20 *d*) du Code de la Libération [C (54) 110 (Final)].

a) Le paragraphe 1 de la Décision prévoyait l'abrogation du paragraphe *d*) de l'article 3 et du paragraphe *d*) de l'article 20 du Code tels qu'ils existaient au moment où la Décision a été adoptée. Ce paragraphe est donc désormais superflu et il conviendrait de le supprimer.

b) Il conviendrait aussi de supprimer au paragraphe 2 la référence à l'article 2 du Code, puisque le Titre I est supprimé, et de corriger les références aux articles 13 et 19, pour tenir compte du remplacement de l'ancien Code de la Libération par le nouveau Code de la Libération des Opérations Invisibles Courantes.

c) Au paragraphe 3, la référence au Comité de Direction des Échanges devrait être amendée en fonction des modifications de la structure institutionnelle résultant du passage de l'O.E.C.E. à l'O.C.D.E.

86. De plus, le Comité attire l'attention sur le fait suivant: si, par la suite, le Conseil décide de proroger sous sa forme actuelle ou sous une forme amendée l'*Acte traitant de la situation spéciale de la Turquie:*

– Résolution du Conseil en date du 17 juin 1960, relative à la suspension, jusqu'au 31 décembre 1960, de la procédure de notification et d'examen résultant du recours de la Turquie aux dispositions de l'article 20 *a*) du Code de la Libération [C/M (60) 14, Point 113 B *d*)],

qui viendra à expiration en décembre 1960, il faudra, pour décider du maintien de cet Acte dans l'O.C.D.E., suivre la même procédure que celle qui sera appliquée à tous les Actes adoptés par l'O.E.C.E. entre le 1er octobre 1960 et la date d'entrée en vigueur de la Convention sur l'O.C.D.E.

87. Il a été convenu que la question d'une Convention multilatérale pour la protection des investissements étrangers devrait continuer à être étudiée par l'O.C.D.E.

Chapitre 5

Agriculture, pêche et alimentation

88. Dans la Partie I de ce rapport, le Comité Préparatoire a convenu que les activités de l'Organisation en matière d'agriculture, de pêche et d'alimentation devraient être renforcées et intégrées étroitement aux autres activités de l'Organisation orientées vers les objectifs de la Convention. Dans ce but, des liaisons étroites devront exister entre l'organisme ou les organismes agricoles et les Comités qui seront chargés des politiques économiques, des questions commerciales et de l'aide aux pays en voie de développement économique, tout en maintenant l'unité de travail nécessaire dans le secteur de l'agriculture, de la pêche et de l'alimentation.

89. L'examen des Actes relatifs à ce secteur a amené le Comité Préparatoire à recommander que les activités suivantes continuent à figurer dans le programme de travail dont l'exécution sera assurée par l'organisme ou les organismes agricoles de l'Organisation, sans pour autant exclure la possibilité d'y ajouter ultérieurement d'autres activités en fonction de directives résultant de nécessités nouvelles:

a) Confrontations et consultations en matière de politique agricole et alimentaire et de politique de pêche sous leurs différents aspects afin de faciliter l'évolution harmonieuse de ces politiques entre pays Membres,

85. The Preparatory Committee recommend finally that the following Act should be continued subject to the amendments indicated below:

Act dealing with the Special Position of Greece

- Decision of the Council of 21st May, 1954, repealing Article 3 *d*) and 20 *d*) of the Code of Liberalisation [C(54)110(Final)].

a) Paragraph 1 of the Decision repealed paragraph *d*) of Article 3 and paragraph *d*) of Article 20 of the Code as they were when the Decision was adopted. The paragraph is thus redundant and should be deleted.

b) Reference in paragraph 2 to Article 2 of the Code should be deleted consequential to the discontinuation of its Part I, and the reference to Articles 13 and 19 should be adapted to the substitution of the new Code of Liberalisation of Current Invisible Operations for the old Code of Liberalisation.

c) The reference to the Steering Board for Trade in paragraph 3 should be amended in the light of the revision of the institutional structure resulting from the passage from the O.E.E.C. to the O.E.C.D.

86. The Preparatory Committee draw attention to the fact, moreover, that if the Council decides in due course upon the renewal in its present or in an amended form of the *Act dealing with the Special Position of Turkey:*

- Resolution of the Council of 17th June, 1960, concerning the suspension until 31st December, 1960, of the notification and examination procedure arising out of the invocation by Turkey of Article 20 *a*) of the Code of Liberalisation [C/M(60)14, item 113 B *d*)],

which will expire in December 1960, the same procedure will have to apply in respect of its retention in the O.E.C.D. as that applying to all Acts of the O.E.E.C. which are adopted between 1st October, 1960, and the date on which the O.E.C.D. Convention enters into force.

87. It was agreed that the question of a multilateral Convention for the protection of foreign investments should continue to be studied by the O.E.C.D.

Chapter 5

Agriculture, Fisheries and Food

88. In Part I of this Report, the Preparatory Committee agreed that activities of the Organisation in the Agriculture, Fisheries and Food sector should be strengthened and closely integrated with the Organisation's other activities in pursuit of the objectives of the Convention. For this purpose it will be desirable to have close links between the agricultural body or bodies and the Committees which will be responsible for economic policies, trade questions, and aid to countries in the process of economic development, while at the same time maintaining the necessary unity of work in the sector of Agriculture, Fisheries and Food.

89. As a result of the review of the Acts in this sector, the Committee recommend that the following activities should continue to feature in the programme of work to be carried out by the agricultural body or bodies of the Organisation, without, however, excluding the possibility that other activities might be added at a later stage in the light of directives resulting from new requirements:

a) confrontation and consultations on agricultural, food and fishery policies under their different aspects with a view to promoting the harmonious development of these policies among Member countries in conformément aux objectifs de l'Organisation et aux engagements pris dans le cadre de la Convention.

b) Examen de la situation d'ensemble de l'agriculture et de la pêche des pays Membres et de ses perspectives, l'examen de l'évolution de l'offre et de la demande y compris.

c) Études des possibilités d'améliorer la commercialisation et la distribution des produits agricoles et alimentaires et de ceux de la pêche, en vue de déterminer des mesures à adopter sur le plan national et international; études similaires dans le domaine des moyens de production.

d) Examen de la situation des marchés des principaux produits de l'agriculture et de la pêche et élaboration, en coopération avec le Comité des Échanges si nécessaire, de propositions de mesures appelées à remédier à la situation en cas de difficultés sur les marchés en question.

e) Examen, en liaison et en coopération avec le Comité des Échanges, des problèmes commerciaux directement liés aux problèmes agricoles et de pêche, et relevant du mandat de l'Organisation en matière commerciale, tel qu'il est décrit dans le présent rapport.

f) Contribution dans le domaine agricole aux activités économiques, commerciales et techniques des autres organes de l'Organisation destinées à atteindre les objectifs de la Convention concernant les pays et, dans des cas particuliers, les régions en voie de développement économique.

g) Actions destinées à faciliter une meilleure utilisation des facteurs de production et à stimuler le progrès technique dans les secteurs de l'agriculture et de la pêche, y compris la commercialisation et la distribution. La nature et la portée de ces activités ainsi que la manière dont elles seront exécutées seront décidées ultérieurement. Dans la mesure où elles auraient des conséquences budgétaires, des règles adéquates seront établies au paragraphe 39 de la Partie I.

90. Le Comité a examiné les Actes et les Rapports relatifs aux politiques agricoles en Europe et en Amérique du Nord, le dernier programme de travail des organes agricoles ainsi que les procédures de confrontation et de consultation élaborées dans l'O.E.C.E. Bien qu'il ne considère pas nécessaire le maintien de ces Actes comme tels, le Comité Préparatoire estime que l'ensemble de ces travaux a été très utile et recommande que les principes et méthodes qui sont contenus dans ces Actes, dans la mesure où ils sont compatibles avec les objectifs et la structure de l'Organisation, servent de guide aux travaux futurs de l'O.C.D.E. Les aspects commerciaux de ces Actes devront être examinés par l'Organisation en vue de déterminer dans quelle mesure et sous quelle forme l'expérience acquise pourrait être utilisée par l'O.C.D.E.

91. En ce qui concerne les deux Actes suivants: Résolution du Comité Ministériel de l'Agriculture et de l'Alimentation relative à la poursuite des travaux dans le secteur des produits laitiers [CMA(58)13] et le texte d'application relatif à la procédure d'urgence, établi par le Comité des Suppléants [CSA(58)39], le Comité considère qu'il n'y a pas lieu de retenir ces Actes, mais recommande que la procédure telle qu'elle est définie dans ces Actes, qui assure un examen rapide de la situation du marché des produits laitiers en cas de risque de crise, soit retenue pour les pays Membres européens. Ceci ne préjuge pas de la pleine participation des États-Unis et du Canada aux discussions.

92. Le Comité recommande le maintien de l'Acte suivant:

– Résolution du Conseil relative aux politiques des pays Membres en matière de pêche [C(60)178].

Il recommande en outre le maintien des Actes particuliers suivants qui, bien que de portée limitée, présentent un certain intérêt technique:

– Décision du Conseil relative à l'établissement d'un système de l'O.E.C.E. pour la certification variétable des semences fourragères destinées au commerce international [C (58)106(Final)];

accordance with the objectives of the Organisation and the undertakings entered into under the Convention;

b) examination of the overall situation of agriculture and fisheries in Member countries and of the prospects including examination of the trend of supply and demand;

c) study of the possibilities for improving the marketing and distribution of agricultural, fishery and food products with a view to determining measures which could be adopted nationally and internationally; similar studies in the field of means of production;

d) surveys of the market situation for the main agricultural and fisheries products and formulation, in co-operation where necessary with the Trade Committee, of proposals for remedial measures in the event of market difficulties;

e) examination in liaison and co-operation with the Trade Committee of trade problems directly connected with agricultural and fishery policies and falling within the mandate of the Organisation in trade matters as described in this Report;

f) assistance in the agricultural field to the economic, trade and technical activities of other bodies of the Organisation in implementing the aims of the Organisation concerning countries, or in special cases, areas in process of economic development;

g) practical work designed to promote a better use of production factors and to promote technical progress in the sectors of agriculture and fisheries including marketing and distribution. The nature and extent of such activities and the way in which they will be performed will be decided later. Insofar as they have budgetary implications appropriate rules will be drawn up in accordance with the principles agreed in Part I, paragraph 39.

90. The Committee examined the Acts and the Reports on Agricultural Policies in Europe and North America, the latest programme of work of the agricultural bodies as well as the confrontation and consultation procedures developed in the O.E.E.C. While they do not consider it necessary to retain these Acts as such, the Preparatory Committee consider that this work, taken as a whole, has been very useful and recommend that the principles and methods which are included in these Acts, to the extent that they are relevant to the objectives and structure of the Organisation, should serve to guide the future work of the O.E.C.D. The trade aspects of these acts should be examined by the Organisation with a view to determining to what extent and in what form this experience might be utilised by the O.E.C.D.

91. With regard to the two following Acts: Resolution of the Ministerial Committee for Agriculture and Food relating to the continuance of work in the dairy products sector [CMA(58)13] and the emergency procedure established by the Committee of Deputies in conformity with that Resolution [CSA(58)39] the Committee consider that these Acts should not be retained but recommend that the procedure as set forth in these Acts ensuring speedy consideration of the situation in the dairy market in the event of a threatened crisis should be retained among European Members, without prejudice to the full participation of the United States and Canada in the discussions.

92. The Committee recommend the retention of the following Act:

- Resolution of the Council relating to the policies of Member countries in fishery matters [C(60)178)].

Furthermore, they recommend the retention of the following specific Acts which, although they are of limited scope, have a certain technical value:

- Decision of the Council concerning the establishment of an O.E.E.C. scheme for the varietal certification of herbage seed moving in international trade [C(58)106(Final)];

- **Décision du Conseil relative à l'établissement d'un Code normalisé de l'O.E.C.E. pour les essais officiels de tracteurs agricoles [C(59)76 (Final)];**
- **Résolution du Comité des Suppléants relative aux indices des prix agricoles [CSA(57)10 (Final)];**
- **Résolution du Comité Ministériel de l'Agriculture et de l'Alimentation relative à l'amélioration des méthodes de prévision de la production porcine à court terme [CMA(58)12 (Final)];**
- Résolution du Comité Ministériel de l'Agriculture et de l'Alimentation relative aux statistiques de la main-d'œuvre agricole [CMA(57)8 (Final)].

Chapitre 6

Science et technologie

93. Le Comité Préparatoire recommande le maintien des Actes suivants:

a) *Recommandation C(56)62 (Final)* tendant à développer la coopération internationale dans le domaine de la recherche appliquée.

b) *Recommandation C(58)143* aux Organisations nationales chargées des questions de personnel scientifique et technique.

94. Le Comité Préparatoire ne recommande pas le maintien de la *Recommandation C(58)142*, mais il estime que les pays Membres de l'Organisation devraient utiliser les recensements généraux pour recueillir des informations sur le personnel scientifique et technique, ainsi que l'indiquait cette Recommandation en ce qui concerne les recensements prévus en 1960.

Chapitre 7

Énergie nucléaire

95. Le Comité Préparatoire recommande le maintien de la *Décision C (57) 255* créant l'Agence Européenne pour l'Énergie Nucléaire avec l'amendement suivant:

> ,,*Article 21*
> Les dispositions du Protocole Additionnel no. 1 à la Convention relative à l'Organisation de Coopération et de Développement Économiques s'appliquent à la représentation de la Communauté Européenne de l'Énergie Atomique (EURATOM) dans l'Agence et son Comité de Direction, ainsi qu'à la participation de la Commission de ladite Communauté aux travaux de l'Agence et de son Comité de Direction".

L'adoption de cette Décision par le Conseil de l'Organisation avec l'approbation du Canada et des États-Unis n'aura pas pour effet de modifier le statut actuel de Membre Associé que ces deux pays ont à l'égard de l'Agence.

96. Le Comité Préparatoire recommande, en outre, le maintien des Actes suivants:

a) *Décision C(59)109(Final)* sur l'adoption de normes de base pour la protection contre les radiations.

b) *Résolution C(60)20(Final)* portant désignation des membres du Tribunal créé par la Convention sur l'établissement d'un contrôle de sécurité dans le domaine de l'énergie nucléaire.

c) *Décision du Conseil C/M(60)20* approuvant le Projet d'Accord entre l'O.E.C.E. et l'Agence Internationale de l'Énergie Atomique figurant en annexe au Rapport C(60)141.

- Decision of the Council concerning the establishment of an O.E.E.C. Standard Code for the official testing of agricultural tractors [C(59)76 (Final)];
- Resolution of the Committee of Deputies on farm price indices [CSA(57) 10(Final)]; Resolution of the Ministerial Committee for Agriculture and Food concerning the improvement of short-term forecasting methods for pig production [CMA(58)12(Final)];
- Resolution of the Ministerial Committee for Agriculture and Food on Agricultural manpower statistics [CMA(57)8(Final)].

Chapter 6

Science and Technology

93. The Preparatory Committee recommend the retention of the following Acts:

a) *Recommendation C(56)62)(Final*) on international co-operation in the field of applied research.

b) *Recommendation C(58)143* on the national Organisations responsible for questions of scientific and technical personnel.

94. While not recommending the retention of *Recommendation C(58) 142*, the Preparatory Committee think that Member countries of the Organisation should use the general census to collect information about scientific and technical personnel, as indicated in that Recommendation with regard to the censuses planned for 1960.

Chapter 7

Nuclear Energy

95. The Preparatory Committee recommend the retention of *Decision C(57)255* establishing the European Nuclear Energy Agency with the following amendment:

"*Article 21*

The provisions of Supplementary Protocol No. 1 to the Convention on the Organisation for Economic Co-operation and Development shall apply to the representation of the European Atomic Energy Community (EURATOM) in the Agency and in its Steering Committee as well as to the participation of the Commission of the said Community in the work of the Agency and of its Steering Committee".

The adoption of this Decision by the Council of the Organisation with the approval of Canada and the United States will not have the effect of modifying the present status of these two countries as Associate Members of the Agency.

96. The Preparatory Committee further recommend the retention of the following Acts:

a) *Decision C(59)109(Final*) on the adoption of radiation protection norms.

b) *Resolution C(60)20(Final*) nominating the members of the Tribunal set up by the Convention on the establishment of a Security Control in the field of nuclear energy.

c) *Council Decision C/M(60)20* approving the draft agreement between the O.E.E.C. and the International Atomic Energy Agency set out in the Annex to Report C(60)141.

97. Les trois Actes indiqués ci-dessus peuvent ne pas s'appliquer aux États-Unis, la question de leur application faisant encore l'objet d'un examen par les autorités américaines. Ils ne s'appliquent pas au Canada.

Chapitre 8

Énergie

DÉCISION GÉNÉRALE

98. Le Comité Préparatoire recommande le maintien de la *Recommandation C(59)172* concernant les mesures à prendre dans le domaine de l'énergie et portant création d'une Commission Consultative de l'Énergie et d'un Comité de l'Énergie. Le Comité Préparatoire recommande que les dispositions de cet Acte qui concernent la structure soient amendées conformément aux décisions qui seront prises ultérieurement en matière de structure.

99. Cet Acte ne s'applique pas, sous sa forme actuelle, au Canada et aux États-Unis qui participeront toutefois dans les cas appropriés aux activités de l'Organisation dans le domaine de l'énergie.

PÉTROLE

100. Le Comité Préparatoire estime qu'il n'est pas nécessaire de maintenir la *Décision C(53)196(Final)*, amendée par la *Décision C(54)92(Final)*, sur la procédure à suivre pour la coordination dans l'industrie du pétrole, qui ne correspond plus aux données de la situation actuelle. Il recommande cependant que les pays Membres de l'Organisation fournissent les renseignements nécessaires concernant leurs projets de raffinage à l'organe compétent de cette Organisation qui transmettra ses observations au Conseil en tant que de besoin.

101. Le Comité Préparatoire propose de maintenir les *recommandations du Rapport C(58)137* sur les stocks et le stockage du pétrole (approuvé dans le document C/M(58)21, Point 195). Ces recommandations ne s'appliquent pas au Canada et aux États-Unis qui, en tant que pays producteurs, ne sont pas placés dans la même situation que la presque totalité des pays Membres de l'O.E.C.E.

102. Le Comité recommande aussi le maintien de la *Recommandation C(60)83(Final)* concernant la répartition des approvisionnements en pétrole en cas de crise et les *Conclusions du Rapport C(60)153* sur la méthode de répartition (approuvé dans le document C/M(60)20, Point 177). Ces Actes ne s'appliquent pas au Canada et aux États-Unis en raison de la situation particulière de ces pays du point de vue des approvisionnements en pétrole. Ces deux pays sont néanmoins prêts à continuer de collaborer avec les pays Membres au cas où ceux-ci auraient à faire face à une crise d'approvisionnement.

103. Le Comité Préparatoire recommande le maintien d'un Comité du Pétrole qui sera notamment chargé de la mise en œuvre des recommandations ci-dessus.

ÉLECTRICITÉ

104. Le Comité Préparatoire recommande le maintien de la *Décision C(56)183* relative aux fournitures occasionnelles et saisonnières d'énergie électrique entre pays à réseaux interconnectés, amendée par la *Décision C(59)125(Final)*. Ces Actes ne s'appliquent pas au Canada et aux États-Unis.

105. Le Comité Préparatoire est convenu de ne pas maintenir la *Recommandation C(56)119(Final)* relative à la production d'électricité

97. The three Acts specified above may not apply to the United States, the question of their application to the United States still being under consideration by the United States authorities. They will not apply to Canada.

Chapter 8

Energy

General Decision

98. The Preparatory Committee recommend the retention of *Recommendation C(59)172* concerning measures to be taken in the field of energy and establishing an Energy Advisory Commission and an Energy Committee. The Preparatory Committee recommend that any provision of this Act relating to structure should be amended in accordance with future decisions concerning structure.

99. Although the Act in its present form will not apply to Canada and the United States, they will take part as appropriate in the energy activities of the Organisation.

Oil

100. The Preparatory Committee do not think it necessary to retain *Decision C(53)196(Final)* amended by Decision C(54)92(Final) on the procedure to be applied in respect of co-ordination in the oil industry; this Decision is no longer appropriate to the current facts. The Committee nevertheless recommend that Member countries of the Organisation should furnish appropriate information about their refinery projects to the competent body of the Organisation which will submit comments to the Council where necessary.

101. The Preparatory Committee recommend the retention of the *recommendations in the Report C(58)137* on oil stocks and storage capacity (approved in C/M(58)21, item 195). These recommendations will not apply to Canada and the United States who as producing countries are in a different situation from almost all the O.E.E.C. Member countries.

102. The Committee also recommend the retention of *Recommendation C(60)83(Final)* concerning the apportionment of oil supplies in an emergency and the *conclusions of the Report C(60)153* on the method of apportionment (approved in C/M(60)20 item, 177). These Acts will not apply to Canada and the United States in view of the special position of these two countries in the matter of oil supplies. These two countries are nevertheless ready to continue to co-operate with other Member countries if they have to face a supply crisis.

103. The Preparatory Committee recommend the maintenance of an Oil Committee to be responsible, *inter alia*, for implementing the above recommendations.

Electricity

104. The Preparatory Committee recommend the retention of *Decision C(56)183* relating to occasional and seasonal supplies of electric power between inter-connected countries, amended by *Decision C(59)125(Final)*. These Acts will not apply to Canada and the United States.

105. The Preparatory Committee agreed not to retain *Recommendation C(56)119(Final)* relating to the generation of electricity in backpressure

dans les installarions à contre-pression mais estime qu'il pourrait être utile qu'une Recommandation semblable soit adoptée par l'Organisation.

CHARBON

106. Le Comité Préparatoire estime qu'il n'est pas nécessaire de maintenir la *Résolution C(51)152(Final)* sur la distribution des combustibles solides, qui portait création du Sous-Comité des Approvisionnements et de la Distribution du Comité du Charbon. Il considère que l'Organisation a la compétence nécessaire pour procéder, en tant que de besoin et compte tenu des obligations internationales de ses Membres, à une répartition des combustibles solides entre les pays Membres européens en cas de pénurie d'approvisionnements.

Chapitre 9

Industrie

DÉCISION GÉNÉRALE RELATIVE AUX INVESTISSEMENTS

107. Le Comité Préparatoire considère qu'il n'est pas nécessaire de maintenir la *Décision C(49)123(Final)* relative à la coordination des investissements ainsi que la *Décision CE(49)76(Final)* relative aux Directives du Comité de la Sidérurgie.

108. Ces deux Décisions ont permis d'effectuer au sein de l'O.E.C.E. un échange d'information dans certains secteurs (pétrochimie, azote, ciment) et de procéder en outre à une confrontation des projets d'investissements dans les industries de la sidérurgie et du pétrole.

109. Le Comité Préparatoire estime qu'un échange régulier d'information et une discussion en commun des projets d'investissement devraient avoir lieu au sein de l'Organisation. Il recommande en conséquence que le Conseil de l'Organisation prenne des dispositions en vue d'assurer la poursuite de ces activités dans l'industrie sidérurgique et dans les autres secteurs industriels et énergétiques où elles se révéleraient nécessaires.

ÉQUIPEMENT

110. Le Comité Préparatoire recommande le maintien de la *Recommandation C(52)137* amendée par la *Résolution C(55)139(Final)* concernant la production de matériel lourd pour centrales électriques.

111. Ces Actes s'appliquent au Canada avec une réserve en ce qui concerne les dispositions prévoyant que les Gouvernements feront des recommandations aux entreprises d'intérêt public.

PLOMB ET ZINC

112. Le Comité Préparatoire estime qu'il n'est pas nécessaire de maintenir la *Recommandation C(58)49(Final)* relative à la production minière de plomb et de zinc. Il a noté que depuis l'adoption de cette Recommandation le déséquilibre persistant du marché mondial a conduit les Nations Unies à créer un Groupe d'Étude du Plomb et du Zinc. Ce Groupe se préoccupe des mesures propres à rétablir un équilibre sain entre l'offre et la demande. Le Comité Préparatoire considère qu'il est souhaitable que les pays Membres de l'Organisation procèdent, dans ce domaine, à une discussion de leurs points de vue et fassent tous leurs efforts pour encourager les échanges internationaux de ces métaux.

plant, but thought it might be useful for a similar Recommendation to be adopted by the Organisation.

COAL

106. The Preparatory Committee do not think it necessary to retain *Resolution C(51)152(Final)* on the distribution of solid fuels creating the Supply and Distribution Sub-Committee of the Coal Committee. They consider that the Organisation is competent to organise distribution of solid fuels as necessary, and in the light of the international obligations of its Members, between European Member countries in the event of a critical shortage of supplies.

Chapter 9

Industry

GENERAL DECISION ON INVESTMENTS

107. The Preparatory Committee do not think it necessary to retain *Decision C(49)123(Final)* relating to the co-ordination of investments or *Decision CE(49)76(Final)* relating to the directives for the Iron and Steel Committee.

108. These two Decisions made it possible to establish, within the O.E.E.C., an exchange of information in certain sectors (petroleum chemicals, nitrogen and cement) and, in addition, to proceed to a confrontation of investment projects in the iron and steel and oil industries.

109. The Preparatory Committee think that a regular exchange of information and a joint discussion of investment projects should be carried out within the Organisation. They therefore recommend that the Council of the Organisation should take steps to pursue these activities in the iron and steel industry and in such other industrial and energy sectors as prove necessary.

MACHINERY

110. The Preparatory Committee recommend the retention of *Recommendation C(52)137* amended by *Resolution C(55)139(Final)* concerning the production of heavy equipment for electric power stations.

111. These Acts will apply to Canada subject to a reservation with respect to provisions calling upon Governments to make recommendations to public utility enterprises.

LEAD AND ZINC

112. The Preparatory Committee do not think it necessary to retain *Recommendation C(58)49(Final)* relating to the output of lead and zinc mines. They note that since the adoption of this Recommendation, the persistent disequilibrium of the world market has led the United Nations to set up a Lead and Zinc Study Group. This Group is concerned with appropriate measures to restore sound equilibrium between supply and demand. The Preparatory Committee think it desirable that Member countries of the Organisation should discuss their points of view in this field and should do everything possible to encourage international trade in these metals.

INDUSTRIE TEXTILE

113. Le Comité Préparatoire estime qu'il n'est pas nécessaire de maintenir la *Résolution C(58)82(Final)* relative au Rapport sur l'avenir de l'industrie cotonnière européenne qui a été prise en considération par les pays Membres et assez largement suivie. Il pense toutefois que la situation de l'industrie textile devrait retenir l'attention de l'Organisation, au cas où des problèmes particuliers se feraient jour.

TRANSPORTS MARITIMES

114. Le Comité Préparatoire recommande le maintien de la *Recommandation C(59)198(Final)* sur l'application du principe de la liberté des transports maritimes en cas d'accord d'aide financière. Cet Acte peut ne pas s'appliquer au Canada. Cet Acte ne s'applique pas aux États-Unis.

Chapitre 10

Main-d'oeuvre

115. Le Comité Préparatoire recommande le maintien des neuf Actes qui figurent dans la liste ci-dessous et qui concernent la libération des mouvements de main-d'œuvre. Ces Actes ne s'appliquent pas à la Turquie. Ces Actes, à l'exception de la Recommandation C(59)273(Final), ne s'appliquent pas aux États-Unis. Ils peuvent ne pas s'appliquer au Canada qui réexaminera sa position, compte tenu de la consolidation des Actes prévue au paragraphe 116 ci-après.

a) *Décision C(56)258* régissant l'emploi des ressortissants des pays Membres. Cet Acte ne s'applique pas au Portugal.

b) *Recommandation C(55)295(Final)* concernant les réglementations et pratiques administratives régissant l'introduction et l'emploi des ressortissants des pays Membres.

c) *Recommandation C(57)37(Final)* relative à l'abolition des visas d'entrée pour les ressortissants des pays Membres rejoignant leur lieu d'emploi.

d) *Recommandations C(57)79* et *C(59)273(Final)* concernant la suppression des restrictions à l'emploi en faveur de certaines catégories de ressortissants des pays Membres. Le second Acte ne s'applique pas au Portugal et à la Grèce.

e) *Recommandation C(58)196(Final)* relative aux réglementations et pratiques administratives régissant le mouvement et l'emploi des réfugiés.

f) *Recommandation C(59)272(Final)* relative aux réglementations et pratiques administratives régissant l'introduction et l'emploi des familles de travailleurs ressortissants des pays Membres.

g) *Recommandation C(60)65(Final)* relative aux réglementations et pratiques administratives régissant les mouvements et l'emploi des réfugiés.

h) *Recommandation C(60)113(Final)* relative au système de compensation internationale des offres et des demandes d'emploi. Cet Acte ne s'applique pas à l'Irlande.

116. Le Comité Préparatoire recommande que les Actes ci-dessus, à l'exception de l'Acte mentionné sous *a*), soient consolidés en un seul Acte.

117. Le Comité Préparatoire recommande aussi le maintien des huit Actes figurant dans la liste ci-après. Les Actes indiqués aux alinéas *a*) à *e*) ci-dessous ne s'appliquent pas aux États-Unis. L'Acte indiqué à l'alinéa *c*) ne s'applique pas au Canada. Les Actes indiqués à l'alinéa *a*) s'appliquent au Canada avec une réserve visant les dispositions de la

TEXTILE INDUSTRY

113. The Preparatory Committee do not think it necessary to retain *Resolution C(58)82(Final)* relating to the Report on the future of the European cotton industry which has been noted by the Member countries and quite widely followed. The Committee nevertheless think that the situation of the textile industry should receive the attention of the Organisation, should any particular problem arise.

MARITIME TRANSPORT

114. The Preparatory Committee recommend the retention of *Recommendation C(59)198(Final)* on the application of the principle of freedom of maritime transport in the case of financial aid agreements. This Act may not apply to Canada. This Act will not apply to the United States.

Chapter 10

Manpower

115. The Preparatory Committee recommend the retention of the nine Acts listed below, which relate to the liberalisation of manpower movements. These Acts will not apply to Turkey. These Acts, with the exception of Recommendation C(59)273(Final), will not apply to the United States. They may not apply to Canada, whose position will be reviewed in connection with the consolidation of the Acts mentioned in paragraph 116 below.

a) *Decision C(56)258* governing the employment of nationals of Member countries. This Act will not apply to Portugal.

b) *Recommendation C(55)295(Final)* on regulations and administrative practices governing the entry and employment of nationals of Member countries.

c) *Resolution C(57)37(Final)* on the abolition of entry visas for nationals of Member countries travelling to their place of work.

d) *Recommendation C(57)79* and *C(59)273(Final)* concerning the abolition of restrictions on employment of certain categories of nationals of Member countries. The second of these Acts will not apply to Portugal and Greece.

e) *Recommendation C(58)196(Final)* on the regulations and administrative practices governing the movement and employment of refugees.

f) *Recommendation C(59)272(Final)* on the regulations and administrative practices governing the entry and employment of the families of workers who are nationals of Member countries.

g) *Recommendation C(60)65(Final)* on the regulations and administrative practices governing the movements and employment of refugees.

h) *Recommendation C(60)113(Final)* on the international clearing system for vacancies and applications for employment. This Act will not apply to Ireland.

116. The Preparatory Committee recommend that the above Acts other than that mentioned under *a*) above should be consolidated in a single Act.

117. The Preparatory Committee also recommend the retention of the eight Acts listed below. The Acts listed under *a*) to *e*) will not apply to the United States. The Act listed under *c*) will not apply to Canada. The Acts listed under *a*) will apply to Canada subject to a reservation with respect to those parts of C(54)99(Final) relating to the

Recommandation C(54)99(Final) qui concernent la classification internationale des emplois et les dispositions de la Recommandation C(58) 197(Final) relatives au bureau central chargé de recueillir et de rassembler les informations concernant le marché de l'emploi. Les Actes indiqués aux alinéas *b*), *d*) et *e*) s'appliquent au Canada sous réserve des limites imposées par la juridiction fédérale concernant les parties de ces Actes qui prévoient la mise en œuvre de dispositions visant l'amélioration et l'extension des possibilités de formation professionnelle.

a) *Recommandations C(54)99 (Final)* et *C(58)197(Final)* concernant les normes à atteindre dans l'organisation des services de l'emploi.

b) *Recommandation C(59)124(Final)* concernant l'extension et l'amélioration des possibilités de formation professionnelle offertes aux jeunes travailleurs.

c) *Recommandation C(59)169* sur la mise au point des dispositions d'entraide en matière de formation de jeunes travailleurs.

d) *Recommandation C(59)170* sur l'organisation des services d'orientation professionnelle.

e) *Recommandation C(59)171* sur les mesures susceptibles d'être prises pour faciliter le recrutement de jeunes travailleurs dans certaines professions.

f) *Recommandation C(56)59(Final)* sur les statistiques de main-d'œuvre.

g) *Recommandation C(52)227(Final)* relative aux enquêtes par sondage sur la situation de la main-d'œuvre.

Chapitre 11

Tourisme

118. Le Comité Préparatoire recommande le maintien des Actes indiqués dans la liste ci-dessous compte tenu des mentions qui y figurent:

a) *Recommandation C (55) 149 (Final)* concernant les facilités à consentir en matière de visas et de passeports. Cet Acte ne s'applique qu'en partie au Canada et aux États-Unis en raison de la réserve générale qu'ils ont faite.

b) *Recommandation C (56) 131 (Final)* concernant la simplification des formalités exigées en matière de passeport au passage des frontières. Cet Acte ne s'applique pas au Canada et aux États-Unis.

c) *Décision C (57) 56 (Final)* tendant à l'établissement d'une carte d'identité uniforme pour les pays Membres. Cet Acte ne s'applique pas au Canada et aux États-Unis.

d) *Décision C (57) 104 (Final)* relative à la circulation internationale des véhicules routiers de tourisme à moteur en location. Cet Acte ne s'applique pas aux États-Unis.

e) *Recommandation C (58) 42 (Final)* sur l'importation temporaire dans les pays Membres des véhicules automobiles à usage privé. Cet Acte ne s'applique pas au Canada.

f) *Décision C (58) 36* concernant certaines facilités douanières en faveur des touristes et *Décision C (58) 37* concernant les facilités douanières en faveur de certaines catégories de touristes. Ces Actes s'appliquent au Canada avec une réserve visant les dispositions de ces Actes concernant les vins et liqueurs et le tabac. Ces Actes ne s'appliquent pas aux États-Unis.

g) *Décision C (58) 14 (Final)* concernant l'importation de documents et de matériel de propagande touristique. Cet Acte ne s'applique pas au Canada et aux États-Unis.

h) *Recommandation C (58) 219 (Final)* concernant certaines facilités douanières en faveur des touristes résidant sur le territoire d'un des pays international classification of occupations and of C(58)197(Final) relating to a central agency for the collection and collation of employment market information. The Acts listed under *b*), *d*) and *e*) will apply to Canada subject to limitations of Federal jurisdiction with respect to those parts of the Acts calling for implementation of provisions concerning the improvement and extension of existing facilities in the field of vocational training.

a) *Recommendation C(54)99(Final)* and *C(58)197(Final)* on the standards of organisation for employment services.

b) *Recommendation C(59)124(Final)* on the extension and improvement of vocational training facilities for young workers.

c) *Recommendation C(59)169* on the implementation of provisions for mutual help in the training of young workers.

d) *Recommendation C(59)170* on the organisation of vocational guidance services.

e) *Recommendation C(59)171* on measures that might be taken to facilitate the recruitment of young workers in certain trades.

f) *Recommendation C(56)59(Final)* on manpower statistics.

g) *Recommendation C(52)227(Final)* on sample surveys into the manpower situation.

Chapter 11

Tourism

118. The Preparatory Committee recommend the retention of the Acts listed below with the qualifications indicated:

a) *Recommendation C(55)149(Final)* on visa and passport facilities. This Act will apply only in part to Canada and the United States, since they have entered a general reservation.

b) *Recommendation C(56)131(Final)* on the simplification of identity control at frontiers. This Act will not apply to Canada and the United States.

c) *Decision C(57)56(Final)* on the establishment of a uniform identity card for Member countries. This Act will not apply to Canada and the United States.

d) *Decision C(57)104(Final)* on the international circulation of hired private road motor vehicles. This Act will not apply to the United States.

e) *Recommendation C(58)42(Final)* on the temporary import of private cars into Member countries. This Act will not apply to Canada.

f) *Decision C(58)36* on Customs facilities for tourists and *Decision C(58)37* on Customs facilities for certain categories of tourists. These Acts will apply to Canada subject to a reservation with respect to those provisions of the Acts relating to wines, spirits and tobacco. These Acts will not apply to the United States.

g) *Decision C(58)14(Final)* on the import of tourist publicity documents and material. This Act will not apply to Canada and to the United States.

h) *Recommendation C(58)219(Final)* relating to certain Customs facilities for tourists resident in one Member country returning home

Membres et rentrant dans leur pays de résidence après un long voyage à l'étranger. Cet Acte s'applique au Canada avec une réserve visant les dispositions de cet Acte relative aux vins et liqueurs et au tabac, et aux limites concernant les exemptions douanières. Cet Acte s'applique aux États-Unis avec une réserve en ce qui concerne les dispositions dont l'application ne serait pas conforme à la réglementation des États-Unis en matière de marques de fabrique.

i) *Recommandation C (53) 257 (Final)* concernant la pollution des eaux côtières. Cet Acte ne s'applique pas au Canada et aux États-Unis.

j) *Décision C (60) 118 (Final)* relative à la continuation, au cours de l'année 1961, de la campagne de publicité collective aux États-Unis pour le développement du tourisme américain en Europe. Cet Acte ne s'applique pas au Canada et aux États-Unis.

119. Le Comité Préparatoire recommande, pour des raisons d'ordre pratique, le maintien jusqu'au 31 décembre 1961 des programmes actuellement financés par le Fonds de Publicité Collective pour le développement du tourisme américain en Europe pendant la période hors saison. Certaines dépenses sont en effet déjà engagées et certaines obligations assumées en application de la Décision C(60)118(Final). Le Comité n'estime cependant pas nécessaire de maintenir la *Décision C(49)205 (Final)* concernant la création de ce Fonds. Le Comité Préparatoire reconnaît que ce Fonds a joué un rôle utile dans le développement du tourisme américain en Europe au cours des dix dernières années et que cette question garde son importance. Il estime toutefois que le caractère unilatéral de ses activités rend difficile le maintien du Fonds sous sa forme actuelle dans le cadre de l'Organisation. Il serait donc nécessaire que le Conseil de l'Organisation réexamine le problème en tenant compte de l'intérêt porté par les États-Unis et le Canada au développement du tourisme sur leur territoire.

120. Le Comité Préparatoire estime qu'il n'est pas nécessaire de maintenir la *Recommandation C(55)148* relative à l'établissement dans les pays Membres de caisses d'épargne de vacances mais considère que cette question mérite d'être étudiée à nouveau au sein de l'Organisation.

Chapitre 12

Fiscalité

121. Le Comité Préparatoire recommande le maintien de la *Recommandation C(59)147(Final)* relative à la suppression des doubles impositions ainsi que de la *Recommandation C(60)157(Final)* qui complète la précédente. Cet Acte peut ne pas s'appliquer au Canada.

Chapitre 13

Actes administratifs et financiers

122. Ces Actes [1] concernent essentiellement quatre grandes catégories de questions: le Statut du personnel, le Règlement financier, le contrôle des comptes et les contributions des Membres. Le Comité Préparatoire examinera ces Actes après la signature de la Convention, sur la base de propositions qui seront soumises par le Secrétaire Général.

123. Le Comité Préparatoire a eu un échange de vues au sujet du vote majoritaire des Actes concernant les questions administratives et financières, et examinera de nouveau cette question après la signature

[1] *Cf.* Liste figurant à l'annexe 4 du Rapport O.C.D.E. (60)5, IIIe Partie.

after foreign travel. This Act will apply to Canada subject to reservations with respect to those provisions of the Act relating to wines, spirits and tobacco and to limitations on customs exemptions. This Act will apply to the United States subject to a reservation with respect to any provisions of which the application would not be in conformity with United States regulations on trade marks.

i) *Recommendation C(53)257(Final)* on the pollution of coastal waters. This Act will not apply to Canada and the United States.

j) *Decision C(60)118(Final)* on the continuance in 1961 of the joint publicity campaign in the United States for the development of United States tourism in Europe. This Act will not apply to Canada and the United States.

119. The Preparatory Committee recommend for practical reasons the retention until 31st December, 1961, of the programmes at present financed by the Joint Publicity Fund for the expansion of United States tourism in Europe during the off-season. Certain expenditure has in fact already been incurred and certain obligations entered into under Decision C(60)118(Final). The Committee, however, do not think it necessary to retain *Decision C(49)205(Final)* establishing this fund. The Preparatory Committee recognise that the Fund has played a valuable part in the development of United States tourism in Europe during the last ten years and that this question remains important. The Committee nevertheless think that the Fund's one-way activities make it difficult to maintain it in its present form within the framework of the Organisation. It would therefore be necessary for the Council of the Organisation to reconsider the question, bearing in mind the interest taken by Canada and the United States in developing tourism in their countries.

120. The Preparatory Committee do not think it necessary to retain *Recommendation C(55)148* relating to the establishment of holiday savings funds in the Member countries but consider that this question deserves reconsideration in the Organisation.

Chapter 12

Fiscal Questions

121. The Preparatory Committee recommend that *Recommendation C(59)147(Final)* on the suppression of double taxation and *Recommendation C(60)157(Final)*, which supplements it, should be retained. This Act may not apply to Canada.

Chapter 13

Administrative and Financial Acts

122. These Acts [1] mainly concern four major topics: the Staff Regulations, the Financial Regulations, the audit of accounts and the contributions of Member countries. The Preparatory Committee will consider these Acts after the signature of the Convention, on the basis of proposals to be submitted by the Secretary-General.

123. The Preparatory Committee have exchanged views on the question of majority voting on Acts dealing with administrative and financial questions, and will consider this further following signature of the Con-

[1] *Cf.* List in Annex 4 to O.E.C.D.(60)5, Part III.

de la Convention. Il a noté qu'une procédure de vote majoritaire existe déjà pour l'adoption des projets opérationnels, dans le cadre des budgets préalablement approuvés par le Conseil.

124. Le Comité Préparatoire a également convenu que le mode de calcul des contributions devrait être déterminé en tenant compte de l'accession des nouveaux Membres.

125. La question des langues officielles de l'Organisation a été soulevée et le Comité Préparatoire est convenu de l'examiner après la signature de la Convention.

Partie III

RELATIONS AVEC LES PARLEMENTAIRES, LES PAYS NON-MEMBRES ET LES AUTRES ORGANISATIONS [1]

Relations avec les Parlementaires

126. Conformément aux directives qui lui ont été données lors de la Réunion ministérielle des 22–23 juillet 1960, le Comité Préparatoire a poursuivi d'une manière plus approfondie l'examen de la Recommandation 245 de l'Assemblée Consultative du Conseil de l'Europe [2] et des commentaires présentés sur cette Résolution à la Réunion par la Délégation du Conseil de l'Europe. Bien que la plupart des Délégations aient estimé souhaitable l'établissement des liens étroits entre l'O.C.D.E. et les Parlementaires de tous les pays Membres, il n'a pas été possible à ce stade d'étudier la question sous tous ses aspects. Le Comité a conclu qu'il pourrait reprendre l'examen de la question après la signature de la Convention; il appartiendra évidemment au Conseil de l'O.C.D.E. de prendre telles mesures qu'il jugera utile.

Relations avec les pays non-membres

127. Le Comité a pris acte des déclarations du Représentant de la Yougoslavie qui a demandé le maintien des arrangements actuels et proposé d'étudier leur remplacement par un accord général plus large. Le Comité estime que les relations avec la Yougoslavie devraient être maintenues et a convenu que la question de leur adaptation devrait être examinée par lui après la signature de la Convention, afin que l'Organisation puisse prendre les décisions nécessaires.

128. Le Comité recommande le maintien de la *Résolution C(59)290* (*Final*) concernant la participation de la Finlande aux travaux du Comité des Transports Maritimes. Le Comité est d'accord pour que soit laissée à la Finlande la faculté de continuer à s'associer à d'autres activités de l'Organisation.

Relations avec les autres organisations

129. Après avoir examiné les Actes relatifs aux relations de l'O.E.C.E. avec d'autres organisations internationales, le Comité Préparatoire a convenu que, d'une façon générale, les rapports avec les autres organisations internationales avec lesquelles l'O.E.C.E. entretient des relations devraient être maintenus. Le Comité Préparatoire est aussi d'accord sur le maintien des relations établies par l'Agence Européenne pour l'Énergie Nucléaire avec d'autres organisations. Le Comité Préparatoire examinera après la signature de la Convention tout les Actes ayant trait à ces relations, en vue de faire les recommandations appropriées.

---

[1] *Cf.* Liste des Actes correspondants, figurant à l'annexe 4 du Rapport O.C.D.E.(60)5, 1re Partie, à l'exception de la Section C (Structure et Organisation).

[2] *Cf.* Document no. 12, page 113.

vention. They have noted that a procedure for a majority voting already exists for the adoption of operational projects within budgets previously approved by the Council.

124. The Preparatory Committee have also agreed that the method of calculating contributions should be determined in the light of the accession of the new Members.

125. The question of the official languages of the Organisation has been raised and the Preparatory Committee have agreed to consider it after the Convention is signed.

PART III

RELATIONS WITH PARLIAMENTARIANS, NON-MEMBER COUNTRIES AND OTHER ORGANISATIONS [1]

RELATIONS WITH PARLIAMENTARIANS

126. Following the directives of the Ministerial Meeting of 22nd–23rd July, 1960, the Preparatory Committee have further considered Recommendation 245 of the Consultative Assembly of the Council of Europe [2] and the comments on this Resolution made to the Meeting by the Delegation from the Council of Europe. While most Delegations thought it desirable to establish close links between the O.E.C.D. and Parliamentarians from all Member countries, it was not possible to explore the matter thoroughly at this stage. The Committee concluded that they might study the matter further after signature of the Convention; it will, of course, be for the O.E.C.D. Council to take such action as it thinks fit.

RELATIONS WITH NON-MEMBER COUNTRIES

127. The Committee have noted the statements of the Yugoslav Representative asking that the existing arrangements should be retained and proposing that consideration should be given to replacing them by a wider general agreement. The Committee consider that relations with Yugoslavia should be maintained and agree that the question of adapting them should be reviewed by the Preparatory Committee after the Convention has been signed so that the Organisation can take the necessary decisions.

128. The Committee recommend the retention of *Resolution C(59)290 (Final)* on the participation of Finland in the work of the Maritime Transport Committee. The Committee agree that it should remain open for Finland to continue to be associated with other activities of the Organisation.

RELATIONS WITH OTHER ORGANISATIONS

129. After considering the Acts concerning relations between the O.E.E.C. and other international Organisations, the Preparatory Committee agree in general that relations should be maintained with the other international Organisations with which O.E.E.C. has relations. The Preparatory Committee also agree that the relations established by the European Nuclear Energy Agency with other Organisations should be maintained. The Preparatory Committee will review all relevant Acts after signature of the Convention with a view to making appropriate recommendations.

---

[1] *Cf.* List of relevant Acts contained in Annex 4 to O.E.C.D.(60)5, Part I, with the exception of Section C (Structure and Organisation).

[2] *Cf.* Document No. 12, page 113.

130. En ce qui concerne les relations avec les Communautés Européennes, le Protocole Additionnel no. 1 à la nouvelle Convention a pour effet d'assurer la représentation de ces Communautés au sein de l'O.C.D.E.; de ce fait, les arrangements conclus avec ces Communautés et qui sont actuellement en vigueur devront être révisés. Il conviendra aussi de donner effet à la Résolution ministérielle du 23 juillet 1960 prévoyant la participation du Secrétaire Général de l'Association Européenne de Libre-Échange aux travaux de l'O.C.D.E.

131. Après avoir pris connaissance d'une note exposant les vues de la Conférence Européenne des Ministres des Transports, le Comité Préparatoire a conclu au maintien des relations établies avec la Conférence Européenne des Ministres des Transports telles qu'elles existent actuellement, sous réserve de modifications de forme.

132. Le Comité Préparatoire a pris connaissance des vues de la Commission Syndicale Consultative Mixte auprès de l'O.E.C.E., et notamment de sa proposition de créer un Conseil Consultatif composé de représentants des travailleurs et des employeurs. Le Comité Préparatoire a reconnu la nécessité de maintenir et de développer les consultations avec les représentants des travailleurs et des employeurs. Le Comité Préparatoire a l'intention de faire des propositions concrètes à cette fin, après la signature de la Convention.

Partie IV

COMMENTAIRES SUR LA CONVENTION ET LES INSTRUMENTS ADDITIONNELS

133. Les commentaires, interprétations convenues et déclarations faites au sujet de la Convention et des Instruments Additionnels figurent ci-après.

Article 2

134. Les interprétations suivantes ont été convenues en ce qui concerne ce paragraphe:

(*i*) La référence aux obligations internationales figurant dans l'article 1 *c*) couvre l'article 2 *d*) dans son ensemble, y compris la mention des paiements courants et des mouvements de capitaux. Il en résulte que l'étendue géographique du principe de non-discrimination et les dérogations qu'il comporte sont celles qui découlent des obligations résultant des conventions internationales applicables dans les différents domaines visés par l'article 2 *d*).

(*ii*) Le terme ,,services" vise les transactions invisibles courantes et les transferts y afférents.

Article 6

135. La rédaction de l'article 6, qui prévoit la possibilité de déroger au principe de l'accord mutuel de tous les membres pour des cas spéciaux, permet que des décisions soient prises par un vote majoritaire toutes les fois que l'Organisation aura décidé à l'unanimité que, dans un domaine ou pour un cas déterminé, les décisions ou les recommandations sont prises à la majorité.

Article 7

136. La rédaction de l'article 7 maintient la possibilité de convocation du Conseil soit au niveau des ministres, soit au niveau des représentants permanents et elle n'exclut pas qu'un pays puisse se faire représenter comme il l'estime utile à l'une ou l'autre réunion.

130. With regard to relations with the European Communities, Supplementary Protocol No. 1 to the new Convention ensures that these Communities will be represented within the O.E.C.D., and the existing arrangements made with them will therefore require review. Action will also be taken to follow up the Ministerial Resolution of 23rd July deciding that the Secretary-General of the European Free Trade Association should take part in the work of the O.E.C.D.

131. After considering a note setting out the views of the European Conference of Ministers of Transport, the Preparatory Committee agree to the retention in their existing form of the relations established with the European Conference of Ministers of Transport, subject to formal modifications.

132. The Preparatory Committee have heard the views of the Joint Trade Union Advisory Committee to the O.E.E.C., including their proposal to establish an Advisory Council representing Labour and Management. The Preparatory Committee recognise the need to maintain and develop consultations with representatives of Labour and Management. The Preparatory Committee intend to make specific proposals to this end after the signature of the Convention.

Part IV

COMMENTS ON THE CONVENTION AND SUPPLEMENTARY INSTRUMENTS

133. The comments, agreed interpretations and declarations made in respect of the Convention and the Supplementary Instruments are set out below.

Article 2

134. The following interpretations relating to this paragraph have been agreed upon:

(*i*) The reference to international obligations in Article 1 *c*) extends to the whole of Article 2 *d*), including the reference to current payments and capital movements. It follows that the geographical scope of the principle of non-discrimination and the derogations which it carries with it are those resulting from commitments introduced by the international conventions applying in the various fields referred to in Article 2 *d*).

(*ii*) The term "services" covers current invisible transactions and transfers.

Article 6

135. The wording of Article 6, which admits exceptions to the principle of mutual agreement of all the Members in special cases, allows decisions to be taken by majority vote wherever the Organisation unanimously decides that, in a specific field or on a specific matter, decisions or recommendations shall be taken by majority vote.

Article 7

136. The wording of Article 7 leaves it open to the Council to meet either at Ministerial level or at the level of Permanent Representatives without excluding the possibility, as in the past, of a country being represented as it deems fit at either type of meeting.

Article 9

137. Le Comité a admis que la question de la participation aux discussions du Comité Exécutif, s'il est créé comme organe restreint, ou de tout autre organe restreint de l'Organisation, des pays qui n'y sont pas représentés, ou qui n'y ont pas de ressortissants, sera réglée par le Règlement de Procédure, compte tenu des dispositions des accords internationaux qui seraient applicables.

138. La présidence du Comité Exécutif, s'il est créé, dépendra de ses fonctions et de sa composition. Une décision sera prise le moment venu à ce sujet; dès maintenant, certaines Délégations ont indiqué que, pour des raisons de principe, elles pourraient être amenées à s'en tenir à une formule en vertu de laquelle la présidence du Comité ne pourrait être, de toute manière, assurée que par le représentant d'un pays Membre ou par le Secrétaire Général en personne.

Article 10

139. La deuxième phrase du paragraphe 1 de l'article 10 permet au Secrétaire Général d'être assisté soit par un ou plusieurs Secrétaires Généraux suppléants ou adjoints, soit par un ou plusieurs Secrétaires Généraux appartenant à l'une et à l'autre de ces deux catégories.

Article 11

140. Le Comité a admis que le Statut du personnel devra prévoir que le Secrétaire Général, tout en tenant compte, lors du recrutement des agents, de la nécessité de faire appel aux services des personnes les plus compétentes, devra assurer, autant que possible, une équitable répartition des emplois entre les ressortissants des pays Membres de l'Organisation.

141. Le Comité a admis que le Statut du personnel devra prévoir qu'en principe les agents titulaires ne peuvent recevoir aucune rémunération d'un Gouvernement ou d'une autre source extérieure à l'organisation, sauf autorisation du Secrétaire Général qui tiendra le Conseil informé des cas ou catégories pour lesquels une dérogation s'avérerait nécessaire et des motifs de cette dérogation.

Article 14

142. La formule „pourront participer" utilisée au paragraphe 4 donne aux signataires un droit à participer aux travaux de l'Organisation sans leur en faire une obligation. Les accords à conclure en vertu de ce paragraphe pourraient d'ailleurs limiter cette participation dans le temps pour éviter de trop longs délais dans les ratifications. Ces accords devront en principe comporter, comme condition à la participation aux travaux de l'O.C.D.E. des signataires n'ayant pas ratifié:

(*i*) que ces signataires appliqueront, à titre provisoire les Actes de l'O.E.C.E. dont le Conseil aura voté l'approbation;

(*ii*) que ces signataires seront réputés adhérer aux autres décisions et recommandations de l'O.C.D.E. par le dépôt de leur instrument de ratification ou d'approbation, sauf s'ils notifient leur intention de s'abstenir dans les dix jours de ce dépôt.

143. Le Comité a constaté qu'un signataire n'ayant pas encore ratifié ne pourrait participer au vote que dans les cas où sa Constitution le permet. Dans ce cas, cette participation pourrait être prévue dans les accords à conclure en vertu du paragraphe 4, en la limitant éventuellement à certaines matières; dans la mesure où un pays aurait le droit de vote, la condition prévue au paragraphe 142 (*ii*) ci-dessus serait inutile. Le Comité a noté cependant que l'octroi du droit de vote aux pays n'ayant pas ratifié la Convention lors de son entrée en vigueur risque d'enlever à ces pays un motif de hâter leur ratification.

Article 9

137. The Committee agreed that the question of participation in discussions of the Executive Committee, if one is established as a restricted body, or of any other restricted body of the Organisation, by countries not represented, or not having nationals, on these bodies, shall be dealt with in the Rules of Procedure, taking into account the international agreements which may be applicable.

138. The chairmanship of the Executive Committee, if one is established, will depend on its functions and composition. A decision will be taken on this matter at the appropriate time; certain Delegations have already indicated that, as a matter of principle, they might have to insist on a formula according to which the chairmanship of the Committee could only be held by the Representative of a Member country or by the Secretary-General himself.

Article 10

139. The second sentence in paragraph 1 of Article 10 permits the Secretary-General to be assisted by a single Deputy Secretary-General, by a single Assistant Secretary-General, or by one or more of both.

Article 11

140. The Committee agreed that the Staff Regulations should provide that, in recruiting staff, the Secretary-General, while bearing in mind the need to call on the services of the most highly qualified persons, should so far as possible ensure a fair distribution of posts among nationals of Member countries of the Organisation.

141. The Committee agreed that the Staff Regulations should provide that, in principle, established members of the staff may not receive any remuneration from any Government or other source external to the Organisation without permission of the Secretary-General and that the latter shall keep the Council informed of the cases or categories of cases in respect of which an exception has proved necessary and the grounds for such exception.

Article 14

142. The words "may take part" in paragraph 4 give Signatories the right to take part in the work of the Organisation without obliging them to do so. The agreements to be concluded under this paragraph could, however, make such participation subject to a time-limit in order to avoid undue delay in ratification. These agreements should, in principle, include as a condition of participation in the work of the O.E.C.D. of Signatories which have not ratified that:

(*i*) such Signatories shall apply provisionally the Acts of the O.E.E.C. which the Council has voted for approval:

(*ii*) these Signatories shall be deemed to have acceded to the other decisions and recommendations of the O.E.C.D. by the deposit of their instruments of ratification or acceptance, unless within ten days thereafter they give notice of their intention to abstain.

143. The Committee noted that a Signatory which had not yet ratified could vote on decisions of the O.E.C.D. only in cases where its constitution allowed it do to so. In such cases, voting could be provided for in the agreements to be concluded under paragraph 4, limiting it, where appropriate, to certain matters. To the extent that the country concerned is accorded the right to vote, the condition in paragraph 142 (*ii*) would then be unnecessary. The Committee noted, however, that if such countries had the right to vote they might be less inclined to ratify the Convention quickly.

Article 15 et Memorandum d'Accord pour l'application de l'article 15

144. La Résolution ministérielle a chargé le Comité Préparatoire „de rédiger l'instrument relatif à l'article 15 de la Convention" en vertu duquel les Gouvernements s'engageront à approuver les décisions, recommandations ou résolutions de l'O.E.C.E. dont le maintien dans le cadre de la nouvelle Organisation aura été recommandé par le Comité Préparatoire. Dans la rédaction de cet instrument, auquel il propose de donner la forme d'un Memorandum d'Accord, le Comité Préparatoire s'est fondé sur le document approuvé à la Réunion ministérielle (Add. 1 à l'O.C.D.E. (60)5–1re Révision).

145. La référence aux recommandations du Comité Préparatoire qui figure dans le paragraphe 1 du Memorandum d'Accord permet d'éviter que celui-ci ne soit accompagné d'annexes reprenant l'ensemble des Actes dont la confirmation est proposée. Cette formule permet aussi de couvrir les recommandations qui seraient faites par le Comité Préparatoire postérieurement à la signature du Memorandum d'Accord. Si la Réunion ministérielle complète ou modifie les recommandations du Comité Préparatoire, il suffira, pour qu'elles tombent sous le coup du paragraphe 1, que ces modifications ou compléments soient repris pour la forme dans une recommandation du Comité Préparatoire. Le Memorandum d'Accord ne vise que les recommandations du Comité Préparatoire concernant le maintien ou la modification d'Actes de l'O.E.C.E.

146. Quelques Délégations ont indiqué qu'elles interprétaient le document approuvé à la Réunion ministérielle de juillet 1960 et par conséquent le Memorandum d'Accord comme signifiant qu'au cas où un signataire demande le réexamen d'une recommandation ayant fait l'objet d'une notification, cette demande entraîne une dérogation à l'engagement prévu au paragraphe 1 du Memorandum d'Accord au cas où le réexamen n'aboutirait pas à une nouvelle recommandation. Certaines Délégations ne se sont pas déclarées d'accord avec cette interprétation. Dans ces conditions, le Comité Préparatoire a convenu de laisser cette question ouverte étant donné qu'il y a très peu de chances pour qu'elle se pose en pratique.

147. Il résulte du paragraphe 5 du Memorandum d'Accord que, pour les pays qui n'auraient pas ratifié la nouvelle Convention lors de son entrée en vigueur, l'engagement prévu au paragraphe 1 du Memorandum d'Accord deviendra effectif dès le dépôt de leur instrument de ratification ou d'approbation de la Convention et ils devront alors adhérer aux Actes confirmés par le Conseil, conformément aux recommandations du Comité Préparatoire, sauf dans la mesure où la procédure des paragraphes 2 et suivants aurait été appliquée.

Article 16

148. La rédaction de l'article 16, qui règle l'accession de nouveaux Membres, fait apparaître que la dérogation au principe de l'unanimité doit être, en cette matière, décidée cas par cas.

Article 19

149. La question de l'institution d'un prélèvement sur les traitements et émoluments du personnel de l'O.C.D.E. a été soulevée au Comité Préparatoire. Il a été convenu que le Comité continuerait d'étudier cette question.

Article 20

150. La rédaction du paragraphe 2 distingue entre les „dépenses

Article 15 and Memorandum of Understanding on the Application of Article 15

144. The Ministerial Resolution instructed the Preparatory Committee" to draft the instrument relating to Article 15" of the Convention by which the Governments would bind themselves to approve the decision, recommendations and resolutions of the O.E.E.C. the retention of which has been recommended by the Preparatory Committee. In drafting this instrument, for which the Preparatory Committee propose the form of a Memorandum of Understanding, the Committee have followed the lines of the document approved at the Ministerial Meeting (Addendum 1 to O.E.C.D.(60)5–1st Revision).

145. The reference to the recommendations of the Preparatory Committee which appears in paragraph 1 of the Memorandum of Understanding makes it possible to avoid attaching to the Memorandum Annexes setting out all the Acts which it is proposed to confirm. This formula also makes it possible to cover recommendations which may be made by the Preparatory Committee after the signature of the Memorandum of Understanding. If the Ministerial Meeting supplements or modifies any recommendation of the Preparatory Committee it will be enough to bring such supplements or modifications within the scope of paragraph 1 if they are formally embodied in a recommendation of the Preparatory Committee. The Memorandum of Understanding refers solely to the recommendations of the Preparatory Committee relating to the retention or amendment of the Acts of the O.E.E.C.

146. Some delegations indicated that they interpreted the document approved at the Ministerial Meeting in July 1960 and, consequently, the Memorandum of Understanding, as meaning that, in the event of a Signatory requesting the reconsideration of a recommendation which had been the subject of a notification, this request would entail a derogation from the undertaking provided for in paragraph 1 of the Memorandum of Understanding if the re-examination did not result in a new recommendation. Other delegations could not agree to this interpretation. In these circumstances, the Preparatory Committee agreed to leave this question open since there was little likelihood that it would arise in practice.

147. It follows from paragraph 5 of the Memorandum of Understanding that in the case of countries which have not ratified the new Convention at the time it comes into force, the commitment provided for in paragraph 1 of the Memorandum of Understanding will take effect as from the deposit of their instrument of ratification or acceptance of the Convention and they will then have to accede to the Acts confirmed by the Council in accordance with the recommendations of the Preparatory Committee, except in so far as the procedure in paragraph 2 and the following paragraph has been applied.

Article 16

148. The wording of Article 16, which governs the accession of new Members, makes it clear that derogations from the principle of unanimity in this field must be decided upon case by case.

Article 19

149. The question of introducing an assessment on the salary and emoluments of O.E.C.D. staff has been raised in the Preparatory Committee. It was agreed that the question should be studied further by the Committee.

Article 20

150. The wording of paragraph 2 distinguishes between "general

générales" et les „autres dépenses" financées sur une base spéciale, en laissant au Règlement financier la définition du critère de cette distinction. Le mode de financement des „autres dépenses" devra être également déterminé par le Règlement financier.

Protocole Additionnel no. 2

151. La question des privilèges et immunités qui pourraient être accordés aux représentants des Commissions de la Communauté Économique Européenne et de la Communauté Européenne de l'Énergie Atomique, de la Haute Autorité de la Communauté Européenne du Charbon et de l'Acier, et de l'Association Européenne de Libre-Échange, qui participeront aux travaux de l'organisation, a été soulevée au Comité Préparatoire. Le Comité estime que cette question devra être réglée par des accords ou arrangements conclus à cet effet.

Protocole relatif à la révision de la Convention de Coopération Économique Européenne du 16 avril 1948

152. Le Comité a constaté que la Constitution de certains pays ne leur permet pas de mettre fin à la Convention de 1948 sans l'approbation de leur Parlement. Il a admis que les Gouvernements qui y seraient tenus pour des raisons d'ordre constitutionnel pourront signer le Protocole sous réserve de ratification ou d'approbation. C'est seulement si ces Gouvernements se trouvaient ne pas avoir ratifié ou approuvé le Protocole lors de l'entrée en vigueur de la nouvelle Convention qu'ils resteraient juridiquement parties à la Convention de 1948 jusqu'à la date de leur ratification ou approbation.

ANNEXE I

ACTES COMMERCIAUX DE L'O.E.C.E.[1] VISÉS AU CHAPITRE 2, PARTIE II

RÉFÉRENCE	TITRE
	I. Libération des échanges
Code de la Libération [2]	Dispositions de la Section II du Titre I, des Titres III, IV, VI et VII, et de l'Annexe A, dans la mesure où elles se rapportent aux échanges et à l'exception de l'article 25 *bis* et de la Section II *bis* de l'Annexe A (*voir* VII. Suspension de mesures de libération).
C(55)56–*4 mars 1955*	Texte de la déclaration d'intention des pays Membres de l'Organisation concernant les objectifs de la libération.
C(56)77–*23 mars 1956*	Résolution du Conseil concernant la procédure à suivre pour les recours exercés en vertu du Code de la Libération.

[1] Pour les Actes marqués d'un astérisque, *voir* Partie II, chapitre 2, paragraphe 70.

[2] Il est rappelé que les engagements du Code en matière de libération des échanges (Titre I, Section I) n'ont pas été examinés. Les Titres II et V et les annexes B et C se réfèrent exclusivement aux transactions invisibles.

expenses" and "other expenditure" financed on a special basis, leaving the definition of criteria for this distinction to the Financial Regulations. The methods of financing "other expenditure" should also be determined by the Financial Regulations.

Supplementary Protocol No. 2

151. The question of privileges and immunities which might be accorded to the representatives of the Commissions of the European Economic Community and the European Atomic Energy Community, of the High Authority of the European Coal and Steel Community, and of the European Free Trade Association, which will participate in the work of the Organisation, has been raised in the Preparatory Committee. The Committee consider that this question will have to be settled by agreements or arrangements concluded for the purpose.

Protocol relating to the Revision of the Convention for European Economic Co-operation of 16th April, 1948

152. The Committee note that the constitution of certain countries did not allow them to terminate the 1948 Convention without the approval of their Parliaments. They agreed that Governments which were bound to do so for constitutional reasons might sign the Protocol subject to ratification or acceptance. Only if these Governments had still not ratified or accepted the Protocol at the time when the new Convention came into force would they formally remain Parties to the 1948 Convention until the date of their ratification or acceptance.

ANNEX I

TRADE ACTS OF THE O.E.E.C.[1] REFERRED TO IN CHAPTER 2 OF PART II

REFERENCE	TITLE
	I. Liberalisation of Trade
Code of Liberalisation [2]	The Provisions of Section II of Part I and Parts III, IV, VI and VII and Annex A, so far as they relate to trade, and with the exception of Article 25 *bis* and Section II *bis* of Annex A (*see* VII. Suspension of measures of liberalisation).
C(55)56 – *4th March, 1955*	Declaration of intention of Member countries concerning the aims of liberalisation.
C(56)77 – *23rd March, 1956*	Resolution of the Council concerning the procedure for references submitted under the Code of Liberalisation.

[1] For Acts marked with an asterisk, *see* Part II, Chapter 2, paragraph 70.

[2] It is recalled that the undertakings of the Code relating to liberalisation of trade (Part I, Section I) have not been considered. Parts II and V and Annexes B and C relate solely to invisible transactions.

RÉFÉRENCE	TITRE
C(56)223(Final)-*26 octobre 1956* ..	Recommandation du Conseil sur de nouveaux progrès dans la libération des échanges et l'assouplissement des restrictions quantitatives.
C(56)240-*26 octobre 1956*.........	Décision du Conseil concernant la prolongation de la libération à 90% et le problème tarifaire.
C(57)206(Final)	Décision du Conseil amendant la Décision C(56)240 ci-dessus.
C(58)157(Final)	d°
C(59)136(Final)	d°
C(57)57(Final-*10 mai 1957*	Résolution du Conseil sur les progrès dans la libération des échanges et l'assouplissement des restrictions quantitatives à l'importation.
C(59)241-*16 octobre 1959*.........	Résolution du Conseil relative à de nouveaux aspects de la contribution de l'Organisation à la libération des échanges.
C(60)35-*2 février 1960*	Recommandation du Conseil relative aux Échanges et Paiements.
C/M(60)17(Final) point 139-*1er juillet 1960*	Inscription au procès-verbal du Conseil, à la suite des discussions sur la prolongation des obligations de libération à 90%.
C(53)9(Final)-*7 février 1953*	Décision du Conseil concernant les États Membres de la Communauté Européenne du Charbon et de l'Acier.

II. Libération et assouplissement des importations vis-à-vis de la zone dollar

C(54)317-*22 décembre 1954*	Recommandation du Conseil relative à l'assouplissement des restrictions quantitatives aux importations de biens (et des restrictions aux transactions invisibles et aux transferts) appliquées à la zone dollar.

III. Échanges avec les territoires d'outre-mer des pays Membres

C(54)113-*13 avril 1954*	Recommandation du Conseil concernant l'expansion des échanges entre les pays Membres et les territoires d'Outre-Mer.

IV. Mesures d'aide aux exportations

C(59)202*-*17 juillet 1959*	Décision du Conseil sur les mesures d'aide aux exportations.

REFERENCE	TITLE
C(56)223(Final) – *26th October, 1956*	Recommendation of the Council concerning further progress in the liberalisation of trade and the relaxation of quantitative restrictions.
C(56)240 – *26th October, 1956*	Decision of the Council concerning the extension of 90 per cent liberalisation and the tariff problem.
C(57)206(Final)	Decision of the Council amending Decision C(56)240 above.
C(58)157(Final)	Decision of the Council amending Decision C(56)240 above.
C(59)136(Final)	do.
C(57)57(Final) – *10th May, 1957* ..	Resolution of the Council concerning progress in the liberalisation of trade and the relaxation of quantitative restrictions on imports.
C(59)241 – *16th October, 1959*	Resolution of the Council on new aspects of the Organisation's contribution towards freeing trade.
C(60)35 – *2nd February, 1960*	Recommendation of the Council on Trade and Payments.
C/M(60)17(Final) Item 139 – *1st July, 1960*	Entry in the Council Minutes after discussion on the extension of 90 per cent liberalisation obligations.
C(53)9(Final) – *7th February, 1953*.	Decision of the Council concerning the Member States of the European Coal and Steel Community.

II. Liberalisation and Relaxation of Restrictions on Imports vis-à-vis the Dollar Area

C(54)317 – *22nd December, 1954* ..	Recommendation of the Council concerning the relaxation of quantitative restrictions on imports of goods (and restrictions on invisible transactions and transfers) relating to the dollar area.

III. Trade with the Overseas Territories of Member Countries

C(54)113 – *13th April, 1954*	Recommendation of the Council concerning the expansion of trade between Member countries and Overseas Territories.

IV. Export Aids

C(59)202* – *17th July, 1959*	Decision of the Council on export aids.

RÉFÉRENCE	TITRE
C(60) 130*	Décision du Conseil portant amendement à la Décision C(59)202 ci-dessus.
C(60) 145	d°
C/M(60) 15* point 121 B–*24 juin 1960*	Inscription au procès-verbal relative à l'application dans le cas de l'Autriche de l'amendement apporté à la Décision C(59) 202, par la Décision C(60) 130.
CMA(58) 10 (Final)*–*9 octobre 1958*	Résolution du Comité Ministériel de l'Agriculture et de l'Alimentation relative à la procédure de notification des mesures d'aide à l'exportation.

V. Restrictions quantitatives aux exportations

C(55)*297–*7 février 1953* et *18 novembre 1955*	Décision du Conseil concernant les restrictions quantitatives aux exportations de marchandises.
C(57) 17(Final)*–*1er mars 1957*	Recommandation du Conseil concernant l'élimination des restrictions quantitatives à l'exportation des déchets de plomb et de zinc.

VI. Réglementations administratives et techniques faisant obstacle aux échanges

C(58) 11(Final)*–*28 février 1958* ...	Recommandation du Conseil relative aux réglementations administratives et techniques faisant obstacle au développement des échanges intra-européens.
C(59) 143(Final)*–*16 octobre 1959* ..	Recommandation du Conseil concernant les réglementations techniques faisant obstacle au développement des échanges intra-européens.
C(55) 162(Final)–**29 septembre 1955*	Recommandation du Conseil concernant l'amélioration du régime des échanges de pièces de rechange entre les pays Membres.

VII. Suspension de mesures de libération

A. Suspension de mesures de libération pour des raisons de difficultés de balance de paiement

Code de la Libération	
Article 25 *bis**	Procédures.
Annexe A, Section II *bis**........	Principes guides.

B. Produits ex-libérés

C(52)244*–*13 août 1952*	Décision du Conseil relative au régime d'importation des produits ex-libérés.

REFERENCE	TITLE
C(60)130*	Decision of the Council amending Decision C(59)202 above.
C(60)145	do.
C/M(60)15* item 121 B – *24th June, 1960*	Entry in the Minutes relating to the application in the case of Austria of the amendment made to Decision C(59)202 by Decision C(60)130.
CMA(58)10(Final)* – *9th October, 1958*	Resolution of the Ministerial Committee for Agriculture and Food concerning the notification procedure for aids to exports.

V. Quantitative Restrictions on Exports

C(55)297* – *7th February, 1953* and *18th November, 1955*	Decision of the Council concerning quantitative restrictions on the export of goods.
C(57)17(Final)* – *1st March, 1957*.	Recommendation of the Council concerning the elimination of quantitative restrictions on the export of lead and zinc scrap.

VI. Administrative and Technical Regulations Hampering Trade

C(58)11(Final)* – *28th February, 1958*	Recommendation of the Council relating to administrative and technical regulations hampering the expansion of intra-European trade.
C(59)143(Final)* – *16th October, 1959*	Recommendation of the Council concerning technical regulations hampering the expansion of intra-European trade.
C(55)162(Final)* – *29th September, 1955*	Recommendation of the Council concerning the improvement of regulations applying to trade in replacement parts between Member countries.

VII. Suspension of Measures of Liberalisation

A. Suspension of measures of liberalisation on the ground of balance-of-payments difficulties

Code of Liberalisation	
Article 25 *bis* *	Procedures.
Annex A – Section II *bis* *	Guiding principles.

B. Ex-freed commodities

C(52)244 * – *13th August, 1952* ...	Decision of the Council concerning the import regime for ex-freed commodities.

RÉFÉRENCE	TITRE

VIII. Échanges dans le domaine de l'énergie nucléaire

C(59)282(Final)*–*29 janvier 1960*..	Décision du Conseil relative aux mesures conservatoires concernant les échanges intra-européens dans le domaine de l'énergie nucléaire.

IX. Cas particuliers de pays [1]

A. Espagne

C(59)192–*20 juillet 1959*	Décision du Conseil relative à l'application à l'Espagne du Code de la Libération et de Décisions connexes.
C(60)174–*19 juillet 1960*	Décision du Conseil relative à l'application par l'Espagne des dispositions de l'article 3 *d*) du Code de la Libération.

B. Grèce

C(54)110(Final)–*21 mai 1954*	Décision du Conseil abrogeant les articles 3 *d*) et 20 *d*) du Code de la Libération.
C(54)202(Final)–*30 juillet 1954*	Recommandation du Conseil relative au développement des exportations de la Grèce.

C. Italie

C(57)205(Final)–*28 février 1958*...	Recommandation du Conseil sur les obstacles aux exportations de produits agricoles italiens.

D. Turquie

C(57)215–*11 octobre 1957*	Décision du Conseil concernant la situation de la Turquie à l'égard de ses obligations découlant du Code de la Libération.

X. Agriculture

CMA(56)6*–*3 mai 1956*	Résolution du Comité Ministériel de l'Agriculture et de l'Alimentation relative au choix des méthodes d'assouplissement des régimes d'importation de pommes, de poires et de tomates.

[1] Les Actes relatifs à des cas particuliers de pays qui bénéficient de crédits sur le Fonds Européen sont traités à la Partie II, chapitre 3 sur l'Accord Monétaire Européen et les Actes de l'O.E.C.E. relatifs à cet Accord (*voir* également Partie II, chapitre 2, paragraphe 65).

REFERENCE	TITLE

VIII. Trade in the Field of Nuclear Energy

C(59)282(Final)* – *29th January, 1960*	Decision of the Council concerning standstill measures in respect of intra-European trade in the field of nuclear energy.

IX. Special Cases of Certain Countries [1]

A. Spain

C(59)192 – *20th July, 1959*	Decision of the Council concerning the application to Spain of the Code of Liberalisation and related Decisions.
C(60)174 – *19th July, 1960*	Decision of the Council concerning the application by Spain of the provisions of Article 3 *d*) of the Code of Liberalisation.

B. Greece

C(54)110(Final) – *21st May, 1954* .	Decision of the Council repealing the former Articles 3 *d*) and 20 *d*) of the Code of Liberalisation.
C(54)202(Final) – *30th July, 1954* .	Recommendation of the Council concerning the development of exports of Greek products.

C. Italy

C(57)205(Final) – *28th February, 1958*	Recommendation of the Council concerning obstacles to exports of Italian agricultural products.

D. Turkey

C(57)215 – *11th October, 1957*	Decision of the Council concerning the situation of Turkey in relation to her obligations under the Code of Liberalisation.

X. Agriculture

CMA(56)6* – *3rd May, 1956*......	Resolution of the Ministerial Committee for Agriculture and Food concerning the choice of methods for relaxing import regimes for apples, pears and tomatoes.

[1] The Acts relating to special cases of countries enjoying credits from the European Fund are dealt with in Part II Chapter 3 "The European Monetary Agreement and the related Acts of the O.E.E.C." (*See* also paragraph 65 of Part II, Chapter 2).

ANNEXE II

ACTES DE L'O.E.C.E. SE RAPPORTANT A L'A.M.E. ET DONT LE COMITÉ PRÉPARATOIRE RECOMMANDE L'APPROBATION PAR LE CONSEIL DE L'O.C.D.E.

1. Recommandation du Conseil, en date du 29 juillet 1955, relative à l'Accord Monétaire Européen et au Protocole d'Application Provisoire dudit Accord. *En vertu de cette Recommandation, le Conseil „décide de prendre les mesures et d'assumer les fonctions prévues par l'Accord".*	C(55)221
2. Décision du Conseil, en date du 29 juillet 1955, portant Directives pour l'application de l'A.M.E.[1]	C(55)222
3. Insertion dans le procès-verbal de la 296e séance du Conseil tenue du 28 au 30 juillet 1955, relative à l'approbation de l'échange de lettres entre le Représentant des États-Unis et le Secrétaire Général de l'O.E.C.E. [*cf.* Annexes II et III au document C(55)234] au sujet des modalités du transfert des avoirs de l'U.E.P. au Fonds Européen.	C/M(55)27, 1re partie, Point 213 *b*)
4. Recommandation du Conseil, en date du 31 juillet 1958, relative à la procédure qui permettra de suivre l'exécution et l'application du Programme de Stabilisation de la Turquie.	C(58)214
5. Insertion dans le procès-verbal de la 426e séance du Conseil, tenue le 6 janvier 1959, autorisant le Secrétaire Général à envoyer au Représentant permanent des États-Unis la lettre dont le projet est joint en addendum au document C(58)280. *Dans cette lettre, le Secrétaire Général accuse réception d'une lettre du Représentant des États-Unis approuvant le transfert au Fonds Européen du reliquat de la contribution des États-Unis à l'Union Européenne de Paiements.*	C/M(59)1, Point 5
6. Décision du Conseil, en date du 30 décembre 1958, relative à la terminaison de l'Accord sur l'établissement d'une Union Européenne de Paiements et à l'application de l'Accord Monétaire Européen. *Dans cette Décision, le Conseil constate que l'A.M.E. est entré en application à la clôture des comptes le 27 décembre 1958.*	C(58)281(Final)
7. Décision du Conseil, en date du 30 janvier 1959, relative à l'exécution des clauses de liquidation de l'U.E.P. *En vertu de cette Décision, chacune des Parties Contractantes à l'Accord U.E.P. a approuvé expressément, en ce qui la concerne, les chiffres relatifs à l'exécution des clauses de liquidation de l'U.E.P. et, en particulier, les crédits bilatéraux découlant des crédits ordinaires et spéciaux de l'U.E.P.*	C(59)16(Final)

---

[1] Telle qu'elle aura été amendée à la date de l'entrée en vigueur de la Convention relative à l'O.C.D.E.

ANNEX II

ACTS OF THE O.E.E.C. RELATING TO THE E.M.A. WHICH THE PREPARATORY COMMITTEE RECOMMEND FOR APPROVAL BY THE COUNCIL OF THE O.E.C.D.

1. Recommendation of the Council of 29th July, 1955, relating to the E.M.A. and the Protocol of Provisional Application of that Agreement. *Under which the Council "decides to take such action and perform such duties as are provided for in the Agreement".*	C(55)221
2. Decision of the Council of 29th July, 1955, giving Directives for the Application of the E.M.A.[1]	C(55)222
3. Entry in the Minutes of the 296th Meeting of the Council, held on 28th–30th July, 1955, approving the exchange of letters between the Representative of the United States and the Secretary-General of the O.E.E.C. concerning the transfer of E.P.U. assets to the European Fund [*see* Annexes II and III to C(55)234].	C/M(55)27, Part I, Item 231 *b*)
4. Recommendation of the Council of 31st July, 1958, concerning the execution and development of the Turkish Stabilization Programme.	C(58)214
5. Entry in the Minutes of the 426th Meeting of the Council, held on 6th January, 1959, authorising the Secretary-General to send to the Permanent United States Representative the letter as drafted in the Addendum to C(58)280. *In this letter the Secretary-General acknowledges a letter from the United States Representative approving the transfer to the European Fund of the remaining portion of the amount of dollars contributed by the United States towards the founding of the E.P.U.*	C/M(59)1, Item 5
6. Decision of the Council of 30th December, 1958, relating to the termination of the Agreement for the Establishment of a European Payments Union and the application of the E.M.A. *Establishes that the E.M.A. began to apply at the close of business on 27th December, 1958.*	C(58)281(Final)
7. Decision of the Council of 30th January, 1959, concerning the execution of the liquidation provisions of the E.P.U. *Under which each Contracting Party to the E.P.U. Agreement signified its express agreement with the figures, insofar as it was concerned, relating to the execution of the liquidation provisions of the E.P.U. and, in particular, the bilateral credits arising out of the ordinary and the special E.P.U. credits.*	C(59)16(Final)

[1] As amended up to the date on which the O.E.C.D. Convention comes into force.

8. Décision du Conseil, en date du 30 janvier 1959, concernant la mise en oeuvre et le développement du Programme de Stabilisation de la Turquie et l'octroi à ce pays d'un crédit par le Fonds Européen.	C(59)36
9. Décision du Conseil, en date du 21 avril 1959, relative à l'exercice financier de l'Accord Monétaire Européen – paragraphe premier seulement.	(C59)54(Final)
10. Résolution du Conseil, en date du 21 avril 1959, relative à l'approbation finale des rapports périodiques établis par l'Agent sur l'exécution des opérations financières effectuées en vertu de l'Accord Monétaire Européen. *Selon la procédure définie dans cette Résolution, chacune des Parties Contractantes approuve expressément, en ce qui la concerne, les chiffres figurant dans les rapports de l'Agent lorsque ceux-ci reçoivent l'approbation finale du Conseil; ainsi se trouvent confirmés tous les paiements déjà reçus ou effectués par le Fonds Européen.*	C(59)61(Final)
11. Décision du Conseil, en date du 21 avril 1959, concernant le taux d'intérêt des avances accordées au titre du financement intérimaire en vertu de l'article 10 de l'Accord Monétaire Européen – paragraphe 3 seulement. *Cette Décision charge le Comité Directeur de suivre constamment la mise en oeuvre des dispositions de financement intérimaire et d'examiner périodiquement s'il convient de modifier le taux d'intérêt assortissant ces avances.*	C(59)91(Final)
12. Insertion dans le procès-verbal de la 447e séance du Conseil tenue le 12 juin 1959 confirmant l'interprétation de l'article 4 *b*) de l'A.M.E. donnée dans le document C(59)121, en vue de fixer l'échelonnement dans le temps des annuités et des intérêts semestriels à verser au titre des prêts attribués à la Norvège et à la Turquie par l'Union Européenne de Paiements et transférés à l'Accord Monétaire Européen.	C/M(59)15, Point 127
13. Décision du Conseil, en date du 12 juin 1959, concernant les dispositions relatives au remboursement des prêts bilatéraux consentis à la Turquie ou par elle lors de la liquidation de l'Union Européenne de Paiements. *Cette Décision fixe l'échelonnement dans le temps des mensualités à verser par la Turquie au Fonds Européen et par le Fonds à chacun des créanciers bilatéraux ainsi que des paiements semestriels d'intérêts.*	C(59)137(Final)
14. Résolution du Conseil, en date du 20 juillet 1959, relative à l'exécution, à l'examen et au renforcement du Programme de Stabilisation de l'Espagne.	C(59)193
15. Décision du Conseil, en date du 20 juillet	C(59)194

8. Decision of the Council of 30th January, 1959, concerning the execution and development of the Turkish Stabilization Programme and the granting by the European Fund of credit to Turkey. C(59)36

9. Decision of the Council of 21st April, 1959, concerning the financial year of the E.M.A. – paragraph 1 only. C(59)54(Final)

10. Resolution of the Council of 21st April, 1959, concerning "final approval" of the periodic reports of the Agent on the execution of financial operation under the E.M.A. C(59)61(Final)

Establishes the procedure under which each Contracting Party signifies its express agreement, as far as it is concerned, with the figures in the Agent's Reports when these Reports are given final approval by the Council thus confirming all payments already made by or to the European Fund.

11. Decision of the Council of 21st April, 1959, concerning the rate of interest on drawings of interim finance under Article 10 of the E.M.A. – paragraph 3 only. *Instructs the Board of Management to keep the interim finance provisions under constant review and to determine from time to time whether the rate of interest thereon should be modified.* C(59)91(Final)

12. Entry in the Minutes of the 447th Meeting of the Council, held on 12th June, 1959, confirming the interpretation of Article 4 *b*) of the E.M.A. given in the report C(59)121, which determines schedules for the payment of annual instalments and half-yearly interest in respect of loans granted to Norway and Turkey by the European Payments Union and transferred to the European Fund. C/M(59)15, Item 127

13. Decision of the Council of 12th June, 1959, concerning arrangements for the repayment of bilateral credits granted to or by Turkey upon the liquidation of the European Payments Union. C(59)137(Final)

Lays down schedules for the monthly instalments to be paid by Turkey to the European Fund and by the latter to each of the bilateral creditors and for the half-yearly interest payments.

14. Resolution of the Council of 20th July, 1959, concerning the carrying out, review and reinforcement of Spain's Stabilization Programme. C(59)193

15. Decision of the Council of 20th July, 1959, C(59)194

1959, relative à l'appel des contributions de certaines Parties Contractantes à l'Accord Monétaire Européen.

Cette Décision stipule que le Danemark, l'Espagne, la Grèce, l'Islande, la Norvège et la Turquie bénéficient des dispositions de l'article 4 d) prévoyant le paiement différé des contributions et qu'en conséquence ces pays ne seront appelés à payer leur contribution qu'après le paiement total des contributions des autres pays.

16. Décision du Conseil, en date du 20 juillet 1959, relative à l'assistance financière à l'Espagne. — C(59)195

17. Décision du Conseil, en date du 29 janvier 1960, relative au Programme de Stabilisation islandais et à l'aide financière à l'Islande. — C(60)32

18. Décision du Conseil, en date du 12 février 1960, relative à l'exécution du Programme espagnol de Stabilisation et à l'assistance financière à l'Espagne. — C(60)39(Final)

19. Résolution du Conseil, en date du 7 avril 1960, concernant la nomination des Commissaires aux Comptes du Fonds Européen et leur mandat pour le premier exercice financier de l'Accord Monétaire Européen. — C(60)53(Final)

20. Décision du Conseil, en date du 19 juillet 1960, relative à l'exécution du Programme de Stabilisation islandais et à l'aide financière à l'Islande. — C(60)166

21. Résolution du Conseil, à prendre en janvier 1961 nommant, pour l'année 1961, le Président, les Vice-Présidents et les Membres du Comité Directeur de l'Accord Monétaire Européen.

c) DOCUMENTS ANNEXES

(I) Chronologie des Négociations

21 décembre 1959: Réunion à Paris des Chefs d'État et de Gouvernement de la France, des États-Unis d'Amérique, de la République Fédérale d'Allemagne et du Royaume-Uni qui décident de mettre à l'étude la réforme de la coopération économique entre les pays du monde libre (document no. 1).

12–13 janvier 1960: Réunion à Paris d'un Comité Économique Spécial, composé des Ministres de treize pays [1] et d'un Représentant de la Commission de la Communauté Économique Européenne, qui adopte une Résolution (document no. 2) créant un Groupe de quatre personnes et le chargeant de préparer un rapport sur la réforme de l'O.E.C.E., une Résolution concernant l'aide au développement (document no. 3) et une Résolution concernant certains problèmes commerciaux (document no. 4).

Ces Résolutions sont approuvées le 14 janvier par les Ministres des vingt pays Membres et Associés de l'O.E.C.E.

---

[1] Allemagne, Belgique, Canada, Danemark, États-Unis, France, Grèce, Italie, Pays-Bas, Portugal, Royaume-Uni, Suède et Suisse.

concerning the calling up of the contributions of certain Contracting Parties to the E.M.A.

Provides that the contributions of Denmark, Spain, Greece, Iceland, Norway and Turkey shall be covered by the deferment rule in Article 4 d), i.e. *shall be called up after all the other contributions.*

16. Decision of the Council of 20th July, 1959, concerning financial assistance to Spain.	C(59)195
17. Decision of the Council of 29th January, 1960, concerning Iceland's Stabilization Programme and financial assistance to Iceland.	C(60)32
18. Decision of the Council of 12th February, 1960, concerning the carrying out of Spain's Stabilization Programme and financial assistance to Spain.	C(60)39(Final)
19. Resolution of the Council of 7th April, 1960, concerning the appointment of auditors to the European Fund and their terms of reference for the first financial year of the E.M.A.	C(60)53(Final)
20. Decision of the Council of 19th July, 1960, concerning the carrying out of Iceland's Stabilization Programme and financial assistance to Iceland.	C(60)166
21. Resolution of the Council to be taken in January 1961, appointing, for the year 1961, the Chairman, Vice-Chairmen and Members of the Board of Management of the E.M.A.	

c) RELATED DOCUMENTS

(I) Short History of the Negotiations

21st December, 1959: Meeting in Paris between the Heads of State and Government of France, the United States of America, the Federal Republic of Germany and the United Kingdom who decided to initiate a review of the principles of economic co-operation between the countries of the free world (Document No. 1).

12th–13th January, 1960: Meeting in Paris of a Special Economic Committee consisting of the Ministers of thirteen countries [1] and a Representative of the Commission of the European Economic Community who adopted a Resolution (Document No.2) appointing a group of four persons to prepare a report on the reorganisation of the O.E.E.C., a Resolution on development assistance (Document No. 3) and a Resolution on certain trade problems (Document No. 4). These Resolutions were approved on 14th January by the Ministers of the twenty Member and Associate countries of the O.E.E.C.

---

[1] Belgium, Canada, Denmark, France, Germany, Greece, Italy, Netherlands, Portugal, Sweden, Switzerland, United Kingdom and United States.

7 avril 1960: Le Groupe des Quatre dépose son rapport: „Une organisation économique rénovée".

24–25 mai 1960: Réunion à Paris de la Conférence des Représentants des vingt Gouvernements et des Communautés Européennes, qui adopte une Résolution relative à la réorganisation de l'O.E.C.E. (document no. 5).

31 mai–9 juillet 1960: Session du Groupe de Travail créé par la Résolution ci-dessus.

22–23 juillet 1960: Les Ministres des vingt Gouvernements et les Représentants des Communautés Européennes adoptent une Résolution portant création d'un Comité Préparatoire (document no. 6), une Résolution relative aux échanges (document no. 7), une Résolution relative à l'aide aux pays en voie de développement (document no. 8) ainsi qu'une Résolution relative à la participation aux travaux de l'O.C.D.E. du Secrétaire Général de l'Association Européenne de Libre-Échange (document no. 9).

14 sept.–23 nov. 1960: Session du Comité Préparatoire.

13–14 décembre 1960: Les Ministres des vingt Gouvernements et les Représentants des Communautés Européennes signent la Convention de l'O.C.D.E., adoptent une Résolution relative au Rapport du Comité Préparatoire (document no. 10) ainsi qu'un Communiqué de Presse (document no. 11).

(II) Documents

Document no. 1

Communiqué du 21 décembre 1959

des Chefs d'État et de Gouvernement de la France, des États-Unis d'Amérique, de la République Fédérale d'Allemagne et du Royaume-Uni.

Les Chefs d'État et de Gouvernement se sont entretenus des importantes modifications qui se sont produites dans la situation économique internationale. Reconnaissant les grands progrès économiques réalisés par l'Europe Occidentale, ils ont convenu que, pratiquement, tous les pays industrialisés du monde libre sont maintenant en état de consacrer, dans une mesure accrue, leurs énergies à des tâches nouvelles et importantes de coopération qui auraient pour objet:

a) de favoriser le développement des pays moins développés, et

b) de mener des politiques commerciales fixées sur l'utilisation rationnelle des ressources économiques et le maintien d'harmonieuses relations internationales, contribuant ainsi au progrès et à la stabilité de l'économie mondiale et à une amélioration générale du niveau de vie.

A leur avis, ces principes de coopération devraient aussi régir les discussions relatives aux problèmes commerciaux découlant de l'existence d'organisations économiques régionales européennes qui sont ou seront établies dans le cadre de l'Accord Général sur les Tarifs douaniers et le Commerce, telles que la Communauté Économique Européenne et l'Association Européenne de Libre-Échange. Leurs relations, tant entre elles qu'avec les autres pays, devraient être discutées dans cet esprit.

Les Chefs d'État et de Gouvernement, reconnaissant que les méthodes nécessaires pour mettre en œuvre ces principes exigent une étude très poussée, sont convenus de convoquer une réunion officieuse qui se tiendra à Paris dans un proche avenir. Ils proposent que les pays et organisations siégeant au Comité Exécutif de l'O.E.C.E. et les Gouvernements

7th April, 1960: The Group of Four submitted its report "A Remodelled Economic Organisation".

24th–25th May, 1960: Meeting in Paris of the Conference of Representatives of the Twenty Governments and of the European Communities who adopted a Resolution on the reorganisation of the O.E.E.C. (Document No. 5).

31st May–9th July, 1960: Meetings of the Working Party set up by the above Resolution.

22nd–23rd July, 1960: The Ministers of the Twenty Governments and the Representatives of the European Communities adopted a Resolution creating a Preparatory Committee (Document No. 6), a Resolution on trade (Document No. 7), a Resolution on aid to developing countries (Document No. 8) and a Resolution concerning the participation of the Secretary-General of the European Free Trade Association in the work of the O.E.C.D. (Document No. 9).

14th Sept.–23rd Nov., 1960: Meetings of the Preparatory Committee.

13th–14th December, 1960: The Ministers of the Twenty Governments and the Representatives of the European Communities signed the Convention on the O.E.C.D. and adopted a Resolution on the Report of the Preparatory Committee (Document No. 10) and a Press Communiqué (Document No. 11).

(II) Documents

Document No. 1

Communiqué of 21st December, 1959

by the Heads of State and Government of France, the United States of America, the Federal Republic of Germany and the United Kingdom.

The Heads of State and Government have discussed the important changes that have taken place in the international economic situation. Recognising the great economic progress of Western Europe, they have agreed that virtually all of the industrialised part of the free world is now in a position to devote its energies in increased measure to new and important tasks of co-operative endeavour with the object of:

a) furthering the development of the less developed countries, and

b) pursuing trade policies directed to the sound use of economic resources and the maintenance of harmonious international relations, thus contributing to growth and stability in the world economy and to a general improvement in the standard of living.

In their view these co-operative principles should also govern the discussions on commercial problems arising from the existence of European economic regional organisations, which are or will be constituted within the framework of the G.A.T.T., such as the European Economic Community and the European Free Trade Association. Their relations both with other countries and with each other should be discussed in this spirit.

The Heads of State and Government, recognising that the method of furthering these principles requires intensive study, have agreed to call an informal meeting to be held in Paris in the near future. They suggest that the members and participants of the Executive Committee of the O.E.E.C. and the Governments whose nationals are members of the dont les ressortissants sont membres du Comité de Direction des Échanges de l'O.E.C.E. soient représentés à cette réunion.

Il est suggéré que l'un des objectifs de cette réunion serait d'examiner dans quelle mesure il est besoin de consultations constantes et quelles méthodes peuvent être employées pour traiter les problèmes ci-dessus mentionnés.

Document no. 2

Résolution concernant l'examen de la réorganisation de l'O.E.C.E.

adoptée par le Comité Économique Spécial lors d'une réunion les 12 et 13 janvier 1960 et approuvée par les Ministres des pays Membres et Associés de l'O.E.C.E. le 14 janvier 1960

Les représentants des Gouvernements de la Belgique, du Canada, de la France, du Danemark, de la République Fédérale d'Allemagne, de la Grèce, de l'Italie, des Pays-Bas, de la Suisse, de la Suède, du Portugal, du Royaume-Uni et des États-Unis, ainsi que le représentant de la Commission de la Communauté Économique Européenne:

a) appréciant pleinement l'œuvre de coopération accomplie par l'O.E.C.E.;

b) soucieux d'assurer la permanence de la coopération dans les domaines où aucun changement n'est requis;

c) décidés à poursuivre des politiques économiques qui contribueront à la stabilité et à l'expansion de l'économie mondiale, notamment des politiques commerciales visant à l'utilisation rationnelle des ressources naturelles et au maintien des relations internationales harmonieuses;

d) conscients de la nécessité de consacrer des efforts accrus au développement des pays sous-développés;

e) reconnaissant l'importance d'une coopération continue pour atteindre ces objectifs;

f) constatant la nécessité d'arrangements qui permettraient la pleine participation non seulement des dix-huit Membres actuels de l'Organisation Européenne de Coopération Économique mais également des deux Membres Associés, États-Unis et Canada;

g) désireux de procéder à l'examen d'arrangements institutionnels améliorés susceptibles d'atteindre au mieux ces objectifs;

h) reconnaissant que tous les Gouvernements Membres de l'Organisation Européenne de Coopération Économique et les Gouvernements qui lui sont Associés ont un égal intérêt en la matière:

Proposent:

1. De réunir à Paris le 19 avril 1960 une Conférence de hauts fonctionnaires des vingt Gouvernements Membres ou Associés de l'O.E.C.E. à laquelle les Communautés Européennes sont également invitées, afin d'étudier les dispositions appropriées qui permettraient d'atteindre les objectifs précités;

2. Qu'afin de faciliter le travail de cette Conférence, il soit créé un Groupe de quatre personnes pour préparer un rapport dans lequel:

a) seraient étudiées les méthodes les plus efficaces pour atteindre les objectifs précités et présenter à cet égard toutes recommandations utiles;

b) seraient présentés, en projet, des articles d'accord, au cas où l'examen de la question ferait apparaître la nécessité d'une organisation de coopération économique convenablement améliorée;

Steering Board for Trade of the O.E.E.C. should be represented at this meeting.

It is proposed that an objective of such a group should be to consider the need for and methods of continuing consultations dealing with the above-mentioned problems.

Document No. 2

Resolution on the Study of the Reorganisation of O.E.E.C.

adopted by the Special Economic Committee at a meeting on 12th–13th January, 1960, and approved by Ministers of Members and Associate Members of O.E.E.C. on 14th January, 1960

The representatives of the Governments of Belgium, Canada, France, Denmark, the Federal Republic of Germany, Greece, Italy, the Netherlands, Sweden, Switzerland, Portugal, the United Kingdom, and the United States and the representative of the Commission of the European Economic Community:

a) fully appreciating the co-operative work accomplished by the O.E.E.C.;

b) wishing to ensure the continuity of co-operation in the fields where no change is called for;

c) determined to pursue economic policies which will contribute to stability and growth in the world economy, including trade policies directed to the sound use of economic resources and the maintenance of harmonious international relations;

d) conscious of the need to devote increased efforts towards furthering the development of less developed countries;

e) recognising the importance of continued co-operation to ensure the achievement of these objectives;

f) noting the desirability of arrangements which would enable full participation not only by the present eighteen Members of the Organisation for European Economic Co-operation but also by the two Associate Members, the United States and Canada;

g) desiring to proceed with an examination of improved organisational arrangements which could best accomplish these purposes;

h) recognising the equal interest of all Member and Associate Member Governments of the Organisation for European Economic Co-operation in this matter;

Propose:

1. That a meeting of senior officials of the twenty Governments, Members or Associate Members of the O.E.E.C., and to which the European Communities should also be invited, be convened in Paris on 19th April, 1960, to consider the question of appropriate arrangements to achieve the objectives stated above;

2. That, in order to facilitate the work of such a meeting, a group of four persons should be appointed to prepare a report which would:

a) examine the most effective methods for achieving the objectives referred to above and make appropriate recommendations with respect thereto;

b) submit a draft of articles of agreement, should their examination of this question indicate the desirability of bringing about an appropriately improved organisation for economic co-operation;

c) seraient déterminées, parmi les fonctions actuellement assumées par l'O.E.C.E., celles qui devraient continuer à faire l'objet d'une coopération économique internationale sous l'égide de toute organisation améliorée qui serait proposée, y compris les arrangements institutionnels qu'il conviendrait de prendre à cet égard;

3. Que le groupe désigné ci-dessus consulte les vingt Gouvernements, les Communautés Européennes, et les organisations internationales appropriées, pendant la préparation de son rapport, sans toutefois engager aucun Gouvernement quant à la teneur de celui-ci. Ce rapport sera soumis par les membres du groupe en leur nom personnel; il sera discuté et négocié au cours de la Conférence envisagée au paragraphe 1 ci-dessus.

Document no. 3

Résolution sur l'aide au développement économique

adoptée par le Comité Économique Spécial lors d'une réunion les 12 et 13 janvier 1960 et approuvée par les Ministres des pays Membres et Associés de l'O.E.C.E. le 14 janvier 1960

Le Comité Économique Spécial

Ayant été informé du désir exprimé par les Gouvernements de la Belgique, du Canada, de la France, de l'Italie, du Portugal, de la République Fédérale d'Allemagne, du Royaume-Uni et des États-Unis, ainsi que par la Commission Économique Européenne, qui en sus de leurs contributions aux organisations internationales mettent, ou sont en mesure de mettre, à la disposition des régions sous-développées des capitaux à long terme d'un montant substantiel, de discuter entre eux des techniques propres à faciliter ces apports de capitaux, tout en prenant en considération les autres méthodes d'aide aux pays en voie de développement.

Prend note de ce que ces huit Gouvernements ainsi que la Commission de la Communauté Économique Européenne ont l'intention de se réunir pour discuter des divers aspects de leur coopération dans ce domaine, d'inviter d'autres pays exportateurs de capitaux à participer à leurs travaux ou à se réunir avec eux en tant que de besoin et, de tenir des consultations avec des organisations multilatérales, telles que la Banque Internationale pour la Reconstruction et le Développement et la Banque Européenne d'Investissements.

Document no. 4

Résolution au sujet de certains problèmes commerciaux

adoptée par le Comité Économique Spécial lors d'une réunion les 12 et 13 janvier 1960 et approuvée par les Ministres des pays Membres et Associés de l'O.E.C.E. le 14 janvier 1960

Le Comité Économique Spécial,

Reconnaissant que certains problèmes de politique commerciale préoccupent particulièrement les vingt Gouvernements Membres ou Associés de l'O.E.C.E.;

Prenant note de l'existence de la C.E.E. et de la Convention portant création d'une A.E.L.E.;

c) identify those functions at present performed by the O.E.E.C. which should continue to be the subject of international economic co-operation under the aegis of the proposed improved organisation, including appropriate organisational arrangements with respect thereto;

3. That the group named above should consult with all twenty Governments and the European Communities and appropriate international organisations during the preparation of their report without, however, committing any Government as to the content of the report, which would be submitted by them in their personal capacities and which would be open for discussion and negotiation at the meeting envisaged in paragraph 1 above.

Document No. 3

Resolution on Development Assistance

adopted by the Special Economic Committee at a meeting on 12th–13th January, 1960, and approved by Ministers of Members and Associate Members of O.E.E.C. on 14th January, 1960

The Special Economic Committee,

Having been informed of the desire of the Governments of Belgium, Canada, France, Germany, Italy, Portugal, the United Kingdom, and the United States, and the Commission of the European Economic Community, who, in addition to their contribution to international organisations, are making available or may be in a position to make available a significant flow of long term funds to underdeveloped areas, to discuss among themselves the question of techniques to facilitate such flow of funds, taking into consideration other means of assistance to developing countries;

Notes that these eight Governments and the Commission of the European Economic Community intend to meet together to discuss various aspects of co-operation in their efforts, and to invite other additional capital exporting countries to participate in their work or to meet with them as may from time to time appear desirable, and to consult with such multilateral organisations as the International Bank for Reconstruction and Development and the European Investment Bank.

Document No. 4

Resolution on Certain Trade Problems

adopted by the Special Economic Committee at a meeting on 12th–13th January, 1960, and approved by Ministers of Members and Associate Members of O.E.E.C. on 14th January, 1960

The Special Economic Committee,

Recognising that there are problems of commercial policy of particular concern to the twenty governments who are members of, or associated with, the O.E.E.C.;

Taking note of the existence of the E.E.C. and of the convention for an E.F.T.A.;

Tenant compte des rapports entre les dispositions de ces accords et l'ensemble de la politique commerciale internationale;

Considérant la nécessité d'examiner par priorité les rapports entre la Communauté Économique Européenne et l'Association Européenne de Libre-Échange, compte dûment tenu des intérêts commerciaux des pays tiers, et des principes et obligations du G.A.T.T;

Décide:

1. D'établir un ou plusieurs groupes de travail officieux, afin d'étudier ces problèmes sans empiéter sur les attributions des institutions internationales existantes tels que le G.A.T.T. ou l'O.E.C.E. Ces groupes devraient faire rapport au Comité;

2. D'inviter le Secrétariat Exécutif du G.A.T.T. à participer à ces discussions.

Document no. 5

Résolution relative a la réorganisation de l'O.E.C.E.

adoptée par la Conférence sur la Réorganisation de l'O.E.C.E. le 25 mai 1960

Les Représentants des Gouvernements des pays suivants: Autriche Belgique, Canada, Danemark, République Fédérale d'Allemagne, France, Grèce, Islande, Irlande, Italie, Luxembourg, Pays-Bas, Norvège, Portugal, Espagne, Suède, Suisse, Turquie, Royaume-Uni, États-Unis d'Amérique et des Communautés Européennes, réunis à Paris les 24 et 25 mai 1960;

Vu la Résolution en date du 14 janvier 1960 sur la réorganisation de l'O.E.C.E.;

Désireux de poursuivre activement leurs efforts en vue de réorganiser l'O.E.C.E.;

Vu que l'accord s'est fait dans une large mesure sur les principales idées exprimées dans le Rapport soumis en avril 1960 par le Groupe des Quatre créé par ladite Résolution;

1. Décide:

1. D'instituer un Groupe de Travail comprenant des représentants des vingt Gouvernements et des Communautés Européennes;

2. De charger ce Groupe de Travail:

a) d'élaborer un projet de convention rénovant l'O.E.C.E.;

b) de prendre comme base pour ses travaux le Rapport du Groupe des Quatre en tenant compte des propositions formulées par la Délégation de la Suisse [O.C.D.E.(60)3] ainsi que toutes autres observations présentées au cours des réunions des 24 et 25 mai ou ultérieurement;

c) de dresser, avec la collaboration du Secrétariat de l'O.E.C.E., la liste des Actes de cette Oranisation en vigueur à la date du 1er juin 1960;

d) de définir les critères à appliquer et la procédure à suivre pour l'examen des Actes de l'O.E.C.E. et de chercher à parvenir à un accord général sur ceux qui ont un caractère fondamental ou, à la requête de tout membre du Groupe de Travail, sur tout autre Acte de l'O.E.C.E.;

e) de faire rapport avant le 10 juillet 1960 sur l'exécution du Mandat ci-dessus;

f) de procéder, le cas échéant, à des consultations avec les organisations internationales intéressées.

BEARING IN MIND the relationship between the provisions of these agreements and general international commercial policy;
CONSIDERING the need to examine, as a matter of priority, the relationship between the E.E.C. and the E.F.T.A. with due regard to the commercial interests of third countries and the principles and obligations of the G.A.T.T.;

DECIDES:

To propose to the twenty governments that they constitute themselves, together with the E.E.C., a committee with power to:
1. Establish one or more informal working groups for the consideration of these problems without infringing the competence of the existing international institutions such as the G.A.T.T. or the O.E.E.C.; these groups should report back to the Committee;
2. Transmit an invitation to the Executive Secretary of the G.A.T.T. to participate in these discussions.

Document No. 5

RESOLUTION PERTAINING TO THE RECONSTITUTION OF THE O.E.E.C.

adopted by the Conference on the Reorganisation of the O.E.E.C. on 25th May, 1960

REPRESENTATIVES of the Governments of Austria, Belgium, Canada, Denmark, the Federal Republic of Germany, France, Greece, Iceland, Ireland, Italy, Luxembourg, the Netherlands, Norway, Portugal, Spain, Sweden, Switzerland, Turkey, the United Kingdom, the United States of America, and the European Communities, meeting in Paris on 24th and 25th May, 1960;
HAVING regard to the Resolution of 14th January, 1960, on the reorganisation of the O.E.E.C.;
DESIROUS of actively pursuing their efforts to reorganise the O.E.E.C.;

HAVING regard to the large measure of agreement expressed with the main ideas in the Report of April 1960 of the Group of Four set up by the said Resolution;

I. DECIDE:

1. To set up a Working Party of Representatives of the Twenty Governments and the European Communities;
2. To instruct the Working Party:
a) to draw up a Draft Convention remodelling the O.E.E.C.;
b) to base its work on the Report of the Group of Four, taking into account the proposals submitted by the Swiss Delegation [O.E.C.D.(60)3], as well as all other comments made during the meetings on 24th and 25th May or subsequently;
c) to draw up in co-operation with the Secretariat of the O.E.E.C. a list of the Acts of that Organisation in force on 1st June, 1960;
d) to establish criteria and procedure for the review of the Acts of the O.E.E.C., and to seek general agreement on those which have a fundamental character and, at the request of any Member of the Working Party, on any other Act of the O.E.E.C.;
e) to report before 10th July on the execution of the above mandate;
f) to consult, as appropriate, with the relevant international organisations.

II. Recommande qu'une Conférence ministérielle soit convoquée à Paris avant la fin de juillet 1960, avec pour objet, sous réserve que les travaux du Groupe de Travail aient progressé de façon satisfaisante, de traiter des questions suivantes:

1. Examiner le Rapport visé au paragraphe 2 *e*) de la Section I ci-dessus;

2. Examiner, en vue de l'approuver à titre provisoire, une Convention transformant l'O.E.C.E. en Organisation de Coopération Économique et de Développement;

3. Nommer un Secrétaire Général désigné de l'O.C.D.E.;

4. Constituer un Comité préparatoire, présidé par le Secrétaire Général désigné, et chargé de poursuivre l'examen des Actes du Conseil de l'O.E.C.E. prévu au paragraphe 2 *d*) de la Section I ci-dessus et réexaminer, le cas échéant, le projet de Convention;

5. Définir les fonctions générales et les caractéristiques qu'aura l'O.C.D.E. en ce qui concerne le développement des régions en voie de développement aussi bien dans les pays Membres qu'ailleurs, et pour la période transitoire, autoriser le Secrétaire Général désigné à organiser la liaison avec l'actuel Groupe d'Aide au Développement;

En vue de la convocation d'une seconde Conférence ministérielle à Paris avant la fin de 1960 pour examiner les travaux effectués par le Comité Préparatoire et pour signer la Convention de l'Organisation de Coopération Économique et de Développement.

Document no. 6

Résolution relative au Comité Préparatoire

adoptée par les Ministres lors de la réunion du 23 juillet 1960
O.C.D.E.(60)14(Final).

Les Représentants des Gouvernements des pays suivants: République Fédérale d'Allemagne, Autriche, Belgique, Canada, Danemark, Espagne, États-Unis, France, Grèce, Irlande, Islande, Italie, Luxembourg, Norvège, Pays-Bas, Portugal, Royaume-Uni, Suède, Suisse, Turquie et les Représentants des Communautés Européennes réunis à Paris les 22 et 23 juillet 1960;

Vu la Résolution du 25 mai 1960 relative à la Réorganisation de l'Organisation Européenne de Coopération Économique;

Vu le Rapport du Groupe de Travail créé le 25 mai 1960 et ses Addendums:

Décident:

1. Le Comité Préparatoire, prévu dans la Résolution du 25 mai 1960, mentionnée ci-dessus, est créé. Le Secrétaire Général Désigné le préside. Le Comité Préparatoire accomplit sa tâche conformément aux autres Résolutions et Décisions adoptées par la présente Réunion Ministérielle.

2. Le Comité Préparatoire est chargé:

a) de parfaire le Projet de Convention relative à l'Organisation de Coopération et de Développement Économiques;

b) de poursuivre l'examen des Actes de l'Organisation Européenne de Coopération Économique; de déterminer les Actes dont il convient de recommander l'approbation au Conseil de l'Organisation rénovée; et de proposer, le cas échéant, les modifications nécessaires en vue d'adapter ces Actes aux fonctions de l'Organisation rénovée, telles qu'elles sont actuellement convenues par les Gouvernements.

II. Recommend that a Ministerial Conference be convened in Paris before the end of July 1960, in order, subject to satisfactory progress in the Working Party, to deal with the following questions:

1. To consider the Report referred to at I. 2 *e*) above;
2. To consider, with a view to approving provisionally, a Convention reconstituting the O.E.E.C. as the Organisation for Economic Co-operation and Development;
3. To name a Secretary-General-Designate of the O.E.C.D.;
4. To establish a Preparatory Committee, chaired by the Secretary-General-Designate, to carry further the review of the Acts of the O.E.E.C. Council, as provided for under paragraph 2 *d*) of Section I above, and to re-examine the draft Convention if necessary;
5. To set forth the future general functions and characteristics of the O.E.C.D. in connection with the development of less-developed areas, both in Member countries and elsewhere, and for the interim authorise the Secretary-General-Designate to establish appropriate liaison with the present Development Assistance Group;

with a view to convening a second Ministerial Conference in Paris before the end of 1960 to consider the work done by the Preparatory Committee and to sign the Convention of the Organisation for Economic Co-operation and Development.

Document No. 6

Resolution relating to the Preparatory Committee

adopted at the Ministerial Meeting on 23rd July, 1960
O.E.C.D.(60)14(Final)

The Representatives of the Governments of Austria, Belgium, Canada, Denmark, the Federal Republic of Germany, France, Greece, Iceland, Ireland, Italy, Luxembourg, the Netherlands, Norway, Portugal, Spain, Sweden, Switzerland, Turkey, the United Kingdom, the United States of America and Representatives of the European Communities, meeting in Paris on 22nd and 23rd July, 1960;

Having regard to the Resolution of 25th May, 1960, on the Reorganisation of the Organisation for European Economic Co-operation;

Having regard to the Report by the Working Party established on 25th May, 1960, and its Addenda;

Decide:

1. The Preparatory Committee provided for in the Resolution of 25th May, 1960, referred to above, is established. The Secretary-General Designate shall act as its Chairman. The Preparatory Committee shall perform its work in conformity with the other Resolutions and Decisions adopted by this Ministerial Meeting.
2. The Preparatory Committee is instructed:

a) to complete the Draft Convention on the O.E.C.D.;

b) to carry further the review of the Acts of the O.E.E.C.; to determine which Acts should be recommended to the Council of the reconstituted Organisation for approval; and to propose, where necessary, the modifications required in order to adapt these Acts to the functions of the reconstituted Organisation as currently agreed by governments;

c) de définir la structure de l'Organisation rénovée et d'établir le mandat des principaux organes nécessaires à l'accomplissement des tâches actuellement convenues pour l'Organisation rénovée;

d) de rédiger l'instrument relatif à l'article 15 de la Convention;

e) d'établir une liste et une description succincte de tous les accords et contrats de l'Organisation Européenne de Coopération Économique qui resteront en vigueur après le 30 juin 1961;

f) d'établir un Rapport sur ses travaux avant le 10 novembre 1960;

g) d'organiser une Réunion Ministérielle, en vue d'examiner le Rapport du Comité Préparatoire et de parvenir à un accord sur les dispositions de la Convention avant la fin de 1960.

Document no. 7

Résolution relative aux échanges [1]

adoptée par les Ministres lors de la réunion du 23 juillet 1960
O.C.D.E.(60)9(Final)

Les Représentants des Gouvernements des pays suivants: République Fédérale d'Allemagne, Autriche, Belgique, Canada, Danemark, Espagne, États-Unis, France, Grèce, Irlande, Islande, Italie, Luxembourg, Norvège, Pays-Bas, Portugal, Royaume-Uni, Suède, Suisse, Turquie et les Représentants des Communautés Européennes réunis à Paris les 22 et 23 juillet 1960;

Ayant examiné les dispositions sur les échanges, contenues dans le projet de Convention relative à l'Organisation de Coopération et de Développement Économiques, qui a été soumis par le Groupe de Travail institué le 25 mai 1960, ainsi que les commentaires y relatifs figurant dans le Rapport de ce Groupe de Travail;

Sont convenus de ce qui suit:

1. Le Projet de Protocole additionnel no. . . . au projet de Convention s'établit comme suit:

,,Les signataires de la Convention relative à l'Organisation de Coopération et de Développement Économiques;

Vu le paragraphe *c*) de l'Article 1 de la Convention;

Sont convenus de ce qui suit:

Il est institué au sein de l'Organisation de Coopération et de Développement Économiques un Comité des Échanges qui assume notamment les fonctions suivantes:

a) Confrontation à intervalles réguliers ou à la demande d'un Membre des politiques commerciales générales et des pratiques en matière d'échanges, compte tenu de la nécessité de maintenir un système de commerce multilatéral permettant aux Membres d'échanger librement des biens et des services entre eux et avec les pays tiers, tout en maintenant un équilibre raisonnable des balances internationales de paiements.

b) Examen de problèmes spécifiques en matière d'échanges intéressant principalement les Membres et leurs territoires d'outre-mer.

c) Examen de ceux des problèmes commerciaux à court et à long terme actuellement étudiés par le Comité des Questions commerciales, créé lors de la réunion ministérielle des 13 et 14 janvier 1960, qui ne sont pas encore réglés''.

[1] Lors de la réunion du 13 décembre 1960, les Ministres ont décidé que le mandat du Comité des Échanges serait inclus dans le Rapport du Comité Préparatoire (*voir* parag. 16 du Rapport, page 32).

c) to define the structure of the reconstituted Organisation and to draw up the terms of reference of the main organs necessary for the accomplishment of the tasks currently agreed for the reconstituted Organisation;

d) to draft the instrument relating to Article 15 of that Convention;

e) to prepare a list and summary description of all agreements and contracts of the O.E.E.C. which will remain in force after 30th June, 1961;

f) to prepare a Report on its work by 10th November, 1960;

g) to arrange for a Ministerial Meeting to consider the Report of the Preparatory Committee and reach agreement on the Articles of the Convention before the end of 1960.

Document No. 7

RESOLUTION ON TRADE [1]

adopted at the Ministerial Meeting on 23rd July, 1960
O.E.C.D.(60)9(Final)

Representatives of the Governments of Austria, Belgium, Canada, Denmark, the Federal Republic of Germany, France, Greece, Iceland, Ireland, Italy, Luxembourg, the Netherlands, Norway, Portugal, Spain, Sweden, Switzerland, Turkey, the United Kingdom, the United States of America and Representatives of the European Communities, meeting in Paris on 22nd and 23rd July, 1960;

HAVING EXAMINED the provisions on trade of the Draft Convention on the Organisation for Economic Co-operation and Development submitted by the Working Party established on 25th May, 1960, as well as the related comments of the Working Party;

HAVE AGREED AS FOLLOWS:

1. Draft Supplementary Protocol No. ... to the Draft Convention shall read as follows:

"THE SIGNATORIES of the Convention on the Organisation for Economic Co-operation and Development;

HAVING REGARD to paragraph *c*) of Article 1 of that Convention;

HAVE AGREED:

There shall be established within the Organisation for Economic Co-operation and Development a Trade Committee which shall carry out, in particular, the following functions:

a) Confrontation of the general trade policies and practices at regular intervals or whenever requested by a Member, having in mind the need for maintaining a system of multilateral trade which would enable Members to exchange goods and services freely with each other and with other countries under conditions of reasonable overall equilibrium in international balance of payments;

b) Examination of specific trade problems primarily of interest to Members and their overseas territories; and

c) Consideration of any short and long-term trade problems currently being considered by the Committee on Trade Problems established by the Ministerial Meeting of 13th–14th January, 1960, which remain outstanding".

---

[1] At the meeting on 13th December, 1960, the Ministers decided that the mandate of the Trade Committee should be included in the Report of the Preparatory Committee (*see* paragraphe 16 of the Report, page 32).

2. Il est entendu que les dispositions relatives au Comité des Échanges prévu dans le Projet de Protocole mentionné au paragraphe 1 ci-dessus permettraient à tout pays Membre d'obtenir que le Comité examine et discute rapidement les mesures prises par un autre Membre dans le domaine des échanges et qui porteraient préjudice à ses intérêts, en vue de supprimer ou d'atténuer le préjudice en question.

3. Les engagements du Code de la Libération en matière de libération des échanges ne devraient pas être maintenus dans l'O.C.D.E. Les actes commerciaux autres que le Code de la Libération seront examinés par le Comité Préparatoire.[1]

4. Le Comité Préparatoire est chargé d'élaborer les méthodes et moyens par lesquels le Comité des Échanges exercera ses fonctions.

Document no. 8

Résolution relative a l'aide aux pays en voie de développement

adoptée par les Ministres lors de la réunion du 23 juillet 1960
O.C.D.E.(60)13

Les Représentants ministériels des Gouvernements des pays suivants: Autriche, Belgique, Canada, Danemark, République Fédérale d'Allemagne, France, Grèce, Irlande, Islande, Italie, Luxembourg, Pays-Bas, Norvège, Portugal, Espagne, Suède, Suisse, Turquie, Royaume Uni, États-Unis d'Amérique et les Représentants des Communautés Européennes, réunis à Paris le 22 juillet 1960;

Vu la Résolution du Comité Économique Spécial en date du 14 janvier 1960 sur la réorganisation de l'O.E.C.E. qui indiquait „la nécessité de consacrer des efforts accrus au développement des pays sous-développés" et la Résolution de la Conférence sur la réorganisation de l'O.E.C.E., en date du 25 mai 1960;

Prenant note de la constitution, en janvier 1960, d'un Groupe d'Aide au Développement;

Prenant note de l'intention du Groupe d'Aide au Développement de limiter ses discussions aux questions d'intérêt général et aux moyens d'améliorer et d'augmenter l'aide, et de ne pas examiner l'assistance à des régions, pays ou projets particuliers;

Décide:

1. L'un des principaux objectifs de l'O.C.D.E. sera de mettre en œuvre la coopération et les consultations tendant à faciliter le développement économique des pays moins développés du monde par les moyens appropriés.

2. Le Secrétaire Général désigné sera habilité à établir la liaison nécessaire avec le présent Groupe d'Aide au Développement mentionné dans le Préambule ci-dessus.

3. Ce Groupe d'Aide au Développement sera, lors de la création de l'O.C.D.E., constitué en un Comité d'Aide au Développement qui conservera les fonctions et les caractéristiques actuelles du Groupe d'Aide au Développement. Les activités de l'O.C.D.E. à cet égard seront menées en tenant dûment compte des activités des autres organisations internationales.

---

[1] La Délégation suisse propose de reprendre le texte intégral du paragraphe 40 du document O.C.D.E.(60)5.

2. It is understood that the provisions relating to the Trade Committee provided for in the Draft Protocol set out in paragraph 1 would enable any Member country to obtain prompt consideration and discussion by the Committee of trade measures by another Member which adversely affect its interests, with a view to removing or minimising such adverse effects.

3. The undertakings of the Code of Liberalisation with regard to Liberalisation of Trade should not be continued in the Organisation for Economic Co-operation and Development. All other Acts on Trade in the Organisation for European Economic Co-operation shall be studied by the Preparatory Committee.[1]

4. The Preparatory Committee shall be responsible for working out ways and means in accordance with which the Trade Committee shall exercise its functions.

Document No. 8

Resolution on Aid to Developing Countries

adopted at the Ministerial meeting on 23rd July, 1960
O.E.C.D.(60)13

Ministerial Representatives of the Governments of Austria, Belgium, Canada, Denmark, the Federal Republic of Germany, France, Greece, Iceland, Ireland, Italy, Luxembourg, the Netherlands, Norway, Portugal, Spain, Sweden, Switzerland, Turkey, the United Kingdom, the United States of America and the Representatives of the European Communities, meeting in Paris the 22nd July, 1960;

Having regard to the Resolution of the Special Economic Committee of 14th January, 1960, on the reorganisation of the O.E.E.C. which expressed "the need to devote increased efforts towards furthering the development of less-developed countries" and to the Resolution of 25th May, 1960, of the Conference on the Reorganisation of the O.E.E.C.;

Taking note of the formation in January 1960, of a Development Assistance Group;

Taking note of the intention of the Development Assistance Group to confine its discussion to matters of general principle and methods of improving and expanding aid and not to discuss aid for particular areas, countries or projects;

Decide:

1. That the O.E.C.D. shall have as one of its major objectives the carrying out of economic co-operation and consultation designed to facilitate the economic development of less-developed countries in the world by appropriate means;

2. That the Secretary-General Designate shall be authorised to establish appropriate liaison with the present Development Assistance Group referred to in the Preamble above;

3. That this Development Assistance Group shall, upon the inception of the O.E.C.D., be constituted as a Development Assistance Committee continuing the present functions and characteristics of the Development Assistance Group. The activities of the O.E.C.D. in this respect shall be conducted with due regard to the activities of other international organisations.

---

[1] The Swiss Delegation would prefer the whole text of paragraph 40 of Document O.E.C.D.(60)5.

4. L'aide particulière, sous quelque forme que ce soit, accordée aux pays Membres moins développés sera du ressort d'organes de l'Organisation rénovée autres que le Comité mentionné au paragraphe 3 ci-dessus.

5. Le Comité Préparatoire sera chargé de préciser les modalités d'application des décisions des paragraphes ci-dessus, en tenant compte particulièrement du paragraphe 4.

Document no. 9

Résolution sur la participation aux travaux de l'O.C.D.E. du Secrétaire Général de l'Association Européenne de Libre-Échange

adoptée par les Ministres lors de la réunion du 23 juillet 1960
O.C.D.E.(60)15(Final)

Les Représentants ministériels des Gouvernements des pays suivants: Autriche, Belgique, Canada, Danemark, République Fédérale d'Allemagne, France, Grèce, Irlande, Islande, Italie, Luxembourg, Pays-Bas, Norvège, Portugal, Espagne, Suède, Suisse, Turquie, Royaume-Uni, États-Unis d'Amérique et les Représentants des Communautés Européennes sont convenus de ce qui suit:

Le Secrétaire Général de l'Association Européenne de Libre-Échange participera aux travaux de l'O.C.D.E.

Document no. 10

Résolution concernant le Rapport du Comité Préparatoire

adoptée par les Ministres lors de la réunion du 13 décembre 1960

Les Représentants des Gouvernements des pays suivants: République Fédérale d'Allemagne, Autriche, Belgique, Canada, Danemark, Espagne, États-Unis, France, Grèce, Irlande, Islande, Italie, Luxembourg, Norvège, Pays-Bas, Portugal, Royaume-Uni, Suède, Suisse et Turquie:

Vu la Résolution relative au Comité Préparatoire adoptée à la Réunion ministérielle du 23 juillet 1960;

Vu la Convention relative à l'Organisation de Coopération et de Développement Économiques;

Désireux de donner effet aux recommandations du Comité Préparatoire;

Approuvent le Rapport du Comité Préparatoire et acceptent les recommandations qu'il contient.

Document no. 11

Communiqué de presse

adopté par les Ministres lors de la réunion du 13 décembre 1960

Le Canada et les États-Unis se sont joints aujourd'hui aux dix-huit pays européens Membres de l'Organisation Européenne de Coopération Économique (O.E.C.E.) [1] pour décider de signer le 14 décembre une

[1] Allemagne, Autriche, Belgique, Danemark, Espagne, France, Grèce, Irlande, Islande, Italie, Luxembourg, Norvège, Pays-Bas, Portugal, Royaume-Uni, Suède, Suisse, Turquie.

4. That specific assistance, of whatever category, extended to less-developed Member countries shall be considered by bodies in the reconstituted Organisation other than the Committee refered to in paragraph 3;

5. That the Preparatory Committee shall work out in detail how the provisions of the preceding paragraphs should be implemented, with particular reference to paragraph 4.

Document No. 9

Resolution concerning the Participation of the Secretary-General of the European Free Trade Association in the work of the O.E.C.D.

adopted at the Ministerial meeting on 23rd July, 1960

O.E.C.D.(60)15(Final)

The Ministerial Representatives of the Governments of Austria, Belgium, Canada, Denmark, the Federal Republic of Germany, France, Greece, Iceland, Ireland, Italy, Luxembourg, the Netherlands, Norway, Portugal, Spain, Sweden, Switzerland, Turkey, the United Kingdom, the United States of America and the Representatives of the European Communities have agreed as follows:

The Secretary-General of the European Free Trade Association shall take part in the work of the O.E.C.D.

Document No. 10

Resolution concerning the Report of the Preparatory Committee

adopted at the Ministerial Meeting on 13th December, 1960

Representatives of the Governments of the following countries: Austria, Belgium, Canada, Denmark, the Federal Republic of Germany, France, Greece, Iceland, Ireland, Italy, Luxembourg, the Netherlands, Norway, Portugal, Spain, Sweden, Switzerland, Turkey, the United Kingdom, and the United States of America;

Having regard to the Resolution relating to the Preparatory Committee adopted at the Ministerial Meeting of 23rd July, 1960;

Having regard to the Convention on the Organisation for Economic Co-operation and Development;

Desiring that effect be given to the recommendations of the Preparatory Committee;

Approve the Report of the Preparatory Committee and accept the recommendations contained therein.

Document No. 11

Press Communiqué

adopted at the Ministerial Meeting on 13th December, 1960

Canada and the United States today joined with the eighteen European countries Members of the Organisation for European Economic Co-operation (O.E.E.C.) [1] in deciding to sign on the 14th December a Con-

[1] Austria, Belgium, Denmark, France, Germany, Greece, Iceland, Ireland, Italy, Luxembourg, the Netherlands, Norway, Portugal, Spain, Sweden, Switzerland, Turkey, the United Kingdom.

Convention créant l'Organisation de Coopération et de Développement Économiques (O.C.D.E.) qui succèdera à l'O.E.C.E.

Les Ministres des vingt pays, qui se sont réunis à Paris le 13 décembre 1960, ont aussi approuvé un Rapport définissant les activités et la structure de l'O.C.D.E.

Les Représentants des Communautés Européennes, qui ont pris part aux négociations, ont participé à la réunion; le Secrétaire Général de l'A.E.L.E. et des observateurs du G.A.T.T., de la B.I.R.D. et du F.M.I. étaient aussi présents.

Le rétablissement et les progrès de l'économie européenne, soutenus par l'aide généreuse des États-Unis, ainsi que par celle du Canada, et réalisés grâce à la coopération établie au sein de l'O.E.C.E., permettent à présent aux pays d'Europe de faire face, en pleine et étroite coopération avec le Canada et les États-Unis, aux tâches nouvelles et importantes et aux objectifs plus amples d'aujourd'hui.

Ces objectifs sont définis par la Convention dans les termes suivants:

- réaliser la plus forte expansion possible de l'économie et de l'emploi et une progression du niveau de vie dans les pays Membres, tout en maintenant la stabilité financière, et contribuer ainsi au développement de l'économie mondiale;
- contribuer à une saine expansion économique dans les pays Membres et les pays non-membres en voie de développement économique;
- contribuer à l'expansion du commerce mondial sur une base multilatérale et non discriminatoire conformément aux obligations internationales.

La Convention prévoit la création d'un Conseil qui sera l'instance suprême de l'Organisation et qui aura le pouvoir de prendre des décisions et de faire des recommandations par accord mutuel de tous ses membres. En outre, les Ministres ont approuvé l'établissement d'un ensemble de Comités qui aidera à atteindre les objectifs et à accomplir les tâches de l'Organisation.

L'O.C.D.E. développera et renforcera la procédure de consultations relatives à la situation et à la politique des pays Membres, déjà pratiquée par l'O.E.C.E. Elle se préoccupera particulièrement des conséquences internationales des politiques nationales afin de créer la compréhension mutuelle qui permettra un ajustement harmonieux de ces politiques. Ces consultations constitueront une activité majeure de l'Organisation en vue de réaliser l'expansion économique qui est essentielle pour permettre aux pays Membres d'assumer les responsabilités qui sont les leurs à l'égard de l'économie mondiale.

D'importantes fonctions sont dévolues à l'O.C.D.E. dans le domaine de l'aide aux pays en voie de développement. Les vingt Gouvernements sont convenus dans la Convention de contribuer au développement économique des pays Membres ainsi que des pays non-membres en voie de développement économique par des moyens appropriés, et, en particulier, par l'apport à ces pays de capitaux, en tenant en outre compte de l'importance que présentent pour leur économie la fourniture d'assistance technique et l'élargissement des débouchés offerts à leurs produits d'exportation. La plupart des instances de l'O.C.D.E. auront un rôle à jouer dans la réalisation de cette tâche.

Le Groupe d'Aide au Développement, créé au début de cette année, et qui comprend actuellement onze membres, sera, dès l'entrée en fonction de l'O.C.D.E., constitué en un Comité d'Aide au Développement. Ce Comité poursuivra les consultations destinées à rendre disponible pour aide aux pays et régions en voie de développement une part des ressources nationales, et à accroître et améliorer l'apport de capitaux à long terme ainsi que toute autre forme d'aide au développement, en faveur de ces pays et régions.

vention setting up the Organisation for Economic Co-operation and Development (O.E.C.D.) which will take the place of the O.E.E.C.

Ministers of the twenty countries, who met in Paris on 13th December, 1960, also approved a Report setting forth the activities and structure of the O.E.C.D.

The Representatives of the European Communities, who have taken part in the negotiations, participated in the meeting; also present were the Secretary-General of the E.F.T.A. and observers from the G.A.T.T., I.B.R.D. and I.M.F.

With the recovery and progress of the European economy, sustained by the generous aid of the United States as well as of Canada, and furthered by the co-operation established within the O.E.E.C., the European countries are now in a position to face, in full and close co-operation with Canada and the United States, the important new tasks and the broader objectives of today.

These objectives are set forth in the Convention in these terms:

- to achieve the highest sustainable economic growth and employment and a rising standard of living in the Member countries while maintaining financial stability and thus to contribute to the development of the world economy;
- to contribute to sound economic expansion in Member as well as non-member countries in the process of economic development; and
- to contribute to the expansion of world trade on a multilateral non-discriminatory basis in accordance with international obligations.

The Convention provides for the establishment of a Council, the supreme body of the Organisation, with power to take decisions and make recommendations with the unanimous agreement of its Members. In addition, the Ministers agreed on a committee structure to assist in implementing the aims and carrying out the activities of the Organisation.

The O.E.C.D. will extend and strengthen the O.E.E.C. practice of consultation on the economic situation and policies of Member countries. It will pay special attention to the international effects of national policies, with a view to establishing a climate of mutual understanding conducive to the harmonious adjustment of policies. These consultations will be a major activity in pursuing the objective of economic growth, essential to enable the Member countries to fulfil their responsibilities in the world economy.

The O.E.C.D. will have important functions in the matter of assistance to developing countries. The twenty Governments have agreed in the Convention to contribute to the economic development of both Member and non-member countries in the process of economic development by appropriate means and, in particular, by the flow of capital to those countries, having regard to the importance to their economies of receiving technical assistance and of securing expanding export markets. Most of the organs of O.E.C.D. will have a part to play in the realisation of this undertaking.

The eleven-member Development Assistance Group, set up earlier this year, will, upon the inception of the O.E.C.D., be constituted as the Development Assistance Committee. This Committee will continue to consult on the methods for making national resources available for assisting countries and areas in the process of economic development, and for expanding and improving the flow of long-term funds and other development assistance to them.

Dans le domaine des échanges, l'O.C.D.E. remplira les fonctions suivantes: confrontation des politiques commerciales générales et des pratiques en matière d'échanges, à intervalles réguliers ou à la demande d'un pays Membre; examen des problèmes spécifiques intéressant au premier chef les pays Membres; examen des problèmes commerciaux à court et à long terme que le Comité des Questions Commerciales, établi en janvier 1960, a reçu mandat de traiter et qui n'auraient pas encore été réglés par lui.

Outre ces tâches, l'O.C.D.E. développera et renforcera, en les adoptant aux objectifs qui lui sont assignés, les tâches de l'O.E.C.E., dont une expérience de plus de dix années a prouvé l'utilité.

L'O.C.D.E. sera ainsi capable de réaliser les voeux des pays qui l'ont créée: devenir le lieu où vingt pays se consulteront, coopéreront étroitement et, le cas échéant, coordonneront leur action en vue de faire face aux tâches économiques qui les confrontent aujourd'hui.

Document no. 12

Recommandation 245 (1960) de l'Assemblée Consultative du Conseil de l'Europe [1]

relative à un organe consultatif de l'Organisation de Coopération et de Développement Économiques

L'Assemblée,

Vu sa Résolution 172;

Ayant pris connaissance des suggestions faites par son Groupe spécial au „Groupe des Quatre" chargé d'établir un rapport sur la réorganisation de l'O.E.C.E., en vue d'assurer que les Représentants à l'Assemblée Consultative puissent, dans des réunions régulières se plaçant en dehors du cadre statutaire du Conseil de l'Europe, exercer, avec les Représentants des Parlements ou des Assemblées prévus par les constitutions ou lois organiques des cinq États qui feront partie de l'O.C.D.E. sans être membres du Conseil de l'Europe, des fonctions consultatives au sujet des activités de l'O.C.D.E.;

Recommande au Comité des Ministres:

1. D'inviter les Gouvernements membres à soumettre aux Conférences internationales chargées d'élaborer la Convention sur l'Organisation de Coopération et de Développement Économiques, le texte ci-après, soit pour l'inclure dans la Convention, soit pour en faire un Protocole additionnel, destiné à être annexé à ladite Convention sur l'O.C.D.E.:

„*a*) en vue d'exercer les fonctions d'organe consultatif de l'O.C.D.E. les membres de l'Assemblée Consultative du Conseil de l'Europe se réunissant au moins une fois par an, avec les représentants des Parlements ou Assemblées prévus par les constitutions ou lois organiques des cinq États qui font partie de l'O.C.D.E. sans être membres du Conseil de l'Europe.

b) les modalités de fonctionnement de ces réunions qui se tiendront en dehors du cadre statutaire du Conseil de l'Europe seront réglées d'un commun accord entre les organes de l'O.C.D.E. et du Conseil de l'Europe".

2. De tenir le Président de l'Assemblée au courant des mesures prises à ce sujet et de faire rapport à l'Assemblée Consultative au cours de la 2e partie de sa 12e Session.

[1] Discussion par l'Assemblée les 26, 27 et 29 avril 1960 (3e, 4e et 8e séances) (*voir* Doc. 1137, Rapport de la Commission politique.)
Texte adopté par l'Assemblée le 29 avril 1960 (8e séance).

In the field of trade the O.E.C.D. will carry out the following functions: confrontations on general trade policies and practices at regular intervals or when requested by a Member; examination of specific trade problems primarily of interest to Members; and consideration of any outstanding short and long-term problems falling within the terms of reference of the Committee on Trade Problems established in January, 1960.

In addition to these activities, the O.E.C.D. will expand and strengthen those activities of the O.E.E.C. which have proved their practical value for more than a decade and which are to be taken over by the O.E.C.D. in pursuance of its objectives.

The O.E.C.D. will thus be able to fulfil the desire of the countries which have created it by becoming the forum in which twenty countries will consult, co-operate closely and, where appropriate, take co-ordinated action to meet the economic tasks which face them today.

Document No. 12

RECOMMENDATION 245 (1960) OF THE CONSULTATIVE ASSEMBLY OF THE COUNCIL OF EUROPE [1]

concerning an advisory body for the Organisation for Economic Co-operation and Development

THE ASSEMBLY,

HAVING REGARD to its Resolution 172;

Having noted the suggestion made by its special group to the "Group of Four" instructed to report on the reorganisation of O.E.E.C. that Representatives of the Consultative Assembly be enabled, outside the official proceedings of that body, to hold regular meetings with representatives of the Parliaments or Assemblies established under the constitutions or basic laws of the five countries not Members of the Council of Europe which will be Members of O.E.C.D., for the purpose of exercising advisory functions in regard to the activities of the latter Organisation;

RECOMMENDS that the Committee of Ministers:

1. Invite Member Governments to submit to the international conferences instructed to prepare the Convention on the Organisation for Economic Co-operation and Development the text given hereunder, either for inclusion in the Convention, or as a Protocol thereto:

a) "for the purpose of acting as an advisory body to O.E.C.D., members of the Consultative Assembly of the Council of Europe shall hold meetings at least once a year with representatives of the Parliaments or Assemblies established under the constitutions or basic laws of the five States not Members of the Council of Europe which are Members of O.E.C.D.

b) Details of the way in which such meetings will be held shall be settled by agreement between the institutions of O.E.C.D. and those of the Council of Europe. They shall take place outside the official proceedings of the Council of Europe".

2. Keep the President of the Assembly regularly informed of action taken in this matter and report to the Consultative Assembly at the second part of its 12th Session.

---

[1] Assembly debate on 26th, 27th and 29th April, 1960, (3rd, 4th and 8th Sittings) (*see* Document 1137, Report of the Political Committee)
Text adopted by the Assembly on 29th April, 1960, (8th Sitting).

C. PUBLICATIONS 1960

AVANT-PROPOS

La plupart de nos lecteurs auront appris par les informations diffusées dans la presse que l'Organisation Européenne de Coopération Économique doit faire l'objet d'une profonde réforme destinée à „rénover" à la fois sa structure et ses attributions. Le Canada et les États-Unis seront membres de plein exercice de la nouvelle organisation, cependant que d'autres pays situés hors d'Europe pourront être plus étroitement liés à son activité. Il serait prématuré, à l'heure où nous mettons sous presse, de donner d'autres informations sur ce sujet, mais, en ce qui concerne nos publications, aucun ralentissement d'activité n'est à prévoir pendant la période de transition. Nos ouvrages continueront donc de constituer une source unique de renseignements sur tous les aspects de la vie économique en Europe et en Amérique du Nord.

I. ÉCONOMIE, FINANCE, STATISTIQUES

Publié sous le titre *l'Europe et l'économie mondiale*, le Onzième Rapport annuel de l'O.E.C.E. faisait déjà état de préoccupations plus larges de celle-ci. Contrairement aux rapports annuels précédents, qui s'attachaient aux résultats internes de la coopération économique entre pays Membres et Associés, le Onzième Rapport s'efforçait de replacer la situation de ces pays dans le contexte mondial. Les chapitres par pays publiés à l'occasion de l'examen annuel ont toutefois continué de mettre l'accent sur la situation à l'intérieur de chaque pays, examinée d'un point de vue européen.

D'autres publications méritent une mention particulière dans le domaine économique: le *Code de la libération* grâce auquel le commerce intra-européen a pris une extension considérable au cours des douze dernières années – a fait l'objet d'une nouvelle édition révisée et mise à jour; le Comité fiscal de l'O.E.C.E. a publié son troisième rapport sur *l'Élimination des doubles impositions*, et le Comité de direction de l'Accord Monétaire Européen son *Premier Rapport annuel*. Un nouveau pas a été fait avec la signature du *Code de la libération des mouvements de capitaux*, dont le texte fut publié en janvier, puis révisé en juin; enfin les études menées par l'O.E.C.E. en matière de comptabilité nationale ont donné lieu à deux nouvelles publications, dont le très grand intérêt n'échappera pas aux spécialistes: *Statistics of Sources and Uses of Finance* (publié seulement en anglais) et *Systèmes de comptes nationaux en Afrique*. Ce dernier ouvrage a été réalisé avec le concours de la Commission de coopération technique en Afrique au sud du Sahara.

II. INDUSTRIE ET COMMERCE

Dans cette catégorie d'ouvrages, celui qui a eu le plus grand retentissement est sans doute le rapport publié par la Commission consultative pour l'énergie de l'O.E.C.E. sous le titre *l'Énergie en Europe: Nouvelles perspectives*. Mentionnons également la série *la Situation dans les secteurs économiques*, qui a inauguré sa septième année de publication, et la parution entre janvier et juin des volumes II à IV du compte rendu de la Conférence de Stresa sur *l'Industrie devant l'énergie nucléaire*.

Le Bureau du Personnel Scientifique et Technique de l'O.E.C.E., organisme récemment créé, a débuté une nouvelle collection en publiant *l'Enseignement par la télévision* et *Prévoir les cadres de demain*. Parmi les nombreux titres publiés pour l'Agence Européenne de Productivité, *l'Étude des marchés en Europe* et le *Guide de la législation sur les pratiques commerciales restrictives* ont soulevé un très large intérêt.

C. PUBLICATIONS 1960

FOREWORD

As most of our readers will have learned from reports in the Press, the Organisation for European Economic Co-operation is shortly to be "re-modelled" into a new organisation, of which Canada and the United States of America will become full Members, while other countries outside Europe may also be more closely linked with its activities. It is too early, at the time of going to press, to make detailed forecasts of the future shape of the organisation but we can say, as far as our publications are concerned, that there are no signs of any slackening of activity, and there is every reason to believe that they will continue to be a unique source of information on all aspects of economic life in Europe and North America.

I. ECONOMY, FINANCE AND STATISTICS

The widening interests of the Organisation were foreshadowed in April 1960 when the Eleventh Annual Economic Review was published under the title *Europe and the World Economy*. As the title implies, this report attempted to show the situation of the European countries, both separately and as a whole, in the overall economic context, whereas previous Annual Reviews had been mainly concerned with the internal effects of economic co-operation between the Member and Associated Countries of O.E.E.C. The country chapters published in connection with the Annual Review continued, however, to place their emphasis on the domestic situation within each country.

Other noteworthy publications were a new and up-to-date edition of the *Code of Liberalisation*, which is the framework within which the freeing of intra-European trade has made such considerable progress over the past twelve years, the O.E.E.C. Fiscal Committee's Third Report on *The Elimination of Double Taxation*, the *First Annual Report of the Board of Management of the European Monetary Agreement*, the *Code of Liberalisation of Capital Movements* and two further contributions to the study of national accounts with *Statistics of Sources and Uses of Finance*, and *Systems of National Accounting in Africa*, the latter being published in co-operation with the Commission for Technical Co-operation in Africa South of the Sahara.

II. INDUSTRY AND COMMERCE

Towards a New Energy Pattern in Europe – a report of the O.E.E.C.'s Consultative Commission for Energy, under the chairmanship of Professor Austin ROBINSON, was perhaps the highlight of our publishing programme in the industrial field and was reviewed extensively in the World Press. The regular series *Trends in Economic Sectors* reached its seventh year, and the report on the Stresa Conference on *The Industrial Challenge of Nuclear Energy* was concluded with the publication of Volumes II–IV between January and June.

The O.E.E.C.'s recently created Office for Scientific and Technical Personnel issued *Teaching through Television* and *Forecasting Manpower Needs for the Age of Science*. Among the titles published on behalf of the European Productivity Agency, the one dealing with *Market Research on a European Scale* and the *Guide to Legislation on Restrictive Business Practices* aroused particularly wide interest.

III. AGRICULTURE ET ALIMENTATION

Le *Quatrième Rapport sur les politiques agricoles en Europe et en Amérique du Nord*, préparé par le Comité ministériel pour l'alimentation et l'agriculture de l'O.E.C.E., a paru en mars, suivi en septembre par *Politiques de pêche en Europe occidentale et en Amérique du Nord.*

Dix titres nouveaux sont venus s'ajouter à la série *Documentation, Agriculture et Alimentation*, allant de *la Contribution apportée par l'économie domestique aux plans agricoles de mise en valeur* à *l'Organisation du marché des fruits et légumes en Espagne et en Turquie.* Dans cette même série, le rapport sur *les Grandes Régions agricoles de la C.E.E.* a été réalisé avec la Communauté Économique Européenne.

I. ÉCONOMIE, FINANCE, STATISTIQUES

Sous cette rubrique, on trouvera des études de théorie et de politique économique, des accords internationaux, les rapports généraux de l'Organisation et les ouvrages statistiques intéressant tous les secteurs de l'économie. Les titres concernant les aspects économiques de secteurs particuliers se trouvent aux parties II ou III de ce catalogue.

L'Europe et l'économie mondiale
Onzième examen annuel de la situation économique (avril 1960) 146 pp.

Situation et problèmes de l'économie des pays membres et associés de l'O.E.C.E. 1959–1960:
Autriche – Canada – Danemark – Espagne – États-Unis – France – Grèce – Irlande – Islande – Italie – Norvège – Pays-Bas – Portugal – République Fédérale d'Allemagne – Royaume-Uni – Suède – Suisse – Union économique belgo-luxembourgeoise.

Fascicules publiés dans le cadre du 12e examen annuel de l'O.E.C.E.
Canada – République Fédérale d'Allemagne – États-Unis – Suisse.

Code de la libération
Nouvelle édition mise à jour au 1er juillet 1960 (juillet 1960) 252 pp.

Accord monétaire européen
Premier rapport annuel du Comité directeur (mai 1960) 68 pp.

Accord monétaire européen du 5 aout 1955 (septembre 1960) 58 pp.

Directives pour l'application de l'accord monétaire européen (août 1960) 28 pp.

L'Élimination des doubles impositions
Troisième rapport du Comité fiscal (août 1960) 54 pp.

Zone pilote en Sardaigne (juillet 1960) 36 pp.

Code de la libération des mouvements de capitaux (janvier 1960) 48 pp.

Code de la libération des mouvements de capitaux
Nouvelle édition mise à jour au 1er juin 1960 (juin 1960) 56 pp.

Prévoir les cadres de demain (octobre 1960) 142 pp.

Systems of national accounts in Africa (décembre 1960) 200 pp.

III. AGRICULTURE AND FOOD

March saw the publication of the *Fourth Report on Agricultural Policies in Europe and North America*, prepared by the O.E.E.C. Committee of Food and Agriculture Ministers. This was followed in September by a new report on *Fishery Policies in Western Europe and North America*.

A further ten titles were added to the *Documentation in Food and Agriculture* series, ranging from *The Contribution of Home Economics Towards Rural Development Projects* to *Marketing of Fruit and Vegetables in Spain and Turkey*. In this series, *The Agricultural Regions of the E.E.C.* was issued in co-operation with the European Economic Community.

I. ECONOMY, FINANCE, STATISTICS

Under this heading will be found titles dealing with economic theory and policy, international agreements, the general reports of the Organisation and statistical works of interest to all sectors of economic activity. Those titles which deal with the economic aspects of particular sectors will be found in sections II or III of this catalogue.

Europe and the world economy
Eleventh Annual Economic Review (April 1960) 138 pp.

Economic conditions in Member and associated countries of the O.E.E.C. 1959–1960
Austria – Belgo-Luxembourg Economic Union – Canada – Denmark – Federal Republic of Germany – France – Greece – Iceland – Ireland – Italy – Netherlands – Norway – Portugal – Spain – Sweden – Switzerland – United Kingdom – United States

Country studies issued in connection with the O.E.E.C.'s 12th Annual economic review
Published late in 1960:
Canada – Federal Republic of Germany – Switzerland – United States.

Code of liberalisation
New edition brought up to date 1st July, 1960 (July 1960) 252 pp.

European Monetary Agreement
First Annual Report of the Board of Management (May 1960) 66 pp.

European Monetary Agreement of 5th August, 1955 (September 1960) 58 pp.

Directives for the application of the European Monetary Agreement (August 1960) 28 pp.

The elimination of double taxation
Third report of the Fiscal Committee (August 1960) 52 pp.

Pilot-area in Sardinia (July 1960) 32 pp.

Code of liberalisation of capital movements (January 1960) 48 pp.

Code of liberalisation of capital movements
New edition brought up to date 1st June 1960 (June 1960) 56 pp.

Forecasting
Manpower needs for the age of science (September 1960) 142 pp.

Systems of national accounts in Africa (December 1960) 200 pp.

Statistiques de base de l'énergie pour les pays de l'O.E.C.E., 1950–1959 (déc. 1960) 84 pp.

Statistiques industrielles 1900–1959 (décembre 1960) 190 pp.

Statistics of sources and uses of finance 1948–1958 (février 1960) 194 pp.

Le régime fiscal des investissements dans les pays d'outre-mer associés aux pays membres de l'O.E.C.E. au 31 décembre 1959 (décembre 1960) Volume I. Congo belge et Ruanda-Urundi, Somalie sous tutelle italienne. Provinces portugaises, Surinam, Territoires britanniques (partie générale) 104 pp.

Une organisation économique rénovée (avril 1960) 78 pp.

BULLETINS STATISTIQUES DE L'O.E.C.E.

1. *Statistiques générales*

Bimestrielles (janvier, mars, etc.).

Production industrielle, Production agricole, Population, Main-d'oeuvre, Échanges, Indices des prix de gros et de détail. Salaires, Économie et Finance.

2. *Statistiques du commerce extérieur*

Série A. Bimestrielle (février, avril, etc.).

Informations sommaires et récentes sur la situation d'ensemble du commerce extérieur, en valeur, des divers pays d'Europe et d'Amérique du Nord.

Série B. Trimestrielle.

Analyse, pour chaque pays, des données essentielles du commerce par grandes catégories de produits. Sa forme condensée conviendra particulièrement aux services d'études des banques et à tous les spécialistes de l'analyse économique.

Série C. Trimestrielle.

Ventilation complète, par pays d'origine et de destination, du commerce de 272 catégories de produits, en quantité et en valeur. Elle apporte aux divers secteurs d'activité un tableau complet du marché de leurs produits dans les relations de chacun des pays membres et associés de l'O.E.C.E. avec le reste du monde.

II. INDUSTRIE ET COMMERCE

L'Industrie devant l'énergie nucléaire

Volume III. *Conférence de Stresa.*

Partie 1. Bilan des programmes européens. Économie de l'énergie nucléaire. Financement des programmes (octobre 1959) 288 pp.

Partie 2. Droit atomique: Législation et administration (janvier 1960) 272 pp.

Partie 3. Le marché des matières nucléaires: combustibles, modérateurs, métaux spéciaux (février 1960) 306 pp.

Partie 4. Le marché des équipements et des instruments nucléaires (juin 1960) 296 pp.

L'Énergie en Europe

Nouvelles perspectives (janvier 1960) 142 pp.

Basic statistics of energy for O.E.E.C. countries 1950–1959 (December 1960) 84 pp.

Industrial statistics 1900–1959 (December 1960) 190 pp.

Statistics of sources and uses of finance 1948–1958 (February 1960) 194 pp.

A remodelled economic organisation (April 1960) 78 pp.

O.E.E.C. STATISTICAL BULLETINS

1. *General statistics*

Alternate months starting January

Industrial Production, Agricultural Production, Population, Manpower, Trade, Wholesale and Retail Price Indexes, Salaries and Wages, Finance, Economics.

2. *Foreign trade statistics*

Series A. Alternate months starting February

An up-to-date summary, expressed in values, of the foreign trade position for each of the European and North American countries.

Series B. Quarterly

Basic trade data for main categories of products. Of particular interest to those specialised in economic analysis, such as intelligence departments in banks and similar institutions.

Series C. Quarterly

Two quarterly volumes, one for exports and one for imports, giving a complete breakdown by countries of origin and destination (both quantities and values being shown) for 272 commodity categories. This series thus offers to the businessman a complete picture of commodity trade for each of the O.E.E.C. Member and Associated countries with the rest of the world.

II. INDUSTRY AND COMMERCE

The industrial challenge of nuclear energy

Volume III. *Stresa conference*

Part. 1. Survey of European Programmes. Economics of Nuclear Power. Financing of Programmes (October 1959) 274 pp.

Part 2. Atomic Law and Administration (January 1960) 264 pp.

Part. 3. The Market for Nuclear Materials: Fuels, Moderators, Special Metals (February 1960) 298 pp.

Part 4. The Market for Nuclear Equipment and Instrumentation (June 1960) 272 pp.

Towards a new energy pattern in Europe (January 1960) 126 pp.

Le Gaz en Europe, 1960
Production, disponibilités, consommation (octobre 1960) 120 pp.

L'Industrie de l'électricité en Europe
10e enquête. Réalisations 1948–1958. Prévisions 1959–1975 (février 1960) 210 pp.

L'Industrie du charbon en Europe
La situation en 1958–1959. Tendance et perspectives (juin 1960) 128 pp.

L'Industrie sidérurgique en Europe 1958–1959 (mai 1960) 192 pp.

L'Industrie du ciment en Europe
Statistiques 1959 (juillet 1960) 38 pp.

Statistiques du bois (juillet 1960) 68 pp.

Statistiques des bois tropicaux 1958 (juin 1960) 102 pp.

Pâtes et papiers
Statistiques 1959. Tendance 1960 (juillet 1960) 90 pp.

Les transports maritimes 1959 (mars 1960) 64 pp.

Le tourisme en Europe 1960 (octobre 1960) 100 pp.

13e Enquête sur l'équipement électrique
Réalisations et prévisions au 1er janvier 1960 (octobre 1960) 136 pp.

L'Industrie textile en Europe
Étude statistique 1959, tendance 1960 (novembre 1960) 116 pp.

Métaux non ferreux
Statistiques 1959. Tendance 1960 (novembre 1960) 128 pp.

L'Industrie des cuirs et peaux en Europe
Statistiques 1959 (novembre 1960) 36 pp.

L'Industrie chimique en Europe 1959–1960 (décembre 1960) 220 pp.

Petites usines de pâtes à papier
Enquête économique (février 1960)
Projet A.E.P. no. 419 294 pp.

Dragon
Projet de réacteur à haute température
Premier rapport annuel 1959–1960 (octobre 1960) 300 pp.

Guide de la législation sur les pratiques commerciales restrictives en Europe et en Amérique du Nord
Projets A.E.P. nos. 5/19 et 6/22.
Volume I: Danemark, France, Allemagne, Irlande et Italie (avril 1960) 330 pp.
Volume II: Pays-Bas, Norvège, Suède, Royaume-Uni, et États-Unis d'Amérique (février 1960) 438 pp.
Volume III: Contient des informations sur l'Autriche, le Canada, le Portugal, la Communauté Européenne du Charbon et de l'Acier, la Com-

Gas in Europe, 1960
Production, Availabilities. Consumption (Otober 1960) 112 pp.

The electricity supply industry in Europe
10th Enquiry. Achievements 1948–1958. Forecasts 1959–1975 (February 1960) 200 pp.

The coal industry in Europe 1960
The situation in 1958 and 1959 and outlook on future trends (June 1960) 122 pp.

The iron and steel industry in Europe 1958–1959 (May 1960) 186 pp.

The cement industry in Europe
1959 Statistics (July 1960) 38 pp.

Timber statistics 1959 (July 1960) 68 pp.

Statistics on tropical timber 1958 (July 1960) 102 pp.

Pulp and paper
Statistics 1959. Trend 1960 (July 1960) 90 pp.

Maritime transport 1959 (March 1960) 64 pp.

Tourism in Europe 1960 (September 1960) 98 pp.

The chemical industry in Europe 1959–1960 (December 1960) 208 pp.

13th Survey of electric power equipment
Situation and Prospects as at 1st January, 1960 (October 1960) 136 pp.

The textile industry in Europe
Statistical Study 1959, Trend in 1960 (November 1960) 116 pp.

Non-Ferrous metals
Statistics 1959, Trend 1960 (November 1960) 128 pp.

The hides and skins industry in Europe
1959 Statistics (November 1960) 36 pp.

Small pulp mills
An Economic Enquiry (February 1960)
E.P.A. Project No. 419 294 pp.

Dragon
High Temperature Reactor Project
First Annual Report 1959–1960 (July 1960) 296 pp.

Guide to legislation on restrictive business practices in Europe and North America
E.P.A. Projects Nos. 5/19 and 6/22
Volume I. Denmark, France, Germany, Ireland and Italy (February 1960) 330 pp.
Volume II. Netherlands, Norway, Sweden, United Kingdom and United States of America (February 1960) 438 pp.
Volume III. Austria, Canada, Portugal, the European Coal and Steel Community, the European Economic Community and a selected inter-

munauté Économique Européenne ainsi qu'une bibliographie succincte des ouvrages publiés dans divers pays sur les pratiques commerciales restrictives (novembre 1960) 386 pp.

Adaptation du travail à l'homme
Conférence internationale de Zürich, 2–6 mars 1959 (mars 1960)
Projet A.E.P. no. 6/07 E 116 pp.

Services techniques rendus par les fournisseurs aux petites et moyennes entreprises
Études de cas dans les industries américaines et européennes (avril 1960)
Projet A.E.P. no. 296/2 48 pp.

L'Étude des marchés européens
Conférence de Paris, 29 juin–1er juillet 1959 (juin 1960)
Projet A.E.P. no. 5/39 142 pp.

Catalogue européen des programmes généraux d'enseignement d'administration des entreprises (juin 1960) 656 pp.

La formation professionnelle accélérée de la main-d'oeuvre non qualifiée ou semi-qualifiée (juin 1960)
Projet A.E.P. no. 6/08 496 pp.

La télévision au service de l'enseignement scientifique (juillet 1960) 76 pp.

La recherche sociale et l'industrie en Europe
Problèmes et perspectives (février 1960)
Projet A.E.P. no. 6/07 C 100 pp.

Répertoire des recherches et des instituts dans les sciences humaines appliquées aux problèmes du travail (mai 1960)
7 fascicules: Allemagne, Belgique, Danemark - Norvège - Suède, France, Pays-Bas, Royaume-Uni, Suisse.

Le libre service en Europe et son rendement (octobre 1960)
Projet A.E.P. no. 5/33 (octobre 1960) 132 pp.

Acheter mieux
L'information objective du consommateur (décembre 1960)
Projet A.E.P. no. 6/03 G 96 pp.

Le traitement intégré des informations et les calculateurs électroniques (novembre 1960)
Projet A.E.P. no. 6/02 B 68 pp.

European Technical Digests

Choix d'articles publiés chaque mois, *en anglais*, à partir d'un millier de périodiques techniques rédigés en plus de dix langues différentes. Chaque article décrit sous une forme succincte mais claire les machines ou les méthodes les plus récentes. L'article est, en général, abondamment illustré.

Cette revue présente un intérêt évident pour toute entreprise soucieuse de connaître les dernières innovations adoptées dans le monde pour améliorer la production en quantité et en qualité. La série comprend un index publié chaque année.

national bibliography on restrictive business practices (December 1960) 300 pp.

Fitting the job to the worker
International Conference of Zurich, 2nd–6th March, 1959 (March, 1960)
E.P.A. Project No. 6/07 E 116 pp.

Technical services to the smaller firm by basic suppliers
Case studies of European and American Industry (April 1960)
E.P.A. Project No. 296/2 42 pp.

Market research on a European scale
Paris Conference, 29th June – 1st July, 1959 (June 1960)
E.P.A. Project No. 5/39 136 pp.

European guide to general courses in business management (June 1960) 640 pp.

Accelerated vocational training for unskilled and semi-skilled manpower (October 1960)
E.P.A. Project No. 6/08 496 pp.

Vocational training in the footwear industry (December 1960)
E.P.A. Projects Nos. 5/10 and 6/08 196 pp.

Teaching through television (July 1960) 72 pp.

Social research and industry in Europe
Problems and Perspectives (February 1960) 96 pp.

Register of research in the human sciences applied to problems of work and directory of relevant research institutions
6 booklets: Belgium, Denmark - Norway - Sweden, France, Netherlands, Switzerland, United Kingdom.

The economic performance of self service in Europe (Otober 1960)
E.P.A. Project No. 5/33 132 pp.

Better buying through consumer information (December 1960)
E.P.A. Project No. 6/03 G 92 pp.

Integrated data processing and computers (November 1960)
E.P.A. Project No. 6/02 B 68 pp.

European Technical Digests

A monthly selection in English of articles taken from over 1,000 technical journals published in a dozen different languages. Each digest gives a full though concise account of the machine or method described, with illustrations where applicable.

No firm can afford to neglect this publication which draws attention to the latest devices by which output can be improved in quantity and quality. Indexes are published each year.

Revue de la Mesure de la Productivité

Ce périodique a pour objet essentiel de montrer aux chefs d'entreprises le parti pratique qu'ils peuvent tirer de la mesure scientifique de la productivité. Il intéresse également les membres de l'enseignement, les dirigeants syndicaux et tous les spécialistes de la productivité auxquels des informations précises et des statistiques sûres sont indispensables.

III. AGRICULTURE ET ALIMENTATION

4e Rapport sur les politiques agricoles en Europe et en Amérique du Nord
Volume 1: Suite des études sur les politiques agricoles (mars 1960) 386 pp.
Volume 2: Problèmes de politique laitière (mars 1960) 496 pp.

Politiques de pêche en Europe occidentale et en Amérique du Nord (août 1960) 332 pp.

Les engrais
9e étude 1957–1960. Production, consommation, prix et commerce en Europe et aux États-Unis (mars 1960) 112 pp.

La modernisation des bâtiments de ferme
Volume II: *Europe* (avril 1960) 154 pp.

SÉRIE DOCUMENTATION 1960

„ALIMENTATION ET AGRICULTURE"

La série Documentation dans l'alimentation et l'agriculture a été inaugurée en 1959. Pendant la première année il a été publié les numéros 1 à 20 et en 1960 ont été ajoutés 10 nouveaux titres numérotés de 21 à 30, dont on trouvera l'énumération ci-dessous.

Commercialisation et consommation du poisson surgelé (mai 1960)
Documentation, Série 1960, no. 21 142 pp.

La consommation des fruits et légumes dans les pays de l'O.E.C.E. (juin 1960)
Documentation, Série 1960, no. 22 244 pp.

Essais de comportement des variétés de graminées, de trèfle et de luzerne dans les pays de l'O.E.C.E. (juin 1960)
Documentation, Série 1960, no. 23 244 pp.

Marges de commercialisation pour le lait et les produits laitiers dans les pays de l'O.E.C.E. (juillet 1960)
Documentation, Série 1960, no. 24 146 pp.

Normalisation des emballages en bois pour fruits et légumes (mai 1960)
Documentation, Série 1960, no. 25 204 pp.

La contribution apportée par l'économie domestique aux plans agricoles de mise en valeur (juillet 1960)
Documentation, Série 1960, no. 26 84 pp.

Les grandes régions agricoles dams la Communauté économique européenne (juillet 1960)
Documentation, Série 1960, no. 27 60 pp.

Productivity Measurement Review

This quarterly periodical is intended principally for managers who want to use productivity measurement to assess and improve productivity in their firm. The Review is also addressed to the wider circle of government officials, university teachers, trade unionists and other specialists concerned with productivity problems and who need precise information and reliable statistics in their work.

In addition to the regular quarterly numbers, "Special Numbers" or "Supplements" are issued once or twice a year. These give more comprehensive discussion of a special subject.

III. AGRICULTURE AND FOOD

4th Report on agricultural policies in Europe and North America
Volume 1. Further problems in agricultural policy (March 1960) 352 pp.
Volume 2. Problems in dairy (March 1960) 464 pp.

Fishery policies in Western Europe and North America (September 1960) 302 pp.

Fertilizers
9th Study 1957–1960. Production. Consumption, Prices and Trade in Europe and U.S.A. (March 1960) 108 pp.

Farm buildings including their remodelling and adaptation
Volume II. *Europe* (April 1960) 148 pp.

FOOD AND AGRICULTURE DOCUMENTATION SERIES 1960

The Documentation in Food and Agriculture Series started in 1959 with the publication of numbers 1 to 20 and continued with the issue during 1960 of numbers 21 to 30 which are listed hereunder.

Marketing and consumption of frozen fish (May 1960)
Documentation. 1960 Series, No. 21 114 pp.

The consumption of fruit and vegetables in O.E.E.C. countries (August 1960)
Documentation, 1960 Series, No. 22 228 pp.

Grass, clover and lucerne trials (May 1960)
Documentation, 1960 Series, No. 23 236 pp.

Marketing and distribution margins for milk and milk products in O.E.E.C. countries (July 1960)
Documentation, 1960 Series, No. 24 148 pp.

Standardisation of wooden packaging for fruit and vegetables (August 1960)
Documentation, 1960 Series, No. 25 210 pp.

The contribution of home economics towards rural development projects (July 1960)
Documentation, 1960 Series, No. 26 78 pp.

Agricultural regions in the European Economic Community (September 1960)
Documentation, 1960 Series, No. 27 54 pp.

Répertoire des quotidiens et périodiques agricoles dans les pays membres de l'O.E.C.E. (février 1960)
Documentation, Série 1960, no. 28 144 pp.
Edition révisée du no. 11 de la série 1959

Organisation du marché des fruits et légumes en Espagne et en Turquie (octobre 1960)
Documentation, Série 1960, no. 29 98 pp.

L'Enseignement agricole au niveau universitaire (octobre 1960)
Documentation, Série 1960, no. 30 124 pp.

La Revue Fatis

(SERVICE D'INFORMATION TECHNIQUE
SUR LES QUESTIONS D'ALIMENTATION ET D'AGRICULTURE)

Projet A.E.P. no. 160 Bimestrielle

Bien que cette revue soit rédigée à l'intention des Services de vulgarisation agricole, de nombreux lecteurs s'intéresseront à une publication dans laquelle ils pourront trouver une vue d'ensemble des principaux problèmes de l'agriculture européenne et dont l'objet essentiel est d'encourager l'accroissement de la productivité agricole.

List of agricultural press and periodicals in O.E.E.C. Member countries (February 1960)
Documentation, 1960 Series, No. 28 144 pp.
(Revised edition of No. 11 in the 1959 Series)

Marketing of fruit and vegetables in Spain and Turkey (October 1960)
Documentation, 1960 Series, No. 29 94 pp.

Higher education in agriculture (October 1960)
Documentation, 1960 Series, No. 30 118 pp.

The Fatis review

(FOOD AND AGRICULTURE TECHNICAL INFORMATION SERVICE)

E.P.A. Project No. 160
Bi-monthly.

Although the Review is intended mainly for agricultural advisory workers, it has attracted a wider circle of readers by the broad picture which it affords of European agriculture as a whole and by its general approach to the problem of improving agricultural productivity.

CHAPITRE V

CONSEIL DE L'EUROPE

A. ÉPHÉMÉRIDES

1960

18–22 janvier: Troisième partie de la Onzième Session ordinaire de l'Assemblée Consultative. M. Selwyn LLOYD, Ministre des Affaires Étrangères de Grande Bretagne, prononce son premier discours devant l'Assemblée. Au nombre des recommandations adaptées, il y a le projet de *Charte Sociale Européenne* ainsi que, des textes relatifs au développement de l'Afrique et aux relations économiques européennes.

25–28 janvier: Troisième session de la Conférence Européenne des Pouvoirs Locaux. La Conférence adopte la Charte lui donnant un satut et des activités permanentes qui doit être soumise à l'Assemblée et au Comité des Ministres.

4 avril: La Commission Européenne des Droits de l'Homme porte l'affaire LAWLESS contre la République d'Irlande devant la Cour Européenne.

18 avril: La *Convention Européenne d'Extradition*, ratifiée par la Norvège, la Suède et la Turquie, entre en vigueur.

25–29 avril: Première partie de la Douzième Session ordinaire de l'Assemblée Consultative. M. Per FEDERSPIEL (libéral modéré danois) est élu président, il succède à M. John EDWARDS, décédé. Adoption de deux recommandations sur l'organisation et les compétences de l'O.C.D.E. contenant une proposition tendant à la création d'une „Assemblée *ad hoc*", à partir de l'Assemblée Consultative. L'Assemblée des 20 examinerait les rapports et activités de l'O.C.D.E. L'Assemblée condamne la collectivisation forcée des entreprises agricoles en la zône soviétique d'Allemagne.

28 avril: Le Comité des Ministres se réunit, à l'échelon ministériel, sous la présidence de M. Jens Otto KRAG, Ministre des Affaires étrangères danois. Élection des sept membres de la Commission Européenne des Droits de l'Homme. Le Comité prend connaissance du Rapport Annuel du Secrétaire Général. Le Comité spécial pour la simplification des formalitées de frontières est autorisé à tenir une nouvelle réunion. *L'accord pour l'importation temporaire en franchise de douane, à titre de prêt gratuit, et à des fins diagnostiques ou thérapeutiques, de matériel médico-chirurgical destiné aux établissements sanitaires* est ouvert à la signature des Membres.

29 avril: La Commission Européenne des Droits de l'Homme envoie l'Affaire Raymond de BECKER contre la Belgique à la Cour Européenne.

18 mai: Transfert des activités culturelles de l'U.E.O. au Conseil de l'Europe.

fin mai: Le président de la Cour Européenne des Droits de l'Homme tire au sort les noms des juges qui devront examiner les deux premières affaires soumises à la Cour.

7–10 juin: Réunion inaugurale du Comité Européen pour l'Enseignement Supérieur et la Recherche sous la présidence de M. le Dr. CALS, Ministre néerlandais de l'Education.

24–25 juin: Septième réunion jointe des membres de l'Assemblée Consultative et de l'Assemblée Parlementaire Européenne. Discours des Présidents des trois Communautés des „Six".

CHAPTER V

COUNCIL OF EUROPE

A. DIARY OF PRINCIPAL EVENTS

1960

18–22 January: Third Part of the Eleventh Ordinary Session of the Consultative Assembly. Mr. Selwyn LLOYD, then Foreign Secretary, makes his first speech to the Assembly. Recommendations adopted include the draft *European Social Charter* and texts on the development of Africa and European economic relations.

25–28 January: Third Session of the European Conference of Local Authorities. The Conference adopts its Charter, which would give it permanent status and functions, for submission to the Assembly and Committee of Ministers.

4 April: European Commission of Human Rights refers LAWLESS case against the Republic of Ireland to the European Court.

18 April: European Convention on Extradition, ratified by Norway, Sweden and Turkey, enters into force.

25–29 April: First Part of the Twelfth Ordinary Session of the Consultative Assembly, Mr. Per FEDERSPIEL, Danish Moderate Liberal, elected President in succession to the late Rt. Hon. John EDWARDS. Adoption of two recommendations on the organisation and competence of O.E.C.D., including a proposal that an *ad hoc* 20-nation Assembly be formed, of which the nucleus would be exhibited by the Consultative Assembly, to review O.E.C.D.'s reports and activities. Assembly energetically condemns enforced collectivisation of agriculture in the Soviet Zone of Germany.

28 April: Committee of Ministers meets at full ministerial level with Mr. Jens Otto KRAG, Danish Foreign Minister, in the Chair. Elects seven members to the European Commission of Human Rights. Takes note of the Secretary-General's Annual Report. Authorises a further meeting of the Special Committee for the Simplification of Frontier Formalities. Opens for signature the *European Agreement on the temporary Importation, free of Duty, of medical, surgical and laboratory Equipment for use on free Loan in Hospitals and other medical Institutions for Purposes of Diagnosis or Treatment.*

29 April: European Commission of Human Rights refers case of Raymond De BECKER against Belgium to European Court.

18 May: Transfer of the exercise of competence for Western European Union's cultural activities to the Council of Europe.

end May: The President of the European Court of Human Rights draws by lot the names of judges to hear the first two cases referred to the Court.

7–10 June: Committee for Higher Education and Research holds its inaugural meeting with Dr. CALS, Netherlands Minister of Education, in the Chair.

24–25 June: Seventh Joint Meeting between the members of the Consultative and European Parliamentary Assemblies, addressed by the Presidents of the three Six-Power Communities.

2 juillet: Signature d'un arrangement entre le Fonds Culturel du Conseil de l'Europe et la Fondation Européenne de la Culture, en vue de constituer un mécanisme commun pour recueillir les fonds et d'établir un programme commun.

11 juillet: Troisème requête gouvernementale (Autriche contre Italie) introduite devant la Commission Européenne des Droits de l'Homme. Elle a trait au verdict prononcé contre six jeunes gens du village de Pfunders pour meurtre d'un douanier en août 56. Des irrégularités contraires aux prescriptions de l'article 6 relatif à l'administration de la justice sont alléguées.

19 juillet: Le Prix Européen attribué pour 1960 à Aarhus (Danemark) et Bruges (Belgique).

31 août: Les Pays-Bas deviennent le 10ème État membre acceptant le droit de recours individuel devant la Commission Européenne des Droits de l'Homme.

21–29 septembre: Deuxième Partie de la Douzième Session ordinaire de l'Assemblée Consultative. Grands débats: situation politique, relations économiques européennes, politique énergétique et coopération européenne dans le domaine scientifique et technique. L'Assemblée demande un accord d'association entre les „Six" et les „Sept", un ouvrage d'art reliant la Grande-Bretagne à la France, un programme spatial européen et une relance du Conseil de l'Europe. La Suisse accepte l'invitation de l'Assemblée Consultative et enverra des observateurs aux débats économiques.

3–4 octobre: Premières audiences publiques de la Cour Européenne des Droits de l'Homme. Examen des objections préliminaires soulevées par le Gouvernement Irlandais et des questions de procédure dans l'affaire LAWLESS envoyée à la Cour par la Commission Européenne.

4 novembre: Inauguration à Paris de la 6° Exposition du Conseil de l'Europe, les *Sources du 20° siècle: les Arts en Europe de 1884 à 1914.*

11 novembre: Sur les questions préliminaires, la Cour Européenne rend son premier arrêt dans l'affaire LAWLESS. Par 6 voix contre 1, elle entérine la décision de la Commission qui a envoyé une copie de son rapport au requérant qu'elle-même pourra éventuellement entendre à un stade ultérieur selon une procédure qui reste à fixer. Le juge de nationalité grecque émet une opinion différente. A l'unanimité, la Cour décide de passer à l'examen du fond.

12 décembre: Le Comité des Ministres se réunit, à l'échelon ministériel, sous la présidence de M. Maurice COUVE DE MURVILLE, Ministre des Affaires étrangères français. Adoption d'une communication à l'Assemblée consacrée à l'examen des réalisations passées et des activités futures se prononce en faveur d'un programme de coopération culturelle et scientifique. Un Comité d'experts, chargé de préparer ce programme sera réuni après la Conférence que tiendront en avril 1961 les ministres responsables des questions d'éducation.

B. DROITS DE L'HOMME

Avis de l'éditeur.

Volume VII de *l'Annuaire européen* – Section documentaire, Conseil de l'Europe – contient (pages 308–336) le Règlement de la Cour européenne, ratifié le 18 septembre 1959.

L'établissement de la Cour a nécessité une addition aux Règlement intérieur de la Commission européenne des Doits de l'Homme qui jusque là avaient consisté en 70 règles (2 titres).

Une publication de la Section des Droits de l'Homme du Secrétariat du Conseil de l'Europe de novembre 1960 donne un exposé complet du Règlement intérieur de la Commission. Afin de compléter les données qui se trouvent dans ce volume VII concernant le fonctionnement de la Cour on publie ci-dessous le texte de ce Règlement.

2 July: Co-operation agreement signed by Council of Europe Cultural Fund and European Cultural Foundation, providing for joint projects and joint national fund-raising committees.

11 July: Third Governmental petition (Austria against Italy) lodged with the European Commission of Human Rights. The application concerns sentence imposed on six young men from the village of Pfunders for the murder of a customs officer in August 1956. It alleges irregularities, contrary to the provisions of Article 6 relating to the administration of justice.

19 July: Announcement of award of European Prize for 1960 to Aarhus (Denmark) and Bruges (Belgium).

31 August: Netherlands becomes tenth Member State to accept the right of individual application to the European Commission of Human Rights.

21–29 September: Second Part of the Twelfth Ordinary Session of the Consultative Assembly. The debates centred on the political situation, European economic relations, energy problems and European scientific and technical co-operation. Assembly proposed a modified customs union linking the Common Market with E.F.T.A., the building of a tunnel or bridge linking Britain to France, a European space programme and steps to improve the effectiveness of the Council. Switzerland accepts invitation to send observers to the Assembly to participate in economic debates.

3–4 October: First public hearings of the European Court of Human Rights. Examination of preliminary objections raised by the Irish Government and procedural questions in the case of Gerard Richard LAWLESS, referred to the Court by the European Commission.

4 November: Inauguration in Paris of the Sixth Council of Europe Art Exhibition, *Twentieth Century Sources: the Arts in Europe from 1884–1914.*

11 November: European Court gives its judgment on the preliminary issues of the LAWLESS case. By six votes to one, it endorses the Commission's action in sending a copy of its report to the applicant and decides that it might call the applicant, but reserves its decision as to whether it will receive the applicant's comments on the report or hear him in person. The judge of Greek nationality enters a dissenting opinion. The Court decides unanimously to proceed with examination of the merits of the case.

12 December: Committee of Ministers meets at full Ministerial level with Mr. Maurice COUVE DE MURVILLE, French Foreign Minister, in the Chair. Adopts a Communication to the Assembly reviewing past achievements and future plans and decides in particular on a full programme of cultural co-operation. Appoints special committee of experts to draw up a programme following projected meeting in April (1961) of Ministers responsible for educational questions.

B. HUMAN RIGHTS

Editors' Note

Volume VII of the *European Yearbook* – Documentary Section, Council of Europe – included (pp. 309–337) the Rules of Court of the European Court of Human Rights as approved on 18th September, 1959.

The establishment of the Court has necessitated an addition to the Rules of Procedure of the European *Commission* of Human Rights which had up to then been set out in 70 Rules (two titles).

A publication of the Human Rights Department of the Council of Europe Secretariat dated November 1960 sets out the complete body of Rules of Procedure of the Commission. In order to amplify the information given in Volume VII concerning the functioning of the Court the text of these rules is given below.

1. RÈGLEMENT INTÉRIEUR DE LA COMMISSION EUROPÉENNE DES DROITS DE L'HOMME [1]

La Commission,

Vu la Convention de sauvegarde des Droits de l'Homme et des Libertés fondamentales et son Protocole additionnel, ci-après dénommés la Convention;
Agissant en vertu de l'article 36 de la Convention;
Arrête le présent Règlement:

TITRE I

ORGANISATION ET FONCTIONNEMENT DE LA COMMISSION

CHAPITRE I

Des Membres de la Commission

Article 1

1. La durée du mandat des membres de la Commission élus le 18 mai 1954 est comptée à partir de cette date. De même, la durée du mandat de tout membre élu du fait qu'un État est devenu Partie à la Convention après le 18 mai 1954 est comptée à partir de l'élection de ce membre.

2. Toutefois, si un membre est réélu à l'expiration de son mandat, ou élu en remplacement d'un membre dont le mandat est expiré ou va expirer, la durée de son mandat est comptée à partir de cette expiration.

3. Conformément à l'article 22, paragraphe 3, de la Convention, le membre élu en remplacement d'un membre dont le mandat n'est pas expiré achève le mandat de son prédécesseur.
4. Conformément à l'article 22, paragraphe 4, de la Convention, les membres restent en fonctions jusqu'à remplacement. Après ce remplacement, ils continuent de connaître des affaires dont ils sont déjà saisis.

Article 2

Avant d'entrer en fonctions, tout membre de la Commission, à la première séance de la Commission à laquelle il assiste après son élection, doit prêter le serment suivant ou faire la déclaration solennelle suivante:
„Je jure" – ou „je déclare solennellement" – „que j'exercerai tous mes devoirs et attributions en tout honneur et dévouement, en pleine impartialité et en toute conscience, et que j'observerai le secret des délibérations".

Article 3

1. Les membres de la Commission prennent rang, après le Président et le Vice-président, suivant leur ancienneté de fonctions.
2. Les membres ayant la même ancienneté de fonctions prennent rang d'après leur ancienneté d'âge.
3. Les membres réélus prennent rang compte tenu de la durée de leurs mandats antérieurs.

---

[1] Tel que la Commission l'a révisé lors de sa 24ème session plénière, tenue à Strasbourg du 1er au 5 août 1960. En ce qui concerne le texte primitif et les amendements subséquents, *cf.* les documents DH (55) 8 déf. (annexe II), DH (55) 13 (pp. 3–5), DH (57) 7 (pp. 7–8), DH (58) 6 déf. (pp. 2–3), DH (59) 1 (pp. 2–3), DH (59) 7 (pp. 7–8), DH (60) 7 déf. (pp. 3–5) et DH (60) 10 (pp. 3–4 et annexe II).

1. RULES OF PROCEDURE OF THE EUROPEAN COMMISSION OF HUMAN RIGHTS [1]

The Commission,

Having regard to the Convention for the Protection of Human Rights and Fundamental Freedoms and Protocol, hereinafter called the Convention;

Pursuant to Article 36 of the Convention;

Adopts the present Rules:

TITLE I

ORGANISATION AND WORKING OF THE COMMISSION

CHAPTER I

Members of the Commission

Rule 1

1. The duration of the term of office of members of the Commission elected on 18th May, 1954, shall be calculated as from this date. Similarly, the duration of the term of office of any member elected as a consequence of a State becoming a Party to the Convention after 18th May, 1954, shall be calculated as from his election.

2. However, when a member is re-elected on the expiry of his term of office or is elected to replace a member whose term of office has expired or is about to expire, the duration of his term of office shall, in either case, be calculated as from the date of such expiry.

3. In accordance with Article 22, paragraph 3, of the Convention, a member elected to replace a member whose term of office has not expired shall hold office for the remainder of his predecessor's term.

4. In accordance with Article 22, paragraph 4, of the Convention, members shall hold office until replaced. After having been replaced, they shall continue to deal with such cases as they already have under consideration.

Rule 2

Before taking up his duties, each member of the Commission shall, at the first meeting of the Commission at which he is present after his election, make the following oath or solemn declaration:

"I swear", or "I solemnly declare" – "that I will exercise all my powers and duties honourably and faithfully, impartially and conscientiously and that I will keep secret all deliberations".

Rule 3

1. Members of the Commission shall take precedence after the President and Vice-President according to the length of time they have been in office.

2. Members having the same length of time in office shall take precedence according to age.

3. Re-elected members shall take precedence having regard to the duration of their previous terms of office.

---

[1] As amended by the Commission during its 24th Plenary Session held at Strasbourg from 1st to 5th August, 1960. For the original text and subsequent amendments, *see* documents DH (55) 8 Final (Appendix II), DH (55) 13 (pp. 3–5), DH (57) 7 (pp. 7–8), DH (58) 6 Final (pp. 2–3), DH (59) 1 (pp. 2–3), DH (59) 7 (pp. 7–8), DH (60) 7 Final (pp. 3–5) and DH (60) 10 (pp. 3–4 and Appendix II).

Article 4

La démission d'un membre est adressée au Président qui la transmet au Secrétaire Général du Conseil de l'Europe. Sous réserve de l'application de l'article 1, paragraphe 4, du présent Règlement, elle emporte vacance de siège.

CHAPITRE II

De la présidence de la Commission

Article 5

1. La Commission procède à l'élection du Président et du Vice-président dans le mois qui suit le point de départ du mandat des membres élus lors d'un renouvellement partiel effectué conformément à l'article 22, paragraphe 1, de la Convention.

2. Si le Président ou le Vice-président cesse de faire partie de la Commission, ou résigne ses fonctions de Président ou de Vice-président, avant le terme normal de celles-ci, la Commission élit un successeur pour la période restant à courir.

3. Les élections visées au présent article ont lieu au scrutin secret; seuls y participent les membres présents. Le membre qui obtient la majorité absolue est élu.

Si aucun membre ne réunit la majorité absolue, il est procédé à un second tour de scrutin. Le membre ayant le plus grand nombre de voix est élu. En cas de parité des suffrages, est élu le membre qui a préséance aux termes de l'article 3 du présent Règlement.

Article 6

Le Président dirige les travaux et préside les séances de la Commission.

Article 7

Le Vice-président remplace le Président en cas d'empêchement de celui-ci et en cas de vacance de la présidence.

Article 8

En cas d'empêchement simultané du Président et du Vice-président, ou en cas de vacance simultanée de leurs fonctions, la présidence est exercée par un autre membre selon l'ordre de préséance établi à l'article 3 du présent Règlement.

Article 9

1. Si le Président est le ressortissant d'une Haute Partie Contractante en cause dans une affaire soumise à la Commission, il cède la présidence pour cette affaire.

2. Le Président cède également la présidence pour toute affaire dont il a connu en Sous-commission en qualité de membre désigné par une partie conformément à l'article 29, paragraphe 2, de la Convention.

Article 10

Si, pour une raison spéciale, le Président de la Commission estime devoir céder la présidence dans une affaire déterminée, il en informe le Vice-président ou son remplaçant.

Rule 4

Resignation of a member shall be notified to the President who shall transmit it to the Secretary-General of the Council of Europe. Subject to the provisions of Rule 1, paragraph 4, it shall constitute vacation of office.

CHAPTER II

Presidency of the Commission

Rule 5

1. The Commission shall elect the President and Vice-President during the month following the date of the entry into office of members elected at periodical elections of part of the Commission in accordance with paragraph 1 of Article 22 of the Convention.

2. If the President or Vice-President, before the normal expiry of his term of office as President or Vice-President, ceases to be a member of the Commission or resigns his office, the Commission shall elect a successor to hold office for the remainder of the said term.

3. The elections referred to in this Rule shall be by secret ballot; only the members present shall take part. Election shall be by an absolute majority of votes.

If no member receives an absolute majority, a second ballot shall take place. The member receiving the most votes shall then be elected. In the case of equal voting the member having precedence under Rule 3 shall be elected.

Rule 6

The President shall direct the work and preside at the meetings of the Commission.

Rule 7

The Vice-President shall take the place of the President if the latter is unable to carry out his duties or if the office of President is vacant.

Rule 8

If the President and Vice-President are at the same time unable to carry out their duties or if their offices are at the same time vacant, the duties of President shall be carried out by another member according to the order of precedence laid down in Rule 3.

Rule 9

1. If the President is a national of a High Contracting Party which is party to a case brought before the Commission, he shall relinquish the office of President in respect of that case.

2. The President shall also relinquish the office of President in respect of any case in which he has acted in a Sub-commission as member appointed by a party pursuant to Article 29, paragraph 2, of the Convention.

Rule 10

If the President of the Commission for some special reason considers that he should relinquish the office of President in a particular case, he shall so inform the Vice-President or the member acting in his place.

CHAPITRE III

Du secrétariat de la Commission

Article 11

1. Conformément à l'article 37 de la Convention, le secrétariat de la Commission est assuré par le Secrétaire Général du Conseil de l'Europe.
2. Le Secrétaire Général désigne le Secrétaire de la Commission.

Article 12

Le Secrétaire de la Commission

a) assiste la Commission, les Sous-commissions et les membres de la Commission dans l'exercice de leurs fonctions;

b) sert d'intermédiaire pour toutes les communications concernant la Commission;

c) a la garde des sceaux, cachets et archives de la Commission.

Article 13

1. Il est tenu au secrétariat un registre spécial sur lequel sont inscrits à la suite, sans blancs ni ratures, toutes les causes, les actes de procédure y afférents et les pièces déposées à l'appui dans l'ordre de leur production. Dans le registre, il n'est rien écrit par abréviation.
2. Mention de l'inscription au registre est faite par le Secrétaire de la Commission sur les originaux et, à la demande des parties, sur les copies qu'elles présenteront à cet effet.
3. Le registre fait foi des inscriptions et mentions prévues au paragraphe 2 du présent article.
4. Les modalités suivant lesquelles le registre est tenu sont déterminées par le Président en accord avec le Secrétaire de la Commission.

Article 14

Les attributions du secrétariat sont réglées par le Président en accord avec le Secrétaire Général du Conseil de l'Europe.

CHAPITRE IV

Des Sous-commissions

Article 15

1. Toute partie qui entend exercer la faculté de désigner un membre de son choix pour faire partie d'une Sous-commission, conformément à l'article 29, paragraphe 2, de la Convention, doit notifier le nom du membre choisi dans le délai approprié fixé par le Président.
2. Si, avant la constitution de la Sous-commission, le membre ainsi désigné se trouve empêché d'accepter sa désignation, le Président en informe la partie intéressée et lui fixe un nouveau délai approprié pour désigner, si elle le désire, un autre membre.

Article 16

Si la Commission estime que plusieurs parties ont le même intérêt, elle leur fixe un délai pour désigner d'un commun accord un seul membre de leur choix. En cas de contestation sur l'existence d'un tel intérêt, la

CHAPTER III

Secretariat of the Commission

Rule 11

1. Pursuant to Article 37 of the Convention, the Secretariat of the Commission shall be provided by the Secretary-General of the Council of Europe.

2. The Secretary-General shall appoint the Secretary of the Commission.

Rule 12

The Secretary of the Commission

a) shall assist the Commission, Sub-commissions and the members of the Commission in the fulfilment of their duties;

b) shall be the channel for all communications concerning the Commission;

c) shall have custody of the seals, stamps and archives of the Commission.

Rule 13

1. A special register shall be kept at the Secretariat in which all cases, relevant pleadings and exhibits shall be entered in the order of their submission and without intervening spaces or deletions. Nothing shall be written in the register in abbreviated form.

2. A note of the entry in the register shall be endorsed by the Secretary of the Commission on the original documents and, at the request of the parties, on copies presented by them for that purpose.

3. Entries in the register and the notes of entries provided for in paragraph 2 of this Rule shall have effect as certified matters of record.

4. The manner of keeping the register shall be laid down by the President in agreement with the Secretary of the Commission.

Rule 14

The duties of the Secretariat shall be laid down by the President in agreement with the Secretary-General of the Council of Europe.

CHAPTER IV

Sub-commissions

Rule 15

1. Any party wishing to exercise the right, provided for in paragraph 2 of Article 29 of the Convention, to appoint a member of its choice as a member of a Sub-commission shall give notice of the name of such member within an appropriate time-limit to be laid down by the President.

2. If, before the Sub-commission has been constituted, a member so appointed is unable to accept the appointment, the President shall notify the party concerned and shall lay down a new and appropriate time-limit within which such party shall, if it so desires, appoint another member.

Rulc 16

If the Commission considers that several parties have the same interest, it shall lay down a time-limit within which such parties shall, acting in agreement, appoint a single member of their choice. In the event of a

Commission décide après avoir recueilli, s'il y a lieu, les explications des parties.

Article 17

En cas de non-désignation d'un membre dans le délai fixé par le Président ou par la Commission conformément à l'article 15 ou à l'article 16 du présent Règlement, la procédure prévue à l'article 18 du présent Règlement est immédiatement appliquée.

Article 18

1. A l'expiration des délais visés aux articles 15 et 16 du présent Règlement, le nombre requis de membres de la Sous-commission est atteint au moyen d'un tirage au sort que le Président effectue avec l'assistance du Secrétaire de la Commission.

2. Les membres restants de la Commission sont, en cas de besoin, appelés à siéger en qualité de suppléants suivant l'ordre établi par un tirage au sort effectué de la manière prévue au paragraphe 1.

3. Dès constitution d'une Sous-commission, le Secrétaire de la Commission en notifie la composition à tous les membres de la Commission ainsi qu'aux parties.

Article 19

Si, après la constitution de la Sous-commission, le membre désigné par une partie est empêché de remplir ses fonctions, le Président en informe la partie et lui fixe un nouveau délai approprié pour désigner, si elle le désire, un autre membre. En cas de non-désignation d'un membre dans le délai ainsi fixé par le Président, il est fait appel à l'un des suppléants visés à l'article 18, paragraphe 2 du présent Règlement, suivant l'ordre établi par le tirage au sort.

Article 20

1. Parmi les membres désignés par le sort conformément à l'article 18, paragraphe 1, du présent Règlement, celui qui a préséance aux termes de l'article 3 dudit Règlement préside la Sous-commission.

2. Si, pour une raison spéciale, le Président de la Sous-commission estime devoir céder la présidence, il en informe la Sous-commission. Il cède la présidence dans le cas prévu à l'article 9, paragraphe 1, du présent Règlement.

Article 21

Si le Président de la Sous-commission cède la présidence, celle-ci est assumée par un autre membre de la Sous-commission selon l'ordre de préséance établi à l'article 3 du présent Règlement.

CHAPITRE V

Du fonctionnement de la Commission et des Sous-commissions

Article 22

Le siège de la Commission est fixé à Strasbourg, siège du Conseil de l'Europe. La Commission et ses organes peuvent toutefois, lorsqu'ils le jugent utile, exercer leurs fonctions en d'autres lieux.

dispute that the same interest exists, the Commission shall decide, if necessary, after receiving the observations of the parties.

Rule 17

In the event of the non-appointment of a member within the time-limit laid down by the President or the Commission, as the case may be, under Rule 15 or 16, the procedure in Rule 18 shall immediately be applied.

Rule 18

1. On the expiry of the time-limits referred to in Rules 15 and 16, the prescribed number of members of the Sub-commission shall be achieved by a drawing of lots which the President shall carry out with the assistance of the Secretary of the Commission.

2. The remaining members of the Commission shall, if necessary, be called upon to sit as substitute members in the order in which they have been chosen by lot in the same manner as provided for in paragraph 1.

3. As soon as a Sub-commission has been constituted the Secretary of the Commission shall communicate its composition to all members of the Commission and to the parties.

Rule 19

If, after the Sub-commission has been constituted, a member appointed by a party is prevented from carrying out his duties, the President shall notify the party concerned and shall lay down a new and appropriate time-limit within which such party shall, if it so desires, appoint another member. In the event of the non-appointment of a member within the time-limit laid down by the President, one of the substitute members provided for in Rule 18, paragraph 2, shall be called upon in accordance with the order in which these members have been chosen by lot.

Rule 20

1. Of those members chosen by lot according to paragraph 1 of Rule 18, the member having precedence under Rule 3 shall preside at the Sub-commission.

2. If the President of the Sub-commission for some special reason considers that he should relinquish the office of President, he shall so inform the Sub-commission. He shall relinguish the office of President in the circumstances set out in paragraph 1 of Rule 9.

Rule 21

If the President of the Sub-commission relinquishes the office of President, that office shall be assumed by another member of the Sub-commission in accordance with the order of precedence laid down in Rule 3.

CHAPTER V

The working of the Commission and Sub-commissions

Rule 22

The seat of the Commission shall be at the seat of the Council of Europe at Strasbourg. The Commission or any of its organs may, however, if they think fit, carry out their duties elsewhere.

Article 23

1. La Commission se réunit sur décision de son Président, chaque fois que celui-ci estime que les circonstances l'exigent. Elle doit en outre être réunie si un tiers au moins de ses membres le demandent.
2. Conformément à l'article 35 de la Convention, la Commission est convoquée par le Secrétaire Général du Conseil de l'Europe.

Article 24

1. Les dates et heures des séances sont fixées par le Président de la Commission.
2. Les dates et heures des séances d'une Sous-commission sont fixées par son Président.

Article 25

Le quorum de neuf membres est exigé pour le fonctionnement de la Commission. Toutefois, la Commission peut siéger valablement en présence de sept de ses membres lorsqu'elle examine la recevabilité d'une requête introduite en vertu de l'article 25 de la Convention et que le groupe de trois membres visé à l'article 34 du présent Règlement est unanime à estimer, dans son rapport, que cette requête semble irrecevable.

Article 26

La Commission et les Sous-commissions siègent à huis clos.

Article 27

1. La Commission et les Sous-commissions délibèrent en chambre du conseil. Leurs délibérations sont et restent secrètes.
2. Seuls les membres de la Commission prennent part aux délibérations de la Commission. Seuls les membres d'une Sous-commission prennent part aux délibérations de cette Sous-commission.
3. Le Secrétaire de la Commission est, en principe, présent en chambre du conseil. Aucune autre personne ne peut y être admise qu'en vertu d'une décision de la Commission ou de la Sous-commission.

Article 28

Chacun des membres présents à la délibération exprime son opinion motivée. Le membre dernier en rang, selon l'ordre de préséance établi à l'article 3 du présent Règlement, a la parole le premier.

Article 29

1. Conformément à l'article 34 de la Convention, les décisions de la Commission sont prises à la majorité des membres présents et votant, et celles d'une Sous-commission à la majorité de ses membres.
2. Les votes sont émis dans l'ordre inverse de l'ordre de préséance établi à l'article 3 du présent Règlement.
3. En cas de partage des voix, la voix du Président est prépondérante.

Article 30

Les procès-verbaux des délibérations sont secrets; ils se bornent à mentionner l'objet des débats, les votes et le nom de ceux qui ont voté pour ou contre une proposition, ainsi que les déclarations expressément faites en vue d'y être insérées.

Rule 23

1. The Commission shall meet at the decision of the President when the latter considers that circumstances so require. It shall also meet if at least one-third of its members so request.
2. Pursuant to Article 35 of the Convention, the Commission shall be convened by the Secretary-General of the Council of Europe.

Rule 24

1. The date and time of meetings shall be laid down by the President of the Commission.
2. The date and time of meetings of a Sub-commission shall be laid down by its President.

Rule 25

A quorum of the Commission shall be nine members. However, seven members shall constitute a quorum when the Commission considers the admissibility of an application submitted under Article 25 of the Convention and provided that the group of three members referred to in Rule 34 has unanimously reported that the application appears to be inadmissible.

Rule 26

Sessions of the Commission and Sub-commissions shall be held in camera.

Rule 27

1. The Commission and Sub-commissions shall deliberate in private. Their deliberations shall be and shall remain secret.
2. Only the members of the Commission shall take part in the deliberations of the Commission. Only the members of a Sub-commission shall take part in the deliberations of such Sub-commission.
3. The Secretary of the Commission shall as a rule be present at the deliberations. No other person may be admitted except by decision of the Commission or Sub-commission.

Rule 28

Every member present at the deliberations shall state his opinion and the reasons therefor. The junior member according to the order of precedence laid down in Rule 3 shall speak first.

Rule 29

1. Pursuant to Article 34 of the Convention, decisions of the Commission shall be taken by a majority of members present and voting and decisions of a Sub-commission shall be taken by a majority of its members.
2. The votes shall be cast in the inverse order to the order of precedence laid down in Rule 3.
3. If the voting is equal, the President shall have a casting vote.

Rule 30

The minutes of deliberations shall be secret; they shall be limited to a record of the subject of the discussions, the votes taken, the names of those voting for and against a motion and any statements expressly made for insertion in the minutes.

Article 31

Les membres empêchés, par suite de maladie ou de circonstances graves, de participer aux séances, en font part, dans le plus bref délai, au Secrétaire de la Commission qui en informe le Président.

Article 32

1. Si, pour une raison spéciale, un membre estime devoir ne pas participer à l'examen d'une affaire déterminée, le Président et ledit membre confrontent leurs vues à ce sujet. S'il y a désaccord, la décision incombe à la Commission ou à la Sous-commission, suivant le cas.

2. Si le Président estime qu'un membre ne doit pas, pour une raison spéciale, participer à l'examen d'une affaire déterminée, il en avise ledit membre et soumet la question, pour décision, à la Commission ou à la Sous-commission, suivant le cas.

Article 33

Les membres de la Commission ne peuvent participer à l'examen d'aucune affaire dans laquelle ils sont antérieurement intervenus comme agent, conseil ou avocat de l'une des parties, ou sur laquelle ils ont été appelés à se prononcer comme membre d'un tribunal, d'une commission d'enquête ou à tout autre titre. S'il y a doute ou contestation, la décision incombe à la Commission ou à la Sous-commission, suivant le cas.

Article 34

1. La Commission constitue, suivant les nécessités, un ou plusieurs groupes composés chacun de trois de ses membres et appelés à exercer les fonctions prévues à l'article 45 du présent Règlement. Elle désigne en outre deux membres suppléants pour chaque groupe.

2. Dans l'intervalle entre les sessions de la Commission, le Président peut, en cas de besoin, procéder soit à la constitution d'un tel groupe, soit au remplacement de tout membre qui se trouverait empêché de participer aux travaux d'un groupe déjà constitué.

3. Chaque groupe est présidé par celui de ses membres qui a préséance aux termes de l'article 3 du présent Règlement.

TITRE II

DE LA PROCÉDURE

CHAPITRE I

Règles générales

Article 35

1. Les langues officielles de la Commission sont le français et l'anglais.

2. Le Président peut autoriser un membre à s'exprimer dans une autre langue.

Article 36

1. Les Hautes Parties Contractantes sont représentées devant la Commission par leurs agents, qui peuvent se faire assister par des conseils ou des avocats.

Rule 31

Members who are prevented by illness or other serious reason from taking part in the meetings shall as soon as possible give notice thereof to the Secretary of the Commission who shall inform the President.

Rule 32

1. If a member for some special reason considers that he should not take part in the examination of a particular case, the President and the member concerned shall consult together. In the event of disagreement, the Commission or Sub-commission, as the case may be, shall decide.
2. If the President considers that a member should not, for some special reason, take part in the examination of a particular case, he shall so notify the member concerned and refer the question for a decision by the Commission or Sub-commission, as the case may be.

Rule 33

Members of the Commission may not take part in the examination of any case in which they have previously acted as the agents, advisers or legal representatives of one of the parties or concerning which they have been required to state an opinion as members of a tribunal, commission of enquiry, or in any other capacity. In the event of doubt or dispute, the Commission or Sub-commission, as the case may be, shall decide.

Rule 34

1. The Commission shall, as circumstances require, constitute one or more groups, each consisting of three of its members, to carry out the duties laid down in Rule 45. It shall also appoint two substitute members for each group.
2. During the interval between sessions of the Commission, the President may, if necessary, either constitute a group or replace any member who is unable to take part in the work of a group already constituted.
3. The President of each group shall be the member of that group who has precedence under Rule 3.

TITLE II

PROCEDURE

CHAPTER I

General Rules

Rule 35

1. The official languages of the Commission shall be French and English.
2. The President may authorise a member to speak in another language.

Rule 36

1. The High Contracting Parties shall be represented before the Commission by their agents who may have the assistance of counsel or advocates.

2. Les personnes physiques, les organisations non-gouvernementales et les groupes de particuliers, visés à l'article 25 de la Convention, peuvent défendre eux-mêmes leur cause devant la Commission; ils peuvent être assistés ou représentés par un avocat, un avoué ou un professeur de droit, ainsi que par tout autre juriste agréé par la Commission.

Article 37

La Commission ou une Sous-commission peut, à la demande d'une partie ou de toute personne qui représente ou assiste cette partie, autoriser l'emploi, par cette partie ou personne, d'une langue autre que le français et l'anglais.

Article 38

1. La Commission traite les affaires dont elle est saisie suivant l'ordre dans lequel elles sont en état. Elle peut toutefois décider de traiter une affaire par priorité.
2. La Commission ou une Sous-commission ou, si elle ne siège pas, son Président, peut, à la demande d'une partie ou d'office, ordonner la remise d'une affaire.

Article 39

La Commission peut, si elle le juge nécessaire, ordonner la jonction de deux ou plusieurs affaires.

CHAPITRE II

De l'introduction de l'instance

Article 40

1. Toute demande présentée en vertu de l'article 24 ou de l'article 25 de la Convention doit l'être sous forme de requête écrite, et être signée par le requérant ou la personne qui le représente.
2. Lorsque la requête est présentée par une organisation non-gouvernementale ou par un groupe de particuliers, elle est signée par les personnes habilitées à représenter l'organisation ou le groupe, si ceux-ci sont régulièrement constitués selon la loi de l'État dont ils relèvent. Dans le cas contraire, la requête doit être signée par les personnes physiques formant le groupe requérant.

Article 41

1. La requête doit indiquer:
a) la partie requérante;
b) la Haute Partie Contractante contre laquelle la demande est formée;
c) l'objet de la demande;
d) autant que possible, la disposition de la Convention dont la violation est alléguée;
e) l'exposé des faits et des moyens;
f) les pièces annexées.
2. La partie requérante doit fournir des éléments permettant d'établir que les conditions de l'article 26 de la Convention se trouvent remplies.

Article 42

Si la partie requérante entend poursuivre la réparation d'un dommage prétendument subi, elle peut indiquer dans la requête le montant de l'indemnité réclamée.

2. The persons, non-governmental organisations and groups of individuals referred to in Article 25 of the Convention may represent their case in person before the Commission. They may be assisted or represented by a member of the Bar, by a solicitor or by a professor of law, or by any other lawyer approved by the Commission.

Rule 37

The Commission or a Sub-commission may, at the request of a party or of a person representing or assisting that party, permit the use by such party or person of a language other than French or English.

Rule 38

1. The Commission shall deal with cases in the order in which they become ready for hearing. It may, however, decide to give precedence to a particular case.

2. The Commission or a Sub-commission or, if it is not in session, its President may at the request of a party or *ex officio* order a case to be adjourned.

Rule 39

The Commission may, if it considers necessary, order the joinder of two or more cases.

CHAPTER II

Institution of proceedings

Rule 40

1. Any claims submitted under Article 24 or 25 of the Convention shall be submitted in the form of an application in writing and shall be signed by the applicant or his representative.

2. Where an application is submitted by a non-governmental organisation or by a group of individuals, it shall be signed by those persons competent to represent such organisation or group, if such organisation or group is properly constituted according to the laws of the State to which it is subject. The application shall in all other cases be signed by the persons composing the group submitting the application.

Rule 41

1. The application shall mention:

a) the name of the applicant;

b) the name of the High Contracting Party against which the claim is made;

c) the object of the claim;

d) as far as possible the provision of the Convention alleged to have been violated;

e) a statement of the facts and arguments;

f) any attached documents.

2. The applicant shall provide information enabling it to be shown that the conditions laid down in Article 26 of the Convention have been satisfied.

Rule 42

Where the applicant intends to claim damages for an alleged injury, the amount of damages claimed may be stated in the application.

Article 43

Le Secrétaire Général du Conseil de l'Europe transmet au Président de la Commission la requête et les pièces s'y rapportant.

Article 44

Si la Commission est saisie par une Haute Partie Contractante, en vertu de l'article 24 de la Convention, le Président de la Commission, par l'intermédiaire du Secrétaire Général du Conseil de l'Europe, donne connaissance de la requête à la Haute Partie Contractante mise en cause et invite celle-ci à présenter à la Commission ses observations écrites sur la recevabilité de ladite requête.

Article 45

1. Toute requête présentée en vertu de l'article 25 de la Convention est soumise par le Président de la Commission au groupe de trois membres visé à l'article 34 du présent Règlement, aux fins d'examen préalable de sa recevabilité. Le résultat de cet examen préalable fait l'objet d'un rapport à la Commission.

2. Si le groupe de trois membres, dans son rapport, est unanime à estimer que la requête semble recevable, le Président de la Commission, par l'intermédiaire du Secrétaire Général du Conseil de l'Europe, donne connaissance de la requête à la Haute Partie Contractante mise en cause et invite celle-ci à présenter à la Commission ses observations écrites sur la recevabilité de ladite requête.

3. Si le groupe de trois membres, dans son rapport, n'est pas unanime à estimer que la requête semble recevable, la Commission examine la requête et peut

a) soit la déclarer *de plano* irrecevable.

b) soit, par l'intermédiaire du Secrétaire Général du Conseil de l'Europe, donner connaissance de la requête à la Haute Partie Contractante mise en cause et inviter celle-ci à présenter à la Commission ses observations écrites sur la recevabilité de ladite requête.

Article 46

1. Sauf dans le cas visé au paragraphe 3, alinéa *a*), de l'article 45 du présent Règlement, la Commission, avant de prendre une décision sur la recevabilité, peut inviter les parties, si elle l'estime utile, à lui présenter des observations écrites complémentaires. Elle peut également inviter les parties à lui donner des explications orales.

2. Dans l'intervalle entre les sessions de la Commission, le Président peut, s'il l'estime utile, exercer les pouvoirs définis au paragraphe 1 du présent article.

3. La décision de la Commission sur la recevabilité de la requête est motivée. Le Secrétaire de la Commission la communique à la partie requérante et, sauf dans le cas visé au paragraphe 3, alinéa *a*), de l'article 45 du présent Règlement, à la partie défenderesse.

Article 47

1. Si la Commission retient la requête, elle procède à la constitution d'une Sous-commission, suivant les prescriptions du Titre I, chapitre IV, du présent Règlement.

2. Si la Commission retient une requête dont les faits sont connexes à ceux d'une affaire opposant les mêmes parties et pour laquelle une Sous-commission a déjà été constituée, elle peut, avec l'accord des parties, renvoyer la nouvelle affaire à ladite Sous-commission.

Rule 43

The Secretary-General of the Council of Europe shall transmit the application and any relevant documents to the President of the Commission.

Rule 44

Where, pursuant to Article 24 of the Convention, an application is brought before the Commission by a High Contracting Party, the President of the Commission shall through the Secretary-General of the Council of Europe give notice of such application to the High Contracting Party against which the claim is made and shall invite it to submit to the Commission its observations in writing on the admissibility of such application.

Rule 45

1. Any application submitted pursuant to Article 25 of the Convention shall be referred by the President of the Commission to the group of three members mentioned in Rule 34, which shall make a preliminary examination as to its admissibility. The group of three members shall then submit to the Commission a Report on such preliminary examination.

2. If the group of three members unanimously reports that the application appears to be admissible, the President of the Commission shall through the Secretary-General of the Council of Europe give notice of such application to the High Contracting Party against which the claim is made and shall invite it to submit to the Commission its observations in writing on the admissibility of such application.

3. If the group of three members does not unanimously report that the application appears to be admissible, the Commission shall consider the application and may

a) either, declare at once that the application is inadmissible,

b) or, through the Secretary-General of the Council of Europe give notice of such application to the High Contracting Party against which the claim is made and invite it to submit to the Commission its observations in writing on the admissibility of such application.

Rule 46

1. Except for the case provided for in Rule 45, paragraph 3 *a*), the Commission, before it decides as to the admissibility of an application, may, if it thinks fit, invite the parties to submit to it their further comments in writing. It may also invite the parties to make oral explanations.

2. During the interval between sessions of the Commission, the President may, if he thinks fit, exercise the powers mentioned in paragraph 1 of this Rule.

3. The decision of the Commission in regard to the admissibility of the application shall be accompanied by reasons. The Secretary of the Commission shall communicate such decision to the applicant and, except for the case provided for in Rule 45, paragraph 3 *a*), to the respondent party.

Rule 47

1. The Commission shall, if it accepts an application, set up a Subcommission according to the provisions of Chapter IV of Title I of the present Rules.

2. If the Commission accepts an application, the facts of which are connected with those of a case between the same parties for which a Sub-commission has already been set up it may refer the new case to the said Sub-commission with the agreement of the parties.

3. Le Président fixe les délais dans lesquels les parties auront à présenter leurs moyens, offres de preuve et conclusions.

Article 48

1. L'original de tout acte de procédure est signé par la partie ou la personne qui la représente.

2. Tous les actes de procédure sont datés. Pour la computation des délais, seule la date du dépôt au Secrétariat Général du Conseil de l'Europe est prise en considération.

3. Tout document produit en annexe et rédigé en une langue autre que les langues officielles doit être accompagné d'une traduction dans une de ces langues, sauf dérogation accordée par le Président. Toutefois, dans le cas de documents volumineux, des traductions en extrait peuvent être présentées. A tout moment, la Commission peut exiger une traduction plus complète ou une traduction certifiée conforme.

Article 49

Dès qu'une Sous-commission est constituée, le dossier de l'affaire lui est transmis pour qu'elle remplisse les fonctions prévues à l'article 28 de la Convention.

CHAPITRE III

De la procédure devant les Sous-commissions

Article 50

1. Chaque Sous-commission peut prendre toutes mesures utiles à l'accomplissement des fonctions prévues à l'article 28 de la Convention.

2. En cas de refus d'une partie de se conformer à une telle mesure, la Sous-commission en prend acte.

Article 51

La Sous-commission peut charger un on plusieurs de ses membres de procéder à une enquête ou à toute autre mesure d'instruction. Elle peut également désigner un de ses membres comme rapporteur.

Article 52

Le Président de la Sous-commission dirige les débats.

Article 53

1. La Sous-commission peut poser des questions aux parties et leur demander des éclaircissements.

2. La même faculté appartient à chaque membre de la Sous-commission qui, pour l'exercer, fait connaître son intention au Président.

Article 54

1. La Sous-commission peut, à la demande d'une partie ou d'office, ordonner l'audition, en qualité de témoin ou d'expert ou à un autre titre, de toute personne dont les dépositions, dires ou déclarations lui paraissent utiles à l'accomplissement de sa tâche.

2. Tout témoin, expert ou autre personne dont la Sous-commission ordonne l'audition est convoqué par le Secrétaire de la Commission. La convocation indique:

3. The President shall lay down the time-limits within which the parties shall submit their arguments, evidence and submissions.

Rule 48

1. Each pleading shall be signed in the original by the party or its representative.
2. Each pleading shall be dated. For the purpose of determining any time-limits, the date of the filing of the pleading with the Secretariat-General of the Council of Europe shall alone be taken into consideration.
3. Any document submitted as an appendix and written in a language other than the official languages shall, unless the President otherwise decides, be accompanied by translation into one of the official languages. Translations of extracts may be submitted, however, in the case of lengthy documents. The Commission may at any time require a more complete translation or a certified translation to be submitted.

Rule 49

As soon as a Sub-commission has been set up the file shall be sent to it to enable it to carry out the duties laid down in Article 28 of the Convention.

CHAPTER III

Procedure before Sub-commissions

Rule 50

1. A Sub-commission may take any measure which it considers expedient in order to carry out the duties laid down in Article 28 of the Convention.
2. A Sub-commission shall take formal note of the refusal of a party to comply with such measures.

Rule 51

A Sub-commission may instruct one or more of its members to undertake an enquiry or any other form of investigation. It may also appoint one of its members as rapporteur.

Rule 52

The President of a Sub-commission shall direct the proceedings.

Rule 53

1. A Sub-commission may put questions to the parties and request them to give explanations.
2. Each member of a Sub-commission shall have the same right and shall give notice to the President if he wishes to exercise it.

Rule 54

1. A Sub-commission may, at the request of a party or *proprio motu*, decide to hear as a witness or expert or in any other capacity any person whose evidence or statements seem likely to assist it in the carrying out of its task.
2. Any witness, expert or other person whom a Sub-commission decides to hear shall be summoned by the Secretary of the Commission. The summons shall indicate:

- les nom, prénoms, profession et domicile des parties en cause;
- les faits ou points sur lesquels portera l'audition;
- les dipositions prises, conformément au paragraphe 3, au paragraphe 4 ou au paragraphe 5 du présent article, pour le remboursement des frais encourus par l'intéressé.

3. Les frais encourus par tout témoin, expert ou autre personne dont la Sous-commission ordonne l'audition à la demande d'une Haute Partie Contractante incombent à cette Partie.

4. Les frais encourus par tout témoin, expert ou autre personne dont la Sous-commission ordonne l'audition à la demande d'une personne physique, d'une organisation non-gouvernementale ou d'un groupe de particuliers qui a saisi la Commission en vertu de l'article 25 de la Convention incombent soit à la partie requérante, soit au Conseil de l'Europe, selon ce que la Sous-commission en décide. Dans le second cas, ils sont fixés par le Président de la Sous-commission.

5. Les frais encourus par tout témoin, expert ou autre personne dont la Sous-commission ordonne d'office l'audition sont fixés par le Président de la Sous-commission et incombent au Conseil de l'Europe.

6. Tout témoin, expert ou autre personne dont la Sous-commission ordonne l'audition peut, s'il ne connaît pas suffisamment le français ni l'anglais, être autorisé par le Président à s'exprimer dans une autre langue.

Article 55

1. Après vérification de l'identité des témoins et experts, le Président de la Sous-commission, ou le ou les membres prévus à l'article 51 du présent Règlement, invitent les témoins et experts à prêter le serment suivant:

a) pour les témoins: „Je jure que je dirai la vérité, toute la vérité et rien que la vérité".

b) pour les experts: „Je jure que mon exposé correspondra à ma conviction sincère".

2. Les témoins et experts peuvent, au lieu de prêter le serment mentionné au paragraphe précédent, faire la déclaration suivante:

a) pour les témoins: „Je déclare solennellement, en tout honneur et en toute conscience, que je dirai la vérité, toute la vérité et rien que la vérité."

b) pour les experts: „Je déclare solennellement, en tout honneur et en toute conscience, que mon exposé correspondra à ma conviction sincère."

Article 56

Les témoins, experts et autres personnes visés à l'article 54, paragraphe 1, du présent Règlement peuvent être interrogés:

a) par le Président ou tout autre membre de la Sous-commission;

b) par une partie, sur autorisation du Président de la Sous-commission ou du ou des membres prévus à l'article 51 du présent Règlement.

Article 57

Lorsque, sans motif légitime, un témoin, expert ou autre personne, dûment invité à comparaître, ne se présente pas ou refuse de déposer, le Secrétaire Général du Conseil de l'Europe, à la demande du Président, signale le fait à la Haute Partie Contractante de la juridiction de laquelle relève l'intéressé. Il en va de même lorsqu'un témoin ou un expert a, de l'avis de la Sous-commission, violé le serment ou la déclaration solennelle prévus à l'article 55 du présent Règlement.

- the names, first names, occupation and domicile of the parties in the case;
- the facts or points regarding which the person concerned will be heard;
- the arrangements made, in accordance with paragraph 3, paragraph 4 or paragraph 5 of this Rule, to reimburse the person concerned for any expenses incurred by him.

3. The expenses incurred by any witness, expert or other person whom a Sub-commission decides to hear at the request of a High Contracting Party shall be borne by that Party.

4. The expenses incurred by any witness, expert or other person whom a Sub-commission decides to hear at the request of a person, non-governmental organisation or group of individuals, which has referred a matter to the Commission under Article 25 of the Convention, shall be borne either by the applicant or by the Council of Europe as the Sub-commission may decide. In the latter case they shall be fixed by the President of the Sub-commission.

5. The expenses incurred by any witness, expert or other person whom a Sub-commission *proprio motu* decides to hear shall be fixed by the President of the Sub-commission and be borne by the Council of Europe.

6. Any witness, expert or other person whom a Sub-commission decides to hear may, if he has not sufficient knowledge of French or English, be authorised by the President to speak in another language.

Rule 55

1. After establishing the identity of the witnesses or experts, the President of a Sub-commission or the member or members mentioned in Rule 51 shall request them to take the following oath:

a) for witnesses: "I swear that I will speak the truth, the whole truth and nothing but the truth".

b) for experts: "I swear that my statement will be in accordance with my sincere belief".

2. Instead of taking the oath in the terms set out in paragraph 1 of this Rule, the witnesses or experts may make the following declaration:

a) for witnesses: "I solemnly declare upon my honour and conscience that I will speak the truth, the whole truth and nothing but the truth".

b) for experts: "I solemnly declare upon my honour and conscience that my statement will be in accordance with my sincere belief".

Rule 56

Questions may be put to the witnesses, experts or other persons mentioned in Rule 54, paragraph 1:

a) by the President or any member of a Sub-commission;

b) by a party, with the permission of the President of the Sub-commission or of the member or members mentioned in Rule 51.

Rule 57

Where, without good reason, a witness, expert or other person who has been duly required to appear, fails to appear or refuses to give evidence, the Secretary-General of the Council of Europe shall, at the request of the President, so inform that High Contracting Party to whose jurisdiction the person concerned is subject. The same provisions shall apply where a witness or expert has, in the opinion of a Sub-commission, violated the oath or solemn declaration mentioned in Rule 55.

Article 58

Si la Sous-commission juge utile de poursuivre l'examen d'une affaire en dehors du siège du Conseil de l'Europe, elle demande à toute Haute Partie Contractante que cela concerne, par l'intermédiaire du Secrétaire Général du Conseil de l'Europe, de lui fournir toutes les facilités nécessaires à l'accomplissement de sa mission, comme prévu à l'article 28 *a*) de la Convention.

Article 59

Le Secrétariat de la Commission établit le procès-verbal des audiences. Ce procès-verbal est signé par le Président et par le Secrétaire de la Commission. Il fait foi de son contenu.

Article 60

Le rapport prévu à l'article 30 de la Convention comprend:
- la date à laquelle il est dressé;
- les noms du Président et des membres de la Sous-commission;
- l'indication des parties;
- les noms des représentants et des conseils des parties;
- l'exposé des faits;
- la solution adoptée.

Article 61

Le rapport visé au précédent article est signé par le Président de la Sous-commission et par le Secrétaire de la Commission. Il est transmis aux Hautes Parties Contractantes intéressées, au Comité des Ministres et au Secrétaire Général du Conseil de l'Europe aux fins de publication.

Article 62

Si elle ne parvient pas à un règlement amiable, la Sous-commission dresse, à l'usage exclusif de la Commission, un rapport contenant notamment:

a) l'établissement des faits de la cause, y compris un exposé de la procédure suivie;

b) le résultat de la tentative de règlement amiable.

CHAPITRE IV

Procédure devant la Commission

Article 63

Les dispositions du chapitre III du présent Titre s'appliquent, *mutatis mutandis*, aux procédures devant la Commission.

CHAPITRE V

Du rapport de la Commission

Article 64

Si, en vue de l'établissement du rapport prévu à l'article 31 de la Convention, la Commission juge nécessaire de réunir des renseignements complémentaires, elle détermine, dans chaque cas, la voie à suivre.

Rule 58

If a Sub-commission considers that it is expedient to examine a case in a place other than the seat of the Council of Europe, it shall, through the Secretary-General of the Council of Europe, request any High Contracting Party concerned to grant it all necessary facilities, as mentioned in paragraph *a*) of Article 28 of the Convention, in order that it may carry out its task.

Rule 59

The secretariat of the Commission shall draw up the minutes of the hearings. The minutes shall be signed by the President and by the Secretary of the Commission. The minutes shall constitute certified matters of record.

Rule 60

The Report provided for in Article 30 of the Convention shall contain:
- the date on which it was drawn up;
- the names of the President and members of a Sub-commission;
- a description of the parties;
- the names of the representatives and counsel of the parties;
- a statement of the facts;
- the terms of the solution reached.

Rule 61

The Report referred to in the preceding Rule shall be signed by the President of a Sub-commission and by the Secretary of the Commission. The Report shall be sent to the High Contracting Parties concerned, to the Committee of Ministers and to the Secretary General of the Council of Europe for publication.

Rule 62

If a Sub-commission fails to effect a friendly settlement, it shall make a Report for the sole use of the Commission. That Report shall, in particular, include:

a) the facts established, including an account of the proceedings;
b) the result of the attempt to reach a friendly settlement.

CHAPTER IV

Procedure before the Commission

Rule 63

The provisions of Chapter III of the present Title shall apply, *mutatis mutandis*, to proceedings before the Commission.

CHAPTER V

The Report of the Commission

Rule 64

If, with a view to the preparation of the Report provided for in Article 31 of the Convention, the Commission considers it necessary to obtain additional information, it shall in each case determine the manner in which this shall be done.

Article 65

Le rapport prévu à l'article 31 de la Convention est établi après délibération de la Commission en séance plénière.

Article 66

Le rapport comprend:
- la date à laquelle il est dressé;
- les noms du Président et des membres qui ont pris part à la délibération prévue à l'article 65 du présent Règlement;
- l'indication des parties;
- les noms des représentants et des conseils des parties;
- l'exposé de la procédure;
- l'exposé des faits;
- l'avis de la Commission sur le point de savoir si les faits constatés révèlent, de la part de la Haute Partie Contractante intéressée, une violation des obligations qui lui incombent aux termes de la Convention;
- les motifs sur lesquels se fonde cet avis;
- l'indication du nombre des membres ayant constitué la majorité;
- éventuellement, les propositions que la Commission jugerait appropriées de formuler.

Article 67

Conformément à l'article 31, paragraphe 1, de la Convention, tout membre peut faire inclure dans le rapport l'exposé de son opinion.

Article 68

Si la Commission décide de formuler des propositions relatives à la réparation prévue à l'article 42 du présent Règlement, elle le fait conformément à l'article 31, paragraphe 3, de la Convention.

Article 69

Le rapport et les propositions éventuelles sont signés par le Président et par le Secrétaire de la Commission. Par l'intermédiaire du Secrétaire Général du Conseil de l'Europe, ils sont transmis au Comité des Ministres et communiqués aux seules Hautes Parties Contractantes intéressées.

Article 70

Dans les trois mois qui suivent la transmission de son rapport au Comité des Ministres, la Commission, siégeant en séance plénière, examine s'il y a lieu ou non de saisir la Cour européenne des Droits de l'Homme de l'affaire en vertu de l'article 48 *a*) de la Convention.

TITRE III

DES RELATIONS DE LA COMMISSION AVEC LA COUR

Article 71

La Commission assiste la Cour européenne des Droits de l'Homme dans toute affaire soumise à celle-ci. A cet effet, et conformément à l'article 29, paragraphe 1, du Règlement de la Cour, elle désigne en séance plénière, dès que possible, un ou plusieurs de ses membres chargés de participer, en qualité de délégués, à l'examen de l'affaire devant la Cour. Ces délégués peuvent se faire assister de toute personne désignée par la

Rule 65

The Report provided for in Article 31 of the Convention shall be drawn up after deliberation by the Commission in plenary session.

Rule 66

The Report shall contain:
- the date on which it was drawn up;
- the names of the President and members who took part in the deliberation mentioned in Rule 65;
- a description of the parties;
- the names of the representatives and counsel of the parties;
- a statement of the proceedings;
- a statement of the facts;
- the opinion of the Commission as to whether the facts found disclose a breach by the High Contracting Party concerned of its obligations under the Convention;
- the reasons on which that opinion is based;
- a statement of the number of members forming the majority;
- any proposal which the Commission may consider appropriate.

Rule 67

Each member may, in accordance with paragraph 1 of Article 31 of the Convention, include in the Report a statement of his opinion.

Rule 68

Where the Commission decides to make proposals concerning damages as envisaged in Rule 42, it shall make them in pursuance of paragraph 3 of Article 31 of the Convention.

Rule 69

The Report and any proposals shall be signed by the President and by the Secretary of the Commission. They shall be sent through the Secretary-General of the Council of Europe to the Committee of Ministers and only to those High Contracting Parties which are concerned.

Rule 70

During the period of three months following the transmission of the Report of the Committee of Ministers, the Commission shall consider at a plenary session whether or not to bring the case before the European Court of Human Rights in pursuance of Article 48, paragraph *a*), of the Convention.

TITLE III

RELATIONS OF THE COMMISSION WITH THE COURT

Rule 71

The Commission shall assist the European Court of Human Rights in any case brought before the Court. For this purpose and in accordance with Rule 29, paragraph 1 of the Rules of Court, the Commission shall as soon as possible appoint, at a plenary session, one or more of its members to take part, as a delegate, in the consideration of the case before the Court. These delegates may be assisted by any person appointed by the

Commission. Dans l'accomplissement de leurs fonctions, ils se conforment aux directives que la Commission peut leur donner.

Article 72

1. Lorsque, en vertu de l'article 48 *a*) de la Convention, la Commission décide de saisir la Cour, elle établit, conformément à l'article 31, paragraphe 2, du Règlement de la Cour, une demande indiquant notamment:

a) les parties à la procédure suivie devant elle;

b) la date à laquelle elle a adopté son rapport;

c) la date à laquelle, suivant certificat du Secrétaire de la Commission joint à la demande, ledit rapport a été transmis au Comité des Ministres;

d) les nom et adresse de ses délégués.

2. Le Secrétaire de la Commission dépose auprès du Greffe de la Cour l'original et trente copies de la demande prévue au paragraphe 1er du présent article.

Article 73

Lorsque, en vertu de l'article 48 *b*), *c*) ou *d*) de la Convention, une Haute Partie Contractante saisit la Cour, le Secrétaire de la Commission communique au Greffe de la Cour, dès que possible:

a) les nom et adresse des délégués de la Commission;

b) tout autre renseignement ou information que la Commission estimerait utile de fournir à la Cour.

Article 74

Dès transmission de la demande visée à l'article 72, paragraphe 2, du présent Règlement, ou dès réception de la communication prévue à l'article 32, paragraphe 1 *c*) du Règlement de la Cour, le Secrétaire de la Commission dépose auprès du Greffe de la Cour un nombre suffisant d'exemplaires du rapport de la Commission.

Article 75

La Commission communique à la Cour, sur demande de celle-ci, tout mémoire, pièce, document ou renseignement concernant le dossier de l'affaire, à l'exception des documents relatifs à la tentative de règlement amiable effectuée conformément à l'article 28 *b*) de la Convention, dont la communication reste subordonnée, dans chaque cas, à une décision de la Commission.

Article 76

Lorsqu'une affaire portée devant la Commission en vertu de l'article 25 de la Convention est déférée ensuite à la Cour, le Secrétaire de la Commission en avise immédiatement le requérant. Sauf décision de la Commission en sens contraire, il lui communique également, en temps utile, le rapport de la Commission, en l'informant qu'il a la faculté de présenter à la Commission, dans un délai fixé par le Président, ses observations écrites sur ledit rapport. La Commission décide de la suite à donner à ces observations.

Commission. In discharging their functions they shall act in accordance with such directives as they may receive from the Commission.

Rule 72

1. When, in pursuance of Article 48, paragraph *a*) of the Convention, the Commission decides to bring a case before the Court, it shall, in accordance with Rule 31, paragraph 2 of the Rules of Court, draw up a request indicating in particular:
a) the parties to the proceedings before the Commission;
b) the date on which the Commission adopted its Report;
c) the date on which, as certified by the Secretary of the Commission in a document attached to the request, the Report was transmitted to the Committee of Ministers;
d) the names and addresses of its delegates.
2. The Secretary of the Commission shall transmit to the Registry of the Court thirty copies of the request referred to in paragraph 1 of this Rule.

Rule 73

When, in pursuance of Article 48, paragraph *b*), *c*) or *d*) of the Convention, a High Contracting Party brings a case before the Court, the Secretary of the Commission shall communicate to the Registry of the Court as soon as possible:
a) the names and addresses of the Commission's delegates;
b) any other information which the Commission may consider appropriate.

Rule 74

The Secretary of the Commission shall, as soon as he has transmitted the request referred to in Rule 72, paragraph 2 above, or has received the communication mentioned in Rule 32, paragraph 1 *c*) of the Rules of Court, file with the Registry of the Court an adequate number of copies of the Commission's Report.

Rule 75

The Commission shall communicate to the Court, at its request, any memorial evidence, document or information concerning the case, with the exception of documents relating to the attempt to secure a friendly settlement in accordance with Article 28, paragraph *b*) of the Convention. The communication of those documents shall be subject in each case to a decision of the Commission.

Rule 76

When a case brought before the Commission in pursuance of Article 25 of the Convention is subsequently referred to the Court, the Secretary of the Commission shall immediately notify the applicant. Unless the Commission shall otherwise decide, the Secretary shall also in due course communicate to him the Commission's Report, informing him that he may, within a time-limit fixed by the President, submit to the Commission his written observations on the said Report. The Commission shall decide what action, if any, shall be taken in respect of those observations.

2. COUR EUROPÉENNE DES DROITS DE L'HOMME

14 novembre 1960

Affaire „LAWLESS"
(exceptions préliminaires et questions de procédure)

ARRÊT

En l'affaire „LAWLESS",

La Cour européenne des Droits de l'Homme, constituée, conformément aux dispositions de l'article 43 de la Convention européenne de Sauvegarde des Droits de l'Homme et des Libertés fondamentales (ci-après dénommée „la Convention"), et des articles 21 et 22 du Règlement de la Cour, en une Chambre composée de:

M. R. CASSIN, *Président*
et de MM. G. MARIDAKIS
E. RODENBOURG
R. MCGONIGAL, membre d'office
G. BALLADORE PALLIERI
E. ARNALDS
K. F. ARIK, *Juges*,
P. MODINOS, *Greffier*,

rend l'arrêt suivant sur les exceptions préliminaires et questions de procédure soulevées par le mémoire de la Commission et le contre-mémoire du Gouvernement irlandais ainsi que par les conclusions prises en audience publique:

Procédure:

Le 13 avril 1960, le Secrétaire de la Commission européenne des Droits de l'Homme (ci-après dénommée „la Commission") a transmis au Greffier de la Cour une demande de la Commission en date du 12 avril 1960, déférant à la Cour l'affaire introduite devant la Commission, en vertu de l'article 25 de la Convention, par une requête datée du 8 novembre 1957 de Gerard Richard LAWLESS, ressortissant de la République d'Irlande, contre le Gouvernement de ladite République.

La demande, qui se réfère à la déclaration faite par le Gouvernement de la République d'Irlande en vertu de l'article 46 de la Convention européenne des Droits de l'Homme le 18 février 1953, ainsi qu'aux pouvoirs conférés à la Commission par les articles 44 et 48 de la Convention, a été transmise, conformément à l'article 32 du Règlement de la Cour, au Gouvernement irlandais le 14 avril 1960. Par application de l'article 21 § 2 du Règlement, le Greffier a, en outre, invité ledit Gouvernement à lui faire savoir, dans les trente jours, s'il désirait comparaître comme Partie dans cette affaire. Comme prévu à l'article 32 § 1 *in fine* du Règlement, le Greffier a informé, également le 14 avril 1960, le Comité des Ministres du dépôt de la demande.

Par télégramme du 12 mai 1960, confirmé par lettre en date du même jour, le Gouvernement irlandais a fait savoir au Greffier qu'il désirait comparaître comme Partie au procès relatif à l'affaire „LAWLESS" et qu'il avait désigné comme son agent M. T. WOODS, Représentant Permanent d'Irlande au Conseil de l'Europe.

A la suite de cette communication, Lord MCNAIR, Président de la Cour, a procédé, en présence du Greffier adjoint, le 18 mai 1960 à Londres, au tirage au sort des noms de six juges appelés à siéger dans la Chambre susmentionnée, M. Richard MCGONIGAL, juge élu de nationalité irlandaise, siégeant d'office, conformément à l'article 43 de la Convention. La com-

2. EUROPEAN COURT OF HUMAN RIGHTS

14th November, 1960

"LAWLESS" case
(preliminary objections and questions of procedure)

JUDGMENT

In the "LAWLESS" case,

The European Court of Human Rights, sitting, in accordance with the provisions of Article 43 of the European Convention for the Protection of Human Rights and Fundamental Freedoms (hereinafter referred to as "the Convention") and of Rules 21 and 22 of the Rules of Court, as a Chamber composed of:

Mr. R. CASSIN, *President*
and MM. G. MARIDAKIS
E. RODENBOURG
R. MCGONIGAL, *ex officio* member
G. BALLADORE PALLIERI
E. ARNALDS
K. F. ARIK, *Judges*
P. MODINOS, *Registrar*

delivers the following judgment on the preliminary objections and questions of procedure raised in the Memorial of the Commission, the Counter-Memorial of the Irish Government and the submissions at the public hearing of the case:

Procedure:

On 13th April, 1960, the Secretary of the European Commission of Human Rights (hereinafter called "the Commission") transmitted to the Registrar of the Court a Request from the Commission, dated 12th April, 1960, submitting to the Court the case brought before the Commission under Article 25 of the Convention, by an Application dated 8th November, 1957, and filed by Gerard Richard LAWLESS, a national of the Republic of Ireland, against the Government of the said Republic.

The Request, which refers to the declaration made on 18th February, 1953, by the Irish Government under Article 46 of the European Convention on Human Rights and to the powers vested in the Commission by Articles 44 and 48 of that Convention, was transmitted to the Irish Government on 14th April, 1960, in accordance with Rule 32 of the Rules of Court. In conformity with Rule 21, paragraph 2 of the Rules of Court, the Registrar furthermore invited the said Government to inform him, within thirty days, whether it wished to appear as a Party to the case. As prescribed in the concluding sub-paragraph of Rule 32, paragraph 1 of the Rules of Court, the Registrar also informed the Committee of Ministers, on 14th April, 1960, of the filing of the Request.

By a telegram of 12th May, 1960, confirmed by a letter of the same date, the Irish Government informed the Registrar that it desired to appear as a Party in the proceedings relating to the LAWLESS case and that it had appointed as its Agent Mr. T. WOODS, Irish Permanent Representative to the Council of Europe.

Following upon this communication, Lord MCNAIR, President of the Court, proceeded on 18th May, 1960, in London, in the presence of the Deputy Registrar to choose by lot the names of six judges to constitute the above-mentioned Chamber – Mr. Richard MCGONIGAL, an elected Judge of Irish nationality, being the *ex officio* member required by position de la Chambre a été notifiée par le Greffier, le 23 mai 1960 aux juges et à l'agent du Gouvernement irlandais ainsi que le 24 mai au Président de la Commission.

Après avoir recueilli, conformément à l'article 35 § 1 du Réglement, l'opinion de l'agent de la Partie ainsi que des délégués de la Commission au sujet de la procédure à suivre, le 1er juin 1960 à Strasbourg, le Président de la Chambre, par ordonnance en date du même jour, a fixé au 30 juin 1960 le terme du délai pour le depôt du mémoire de la Commission, et au 20 août 1960 le terme du délai pour le dépôt du contre-mémoire du Gouvernement irlandais. A la demande de la Partie, le terme de ce dernier délai a été reporté au 30 août 1960, et ceci en vertu d'une ordonnance du Président de la Chambre en date du 16 août 1960. Le mémoire et le contre-mémoire – l'un et l'autre soulevant essentiellement des exceptions préliminaires et questions de procédure – ont été présentés aux dates prévues. Conformément à l'article 35 § 3, du Règlement de la Cour, le mémoire de la Commission a été transmis aux juges et à l'agent du Gouvernement irlandais, le 30 juin 1960, le contre-mémoire a été communiqué aux juges et aux délégués de la Commission, le 30 août 1960. En ce qui concerne les exceptions préliminaires, l'affaire se trouve donc en état depuis le 30 août 1960.

Une audience publique a été tenue les 3 et 4 octobre 1960, à laquelle ont comparu:

pour la Commission:

M. C. H. M. Waldock, Président de la Commission, *délégué principal*,
M. C. Th. Eustathiades, Vice-Président,
et M. S. Petren, Membre de la Commission, *délégués adjoints*,

pour le Gouvernement irlandais, Partie:

M. T. Woods, Représentant permanent auprès du Conseil de l'Europe, *Agent*, assisté de
MM. A. O'Keeffe, Attorney-General d'Irlande,
S. Morrissey, Barrister-at-Law, Legal Adviser, Ministère des Affaires étrangères,
P. Reuter, Professeur à la Faculté de Droit de Paris,
A. J. Heddermann, Barrister-at-Law, *Conseils*, et de
MM. D. O'Donovan, Chief State Solicitor,
P. Berry, Assistant Secretary-General, Department of Justice.

A cette audience, la Cour a entendu, en leurs déclarations, réponses et conclusions, pour la Commission: M. C. H. M. Waldock, délégué principal; pour le Gouvernement irlandais: M. A. O'Keeffe, Attorney-General.

La Cour a, les 3 et 4 octobre 1960, limité les débats aux exceptions préliminaires et questions de procédure.

EN FAIT

La demande de la Commission – à laquelle se trouve joint le rapport établi par la Commission conformément aux dispositions de l'article 31 de la Convention – a pour objet de soumettre l'affaire G. R. Lawless à la Cour afin que celle-ci puisse décider si les faits de la cause relèvent ou non, de la part du Gouvernement défendeur, une violation des obligations qui lui incombent aux termes de la Convention.

Ainsi qu'il ressort de la demande et du mémoire de la Commission, M. Lawless allègue dans sa requête une violation de la Convention à son

Article 43 of the Convention. The Composition of the Chamber was notified by the Registrar to the judges and to the Agent of the Irish Government on 23rd May, 1960, and to the President of the Commission on 24th May.

After having, at Strasbourg on 1st June, 1960, ascertained the views of the Agent of the Party and the delegates of the Commission upon the procedure to be followed, as required by Rule 35, paragraph 1, of the Rules of Court, the President of the Chamber, by an Order of the same date, appointed 30th June, 1960, as the final date for the filing of the Commission's Memorial and 20th August, 1960, as the final date for the filing of the Counter-Memorial by the Irish Government. At the request of the Party, this latter time-limit was extended to 30th August, 1960, by an order of the President of the Chamber dated 16th August, 1960. The Memorial and Counter-Memorial – both raising principally preliminary objections and questions of procedure – were filed on the appointed dates. In accordance with Rule 35, paragraph 3 of the Rules of Court, the Memorial of the Commission was transmitted to the judges and to the Agent of the Irish Government on 30th June, 1960, and the Counter-Memorial was communicated to the judges and to the delegates of the Commission on 30th August, 1960. So far as concerns the preliminary objections, the case has thus been ready for hearing since 30th August, 1960.

Public hearings were held on 3rd and 4th October, 1960, at which there appeared:

for the Commission:

Mr. C. H. M. Waldock, President of the Commission, *principal delegate*
Mr. C. Th. Eustathiades, Vice-President,
and Mr. S. Petren, Member of the Commission, *assistant delegates*,

for the Irish Government, Party to the case:

Mr. T. Woods, Permanent Representative to the Council of Europe, *Agent*, assisted by
MM. A. O'Keeffe, Attorney-General of Ireland,
S. Morrissey, Barrister-at-Law, Legal Adviser, Ministry of Foreign Affairs,
P. Reuter, Professor of the Faculty of Law of Paris,
A. J. Heddermann, Barrister-at-Law,
Counsel, and by
MM. D. O'Donovan, Chief State Solicitor,
P. Berry, Assistant Secretary-General, Department of Justice.

At this hearing the Court heard the following statements, replies and submissions: for the Commission: from Mr. C. H. M. Waldock, principal delegate; for the Irish Government: Mr. A. O'Keeffe, Attorney-General.

On 3rd and 4th October, 1960, the Court confined its debate to the preliminary objections and questions of procedure.

AS TO THE FACTS:

The purpose of the Commission's Request – to which is appended the Report drawn up by the Commission in accordance with the provisions of Article 31 of the Convention – is to submit the case of G. R. Lawless to the Court so that it may decide whether or not the facts of the case disclose that the Respondent Government has failed in its obligations under the Convention.

As appears from the Commission's Request and from its Memorial, Mr. Lawless alleges in his Application that there has been a violation of

égard, par les autorités de la République d'Irlande, du fait de sa détention sans jugement du 13 juillet au 11 décembre 1957 dans un camp de détention militaire situé sur le territoire de la République d'Irlande, en exécution d'une ordonnance prise par le Ministre de la Justice en vertu de l'article 4 de la Loi de 1940 modifiant la Loi relative aux atteintes à la sûreté de l'État. Les pouvoirs spéciaux d'arrestation et de détention conférés par cette loi aux Ministres de l'État auraient été mis en vigueur le 8 juillet 1957 sur la base d'une proclamation publiée par le Gouvernement irlandais le 5 juillet 1957.

La Commission, après avoir déclaré la requête recevable, le 30 août 1958, l'a examinée conformément à la procédure prévue aux articles 28 et 29 de la Convention. Un règlement amiable n'ayant pu intervenir, la Commission a établi le rapport prévu à l'article 31 de la Convention. Ledit rapport a été adopté par la Commission le 19 décembre 1959, la majorité ayant été d'avis qu'il n'y a pas de violation de la Convention de la part du Gouvernement irlandais et qu'aucune suite ne devait être donnée à la demande de dommages-intérêts formulée par le requérant.

Après avoir transmis ledit rapport au Comité des Ministres du Conseil de l'Europe le 1er février 1960, et ceci conformément à l'article 31, paragraphe 2 de la Convention, la Commission, à sa séance du 1er avril 1960, a décidé de se prévaloir de la faculté qui lui est offerte aux articles 44 et 46 de la Convention et de déférer l'affaire LAWLESS à la Cour pour décision définitive.

A l'appui de sa décision, la Commission a fait valoir, dans son mémoire, qu'un avis formulé par elle en vertu de l'article 31 de la Convention sur le point de savoir si les faits constatés révèlent une violation de celle-ci, ne mettait pas fin au litige. La Commission a, en effet, souligné qu'aux termes de l'article 32, paragraphe 1 de la Convention, si l'affaire n'est pas déférée à la Cour, c'est au Comité des Ministres qu'il incombe de prendre, par un vote à la majorité des deux tiers, une décision sur la question de savoir s'il y a eu ou non violation de la Convention.

Or, en raison de l'importance fondamentale des problèmes juridiques qui se posent dans cette affaire – notamment en ce qui concerne les questions relevant de l'article 15 de la Convention – la Commission a jugé opportun de la soumettre à la Cour, sans pour autant modifier sa propre opinion à ce sujet telle qu'elle a été consignée dans le rapport.

A la réunion tenue, conformément à l'article 35, paragraphe 1, du Règlement de la Cour, le 1er juin 1960, ainsi que dans son mémoire du 27 juin 1960, la Commission a fait savoir que, conformément à l'article 76 de son Règlement intérieur, elle avait, le 13 avril 1960 – donc après avoir déféré la présente affaire à la Cour – transmis le rapport au requérant en l'invitant à soumettre à la Commission ses observations. En transmettant le rapport du requérant, la Commission a souligné que ce document devait rester secret et que le requérant n'avait pas la faculté de le publier.

L'article 76 du Règlement de la Commission est ainsi libellé:

> „Lorsqu'une affaire portée devant la Commission en vertu de l'article 25 de la Convention est déférée ensuite à la Cour, le Secrétaire de la Commission en avise immédiatement le requérant. Sauf décision de la Commission en sens contraire, il lui communique également, en temps utile, le rapport de la Commission, en l'informant qu'il a la faculté de présenter à la Commission, dans un délai fixé par le Président, ses observations écrites sur ledit rapport. La Commission décide de la suite à donner à ces observations".

Dans son mémoire, la Commission a souligné qu'elle était prête „à communiquer à la Cour les observations du requérant sur le rapport, en tant que document concernant le dossier de l'affaire". Toutefois, au lieu the Convention in his case, by the authorities of the Repubilc of Ireland, inasmuch as he was detained without trial, between 13th July and 11th December, 1957, in a military detention camp situated in the territory of the Republic of Ireland, in pursuance of an Order made by the Minister of Justice under Section 4 of the Offences against the State (Amendment) Act, 1940. The special powers of arrest and of detention allowed to Ministers of State by this Act are said to have been brought into force on 8th July, 1957, by a proclamation made and published by the Irish Government on 5th July, 1957.

After being declared admissible on 30th August, 1958, the Request was dealt with by the Commission according to the procedure laid down in Articles 28 and 29 of the Convention. It proved impossible to secure a friendly settlement, and the Commission therefore drew up the Report called for by Article 31 of the Convention. This Report was adopted by the Commission on 19th December, 1959, the majority holding that there had been no breach of the Convention on the part of the Irish Government and that no action should be taken on the Applicant's suit for damages.

After transmitting this Report to the Committee of Ministers of the Council of Europe on 1st February, 1960, in accordance with Article 31, paragraph 2, of the Convention, the Commission decided, at its meeting of 1st April, 1960, to avail itself of the possibility offered by Articles 44 and 46 of the Convention, and refer the LAWLESS case to the Court for final decision.

In support of this step, the Commission recalled in its Memorial that an opinion stated by it under Article 31 of the Convention as to whether or not the facts found disclosed a breach of the Convention would not be conclusive. The Commission pointed out that under Article 32, paragraph 1, of the Convention, if a question were not referred to the Court, it rested with the Committee of Ministers to decide, by a majority of two-thirds, whether or not there had been a violation of the Convention.

In view of the fundamental importance of the legal problems raised in this case – and particularly of the questions arising in relation to Article 15 of the Convention – the Commission deemed it advisable to refer the case to the Court, though without qualifying in any way its own opinion on the subject as expressed in the Report.

At the meeting held on 1st June, 1960, in accordance with Rule 35, paragraph 1, of the Rules of Court, and in its Memorial of 27th June, 1960, the Commission stated that in conformity with Rule 76 of its Rules of Procedure, it had, on 13th April, 1960 – that is, after referring the case to the Court – transmitted the Report to the Applicant, inviting him to submit his observations to the Commission. In submitting the Report to the Applicant the Commission pointed out that that document must be kept secret and that the Applicant was not entitled to publish it.

Rule 76 of the Rules of Procedure of the Commission runs as follows:

> "When a case brought before the Commission in pursuance of Article 25 of the Convention is subsequently referred to the Court, the Secretary of the Commission shall immediately notify the Applicant. Unless the Commission shall otherwise decide, the Secretary shall also in due course communicate to him the Commission's Report, informing him that he may, within a time-limit fixed by the President, submit to the Commission his written observations on the said Report. The Commission shall decide what action, if any, shall be taken in respect of these observations".

In its Memorial, the Commission declared its readiness "to submit to the Court the Applicant's comments upon the Report as a document relevant in the present proceedings". However, instead of communicating de faire cette communication de sa propre initiative, elle a cru devoir, à ce stade préliminaire de la procédure, demander à la Cour l'autorisation de déposer le mémoire contenant les observations du requérant en tant que document soumis par la Commission.

Au cours de la procédure écrite, les conclusions ci-après ont été prises en ce qui concerne la procédure seulement;

par la Commission, dans son mémoire:

,,Plaise à la Cour:

1. d'autoriser la Commission à lui soumettre les observations du requérant sur son rapport comme l'un des documents de la Commission concernant l'affaire;

2. d'une manière générale, de donner des instructions quant au droit de la Commission de lui communiquer les observations du requérant sur les questions qui se posent dans la présente procédure.''

Par le Gouvernement irlandais, dans son contre-mémoire:

,,Qu'il plaise à la Cour:

1. de se refuser à connaître de la présente affaire, à moins que la Commission n'établisse que, entre le 19 décembre 1959 et le 1er février 1960, elle n'a nullement examiné la question de la saisine de la Cour;

2. de se refuser à retenir l'affaire tant que n'aura pas été justifié le délai de transmission du rapport de la Commission au Comité des Ministres et au Gouvernement;

3. de déclarer que toute publication du rapport par la Commission en dehors des cas expressément autorisés par la Convention, constitue un acte contrevenant aux obligations imposées à la Commission par la Convention;

4. de décider de ne pas retenir les observations du requérant sur le rapport de la Commission et sur les questions qui se posent dans la présente procédure par les motifs:

a) que la Commission n'a fourni aucun argument en faveur de leur recevabilité;

b) que le fait de retenir de telles observations constituerait un moyen oblique d'amender la Convention;

c) que ces observations n'ont pu être formulées qu'à la suite de la non-observation, par la Commission, de son obligation de secret;

d) que, en l'état de la procédure, ces observations sont hors de propos;

5. de déclarer que l'interprétation correcte de la Convention n'autorise pas la Commission à agir comme elle l'envisage à l'article 76 de son Règlement intérieur.''

A l'audience du 3 octobre 1960, la Commission a présenté les conclusions suivantes:

,,A. *Quant à l'exception portant sur la compétence de la Cour:*

Plaise à la Cour de rejeter les exceptions préliminaires formulées contre la compétence de la Cour au paragraphe 4 du Contre-mémoire du Gouvernement défendeur.

B. *Quant à l'exception concernant la publication du rapport:*

Plaise à la Cour de décider que les dispositions de l'article 76 du Règlement intérieur de la Commission et la communication au requérant par la Commission de son rapport sur la présente affaire relèvent de la compétence conférée à la Commission par la Convention, et de rejeter l'exception préliminaire formulée au paragraphe 5 du contre-mémoire présenté par le Gouvernement défendeur.

these comments on its own initiative, the Commission thought appropriate, at this preliminary stage of the procedure, to request the Court for leave to file the memorandum containing the Applicant's comments as a document submitted by the Commission.

In the pleadings, the following submissions were made in regard to the procedure alone:

By the Commission, in its Memorial:

"May it please the Court:

1. To give leave for the Commission to submit to the Court the Applicant's comments on the Commission's Report as one of the Commission's documents in the case; and

2. in general, to give directions as to the right of the Commission to communicate to the Court the comments of the Applicant in regard to matters arising in the present proceedings".

By the Irish Government, in their Counter-Memorial:

"May it please the Court:

1. To decline jurisdiction in the present case unless the Commission satisfies the Court that between 19th December ,1959, and 1st February, 1960, the question of reference of the case to the Court was not discussed in any way by the Commission;

2. To refuse to entertain the case while the delay on the part of the Commission in transmitting its Report to the Committee of Ministers and to the Government has not been satisfactorily explained;

3. To declare that any publication by the Commission of its Report other than that expressly authorised by the Convention, is a breach of the obligations imposed on the Commission by the Convention;

4. To rule that the comments of the Applicant on the Report of the Commission and the further comments of the Applicant on matters arising in the present proceedings be not received by the Court,

a) because no argument in favour of their admission has been submitted by the Commission, and

b) because the admission of such comments would be an oblique method of amending the Convention, and

c) because such comments have come into existence only through a breach by the Commission of its obligations of secrecy, and

d) because in the circumstances of the present proceedings such comments are not material;

5. To declare that a correct interpretation of the Convention does not permit of action of the nature contemplated by Rule 76 of the Rules of the Commission".

At the hearing of 3rd October, 1960, the Commission made the following submissions:

"A. *As to the objection to the Court's jurisdiction:*

May it please the Court to reject the preliminary objections to the Court's jurisdiction formulated in paragraph 4 of the Respondent Government's Counter-Memorial.

B. *As to the objection concerning the publication of the Report:*

May it please the Court to decide that the provisions of Rule 76 of the Commission's Rules of Procedure and the Commission's communication of its Report on the present case to the Applicant fall within the competence conferred upon the Commission by the Convention, and to reject the preliminary objection formulated in paragraph 5 of the Respondent Government's Counter-Memorial.

C. *Quant à l'exeption concernant le rôle du requérant dans la procédure devant la Cour:*

Plaise à la Cour:

a) de permettre à la Commission de lui transmettre les observations écrites du requérant sur le rapport de la Commission;

b) de donner telles directives qu'elle peut juger appropriées quant au droit de la Commission de communiquer à la Cour les observations du requérant en ce qui concerne les questions surgissant au cours de la présente procédure;

c) de rejeter les conclusions formulées au paragraphe 6 du contre-mémoire du Gouvernement défendeur".

A l'audience du 3 octobre 1960, l'Agent du Gouvernement irlandais, tenant compte des explications fournies par le Délégué de la Commission au cours de sa plaidoirie orale, a retiré les exceptions préliminaires figurant sous les numéros 1 et 2 du contre-mémoire de son Gouvernement.

Les conclusions suivantes, portant sur les exceptions préliminaires et les questions de procédure soulevées en la présente instance, ont été prises par l'Agent du Gouvernement irlandais, à l'audience du 4 octobre 1960:

„Qu'il plaise à la Cour:

1. de déclarer que toute publication du rapport par la Commission en dehors des cas expressément autorisés par la Convention constitue un acte contrevenant aux obligations imposées à la Commission par la Convention;

2. de décider de ne pas recevoir les observations du requérant sur le rapport de la Commission;

3. de décider de ne pas recevoir les observations formulées d'autre part, par le requérant sur les questions qui se posent dans la présente procédure;

4. de déclarer que l'interprétation correcte de la Convention n'autorise pas la Commission à agir comme elle l'envisage à l'article 76 de son Règlement intérieur."

EN DROIT

Considérant, qu'en réponse aux questions de procédure soulevées par la Commission dans son mémoire, le Gouvernement irlandais s'est conformé aux prescriptions de l'article 46 du Règlement de la Cour en formulant ses exceptions préliminaires et objections de procédure dans le contre-mémoire qui constitue la première pièce de la procédure écrite déposée par cette Partie, contre-mémoire dans lequel il a joint ses objections de procédure; qu'à l'audience du 3 octobre 1960, la Cour a pris acte de ce que l'Agent du Gouvernement irlandais a retiré les exceptions préliminaires figurant aux paragraphes 1 et 2 des conclusions prises par ce Gouvernement dans son contre-mémoire; que, d'autre part, le Gouvernement irlandais n'a pas maintenu, dans ses conclusions prises à l'audience du 4 octobre, les objections qu'il avait soulevées au paragraphe 7 de son contre-mémoire, relatives à la forme interrogative des conclusions prises par la Commission sur le fond de l'affaire; qu'il n'y a donc plus lieu pour la Cour de se prononcer sur ces questions;

Considérant, suivant les conclusions finales prises par la Commission et par le Gouvernement irlandais à l'audience des 3 et 4 octobre 1960, que la Cour n'est appelée à se prononcer que sur les trois questions suivantes:

(*i*) L'article 76 du Règlement de la Commission est-il, en général, contraire à la Convention?

(*ii*) La Commission pouvait-elle, après avoir déféré l'affaire à la Cour, communiquer son rapport à G. R. Lawless, requérant, dans les conditions énoncées par le Délégué de la Commission, sans contrevenir aux prescriptions de la Convention?

C. *As to the objection in regard to the role of the Applicant in the proceedings before the Court:*

May it please the Court:

a) to give leave to the Commission to transmit to the Court the written comments of the Applicant upon the Commission's Report;

b) to give such directions as the Court may consider appropriate *as to the right* of the Commission to communicate to the Court *the comments of the Applicant* in regard to matters arising in the present proceedings;

c) to reject the submissions formulated in paragraph 6 of the Respondent Government's Counter-Memorial".

At the hearing of 3rd October, 1960, the Agent of the Irish Government, in view of the explanations furnished by the Delegate of the Commission during his oral pleading, withdrew the preliminary objections appearing as Nos. 1 and 2 in his Government's Counter-Memorial.

The following submissions, relating to the preliminary objections and questions of procedure raised during the present proceedings, were presented by the Agent of the Irish Government at the hearing of 4th October, 1960:

"May it please the Court:

1. to declare that any publication by the Commission of its Report, other than that expressly authorised by the Convention, is a breach of the obligations imposed on the Commission by the Convention.

2. To rule that the comments of the Applicant on the Report of the Commission be not received by the Court.

3. To rule that no further comments of the Applicant on matters arising in the present proceedings may be received by the Court.

4. To declare that a correct interpretation of the Convention does not permit of action of the nature contemplated by Rule 76 of the Rules of the Commission".

AS TO THE LAW:

Whereas the Irish Government, in reply to the questions of procedure raised in the Commission's Memorial, complied with Rule 46 of the Rules of Procedure of the Court in raising their preliminary and procedural objections in the Counter-Memorial which constitutes the first written document in their case; and whereas at the hearing of 3rd October, 1960, the Court took formal note of the Irish Government's withdrawal of their preliminary objections set out in paragraphs 1 and 2 of the final submissions of their Counter-Memorial; whereas furthermore, in their submissions at the hearing of 4th October the Irish Government did not press the objections raised in paragraph 7 of the Counter-Memorial, concerning the interrogative form of the Commission's findings on the substance of the case; whereas accordingly there is no need for the Court to consider these matters;

Whereas, in the light of the final submissions of the Commission and of the Irish Government at the hearings of 3rd and 4th October, 1960, the Court is called upon to decide the following three points only:

(*i*) Is Rule 76 of the Rules of Procedure of the Commission in general contrary to the terms of the Convention?

(*ii*) Could the Commission, after bringing the case before the Court, communicate its Report to G. R. LAWLESS, the Applicant, in the manner described by the Commission's delegate, without infringing the terms of the Convention?

(*iii*) La Cour devrait-elle, soit sur l'initiative de la Commission prise *de plano*, soit après autorisation donnée par elle à la Commission, recevoir par l'intermédiaire de celle-ci, communication des observations écrites du requérant LAWLESS sur le rapport de la Commission ou sur les questions surgissant au cours de la présente procédure?

(*i*) *Sur la prétendue contradiction „in genere" entre l'article 76 du Règlement de la Commission et la Convention*

Considérant que parmi les moyens préliminaires soulevés par le Gouvernement irlandais au sujet du déroulement de la procédure devant la Cour, celui qui figure au paragraphe 4 des conclusions finales de ce Gouvernement tend à ce que la Cour se prononce, de manière générale, sur la conformité de l'article 76 du Règlement de la Commission avec les dispositions de la Convention;

Considérant que la Convention a, par son article 19, institué la Commission ainsi que la Cour „afin d'assurer le respect des engagements résultant pour les Hautes Parties Contractantes de la Convention"; que, pour la sauvegarde des droits de l'homme, elle a confié à chacun de ces deux organes des fonctions déterminées; qu'elle a doté la Commission d'attributions différant dans le temps; que dans la phase initiale de la procédure – principalement couverte par les dispositions du Titre III de la Convention – la Commission reçoit essentiellement une mission indépendante d'enquête, de conciliation et éventuellement d'initiative pour saisir la Cour; qu'à la vérité, une fois la Cour saisie d'une affaire, la Commission devient principalement une aide de la Cour et est associée au fonctionnement de celle-ci, mais que même dans cette phase de la procédure, elle exerce des attributions qui dérivent directement de la Convention et ne sont pas fixées par la Cour;

Considérant qu'il résulte de l'ensemble des règles régissant les pouvoirs de la Cour que celle-ci ne peut interpréter les dispositions de la Convention de manière abstraite, mais seulement en fonction du cas déterminé qui lui est déféré; qu'en effet, aux termes de l'article 45 de la Convention, la compétence de la Cour „s'étend à toutes les affaires concernant l'interprétation et l'application de la Convention"; que la portée de cette disposition est précisée et délimitée par d'autres dispositions de la Convention, à savoir: *a*) l'article 47 aux termes duquel „la Cour ne peut être saisie d'une affaire qu'après la constatation, par la Commission, de l'échec du règlement amiable et dans le délai de trois mois prévu à l'article 32"; *b*) l'article 53 en vertu duquel seules les Hautes Parties Contractantes qui sont „parties au litige" sont liées par les décisions de la Cour;

Considérant qu'il résulte de ce qui précède que la Cour n'a pas compétence pour prendre des décisions telle que l'annulation d'un article du Règlement de la Commission, produisant des effets à l'égard de tous les intéressés à la Convention, compétence qui ressemblerait au pouvoir soit de rendre des arrêts de règlement, soit d'émettre des avis consultatifs; que dès lors la Cour ne peut entrer dans l'examen d'un problème qui lui est posé d'une manière générale par les deux concluants;

Considérant, néanmoins, que dans l'exercice de ses fonctions, la Cour a le devoir de veiller au respect de la Convention dans le cas déterminé qui lui est déféré et, éventuellement, de relever les irrégularités qui auraient pu être commises ainsi que de refuser l'application dans ledit cas de toute disposition réglementaire ou autre, prise en contravention avec la Convention; qu'à ce titre la Cour doit entrer dans l'examen du moyen particulier qui suit;

(*ii*) *Sur la communication, par la Commission, de son rapport à* G. R. LAWLESS

Considérant qu'il a été établi, au cours de la procédure, que la Commission a transmis, un jour après avoir saisi la Cour de la présente affaire, (*iii*) Should the Court, either at the instance of the Commission acting on its own authority, or through the Commission after authorisation by the Court, receive the written observations of G. R. LAWLESS, the Applicant, on the Commission's Report or on points arising during the proceedings?

(*i*) *As regards the alleged incompatibility "in genere" of Rule 76 of the Rules of Procedure of the Commission with the Convention*

Whereas among the preliminary points raised by the Irish Government th regard to the proceedings before the Court, that set out in paragraph 4 of their conclusions calls for a general decision by the Court on the compatibility of Rule 76 of the Commission with the terms of the Convention;

Whereas in Article 19, the Convention sets up both the Commission and the Court "to ensure the observance of the engagements undertaken by the High Contracting Parties in the Convention" and assigns to each of these bodies specific functions in the safeguarding of human rights; whereas those of the Commission differ according to the stage reached in the proceedings; whereas, in the initial stage – governed mainly by Section III of the Convention – the Commission's chief function is to carry out an independent inquiry, to seek a friendly settlement and, if need be, to bring the case before the Court: whereas, once this has been done, the Commission's main function is to assist the Court, and it is associated with the proceedings; whereas, however, even at this stage its action is determined not by a decision of the Court, but directly by the terms of the Convention;

Whereas it follows from the whole body of rules governing the powers of the Court, that it cannot interpret the Convention in an abstract manner, but only in relation to such specific cases as are referred to it; whereas, according to Article 45 of the Convention, the jurisdiction of the Court "shall extend to all cases concerning the interpretation and application of the Convention"; and whereas the exact meaning of this clause is defined in other articles of the Convention, namely: *a*) Article 47, according to which "the Court may only deal with a case after the Commission has acknowledged the failure of efforts for a friendly settlement and within the period of three months provided for in Article 32"; *b*) Article 53, which states that only High Contracting Parties which are "parties to the case" are bound by the decision of the Court;

Whereas it follows from the foregoing that the Court is not competent to take decisions such as that to delete a rule from the Commission's Rules of Procedure – a step which would affect all Parties to the Convention – since this would amount to having power to make rulings on matters of procedure or to render advisory opinions; that accordingly the Court has no power to consider a point raised in a general manner by the Commission and the Irish Government;

Whereas, notwithstanding, it is the duty of the Court, in the exercise of its functions, to ensure that the Convention is respected and, if need be, to point to any irregularities and to refuse to apply in such a case any provisions or regulations which are contrary to the Convention; whereas it follows that the Court must consider the specific point which follows;

(*ii*) *As regards the communication of the Commission's Report to* G. R. LAWLESS

Whereas, it was established, in the course of the proceedings, that the Commission transmitted the Report drawn up in accordance with Article soit le 13 avril 1960, le rapport qu'elle avait rédigé, conformément à l'article 31 de la Convention, à G. R. Lawless, requérant;

Considérant que le Gouvernement irlandais a soutenu: que la Commission, en donnant connaissance de son rapport à G. R. Lawless, a violé les dispositions de la Convention; qu'aux termes de l'article 31 de la Convention, il est expressément interdit aux États Contractants de publier le rapport de la Commission; qu'il en est de même pour le Comité des Ministres, sauf si la Partie contractante mise en cause n'a pas adopté les mesures donnant satisfaction à la décision du Comité des Ministres; que si l'affaire est déférée à la Cour, le rapport reste sous la sauvegarde de la Cour et demeure secret, à moins que la Cour n'en autorise expressément la publication; que les États Contractants s'étant, en vertu de la Convention, imposé de garder secret le rapport de la Commission, celle-ci, qui tire uniquement sa compétence de l'adhésion volontaire des États à la Convention, ne peut corrélativement bénéficier de la liberté de publier le rapport au moment qui lui conviendrait et de le communiquer à qui elle jugerait bon de le faire; que, sinon, les États Contractants se trouveraient placés dans une position inférieure à celle de la Commission quant à l'obligation du secret; que le fait que les auteurs de la Convention n'ont pas inséré une disposition interdisant formellement à la Commission de publier le rapport, n'est pas dû à un simple hasard; qu'aux termes de la Convention, l'individu n'a aucun rôle à remplir, ni devant le Comité des Ministres, ni devant la Cour; qu'une fois le rapport adopté par la Commission, l'individu „disparaît" de la procédure;

Considérant que la Commission, afin de justifier la communication du rapport au requérant, a soutenu: que les États Contractants, sous réserve des dispositions expresses de la Convention, ont conféré à la Commission les pouvoirs nécessaires pour l'exécution effective de la tâche qui lui est confiée par l'article 19 de la Convention; que notamment celle-ci ne contient aucune disposition interdisant à la Commission de publier ou de communiquer à quiconque son rapport lorsqu'elle estime qu'une telle publication ou communication est nécessaire à l'accomplissement de sa tâche; qu'en l'espèce, la Commission a transmis le rapport à G. R. Lawless, après que la Cour avait été saisie de l'affaire, et ce afin d'être en mesure de présenter l'affaire objectivement à la Cour; qu'en transmettant le rapport au requérant, la Commission a pris en considération que l'affaire avait été introduite devant elle par le requérant;

Considérant que, de l'avis de la Cour, la procédure suivie devant elle dans une affaire engagée selon les règles de la Convention se distingue de la procédure en vigueur devant la Commission ou encore devant le Comité des Ministres;

Considérant que les procédures visées par les dispositions du Titre III de la Convention ont un caractère secret; que la procédure devant la Commission, à laquelle le requérant est associé, se déroule à huis clos en vertu de l'article 33; que, lorsque la Commission a transmis son rapport au Comité des Ministres et aux États intéressés, ceux-ci sont privés, par l'article 31, alinéa 2, de la faculté de le publier;

Considérant que, dès que l'affaire a été soumise à la Cour, conformément aux dispositions de l'article 48 de la Convention, la procédure acquiert un caractère judiciaire; que, dans toute société démocratique au sens du Préambule et des autres dispositions de la Convention, la procédure devant un organe judiciaire doit avoir un caractère contradictoire et public; que ce principe fondamental se trouve consacré, en ce qui concerne les juridictions nationales de caractère civil et pénal, par l'article 6 de la Convention; qu'en outre, le Titre IV de la Convention régissant l'organisation et la compétence de la Cour n'édicte aucune disposition analogue à celle de l'article 33 prescrivant que la Commission siège à huis clos; qu'au surplus, la Cour elle-même a confirmé, à l'article 18 de son Règlement,

31 of the Convention to G. R. LAWLESS, the Applicant, on 13th April, 1960, that is to say one day *after* bringing the case before the Court;

Whereas the Irish Government claimed that the Commission committed a breach of the Convention in communicating its Report to G. R. LAWLESS, arguing that Article 31 of the Convention expressly forbade Contracting States to publish the Commission's Report; that this applied also to the Committee of Ministers unless the State concerned did not take the measures required by the decision of the Committee of Ministers; that if the case were brought to the Court, the Report had to remain with the Court and be kept secret unless the Court expressly authorised its publication; that just as the Contracting Parties undertook, by virtue of the Convention, to keep the Report secret, so the Commission, which derived its competence solely from the Convention to which those States were voluntary Parties, was correspondingly not at liberty to publish the Report when it wished, or to communicate it to whomsoever it thought fit, otherwise the Contracting Parties would be in a position subordinate to that of the Commission with regard to the secrecy of the Report; that it was not by a fortuitous omission that the authors of the Convention did not include a clause expressly forbidding the Commission to publish the Report; that under the terms of the Convention, the individual had no part in the proceedings either before the Committee of Ministers or before the Court; and that once the Commission had adopted its Report, the individual dropped out of the proceedings altogether;

Whereas the Commission, in justification of its action in communicating the Report to the Applicant, maintained that the Contracting States, subject to the express provisions of the Convention, had conferred on it the necessary powers to fulfil effectively the functions entrusted to it by Article 19 of the Convention; whereas, moreover, the latter contained no provision forbidding the Commission to publish its Report or communicate it to whomsoever it wished when it considered that the fulfilment of its functions so required; whereas, furthermore, in the present case, the Commission had communicated the Report to G. R. LAWLESS after the case had been referred to the Court in order to be in a position to present the case impartially and, in so doing, had borne in mind that it was the Applicant who had first brought the case before the Commission;

Whereas in the opinion of the Court the procedure, in a case brought before it under the terms of the Convention, differs from that applicable either before the Commission or before the Committee of Ministers;

Whereas the procedures referred to in Section III of the Convention are secret and the proceedings before the Commission which involve the Applicant, are conducted *in camera* in accordance with Article 33; whereas moreover, when the Commission transmits its Report to the Committee of Ministers and to the States concerned, they are prevented, by Article 31 (2), from publishing it;

Whereas, as soon as the case has been referred to the Court, in accordance with Article 48 of the Convention, the proceedings assume a judicial character; whereas, furthermore, in any democratic society, within the meaning of the Preamble and the other clauses of the Convention, proceedings before the judiciary should be conducted in the presence of the Parties and in public; whereas this fundamental principle with regard to domestic civil and criminal law, is upheld in Article 6 of the Convention and whereas Section IV of the Convention, governing the organisation and competence of the Court, contains no such provision as Article 33 which stipulates that the Commission shall meet *in camera;* whereas Rule 18 of the Rules of Court in fact states that hearings shall be que l'audience devant elle est publique, ,,à moins que la Cour n'en décide autrement en raison de circonstances exceptionnelles''; qu'enfin il est prévu, à l'article 51 dudit Règlement, que l'arrêt de la Cour ,,est lu en audience publique''; qu'ainsi la procédure devant la Cour a un caractère public;

Considérant, il est vrai, que ce caractère public de la procédure concerne les débats à l'audience et le texte de l'arrêt, et que les autres documents de la procédure ne peuvent être publiés, conformément à l'article 52 du Règlement, qu'en vertu d'une autorisation expresse de la Cour, mais que cette dernière disposition ne saurait faire échec au caractère contradictoire de la procédure et n'exclut pas la communication, assortie d'une interdiction de publication faite soit par la Commission, soit par une des Parties, des pièces écrites du dossier aux personnes physiques ou morales directement intéressées au litige; qu'il y a donc lieu de distinguer entre, d'une part, la publication des pièces écrites qui doit faire l'objet d'une autorisation de la Cour, et, d'autre part, la communication desdites pièces au requérant, laquelle ne requiert aucune autorisation semblable;

Considérant, en l'espèce, que le requérant, G. R. Lawless, bien qu'il ne soit pas habilité à saisir la Cour, à comparaître juridiquement devant elle, ou encore à formuler des conclusions par un représentant choisi par lui, est cependant directement intéressé à la procédure qui se déroule devant la Cour; qu'il ne faut pas perdre de vue que le requérant est l'initiateur de l'instance engagée devant la Commission; que, dans le cas où la Cour reconnaîtrait le bien-fondé de ses griefs, il pourrait être directement affecté par toute décision que la Cour serait amenée à prendre en vertu de l'article 50 de la Convention, sur le fond de l'affaire; que l'article 38 de son Règlement autorise la Cour à entendre toute personne dont la déposition lui paraît utile à l'accomplissement de sa tâche, ce que, par ailleurs, le Gouvernement irlandais et la Commission reconnaissent;

Considérant que la Commission, en communiquant à G. R. Lawless son rapport, n'a pas manqué d'attirer expressément son attention sur le caractère confidentiel de ce document en lui faisant défense de le publier;

Considérant que, compte tenu de ce qui précède, la Cour est d'avis qu'en vertu de la Convention, la Commission a la faculté de communiquer au requérant, avec interdiction de publication, son rapport ou partie de ce rapport ou un sommaire de ce rapport chaque fois que pareille communication lui paraît utile; qu'en conséquence, dans la présente affaire, la Commission n'a pas, en communiquant son rapport à G. R. Lawless, requérant, dépassé les limites de ses pouvoirs;

(*iii*) *Sur la soumission par la Commission à la Cour, des observations du requérant concernant le rapport de la Commission ou d'autres questions surgissant au cours de la procédure*

Considérant que la Commission demande à la Cour l'autorisation de lui soumettre comme document du dossier, les observations que le requérant a faites sur le rapport de la Commission après en avoir reçu communication dans les conditions susmentionnées; que la Commission, d'une manière générale, demande à la Cour ,,de donner telles directives qu'elle peut juger appropriées quant au droit de la Commission de communiquer à la Cour les observations du requérant en ce qui concerne les questions surgissant au cours de la présente procédure''; que la Commission, tout en reconnaissant que le requérant n'est pas Partie au procès devant la Cour, a fait valoir que sa demande tend à soumettre à la Cour les observations du requérant sur les points essentiels de la procédure le concernant; que la Commission invoque certains précédents empruntés à la procédure d'avis consultatif suivie devant la Cour permanente de Justice internationale, et, après elle, devant la Cour internationale de public "unless the Court shall in exceptional circumstances decide otherwise"; whereas likewise, Rule 51 states that the Court's judgments "shall be read at a public hearing" and whereas it follows, therefore, that proceedings before the Court are public;

Whereas it is true that the debates and the judgment alone are public and that other documents in the case can only be published, in accordance with Rule 52 of the Rules of Court, if the Court expressly authorises such publication; whereas, however, this provision cannot alter the fact that the proceedings take place in the presence of the Parties ("le caractère contradictoire de la procédure"), nor does it prevent the communication of the documents in the case to the persons or bodies directly concerned, with the proviso, made either by the Commission or by one of the Parties, that they should not be published; whereas, therefore, there is a distinction between the publication of documents for which the authorisation of the Court is required and the communication of the said documents to the Applicant, which requires no such authorisation;

Whereas, in the present case, G. R. LAWLESS, the Applicant, although he is not entitled to bring the case before the Court, to appear before the Court or even to make submissions through a representative appointed by him, is nevertheless directly concerned in the proceedings before the Court; whereas it must be borne in mind that the Applicant instituted the proceedings before the Commission and that, if the Court found that his complaints were justified, he would be directly affected by any decision, in accordance with Article 50 of the Convention, on the substance of the case; whereas Article 38 of the Rules of Court authorise it to hear any person whose deposition seems to it useful in the fulfilment of its task, as is admitted, moreover, both by the Irish Government and by the Commission;

Whereas in communicating its Report to LAWLESS, the Commission did not fail to draw attention to its confidential character in expressly forbidding its publication;

Whereas it follows from the foregoing that the Court is of the opinion that the Commission is enabled under the Convention to communicate to the Applicant, with the proviso that it must not be published, the whole or part of its Report or a summary thereof, whenever such communication seems appropriate; whereas, therefore, in the present case, the Commission, in communicating its Report to G. R. LAWLESS, the Applicant, did not exceed its powers;

(*iii*) *As regards the presentation to the Court by the Commission, of the Applicant's observations on the Report and other points arising during the proceedings*

Whereas the Commission asked the Court for authorisation to submit, as a document in the case, the Applicant's observations on the Report following its communication to him under the conditions referred to above; whereas the Commission requests a general ruling on its right to communicate to the Court the Applicant's observations on points arising in the course of the preceedings;

Whereas, while realising that the Applicant is not a party to the proceedings before the Court, the Commission has stated that it wishes to submit to the Court the Applicant's views on the main points of the proceedings with which he is concerned; whereas the Commission has invoked various precedents drawn from advisory opinion procedure at the Permanent Court of International Justice and, subsequently at the International Court of Justice, where observations by individuals submitted through the international organisations who applied for the

Justice, procédure au cours de laquelle ont été prises en considération des observations formulées par des individus et soumises aux susdites juridictions par l'intermédiaire des organisations internationales ayant sollicité l'avis consultatif, bien qu'en vertu du Statut de ces juridictions, les États aient seuls qualité pour se présenter devant elles; qu'en outre, la Commission invoque l'ensemble des dispositions de la Convention, et notamment la version anglaise de l'article 44, pour soutenir que les auteurs de la Convention n'ont pas eu l'intention de dissocier complètement l'individu (requérant devant la Commission) de la procédure devant la Cour, mais ont simplement voulu lui interdire de porter lui-même une affaire devant la Cour;

Considérant que le Gouvernement irlandais soutient que si la Cour acceptait de recevoir, de la Commission, les observations du requérant, ce fait constituerait une violation des dispositions de la Convention, notamment de son article 44, aux termes duquel, dans la version française, seules les Hautes Parties Contractantes et la Commission ont qualité pour se „présenter" devant la Cour; que, d'autre part, si la Commission était autorisée à soumettre les observations du requérant comme un document émanant d'elle, son impartialité et son objectivité seraient mises en cause; que le Gouvernement irlandais a fait valoir, au surplus, qu'une transmission des observations du requérant à la Cour offrirait à l'individu des possibilités d'utiliser la procédure à des fins de propagande contre son propre Gouvernement;

Considérant qu'il n'y a pas lieu, pour la Cour, d'entrer dans un examen approfondi des précédents invoqués par la Commission au sujet du rôle de l'individu devant d'autres juridictions internationales; que, sans méconnaître la valeur des précédents invoqués, la Cour doit tenir compte du fait qu'aucun des exemples cités ne concernait le cas de griefs formulés par un individu contre l'État dont il est le ressortissant; que la présente affaire a son origine dans une requête soumise à la Commission par G. R. LAWLESS contre l'État dont il est le ressortissant; que, dès lors, il convient de rechercher la réponse aux questions posées dans les particularités de la procédure instituée par la Convention; qu'en effet, en vertu de l'article 44 de la Convention, seuls les États Contractants et la Commission ont le droit de saisir la Cour ainsi que de comparaître juridiquement devant elle; que, toutefois, la Cour doit avoir notamment égard au devoir lui incombant de sauvegarder les intérêts de l'individu qui ne peut être Partie devant elle; que la procédure organisée devant la Cour, tant par la Convention que par le Règlement de la Cour, est tournée vers des fins qui concernent le requérant; qu'il est dans l'intérêt d'une bonne administration de la justice que la Cour puisse connaître et, le cas échéant, prendre en considération le point de vue du requérant; qu'à cette fin elle dispose: dans tous les cas et en premier lieu, du rapport de la Commission lequel fait nécessairement état, même si elle ne les fait pas siennes, des allégations de fait ou des prétentions de droit du requérant; en second lieu, des observations écrites ou orales des délégués, et conseils de la Commission qui, en vertu de sa mission d'intérêt général, a le droit, même si elle ne les prend pas à son compte, de faire état devant la Cour, sous sa propre responsabilité, des considérations du requérant en tant qu'élément propre à éclairer celle-ci; qu'en troisième lieu la Cour peut encore entendre le requérant en vertu de l'article 38 de son Règlement et qu'elle a encore le droit, à titre de mesure d'instruction, soit d'inviter d'office la Commission, soit d'autoriser celle-ci, sur sa demande, à lui soumettre les observations du requérant concernant le rapport ou toute autre question déterminée ayant surgi au cours des débats;

Considérant, en l'espèce, qu'il y a lieu de donner acte à la Commission de sa demande tendant à être autorisée à soumettre les observations du requérant sur le rapport, mais que la Cour, n'ayant pu encore aborder advisory opinions have been taken into consideration, although the Statutes of both these bodies provide that States alone may be represented in Court; whereas the Commission also invokes the terms of the Convention as a whole and, in particular, the English version of Article 44, to show that the authors of the Convention did not intend to disassociate entirely the individual who had applied to the Commission from the proceedings before the Court, but simply to prevent him from bringing a case to Court himself.

Whereas the Irish Government maintained that if the Court agreed to receive the Applicant's observations from the Commission, this would constitute a breach of the Convention since, according to the French version of Article 44, the High Contracting Parties and the Commission alone were entitled to appear before the Court ("se présenter devant la Cour"); and that, moreover, if the Commission were authorised to submit the Applicant's observations as a Commission document, the impartiality and objectivity required of the Commission under the terms of the Convention would be impaired; and furthermore, that to allow the Applicant to submit his observations to the Court would be to give an individual the opportunity of using the proceedings as a means of propaganda against his own Government;

Whereas the Court, is not called upon to examine in detail the precedents invoked by the Commission with regard to the part to be played by the individual before an international judicial body; whereas, though recognising their force, the Court must bear in mind the fact that none of the examples cited is that of an individual appealing against the action of his own Government, while in the present case, proceedings were instituted by LAWLESS against the State of which he is a national; whereas accordingly, the solution to this question must be sought in the special nature of the procedure laid down in the Convention; whereas, according to Article 44 of the Convention, Contracting States and the Commission are alone empowered to bring a case before the Court or to appear in Court; whereas, nevertheless, the Court must bear in mind its duty to safeguard the interests of the individual, who may not be a party to any court proceedings, and whereas the whole of the proceedings in the Court, as laid down by the Convention and the Rules of Court, are upon issues which concern the Applicant; whereas, accordingly, it is in the interests of the proper administration of justice that the Court should have knowledge of and, if need be, take into consideration, the Applicant's point of view; whereas to this end the Court has at its disposal: in the first place, and in any event, the Commission's Report, which of necessity sets out the Applicant's allegations with regard to the facts and his legal arguments, even if it does not endorse them; secondly, the written and oral observations of the delegates and Counsel of the Commission which, as the defender of the public interest, is entitled of its own accord, even if it does not share them, to make known the Applicant's views to the Court as a means of throwing light on the points at issue; and thirdly, the Court may also hear the Applicant in accordance with Rule 38 of the Rules of Court, and, as part of the enquiry, may invite the Commission, ex officio, or authorise the Commission at its request, to submit the Applicant's observations on the Report or on any specific point arising in the course of the debates;

Whereas, in the present case, formal note must be taken of the Commission's request for authorisation to submit the Applicant's observations on the Report, but whereas the Court having been unable as yet to l'examen du fond, ne dispose pas, en l'état, d'éléments suffisants pour lui permettre de statuer sur cette demande; qu'elle se réserve d'y statuer au moment opportun;

Par ces motifs,

LA COUR,

donne acte au Gouvernement irlandais du retrait des exceptions préliminaires formulées aux alinéas 1 et 2 des conclusions de son contre-mémoire et de ses objections soulevées au paragraphe 7 de son contre-mémoire;

par 6 voix contre 1,

écarte les objections de procédure formulées aux paragraphes 1, 3 et 4 des conclusions finales dudit Gouvernement,

déclare qu'à ce stade, il n'y a pas lieu d'autoriser la Commission à lui transmettre les observations écrites du requérant sur le rapport de la Commission

et décide, à l'unanimité, de passer à l'examen du fond de l'affaire.

Fait en français et en anglais, le texte français faisant foi, au Conseil de l'Europe, à Strasbourg, le quatorze novembre mil neuf cent soixante.

Le Président
(signé) R. Cassin
Le Greffier
(signé) P. Modinos

M. G. Maridakis, juge, se prévalant du droit que lui confère l'article 50, § 2 du Règlement de la Cour, joint à l'arrêt l'exposé de son opinion dissidente.

(Paraphé) R. C.
(Paraphé) P. M.

Opinion Dissidente de M. G. Maridakis.

D'après l'art. 28 de la Convention, la Commission, afin d'établir les faits, procède à un *examen contradictoire* de la requête avec les représentants des parties et, s'il y a lieu, à une *enquête*...

D'après l'art. 31, si une solution n'a pu intervenir, la Commission rédige un rapport dans lequel elle *constate* les faits et formule un avis sur le point de savoir si les faits constatés révèlent, de la part de l'État intéressé, une violation des obligations... Les opinions de tous les membres de la Commission sur ce *point* peuvent être exprimées dans ce rapport.

D'après l'al. 2 de ce même art. 31, le rapport est transmis au Comité des Ministres; il est également *communiqué aux États intéressés*, qui n'ont pas la faculté *de le publier*. Par „communiquer" on entend au sens et aux fins de la Convention, délivrer une copie exacte du rapport au Comité des Ministres et aux États intéressés.

On peut déduire de ces dispositions:

1. Que la Commission a pour juridiction d'établir les faits.
2. Qu'à cette fin elle procède à un examen *contradictoire* de la requête avec les représentants des Parties et, s'il y a lieu, à une *enquête*.
3. Qu'elle *rédige un rapport* dans lequel elle *constate les faits* et formule un *avis*...
4. Qu'elle transmet le rapport au Comité des Ministres.
5. Qu'elle communique *également* le rapport aux États intéressés, *qui n'ont pas la faculté de le publier.*

examine the merits of the case, is not in a position to reach a decision on this request and reserves its right to do so when it deems fit;

For these reasons,

THE COURT,

Takes note of the withdrawal by the Irish Government of the preliminary objections set out in paragraphs 1 and 2 of their final submissions in their Counter-Memorial and of the objections raised in paragraph 7 of the same Counter-Memorial;

By 6 votes to 1,
rejects the objections relating to procedure raised by the said Government in paragraphs 1, 3 and 4 of their final submissions,
declares that at this stage there is no reason to authorise the Commission to transmit to it the Applicant's written observations on the Commission's Report;
Decides unanimously to proceed to the examination of the merits of the case.
Done in French and in English, the French text being authentic, at the Council of Europe, Strasbourg, this fourteenth day of November 1960.

(Signed) R. CASSIN
President
(Signed) P. MODINOS
Registrar

Judge G. MARIDAKIS, availing himself of his right under the terms of Rule 50 (2) of the Rules of Court, annexes his dissenting opinion to the present judgment.

(Initialled) R.C.
(Initialled) P.M.

DISSENTING OPINION OF MR. G. MARIDAKIS

According to Article 28 of the Convention, the Commission shall, with a view to ascertaining the facts, undertake together with the representatives of the Parties an *examination of the petition* and, if need be, an *investigation*....

Under Article 31, if a solution is not reached, the Commission shall draw up a *report on the facts* and state its opinion as to whether the facts found disclose a breach by the State concerned of its obligations .... The opinions of all the members of the Commission on this *point* may be stated in the Report.

According to paragraph 2 of the said Article 31, the Report shall be transmitted to the Committee of Ministers. It shall also be *transmitted to the States concerned* who shall not be at liberty *to publish it*. For the purposes of the Convention the word "transmitted" shall be understood to mean hand over an exact copy of the Report to the Committee of Ministers and the States concerned.

From these provisions it can be deduced:

1. that the duty of the Commission is to ascertain the facts;
2. that, to this end, it shall undertake with the representatives of the Parties an *examination of the petition* and if need be, *an investigation;*
3. that it shall *draw up a report on the facts* and state its *opinion*....;
4. that it shall transmit the Report to the Committee of Ministers;
5. that it shall *also* transmit the Report to the States concerned, *who shall not be at liberty to publish it.*

Il ressort de ces dispositions combinées que la juridiction de la Commission, en tant qu'organe chargé d'établir les faits et de rédiger un rapport, cesse dès que ce rapport est transmis au Comité des Ministres.

Dès ce moment commence à courir le délai de trois mois dans lequel, conformément à l'art. 32 de la Convention, la Commission peut saisir la Cour.

La disposition de l'art. 76 du Règlement de la Commission, aux termes duquel, lorsqu'une affaire est déférée à la Cour, le Secrétaire de la Commission communique également, en temps utile (?) au requérant le rapport de la Commission, *contrevient à la Convention*. Si, après la transmission du rapport au Comité des Ministres, la Commission n'a plus les pouvoirs qu'elle tire des articles 28 et 31 al. 1, à plus forte raison ne conserve-t-elle plus aucun pouvoir après que l'affaire a été déférée à la Cour par application de l'art. 48 de la Convention. A partir de ce moment, l'affaire, *dans son ensemble, appartient à la Cour*. Si la Cour estime que certains points du rapport ont besoin d'être precisés et que seul le requérant pourrait les éclaircir, la Cour, en tant que *juge souverain* de l'affaire, a la faculté de convoquer le requérant et de l'entendre conformément à l'article 38 du Règlement de la Cour.

D'après l'art. 76 précité du Règlement de la Commission, le requérant a la faculté de présenter à la Commission ses observations écrites sur ledit rapport et la Commission décide de la suite à donner à ces observations.

Or, d'après l'art. 28 de la Convention, la Commission procède à un examen *contradictoire* et, s'il y a lieu, à une *enquête*.

Par conséquent, dès lors que la Commission accomplit sa tâche suivant la procédure précitée et que, d'autre part, elle ne peut modifier son rapport après qu'elle l'a transmis au Comité des Ministres, et qu'au surplus l'affaire a été déférée *dans son ensemble à la Cour*, par quelle voie sera-t-il possible à la Commission de donner suite aux observations du requérant sur ledit rapport? Si la Commission présente ces observations simplement en tant qu'elles lui furent soumises par le requérant, elle n'a point qualité pour le faire puisque, d'après l'art. 19 de la Convention, elle agit et se tient *au-dessus des parties*. Si elle *adopte* ces observations pour les présenter comme siennes, il en résulte que le requérant se présente, devant la Cour, *sous le couvert de la Commission*. Or, l'article 44 de la Convention prescrit que „seules les Hautes Parties Contractantes et la Commission ont qualité pour se présenter devant la Cour".

Ainsi libellé, cet article implique un sens *plus profond*. Il signifie que la Cour n'est pas instituée pour trancher un *différend* entre le requérant et l'État auquel il reproche d'avoir violé en sa personne les obligations assumées en vertu de la Convention. Il signifie que la Cour agit en organe de haute surveillance, afin d'assurer l'ordre européen tel qu'il est institué par la Convention. (*Voir* Statut du Conseil de l'Europe, Art. 1, *b*).

Telle étant l'idée que la Convention se fait de la tâche dévolue à la Cour, il est naturel que la comparution du requérant devant ce tribunal soit exclue. Si le droit de comparaître devant la Cour était accordé au requérant, il est évident que la procédure qui se déroulerait devant la Cour risquerait de dégénérer en un simple procès entre le requérant et l'État incriminé, alors que, dans l'esprit de la Convention, la Cour est instituée, non pas pour statuer sur des différends, mais „afin d'assurer le respect des engagements résultant de la présente Convention" (art. 19).

C'est ainsi seulement que s'explique et se justifie la disposition de l'art. 31 al. 2 de la Convention d'après laquelle le rapport de la Commission n'est communiqué qu'aux États intéressés. Le requérant est bien la personne qui prétend avoir été lésée par l'État, mais son allégation ne fait que donner l'occasion – et il n'en saurait être autrement – d'examiner si

It is apparent from these provisions read together that the jurisdiction of the Commission as the body responsible for ascertaining the facts and drawing up a Report ceases as soon as the Report has been transmitted to the Committee of Ministers.

From this date begins the period of three months during which, under Article 32 of the Convention, the Commission may refer the question to the Court.

The provision contained in Rule 76 of the Rules of Procedure of the Commission, that when a case is referred to the Court, the Secretary of the Commission shall also in due course(?) communicate to the Applicant the Commission's Report, *is contrary to the Convention.* If, after the Report has been transmitted to the Committee of Ministers, the Commission no longer has the powers conferred on it by Articles 28 and 31 (1) *a fortiori* it has no further powers after the case has been referred to the Court in accordance with Article 48 of the Convention. From this moment *the Court has sole jurisdiction in the case.* If the Court considers that certain points of the Report need to be clarified and that the Applicant is the only person capable of doing so, the Court may, as *sole judge* call the Applicant and hear him, in accordance with Rule 38 of the Rules of the Court.

Under Rule 76, referred to above, of the Rules of Procedure of the Commission, the Applicant may submit to the Commission his written observations on the said Report and the Commission shall decide what action, if any, shall be taken in respect of those observations.

Now, under Article 28 of the Convention, the Commission undertakes an *examination of the petition* and, if need be, an investigation.

Consequently, if the Commission acts in accordance with the procedure described above, since it may not amend its Report once it has been transmitted to the Committee of Ministers and since furthermore, the case as a whole has been placed in the hands of the Court, what kind of action could the Commission take in respect of the Applicant's observations on the said Report? It is not entitled to present them simply as they come from the Applicant, since Article 19 of the Convention places the Commission above the Parties. If it were to *adopt* these observations and submit them as its own, the Applicant would be appearing before the Court *under cover of the Commission.* But Article 44 of the Convention states that "only the High Contracting Parties and the Commission shall have the right to bring a case before the Court".

The wording of this Article brings out its *deeper* significance. It means that the Court has not been set up to settle *disputes* between the Applicant and the State which he is accusing of having violated, in his regard, its obligations under the Convention. It means that the Court is a high supervisory authority set up to guarantee the European order established by the Convention (*cf.* Statute of the Council of Europe, Article 1 *b*)).

Such being the conception contained in the Convention of the duties devolving upon the Court, it is natural that the Applicant should not be entitled to appear before it. If he had this right, it is clear that the proceedings might degenerate into a simple legal action between the Applicant and the State involved, whereas, in the spirit of the Convention, the Court was set up not to judge disputes but "to ensure the observance of the engagements undertaken in the present Convention" (Article 19).

This is the only way of interpreting Article 31 (2) and justifying the provision that the Commission's Report may be transmitted only to the States concerned. The Applicant is the person who claims to have been injured by the State concerned, but his allegation only provides an opportunity – it could not be otherwise – of considering whether or not l'État respecte ou non les obligations découlant de la Convention. Ainsi s'explique aussi la disposition de l'al. 2 du même article 31 selon laquelle les États n'ont pas la faculté de publier le rapport qui leur est communiqué, ainsi que la disposition de l'al. 3 de l'Article 32 d'après laquelle la publication du rapport est interdite même au Comité des Ministres.

Mais, si ni les États auxquels le rapport est communiqué ni le Comité des Ministres n'ont la faculté de publier le rapport, à plus forte raison la Commission n'est-elle pas en droit de le faire. Or, en substance, c'est publier le rapport que de le communiquer au requérant comme le prévoit l'art. 76 du Règlement de la Commission.

La disposition de la Convention qui interdit la publication du rapport répond à un objet important. Lorsqu'un État est accusé d'avoir enfreint les obligations qu'il a assumées en vertu de la Convention, le prestige de cet État s'en trouve atteint. Les auteurs de la Convention ont estimé nécessaire de sauvegarder le prestige de l'État pendant la durée de la procédure. Aussi ont-ils interdit la publication du rapport, qui contient les opinions des membres (art. 31) et ne fait que préparer l'appréciation définitive que la Convention réserve à la Cour et, le cas échéant, au Comité des Ministres.

L'unité de la procédure est un principe général qui s'applique à toute procédure. En vertu de ce principe, la valeur à donner aux observations du requérant sur le rapport de la Commission appartient exclusivement à la Cour.

Or, la disposition de l'art. 76 du Règlement de la Commission selon laquelle la Commission décide de la suite à donner aux observations du requérant est contraire à ce principe puisqu'elle confère à la Commission un pouvoir discrétionnaire incompatible avec les pouvoirs qui incombent à la Cour, seule souveraine de l'affaire.

Par les motifs qui précèdent, l'article 76 du Règlement de la Commission contrevient à la Convention.

Toutefois, de ce que la Commission ne possède pas le pouvoir de communiquer le rapport au requérant, il ne s'ensuit pas que ce dernier ne doit pas en prendre connaissance au cours de la procédure contentieuse.

Du moment que le requérant accuse un des États contractants de la Convention d'avoir violé les obligations qui en découlent pour cet État, il est conforme à l'équité et aux principes généraux du droit qu'aucun moyen lui permettant de prendre connaissance du rapport ne lui soit dénié. Or, ce moyen ne peut être que celui par lequel le Greffier de la Cour inviterait le requérant à lire le rapport en sa présence. Et, au cas où le requérant demanderait à formuler des observations, il appartient à la Cour, et à elle seule, de déterminer les formes dans lesquelles ces observations devront lui être présentées.

Cette manière de voir ne procède pas d'une interprétation de la Convention faite *in abstracto*. Elle n'a pas davantage pour effet d'aboutir à une annulation, prononcée par cette Cour, de l'article 76 du Règlement de la Commission. Les conclusions de la Commission, aussi bien que celles introduites par le Gouvernement irlandais, invoquent toutes les deux l'article 76 du susdit Règlement. Mais on ne peut apprécier le bien-fondé de ces conclusions sans rechercher si l'article 76 est conforme à la Convention ou s'il y contrevient. Et il est évident que cette question ne peut être tranchée que par l'interprétation du texte de la Convention.

Il est vrai que la Cour n'a point le pouvoir de déclarer nul et non avenu la disposition de l'article 76 du Règlement de la Commission. Mais il est également hors de doute qu'elle a le pouvoir en même temps que le devoir, de refuser d'appliquer toute disposition de ce Règlement qui, dans l'opinion de la Cour, est contraire à la Convention, en vertu de ce même principe qui, dans les droits internes, fait un devoir au juge de ne point that State respects its obligations under the Convention. This is the explanation, too, of Article 31 (2), whereby States are not at liberty to publish the Report transmitted to them, and also of the provision in Article 32 (3) that the Committee of Ministers is not entitled to publish the Report.

But, if neither the States to whom the Report has been transmitted, nor the Committee of Ministers are at liberty to publish the Report *a fortiori* the Commission has no right to do so. And, in substance, to communicate the Report to the Applicant in the manner described in Rule 76 of the Rules of Procedure of the Commission is to publish it.

The provision in the Convention prohibiting publication of the Report has been inserted for a good purpose. When a State is accused of a breach of its obligations assumed under the Convention, its prestige suffers prejudice. The authors of the Convention thought that steps should be taken to safeguard the prestige of such a State during the proceedings. They therefore prohibited publication of the Report which contains the opinions of the members (Article 31) and merely prepares the ground for the final judgment to be rendered, in accordance with the Convention, by the Court or, in some cases by the Committee of Ministers.

Unity is an important principle in all legal proceedings and by virtue of this principle the weight to be given to the Applicant's observations on the Commission's Report must be determined by the Court alone.

The provision contained in Rule 76 of the Rules of Procedure of the Commission, whereby the Commission decides what action, if any, shall be taken in respect of the Applicant's observations, is contrary to the above principle, since it confers on the Commission a discretionary power incompatible with the powers of the Court which has sole jurisdiction at the present stage.

For the above reasons, therefore, Rule 76 of the Rules of Procedure of the Commission is contrary to the terms of the Convention.

However, although the Commission has no authority to communicate the Report to the Applicant, it does not follow that the latter may not take cognizance of it (in the course of contentious proceedings).

Since the Applicant has accused one of the Contracting Parties of a breach of the undertakings given in the Convention, it is a principle of equity (and of law in general) that he should not be denied any means of taking cognizance of the Report. The only way to acquaint him with the contents of the Report would be for the Registrar to invite him to read it in his presence. Should he wish to make any observations on it, the Court alone has power to decide in what form they are to be presented.

This view does not derive from an abstract interpretation of the Convention, nor does it amount to the Court declaring null and void Rule 76 of the Rules of Procedure of the Commission. Both the Commission and the Irish Government in their submissions, refer to Rule 76 of the Commission's Rules of Procedure, but in order to weigh up their respective arguments it must first be determined whether Rule 76 complies with the terms of the Convention or not. It is clear that this cannot be decided without interpreting the text of the Convention.

True, the Court is not empowered to declare null and void Rule 76 of the Commission's Rules of Procedure, but there is no doubt that the Court has the right, and is in duty bound, to refuse to apply any of these rules which it regards as contrary to the terms of the Convention, in accordance with the principle of domestic law, whereby it is a judge's appliquer la disposition légale qui se trouve en contradiction avec la Constitution ou celle, simplement réglementiare, qui contrevient à une loi formelle.

En procédant, dans ce but, à l'interprétation de la Convention, il est clair que la Cour n'émet point un avis consultatif détachable du jugement du litige qui lui a été déféré: elle étaye purement et simplement sur l'interprétation de la Convention le raisonnement sur lequel elle fonde la solution proprement dite du litige et des questions préliminaires ou incidentes, ce qui est l'objet même de sa juridiction aux termes de l'article 45.

(signé) G. MARIDAKIS

C. CONFÉRENCE EUROPÉENNE DES ORGANISATIONS PROFESSIONNELLES DES PRODUITS DE LA VIGNE, DES SPIRITUEUX ET DE LA BIÈRE

Les associations nationales de négoce des vins, spiritueux et bières ont été convoquées par le Conseil de l'Europe pour une Conférence qui s'est tenue à la Maison de l'Europe les 4 et 5 avril 1960. L'initiative en est partie de la Commission de l'Agriculture de l'Assemblée Consultative, qui, après enquêtes préliminaires, avait recommandé, en octobre 1958, qu'un groupe d'experts soit appelé à élaborer le projet d'une Convention fixant les lignes d'une politique générale de production et de commercialisation des produits de la vigne et des spiritueux, ainsi que d'une protection des appellations d'origine. Cette même Commission avait également proposé la convocation d'une Conférence des associations nationales intéressées, afin que les milieux professionnels soient informés du travail entrepris dans ce domaine à l'échelle gouvernementale. L'Assemblée Consultative a adopté, en conséquence, le 16 octobre 1958 sa Recommendation 182.

Le Comité des Ministres, après avoir consulté l'O.E.C.E., a désigné un Comité d'Experts chargé d'élaborer une politique commune de production et de commercialisation des produits de la vigne et des spiritueux, et de protection des raisons sociales qui sont des garanties d'origine. Après que ce Comité se fût réuni deux fois en 1959 et eût prévu une troisième réunion pour avril 1961, l'Assemblée Consultative estima (janvier 1960) que le moment était venu de convoquer ladite Conférence des Associations nationales.

Dix des quinze États membres du Conseil envoyèrent ces délégations. Assistèrent également à cette Conférence des représentants de trois pays non membres: la Suisse, l'Espagne et le Portugal, ainsi que des observateurs de la Commission de la C.E.E. (Division des Relations Extérieures), de l'Organisation de l'Agriculture et de l'Alimentation (F.A.O.) et de l'Office International du Vin.

Il semble utile de donner ici le texte des principales Recommandations de cette Conférence.

1. RECOMMANDATION SUR LES VINS ET SPIRITUEUX (adoptée à l'unanimité le 5 avril 1960)

La Conférence des Organisations nationales européennes des Vins, Spiritueux et de la Bière, réunie à Strasbourg, les 4 et 5 avril 1960,

– ADRESSE ses vifs remerciements au Conseil de l'Europe et plus particulièrement à la Commission de l'Agriculture de l'Assemblée Consultative;
– SE FÉLICITE de l'occasion qui a été donnée aux professionnels des Vins et Spiritueux des divers pays de procéder à un large échange de vues sur des problèmes dont l'importance est considérable sur le plan de l'économie européenne;

duty to refrain from applying any legal provision which contravenes the Constitution or any regulation which is contrary to law.

In interpreting the Convention with this end in view, it is clear that the Court is not rendering an advisory opinion which could have any force outside the context of the present case, but is simply interpreting the Convention to support the arguments on which its judgment of the case itself and its decisions in respect of the preliminary objections and other incidental points are based, in accordance with the definition of its jurisdiction in Article 45.

(Signed) G. MARIDAKIS

C. EUROPEAN CONFERENCE OF NATIONAL ASSOCIATIONS CONCERNED WITH WINE, SPIRITS AND BEER

A Conference of National Associations concerned with wines, spirits and beer was convened by the Council of Europe and held on its premises on April 4th and 5th, 1960. The initiative came from the Committee on Agriculture of the Consultative Assembly, which, after preliminary investigation, had recommended, in October 1958, that a group of experts be instructed to prepare the draft of a Convention laying down the broad lines of a common policy for the production and marketing of wine and the protection of appellations of origin – and had also proposed the calling of a conference of the national associations concerned, in the various European countries, so that professional circles might be informed of the work being undertaken at governmental level. The Assembly adopted Recommendation 182 in consequence on 16th October, 1958.

The Committee of Ministers – after consulting the O.E.E.C. – duly appointed a Committee of Experts to work out a common policy of the production and marketing of vine products and spirits and for the protection of trade names which are warranties of origin. After this Committee of Experts had met twice in 1959 – and had arranged a third meeting for April 1961 – the Assembly Committee decided (January 1960) that the time had come to hold the proposed Conference of National Associations.

Ten of the fifteen Member States of the Council sent delegations, and representatives of three non-member countries – Switzerland, Spain and Portugal – also attended, together with observers on the part of the E.E.C. Commission (Foreign Relations Section), the F.A.O. and the International Wine Office. It may be useful to give here the text of the main Recommendations of the Conference.

1. RECOMMENDATION ON WINES AND SPIRITS
(adopted unanimously on April 5th, 1960)

The European Conference of National Associations concerned with Wines, Spirits and Beer, meeting in Strasbourg on 4th and 5th April, 1960,

- Expresses its gratitude to the Council of Europe and in particular to the Committee on Agriculture of the Consultative Assembly;

- Welcomes the opportunity afforded to the professional associations concerned with wines, spirits and beers of the different countries to hold a broad exchange of views on problems of such importance to the economy of Europe;

- **Manifeste** sa gratitude au Comité des Experts et les encourage à poursuivre leurs travaux;
- **Suggère** qu'une Commission chargée d'étudier les problèmes du cidre et autres boissons fermentées de fruits soit constituée lors de la prochaine réunion;

Recommande:

A. Pour les vins

I. *Sur un plan général*

a) la stabilisation momentanée de la production vinicole;
b) d'orienter la politique viti-vinicole des pays producteurs vers une production de qualité grâce notamment à la protection rigoureuse des appellations d'origine et une politique d'encépagement dirigée;
c) d'interdire toutes pratiques pouvant aboutir à une altération des produits récoltés;
d) d'éliminer pour la consommation les produits du surpressurage et des lies;
e) d'assurer cette production saine et de qualité par:
1. le classement descépages en cépages recommandés, tolérés et interdits, l'arrachage et le remplacement éventuel des plants interdits;
2. le contrôle des pépinières.

II. *Sur le plan de l'économie générale*

a) l'établissement d'un cadastre viticole;
b) la détermination des zones à vocation viticole traditionnelle, en tenant compte notamment des éléments de qualité et de prix de revient;
c) l'établissement, par déclarations annuelles, des superficies, des récoltes et des stocks à la propriété et au commerce de gros;
d) en ce qui concerne les vins à appellation d'origine, la détermination de leur condition de production et notamment la limitation de leur aire de production;
e) l'harmonisation de la réglementation concernant les méthodes de production et de vinification des diverses catégories de vins, c'est-à-dire les vins proprement dits, les vins spéciaux et les mistelles;
f) l'uniformisation des méthodes d'analyse sur la base des travaux de l'Office International du Vin.

III. *Sur le plan de la commercialisation*

a) l'interdiction de commercialisation des produits ne correspondant pas aux normes définies par l'Office International du Vin, et la fixation de degrés minima à la sortie de la propriété pour la consommation et la commercialisation;
b) le contrôle du mouvement des vins;
c) l'établissement d'un répertoire général européen des appellations d'origine, mis à jour périodiquement.

B. Pour les spiritueux

1. Une harmonisation effective des réglementations et l'atténuation des disparités existant présentement entre les législations nationales;

- Expresses its gratitude to the Committee of Experts and hopes they will continue their work;
- Suggests that a committee be set up at the next meeting to study the problems of cider and other fermented fruit drinks;

RECOMMENDS:

A. As regards wines

I. *General*

a) a temporary stabilisation of wine production;

b) that the wine policy of producing countries should be directed towards the production of quality wine and should embrace the strict protection of warranties of origin and the control of vine-planting;

c) that all practices which might lead to adulteration of the products harvested should be forbidden;

d) that it shoud be forbidden to offer for consumption the products of second pressings and lees;

e) that such a healthy and high-quality production should be assured by means of:

1. a classification of growths into recommended, tolerated and forbidden growths, and the uprooting and replacement where necessary of the forbidden plants;

2. a control over the production of vine seedlings and plants.

II. *General economy*

a) that an ordnance survey be made of vine-growing areas;

b) that the traditional vine-growing areas should be defined with full allowance for quality factors and production costs;

c) that annual declarations be made of areas, harvests and stocks held by vineyard owners and by whole-salers;

d) that the production conditions of wines of certified origin, and in particular the geographical delimitation of the area in which they are produced, should be determined;

e) that regulations governing production and vinification methods for the various categories of wine, *i.e.* wines proper, special wines and 'mistelles', should be standardised;

f) that methods of analysis should be standardised on the basis of the work of the International Wines Office.

III. *Marketing*

a) that products which do not conform to the standards laid down by the International Wine Office should not be offered for sale, and that the minimum alcohol content on leaving the vineyard for sale and consumption should be fixed;

b) that the movement of wines should be controlled;

c) that a general European register of warranties of origin ('controlled appellations') should be prepared and kept up to date.

B. As regards spirits

1. harmonisation of regulations and reduction of the present disparities between national legislations;

2. un accord international sur les définitions spécifiques; appellations, et critères de qualité des produits, ainsi que sur les techniques et méthodes d'analyse [1];

3. l'harmonisation des terminologies afin que les produits mis sur le marché sous la même dénomination correspondent effectivement à des définitions identiques; [1]

4. l'établissement des droits de douane dans le commerce international au degré d'alcool et non *ad valorem;*

5. l'unification, sur le plan européen, des degrés minima d'alcool imposés pour la commercialisation des spiritueux;

6. la protection des appellations d'origine dont bénéficient certains spiritueux, et la répression de toute tentative de tromperie sur l'origine géographique de tout spiritueux.

* * *

La Conférence, n'ayant pas été suffisamment informée préalablement, n'a pas été en mesure d'étudier les propositions finales du Rapport de MM. SOURBET et BOURGOIN.

Elle serait heureuse de pouvoir se réunir à nouveau, pour être tenue informée des travaux du Comité d'Experts et pouvoir examiner les questions laissées en suspens qui méritent d'être approfondies.

2. RÉSOLUTION SUR LA BIÈRE
(approuvée le 5 avril 1960, par 19 voix à 16)

Les délégués des Groupements professionnels de brasseries,

Considérant que la bière est un produit industriel de deuxième transformation;

Considérant que la bière est un produit spécifique dont les processus et les règles de fabrication sont tout à fait différents de ceux qui sont à l'origine de la production des vins et des spiritueux;

Considérant que dans la plupart des pays d'Europe, les règles qui s'appliquent à la fabrication et au commerce des bières, n'ont rien de commun avec celles qui visent les vins et les spiritueux;

Considérant enfin que les matières premières de bases sont elles aussi spécifiques et différentes des produits agricoles d'où découlent les vins et la plupart des spiritueux;

Remercient le Conseil de l'Europe de sa sollicitude à leur égard;

Émettent, cependant, le voeu que l'examen de leur futur statut européen soit dissocié de celui des vins et des spiritueux;

Marquent leur accord de principe sur la nécessité d'une unification du Statut de la Bière en Europe et se proposent de consulter leurs organisations nationales respectives sur un projet qui pourrait concerner:

1. la définition du produit;
2. les matières premières entrant dans sa fabrication;
3. les opérations et traitements autorisés dans les brasseries;
4. la définition des unités de densités et des méthodes d'analyse.

D. CONVENTIONS EUROPÉENNES

1. ACCORD POUR L'IMPORTATION TEMPORAIRE EN FRANCHISE DE DOUANE, A TITRE DE PRÊT GRATUIT ET A DES FINS DIAGNOSTIQUES OU THÉRAPEUTIQUES, DE MATÉRIEL MÉDICO-CHIRURGICAL ET DE LABORATOIRE DESTINÉ AUX ÉTABLISSEMENTS SANITAIRES

Les Gouvernements signataires, Membres du Conseil de l'Europe,

---

[1] La Commission souhaite examiner les définitions, terminologies *etc.* lors d'une seconde session de la Conférence.

2. an international agreement on specific definitions, appellations, criteria of quality, techniques and methods of analysis [1];

3. standardisation of terminology, so that products marketed under the same name shall answer to the same specifications [1];

4. that customs duties in international trade should be based on alcoholic strength and not on value;

5. unification at European level of the minimum alcoholic strength at which spirits should be marketed;

6. the protection of the appellations of origin to which certain spirits are entitled and the suppression of false or misleading indications of the geographical origin of any spirits.

* * *

The Conference was unable to study the final proposals in the report of MM. Sourbet and Bourgoin as it had not had sufficient time to consider the matter in advance.

The Conference would like to meet again in order to be kept informed of the work of the Committee of Experts and to examine those questions which are outstanding and require further consideration.

2. RESOLUTION ON BEER
(approved by 19 votes to 16 on April 5th, 1960)

The delegates of the Brewers' Associations,

Whereas beer is an industrial product obtained by a second processing;

Whereas beer is a specific product and the principles and processes of its production are altogether distinct from those applying to wines and spirits;

Whereas in most European countries the rules which apply to the production of, and trade in, beers have nothing in common with those which apply to wines and spirits;

Whereas the primary materials are also distinct from the agricultural products from which wines and most spirits are derived;

Thank the Council of Europe for its solicitude on their behalf;

Nevertheless express their desire that their future European statute should be dissociated from that relating to wines and spirits;

Signify their agreement in principle on the need for unified regulations governing the beer trade in Europe and propose to consult their national associations on a draft relating to:

1. definition of the product;
2. raw materials used in its manufacture;
3. authorised operations and treatments in breweries;
4. definition of units of specific gravity and methods of analysis.

D. EUROPEAN CONVENTIONS

1. AGREEMENT ON THE TEMPORARY IMPORTATION, FREE OF DUTY, OF MEDICAL, SURGICAL AND LABORATORY EQUIPMENT FOR USE ON FREE LOAN IN HOSPITALS AND OTHER MEDICAL INSTITUTIONS FOR PURPOSES OF DIAGNOSIS OR TREATMENT

The Governments signatory hereto, being Members of the Council of Europe,

[1] The Committee hopes to review the definitions, terminology, *etc.*, at a second Session of the Conference.

Considérant que, par suite de circonstances exceptionnelles, un État peut se trouver subitement démuni du matériel médico-chirurgical et de laboratoire qui lui permettrait de satisfaire aux besoins les plus urgents de sa population;

Considérant qu'il est souhaitable de faciliter le franchissement des frontières au matériel médico-chirurgical et de laboratoire que des États membres seraient susceptibles de mettre à la disposition d'autres États membres;

Considérant d'autre part que le but du Conseil de l'Europe est de réaliser une union plus étroite entre ses Members et de favoriser leur progrès économique et social, notamment par la conclusion d'accords européens;

Reconnaissant qu'un accord permettant la libre circulation du matériel médico-chirurgical et de laboratoire serait un moyen efficace d'atteindre ce but,

Sont convenus de ce qui suit:

Article 1er

1. Les Parties Contractantes, pour autant qu'elles disposent de réserves suffisantes pour leurs propres besoins, mettront du matériel médico-chirurgical et de laboratoire, à titre de prêt gratuit, à la disposition des autres Parties Contractantes qui, se trouvant dans des circonstances exceptionnelles, en ont un besoin urgent; ce matériel sera envoyé sur demande de la Partie intéressée et sera rendu ultérieurement.

2. Toute Partie Contractante bénéficiaire des dispositions du paragraphe précédent accordera toutes les facilités possibles pour l'importation temporaire, sur son territoire, du matériel prêté.

Article 2

1. La durée de l'importation temporaire ne dépassera pas six mois; elle est renouvelable dans les mêmes conditions en accord avec le pays d'exportation.

2. Ces facilités concerneront uniquement le matériel médico-chirurgical et de laboratoire destiné aux hôpitaux et aux autres établissements sanitaires. Elles comporteront l'octroi de licences éventuellement nécessaires pour la mise sous régime d'importation temporaire et la suspension des droits et taxes à l'importation (y compris tous les droits et taxes perçus à l'occasion de l'importation). Cependant, les autorités du pays d'importation temporaire peuvent se faire rembourser les frais correspondant au coût des services rendus.

Article 3

Les dispositions des articles 1er et 2 n'empêcheront pas les autorités compétentes de l'État d'importation de prendre les mesures nécessaires, soit pour s'assurer que les objets admis temporairement seront réexportés dès que les circonstances exceptionnelles ou que la période limite prévue au paragraphe 1 de l'article 2 auront pris fin, soit pour garantir le paiement des droits et taxes en cas de non-réexportation.

Article 4

Les dispositions du présent Accord ne portent pas atteinte aux dispositions plus favorables à l'importation temporaire du matériel visé à l'article 1er, contenues soit dans la législation ou les règlements de toute Partie Contractante, soit dans tout autre convention, traité ou accord en vigueur entre deux ou plusieurs des Parties Contractantes.

Considering that a State may in exceptional circumstances find itself suddenly to be without sufficient stocks of medical, surgical and laboratory equipment to satisfy the most urgent requirements of the population;

Considering that it is desirable to facilitate the crossing of frontiers for medical, surgical and laboratory equipment which one Member State may be able to make available to another;

Considering, further, that the aim of the Council of Europe is to achieve a greater unity between its Members and to facilitate their economic and social progress by various means including the conclusion of European agreements;

Recognising that a practical way of achieving that aim would be the conclusion of an agreement providing for the free passage of medical, surgical and laboratory equipment on loan,

Have agreed as follows:

Article 1

1. The Contracting Parties shall, provided that they have sufficient stocks for their own needs, make medical, surgical and laboratory equipment available on free loan to such other Contracting Parties as may, in exceptional circumstances, have urgent need of it; such equipment shall, upon request, be sent to the Party concerned and shall subsequently be returned.

2. Each Contracting Party benefiting under the terms of the previous paragraph shall grant all possible facilities for the importation on a temporary basis of the equipment loaned.

Article 2

1. The period of temporary importation shall not exceed six months in the first instance but may, with the agreement of the exporting country, be extended for a further period subject to the same conditions.

2. The above facilities shall be granted only in respect of medical, surgical and laboratory equipment for use in hospitals and other medical institutions. They shall include the issue of any licences required for the temporary importation of such equipment and the suspension of import duties and import taxes (including all duties and taxes whatsoever chargeable by reason of importation) other than charges for actual expenses incurred by the authorities of the country of temporary importation.

Article 3

Notwithstanding the provisions of Articles 1 and 2 above, the competent authorities of the importing State may take such measures as may be necessary either to ensure the re-exportation of any such equipment imported on a temporary basis, once the exceptional circumstances shall have ceased to exist or the time-limit provided for under paragraph 1 of Article 2 above has elapsed, whichever is the earlier, or to ensure payment of any import duties and import taxes which become payable in the case of any failure to re-export the equipment.

Article 4

The provisions of this Agreement shall not prejudice more favourable provisions for the temporary importation of the equipment referred to in Article 1, contained in the laws or regulations of any Contracting Party or in any Convention, Treaty or Agreement in force between two or more Contracting Parties to the present Agreement.

Article 5

1. Le présent Accord est ouvert à la signature des Membres du Conseil de l'Europe qui peuvent en devenir Parties par:

a) la signature sans réserve de ratification, ou

b) la signature sous réserve de ratification suivie de ratification.

2. Les instruments de ratification seront déposés près le Secrétaire Général du Conseil de l'Europe.

Article 6

1. Le présent Accord entrera en vigueur trois mois après la date à laquelle trois Membres du Conseil, conformément aux dispositions de l'article 5, auront signé l'Accord sans réserve de ratification ou l'auront ratifié.

2. Pour tout Membre qui, ultérieurement, signera l'Accord sans réserve de ratification ou le ratifiera, l'Accord entrera en vigueur trois mois après la signature ou le dépôt de l'instrument de ratification.

Article 7

Le Comité des Ministres du Conseil de l'Europe peut inviter tout État non membre du Conseil à adhérer au présent Accord. L'adhésion prendra effet trois mois après le dépôt de l'instrument d'adhésion auprès du Secrétaire Général du Conseil de l'Europe.

Article 8

Le Secrétaire Général du Conseil de l'Europe notifiera aux Membres du Conseil et aux États adhérents:

a) la date de l'entrée en vigueur du présent Accord et les noms des Membres l'ayant signé sans réserve de ratification ou l'ayant ratifié;

b) le dépôt de tout instrument d'adhésion effectué en application des dispositions de l'article 7.

Article 9

1. Le présent Accord demeurera en vigueur sans limitation de durée.

2. Toute Partie Contractante pourra mettre fin, en ce qui la concerne, à l'application du présent Accord, en donnant un préavis d'un an à cet effet au Secrétaire Général du Conseil de l'Europe.

En foi de quoi, les soussignés, dûment autorisés à cet effet, ont signé le présent Accord.

Fait à Strasbourg, le 28 avril 1960 en français et en anglais, les deux textes faisant également foi, en un seul exemplaire, qui sera déposé dans les archives du Conseil de l'Europe. Le Secrétaire Général en communiquera des copies certifiées conformes à tous les gouvernements signataires et adhérents.

Pour le Gouvernement de la République d'Autriche:

Pour le Gouvernement du Royaume de Belgique:
sous réserve de ratification

Article 5

1. This Agreement shall be open to the signature of Members of the Council of Europe, who may become Parties to it by:

a) signature without reservation in respect of ratification, or

b) signature with reservation in respect of ratification, followed by ratification.

2. Instruments of ratification shall be deposited with the Secretary-General of the Council of Europe.

Article 6

1. This Agreement shall enter into force three months after the date on which three Members of the Council shall, in accordance with Article 5, have signed the Agreement without reservation in respect of ratification or shall have ratified it.

2. In the case of any Member of the Council who subsequently shall sign the Agreement without reservation in respect of ratification or who shall ratify it, the Agreement shall enter into force three months after the date of such signature or of the deposit of the instrument of ratification.

Article 7

The Committee of Ministers of the Council of Europe may invite any non-Member State to accede to this Agreement. Such accession shall take effect three months after the date on which the instrument of accession was deposited with the Secretary-General of the Council of Europe.

Article 8

The Secretary-General of the Council of Europe shall notify Members of the Council and acceding States:

a) of the date of entry into force of this Agreement and the names of any Members who have signed without reservation in respect of ratification or who have ratified it;

b) of the deposit of any instrument of accession in accordance with Article 7.

Article 9

1. This Agreement shall remain in force indefinitely.

2. Any Contracting Party may withdraw from the Agreement by giving one year's notice to that effect to the Secretary-General of the Council of Europe.

In witness whereof the undersigned, being duly authorised thereto, have signed this Agreement.

Done at Strasbourg, this 28th day of April, 1960, in English and French, both texts being equally authoritative, in a single copy which shall remain deposited in the archives of the Council of Europe. The Secretary-General shall send certified copies to each of the signatory and acceding Governments.

For the Government of the Republic of Austria:

For the Government of the Kingdom of Belgium:
with reservation in respect of ratification

Pour le Gouvernement du Royaume de Danemark:
sous réserve de ratification
J. O. Krag

Pour le Gouvernement de la République française:
Lecompte Boinet

Pour le Gouvernement de la République Fédérale d'Allemagne:
sous réserve de ratification
Dr. Hans Joachim von Merkatz

Pour le Gouvernement du Royaume de Grèce:
sous réserve de ratification
Cambalouris

Pour le Gouvernement de la République islandaise:

Pour le Gouvernement d'Irlande:
Thomas Woods

Pour le Gouvernement de la République italienne:
sous réserve de ratification
Bombassei de Vettor

Pour le Gouvernement du Grand-Duché de Luxembourg:
sous réserve de ratification
Pierre Wurth

Pour le Gouvernement du Royaume des Pays-Bas:

Pour le Gouvernement du Royaume de Norvège:
Hans Engen

Pour le Gouvernement du Royaume de Suède:
sous réserve de ratification
Leif Belfrage

Pour le Gouvernement de la République turque:
sous réserve de ratification

Pour le Gouvernement du Royaume-Uni de Grande-Bretagne et d'Irlande du Nord:
John H. Peck

Pour le Secrétaire Général du Conseil de l'Europe:
Gerrit v. Haeften
Chef du Service juridique

2. ARRANGEMENT EUROPÉEN POUR LA PROTECTION DES ÉMISSIONS DE TÉLÉVISION

Les Gouvernements signataires, Membres du Conseil de l'Europe,

Considérant que le but du Conseil de l'Europe est de réaliser une union plus étroite entre ses Membres;

Considérant que les échanges de programmes de télévision entre les pays européens sont de nature à contribuer à la réalisation de ce but;

For the Government of the Kingdom of Denmark:
with reservation in respect of ratification
J. O. KRAG

For the Government of the French Republic:
LECOMPTE BOINET

For the Government of the Federal Republic of Germany:
with reservation in respect of ratification
Dr. Hans Joachim VON MERKATZ

For the Government of the Kingdom of Greece:
with reservation in respect of ratification
CAMBALOURIS

For the Government of the Icelandic Republic:

For the Government of Ireland:
Thomas WOODS

For the Government of the Italian Republic:
with reservation in respect of ratification
BOMBASSEI DE VETTOR

For the Government of the Grand Duchy of Luxembourg:
with reservation in respect of ratification
Pierre WURTH

For the Government of the Kingdom of the Netherlands:

For the Government of the Kingdom of Norway:
Hans ENGEN

For the Government of the Kingdom of Sweden:
with reservation in respect of ratification
Leif BELFRAGE

For the Government of the Turkish Republic:
with reservation in respect of ratification

For the Government of the United Kingdom of Great Britain and Northern Ireland:
John H. PECK

For the Secretary-General of the Council of Europe
Gerrit v. HAEFTEN

2. EUROPEAN AGREEMENT ON THE PROTECTION OF TELEVISION BROADCASTS

The Governments signatory hereto, being Members of the Council of Europe,

Considering that the object of the Council is to achieve a greater unity between its Members;

Considering that exchanges of television programmes between the countries of Europe are calculated to further the achievement of that object;

Considérant que ces échanges sont entravés par l'impossibilité où se trouvent la plupart des organismes de télévision d'interdire la réémission, la fixation et la communication au public de leurs émissions, alors que, notamment, les organisateurs de manifestations artistiques ou les promoteurs d'événements sportifs subordonnent l'autorisation de diffusion vers d'autres pays à la garantie que les relais ne seront utilisés à d'autres fins que la réception privée;

Considérant que la protection internationale des émissions de télévision n'affectera d'aucune façon les droits des tiers pouvant exister au sujet de ces émissions;

Considérant que ce problème revêt un caractère d'urgence, compte tenu de la mise en place, à travers l'Europe, d'installations et de liaisons rendant dès maintenant techniquement aisés les échanges de programmes entre organismes européens de télévision;

Considérant qu'en attendant l'établissement d'une convention à vocation universelle sur les droits dits ,,voisins'' actuellement envisagée, il sied que soit conclu un arrangement régional, restreint dans son objet aux émissions de télévision et limité dans sa durée,

Sont convenus de ce qui suit:

Article 1er

Les organismes de radiodiffusion constitués sur le territoire d'une Partie à l'Arrangement en conformité de la loi de celle-ci ou effectuant des émissions sur un tel territoire jouissent, en ce qui concerne toutes leurs émissions de télévision:

1. sur le territoire de toutes les Parties à l'Arrangement, du droit d'autoriser ou d'interdire:

a) la réémission de ces émissions;

b) la distribution au public de ces émissions par fil;

c) la communication au public de ces émissions par tout instrument transmetteur de signes, de sons ou d'images;

d) toute fixation de ces émissions ou de leurs images isolées et toute reproduction de cette fixation; et

e) la réémission, la distribution par fil ou la communication au public au moyen des fixations ou reproductions visées à la lettre *d*) ci-dessus, sauf si l'organisme titulaire du droit a autorisé la vente au public de ces fixations ou reproductions;

2. sur le territoire de toute autre Partie à l'Arrangement, de la même protection que cette autre Partie accorde aux organismes de radiodiffusion constitués sur son territoire en conformité de sa loi ou effectuant des émissions sur son territoire, lorsque cette protection est plus large que celle prévue au chiffre 1 ci-dessus.

Article 2

1. Sous réserve de l'application des dispositions du chiffre 2 de l'article 1er, et des articles 13 et 14, la protection prévue au chiffre 1 de l'article 1er prendra fin à l'expiration de la dixième année civile qui suit celle au cours de laquelle la première émission a été effectuée sur le territoire d'une Partie à l'Arrangement.

2. Aucune Partie à l'Arrangement n'est tenue, en vertu des dispositions du chiffre 2 de l'article 1er, d'accorder aux émissions des organismes de radiodiffusion constitués sur le territoire d'une autre Partie à l'Arrangement en conformité de la loi de celle-ci ou effectuant des émissions sur le territoire de cette même Partie, une protection plus longue que celle accordée par cette autre Partie.

Considering that these exchanges are hampered by the fact that the majority of television organisations are at present powerless to restrain the re-broadcasting, fixation or public performance of their broadcasts, whereas the organisers of musical or dramatic performances or the like, and the promoters of sports meetings, make their consent to broadcasting to other countries conditional upon an undertaking that the relays will not be used for purposes other than private viewing;

Considering that the international protection of television broadcasts will in no way affect any rights of third parties in these broadcasts;

Considering that the problem is one of some urgency, in view of the installations and links now being brought into service throughout Europe, which are such as to make it easy from the technical point of view for European television organisations to exchange their programmes;

Considering that, pending the conclusion of a potentially universal Convention on "neighbouring rights" at present in contemplation, it is fitting to conclude a regional Agreement restricted in scope to television broadcasts and of limited duration,

Have agreed as follows:

Article 1

Broadcasting organisations constituted in the territory and under the laws of a Party to this Agreement or transmitting from such territory shall enjoy, in respect of all their television broadcasts;

1. in the territory of all Parties to this Agreement, the right to authorise or prohibit:

a) the re-broadcasting of such broadcasts;

b) the diffusion of such broadcasts to the public by wire;

c) the communication of such broadcasts to the public by means of any instrument for the transmission of signs, sounds or images;

d) any fixation of such broadcasts or still photographs thereof, and any reproduction of such a fixation; and

e) re-broadcasting, wire diffusion or public performance with the aid of the fixations or reproductions referred to in sub-paragraph *d*) of this paragraph, except where the organisation in which the right vests has authorised the sale of the said fixations or reproductions to the public;

2. in the territory of any other Party to this Agreement, the same protection as that other Party may extend to organisations constituted in its territory and under its laws or transmitting from its territory, where such protection is greater than that provided for in paragraph 1 above.

Article 2

1. Subject to paragraph 2 of Article 1, and Articles 13 and 14, the protection provided for in paragraph 1 of Article 1 shall continue until the end of the tenth calendar year following the year in which the first broadcast was made from the territory of a Party to this Agreement.

2. No Party to this Agreement shall be required, in pursuance of paragraph 2 of Article 1, to accord to the broadcasts of any broadcasting organisations constituted in the territory and under the laws of another Party to this Agreement or transmitting from the territory of another Party longer protection than that granted by the said other Party.

Article 3

1. Les Parties à l'Arrangement ont la faculté, moyennant la déclaration prévue à l'artcle 10, et en ce qui concerne leur territoire:

a) d'exclure la protection prévue au chiffre 1, lettre *b*), de l'article 1er;

b) d'exclure la protection prévue au chiffre 1, lettre *c*), de l'article 1er, lorsque la communication au public n'est pas faite contre paiement au sens de leur loi interne;

c) d'exclure la protection prévue au chiffre 1, lettre *d*), de l'article 1er, lorsqu'il y a fixation ou reproduction de cette fixation pour un usage privé ou dans le seul but d'enseignement;

d) d'exclure la protection prévue au chiffre 1, lettres *d*) et *e*), de l'article 1er, lorsqu'il y a fixation d'images isolées ou reproduction d'une telle fixation;

e) d'exclure de la protection prévue par l'Arrangement les émissions de télévision des organismes de radiodiffusion constitués sur leur territoire en conformité de leur loi ou effectuant des émissions sur ce territoire, lorsque ces émissions bénéficient d'une protection selon leur loi interne;

f) de limiter l'application de l'Arrangement aux organismes de radiodiffusion qui, constitués sur le territoire d'une Partie à l'Arrangement en conformité de la loi de celle-ci, effectuent des émissions sur le territoire de cette Partie.

2. Les mêmes Parties ont la faculté de prévoir, en ce qui concerne leur territoire, des exceptions à la protection des émissions de télévision:

a) lorsque, à l'occasion du compte rendu d'un événement d'actualité, il y a réémission, fixation ou reproduction de la fixation, distribution par fil ou communication au public de courts fragments d'une émission constituant elle-même tout ou partie de cet événement;

b) lorsqu'il y a fixation éphémère d'émissions de télévision réalisée par un organisme de radiodiffusion par ses propres moyens et pour ses émissions.

3. Les mêmes Parties ont la faculté, en ce qui concerne leur territoire, de désigner un organe qui pourra être saisi des cas où le droit de communication au public visé au chiffre 1, lettre *c*), de l'article 1er, aura été refusé arbitrairement ou accordé à des conditions excessives par l'organisme de radiodiffusion titulaire de ce droit.

Article 4

1. Les fixations d'une émission protégée par l'Arrangement ou d'une image isolée de celle-ci, ainsi que les reproductions de ces fixations, réalisées sur un territoire auquel l'Arrangement ne s'applique pas et importées dans le territoire d'une Partie à l'Arrangement sur lequel elles seraient illicites sans l'autorisation de l'organisme de radiodiffusion titulaire du droit, pourront y être saisies.

2. La disposition de l'alinéa précédent est applicable à l'importation dans le territoire d'une Partie à l'Arrangement de fixations de l'image isolée d'une émission protégée par l'Arrangement ainsi que de reproductions de ces fixations, lorsqu'elles sont réalisées sur le territoire d'une autre Partie à l'Arrangement en vertu des dispositions de l'alinéa 1, lettre *d*), de l'article 3.

3. La saisie a lieu conformément à la loi interne de chaque Partie à l'Arrangement.

4. Aucune Partie à l'Arrangement n'est tenue de prévoir une protection contre la fixation d'images isolées, ni la reproduction de cette fixation, des émissions d'un organisme de radiodiffusion constitué sur le territoire d'une autre Partie à l'Arrangement en conformité de la loi de celle-ci ou effectuant des émissions sur un tel territoire, lorsque cette autre Partie a fait usage de la réserve prévue à l'alinéa 1, lettre *d*), de l'article 3.

Article 3

1. Parties to this Agreement, by making a declaration as provided in Article 10, and in respect of their own territory, may:

a) withhold the protection provided for in sub-paragraph 1 *b*) of Article 1;

b) withhold the protection provided for in sub-paragraph 1 *c*) of Article 1, where the communication is not to a paying audience within the meaning of their domestic law;

c) withhold the protection provided for in sub-paragraph 1 *d*) of Article 1, where the fixation or reproduction of the fixation is made for private use, or solely for educational purposes;

d) withhold the protection provided for in sub-paragraphs 1 *d*) and *e*) of Article 1, in respect of still photographs or reproductions of such photographs;

e) withhold the protection provided for in this Agreement from television broadcasts by broadcasting organisations constituted in their territory and under their laws or transmitting from such territory, where such broadcasts enjoy protection under their domestic law;

f) restrict the operation of this Agreement to broadcasting organisations constituted in the territory and under the laws of a Party to this Agreement and also transmitting from the territory of such Party.

2. It shall be open to the aforesaid Parties, in respect of their own territory, to provide exceptions to the protection of television broadcasts:

a) for the purpose of reporting current events, in respect of the re-broadcasting, fixation or reproduction of the fixation, or reproduction of the fixation, wire diffusion or public performance of short extracts from a broadcast which itself constitutes the whole or part of the event in question;

b) in respect of the making of ephemeral fixations of television broadcasts by a broadcasting organisation by means of its own facilities and for its own broadcasts.

3. The aforesaid Parties may, in respect of their own territory, provide for a body with jurisdiction over cases where the right of communication to the public referred to in sub-paragraph 1 *c*) of Article 1 has been unreasonably refused, or granted on unreasonable terms, by the broadcasting organisation in which the said right vests.

Article 4

1. Fixations of a broadcast in which protection under this Agreement subsists, or still photographs thereof, as well as reproductions of such photographs, made in a territory to which this Agreement does not apply and imported into the territory of a Party to this Agreement where they would be unlawful without the consent of the broadcasting organisation in which the right vests, shall be liable to seizure in the latter territory.

2. The provisions of the last preceding paragraph shall apply to the importation into the territory of a Party to this Agreement of still photographs of a broadcast in which protection under this Agreement subsists and of reproductions of such photographs, where such photographs or reproductions are made in the territory of another Party to this Agreement by virtue of sub-paragraph 1 *d*) of Article 3.

3. Seizure shall be effected in accordance with the domestic law of each Party to this Agreement.

4. No Party to this Agreement shall be required to provide protection in respect of still photographs, or the reproduction of such photographs, of broadcasts made by a broadcasting organisation constituted in the territory and under the laws of another Party to this Agreement or transmitting from such territory, if the said other Party has availed itself of the reservation provided for in sub-paragraph 1 *d*) of Article 3.

Article 5

La protection prévue par l'Arrangement s'applique à l'émission de télévision, à la fois dans son élément visuel et dans son élément sonore. Elle ne vise pas l'élément sonore diffusé séparément.

Article 6

1. La protection prévue à l'article 1er n'affecte aucun des droits pouvant exister au regard d'une émission de télévision au profit de tiers, notamment ceux des auteurs, artistes exécutants ou interprètes, des producteurs de films ou de phonogrammes et des organisateurs de spectacles.
2. Elle laisse également intacte la protection des émissions de télévision résultant d'autres sources de droit.

Article 7

1. L'Arrangement est ouvert à la signature des Membres du Conseil de l'Europe, qui peuvent y devenir Parties:
a) par la signature sans réserve de ratification; ou
b) par la signature sous réserve de ratification suivie du dépôt d'un instrument de ratification.
2. Les instruments de ratification seront déposés près le Secrétaire Général du Conseil de l'Europe.

Article 8

1. L'Arrangement entrera en vigueur un mois après la date à laquelle trois Membres du Conseil de l'Europe auront, conformément aux dispositions de l'article 7, signé l'Arrangement sans réserve de ratification ou l'auront ratifié.
2. Pour tout Membre qui, ultérieurement, signera l'Arrangement sans réserve de ratification ou le ratifiera, l'Arrangement entrera en vigueur un mois après la date de la signature ou du dépôt de l'instrument de ratification.

Article 9

1. Après l'entrée en vigueur de l'Arrangement, tout gouvernement européen non Membre du Conseil de l'Europe ou tout gouvernement d'un pays non européen ayant des liens politiques avec un Membre du Conseil pourra y adhérer avec l'accord préalable du Comité des Ministres du Conseil de l'Europe.
2. L'adhésion s'effectuera par le dépôt, près le Secrétaire Général du Conseil de l'Europe, d'un instrument d'adhésion qui prendra effet un mois après la date du dépôt.

Article 10

La signature, la ratification ou l'adhésion emportera de plein droit l'acceptation de toutes les dispositions de l'Arrangement. Chaque Partie devra spécifier, au moment de la signature ou du dépôt de l'instrument de ratification ou d'adhésion, quelles sont les réserves prévues à l'alinéa 1 de l'article 3 dont elle entend faire usage.

Article 11

Le Secrétaire Général du Conseil de l'Europe notifiera aux Membres du Conseil, aux gouvernements des pays qui auront adhéré à l'Arrangement ainsi qu'au Directeur du Bureau de l'Union internationale pour la protection des oeuvres littéraires et artistiques:

Article 5

The protection afforded by this Agreement shall apply both in relation to the visual element and in relation to the sound element of a television broadcast. It shall not affect the sound element when broadcast separately.

Article 6

1. The protection provided for in Article 1 shall not affect any rights in respect of a television broadcast that may accrue to third parties, such as authors, performers, film makers, manufacturers of phonographic records or organisers of entertainments.

2. It shall likewise be without prejudice to any protection of television broadcasts that may be accorded apart from this Agreement.

Article 7

1. This Agreement shall be open to signature by the Members of the Council of Europe, who may become Parties to it either by:

a) signature without reservation in respect of ratification; or

b) signature with reservation in respect of ratification, followed by the deposit of an instrument of ratification.

2. Instruments of ratification shall be deposited with the Secretary-General of the Council of Europe.

Article 8

1. This Agreement shall enter into force one month after the date on which three Members of the Council of Europe shall, in accordance with Article 7 thereof, have signed it without reservation in respect of ratification or shall have ratified it.

2. In the case of any Member of the Council of Europe who shall subsequently sign the Agreement without reservation in respect of ratification or who shall ratify it, the Agreement shall enter into force one month after the date of such signature or deposit of the instrument of ratification.

Article 9

1. After this Agreement has come into force, any European Government which is not a Member of the Council of Europe or any non-European Government having political ties with a Member of the Council of Europe may accede to it, subject to the prior approval of the Committee of Ministers of the Council of Europe.

2. Such accession shall be effected by the deposit of an instrument of accession with the Secretary-General of the Council of Europe and shall take effect one month after the date of deposit.

Article 10

Signature, ratification or accession shall imply full acceptance of all the provisions of this Agreement; provided always that any country may declare, at the time of signature or of deposit of its instrument of ratification or accession, that it intends to avail itself of one or more of the options in paragraph 1 of Article 3 above.

Article 11

The Secretary-General of the Council of Europe shall notify Members of the Council, the Governments of any countries which may have acceded to this Agreement and the Director of the Bureau of the International Union for the Protection of Literary and Artistic Works:

a) toute signature avec les réserves éventuelles de ratification, le dépôt de tout instrument de ratification et la date de l'entrée en vigueur de l'Arrangement:

b) le dépôt de tout instrument d'adhésion effectué en application des dispositions de l'article 9;

c) toute déclaration et toute notification reçues en application des dispositions des articles 12, 13 ou 14.

d) toute décision du Comité des Ministres intervenue en application de l'alinéa 2 de l'article 13.

Article 12

1. L'Arrangement s'applique aux territoires métropolitains des Parties.
2. Toute Partie peut, au moment de la signature, du dépôt de son instrument de ratification ou d'adhésion, ou à tout autre moment par la suite, déclarer, par notification adressée au Secrétaire Général du Conseil de l'Europe, que l'Arrangement s'appliquera à l'ensemble ou à l'un des territoires dont elle assure les relations internationales.
3. Tout gouvernement qui, en vertu de l'alinéa 2 du présent article, aura fait une déclaration étendant l'application de l'Arrangement à un territoire dont il assure les relations internationales, peut dénoncer l'Arrangement séparément pour ce territoire, conformément à l'article 14 ci-dessous.

Article 13

1. L'Arrangement cessera de déployer ses effets, excepté en ce qui concerne les fixations déjà réalisées, lorsqu'une convention sur les droits dits „voisins", comportant une protection des émissions de télévision et ouverte, entre autres, aux pays européens, sera entrée en vigueur à l'égard d'au moins la majorité des Membres du Conseil de l'Europe et Parties à l'Arrangement.
2. Le Comité des Ministres du Conseil de l'Europe constatera en temps voulu l'accomplissement des conditions prévues à l'alinéa précédent pour la cessation des effets de l'Arrangement.

Article 14

Toute Partie pourra mettre fin, en ce qui la concerne, à l'Arrangement en donnant un préavis d'un an notifié à cet effet au Secrétaire Général du Conseil de l'Europe.

En foi de quoi, les soussignés, dûment autorisés à cet effet, ont signé le présent Arrangement.

Fait à Strasbourg, le 22 juin 1960, en français et en anglais, les deux textes faisant également foi, en un seul exemplaire, qui sera déposé dans les archives du Conseil de l'Europe. Le Secrétaire Général en communiquera des copies certifiées conformes à tous les Gouvernements signataires et adhérents, ainsi qu'au Directeur du Bureau de l'Union internationale pour la protection des oeuvres littéraires et artistiques.

Pour le Gouvernement de la République d'Autriche:

Pour le Gouvernement du Royaume de Belgique:
sous réserve de ratification

a) of any signatures, together with any reservations as to ratification, of the deposit of instruments of ratification and of the date of entry into force of this Agreement;

b) of the deposit of any instruments of accession in accordance with Article 9;

c) of any declaration or notification received in accordance with Articles 12, 13 or 14.;

d) of any decision of the Committee of Ministers taken in pursuance of paragraph 2 of Article 13.

Article 12

1. This Agreement shall apply to the metropolitan territories of the Parties.

2. Any Party may, at the time of signature, of the deposit of its instrument of ratification or accession, or at any later date, declare by notice addressed to the Secretary-General of the Council of Europe that this Agreement shall extend to any or all of the territories for whose international relations it is responsible.

3. Any Government which has made a declaration under paragraph 2 of this Article extending this Agreement to any territory for whose international relations it is responsible may denounce the Agreement separately in respect of that territory in accordance with Article 14 thereof.

Article 13

1. This Agreement shall cease to be effective, except in regard to fixations already made, at such time as a Convention on "neighbouring rights", including the protection of television broadcasts and open to European countries, amongst others, shall have entered into force for at least a majority of the Members of the Council of Europe that are themselves Parties to the Agreement.

2. The Committee of Ministers of the Council of Europe shall at the appropriate time declare that the conditions laid down in the preceding paragraph have been fulfilled, thereby entailing the termination of this Agreement.

Article 14

Any Contracting Party may denounce this Agreement by giving one year's notice to that effect to the Secretary-General of the Council of Europe.

In witness whereof, the undersigned, being duly authorised thereto, have signed this Agreement.

Done at Strasbourg, this 22th day of June, 1960, in English and French, both texts being equally authoritative, in a single copy, which shall remain in the archives of the Council of Europe and of which the Secretary-General shall send certified copies to each of the signatory and acceding Governments and to the Director of the Bureau of the International Union for the Protection of Literary and Artistic Works.

For the Government of the Republic of Austria:

For the Government of the Kingdom of Belgium:
with reservation in respect of ratification

Pour le Gouvernement du Royaume de Danemark:
sous réserve de ratification
V. U. HAMMERSHAIMB

Pour le Gouvernement de la République française:
LECOMPTE BOINET

Pour le Gouvernement de la République Fédérale d'Allemagne:
sous réserve de ratification

Pour le Gouvernement du Royaume de Grèce:
sous réserve de ratification
N. CAMBALOURIS

Pour le Gouvernement de la République islandaise:

Pour le Gouvernement d'Irlande:
sous réserve de ratification:
Thomas WOODS

Pour le Gouvernement de la République italienne
sous réserve de ratification
BOMBASSEI DE VETTOR

Pour le Gouvernement du Grand-Duché de Luxembourg:
sous réserve de ratification

Pour le Gouvernement du Royaume des Pays-Bas:

Pour le Gouvernement du Royaume de Norvège:

Pour le Gouvernement du Royaume de Suède:
sous réserve de ratification:

Pour le Gouvernement de la République turque:
sous réserve de ratification
M. BOROVALI

Pour le Gouvernement du Royaume-Uni de Grande-Bretagne et d'Irlande du Nord:
sous réserve de ratification

E. RECOMMANDATIONS DE L'ASSEMBLÉE CONSULTATIVE

COMMUNICATION DU COMITÉ DES MINISTRES À L'ASSEMBLÉE CONSULTATIVE

1. RECOMMANDATION 243 (1960) [1]
RELATIVE AUX RELATIONS ÉCONOMIQUES EUROPÉENNES
(assistance aux pays européens moins développés)

1. L'Assemblée,
2. Rappelant ses Recommandations 91 et 95, dans lesquelles elle attirait l'attention sur les besoins des régions moins développées de l'Italie méridionale, de la Grèce et de la Turquie;

---

[1] *Discussion par l'Assemblée* les 26, 27 et 29 avril 1960 (3e, 4e et 8e séances) (*voir* Doc. 1133, rapport de la Commission économique).
Texte adopté par l'Assemblée le 29 avril 1960 (8e séance).

For the Government of the Kingdom of Denmark:
with reservation in respect of ratification
V. U. HAMMERSHAIMB

For the Government of the French Republic:
LECOMPTE BOINET

For the Government of the Federal Republic of Germany:
with reservation in respect of ratification

For the Government of the Kingdom of Greece:
with reservation in respect of ratification:
N. CAMBALOURIS

For the Government of the Icelandic Republic:

For the Government of Ireland:
with reservation in respect of ratification
Thomas WOODS

For the Government of the Italian Republic:
with reservation in respect of ratification
BOMBASSEI DE VETTOR

For the Government of the Grand Duchy of Luxembourg:
with reservation in respect of ratification

For the Government of the Kingdom of the Netherlands:

For the Government of the Kingdom of Norway:

For the Government of the Kingdom of Sweden:
with reservation in respect of ratification

For the Government of the Turkish Republic:
with reservation in respect of ratification:
M. BOROVALI

For the Government of the United Kingdom of Great Britain and Northern Ireland:
with reservation in respect of ratification

E. RECOMMENDATIONS OF THE CONSULTATIVE ASSEMBLY

COMMUNICATION OF THE COMMITTEE OF MINISTERS TO THE CONSULTATIVE ASSEMBLY

1. RECOMMENDATION 243 (1960) [1]
ON EUROPEAN ECONOMIC RELATIONS
(assistance to the less developed countries of Europe)

1. The Assembly,
2. Recalling its Recommendations 91 and 95, which drew attention to the needs of the less developed regions of Southern Italy, Greece and Turkey;

---

[1] ***Assembly debate*** on 26th, 27th and 29th April, 1960 (3rd, 4th and 8th Sittings) (*see* Doc. 1133, Report of the Economic Committee).
Text adopted by the Assembly on 29th April, 1960 (8th Sitting).

3. Considérant que l'écart entre les pays plus développés et les pays moins développés continue à s'étendre, et que cette situation ne pourrait se prolonger sans que la paix et la construction européenne risquent d'être sérieusement menacées;

4. Rappelant qu'une action multilatérale vient d'être préconisée afin de préparer un programme pour une aide efficace aux pays et régions en voie de développement;

5. Considérant que des problèmes économiques particulièrement urgents se posent aux cinq États membres de l'O.E.C.E. qui ne sont membres ni de la Communauté Économique Européenne ni de l'Association Européenne de Libre-Échange;

6. Tenant compte des Résolutions (56) 15 et (59) 31 du Comité des Ministres,

7. Recommande au Comité des Ministres:

a) de demander aux gouvernements membres de la Communauté Économique Européenne et de l'Association Européenne de Libre-Échange de prendre des mesures immédiates pour contribuer, par un effort commun, à résoudre les difficultés, dues aux Traités de Rome et de Stockholm, auxquelles se heurtent les cinq États membres de l'O.E.C.E. qui ne sont pas membres de la Communauté Économique Européenne ni de l'A.E.L.E., en particulier par l'adoption de mesures propres à accroître les échanges avec ces pays et à favoriser les exportations de ceux-ci;

b) de créer un Fonds européen spécial de developpement chargé de fournir des capitaux, sous forme de subventions, de prêts ou de garanties, en vue du financement de projets de développement dans les États membres moins développés de l'O.E.C.E.

2. RECOMMANDATION 251 (1960) [1]

RELATIVE À LA COOPÉRATION EUROPÉENNE DANS LE DOMAINE DE LA RECHERCHE SPATIALE ET DE LA TECHNOLOGIE SPATIALE

L'Assemblée,

Considérant les progrès spectaculaires accomplis ces dernières années par les États-Unis et l'Union Soviétique dans le domaine de la recherche scientifique concernant l'espace extra-atmosphérique et des techniques spatiales;

Convaincue qu'il est essentiel que les États membres du Conseil de l'Europe entreprennent dans ce domaine des recherches, afin de maintenir la qualité de leurs propres recherches relatives aux sciences exactes et naturelles, de permettre à leurs industries de participer au progrès commercial auquel donneront lieu les techniques spatiales et d'assurer l'application de ces connaissances nouvelles au profit de leurs populations et de leurs économies;

Consciente que ces recherches exigent des moyens économiques et scientifiques supérieurs à ceux de la plupart des États membres, s'ils doivent agir individuellement;

Ayant à l'esprit les exemples du succès de la coopération scientifique européenne fournis par l'Agence européenne pour l'Énergie nucléaire et l'Organisation européenne pour la Recherche nucléaire,

Recommande au Comité des Ministres:

1. d'étudier de toute urgence la possibilité et le coût de l'établissement d'une agence européenne qui aurait pour tâche d'entreprendre un programme de recherches spatiales en prenant pour base un véhicule spatial conçu et construit en Europe, et de stimuler l'utilisation pacifique de l'espace extra-atmosphérique;

[1] *Discussion par l'Assemblée* les 23 et 24 septembre 1960 (13e et 14e séances) (*voir* Doc. 1175, rapport de la Commission économique).
Texte adopté par l'Assemblée le 24 septembre 1960 (14e séance).

3. Considering that the gap between more developed and less developed countries is still widening and that this situation cannot be allowed to continue without becoming a serious threat to peace and to the building of Europe;

4. Recalling that multilateral action has recently been advocated to prepare a programme of effective aid to countries and regions in course of development;

5. Considering that there are particularly urgent economic problems arising for the five Member States of the O.E.E.C. which are not Members either of the European Economic Community or of the European Free Trade Association;

6. Taking into account Resolutions (56) 15 and (59)31 of the Committee of Ministers,

7. Recommends that the Committee of Ministers:

a) should ask Member Governments of both the E.E.C. and the E.F.T.A. to take immediate steps to assist in a joint effort the five Member States of O.E.E.C. that are not Members of the E.E.C. or the E.F.T.A. in overcoming the difficulties created for them by the Rome and Stockholm Treaties; in particular by promoting measures for increasing trade with and stimulating exports from these countries;

b) should set up a special European Development Fund to provide capital for development projects in less developed Member States of O.E.E.C. in the form of grants or loans or guarantees.

2. RECOMMENDATION 251 (1960) [1]
ON EUROPEAN CO-OPERATION ON SPACE RESEARCH AND SPACE TECHNOLOGY

The Assembly,

Considering the spectacular progress made in recent years by the U.S.A., and the U.S.S.R. in scientific research in outer space and in space technology;

Believing that it is essential for Member States to conduct research in outer space, in order to maintain their own high standards of research in the natural sciences; to enable their industries to participate in the commercial developments resulting from space technology; and to ensure the application of this new knowledge to the benefit of their peoples and of their economies;

Realising that such research would be beyond the economic and scientific resources of most Member States acting individually;

Bearing in mind the successful examples of European co-operation in the scientific field furnished by the European Nuclear Energy Agency and the European Organisation for Nuclear Research,

Recommends to the Committee of Ministers:

1. that they study as a matter of urgent policy the possibilities and cost of setting up a European agency to undertake a space programme, based upon a space vehicle developed and built in Europe, and to promote the peaceful uses of outer space;

1. ***Assembly debate*** **on 23rd and 24th September, 1960 (13th and 14th Sittings) (*****see*** **Doc. 1175, Report of the Economic Committee).**
Text adopted by the Assembly **on 24th September, 1960 (14th Sitting).**

2. de s'informer auprès des États membres de leur volonté de principe de participer à un programme européen de recherches spatiales et de l'importance des engagements que chaque État participant serait disposé à prendre dans les domaines financier et scientifique;

3. si cette étude et cette enquête le justifient, d'élaborer un plan précis portant sur la création d'une agence spatiale européenne et de le soumettre aux gouvernements membres aux fins de ratification rapide;

4. de soumettre toute agence spatiale européenne qu'ils auront créée au contrôle souverain d'un comité de ministres compétents et à l'influence parlementaire de l'Assemblée Consultative;

5. de tenir l'Assemblée informée des progrès obtenus et de la consulter sur les développements ultérieurs de ce programme.

3. RECOMMANDATION 266 (1960) [1]
RELATIVE AUX RELATIONS ÉCONOMIQUES EUROPÉENNES

1. L'Assemblée,

2. Réaffirmant sa foi dans l'idéal d'unité de toute l'Europe démocratique, dont la Communauté des Six et l'Association Européenne de Libre-Échange constituent des étapes;

3. Prenant acte, d'une part, de la décision de la Communauté Économique Européenne d'accélérer la réalisation du marché commun et de la possibilité que l'Association Européenne de Libre-Échange (A.E.L.E.) en fasse de même et, d'autre part, de ce que la compétence du Comité des problèmes commerciaux des Vingt et un se borne à rechercher des solutions pragmatiques aux difficultés à court terme du commerce intra-européen; et craignant en conséquence que le problème à long terme puisse rester sans solution;

4. Reconnaissant la nécessité de réduire les divergences résultant de l'existence de la Communauté Économique Européenne et de l'Association Européenne de Libre-Échange, et se félicitant de la volonté de renforcer l'unité européenne récemment exprimée par certains chefs de gouvernement européens;

5. Convaincue qu'il est possible, suivant les modalités d'association prévues à l'article 238 du Traité de Rome et à l'article 41 de la Convention de Stockholm, d'aboutir, pourvu qu'il existe une volonté sincère, à un accord d'association entre la Communauté Économique Européenne, l'A.E.L.E. et, le cas échéant, les autres États membres du Conseil de l'Europe;

6. Rappelant les suggestions formulées dans le paragraphe 1 des dispositifs de sa Recommandation 229,

7. Recommande au Comité des Ministres:

8. que des pourparlers préliminaires soient engagés, dès que possible, sur les conditions dans lesquelles pourrait être négocié un tel accord d'association, respectant pleinement les obligations incombant aux pays membres en vertu du Traité de Rome, de la Convention de Stockholm et de l'Accord général sur les Tarifs douaniers et le Commerce (G.A.T.T.);

9. que cet accord comporte les dispositions générales suivantes:

a) l'élimination progressive des droits de douane et des contingents appliqués aux échanges de produits industriels entre les pays membres de cette association, selon des échéances convenues;

b) l'harmonisation des droits de douane, avec l'adoption d'un tarif commun dans certains secteurs, l'utilisation de certificats d'origine

---

[1] *Discussion par l'Assemblée* le 27 septembre 1960 (17e et 18e séances) (*voir* Doc. 1176, rapport de la Commission politique, 1179, rapport de la Commission économique, et 1216, projet de recommandation révisé présenté conjointement par les Présidents et les rapporteurs des deux Commissions).
Texte adopté par l'Assemblée le 29 septembre 1960 (20e séance).

2. that they ascertain which Member States would be willing in principle to take part in a European programme of space research and the limit of the financial and scientific commitments which each participating State would be willing to undertake;

3. that, if warranted by these studies and investigations, they prepare a specific plan for the creation of a European space agency and submit it to Member Governments for early ratification;

4. that any European space agency which they may create should be subject to overall control by a committee of the appropriate Ministers and to the parliamentary influence of this Assembly;

5. that they keep this Assembly informed of the progress made and that this Assembly be consulted as to the future development of this programme.

3. RECOMMENDATION 266 (1960) [1]
ON EUROPEAN ECONOMIC RELATIONS

1. The Assembly,

2. Reaffirming its faith in the concept of the unity of the whole of democratic Europe, of which the six-Power Community and the European Free Trade Association represent stages;

3. Noting, on the one hand, the decision of the European Economic Community to accelerate the implementation of the Common Market and the possibility that the European Free Trade Association (E.F.T.A.) may do the same, and, on the other hand, that the Committee on Trade Problems of the Twenty-one is exclusively concerned with seeking practical solutions to the short-term difficulties in intra-European trade; and fearing therefore that the problem of a long-term solution may remain unresolved;

4. Recognising the need for diminishing the divergences resulting from the separate existence of the European Economic Community and the European Free Trade Association and welcoming the determination recently expressed by European Heads of Governments to strengthen European unity;

5. Convinced that it is possible, with a sincere will, to reach an association agreement between the E.E.C, the E.F.T.A. and, where appropriate, the other Member States of the Council of Europe, in accordance with the provisions contained in Article 238 of the Treaty of Rome and Article 41 of the Stockholm Convention;

6. Recalling the suggestions contained in paragraph 1 of the operative part of Recommendation 229,

7. Recommends to the Committee of Ministers:

8. that exploratory conversations should begin as soon as possible on the conditions under which such an Association Agreement could be negotiated, fully respecting the obligations of Member countries under the Rome Treaty, the Stockholm Convention and the General Agreement on Tariffs and Trade (G.A.T.T.);

9. that the Agreement should embody the following general features:

a) Gradual elimination of customs duties and quotas in industrial goods between Member countries of this Association, in accordance with an agreed time-table;

b) Harmonisation of customs duties, with the adoption of a common tariff in some sectors, certificates of origin being used to avoid deflection

---

[1] *Assembly debate* on 27th September, 1960 (17th and 18th Sittings) (*see* Docs. 1176, Report of the Political Committee, 1179, Report of the Economic Committee, and 1216, revised draft Recommendation presented jointly by the Chairmen and Rapporteurs of the two Committees).
Text adopted by the Assembly on 29th September, 1960 (20th Sitting).

destinés à éviter des détournements de trafic étant limitée aux seuls cas où il n'aura pas été possible d'établir une harmonisation satisfaisante des droits;

c) des dispositions prévoyant des consultations relatives aux échéances de la réduction des obstacles aux échanges à l'intérieur de la Communauté Économique Européenne et de l'A.E.L.E. effectuée conformément au Traité de Rome et à la Convention de Stockholm, et, dans la mesure du possible, la synchronisation de ces échéances;

d) la coordination des politiques commerciales à l'égard des pays tiers;

e) des dispositions destinées à faciliter l'expansion des échanges de produits agricoles parallèlement à celle des produits industriels, tout en respectant les objectifs des politiques agricoles des États membres et la politique agricole commune de la Communauté Économique Européenne;

f) des dispositions permettant au Royaume-Uni et aux autres pays membres de garder des relations commerciales et économiques spéciales avec leurs territoires d'outre-mer, les pays associés et le Commonwealth; dans les cas où les préférences existantes constituent un obstacle à l'harmonisation des tarifs, cette difficulté pourrait être surmontée en substituant aux droits préférentiels des contingents tarifaires en accord avec les dispositions du G.A.T.T., ou éventuellement par l'octroi de la part des autres membres de l'association de préférences identiques;

g) des dispositions permettant aux pays européens qui ne sont membres ni de la Communauté Économique Européenne, ni de l'A.E.L.E., de devenir membres de la nouvelle association en devenant membres ou associés de l'un ou l'autre des deux groupes, compte étant tenu des besoins spéciaux de développement de ces pays;

h) la confrontation régulière et la coordination accrue des politiques économiques, financières et sociales des pays membres, en vue d'assurer un fonctionnement équilibré de l'association et de parvenir progressivement au degré d'harmonisation nécessaire à un marché européen unifié;

i) des dispositions en matière de primes et de subventions, de dumping, d'entreprises publiques, de transactions invisibles, de mouvements de capitaux, de pratiques commerciales restrictives et de droit d'établissement, imposant de suivre des règles au moins aussi libérales que celles qui sont définies dans la Convention de Stockholm;

j) l'application des politiques mentionnées ci-dessus par des organismes appropriés, qui ne devraient entraver le fonctionnement d'aucune des institutions régionales existantes.

4. RÔLE DU CONSEIL DE L'EUROPE

Communication du Comité des Ministres à l'Assemblée Consultative

1. Le Comité des Ministres cherche actuellement à déterminer quels seraient pour lui, dans les circonstances présentes, les moyens les meilleurs de s'acquitter des obligations que lui confère le Statut du Conseil de l'Europe.

2. Tandis que les Ministres s'efforcent de trouver une solution aux problèmes économiques européens qui font l'objet de discussions et de négociations devant plusieurs instances, ils estiment que leur tâche la plus importante est de trouver les moyens pratiques de renforcer l'unité des quinze pays membres du Conseil de l'Europe et de fortifier chez eux l'esprit européen.

3. Le Comité des Ministres considère l'Assemblée Consultative – élément moteur de l'Europe – comme le forum où sont échangées, sur les

---

[1] C.M. (60) C.R. 2 Prov. Annexe II.

of trade only where satisfactory harmonisation of tariffs has proved impossible;

c) Provisions for consultation concerning the time-tables for the reduction of internal trade barriers in accordance with the Rome Treaty and the Stockholm Convention, and, insofar as possible, the synchronisation of these time-tables;

d) Co-ordination of commercial policies towards third countries;

e) Provisions for facilitating expansion of trade in agricultural products, parallel to that of trade in industrial goods, respecting the aims of the agricultural policies of Member States and the common policy of the E.E.C.;

f) Provisions allowing the United Kingdom and other Member countries to maintain special commercial and economic relations with their overseas territories, associated countries, and with the Commonwealth; where existing preferences stand in the way of the harmonisation of tariffs, this difficulty might be overcome by replacing the preferences by tariff quotas in accordance with G.A.T.T. rules, or, possibly, by the other countries of the Association accepting to grant the same preferences;

g) Provisions making it possible for the European countries which are neither members of E.E.C. nor of E.F.T.A. to become Members of the new Association by becoming Members or Associated Members of one or the other of the two groupings, taking into account the special development needs of these countries;

h) Regular confrontation and increasing co-operation of economic, financial and social policies of Member countries to ensure the balanced functioning of the Association and to achieve gradually the degree of harmonisation necessary for a unified European market;

i) Undertaking of obligations to apply rules at least as liberal as those laid down in the Stockholm Convention in the matter of bonuses and subsidies, dumping, public undertakings, invisible transactions, movement of capital, restrictive practices and the right of establishment;

j) The promotion of the above-mentioned policies by appropriate bodies which should not impede the functioning of any of the regional institutions.

4. RÔLE OF THE COUNCIL OF EUROPE

Communication of the Committee of Ministers to the Consultative Assembly

1. The Committee of Ministers is in process of reviewing the best means in present conditions of carrying out its obligations under the Statute of the Council of Europe.

2. While the Ministers are seeking means of resolving European economic problems in Europe which are the subject of discussion and negotiations by several bodies, they consider that the most important task confronting them is to seek practical means of strengthening the unity, and the European spirit among the Fifteen Member nations of the Council of Europe.

3. The Committee of Ministers regards the Consultative Assembly – driving force of Europe – as the forum for the interchange of ideas for

[1] C.M. (60) C.R. 2 prov. Appendix II.

problèmes de son développement, des idées qui peuvent ensuite, par l'intermédiaire des parlements nationaux, s'imposer à la conscience nationale des pays membres; l'Assemblée constitue également la source de propositions constructives en vue de la mise en oeuvre de ces idées. De telles propositions méritent d'être étudiées attentivement par le Comité des Ministres lui-même et par les autres organismes intergouvernementaux auxquels le Comité pourrait les transmettre.

4. De l'avis du Comité des Ministres de grands progrès ont déjà été réalisés, depuis la création du Conseil de l'Europe, vers l'établissement d'une base pour la coopération intergouvernementale en Europe.

a) La liste des conventions, accords et protocoles qui ont été conclus jusqu'à ce jour par le Conseil de l'Europe et dont le nombre est maintenant de 30, vient à l'appui de ce point de vue. Vingt-trois de ces instruments sont actuellement en vigueur, dont les plus importants sont les suivants:

- Convention européenne de sauvegarde des Droits de l'Homme et des Libertés fondamentales, en vertu de laquelle les droits de l'homme ont été, pour la première fois dans l'histoire, non seulement définis mais garantis par un mécanisme juridique indépendant sous la forme d'une Commission européenne et d'une Cour européenne;
- Accords intérimaires européens concernant la Sécurité sociale et l'assistance médicale qui ont entendu sur le plan multilatéral les dispositions d'une série d'accords bilatéraux conclus entre des États membres de sorte que les citoyens de tous les États membres peuvent en bénéficier;
- Conventions européennes concernant les demandes de brevets et la classification de ces derniers qui, en dehors de l'intérêt pratique immédiat qu'elles présentent pour les inventeurs des États membres, sont également ouvertes à l'adhésion des pays qui ne sont pas parties aux conventions du Conseil de l'Europe. L'Union Sud-Africaine et la Suisse ont adhéré à la Convention relative aux demandes de brevets et l'Australie à celle concernant la classification de ces derniers;
- Convention culturelle européenne et autres conventions dans le domaine culturel

  sur l'équivalence des diplômes donnant accès aux établissements universitaires;

  sur l'équivalence des périodes d'études universitaires;

  sur la reconnaissance académique des qualifications universitaires;

  qui toutes, ainsi que l'institution du Fonds Culturel européen et la création du Comité de l'Enseignement supérieur et de la Recherche, ont permis au Conseil de l'Europe de jouer un rôle prééminent dans le développement de la compréhension entre les pays européens;
- Conventions européennes sur le règlement pacifique des différends, l'extradition, l'entraide judiciaire en matière pénale, l'assurance des véhicules et l'établissement, qui ont toutes apporté une contribution réelle à une harmonisation plus complète des règles et pratiques européennes dans le domaine juridique;
- Une convention européenne et un accord dans le domaine de la Santé publique

  sur l'échange des mutilés de guerre aux fins de traitement médical;

  sur l'échange de substances thérapeutiques d'origine humaine;

  sur l'importation temporaire en franchise de douane, à titre de prêt gratuit et à des fins diagnostiques ou thérapeutiques, de matériel médico-chirurgical et de laboratoire destiné aux établissements sanitaires;
- Accords européens sur le régime de la circulation des personnes entre les pays membres et la suppression des visas pour les réfugiés – dont le premier a supprimé l'obligation du passeport et des carnets de passage pour le franchissement de la frontière en faveur d'un grand nombre d'Européens;

the development which may then be extended through national Parliaments into the national consciousness of Member nations; the Assembly is also the source of constructive proposals for putting these ideas into effect. Such proposals merit careful study by the Committee of Ministers itself and by other intergovernmental agencies to which it may transmit them.

4. It appears to the Committee of Ministers that considerable progress has already been made since the inception of the Council of Europe in the task of building up a foundation for intergovernmental co-operation in Europe.

a) The current list of Conventions, Agreements and Protocols concluded by the Council of Europe – now numbering thirty – bears witness to this fact. Twenty-three of them are now in force, among the most important of which are the following:

- the European Convention of Human Rights and Fundamental Freedoms whereby for the first time in history, human rights are not only defined but guaranteed by independent legal machinery in the form of the European Commission and the European Court;

- European Interim Agreements on Social Security and Medical Assistance which have extended multilaterally the provisions of a series of bilateral agreements concluded between Member States so that the citizens of all Member States may benefit therefrom;

- European Convention on Patent Application and Classification, which apart from their immediate practical value to inventors in Member countries, are also open to adherence by third countries. South Africa and Switzerland have adhered to the Convention on Applications, and Australia to that on Classification;

- the European Cultural Convention and other cultural conventions; on the equivalence of diplomas leading to University admission; on the equivalence of periods of University study; on the academic recognition of University qualifications; all of which, together with the setting up of the European Cultural Fund, and the establishment of the Committee for Higher Education and Research have given the Council of Europe a pre-eminent rôle in the promotion of intra-European understanding;

- the European Conventions on the Peaceful Settlement of Disputes, Extradition, Assistance in Criminal Matters, Vehicle Insurance, and Establishment – which have each made a real contribution to a closer harmonisation of European rules and practice in the legal field;

- a European Convention and Agreement in the field of Public Health: on the exchange of War Cripples for medical treatment; on the exchange of therapeutic substances of human origin; on the temporary importation, free of duty, of Medical, Surgical and Laboratory equipment for use on free loan in Hospitals and other Medical Institutions for purposes of Diagnosis or Treatment;

- European Agreements on Regulations governing the movement of persons between Member States and on the abolition of visas for refugees – the first of which has removed the necessity of passports and *carnets de passage* when crossing frontiers for the citizens of a number of European countries;

- Arrangements européens concernant l'échange des programmes au moyen de films de télévision et la protection des émissions de télévision – mesures par lesquelles le Conseil a exercé son influence unificatrice sur le moyen actuellement le plus puissant de l'échange des idées.

b) En outre, d'importants travaux sont en cours. A cet égard il convient d'appeler l'attention sur l'activité des comités d'experts chargés d'élaborer:

- le projet de Charte sociale européenne, qui est maintenant en voie d'achèvement et qui tend à harmoniser les politiques sociales des pays membres;
- le projet de Code européen de sécurité sociale, qui vise à relever les niveaux de sécurité sociale dans les pays membres et à harmoniser leurs charges sociales;
- un projet de convention européenne concernant les personnes morales, en vertu duquel il est envisagé d'ajouter aux dispositions de la Convention européenne d'établissement un nouvel accord visant les sociétés et les personnes morales;
- un projet de convention consulaire européenne;
- un projet de convention portant loi uniforme sur l'arbitrage en matière civile et commerciale;
- un projet de convention sur la réduction des cas de pluralité de nationalités;
- un projet de convention concernant la production et la commercialisation des produits de la vigne et des spiritueux.

D'autre part, il y a lieu de mentionner les importants travaux actuellement en cours:

- dans le domaine de la culture;
- dans le domaine de la santé publique, spécialement en ce qui concerne les bourses médicales du Conseil de l'Europe;
- au sein du Groupe de travail de la fonction publique européenne, auquel participent plusieurs organisations européennes et dont le Conseil de l'Europe assume la présidence;
- au sein du Comité européen pour les problèmes criminels qui s'occupe actuellement, *inter alia*, de la conclusion d'une convention pour la répression des infractions routières.

D'autres exemples de travaux courants présentant une grande utilité sont fournis:

- par la mise en place de la Conférence européenne des Pouvoirs locaux;
- par l'Arrangement entre l'Organisation internationale du Travail et le Conseil de l'Europe concernant la création et le fonctionnement du Centre international d'information et de recherche sur la formation professionnelle.

5. Par ailleurs, il est évident que, dans la recherche de nouveaux champs d'action collective, il reste encore de nombreuses tâches à définir et à accomplir avant que l'Europe puisse être considérée comme harmonisée et étroitement unie.

Les Ministres espèrent que l'Assemblée Consultative coopérera avec eux à l'étude et à la mise en oeuvre de projets appropriés.

Ils poursuivront, pour leur part, leurs propres efforts dans les divers domaines où la coopération intergouvernementale est possible. Ils se proposent d'inviter l'Assemblée à faire connaître son avis lorsque leurs travaux auront atteint un stade suffisamment avancé.

6. En particulier, comme l'unité de l'Europe est pour une large part le fruit de son histoire et de sa culture, c'est dans une large mesure par un accroissement d'activité dans le vaste domaine de l'éducation, de la science et de la culture que cette unité pourra être renforcée et étendue.

- European Agreements concerning Programme Exchanges by means of Television films and on the protection of copyright in the context of television broadcasts – measures whereby the Council has brought its unifying influence to bear upon the most powerful contemporary medium for the exchange of ideas.

b) Moreover, there is considerable volume of work in progress. In this connection it is appropriate to draw attention to the work of the Committee of Experts dealing with:
- the draft European Social Charter, which is now nearing completion and which aims at harmonising the social policies of Member countries;
- the draft European Code of Social Security, which aims at raising the Social Security standards of Member countries and harmonising their social charges;
- a proposed European Convention on Moral Persons, whereby it is intended to add to the provisions of the European Convention on Establishment a further agreement covering companies and corporate bodies;
- a proposed European Consular Convention;
- a proposed Convention on a uniform law concerning arbitration in civil and commercial matters;
- a proposed Convention on the reduction of the number of cases of multiple nationality;
- a proposed Convention on the production and marketing of vine products and spirits.

Secondly, note should be taken of the important work in progress:
- in the field of culture;
- in the field of public health, with special emphasis on the Council of Europe Médical Fellowships;
- in the Working Party on the European Civil Service; a number of European organisations participate and of which the Council of Europe assumes the chairmanship;
- in the European Committee on Crime Problems which is working among other things, on the conclusion of a convention covering traffic offences.

Further examples of current useful work are provided:
- by the installation of the European Conference of Local Authorities;
- by the Agreement between the I.L.O. and the Council of Europe on the creation and activities of the International Centre for Vocational Training, Information and Research.

5. In addition, it is clear that in seeking fields of collective action there are still many new tasks to be defined and accomplished before Europe can be regarded as harmonious and closely united.

The Ministers hope that the Consultative Assembly will co-operate with them in the study and implementation of suitable projects.

They for their part will pursue their own efforts in various directions in which intergovernmental co-operation is practicable. They propose to invite the opinion of the Assembly in these matters when they have reached a sufficiently advanced stage.

6. In particular, since the unity of Europe derives largely from its history and its culture, it is chiefly through increased activity in the broad field of education, science and culture that this unity may be strengthened and extended.

Le Comité des Ministres appelle donc l'attention de l'Assemblée Consultative sur les plus récentes décisions qui sont intervenues et sur les plus recents développements qui se sont produits dans ces domaines; il a réaffirmé aujourd'hui sa volonté de promouvoir une action plus étendue et plus systématique de la part du Conseil de l'Europe, en recommandant d'accroître substantiellement le montant des contributions au Fonds Culturel, en invitant les Ministres de l'Éducation à faire connaître leurs vues sur un programme et en convoquant ensuite un comité ad hoc de hauts fonctionnaires ayant pour mandat de présenter un rapport détaillé.

7. Pour que l'esprit d'unité de l'Europe se traduise par des réalisations pratiques, il est indispensable de disposer de l'appui des populations, de leurs représentants élus et des gouvernements de tous les pays membres du Conseil de l'Europe. Mieux l'Assemblée Consultative et le Comité des Ministres réussiront à stimuler et à mettre en oeuvre ce programme par une action positive, même si celle-ci s'exerce sur une échelle réduite, plus il sera facile au Comité des Ministres d'harmoniser progressivement sa politique sur le plan plus vaste des affaires mondiales dans l'esprit du Statut du Conseil de l'Europe.

Le Comité se propose donc de se concentrer sur l'ensemble d'un programme d'action pratique et à cette fin il compte sur l'étroite et fructueuse collaboration du Président, du Bureau et des membres de l'Assemblée Consultative.

F. PUBLICATIONS

(décembre 1960)

1. PUBLICATIONS DE L'ASSEMBLÉE CONSULTATIVE

A la fin de chaque session ou partie de session, les services de l'Assemblée éditent les quatre séries suivantes de recueils:

Compte-rendu des Débats

Sténogramme des discours prononcés au cours de chaque séance. Édition unilingue, depuis 1955; dans les années précédentes bilingue (une page anglaise, une page française).

Documents de Séance

Rapports, propositions de résolution et de recommandation, motions, amendements, *etc.*: tous les documents qui servent de base à la discussion de l'Assemblée.

Texte bilingue (une colonne anglaise, une colonne française).

Textes adoptés

Recueil des textes (recommandations, résolutions, avis, *etc.*) adoptés par l'Assemblée.

Texte bilingue (une colonne anglaise, une colonne française).

Ordres du Jour – Procès-Verbaux

Texte bilingue (une colonne anglaise, une colonne française).

Réunions Jointes: Compte Rendu des Débats

Depuis 1953, les membres de l'Assemblée Consultative du Conseil de l'Europe et les membres de l'Assemblée Commune de la Communauté Européenne du Charbon et de l'Acier (maintenant Assemblée Parlementaire Européenne) tiennent des réunions jointes, dont cette publication donne le compte rendu sténographique (Texte anglais ou français).

The Committee of Ministers therefore invites the attention of the Consultative Assembly to the latest decisions and developments in this field. It has today reasserted its will to promote broader and more systematic action on the part of the Council of Europe, by recommending a substantial increase in contributions to the Cultural Fund, by inviting the Ministers for Education to formulate views on a programme and, thereafter, by convening an *ad hoc* committee of senior officials with the mandate of presenting a detailed Report.

7. The task of giving practical effect to the spirit of unity of Europe requires the support of the people, their elected representatives, and the Governments of all the Member nations of the Council of Europe. The more successful the Consultative Assembly and the Committee of Ministers are in stimulating and carrying out this programme with effective action even on a limited scale, the easier it will be for the Committee of Ministers to harmonise progressively its policies over the broader field of world affairs in the spirit of the Statute of the Council of Europe.

The Committee of Ministers therefore proposes to concentrate upon a full programme of practical tasks and to this end it relies upon close and fruitful collaboration with the President, the Bureau and the members of the Consultative Assembly.

F. PUBLICATIONS

(December 1961)

1. PUBLICATIONS OF THE CONSULTATIVE ASSEMBLY

At the end of each Session, or part-Session, the Assembly Services publish the following four series:

Official Report of Debates

Verbatim record of the speeches made at each Sitting.

Separate editions in English and French, from 1955; previously bilingual (one English and one French page).

Documents (Working Papers)

Reports, draft Resolutions and Recommendations, motions, amendments, *etc.*; all documents used as a basis for discussion in the Assembly.

Bilingual (one English and one French column).

Texts adopted

Compilation of motions (Recommendations, Resolutions, Opinions, *etc.*) adopted by the Assembly.

Bilingual (one English and one French column).

Orders of the Day – Minutes of Proceedings

Bilingual (one English and one French column).

"Joint Meeting": Official Report of the Debate

Since 1953 the members of the Consultative Assembly of the Council of Europe and the members of the Common Assembly of the European Coal and Steel Community (now the European Parliamentary Assembly) have held joint meetings, of which this publication gives the verbatim report. English and French separate editions).

2. TRAITÉS ET CONVENTIONS EUROPÉENS

Dans cette série sont imprimés les textes de tous les accords et conventions conclus entre les Membres du Conseil de l'Europe.

Statut du Conseil de l'Europe

1.
6.
7.
8.
11.

Le texte du Statut (no. 1) et les amendements qui y ont été apportés par la suite (nos. 6, 7 et 11) sont réunis dans une seule brochure (no. 8).

Convention de sauvegarde des Droits de l'Homme et des Libertés fondamentales

5.
9.

Le texte de la Convention (no. 5) et de son Protocole (no. 9) sont réunis dans une seule brochure.

2. *Accord Général sur les Privilèges et Immunités.*
3. *Accord Spécial relatif au Siège du Conseil de l'Europe.*
4. *Accord Complémentaire à l'Accord Général sur les Privilèges et Immunités du Conseil de l'Europe.*

10. *Protocole additionnel à l'Accord Général sur les Privilèges et Immunités du Conseil de l'Europe.*
12. *Accord intérimaire européen concernant les Régimes de Sécurité Sociale relatifs à la Vieillesse, à l'Invalidité et aux Survivants, avec Protocole additionnel.*
13. *Accord intérimaire européen concernant la Sécurité Sociale à l'exclusion des Régimes relatifs à la Vieillesse, à l'Invalidité et aux Survivants, avec Protocole additionnel.*
14. *Convention Européenne d'Assistance Sociale et Médicale, avec Protocole additionnel.*
15. *Convention Européenne relative à l'Équivalence des Diplômes donnant accès aux Établissements Universitaires.*
16. *Convention Européenne relative aux Formalités prescrites pour les Demandes de Brevets.*
17. *Convention Européenne sur la Classification Internationale des Brevets d'Invention.*
18. *Convention Culturelle Européenne.*
19. *Convention Européenne d'Établissement.*
20. *Accord Européen sur l'Échange de Mutilés de Guerre aux fins de traitement médical.*
21. *Convention Européenne sur l'Équivalence des Périodes d'Études Universitaires.*
22. *Deuxième Protocole additionnel à l'Accord Général sur les Privilèges et Immunités du Conseil de l'Europe.*
23. *Convention Européenne pour le Règlement pacifique des Différends.*
24. *Convention Européenne d'Extradition.*
25. *Accord Européen sur le Régime de la libre Circulation des Personnes entre les pays membres du Conseil de l'Europe.*
26. *Accord Européen relatif à l'Échange de Substances thérapeutiques d'origine humaine.*
27. *Arrangement Européen sur l'Échange des Programmes au moyen de Films de Télévision.*
28. *Troisième Protocole additionnel à l'Accord Général sur les Privilèges et Immunités du Conseil de l'Europe.*
29. *Convention Européenne relative à l'Assurance obligatoire de la Responsabilité Civile en matière de Véhicules Automoteurs.*
30. *Convention Européenne d'Entraide judiciaire en matière pénale.*
31. *Accord Européen relatif à la Suppression des Visas pour les Réfugiés.*

2. EUROPEAN TREATY SERIES

The texts of Agreements and Conventions concluded between Members of the Council of Europe are published in the European Treaty Series.

The Statute of the Council of Europe.

1.
6. The original text of the Statute (no. 1) and any subsequent amendments (no.6, 7 and 11) are issued together (no. 8).
7.
8.
11.

The Convention for the Protection of Human Rights and Fundamental Freedoms.

5. The text of the Convention (no. 5) and its Protocol (no. 9) are
9. issued together.
2. *The General Agreement on Privileges and Immunities.*
3. *The Special Agreement relating to the Seat of the Council of Europe.*
4. *The Supplementary Agreement amending certain provisions of the General Agreement on Privileges and Immunities of the Council of Europe.*
10. *The Protocol to the General Agreement on Privileges and Immunities of the Council of Europe.*
12. *Interim Agreement on Social Security Schemes relating to Old Age, Invalidity and Survivors, with Protocol.*
13. *Interim Agreement on Social Security other than Schemes for Old Age, Invalidity and Survivors, with Protocol.*
14. *The Convention on Social and Medical Assistance, with Protocol.*
15. *The Convention on the Equivalence of Diplomas leading to Admission to Universities.*
16. *The Convention relating to the formalities required for Patent Applications.*
17. *The Convention on the International Classification of Patents for Invention.*
18. *European Cultural Convention.*
19. *European Convention on Establishment.*
20. *European Agreement on the Exchange of War Cripples with a view to Medical Treatment.*
21. *European Convention on the Equivalence of Periods of University Study.*
22. *Second Protocol to the General Agreement on Privileges and Immunities of the Council of Europe.*
23. *European Convention for the Peaceful Settlement of Disputes.*
24. *European Convention on Extradition.*
25. *European Agreement on Regulations governing the Movement of Persons between Member States of the Council of Europe.*
26. *European Agreement on the Exchange of Therapeutic Substances of Human Origin.*
27. *European Agreement concerning Programme Exchanges by means of Television Films.*
28. *Third Protocol to the General Agreement on Privileges and Immunities of the Council of Europe.*
29. *European Convention on Compulsory Insurance against Civil Liability in respect of Motor Vehicles.*
30. *European Convention on Mutual Assistance in Criminal Matters.*
31. *European Agreement relating to the Suppression of Visas for Refugees.*

32. *Convention Européenne sur la Reconnaissance académique des Qualifications Universitaires.*
33. *Accord relatif à l'Importation temporaire en franchise de douane, à titre de prêt gratuit et à des fins diagnostiques ou thérapeutiques, de Matériel médico-chirurgical et de Laboratoire destiné aux Établissements sanitaires.*
34. *Arrangement Européen pour la Protection des Émissions de Télévision.*

3. PUBLICATIONS DE CARACTÈRE GÉNÉRAL

L'union de l'Europe: ses progrès, ses problèmes, ses perspectives, sa place dans le monde occidental.
Conférence de Strasbourg entre les délégations du Congrès des États-Unis d'Amérique et de l'Assemblée Consultative du Conseil de l'Europe.

Les objectifs de plein emploi dans le cadre du problème de la Coopération européenne.
„Low Tariff Club".
Le Plan de Strasbourg: Pour une amélioration des relations économiques entre les États membres du Conseil de l'Europe et les pays avec lesquels ils ont des liens constitutionnels.
Procédure de l'Assemblée Consultative (Édition 1961).
Procédure en Commission – Manuel du Président.
Réfugiés et Excédents de Population.
Que faire pour eux?...
Le Statut futur de la Sarre.
Vers un Parlement européen – par Kenneth LINDSAY. – Introduction par Sir Robert BOOTHBY, M.P.
La Commission Européenne des Droits de l'Homme. – Premier supplément au Manuel de Procédure de l'Assemblée Consultative, 1956.
Les Commissions de l'Assemblée Consultative. – Deuxième supplément au Manuel de Procédure de l'Assemblée Consultative, 1956.
Coopération européenne en 1958. – Ière et IIème parties. Rapport du Secrétaire Général, 1959.
Coopération européenne en 1959. – Rapport du Secrétaire Général à l'Assemblée Consultative, 1960.
Coopération européenne en 1960. – Rapport du Secrétaire Général à l'Assemblée Consultative, 1961.
La délinquance juvénile dans l'Europe d'après-guerre.
Rapport annuel du Fonds Culturel du Conseil de l'Europe.
Europe et Afrique.
Hygiène du Camping.

4. BROCHURES ÉDITÉES PAR LA DIRECTION DE L'INFORMATION

Le Conseil de l'Europe (1959) (Remplace le Petit Manuel)
Existe en français, anglais, allemand, néerlandais, italien, suédois, norvégien, danois, islandais, grec, turc, irlandais.
Convention Européenne des Droits de l'Homme
Éditions en français, anglais, allemand.
La Culture européenne et le Conseil de l'Europe
Deuxième édition disponible en anglais et allemand seulement.

5. PUBLICATIONS PÉRIODIQUES

La Direction de l'Information du Conseil de l'Europe publie aussi chaque mois, dans les deux langues officielles, *Les Nouvelles du Conseil de l'Europe,*

32. *European Convention on the Academic Recognition of University Qualifications.*
33. *Agreement on the Temporary Importation, free of duty, of Medical Surgical and Laboratory Equipment for use on Free Loan in Hospitals and other Medical Institutions for Purposes of Diagnosis or Treatment.*
34. *European Agreement on the Protection of Television Broadcasts.*

3. GENERAL LIST

The Union of Europe: its progress, problems, prospects, and place in the Western World.
Conference of Strasbourg between delegations of the Congress of the United States of America and of the Consultative Assembly of the Council of Europe.
Full employment objectives *in relation to the problem of European co-operation.*
Low Tariff Club.
The Strasbourg Plan: proposals for improving the economic relations between Member States of the Council of Europe and the overseas countries with which they have constitutional links.
Procedure of the Consultative Assembly (Edition 1961).
Committee Practice and Procedure: a Chairman's Handbook.
Refugees and Surplus Elements of Population.
No Room for Them?...
The Future Position of the Saar.
Towards a European Parliament – by Kenneth LINDSAY. – Introduction by Sir Robert BOOTHBY, M.P.
The European Commission of Human Rights. – 1st Supplement to the Manual of Procedure of the Consultative Assembly, 1956.
Committees of the Consultative Assembly. – 2nd Supplement to the Manual of Procedure of the Consultative Assembly, 1956.
European Co-operation in 1958. – First and Second Part. Report of the Secretary-General, 1959.
European Co-operation in 1959. – Report of the Secretary-General, 1960.
European Co-operation in 1960. – Report of the Secretary-General, 1961.
Juvenile Delinquency in Post-war Europe.
Annual Report of the Cultural Fund of the Council of Europe.
Europe and Africa.
Camping Hygiene.

4. BOOKLETS PUBLISHED BY THE DIRECTORATE OF INFORMATION

The Council of Europe (1959) (replacing the Concise Handbook).
Obtainable in French English, German, Dutch, Italian, Swedish, Norwegian, Danish, Icelandic, Greek, Turkish and Irish.
European Convention on Human Rights
French, English and German editions.
European Culture and the Council of Europe
Second edition available in English and German.

5. PERIODICAL PUBLICATIONS

Council of Europe News. – Information bulletin on the activities of the Council of Europe, published monthly in the two official languages bulletin d'information sur les activités du Conseil. Depuis avril 1959 (en anglais seulement) cette Direction publie un bulletin bi-mensuel, destiné à un public plus large, sous le titre de *Forward in Europe*.

La Section documentaire de la Bibliothèque du Conseil de l'Europe, de son côté, fait paraître: *Recherches*, périodique d'information bibliographique et documentaire.

Données Statistiques, recueil de statistiques européennes (publication annuelle).

Documentation sur les problèmes sociaux (bulletin multilingue paraissant tous les trois mois).

G. LISTE DES POSTES SUPÉRIEURS AU SECRÉTARIAT GÉNÉRAL

au 31 décembre 1960

Le siège du Conseil de l'Europe est établi à la Maison de l'Europe, Strasbourg, France. – Bureau à Paris: 55, Avenue Kléber, Paris, 16e.

Secrétaire Général:	M. Lodovico BENVENUTI (Italien)
Secrétaire Général adjoint:	M. Dunstan CURTIS (Britannique)
Greffier de l'Assemblée:	M. Gerhart SCHLOESSER (Allemand)
Directeur Politique:	(*vacant*)
Directeur de l'Information et de la Presse:	M. Paul M. G. LEVY (Belge)
Directeur des Droits de l'Homme et Greffier de la Cour Européenne:	M. Polys MODINOS (Grec)
Directeur des Affaires Économiques et Sociales:	M. Ömer SARC (Turc)
Directeur des Affaires Administratives:	M. Armand DAUSSIN (Belge)
Chef du Service Juridique:	M. Gerrit von HAEFTEN (Allemand)
Chef du Service des Relations Extérieures:	M. Sf. SFORZA (Italien) (a.i.)
Chef des Services Généraux:	M. Georges CUNIN (Français)

by the Directorate of Information. Since April 1959, this Directorate has published (in English only) a bi-monthly bulletin designed for a wider public under the title *Forward in Europe.*

The Documentation Section of the Library of the Council of Europe has published:

Research: Bibliographical and documentary bulletin.

Statistical Data: European statistics compilation (annual edition).

Documentary Material on Social Problems (multi-lingual bibliographical bulletin appearing quarterly).

G. LIST OF PRINCIPAL OFFICERS OF THE SECRETARIAT-GENERAL

as at 31st Decemcer, 1960

The Seat of the Council of Europe is the House of Europe, Strasbourg, France. - Paris Office: 55, Avenue Kléber, Paris 16e.

Secretary-General:	M. Lodovico BENVENUTI (Italian)
Deputy Secretary-General:	M. Dunstan CURTIS (British)
Clerk of the Assembly:	M. Gerhart SCHLOESSER (German)
Political Director:	(*Vacant*)
Director of Press and Information:	M. Paul M.G. LEVY (Belgian)
Director of Human Rights and Registrar of the European Court:	M. Polys MODINOS (Greek)
Director of Economic and Social Affairs:	M. Ömer SARC (Turkish)
Director of Administration:	M. Armand DAUSSIN (Belgian)
Head of the Legal Department:	M. Gerrit von HAEFTEN (German)
Head of the External Relations Department:	M. Sf. SFORZA (Italian) (acting)
Head of General Services:	M. Georges CUNIN (French)

H. ÉTAT DES DÉPÔTS DES RATIFICATION

1. Accord Général sur les Privilèges et Immunités du Conseil de l'Europe.
2. Protocole additionnel à l'Accord Général sur les Privilèges et Immunités du Conseil de l'Europe.
3. Deuxième Protocole additionnel à l'Accord Général sur les Privilèges et Immunités du Conseil de l'Europe (Dispositions relatives aux membres de la Commission européenne des Droits de l'Homme).
4. Troisième Protocole additionnel à l'Accord Général sur les Privilèges et Immunités du Conseil de l'Europe (Fonds de Réétablissement pour les Réfugiés nationaux et les Excédents de population en Europe).
5. Convention de sauvegarde des Droits de l'Homme et des Libertés fondamentales.
6. Protocole additionnel à la Convention de sauvegarde des Droits de l'Homme et des Libertés fondamentales.
7. Déclaration relative à l'article 25 de la Convention de sauvegarde des Droits de l'Homme et des Libertés fondamentales (Droit de recours individuel).
8. Déclaration relative à l'article 46 de la Convention de sauvegarde des Droits de l'Homme et des Libertés fondamentales (Juridiction de la Cour).
9. Accord intérimaire européen concernant la Sécurité Sociale à l'exclusion des régimes relatifs à la vieillesse, à l'invalidité et aux survivants.
10. Protocole additionnel à l'Accord intérimaire européen concernant la Sécurité Sociale à l'exclusion des régimes relatifs à la vieillesse, à l'invalidité et aux survivants.
11. Accord intérimaire européen concernant les régimes de Sécurité Sociale relatifs à la vieillesse, à l'invalidité et aux survivants.
12. Protocole additionnel à l'Accord intérimaire européen concernant les régimes de Sécurité Sociale relatifs à la vieillesse, à l'invalidité et aux survivants.
13. Convention européenne d'Assistance sociale et médicale.
14. Protocole additionnel à la Convention européenne d'Assistance sociale et médicale.
15. Convention européenne relative à l'Équivalence des Diplômes donnant accès aux établissements universitaires.

	PRIVILÈGES ET IMMUNITÉS *			
(*voir titres ci-contre*)	**1**	**2**	**3**	**4**
Date et lieu de la signature	Paris 2.IX.1949	Strasbourg 6.XI.1952	Paris 15.XII.1956	Strasbourg 6.III.1959
Conditions d'entrée en vigueur	7 ratifications	Ratification par tous les Membres ayant ratifié l'Accord	3 ratifications	3 ratifications
Date d'entrée en vigueur...	**10.IX.1952**	**11.VII.1956**	**15.XII.1956**	
Autriche	Adhésion 9.V.1957	Adhésion 9.V.1957	13.XI.1958	non membre du Fonds
Belgique	5.IV.1951	24.VII.1953	**n.r.**	**n.r.**
Danemark ...	2.IX.1953	2.IX.1953	15.XII.1956	non membre du Fonds
France	**n.r.**	**n.r.**	**n.r.**	signé le 17.III.1959 **n.r.**
République Fédér. d'Allemagne	*a*) Adhésion 10.IX.1954	*a*) Adhésion 10.IX.1954	7.VII.1960	signé le 18.III.1959 **n.r.**
Grèce	17.XI.1953	17.XI.1953	2.II.1961	signé le 18.III.1959 **n.r.**
Islande	*a*) Adhésion 11.III.1955	*a*) Adhésion 11.III.1955	15.XII.1956	signé le 20.IV.1959 **n.r.**
Irlande	**n.r.**	**n.r.**	non signé	non membre du Fonds
Italie	7.II.1952	11.VII.1956	4.VI.1958	**n.r.**
Luxembourg .	10.IX.1952	29.VI.1953	8.I.1960	13.IX.1960
Pays-Bas	18.III.1950	19.VI.1953	29.IV.1957	non membre du Fonds
Norvège......	1.XII.1949	24.IV.1953	15.XII.1956	non membre du Fonds
Suède	25.IX.1950	30.IV.1953	15.XII.1956	non membre du Fonds
Turquie	7.I.1960	7.I.1960	7.I.1960	signé le 31.III.1959
Royaume-Uni.	25.IX.1950	19.XI.1954	8.VII.1958	non membre du Fonds

* n.r. = non ratifié ou Déclaration non faite
a) Entré en vigueur le 11.VII.1956.

ES CONVENTIONS ET ACCORDS DU CONSEIL DE L'EUROPE

DROITS DE L'HOMME * ET LIBERTÉS FONDAMENTALES				SÉCURITÉ SOCIALE *			
5	**6**	**7**	**8**	**9**	**10**	**11**	**12**
Rome 4.XI.1950	Paris 20.III.1952	Rome 4.XI.1950	Rome 4.XI.1950	Paris 11.XII.1953	Paris 11.XII.1953	Paris 11.XII.1953	Paris 11.XII.1953
10 ratifications	10 ratifications	6 déclarations	8 déclarations	2 ratifications	2 ratifications	2 ratifications	2 ratifications
3.IX.1953	**18.V.1954**	**5.VII.1955** c)	**3.IX.1958** c)	**1.VII.1954**	**1.X.1954**	**1.VII.1954**	**1.X.1954**
3.IX.1958	3.IX.1958	3 ans oui 3.IX.1958	3 ans	non signé	non signé	non signé	non signé
14.VI.1955	14.VI.1955	oui 5 ans 30.VI.1959	5 ans 29.VI.1955	3.IV.1957	3.IV.1957	3.IV.1957	3.IV.1957
13.IV.1953	13.IV.1953	oui 5 ans 7.IV.1957	oui 3 ans 7.IV.1959	30.VI.1954	non signé	30.VI.1954	non signé
n.r.	**n.r.**	**n.r.**	**n.r.**	18.XII.1957	18.XII.1957	18.XII.1957	18.XII.1957
5.XII.1952	13.II.1957	3 ans oui 1.VII.1958	3 ans	24.VIII.1956	24.VIII.1956	24.VIII.1956	24.VIII.1956
28.III.1953	28.III.1953	**n.r.**	**n.r.**	**n.r.**	**n.r.**	**n.r.**	**n.r.**
29.VI.1953	29.VI.1953	oui 25.III.1960	oui 3 ans 23.VIII.1958	**n.r.**	**n.r.**	**n.r.**	**n.r.**
25.II.1953	25.II.1953	oui 25.II.1953		31.III.1954	31.III.1954	31.III.1954	31.III.1954
26.X.1955	26.X.1955	**n.r.**	**n.r.**	26.VIII.1958	26.VIII.1958	26.VIII.1958	26.VIII.1958
3.IX.1953	3.IX.1953	3 ans oui 18.IV.1958	3 ans	18.XI.1958	18.XI.1958	18.XI.1958	18.XI.1958
31.VIII.1954 b)	31.VIII.1954 b)	oui d)	oui 5 ans 31.VIII.1954	11.III.1955	11.III.1955	11.III.1955	11.III.1955
15.I.1952	18.XII.1952	oui 2 ans 9.XII.1959	**n.r.**	9.IX.1954	9.IX.1954	9.IX.1954	9.IX.1954
4.II.1952	22.VI.1953	oui 4.II.1952	**n.r.**	2.IX.1955	2.IX.1955	2.IX.1955	2.IX.1955
18.V.1954	18.V.1954	**n.r.**	**n.r.**	**n.r.**	**n.r.**	**n.r.**	**n.r.**
8.III.1951 a)	3.XI.1952	**n.r.**	**n.r.**	7.IX.1954	7.IX.1954	7.IX.1954	7.IX.1954

n.r. = non ratifié ou Déclaration non faite
La Convention a été étendue le 23.X.1953 à 42 territoires.
La Convention, à l'exclusion de l'article 6 paragr. 3*c*, et le Protocole ont été étendus le 1.XII.1955 au Surinam et aux Antilles néerlandaises.
Dates à partir desquelles les délais indiqués dans les déclarations ont commencé à courir.
A partir du 28 juin 1960 jusqu'au 31 août 1964.

H. ÉTAT DES DÉPÔTS DES RATIFICATION

	ASSISTANCE SOCIALE * ET MÉDICALE		DIPLÔMES *	CULTU- * RELLE	ÉQUI- * VALENCE ÉTUDES	QUALIFI- * CATIONS UNIVER- SITAIRES	BREVETS *
voir titres ci-contre)	**13**	**14**	**15**	**16**	**17**	**18**	**19**
Date et lieu de la signature	Paris 11.XII.1953	Paris 11.XII.1953	Paris 11.XII.1953	Paris 19.XII.1954	Paris 15.XII.1956	Paris 14.XII.1959	Paris 11.XII.1953
Conditions d'entrée en vigueur	2 ratifications	2 ratifications	3 ratifications	3 ratifications	3 ratifications	3 ratifications	4 ratifications
Date d'entrée en vigueur	**1.VII.1954**	**1.VII.1954**	**20.IV.1954**	**5.V.1955** [a]	**18.IX.1957**		**1.VI.1955** [b]
Autriche	non signé	non signé	Adhésion 9.X.1956	4.III.1958	2.X.1957	6.XII.1960	non signé
Belgique	24.VII.1956	24.VII.1956	14.VI.1955	11.V.1955	**n.r.**	**n.r.**	**n.r.**
Danemark	30.VI.1954	30.VI.1954	20.IV.1954	7.V.1955	23.VI.1958	non signé	3.IX.1956
France	30.X.1957	30.X.1957	11.III.1955	19.III.1955	19.II.1958	**n.r.**	**n.r.**
République Fédér. d'Allemagne.....	24.VIII.1956	24.VIII.1956	3.III.1955	17.XI.1955	**n.r.**	non signé	17.V.1955
Grèce	23.VI.1960	23.VI.1960	5.XII.1955	**n.r.**	signé le 16.IX.1960 **n.r.**	**n.r.**	15.VI.1955
Islande	**n.r.**	**n.r.**	5.VIII.1954	1.III.1956	**n.r.**	**n.r.**	
Irlande	31.III.1954	31.III.1954	31.III.1954	11.III.1955	20.II.1957	non signé	17.VI.1954
Italie	1.VII.1958	1.VII.1958	31.X.1956	16.V.1957	29.III.1958	**n.r.**	17.X.1958
Luxembourg	18.XI.1958	18.XI.1958	12.I.1955	30.VII.1956	**n.r.**	**n.r.**	4.VII.1957
Pays-Bas	20.VII.1955	20.VII.1955	27.VIII.1956	8.II.1956	10.XII.1959	**n.r.**	9.V.1956
Norvège	9.IX.1954	9.IX.1954	21.V.1954	24.I.1956	14.III.1957	**n.r.**	21.V.1954
Suède	2.IX.1955	2.IX.1955	27.V.1960	16.VI.1958	**n.r.**	non signé	28.VI.1957
Turquie	**n.r.**	**n.r.**	10.X.1957	10.X.1957	18.II.1960	**n.r.**	22.X.1956
Royaume-Uni	7.IX.1954	7.IX.1954	22.III.1954	5.V.1955	18.IX.1957	13.II.1961	5.V.1955

* n.r. = non ratifié ou Déclaration non faite.
a) L'Espagne a adhéré à cette Convention le 4.VII.1957.
b) L'Afrique du Sud a adhéré à cette Convention le 28.XI.1957 et la Suisse le 28.XII.1959.

ES CONVENTIONS ET ACCORDS DU CONSEIL DE L'EUROPE

BREVETS *	FILMS DE TÉLÉVISION *	PROTECTION ÉMISSIONS TÉLÉVISION *	ÉTABLISSEMENT *	RÈGLEMENT PACIFIQUE *	EXTRADITION *	ENTRAIDE PÉNALE *	ASSURANCE VÉHICULES *
20	**21**	**22**	**23**	**24**	**25**	**26**	**27**
Paris 19.XII.1954	Paris 15.XII.1958	Strasbourg 22.VI.1966	Paris 13.XII.1955	Strasbourg 29.IV.1957	Paris 13.XII.1957	Strasbourg 20.IV.1959	Strasbourg 20.IV.1959
4 ratifications	3 ratifications	3 ratifications	5 ratifications	2 ratifications	3 ratifications	3 ratifications	4 ratifications
1.VIII.1955 *a)*				**30.IV.1958**	**18.IV.1960**		
non signé	non signé	non signé	signé le 13.XII.1957 **n.r.**	15.I.1960	**n.r.**	**n.r.**	**n.r.**
16.V.1955	**n.r.**	signé le 13.IX.1960 **n.r.**	**n.r.**	**n.r.**	**n.r.**	**n.r.**	**n.r.**
23.IX.1957	**n.r.**	**n.r.**	**n.r.**	17.VII.1959	**n.r.**	**n.r.**	non signé
1.VII.1955	15.XII.1958	22.VI.1960	**n.r.**	**n.r.**	**n.r.**	non signé	**n.r.**
28.XI.1955	non signé	signé le 11.VII.1960 **n.r.**	**n.r.**	**n.r.**	**n.r.**	**n.r.**	**n.r.**
n.r.	**n.r.**	**n.r.**	**n.r.**	**n.r.**	**n.r.**	**n.r.**	**n.r.**
non signé	non signé	non signé	**n.r.**	**n.r.**	non signé	non signé	non signé
11.III.1955	non signé	**n.r.**	non signé	**n.r.**	non signé	non signé	non signé
9.I.1957	**n.r.**	**n.r.**	**n.r.**	29.I.1960	**n.r.**	**n.r.**	**n.r.**
non signé	**n.r.**	signé le 13.IX.1960 **n.r.**	**n.r.**	**n.r.**	**n.r.**	**n.r.**	**n.r.**
12.I.1956	non signé	non signé	**n.r.**	7.VII.1958	non signé	non signé	non signé
11.III.1955	signé le 17.XI.1959 **n.r.**	non signé	20.XI.1957	27.III.1958	19.I.1960	non signé	**n.r.**
28.VI.1957	**n.r.**	signé le 3.VIII.1960 **n.r.**	**n.r.**	30.IV.1958	22.I.1959	**n.r.**	**n.r.**
22.X.1956	**n.r.**	**n.r.**	**n.r.**	signé le 8.V.1958 **n.r.**	7.I.1960	signé le 23.X.1959 **n.r.**	non signé
28.X.1955	15.XII.1958	signé le 13.VII.1960 **n.r.**	signé le 24.II.1956 **n.r.**	7.XII.1960	non signé	non signé	non signé

* n.r. = non ratifié ou Déclaration non faite.
a) L'Australie a adhéré à cette Convention le 7.III.1958 (entrée en vigueur: 24.V.1958).

H. ÉTAT DES DÉPÔTS DES RATIFICATIONS DES CONVENTIONS ET ACCORDS DU CONSEIL DE L'EUROPE

	MUTILÉS * DE GUERRE	SANG * HUMAIN	MATÉRIEL * MÉDICO-CHIRURGICAL	CIRCULATION * PERSONNES	VISAS * RÉFUGIÉS
(*voir titres ci-contre*)	**28**	**29**	**30**	**31**	**32**
Date et lieu de la signature	Paris 13.XII.1955	Paris 15.XII.1958	Strasbourg 28.IV.1960	Paris 13.XII.1957	Strasbourg 20.IV.1959
Conditions d'entrée en vigueur	3 ratifications	3 ratifications	3 ratifications	3 ratifications	3 ratifications
Date d'entrée en vigueur...	**1.I.1956**	**1.I.1959**	**29.VII.1960**	**1.I.1958**	**3.IX.1960**
Autriche	13.XII.1957	**n.r.**	non signé	30.V.1958	non signé
Belgique	29.IV.1959	15.XII.1958	8.VI.1960	13.XII.1957	20.IV.1959
Danemark ...	5.VI.1957	non signé	**n.r.**	non signé	*b)* 30.XI.1960
France	13.XII.1955	2.VI.1960	28.IV.1960	13.XII.1957	20.IV.1959
République Fédér. d'Allemagne	13.XII.1955	**n.r.**	**n.r.**	30.V.1958	**n.r.**
Grèce	5.VI.1959	2.II.1961	**n.r.**	*a)* 13.XII.1957	non signé
Islande	non signé	non signé	non signé	non signé	non signé
Irlande	13.XII.1955	15.XII.1958	28.IV.1960	non signé	non signé
Italie	17.I.1957	**n.r.**	**n.r.**	13.XII.1957	non signé
Luxembourg .	26.III.1958	**n.r.**	**n.r.**	**n.r.**	**n.r.**
Pays-Bas	22.X.1958	signé le 26.II.1959	non signé	24.II.1961	3.VIII.1960
Norvège......	21.IX.1956	15.XII.1958	28.IV.1960	non signé	*b)* 25.XI.1960
Suède	3.III.1956	15.XII.1958	**n.r.**	non signé	*b)* 30.XI.1960
Turquie	7.X.1959	**n.r.**	non signé	non signé	non signé
Royaume-Uni.	13.VII.1956	non signé	28.IV.1960	non signé	non signé

16. Convention culturelle eurc péenne.
17. Convention européenne su l'Équivalence des Périodes d'é tudes universitaires.
18. Convention européenne sur l Reconnaissance académique de Qualifications universitaires.
19. Convention européenne relativ aux Formalités prescrites pou les Demandes de Brevets.
20. Convention européenne sur l Classification internationale de Brevets d'invention.
21. Arrangement européen sur l'É change des Programmes au moyen de Films de télévision
22. Arrangement européen pou la protection des émissions d télévision.
23. Convention européenne d'Éta blissement.
24. Convention européenne pour l Règlement pacifique des dif férends.
25. Convention européenne d'Ex tradition.
26. Convention européenne d'En traide judiciaire en matière pénale.
27. Convention européenne relative à l'Assurance obligatoire de la Responsabilité civile en matière de véhicules automoteurs.
28. Accord sur l'Échange des Mutilés de guerre entre les pays membres du Conseil de l'Europe aux fins de traite ment médical.
29. Accord européen relatif à l'Échange de Substances thé rapeutiques d'origine humaine
30. Accord pour l'importation temporaire en franchise de douane, à titre de prêt gratuit et à des fins diagnostiques ou thérapeutiques, de matériel médico-chirurgical et de labo ratoire destiné aux établisse ments sanitaires.
31. Accord européen sur le Régime de la Circulation des personnes entre les pays membres du Conseil de l'Europe.
32. Accord européen relatif à la Suppression des Visas pour les Réfugiés.

* n.r. = non ratifié ou Déclaration non faite.

a) La Grèce a fait application de la faculté prévue à l'article 7 qui permet de ne pas appliquer immédiatement le présent Accord. Toutefois, l'entrée en Grèce pour une période de 3 mois est accordée aux ressortissants de l'Autriche, de la Belgique, de la France, de la Rép. Fédér. d'Allemagne, de l'Italie et du Luxembourg, qui sont munis d'un des documents visés à l'Accord.

b) Entrée en vigueur: 1.I.1961.

CHART SHOWING THE DEPOSIT OF RATIFICATIONS OF COUNCIL OF EUROPE CONVENTIONS AND AGREEMENTS

1. General Agreement on Privileges and Immunities of the Council of Europe.
2. Protocol to the General Agreement on Privileges and Immunities of the Council of Europe.
3. Second Protocol to the General Agreement on Privileges and Immunities of the Council of Europe (Provisions regarding members of the European Commission of Human Rights).
4. Third Protocol to the General Agreement on Privileges and Immunities of the Council of Europe (Resettlement Fund for National Refugees and Over-population in Europe).
5. Convention for the Protection of Human Rights and Fundamental Freedoms.
6. Protocol to the Convention for the Protection of Human Rights and Fundamental Freedoms.
7. Declaration regarding Article 25 of the Convention for the Protection of Human Rights and Fundamental Freedoms (Right of Individual Petition).
8. Declaration regarding Article 46 of the Convention for the Protection of Human Rights and Fundamental Freedoms (Jurisdiction of the Court).
9. European Interim Agreement on Social Security other than Schemes for Old Age, Invalidity and Survivors.
10. Protocol to the European Interim Agreement on Social Security other than Schemes for Old Age, Invalidity and Survivors.
11. European Interim Agreement on Social Security Schemes relating to Old Age, Invalidity and Survivors.
12. Protocol to the European Interim Agreement on Social Security Schemes relating to Old Age, Invalidity and Survivors.
13. European Convention on Social and Medical Assistance.
14. Protocol to the European Convention on Social and Medical Assistance.
15. European Convention on the Equivalence of Diplomas leading to Admission to Universities.

	PRIVILEGES * AND IMMUNITIES			
(*see titles opposite*)	1	2	3	4
Date and place of signature..	Paris 2.IX.1949	Strasbourg 6.XI.1952	Paris 15.XII.1956	Strasbourg 6.III.1959
Conditions of entry into force........	7 ratifications	Ratification by all Members which have ratified the Agreement	3 ratifications	3 ratifications
Date of entry into force....	**10.IX.1952**	**11.VII.1956**	**15.XII.1956**	
Austria	Accession 9.V.1957	Accession 9.V.1957	13.XI.1958	not a Member of the Fund
Belgium......	5.IV.1951	24.VII.1953	**n.r.**	**n.r.**
Denmark	2.IX.1953	2.IX.1953	15.XII.1956	not a Member of the Fund
France	**n.r.**	**n.r.**	**n.r.**	signed 17.III.1959 **n.r.**
Federal Republic of Germany	*a*) Accession 10.IX.1954	*a*) Accession 10.IX.1954	7.VII.1960	signed 18.III.1959 **n.r.**
Greece	17.XI.1953	17.XI.1953	2.II.1961	signed 18.III.1959 **n.r.**
Iceland	*a*) Accession 11.III.1955	*a*) Accession 11.III.1955	15.XII.1956	signed 20.IV.1959 **n.r.**
Ireland	**n.r.**	**n.r.**	not signed	not a Member of the Fund
Italy	7.II.1952	11.VII.1956	4.VI.1958	**n.r.**
Luxembourg .	10.IX.1952	29.VI.1953	8.I.1960	13.IX.1960
Netherlands ..	18.III.1950	19.VI.1953	29.IV.1957	not a Member of the Fund
Norway	1.XII.1949	24.IV.1953	15.XII.1956	not a Member of the Fund
Sweden	25.IX.1950	30.IV.1953	15.XII.1956	not a Member of the Fund
Turkey	7.I.1960	7.I.1960	7.I.1960	signed 30.III.1959
United Kingdom	25.IX.1950	19.XI.1954	8.VII.1958	not a Member of the Fund

* n.r. = not ratified or no Declaration made.

a) Entered into force on 11.VII.1956.

H. CHART SHOWING THE DEPOSIT OF RATIFICATION

	HUMAN RIGHTS * AND FUNDAMENTAL FREEDOMS				SOCIAL SECURITY *		
(see titles opposite)	**5**	**6**	**7**	**8**	**9**	**10**	**11**
Date and place of signature	Rome 4.XI.1950	Paris 20.III.1962	Rome 4.XI.1950	Rome 4.XI.1950	Paris 11.XII.1953	Paris 11.XII.1953	Paris 11.XII.1953
Conditions of entry into force	10 ratifications	10 ratifications	6 acceptances	8 acceptances	2 ratifications	2 ratifications	2 ratifications
Date of entry into force	**3.IX.1953**	**18.V.1954**	**5.VII.1955** c)	**3.IX.1958** c)	**1.VII.1954**	**1.X.1954**	**1.VII.1954**
Austria	3.IX.1958	3.IX.1958	3 years yes 3.IX.1958	3 years	not signed	not signed	not signed
Belgium	14.VI.1955	14.VI.1955	yes 5 years 30.VI.1959	5 years 29.VI.1955	3.IV.1957	3.IV.1957	3.IV.1957
Denmark	13.IV.1953	13.IV.1953	yes 5 years 7.IV.1957	yes 3 years 7.IV.1959	30.VI.1954	not signed	30.VI.1954
France	**n.r.**	**n.r.**	**n.r.**	**n.r.**	18.XII.1957	18.XII.1957	18.XII.1957
Federal Republic of Germany	5.XII.1952	13.II.1957	yes 3 years I.VII.1953	3 years	24.VIII.1956	24.VIII.1956	24.VIII.1956
Greece...........	28.III.1953	28.III.1953	**n.r.**	**n.r.**	**n.r.**	**n.r.**	**n.r.**
Iceland	29.VI.1953	29.VI.1953	yes 25.III.1955	yes 3 years 23.VIII.1958	**n.r.**	**n.r.**	**n.r.**
Ireland	25.II.1953	25.II.1953	yes 25.II.1953		31.III.1954	31.III.1954	31.III.1954
Italy	26.X.1955	26.X.1955	**n.r.**	**n.r.**	26.VIII.1958	26.VIII.1958	26.VIII.1958
Luxembourg	3.IX.1953	3.IX.1953	3 years yes 18.IV.1958	3 years	18.XI.1958	18.XI.1958	18.XI.1958
Netherlands	31.VIII.1954 b)	31.VIII.1954 b)	yes d)	yes 5 years 31.VIII.1954	11.III.1955	11.III.1955	11.III.1955
Norway	15.I.1952	18.XII.1952	yes 2 years 9.XII.1959	**n.r.**	9.IX.1954	9.IX.1954	9.IX.1954
Sweden	4.II.1952	22.VI.1953	yes 4.II.1952	**n.r.**	2.IX.1955	2.IX.1955	2.IX.1955
Turkey	18.V.1954	18.V.1954	**n.r.**	**n.r.**	**n.r.**	**n.r.**	**n.r.**
United Kingdom..	8.III.1951 a)	3.XI.1962	**n.r.**	**n.r.**	7.IX.1954	7.IX.1954	7.IX.1954

* n.r. = not ratified or no Declaration made.

a) The Convention was extended to 42 territories on 23.X.1953.

b) The Convention, with the exception of Article 6, paragraph 3*c*, and the Protocol were extended on 1.12.1955 to Surinam and the Netherlands Antilles.

c) Dates from which the time-limits indicated in the declarations began to run.

d) From 28th June, 1960 until 31st August, 1964.

F COUNCIL OF EUROPE CONVENTIONS AND AGREEMENTS

	SOCIAL and MEDICAL * ASSISTANCE		DIPLOMAS *	CULTURAL *	EQUIVA- * LENCE OF PERIODS OF STUDY	UNI- * VERSITY QUALIFI- CATIONS	PATENTS *
12	**13**	**14**	**15**	**16**	**17**	**18**	**19**
Paris 11.XII.1953	Paris 11.XII.1953	Paris 11.XII.1953	Paris 11.XII.1953	Paris 19.XII.1954	Paris 15.XII.1956	Paris 14.XII.1959	Paris 11.XII.1953
2 ratifications	2 ratifications	2 ratifications	3 ratifications	3 ratifications	3 ratifications	3 ratifications	4 ratifications
1.X.1954	**1.VII.1954**	**1.VII.1954**	**20.IV.1954**	**5.V.1955**[a]	**18.IX.1957**		**1.VI.1955**[b]
not signed	not signed	not signed	Accession 9.X.1956	4.III.1958	2.X.1957	6.XII.1960	not signed
3.IV.1957	24.VII.1956	24.VII.1956	14.VI.1955	11.V.1955	**n.r.**	**n.r.**	**n.r.**
not signed	30.VI.1954	30.VI.1954	20.IV.1954	7.V.1955	23.VI.1958	not signed	3.I.X1956
18.XII.1957	30.X.1957	30.X.1957	11.III.1955	19.III.1955	19.II.1958	**n.r.**	**n.r.**
24.VIII.1956	24.VIII.1956	24.VIII.1956	3.III.1955	17.XI.1955	**n.r.**	not signed	17.V.1955
n.r.	23.VI.1960	23.VI.1960	5.XII.1955	**n.r.**	not signed 16.IX.1960 **n.r.**	**n.r.**	15.VI.1955
n.r.	**n.r.**	**n.r.**	5.VIII.1954	1.III.1956	**n.r.**	**n.r.**	
31.III.1954	31.III.1954	31.III.1954	31.III.1954	11.III.1955	20.II.1957	not signed	17.VI.1954
26.VIII.1958	1.VII.1958	1.VII.1958	31.X.1956	16.V.1957	29.III.1958	**n.r.**	17.X.1958
18.XI.1958	18.XI.1958	18.XI.1958	12.I.1955	30.VII.1956	**n.r.**	**n.r.**	4.VII.1957
11.III.1955	20.VII.1955	20.VII.1955	27.VIII.1956	8.II.1956	10.XII.1958	**n.r.**	9.V.1956
9.IX.1954	9.IX.1954	9.IX.1954	21.V.1954	24.I.1956	14.III.1957	**n.r.**	21.V.1954
2.IX.1955	2.IX.1955	2.IX.1955	27.V.1960	16.VI.1958	**n.r.**	not signed	28.VI.1957
n.r.	**n.r.**	**n.r.**	10.X.1957	10.X.1957	18.II.1960	**n.r.**	22.X.1956
7.IX.1954	7.IX.1954	7.IX.1954	22.III.1954	5.V.1955	18.IX.1957	13.II.1961	5.V.1955

n.r. = not ratified or no Declaration made.
) Spain adhered to this Convention on 4.VII.1957.
South Africa adhered to this Convention on 28.XI.1957 and Switzerland on 28.XII.1959

H. CHART SHOWING THE DEPOSIT OF RATIFICATIO

	PATENTS *	TELE- * VISION FILMS	PRO. TECTION * TELEVISION BROAD-CASTS	* ESTABLISH-MENT	PEACEFUL * SETTLE-MENT	EXTRA- * DITION	AS- * SISTANCI CRIMINAI MATTERS
see titles opposite)	**20**	**21**	**22**	**23**	**24**	**25**	**26**
Date and place of signature	Paris 19.XII.1954	Paris 15.XII.1958	Strasbourg 22.VI.1960	Paris 13.XII.1955	Strasbourg 29.IV.1957	Paris 13.XII.1957	Strasbourg 20.IV.1959
Conditions of entry into force	4 ratifications	3 ratifications	3 ratifications	5 ratifications	2 ratifications	3 ratifications	3 ratification
Date of entry into force	**1.VIII.1955** a)				**30.IV.1958**	**18.IV.1960**	
Austria	not signed	not signed	not signed	signed 13.XII.1957 **n.r.**	15.I.1960	**n.r.**	**n.r.**
Belgium	16.V.1955	**n.r.**	signed 13.IX.1960 **n.r.**	**n.r.**	**n.r.**	**n.r.**	**n.r.**
Denmark	23.IX.1957	**n.r.**	**n.r.**	**n.r.**	17.VII.1959	**n.r.**	**n.r.**
France	1.VII.1955	15.XII.1958	22.VI.1960	**n.r.**	**n.r.**	**n.r.**	not signed
Federal Republic of Germany	28.XI.1955	not signed	**n.r.** signed 11.VII.1960	**n.r.**	**n.r.**	**n.r.**	**n.r.**
Greece...........	**n.r.**	**n.r.**	**n.r.**	**n.r.**	**n.r.**	**n.r.**	**n.r.**
Iceland	not signed	not signed	not signed	**n.r.**	**n.r.**	not signed	not signed
Ireland	11.III.1955	not signed	**n.r.**	not signed	**n.r.**	not signed	not signed
Italy	9.I.1957	**n.r.**	**n.r.**	**n.r.**	29.I.1960	**n.r.**	**n.r.**
Luxembourg	not signed	**n.r.**	signed 13.IX.1960 **n.r.**	**n.r.**	**n.r.**	**n.r.**	**n.r.**
Netherlands	12.I.1956	not signed	not signed	**n.r.**	7.VII.1958	not signed	not signed
Norway	11.III.1955	signed 17.XI.1959	not signed	20.XI.1957	27.III.1958	19.I.1960	not signed
Sweden	28.VI.1957	**n.r.**	signed 3.VIII.1960 **n.r.**	**n.r.**	30.IV.1958	22.I.1959	**n.r.**
Turkey	22.X.1956	**n.r.**	**n.r.**	**n.r.**	signed 8.V.1958	7.I.1960	signed 23.X.1959 **n.r.**
United Kingdom..	28.X.1955	15.XII.1958	signed 13.VII.1960 **n.r.**	signed 24.II.1956	7.XII.1960	not signed	not signed

* n.r. = not ratified or no Declaration made.
a) Australia adhered to this Convention on 7.III.1958 (entry into force: 24.V.1958).

? COUNCIL OF EUROPE CONVENTIONS AND AGREEMENTS

VEHICLE * NSURANCE	WAR * CRIPPLES	HUMAN * BLOOD	MEDICAL * SURGICAL EQUIPMENT	* MOVEMENT PERSONS	REFUGEE * VISAS
27	**28**	**29**	**30**	**31**	**32**
Strasbourg 20.IV.1959	Paris 13.XII.1955	Paris 15.XII.1958	Strasbourg 28.IV.1960	Paris 13.XII.1957	Strasbourg 20.IV.1959
4 ratifications	3 ratifications	3 ratifications	3 ratifications	3 ratifications	3 ratifications
	1.I.1956	**1.I.1959**	**29.VII.1960**	**1.I.1958**	**3.IX.1960**
n.r.	13.XII.1957	**n.r.**	not signed	30.V.1958	not signed
n.r.	29.IV.1959	15.XII.1958	8.VI.1960	13.XII.1957	20.IV.1959
not signed	5.VI.1957	not signed	**n.r.**	not signed	*b)* 30.XI.1960
n.r.	13.XII.1955	2.VI.1960	28.IV.1960	13.XII.1957	20.IV.1959
n.r.	13.XII.1955	**n.r.**	**n.r.**	30.V.1958	**n.r.**
n.r.	5.VI.1959	2.II.1961	**n.r.**	*a)* 13.XII.1957	not signed
not signed	not signed	not signed	not signed	not signed	not signed
not signed	13.XII.1955	15.XII.1958	28.IV.1960	not signed	not signed
n.r.	17.I.1957	**n.r.**	**n.r.**	13.XII.1957	not signed
n.r.	26.III.1958	**n.r.**	**n.r.**	**n.r.**	**n.r.**
not signed	22.X.1958	signed 26.II.1959 **n.r.**	not signed	24.II.1961	3.VIII.1960
n.r.	21.IX.1956	15.XII.1958	28.IV.1960	not signed	*b)* 25.XI.1960
n.r.	3.III.1956	15.XII.1958	**n.r.**	not signed	*b)* 30.XI.1960
not signed	7.X.1959	**n.r.**	not signed	not signed	not signed
not signed	13.VII.1956	not signed	28.IV.1960	not signed	not signed

16. European Cultural Convention.

17. European Convention on the Equivalence of Periods of University Study.

18. European Convention on the Academic Recognition of University Qualifications.

19. European Convention relating to the Formalities required for Patent Applications.

20. European Convention on the International Classification of Patents for Invention.

21. European Agreement concerning Programme Exchanges by means of Television Films.

22. European Agreement on the Protection of Television Broadcasts.

23. European Convention on Establishment.

24. European Convention for the Peaceful Settlement of Disputes.

25. European Convention on Extradition.

26. European Convention on Mutual Assistance in Criminal Matters.

27. European Convention on Compulsory Insurance against civil Liability in respect of Motor Vehicles.

28. Agreement on the Exchange of War Cripples between Member Countries of the Council of Europe with a view to Medical Treatment.

29. European Agreement on the Exchange of Therapeutic Substances of Human Origin.

30. Agreement on the temporary Importation, free of Duty, of Medical, Surgical and Laboratory Equipment for use on free loan in Hospitals and other Medical Institutions for purposes of Diagnosis or Treatment.

31. European Agreement on Regulations governing the movement of persons between Member States of the Council of Europe.

32. European Agreement on the Abolition of Visas for Refugees.

n.r. = not ratified or no Declaration made.

Greece has availed itself of the option offered by Article 7 whereby the entry into force of this Agreement can be delayed. However, entry into Greece for a period of 3 months is granted to nationals of Austria, Belgium, France, the Fed. Rep. of Germany, Italy and Luxembourg, in possession of one of the documents referred to in the Agreement.

Entry into force: 1.I.1961.

CHAPITRE VI

COMMUNAUTÉS EUROPÉENNES

A. CHRONOLOGIE DE L'ANNÉE 1960

11–12 janvier: 15e session du Comité Monétaire.

11–15 janvier: Session de l'Assemblée Parlementaire à Strasbourg sous la présidence de M. Robert SCHUMAN.

1–2 février: Le Conseil confirme sa volonté d'entamer des négociations en vue de l'association de la Grèce à la C.E.E.

12–13 février: Conférence des Représentants des gouvernements des États membres à Bruxelles.

16 février: Des recommandations relatives à une accélération de la mise en place de la C.E.E. sont déposées au Conseil par la Commission.

mars: Au cours de sa session mars–avril, l'Assemblée Parlementaire Européenne, au cours du débat de politique générale, adopte une résolution favorable à l'accélération du rythme du Traité.

2 mars: Les représentants des États membres, réunis à Rome, signent un accord portant sur l'ensemble des produits de la Liste G, à l'exception de 4 rubriques correspondant aux produits pétroliers. Cet accord met un point final à l'élaboration du Tarif Extérieur Commun.

10 avril: Création d'une mission canadienne auprès d'Euratom.

21 avril: Création d'une mission canadienne auprès de la Communauté Économique Européenne.

28 avril: Création d'une mission de la Nouvelle-Zélande auprès de la Communauté Économique Européenne.

mai: Le Conseil, sur la base d'une recommandation de la Commission, décide d'accélérer le rythme de réalisation du Traité.

10–17 mai: Session plénière à Strasbourg de l'Assemblée Parlementaire Européenne. Le projet de Convention sur l'élection de l'Assemblée au suffrage universel direct est adopté.

13 juin: Création d'une mission de l'Australie auprès de la Communauté Économique Européenne.

14 juin: Création d'une mission du Brésil auprès de la Communauté Économique Européenne.

20–21 juin: Le Conseil de la Communauté Économique Européenne, en accord avec la Commission, convient de prendre acte avec un grand intérêt de la volonté des Gouvernements des Républiques Central-africaine, de la Côte d'Ivoire, du Congo (Brazzaville), Gabonaise, de la Haute Volta, Malgache, du Niger, du Sénégal, du Tchad et du Togo de maintenir l'Association, décide de leur faire connaître que, de l'avis de la Communauté, les relations existantes fondées sur la 4ème partie du Traité et sur la Convention d'application peuvent être maintenues d'un commun accord jusqu'à nouvel ordre.

24–25 juin: Réunion conjointe des membres de l'Assemblée Consultative du Conseil de l'Europe et des membres de l'Assemblée Parlementaire Européenne.

30 juin: La Commission de la Communauté Économique Européenne transmet au Conseil ses propositions définitives en matière de politique agricole commune.

CHAPTER VI

EUROPEAN COMMUNITIES

A. LEADING EVENTS IN 1960

11–12 January: Fifteenth session of the Monetary Committee.

11–15 January: Session of the European Parliament in Strasbourg under the presidency of M. Robert SCHUMAN.

1–2 February: The Council re-affirms its readiness to begin negotiations on the association of Greece with the E.E.C.

12–13 February: Conference of the representatives of the Governments of the Member States in Brussels.

16 February: Recommendations for speeding up the time-table of the establishment of the E.E.C. are submitted to the Council by the Commission.

March: In its March–April session, the European Parliament, during the debate on general policy, adopts a resolution in favour of the speedier implementation of the Treaty.

2 March: The Representatives of the Member States, meeting in Rome, sign an agreement covering all the products in List G, except four groups of items connected with petroleum products. This agreement puts the finishing touches to the drafting of the common external tariff.

10 April: Establishment of a Canadian Mission to Euratom.

21 April: Establishment of a Canadian Mission to the European Economic Community.

28 April: Establishment of a New Zealand Mission to the European Economic Community.

May: The Council, on the basis of a recommendation by the Commission, decides to speed up the implementation of the Treaty.

10–17 May: Plenary session of the European Parliament in Strasbourg. The draft convention on election to the Parliament by direct universal suffrage is adopted.

13 June: Establishment of an Australian Mission to the European Economic Community.

14 June: Establishment of a Brazilian Mission to the European Economic Community.

20–21 June: The Council decides to take note with great interest of the wishes of the Governments of the Central African Republic, the Republics of Ivory Coast, of Congo (Brazzaville), of Gaboon, of Upper Volta, of Madagascar, of Niger, of Chad, of Senegal and of Togo to maintain the association with the E.E.C. The Council decides to inform these Governments that in the opinion of the Community the existing relationships based on Part Four of the Treaty and on the Implementing Convention can be maintained by common agreement until further notice.

24–25 June: Joint meeting of the members of the Consultative Assembly of the Council of Europe with the members of the European Parliament.

30 June: The Commission of the European Economic Community transmits to the Council its final proposals in the field of the common agricultural policy.

1 juillet: Désarmement douanier: réduction de 10% des droits de douane intervient entre les États membres de la Communauté Économique Européenne.

22–23 juillet: La Commission participe à la Conférence Ministérielle de Paris sur la réorganisation de l'O.E.C.E.

26 juillet: Création d'une mission du Maroc auprès de la Communauté Économique Européenne.

28 juillet: La Commission remet au Conseil le projet de programme général pour la suppression des restrictions à la libre prestation des services à l'intérieur de la Communauté. Ce programme est transmis pour avis à l'Assemblée et au Comité Économique et Social.

6 septembre: Les représentants des Gouvernements des États membres nomment M. Jacques RUEFF membre de la Cour de Justice des Communautés européennes.

6–7 septembre: Les Conseils de la C.E.E. et de la C.E.E.A. arrêtent un projet de statut pour les fonctionnaires des Communautés.

27 septembre: La Commission de la Communauté Économique Européenne désigne M. PETRILLI comme Président du Comité du Fonds Social Européen.

28 septembre: La Commission de la Communauté Économique Européenne transmet au Conseil les propositions sur l'accélération de la mise en oeuvre du Traité applicables aux pays associés.

29 septembre: M. ROSENBERG est élu Président du Comité Économique et Social.

12–18 octobre: Session plénière de l'Assemblée sous la présidence de M. Hans FURLER. En particulier, débats sur l'incidence des récents échanges de vues entre les Gouvernements des Six sur le rôle des Institutions européennes.

8 novembre: La Commission de la Communauté Économique Européenne transmet au Conseil son premier projet de règlement pour l'application des articles 85 et 86 du Traité de Rome (concurrence).

9 décembre: Création d'une mission de l'Afrique du Sud auprès de la Communauté Économique Européenne.
Création d'une mission de l'Espagne auprès de la Communauté Économique Européenne.

31 décembre: L'abaissement des droits de douane à l'intérieur de la Communauté atteint 30%.
Premier rapprochement vers le Tarif Extérieur Commun.

B. TEXTES FONDAMENTAUX

Note de la rédaction

L'Assemblée Parlementaire Européenne s'est préoccupée continuellement de faire accepter par les Gouvernements l'élection directe au suffrage universel de ses Représentants. (A l'heure qu'il est, les membres de chaque délégation sont désignés par les Parlements nationaux, compte tenu des effectifs des divers partis).

L'Assemblée, en effet, est tenue, d'après les termes des traités relatifs aux trois Communautés, de faire des propositions à cet effet. A la suite des travaux préparatoires incombant à une commission dont M. DEHOUSSE *fut le Président et le rapporteur, l'Assemblée adopta à l'unanimité, avec 12 abstentions, en juin 1960, un projet de convention élaborant les modalités d'une telle élection, ainsi que plusieurs résolutions. Le dispositif de ce texte se trouve imprimé ci-dessous – avec traduction ,,officieuse'' en anglais. Ce projet de convention est dès maintenant soumis aux Conseils de Ministres des trois Communautés. Ceux-ci doivent l'approuver et le faire ratifier par les six Parlements nationaux; et c'est seulement alors que le système pourra entrer en vigueur. L'Assemblée, du reste, a exprimé le voeu que les premières élections européennes aient lieu en 1962 ou 1963.*

1 July: Customs disarmament: customs duties between the Member States of the European Economic Community reduced by 10%.

22–23 July: The Commission takes part in the Paris Ministerial Conference on the re-organization of the O.E.E.C.

26 July: Establishment of a Moroccan Mission to the European Economic Community.

28 July: The Commission submits to the Council the draft general programme for the abolition of restrictions on the free supply of services within the Community. This programme is transmitted for an opinion to the Parliament and to the Economic and Social Committee.

6 September: The Representatives of the Governments of the Member States appoint M. Jacques RUEFF a member of the Court of Justice of the European Communities.

6–7 September: The Councils of the E.E.C. and Euratom decide on a draft Statute of service for the staff of the Communities.

27 September: The Commission of the European Economic Community appoints M. PETRILLI to be Chairman of the Committee of the European Social Fund.

28 September: The Commission of the European Economic Community transmits to the Council the proposals on speedier implementation of the Treaty which affect the associated countries.

29 September: M. ROSENBERG is elected Chairman of the Economic and Social Committee.

12–18 October: Plenary session of the Parliament under the presidency of M. Hans FURLER. In particular, there are debates on the effects of the recent discussions between the Governments of the Six on the rôle played by the European Institutions.

8 November: The Commission of the European Economic Community transmits to the Council its first draft of the regulation for the application of Articles 85 and 86 of the Treaty of Rome (competition).

9 December: Establishment of a South African Mission to the European Economic Community.
Establishment of a Spanish Mission to the European Economic Community.

31 December: The reduction of customs duties within the Community reaches 30%.
First approximation towards the common external tariff.

B. BASIC TEXTS

Editors' Note

The possibility of securing direct election of members has been a constant preoccupation of the European Parliamentary Assembly. (At present the members of each delegation are nominated by the six national Parliaments in proportion of party strengths). The Assembly was indeed required by the three Community treaties to submit draft proposals on this matter. Following on the spade-work of a Commission, of which M. DEHOUSSE *was Chairman and Rapporteur, the Assembly adopted unamimously with 12 abstentions, in May 1960, a draft convention to this end, together with a number of Resolutions. The substantive text is printed below, with an unofficial English translation. It was sent forward to the Councils of Ministers for approval. Ratification by the six national Parliaments will be required before the arrangements can come into effect. The Assembly has expressed the hope that the first European elections may take place in 1962 or 1963.*

RÉSOLUTION

portant adoption d'un projet de convention
sur l'élection de l'Assemblée Parlementaire Européenne
au suffrage universel direct.

L'Assemblée Parlementaire Européenne,

- considérant que le moment est venu d'associer directement les peuples à l'édification de l'Europe,
- consciente de ce qu'une Assemblée élue au suffrage universel direct constituera un élément essentiel de l'unification européenne,
- en exécution du mandat qui lui a été confié par les traités instituant les Communautés européennes,

approuve le texte suivant du

PROJET DE CONVENTION

Portant application de l'article 21, paragraphe 3, du Traité instituant la Communauté Européenne du Charbon et de l'Acier, de l'article 138, paragraphe 3, du Traité instituant la Communauté Économique Européenne et de l'article 108, paragraphe 3, du Traité instituant la Communauté Européenne de l'Énergie Atomique,

sur

L'élection de l'Assemblée Parlementaire Européenne au suffrage universel direct

Le Conseil spécial de Ministres de la Communauté Européenne du Charbon et de l'Acier,

Le Conseil de la Communauté Économique Européenne,

Le Conseil de la Communauté Européenne de l'Énergie Atomique,

résolus à donner pour fondement à la mission dévolue à l'Assemblée Parlementaire Européenne la volonté librement exprimée des populations des États membres des Communautés Européennes,

soucieux d'accroître le caractère représentatif de l'Assemblée Parlementaire Européenne,

Vu l'article 21 du Traité instituant la Communauté Européenne du Charbon et de l'Acier,

Vu l'article 138 du Traité instituant la Communauté Économique Européenne,

Vu l'article 108 du Traité instituant la Communauté Européenne de l'Énergie Atomique,

Vu le projet élaboré par l'Assemblée Parlementaire Européenne et adopté par elle le 17 mai 1960,

arrêtent les dispositions suivantes dont ils recommandent l'adoption par les États membres:

CHAPITRE I

DE L'ASSEMBLÉE ÉLUE

Article premier

Les représentants des peuples à l'Assemblée Parlementaire Européenne sont élus au suffrage universel direct.

Unofficial translation

RESOLUTION

embodying a draft Convention on the election of the European Parliamentary Assembly by direct universal suffrage

The European Parliamentary Assembly:

- considering that the time has come to bring the peoples of Europe into direct association in the task of European construction,
- aware that an Assembly elected on a basis of direct universal suffrage is likely to be an essential element in the pattern of European unification,
- in implementation of the mandate conferred on it by the treaties establishing the European Communities,

approves the following text of a

DRAFT CONVENTION

In application of Article 21, paragraph 3, of the Treaty setting up the European Coal and Steel Community, Article 138, paragraph 3, of the Treaty setting up the European Economic Community and Article 108, paragraph 3, of the Treaty setting up the European Atomic Energy Community.

on

The election of the European Parliamentary Assembly by direct universal suffrage.

"The Special Council of Ministers of the Coal and Steel Community,
The Council of the Economic European Community,
The Council of the European Atomic Energy Community,
Resolved to lay firm foundations for the work of the European Parliamentary Assembly in the freely expressed will of the peoples of the Member States of the European Communities,
Anxious to enhance the representative character of the European Parliamentary Assembly,
By virtue of Article 21 of the Treaty establishing the Coal and Steel Community,
By virtue of Article 138 of the Treaty establishing the European Economic Community,
By virtue of Article 108 of the Treaty establishing the European Atomic Energy Community,
In accordance with a draft prepared by the European Parliamentary Assembly and adopted by it on 17th May, 1960,
Hereby set forth the following provisions which are recommended for adoption by the Member States:

CHAPTER I

PATTERN OF THE ELECTED ASSEMBLY

Article 1

The representatives of the peoples in the European Parliamentary Assembly shall be elected direct by universal suffrage.

Article 2

Le nombre des représentants élus dans chaque État membre est fixé ainsi qu'il suit:

Belgique	42
Allemagne	108
France	108
Italie	108
Luxembourg	18
Pays-Bas	42

Article 3

Pendant une période transitoire, un tiers de ces représentants est élu par les Parlements en leur sein selon une procédure qui assure aux groupes politiques une représentation équitable.

Article 4

La période transitoire commence à la date de l'entrée en vigueur de la présente Convention.

Son terme est fixé par l'Assemblée Parlementaire Européenne. Il ne peut être antérieur à la fin de la troisième étape de l'établissement du marché commun, définie à l'article 8 du Traité instituant la Communauté Économique Européenne; il ne peut être postérieur à l'expiration de la législature au cours de laquelle cette troisième étape aura pris fin.

Article 5

1. Les représentants sont élus pour cinq ans.

Toutefois, le mandat des représentants élus par les Parlements prend fin par la perte du mandat parlementaire national ou au terme de la période pour laquelle ils ont été élus par leurs Parlements respectifs. Tout représentant dont le mandat se termine de la sorte reste en fonctions jusqu'à validation de son successeur à l'Assemblée Parlementaire Européenne.

2. La législature quinquennale commence à l'ouverture de la première session tenue après chaque élection.

Article 6

Les représentants votent individuellement et personnellement. Ils ne peuvent recevoir ni instructions ni mandat impératif.

Article 7

Pendant la période transitoire, la qualité de représentant à l'Assemblée Parlementaire Européenne est compatible avec celle de membre d'un Parlement.

L'Assemblée décidera si la compatibilité de ces mandats est applicable après la fin de la période transitoire.

Article 8

1. Pendant la période transitoire:

a) La qualité de représentant à l'Assemblée Parlementaire Européenne est incompatible avec celle de:

– membre du gouvernement d'un État membre,

Article 2

The number of Representatives elected in each Member State will be fixed as follows:

Belgium	42
Germany	108
France	108
Italy	108
Luxembourg	18
Netherlands	42

Article 3

During a transitional period one-third of these Representatives will be elected by the Member Parliaments in accordance with a mode of procedure designed to ensure equitable representation for the several political groups.

Article 4

The transitional period will run from the date of the entry into force of this Convention.

The end-date will be fixed by the European Parliamentary Assembly. It cannot be before the end of the third stage of the establishment of the common market, as prescribed in Article 8 of the Treaty establishing the European Economic Community, it cannot be after the expiry of the legislative period marking the end of that third stage.

Article 5

1. The Representatives shall be elected for 5 years.

Nevertheless, the mandate of the Representatives elected by the parliaments shall lapse if a member ceases to sit in his national Parliament or, alternatively, at the end of the period for which they have been elected by their respective Parliaments. Any Representative whose mandate comes to an end in this way shall remain a member until his successor's credentials have been confirmed by the European Parliamentary Assembly.

2. The five years period of a legislature shall begin to run from the opening of the first session to be held after the election.

Article 6

Representatives shall vote individually and personally. They shall not receive instructions nor shall they take orders from anyone.

Article 7

During the transitional period the status of Representative to the European Parliamentary Assembly will be compatible with that of a national member of Parliament.

The Assembly will decide if the two functions are still compatible after the end of the transitional period.

Article 8

1. During the transitional period:

a) The status of Representative to the European Parliamentary Assembly shall be incompatible with:

– membership of one of the Governments of the Member States;

- membre de la Haute Autorité de la Communauté Européenne du Charbon et de l'Acier, de la Commission de la Communauté Économique Européenne ou de la Commission de la Communauté Européenne de l'Énergie Atomique,
- juge, avocat général ou greffier de la Cour de Justice des Communautés Européennes,
- membre du Comité Consultatif de la Communauté Européenne du Charbon et de l'Acier ou membre du Comité Économique et Social de la Communauté Économique Européenne et de la Communauté Européenne de l'Énergie Atomique.
- commissaire aux comptes prévu à l'article 78 du Traité instituant la Communauté Européenne du Charbon et de l'Acier ou membre de la Commission de contrôle prévue à l'article 206 du Traité instituant la Communauté Économique Européenne et à l'article 180 du Traité instituant la Communauté Européenne de l'Énergie Atomique,
- membre des comités ou organismes créés en vertu ou en application des Traités instituant la Communauté Européenne du Charbon et de l'Acier, la Communauté Économique Européenne et la Communauté Européenne de l'Énergie Atomique en vue de l'administration de fonds des Communautés ou d'une tâche permanente et directe de gestion administrative,
- membre du Conseil d'administration, du comité de direction ou employé de la Banque Européenne d'Investissement,
- fonctionnaires ou agents en activité des institutions des Communautés européennes ou des organismes spécialisés qui leur sont rattachés.

Les représentants à l'Assemblée Parlementaire Européenne qui, au cours d'une législature, sont appelés à une des fonctions prévues ci-dessus sont remplacés conformément aux dispositions de l'article 17.

b) Chaque État membre détermine si, et dans quelle mesure, les incompatibilités édictées par sa législation pour l'exercice du mandat parlementaire national sont applicables pour l'exercice du mandat à l'Assemblée Parlementaire Européenne.

2. L'Assemblée décidera du régime des incompatibilités applicable après la fin de la période transitoire.

Chapitre II

DU RÉGIME ÉLECTORAL

Article 9

L'Assemblée Parlementaire Européenne arrête les dispositions qui régiront, selon une procédure aussi uniforme que possible, l'élection des représentants après l'expiration de la période transitoire prévue à l'article 4.

Jusqu'à l'entrée en vigueur de celles-ci, le régime électoral relève de la compétence de chaque État membre, sous réserve des dispositions de la présente convention.

Article 10

Sont électeurs, dans chaque État membre, sous réserve des dispositions de l'article 11, les hommes et les femmes qui satisfont aux conditions nécessaires dans cet État membre pour participer aux élections au suffrage universel direct pour la désignation du Parlement.

Article 11

L'âge à partir duquel le droit de vote est exercé est de vingt et un ans accomplis.

- membership of the High Authority of the Coal and Steel Community;
- the Commission of the European Economic Community, or of the Commission of the European Atomic Energy Community;
- the position of Judge, public prosecutor or Registrar of the Court of Justice of the Communities;
- membership of the Consultative Committee of the Coal and Steel Community or of the Economic and Social Committee of the European Economic Community or of the European Atomic Energy Community;
- the status of auditor, as described in Article 78 of the Treaty establishing the Coal and Steel Community, or membership of the Control Commission referred to in Article 206 of the Treaty establishing the European Economic Community and Article 180 of the Treaty establishing the European Atomic Energy Community.
- membership of Committees or bodies set up in virtue of or in application of the Treaties establishing the Coal and Steel Community, the European Economic Community and the European Atomic Energy Community and responsible for the administering of funds of the Communities or any permanent and direct task of administrative management.
- membership of the Board of Directors or of the management or of the staff of the European Investment Bank,
- the status of officials of any institutions of the European Communities or specialised bodies connected with them.

Representatives to the European Parliamentary Assembly appointed to discharge any of the functions specified above during a statutory period shall be duly replaced in accordance with the provisions of Article 17.

b) Each Member State shall determine whether and to what extent incompatibilities under its own laws in respect of the position of a member of a national Parliament shall be applicable for the exercise of parliamentary functions in the European Parliamentary Assembly.

2. The Assembly shall make its own decisions as to the *régime* in the matter of incompatibilities that shall be applicable after the end of the transitional period.

CHAPTER II

ELECTORAL RÉGIME

Article 9

The European Parliamentary Assembly shall fix the rules governing, with the maximum possible uniformity, the election of Representatives at the conclusion of the transitional period mentioned in Article 4.

Until such provisions come into force the electoral *régime* will remain within the competence of each Member State, subject to the provisions of the present Convention.

Article 10

The electorate in each Member State, subject to the provisions of Article 11, shall consist of those persons, male and female, who satisfy the necessary conditions in each State for participation in elections by direct universal suffrage for the designation of its parliament.

Article 11

The age for the exercise of the right of vote shall be 21 years.

Les ressortissants d'un État membre qui résident sur le territoire d'un autre État membre ont la faculté d'exercer le droit de vote dans leur pays d'origine, qui institue à cet effet les mesures appropriées.

Au cas où l'État de résidence permet également l'exercice du droit de vote aux personnes visées à l'alinéa précédent, celles-ci ne peuvent voter qu'une seule fois. Toute infraction à cette règle sera passible des sanctions édictées par la loi du pays d'origine.

Article 12

Sont éligibles dans chaque État membre les hommes et les femmes âgés de vingt-cinq ans accomplis, ressortissant de l'un des États signataires des Traités instituant les Communautés, sous réserve des cas d'inégibilité traditionnelle déterminés par la loi nationale.

Les incompatibilités prévues à l'article 8 n'entraînent pas l'inégibilité.

Article 13

Les dispositions qui règlent constitutionnellement dans chaque État membre l'admission des partis politiques aux élections s'appliquent à l'élection à l'Assemblée Parlementaire Européenne.

Article 14

L'élection à l'Assemblée Parlementaire Européenne a lieu le même jour dans les six États membres; la date sera fixée de manière que les élections nationales ne coïncident pas avec Celles de l'Assemblée Parlementaire Européenne.

Toutefois, pour des motifs tenant à la tradition ou aux conditions géographiques, tout État membre peut décider que les opérations de vote auront lieu la veille ou le lendemain du jour fixé ou seront étendues à ces deux jours.

Article 15

1. L'élection à l'Assemblée Parlementaire Européenne a lieu au plus tard un mois avant la fin de chaque législature.
2. L'Assemblée Parlementaire Européenne se réunit de plein droit le premier mardi qui suit l'expiration d'un délai d'un mois à compter de la date de l'élection.
3. L'Assemblée Parlementaire Européenne sortante reste en fonctions jusqu'à la première réunion de la nouvelle Assemblée.

Article 16

L'Assemblée Parlemenatire Européenne vérifie les pouvoirs des représentants et statue sur les contestations qui s'élèvent à ce sujet.

Article 17

En cas de vacance d'un siège pourvu au suffrage universel direct, il n'est pas procédé à une élection partielle.

Pour la période transitoire, la loi nationale doit établir les dispositions électorales qui permettent, tout en satisfaisant à cette condition, d'attribuer le siège à un nouveau titulaire.

En cas de vacance d'un siège pourvu conformément à l'article 3, le Parlement de l'État membre procède à l'élection du successeur.

The nationals of a Member State who live in the territory of another Member State shall have the opportunity of exercising the right of vote in their country of origin, and the latter will take all appropriate measures to make this possible.

In the event of the "residence" State also allowing the exercise of the European vote for persons such as those referred to in the previous paragraph, the latter shall not, however, be able to vote more than once. Any infringement of this rule will be liable to whatever penalties are imposed by the law of the country of origin.

Article 12

Persons eligible for election in each Member State, will be men and women of 25 years of age or over who are nationals of one of the signatory States of the Treaties setting up the Communities, subject always to any criteria of ineligibility laid down in their national laws.

The incompatibilities set forth in Article 8 do not necessarily involve ineligibility.

Article 13

The constitutional precepts in each Member State governing the admission of political parties to election shall be equally applicable to elections for the European Parliamentary Assembly.

Article 14

Elections for the European Parliamentary Assembly will take place on the same day in the six Member States; the date will be fixed so as not to coincide with national elections.

Notwithstanding, for reasons connected with tradition or geography any Member State may decide that the voting operations take place on the day before or the day after the scheduled date, or may be spread over the two days.

Article 15

1. Election to the European Parliamentary Assembly shall take place not later than a month before the end of each legislature.

2. The European Parliamentary Assembly will meet, by law, on the first Tuesday in the second calendar month after the elections.

3. The European Parliamentary Assembly whose mandate has expired will remain in being until the first meeting of the new Assembly.

Article 16

The European Parliamentary Assembly shall examine the credentials of all Representatives and shall give judgment on any contested election.

Article 17

Whenever any seat to which a candidate has been elected by direct universal suffrage falls vacant, it shall be left vacant, and there will not be a by-election.

For the transitional period the national law is required to arrange for electoral rules which will make it possible, subject to the above, to allocate the seat to someone else.

When a vacancy occurs in accordance with Article 3, the Parliament of a Member State shall take steps to provide for a replacement.

Article 18

Les candidats ou les listes ayant obtenu au minimum 10% des suffrages exprimés du collège électoral qu'ils auront sollicité pourront obtenir le remboursement de certains frais électoraux.

Il sera prévu à cet effet au budget de l'Assemblée Parlementaire Européenne les crédits nécessaires pour permettre ce remboursement suivant les modalités fixées d'avance par le bureau de ladite Assemblée.

. . . .

CHAPITRE III

(*Suivent quelques dispositions procédurales*)

. . . .

Article 18

Candidates or lists having obtained at least 10% of the votes cast in the electoral college to which they belong may obtain re-imbursement of certain election expenses.

Provision will be made for this in the budget of the European Parliamentary Assembly and repayment will be made in accordance with regulations fixed in advance by the *Bureau* of that Assembly.

. . . .

CHAPTER III

(*Some procedural provisions follow.*)

. . . .

I. COMMUNAUTÉ ÉCONOMIQUE EUROPÉENNE

A. TEXTES FONDAMENTAUX

1. DÉCISION

DES REPRÉSENTANTS DES GOUVERNEMENTS DES ÉTATS MEMBRES DE LA COMMUNAUTÉ ÉCONOMIQUE EUROPÉENNE RÉUNIS AU SEIN DU CONSEIL, CONCERNANT L'ACCÉLÉRATION DU RYTHME DE RÉALISATION DES OBJETS DU TRAITÉ

LES REPRÉSENTANTS DES GOUVERNEMENTS DES ÉTATS MEMBRES DE LA COMMUNAUTÉ ÉCONOMIQUE EUROPÉENNE RÉUNIS AU SEIN DU CONSEIL,

vu les dispositions du Traité instituant la Communauté Économique Européenne,

vu la recommandation de la Commission,

DÉCIDENT:

I.

Article premier

1. Sans préjudice de l'application des réductions prévues par l'article 14 du Traité, les États membres mettent en vigueur entre eux à compter du 1er juillet 1960 pour chaque produit un droit de douane égal au droit de base diminué de 30%.

L'abaissement à intervenir le 31 décembre 1961 sera au minimum de 10% conformément à l'article 14 du Traité. Le Conseil décidera avant le 30 juin 1961 si un abaissement supplémentaire de 10% est possible le 31 décembre de la même année, compte tenu de la conjoncture économique.

2. Les États membres de la Communauté Économique Européenne procéderont au plus tard le 31 décembre 1960 au premier rapprochement vers le tarif douanier commun selon les modalités de l'article 23, paragraphe 1, *a*) et *b*), du Traité. Ce rapprochement sera effectué sur la base de calcul du tarif douanier commun réduit de 20%, sans pour autant pouvoir ramener les droits applicables à un niveau inférieur à celui du tarif douanier commun.

3. Les produits de la liste G seront soumis à la procédure prévue au paragraphe 2. Toutefois, sur demande de l'État membre intéressé, la Commission pourra décider que, pour des produits particulièrement sensibles de la liste G, le rapprochement vers le tarif douanier commun sera effectué sur la base des droits fixés le 2 mars 1960.

Article 2

1. Sans préjudice de l'application des réductions prévues à l'article 14 du Traité, les dispositions nécessaires devront être prises par les États membres pour assurer la mise en application des mesures énoncées à l'article premier, paragraphe 1, alinéa 1, et paragraphes 2 et 3, au plus tard le 31 décember 1960.

2. En ce qui concerne la République Fédérale d'Allemagne, le rapprochement vers le tarif douanier commun effectué conformément à l'article 23 du Traité pourra ne comporter au 31 décembre 1960 que la résorption de 50% des baisses conjoncturelles affectant certains droits.

I. EUROPEAN ECONOMIC COMMUNITY

A. BASIC TEXTS

Unofficial Translation

1. DECISION ON THE ACCELERATION OF THE IMPLEMENTATION OF THE TREATY TAKEN BY THE REPRESENTATIVES OF THE GOVERNMENTS OF THE MEMBER STATES OF THE EUROPEAN ECONOMIC COMMUNITY MEETING IN THE COUNCIL

THE REPRESENTATIVES OF THE GOVERNMENTS OF THE MEMBER STATES OF THE EUROPEAN ECONOMIC COMMUNITY, MEETING IN THE COUNCIL,

Considering the provisions of the Treaty establishing the European Economic Community,

Considering the recommendation submitted by the Commission,

DECIDE:

I.

Article 1

1. Without prejudice to the implementation of the reductions stipulated in Article 14 of the Treaty, the Member States shall, as from 1st July, 1960, apply among themselves for each product a customs duty equal to the basic duty reduced by 30%.

Under Article 14 of the Treaty the reduction to be effected on 31st December, 1961, will amount to no less than 10%. Before 30th June, 1961, the Council shall decide whether, in the light of economic developments, a further reduction of 10% will be possible on 31st December of the same year.

2. At the latest on 31st December, 1960, the Member States of the European Economic Community shall undertake the first approximation to the common external tariff in accordance with the particulars contained in Article 23 (1*a*) and *b*)). The approximation will be made on the basis of the common external tariff reduced by 20%, but the duties to be applied may not thereby be reduced to a level below that shown in the common external tariff.

3. The commodities on List G shall be subjected to the procedure outlined in paragraph 2 above. Nevertheless, upon request of a Member State, the Commission may decide that for the particularly sensitive commodities of List G the approximation towards the common external tariff shall be effected on the basis of the duties fixed on 2nd March, 1960.

Article 2

1. Without prejudice to the implementation of the reductions provided for in Article 14 of the Treaty, the Member States shall take the steps necessary to ensure the application of the measures outlined in Article 1, (paragraph 1, sub-paragraph 1) and paragraphs 2 and 3 not later than 31st December, 1960.

2. For the Federal Republic of Germany, approximation towards the common external tariff on 31st December, 1960, in accordance with Article 23 of the Treaty shall not be required to involve the reabsorption of more than 50% of the reduction in certain duties which was made to meet economic developments.

Article 3

1. Les différentes réductions tarifaires effectuées au profit des pays tiers le seront à titre provisoire.

2. La Communauté Économique Européenne se déclare prête à discuter avec les États intéressés les modalités de la réciprocité qui pourrait lui être accordée.

3. Les États membres pourront procéder à une extension *erga omnes* des baisses nationales dans la limite du tarif douanier commun, compte tenu de la réciprocité qui serait accordée par les États tiers. Il devra être tenu compte aussi des extensions *erga omnes* déjà effectuées.

4. Il sera procédé à la consolidation de toute ou partie de la réduction de 20% utilisée dans le calcul du rapprochement vers le tarif douanier commun au cours des négociations tarifaires prévues dans le cadre du G.A.T.T. pour le début de l'année 1961.

Article 4

Sans préjudice des dispositions du Traité, les États membres supprimeront dans les meilleurs délais, dans le cadre des obligations stipulées dans l'Accord général sur les Tarifs et le Commerce et compte tenu des recommandations pertinentes du Fonds monétaire international, les restrictions quantitatives à l'importation sur les produits industriels.

En tout état de cause, chaque État membre supprimera, à la date du 31 décembre 1961 toutes les restrictions quantitatives s'appliquant aux importations de produits industriels des autres États membres de la Communauté Économique Européenne.

II.

AGRICULTURE

Article 5

1. Les mesures prévues par le Traité, dont l'application a été jusqu'à présent différée, devront avoir été mises en vigueur avant le 31 décembre 1960.

2. La préparation de la politique agricole commune sera poursuivie conformément au paragraphe 4 de l'article 38 du Traité, en vue d'accélérer sa mise en oeuvre.

3. Les dispositions prévues aux articles 6 et 7 seront, sans préjudice des mesures qui résultent de l'application du Traité dans le secteur agricole, applicables au premier janvier 1961, compte tenu des modalités ci-après.

4. Le Conseil tiendra, d'ici le 31 décembre 1960, une ou plusieurs sessions pour délibérer sur les propositions visées à l'article 43, paragraphe 2, du Traité, relatives à la politique agricole commune, notamment en vue de dégager une première solution communautaire aux difficultés résultant de conditions différentes de concurrence dues à des différences de politique générale agricole, dans les secteurs agricole et alimentaire.

A cet effet, le Conseil arrête le calendrier suivant des travaux relatifs à la politique agricole commune:
- dépôt des propositions finales de la Commission avant le 30 juin;
- première discussion générale par le Conseil avant le 31 juillet;
- création immédiate après cette discussion générale, par le Conseil, d'un comité spécial pour préparer ses décisions;
- premier rapport du comité spécial au Conseil avant le 15 octobre.

5. Le Conseil constatera, avant le 31 décembre 1960, les progrès réalisés sur les points visés au paragraphe 4, alinéa 1.

Article 3

1. The various tariff reductions benefiting non-member States shall be of a provisional nature.

2. The European Economic Community declares its readiness to discuss with the countries concerned the terms of any reciprocity which could be granted to it.

3. The Member States shall be entitled to extend the national reductions to all countries, within the limits of the common external tariff, account being taken of the reciprocity granted by the non-member states. Any extension to all countries already granted will also have to be taken into account.

4. At the tariff negotiations to be held in G.A.T.T. at the beginning of 1961, action will be taken to consolidate, wholly or in part, the 20% reduction used in calculating the approximation to the common external tariff.

Article 4

Without prejudice to the provisions of the Treaty, the Member States shall, in accordance with their obligations under the General Agreement on Tariffs and Trade and with due regard to the pertinent recommendations of the International Monetary Fund, abolish as soon as possible all quantitative restrictions on the import of industrial goods.

On 31st December, 1961, all Member States shall in any case abolish all quantitative restrictions on the import of industrial goods from the other Member States of the E.E.C.

II.

AGRICULTURE

Article 5

1. The measures provided for in the Treaty but not yet implemented shall be put into effect before 31st December, 1960.

2. In compliance with Article 38(4) of the Treaty, preparation of the common agricultural policy will be pressed forward with a view to speeding its implementation.

3. Subject to the particulars below, the provisions of Articles 6 and 7 shall, without prejudice to measures resulting from the application of the Treaty in the agricultural sector, enter into effect on 1st January, 1961.

4. By 31st December, 1960, the Council shall hold one or more sessions to consider the proposals concerning the common agricultural policy referred to in Article 43(2) of the Treaty, particularly with a view to working out a first solution at the Community level for the difficulties caused, in the agricultural and foodstuffs sectors, by different conditions of competition due to differences in general agricultural policy.

To this end the Council hereby lays down the following time-table for work on the common agricultural policy:

- Submission of the Commission's final proposals before 30th June;
- First general discussion by the Council before 31st July;
- Immediately after this general discussion, creation by the Council of a special committee to prepare its decisions;
- First report of this special committee to the Council before 15th October.

5. Before 31st December, 1960, the Council will review the progress made on the points referred to in paragraph 4, sub-paragraph 1.

En fonction de ces constatations, la Commission formulera, en tant que de besoin, les propositions appropriées pour l'exécution ou la révision éventuelle des dispositions énoncées au paragraphe 3, ci-dessus.

Ces propositions, qui pourront être modifiées à l'unanimité conformément à l'article 149 du Traité, seront adoptées par le Conseil à la majorité qualifiée prévue à l'article 148, paragraphe 2, alinéa 2, première alternative.

Article 6

1. En ce qui concerne les produits agricoles non libérés, la réduction supplémentaire sera de 5%, de telle sorte que la réduction des droits applicables entre les États membres prévue à l'article premier, paragraphe 1, soit de 25% par rapport aux droits de base.

2. Les mesures concernant le rapprochement vers le tarif douanier commun prévues à l'article premier, paragraphe 2, ne s'appliqueront pas aux produits agricoles, une politique commune étant prévue pour ces produits.

Article 7

1. Les contingents globaux ouverts au titre de l'article 33, paragraphe 1, du Traité seront augmentés annuellement, jusqu'à la fin de la première étape, de 20% par rapport à l'année précédente.

2. Chaque contingent global ouvert au titre de l'article 33, paragraphe 2, du Traité sera, pour l'année 1961, fixé à 5,2% de la production nationale.

3. En ce qui concerne les produits pour lesquels les dispositions visées aux paragraphes 1 et 2, ci-dessus, ne seraient pas appliquées et en ce qui concerne les produits pour lesquels un contrat ou accord à long terme n'aurait pas été déjà conclu, les États membres devront accorder des possibilités totales d'importations égales à la moyenne des importations réalisées pendant les trois années avant l'entrée en vigueur du Traité, majorée de 10% chaque année au titre des années 1959, 1960 et jusqu'à la fin de la première étape.

4. Les mesures visées aux paragraphes 1, 2, et 3, ne s'appliqueront plus dans les cas où les États membres pratiqueraient des mesures préparant l'établissement de la politique agricole commune, qui comporteraient l'abolition des restrictions quantitatives et des tarifs entre eux.

III.

Article 8

La présente décision consignée au procès-verbal de la session du Conseil sera publiée au *Journal officiel des Communautés européennes*.

Les gouvernements des États membres notifieront au Secrétaire Général du Conseil dans un délai d'un mois si des procédures sont requises par leurs droits internes pour assurer l'application de la présente décision; le cas échéant, ils lui notifieront sans délai l'accomplissement de ces procédures.

Fait à Bruxelles, le 12 mai 1960.

ANNEXE

Au cours de la même session, les États membres de la Communauté Économique Européenne réunis au sein du Conseil ont adopté les déclarations d'intention suivantes:

In the light of this review the Commission shall draft such proposals as may be necessary for the execution or revision of the provisions listed in paragraph 3 above.

These proposals, which may be amended by a unanimous vote in accordance with Article 149, shall be adopted by the Council by a qualified majority as laid down in Article 148(2), sub-paragraph 2, first alternative.

Article 6

1. For the non-liberalized agricultural products the additional reduction shall amount to 5%, operated in such a way that the reduction of duties applicable amongst the Member States in accordance with Article 1, paragraph 1, shall amount to 25% in relation to the basic duty.

2. The measures for the approximation to the common external tariff to which Article 1 (2) refers will not apply to agricultural products, since a common policy is envisaged for these products.

Article 7

1. The global quotas opened under Article 33(1) of the Treaty shall be increased annually, until the end of the first stage, by 20% in relation to the previous year.

2. All global quotas opened under Article 33(2) of the Treaty will for the year 1961 be set at 5.2% of national production.

3. For products to which the provisions of paragraphs 1 and 2 above have not been applied and for products in respect of which no contract or long-term agreement has been concluded, the Member States shall be required to allow overall imports equal to the average imports for the three years before the entry into force of the Treaty, increased by 10% each year for 1959 and 1960 and until the end of the first stage.

4. The measures referred to in paragraphs 1, 2 and 3 shall no longer apply in cases where the Member States are already applying measures in aid of the establishment of a common agricultural policy which would involve the abolition of quotas and tariffs amongst them.

III.

Article 8

The present decision shall be recorded in the Minutes of the session of the Council and published in the *Official Gazette of the European Communities*.

The Governments of the Member States shall, within one month, inform the Secretary-General of the Council whether under their municipal legislation special procedures are required in order to implement the present decision; where this is the case, they will inform the Secretary-General without delay when these procedures have been completed.

Done at Brussels on 12th May, 1960.

APPENDIX

In the course of the same session the Member States of the European Economic Community, meeting in the Council, adopted the following declarations of intention:

DÉCLARATION D'INTENTION QUANT À L'ACCÉLÉRATION INTERNE

Le Conseil confirme son intention de poursuivre le plus rapidement possible l'accélération du Traité non seulement dans le domaine de l'union douanière, mais parallèlement dans tous les secteurs de l'intégration économique.

Il affirme particulièrement sa volonté de hâter la mise en oeuvre des mesures de caractère social et qui sont notamment relatives à la formation professionnelle des travailleurs, à leur libre circulation et à l'application des régimes de sécurité sociale aux catégories de travailleurs le plus directement intéressés et à l'égalité des salaires masculins et féminins.

Il rappelle son intention de poursuivre en matière de concurrence, de transports et de droit d'établissement une politique qui suive le rythme du développement des autres domaines du marché commun.

Il attache une attention particulière au développement économique des pays et territoires d'outre-mer associés et veillera à prendre les mesures nécessaires pour qu'ils puissent profiter pleinement des bénéfices de l'association.

Il invite la Commission à lui faire, dans ces divers domaines, des propositions concrètes dans le délai de trois mois.

DÉCLARATION D'INTENTION DANS LE DOMAINE DES RELATIONS EXTÉRIEURES

Il est dans l'esprit et les intentions de la Communauté Économique Européenne, tout en veillant aux nécessités de son développement interne, de poursuivre à l'égard des pays tiers et notamment des autres pays européens une politique libérale qui tienne compte de leurs préoccupations. Le Conseil confirme à cet égard ses intentions manifestées dans sa décision du 24 novembre 1959.

La Communauté est prête à poursuivre activement des négociations avec tous les États ou groupes d'États membres du Comité des Questions commerciales.

Dans ce cadre, les négociations à entreprendre en particulier avec les pays membres de l'Association Européenne de Libre-Échange devraient être de préférence orientées vers le maintien du commerce traditionnel entre la Communauté Économique Européenne et les pays de l'Association Européenne de Libre-Échange, en conformité avec les règles de l'Accord général sur les Tarifs douaniers et le Commerce, et si possible vers l'augmentation de ce commerce.

La recherche d'une telle coopération en vue d'une réduction réciproque des barrières aux échanges doit s'inscrire dans le respect des principes de l'Accord général sur les Tarifs douaniers et le Commerce. C'est sur une telle base, ne mettant pas en cause, en ce qui concerne la Communauté Économique Européenne, la constitution de l'union douanière sur laquelle elle se fonde, que la coopération peut être recherchée, notamment dans le domaine tarifaire.

La Communauté Économique Européenne rappelle sa décision du 24 novembre 1959 dans laquelle elle proposait la création d'une commission de contact qui permettra de surveiller l'évolution des courants d'échanges et de trouver les moyens appropriés de répondre aux difficultés qui se présenteraient. Le Comité des questions commerciales en est saisi.

2. RÈGLEMENT NO. 9 CONCERNANT LE FONDS SOCIAL EUROPÉEN

LE CONSEIL DE LA COMMUNAUTÉ ÉCONOMIQUE EUROPÉENNE,

vu les dispositions du Traité instituant la Communauté Économique Européenne, et notamment l'article 127,

DECLARATION OF INTENTION CONCERNING INTERNAL ACCELERATION

The Council confirms its intention to proceed as expeditiously as possible with a more rapid implementation of the Treaty, not only so far as the customs union is concerned but concurrently in all sectors of economic integration.

The Council lays special emphasis on its desire to hasten the implementation of measures in the social field, especially in connection with the vocational training of workers and their freedom of movement, with the application of social security provisions to those categories of workers most immediately concerned, and with equal pay for men and women workers.

The Council recalls its intention to pursue in the fields of competition, transport and the right of establishment a policy in step with developments in the other sectors of the common market.

The Council attaches particular importance to the economic development of the associated overseas countries and territories and will ensure that the necessary measures will be taken to enable these countries to draw the fullest benefit from their association.

The Council requests the Commission to submit to it within three months concrete proposals on these matters.

DECLARATION OF INTENTION CONCERNING EXTERNAL RELATIONS

It is in the spirit and the intention of the European Economic Community, whilst safeguarding the needs of its internal development, to pursue, *vis-à-vis* non-member countries, and in particular *vis-à-vis* the other European countries, a liberal policy which takes their anxieties into account. In this respect the Council re-affirms the intentions set forth in its decision of 24th November, 1959.

The Community is ready to undertake active negotiations with all the States or groups of States who are members of the Committee on Trade Problems.

In this context, the negotiations to be opened with the Member countries of the European Free Trade Association, in particular, should be directed towards maintaining and, if possible, increasing the traditional trade between the European Economic Community and the countries of the European Free Trade Association, subject always to conformity with the rules of the General Agreement on Tariffs and Trade.

Efforts at co-operation on these lines, with a view to the reciprocal reduction of trade barriers, must respect the principles of the General Agreement on Tariffs and Trade. It is on this basis, and without calling into question the European Economic Community's establishment of the customs union on which it is founded, that co-operation can be sought, largely in the field of tariffs.

The European Economic Community recalls its decision of 24th November, 1959, in which it proposed that a Contact Committee be set up which could be used to observe trade trends and through which the appropriate means to meet any difficulties could be found. This matter has been referred to the Committee on Trade Problems.

2. REGULATION NO. 9 CONCERNING THE EUROPEAN SOCIAL FUND

THE COUNCIL OF THE EUROPEAN ECONOMIC COMMUNITY,

Considering the provisions of the Treaty establishing the European Economic Community, and in particular Article 127,

vu la proposition de la Commission,
vu l'avis du Comité économique et social,
vu l'avis de l'Assemblée Parlementaire Européenne,

considérant que le Fonds social européen doit apporter une contribution essentielle au relèvement du niveau de vie des travailleurs, en améliorant leurs possibilités d'emploi ainsi que leur mobilité géographique et professionnelle,

considérant que, dans le cadre de cette mission, une tâche immédiate a été confiée au Fonds par les dispositions de l'article 125 du Traité,

considérant que les dispositions du Protocole concernant l'Italie, annexé au Traité, recommendant de recourir à un emploi adéquat des ressources du Fonds, en vue de faciliter au Gouvernement italien son action pour diminuer le chômage,

considérant que le Règlement ci-après a pour objet de régler les modalités d'action et de fonctionnement du Fonds dans la réalisation de ses tâches immédiates, sans préjuger les autres missions qui seront confiées au Fonds dans les conditions prévues au Traité,

considérant qu'en raison de la diversité des législations nationales et pour donner plein effet à l'action du Fonds en conformité des objectifs généraux de la Communauté, la mise en oeuvre des dispositions du Traité impose de définir d'une manière uniforme les notions à partir desquelles le Fonds apportera son concours dans les domaines visés à l'article 125,

considérant que seules des définitions uniformes permettent d'éviter que le Fonds ne rembourse pas des dépenses résultant d'opérations qui ne correspondent pas à sa mission,

considérant qu'il convient de préciser les limites dans lesquelles le concours du Fonds est accordé ainsi que le régime transitoire pour le remboursement des dépenses effectuées entre le premier janvier 1958 et la date d'entrée en vigueur du présent Règlement,

considérant que pour faciliter l'instruction des demandes de remboursement les États membres doivent accorder à la Commission leur plein concours, notamment en permettant à celle-ci de disposer de tous les éléments d'information nécessaires,

A ARRÊTÉ LE PRÉSENT RÈGLEMENT:

PREMIÈRE PARTIE

CONDITIONS DU CONCOURS DU FONDS

Champ d'application

Article premier

Le Fonds, dont la fonction est de promouvoir, à l'intérieur de la Communauté, les facilités d'emploi et la mobilité géographique et professionnelle des travailleurs, rembourse, dans les conditions et les limites du Traité et du présent Règlement, 50% des dépenses consacrées par les États membres ou par des organismes de droit public:

- à la rééducation professionnelle des travailleurs en chômage;
- à la réinstallation des travailleurs en chômage;
- au maintien du même niveau de rémunération des travailleurs touchés par une reconversion.

Toutefois, le Fonds ne rembourse par les dépenses supportées par les États membres ou par des organismes de droit public, concernant le personnel participant à l'exercice de l'autorité publique.

De même, le Fonds ne participe pas aux dépenses visées au paragraphe 1 du présent article, si les dépenses effectuées répondent aux conditions

Considering the proposal of the Commission,
Considering the opinion of the Economic and Social Committee,
Considering the opinion of the European Parliament,
Whereas the European Social Fund is to make an essential contribution to raising the living standard of workers by improving their opportunities for employment and their geographical and occupational mobility,
Whereas an immediate task in connection with this objective has been entrusted to the Fund under Article 125 of the Treaty,
Whereas the provisions of the Protocol concerning Italy, appended to the Treaty, recommend the adequate utilization of the Fund's resources to facilitate the task of the Italian Government in reducing unemployment,
Whereas the object of the following Regulation is to fix the procedure for the activities and operation of the Fund in the discharge of its immediate tasks, without prejudice to other tasks which will be entrusted to it as provided for in the Treaty.
Whereas, by reason of the diversity of national legislative provisions and to give full effect to the action of the Fund in conformity with the general objectives of the Community, the implementation of the provisions of the Treaty makes it imperative to define in a uniform manner the concepts which shall underlie the granting by the Fund of assistance in the fields covered by Article 125,
Whereas uniform definitions alone make it possible to avoid the Fund reimbursing expenses in respect of operations incompatible with its task,
Whereas there is need to specify the limits within which the assistance of the Fund shall be granted as well as the transitional system for the reimbursement of expenses effected between 1 January, 1958, and the date of the entry into force of this Regulation,
Whereas, in order to facilitate the examination of applications for reimbursement, the Member States must grant the Commission their full assistance, in particular by enabling the Commission to have all necessary information at its disposal.

HAS AGREED ON THE FOLLOWING REGULATION:

PART ONE

CONDITIONS FOR THE GRANTING OF AID BY THE FUND

Field of application

Article 1

The Fund, whose function is to promote within the Community employment facilities and the geographical and occupational mobility of workers, shall reimburse, under the conditions and within the limits laid down by the Treaty and by this Regulation, 50% of the expenses incurred by the Member States or by bodies under public law for:
- the occupational re-training of unemployed workers;
- the resettlement of unemployed workers;
- the maintenance of the same wage level for workers affected by conversion operations.

However, the Fund shall not reimburse expenses incurred by the Member States or by bodies under public law in respect of personnel participating in the exercise of public authority.

Similarly, the Fund shall not assist in covering the expenses referred to in paragraph 1 of this Article if the expenses incurred fulfil the conditions de l'octroi, par la Haute Autorité, d'une aide non remboursable au titre des dispositions du Traité instituant la Communauté Européenne du Charbon et de l'Acier ou de la Convention relative aux dispositions transitoires.

Le Conseil, sur proposition de la Commission, peut confier au Fonds, conformément au Traité, toute mission dans le cadre d'initiatives visant à améliorer les possibilités d'emploi et la mobilité géographique et professionnelle des travailleurs, ainsi que dans la mise en oeuvre, en application de l'article 128 du Traité, d'une politique commune de formation professionnelle.

Travailleurs en chômage

Article 2

Par travailleur en chômage, au sens de l'article premier du présent Règlement, on entend toute personne, âgée d'au moins seize ans, inscrite à un bureau officiel de main-d'oeuvre en qualité de demandeur d'emploi et privée de tout emploi salarié ou indépendant.

Toutefois, un délai d'inscription de trois mois consécutifs est requis pour les travailleurs de moins de dix-huit ans.

Est également considérée comme travailleur en chômage toute personne qui se trouve dans l'un des cas suivants, constaté par le bureau officiel de main-d'oeuvre compétent:

a) Être comme travailleur salarié ou travailleur indépendant dans une situation manifeste de sous-emploi prolongé, et être inscrite auprès d'un bureau officiel de main-d'oeuvre compétent, comme demandeur d'un emploi s'exerçant à temps plein, ou – pendant une période de deux ans à partir de la mise en vigueur du présent Règlement, et à défaut d'une pareille inscription pour les travailleurs âgés d'au moins dix-huit ans – faire l'objet d'une attestation du bureau officiel compétent constatant qu'elle est dans cette situation de sous-emploi depuis au moins six mois;

b) Être touchée par une reconversion au sens de l'article 9 du présent Règlement, pour autant que cette reconversion nécessite corrélativement sa rééducation professionnelle.

Rééducation professionnelle

Article 3

Par rééducation professionnelle des travailleurs en chômage, au sens de l'article premier du présent Règlement, on entend toute formation dispensée suivant un programme préétabli, définissant entre autres conditions son étendue et sa durée, dans le but d'assurer aux travailleurs en chômage un emploi productif salarié, impliquant soit une réadaptation, soit un changement de profession, métier ou poste de travail. Ce changement peut porter sur la nature de l'emploi exercé antérieurement ou sur son niveau de qualification et s'appliquer à tous les travailleurs, quelle que soit leur qualification existante, qui ne peuvent être employés qu'après avoir fait l'objet d'une action éducative tendant à transformer ou à élever leur qualification professionnelle.

Ne sont pas visés par le présent article les systèmes normaux d'enseignement s'adressant spécialement aux jeunes.

Article 4

Le concours du Fonds à la rééducation professionnelle des travailleurs en chômage ne peut être accordé que si les travailleurs en cause remplissent les conditions suivantes:

for the granting by the High Authority of nonreimbursable aid under the provisions of the Treaty establishing the European Coal and Steel Com munity or of its Convention containing the transitional provisions.

On a proposal of the Commission and in conformity with the Treaty, the Council shall have power to entrust the Fund with any task connected with action to improve opportunities of employment and the geographical and occupational mobility of workers or the implementation, in application of Article 128 of the Treaty, of a common occupational training policy.

Unemployed workers

Article 2

An unemployed worker within the meaning of Article 1 of this Regulation shall be any person aged at least sixteen registered with an official employment exchange as an applicant for employment and having no paid or independent employment.

However, a period of registration of three consecutive months is required in the case of workers under eighteen.

Any person noted by the official employment exchange concerned as falling within one of the categories in *a*) and *b*) below shall also be considered as an unemployed worker:

a) Any wage-earner or independent worker in a manifest situation of prolonged under-employment and registered with an official employment exchange as an applicant for full-time employment or – for a period of two years beginning with the entry into force of this Regulation, and failing a similar registration in the case of workers under eighteen – certified by the official exchange concerned as having been in this situation of under-employment for at least six months;

b) Any person affected by a conversion, within the meaning of Article 9 of this Regulation, to the extent that this conversion at the same time necessitates his occupational re-training.

Occupational re-training

Article 3

Occupational re-training of unemployed workers within the meaning of Article 1 of this Regulation shall be any training provided under a pre-established programme which defines, among other conditions, its scope and duration for the purpose of ensuring to unemployed workers productive paid employment, implying either resettlement or change of occupation, trade, or work position. This change may concern either the nature of the employment previously carried on or the requisite degree of qualification, and apply to all workers, whatever their existing qualifications may be, who cannot be employed before they have undergone instruction to transform or improve their occupational qualifications.

This Article does not cover normal systems of teaching provided especially for young people.

Article 4

The assistance of the Fund for the occupational re-training of unemployed workers shall only be granted if the workers concerned fulfil the following conditions:

1. N'avoir pu obtenir d'emploi dans une activité de nature analogue et de niveau équivalent à ceux de l'activité antérieurement exercée, ou correspondant à leurs possibilités normales de travail s'ils n'ont pas déjà exercé une activité salariée;

2. Occuper, après leur rééducation, à l'intérieur de la Communauté, un nouvel emploi productif salarié dans la profession, métier, poste de travail, pour lequel ils ont été rééduqués, ou dans une activité similaire;

3. Avoir exercé cet emploi productif pendant au moins six mois au cours des douze mois suivant la fin du stage de rééducation.

Article 5

Le concours du Fonds en matière de rééducation professionnelle, dans la limite de l'article premier du présent Règlement, est accordé:

a) En ce qui concerne les dépenses supportées par un État ou un organisme de droit public pour l'exécution de programmes de rééducation professionnelle dans les centres collectifs de l'État, des organismes de droit public, ou dans les centres collectifs privés placés sous leur contrôle effectif, pour:

1. Les indemnités de séjour, frais d'hébergement, frais de voyage, primes de travail, frais relatifs au maintien intégral des droits aux prestations familiales et de sécurité sociale de même que les indemnités de chômage et tout autre avantage accordés aux personnes rééduquées pendant la période de leur rééducation et en fonction des nécessités de celle-ci;

2. Les salaires et les charges sociales y afférentes consacrés au personnel des centres;

3. Les dépenses de matériel d'équipement;

4. Les dépenses de matériaux;

5. Les frais d'administration, location de locaux, assurances, entretien, chauffage, éclairage;

6. Les frais d'amortissement;

Le total des coûts mentionnés sous *a*) sera estimé chaque fois forfaitairement à 135% des dépenses effectuées qui sont visées aux paragraphes 1 et 2;

b) En ce qui concerne les dépenses supportées par un État ou un organisme de droit public pour l'exécution, sous son contrôle effectif, d'un programme de rééducation professionnelle auprès d'une ou plusieurs entreprises privées, pour:

- les dépenses figurant au paragraphe 1 sous *a*) ci-dessus;
- le cas échéant, les salaires et les charges sociales y afférentes consacrés au personnel assurant la rééducation, ainsi que les autres dépenses figurant aux paragraphes 3 à 5 sous *a*) effectivement supportées par l'État ou un organisme de droit public, à condition qu'il s'agisse d'une gestion séparée.

Au cas où les travaux pratiques de rééducation professionnelle comportent une participation directe à la production, la valeur en résultant sera déduite du total des coûts susvisés.

Réinstallation

Article 6

Par réinstallation d'un travailleur en chômage, au sens de l'article premier du présent Règlement, on entend le changement de lieu de résidence à l'intérieur de la Communauté, rendu nécessaire pour occuper un nouvel emploi productif salarié à caractère non saisonnier offert ou agréé par le ou les services de main-d'oeuvre compétents. L'ancien et le nouveau

1. That they have been unable to obtain employment in an activity of a similar nature and equivalent level to those of the activity previously exercised, or corresponding to their normal qualifications for work if they have not already been in paid employment;

2. That after their re-training they take up a new paid productive employment within the Community, in the occupation, trade, or work position for which they have been re-trained, or in a similar activity;

3. That they have been in this productive employment for at least six months in the course of the twelve months following the end of the re-training period.

Article 5

Within the limits laid down in Article 1 of this Regulation, the assistance of the Fund for occupational re-training shall be granted:

a) In respect of the expenses incurred by a State or a body under public law in the carrying out of group occupational re-training programmes in State establishments, bodies under public law, or private establishments placed under their effective supervision, for:

1. Allowances for residence, board and lodging, travel expenses, bonuses for work, expenditure in connection with the complete maintenance of rights to family and social security benefits and also to unemployment benefits and any other benefit granted to the persons being re-trained during the period of such re-training and in the light of its requirements;

2. Salaries and related social costs for the personnel of the centres;

3. Expenditure on equipment;

4. Expenditure on materials;

5. Costs of administration, rent of premises, insurance, maintenance, heating, light;

6. Amortization costs;

The total of the expenses referred to under *a*) shall be estimated on each occasion as a lump sum equal to 135% of those expenses incurred which are covered under sub-paras 1 and 2;

b) In respect of expenses borne by a State or a body under public law for the carrying out, under its effective supervision, of a programme of occupational re-training with one or several private enterprises, for:

- expenses referred to in para *a*) sub-para 1 above;
- where applicable, the wages and related social costs for the personnel providing the re-training, and the other expenses shown in paragraph *a*) sub-paras 3 to 5 actually borne by the State or by a body under public law, on condition that this is under independent management.

Should the practical work of occupational re-training necessitate direct participation in production, the value resulting from this shall be deducted from the total of the above-mentioned costs.

Resettlement

Article 6

Resettlement of an unemployed worker within the meaning of Article 1 of this Regulation shall mean any change in the place of residence within the Community required to occupy a new paid productive employment of a non-seasonal nature offered or approved by the competent employment service(s). The old and the new place of residence shall be those lieu de résidence sont ceux qui sont reconnus comme tels par le ou les États membres qui présentent la demande visant le concours du Fonds en application de l'article 17 du présent Règlement.

Article 7

Le concours du Fonds à la réinstallation des travailleurs en chômage ne peut être accordé qui si les travailleurs en cause remplissent les conditions suivantes:

1. N'avoir pu, lorsqu'ils demeuraient dans leur ancien lieu de résidence, obtenir d'emploi dans une activité de nature analogue et de niveau équivalent à ceux de l'activité exercée ou correspondant à leurs possibilités normales de travail, s'ils n'ont pas déjà exercé une activité salariée;

2. Dans un délai de six mois, à compter du départ de l'ancienne résidence, avoir trouvé un nouvel emploi productif salarié dans un nouveau lieu de résidence ou effectuer dans celui-ci un stage de rééducation professionnelle au sens de l'article 3 du présent Règlement;

3. Avoir exercé dans cette nouvelle résidence un ou plusieurs emplois productifs salariés pendant au moins six mois au cours des douze mois suivant leur départ de l'ancienne résidence ou suivant la fin de leur stage de rééducation.

Article 8

Le concours du Fonds, dans la limite de l'article premier du présent Règlement, est accordé pour les dépenses résultant de la réinstallation, c'est-à-dire:

1. Les frais de voyage du travailleur et des personnes à sa charge, reconnues comme telles par le ou les États membres qui présentent la demande visant le concours du Fonds en application de l'article 17 du présent Règlement;

2. Les frais de transport de son mobilier ou une indemnité forfaitaire correspondante;

3. Une indemnité couvrant les autres frais résultant de la réinstallation, y compris les frais de séparation éventuelle, à concurrence d'un montant égal au maximum à trois fois la moyenne du salaire hebdomadaire effectivement perçu par le travailleur pendant les six premiers mois d'activité dans sa nouvelle résidence, majoré d'autant de fois une fois et demie ce salaire qu'il a de personnes à sa charge; l'indemnité ainsi calculée ne pourra toutefois dépasser douze fois la moyenne du salaire hebdomadaire effectivement perçu.

Reconversion

Article 9

Par reconversion, au sens de l'article premier du présent Règlement, on entend tout changement non provisoire du programme de production d'une entreprise ou partie d'entreprise ayant son propre programme de production, affectant les élements déterminants de ce programme et ayant pour but la production de nouveaux produits se différenciant des anciens autrement que par des améliorations ou des compléments.

Ce changement doit être accompagné d'une suspension temporaire ou d'une réduction de l'activité rétribuée du personnel, après qu'auront été épuisées les possibilités d'emploi approprié offertes par l'entreprise elle-même, et doit permettre le réemploi de tout ou partie de ce personnel après la période de reconversion.

recognized as such by the Member State(s) submitting the application for the assistance of the Fund under Article 17 of this Regulation.

Article 7

The assistance of the Fund in the resettlement of unemployed workers shall only be granted if the workers in question fulfil the following conditions:

1. That they have been unable, while they remained in their previous place of residence, to obtain employment in an activity of a similar nature and of equivalent level to those of the activity previously exercised or corresponding to their normal qualifications for work, if they have not already been in paid employment;

2. That, within six months reckoned from the time of leaving the previous place of residence, they have found a new paid productive employment in a new place of residence or have there undergone a period of occupational re-training within the meaning of Article 3 of this Regulation;

3. That in this new place of residence they have been in paid productive employment in one or more activities for at least six months of the twelve months following their departure from the previous place of residence or following the termination of their period of re-training.

Article 8

Within the limits laid down in Article 1 of this Regulation, the assistance of the Fund shall be granted for expenses arising from resettlement, *i.e.*:

1. Travelling expenses of the worker and those dependents who are recognized as such by the Member State(s) submitting the application for the assistance of the Fund under Article 17 of this Regulation;

2. Costs of furniture removal or a corresponding lump sum payment;

3. Compensation to cover the other expenses arising from the resettlement, including a possible separation allowance up to a maximum amount equal to three times the average weekly wage actually paid to the worker during the first six months of activity in his new place of residence, plus one and a half times this wage for every dependent; the compensation thus calculated may not, however, exceed twelve times the average of the weekly wage actually received.

Conversion

Article 9

Within the meaning of Article 1 of this Regulation, conversion shall be any change, which is not of a temporary nature, in the production programme of an enterprise or part of an enterprise having its own production programme, which affects the determinant elements of this programme and the purpose of which is the production of new commodities differing from the old otherwise than by improvements or additions.

This change must be accompanied by a temporary suspension or reduction of the paid activity of the personnel once the opportunities of appropriate employment offered by the enterprise itself are exhausted, and it must permit the re-employment, completely or in part, of this personnel after the conversion period.

Article 10

Par travailleur touché par une reconversion, au sens de l'article premier du présent Règlement, on entend tout travailleur salarié occupant, précédemment à celle-ci, un emploi à caractère permanent dans une entreprise ou partie d'entreprise effectuant une reconversion dans les conditions prévues à l'article 9 et dont l'emploi est temporairement réduit ou suspendu.

Article 11

Par maintien du même niveau de rémunération des travailleurs touchés par une reconversion au sens de l'article premier du présent Règlement, on entend le maintien du salaire brut, à concurrence de 90%, et des versements nécessaires pour conserver les avantages légaux et extra-légaux y attachés, auxquels ces travailleurs avaient droit pour une période de paye normale. Le salaire brut calculé à l'aide des bulletins et livres de paye de l'entreprise s'entend du salaire avant toute déduction obligatoire pour cotisations de sécurité sociale et retenues fiscales à la charge des travailleurs, pour autant que cette déduction ne soit pas interrompue en tout ou en partie pendant la période de reconversion.

Il comprend:

1. Le salaire en espèces au temps, à la tâche ou au rendement;
2. Les primes individuelles et collectives à caractère conventionnel, à condition qu'elles constituent un complément direct du salaire, mais à l'exclusion de toutes primes et indemnités en espèces ou en nature octroyées pour défrayer des dépenses relatives aux déplacements occasionnés par le travail et à l'exercice d'un travail collectif;
3. La valeur représentative des avantages en nature qui, étant accordés en contrepartie d'un travail effectif, ne sont pas maintenus durant la période de reconversion.

Pour les travailleurs au temps, le salaire en espèces sera calculé suivant les taux horaires de la dernière période de paye précédant la présentation du projet de reconversion, prévue à l'article 15, et sur la base de l'horaire normal pour chaque travailleur, tel qu'il est habituellement pratiqué dans l'entreprise. Toutefois, ce calcul ne pourra être fait sur une durée de travail supérieure à 48 heures par semaine, sauf dérogation légale ou réglementaire de caractère permanent autorisant pour des professions ou des travaux déterminés un horaire plus élevé.

Pour les travailleurs au rendement ou à la tâche, la partie salaire de base sera également calculée de cette façon; la partie rendement sera évaluée sur la base du rendement moyen des six derniers mois précédant le dépôt du projet de reconversion.

Article 12

Le concours du Fonds, dans la limite de l'article premier du présent Règlement, est accordé pour toutes les dépenses résultant du maintien du même niveau de rémunération des travailleurs touchés par une reconversion, à savoir:

a) En ce qui concerne les travailleurs dont l'emploi est suspendu entièrement et qui n'ont aucun autre emploi temporaire:

l'ensemble du salaire brut et les versements nécessaires pour conserver les avantages légaux et extra-légaux y attachés, calculé comme indiqué à l'article 11;

b) En ce qui concerne les travailleurs dont l'emploi est réduit ou qui sont temporairement occupés à un autre emploi moins lucratif:

la différence entre l'ensemble prévu sous *a*) et la rémunération effectivement perçue.

Article 10

Within the meaning of Article 1 of this Regulation, a worker affected by conversion shall be any wage-earner who, before this conversion, was in permanent employment in an enterprise or part of an enterprise carrying out a conversion under the conditions laid down in Article 9 and whose employment is temporarily reduced or suspended.

Article 11

Within the meaning of Article 1 of this Regulation, the maintenance of the same wage level for workers affected by conversion shall be the maintenance of up to 90% of the gross salary and of the payments necessary to preserve the statutory and fringe benefits attached thereto, to which these workers were entitled for a normal pay period. The gross salary calculated on the basis of the pay-slips and payrolls of the enterprise shall be the salary before any obligatory deduction for social security contributions or stoppages for taxation borne by the workers, to the extent that this deduction is not wholly or partly suspended during the conversion period.

It shall include:

1. The cash wage at time, piece or performance rates;
2. Individual and collective bonuses based on agreements, on condition that they constitute a direct addition to the wage, but excluding all bonuses and compensations in cash or in kind granted to defray expenses in connection with travel necessitated by the work or in connection with the carrying out of a collective task;
3. The equivalent value of benefits in kind which, since they are granted as a counterpart for work actually carried out, are not continued during the conversion period.

For workers paid at time rates, the cash wage shall be calculated in accordance with the hourly rates of the last pay-period preceding the submission under Article 15 of the conversion project, and on the basis of the normal working hours for each worker customary in the enterprise. Nevertheless, this calculation may not be based on a working week longer than 48 hours, except where statutory or administrative exceptions of a permanent nature authorize a longer working week for specific tasks or occupations.

For workers on performance or piece rates, the basic salary element shall also be calculated in this way; the performance element shall be calculated on the basis of the average performance of the six months preceding the submission of the conversion project.

Article 12

The assistance of the Fund, within the limits of Article 1 of this Regulation, shall be granted for all expenses resulting from the maintenance of the same wage level of workers affected by a conversion, *i.e.*:

a) In respect of workers whose employment is entirely suspended and who have no other temporary employment:

the whole of the gross wage and the payments necessary to preserve the statutory and fringe benefits attached to it calculated as indicated in Article 11;

b) In respect of workers whose employment is reduced or who are temporarily occupied in another less lucrative employment:

the difference between the total provided for under *a*) and the remuneration actually received.

Le recours au Fonds au titre de l'alinéa *a*) ci-dessus implique que l'État intéressé s'est assuré que les travailleurs touchés par la reconversion se sont fait inscrire à un bureau officiel de main-d'oeuvre et qu'aucune prestation en vue du maintien du même niveau de rémunération au sens de l'article 11 du présent Règlement n'a été versée pour une période de 4 semaines au minimum, dans le cas où les travailleurs se sont refusés à exercer, sans raison suffisante, un emploi approprié qui leur a été offert.

Article 13

Dans le cas où la reconversion d'une entreprise ou partie d'entreprise nécessite corrélativement la rééducation professionnelle des travailleurs, le Fonds accorde son concours à cette rééducation, à condition que le projet de reconversion prévu à l'article 15 en justifie l'opportunité et que cette rééducation intervienne suivant les dispositions des articles 3 et 4 du présent Règlement.

Ce concours est accordé conformément aux dispositions de l'article 5 du présent Règlement, en excluant cependant des dépenses prises en considération les indemnités de séjour, primes de travail, frais relatifs au maintien intégral des droits aux prestations familiales et de sécurité sociale de même que les indemnités de chômage et tout autre avantage accordé aux personnes rééduquées pendant la période de leur rééducation.

Article 14

Pour l'application des articles 10 à 13 du présent Règlement, ne seront pris en considération que les cas de reconversion d'une entreprise ou partie d'entreprise, au sens de l'article 9, dans laquelle, pendant ou immédiatement avant les opérations de reconversion, l'horaire moyen pratiqué a effectivement été réduit d'au moins 10% ou l'effectif d'au moins 5%, pour l'ensemble des travailleurs qui y sont occupés.

Article 15

En cas de reconversion, le concours du Fonds ne peut être accordé:

1. Que si le gouvernement intéressé a présenté préalablement à la Commission un projet établi par l'entreprise en question, relatif à la reconversion en cause et à son financement, et
2. Que si la Commission a donné son approbation préalable à ce projet.

Le concours n'est accordé que pour ceux des travailleurs touchés par la reconversion qui ont été pleinement réoccupés dans cette entreprise pendant au moins six mois.

DEUXIÈME PARTIE

PROCÉDURE RELATIVE A L'OCTROI DU CONCOURS DU FONDS

Dispositions générales

Article 16

Le premier juillet de chaque année au plus tard, chaque État membre présente au Fonds l'estimation motivée du montant approximatif des demandes qu'il soumettra à la Commission au cours de l'exercice suivant.

Article 17

Toute demande visant le concours du Fonds doit être présentée à la Commission par un ou plusieurs États membres et doit se référer à des

Recourse to the Fund under sub-para *a*) above implies that the State concerned has made sure that the workers affected by the conversion have registered with an official employment exchange and that the payment of remunerations has been suspended for a minimum period of four weeks in cases where the workers have refused, without sufficient grounds, to take up suitable employment offered them.

Article 13

Should the conversion of an enterprise or part of an enterprise involve occupational re-training of the workers, the Fund shall grant its assistance for this re-training on condition that the conversion project, as provided for in Article 15, establishes that it is opportune and that the re-training takes place in accordance with the provisions of Articles 3 and 4 of this Regulation.

This assistance shall be granted in conformity with the provisions of Article 5 of this Regulation, excluding, however, from the expenses taken into account, residence allowances, bonuses for work, expenses in connection with the complete maintenance of rights to family and social security benefits and also unemployment benefits and any other advantage granted to the persons re-trained during the period of their re-training.

Article 14

In applying Articles 10 to 13 of this Regulation, account shall be taken only of cases of conversion of an enterprise or part of an enterprise within the meaning of Article 9, in which, during or immediately before the conversion operations, the average working hours have actually been reduced by at least 10% or the labour force by at least 5% for the whole body of workers employed.

Article 15

In the event of conversion, the assistance of the Fund shall only be granted if:

1. The government concerned has previously submitted to the Commission a project drawn up by the enterprise involved for the conversion in question and its financing, and if
2. The Commission has given its previous approval to this project.

The assistance shall only be granted for those of the workers affected by the conversion who have been fully re-employed in the enterprise for at least six months.

PART TWO

Procedure for the Granting of Assistance by the Fund

General provisions

Article 16

At the latest on 1 July of each year, each Member State shall submit to the Fund a reasoned estimate of the approximate amount of the applications which it intends to submit to the Commission in the course of the following financial year.

Article 17

Every application for the assistance of the Fund must be submitted to the Commission by one or several Member States and must refer to dépenses supportées par les États membres ou par des organismes de droit public à partir du premier janvier 1958.

Article 18

Par organisme de droit public, au sens de l'article premier du présent Règlement, on entend, outre les collectivités publiques décentralisées, tout organisme créé ou reconnu comme organisme de droit public par la législation nationale, doté de la personnalité juridique et de l'autonomie de gestion financière et contrôlé par l'État ou par une collectivité publique décentralisée, à la condition que cet organisme ait parmi ses objectifs des activités relevant de la compétence du Fonds.

La Commission établit et tient à jour la liste des organismes de droit public visés au présent Règlement, après avoir recueilli l'opinion du Comité du Fonds social européen prévu à l'article 27.

Ne devront pas être inclus dans cette liste les entreprises et services à caractère essentiellement industriel et commercial, constitués sous forme d'organismes de droit public.

Cette liste et toute modification éventuelle seront publiées au *Journal officiel des Communautés européennes.*

Présentation des demandes concernant la rééducation professionnelle et la réinstallation

Article 19

Les demandes des États membres relatives à l'obtention de concours du Fonds doivent être présentées à la Commission:

a) Pour la rééducation professionnelle, dans le délai maximum de six mois, à compter de l'expiration du douzième mois après la fin du stage de rééducation.

b) Pour la réinstallation, dans le délai maximum de six mois, à compter de l'expiration du douzième mois après le départ de l'ancien lieu de résidence ou après la fin du stage de rééducation effectué dans la nouvelle résidence.

Les demandes introduites après l'expiration des délais fixés ci-dessus ne sont plus prises en considération.

Article 20

Toute demande visant le concours du Fonds pour un programme de rééducation professionnelle réalisé doit faire ressortir que les dépenses présentées sont conformes aux dispositions du présent Règlement.

Elle doit, à cet effet, contenir au moins les indications suivantes:

- l'origine, la nature et le but du programme;
- tous les renseignements utiles sur les caractéristiques du programme, notamment l'étendue et le contenu, la durée, les horaires, le niveau de qualification visé, les épreuves d'examen, l'importance numérique du personnel formateur et ses conditions d'emploi;
- tous renseignements établissant que la demande porte sur des travailleurs en chômage au sens de l'article 2;
- le nombre total des travailleurs intéressés par le programme et le nombre de travailleurs rééduqués ayant effectivement occupé, dans les conditions de l'article 4, un emploi productif salarié pendant au moins six mois;
- les dépenses détaillées relatives:

1. Aux indemnités de séjour, frais d'hébergement, frais de voyage, primes de travail, frais relatifs au maintien intégral des droits aux prestations familiales et de sécurité sociale, de même qu'aux indemnités de

expenses incurred by the Member States or by bodies under public law on or after 1 January, 1958.

Article 18

Within the meaning of Article 1 of this Regulation, a body under public law shall be, in addition to decentralized public authorities, any body established or recognized as a body under public law by the national legislation, possessing legal entity and autonomous financial management, and supervised by the State or a decentralized public authority, on condition that this body has among its objectives activities which are within the purview of the Fund.

The Commission shall establish and keep up-to-date the list of bodies under public law covered by this Regulation, after having obtained the opinion of the Committee of the European Social Fund as provided in Article 27.

Enterprises and services of an essentially industrial and commercial character constituted in the form of bodies under public law shall not be included in this list.

The list and any possible amendments thereto shall be published in the *Official Gazette of the European Communities.*

Submission of applications concerning occupational re-training and resettlement

Article 19

Applications from the Member States to obtain the assistance of the Fund must be presented to the Commission:

a) In respect of occupational re-training, at the latest within six months reckoned from the end of the twelfth month after the termination of the re-training period;

b) In respect of resettlement, at the latest within six months reckoned from the end of the twelfth month after the departure from the previous place of residence or after the termination of the re-training period carried out in the new place of residence.

Applications submitted after the expiry of the time limits fixed above shall not be considered.

Article 20

Any application for the assistance of the Fund for a programme of occupational re-training which has been completed must show that the expenses as submitted conform with the provisions of this Regulation.

To this end, it must contain at least the following details:

- The origin, nature and purpose of the programme;
- All necessary information on the characteristics of the programme, in particular its scope and content, duration, time-table, degree of proficiency aimed at, examination papers, numbers of training staff and their conditions of employment;
- All information necessary to establish that the application concerns unemployed workers within the meaning of Article 2;
- The total number of workers concerned in the programme and the number of re-trained workers who have actually been in paid productive employment for at least six months under the conditions laid down in Article 4;
- Detailed expenses in connection with:

1. Residence allowances, board and lodging, travel expenses, bonuses for work, expenditure in connection with the complete maintenance of rights to family and social security benefits and also unemployment

chômage et à tout autre avantage accordés aux personnes rééduquées pendant la période de leur rééducation et en fonction des nécessités de celle-ci;

2. Aux salaires et charges sociales y afférentes consacrés au personnel visé à l'article 5;

3. Le cas échéant, au matériel d'équipement, aux matériaux, aux frais d'administration, à la location de locaux, aux assurances, à l'entretien, au chauffage et à l'éclairage;

– la valeur des travaux pratiques de rééducation professionnelle comportant une participation directe à la production.

Article 21

Toute demande visant le concours du Fonds pour une indemnité de réinstallation doit faire ressortir que les dépenses présentées sont conformes aux dispositions du présent Règlement.

Elle doit, à cet effet, contenir au moins les indications suivantes:

– tous renseignements établissant que la demande porte sur les travailleurs en chômage au sens de l'article 2;
– tous renseignements établissant la réalité du déplacement et la nécessité de la réinstallation du travailleur, notamment ses ancien et nouveau lieux de résidence, la date de son départ et celle de sa réinstallation, le nouvel emploi offert ou agréé par le ou les services de main-d'oeuvre compétents et la date à laquelle le travail a été effectivement commencé;
– tous renseignements susceptibles de montrer que les travailleurs qui se sont déplacés ont occupé, dans les conditions de l'article 7, un emploi productif salarié pendant au moins six mois;
– le détail des dépenses énumérées à l'article 8.

Présentation des demandes concernant la reconversion

Article 22

Les États membres doivent présenter à la Commission une demande d'approbation préalable pour tout projet de reconversion pour lequel le concours du Fonds est envisagé. Cette demande doit contenir, outre l'avis motivé du gouvernement intéressé, toute donnée permettant de juger du plan de reconversion envisagé, et au moins les indications suivantes:

– nécessité, but, ampleur et financement de la reconversion;
– durée prévue des opérations de reconversion et leur rythme d'exécution;
– nombre de travailleurs dont l'emploi sera maintenu à la suite de mesures prises par l'entreprise elle-même;
– nombre de travailleurs dont l'emploi sera temporairement réduit ou suspendu en tout ou en partie et description des nouveaux emplois prévus; échelonnement des réductions et des réemplois;
– incidences financières du maintien, selon les dispositions de l'article 11, du même niveau de rémunération des travailleurs touchés;
– justification de l'opportunité d'un programme éventuel de rééducation professionnelle et nombre de travailleurs intéressés;
– incidences financières de l'exécution de ce programme de rééducation professionnelle.

Article 23

Les demandes des États membres relatives à l'obtention du concours du Fonds pour une reconversion réalisée doivent être présentées à la Commission dans les douze mois suivant la fin des opérations de reconbenefits and any other benefit granted to the persons being re-trained during the period of such re-training and in the light of its requirements;

2. The salaries and related social costs for the personnel referred to in Article 5;

3. Expenses for equipment, materials, administrative costs, rent of premises, insurance, maintenance, heating and light, as the case may be;

– The value of practical work involving direct participation in production in the course of occupational re-training.

Article 21

Any application for the assistance of the Fund in respect of compensation for resettlement must show that the expenses as presented conform with the provisions of this Regulation.

To this end, it must contain at least the following details:

– All information necessary to establish that the application concerns unemployed workers within the meaning of Article 2;
– All information to establish the fact of the movement and the necessity for the resettlement of the worker, in particular his old and new place of residence, the date of his departure and that of his resettlement, the new employment offered or approved by the employment service(s) concerned and the date on which the work actually began;
– All information likely to show that the workers who have moved have been in paid productive employment for at least six months under the conditions in Article 7;
– Details of the expenses listed in Article 8.

Submission of applications concerning conversion

Article 22

The Member States shall submit to the Commission an application for prior approval in respect of any conversion project for which the assistance of the Fund is envisaged. This application shall contain, in addition to the reasoned opinion of the Government concerned, any data to make possible an appraisal of the conversion plan envisaged, and at least the following information:

– Need, purpose, scope and financing of the conversion;
– Planned duration of the conversion operations and pace at which they are to be carried out;
– Number of workers whose employment will be maintained by measures taken by the enterprise itself;
– Number of workers whose employment will be temporarily reduced or suspended wholly or in part, and description of the new employment planned for them; staggering of cuts in staff and re-employment;
– Financial repercussions of the maintenance, according to the provisions of Article 11, of the same wage level for the workers affected;
– Reasons why the programme of occupational re-training seems called for, and the number of workers concerned;
– Financial repercussions of carrying out this programme of occupational re-training.

Article 23

Applications from the Member States for the assistance of the Fund for a conversion already carried out shall be submitted to the Commission within the twelve months following termination of the conversion operversion approuvées. Les demandes introduites après l'expiration du délai fixé ci-dessus ne sont plus prises en considération.

Toute demande doit faire ressortir que les dépenses présentées sont conformes aux dispositions du présent Règlement. Elle doit, à cet effet, contenir notamment les indications suivantes:

- tous renseignements indiquant que la reconversion a été réalisée en concordance avec le projet approuvé par la Commission;
- tous renseignements indiquant que les travailleurs bénéficiaires sont pleinement réoccupés dans l'entreprise depuis au moins six mois;
- les dépenses détaillées relatives;

1. Au maintien du salaire brut et des versements nécessaires pour conserver les avantages légaux et extra-légaux y attachés;

2. Éventuellement, en cas de rééducation professionnelle des travailleurs:

aux salaires et charges sociales y afférentes consacrés au personnel visé à l'article 5, aux frais d'hébergement et de voyage des travailleurs rééduqués;

au matériel d'équipement, aux matériaux, aux frais d'administration, à la location de locaux, aux assurances, à l'entretien, au chauffage et à l'éclairage.

Examen des demandes et enquêtes éventuelles

Article 24

Les États membres accordent toute leur collaboration à la Commission pour lui permettre de recueillir toute information complémentaire qu'elle juge utile pour vérifier le bienfondé des éléments contenus dans les demandes visant le concours du Fonds. Ils facilitent le cas échéant des contacts avec les organismes ou entreprises intéressés.

Article 25

La Commission examine la conformité des demandes aux dispositions du présent Règlement. A cet examen, elle associe le Comité du Fonds dans les conditions prévues aux articles 28 à 30.

Opérations financières

Article 26

Les modalités et la procédure des opérations financières ainsi que celles de la mise à la disposition des contributions des États membres destinées à faire face aux dépenses du Fonds sont fixées dans le règlement financier prévu par l'article 207 du Traité. Ce règlement fixe également les modalités relatives à la reddition et à la vérification des comptes ainsi que les règles de contrôle de la responsabilité des ordonnateurs et comptables.

TROISIÈME PARTIE

Comité du Fonds Social Européen

Article 27

La Commission est assistée dans sa tâche par un Comité composé de représentants des gouvernements et des organisations syndicales de travailleurs et d'employeurs, dont le statut sera arrêté par le Conseil.

ations approved. Applications submitted after the expiry of the above time limit shall not be considered.

Every application must show that the expenses submitted conform with the provisions of this Regulation. To this effect they shall, in particular, contain the following details:

- All information showing that the conversion has been carried out in accordance with the project approved by the Commission;
- All information indicating that the workers who have benefited have been fully re-employed in the enterprise for at least six months;
- Detailed expenses in connection with:

1. The maintenance of the gross wage and of the payments necessary to preserve the statutory and fringe benefits attached thereto;

2. Where necessary, in cases of occupational re-training of workers:

wages and social costs in connection therewith paid to personnel referred to in Article 5, lodging and travel expenses of the workers re-trained;

equipment, materials, administrative costs, rent of premises, insurance, maintenance, heating and light.

Examination of applications and possible enquiries

Article 24

The Member States shall give every aid to the Commission to enable it to assemble all further information which it deems necessary to verify the details contained in the applications for assistance from the Fund. Where necessary, they shall facilitate contacts with the bodies or enterprises concerned.

Article 25

The Commission shall examine whether applications conform with the provisions of this Regulation. The Committee of the Fund shall be associated with it in this examination in the manner laid down in Articles 28 to 30.

Financial operations

Article 26

The financial regulations provided for in Article 207 of the Treaty lay down the methods and procedure of the financial operations as well as those whereby the contributions of Member States to meet the expenses of the Fund are made available. These regulations also establish the procedure for rendering and auditing accounts and fix the responsibility and relevant supervision of pay-commissioners and accountants.

PART THREE

COMMITTEE OF THE EUROPEAN SOCIAL FUND

Article 27

The Commission shall be assisted in its task by a Committee, consisting of representatives of the Governments and of trade union and employers' organizations, the statutes of which shall be decided upon by the Council.

Article 28

Le Comité est consulté sur toutes les questions d'importance générale ou de principe concernant l'administration du Fonds. A cet effet, il reçoit tous documents et informations nécessaires.

Il a également sur ces mêmes questions la faculté de présenter de sa propre initiative à la Commission des avis suivant les modalités de son statut.

En outre, il est régulièrement informé de l'activité du Fonds ainsi que des divers aspects de la politique générale de la Commission en matière économique et sociale intéressant cette activité.

Article 29

L'avis préalable du Comité est obligatoirement recueilli en ce qui concerne:

1. L'avant-projet de budget annuel du Fonds;
2. La liste des organismes de droit public et sa mise à jour;
3. Les demandes visant le concours du Fonds ou l'approbation préalable par la Commission d'un projet de reconversion;
4. Les problèmes que pose l'intervention du Fonds dans la réalisation d'une politique commune de formation professionnelle;
5. Les mesures d'exécution nécessaires à l'application du présent Règlement;
6. L'opportunité d'une révision du présent Règlement et les éventuelles propositions de révision;
7. Les modifications éventuelles des tâches du Fonds à l'expiration de la période de transition.

Article 30

Le Comité peut émettre des avis d'ordre général sur des demandes ou des catégories de demandes, visant le concours du Fonds, qu'il estime ne plus devoir lui être présentées séparément, de façon à éviter de sa part la répétition des avis.

Dispositions finales

Article 31

La Commission est chargée de prendre les mesures d'exécution résultant des dispositions du présent Règlement.

Article 32

La Commission examine, dans la limite de deux ans après la mise en vigueur du présent Règlement, l'opportunité de procéder à sa révision. Elle soumet au Conseil dans ce délai, éventuellement sous forme de proposition, les conclusions de cet examen.

Disposition transitoire

Article 33

Les délais de six mois prévus à l'article 19 sont prorogés jusqu'à l'expiration du sixième mois après la mise en vigueur du présent Règlement, dans les cas où l'expiration du douzième mois après la fin du stage de rééducation ou après le départ de l'ancien lieu de résidence est intervenue

Article 28

The Committee shall be consulted on all questions of general importance or of principle concerning the administration of the Fund. To this end it shall receive all necessary documents and information.

According to its statutes it is also empowered to express opinions to the Commission on its own initiative.

Furthermore, the Committee shall be regularly informed of the activities of the Fund and of the various aspects of the general policy of the Commission in economic and social matters relating to such activities.

Article 29

The prior opinion of the Committee must be obtained in the following matters:

1. The advance draft of the annual budget of the Fund;
2. The establishment and keeping up to date of the list of bodies under public law.
3. Applications for the assistance of the Fund, or the prior approval by the Commission of a conversion project;
4. Problems arising from any action by the Fund intended to achieve a common policy on occupational training;
5. Any action required for applying this Regulation;
6. The advisability of a revision of this Regulation and any proposals for such revision;
7. Any changes in the tasks of the Fund after the end of the transition period.

Article 30

The Committee may formulate opinions of a general nature on applications or categories of applications to the Fund for assistance when, to save repetition of the Committee's opinions, they are no longer considered to need separate submission.

Final Provisions

Article 31

The Commission shall take the action required by this Regulation.

Article 32

Within two years of this Regulation coming into force, the Commission shall consider the advisability of revising it. It shall submit the conclusions of this examination to the Council within this time limit, in the form of a proposal if appropriate.

Transitory Provision

Article 33

The six-month time limits provided for in Article 19 shall be extended until the expiry of the sixth month after this Regulation comes into force in those cases where the expiry of the twelfth month after the conclusion of the re-training period or the departure from the old place of avant cette mise en vigueur, pour autant que le stage de rééducation ou la réinstallation ait eu lieu après le premier janvier 1958.

Le présent Règlement est obligatoire dans tous ses éléments et directement applicable dans tout État membre.

Fait à Bruxelles, le 25 août 1960.

Par le Conseil, Le président
J. M. A. H. LUNS

STATUT DU COMITÉ DU FONDS SOCIAL EUROPÉEN

LE CONSEIL DE LA COMMUNAUTÉ ÉCONOMIQUE EUROPÉENNE,

vu les dispositions du Traité instituant la Communauté Économique Européenne et notamment les articles 124 et 153,

après avoir recueilli l'avis de la Commission,

DÉCIDE:

Article premier

Le Comité du Fonds social européen assiste la Commission dans l'administration du Fonds, selon les conditions fixées par le présent Statut et par le Règlement prévu à l'article 127 du Traité.

Article 2

Le Comité est composé de trente-six membres, à raison de deux représentants du gouvernement, deux représentants des organisations syndicales de travailleurs et deux représentants des organisations syndicales d'employeurs pour chacun des six États membres.

Article 3

Le Comité est présidé par un membre de la Commission qui ne participe pas au vote.

Article 4

Il est nommé un suppléant pour chacun des six États membres et pour chaque catégorie au sens de l'article 2.

En l'absence de l'un ou des deux membres, leur suppléant participe de plein droit aux délibérations du Comité.

Lorsque les deux membres sont présents, leur suppléant peut assister aux réunions du Comité. Il peut intervenir dans la discussion lorsqu'il y est invité par le président en accord avec les membres titulaires dont il est suppléant.

Article 5

La durée du mandat des membres et des suppléants est de deux ans. Le mandat est renouvelable.

Article 6

Seuls les ressortissants des États membres peuvent être nommés membres du Comité ou suppléants.

Les fonctions de membre ou de suppléant sont incompatibles avec celles de membre d'une institution de la Communauté Économique Européenne ainsi qu'avec celles de fonctionnaire des Communautés Européennes.

residence occurred before it came into force, if the re-training period or the resettlement were subsequent to 1 January, 1958.

This Regulation is mandatory in all its parts and directly applicable in every Member State.

Done at Brussels, on this 25th day of August, 1960.

By the Council, The President
J. M. A. H. LUNS

STATUTES OF THE COMMITTEE OF THE EUROPEAN SOCIAL FUND

THE COUNCIL OF THE EUROPEAN ECONOMIC COMMUNITY

Having Regard to the provisions of the Treaty establishing the European Economic Community, in particular Articles 124 and 153 thereof,

Having heard the opinion of the Commission,

DECIDES:

Article 1

The Committee of the European Social Fund shall assist the Commission in the administration of the Fund in the conditions laid down by these Statutes and by the Regulation provided for under Article 127 of the Treaty.

Article 2

The Committee shall consist of 36 members, being two representatives of the Government, two representatives of the trade unions' and two representatives of the employers' organizations for each of the six Member States.

Article 3

The Chairman of the Committee shall be a member of the Commission, he shall have no voting rights.

Article 4

An alternate shall be appointed for each of the six Member States and for each category within the meaning of Article 2.

In the absence of one or both members, their alternate shall take part with full rights in the deliberations of the Committee.

When the two members are present, their alternate may attend the meetings of the Committee. He may intervene in the discussion when invited to do so by the Chairman in agreement with the regular members whose alternate he is.

Article 5

The duration of the office of members and alternates shall be two years. They may be reappointed.

Article 6

Only nationals of Member States shall be eligible for appointment as members of the Committee or as alternates.

The position of member or alternate shall be incompatible with that of member of an Institution of the European Economic Community and with that of official of the European Communities.

Article 7

Les membres et les suppléants sont nommés par le Conseil. Le Conseil s'efforce de réaliser dans la composition du Comité une représentation équitable des différents secteurs intéressés.

La liste des membres et suppléants du Comité est publiée par le Conseil au *Journal officiel des Communautés européennes* pour information.

Article 8

En règle générale, le Comité se réunit au moins quatre fois par an.

Il est convoqué par son président, soit à l'initiative de celui-ci, soit à la demande d'au moins un tiers des membres.

Les réunions du Comité ne sont pas publiques.

Article 9

Dans la convocation, le président fixe la liste des questions à examiner par le Comité. Toutefois, celui-ci examine également d'autres questions de sa compétence si la majorité des membres est d'accord.

Article 10

A la fin de chaque réunion, le Comité présente à la Commission pour toutes les questions examinées un résumé des avis qu'il a formulés ou des conclusions auxquelles il a abouti.

Dans les cas où le Comité a formulé un avis, le résumé visé à l'alinéa précédent énonce également les diverses opinions éventuellement exprimées en conclusion des débats.

Article 11

Sauf disposition contraire du présent Statut, les décisions du Comité sont acquises à la majorité absolue des suffrages valablement exprimés.

Article 12

En cas de décès ou de démission d'un membre ou d'un suppléant ou si les conditions nécessaires à l'exercice du mandat ne sont plus remplies, le Conseil procède, selon la procédure prévue à l'article 7 du présent Statut, au remplacement du membre ou du suppléant pour la durée du mandat restant à courir.

Article 13

Sur proposition de son président, le Comité peut entendre des experts

Article 14

Le Comité établit, à la majorité de ses membres, son règlement intérieur précisant ses méthodes de travail.

Le règlement intérieur est approuvé par le Conseil après avis de la Commission.

Article 15

Le secrétariat du Comité est assuré par les services de la Commission. Celle-ci met à la disposition du Comité les locaux et les moyens nécessaires à son fonctionnement.

Article 7

The members and alternates shall be appointed by the Council, which shall endeavour when choosing them to provide equitable representation of the various sectors concerned.

The list of members and alternates of the Committee shall be published by the Council for information in the *Official Gazette*.

Article 8

As a general rule, the Committee shall meet at least four times a year.

It shall be convened by the Chairman, either on his own initiative or at the request of at least one third of the members.

Meetings of the Committee shall not be public.

Article 9

In the notice of meeting, the Chairman shall specify the list of questions to be examined by the Committee. Nevertheless, the Committee may also study other questions within its competence if a majority of the members agrees to do so.

Article 10

After each meeting, the Committee shall submit to the Commission a summary of any opinion adopted or any conclusion reached on all the questions discussed.

In cases where the Committee has adopted an opinion, the summary referred to in the preceding sub-paragraph shall also state the various opinions which may have been expressed at the conclusion of the discussion.

Article 11

Except where otherwise provided in these Statutes, the decisions of the Committee shall be taken by an absolute majority of the votes validly cast.

Article 12

In the event of the decease or resignation of a member or alternate, or where the necessary conditions for him to exercise his office are no longer fulfilled, the Council shall replace him for the remainder of his term of office, in accordance with the procedure laid down in Article 7 of these Statutes.

Article 13

On the proposal of the Chairman, the Committee shall be entitled to hear experts.

Article 14

The Committee shall lay down, by majority vote of its members, rules of procedure fixing its methods of work.

The rules of procedure shall be approved by the Council after the Commission has given an opinion on them.

Article 15

The Secretariat of the Committee shall be provided by the staff of the Commission. The Commission shall place at the disposal of the Committee the accommodation and the means necessary for its work.

Article 16

Les dépenses de fonctionnement du Comité sont imputées suivant les dispositions des règlements financiers prévus à l'article 209 du Traité instituant la Communauté Économique Européenne.

Fait à Bruxelles, le 25 août 1960.

Par le Conseil, Le président
J. M. A. H. LUNS

3. RÈGLEMENT NO. 11 CONCERNANT LA SUPPRESSION DE DISCRIMINATIONS EN MATIÈRE DE PRIX ET CONDITIONS DE TRANSPORT, PRIS EN EXÉCUTION DE L'ARTICLE 79, PARAGRAPHE 3, DU TRAITÉ INSTITUANT LA COMMUNAUTÉ ÉCONOMIQUE EUROPÉENNE

LE CONSEIL DE LA COMMUNAUTÉ ÉCONOMIQUE EUROPÉENNE,

vu le Traité instituant la Communauté Économique Européenne, et notamment son article 79,

vu la proposition de la Commission,

vu l'avis du Comité économique et social,

considérant qu'en vertu de l'article 79, paragraphe 3, le Conseil doit établir une réglementation assurant dans le trafic à l'intérieur de la Communauté la suppression des discriminations visées à l'article 79, paragraphe premier;

considérant que, pour assurer cette suppression, il est nécessaire d'interdire ces discriminations, y compris l'établissement de tarifs ou la fixation sous quelque forme que ce soit de prix et conditions de transport dont l'application constituerait une discrimination;

considérant que, pour permettre de vérifier les prix et conditions de transport pratiqués et de déceler les discriminations éventuelles, les transporteurs et intermédiaires doivent être tenus de fournir les informations nécessaires et d'établir un document de transport permettant de les vérifier, ainsi que de se soumettre à contrôle;

considérant enfin qu'un mécanisme de sanctions doit, sous le contrôle de pleine juridiction de la Cour de justice prévu par l'article 172 du Traité, assurer le respect de ces prescriptions;

A ARRÊTÉ LE PRÉSENT RÈGLEMENT:

Article premier

Les dispositions du présent Règlement s'appliquent aux transports de toutes les marchandises par chemin de fer, par route et par voie navigable, à l'intérieur de la Communauté, à l'exclusion des transports des marchandises désignées aux annexes I et III du Traité instituant la Communauté Européenne du Charbon et de l'Acier.

Article 2

1. Les dispositions de ce Règlement s'appliquent à tous les transports dont le lieu de départ ou de destination du produit transporté est situé sur le territoire d'un État membre, y compris les transports entre les États membres et des pays tiers ou associés.

2. Les dispositions du présent Règlement ne s'appliquent qu'aux parties de parcours situées à l'intérieur de la Communauté.

3. Elles s'appliquent également aux parcours par chemin de fer, par route ou par voie navigable dans le cas où les marchandises, sur d'autres parties du parcours, sont transportées par d'autres modes de transport.

Article 16

The operating expenses of the Committee shall be provided in accordance with the financial regulations referred to in Article 209 of the Treaty establishing the European Economic Community.

Done at Brussels, this 25th day of August, 1960.

The Council, The President
J. M. A. H. LUNS

3. REGULATION NO. 11 CONCERNING THE ABOLITION OF DISCRIMINATION IN RESPECT OF TRANSPORT RATES AND CONDITIONS, ISSUED IN PURSUANCE OF ARTICLE 79, PARA. 3, OF THE TREATY ESTABLISHING THE EUROPEAN ECONOMIC COMMUNITY

THE COUNCIL OF THE EUROPEAN ECONOMIC COMMUNITY,

Having regard to the Treaty establishing the European Economic Community, in particular Article 79,

Having regard to the proposal of the Commission,

Having regard to the opinion of the Economic and Social Committee,

Whereas under Article 79, para. 3 the Council is called upon to lay down rules for the abolition of the cases of discrimination referred to in Article 79, para. 1, in the traffic within the Community;

Whereas such abolition entails prohibiting the said cases of discrimination, including the establishment of schedules or the fixing in any form whatsoever of transport rates and conditions the application of which would constitute discrimination;

Whereas, to enable transport rates and conditions to be checked and any cases of discrimination to be detected, carriers or their agents must be required to supply the necessary information and to complete and produce on request transport forms for this purpose;

Whereas, lastly, a system of penalties, under the full jurisdiction of the Court of Justice provided for in Article 172 of the Treaty is necessary to ensure the observance of these rules;

HEREBY ISSUES THE FOLLOWING REGULATION:

Article 1

The provisions of this Regulation shall apply to the conveyance by rail, road, inland waterway within the Community of all goods with the exception of the goods listed in Annexes I and III to the Treaty constituting the European Coal and Steel Community.

Article 2

1. The terms of this Regulation shall apply to the conveyance of all goods from or to any place in the territory of a Member State, including carriage between Member States and third countries or associated countries.

2. The terms of this Regulation shall apply only to those sections of the route situated within the Community.

3. They shall also apply to stretches covered by rail, road or inland waterway in the case of goods carried by other means over other sections of the route.

Article 3

Lorsqu'un transport régi par un contrat unique est effectué par des transporteurs successifs, chaque transporteur est soumis, sur le parcours qu'il effectue, aux dispositions du présent Règlement.

Article 4

1. Sont interdites, dans le trafic à l'intérieur de la Communauté, les discriminations qui consistent en l'application par un transporteur, pour les mêmes marchandises sur les mêmes relations de trafic, de prix et conditions de transport différents en raison du pays d'origine ou de destination des produits transportés.

Cette interdiction n'affecte pas la validité des contrats de droit privé.

2. Est également interdit l'établissement de tarifs, ou la fixation, sous quelque forme que ce soit, de prix et conditions de transport dont l'application constituerait une discrimination au sens du paragraphe premier.

3. Les interdictions énoncées dans le présent article prennent effet le 1er juillet 1961.

Article 5

1. Les gouvernements signalent à la Commission, avant le 1er juillet 1961, les tarifs, les conventions, les accords de prix et conditions de transport, en vigueur dans leur pays respectif, qui prévoient à l'intérieur de la Communauté, sur les mêmes relations de trafic et pour les mêmes marchandises, des prix et conditions de transport différents *selon* le pays d'origine ou de destination de ces marchandises. Sera également portée sans délai à la connaissance de la Commission toute mesure de ce genre qui pourrait être adoptée ultérieurement.

2. Les entreprises qui effectuent des transports sont tenues de fournir à leur gouvernement respectif, avant le 1er janvier 1961, les renseignements utiles relatifs aux tarifs, conventions, accords de prix et conditions de transport visés au paragraphe premier et de leur signaler sans délai toute mesure de ce genre qui pourrait être adoptée ultérieurement.

3. Les dispositions du présent article s'appliquent aux transports dont le lieu de départ ou d'arrivée est situé sur le territoire d'un État membre.

Article 6

1. Chaque transport à l'intérieur de la Communauté fait l'objet d'un document de transport comportant les indications suivantes:

- le nom et l'adresse de l'expéditeur,
- la nature et le poids de la marchandise,
- la localité et la date d'acceptation des marchandises au transport,
- la localité prévue pour la livraison de la marchandise,
- l'itinéraire d'acheminement ou la distance, dans la mesure où ces éléments justifient un prix différent du prix de transport normalement applicable,
- le cas échéant, les points de passage aux frontières.

2. Le document de transport est établi en double exemplaire et numéroté. Un exemplaire accompagne la marchandise; l'autre est conservé par le transporteur pendant deux ans à compter de la date du transport et classé par ordre numérique. Ce dernier exemplaire comporte les prix de transport définitifs sous quelque forme que ce soit, les autres frais et, le cas échéant, les ristournes et toutes les autres conditions influençant les prix et conditions de transport.

3. Lorsque les documents existants comportent toutes les indications visées au paragraphe premier et rendent possible, conjointement avec le système d'enregistrement et la comptabilité des transporteurs, une

Article 3

When a consignment under a single contract is transported in successive stages by more than one carrier, each carrier shall observe the terms of this Regulation in respect of the section of the route for which he is responsible.

Article 4

1. Any discrimination which consists in the application by a carrier, in respect of the same goods conveyed in the same circumstances, of transport rates and conditions which differ on the ground of country of origin or destination of the goods carried is prohibited in the traffic within the Community.

This prohibition shall not affect the validity of private law contracts.

2. The establishment of schedules or the fixing in any form whatsoever of transport rates or conditions the application of which would constitute discrimination within the meaning of paragraph 1 is likewise prohibited.

3. The prohibitions set forth in this Article shall come into force on 1st July, 1961.

Article 5

1. Governments shall notify the Commission by 1st July, 1961, of any schedules, arrangements and agreements regarding transport rates and conditions, in force in their respective countries, whereby transport rates and conditions within the Community differ in respect of the same goods, conveyed in the same circumstances, according to the country of origin or destination of such goods. Any such measure introduced subsequently shall also be reported to the Commission without delay.

2. Carriers must supply to their Governments by 1st January, 1961, the required information concerning any schedules, arrangements and agreements regarding transport rates and conditions referred to in paragraph 1 above and report without delay any such measures introduced subsequently.

3. The terms of this Article shall apply to the conveyance of goods from or to any place in the territory of a Member State.

Article 6

1. A transport form shall be completed for every consignment of goods within the Community. It shall show:

- the name and address of the sender,
- the nature and weight of the goods,
- the place and date of acceptance of the goods for transport,
- the place of delivery,
- the route or distance, insofar as these may justify a price differing from that normally charged,
- the points at which frontiers are to be crossed, where appropriate.

2. The transport form shall be made out in duplicate and numbered. One copy shall accompany the goods; the other shall be kept by the carrier for two years from the date of the consignment and filed in numerical order. The latter copy shall show the final charge for carriage in whatsoever form, the additional charges made and, where appropriate, any discounts or other conditions affecting the transport rates and conditions.

3. When the existing forms give all the information specified in paragraph 1 above and, in conjunction with the carrier's own records and accounts, enable a complete check to be made on transport rates and

vérification complète des prix et conditions de transport permettant de supprimer ou d'éviter les discriminations visées à l'article 79, paragraphe 1, du Traité, les transporteurs ne sont pas tenus de mettre en service de nouveaux documents.

4. Le transporteur est responsable de l'établissement régulier des documents de transport.

Article 7

1. Les dispositions de l'article 6 entrent en vigueur le 1er juillet 1961.

2. Toutefois, pour certaines catégories de transports à déterminer, la Commission peut, avant la date précitée, différer cette entrée en vigueur jusqu'au 1er janvier 1964 au plus tard, par un règlement pris après consultation du Conseil.

Article 8

Les dispositions de l'article 6 ne s'appliquent pas:

a) Aux transports de marchandises adressées par un expéditeur à un même destinataire, lorsque le poids total ne dépasse pas cinq tonnes;

b) Aux transports de marchandises à l'intérieur d'un État membre, effectués sur un parcours total ne dépassant pas cent kilomètres;

c) Aux transports de marchandises entre les États membres, effectués sur un parcours total ne dépassant pas trente kilomètres.

Article 9

Les dispositions de l'article 6 ne s'appliquent pas aux transports de marchandises effectués par une entreprise pour ses propres besoins, dans la mesure où les conditions suivantes sont remplies:

- les transports doivent être effectués avec des moyens de transport lui appartenant ou qu'elle a achetés à crédit et qui sont conduits par son propre personnel,
- le transport ne doit constituer qu'une activité accessoire dans le cadre de l'ensemble de l'activité de l'entreprise,
- les marchandises transportées doivent appartenir à cette entreprise ou avoir été vendues, achetées, prêtées, empruntées, données ou prises en location, produites, transformées ou réparées par elle,
- le transport doit servir à amener les marchandises vers l'entreprise, à les expédier de cette entreprise, à les déplacer soit à l'intérieur de l'entreprise soit, pour ses propres besoins, à l'extérieur de l'entreprise.

Article 10

Si la publicité des prix et conditions de transport n'a pas fait l'objet, avant le 1er juillet 1963, d'une réglementation prise dans le cadre de l'article 74 et en application de l'article 75 du Traité, des décisions relatives à la nature, à la forme et à l'étendue de cette publicité, ainsi que toutes autres dispositions utiles, seront prises dans les limites et conditions de l'article 79, paragraphes 1 et 3, du Traité, en tenant compte de ce qu'elles devront en tout cas s'encadrer dans la politique commune des transports.

Article 11

1. Sans préjudice de l'application de l'article 5 du présent Règlement les gouvernements et les entreprises fournissent, sur la demande de la Commission, toutes les informations supplémentaires nécessaires relatives aux tarifs, conventions, accords de prix et conditions de transport.

2. La Commission peut fixer un délai minimum d'un mois pour la communication de ces informations.

conditions with a view to abolishing or preventing the cases of discrimination referred to in Article 79, para. 1 of the Treaty, carriers shall not be required to introduce new forms.

4. Carriers shall be responsible for the proper completion of transport forms.

Article 7

1. The provisions of Article 6 shall come into force on 1st July, 1961.

2. However, the Commission may, before the above-mentioned date, defer their entry into force for such categories of transport as may be determined until 1st January, 1964, at latest, by means of a regulation issued after consultation with the Council.

Article 8

The provisions of Article 6 shall not apply:

a) to consignments of goods despatched to the same addressee, provided the total weight does not exceed five tons;

b) to the carriage of goods inside a Member State over a distance not exceeding one hundred kilometres;

c) to the carriage of goods between Member States over a distance not exceeding thirty kilometres.

Article 9

The provisions of Article 6 shall not apply to goods conveyed by firms for their own use, insofar as the following conditions are complied with:

- the goods must be conveyed in vehicles belonging to the firm or acquired on credit terms, and driven by its own staff;
- the transport of goods must be only a subsidiary activity of the firm;
- the goods conveyed must be the property of the firm or have been sold, purchased, lent, borrowed, rented, hired, produced, processed or repaired by the firm;
- the object of conveying the goods must be to bring them to the firm, to despatch them from the firm, or to move them from one of the firm's premises to another or to another place for the firm's own purposes.

Article 10

If by 1st July, 1963, no regulation has been issued within the framework of Article 74 and in implementation of Article 75 of the Treaty regarding the publication of transport rates and conditions, decisions as to the form and extent of such publication and any other appropriate measures, shall be taken within the limits and in accordance with the terms of Article 79, paras. 1 and 3, of the Treaty, bearing in mind that such decisions and measures must be in harmony with the common transport policy.

Article 11

1. Without prejudice to Article 5 of the present Regulations, Governments and firms shall supply, on request by the Commission, such additional information as may be required concerning schedules, arrangements and agreements regarding transport rates and conditions.

2. The Commission may fix a time-limit of not less than one month for the production of this information.

3. Si la Commission demande à une entreprise de lui fournir des renseignements, elle en informe aussitôt le gouvernement de l'État membre dans lequel se trouve le siège de l'entreprise, en lui adressant copie de la demande de renseignements.

4. Un renseignement peut être refusé si celui-ci entraîne la divulgation de faits dont la communication est, de l'avis d'un État membre, contraire aux intérêts essentiels de sa sécurité.

Article 12

1. Les transporteurs qui appliquent pour les mêmes marchandises et sur les mêmes relations de trafic, des prix et conditions de transport différents selon le pays d'origine ou de destination des produits transportés, sont tenus, sur la demande de la Commission, de justifier que cet agissement ne constitue pas une violation des dispositions du présent Règlement.

2. Ne constitue pas une violation des dispositions du présent Règlement l'application de prix et conditions de transport différents résultant exclusivement de la situation de concurrence entre transporteurs ou de caractéristiques techniques ou économiques d'exploitation propres aux transports effectués sur la relation de trafic considérée.

Article 13

1. Les commissionnaires et intermédiaires de transport sont tenus de communiquer, sur la demande de leur gouvernement ou de la Commission, toutes les informations relatives aux prestations fournies ainsi qu'aux prix et conditions appliqués.

2. Cette obligation est également applicable aux entreprises qui fournissent directement des prestations accessoires de transport, pourvu que leur rémunération et la rémunération des transporteurs soient contenues dans un prix global.

3. Les dispositions de l'article 11, paragraphes 2, 3 et 4, sont également applicables aux demandes de communications faites en vertu du présent article.

Article 14

1. Les États membres assurent le contrôle de l'exécution des obligations imposées aux transporteurs à l'article 5, paragraphe 2, et aux articles 6 et 11 du présent Règlement, ainsi que de l'obligation de communication prévue à l'article 13.

A cet effet ils prennent les mesures nécessaires avant le 1er juillet 1961, après consultation de la Commission.

2. La Commission peut, dans la mesure où l'exécution du présent Règlement le rend nécessaire, charger ses agents ou des experts de missions de contrôle en vue de vérifier et de surveiller l'exécution des obligations incombant aux entreprises en vertu des articles 5, 6, 11 et 13 de ce Règlement.

A cet effet, les mandataires de la Commission disposent des droits et pouvoirs suivants:

a) Vérifier les livres et autres documents professionnels des entreprises,

b) Prendre sur place des copies ou extraits de ces livres et documents,

c) Avoir accès à l'ensemble des locaux, terrains et véhicules des entreprises,

d) Exiger toutes explications sur les livres et documents.

Les mandataires de la Commission exercent ces droits sur présentation d'un laissez-passer indiquant qu'ils sont chargés de procéder, dans toute la mesure nécessaire, à des contrôles en vertu du présent article. Ils doivent être porteurs d'un ordre de mission désignant l'entreprise à contrôler

3. When the Commission requests a firm to supply information, it shall immediately notify the Government of the Member State in whose territory the company's registered office is situated, forwarding a copy of the request for information.

4. Information may be refused if it would involve the disclosure of facts the communication of which, in the opinion of the Member State concerned, would be contrary to its security.

Article 12

1. Carriers who, in respect of the same goods conveyed in the same circumstances, apply transport rates and conditions which differ according to the country of origin or destination of the goods shall be required to show, on request by the Commission that this proceeding does not constitute a breach of the present Regulation.

2. The application of transport rates and conditions whose differences are due solely to competition between carriers or to technical or economic features peculiar to conveyance in the circumstances in question shall not be deemed a breach of the present Regulation.

Article 13

1. Forwarding agents and contractors shall be required, at the request of their Government or of the Commission, to supply full details of services rendered and of rates and conditions applied.

2. Firms which directly supply services in support of transport, provided that their remuneration and that of the carriers are included in the overall charge, shall be under the same obligation.

3. The provisions of Article 11, paras. 2, 3 and 4, are likewise applicable to requests for information under the terms of the present Article.

Article 14

1. Member States shall be responsible for ensuring the fulfilment of the obligations imposed on carriers under Article 5, para. 2, and Articles 6 and 11 of the present Regulation, as well as of the obligation to supply information under Article 13.

They shall take steps to this end, after consultation with the Commission, before 1st July, 1961.

2. The Commission may, as required for the enforcement of the present Regulation, instruct its officials or appoint experts to inspect and supervise the fulfilment of the obligations imposed on companies under Articles 5, 6, 11 and 13 of this Regulation.

For this purpose, the Commission's representatives shall be entitled and empowered:

a) to investigate the books and other commercial records of firms;

b) to take copies of or extracts from such books and records on the spot;

c) to have access to all premises, grounds and vehicles of firms;

d) to require explanations regarding books and records.

The Commission's representatives shall exercise these rights on presentation of a pass stating that they are empowered under this Article to carry out any inspections that may be necessary. They must produce a movement order specifying the company to be inspected and the purpose et l'objet du contrôle. L'ordre de mission et la qualité des personnes chargées de son exécution sont dûment notifiés au préalable à l'État membre intéressé.

Des agents de cet État peuvent, sur la demande de celui-ci ou de la Commission, assister les mandataires de la Commission dans l'accomplissement de leur mission.

Lorsqu'une entreprise s'oppose à un contrôle prévu dans le présent Règlement, l'État membre intéressé est tenu de fournir l'aide et l'appui nécessaires aux mandataires de la Commission pour leur permettre d'effectuer les missions de contrôle dont ils sont chargés. À cet effet, les États membres prennent les mesures nécessaires avant le 1er juillet 1961, après consultation de la Commission.

3. Toutes les personnes participant aux opérations de contrôle prévues au présent article sont tenues au secret professionnel, conformément à l'article 214 du Traité.

Article 15

1. Sans préjudice de l'application de l'article 79, paragraphe 4, du Traité, la Commission et les États membres veillent à ce que tous les faits dont ils ont pris connaissance en vertu des articles 5, 11, 13 et 14 conservent leur caractère confidentiel.

2. Sauf décision contraire unanime du Conseil, les renseignements ainsi obtenus ne peuvent être utilisés qu'en vue de l'exécution du présent Règlement.

Article 16

Les États membres déterminent, après consultation de la Commission et dans le délai prévu à l'article 14, paragraphe 1, les sanctions appropriées, applicables:

a) Aux transporteurs qui se sont soustraits aux mesures de contrôle prévues à l'article 5, paragraphe 2, et à l'article 6;

b) Aux entrepreneurs qui, après en avoir été requis, n'ont pas fourni à leur gouvernement, dans le délai imparti, les renseignements prévus aux articles 11 et 13;

c) Aux entrepreneurs qui ont fourni sciemment des informations fausses à leur gouvernement.

Article 17

1. Si l'entrepreneur ne fournit pas dans le délai imparti les informations demandées par la Commission en application des articles 11 ou 13, ou s'il lui fournit sciemment des informations fausses, celle-ci peut, conformément à l'article 79, paragraphe 3, alinéa 2, du Traité, prendre à son encontre une décision prononçant une sanction dont le maximum est de cinq cents unités de compte, et fixer un nouveau délai pour la communication des informations demandées. Si l'entrepreneur n'a pas fourni ces informations à l'expiration de ce nouveau délai, la décision peut être renouvelée.

2. Toutefois, ces sanctions ne peuvent être prononcées que si la demande d'informations a été présentée sous forme de décision se référant expressément aux sanctions prévues au présent article.

Article 18

1. La Commission, après avoir constaté l'existence d'une discrimination au sens de l'article 79, paragraphe 1, du Traité, peut, pour chaque cas de discrimination et dans le cadre des décisions prévues à l'article 79, paragraphe 4, prononcer à l'encontre du transporteur responsable une

of the inspection. The Member State concerned shall be duly notified in advance of the movement order and the particulars of the persons to whom it has been issued.

Officials of that State may, at the request of the State or of the Commission, assist the Commission's representatives in their appointed task.

When a firm opposes an inspection under the present Regulation, the Member State concerned is required to provide any assistance and support that the Commission's representatives may need to carry out their inspection. Member States shall make the necessary arrangements to this end, after consultation with the Commission, by 1st July, 1961.

3. All persons taking part in inspections carried out under the present Regulation shall be bound to professional secrecy in accordance with Article 214 of the Treaty.

Article 15

1. Without prejudice to Article 79, para. 4 of the Treaty, the Commission and the Member States shall ensure that all facts that come to their knowledge by virtue of Articles 5, 11, 13 and 14 shall remain confidential.

2. Unless otherwise unanimously decided by the Council, information so obtained may be used only for the purpose of enforcing this Regulation.

Article 16

Member States, after consultation with the Commission and within the time-limit laid down in Article 14, para. 1, shall prescribe penalties applicable:

a) to carriers who evade the measures of control laid down in Article 5, para. 2, and Article 6;

b) to firms which, after having been required to do so, fail to supply to their Governments within the prescribed time-limit the information specified in Articles 11 and 13;

c) to firms which knowingly supply their Governments with false information.

Article 17

1. If a firm fails to supply within the prescribed time-limit the information requested by the Commission in accordance with Articles 11 and 13, or if it knowingly supplies false information, the Commission may make an order against it, in accordance with Article 79, para. 3, sub-para. 2 of the Treaty, imposing a fine not exceeding five hundred units of account, and may fix a new time-limit for the communication of the information requested. If, on the expiry of this further period, the firm has not supplied the said information, another order may be made.

2. Such fines may not be imposed, however, unless the request for information was presented in the form of a decision referring expressly to the penalties provided for in the present Article.

Article 18

1. The Commission, after establishing the existence of discrimination within the meaning of Article 79, para. 1 of the Treaty, may in respect of each case of discrimination and within the framework of the decisions provided for in Article 79, para. 4, impose on the carrier responsible

sanction dont le maximum est de vingt fois le prix du transport perçu ou demandé.

2. Si une discrimination au sens de l'article 79, paragraphe 1, du Traité subsiste malgré une décision de la Commission enjoignant d'y mettre fin, la Commission peut prononcer, à l'encontre du transporteur responsable, pour chaque cas de discrimination et conformément à l'article 79, paragraphe 4, du Traité, une sanction dont le maximum sera de dix mille unités de compte.

3. Avant de prendre une sanction dans le cadre de l'article 17, la Commission consulte tout État membre intéressé auquel elle communique sous forme de copie tous les documents et éléments d'information réunis dans le cadre de l'examen auquel elle a procédé en application de l'article 79, paragraphe 4, du Traité. Chaque État membre consulté peut demander l'avis d'une autorité nationale indépendante et répond dans un délai de deux mois.

Article 19

Les décisions prises en vertu des articles 17 et 18 n'ont pas un caractère pénal.

Article 20

La décision à prendre en application des articles 17 et 18 est précédée d'une notification, à l'entrepreneur intéressé, de la mesure envisagée.

La Commission transmet pour information aux États membres intéressés copie des décisions prises sur la base des articles 17 et 18.

Article 21

Pour l'application des articles précédents, l'unité de compte est celle retenue pour l'établissement du budget de la Communauté, en vertu des articles 207 et 209 du Traité.

Article 22

Les entreprises, que leur statut juridique soit public ou privé, sont responsables du fait de leurs agents en ce qui concerne l'exécution des dispositions du présent Règlement. Cette disposition est également applicable aux sanctions prévues dans ce Règlement.

Article 23

Les sanctions prononcées par la Commission en application des articles 17 et 18 sont exécutées dans les conditions prévues à l'article 192 du Traité. Les sommes perçues en exécution des décisions prononçant ces sanctions sont versées à la Communauté Économique Européenne et figurent en recette à son budget.

Article 24

L'État membre qui, au titre de l'article 79, paragraphe 4, du Traité, demande l'examen d'un cas qu'il estime discriminatoire, doit motiver sa demande.

Article 25

1. Avant de prendre une décision ou de prononcer une sanction au titre de l'article 18 du présent Règlement, la Commission entend les explications de l'intéressé ou de son mandataire; elle peut déléguer un de ses agents pour recevoir ces explications.

a fine not exceeding twenty times the transport charge received or demanded.

2. If discrimination within the meaning of Article 79, para. 1, of the Treaty persists in spite of the Commission's order enjoining its termination the Commission may impose on the carrier responsible, in respect of each case of discrimination and in accordance with Article 79, para. 4 of the Treaty, a fine not exceeding ten thousand units of account.

3. Before imposing a fine under Article 17, the Commission shall consult the Member State concerned and transmit to it copies of all documents and information assembled in the course of the enquiry carried out in accordance with Article 79, para. 4, of the Treaty. Any Member State so consulted may seek the opinion of an independent national authority and shall reply to the Commission within two months.

Article 19

Orders made in accordance with Articles 17 and 18 shall have no penal character.

Article 20

An order made in accordance with Article 17 or 18 shall be preceded by notification to the firm concerned of the measure contemplated.

The Commission shall transmit to Member States for information copies of orders made in accordance with Articles 17 and 18.

Article 21

For the purposes of the above Articles, the unit of account shall be that adopted for the Budget of the Community in accordance with Articles 207 and 209 of the Treaty.

Article 22

Firms, whether public or private, shall be responsible for the actions of their staff in regard to the observance of this Regulation. This provision also applies to the penalties imposed under this Regulation.

Article 23

Fines imposed by the Commission under Articles 17 and 18 shall be enforced as laid down in Article 192 of the Treaty. The sums so collected shall be credited to the European Economic Community and shall appear in the budget of receipts.

Article 24

A Member State which, under Article 79, para. 4, of the Treaty, requests an enquiry into what it regards as a case of discrimination shall give reasons in support of its request.

Article 25

1. Before making an order or imposing a fine under Article 18 of this Regulation, the Commission shall hear the explanations of the interested party or his representative; it may designate one of its own officials to receive such explanations.

2. En application de l'article 172 du Traité, une compétence de pleine juridiction est attribuée à la Cour de Justice en ce qui concerne toute sanction prise en vertu des articles 17 et 18. La Commission ne peut poursuivre l'exécution de la sanction qu'après l'expiration du délai de recours.

Article 26

La Commission est chargée de prendre les mesures d'application nécessaires à l'exécution du présent Règlement.

Le présent Règlement est obligatoire en tous ses éléments et directement applicable dans tous les États membres.

Fait à Bruxelles, le 27 juin 1960.

Par le Conseil, Le président
P. GRÉGOIRE

B. PUBLICATIONS DE LA C.E.E.

Texte unique pour les deux langues

Ce liste contient les titres de toutes les publications, périodiques ou non, éditées par la C.E.E. depuis ses origines. Les publications de l'office statistique des Communautés européennes et celles du service de presse-information des Communautés européennes y sont également mentionnées.

Pour une raison d'ordre systématique, les publications C.E.E. ont été réparties en plusieurs rubriques, suivant leur caractére et les matières traitées.

Une mention à part est faite pour le *Journal officiel des Communautés européennes.*

Les publications de la C.E.E. sont éditées, en général, dans les quatre langues officielles de la Communauté; par ailleurs, pour certaines d'entre elles, il existe une édition dans les langues anglaise et espagnole.

Des signes abréviatifs figurant à la suite de chaque titre indiquent les langues dans lesquelles chaque publication a été publiée: f = langue française; d = langue allemande; i = langue italienne; n= langue néerlandaise; e = langue anglaise; s = langue espagnole.

Pour les publications bilingues, quadrilingues ou multilingues, l'indication est donnée par les mêmes signes, séparés d'une barre au lieu d'une virgule.

Journal officiel des Communautés européennes

Publication commune aux trois institutions: C.E.C.A., C.E.E., C.E.E.A.

Le „Journal officiel des Communautés européennes" publie notamment:

- le calendrier des sessions et des réunions des Commissions, les procès-verbaux des séances de l'Assemblée parlementaire européenne, les réponses aux questions écrites;
- les recours et arrêts de la Cour de justice;
- les règlements, décisions, avis, statuts, les accords et autres délibérations ainsi que les états prévisionnels des dépenses administratives et les budgets des trois Communautés.

Plus particulièrement, en ce qui concerne la C.E.E.;

- le rapport trimestriel sur la situation économique de la Communauté et les perspectives pour le trimestre suivant;
- les conventions de financement, le financement, les avis d'adjudication,

2. In pursuance of Article 172 of the Treaty, the Court of Justice shall have full jurisdiction in respect of any penalty imposed under Articles 17 and 18 of this Regulation. The Commission may not proceed to enforcement of the penalty until after the expiry of the time-limit for appeal.

Article 26

The Commission shall take measures for the enforcement of this Regulation.

This Regulation shall be binding in all its provisions and shall be directly applicable in all Member States.

Done at Brussels, this 27th day of June, 1960

By the Council, The Chairman
P. Grégoire

B. PUBLICATIONS OF THE E.E.C.

See French text

les projets d'investissement économique et social du fonds de développement pour les pays et territoires d'outre-mer;
- les décisions de la commission administrative pour la sécurité sociale des travailleurs migrants et du comité du fonds social européen.
(f, d, i, n).

PREMIÈRE PARTIE

TEXTES INSTITUTIONNELS, RAPPORTS D'ACTIVITÉ, PUBLICATIONS DE CARACTÈRE GÉNÉRAL

Textes institutionnels

Traité instituant la Communauté économique européenne et documents annexes.
Février 1957. 345 pp. (f, d, i, n).
Treaty Establishing the European Economic Community and Connected Documents.
1957. 378 pp. (édition anglaise).

Rapports d'activité

Premier rapport général sur l'activité de la Communauté.
(1er janvier – 17 september 1958) 156 pp. (f, d, i, n, e).
Deuxième rapport général sur l'activité de la Communauté.
(18 septembre 1958 – 20 mars 1959) 155 pp. (f, d, i, n, e)
Troisième rapport général sur l'activité de la Communauté.
(21 mars 1959–15 mai 1960) 268 pp. (f, d, i, n, e)
Exposé sur la situation sociale de la Communauté (joint au „Premier rapport général sur l'activité de la Communauté" en application de l'article 122 du Traité).
Septembre 1958. 129 pp. (f, d, i, n).
Exposé sur l'évolution de la situation sociale dans la Communauté (joint au „Deuxième rapport général sur l'activité de la Communauté" en application de l'article 122 du Traité.
Mai 1959. 137 pp. (f, d, i, n).
Exposé sur l'évolution de la situation sociale dans la Communauté en 1959 (joint au „Troisième rapport général sur l'activité de la Communauté" en application de l'article 122 du Traité).
Juin 1960. 396 pp. (f, d, i, n).

Allocutions et Discours

Allocution de M. Walter HALLSTEIN, *président de la Commission devant l'Assemblée Parlementaire Européenne à Strasbourg.*
20 mars 1958. 42 pp. (f, d, n, e; *i*: épuisé).
Déclaration faite par M. Walter HALLSTEIN, *président de la Commission de la Communauté économique européenne devant l'Assemblée Parlementaire Européenne à Strasbourg.*
21 octobre 1958. 38 pp. (f, d, i, n).
Erklärung des Präsidenten der Kommission der Europäischen Wirtschaftsgemeinschaft, Professor Dr. Walter HALLSTEIN, *vor dem Europäischen Parlament in Strasburg.*
13 janvier 1959. 27 pp. (*d*).
Erklärung des Präsidenten der Kommission der Europäischen Wirtschaftsgemeinschaft, Professor Dr. Walter HALLSTEIN, *vor der Beratenden Versammlung des Europarates in Strasburg im Verlauf der Debatte über die europäischen Wirtschaftsbeziehungen.*
20 janvier 1960. 28 pp. (d).

Publications de caractère général

Bulletin de la Communauté économique européenne.
Périodique: environ 10 numéros par an (f, d, i, n, e, s).

DEUXIÈME PARTIE

ÉTUDES ET AUTRES PUBLICATIONS PAR SECTEUR

Relations extérieures

Premier mémorandum de la Commission de la Communauté économique européenne au Conseil de Ministres de la Communauté 26 février 1959. 42 pp. plus 7 annexes. (f, d, n, e, s; *i*: épuisé).

Économie et finances

Rapport sur la situation économique dans les pays de la Communauté.
Septembre 1958. 608 pp.
(f, d, i, n; éditions reliées en pleine toile) (e: édition brochée).
L'évolution récente de la situation économique.
15 septembre 1958. 67 pp. (f, d, i, n).
Premier rapport d'activité du Comité monétaire.
28 février 1959. 17 pp. plus 4 annexes. Édition ronéotée (f, d, i, n).
Deuxième rapport d'activité du Comité monétaire.
1er février 1960. 33 pp. (f, d, i, n).
Graphiques et notes rapides sur la conjoncture dans la Communauté.
Mensuel. (Édition bilingue: f/i et d/n).
La situation économique de la Communauté et les perspectives d'évolution.
Trimestriel. (f, d, i, n).

Industrie - Artisanat - Commerce - Douanes

Répertoire des organismes communs créés dans le cadre de la C.E.E. par les associations industrielles, artisanales et commerciales des six pays.
1960, 513 pp. (Édition quadrilingue: f/d/i/n).
Tarif douanier des Communautés européennes.
Tableau complet des droits de douane fixés à l'égard des pays tiers ou non associés, dans le cadre des trois Communautés européennes.
Janvier 1961. 298 pp. (f, d, i, n).

Affaires sociales

Exposé sur l'évolution de la situation sociale (rapport annuel joint aux rapports généraux sur l'activité de la Communauté).
L'évolution de l'emploi dans les États membres (1954–1958).
Mars 1961. 277 pp. (f, d, i, n).

Commission administrative de la C.E.E. pour la Sécurité Sociale des Travailleurs Migrants

Modèles des formules arrêtés par la Commission administrative pour la Sécurité Sociale des Travailleurs Migrants en vue de l'application des Règlements no. 3 et no. 4 (f, d, i, n).

E 1 *Certificat de détachement.*

E 2 *Demande de prolongation de détachement.*

E 3 *Option* (*ambassades, légations, consulats,* etc.).

E 4 *Attestation concernant la totalisation des périodes d'assurance maladie - maternité-décès* (*allocations*) *- tuberculose.*

E 5 *Attestation concernant les membres de la famille du travailleur pouvant être pris en considération pour le calcul des prestations en espèces.*

E 6 *Attestation concernant le droit aux prestation en nature.*

E 7 *Instruction d'une demande de prestations en nature.*

E 8 *Notification d'hospitalisation d'urgence* (*nécessité de soins immédiats*).

E 9 *Notification de sortie d'hôpital.*

E 10 *Demande concernant l'octroi de prothèses, grand appareillage,* etc.

E 11 *Notification de l'octroi d'urgence de prothèses, de grand appareillage,* etc.

E 12 *Demande de prestations en espèces en cas d'incapacité de travail.*

E 13 *Notification de fin d'incapacité de travail.*

E 14 *Attestation concernant le maintien des prestations en cours en cas de transfert de résidence.*

E 15 *Certificat médical en cas d'accident du travail.*

E 16 *Demande d'allocation de décès.*

E 17 *Attestation concernant les périodes à prendre en compte pour l'octroi des prestations de chômage.*

E 18 *Attestation concernant les membres de la famille, pouvant être pris en considération pour le calcul des prestations de chômage.*

E 19 *Attestation concernant le maintien du droit aux prestations de chômage en cas de transfert de résidence.*

E 20 *Attestation concernant l'état de famille en vue de l'octroi des allocations familiales.*

E 21 *Demande d'allocations familiales en cas de décès du soutien de famille pour les enfants résidant ou élevés sur le territoire d'un autre État membre.*

E 22 *Attestation concernant la totalisation des périodes d'assurances.*

E 23 *Instruction d'une demande de pension de vieillesse.*

E 24 *Instruction d'une demande de pension de survivant.*

E 25 *Instruction d'une demande de pension d'invalidité.*

E 26 *Renseignements concernant la carrière d'assurance en Belgique, Allemagne, France, Italie, au Luxembourg et aux Pays-Bas.*

E 27 *Relevé des services dans les mines ou exploitations assimilées.*

E 28 *Questionnaire concernant les occupations exercées.*

E 29 *Détermination de la pension.*

E 30 *Rapport médical détaillé.*

E 31 *Bordereau de paiement pour pensions ou rentes.*

E 32 *Avis de versement.*

E 33 *Attestation concernant le droit aux prestations en nature.*

E 34 *Attestation pour l'octroi des prestations en nature aux membres de la famille des titulaires de pensions ou rentes.*

E 35 *Avis de suspension ou de suppression du droit aux prestations en nature des titulaires de pensions ou rentes.*

E 36 *Attestation concernant l'inscription des membres de la famille du travailleur pour la tenue des inventaires.*

E 37 *Attestation pour l'inscription des membres de la famille du travailleur et la tenue des inventaires en cas d'application de la procédure prévue à l'article 22, paragraphe 3, du Réglement no. 4.*

E 38 *Certificat de poursuite d'études en vue de l'octroi des allocations familiales – Inscription.*

E 39 *Certificat de poursuite d'études en vue de l'octroi des allocations familiales – Fréquentation.*

E 40 *Certificat d'apprentissage en vue de l'octroi des allocations familiales.*

E 41 *Déclaration en vue de l'octroi des allocations familiales aux enfants incapables de travailler.*

E 42 *Certificat médical en vue de l'octroi des allocations familiales aux enfants incapables de travailler* – Confidentiel.

E 43 *Attestation en vue de l'octroi des allocations familiales à la jeune fille ménagère restant au foyer.*

E 44 *Avis de cessation du paiement de prestations d'assurance invalidité, vieillesse, décès (pensions) ou d'une rente d'accident du travail ou maladie professionnelle servies pour le compte de l'institution compétente par l'organisme de liaison du pays de résidence du titulaire, conformément aux dispositions des articles 41 ou 58 du Règlement no. 4.*

Agriculture

Recueil des documents de la Conférence agricole des États membres de la Communauté économique européenne, à Stresa, du 3 au 12 juillet 1958.
Juillet 1958. 250 pp. (f, d, i, n).

Document de travail sur la situation de l'agriculture dans la Communauté établi à l'intention des membres de l'Assemblée Parlementaire Européenne.
15 septembre 1958. 50 pp. (f, d, i, n).

Répertoire des organisations agricoles non gouvernementales groupées dans le cadre de la Communauté économique européenne 1960. 200 pp.
Réédition quadrilingue: f/d/i/n, avec mise a jour.

La politique agricole commune.
Extrait du ,,Bulletin de la Communauté économique européenne'' no. 5, 1959. 29 pp. (f, d, i, n).

Études – Série agriculture

Les grandes régions agricoles dans la C.E.E.
(Étude réalisée en commun par la C.E.E. et l'O.E.C.E.).
1960. 60 pp. plus 5 documents cartographiques (f, d).

Tendances de la production et de la consommation en denrées alimentaires dans la C.E.E. (1956–1965).
1960. 120 pp. (rapport) plus 145 p. (annexes).

Pays et Territoires d'Outre-Mer

Discours prononcé par M. Robert LEMAIGNEN, *membre de la Commission de la C.E.E., à l'Assemblée annuelle des Comités nationaux allemands de la Chambre de commerce internationale, à Hambourg.*
17 septembre 1959. 19 pp. (f, d).

Missions et objectifs de la C.E.E. en Afrique par M. le directeur général ALLARDT.
(Direction générale des pays et territoires d'outre-mer de la Communauté économique européenne).
Hanovre, 30 avril 1959. 30 pp. (f, d, e).

Fonds européen de Développement pour les pays et territoires d'outre-mer. But et fonctionnement.
Extrait du ,,Bulletin de la Communauté économique européenne'' no. 2/1960. 12 pp. (f; *d, i, n = épuisés*).

Rapport sur la situation sociale dans les pays d'outre-mer associés à la Communauté économique européenne.
Septembre 1960. 254 pp. (f, d, i, n).

Commentaire sur les directives fixant les modalités d'application pro-

gressive du droit d'établissement dans les pays et territoires d'outre-mer et les départemens français d'outre-mer, arrêtées par le Conseil de la C.E.E. le 23 novembre 1959 et publiées au "Journal officiel des Communautés européennes" du 10 février 1960, no. 7. 13 pp. (f, d, i, n).

TROISIÈME PARTIE

STATISTIQUES

A. Publications annuelles et occasionnelles

Mémento de statistiques – Énergie (charbon et autres sources d'énergie) – Sidérurgie.
15 décembre 1960. 138 pp. (f, d, i, n).
Statistiques de base de douze pays européens.
Octobre 1958. 100 pp. (f, d, i, n).
Commerce extérieur par pays, 1953–1958.
Édition multilingue (f/d/i/n/e).
Octobre 1959. 188 pp.
Classification statistique et tarifaire (C.S.T.) pour le commerce international.
Janvier 1961. 56 pp. (f; réédition revisée, d, i, n).

B. Publications périodiques

1. *Bulletin général de statistiques (série violette)* 11 numéros par an f/d).
2. *Informations statistiques (série orange)* Trimestriel (f, d, i, n).
   Séries supplémentaires
   aux informations statistiques
   a) *Statistiques industrielles (série bleue).*
   Trimestriel (f/d).
   b) *Statistique agricole (série verte).*
   Minimum 4 numéros par an (f/d).
   c) *Statistiques sociales (série jaune).*
   Minimum 2 numéros par an (d, f, i, n).
3. *Commerce extérieur (série rouge).*
   a) *Statistique mensuelle.*
   Cette série remplace l'ancien bimestriel „Tableaux synoptiques" (parus en 1960. 11 numéros par an (f/d avec supplément méthodologique pentalingue: f, d, i, n, e).
   b) *Tableaux analytiques.*
   Données détaillées par produits et par pays sur le commerce des pays de la C.E.E. (pour chaque période: 1 tome „Importation" et 1 tome „Exportation").
   Éditions rétrospectives:
   1958 et 1959, annuel (f/d).
   c) *Associés d'outre-mer.*
   Données détaillées sur tous les produits importés et exportés par 25 pays d'outre-mer (pour chaque période: 1 tome „Importation" et 1 tome „Exportation").
   Éditions rétrospectives:
   1959, annuel (f/d).
4. *Bulletin statistique charbon et acier.*
   Trimestriel (f/i; d/n).

QUATRIÈME PARTIE

BROCHURES ET MATÉRIEL DE VULGARISATION

Dans le cadre de son activité d'information et de vulgarisation, le „*Service de Presse et d'Information des Communautés européennes*" en étroite collaboration avec ses bureaux de Paris, Bonn, Rome, La Haye, Londres et Washington, édite périodiquement des brochures sur les trois Communautés (C.E.C.A., C.E.E., Euratom).

Ces brochures visent à présenter, d'une façon synthétique et à l'aide de graphiques et d'autres moyens visuels, les différents aspects, problèmes, étapes de réalisation de l'intégration économique de l'Euorpe des Six.

Il n'est pas possible de donner dans ce catalogue une liste à jour de ces publications, qui, en raison de la large diffusion dont elles font l'objet, sont rapidement épuisées et remplacées par d'autres au fur et à mesure.

Ces publications sont gratuites et peuvent être obtenues sur simple demande adressée aux bureaux centraux de Bruxelles et de Luxembourg ou aux bureaux nationaux.

SERVICE DE PRESSE ET D'INFORMATION DES COMMUNAUTÉS EUROPÉENNES

244, rue de la Loi
Bruxelles
Tel.: 35.00.40

18, rue Aldringer
Luxembourg
Tel.: 2.92.41

Publications:

Brochures, dépliants, panneaux muraux, pochettes cartographiques, *etc.* en f, d, i, n, e, s.

France:
Bureau d'information des Communautés européennes.
61, rue des Belles Feuilles.
Paris XVIe, KLEber 53–26.
Publication périodique:
,,Communauté européenne'', mensuel.
Publications non-périodiques:
a. Série ,,Les cahiers de *Communauté européenne*''.
b. Série ,,En bref''.
c. Série ,,Les documents de *Communauté européenne*''.

Deutschland:
Verbindungsbüro der Europäischen Gemeinschaften.
Zitelmannstraße 11.
Bonn
Tel.: 2.60.41.
Periodische Veröffentlichung:
,,Europäische Gemeinschaft'', wöchentlich.
Nichtperiodische Veröffentlichungen:
Broschüren, Karten usw.

Italia:
Ufficio Stampa e Informazione delle Comunità Europee
Via Poli, 29.
Roma.
Tel.: 670.696/688/182.
Publicazione periodica:
,,Comunità Europee'', mensile.
Pubblicazioni non periodiche:
a. Serie ,,Quaderni di *Comunità Europee*''.
b. Serie ,,Notizie in breve''.
c. Opuscoli vari.

Nederland:
Voorlichtingsdienst van de Europese Gemeenschappen.
Mauritskade 39.
Den Haag.
Tel.: 184.815.

Periodieke publikatie:
„Europese Gemeenschap", maandelijks.
Niet-periodieke publikaties:
Brochures, wandkaarten, enz.
England:
Information Service of the European Community.
26 Chesham Street.
London S.W. 1.
Tel.: SLOane 0456/0457/0458.
Publications:
„Bulletin from the European Community", irregular.
Brochures, folders, pamphlets, maps, etc.
United States of America:
European Community Information Service.
236 Southern Building.
Washington 5, D.C.
Tel.: National 8–5070.
Publications; see: England.

BUREAUX DE VENTE ET D'ABONNEMENT

BELGIQUE – BELGIË

Moniteur Belge – 40, rue de Louvain, BRUXELLES
Belgisch Staatsblad – Leuvensestraat, 40 BRUSSEL

DEUTSCHLAND

Bundesanzeiger – Postfach – Köln 1 – Fernschreiber:
Anzeiger Bonn 8 882 595

FRANCE

Service de vente en France des publications des Communautés Européennes
26, rue Desaix – Paris 15e – Compte courant postal: Paris 23–96

GRAND-DUCHÉ DE LUXEMBOURG

Service de diffusion du Mémorial – 8, avenue Pescatore – LUXEMBOURG

GREAT BRITAIN AND COMMONWEALTH

H.M. Stationery Office P.O. Box 569 – LONDON S.E. 1

ITALIA

Libreria dello Stato – Piazza G. Verdi, 10 – Roma
– *Agenzie:*
– ROMA – Via del Tritone, 61/A e 61/B
– ROMA – Via XX Settembre (Palazzo Ministero delle Finanze)
– MILANO – Galleria Vittorio Emanuele, 3
– NAPOLI – Via Chiaia, 5
– FIRENZE – Via Cavour, 46/r

NEDERLAND

Staatsdrukkerij- en Uitgeverijbedrijf – Fluwelen Burgwal, 18, DEN HAAG

AUTRES PAYS

Service des Publications des Communautés Européennes
Bureau de vente: 2, place de Metz-LUXEMBOURG (C.C.P. no. 191–90).

CHAPITRE VII

CONFÉRENCE EUROPÉENNE DES MINISTRES DES TRANSPORTS

A. SEPTIÈME RAPPORT ANNUEL

Extrait

.I EXPOSÉ GÉNÉRAL SUR LE FONCTIONNEMENT DE LA CONFÉRENCE ET SES RELATIONS EXTÉRIEURES

Pendant l'année 1960, le Conseil des Ministres des Transports a tenu deux sessions: à Paris le 24 mai et à La Haye le 5 octobre. Elles ont été préparées par des réunions du Bureau du Conseil : à Vienne, du 29 février au 2 mars; à Paris, le 23 septembre.

Au cours de sa séance du 5 octobre 1960, le Conseil des Ministres des Transports a procédé, conformément à son Règlement intérieur, au renouvellement de son Bureau, qui se trouve composé, pour l'exercice en cours, des Ministres des Transports de l'Autriche (Président), de la Norvège (1er Vice-Président) et de la Belgique (2e Vice-Président).

Pendant l'année 1960, le Comité des suppléants a tenu sept sessions.

. . . .

Les Groupes restreints, constitués sur la base de l'article 8 du Protocole instituant la Conférence, ont poursuivi leur activité, ainsi qu'il est indiqué dans la suite du rapport. Ils ont pour objet:

a) le premier, qui comprend tous les pays Membres à une exception près, de suivre l'activité de la Société Eurofima (*voir* chapitre IV *c*);

b) le deuxième, qui groupe les pays Membres de la Communauté Économique Européenne (C.E.E.), de préparer les informations à donner à la C.E.M.T. sur les problèmes de transport qui sont traités dans le cadre de la C.E.E. et de recueillir, sur ces problèmes, l'avis des membres de la C.E.M.T. qui ne font pas partie de la C.E.E. Au cours de l'année 1960, ce groupe s'est réuni deux fois au niveau des ministres;

c) le troisième, qui est nouveau, de poursuivre les études entreprises par huit pays de la C.E.M.T. dans un cadre *ad hoc*, en vue de l'uniformisation des règles de circulation routière (*voir* chapitre V *d*);

d) les autres, au nombre de seize, de veiller au développement des grandes liaisons routières entre pays limitrophes.

. . . .

II. EXPOSÉ GÉNÉRAL SUR LA SITUATION DES TRANSPORTS

a) *RÉSULTATS D'ENSEMBLE DE LA PÉRIODE 1956-1960*

Ainsi que le rappelaient les précédents Rapports, des prévisions relatives à l'évolution de la demande des transports pour la période 1956–1960 avaient été faites par la C.E.M.T., sur la base des estimations suivantes de l'O.E.C.E. pour l'ensemble de l'économie: augmentation de 17,4% du produit national brut et de 25% de la production industrielle pour l'ensemble de ses pays membres. (En fait, les pourcentages réels constatés pour cette période ont été de 22 et 30%.)

Quant aux prévisions de la C.E.M.T., elles étaient les suivantes:

- pour les chemins de fer: augmentation de 7% les voyageurs-kilomètres et de 14% pour les tonnes-kilomètres;
- pour les voies navigables: 16% de majoration sur les tonnes-kilomètres (24% sur le Rhin);

CHAPTER VII

EUROPEAN CONFERENCE OF MINISTERS OF TRANSPORT

A. SEVENTH ANNUAL REPORT

Extracts

I. GENERAL REVIEW OF THE WORKING OF THE CONFERENCE AND ITS EXTERNAL RELATIONS

During 1960, the Council of Ministers of Transport held two sessions: in Paris on 24th May and in The Hague on 5th October. Preparations for these sessions had been made at meetings of the officers held in Vienna from 29th February to 2nd March and in Paris on 23rd September.

At its meeting on 5th October, 1960, the Council of Ministers of Transport elected its officers for the current year, in accordance with its Rules of Procedure. The officers are the Ministers of Transport of Austria (Chairman), Norway (1st Vice-Chairman) and Belgium (2nd Vice-Chairman).

During 1960, the Committee of Deputies held seven sessions.

. . . .

The Restricted Groups, formed in accordance with Article 8 of the Conference Protocol, have continued their activities, as is shown later in this report. Their aims are as follows:

a) One group, which consists of all Member countries except one, follows the activities of the Eurofima Company (*see* Chapter IV *c*);

b) The second group, which consists of the Member countries of the European Economic Community (E.E.C.), prepares information for communication to the E.C.M.T. on transport problems dealt with in the E.E.C. and assembles the views of E.C.M.T. countries which are members of the E.E.C. on these problems. During 1960, this Group met twice at ministerial level;

c) The third, which is new, continues the studies begun on an "ad hoc" basis by eight Member countries of the E.C.M.T. to co-ordinate road traffic regulations (*see* Chapter V *d*);

d) The other sixteen groups keep under review the development of the main road links between adjacent countries.

. . . .

II. GENERAL REVIEW OF THE TRANSPORT SITUATION

a) *OVERALL RESULTS FOR THE PERIOD 1956–1960*

As recalled in the previous reports, forecasts of the trend of the demand for transport for the period 1956–1960 were established by the E.C.M.T. on the basis of the following estimates of the O.E.E.C. for the economy as a whole: increase of 17,4 per cent in the gross national product and 25 per cent in industrial production for Member countries as a whole (the actual percentages for this period were in fact 22 and 30 per cent).

The E.C.M.T. forecasts were as follows:

- Railways: increase of 7 per cent in passenger-kilometres, and of 14 per cent in ton-kilometres;
- Inland waterways: increase of 16 per cent in ton-kilometres (24 per cent for Rhine traffic);

- pour les transports routiers: augmentation du parc de 50% (à défaut de statistiques portant sur les tonnes-kilomètres).

Ces prévisions ont été atteintes et même dépassées pour ce qui concerne le parc automobile, qui s'est développé très régulièrement à une cadence annuelle supérieure à 10%: par rapport à 1956, l'augmentation du parc à la fin de 1960 représente une augmentation d'environ 60%.

Dans les dernières années, l'évolution du trafic des marchandises par chemin de fer pour l'ensemble des pays de la C.E.M.T., mesuré en tonnes-kilomètres, a été la suivante: 1953: 100; 1954: 103; 1955: 112; 1956: 117; 1957: 119; 1958: 111; 1959: 112,5; 1960 (9 mois): 121. Les années 1958 et 1959 ont donc été des périodes de régression; la situation s'est renversée vers la fin de 1959 et cette reprise s'est affirmée en 1960, qui a été une année record. Néanmoins, l'augmentation du trafic des marchandises par chemin de fer pour l'ensemble de la période 1956–1960 n'a pas atteint les prévisions.

Quant au trafic des voyageurs par chemin de fer (mesuré en voyageurs-kilomètres), il a d'abord été en progression de 4% de 1956 à 1957, mais il accuse depuis une tendance à la stagnation, dont une des causes peut être attribuée au développement de l'automobile.

Mesuré en tonnes, le trafic sur les voies navigables a d'abord augmenté de 5% de 1956 à 1957, puis fléchi de 3% de 1957 à 1958. En 1959, il s'est relevé de 3,9%, et cette progression s'est considérablement amplifiée en 1960, puisqu'elle atteint 18% environ pour l'ensemble du trafic. Ainsi, pour la période 1956–1960, l'augmentation totale du tonnage transporté aura dépassé les prévisions.

En ce qui concerne le Rhin, on constate que le trafic rhénan traditionnel est passé de 104,5 millions de tonnes en 1956 à environ 130 millions de tonnes en 1960, soit une augmentation de 24,4%, qui correspond exactement à la prévision faite en 1957 par la C.E.M.T. Toutefois, cette augmentation a été loin d'être progressive, le trafic des années 1957, 1958 et 1959 ayant été respectivement de 108,1, 105,6 et 109,7 millions de tonnes. Les causes du bond constaté en 1960 sont expliquées plus loin.

Si, en dépit d'une conjoncture économique devenue très favorable depuis 1959, toutes les prévisions de transport faites en 1956 pour 1960 n'ont pas été atteintes, c'est surtout parce que les corrélations que l'on considérait jusqu'alors comme valables entre certains indices économiques généraux et le volume des transports de marchandises paraissent avoir été perturbées dans les dernières années par les profondes modifications déjà intervenues dans la structure de l'énergie et, à un moindre degré, par le récent développement des transports par oléoducs. C'est principalement le trafic ferroviaire qui paraît avoir été influencé par ces perturbations.

b) ANALYSE DES RÉSULTATS DE L'ANNÉE 1960

Au moment de la rédaction du Rapport, on ne dispose pas encore des résultats complets de l'année 1960. Aussi, les conclusions tirées des chiffres donnés ci-après, qui s'appliquent généralement à une période plus ou moins longue de 1960 (en général neuf mois), ne peuvent-elles avoir qu'un caractère provisoire et approximatif.

Durant l'année 1960, la conjoncture a été particulièrement favorable dans la plupart des pays de l'O.E.C.E.: pour l'ensemble de ceux-ci, on enregistre en effet, par rapport à 1959, un accroissement de 5,8% du produit national brut (chiffre provisoire) et de 9% de la production industrielle, les chiffres correspondants pour les six pays de la C.E.E. étant 7 et 12%. De même, les résultats de la production agricole ont été généralement meilleurs en 1960 qu'en 1959, la Grèce, l'Italie et le Portugal faisant exception.

- Road transport: increase of 50 per cent in the number of vehicles (in the absence of figures showing ton-kilometres).

These forecasts were fulfilled, and even exceeded as regards the number of motor vehicles, which developed very regularly at an annual rate of more than 10 per cent: as compared with 1956, the numbers at the end of 1960 represent an increase of about 60 per cent.

In recent years, the trend of goods traffic by rail for the E.C.M.T. countries as a whole, measured in ton-kilometres, was as follows: 1953: 100; 1954: 103; 1955: 112; 1956: 117; 1957: 119; 1958: 111; 1959: 112.5; 1960 (9 months): 121. The years 1958 and 1959 were therefore periods of regression; the situation was reversed towards the end of 1959 and this recovery was accentuated in 1960, which was a record year. Nevertheless, the increase in goods traffic by rail over the entire period 1956–1960 did not come up to expectations.

Passenger traffic by rail (measured in passenger-kilometres) rose by 4 per cent between 1956 and 1957, but has since shown a tendency to remain unchanged, one of the causes being perhaps the expansion of motor traffic.

Measured in tons, inland waterway traffic first increased by 5 per cent between 1956 and 1957 and then dropped by 3 per cent from 1957 to 1958. This was followed by a 3.9 per cent recovery in 1959 and this progress assumed greater proportions in 1960, when it amounted to about 18 per cent for all traffic. The total increase in the tonnage carried for the period 1956–1960 will thus have exceeded the forecast.

On the Rhine, it was found that normal Rhine traffic increased from 104.5 million tons in 1956 to about 130 million tons in 1960, an increase of 24.4 per cent, which corresponds exactly to the forecast made by the E.C.M.T. in 1957. This increase was, however, by no means progressive, for traffic in 1957, 1958 and 1959 was 108.1, 105.6 and 109.7 million tons respectively. The causes of the jump in 1960 are explained later in this Report.

If, despite the very favourable general economic situation since 1959, the transport forecasts for 1960 made in 1956 have not all been fulfilled, this is mainly because the correlations previous considered valid between certain general economic indices and the volume of goods transport seem to have been disturbed in recent years by deep-seated changes which have already occurred in the energy pattern and, to a lesser extent, by the recent development of pipeline transport. Railway traffic seems to have been principally affected by these disturbances.

b) ANALYSIS OF RESULTS FOR 1960

At the time of writing this Report, no complete results for 1960 are available. Any conclusions drawn from the figures given below, which generally apply to a variable period in 1960 (usually nine months), can therefore be only provisional and approximate.

In 1960, the general economic situation was particularly favourable in most O.E.E.C. countries: as a whole, these show an increase over 1959 of 5.8 per cent in the gross national product (provisional figure) and 9 per cent in industrial production, the corresponding figures for the six E.E.C. countries being 7 and 12 per cent. Similarly, agricultural production was generally better in 1960 than in 1959, with the exception of Greece, Italy and Portugal.

La production de l'acier, qui avait repris depuis le printemps 1959, a atteint en 1960 un nouveau record: par rapport à 1959, l'accroissement a été de + 16,4% pour l'ensemble des pays de l'O.E.C.E. (15,3% pour les six pays de la C.E.E.).

Tout en s'améliorant en 1960 dans certains pays, le marché du charbon connaît toujours des difficultés et défend avec peine sa position concurrentielle vis-à-vis des autres formes de l'énergie: la production des pays de l'O.E.C.E., qui avait baissé de 2% en 1958 et de 4% en 1959, a été en 1960 de nouveau en baisse de 2,8%.

La haute conjoncture qui a caractérisé l'année 1960 a eu pour effet d'accroître, par rapport à l'année précédente, le trafic de marchandises de la plupart des grands ports de mer européens: l'augmentation a été de: 6,1% à Hambourg; 7,6% à Brême; 18,7% à Rotterdam (11 premiers mois); 8,7% à Anvers (11 premiers mois); 23% à Gênes; 9% à Venise; 21% à Trieste; 3,8% à Rijeka (9 premiers mois).

I. Évolution du trafic ferroviaire en 1960

A. Trafic des marchandises

Sous l'influence d'une conjoncture très favorable, le trafic des marchandises de la plupart des pays de la C.E.M.T. a enregistré en 1960 de bons résultats. Pour les 9 premiers mois, l'augmentation a été, dans l'ensemble, de 8,5% pour les tonnes transportées, et de 7,7% pour les tonnes-kilomètres. Elle a été en moyenne du même ordre (9 à 10% en tonnes-kilomètres) pour les pays de la C.E.E. et pour ceux de l'E.F.T.A., ainsi que pour la Yougoslavie. En Espagne, en Grèce et en Turquie, le trafic ferroviaire de marchandises a subi un recul important supérieur à 10%.

En Allemagne, les transports de marchandises par voie ferrée ont à peu près retrouvé en 1960 le niveau le plus élevé atteint depuis la Guerre, dépassant d'environ 10% (en tonnes-kilomètres) le chiffre de l'année précédente. Ce résultat reflète l'augmentation de la production industrielle (+ 11%) et celle de l'acier (+ 15,8%), qui a entraîné une intensification des importations de minerai de fer.

La progression du trafic de 1959 à 1960 a été encore plus forte en Autriche, puisqu'elle atteint 10% pour les tonnes transportées et 20% pour les tonnes-kilomètres.

En Belgique, l'évolution du trafic en 1960, qui fait ressortir une augmentation d'environ 4% (en tonnes-kilomètres) par rapport à 1959, a suivi celle de la conjoncture économique (production industrielle: + 6%; production de l'acier: + 11,2%). Le redressement du trafic s'est toutefois atténué dans le second semestre de 1960.

La situation a été analogue au Luxembourg, où les pourcentages d'augmentation ont été: trafic marchandises (en tonnes-kilomètres): 12%; production industrielle: 10%; production de l'acier: 11,5%.

Au Danemark, on note en 1960 une augmentation de 6,5% en tonnes-kilomètres, due à un degré satisfaisant de la production.

En France, le trafic a été en progression de 6,5% (en tonnes-kilomètres) par rapport à 1959, dépassant ainsi de 5,8% celui de 1957, qui avait été une année record. Néanmoins, la progression reste inférieure à celle des indices économiques (production industrielle: + 10%; production de l'acier: + 13%).

Un sensible fléchissement du trafic a été constaté en Grèce, dû en partie à la diminution des transports de produits agricoles.

La conjoncture particulièrement favorable dont a bénéficié l'Italie (production industrielle: + 15,5%; production de l'acier: + 21,5%) s'est traduite par une très forte augmentation du trafic ferroviaire, qui est de l'ordre de 15% (en tonnes-kilomètres).

Aux Pays-Bas, comme en France, l'amélioration du trafic marchandises

Steel production, which had recovered since the Spring of 1959, set up a new record in 1960: the increase over 1959 was + 16.4 per cent for the O.E.E.C. countries as a whole (15.3 per cent for the six E.E.C. countries).

Though the coal market improved in certain countries in 1960, it is still experiencing difficulties and finds it hard to maintain a competitive position with regard to other forms of energy: the output of the O.E.E.C. countries, which had declined by 2 per cent in 1958 and by 4 per cent in 1959, fell by a further 2.8 per cent in 1960.

The favourable economic situation in 1960 had the effect of increasing the goods traffic handled by most major European seaports, as compared with the previous year: the increase was 6.1 per cent at Hamburg; 7.6 per cent at Bremen; 18.7 per cent at Rotterdam (first 11 months); 8.7 per cent at Antwerp (first 11 months); 23 per cent at Genoa; 9 per cent at Venice; 21 per cent at Trieste; 3.8 per cent at Rijeka (first 9 months).

I. Trend of railway traffic in 1960

A. Goods traffic

Under the influence of highly favourable economic trends, goods traffic in most E.C.M.T. countries showed good results in 1960. As a whole, the increase for the first nine months was 8.5 per cent in terms of tons carried and 7.7 per cent in terms of ton-kilometres. It was the same on average (9 to 10 per cent in ton-kilometres) for E.E.C. countries and E.F.T.A. countries, and also for Yugoslavia. In Greece, Spain and Turkey, goods traffic by rail showed a considerable decline of more than 10 per cent.

In Germany, goods transport by rail in 1960 almost regained the highest level attained since the War and exceeded the figure for the previous year by about 10 per cent (in ton-kilometres). This result reflects the increase in industrial production (+ 11 per cent) and in steel output (+ 15.8 per cent), which led to greater imports of iron ore.

The development of traffic between 1959 and 1960 was greater still in Austria, where the increase was 10 per cent in terms of tons carried and 20 per cent in ton-kilometres.

In Belgium, the trend of traffic in 1960, which shows an increase over 1959 of about 8 per cent (in ton-kilometres), followed the economic trend (industrial production: + 6 per cent; steel output: + 11.2 per cent). Traffic fell off, however, in the second half of 1960.

The situation was similar in Luxembourg, where the percentage increase were: goods traffic (in ton-kilometres): 12 per cent; industrial production: 10 per cent; steel output: 11.5 per cent.

In Denmark, there was an increase of 6,5 per cent (in ton-kilometres) in 1960, due to the satisfactory progress of production.

In France, traffic was 6.5 per cent up on 1959 (in terms of ton-kilometres), which made it 5.8 per cent above the level of the record year 1957. Progress is still lower, however, than for the economic indices (industrial production: + 10 per cent; steel output: + 13 per cent).

There was an appreciable decline in traffic in Greece, which was partly due to a drop in the transport of agricultural products.

The particularly favourable economic situation enjoyed by Italy (industrial production: + 15.5 per cent; steel output: + 21.5 per cent) resulted in a very heavy increase of about 15 per cent in railway traffic (in terms of ton-kilometres).

In the Netherlands, as in France, although the improvement in goods

(+ 8% en tonnes-kilomètres), tout en étant très substantielle, n'a pas entièrement reflété l'augmentation de la production industrielle (13%).

Par suite de la situation peu favorable de l'agriculture, l'évolution du trafic a été assez irrégulière au Portugal, où les résultats de 1960 sont peu différents de ceux de l'année précédente: + 3% (en tonnes-kilomètres).

Le trafic des chemins de fer britanniques a été en sensible augmentation (6% en tonnes-kilomètres) de 1959 à 1960. L'expansion de l'économie britannique (augmentation de 8% de la production industrielle), et particulièrement l'accroissement de la production d'acier, a provoqué des transports supplémentaires: pour les transports de produits métallurgiques et semi-finis, l'augmentation (en tonnes-kilomètres) a été voisine de 14%. Les transports de charbon n'ont guère changé, tout en marquant une très légère tendance à l'amélioration.

En Suisse, les chemins de fer fédéraux ont vu, en 1960, leur trafic (en tonnes-kilomètres) augmenter de 18%: les transports internationaux ont été stimulés par l'augmentation des exportations (bois et machines en particulier), des importations (combustibles liquides, fer et acier, matériaux de construction) et du transit (métaux, machines et véhicules). Le trafic interne, qui a essentiellement profité de l'essor extraordinaire de l'industrie du bâtiment, est également en progrès.

En Suède, le renversement de tendance constaté au cours de l'année 1959 s'est poursuivi en 1960, qui fait ressortir (pour les 9 premiers mois) une augmentation de trafic de 13 à 14%; le rythme de progression s'est toutefois ralenti dans le deuxième semestre.

Par contre, les chemins de fer turcs ont enregistré en 1960 une baisse de trafic d'environ 10% en tonnes-kilomètres, qui paraît due à la situation économique et à la concurrence des transports routiers.

En Yougoslavie, on a relevé en 1960 une augmentation de 7% en tonnes, et de 9,9% en tonnes-kilomètres, par rapport à l'année précédente.

B. Trafic des voyageurs

Dans l'ensemble, le mouvement de lente régression, de l'ordre de 1%, constaté en 1958 et 1959, s'est poursuivi en 1960, mais à un rythme très ralenti: on note en effet en moyenne une diminution de 0,7% pour les voyageurs transportés et une augmentation de 0,5% pour les voyageurs-kilomètres, avec des résultats assez variables suivant les pays. Quelquefois, la tendance à la baisse s'est confirmée: c'est le cas par exemple en Allemagne (— 2% pour les voyageurs-kilomètres); au Luxembourg (— 4% pour les voyageurs transportés et — 5% pour les voyageurs-kilomètres), et au Royaume-Uni (— 4% pour les voyageurs transportés). On ne relève pratiquement pas de changement en Belgique, au Danemark, en France, en Suède (sauf pour les cartes d'abonnement, qui sont en baisse), en Suisse et en Turquie. Il y a eu une amélioration plus ou moins nette en Autriche (+ 2% pour les voyageurs transportés et + 4% pour les voyageurs-kilomètres), en Grèce (+ 5% en voyageurs-kilomètres), en Italie (+ 3,5 et + 8%), en Norvège (+ 3%), aux Pays-Bas (+ 3,4 et + 2,7%) et au Portugal (+ 8 et + 6%). Dans l'ensemble, le trafic des voyageurs paraît stabilisé, l'expansion économique stimulant surtout les transports individuels par voiture automobile. Deux pays font exception à cette règle de relative stabilité: l'Espagne et la Yougoslavie, où l'évolution du trafic (en voyageurs-kilomètres) a été d'ailleurs de sens opposé: — 17% pour l'Espagne et + 13% pour la Yougoslavie.

II. Évolution des transports routiers en 1960

Les statistiques concernant les prestations effectuées par les transports routiers faisant encore défaut dans beaucoup de pays, on a eu recours, traffic was substantial (+ 8 per cent in ton-kilometres), it did not fully reflect the increase in industrial production (13 per cent).

Owing to the unfavourable situation of agriculture, the trend of traffic was rather irregular in Portugal, where results for 1960 do not differ greatly from those of the previous year: + 3 per cent (in ton-kilometres).

Traffic on British Railways was appreciably heavier, rising by 6 per cent (in ton-kilometres) between 1959 and 1960. The expansion of the United Kingdom economy (8 per cent increase in industrial production) and particularly the increase in the output of steel called for additional transport: the gain in the transport of metallurgical products and semi-finished goods was in the neighbourhood of 14 per cent (in ton-kilometres). Coal transport changed little, though it showed a slight tendency to improve.

In Switzerland, traffic on the Federal Railways was about 18 per cent higher in 1960 (in ton-kilometres). International traffic was stimulated by increases in exports (*e.g.* timber and machinery), imports (liquid fuels, iron and steel, building materials) and transit transport (metals, machinery and vehicles). Internal traffic, which benefited mainly from the extraordinary advance made by the building industry, was also heavier.

In Sweden, the reversal of the tendency which had begun in 1959 continued in 1960, when traffic for the first nine months showed an increase of 13 to 14 per cent; the rate of progress was slower, however, in the second six months.

Traffic on the Turkish railways, on the other hand, declined by about 10 per cent (in ton-kilometres) in 1960; this appears to be due to the economic situation and to competition from road transport.

In Yugoslavia, there was an increase in 1960 of 7 per cent (in tons) and 9.9 per cent (in ton-kilometres) compared with the previous year.

B. Passenger traffic

On the whole, the slow decline of about 1 per cent recorded in 1958 and 1959 continued in 1960, but at an even slower rate: there was in fact an average drop of 0.7 per cent in the number of passengers carried and an increase of 0.5 per cent in terms of passenger-kilometres, with results varying considerably according to country. Sometimes the downward tendency was confirmed: this was so, for example, in Germany (— 2 per cent in terms of passenger-kilometres), in Luxembourg (— 4 per cent in terms of passengers carried and — 5 per cent in passenger-kilometres) and in the United Kingdom (— 4 per cent in passengers carried). There was practically no change in Belgium, Denmark, France, Sweden (except for a decline in the number of season tickets), Switzerland and Turkey. There was a fairly definite improvement in Austria (+ 2 per cent in passengers carried and + 4 per cent in passenger-kilometres), Greece (+ 5 per cent), Italy (+ 3.5 and + 8 per cent), the Netherlands (+ 3.4 and + 2.7 per cent), Norway (+ 3 per cent) and Portugal (+ 8 and + 6 per cent). On the whole, passenger traffic seems to have found its level, for the economic expansion stimulates mainly individual transport by private car. Two countries form an exception to this rule of relative stability: Spain and Yugoslavia, where the trend of traffic (in passenger-kilometres) moved in opposite directions: — 17 per cent in Spain and + 13 per cent in Yugoslavia.

II. Trend of road transport in 1960

As statistics on the services rendered by road transport do not yet exist in many countries, the numbers of vehicles and the con-pour avoir une idée approximative de leur tendance, à l'évolution des parcs de véhicules et à la consommation de carburants.

D'une manière générale, les parcs ont poursuivi en 1960 une rapide progression, surtout pour ce qui concerne les voitures privées. L'augmentation a été d'environ 22% (voitures privées) et 6% (camions) en Allemagne; 18 et 4% en Autriche; 9,5 et 0,7% en Belgique; 9 et 10% en Grèce; 12 et 8% en Italie; 12 et 5% au Royaume-Uni; 11% (ensemble du parc) en Suisse; 16 et 17% en Turquie.

L'augmentation de 1959 à 1960 du nombre des véhicules immatriculés — et non plus du parc total - a été d'environ 30% (voitures privées) et 6% (camions) au Danemark; 36% (voitures privées), 20% (véhicules commerciaux) et 35% (camions de plus de 3 tonnes de charge utile au Royaume-Uni (pendant les 10 premiers mois de 1960 pour les voitures et les 9 premiers mois pour les véhicules commerciaux); 12% en France (voitures privées).

La consommation de carburants a suivi également un mouvement ascendant. Par rapport à 1959, on relève en 1960 des augmentations que l'on peut évaluer à 17,5% (essence) et 7,6% (gas-oil) en Allemagne; 13% (essence et gas-oil) en Autriche; 6,8% (essence) et 9,1% (gas-oil) en France; 24% (essence) et 19% (gas-oil) en Italie; 8 et 15% aux Pays-Bas; 20% (gas-oil) en Suède; 14% (au total) en Suisse; 9 et 16% en Turquie, et 19% au total en Yougoslavie. En Belgique, cependant, la consommation n'a pas progressé.

Quelques pays disposent toutefois de statistiques sur les transports routiers qui permettent d'avoir une idée plus précise de leur évolution en 1960.

En Allemagne, les transports publics de marchandises à longue distance et les transports pour compte propre à longue distance (qui représentent à peu près 1/3 en tonnes et 1/5 en tonnes-kilomètres des précédents) ont été en augmentation respectivement de 11 et 12%. Quant aux transports internationaux de marchandises, ils ont continué à progresser (en tonnes) de 31% pendant le 1er semestre de 1960, la part du trafic assuré par des véhicules étrangers, qui représente 57% environ, ayant augmenté davantage (38%) au cours de la même période. En Autriche, le trafic international des marchandises a aussi progressé de 15% pendant les 9 premiers mois de 1960. Au Danemark, l'augmentation du trafic routier de 1959 à 1960 peut être évaluée de 5 à 15%, et même à 20 à 25% sur les routes importantes desservant Copenhague. De même, les Pays-Bas enregistrent en 1960 une augmentation de 15% (en tonnes) et de 18% (en tonnes-kilomètres) pendant le 1er semestre pour les transports intérieurs publics et de 22% (pendant les 9 premiers mois) pour le trafic international. Au Royaume-Uni, on évalue l'augmentation du volume des transports routiers de marchandises à 8% pour les 10 premiers mois de l'année 1960. Mesuré en tonnes-kilomètres, le volume total des transports routiers britanniques dépasse maintenant de 50% celui des transports ferroviaires. En Suisse, le trafic routier s'est aussi développé, et tout particulièrement le trafic international: les transports de bois et de matériaux de construction à destination et au départ de ce pays ont pris une extension extraordinaire en 1960, et le nombre de camions suisses et étrangers ayant franchi les frontières suisses a augmenté, dans le 1er semestre, de 72%. Le trafic international à destination de la Suède s'est considérablement accru (+ 68%). On évalue enfin en Turquie à 20% environ l'augmentation en 1960 des prestations du trafic routier par rapport à 1959. En Yougoslavie, l'augmentation a été de 28% (en tonnes) en trafic intérieur, et 38% (en tonnes) pour le trafic international de marchandises (pendant les 9 premiers mois).

Les transports publics de voyageurs par autobus ou autocar ont marqué en 1960, dans plusieurs pays, une tendance à la stagnation, ou même à la sumption of motor fuels have been used to give an approximate idea of the trend.

Generally speaking, the numbers of vehicles contined to rise rapidly in 1960, particularly as regards private cars. The increase was about 22 per cent (private cars) and 6 per cent (lorries) in Germany; 18 and 4 per cent in Austria; 0.7 per cent (commercial vehicles) in Belgium; 9 and 10 per cent in Greece; 12 and 8 per cent in Italy; 12 and 5 per cent in the United Kingdom; 11 per cent (all vehicles) in Switzerland; and 16 and 17 per cent in Turkey.

The increase in the number of vehicles registered – as opposed to total numbers – between 1959 and 1960 was about 30 per cent (private cars) and 6 per cent (lorries) in Denmark; 36 per cent (private cars), 20 per cent (commercial vehicles) and 35 per cent (lorries of more than 3 tons unladen weight) in the United Kingdom (in the first 10 months of 1960 for private cars and the first 9 months for commercial vehicles); and 12 per cent (private cars) in France.

Fuel consumption also followed an upward movement. As compared with 1959, the increases in 1960 may be assessed at 13 per cent (motor spirit and diesel fuel) in Austria; 6.8 per cent (motor spirit) and 9.1 per cent (diesel fuel) in France; 17.5 per cent (motor spirit) and 7.6 per cent (diesel fuel) in Germany; 24 per cent (motor spirit) and 19 per cent (diesel fuel) in Italy; 8 and 15 per cent in the Netherlands; 20 per cent (diesel fuel) in Sweden; 14 per cent (total) in Switzerland; 9 and 16 per cent in Turkey and 19 per cent (total) in Yugoslavia. Consumption did not rise, however, in Belgium.

A few countries do, however, have road transport statistics which give a more accurate idea of the trend in 1960.

In Germany, long-distance goods transport for hire or reward and long-distance transport on own account (which represents about one-third of the former reckoned in tons and one-fifteenth in ton-kilometres) increased by 11 and 12 per cent respectively. International goods transport continued to progress (in terms of tons) by 31 per cent in the first half of 1960, and the proportion of this traffic accounted for by foreign vehicles (representing about 57 per cent) increased even more (38 per cent) during the same period. In Austria, international goods traffic also increased by 15 per cent in the first nine months of 1960. In Denmark, the increase in road traffic between 1959 and 1960 may be estimated at from 5 to 15 per cent and even 20 to 25 per cent on important roads serving Copenhagen. Similarly, the Netherlands showed an increase of 15 per cent (in tons) and 18 per cent (in ton-kilometres) for public internal transport in the first half of 1960, and 22 per cent (in the first nine months) for international traffic. In the United Kingdom, the increase in the volume of goods traffic by road is assessed at 8 per cent for the first ten months of 1960. Measured in ton-kilometres, the total volume of road transport in the United Kingdom is now 50 per cent higher than that of railway transport. In Switzerland, road traffic also developed, particularly international traffic: the carriage of timber and building materials to and from that country expanded to an extraordinary extent in 1960, and the number of Swiss and foreign lorries crossing the Swiss frontiers increased by 72 per cent in the first six months. International traffic entering Sweden also increased considerably (+ 68 per cent). The increase in road traffic in Turkey is estimated at about 20 per cent as compared with 1959. In Yugoslavia, the increase was 28 per cent (in tons) for internal traffic and 38 per cent (in tons) for international goods traffic, in the first nine months.

Public passenger transport by motor-bus and motor-coach showed a tendency to remain steady in 1960 or even to decline in several countries.

régression. C'est le cas notamment pour l'Allemagne, l'Autriche (pour le trafic international seulement), le Royaume-Uni et la Suisse. L'Autriche (pour le trafic intérieur), l'Italie, la Suède (pour le trafic international), la Turquie et la Yougoslavie annoncent au contraire une augmentation de ces transports.

III. Évolution des transports par voies navigables en 1960

Les voies navigables des pays membres de la C.E.M.T. peuvent être divisées en trois systèmes distincts: le Rhin, ainsi que le réseau de canaux et de rivières canalisées qui y est relié; le Danube; et les autres voies, qui sont à leur tour divisées en plusieurs tronçons d'importance variable. Dans ce qui suit, on a analysé séparément les transports sur le Rhin et sur le Danube, en raison du caractère européen de ces fleuves.

En considérant seulement le trafic ayant franchi la frontière germano-néerlandaise, le trafic rhénan a atteint en 1960 70,6 millions de tonnes, en augmentation de 28,3% sur l'année précédente, le trafic vers l'amont ayant dans l'ensemble augmenté davantage que le trafic vers l'aval. Si on laisse de côté les transports d'huile minérale, l'augmentation été de 30,8%: en effet, cette catégorie de transports fait ressortir en 1950, en raison du développement considérable de la consommation allemande de fuel-oil, un accroissement entièrement dû au transport de produits raffinés, de 12% seulement, qui correspond à un trafic total de 9,6 millions de tonnes, inférieur au chiffre de 1958 (10,5 millions de tonnes). D'ailleurs, si l'on compare les chiffres du 2e semestre de l'année, on constate en 1960 une baisse de 190.000 tonnes (— 4,5%), qui est évidemment à mettre en relation avec la mise en service, le 27 juin 1960, de l'oléoduc Rotterdam-région de Cologne. Les transports de charbon (houille et lignite) ont été en hausse de 35,2% vers l'aval et seulement de 10,1% vers l'amont: la hausse a été également très forte pour les minerais de fer et de manganèse (+ 51,7%), les minerais non ferreux (+ 50,4%) et le sable (+ 34,1%). Par contre, ont été en diminution les transports de céréales (— 14%) et, à un moindre degré, d'engrais (— 1,4%).

Le niveau élevé des transports assurés en 1960 par la navigation rhénane doit toutefois être apprécié avec prudence. Il résulte en effet de l'influence combinée de plusieurs facteurs: exécution, pendant les premiers mois de l'année 1960, de transports que la période de basses eaux de la fin 1959 avait conduit à différer; réapprovisionnement plus accentué des stocks; permanence de conditions particulièrement favorables pour la navigation. Tous ces facteurs confèrent aux résultats en 1960 du trafic rhénan un caractère exceptionnel.

Le trafic sur le Rhin avec la Suisse a atteint en 1960 un niveau record: le volume des marchandises transbordées dans les ports de Bâle est évalué en effet à 7 millions de tonnes en chiffres ronds contre 4,9 millions en 1959, soit une augmentation de 42%; 41,8% du trafic total a été assuré par le pavillon suisse. La part de la navigation rhénane dans le commerce extérieur suisse a été de 36,9% en 1960 contre 32,1% l'année précédente. La forte augmentation des transports de combustibles liquides (56,6% par rapport à 1959) paraît devoir être attribuée en partie à l'installation, dans la région de la Ruhr et de Cologne, des nouvelles raffineries alimentées par oléoducs. L'occupation de la cale des bateaux a été bien meilleure que l'année précédente, où, par suite des basses eaux, il avait fallu stocker en partie les marchandises dans les ports: celles-ci purent être transportées en 1960, ce qui, avec les bonnes conditions de la navigation, a contribué aux excellents résultats d'exploitation.

En Allemagne, le trafic assuré par les voies navigables en 1960 est évalué à 170 millions de tonnes, en augmentation de 20% sur l'année précédente. La part de ce trafic assuré par des bateaux allemands, qui représente maintenant environ 60%, a augmenté pendant les 9 premiers

This is the case particularly in Austria (for international traffic only), Germany, Switzerland and the United Kingdom. Austria (for internal traffic), Italy, Sweden (for international traffic), Turkey and Yugoslavia announce an increase in this form of transport.

III. Trend of inland waterways transport in 1960

The inland waterways of O.E.E.C. Member countries can be divided into three distinct systems: the Rhine together with the network of canals and canalised rivers connected with it; the Danube; and other waterways, which in their turn are divided into several stretches of varying importance. Transport on the Rhine and on the Danube has been analysed separately in this chapter, owing to the European nature of these rivers.

Considering only traffic crossing the German-Netherlands frontier, Rhine traffic amounted to 70.6 million tons in 1960, an increase of 28.3 per cent over the previous year, upstream traffic having on the whole increased more than downstream traffic. Excluding the transport of mineral oil, the increase was 30.8 per cent; owing to the considerable expansion of German consumption of fuel oil, this class of transport showed an increase of only 12 per cent, entirely attributable to the carriage of refined products and corresponding to a total traffic of 9.6 million tons, which is less than the figure for 1958 (10.5 million tons). Furthermore, comparing the figures for the second six months, 1960 shows a drop of 190,000 tons (— 4.5 per cent), which is obviously to be related to the coming into service, on 27th June, 1960, of the pipeline from Rotterdam to the Cologne area. The increase in coal traffic (hard coal and lignite) was 35.2 per cent for downstream traffic and only 10.1 per cent for upstream traffic; the rise was also very pronounced for iron and manganese ores (+ 51.7 per cent), non-ferrous ores (+ 50.4 per cent) and sand (+ 34.1 per cent). On the other hand, there was a drop in transport of cereals (— 14 per cent) and, to a lesser extent, fertilizers (— 1.4 per cent).

The high level of traffic on the Rhine in 1960 must, however, be judged with some reserve. It was in fact due to the combined influence of several factors: the performance in the early months of 1960 of transport operations which had had to be postponed because of the low water levels at the end of 1959; heavier stockpiling; and the persistence of particularly favourable navigating conditions. All these factors make the results of Rhine traffic in 1960 quite exceptional.

Rhine traffic with Switzerland reached a record level in 1960: in round figures, the volume of goods handled in the port of Basle is estimated at 7 million tons, compared with 4.9 millions tons in 1959, an increase of 42 per cent; 41.8 per cent of the total traffic was carried in Swiss barges. Rhine traffic accounted for 36.9 per cent of Swiss foreign trade in 1960, compared with 32.1 per cent in the previous year. The heavy increase in the transport of liquid fuels (56.6 per cent higher than in 1959) seems to be partly attributable to the installation of new refineries supplied by pipeline in the Ruhr and at Cologne. The cargo capacity of the barges was more fully taken up than in the previous year, when, owing to low water levels, some goods had to be stored in the ports: these could be taken away in 1960 and this, together with the good navigating conditions, contributed to the satisfactory operating results.

Inland waterways traffic in Germany in 1960 is estimated at 170 million tons, an increase of 20 per cent over the previous year. The share of this traffic represented by German barges, now about 60 per cent, increased by 12 per cent in the first nine months, while traffic by foreign mois de 12%, et celle des bateaux étrangers de 22%. Pour le trafic intérieur, qui est moins favorisé que l'ensemble du trafic, on note le même phénomène, les pourcentages correspondants étant de 11 et 28%. Le trafic échangé entre les ports fluviaux allemands et l'étranger s'est accru de 23%. Quant au trafic de transit, il s'est relevé de 8%, au bénéfice exclusif de la navigation étrangère, la part assurée par des bateaux allemands ayant diminué de 5%. Dans l'ensemble, l'occupation de la flotte a été satisfaisante et la cale a été suffisante pour absorber la demande de transport, même pendant la période de pointe de juillet.

En Belgique, l'accroissement du trafic des voies navigables de 1959 à 1960 (8 premiers mois) a été aussi très substantiel, puisqu'il atteint 19% en tonnes et 14% en tonnes-kilomètres, effaçant ainsi la chute des deux années précédentes. L'augmentation (en tonnes) a été plus importante en trafic international (+ 40% pour les importations; + 10% pour les exportations; + 20% pour le transit) qu'en trafic intérieur (+ 9%).

Aux Pays-Bas, on a également enregistré en 1960 une augmentation sensible du trafic des voies navigables, qui, pour les 9 premiers mois de l'année, est évaluée à 15% (en tonnes) et 14% (en tonnes-kilomètres). Le tonnage transporté s'est accru davantage en trafic international (+ 19% à l'entrée; + 21% à la sortie; + 13% pour le transit) que le trafic intérieur (+ 11%).

En France, le relèvement du trafic constaté en 1960 (8% pour les tonnes et 13% pour les tonnes-kilomètres), bien que substantiel, a été de moindre amplitude que dans d'autres pays.

Sur le Danube (parcours autrichien), le trafic de 1960 se compare comme suit avec celui de l'année précédente:

	Tonnes transportées		Modifications 1959–60 (%)	Tonnes-kilomètres		Modifications 1959–60 (%)
	1959	1960		1959	1960	
Importations	2.117.923	3.016.233	+42,4	341.451.736	482.376.225	+41,3
Exportations	1.256.298	1.304.402	+ 3,8	160.507.878	152.495.448	— 5,0
Transit	512.050	692.094	+35,2	179.789.550	240.609.492	+33,8
Trafic intérieur	1.078.265	1.189.376	+10,3	65.826.205	86.137.195	+30,9
Ensemble du trafic . . .	4.964.536	6.202.105	+24,9	747.575.369	961.618.360	+28,6

On peut attribuer les bons résultats de l'année 1960 à la persistance d'une haute conjoncture économique et aussi à l'existence, pendant toute l'année, de conditions de navigation favorables sur le Danube.

Sur le Danube (parcours yougoslave), le trafic de 1960 se compare comme suit avec celui de l'année précédente:

	Tonnes transportées		Augmentation (%)	Tonnes-kilomètres (en milliers)		Augmentation (%)
	1959	1960		1959	1960	
Exportations	313.365	416.705	32,9	103.578	130.927	26,4
Importations	129.479	226.193	105,6	137.723	182.138	32,2
Transit	3.229.624	4.151.800	28,5	1.899.019	2.441.549	28,5
Trafic intérieur	2.787.433	3.434.418	23,2	183.945	251.521	36,7
Ensemble du trafic . . .	6.459.901	8.229.116	27,4	2.324.265	3.006.135	29,3

barges increased by 22 per cent. The same phenomenon occurs in internal traffic, which has, however, made less progress than total traffic, the corresponding percentages being 11 and 28. Traffic between German inland ports and foreign countries increased by 23 per cent. Transit traffic was 8 per cent higher, the increase going entirely to foreign barges, for the share of German barges declined by 5 per cent. On the whole, the fleet was satisfactorily employed and cargo capacity was sufficient to absorb the demand for transport, even during the peak period in July.

In Belgium, the increase in waterways traffic was also very substantial between 1959 and 1960 (first 8 months), for it amounted to 19 per cent in terms of tons and 14 per cent in ton-kilometres and thus offset the drop which had occurred in the previous two years. The increase (in tons) was greater for international traffic (+ 40 per cent for imports; + 10 per cent for exports; + 20 per cent for transit) than for internal traffic (+ 9 per cent).

In the Netherlands in 1960, there was an appreciable increase in inland waterways traffic, which was assessed at 15 per cent (in tons) and 14 per cent (in ton-kilometres) during the first nine months of the year. The tonnage carried increased more in international traffic (+ 19 per cent incoming; + 21 per cent outgoing; + 13 per cent transit) than in internal traffic (+ 11 per cent).

In France, although the increase in traffic was substantial in 1960 (8 per cent in tons and 13 per cent in ton-kilometres), it was less striking than in other countries.

On the Danube (Austrian reaches), traffic for 1960 compares with that of the previous year as follows:

	Tons carried		Changes 1959–60 (%)	Ton-kilometres		Changes 1959–60 (%)
	1959	1960		1959	1960	
Imports	2,117,923	3,016,233	+ 42.4	341,451,736	482,376,225	+ 41.3
Exports	1,256,298	1,304,402	+ 3.8	160,507,878	152,495,448	+ 5.0
Transit	512,050	692,094	+ 35.2	179,789,550	240,609,492	+ 33.8
Internal traffic	1,078,265	1,189,376	+ 10.3	65,826,205	86,137,195	+ 30.9
All traffic	4,964,536	6,202,105	+ 24.9	747,575,369	961,618,360	+ 28.6

The good results for 1960 may be attribued to the persistence of a favourable economic situation and also to the existence throughout the the year of excellent navigating conditions.

On the Danube (Yugoslav reaches), traffic in 1960 compares with that of the previous year as follows:

	Tons carried		Increase (%)	Ton-kilometers (in thousands)		Increase (%)
	1959	1960		1959	1960	
Exports	313,365	416,705	32.9	103,578	130,927	26.4
Imports	129,479	226,193	105.6	137,723	182,138	32.2
Transit	3,229,624	4,151,800	28.5	1,899,019	2,441,549	28.5
Internal traffic	2,787,433	3,434,418	23.2	183,945	251,521	36.7
All traffic	6,459,901	8,229,116	27.4	2,324,265	3,006,135	29.3

En Italie, les transports de marchandises par voies navigables ont représenté en 1960 (9 mois) 3,7 millions de tonnes, en augmentation de 9% par rapport à la même période de l'année précédente: ils ont été favorisés par l'installation de nouvelles raffineries et le développement des transports de produits pondéreux.

En Suède, les deux canaux (reliant respectivement les ports des lacs Mälar et Vänern à la mer Baltique et à la mer du Nord) ont assuré en 1960 (9 premiers mois) un trafic total de 3,3 millions de tonnes, en augmentation de 17% sur la même période de l'année précédente, qui s'explique par le renforcement de l'activité industrielle et l'augmentation du commerce extérieur.

....

III. AMÉLIORATION ET DÉVELOPPEMENT DES GRANDES VOIES DE COMMUNICATION EUROPÉENNES COORDINATION ET FINANCEMENT DES INVESTISSEMENTS

a) *APERÇU D'ENSEMBLE*

....

Dans son état actuel, le système des grandes voies de communication européennes a été influencé par de nombreux facteurs: configuration géographique du terrain, répartition de la population, évolution historique de la formation politique des États (à forme centralisée ou fédérative), nature de leur économie (industrielle, agricole), état de leurs ressources énergétiques, importance de leur rôle touristique, *etc.* En outre, tel ou tel de ces facteurs, en exerçant dans certains pays une influence prédominante, les a conduits plus tôt que d'autres à recourir à certaines techniques nouvelles; après quoi, l'état des connaissances a évolué et a offert d'autres solutions qui ont été préférées ailleurs. C'est ce qui explique, en particulier, la diversité des systèmes de courant choisi pour l'électrification des réseaux européens de chemins de fer.

Modelé en quelque sorte par tous ces facteurs, le réseau des grandes voies de communication européennes, au prix d'investissements considérables, a pris peu à peu sa forme actuelle. Celle-ci, comme il ressort des précédents Rapports, va continuer à évoluer en raison des programmes très importants d'amélioration et d'extension qui sont en cours d'exécution et concernent essentiellement:

a) L'électrification des chemins de fer. Achevée en Suisse, elle est pratiquement terminée aux Pays-Bas et en Suède, où les programmes d'électrification ont été entièrement exécutés; elle est enfin activement poursuivie dans d'autres pays (Allemagne, Autriche, Belgique, France, Italie). Compte tenu des travaux en cours, ou dont la réalisation est projetée dans les cinq prochaines années, on peut admettre que d'ici-là sera achevée l'électrification de plusieurs grandes artères très importantes, telles que Paris-Marseille, Paris-Strasbourg(-Vienne), Hambourg-Francfort(-Bâle), Vienne-Tarvis(-Venise). Les progrès réalisés ou escomptés dans ce domaine, qui laissent cependant subsister quelques lacunes, ressortent clairement de la carte du réseau électrifié que la C.E.M.T. a publié en octobre 1960;

b) Le développement du réseau des autoroutes et des grandes liaisons routières à travers les Alpes. Le programme de construction des autoroutes sur lequel renseignaient les précédents rapports, se poursuit conformément aux prévisions et a enregistré en 1960, particulièrement dans les pays du Benelux, en Allemagne, Autriche, et Italie, de nouveaux et substantiels progrès qui concernent des liaisons destinées à jouer un rôle capital pour les transports routiers internationaux: grands ports du Benelux-région de Cologne, Hambourg-Francfort-Bâle, Salzbourg-Vienne, Milan-Venise et Milan-Bologne-Florence („autoroute du soleil").

In 1960 (nine months) goods transport by inland waterways in Italy represented 3.7 million tons, an increase of 9 per cent over the corresponding period of the previous year; it was favoured by the establishment of new refineries and by the development of the transport of bulky goods.

In Sweden, the two canals (connecting ports on Lakes Mälar and Vänern to the Baltic Sea and to the North Sea respectively) carried a total traffic of 3.3 million tons in the first nine months of 1960, an increase of 17 per cent over the same period of the previous year; this is explained by intensified industrial activity and increased foreign trade.

. . . .

III. IMPROVEMENT AND DEVELOPMENT OF EUROPEAN MAIN LINES OF COMMUNICATION CO-ORDINATION AND FINANCING OF INVESTMENT

a) *GENERAL OUTLINE*

. . . .

In its present state, the network of European main lines of communication has been influenced by many factors: configuration of the ground, distribution of population, history of the political formation of States (centralised or federative form), nature of their economy (industrial or agricultural), state of their energy resources, importance from the point of view of tourism, *etc.* Certain countries in which one, or other, of these factors happens to predominate have been led to adopt certain new techniques earlier than other countries; afterwards, more advanced knowledge afforded other solutions which have been preferred elsewhere. This explains in particular the diversity of the types of current used for the electrification of European railways.

To some extent, the network of European main lines of communication has been shaped by all these factors and has gradually assumed its present form at the cost of considerable investment. As shown in previous reports, the network will continue to develop in accordance with current large-scale programmes of improvement and extension in connection with:

a) The electrification of the railways. This is complete in Switzerland and practically completed in the Netherlands and Sweden, where electrification programmes have been carried out in full; it is being actively continued in other countries (Austria, Belgium, France, Germany, Italy). Allowing for work already in hand or planned for the next five years, it may be said that, by then, the electrification of several very important main arteries will be completed, such as Paris-Marseilles; Paris-Strasbourg (-Vienna); Hamburg–Frankfurt (-Basle); Vienna–Tarvisio (-Venice). The progress already made or expected in this field, which still leaves a few gaps however, is clearly shown in the map of the electrified system published by the E.C.M.T. in October 1960;

b) The development of the network of motorways and main road links through the Alps. The motorways building programme, on which information was given in the previous reports, is continuing as planned and has made further substantial progress in 1960, particularly in the Benelux countries, Austria, Germany and Italy. The chief progress has been made in connections which are to play a capital part in international road transport: main Benelux ports-Cologne area; Hamburg–Frankfurt–Basle; Salzburg–Vienna; Milan–Venice; Milan–Bologna–Florence ("Sunshine" Motorway).

En outre, la construction des deux grands tunnels routiers, sous le mont Blanc et sous le col du Grand-Saint-Bernard progressent favorablement et seront achevés dans les délais prévus. Il en est de même de l'aménagement de la partie nord de la route du Brenner, entre le col et Innsbruck.

c) L'exécution de certains grands projets destinés à étendre le réseau des voies navigables au gabarit européen: Meuse jusqu'à la frontière française, Moselle juqsu'à Thionville, Main jusqu'à Nuremberg.

....

e) *TRANSPORTS PAR OLÉODUCS*

Ainsi que le mentionnait le précédent Rapport annuel la C.E.M.T. a publié en octobre 1959 un rapport spécial sur le développement du réseau européen des oléoducs et les problèmes en découlant pour la politique des transports.

Ce rapport spécial donnait un tableau de la situation des oléoducs alors en exploitation, en construction ou en projet: comme il y était annoncé, l'oléoduc pour le transport du pétrole brut entre le port de Rotterdam et la région de la Ruhr et Cologne a été mis en service le 27 juin 1960. On sait que les raffineries de cette région sont déjà desservies, depuis le début de 1959, par un autre oléoduc qui les relie au port de Wilhelmshaven.

La quantité d'huile brute transportée par l'oléoduc Wilhelmshaven-région de la Ruhr-Cologne est passée de 5,8 millions de tonnes en 1959 à 9,5 millions de tonnes en 1960. Quant à l'oléoduc provenant de Rotterdam, il a transporté 2,5 millions de tonnes depuis la date de sa mise en service jusqu'à la fin de 1960, portant ainsi à un total de 12 millions de tonnes la quantité d'huile brute introduite en 1960 par pompage dans la République Fédérale. On a signalé précédemment quelle en avait été l'influence sur les transports de la navigation rhénane.

Pendant l'année 1960, les quantités d'huile brute transportées par les oléoducs italiens les plus importants ont été les suivantes:

Oléoduc Gênes-Rho (Milan).	1,86	million de tonnes
,, Raguse-Augusta (Sicile) . . .	1,20	,, ,, ,,
Vado Ligure-Trecate.	0,94	,, ,, ,,
Total	4	millions de tonnes

Parmi les oléoducs alors à l'étude, le rapport spécial de la C.E.M.T. signalait en premier lieu l'oléoduc devant relier le port de Lavera (près de Marseille) à des raffineries à construire dans la région de Strasbourg, et précisait que sa construction avait été autorisée par décret du 14 octobre 1959 du Gouvernement français. En décembre 1960 a été signé le décret déclarant d'utilité publique les travaux qui vont être entrepris et seront menés de manière à permettre la mise en service au début de 1963. Le prolongement de cet oléoduc est prévu jusqu'à Karlsruhe.

Un commencement d'exécution est également à signaler pour les travaux de construction d'un oléoduc pour produits bruts devant relier le port de Gênes à une raffinerie à construire à Collombey-Aigle, dans le canton suisse du Valais, et que mentionnait également le rapport spécial de la C.E.M.T. Une décision sur la prolongation éventuelle de cette conduite vers l'Allemagne du Sud (Munich) n'interviendra qu'après l'adoption de la loi dont il est question au paragraphe 112; il est possible qu'Aigle constitue son point terminus.

En vue de sauvegarder les intérêts de la navigation suisse sur le Rhin vis-à-vis de la concurrence de l'oléoduc de Collombey-Aigle pour l'approvisionnement du marché suisse, une ,,Société rhénane de transports par pipe-line'', au capital de 200.000 francs suisses, a été constituée à Bâle à la fin de 1960: elle se propose essentiellement d'étudier la construction de

In addition, favourable progress is being made with the construction of the two main road tunnels under Mont Blanc and under the Great St. Bernard Pass, which will be completed within the prescribed time limits. The same applies to the improvement of the northern part of the Brenner road between the pass and Innsbruck;

c) Work on certain main projects to bring the waterways network up to "European" standards: Meuse as far as the French frontier; Moselle as far as Thionville; Main as far as Nuremberg.

. . . .

e) *PIPELINE TRANSPORT*

As stated in the previous Annual Report, in October 1959, the E.C.M.T. published a special report on the development of the European pipeline system and the resulting problems affecting transport policy.

This special report gave a survey of pipelines then in operation, under construction or planned. As announced at the time, the pipeline carrying crude oil from the port of Rotterdam to the Ruhr and Cologne came into service on 27th June, 1960. Since the beginning of 1959, the refineries in this area have of course already been served by another pipeline connecting them to the port of Wilhelmshaven.

The quantity of crude oil carried by the Wilhelmshaven-Ruhr-Cologne pipeline rose from 5.8 million tons in 1959 to 9.5 million tons in 1960. The pipeline running from Rotterdam has carried 2.5 million tons since the date of its coming into service up to the end of 1960, and thus brings the quantity of crude oil brought in to the Federal Republic in 1960 by pumping operations up to a total of 12 million tons. The effect of this on waterway transport on the Rhine has already been pointed out.

During 1960, the quantities of crude oil carried by the main Italian pipelines were as follows:

Genoa-Rho (Milan) line	1.86	million tons
Ragusa-Augusta (Sicily) line	1.20	,, ,,
Vado Ligure-Trecate line	0.94	,, ,,
Total.	4	million tons

Among the pipelines then planned, the E.C.M.T. special report first mentioned the line which was to link the port of Lavera (near Marseilles) to the refineries to be built near Strasbourg, and indicated that its construction had been authorised by a French Government Decree of 14th October, 1959. In December 1960, a Decree was signed declaring the public utility of the work to be undertaken, which is scheduled to come into service at the beginning of 1963. It is planned to extend this pipeline as far as Karlsruhe.

Work has also been started on the building of a pipeline for crude oil to link the port of Genoa to a refinery to be built at Collombey-Aigle in the Swiss Canton of Wallis, also mentioned in the E.C.M.T. special report. No decision on the possible extension of this line towards Southern Germany (Munich) will be taken until after the adoption of the Law referred to in paragraph 112; it is possible that Aigle may become its terminus.

In order to protect the interests of Swiss shipping on the Rhine from competition from the Collombey-Aigle pipeline in bringing supplies to the Swiss market, a "Société Rhénane de Transports par Pipeline", with a capital of Sw.Fr. 200,000, was established at Basle at the end of 1960. Its chief purpose is to study the construction of pipelines for the districonduites pour la distribution en Suisse des produits raffinés, acheminés par la voie rhénane. La construction d'un oléoduc Bâle-région de Zürich, et éventuellement de Berne, est envisagée en premier lieu.

L'approvisionnement en produits bruts de l'Allemagne du Sud par oléoducs continue à faire l'objet d'une compétition entre divers groupes internationaux: un premier projet, patronné par la „Konsortium Karlsruhe-Bayern Ölleitung", constituée en mai 1960, prévoit le prolongement de l'oléoduc Marseille-Strasbourg-Karlsruhe jusqu'en Bavière. Un autre projet, élaboré par la Société „Südpetrol", avec l'appui de l'E.N.I. italienne, paraît, après quelques modifications successives, vouloir en dernier lieu utiliser l'itinéraire Gênes-Milan (section commune avec l'oléoduc conduisant à Aigle) – Suisse orientale (par les cantons du Tessin, des Grisons et de Saint-Gall) – Vorarlberg. A cet effet, des accords ont été passés à la fin de 1960 entre les autorités cantonales suisses et autrichiennes d'une part, la Société italienne S.N.A.M. d'autre part, pour la construction d'un oléoduc, dont la capacité annuelle de transport serait de 8 millions de tonnes de pétrole brut. Il n'est pas possible, à l'heure actuelle, de prévoir si et quand ces projets seront effectivement mis en oeuvre.

Au sujet des oléoducs intéressant le territoire de la Confédération helvétique, le Rapport spécial de la C.E.M.T. avait précisé que „ni la construction d'un oléoduc, ni celle d'une raffinerie de pétrole ne sont subordonnées à une autorisation ou à une concession relevant du droit fédéral". Or, le 23 août 1960, le Conseil fédéral a adressé à l'Assemblée fédérale une disposition selon laquelle „la législation sur les installations de transport par conduites de combustibles ou de carburants liquides ou gazeux est du domaine de la Confédération". L'Assemblée fédérale a voté l'arrêté nécessaire, qui va être soumis le 5 mars 1961 au vote du peuple suisse. Tel qu'il est rédigé, le nouvel article constitutionnel permet d'adopter ultérieurement une loi instituant le régime de la concession.

Il est aussi question, pour l'approvisionnement du marché de l'Allemagne du Sud par conduite partant d'un port méditerranéen, d'un projet d'oléoduc reliant Venise à Munich par Innsbruck. Un autre projet plus vaste, et susceptible d'ailleurs de se combiner avec le précédent, concerne la construction d'une conduite de pétrole brut d'une capacité annuelle pouvant atteindre 8 millions de tonnes, qui partirait de Trieste (ou de Venise) et se diviserait en 2 branches se dirigeant: l'une vers Ingolstadt (Bavière) par Innsbruck (avec une capacité pouvant atteindre 5 millions de tonnes) et l'autre vers Vienne par le Tarvis et le Semmering (avec une capacité pouvant atteindre 3 millions de tonnes). Il n'est toutefois pas certain que la région viennoise soit en état d'utiliser dans les prochaines années une capacité supplémentaire de cet ordre; en effet, on estime que la consommation autrichienne passera probablement de 2,8 millions de tonnes (consommation de 1960) à 4,5 millions de tonnes environ en 1970. La production autrichienne devant être à cette date de l'ordre de 2 millions de tonnes, l'importation totale ne devrait pas dépasser 2,5 millions de tonnes.

Si un oléoduc Trieste-Vienne voyait réellement le jour, il ne subsisterait plus alors qu'une solution de continuité d'environ 60 km jusqu'à l'extrémité (Bratislava) de l'une des branches du système de canalisation en construction destinées à amener le pétrole soviétique dans les pays de l'Europe de l'Est. Du point de vue technique, une liaison entre les deux conduites ne rencontrerait pas de difficultés. Cette éventualité a été évoquée récemment dans certains milieux, à la suite de la conclusion, en novembre 1960, d'un accord de troc prévoyant en particulier la livraison annuelle à l'Italie de 2,5 millions de tonnes de pétrole soviétique pendant cinq ans.

Au début du mois d'août 1960 a été créée à Vienne une „Société autribution, in Switzerland, of the refined products brought in via the Rhine. The construction of a pipeline from Basle to the Zürich area, and possibly to Berne, is envisaged as a first stage.

There is still competition among various international groups for the supply of crude oil to Southern Germany by pipeline; a first project, sponsored by the "Konsortium Karlsruhe-Bayern Ölleitung", constituted in May 1960, would extend the Marseilles-Strasbourg-Karlsruhe line into Bavaria. Another project, drawn up by the "Südpetrol" Company with the support of the Italian E.N.I., seems likely, after several successive changes, to use the route: Genoa-Milan (section in common with the line leading to Aigle)-Eastern Switzerland (via the Cantons of Ticino, Grisons and St. Gallen)-Vorarlberg. For this purpose, agreements were concluded at the end of 1960 between the Austrian and Swiss cantonal authorities, on the one hand, and the Italian S.N.A.M. Company, on the other, for the construction of a pipeline with an annual carrying capacity of 8 million tons of crude. It is not possible at present to say if, and when, these projects will actually be started.

With reference to the pipelines using the territory of the Swiss Confederation, the E.C.M.T. special report had said that "neither the construction of a pipeline nor that of an oil refinery requires an authorisation or a concession by Federal law". On 23rd August, 1960, the Federal Council sent a message to the Federal Assembly proposing the inclusion in the Federal Constitution of provisions whereby "legislation on the carriage of fuels or of liquid or gaseous motor spirit by pipeline shall be under the control of the Confederation". The Federal Assembly voted the necessary Decree, which is to be submitted to the Swiss people on 5th March, 1961. As drafted, the new Article in the Constitution makes it possible subsequently to adopt a law instituting a licensing system.

There is also a question of supplying the South German market from a Mediterranean port by a proposed pipeline linking Venice to Munich via Innsbruck. There is a larger-scale project, which might be combined with the former, for the construction of a crude oil pipeline with an annual capacity of up to 8 million tons, starting from Trieste or Venice and dividing into two branches, one towards Ingolstadt (Bavaria) via Innsbruck, with a capacity of up to 5 million tons, and another towards Vienna, via Tarvisio and the Semmering (with a capacity of up to 3 million tons). It is not certain, however, that the Vienna region will be able to use so much additional capacity in the next few years; it is estimated that Austrian consumption will probably rise from 2.8 million tons in 1960 to 4,5 million tons in 1970. Since Austrian internal production would be about 2 million tons at that date, total imports should not exceed 2.5 million tons.

If a Trieste-Vienna pipeline really came into being, this would leave a distance of only about 60 kilometres to the terminus (Bratislava) of one of the branches of the pipeline system being constructed to bring Soviet oil into the countries of Eastern Europe. From a technical point of view, there would be no difficulty in connecting the two pipelines. This possibility has recently been mentioned in certain quarters as a result of the conclusion, in November 1960, of a barter agreement providing among other things for the annual delivery of 2.5 million tons of Soviet oil to Italy for five years.

At the beginning of August 1960, an "Austrian Pipeline Research chienne d'études de pipe-lines" (Österreichische Pipeline-Studiengesellschaft), au capital d'un million de schillings. Constituée par quatre grandes banques (pour 75% du capital) et par l'administration autrichienne des huiles minérales (Österreichische Mineralölverwaltung) [pour 25% du capital], elle a pour objet l'étude, avec la collaboration des autorités compétentes, des possibilités de construction de conduites d'huile minérale intéressant le territoire autrichien, et elle procède actuellement à l'examen de certains projets qui ont été décrits précédemment. A l'heure actuelle, la construction d'un oléoduc ne nécessite pas, en Autriche, une concession, mais l'opportunité de modifier cet état de choses est à l'examen.

En raison de l'influence que la construction d'oléoducs peut exercer sur le trafic des produits pétroliers des autres modes de transport, la C.E.M.T. suit très attentivement l'évolution de tous les projets de ce genre d'intérêt européen, et en tiendra compte dans l'étude à laquelle elle procède sur les perspectives à long terme de la demande de transport. Elle se tient d'autre part informée de l'évolution des dispositions législatives et réglementaires régissant la construction et l'exploitation des oléoducs dans les pays Membres et considère comme souhaitable de leur donner un certain degré d'uniformité, tout au moins en ce qui concerne l'intervention du Ministre des Transports. Comme le mentionne le rapport spécial, la France est jusqu'à présent le seul pays où existe une législation particulière à l'établissement et à l'exploitation des oléoducs.

f) TUNNEL SOUS LA MANCHE

Ainsi que l'annonçait le précédent Rapport, le Groupement d'études du tunnel sous la Manche a remis aux Gouvernements britannique et français, en mars 1960, son rapport, qui comprend: une étude du trafic; une étude technique des différentes solutions possibles (tunnel foré, tunnel immergé, pont), avec une estimation du prix de revient et des recettes à prévoir pour les divers types d'ouvrages; une analyse financière du projet et un examen des problèmes juridiques qui se poseraient. Ce rapport arrive à la conclusion que „sur le plan technique, la solution la meilleure pour le franchissement du Pas-de-Calais paraît être, en première étape tout au moins, un tunnel ferroviaire, foré ou immergé, assurant par navettes le transport des véhicules routiers".

Les Gouvernements britannique et français procèdent actuellement à l'étude du rapport du Groupement, dont les propositions financières ont été, entre-temps, modifiées.

Au cours de sa séance du 28 septembre 1960, l'Assemblée du Conseil de l'Europe a adopté une Recommandation (no. 260) aux gouvernements intéressés pour qu'ils „donnent une suite favorable au projet créant une voie de communication aussi complète que possible par un tunnel ou par un pont entre la France et la Grande-Bretagne".

En vue d'étudier d'une manière approfondie l'établissement d'une voie de communication par le moyen d'un pont, une „Société d'étude du pont sur la Manche" vient de se constituer à Paris, avec la participation d'entreprises bancaires, industrielles, et de travaux publics.

. . . .

IV. PROBLÈMES CONCERNANT LES CHEMINS DE FER

a) PROBLÈMES ÉCONOMIQUES CONCERNANT LES CHEMINS DE FER

. . . .

Parmi les mesures dont la Conférence a eu connaissance au cours de l'année 1960, figure tout d'abord, dans le sens des conclusions approuvées par la Résolution no. 10, la normalisation des comptes présentée par les administrations ferroviaires, c'est-à-dire l'évaluation séparée des charges

Company" (*Österreichische Pipeline-Studiengesellschaft*) was formed, with a capital of 1 million schillings. 75 per cent of this capital was put up by four large banks and 25 per cent by the Austrian Mineral Oil Administration (*Österreichische Mineralölverwaltung*). The purpose of the Company is to co-operate with the competent authorities in the study of the possible building of mineral oil pipelines on Austrian territory, and it is now considering certain projects which have already been described. At present, the building of a pipeline does not require a licence in Austria, but the advisability of changing this state of affairs is under consideration.

In view of the effects which the building of pipelines may have on the oil traffic of other means of transport, the E.C.M.T. is giving close attention to the development of all such projects of European importance and will take them into account in the study it is making on the long-term prospects of transport demand. The Conference is also being kept informed of the trend of laws and regulations governing the construction and operation of pipelines in Member countries and considers it desirable that these should be given some measure of uniformity, at least so far as the intervention of the Minister of Transport is concerned. As stated in the special report, France is so far the only country in which there is special legislation governing the building and operation of pipelines.

f) CHANNEL TUNNEL

As announced in the previous Report, the Channel Tunnel Study Group submitted its report to the French and United Kingdom Governments in March 1960; this report consists of a traffic study, a technical study of the various possible solutions (bored tube, immersed tube, bridge), with an estimate of costs and anticipated receipts for the various types of project, a financial analysis of the project and an examination of the legal problems which might arise. This report reaches the conclusion that, technically speaking, the best solution for crossing the Channel seems, in the initial stages at least, to be a bored or immersed railway tunnel providing a shuttle service for the carriage of road vehicles.

The French and United Kingdom Governments are now studying the Group's report, the financial proposals of which have been changed in the meantime.

At its meeting on 28th September, 1960, the Consultative Assembly of the Council of Europe adopted a Recommendation (No. 260) to the Governments concerned that "they should take favourable action regarding the construction of as complete a means of communication as possible, either by a tunnel or by a bridge between France and Great Britain".

In order to make a thorough study of the construction of a means of communication by a bridge, a Channel Bridge Study Group has recently been set up in Paris with the participation of banking, industrial and civil engineering undertakings.

. . . .

IV. RAILWAY PROBLEMS

a) ECONOMIC PROBLEMS CONFRONTING THE RAILWAYS

. . . .

Foremost among the measures reported to the Conference in 1960, is the normalization of the accounts of the railway administrations, *i.e.* a separate assessment of abnormal liabilities with a view to their suppression or assumption by the State. In this connection, the 5th and 6th Reports anormales qu'elles supportent, en vue de leur suppression ou de leur prise en charge par l'État. Les 5e et 6e Rapports reproduisaient à cet égard deux tableaux, A et B, établis par l'U.I.C. et indiquant pour les années 1956, 1957 et 1958 les résultats qu'aurait donnés la normalisation des comptes si les demandes des réseaux avaient été entièrement acceptées. Des tableaux analogues furent établis par l'U.I.C., pour 1959.

En 1960, certains gouvernements ont continué à entériner des demandes de normalisation des comptes présentées par leur administration ferroviaire et leur ont donné une réalisation comptable.

Dans la République Fédérale d'Allemagne, la Commission d'enquête sur la Deutsche Bundesbahn, mentionnée à l'annexe III du 5e Rapport, a déposé son rapport au début de l'année 1960. Le Gouvernement Fédéral a adopté, comme premier résultat de cet examen, un programme de mesures immédiates, dont plusieurs exercent déjà une influence sur la normalisation des comptes et sont indiquées ci-après.

Sur la base d'une décision gouvernementale de 1957, les chemins de fer ont été encore remboursés en 1960, moyennant un crédit budgétaire de 280 millions de DM, de dépenses d'assistance au personnel de l'ancienne Reichsbahn ayant servi en dehors du territoire actuel de la République Fédérale. Conformément au programme de mesures immédiates, un crédit de 175 millions de DM est prévu en 1961 afin d'alléger les chemins de fer d'une partie des charges excessives que l'héritage du passé leur fait supporter pour les retraites et pensions.

Un nouveau projet de loi sur les croisements de la voie ferrée prévoyant une répartition plus équitable des frais a été déposé par le Gouvernement fédéral. Dans le cadre du programme de mesures immédiates, les chemins de fer doivent bénéficier, à partir de 1961, d'une subvention fédérale pour l'entretien et l'exploitation des croisements du chemin de fer et des routes fédérales. D'autre part, l'examen ou la mise en oeuvre des mesures propres à assurer la couverture, par chaque mode de transport, de ses frais d'infrastructure se poursuit.

Par application de la décision gouvernementale de 1957, les chemins de fer allemands ont également reçu en 1960 une somme de 34 millions de DM, correspondant à l'intérêt d'obligations mises à leur charge lors de la réforme monétaire de 1948.

Sur la base des propositions de la Commission d'enquête, et aussi pour tenir compte de l'augmentation continuelle de leurs dépenses, les chemins de fer allemands ont pris en 1960 des mesures tarifaires qui non seulement amélioreront le compte d'exploitation, mais contribueront aussi à une normalisation des comptes. On peut mentionner parmi elles:

- l'aménagement des tarifs de subvention à l'agriculture, qui ont été fixés, à la fin de 1960, à un niveau mieux adapté au prix de revient du transport et à la situation du marché. On en attend pour 1961 une recette supplémentaire de 22,2 millions de DM. Ce relèvement ayant pour effet de supprimer à ces tarifs leur caractère de subventions, ils n'apparaîtront plus, à partir de 1961, dans les comptes normalisés.
- le relèvement, depuis le 1er novembre 1960, des cartes d'abonnement pour voyages professionnels. Le taux de relèvement proposé par la Commission d'enquête ayant été jugé trop élevé par le Gouvernement, celui-ci versera aux chemins de fer, à partir de 1961, à titre de compensation partielle, une somme annuelle de 150 millions de DM, qui représente une véritable normalisation des comptes. Sur la base de ce remboursement, les chemins de fer ont alors demandé un relèvement de 46% environ sur les prix des cartes d'abonnement des voyageurs professionnels et de celles des écoliers. Le Gouvernement n'ayant accordé qu'une augmentation de 25% pour les seuls voyageurs professionnels, il subsiste de ce fait, à partir de 1961, une charge de 85 millions de DM pouvant faire l'objet d'une opération de normalisation. A cela

reproduced two tables, A and B, prepared by the U.I.C., showing for the years 1956, 1957 and 1958 the results which could have been achieved through the normalization of accounts if the demands of the railways had been accepted in full. Similar tables were prepared by the U.I.C. for 1959.

In 1960, certain Governments have continued to recognise their railways' claims for the normalization of accounts and have put them into effect.

In the Federal Republic of Germany, the Commission of Enquiry on the Deutsche Bundesbahn, referred to in Annex III to the 5th Report, submitted its report at the beginning of 1960. The Federal Government has adopted, as a first stage, a programme of immediate measures, several of which already have an effect on the normalization of accounts.

Under a governmental decision of 1957, a budget allocation (DM 280 million) has again been devoted in 1960 to the repayment to the railways of expenditure in respect of assistance to employees of the former Reichsbahn who served outside the present territory of the Federal Republic. In accordance with the programme of immediate measures, an allocation of DM 175 million is planned for 1961, to relieve the railways of part of the excessive burden of retirement and other pensions handed down to them from the past.

A new bill on railway crossings, providing for a fairer distribution of costs, has been tabled by the Federal Government. Under the programme of immediate measures, the railways are to receive, from 1961 onwards, a Federal grant for the upkeep and operation of railway crossings with Federal roads. Suitable measures to ensure that each means of transport covers its own infrastructure expenses are still being considered or put into practice.

In application of the governmental decision of 1957, the German railways also received DM 34 million in 1960, to cover interest on the loans for which they were made responsible at the time of the 1948 currency reform.

On the basis of the proposals of the Commission of Enquiry and also to take account of the constant increase in their expenses, the German railways adopted in 1960 measures concerning freight rates and fares, which will not only improve the operating account, but will also contribute to the normalization of accounts. These include:

- an adjustment of the preferential rates for agriculture, which, at the end of 1960, were fixed at a level better adapted to the cost of transport and to the market situation. Additional receipts of DM 22.2 million are expected from this in 1961. Since the effect of this increase will be to remove these rates from the preferential category, they will no longer appear in the normalized accounts from 1961 onwards.
- the increase, as from 1st November 1960, in season ticket fares for business travel. As the Government thought the rate of increase proposed by the Commission of Enquiry too high, it is to pay the railways, as from 1961, partial compensation amounting to DM 150 million annually, which represents a true normalization of accounts. On the basis of this refund, the railways then asked for an increase of about 46 per cent in season ticket fares for commercial travellers and schoolchildren. The Government having granted an increase of only 25 per cent for commercial travellers alone, there is still a liability of DM 85 million as from 1961 which could be normalized. In addition,

s'ajoute encore pour les chemins de fer une charge annuelle de 79 millions de DM du fait de divers tarifs à caractère social.

Selon le programme de mesures immédiates du gouvernement fédéral, d'autres mesures vont être prises pour améliorer les dettes en capital de la Deutsche Bundesbahn: tout d'abord, l'État fédéral renonce à partir de 1961 à l'annuité de 145 millions de DM correspondant à l'intérêt et au remboursement de prêts consentis aux chemins de fer depuis 1956. D'autre part, les créances de l'État fédéral sur la Deutsche Bundesbahn, qui s'élèvent à environ 2.200 millions de DM au 31 décembre 1960, seront consolidées, de telle manière que les chemins de fer en retireront un allégement annuel d'intérêts de 45 millions de DM et une économie annuelle de 47 millions de DM sur le service d'amortissement.

En Belgique, l'État est intervenu effectivement de nombreuses manières pour normaliser les comptes des chemins de fer, ainsi qu'il ressort de l'énumération des mesures prises en 1960.

		Millions de francs belges
a)	Personnel en activité: remboursement par l'État des dépenses résultant des bonifications de temps de services accordées aux invalides de guerre	13,6
b)	Retraites et pensions:	
	– majorations de pension accordées aux anciens combattants	213,9
	– compensation des charges afférentes à l'effectif des pensionnés, excédentaires par rapport à celui correspondant normalement à l'effectif des agents en service	1.284
c)	Abandon à la S.N.C.B. de la taxe sur les transports	266
d)	Interventions de l'État:	
	– dans les charges de renouvellement	1.860
	– dans les dépenses d'amélioration du matériel roulant	80
e)	Intervention de l'État, à concurrence de 50%, dans les charges d'entretien, de desserte et de renouvellement des installations de croisement avec la route	112
f)	Participation de l'État dans les charges d'intérêt des emprunts destinés au financement de l'électrification du réseau	174,5
g)	Allocation d'indemnités destinées à réduire le manque à gagner découlant pour la S.N.C.B. de l'attribution, pour des motifs sociaux, de tarifs réduits:	
	– aux invalides, anciens combattants, familles nombreuses	133,5
	– aux abonnements d'ouvriers et d'employés	1.148
	– aux abonnements scolaires	90
		5.375,5

Les dispositions prises en France dans ce domaine au cours des années antérieures ont été exposées dans les précédents Rapports: aucune mesure nouvelle n'est intervenue en 1960.

En Italie, une loi du 3 juin 1960 a fixé forfaitairement à 50 milliards de lires le remboursement à effectuer par l'État aux chemins de fer pour l'exercice 1959-60, l'application intégrale des dispositions de la loi du 29 novembre 1957, mentionnée à l'annexe III du 5e Rapport annuel, n'ayant pas été possible. En ce qui concerne les charges anormales pour les pensions, une loi du 24 décembre 1959 a élevé la contribution du Trésor de 10 à 15 milliards de lires à partir de l'exercice 1959-60.

Au Grand-Duché de Luxembourg, divers crédits ont été inscrits au budget de 1960, afin de satisfaire les demandes des chemins de fer: 23,2 millions de francs pour le personnel en activité; 38,7 millions pour les retraites et pensions; 8,5 millions pour des réductions tarifaires de caractère social, soit 70,4 millions au total.

the railways have an annual liability of DM 79 million from various reduced fares for social purposes.

Under the Federal Government's programme of immediate measures, other steps will be taken to improve the capital liabilities of the Deutsche Bundesbahn: first, the Federal Government waived its claim, as from 1961, to an annual payment of DM 145 million representing interest and repayment of loans granted to the railways since 1956. Secondly, Federal Government claims on the Deutsche Bundesbahn, amounting to about DM 2,200 million at 31st December, 1960, will be consolidated in such a way as to give the railways an annual relief of DM 45 million on interest and an annual saving of DM 47 million on amortization.

In Belgium, the State has intervened effectively in many ways to normalize the accounts of the railways, as is shown by the following list of measures taken in 1960.

		B. Fr. million
a)	Active staff: State refund of expenditure resulting from bonus years of service granted to war-disabled persons. . .	13,6
b)	Retirement and other pensions:	
	– pension increases granted to ex-servicemen	213,9
	– compensation for liabilities deriving from the number of pensioners, which is in excess of the number normally corresponding to the number of active employees	1,284
c)	Transfer of transport tax to the S.N.C.B..	266
d)	State interventions:	
	– in replacement charges.	1,860
	– in expenditure on improvement of rolling stock	80
e)	State participation up to 50 per cent in cost of maintenance, service and replacement of road crossing works	112
f)	State participation and interest charges on loans to finance the electrification of the railways	174,5
g)	Subsidies to reduce the S.N.C.B.'s loss of earnings arising out of the grant of reduced fares, for social reasons:	
	– to disabled persons, ex-servicemen and large families . .	133.5
	– on workers' season tickets	1,148
	– on schoolchildren's season tickets	90
		5,375.5

The arrangements of this kind made in France in previous years were stated in earlier reports: no new steps were taken in 1960.

In Italy, a Law of 3rd June, 1960, provided for a lump sum refund of 50,000 million lire to the railways by the State for the financial year 1959–60, since it was not possible to apply in full the provisions of the Law of 29th November, 1957, referred to in Annex III to the 5th Annual Report. A Law of 24th December, 1959, raised the Treasury contribution to cover abnormal pension liabilities from 10,000 to 15,000 million lire as from the financial year 1959–60.

In the Grand Duchy of Luxembourg, various allocations were included in the 1960 Budget to meet the demands of the railways: LF 23.2 million for active staff; 38.7 million for retirement and other pensions; 8.5 million to cover reduced rates for social purposes, or 70.4 million in all.

Les opérations de normalisation effectuées en Suède pendant l'année 1960 ont été les suivantes (en millions de couronnes): 1 pour le personnel en activité; 9 pour les pensions; 7 pour les dépenses à concurrence de 50% causées par les passages à niveau; 6 pour les réductions tarifaires de caractère non commercial; 8 pour diverses autres opérations; inversement, en augmentation des dépenses des chemins de fer, 93 millions représentant l'intérêt du capital investi par l'État.

En Yougoslavie, l'État a remboursé en 1960 aux chemins de fer une somme de 10 milliards de dinars, correspondant aux réductions tarifaires qu'ils sont obligés d'accorder par la loi à certaines catégories de voyageurs.

Les chemins de fer fédéraux suisses, qui n'ont pas eu de déficit en 1960, n'ont pris aucune mesure de normalisation, ni pour le personnel en activité ni pour les retraites et pensions, bien qu'ils supportent, de ce dernier chef, certaines charges dépassant leurs obligations statutaires et qui peuvent être chiffrées pour 1960 à 38,5 millions de francs suisses, soit 4,1% des dépenses totales. Ils bénéficient d'autre part d'une exemption quasi totale des impôts directs, en contrepartie des obligations qu'ils assument, comme service public, en faveur de l'économie nationale. La nouvelle loi sur les chemins de fer prévoit un partage équitable des frais de construction de nouveaux croisements entre le rail et la route et des frais de remplacement de croisements à niveau par des passages supérieurs ou inférieurs. Pour ce qui est des frais de gardiennage, les chemins de fer les supportent en totalité, bien qu'ils admettent que la moitié de ces frais, à savoir 4 millions de francs suisses, sont étrangers aux frais qu'ils devraient normalement supporter.

En Autriche, le Comité ministériel institué pour l'examen de la situation financière des chemins de fer fédéraux n'est pas encore arrivé à un résultat quant au but envisagé d'alléger leur budget, et, en particulier, aucune mesure de normalisation des comptes n'a été prise en 1960.

Il en a été de même dans les pays suivants: Danemark, Espagne, Grèce, Norvège, Portugal, Royaume-Uni, Turquie et aussi aux Pays-Bas, où l'équilibre financier des chemins de fer a été réalisé.

La deuxième série de mesures rentrant dans le cadre de la Résolution no. 10 du Conseil des Ministres (16 mai 1957) a trait:

- à la modernisation technique des réseaux;
- à leur évolution vers une gestion plus commerciale;
- à la coordination avec les autres modes de transport.

La modernisation technique a fait de nouveaux progrès en 1960. Abstraction faite du développement de l'électrification et de la dieselisation, que le Rapport a déjà mentionné, elle a porté en particulier, en ce qui concerne les installations fixes, sur la mécanisation des travaux de la voie et l'utilisation plus étendue de rails soudés; le développement des postes de commandes centralisées des signaux et aiguilles ainsi que du bloc automatique à signaux lumineux; le perfectionnement des installations de triage, qui facilite la concentration de la formation des trains, et l'extension du triage automatique; l'équipement de passages à niveau dotés d'une signalisation routière automatique avec demi-barrière et de passages à niveau à feux clignotants; l'amélioration dans les gares des installations de transbordement des colis de détail; l'amélioration des télécommunications; le recours de plus en plus étendu à l'électronique pour la location des places. D'autre part, le renouvellement des voies est souvent effectué avec des rails plus lourds, afin de permettre l'augmentation des vitesses et de la charge par essieu.

Pour ce qui touche au matériel roulant, la modernisation s'applique à l'augmentation du parc de voitures offrant des places couchées; à la substitution du matériel en acier aux vieilles voitures en bois; à l'accroissement du nombre des containers et des wagons de types spéciaux, en particulier pour le chargement et déchargement automatique des mar-

The following normalizations were carried out in Sweden during 1960 (Sw.Kr. million): 1 for active staff; 9 for pensions; 7 to cover up to 50 per cent of expenditure on level crossings; 6 for non-commercial reduced rates and fares; 8 for various other operations; on the other hand, railways expenditure is increased by 93 million, representing interest on capital invested by the State.

In Yugoslavia, the State refunded 10,000 million dinars to the railways in 1960, to cover the fare reductions which they are obliged to allow to certain classes of passengers.

The Swiss Federal Railways, which had no deficit in 1960, have taken no normalization measures either in regard to active staff or to retirement and other pensions, although, under the latter heading, they bear certain liabilities in excess of their statutory obligations, which may be estimated for 1960 at Sw.Fr. 38.5 million, or 4.1 per cent of total expenditure. They are also almost entirely exempt from direct taxation, in return for the obligations they assume as a public service on behalf of the national economy. The new Railway Law provides for a fair division of the cost of building new road and rail crossings and the cost of replacing level crossings by over-pass or under-pass bridges. The railways bear the full cost of crossing-keepers, although they agree, that one-half of this cost, namely Sw.Fr. 4 million, should not normaly be borne by them.

In Austria, the Ministerial Committee set up to examine the financial situation of the Federal Railways has not yet reached any conclusion on the proposed aim of relieving their budget and, in particular, no normalization of accounts has been undertaken in 1960.

This also applies to the following countries: Denmark, Greece, Norway, Portugal, Spain, Turkey and the United Kingdom, as well as to the Netherlands, where, of course, the railways have achieved financial equilibrium.

The second series of measures covered by Resolution No. 10 of the Council of Ministers (16th May, 1957) relates to:

- the technical modernisation of the railways;
- progress towards management on a more strictly commercial basis;
- co-ordination with other means of transport.

Technical modernisation made further progress in 1960. Apart from the development of electrification and dieselisation already referred to in the Report this related particularly, as far as fixed stock is concerned, to the mechanisation of work on the permanent way and the more extensive use of welded rails; the development of centralised control posts for signals and points, and the automatic block warning system; improvements to marshalling yards to facilitate and concentrate the formation of trains and the extension of automatic marshalling arrangements; the equipment of level crossings with automatic road signals with half-gates and "winking light" level crossings; improvement in arrangements for handling parcels at stations; improvement of telecommunications; more extensive use of electronics for the reservation of seats. Tracks are often replaced with heavier rails to allow increased speeds and higher axle loadings.

With regard to rolling stock, modernisation is concerned with the increase in the amount of sleeping accommodation; the replacement of old wooden coaches by steel; the increase in the number of containers and special types of wagons, particularly for the automatic loading and chandises en vrac, ainsi que de wagons à deux étages pour le transport d'automobiles.

Dans le domaine de l'exploitation, il est envisagé d'accélérer l'acheminement international des marchandises, par la création d'un réseau, de trains „Trans-Europ-Express-Marchandises", qui serait l'équivalent du réseau T.E.E. créé pour le transport des voyageurs; pour en retirer tout le bénéfice, l'accélération de ces acheminements devrait aller de pair avec une réduction de la durée des stationnements aux frontières pour les opérations de douane.

Dans le domaine de l'évolution des réseaux vers une gestion plus commerciale et l'assouplissement de leurs obligations de service public, l'action précédemment entreprise en vue de la fermeture de lignes non rentables et la substitution de services automobiles de remplacement a été poursuivie en 1960 dans quelques pays. En Allemagne, 426 km ont été fermés au service des voyageurs et 178 km au service des marchandises; les services supprimés ont été remplacés par des services automobiles en totalité pour les voyageurs, et sur 63 km seulement pour les colis de détail. En Belgique, 36 km de lignes et 28 gares ont été fermées; 156 km ont été fermés à la circulation des trains de voyageurs et le trafic assuré par des autobus. En France, 20 km de lignes ont été fermés à tout trafic des marchandises. En Italie, 67 km de lignes ont été fermés et remplacés par des lignes automobiles concessionnées. Au Royaume-Uni, les services non rentables supprimés en 1960 correspondent à 288 km pour les voyageurs, 166 km pour les marchandises et 43 km portant à la fois sur les voyageurs et les marchandises, entraînant une économie annuelle nette de £ 360.000 au minimum: en outre, pendant les neuf premiers mois de l'année 1960, les services offerts par 172 gares ont été supprimés, l'économie annuelle escomptée étant de £ 152.000 et, dans les trois derniers mois de l'année, il en sera de même pour 40 autres gares. En Suède, pendant l'année budgétaire 1959–60, 121 km de lignes à voie normale et 266 km de lignes à voie étroite ont été fermés totalement, et 31 et 36 km de ces catégories de lignes partiellement. En outre, 170 gares ont été soit fermées totalement, soit transformées en arrêt sans personnel.

L'atténuation des obligations d'exploiter, de transporter, de publier les tarifs, *etc.*, est toujours à l'étude dans de nombreux pays. En Espagne, un arrêté du 14 janvier 1960 a autorisé les chemins de fer à consentir des tarifs spéciaux à prix réduits, applicables sur une partie seulement du réseau, ainsi qu'à conclure des accords particuliers qui entrent en vigueur dans un délai de quinze jours, sauf veto du ministre. Au Royaume-Uni, l'obligation de publier les tarifs de marchandises, autres que les tarifs maximums, est supprimée depuis 1953; quant aux tarifs de voyageurs, ils ont été relevés en mai 1960 et l'obligation d'émettre des billets à prix réduit valables le matin de bonne heure a été supprimée le 1er janvier 1961. Dans le trafic international entre pays Membres, la nouvelle Convention de Berne (C.I.M.) prévoit la possibilité pour les chemins de fer, sous réserve de l'assentiment des gouvernements, de conclure des accords particuliers non publiés, en tant que des conditions comparables sont consenties aux usagers qui se trouvent dans des situations comparables.

La coordination technique entre les chemins de fer et les autres modes de transport, et tout particulièrement l'automobile, s'est encore développée pendant l'année écoulée, notamment sous la forme de l'utilisation toujours plus étendue des containers et des wagons construits spécialement pour le transport de camions ou de voitures de tourisme. Les trains conçus pour le transport de voyageurs accompagnés de leur voiture automobile, qui ont circulé pendant la saison d'été 1960, ont rencontré un grand succès et il est envisagé d'en augmenter le nombre et d'en étendre la fréquence pendant l'année 1961.

Dans le domaine de la coordination réglementaire, tarifaire ou fiscale, unloading of bulk goods and two-storey wagons for the carriage of motor vehicles.

With regard to operation, it is planned to speed up the international carriage of goods by establishing a network of "Trans-Europ-Express-Goods" trains, which would be the equivalent of the T.E.E. passenger network. If the full benefit is to be derived from this, the acceleration of the journey should be accompanied by a reduction in the time spent standing at frontiers for customs operations.

With regard to progress towards the management of the railways on a more strictly commercial basis and the relaxation of their public service obligations, the action already taken to close uneconomic lines and introduce alternative motor services was continued in certain countries in 1960. In Germany, 426 km. of line were closed to passenger services and 178 km. to goods services; all the passenger services withdrawn were replaced by motor services and similar services were provided for small parcels on 63 km. only. In Belgium, 36 km. of line and 28 stations were closed; 156 km. of passenger services were withdrawn and replaced by bus services. In France, 20 km. of line were closed to all goods traffic. In Italy, 67 km. of line were closed and replaced by motor services operating under licence. In the United Kingdom, the uneconomic services withdrawn during 1960 represent 288 route kilometres of passenger services, 166 route kilometres of freight services and 43 kilometres of both passenger and freight services, from which the estimated minimum net annual saving amounts to £360,000: in addition, during the first nine months of 1960, facilities were withdrawn from 172 stations, making an estimated saving of £152,000 per annum, and during the last three months of the year 40 other stations will have been closed. In Sweden, during the budget year 1959–60, 121 km. of normal-gauge track and 266 km. of narrow-gauge track have been permanently closed, and 31 km. and 36 km. of these categories of lines partially closed. In addition, 170 stations were permanently closed or converted into unstaffed halts.

The relaxation of the obligations to operate, to carry, to publish rates, *etc.*, is still being studied in many countries. In Spain, an Order of 14th January, 1960, authorised the railways to grant special reduced rates applicable over only part of the system and to conclude private agreements which will come into force within 15 days unless vetoed by the Minister. In the United Kingdom, the obligation to publish goods rates, other than maximum rates, was abolished in 1953; fares were raised in May 1960 and the obligations to issue early morning tickets at reduced fares ceased on 1st January, 1961. In international traffic between Member countries, the new Berne Convention (C.I.M.) provides for the possibility of the railways' concluding unpublished private agreements, subject to government assent, provided that comparable conditions are granted to users in comparable situations.

Technical co-ordination between the railways and other means of transport, particularly motor transport, developed further during the past year, in particular in the form of the constantly increasing use of containers and wagons specially built to carry lorries or private cars. The trains designed to carry passengers accompanied by their cars, which ran during the 1960 summer season, were a great success and it is planned to increase their number and the frequency of the service in 1961.

There are some new measures to report in the co-ordination of reguquelques mesures nouvelles sont à signaler: en Autriche et en France, le récent relèvement des tarifs marchandises des chemins de fer a été conjugué avec un relèvement des taxes fiscales frappant certaines catégories de transports routiers par camions. Plusieurs dispositions législatives ont été promulguées en Belgique, ouvrant la liberté d'accès à la profession de transporteur routier professionnel et assimilant les chemins de fer à un transporteur routier, ce qui leur permettra d'obtenir des autorisations de transport sans limitation de nombre de véhicules ni de charge utile. La S.N.C.B. est en effet habilitée par la loi du 1er août 1960 à „faire toutes opérations commerciales, industrielles ou financières se rapportant directement ou indirectement en tout ou en partie à son but social, ou qui seraient susceptibles d'en faciliter ou d'en favoriser la réalisation ou le développement". D'autre part, la nouvelle loi belge sur le transport professionnel routier prévoit la possibilité d'instituer, lorsque les circonstances l'exigent, une tarification routière obligatoire, qui serait établie par le Ministre des Transports, assisté d'une Commission consultative. En France, une tarification applicable aux transports routiers d'au moins 5 tonnes à plus de 150 km, élaborée par la profession, a été homologuée par le Ministre des Transports et sera applicable à partir du 1er juillet 1961; d'autre part, une nouvelle réglementation sur la durée de la conduite dans les transports routiers a été adoptée par décret du 17 décembre 1960.

D'importantes mesures sont envisagées par le Gouvernement britannique pour réorganiser les entreprises de transport nationalisées et, en particulier, pour assainir la situation financière des chemins de fer. Ces mesures ont été exposées au Parlement en décembre 1960 sous la forme d'un livre blanc et feront l'objet d'un projet de loi qui sera soumis au Parlement dans sa prochaine session. Elles ont un triple but: remplacer la British Transport Commission par une structure nouvelle remédiant aux inconvénients actuels; assainir les finances de la Commission et, en particulier, celles des chemins de fer; donner aux entreprises plus de liberté dans la gestion de leurs affaires commerciales.

En ce qui concerne la réforme de structure, le Gouvernement britannique propose de scinder la Commission existante en „Boards" séparés, dont l'un pour les chemins de fer (British Railways Board), chacun d'eux devant être responsable de ses dettes en capital et soumis à l'autorité directe du Ministre des Transports, qui en nommerait les membres. Le British Railways Board aura seulement à assurer les fonctions centrales essentielles pour faire marcher les chemins de fer en tant qu'organisme unique, les autres tâches étant confiées à des „Boards" régionaux, responsables de la gestion de leur réseau et autonomes pour les affaires ne concernant que la région.

D'autre part, les dispositions suivantes sont envisagées pour l'assainissement de la situation financière des chemins de fer britanniques: leur dette en capital ayant été évaluée à £ 1.600 millions, une somme de £ 400 millions, représentant les déficits accumulés des dernières années qui ont été financés par des avances de l'État, sera annulée et la dette amortie en conséquence. Sur les £ 1.200 millions restants, le Gouvernement britannique propose qu'une somme de £ 400 millions, équivalant à la valeur comptable des investissements effectués depuis 1955, date du début de la modernisation, continue à être considérée comme emprunt portant intérêt; enfin, le solde (£ 800 millions) sera mis dans un compte d'attente ne portant pas intérêt ni obligation de remboursement. Le sort à donner à ce compte d'attente fera l'objet d'un examen périodique. Par l'effet de ces diverses mesures, les chemins de fer seront allégés du fardeau de la totalité des déficits accumulés, et aussi de la plus grande part de leurs dettes en capital antérieures au début de leur modernisation, à moins qu'ils ne se révèlent capables, ultérieurement, d'assumer à nouveau cette lations governing freight rates and revenue taxes: in Austria and France, the recent increase in railway goods rates was coupled with an increase in the revenue taxes applied to certain categories of road transport by lorry. Several legal provisions have been issued in Belgium, giving freedom of entry into the occupation of road haulier and assimilating the railways to road hauliers, which will enable them to obtain transport licences without limitation as to the number of vehicles or payload. Under the Law of 1st August, 1960, the S.N.C.B. is empowered to "carry out all commercial, industrial or financial operations relating directly or indirectly and in whole or in part to its social aim or which might facilitate or encourage the achievement or development thereof". The new Belgian Law on road haulage also provides the possibility, when circumstances so require, of introducing compulsory road transport rates, which would be drawn up by the Minister of Transport with the assistance of a Consultative Committee. In France, a system of rates for loads of at least 5 tons and hauls over 150 km. has been prepared by the industry and approved by the Minister of Transport and will be applicable as from 1st July, 1961; new regulations governing driving hours in road transport were also adopted by a decree of 17th December, 1960.

Important measures are contemplated by the United Kingdom Government to reorganise the nationalised transport undertakings and, in particular, to rectify the financial situation of the railways. These measures were presented to Parliament in December 1960 in the form of a White Paper and will be embodied in a Bill to be submitted to Parliament during its next session. They have a threefold purpose: to replace the British Transport Commission by a new structure designed to overcome present defects and disadvantages; to reconstruct the finances of the Commission and, in particular, those of the railways; and to give the various undertakings more freedom in the operation of their commercial affairs.

For its structural reform, the United Kingdom Government proposes to split the existing Commission into separate Boards, one of which would manage the railways (British Railways Board), each being responsible for its own capital debt, but directly answerable to the Minister of Transport, who would appoint the members. The British Railways Board will perform only those central functions which are essential to the running of the railways as a single entity; all other functions would be the responsibility of regional Railway Boards responsible for the management and operation of their system and autonomous in all matters concerning their own Regions.

The following arrangements are also contemplated to improve the financial situation of British Railways: their capital liabilities having been assessed at £1,600 million, a sum of £400 million, representing losses accumulated in recent years and financed by State advances, will be written off and the outstanding debt reduced accordingly. Of the remaining £1,200 million, the United Kingdom Government proposes that about £400 million, equivalent to the written-down book value of investments since 1955 when modernisation began, should continue to rank as an interest-bearing loan; finally, the remainder (£800 million) will be placed to suspense account and carry neither fixed interest nor fixed repayment of obligations. The treatment of this account will be subject to review from time to time. The effect of these various measures will be to relieve the railways of the burden of all their accumulated deficits, as well as the greater part of their capital liabilities, before the beginning of modernisation, unless they subsequently prove capable of meeting this liability again. In spite of these substantial reliefs, the task charge. En dépit de ces allégements substantiels, la tâche des chemins de fer britanniques est qualifiée de „formidable" par le Livre blanc, puisqu'ils devront à la fois éliminer leur déficit d'exploitation, qui est actuellement de l'ordre de £ 60 millions par an, et parvenir en cinq ans à couvrir avec leurs propres ressources les charges d'intérêt subsistantes, soit environ £ 60–70 millions. Pendant la période intérimaire, les sommes nécessaires seront fournies par l'État.

Le Livre blanc britannique reconnaît enfin que „dans les nouvelles circonstances il ne serait pas raisonnable de laisser les chemins de fer sujets à des restrictions dépassées quant à leurs activités commerciales". Aussi est-il prévu, afin de leur permettre d'ajuster d'une manière rapide et adéquate leurs tarifs, de les libérer du contrôle statutaire sur ceux-ci, à l'exception des tarifs s'appliquant aux déplacements des personnes dans l'agglomération de Londres.

Dans l'ensemble, si des résultats appréciables ont été obtenus jusqu'ici, ils sont encore insuffisants et il reste une vaste tâche à accomplir pour assainir la situation financière des chemins de fer, dont le déficit demeure toujours important dans les pays membres (à l'exception des Pays-Bas, de la Suède et de la Suisse, où les comptes sont équilibrés). Conscient du caractère non satisfaisant de cette situation, le Conseil des Ministres des Transports a demandé que soit entreprise une relance de l'étude de la situation économique des administrations de chemin de fer, qui portera essentiellement sur la mesure dans laquelle a été mise en oeuvre la Résolution no. 10 de 1957 et qui tendra, compte tenu de l'évolution intervenue entre-temps, à dégager éventuellement d'autres conclusions. Bien entendu, cette nouvelle étude traitera aussi des nombreux aspects du problème de la coordination des transports, qui influent sur la situation financière des chemins de fer. A la demande de la C.E.M.T., l'U.I.C. est en train d'élaborer un mémoire devant servir de base de discussion pour cette question capitale, qui constituera l'un des éléments essentiels des prochains débats des Ministres des Transports.

b) STANDARDISATION DU MATÉRIEL ROULANT

Le précédent Rapport exposait l'état d'avancement de la standardisation du matériel roulant, et notait en particulier qu'après le succès enregistré par la standardisation de 4 classes de locomotives diesel, la standardisation d'une 5e classe très importante (locomotives du type „f", appelées à être utilisées aussi bien sur les lignes principales que sur les lignes secondaires) n'avait pas abouti, et que les efforts avaient dû se limiter à des études de standardisation partielle d'éléments de ces locomotives. Cette situation, qui ne peut être considérée comme satisfaisante, n'a pas subi de changement en 1960.

. . . .

c) ACTIVITÉ DE LA SOCIÉTÉ EUROFIMA

L'Assemblée générale de la Société Eurofima, à laquelle la C.E.M.T. a été représentée, s'est tenue le 21 mai 1960 pour approuver les comptes de l'exercice 1959 (3e exercice social): comme l'année précédente, ils ont permis, après dotation des fonds de réserve, de distribuer aux actions A un dividende de 4% (maximum statutaire).

En application de l'article 6 *b*) de la Convention, la Société a adressé aux gouvernements signataires un rapport sur sa 4e année d'activité (1960). Ce rapport, qui est reproduit à l'annexe IV, expose tout d'abord l'action entreprise par la Société afin de pouvoir accéder à d'autres sources de capitaux que le marché suisse, pratiquement seul à avoir été jusqu'ici mis à contribution.

Le rapport ajoute qu'un nouvel emprunt, d'un montant de 30 millions de francs suisses, a pu être placé sur le marché suisse en octobre 1960 facing British Railways is described in the White Paper as "a very formidable one", since they will have to eliminate their operating loss, now running at about £60 million per year, and manage in the next five years to meet existing interest charges amounting to about £60–70 million out of their own revenues. In the meantime, the necessary amounts will be supplied by the State.

The United Kingdom White Paper recognises that "in the new circumstances it would not be reasonable to leave the Railways subject to out-of-date restrictions on their commercial activities". To enable them to adjust their freight charges and passenger fares quickly and adequately, it is planned to free the railways from statutory control over their charges, except for passenger fares applying to the London area.

On the whole, although appreciable results have been obtained so far, they are still inadequate and there is a vast amount of work to be done to improve the financial situation of the railways, which still have a large deficit in Member countries (except in the Netherlands, Sweden and Switzerland, where their accounts are balanced). Realising the unsatisfactory nature of this situation, the Council of Ministers of Transport has asked for the study on the economic situation of the railway administrations to be renewed, dealing essentially with the extent to which Resolution No. 10 of 1957 has been applied and endeavouring, in the light of the progress made in the meantime, to formulate any other conclusions. This new study will, of course, deal also with the many aspects of the problem of the co-ordination of transport which affect the financial situation of the railways. At the request of the E.C.M.T., the U.I.C. is now preparing a memorandum to serve as a basis of discussion on this vital question, which will be one of the essential items in the future debates of the Ministers of Transport.

b) STANDARDIZATION OF RAILWAY ROLLING STOCK

The previous report gave a progress report on the standardization of rolling stock and noted, in particular, that, after the success of the standardization of 4 classes of diesel locomotives ,the standardization of a very important fifth class (locomotives of type "f", suitable for use on both main and secondary lines) had produced no results, and efforts had to be concentrated on the partial standardization of parts for these locomotives. This situation, which cannot be considered satisfactory, remained unchanged in 1960.

. . . .

c) ACTIVITIES OF THE EUROFIMA COMPANY

The General Assembly of the Eurofima Company, on which the E.C.M.T. was represented, met on 21st May, 1960, to approve the accounts for the financial year 1959 (the Company's third year); as in the previous year, these made it possible, after making the usual transfer to the ordinary reserve, to distribute the statutory maximum dividend of 4 per cent on Class A shares.

In application of Article 6 *b*) of the Convention, the Company sent to signatory Governments a report on its fourth year of activity (1960). This report, which is reproduced as Annex IV, first of all describes the action taken by the Company to obtain access to sources of capital other than the Swiss market, which is practically the only one drawn upon so far.

The report adds that a new loan of Sw.Fr. 30 million was floated on the Swiss market in October 1960 on the following terms: nominal rate, 4.5

aux conditions suivants: taux nominal, 4,5%; durée, dix-sept ans, avec différé d'amortissement de quatre ans; cours d'émission net, 98,60%. Au produit de cet emprunt, qui a été intégralement couvert, ont pu être ajoutés 6 millions de francs suisses, provenant de crédits bancaires suisses, et des fonds propres de la Société: au total, 36 millions ont été mis à la disposition des administrations ferroviaires membres d'Eurofima, au taux moyen de 5,06%. Les commandes correspondantes portent sur des locomotives diesel standards de manoeuvre et de ligne pour les chemins de fer allemands, belges, français, grecs et yougoslaves, et sur des wagons pour les chemins de fer autrichiens et italiens; il reviendra aux chemins de fer portugais trois nouvelles rames triples électriques, dont une partie des équipements proviendra de Suisse.

Le rapport de la Société Eurofima fait aussi mention d'une autre opération de crédit consistant en un prêt de 50 millions de francs suisses, consenti à Eurofima par un groupe suisse et destiné au financement de commandes au profit des chemins de fer allemands.

Ainsi, la Société Eurofima a pu mobiliser dans l'année 1960 un montant de 86 millions de francs suisses, ce qui porte à 272 millions de francs suisses le total des ressources qu'elle a trouvées en quatre ans sur le marché suisse, auxquels s'ajoutent 5 millions de DM.

Ainsi que le signale le rapport de la Société Eurofima, les Ministres des Transports des pays intéressés, pour répondre à sa demande, sont convenus, dans leur réunion de La Haye, le 5 octobre 1960, d'intervenir auprès des autorités compétentes de leurs pays, afin qu'une suite favorable soit donnée aux demandes de la Société Eurofirma tendant à ce que ses obligations puissent être admises en emploi des réserves obligatoires de compagnies d'assurances. L'accord des autorités compétentes a été obtenu en Belgique, France, Pays-Bas et Suisse; il faut espérer que d'autres pays suivront cet exemple.

La ratification par le Parlement autrichien, le 9 novembre 1960, de la Convention internationale ,,Eurofima'' et le dépôt le 6 février 1961 à Berne des instruments de ratification ont mis le point final au processus de la ratification de cette Convention par les pays signataires.

d) INTRODUCTION DE L'ATTELAGE AUTOMATIQUE

Les représentants de l'U.I.C. et des organisations internationales du personnel des transports ont récemment attiré l'attention de la C.E.M.T. sur le fait que le problème de l'introduction de l'attelage automatique du matériel roulant, qui est à l'étude depuis de nombreuses années, allait sans doute présenter un aspect nouveau, en raison de l'intention de certains pays de l'Europe de l'Est de procéder prochainement à l'équipement de leur matériel avec un attelage automatique de traction et de choc. En raison des échanges réciproques de matériel roulant entre les pays de l'Ouest et de l'Est, cette perspective ne peut laisser indifférentes les administrations ferroviaires des pays de la C.E.M.T.; des dispositions ont déjà été prises dans le cadre du Comité des transports intérieurs de la Commission Économique pour l'Europe des Nations Unies, afin d'établir une collaboration pour l'étude technique et économique du problème entre l'ensemble des administrations ferroviaires intéressées, en vue de parvenir à une décision commune, ou, du moins, à des décisions compatibles. De son côté, l'U.I.C. poursuit ses propres études, qui comportent des essais de matériel et l'évaluation du montant des économies d'exploitation que l'on peut espérer en contrepartie des dépenses très élevées d'investissement nécessaires.

Le Conseil des Ministres des Transports a marqué un intérêt spécial pour ce problème, en raison tant des avantages techniques et économiques que peut présenter l'attelage automatique que de son heureuse influence sur la sécurité et l'amélioration des conditions de travail des agents de chemins de fer.

per cent; duration, 17 years, with 4 years deferred amortization; net issue price, 98.60 per cent. The Sw.Fr. 6 million derived from bank credits obtained in Switzerland and from the Company's own funds were added to the net proceeds of this loan, which was fully taken up. In all, Sw.Fr. 36 million were made available to member railways of Eurofima at an average rate of 5.06 per cent. The orders covered by these loans are for standard diesel shunting engines and main-line locomotives for the Belgian, French, German, Greek and Yugoslav railways and goods wagons for the Austrian and Italian railways; the Portuguese railways will receive three new three-coach electric sets, for which part of the equipment will come from Switzerland.

The Eurofima Company's report also mentions another loan operation, amounting to Sw.Fr. 50 million, granted to Eurofima by a Swiss group to finance orders on behalf of the German railways.

During 1960, the Eurofima Company was thus able to collect Sw. Fr. 86 million, bringing the total resources which it has found on the Swiss market in four years to a total of Sw.Fr. 272 million, in addition to DM 5 million.

As stated in the Eurofima Company's report, the Ministers of Transport of the countries concerned, meeting at The Hague on 5th October, 1960, agreed, at the Company's request, to approach the competent authorities in their countries in support of the Eurofima Company's requests that its bonds be accepted for use as compulsory reserves of insurance companies. The assent of the competent authorities has been obtained in Belgium, France, the Netherlands and Switzerland; it is to be hoped that other countries will follow this example.

The ratification of the Eurofima International Convention by the Austrian Parliament, on 9th November, 1960, and the deposit of the instruments of ratification at Berne, on 6th February, 1961, completed the ratification of this Convention by the signatory countries.

d) INTRODUCTION OF AUTOMATIC COUPLINGS

The representatives of the U.I.C. and the international workers' organisations recently drew the attention of the E.C.M.T. to the fact that the problem of the introduction of automatic couplings for railway rolling stock, which has been studied for many years, was likely to assume a new aspect since certain Eastern European countries shortly intend to equip their rolling stock with an automatic buffer coupling system. In view of the interchange of rolling stock between East and West European countries, this prospect cannot be ignored by the railway administrations of the E.C.M.T. countries. Steps have already been taken by the Inland Transport Committee of the United Nations Economic Commission for Europe to encourage co-operation in a technical and economic study of the problem among all the railway administrations concerned, so as to reach a common decision or, at least, compatible decisions. The U.I.C. is also continuing its own studies, which include tests of equipment and an estimate of the savings in operational costs which can be looked for in return for the very heavy investment needed.

The Council of Ministers of Transport showed special interest in this problem because of the possible technical and economic advantages of automatic couplings and also because of their beneficial effects on safety and the improvement of working conditions for railway employees.

V. PROBLÈMES CONCERNANT LES TRANSPORTS ROUTIERS

a) *AMÉLIORATION DES STATISTIQUES ROUTIÈRES*

Le précédent Rapport annuel mentionnait la Résolution concernant l'amélioration des statistiques routières, qui avait été adoptée par le Conseil des Ministres des Transports dans sa session d'octobre 1959.

Pour les transports nationaux de marchandises, elle recommandait de recourir à des sondages portant sur des périodes suffisantes pour parvenir à des résultats valables pour une année entière. Les problèmes de méthode que pose ce genre d'enquêtes sont actuellement suivis dans le cadre du Comité des transports intérieurs de la C.E.E. des Nations Unies, dont le Secrétariat publie chaque année les statistiques en découlant.

La Résolution prévoyait d'autre part, pour les transports internationaux de marchandises, la mise en oeuvre d'un système de collecte, de dépouillement et de publication de fiches statistiques de modèle uniforme, portant sur la totalité du parcours.

Comme l'application d'un tel système a fait apparaître des difficultés, il est envisagé de faire tout d'abord l'essai, pendant l'année 1961, d'autres méthodes (par exemple sur la base des déclarations en douane), sans toutefois que le système des statistiques existant dans les différents pays pour le trafic international par route en soit modifié.

b) *PROBLÈMES RELATIFS AUX DIMENSIONS ET POIDS DES VÉHICULES ROUTIERS*

Les précédents Rapports, et, en dernier lieu, le 6e Rapport ont souligné les sérieux inconvénients de la disparité des réglementations nationales en la matière, aussi bien pour l'exécution des transports internationaux que pour la construction et le commerce des véhicules commerciaux.

Il est rappelé que la République Fédérale d'Allemagne, en application d'un décret du 21 mars 1956, avait mis en vigueur, le 1er janvier 1958, une législation nouvelle qui modifiait dans un sens restrictif les normes applicables dans ce pays: elle fixait par exemple le poids maximum à 8 tonnes pour l'essieu simple, à 12 tonnes pour l'essieu double, à 24 tonnes le poids total maximum en charge pour les véhicules articulés et les trains routiers, et limitait respectivement à 13 m et 14 m la longueur maximum des véhicules articulés et des trains routiers. Sur ce dernier point, elle s'écartait sensiblement de la longueur de 18 m, prévue par l'annexe 7 à la Convention de Genève sur la circulation routière du 19 septembre 1949, dont l'Allemagne n'est pas signataire. En ce qui concerne le poids par essieu, plusieurs autres pays admettaient dans leur législation nationale un poids maximum par essieu simple de 10 tonnes, ou même un chiffre supérieur, et là encore se manifestait une sérieuse divergence.

Dans l'adoption de cette nouvelle législation, le Gouvernement allemand avait été guidé par le souci d'améliorer la sécurité et la capacité des routes existantes, et de ralentir la progression rapide des dépenses entraînées par l'entretien et le développement du réseau routier allemand. Des mesures de transition avaient été consenties pour un certain nombre de véhicules jusqu'au 1er juillet 1960, date limite pour les tolérances admises, tant pour les véhicules allemands que pour les véhicules étrangers.

Consciente de la nécessité de trouver un terrain d'entente sur des normes qui auraient un caractère européen, la C.E.M.T., d'abord au sein d'un groupe de travail créé spécialement à cet effet le 8 mai 1956, puis au cours de nombreuses séances du Comité des suppléants et du Conseil des Ministres, s'est efforcée avec persévérance d'obtenir l'adhésion du plus grand nombre possible de pays à une solution qui, en raison des politiques différentes suivies par les pays intéressés en fonction de leurs

V. ROAD TRANSPORT PROBLEMS

a) *IMPROVEMENT OF ROAD TRANSPORT STATISTICS*

The previous Annual Report referred to the Resolution concerning the improvement of road transport statistics, which had been adopted by the Council of Ministers of Transport at its session in October 1959. This recommended taking sample surveys of national goods transport, covering sufficiently long periods to produce results valid for an entire year. The problems of method involved in this kind of enquiry are being followed in the Inland Transport Committee of the E.C.E., the Secretariat of which publishes statistics on the matter each year.

The Resolution also provided, with regard to national goods transport, for the institution of a system for the collection, analysis and publication of standard statistical forms relating to the entire length of haul.

Since the application of such a system has revealed difficulties, it is proposed to try out other methods in 1961 (based, for instance, on Customs declarations), without changing the statistical systems applied in the various countries to international road traffic.

b) *PROBLEMS CONCERNING THE WEIGHTS AND DIMENSIONS OF ROAD VEHICLES*

Previous reports, culminating in the Sixth Report, emphasized the serious disadvantages of the disparity between national regulations not only in the operation of international transport, but also in the manufacture and marketing of commercial road vehicles.

It is recalled that, in application of a Decree of 21st March, 1956, the Federal Republic of Germany had, on 1st January, 1958, introduced new legislation which reduced the standards applicable in that country: for example, it laid down a maximum loading of 8 tons for single axles and 12 tons for twin axles and a maximum total laden weight of 24 tons for articulated vehicles and combinations of vehicles, and limited the maximum lengths of articulated vehicles and combinations of vehicles to 13 m. and 14 m. respectively. On this last point, it departed appreciably from the length of 18 m. laid down in Annex 7 to the Geneva Convention on Road Traffic of 19th September, 1949, to which Germany was not a signatory. The national legislation of several other countries allowed a maximum loading of 10 tons per single axle or even more, and here again there was a serious divergence.

In adopting its new legislation, the German Government was guided by its anxiety to improve the safety and capacity of existing roads and to curb the rapid rise in the expenditure required for the upkeep and development of the German road network. Transitional arrangements were made for a number of vehicles up to 1st July, 1960, the final date for tolerances for both German and foreign vehicles.

Conscious of the need to find some common ground for agreement on standards of European application, the E.C.M.T. tried persistently, first by means of a Working Party set up for this purpose on 8th May, 1956, and then at numerous meetings of the Committee of Deputies and the Council of Ministers, to obtain the support of the largest possible number of countries for a solution which, owing to the different policies pursued by the countries concerned according to their geographical and economic caractéristiques géographiques et économiques, ne pouvait évidemment que constituer un compromis entre les diverses positions en présence.

Au début de l'année 1960, les Ministres des Transports de la République Fédérale d'Allemagne et de la France ont fait connaître qu'ils s'étaient mis d'accord sur le compromis suivant entre les thèses que leurs pays défendaient jusqu'alors:

Poids maximum par essieu:	
Essieu simple	10 tonnes
Essieu tandem.	16 ,,
Poids total maximum en charge pour les véhicules articulés et trains routiers.	32 ,,
Longueur maximum:	
Véhicules articulés	15 m
Trains routiers.	15,50 m

Cette proposition n'était pas très éloignée des demandes des organisations internationales professionnelles, sauf en ce qui concerne la longueur des trains routiers; elle a donné lieu, de la part de certains pays, à des objections portant principalement sur la réduction de cette longueur par rapport au chiffre de 18 m de l'annexe 7 à la Convention sur la circulation routière de 1949, appliqué par l'Accord européen de 1950, et aussi sur le relèvement de 8 à 10 tonnes du poids maximum par essieu.

A l'appui de leur manière de voir, les pays dont il s'agit ont fait valoir que la réduction proposée de la longueur des trains routiers serait pratiquement sans intérêt pour la sécurité routière et aurait une influence défavorable sur le rendement économique de ces transports en modifiant à leur désavantage les conditions de la concurrence. Quant au relèvement à 10 tonnes du poids maximum par essieu, il soulevait des objections tenant à l'état du réseau routier de certains pays.

Le Conseil des Ministres des Transports a procédé sur ces problèmes, au cours de sa séance du 24 mai 1960, à une discussion approfondie, au cours de laquelle le Ministre des Transports de la Yougoslavie a suggéré, à titre de nouveau compromis, de fixer à 16,5 m la longueur maximum des trains routiers. En conclusion de ses débats, le Conseil a chargé le Comité des suppléants de poursuivre le rapprochement des points de vue en présence.

Dans la séance du 3 juin 1960 du Comité des suppléants plusieurs pays, partisans de la longueur maximum de 18 mètres pour les trains routiers ont fait connaître que, dans un esprit de conciliation, ils seraient disposés, sous réserve de délais transitoires suffisamment longs, à accepter une longueur de 17 mètres. Dans le même esprit, certains pays ont indiqué qu'ils étaient prêts à se rallier à une longueur de 16,50 m, au lieu de la longueur de 15,50 m, en faveur de laquelle ils s'étaient précédemment prononcés. Une entente n'a toutefois pas pu se faire.

. . . .

c) PROBLÈMES CONCERNANT LA SÉCURITÉ ROUTIÈRE

Le précédent Rapport avait exposé les premiers résultats de l'action entreprise par la C.E.M.T. dans le domaine de la sécurité routière, qui s'étaient concrétisés sous la forme d'une Résolution no. 10 (Transports par route) adoptée par le Conseil des Ministres des Transports en octobre 1959, sur la base d'un premier rapport élaboré par le Groupe de travail de la sécurité routière. Les principales questions traitées concernaient les enseignements à tirer des statistiques des accidents de la route et la fixation d'une vitesse maximum uniforme dans les agglomérations.

Pendant l'année 1960, le Groupe de travail de la sécurité routière a poursuivi ses études, avec le concours du directeur de la Division des transports de la C.E.E. des Nations Unies, en concentrant ses efforts sur d'autres problèmes concrets: éducation des usagers, influence de characteristics, could obviously be only a compromise between the various opposing standpoints.

At the beginning of 1960, the Ministers of Transport of France and the Federal Republic of Germany announced that they had agreed on the following compromise between the views which their countries had upheld so far.

Maximum axle loading:	
Single axle	10 tons
Twin axle	16 ,,
Maximum total laden weight for articulated vehicles and combinations of vehicles	32 ,,
Maximum length:	
Articulated vehicles	15 m
Combinations of vehicles	15,50 m

This proposal did not differ greatly from the requests of the international non-governmental organisations, except as regards the length of combinations of vehicles; certain countries raised objections principally to the reduction of this length from the figure of 18 metres given in Annex 7 to the 1949 Convention on Road Traffic and applied by virtue of the European Agreement of 1950, and to the raising of the maximum axle loading from 8 to 10 tons.

In support of their view, the countries in question showed that the proposed reduction of the length of combinations of vehicles would scarcely affect road safety and would have an unfavourable effect on the economic return on such transport by altering competitive conditions to their disadvantage. They objected to the raising of the maximum axle loading to 10 tons because of the state of the road network in certain countries.

At its meeting of 24th May, 1960, the Council of Ministers of Transport discussed these problems in great detail, when the Minister of Transport of Yugoslavia suggested, as a new compromise, that the maximum length of combinations of vehicles should be fixed at 16.5 metres. At the end of its discussion, the Council instructed the Committee of Deputies to continue to try to reconcile the conflicting views.

At the meeting of the Committee of Deputies on 3rd June, 1960, several countries which supported the maximum length of 18 metres for combinations of vehicles announced that, in a spirit of conciliation and subject to sufficiently long transitional periods, they would be prepared to accept a length of 17 metres. In the same spirit, certain countries said they were prepared to support a length of 16.50 m. instead of 15.50 m. which they had previously advocated. It was not possible, however, to reach agreement.

. . . .

c) *ROAD SAFETY PROBLEMS*

The previous report described the first results of the action taken by the E.C.M.T. in the field of road safety, which had been embodied in the form of Resolution No. 10 (Road Transport Problems) adopted by the Council of Ministers of Transport in October 1959, on the basis of a first report prepared by the Working Party on Road Safety. The chief questions dealt with were the lessons to be drawn from road accident statistics and the fixing of a uniform maximum speed limit in built-up areas.

In 1960, the Working Party on Road Safety continued its studies with the assistance of the Director of the Transport Division of the E.C.E., concentrating its efforts on other practical problems: the education of road users, the alcohol problem, conditions for the issue and renewal of l'alcoolisme, conditions de délivrance et de renouvellement du permis de conduire, tenue d'un fichier des infractions. Ces différents aspects du problème de la sécurité routière ont été traités dans un deuxième rapport, qui a été approuvé par le Conseil des Ministres dans sa réunion du 5 octobre 1960, sous la forme de 3 Résolutions nouvelles.

L'étude d'autres aspects du problème de la sécurité routière est en cours: d'abord, en collaboration avec le Comité du Conseil de l'Europe pour l'étude des problèmes criminels, celle des sanctions à appliquer: retrait du permis de conduire, peines privatives de liberté ou amendes; ensuite, l'évaluation de la part incombant aux poids lourds dans les accidents mortels; l'opportunité d'établir des règles restreignant, pendant certaines périodes et sur certaines routes, la circulation des véhicules commerciaux, comme c'est déjà le cas en Allemagne, Autriche, Italie et Suisse. Enfin, plusieurs pays (Allemagne, Autriche, Belgique, France Royaume-Uni, Suède) ont introduit récemment, à titre d'essai, des limitations temporaires de vitesse; l'effet de ces mesures sur le nombre et la gravité des accidents va également faire l'objet d'une étude approfondie.

Les problèmes de la sécurité routière, par leur importance sans cesse grandissante avec le développement de la circulation, et leurs multiples aspects, retiennent l'attention d'un nombre croissant d'organisations internationales, gouvernementales ou privées. Tout en se félicitant de l'intérêt qu'ils suscitent et des initiatives qu'ils provoquent, le Conseil des Ministres des Transports s'est demandé si une certaine coordination ne serait pas désirable, afin d'éviter une trop grande dispersion des efforts ou peut-être même des doubles emplois.

. . . .

d) UNIFORMISATION DES RÈGLES DE LA CIRCULATION ROUTIÈRE

Le précédent Rapport faisait état d'une initiative prise par les pays du Benelux en vue d'uniformiser certaines de leurs règles de circulation routière: pour ces pays, la question présente en effet un grand caractère d'urgence, en raison de l'intensité de la circulation routière entre eux et de la refonte projetée de leurs codes de la route. Cette initiative s'est traduite par la constitution d'une Commission pour l'uniformisation des règles de circulation routière, aux travaux de laquelle ont été invités, en sus des pays du Benelux, l'Allemagne, l'Autriche, la France, l'Italie et la Suisse, et qui a tenu huit sessions.

Dans un rapport provisoire, établi en septembre 1960, la Commission observe tout d'abord qu'elle a été guidée, dans ses études, par le souci de ne pas s'écarter des principes inscrits dans la Convention sur la circulation routière signée à Genève le 19 septembre 1949, mais de préciser la mise en pratique de ces principes, qui sont souvent présentés sous des formules générales. Le but poursuivi est la définition de règles que les gouvernements qui y souscriront introduiront dans leur réglementation nationale, après les avoir adaptées aux conditions particulières de leur pays. Les dispositions retenues par la Commission, qui, en l'état actuel, donnent lieu dans certains cas à des réserves de délégations, ont pour but de déterminer autant que possible les devoirs, obligations et interdictions auxquels doivent se soumettre les usagers de la route. En première étape, la circulation des véhicules sur rails a été laissée de côté, ainsi que d'autres questions, telles que l'usage des feux de véhicules et le comportement des conducteurs aux passages pour piétons.

. . . .

Il est dans les intentions de la C.E.M.T. de poursuivre activement les travaux déjà fructueux de la Commission, avec le souci de les mener à bonne fin le plus rapidement possible; avec le développement remarquable pris par le trafic international, touristique et commercial, l'uni-driving licences, file of offences. These various aspects of the road safety problem were dealt with in a second report, approved by the Council of Ministers at its meeting of 5th October, 1960, in the form of three new Resolutions.

Other aspects of the problem of road safety are being studied: first, in conjunction with the European Committee on Crime Problems of the Council of Europe, the question of the penalties to be imposed: suspension of driving licence, fines or imprisonment; the incidence of heavy vehicles in fatal accidents; the advisability of introducing regulations restricting the movement of commercial vehicles at certain times and on certain roads, as is already done in Austria, Germany, Italy and Switzerland. Finally, several countries (Austria, Belgium, France, Germany, Sweden and the United Kingdom) have recently introduced experimental temporary speed limits; the effect of these measures on the number and severity of accidents will also be studied in detail.

The increasing number of road safety problems as traffic is intensified and the many aspects they may assume attract the attention of a growing number of governmental or private international organisations. Though the Council of Ministers of Transport is very pleased that interest has been aroused in these problems and action taken as a result, it wonders whether some co-ordination would not be desirable to avoid an over-dispersal of efforts and possibly some duplication.

. . . .

d) CO-ORDINATION OF ROAD TRAFFIC REGULATIONS

The previous report referred to the action taken by the Benelux countries to co-ordinate some of their road traffic regulations; the question is extremely urgent for these countries owing to the intensity of road traffic between them and the proposed revision of their Highway Codes. Their action took the form of setting up a Group of Experts for the Co-ordination of Road Traffic Rules; in addition to the Benelux countries, Austria, France, Germany, Italy and Switzerland were invited to take part and the Group held eight sessions.

In a provisional report prepared in September 1960, the Group first of all said that it had been guided in its studies by the need to avoid any departure from the principles laid down in the Convention on Road Traffic signed at Geneva on 19th September, 1949, its aim being to clarify the practical application of these principles, which are often couched in general terms. The aim in view was the definition of the rules which governments subscribing to the Convention would embody in their national regulations after adapting them to the special conditions prevailing in their own countries. The provisions adopted by the Group, in respect of which certain Delegations at present maintain reservations, were to specify as clearly as possible the duties, obligations and prohibitions with which road users must comply. In the first stage, tramcar traffic was omitted, together with other matters, such as vehicle lighting and drivers' behaviour at pedestrian crossings.

. . . .

The E.C.M.T. intends actively to continue the successful work of the Group and to try to reach a satisfactory conclusion as quickly as possible; with the remarkable expansion of international traffic, both tourist and commercial, the co-ordination of road traffic regulations formisation des règles de la circulation routière, qui contribuera à la réduction du nombre des accidents, est devenue en effet une tâche essentielle et urgente.

e) RÉGIME DES TRANSPORTS ROUTIERS INTERNATIONAUX

Le précédent Rapport annonçait qu'un groupe mixte, composé d'experts de l'O.E.C.E. et de la C.E.M.T., avait été chargé d'étudier la possibilité d'assouplir le régime actuel des transports routiers internationaux.

Les travaux de ce groupe ont été suspendus en février 1960 et n'ont pas repris depuis cette date, en raison notamment de la réorganisation de l'O.E.C.E.

f) CONDITIONS D'EMPLOI DU PERSONNEL DANS LES TRANSPORTS ROUTIERS INTERNATIONAUX

Au cours de leur audition, le 21 mai 1960, par le Bureau du Comité des suppléants, les représentants de la Fédération internationale des ouvriers du transport, appuyés par ceux de la Fédération internationale des syndicats chrétiens du personnel des transports, ont demandé l'intervention du Conseil des Ministres des Transports pour faire aboutir les textes élaborés par le Comité des transports intérieurs de Genève sur les conditions de travail de l'équipage des véhicules effectuant des transports internationaux par route. Ces textes faisaient l'objet de l'annexe A à l'Accord général portant réglementation économique des transports routiers internationaux, conclu à Genève en 1954 et non entré en vigueur.

Informé dans sa séance du 24 mai 1960 de la demande des représentants des organisations représentatives des travailleurs des transports, le Conseil des Ministres a marqué son accord à ce que les travaux entrepris dans le cadre du Comité des transports intérieurs de la C.E.E. des Nations Unies aboutissent et qu'ainsi soit réglé un problème qui intéresse à la fois la législation sociale et la sécurité routière.

Dans le cadre de Genève, le Comité des transports intérieurs a approuvé, en décembre 1960, une proposition tendant à ce que les dispositions de l'annexe A fassent l'objet, après avoir été complétées et mises au point, d'un nouvel accord international. Faisant suite à une première discussion qui avait déjà eu lieu en septembre 1960, d'autres réunions sont prévues dans le courant du 1er semestre 1961, en vue d'élaborer un texte définitif.

VI. PROBLÈMES CONCERNANT LES TRANSPORTS PAR VOIES NAVIGABLES

Le précédent Rapport indiquait qu'une Conférence économique de la navigation rhénane, à laquelle la C.E.M.T. a été invitée à se faire représenter, avait été convoquée par la Commission centrale pour la Navigation du Rhin. Cette Conférence s'est réunie à plusieurs reprises à Strasbourg entre le 2 juillet 1959 et le 21 octobre 1960.

Elle a constitué quatre Commissions pour l'étude des problèmes suivants:

Commission I:

a) Détermination des causes de l'inefficacité partielle des recommandations de la Conférence économique de 1952.

b) Examen des causes d'une aggravation de la crise latente de la navigation rhénane.

Commission II:

a) Problèmes du déséquilibre dans les transports rhénans.

b) Problèmes qui se posent en relation avec les mesures et les objectifs du domaine économique des transports des organisations européennes.

c) Problèmes de la nationalité des bateaux.

has become an essential priority, for it will help to reduce the number of accidents.

e) REGULATIONS AFFECTING INTERNATIONAL ROAD TRANSPORT

The previous report announced that a Joint Working Party, consisting of experts of the O.E.E.C. and the E.C.M.T., had been instructed to study the possibilities of relaxing present international road transport regulations.

The Working Party's studies were suspended in February 1960 and have not been resumed since, partly owing to the reorganisation of the O.E.E.C.

f) WORKING CONDITIONS IN INTERNATIONAL ROAD TRANSPORT

At their hearing on 21st May, 1960, by the officers of the Committee of Deputies, the representatives of the International Transport Workers' Federation, supported by the International Federation of Christian Trade Unions of Transport Workers, asked the Council of Ministers of Transport to intervene in order to give practical effect to the texts prepared by the Inland Transport Committee at Geneva on the working conditions of crews of vehicles engaged in international road transport. These texts appeared in Annex A to the General Agreement on Economic Regulations for International Road Transport concluded at Geneva in 1954, which has not come into force.

On being informed, at its meeting of 24th May, 1960, of the request by the transport workers' organisations, the Council of Ministers agreed that the work done by the Inland Transport Committee of the E.C.E. should be followed up, so as to settle a problem of importance both to social legislation and to road safety.

At Geneva in December 1960, the Inland Transport Committee approved a proposal that the provisions of Annex A, supplemented and revised, should be embodied in a new International Agreement. To follow up a preliminary discussion held in September 1960, other meetings are planned for the first half of 1961, with a view to preparing a final text.

VI. PROBLEMS CONCERNING INLAND WATERWAYS TRANSPORT

The previous report stated that an Economic Conference on the Navigation of the Rhine, to which the E.C.M.T. had been invited to send a representative, had been convened by the Central Commission for Navigation of the Rhine. This Conference met several times at Strasbourg between 2nd July, 1959, and 21st October, 1960.

It set up four Committees to study the following problems:

Committee I:

a) Determination of the causes of the partial failure of the recommendations of the 1952 Economic Conference;

b) Causes of the intensification of the latent crisis in Rhine navigation.

Committee II:

a) Disequilibrium in Rhine transport;

b) Problems arising out of the action of European organisations and their objectives concerning the economic aspect of transport.

c) Nationality of vessels.

Commission III:
a) Formation des frets.
b) Capacité de la flotte rhénane.
c) Organisation de la profession et de la batellerie.

Commission IV:
a) Problème de la formation des frets, Accords de Petersberg.
b) Pools et conventions.
c) Action sur la capacité de la flotte.
d) Nouvelle organisation de la navigation du Rhin.
e) Proposition de création d'une communauté d'exploitation.

. . . .

Le 21 octobre 1960, la Conférence économique a décidé de suspendre ses travaux et de transmettre les rapports qu'elle a établis à la Commission centrale en lui demandant d'examiner:

1. si elle estime qu'une organisation sous la forme proposée, ou sous une forme analogue, est justifiée par les besoins économiques;
2. dans quelle mesure elle serait disposée à recommander aux gouvernements d'adopter, sans perdre de vue les principes de la Convention de Mannheim, des mesures propres à permettre à la profession la réalisation d'une organisation englobant toute la navigation, et assurée par elle-même.

Le résultat des travaux de la Conférence économique est en cours d'examen par la Commission centrale.

VII. QUESTIONS DIVERSES

a) *TRANSPORT DE MATIÈRES A HAUT DEGRÉ DE RADIOACTIVITÉ*

L'étude des règles de sécurité pour le transport des matières radioactives, entreprise par l'Agence Internationale de l'Énergie Atomique (A.I.E.A.) de Vienne, et que signalait le précédent Rapport a abouti à un Règlement de transport, publié par l'Agence. En septembre 1960, le Conseil des gouverneurs de celle-ci a approuvé l'application du règlement à ses opérations et a recommandé aux organisations internationales intéressées, dont la C.E.M.T., de le prendre pour base des règlements de transport international des matières radioactives.

Le règlement de l'A.I.E.A. a été élaboré sur le plan mondial et pour tous les modes de transport, y compris les transports maritimes: il convient donc maintenant de l'adapter à l'échelle européenne et aux conditions particulières du transport par chemin de fer, par route et par voies navigables. Les organes compétents (Office central des transports internationaux par chemins de fer de Berne; Commission Économique pour l'Europe des Nations Unies) s'en préoccupent; un petit groupe d'experts a préparé un projet d'adaptation du règlement de l'A.I.E.A. aux dimensions du R.I.D., qui sera examiné en mai 1961 par le Comité d'experts du R.I.D.

. . . .

b) *COLLABORATION ENTRE LES TRANSPORTS DE SURFACE ET LES TRANSPORTS AÉRIENS*

Dans sa Résolution 174 (1960) portant réponse au 6e Rapport annuel de la C.E.M.T., l'Assemblée du Conseil de l'Europe, „estimant que la prévision à long terme de l'évolution des transports de surface et le problème du financement de leurs investissements ne peuvent être dissociés de l'évolution des transports aériens, prie instamment les Ministres des Transports d'établir avec la Commission européenne de l'Aviation civile (C.E.A.C.), et notamment avec son Comité de coordination, les contacts

Committee III:
a) Freight formation;
b) Transport capacity of the Rhine fleet;
c) Organisation of the industry and the waterway transport companies.

Committee IV:
a) Freight formation – Petersberg Agreement;
b) Pools and Conventions;
c) Action on the capacity of the fleet;
d) Reorganisation of the navigation of the Rhine;
e) Proposal to create an operating community.

. . . .

On 21st October, 1960, the Economic Conference decided to suspend its work and submit the reports it had prepared to the Central Commission, which it asked to consider:

1. Whether it thought that an organisation in the form proposed or in any similar form was justified by economic needs;
2. How far it would be prepared to recommend that, bearing in mind the principles of the Mannheim Convention, Governments should adopt suitable measures to enable the industry itself to form and ensure the operation of an organisation covering all navigation on the Rhine.

The results of the work of the Economic Conference are now being considered by the Central Commission.

VII. MISCELLANEOUS PROBLEMS

a) TRANSPORT OF HIGHLY RADIOACTIVE MATERIALS

The study of safety rules for the transport of radioactive materials undertaken by the International Atomic Energy Agency (I.A.E.A.) in Vienna, referred to in the previous report has resulted in the Transport Regulations published by the Agency. In September 1960, the Board of Governors of the Agency approved the application of these Regulations to its own operations and recommended the international organisations concerned, including the E.C.M.T., to use them as a basis for regulations governing the international transport of radioactive materials.

The I.A.E.A. Regulations were prepared on a world scale and for all means of transport, including maritime transport: they therefore need to be adapted to the European scale and to the special conditions of transport by railway, road and inland waterways. The competent bodies (Central Office for International Railway Transport at Berne; Economic Commission for Europe of the United Nations Organisation) are dealing with this matter; a small group of experts has prepared a draft adaptation of the A.I.A.E. regulations to the format of the R.I.D. and this will be considered by the Committee of Experts of the R.I.D. in May 1961.

. . . .

b) CO-OPERATION BETWEEN SURFACE AND AIR TRANSPORT

In its Resolution 174 (1960) in reply to the Sixth Annual Report of the E.C.M.T., the Consultative Assembly of the Council of Europe, "taking in view that the long-term prospects of surface transport and of the problem of financing investments cannot be dissociated from the development of air transport, urges the Ministers of Transport to establish suitable contacts with the European Civil Aviation Conference (E.C.A.C.)

nécessaires pour l'aboutissement dans les meilleures conditions de ces études".

Cette question a fait l'objet, au cours de la séance du 24 mai 1960 du Conseil des Ministres, d'un débat en conclusion duquel les suppléants ont été chargés d'étudier „sous quelle forme la C.E.M.T. pourrait s'intéresser aux transports aériens et quelles seraient les mesures pratiques qu'il serait nécessaire de prendre à cet effet".

Le Comité des suppléants a étudié une note soumise par la Délégation autrichienne. La majorité des délégations a été d'avis que les propositions contenues dans cette note ne pouvaient pas être discutées utilement dans le sein de la C.E.M.T. et a attiré l'attention sur le fait que les transports aériens ne sont pas inclus dans les objectifs de la Conférence.

Néanmoins, l'opinion générale a été qu'une liaison avec la C.E.A.C. en ce qui concerne les problèmes de coopération technique pourrait être fructueuse et, dans ce but, le président du Comité des suppléants a pris un contact préliminaire avec le président de la C.E.A.C.

ANNEXE

NORMALISATION DES COMPTES DES ADMINISTRATIONS FERROVIAIRES

TABLEAUX ÉTABLIS PAR L'UNION INTERNATIONALE DES CHEMINS DE FER

TABLEAU A. RÉSULTATS DE LA NORMALISATION DES COMPTES

Rapport des dépenses aux recettes

Pays	1958			1959		
	Sans indemnités ni contributions	Avec indemnités et contributions	Après normalisation	Sans indemnités ni contributions	Avec indemnités et contributions	Après normalisation
Allemagne	1,13	1,08	0,93	1,09	1,05	0,91
Autriche	1,46	1,46	1,17	1,36	1,36	1,08
Belgique	1,55	1,26	1,12	1,57	1,18	1,09
Danemark [1]	1,18	1,18	1,18	1,14	1,14	1,14
Espagne	1,29	1,29	1,19	1,25	1,25	1,15
France	1,27	1,05	1,01	1,19	1,04	0,98
Grèce	.	.	.	1,68	1,68	1,32
Italie [2]	1,39	1,18	0,96	1,40	1,14	0,98
Luxembourg	1,21	1,14	0,92	1,12	1,07	0,71
Norvège [2]	1,40	1,40	1,35	1,41	1,41	1,36
Pays-Bas	1,00	1,00	0,97	0,98	0,98	0,95
Portugal	1,30	1,30	1,28	1,26	1,26	1,23
Suède [2]	1,04	0,97	1,08 [3]	1,04	0,97	1,08 [3]
Suisse	0,99	0,99	0,93	0,99	0,99	0,93

[1] Exercice budgétaire 1er avril-31 mars.
[2] Exercice budgétaire 1er juillet-30 juin.
[3] Rapport en augmentation du fait de la prépondérance de certaines opérations de normalisation des comptes ayant eu pour effet d'augmenter les dépenses (prise en compte des intérêts calculés sur le capital investi par l'État dans les chemins de fer).

and, in particular, with its Co-ordination Committee, so that these studies may achieve the best results".

At the meeting of the Council of Ministers of 24th May, 1960, this topic was the subject of a debate at the end of which the Deputies were instructed to study "the form in which the E.M.C.T. might concern itself with air transport and what practical measures it would be necessary to take to that effect".

The Committee of Deputies studied a note submitted by the Austrian Delegation. Most delegations considered that the proposals contained in that note could not usefully be discussed by the E.C.M.T. and drew attention to the fact that air transport was not covered by the purposes of the Conference.

The general opinion was, however, that liaison with the E.C.A.C. on problems of technical co-operation might prove fruitful, and the Chairman of the Committee of Deputies has therefore made preliminary contact with the Chairman of the E.C.A.C.

ANNEX

NORMALIZATION OF RAILWAY ACCOUNTS

TABLES DRAWN UP BY THE INTERNATIONAL RAILWAY UNION

TABLE A. RESULTS OF THE NORMALIZATION OF ACCOUNTS

Expenditure-Income Ratio

Countries	1958			1959		
	Without allowances or contributions	With allowances and contributions	After normalization	Without allowances or contributions	With allowances and contributions	After normalization
Germany	1.13	1.08	0.93	1.09	1.05	0.91
Austria	1.46	1.46	1.17	1.36	1.36	1.08
Belgium	1.55	1.26	1.12	1.57	1.18	1.09
Denmark [1]	1.18	1.18	1.18	1.14	1.14	1.14
Spain	1.29	1.29	1.19	1.25	1.25	1.15
France	1.27	1.05	1.01	1.19	1.04	0.98
Greece	—	—	—	1.68	1.68	1.32
Italy [2]	1.39	1.18	0.96	1.40	1.14	0.98
Luxembourg	1.21	1.14	0.92	1.12	1.07	0.71
Norway [2]	1.40	1.40	1.35	1.41	1.41	1.36
Netherlands	1.00	1.00	0.97	0.98	0.98	0.95
Portugal	1.30	1.30	1.28	1.26	1.26	1.23
Sweden [2]	1.04	0.97	1.08 [3]	1.04	0.97	1.08 [3]
Switzerland	0.99	0.99	0.93	0.99	0.99	0.93

[1] Budget year 1st April–31st March.
[2] Budget year 1st July–30th June.
[3] Ratio higher owing to the preponderance of certain normalizations of accounts which had the effect of increasing expenditure (allowance for interest calculated on capital invested in the railways by the State).

TABLEAU B. EFFETS DE CERTAINES CORRECTIONS IMPORTANTES RÉSULTANT DE LA NORMALISATION DES COMPTES

Pays	Réductions tarifaires		Retraites		Entretien et renouvellement	
	Pourcentage des recettes		Pourcentage des dépenses		Pourcentage des dépenses	
	1958	1959	1958	1959	1958	1959
Allemagne	+ 4,02	+ 2,77	— 8,22	— 8,27	—	—
Autriche	+ 6,46	+ 5,50	— 19,33	— 20,10	+ 5,88	+ 4,82
Belgique	+ 16,23	+ 19,57	— 16,14	— 15,87	+ 2,58	+ 1,11
Danemark	—	—	—	—	—	—
Espagne	+ 14,25	+ 14,47	—	—	+ 5,58	+ 5,46
France	+ 13,09	+ 8,09	— 8,83	— 8,84	+ 2,33	+ 0,71
Grèce	—	+ 5,86	—	— 14,99	—	—
Italie [1]	+ 15,18	+ 15,48	— 15,56	— 15,50	— 2,41	— 0,61
Luxembourg	+ 0,67	+ 27,50	— 22,22	— 17,84	—	—
Norvège [1]	+ 0,71	+ 0,70	— 1,97	— 2,07	—	—
Pays-Bas	+ 0,80	+ 0,99	—	—	—	—
Portugal	+ 0,66	+ 0,64	— 2,43	— 5,61	+ 5,07	+ 4,89
Suède [1]	+ 0,44	+ 0,43	—	— 0,55	—	—
Suisse	+ 2,18	+ 2,07	— 3,74	— 3,54	—	—

[1] Exercice budgétaire 1er juillet-30 juin.

B. RÉSOLUTIONS

1. RÉSOLUTION NO. 11 CONCERNANT L'ÉDUCATION DES USAGERS DE LA ROUTE

LE CONSEIL DES MINISTRES DES TRANSPORTS,

Réuni à La Haye, le 5 octobre 1960;

Vu sa Résolution no. 10 (Transports par routes);

Sur la proposition du Comité des Suppléants;

Approuve le Rapport ci-après [CM(60)9final] du Groupe de travail de la Sécurité routière sur l'éducation des usagers en date du 17 septembre 1960.

Constatant avec regret que le nombre des victimes de la circulation routière s'accroît constamment d'une année à l'autre, que chaque année, dans les pays membres de la C.E.M.T., plus de 50.000 personnes sont tuées et que plus d'un million sont blessées dans les accidents;

Se donnant pour tâche d'examiner et de discuter sur le plan international les problèmes posés par la sécurité routière et de rechercher les mesures pouvant compléter l'effort déjà entrepris en vue d'éviter les accidents de la circulation;

Se saisissant à cet effet des questions concernant l'éducation routière et la formation des usagers,

I. EXPRIME l'avis suivant:

1. L'éducation routière et la formation des usagers, c'est-à-dire l'ensemble des mesures qui ont pour objectif:

TABLE B. RESULTS OF CERTAIN IMPORTANT CORRECTIONS FOLLOWING THE NORMALIZATION OF ACCOUNTS

Countries	Reduced rates		Pensions		Maintenance and renewals	
	Percentage of income		Percentage of expenditure		Percentage of expenditure	
	1958	1959	1958	1959	1958	1959
Germany	+ 4.02	+ 2.77	— 8.22	— 8.27	—	—
Austria	+ 6.46	+ 5.50	— 19.33	— 20.10	+ 5.88	+ 4.82
Belgium	+ 16.23	+ 19.57	— 16.14	— 15.87	+ 2.58	+ 1.11
Denmark	—	—	—	—	—	—
Spain	+ 14.25	+ 14.47	—	—	+ 5.58	+ 5.46
France	+ 13.09	+ 8.09	— 8.83	— 8.84	+ 2.33	+ 0.71
Greece	—	+ 5.86	—	— 14.99	—	—
Italy [1]	+ 15.18	+ 15.48	— 15.56	— 15.50	— 2.41	— 0.61
Luxembourg	+ 0.67	+ 27.50	— 22.22	— 17.84	—	—
Norway [1]	+ 0.71	+ 0.70	— 1.97	— 2.07	—	—
Netherlands	+ 0.80	+ 0.99	—	—	—	—
Portugal	+ 0.66	+ 0.64	— 2.43	— 5.61	+ 5,07	+ 4.89
Sweden [1]	+ 0.44	+ 0.43	—	— 0.55	—	—
Switzerland	+ 2.18	+ 2.07	— 3.74	— 3.54	—	—

[1] Budget year 1st July–30th June.

B. RESOLUTIONS

1. RESOLUTION NO. 11 CONCERNING THE EDUCATION OF ROAD USERS

THE COUNCIL OF MINISTERS OF TRANSPORT,
Meeting at The Hague on 5th and 6th October, 1960;
Having regard to its Resolution No. 10 (Road Transport);
On the proposal of the Committee of Deputies;
Approves the Report below [CM(60)9Final] of the Working Party on Road Safety on the Education of Road Users.

Noting with regret that the number of road traffic victims is steadily increasing from year to year, that more than 50,000 people are killed and more than one million are injured in traffic accidents each year in the Member countries of the E.C.M.T.;

Undertaking to consider and discuss road safety at international level and to seek ways and means of furthering the work already done to prevent road accidents;
Concerning itself for this purpose with questions of road safety education and the training of road users;

I. ADOPTS the following views:

1. Road safety education and the training of road users, that is to say all measures designed:

- d'informer les usagers des caractéristiques les plus saillantes de la circulation actuelle et de ses dangers, ainsi que des nécessités auxquelles répond le Code de la route et des mesures prises par l'Administration et la Police de la route;
- de donner aux usagers les connaissances pratiques indispensables pour qu'ils soient à même de se comporter correctement sur les voies publiques;
- d'éveiller et de renforcer chez tous les usagers, par des arguments moraux, sociaux et religieux, l'idée qu'ils sont personnellement responsables du déroulement normal de la circulation, qui est un important aspect de la vie sociale, et qu'ils sont également responsables de leur vie, de leur santé et de celles des autres;

sont considérées, d'une part, comme des moyens très efficaces d'accroître la sécurité routière et de prévenir les accidents de la circulation et, d'autre part, comme un complément indispensable des mesures prises par les autorités publiques dans le domaine de la sécurité routière.

Il est donc absolument indispensable d'obtenir les ressources financières nécessaires pour permettre un travail fructueux dans ce domaine, ainsi que pour doter les autorités des ressources en personnel et en matériel dont elles ont besoin.

2. Il faut attribuer une importance toute particulière à l'éducation routière, non seulement dans les écoles primaires, mais aussi dans les écoles secondaires et techniques, car elle donne des résultats satisfaisants et durables. Cette éducation, qui apprend aux jeunes comment ils doivent se comporter et prendre conscience des responsabilités qui leur incombent en tant qu'usagers de la route, exige que l'enseignement en matière de circulation soit donné régulièrement et méthodiquement par des maîtres compétents. Il est donc nécessaire de faire en sorte que ces conditions soient, autant que possible, partout remplies.

3. L'initiative privée s'est révélée très efficace dans le domaine de l'éducation routière et elle est vivement appréciée. Une importance particulière doit être donnée à la coordination des initiatives officielles et privées. Cette coordination permet de leur donner un maximum d'efficacité.

4. Il conviendrait d'assurer et d'intensifier la collaboration internationale dans le domaine de l'éducation routière et de la formation des usagers, notamment les échanges mutuels de données d'expérience.

Il serait de même indiqué d'organiser, sur des thèmes choisis et en leur conférant un caractère officiel qui pourrait se concrétiser par le patronage des Ministres des Transports, des manifestations internationales pour la mise en oeuvre desquelles il pourrait être fait appel au concours des organisations internationales et nationales de prévention routière.

II. Charge le Comité des Suppléants de poursuivre, en utilisant largement les études faites au sein d'autres organismes internationaux, et notamment le Groupe de travail de la Prévention des Accidents de la Commission Économique pour l'Europe, la préparation de mesures destinées à résoudre de façon aussi uniforme que possible les problèmes qui ont trait à l'éducation des usagers de la route.

2. RÉSOLUTION NO. 12 CONCERNANT LES MESURES PROPRES A COMBATTRE L'ALCOOLISME CHEZ LES USAGERS DE LA ROUTE

Le Conseil des Ministres des Transports,

Réuni à La Haye le 5 octobre 1960;

Vu le Rapport ci-après [CM(60)9final] du Groupe de travail de la Sécurité routière sur le problème de l'alcoolisme;

- to explain to the public the essential facts of modern traffic and its dangers, the purpose of the Highway Code and the necessity of traffic regulations;

- to give practical instruction to road users in the proper use of the public highway;

- to bring home to all road users that on ethical, civic and religious grounds they are personally responsible for the smooth running of road traffic as an important part of community life, and for the lives and safety of themselves and others;

are deemed to be most effective ways of enhancing road safety and preventing traffic accidents and an essential adjunct to the road safety measures taken by the public authorities.

It is therefore absolutely essential to obtain the necessary funds to enable useful work to be done in this field and to provide the authorities with the staff and equipment they require.

2. Particular importance should be attached to road safety education in secondary and technical as well as primary schools, since it generally produces satisfactory and lasting results. This education, which teaches children road behaviour and brings home to them their responsibilities as road users, must be given regularly and methodically by competent teachers. It is therefore essential that these conditions should as far as possible be complied with everywhere.

3. Private initiative has proved very effective in road safety education and is warmly welcomed. Special importance should be attached to the co-ordination of official and private initiatives in the interests of maximum efficiency.

4. International co-operation in road safety education and the training of road users should be established and intensified, particularly by exchanges of experience.

It would also be advisable to organise international demonstrations on selected themes and to give them official status, perhaps in the form of the patronage of the Ministers of Transport. The co-operation of the international and national road safety organisations might be sought in arranging these activities.

II. INSTRUCTS the Committee of Deputies to proceed with the framing of measures with a view to the training of road users on as uniform a basis as possible and, in doing so, to make wide use of the studies made by other international bodies, such as the European Commission for Europe Working Party on Accident Prevention.

2. RESOLUTION NO. 12 CONCERNING THE MEASURES TO COUNTER DRUNKENNESS AMONG ROAD USERS

THE COUNCIL OF MINISTERS OF TRANSPORT,

Meeting at The Hague on 5th and 6th October, 1960;

Constatant:
- que l'absorption de boissons alcoolisées réduit l'aptitude à conduire un véhicule et qu'ainsi l'alcoolisme aggrave sensiblement l'insécurité de la circulation routière;
- que des mesures ont déjà été prises dans tous les pays Membres contre les conducteurs de véhicules se trouvant sous l'influence de l'alcool;

Jugeant nécessaire d'intensifier ces mesures en vue de réduire, autant que possible, les accidents de la route causés par des conducteurs ayant absorbé des boissons alcoolisées;

Estimant utile que ces mesures soient appliquées non seulement aux conducteurs de véhicules, mais aussi à d'autres usagers de la route dont l'état alcoolique pourrait rendre la circulation dangereuse.

Sur la proposition du Comité des Suppléants,

RECOMMANDE aux pays membres:

a) de prévoir des sanctions sévères contre les usagers de la route en état d'ébriété et contre les conducteurs de véhicules sous l'influence de l'alcool, ces sanctions comportant, pour ces derniers, le retrait du permis de conduire;

b) d'adopter des dispositions légales permettant de soumettre à des tests de vérification, pour la recherche du degré d'alcool dans le sang, les conducteurs suspectés d'être sous l'influence de l'alcool et définissant la procédure à suivre et les examens à effectuer;

c) de fixer un taux limite d'alcool dans le sang au-dessus duquel toute personne sera considérée comme inapte à la conduite d'un véhicule à moteur, cette fixation résultant soit de la loi, soit des principes généraux se dégageant de la jurisprudence, étant entendu que l'existence d'une telle limite n'exclut pas la possibilité de poursuivre et de condamner, compte tenu des circonstances de fait, pour conduite sous l'influence de l'alcool, des conducteurs dont le sang aurait une teneur en alcool inférieure au taux limite prévu;

d) de fixer cette limite, sur la base de recherches médicales, à un niveau tel que la grande majorité des conducteurs qui la respectent conservent leur aptitude à conduire un véhicule à moteur;

e) de créer des installations permettant de satisfaire, d'une manière rapide et efficace, aux prescriptions visées au point *b*) ci-dessus;

f) d'intensifier les mesures prises par les pouvoirs publics pour informer et éduquer les usagers de la route, afin de leur mieux faire comprendre la gravité des dangers que l'absorption de l'alcool entraîne pour la sécurité de la circulation routière;

g) de faire appel, autant que possible, à la collaboration de toutes les organisations privées et institutions dans la lutte contre l'alcoolisme des usagers de la route.

3. RÉSOLUTION NO. 13 CONCERNANT LES PERMIS DE CONDUIRE, L'INSTITUTION D'UN FICHIER DES CONDAMNATIONS ET INFRACTIONS AU CODE DE LA ROUTE ET LES PREMIERS SECOURS A DONNER AUX BLESSÉS

LE CONSEIL DES MINISTRES DES TRANSPORTS,

Réuni à La Haye le 5 octobre 1960;

Vu le Rapport ci-après [CM(60)9final] du Groupe de travail de la Sécurité routière sur les conditions de délivrance des permis de conduire et sur le fichier des infractions;

Sur la proposition du Comité des suppléants;

I. *Constatant* que le comportement de certaines catégories de conduc-

Having noted:
- that drinking alcohol reduces ability to drive a vehicle and that the influence of alcohol therefore appreciably increases danger on the road;
- that measures have already been taken in all Member countries against drivers who are under the influence of alcohol;

Judging it necessary to intensify such measures in order to reduce to a minimum the number of road accidents caused by drivers who are under the influence of alcohol;

Considering it valuable that such measures should be applied not only to drivers but to other road users whose alcoholic state might endanger traffic;

On the proposal of the Committee of Deputies;

RECOMMENDS that Member countries:

a) provide for the infliction of severe penalties on road users and drivers of vehicles who are under the influence of alcohol, including, in the case of drivers, withdrawal of the driving licence;

b) adopt legal provisions making it possible to require drivers who are alleged to be under the influence of alcohol to submit to tests to ascertain the concentration of alcohol in the blood and defining procedure for such tests;

c) specify a maximum alcohol content in the blood above which any person will be deemed unfit to drive a motor vehicle, such maximum being determined either by statute or by general principles derived from case law, provided that the existence of such a maximum shall not exclude the possibility, according to the facts of the case, of prosecuting and convicting for driving while under the influence of alcohol any driver the alcohol content of whose blood is less than the said maximum.

d) fix such maximum on the basis of medical research at such a point that the great majority of drivers who conform to it will be fit to drive a motor vehicle;

e) supply suitable facilities for carrying out quickly and efficiently the action recommended under *b*) above;

f) intensify the measures taken by the authorities to inform and educate road users as to the serious danger to road safety involved in the consumption of alcohol;

g) obtain the fullest possible co-operation of all private organisations and institutions in the campaign against the excessive consumption of alcohol by road users.

3. RESOLUTION NO. 13 CONCERNING THE DRIVING LICENCES, THE ESTABLISHMENT OF A FILE OF CONVICTIONS AND INFRINGEMENTS OF THE HIGHWAY CODE AND FIRST AID

THE COUNCIL OF MINISTERS OF TRANSPORT,

Meeting at The Hague on 5th and 6th October, 1960;

I. *Noting* that, owing to the nature of the vehicle driven or to the teurs de véhicules à moteur est susceptible, du fait de la nature du véhicule qu'ils conduisent ou de l'état physique du conducteur, d'entraîner des conséquences particulièrement graves sur la sécurité de la circulation routière;

Est favorable à l'obligation d'un examen médical préalable à la délivrance du permis de conduire pour les conducteurs d'autocars et de taxis ainsi que pour les candidats âgés de plus de 65 ans, et d'un examen simplifié de la vue, à faire passer par l'examinateur;

RECOMMANDE de fixer pour les conducteurs de taxis, de même qu'il est fait pour les conducteurs d'autocars, un âge minimum, plus élevé que pour les conducteurs de véhicules privés.

II. *Constatant:*
- que le retrait du permis de conduire constitue une sanction très efficace, dont la menace peut déjà agir par elle-même;
- que, pour prononcer cette sanction en connaissance de cause, l'autorité compétente doit pouvoir disposer des éléments d'information nécessaires;
- qu'une base valable d'appréciation lui est précisément fournie si elle peut recourir à un fichier des condamnations et infractions au Code de la route;
- qu'un tel fichier, par le seul fait de son existence, exerce sur le public une crainte salutaire;
- qu'il est en même temps capable, par la source de documentation qu'il constitue, de rendre d'autres services, tant au législateur, aux tribunaux et aux autorités administratives qu'aux recherches statistiques ou scientifiques;

RECOMMANDE aux pays membres qui ne le font pas déjà de tenir un tel fichier, en adoptant un système qui évite les risques de double inscription et qui assure que toutes les infractions concernant un conducteur soient bien portées sur le même fichier.

ESTIME souhaitable, afin de faire produire au fichier tous ses effets, d'y inscrire toutes les peines prononcées, quelle qu'en soit la nature.

III. *Conscient* de l'importance des premiers secours à donner aux blessés en cas d'accidents,

RECOMMANDE:
- qu'une documentation à ce sujet soit fournie aux candidats au permis de conduire;
- que des prescriptions administratives obligent les conducteurs d'autocars à avoir une connaissance sommaire de ces premiers secours.

4. CONCLUSIONS ADOPTÉES PAR LES MINISTRES DES TRANSPORTS DE 13 PAYS CONCERNANT LES POIDS ET DIMENSIONS DES VÉHICULES ROUTIERS

LES MINISTRES DES TRANSPORTS des pays suivants:

Allemagne, Autriche, Belgique, Danemark, Espagne, France, Grèce, Luxembourg, Norvège, Portugal, Suède, Turquie et Yougoslavie.

Réunis à La Haye, le 5 octobre 1960,

CONSIDÉRANT qu'il est nécessaire, pour le bon fonctionnement du trafic international routier de marchandises, d'avoir des poids et dimensions uniformes maximums pour camions, trains routiers et véhicules;

ESTIMENT que, dans la mesure où l'état des différents itinéraires dans chaque pays le permet, les normes maximums suivantes devraient être introduites dans les transports internationaux entre les pays membres:

physical state of the driver, the behaviour of certain categories of drivers of motor vehicles is liable to have particularly serious effects on road safety;

Favours a compulsory medical examination prior to the issue of a driving licence for drivers of motor-coaches and taxis, and applicants aged over 65, and a simple sight test to be given by the examiner;

RECOMMENDS the fixing of a minimum age for taxi-drivers, higher than the lower age limit for drivers of private cars, as is already the case for motor-coach drivers.

II. *Noting:*
- that withdrawal of the driving licence is a very effective penalty, the threat of which may be sufficient in itself;
- that, in order to impose this penalty advisedly, the authority responsible must be in possession of all necessary informations;
- that valid grounds for judgment are provided if the authority has access to a file of convictions and infringements of the Highway Code;
- that the very existence of such a file has a salutary effect on the public;
- that such a file may, at the same time, by reason of the information it provides, render other services to legislators, courts of law and administrative authorities, as well as to statistical or scientific research;

RECOMMENDS that Member countries which do not already do so should keep such a file on lines which avoid any risk of duplication of entries, but which will ensure that a driver's offences are all recorded in the same file;

CONSIDERS it desirable, in order to make the file fully effective, to enter all penalties imposed, of whatsoever kind.

III. *Conscious* of the importance of first aid to persons injured in cases of accident;

RECOMMENDS:
- that printed information on this subject be supplied to applicants for driving licences;
- that drivers of motor-coaches should be required by regulation to have some knowledge of first aid.

4. CONCLUSIONS CONCERNING THE WEIGHTS AND DIMENSIONS OF ROAD VEHICLES ADOPTED BY THE MINISTERS OF TRANSPORT OF 13 COUNTRIES

THE MINISTERS OF TRANSPORT of Austria, Belgium, Denmark, France, Germany, Greece, Luxembourg, Norway, Portugal, Spain, Sweden, Turkey and Yugoslavia,

Meeting in The Hague on 5th October, 1960;

CONSIDERING that it is necessary for the efficient operation of international goods transport by road to have uniform maximum weights and dimensions for lorries, combinations of vehicles and articulated vehicles;

BELIEVE that, in so far as the state of the various itineraries in each country allows, the following maximum standards should be introduced for international transport between Member countries:

- charge par essieu simple. . . . . 10 tonnes
- charge par essieu double . . . . 16 tonnes
- poids total des trains routiers et véhicules articulés. . . . 32 tonnes
- longueur des trains routiers . . . . 16,50 m.
- longueur des véhicules articulés . . . . 15 mètres

et

S'EMPLOIERONT à ce que:
- les véhicules ayant des dimensions techniques supérieures à celles mentionnées ci-dessus ne soient plus utilisés dans les transports internationaux au-delà du 31 décembre 1965;
- les mesures nécessaires à l'application des recommandations mentionnées ci-dessus soient prises aussi vite que possible dans leurs pays respectifs.

5. RÉSOLUTION SUR LE PLACEMENT DES OBLIGATIONS D'EUROFIMA DANS LE PORTEFEUILLE DE RÉSERVES DES COMPAGNIES D'ASSURANCES

Le Conseil des Ministres des Transports du Groupe restreint „Eurofima":

Réuni à La Haye le 4 octobre 1960;

Vu le 3e Rapport annuel [1] établi par la Société Eurofima, en application de l'article 6 *b*) de la Convention relative à la constitution d'Eurofima, dans lequel les Gouvernements signataires de ladite Convention sont priés de rechercher une solution favorable aux difficultés rencontrées pour la participation des compagnies d'assurances aux émissions d'obligations d'Eurofima;

Vu la lettre du 7 juillet 1960 par laquelle le Directeur général de la Société Eurofima demande à la C.E.M.T. de suggérer aux Gouvernements intéressés de se concerter, en vue de tenter d'éliminer ces difficultés, qui s'opposent à la poursuite des objectifs de la Société;

Vu l'article 10 de la Convention;

CONSTATANT avec satisfaction que, dans quelques pays signataires de la Convention, les obligations de la Société Eurofima peuvent déjà être admises en emploi de réserves obligatoires de compagnies d'assurances;

RECONNAISSANT que l'application de cette mesure dans le plus grand nombre possible de pays favoriserait considérablement la réalisation des objectifs de la Société;

Sur la proposition du Comité des Suppléants du Groupe restreint;

CONVIENT que les membres du Conseil interviendront, en tant que de besoin, auprès des autorités compétentes de leurs pays, afin qu'une suite favorable soit donnée aux demandes de la Société Eurofima tendant à ce que ses obligations puissent être admises en emploi des réserves obligatoires de compagnies d'assurances;

DÉCIDE que le résultat de ces interventions sera porté, dans le meilleur délai, à la connaissance du Conseil.

---

[1] Ce rapport est reproduit à l'annexe IV du 6e Rapport annuel de la C.E.M.T.

- loading per single axle . . . . 10 tons
- loading per twin axle . . . . 16 tons
- total weight of combinations of vehicles and of articulated vehicles . . . . 32 tons
- length of combinations of vehicles. . . . . 16.50 metres
- length of articulated vehicles . . . . 15 metres

and

SHALL MAKE EVERY EFFORT to ensure that:
- vehicles with specifications greater than those referred to above are no longer used for international transport after 31st December, 1965;
- the necessary measures for the application of the recommendations referred to above are taken as quickly as possible in their respective countries.

5. RESOLUTION ON THE INVESTMENT OF THE RESERVES OF INSURANCE COMPANIES IN EUROFIMA LOANS

The Council of Ministers of Transport of the "Eurofima" Restricted Group:

Having met in the Hague on 4th October, 1960;

Considering the Third Annual Report [1] prepared by the Eurofima Company under Article 6 *b*) of the Convention on the constitution of Eurofima, in which Governments signatories to the said Convention are requested to seek a favourable solution to the difficulties encountered in connection with the participation of insurance companies in the issue of Eurofima loans;

Considering the letter of 7th July, 1960, in which the General Manager of the Eurofima Company requests the E.C.M.T. to suggest to the Governments concerned to enter into consultation with a view to overcoming these difficulties, which prevent the Eurofima Company from attaining its purposes;

Considering Article 10 of the Convention;

NOTING with satisfaction that, in some countries signatories to the Convention, insurance companies may already invest their compulsory reserve funds in loans of the Eurofima Company;

RECOGNISING that the application of this measure in the greatest possible number of countries would be of considerable assistance to the Company in attaining its purposes;

On the proposal of the Committee of Deputies of the Restricted Group;

AGREES that the Members of the Council shall, if need be, take steps with the competent authorities in their countries in order to obtain a favourable reply to the request of the Eurofima Company that insurance companies may invest their compulsory reserve funds in its loans;

DECIDES that the Council shall be informed as soon as possible of the outcome of such steps.

---

[1] This Report is set out in Annex IV of the 6th Annual Report of the E.C.M.T.

C. COMPOSITION DES BUREAUX DE LA C.E.M.T.

BUREAU DU CONSEIL DES MINISTRES

Conformément aux dispositions de l'article 1 *a*) du Règlement intérieur, le Conseil des Ministres a procédé, lors de sa séance du 5 octobre 1960, à l'élection de son Bureau, qui est constitué comme suit:

Présidence (*Autriche*):
M. K. WALDBRUNNER, Ministre Fédéral des Transports et de l'Électricité.
Première Vice-Présidence (*Norvège*):
M. T. BRATTELI, Ministre des Communications.
Deuxième Vice-Présidence (*Belgique*):
M. P. W. SEGERS, Ministre des Communications.

BUREAU DU COMITÉ DES SUPPLÉANTS

Par application de l'article 3 du Règlement intérieur, le Bureau du Comité est constitué comme suit:

Présidence (*Autriche*):
M. R. FISCHER, Directeur Général au Ministère Fédéral des Transports et de l'Électricité.
Première Vice-Présidence (*Norvège*):
M. E. FØIEN, Directeur, Ministère des Communications.
Deuxième Vice-Présidence (*Belgique*):
M. M. MALDEREZ, Secrétaire Général du Ministère des Communications.

C. LIST OF OFFICERS OF THE E.C.M.T.

OFFICERS OF THE COUNCIL OF MINISTERS

In accordance with the provisions of Article 1 *a*) of the Rules of Procedure, the Council of Ministers, at its session of 5th October, 1960, elected the following Officers:

Chairmanship (Austria):
Mr. K. WALDBRUNNER, Federal Minister of Transport and Electricity.
First Vice-Chairmanship (Norway):
Mr. T. BRATTELI, Minister of Communications.
Second Vice-Chairmanship (Belgium):
Mr. P. W. SEGERS, Minister of Communications.

OFFICERS OF THE COMMITTEE OF DEPUTIES

In application of Article 3 of the Rules of Procedure, the Officers of the Committee are the following:

Chairmanship (Austria):
Mr. R. FISCHER, Director General, Federal Ministry of Transport and Electricity.
First Vice-Chairmanship (Norway):
Mr. E. FØIEN, Director, Ministry of Communications.
Second Vice-Chairmanship (Belgium):
Mr. M. MALDEREZ, Secretary-General of the Ministry of Communication..

ORGANISATION EUROPÉENNE POUR LA RECHERCHE NUCLÉAIRE (C.E.R.N.)

A. ACTIVITÉS ET STRUCTURE 1960

1. ÉTAT D'AVANCEMENT DES TRAVAUX

a) Bâtiments, eau, électricité

De nouveaux bâtiments auxiliaires destinés à compléter l'équipement expérimental ont été achevés et sont entrés en service, notamment un bâtiment pour les générateurs. Un bâtiment d'essai pour les grandes chambres à bulles et un petit bâtiment pour loger la nouvelle calculatrice I.B.M. sont actuellement en cours de montage.

Dans le secteur expérimental Sud, un hall a été rendu disponible. Vide, il paraissait très vaste au début de l'année. Maintenant, il est rempli d'appareillage expérimental. Trois chambres à bulles, dont deux sont en service et une en construction, occupent à une extrémité de la salle un secteur qui a subi les modifications nécessaires pour permettre d'y utiliser en sécurité l'hydrogène et le propane. Des cibles d'hydrogène liquide sont disposées dans des cabines spéciales situées à même le sol de la salle; ces cibles, les chambres à bulles et les compteurs de Čerenkov à éthylène sous haute pression constituent un ensemble particulièrement explosif dans une grande salle. De sévères précautions ont été prises contre les accidents possibles. A cet effet, il a été nécessaire de prévoir, entre autres, un système d'éclairage anti-déflagrant et des dispositifs de ventilation spéciaux.

Les projets en cours de réalisation de nouveaux laboratoires, d'un nouvel atelier, d'un nouveau bâtiment pour le montage des appareils, ainsi que les projets relatifs au secteur expérimental Est, permettront progressivement de disposer de plus de place pour les expériences avec le synchrotron à protons en 1961.

Tous ces nouveaux projets de construction ont entraîné la révision complète et le développement des services communs des laboratoires, tels que la distribution d'eau et d'électricité. La consommation d'eau de refroidissement a augmenté de 54% par rapport à 1959. La situation est analogue en ce qui concerne l'électricité, dont la consommation qui a augmenté de 46% en 1960, oblige à prévoir pour l'avenir une puissance maximum instantanée de l'ordre de 30 000 kW.

b) Synchro-cyclotron

Le synchro-cyclotron, le premier des deux accélérateurs qui soit entré en service comme instrument de recherche nucléaire, a été utilisé jusqu'à présent à deux fins. En premier lieu, il a servi à la formation des équipes de recherche expérimentale qui ont effectué cette année des travaux de recherche exploratifs en physique nucléaire avec le synchrotron à protons. Pour la majorité des membres de ces équipes, les expériences effectuées avec le S.C. ont constitué le premier contact avec la recherche dans le domaine des hautes énergies. S'il a été possible cette année de transférer sur la grande machine des équipes compétentes pour effectuer des travaux d'expérimentation, cela est dû principalement à la formation et à l'expérience qu'elles avaient acquises avec la petite machine. En second lieu,

CHAPTER VIII

EUROPEAN ORGANIZATION FOR NUCLEAR RESEARCH (C.E.R.N.)

A. PROGRESS AND STRUCTURE 1960

1. PROGRESS

a) Building, water, electricity

New auxiliary buildings to complete the experimental equipment have been finished and are now in use, in particular a generator building. A test building for the large bubble chambers and a small building for the new I.B.M. computer are now being erected.

A hall has been made available in the South Experimental Area. When standing empty at the beginning of the year this appeared very large, but it has already been filled with experimental equipment. Three bubble chambers, two in operation and one under construction, are at one end of the hall which has been modified to make it safe for the use of hydrogen and propane. Liquid hydrogen targets are placed inside special cubicles standing on the floor of the hall; these targets, with the bubble chambers and the high pressure ethylene Cerenkov counters, create special explosion hazards in a large hall. Strict precautions have been taken against possible accidents. For this purpose it has been necessary to provide explosion-proof lighting and a special ventilation system.

The building of new laboratories, a new workshop and a new building for the assembly of equipment, which are all under way, as well as the plans for the East Experimental Area, will make an increasing amount of room available for experiments with the proton synchrotron in 1961.

All these new building schemes have entailed the complete revision and the development of the laboratory common services, such as water and electricity supplies. The consumption of cooling water was 54% higher than in 1959. The same applied to electricity, consumption having increased by 46% in 1960; it has therefore been necessary to cater for a maximum peak demand of the order of 30 000 kW in future.

b) Synchro-cyclotron

The synchro-cyclotron, the first of the two accelerating machines to come into use as a nuclear tool, has been used so far for two purposes. The first was as a training ground for experimental teams which this year have been carrying out the exploratory nuclear physics work with the proton synchrotron. For the majority of the staff of these teams, the synchro-cyclotron experiments have been their first experience in high energy physics research. That is has been possible this year to switch competent teams over to the experimental work with the big machine has been due mainly to the excellent training and experience they gained with the smaller machine. The second purpose of the synchro-cyclotron twa so carry out fundamental research in pion and muon physics. Such le synchro-cyclotron avait pour objet de permettre d'effectuer des travaux de recherche fondamentale sur la physique des mésons et des muons. Les expériences, telles que celles qui avaient été effectuées sur la désintégration π–e ainsi que la mesure actuelle du moment magnétique anormal du muon, connue sous le nom d'expérience $g-2$, constituent sans doute les meilleurs exemples de ce genre de travail.

Le but de cette dernière expérience était de vérifier dans quelle mesure le muon (ou méson mu) peut être apparenté à l'électron, en dépit de la différence considérable des masses qui caractérisent ces deux particules.

L'expérience „$g-2$", tentée par cinq autres laboratoires dans le monde a nécessité deux ans de préparation. Elle a été menée à bonne fin au C.E.R.N. à la mi-décembre. Elle a montré que la valeur expérimentale du moment magnétique du muon concordait avec les chiffres prédits par la théorie, avec une précision de deux parties dans 100.000.

Cet accord entre la théorie et l'expérience permet de tirer des conclusions très importantes pour la recherche destinée à approfondir la connaissance des lois de la nature, et notamment de considérer le muon comme un électron lourd.

Le canal de muons réalisé par la Division du Synchro-cyclotron paraît être le meilleur de ceux qui existent. Certains membres du groupe qui l'ont construit ont été invités aux États-Unis afin de donner des précisions sur la technique que ce groupe a mis en oeuvre.

En plus des huit groupes de la Division du Synchro-cyclotron, sept équipes nationales de physiciens visiteurs ont effectué des expériences sur cet accélérateur, mettant ainsi à profit les 40% du temps de la machine mis à leur disposition.

c) Synchrotron à protons

Le synchrotron à protons a été inauguré en février 1960 avec toute la solennité qui convenait à un événement aussi important de la vie du C.E.R.N. Parmi les centaines de personnalités invitées, on relevait la présence de quatre ministres: le Professeur BALKE, Ministre de l'Énergie atomique de la République Fédérale allemande, M. CALS, Ministre de l'Éducation, des Beaux-Arts et des Sciences des Pays-Bas, Lord HAILSHAM, Ministre de la Science du Royaume-Uni et M. MEDICI, Ministre de l'Éducation d'Italie. Le monde de la science était représenté par des personnalités telles que les Professeurs Niels BOHR, Francis PERRIN, Edoardo AMALDI, Sir John COCKCROFT, Edwin MCMILLAN, J. R. OPPENHEIMER, W. HEISENBERG, P. M. S. BLACKETT et nombre d'autres savants. La présence de plus de cent représentants de la presse témoignait de l'intérêt suscité par cette cérémonie dans le monde entier. C'est le Professeur C. J. BAKKER qui, au nom du personnel du C.E.R.N., répondit aux discours de M. de ROSE, Président du Conseil du C.E.R.N., du Professeur AMALDI, Président du Comité des Directives scientifiques et des Professeurs MCMILLAN et OPPENHEIMER.

Le synchrotron à protons, qui est entré en service à la fin de 1959, a fonctionné durant toute l'année 1960 et il a été mis à la disposition des groupes de physique nucléaire pour des périodes de plus en plus longues au fur et à mesure que l'année avançait. L'intensité du faisceau a été progressivement améliorée au cours des six premiers mois: elle a passé de 2.10^{10} protons par impulsion au début de l'année à 3.10^{11} protons par impulsion durant l'été. L'intensité moyenne actuelle de 10^{11} protons/sec est la plus élevée qui ait été obtenue jusqu'à présent avec un synchrotron à protons et l'énergie maximale de 25–28 GeV du synchrotron à protons du C.E.R.N. n'est dépassée que par une seule autre machine dans le monde, l'A.G.S. de Brookhaven de 30 GeV qui est entré en service au cours de l'automne.

Bien que le temps disponible pour effectuer des expériences de physique experiments as the π-e decay and the current measurement of the anomalous magnetic moment of the muon, the so-called *g*–2 experiment, are, perhaps, the best examples of such work.

The latter experiment was performed in order to discover how far the muon (or mu meson) resembles the electron, in spite of the considerable difference in the mass of these two particles.

The "*g*–2" experiment, attempted by five other laboratories in various parts of the world, called for two years' preparation. It was successfully carried out at C.E.R.N. in mid-December. It showed that the experimental value of the magnetic moment of the muon tallied with that foreseen theoretically, with an accuracy of two parts in 100,000.

As a result of this agreement between theoretical and experimental findings, conclusions were drawn which have a considerable bearing on research into the laws of nature, and in particular the idea that the muon can be regarded as a heavy electron.

The muon channel constructed by the Synchro-cyclotron Division appears to be the best in existence. Some members of the group responsible were invited to the United States to explain the technique used by the group.

In addition to the eight groups of the Synchro-cyclotron Division, seven national teams of visiting physicists performed experiments on this accelerator, thus taking advantage of the 40% of machine time made available to them.

c) Proton Synchrotron

In February 1960, the C.E.R.N. proton synchrotron was inaugurated with all the dignity appropriate to such an important occassion in the life of the C.E.R.N. laboratory. Amongst the hundreds of guests were four Ministers: Professor BALKE, Minister of Atomic Energy of the German Federal Republic; Mr. CALS, Minister of Education, Arts and Sciences of the Netherlands; Lord HAILSHAM, Minister for Science of the United Kingdom and Mr. MEDICI, Minister of Education of Italy. The world of science was represented by Professors Niels BOHR, Francis PERRIN, Edoardo AMALDI, Sir John COCKCROFT, Edwin MCMILLAN, J. Robert OPPENHEIMER, W. HEISENBERG, P. M. S. BLACKETT and many more. The presence of over one hundred press correspondents showed the interest aroused by this ceremony all over the world. The speeches of Mr. de ROSE, the President of the C.E.R.N. Council; Professor AMALDI, the Chairman of the Scientific Policy Committee; Professors MCMILLAN and OPPENHEIMER, were replied to by Professor C. J. BAKKER, Director-General of C.E.R.N., on behalf of the staff of the whole laboratory.

The proton synchrotron, which came into operation for the first time at the end of 1959, has been operated throughout the whole of 1960, and more and more time has become available for nuclear physics experiments as the year proceeded. A steady improvement in beam intensity was achieved in the first six months and starting with 2.10^{10} protons/pulse at the beginning of the year, the intensity was raised to 3.10^{11} protons/pulse by the summer months. The present mean intensity of 10^{11} protons/sec is the highest of any proton synchrotron so far built and the maximum energy of 25–28 GeV can only be exceeded by one other machine in the world, the Brookhaven 30 GeV AGS which came into operation in the autumn of this year.

Although the time available for nuclear physics experiments this year nucléaire ait été assez restreint cette année, il en a été tiré parti pour mettre au point des techniques d'utilisation des cibles qui permettront d'effectuer simultanément plus d'une expérience, ce qui doublera ou triplera les heures effectivement consacrées à la recherche expérimentale. Les cibles donnant des impulsions courtes de particules secondaires, d'une durée se situant entre 200 et 300 sec, et de faible intensité, peuvent être utilisées pour les expériences avec chambres à bulles, tandis que d'autres cibles produisant de longues impulsions allant jusqu'à 400 ms, de haute intensité, peuvent être utilisées simultanément pour les expériences au moyen de compteurs. Le partage du faisceau accéléré entre plusieurs expériences sera encore intensifié lorsque le secteur expérimental Nord sera libéré pour des expériences et que le secteur expérimental Est deviendra disponible.

d) Études théoriques

La Division d'Études théoriques a deux tâches principales dans l'ensemble des activités scientifiques du C.E.R.N. L'une de ces tâches consiste à poursuivre des travaux de recherche fondamentale dans toutes les branches de la théorie qui ont ou peuvent prendre de l'importance pour les recherches dans le domaine de la physique des hautes énergies. L'autre tâche consiste à fournir aux groupes de recherche expérimentale toutes les données théoriques et tous les conseils dont ils peuvent avoir besoin.

Parmi les travaux de recherche fondamentale, il y a lieu de mentionner ceux qui ont été effectués sur la théorie quantique des champs, notamment en ce qui concerne les aspects mathématiques de cet important sujet. Il convient de mentionner aussi les travaux considérables effectués sur les relations de dispersion en vue de mieux comprendre la physique des mésons μ, nucléons et particules étranges dans la région des énergies relativement basses. Il faut signaler enfin les recherches qui ont trait aux phénomènes électrodynamiques à hautes et basses énergies.

Parmi les activités de la seconde catégorie, la Division a notamment effectué des travaux sur les particules étranges et des calculs étendus basés sur la théorie statistique de production multiple de particules dans des collisions de haute énergie. Elle a également fait des prédictions théoriques approximatives concernant les sections efficaces pour l'impact de neutrinos de haute énergie sur des nucléons. Tous ces travaux présentent de l'importance pour les expériences accomplies ou prévues avec le grand accélérateur.

Au cours des derniers mois de 1960, la Division d'Études théoriques s'est orientée plus qu'auparavant vers des activités qui se rapportent à l'exploitation du synchrotron à protons de 25 GeV. Les travaux dans ce domaine se révèlent difficiles, car la physique théorique donne peu d'indications concernant les événements qui se passent à ces énergies élevées. On est amené à procéder par élaboration de diverses hypothèses permettant d'orienter les travaux.

Les théoriciens attachés au C.E.R.N. ont le privilège de se trouver dans une ambiance où des travaux d'expérimentation extrêmement actifs et intéressants se poursuivent dans une nouvelle gamme d'énergies; le nombre de jeunes boursiers et de visiteurs plus expérimentés qui désirent participer à ces travaux suffit à montrer l'intérêt qu'ils suscitent. Bien qu'il n'y ait que neuf membres du personnel à la Division Théorique, l'effectif de la Division, y compris les boursiers et visiteurs, a été de 40 en moyenne cette année.

e) Services scientifiques et techniques

Au C.E.R.N., comme dans d'autres laboratoires de physique des hautes énergies, il s'agit pour l'instant d'analyser quelques dizaines de milliers has been relatively modest, 95 hours in the first quarter, 180 hours in the second, 300 hours in the third and 600 hours planned in the fourth, good use has been made of the remaining operating time to develop target techniques which enable more than one experiment to be run simultaneously, thus doubling or tripling the effective experiment hours. Targets giving short bursts of secondary particles of 200 to 300 sec duration and low intensity for bubble chamber experiments can be used at the same time as other targets giving long bursts of high intensity of up to 400 ms for counter experiments. This sharing of the accelerated beam between several experiments will be even more extensively used when the North experimental area is freed next year, and later on when the East experimental area becomes available.

d) Theoretical Study

The Theoretical Study Division has two main tasks which form part of C.E.R.N.'s scientific work. One is to do fundamental research in all branches of theory which are or might become important for high energy physics research. The other consists in providing the experimental research groups with all the theoretical data and advice which they may require.

Among the fundamental research work it is necessary to mention that done on quantum field theory, especially concerning the mathematical aspects of that important subject. Mention should also be made of the considerable amount of work done on dispersion relations with the aim of arriving at a better understanding of the physics of μ-mesons, nucleons and strange particles in the relatively low energy region. Finally, mention should be made of research relating to electro-dynamic phenomena at high and low energies.

Among activities in the second category, the Division has in particular done work on strange particles and made extensive calculations based on the statistical theory of multiple particle production in high energy collisions. It has also made approximate theoretical forecasts of cross sections for the impact of high energy neutrinos on nucleons. All this work was of great importance for experiments which have been performed or which are planned with the big accelerator.

During the last months of 1960 the Theoretical Study Division was more concerned than previously with activities relating to the exploitation of the 25 GeV proton synchrotron. Work in this field is proving difficult because theoretical physics gives little information about events occurring at such high energies. It is necessary to proceed by elaborating various hypotheses on which to base the work.

Theoreticians working at C.E.R.N. have the unique opportunity of being in the midst of very active and exciting experimental work in a new energy range and the number of young fellows and experienced visitors wanting to participate in these studies bears witness to the interest aroused. Although the total number of C.E.R.N. staff in the Theoretical Division is only nine, the average population including visitors and fellows has been about forty during the year.

e) Scientific and Technical Services

C.E.R.N., like other high energy physics laboratories, has to analyse some tens of thousands of events per year. For this purpose C.E.R.N.

d'événements par an. A cet effet, le C.E.R.N. a mis au point et construit depuis 1956 ses appareils „Iep" en maintenant une collaboration étroite avec Berkeley où les grandes chambres à bulles sont entrées en service assez longtemps avant celles du C.E.R.N. D'autre part, comme ce genre d'activité a pris au C.E.R.N. un essor plus rapide que dans les laboratoires des pays membres, le C.E.R.N. a été en mesure de renseigner ces derniers.

Le problème est sur le point de devenir plus complexe, car il s'agira bientôt, tant en Europe qu'aux États-Unis, d'analyser chaque année plusieurs centaines de milliers de photographies émanant d'un seul laboratoire possesseur d'accélérateur.

Au C.E.R.N., les activités se sont concentrées sur un moyen terme, et notamment sur un type d'appareil qui permettrait d'opérer plus rapidement qu'avec les instruments actuellement disponibles sans mettre en jeu des principes entièrement nouveaux. Cet appareil est en grande partie dû à l'initiative du Professeur Hough de l'université de Michigan, qui vient de passer un an au C.E.R.N., où un premier prototype a été construit.

Les divers experts en la matière, qui se sont réunis à Berkeley en septembre, ont manifesté un grand intérêt pour le nouveau principe mis en oeuvre dans cet appareil et tout récemment deux laboratoires américains ont décidé de développer chez eux l'appareillage basé sur ce nouveau principe, qui représente probablement la première étape vers la réalisation ultérieure de systèmes plus perfectionnés. Il va sans dire que le C.E.R.N. maintient une collaboration étroite avec ces deux laboratoires.

Comme l'an passé, le Groupe Iep a été l'hôte de nombreux visiteurs, stagiaires, boursiers et travailleurs bénévoles qui désirent acquérir de l'expérience dans les techniques d'instrumentation, de programmation et de mesure. Un physicien et un programmeur du Groupe ont fait un stage de plusieurs semaines à Berkeley en amorçant ainsi une collaboration étroite dans la programmation.

Le C.E.R.N. a présenté plusieurs communications aux séances spécialisées de la Conférence de Berkeley, dont un rapport d'ensemble sur les progrès réalisés en Europe.

Depuis novembre, le C.E.R.N. dispose d'une nouvelle calculatrice I.B.M. 709 qui, pour le moment, est la plus puissante en Europe occidentale. Elle est munie d'une mémoire rapide de 32.000 mots, d'un synchronisateur de données, de huit unités à bande magnétique et de l'équipement d'entrée et de sortie en proportion avec ces moyens d'action, ce qui la rend particulièrement apte à manipuler de grandes masses de données. Pour recevoir cette machine un bâtiment a été installé, doté des sources nécessaires de température constante et de courant stabilisé.

Le groupe de physique de santé, depuis la mise en service du synchrotron à protons, travaille à adapter les normes actuelles de protection au caractère du rayonnement de cet accélérateur.

Le C.E.R.N. a publié 43 rapports et 60 articles scientifiques. En annexe figure la liste des principales publications.

f) Autres activités

Une étude approfondie a été effectuée dans le courant de l'année sur les problèmes que pose l'utilisation des deux accélérateurs du C.E.R.N. et de l'appareillage expérimental du laboratoire par des physiciens européens qui n'appartiennent pas à l'Organisation. Le C.E.R.N. compte parmi son personnel des expérimentateurs et des théoriciens, mais il y a également dans le laboratoire un grand nombre de physiciens qui ne sont pas membres du personnel: certains sont au bénéfice de bourses offertes par le C.E.R.N., tandis que d'autres sont rémunérés par divers laboratoires et instituts de recherche européens sur leurs propres budgets. En since 1956, has developed and constructed its Iep equipment, keeping in close touch with Berkeley, where large bubble chambers went into operation some time before those at C.E.R.N. Moreover, as this kind of work has progressed more rapidly at C.E.R.N. than in the laboratories of the Member countries, C.E.R.N. has been able to provide information to the latter.

The problem is about to become more complex, because, both in Europe and the United States it will soon involve analysing several hundred thousands photographs per year from each laboratory possessing a big accelerator.

At C.E.R.N., activities are planned on a medium-term basis and concentrated on a type of equipment which will be faster than the instruments at present available, without the application of entirely new principles. This equipment is largely due to the initiative of Professor HOUGH of the University of Michigan, who has just spent a year at C.E.R.N., where a first prototype has been built.

The various experts in the matter who met at Berkeley in September showed great interest in the new principle used in this apparatus and quite recently two American laboratories have decided to develop equipment along the same lines, which is probably the first step towards the subsequent development of more advanced systems. C.E.R.N. is of course co-operating closely with these two laboratories.

As last year, many visitors, students, fellows and unpaid scientists stayed with the Iep Group to gain experience in instrumentation, programming and measuring techniques. A physicist and a programmer from the Group spent several weeks at Berkeley and thus laid the foundations of a close co-operation in programming.

Several papers were read at the specialist meetings of the Berkeley Conference, including a general report on progress achieved in Europe.

Since November C.E.R.N. has had a new I.B.M. 709 computer which is at present the most powerful in Western Europe. It possesses a fast memory of 32,000 words, a data synchronizer, 8 magnetic tape units and input and output devices in keeping with these facilities, so that the machine is particularly well suited to handle a large volume of data. To house it, a prefabricated building has been put up with all necessary airconditioning and stabilized power supply facilities.

Since the proton synchrotron came into operation, the Health Physics Group has been working to adapt the present regulations governing protection to the type of radiation emitted by this accelerator.

C.E.R.N. has published 43 reports and 60 scientific articles. A list of the main publications is attached.

f) Other activities

The problem of the utilization of the two accelerating machines of C.E.R.N. and the experimental facilities of the laboratory by European physicists from outside C.E.R.N. has received considerable study this year. C.E.R.N. has on its staff experimental physicists and theoreticians but working at the laboratory are a large number of non-C.E.R.N. staff scientists, some paid by C.E.R.N. through fellowships and some paid by the European laboratories and institutes using their own funds. In

1960, le personnel scientifique des diverses catégories était réparti en moyenne de la manière suivante:

	Phys. exp.	Phys. théor.
Personnel du C.E.R.N. (exécutant le programme de recherche)	60	9
Boursiers et attachés de recherche C.E.R.N. (rémunérés sur le budget du C.E.R.N.) . .	23	25
Boursiers Ford (rémunérés par le C.E.R.N. pour le compte de la Fondation Ford) . . .	10	5
Savants visiteurs (non rémunérés par le C.E.R.N.)	50	0
Total	143	39

Tous ces chercheurs utilisent les installations du C.E.R.N., ses services administratifs et techniques ainsi que les faisceaux de particules produits par les accélérateurs. Il y a lieu de leur trouver la place nécessaire pour exécuter leurs travaux et, dans certains cas, pour installer le matériel qu'ils apportent. L'activité globale du C.E.R.N. est la somme de ces diverses activités et elle ne peut être efficace sans appui technique suffisant. En dehors du C.E.R.N. des équipes universitaires utilisent les installations du laboratoire bien qu'elles ne travaillent pas au C.E.R.N. même, car elles dépendent des activités poursuivies à Meyrin; parmi celles-ci se trouvent les équipes qui analysent les émulsions exposées aux faisceaux de particules du S.P., ainsi que les équipes chargées d'analyser les photographies de chambres à bulles. A tout ce personnel scientifique, le C.E.R.N. fournit l'occasion d'effectuer des travaux de recherche fondamentale intéressants. Il n'est donc pas surprenant que l'utilisation du laboratoire, le choix des expériences et la participation aux travaux de recherche posent une série de problèmes qu'il n'est pas facile de résoudre à la satisfaction de tous les intéressés.

Dans le courant de l'année, de nouvelles dispositions relatives aux travaux de recherche du laboratoire ont été élaborées; elles devraient assurer une participation plus directe des équipes de recherche venant de l'extérieur et sans doute faciliter la solution de ce problème. Ce nouveau système part du point de vue qu'il faut amenuiser la distinction entre le personnel du C.E.R.N., les boursiers et visiteurs, en formant des équipes de recherche qui comprendront des physiciens de toutes ces catégories dans des proportions adaptées aux expériences à effectuer et à l'appareillage à utiliser. Ce système fonctionne déjà très bien pour les expériences avec le synchrotron à protons.

Le synchrotron à protons du C.E.R.N. est une machine exceptionnelle qui doit être utilisée par l'élite des physiciens européens. Il existe toutefois d'autres accélérateurs en Europe et, en plus, de leurs activités universitaires, nombre des meilleurs physiciens sont dans l'obligation de les utiliser. Il convient de trouver une solution permettant à ce personnel de participer plus librement aux travaux de recherche du C.E.R.N., ce qui entraînerait sans doute certaines modifications dans les dispositions relatives au personnel universitaire.

g) Budget

Pour la période triennale 1960 à 1962, le Conseil a fixé le plafond du budget à 65 millions par an. Pour l'année 1960, le budget a été de 65 millions.

1960, the average numbers of scientists in the various categories were as follows:

	Exp. Phys.	Theor. Phys.
C.E.R.N. staff (engaged on research programmes)	60	9
C.E.R.N. fellows & research associates (paid by C.E.R.N. funds)	23	25
Ford fellows (paid by Ford Foundation through C.E.R.N.)	10	5
Visiting scientists (not paid by C.E.R.N.)	50	0
Total	143	39

All these scientists use the facilities of the C.E.R.N. laboratory, the administrative services, the technical facilities and the beams of particles from the accelerating machines. They all have to be found space to work on the site and in some cases space has to be found for the apparatus they bring with them. The total represents the scientific effort of the laboratory and to make this effort effective there must be adequate technical assistance. Outside C.E.R.N., but still using facilities of the laboratory, are the teams in the universities who, in general, do not work at C.E.R.N., but who depend on work done at the laboratory, such as the emulsion teams analysing the plates exposed to the particle beams of the proton synchrotron and the teams analysing the bubble chamber photographs. C.E.R.N. provides interesting fundamental research work for all these scientists. It is no wonder that the utilization of the laboratory, the choice of experiments and the participation in the research work should raise problems that are not easy to solve to everybody's satisfaction.

During this year a new system of arranging the research work of the laboratory has been worked out that brings in the external research teams in a more definite manner, which it is hoped will go a long way to solving this problem. Underlying this new system is the idea that distinctions between C.E.R.N. staff, fellows and visitors should be minimized by the formation of research teams containing all such physicists in proportions appropriate to the experiments being done and the apparatus being used. This system is already working very well with the P.S. experiments.

The C.E.R.N. proton synchrotron is an exceptional machine and should be used by the best European physicists. However, there are other machines in Europe and many of the best physicists are committed to use them in addition to their university teaching duties. Some way must be found to allow these people to participate more freely in the research work of C.E.R.N. and this may involve modifications to the staffing ideas of the universities.

g) Budget

For the three-year period 1960–1962 the Council fixed the budget ceiling at 65 million per year. For 1960, the budget was 65 million.

2. CONSEIL, COMITÉS ET STRUCTURE INTERNE

En 1960, il n'a pas été apporté de modifications à la composition du Conseil et de ses Comités.

Le Professeur BAKKER, Directeur général du C.E.R.N. depuis 1955, est mort le 23 avril 1960 alors qu'il se rendait en service aux États-Unis. M. J. B. ADAMS lui a succédé. Le Professeur L. Van HOVE est devenu chef, à temps partiel, de la Division d'Études théoriques, en septembre.

A partir de 1961, la structure interne subira de profondes modifications. Un Directoire, présidé par le Directeur Général, dirigera l'institution. Un nouveau Directeur Général, le Professeur V. F. WEISSKOPF, succédera à M. J. B. ADAMS le 1er août 1961. Les six divisions actuelles seront scindées en douze divisions pour faire face aux activités scientifiques croissantes.

Enfin le nombre des États membres sera porté à quatorze. En effet, le Conseil, à sa dix-huitième session, le 8 décembre 1960, a admis à l'unanimité l'Espagne comme État membre à partir du 1er janvier 1961.

B. PUBLICATIONS

1960

1. LISTE DES RAPPORTS SCIENTIFIQUES

1. LIST OF SCIENTIFIC REPORTS

C.E.R.N. 60–1 GRATREAU, P. *et* MAISONNIER, CH. *Contributions à l'étude des bétatrons à air.*

C.E.R.N. 60–2 KELLER, R., DICK, L. *et* FIDECARO, M. *Une source de protons polarisés. État actuel de la construction.*

C.E.R.N. 60–3 GOEBEL, K. *and* SCHULTES, H. *The cross-section of the reaction* Al^{27} $(p.\ 3pn)Na^{24}$ *at 590 MeV.*

C.E.R.N. 60–4 *Data sheets and status reports on accelerating machines in the energy range 1 GeV and above and models of new machines, presented at the International conference on high-energy accelerators and instrumentation at C.E.R.N.*

C.E.R.N. 60–5 SEPTIER, A. *Étude et réalisation de biprismes électrostatiques utilisables en optique corpusculaire.*

C.E.R.N. 60–6 SEPTIER, A. *Les lentilles magnétiques quadrupolaires sans fer: réalisation de répartitions d'induction à gradient constant.*

C.E.R.N. 60–7 BÖCK, R. *A computer program for least-squares-fit of position of one or more cameras using film measurements of fiducial marks.*

C.E.R.N. 60–8 YORK, C. M., *A transistorized circuit for limiting and shaping the input pulses to a fast coincidence circuit.*

C.E.R.N. 60–9 HORISBERGER, H. *The C.E.R.N. pneumatic transport system.*

C.E.R.N. 60–10 CERULUS, F. *K-meson production in* N-$\bar{N}$ *annihilation computed with a statistical theory.*

C.E.R.N. 60–11 MACLEOD, G. R. *An input programme for measurements of track chamber photographs.*

C.E.R.N. 60–12 MACLEOD, G. R. *Geometrical reconstruction for digitised protractor measurements.*

C.E.R.N. 60–13 MACLEOD, G. R. *A kinematics programme for the analysis of pion-proton elastic scattering.*

C.E.R.N. 60–14 MACLEOD, G. R. *Digitised protractors for the measurement of track chamber photographs.*

2. COUNCIL, COMMITTEES AND INTERNAL STRUCTURE

In 1960 there was no change in the composition of the Council and its committees.

Professor BAKKER, Director-General of C.E.R.N. since 1955, died on 23 April, 1960, while travelling on duty in the United States. He was succeeded by Mr. J. B. ADAMS.

Professor L. VAN HOVE became Leader of the Theoretical Study Division in September, on a part-time basis.

From 1961 onwards the internal structure will be considerably changed. The organization will be managed by a Directorate, presided over by the Director-General. A new Director-General, Professor V. F. WEISSKOPF, will succeed Mr. J. B. ADAMS on 1st August, 1961. The present 6 divisions will be split up into 12 in order to deal with the increasing amount of scientific work.

Finally the number of Member States will be increased to 14. The Council at its eighteenth session on 8 December, 1960, unanimously admitted Spain as a Member State with effect from 1st January, 1961.

C.E.R.N. 60–15 VOGT-NILSEN, N. *The magnetic guide field and the orbital equations for a fixed field two-way scaling accelerator.*

C.E.R.N. 60–16 *Groupe Iep du C.E.R.N. Un mécanisme de transport de film pour instrument pour l'évaluation des photographies.*

C.E.R.N. 60–17 HARTING, D., KLUYVER, J. C. *and* KUSUMEGI, A. *Absolute intensity measurements on the external proton beam of the C.E.R.N. Synchro-cyclotron. A measurement of the cross-section of the reaction* C^{12} *(p, pn)*C^{11} *at 591 MeV incident proton energy.*

C.E.R.N. 60–18 ØVERÅS, H. *On small angle multiple scattering in confined bodies.*

C.E.R.N. 60–19 Not issued.
(The subject matter of the original draft dealing with the geodetic survey of the C.E.R.N. PS, by DECAE and GERVAISE, will be included in "Regenstreif, E. *The C.E.R.N. Proton Synchrotron*. 3rd Part." to be issued in 1961.)

C.E.R.N. 60–20 BEHR, J. V. *and* HAGEDORN, R. *Graphs of lab.-spectra (at different angles (1°, 3°, 5°, 10°, 20°)) of particles produced in 25 GeV pp collisions according to a statistical theory.*

C.E.R.N. 60–21 DERADO, I. *and* VAN DE WALLE, R. *π-p phase-shift analysis with D-waves.*

C.E.R.N. 60–22 VAN DER MEER, S., *Achromatic beam optics for particle separator.*

C.E.R.N. 60–23 C.E.R.N. Proton Synchrotron Machine Group. *Operation and development.* Quarterly report No. 1. January – March 1960.

C.E.R.N. 60–24 MONTAGUE, B. W. *Phase space analogue computer for beam matching problems.*

C.E.R.N. 60–25 ACHERMANN, A. *Caterpillars for loads of up to 80 tons.*

C.E.R.N. 60–26 REGENSTREIF, E. *The C.E.R.N. Proton Synchrotron.* 2nd Part. Ch. 5. Injection.

C.E.R.N. 60–27 MORPURGO, M., HOFFMANN, L. *and* GIBSON, W. M. *Design and construction of a 200 Kgauss pulsed magnet.*

C.E.R.N. 60–28 KRACHT, U. *The linac RF power system below 400 kW.*

C.E.R.N. 60–29 C.E.R.N. Proton Synchrotron Machine Group. *Operation and development.* Quarterly report No. 2. January – March 1960.

C.E.R.N. 60–30 BÖCK, R. *Application of a generalized method of least squares for kinematical analysis of tracks in bubble chambers.*

C.E.R.N. 60–31 BRAMHAM, P. *A co-axial line variable power divider and phase shifter for high power.*

C.E.R.N. 60–32 SCHIFF, L. I. *Note on the calculation of deuteron production in high energy events.*

C.E.R.N. 60–33 MOORHEAD, W. G. *A programme for the geometrical reconstruction of curbed tracks in a bubble chamber.*

C.E.R.N. 60–34 BARBIER, M. *Les limites physiques de la correction de temps de vol dans un photo-multiplicateur.*

C.E.R.N. 60–35 OHKAWA, T. *Notes on the electrostatic instability of neutralized electron beams.*

C.E.R.N. 60–36 MONTANET, L. *Étude expérimentale des interactions nucléaires de l'ordre de 100 GeV.*

C.E.R.N. 60–37 THIERRY, M. *Mesure de la vitesse de pompage en ultra-vide.*

C.E.R.N. 60–38 HEREWARD, H. G. *and* JOHNSEN, K. *The effect of radio-frequency programme noise on the phase-stable acceleration process.*

C.E.R.N. 60–39 SEPTIER, A. *Aberration sphérique de quelques lentilles électrostatiques à symétrie de révolution pour des faisceaux de grande ouverture.*

C.E.R.N. 60–40 MANDL, F. *Symmetry properties of particles and fields.* (C.E.R.N. lectures).

C.E.R.N. 60–41 FERGER, F. *and* SUSINI, A. *Wide band impedance matching by the root locus method. Application to the design of a high power radio-frequency system for an F.F.A.G. accelerator.*

C.E.R.N. 60–42 C.E.R.N. Proton Synchrotron Machine Group, *Operation and development.* Quarterly report No. 3. July-September 1960.

C.E.R.N. 60–43 KELLER, R., DICK, L. *et* FIDECARO, M. *Les essais d'accélération stochastique dans le synchro-cyclotron de 600 MeV et leur interprétation.*

2. LISTE DE TIRÉS A PART
Janvier – juin 1960

2. LIST OF REPRINTS
January – June 1960

ADAMS, J. B. *The C.E.R.N. Proton Synchrotron.*
Repr. from Nature, *185*, (4713), p. 568–572, 1960.

AMATI, D., FIERZ, M. *and* GLASER, V. *High-energy limit of scattering cross sections.*
Repr. from Physical Review Letters, *4*, (2), p. 89–91, 1960.

ASHKIN, J., FAZZINI, T., FIDECARO, G., LIPMAN, N. H., MERRISON, A. W. *and* PAUL, H., *Search for the decay $\mu \rightarrow e + \gamma$ and observation of the decay $\mu \rightarrow e + \nu + \bar{\nu} + \gamma$.*
Repr. from Nuovo Cimento, ser. 10, *14*, p. 1266–1281, 1959.

BUDDE, R., BURGER, A., FILTHUTH, H., GOLDSCHMIDT-CLERMONT, Y., MAYER, H. M., MORRISON, D. R. O., PEYROU, CH. *and* TREMBLEY, J. *Track distortion in a liquid hydrogen bubble chamber.*
Repr. from Nuovo Cimento, ser. 10, *14*, p. 778–786, 1959.

CERULUS, F. *Consequences of a strong π-π interaction in the statistical theory of p-$\bar{p}$ annihilation.*
Repr. from Nuovo Cimento, ser. 10, *14*, p. 827–835, 1959.

CERULUS, F. *Statistical weights of many-particle systems in spin or isospin space.*
Repr. from Nuovo Cimento, Supplemento, ser. 10, *15*, (3), p. 402–425, 1960.

CHARAP, J. M. *and* FUBINI, S. P. *The field-theoretical definition of nuclear potential – II.*
Repr. from Nuovo Cimento, ser. 10, *15*, p. 73–86, 1960.

DAVIS, D. G., HANNA, R. C., HEYMANN, F. F. *and* WHITEHEAD, C. *An experimental test of parity conservation in π^0-meson production by neutrons.*
Repr. from Nuovo Cimento, ser. 10, *15*, p. 641–641, 1960.

d'ESPAGNAT, B. *et* PRENTKI, J. *Incompatibilité entre l'hypothèse de la symétrie restreinte et certains résultats expérimentaux.*
Repr. from Nuovo Cimento, ser. 10, *15*, p. 130–146, 1960.

FARLEY, F. J. M. *Excited nucleon interpretation of high energy nuclear interactions.*
Repr. from Nuovo Cimento, ser. 10, *16*, p. 209–226, 1960.

FIDECARO, G. *The high frequency properties of a coaxial cable and the distortion of fast pulses.*
Repr. from Nuovo Cimento, Supplemento, ser. 10, *15*, (2), p. 254–263, 1960.

FISCHER, J. *and* LUNDBY, A. *Time-to-pulse height converter of wide range.*
Repr. from Review of Scientific Instruments, *31*, (1), p. 10–14, 1960.

FRONSDAL, C. *Completion and embedding of the Schwarzschild solution.*
Repr. from Physical Review, *116*, (3), p. 778–781, 1959.

FRONSDAL, C. *and* GLASHOW, S. L. *μ-meson decay.*
Repr. from Physical Review Letters, *3*, (12), p. 570–571, 1959.

FUBINI, S. *Meson phenomena.*
Repr. from Nuovo Cimento, Supplemento, ser. 10, *14*, (2), p. 283–309, 1959.

FUBINI, S. *and* WALECKA, D. *Dispersion analysis of possible parity non-conservation in low-energy pion-nucleon scattering.*
Repr. from Physical Review, *116*, (1), p. 194–202, 1959.

GOURDIN, M. *and* MARTIN, A. *K^+-deuterium inelastic and exchange scattering – II.*
Repr. from Nuovo Cimento, ser. 10, *14*, p. 722–734, 1959.

GOURDIN, M. *and* MARTIN, A. *Photoproduction of pions on pions.*
Repr. from Nuovo Cimento, ser. 10, *16*, p. 78–95, 1960.

HAGEDORN, R. *A new derivation of the statistical theory of particle production with numerical results for p-p collisions at 25 GeV.*
Repr. from Nuovo Cimento. ser. 10, *15*, p. 434–461, 1960.

HAGEDORN, R. *Note on the high-energy tail of the pion and γ-spectra in p-p collisions at 25 GeV.*
Repr. from Nuovo Cimento, ser. 10, *15*, p. 462–464, 1960.

HAGEDORN, R. *Particle production in 6.2 GeV p-p collisions treated by a statistical model.*
Repr. from Nuovo Cimento, ser. 10, *15*, p. 246–268, 1960.

HILLMAN, P., MIDDELKOOP, W. C., YAMAGATA, T. *and* ZAVATTINI, E. *The π^-–π^0* mass difference.
Repr. from Nuovo Cimento, ser. 10, *14*, p. 887–894, 1959.

KANELLOPOULOS, TH. *and* WILDERMUTH, K. *Anti-symmetrization of "cluster model" wave functions and their expansion in "shell model" wave functions.*
Repr. from Nuclear Physics, *14*, p. 349–375, 1959/60.

KIRSTEIN, P. T. *Some solutions to the equations of steady space charge flow in magnetic fields.*
Repr. from Journal of Electronics and Control, *7*, (5), p. 417–422, 1959.

LINHART, J. G. *Plasma betatron.*
Repr. from Fourth International Conference on Ionization Phenomena in Gases, Uppsala, 17–21 August, 1959. Proceedings. Amsterdam, North-Holland, 1960. p. 981–985.

LINHART, J. G. *and* ORNSTEIN, L. TH. M. *Compression of radiation fields by a magnetically driven plasma shell.*
Repr. from Fourth International Conference on Ionization Phenomena in Gases, Uppsala, 17–21 August, 1959. Proceedings. Amsterdam, North-Holland, 1960. p. 774–777.

LINHART, J. G. *and* ZYCH, W. *Plasma wave-guides and resonators for cm-waves.*
Repr. from Fourth International Conference on Ionization Phenomena in Gases, Uppsala, 17–21 August, 1959. Proceedings. Amsterdam, North-Holland, 1960. p. 778–785.

LUNDBY, A. *Weak interactions. Experiments on parity, charge conjugation and time reversal symmetries.*
Repr. from Progress in Elementary Particle and Cosmic Ray Physics, *5*, p. 1–96, 1960.

LURIÉ, D. *and* POWER, E. A. *Parity non-conservation in pion production.*
Repr. from Nuovo Cimento, ser. 10, *14*, p. 1145–1148, 1959.

MARTIN, A. *Analytic properties of $e \neq o$ partial wave amplitudes for a given class of potentials.*
Repr. from Nuovo Cimento, ser. 10, *15*, p. 99–109, 1960.

MEYER, PH. *and* SALZMAN, *The $\mu \rightarrow e + \gamma$ decay and the intermediate charged vector boson theory.*
Repr. from Nuovo Cimento, ser. 10, *14*, p. 1310–1321, 1959.

SAWYER, R. F. *Decay of the charged pion.*
Repr. from Physical Review, *116*, (1), p. 231–235, 1959.

SCARF, F. L. *Equations of motion for renormalized fields.*
Repr. from Nuovo Cimento, ser. 10, *14*, p. 849–855, 1959.

SCARF, F. L. *Thirring model with variable interaction.*
Repr. from Physical Review, *117*, (3), p. 868–872, 1960.

TARGONSKI, GY. *Approximation of velocity-dependent potentials by separable kernels.*
Repr. from Nuovo Cimento, ser. 10, *14*, p. 1093–1101, 1959.

THIRRING, W. *Three-field theory of strong interactions.*
Repr. from Nuclear Physics, *14*, p. 565–577, 1959/60.

WESS, J. E. *Investigation of the invariance group in the three fundamental fields model.*
Repr. from Nuovo Cimento, ser. 10, *15*, p. 52–72, 1960.

YAMAGUCHI, Y. *A composite theory of elementary particles.*
Repr. from Progress of Theoretical Physics, Supplement, *11*, p. 1–36, 1959.

YAMAGUCHI, Y. *A model of strong interactions.*
Repr. from Progress of Theoretical Physics, Supplement, *11*, p. 37–51, 1959.

3. LISTE DE TIRÉS A PART
Juillet – décembre 1960

3. LIST OF REPRINTS
July – December 1960

AMATI, D., LEADER, E. *and* VITALE, B. *Theory of low energy nucleon-nucleon scattering – I.*
Repr. from Nuovo Cimento, ser. 10, *17*, p. 68–97, 1960.

ASCOLI, R. *and* MINGUZZI, A. *Analyticity properties of production amplitudes.*
Repr. from Physical Review, *118*, (5), p. 1435–1438, 1960.

ASHKIN, J., FAZZINI, T., FIDECARO, G., GOLDSCHMIDT-CLERMONT, Y., LIPMAN, N. H., MERRISON, A. W. *and* PAUL, H. *A new measurement of the mean life of the positive pion.*
Repr. from Nuovo Cimento, ser. 10, *16*, p. 490–504, 1960.

BACKENSTOSS, G. K., FRAUENFELDER, H., HYAMS, B. D., KOESTER, L. J. *and* MARIN, P. C. *An investigation of the stability of nucleons.*
Repr. from Nuovo Cimento, ser. 10, *16*, p. 749–755, 1960.

BERNSTEIN, J., FUBINI, S., GELL-MANN, M. *and* THIRRING, W. *On the decay rate of the charged pion.*
Repr. from Nuovo Cimento, ser. 10, *17*, p. 757–766, 1960.

BOWCOCK, J., COTTINGHAM, W. N. *and* LURIÉ, D. *Effect of a pion-pion scattering resonance on low energy pion-nucleon scattering.*
Repr. from Nuovo Cimento, ser. 10, *16*, p. 918–938, 1960.

BOWCOCK, J., COTTINGHAM, W. N. *and* LURIÉ, D. *π-π scattering, nucleon structure, and π-N scattering.*
Repr. from Physical Review Letters, *5*, (8), p. 386–398, 1960.

BRIDGE, H., BUDDE, R., BURGER, A., FILTHUTH, H., MORRISON, D. R. O., PEYROU, CH. *and* TREMBLEY, J. *Some vacuum problems at low temperatures.* (Presented at the 1st International Congress on Vacuum Technology, Namur, Belgium, June 1958).
Repr. from "Advances in vacuum science and technology, Vol. 2", London, Pergamon Press, 1960.

CHARPAK, G., LEDERMAN, L. M., SENS, J. C. *and* ZICHICHI, A. *A method for trapping muons in magnetic fields, and its application to a redetermination of the E.D.M. of the muon.*
Repr. from Nuovo Cimento, ser. 10, *17*, p. 288–303, 1960.

CINI, M. *and* FUBINI, S. *Theory of low-energy scattering in field theory.*
Repr. from Annals of Physics, *10*, (3), p. 352–389, 1960.

COCCONI, V. T., FAZZINI, T., FIDECARO, G., LEGROS, M., LIPMAN, N. H., *and* MERRISON, A. W. *Mass analysis of the secondary particles produced by the 25-GeV proton beam of the C.E.R.N. Proton Synchrotron.*
Repr. from Physical Review Letters, *5*, (1), p. 19–21, 1960.

DERADO, I. *Experimental evidence for the pion-pion interaction at 1 GeV.*
Repr. from Nuovo Cimento, ser. 10, *15*, p. 853–855, 1960.

FAISSNER, H. *and* SCHNEIDER, H. *Direct processes and collective effects in high energy proton induced fission.*
Repr. from Nuclear Physics, *19*, p. 346–365, 1960.

FUBINI, S. *and* STROFFOLINI, R. *Some remarks about the spectral representation of the $K^{\pm} \rightarrow 3\pi$ decay amplitude.*
Repr. from Nuovo Cimento, ser. 10, *17*, p. 263–266, 1960.

GOURDIN, M. *and* MARTIN, A. *Pion photon scattering.*
Repr. from Nuovo Cimento, ser. 10, *17*, p. 224–243, 1960.

HAGEDORN, R. *Deuteron production in high-energy collisions.*
Repr. from Physical Review Letters, *5*, (6), p. 276–277, 1960.
HARTING, D., KLUYVER, J. C., KUSUMEGI, A., RIGOPOULOS, R., SACHS, A. M., TIBELL, G., VANDERHAEGHE, G. *and* WEBER, G. *Experiment on charge independence in interactions of nucleons and pions.*
Repr. from Physical Review, *119*, (5), p. 1716–1725, 1960.
KÖHLER, H. S. *Electromagnetic corrections to the ratio* $\sigma(p + d \rightarrow H^3 + \pi^+)/\sigma(p + d \rightarrow He^3 + \pi^\circ)$.
Repr. from Physical Review, *118*, (5), p. 1345–1350, 1960.
MEYER, PH. *and* PRENTKI, J. *On a contradiction between experimental results on nucleon form factors and certain symmetries of strong interactions.*
Repr. from Nuovo Cimento, ser. 10, *18*, p. 203–205, 1960.
MINGUZZI, A. *and* STREATER, R. F. *Some remarks on the vertex function.*
Repr. from Physical Review, *119*, (3), p. 1127–1128, 1960.

D. PERSONNEL SUPÉRIEUR DU C.E.R.N.

1960

Division d'Études théoriques

GLASER V. PETERMANN A. PRENTKI J.

Division du Synchrotron à protons

BONAUDI, F.
DECAE, A.
GERMAIN, P.
GRUETTER, F.
HEREWARD, H. G.
HINE, M. G. N.
JOHNSEN, K.
LAPOSTOLLE, P.
PEYROU, Ch.
RAMM, C. A.
SCHMEISSNER, F.
SCHMELZER, Ch.
SCHOCH, A.
STANDLEY, P. H.
ZILVERSCHOON, C.

Division du Synchro-cyclotron

ASTBURY, P.
CITRON, A.
COCCONI, G.
VON DARDEL, G.
FIDECARO, G.
HEDIN, B.
LUNDBY, A.
PIZER, H. I.

Division des Services scientifiques et techniques

COBLANS, H. GOLDSCHMIDT-CLERMONT, Y.

Division Site et Bâtiments

WEBB, F. A. R.

Division de l'Administration

PENNEY, R. W. SCHOU OLSEN, F. TIÈCHE, C.

MONTANET, L., NEWTH, J. A., PETRUCCI, G., SALMERON, R. A. *and* ZICHICHI, A. *A cloud chamber study of nuclear interactions with energies of about 100 GeV.*
Repr. from Nuovo Cimento, ser. 10, *17*, p. 166–188, 1960.
SALZMAN, F. *and* G. *Pion production from* $\pi^- - p$ *collisions in the long-range interaction model.*
Repr. from Physical Review, *120*, (2), p. 599–608, 1960.
SELLERI, F. *Evidence for two pion-pion resonances.*
Repr. from Nuovo Cimento, ser. 10, *16*, p. 775–779, 1960.
STREATER, R. F. *Double commutator in quantum field theory.*
Repr. from Journal of Mathematical Physics, *1*, (3), p. 231–233, 1960.
YAMAGUCHI, Y. *Classification of composite bosons in the Sakata model.*
Repr. from Progress of Theoretical Physics, *23*, (5), p. 882–886, 1960.
YAMAGUCHI, Y. *Interactions induced by high energy neutrinos.*
Repr. from Progress of Theoretical Physics, *23*, (6), p. 1117–1137, 1960.

D. C.E.R.N. SENIOR STAFF
1960

Theoretical Study Division

GLASER, V. PETERMANN, A. PRENTKI J.

Proton Synchrotron Division

BONAUDI, F.
DECAE, A.
GERMAIN, P.
GRUETTER, F.
HEREWARD, H. G.
HINE, M. G. N.
JOHNSEN, K.
LAPOSTOLLE, P.
PEYROU, CH.
RAMM, C. A.
SCHMEISSNER, F.
SCHMELZER, Ch.
SCHOCH, A.
STANDLEY, P. H.
ZILVERSCHOON, C.

Synchro-cyclotron Division

ASTBURY, P.
CITRON, A.
COCCONI, G.
VON DARDEL, G.
FIDECARO, G.
HEDIN, B.
LUNDBY, A.
PIZER, H. I.

Scientific and Technical Services Division

COBLANS, H. GOLDSCHMIDT-CLERMONT, Y.

Site and Buildings Division

WEBB. F. A. R.

Administration Division

PENNEY, R. W. SCHOU OLSEN, F. TIÈCHE, C.

C. CONSEIL DE L'ORGANISATION

COMPOSITION

BUREAU DU CONSEIL [1] *Président:* M. François de Rose (France)
Vice-Présidents: Professeur W. Heisenberg (République Fédérale allemande)
M. J. Willems (Belgique)

DÉLÉGATIONS (Deux délégués par État membre) [2]												
Autriche	Belgique	Danemark	France	Grèce	Italie	Norvège	Pays-Bas	République Fédérale allemande	Royaume-Uni de Grande-Bretagne et d'Irlande du Nord	Suède	Suisse	Yougoslavie
Dr E. Treu Professeur W. Thirring	M. J. Willems Professeur J. Franeau	Professeur J. K. Bøggild M. O. Obling	M. F. de Rose Professeur F. Perrin	Professeur T. G. Kouyoumzelis M. A. Vlachos	Professeur E. Amaldi M. G. B. Toffolo	Professeur B. Trumpy Professeur J. Holtsmark	M. J. H. Bannier Professeur J. de Boer	Professeur W. Heisenberg Dr A. Hocker	Sir John Cockcroft Sir Harry Melville	Dr G. Funke Professeur I. Waller	Professeur P. Scherrer M. A. de Senarclens	Professeur I. Supek M. D. Baum

COMITÉ DES DIRECTIVES SCIENTIFIQUES

Président Professeur E. Amaldi [1]
Vice-Président Professeur L. Leprince-Ringuet
Membres Professeur N. Bohr
Sir John Cockcroft
Professeur W. Heisenberg
Professeur C. Møller
Professeur F. Perrin
Professeur C. F. Powell
Professeur P. Scherrer

COMITÉ DU CONSEIL

Président
le Président du Conseil
M. F. de Rose (France)
Membres
les Vice-Présidents du Conseil
Professeur W. Heisenberg (République Fédérale allemande)
M. J. Willems (Belgique)
le Président du Comité des Directives scientifiques
Professeur E. Amaldi (Italie)
le Président du Comité des Finances
M. J. H. Bannier (Pays-Bas)
Membres du Conseil [1]
Professeur F. Regler (Autriche)
Professeur B. Trumpy (Norvège)
Sir Harry Melville (Royaume-Uni)

COMITÉ DES FINANCES

Président M. J. H. Bannier (Pays-Bas) [1]
Membres un délégué par État membre

[1] *Depuis le 1er janvier 1961:*
Conseil: Président: M. J. Willems (Belgique); Vice-Présidents: Professeur E. Amaldi (Italie); M. J. H. Bannier (Pays-Bas).
Comité du Conseil: Membres (autres que les membres en faisant partie d'office): Professeur J. K. Bøggild (Danemark); M. F. de Rose (France); Professeur P. Scherrer (Suisse), Professeur I. Supek (Yougoslavie); réélu: Sir Harry Melville (Royaume-Uni).
Comité des Directives Scientifiques: Président: Professeur C. F. Powell (Royaume-Uni). *Es-qualités:* Professeur B. Gregory (France), Président, Comité des Chambres à trajectoires; Professeur G. Salvini (Italie), Président, Comité des Expériences électroniques; Professeur C. F. Powell (Royaume-Uni) Président, Comité des Emulsions.
Comité des Finances: Président: Dr. A. Hocker (République Fédèrale allemande).
Substituts à certaines sessions du Conseil:
Professeur F. Regler (Autriche); Professeur J. Cnops (Belgique); M. J. Tsambiras (Grèce); M. S. C. Sommerfelt, Professeur A. Wergeland (Norvège); Professeur S. A. Wouthuysen (Pays-Bas); Professeur W. Jentschke (République Fédérale allemande); M. T. G. Pickavance, Mr. H. L. Verry (Royaume-Uni); Dr A. [illegible] (Yougoslavie).

C. COUNCIL OF THE ORGANIZATION

STRUCTURE AND MEMBERSHIP

OFFICERS OF THE COUNCIL [1] *President:* Mr. François de Rose (France)
Vice-Presidents: Professor W. Heisenberg (German Federal Republic)
Mr. J. Willems (Belgium)

DELEGATIONS (Two delegates from each Member State) [2]

Austria	Belgium	Denmark	France	German Federal Republic	Greece	Italy	Netherlands	Norway	Sweden	Switzerland	United Kingdom of Great Britain and Northern Ireland	Yugoslavia
Dr E. Treu Professor W. Thirring	Mr. J. Willems Professor J. Franeau	Professor J. K. Bøggild Mr. O. Obling	Mr. F. de Rose Professor F. Perrin	Professor W. Heisenberg Dr. A. Hocker	Professor T. G. Kouyoumzelis Mr. A. Vlachos	Professor E. Amaldi Mr. G. B. Toffolo	Mr. J. H. Bannier Professor J. de Boer	Professor B. Trumpy Professor J. Holtsmark	Dr. G. Funke Professor I. Waller	Professor P. Scherrer Mr. A. de Senarclens	Sir John Cockcroft Sir Harry Melville	Professor I. Supek Mr. D. Baum

SCIENTIFIC POLICY COMMITTEE

Chairman Professor E. Amaldi [1]
Vice-Chairman Professor L. Leprince-Ringuet
Members Professor N. Bohr
Sir John Cockcroft
Professor W. Heisenberg
Professor C. Møller
Professor F. Perrin
Professor C. F. Powell
Professor P. Scherrer

COMMITTEE OF THE COUNCIL

Chairman
the President of the Council
Mr. F. de Rose (France)
Members
the Vice-Presidents of the Council
Professor W. Heisenberg (German Federal Republic)
Mr. J. Willems (Belgium)
the Chairman of the Scientific Policy Committee
Professor E. Amaldi (Italy)
the Chairman of the Finance Committee
Mr. J. H. Bannier (Netherlands)
Members of the Council [1]
Professor F. Regler (Austria)
Professor B. Trumpy (Norway)
Sir Harry Melville (United Kingdom)

FINANCE COMMITTEE

Chairman Mr. J. H. Bannier (Netherlands) [1]
Members one delegate from each Member State

[1] *Since 1st January, 1961:*
Council: President: Mr. J. Willems (Belgium); Vice-Presidents: Professor E. Amaldi (Italy); Mr. J. H. Bannier (Netherlands).
Committee of the Council: (Other than ex officio members); Professor J. K. Bøggild (Denmark); Mr. F. de Rose (France); Professor P. Scherrer (Switzerland); Professor I. Supek (Yugoslavia); re-elected: Sir Harry Melville (United Kingdom).
Scientific Policy Committee: Chairman: Professor C. F. Powell (United Kingdom). *Ex officio:* Professor B. Gregory (France), Chairman, Track Chamber Experiments Committee; Professor G. Salvini (Italy), Chairman, Electronic Experiments Committee; Professor C. F. Powell (United Kingdom), Chairman Emulsion Experiments Committee.
Finance Committee: Chairman: Dr. A. Hocker (German Federal Republic).
[2] *Alternates at certain Council sessions:*
Professor F. Regler (Austria); Professor J. Cnops (Belgium); Professor W. Jentschke (German Federal Republic); Mr. J. Tsambiras (Greece); Professor S. A. Wouthuysen (Netherlands); Mr. S. C. Sommerfelt; Professor A. Wergeland (Norway); Mr. T. G. Pickavance, Mr. H. L. Verry (United Kingdom); Dr. A. Moljk (Yugoslavia).

CHAPITRE IX

CONFÉRENCE EUROPÉENNE DES ADMINISTRATIONS DES POSTES ET DES TÉLÉCOMMUNICATIONS

Note de la rédaction

Un article paraissant dans le Volume VII de** l'Annuaire Européen **a décrit les diverses étapes de l'instauration de cette nouvelle organisation européenne (pp. 100–115) et les textes y afférents se trouvent à la Section documentaire du même volume VII (pp. 636–659). La Conférence a tenu sa première session à Paris du 19–29 octobre 1960. On trouvera ici un résumé des travaux de la session.

SESSION DE PARIS DE LA C.E.P.T.

19–29 octobre 1960

Toutes les Administrations membres de la C.E.P.T. étaient représentées, à l'exclusion de celle de la Turquie, à la Session de Paris qui a réuni 112 Délégués.

Les travaux se sont déroulés, soit en Assemblée plénière pour l'examen de questions d'ordre général ou intéressant à la fois les Postes et les Télécommunications, soit au sein de Commissions spécialisées „Postes" et „Télécommunications".

Une parfaite compréhension et une volonté unanime de parvenir à des résultats positifs se sont manifestées tout au cours des débats dont les principaux sujets sont rappelés ci-après:

QUESTIONS INTÉRESSANT L'ASSEMBLÉE PLÉNIÈRE

Sept études proposées par les Administrations membres ont été retenues et seront entreprises dans les conditions suivantes:

Introduction d'un clearing pour les décomptes de taxes
(proposition suisse)

L'étude de cette question a été confiée à un Groupe de travail dirigé par la Suisse qui s'est déjà réuni au cours de la session et qui formulera des propositions concrètes l'année prochaine.

Échange de publications et d'informations entre les services bibliothécaires
(proposition suisse)

Une Recommandation préconisant l'échange d'informations et de renseignements sur les publications nouvelles a été adoptée.

Un Groupe de traivail dirigé par la Suisse s'emploiera à donner son plein effet à cette Recommandation.

Enquête sur les possibilités d'améliorer les prix de revient
(proposition française)

Une enquête portant sur les conditions de gestion financière des différentes Administrations sera effectuée à la diligence de la France, Rapporteur du Groupe de travail institué pour l'étude de cette question.

Information du public en matière de Postes et de Télécommunications
(proposition française)

Un mémento contenant les méthodes de travail en matière de „relations publiques" sera présenté par la France au cours de la prochaine session.

CHAPTER IX

EUROPEAN CONFERENCE OF POSTAL AND TELECOMMUNICATIONS ADMINISTRATIONS

Editor's Note

An article in Vol. VII of the European Yearbook *(pp. 100–115) described the creation of this new European organisation, while its statutory texts were published in the Documentary Section of Vol. VII (pp. 637–659).*

The Conference held its first session in Paris from 19th to 29th October, 1960, and the following is a summary of the proceedings of the first session.

SESSION IN PARIS OF THE E.C.P.T.

19th–29th October, 1960

With the exception of Turkey, all member Administrations of the E.C.P.T. were represented at the Paris Session, which was attended by a total of 112 delegates.

General questions, or those of interest to both Postal and Telecommunications Administrations, were debated in the Plenary Assembly, while other business was dealt with by the specialised "Postal" or "Telecommunications" Committees.

Complete agreement and a unanimous desire to achieve positive results were evidenced throughout the debates. The subjects chiefly discussed were:

PLENARY ASSEMBLY

Seven surveys proposed by the member Administrations were agreed and will be undertaken as follows:

Introduction of a clearing house for the calculation of charges
(Swiss proposal)

This question is to be studied by a working party under Swiss Chairmanship. It met during the Session and will draw up concrete proposals next year.

Exchange of publications and information between library services
(Swiss proposal)

A Recommendation was adopted advocating the exchange of information on new publications.

A working party, headed by Switzerland, will consider ways and means of giving full effect to this Recommendation.

Enquiry into the possibilities of improving operating costs
(French proposal)

An enquiry into the conditions of financial management in the various Administrations will be carried out on the proposal of France, Rapporteur of the working party set up to study this question.

Keeping the public informed on postal and telecommunication matters
(French proposal)

A memorandum describing "public relations" procedure will be presented by France at the next Session.

Organisation de stages de fonctionnaires européens
(proposition française)

La France a été chargée de définir, au cours des mois à venir, une méthode pratique pour l'organisation de tels stages.

Échanges d'enfants
(proposition française)

Un Groupe de travail – comprenant l'Allemagne, l'Autriche, la Belgique, la France, la Grande-Bretagne et l'Italie – a été chargé de prendre toutes les dispositions pour organiser des échanges dès l'été prochain, de façon que les conclusions pratiques puissent être tirées de cette première expérience au cours de la prochaine session.

QUESTIONS INTÉRESSANT LA COMMISSION „POSTES"

I. TRAVAUX EN COURS DEPUIS LA RÉUNION DE MONTREUX

– Les *résultats* concrets ci-après ont été acquis:

1. Adoption d'une résolution visant à l'émission annuelle d'un „timbre Européen";

Pour l'anneé 1961, il a été décidé que l'émission aurait lieu le lundi 18 septembre dans les Pays qui décideront d'y participer.

2. Simplification des formalités d'exécution visant l'échange des dépêches postales et le service des colis postaux, mesures qui favoriseront l'accélération des relations postales entre les Pays membres;

3. Adoption de deux recommandations:

- l'une invitant les Administrations qui ont déjà rétabli l'échange des envois contre-remboursement à lui donner son plein développement en s'efforçant de porter dès que possible le montant des envois au maximum de 1.000 francs-or prévu par l'Arrangement de l'U.P.U. sur ce service;
- l'autre visant à assimiler à la perte, dans les relations entre les membres de la C.E.P.T., la spoliation totale ou l'avarie du contenu des envois recommandés sous réserve de certaines garanties concernant l'emballage de ces objets.

L'application de ces deux recommandations apportera une amélioration de la qualité du service qui sera certainement appréciée du public européen.

– Par ailleurs, les travaux vont se poursuivre en ce qui concerne:

- le tri automatique des lettres,
- la création d'ambulants transeuropéens,
- l'instauration d'une politique tarifaire européenne,
- l'automation dans le service des chèques postaux,
- la simplification de la poste aérienne,
- l'utilisation en commun des sacs postaux.

II. NOUVEAUX TRAVAUX

Adoption de toutes les possibilités offertes par certaines dispositions facultatives de la Convention Postale Universelle et de ses Arrangements
(proposition autrichienne)

Cette question sera étudiée, sous la direction de l'Autriche, par les Administrations de Belgique, de France, de Grande-Bretagne et de Suisse, avec le concours d'experts qualifiés en matière de poste aux lettres, de poste aérienne et de services financiers.

A noter que, sur une suggestion française, l'extension des échanges réciproques de bons postaux de voyage sera examinée par priorité.

Courses for European civil servants (French proposal)

France was instructed to work out, during the coming months, practical arrangements for such courses.

Exchanges of children (French proposal)

A working party, composed of Germany, Austria, Belgium, France, the United Kingdom and Italy, was instructed to take steps to arrange exchanges next summer, so that practical conclusions might be drawn from this initial experiment at the next Session.

"POSTAL "COMMITTEE

I. CURRENT WORK SINCE THE MONTREUX MEETING

Results:

1. Adoption of a Resolution for the annual issue of a "European stamp";

It was decided that in 1961 the issue would be made on Monday, 18th September, in participating countries.

2. Simplification of formalities for sending telegrams and parcels; procedure for speeding up postal communications between member countries.

3. Adoption of two Recommendations:

- inviting Administrations which have re-introduced cash-on-delivery mail to develop this system to the full by raising, as soon as possible, the sum which can be sent to 1,000 gold francs, as provided for by the relevant U.P.U. Agreement;
- counting as loss, as between members of the E.C.P.T., damage to or theft of the entire contents of registered mail, subject to certain safeguards concerning packaging;

Implementation of these two Recommendations will bring about an improvement in services which will most surely be appreciated by the European public.

Work will continue on the following matters:

- automatic sorting of letters;
- introduction of a trans-European mail-sorting service;
- adoption of a European policy for postal rates;
- automation in the "postal cheque" service;
- simplification of the air-mail service;
- pooling of mail bags.

II. NEW WORK

Adoption of all possibilities offered by certain optional provisions of the Universal Postal Convention and its Arrangements (Austrian proposal)

This question will be discussed, under the Chairmanship of Austria, by the Belgian, French, United Kingdom and Swiss Administrations with the assistance of qualified experts in letter post, air-mail and financial transaction matters.

It should be noted that a French proposal to extend reciprocal exchanges of postal travel vouchers will be given priority consideration.

Création d'un „timbre européen"
(proposition suisse)
Un Groupe de travail composé de la Suisse, Rapporteur, de l'Autriche et de la Grèce va étudier la possibilité de créer un „timbre européen" utilisable dans tous les Pays de la C.E.P.T. et dont la valeur fixé ne correspondrait pas obligatoirement à l'affranchissement exact d'un objet de correspondance.

Problèmes particuliers au service des Cheques Postaux et des Articles d'Argent
Sur l'initiative de la France, diverses questions (comme par exemple la mécanisation des opérations de paiement à domicile, le tri des documents dans le service des chequès postaux, *etc.* ...) vont faire l'objet d'un examen particulier.

Préparation en commun du Congrès Postal Universel de Rio de Janeiro
Conformément aux objectifs que s'est assignés la C.E.P.T., les Administrations membres prépareront en commun le prochain Congrès Postal Universel (Rio de Janeiro, juin 1962).

Une procédure d'examen a été définie en ce qui concerne aussi bien les propositions formulées par les Administrations de la C.E.P.T. que celles émanant des autres Administrations.

QUESTIONS INTÉRESSANT LA COMMISSION „TÉLÉCOMMUNICATIONS"

1. – Six recommandations ont été adoptées, qui permettront la mise en oeuvre de nouvelles procédures ou l'application de nouveaux tarifs, et ceci dans certains cas, dès l'année 1961.

Deux d'entre elles apportent des simplifications dans la comptabilité télégraphique internationale par l'adoption de méthodes de comptabilité simplifiées et la suppression de la notification d'acceptation des comptes télégraphiques entre les Administrations membres de la C.E.P.T.

Une troisième recommandation se rapporte aux locations de circuits par les organismes de radiodiffusion. Elle prévoit un tarif unique pour les circuits de type ancien et ceux de type normal, ce qui présente un intérêt pour les auditeurs. En effet, les organismes de radiodiffusion, n'ayant plus de surtaxe à acquitter pour les circuits de haute qualité, seront portés à nous demander de préférence l'utilisation de ceux-ci.

Le calcul des différentes taxes unitaires a été également modifié et le lien qui existait avec la taxe des conversations téléphoniques a été supprimé.

Deux autres recommandations se rapportent à l'exploitation et à la tarification téléphoniques: l'une prévoit la suppression de la taxe rémunérant l'intervention d'un centre de transit international automatique dans l'exploitation semi-automatique et automatique; l'autre donne des directives, dont l'application pourrait faire l'objet de conventions bilatérales, pour l'introduction d'un tarif de nuit de service automatique intégral.

Enfin, dans le domaine des radiocommunications, une recommandation a été adoptée. Elle se rapporte à la lutte contre les émissions illicites de radiodiffusion faites à partir d'avions ou de navires.

2. – Un quatrième Groupe de travail, intitulé „Transmissions télévisuelles et sonores", qui s'ajoute aux trois Groupes de travail Télégraphe, Téléphone et Radiocommunications existants, a été créé pour l'étude de problèmes techniques ou d'exploitation relatifs aux transmissions visuelles et sonores, et en particulier, de ceux qui peuvent nous être soumis par l'U.E.R.

"European" stamp (Swiss proposal)

A working party, composed of Switzerland (Rapporteur), Austria and Greece, will study the possibility of having a European stamp which can be used in all E.C.P.T. countries, with a fixed value which would not necessarily correspond exactly to the postage required.

Special problems connected with the "postal cheque" service and sending of money

On a French proposal, various questions (such as the mechanisation of arrangements for payments at payee's address, sorting in the "postal cheque" department *etc.*) will be given special consideration.

Joint preparation of the Universal Postal Congress in Rio de Janeiro

In accordance with the aims of the E.C.P.T., the member Administrations will jointly make arrangements for the next Universal Postal Congress (Rio de Janeiro, June 1962).

A procedure has been established for examining proposals put forward by E.C.P.T. Administrations and other Administrations.

"TELECOMMUNICATIONS" COMMITTEE

1. Six Recommendations were adopted for the introduction of new methods or new rates; some of these will come into force in 1961.

Two Recommendations are concerned with simplified methods of international telegraphic accounting and abolishing acknowledgement of telegraphic accounts between E.C.P.T. member Administrations.

A third Recommendation concerns the reserving of lines by broadcasting organisations. It provides for a single rate for old type and normal lines which is advantageous for listeners. Since broadcasting organisations no longer have to pay a surcharge for high quality lines, such lines are likely to be preferred whenever possible.

Calculation of the various unit charges has also been altered and the former relationship with telephone conversation charges has been abolished.

Two other Recommendations refer to telephone charges: one abolishes the charge for using an automatic international exchange in connection with semi-automatic and automatic systems; the other contains rules – which might form the basis of bilateral conventions – for the introduction of a night rate in a completely automatic service.

Finally, a Recommendation was adopted concerning radiocommunications. It refers to suppressing unauthorised transmissions from ships or aircraft.

2. A fourth working party, to be known as "Television and Sound Transmissions", additional to the three working parties already in existence, "Telegraph", "Telephone" and "Radiocommunications", was set up to study technical problems or problems relating to the exploitation of visual or sound broadcasting, in particular those submitted to us by the E.B.U.

Par ailleurs, les travaux vont se poursuivre en ce qui concerne:
- la tarification télégraphique entre les pays de la C.E.P.T.,
- l'introduction d'un service de „téléxogrammes",
- le développement du service mobile terrestre radiotéléphonique en Europe,
- les rayonnements radioélectriques des installations industrielles, scientifiques et médicales,
- le service de radioastronomie,
- les services de radiocommunications „Espace" et „Terre-Espace",
- les mesures à prendre pour empêcher le fonctionnement de stations de radiodiffusion à bord de navires ou d'aéronefs hors des limites des territoires nationaux (suite de la recommandation déjà adoptée).

De plus, les travaux des Groupes de travail en activité ont donné les résultats suivants:

1. *Groupe de travail „Télégraphe":*

- création d'un centre de commutation européen pour l'écoulement du trafic télex avec l'Amérique par câble transatlantique en vue d'augmenter le rendement des circuits télégraphiques intercontinentaux.

2. *Groupe de travail „Téléphone"*

- création d'un centre de commutation européen pour le trafic téléphonique avec l'Amérique en vue également d'augmenter le rendement des circuits téléphoniques intercontinentaux;
- dépôt à l'avance de demandes de communications téléphoniques pendant la période de fin d'année;
- diminution du nombre d'échelons de taxes en exploitation automatique en vue de simplifier les équipements;
- conditions de location (utilisation, tarifs, *etc.* ...) des circuits de télécommunications aux usagers.

3. *Groupe de travail „Radiocommunications":*

- service radioélectrique terrestre d'appel des véhicules;
- stations d'amateur (procédure de délivrance des licences à des radioamateurs étrangers).

Work will also continue on the following:
- telegraphic rates between the E.C.P.T. countries;
- introduction of a "telexogram" service;
- development of the mobile land radio-telephone service in Europe;
- radio-electric radiation from industrial, scientific and medical installations;
- radio-astronomy service;
- "space" and "land-space" radio-communication services;
- action to prevent radio stations on board ships or aircraft from operating outside national territorial limits (following the Recommendation already adopted).

Results of existing working parties:

1. *"Telegraph" Working Party*

- the setting up of a European switchboard to handle telex traffic with America by transatlantic cable, with a view to increasing the throughput of inter-continental telegraph lines.

2. *"Telephone" Working Party*

- the setting up of a European switchboard for telephone traffic with America, also with a view to increasing the throughput of inter-continental telephone lines;
- advance booking of telephone calls during the end-of-the-year period;
- decrease in the number of scales of charges in use in automatic systems, with a view to simplifying equipment;
- conditions for hiring (use, rates *etc.*) of telecommunication lines to users.

3. *"Radio-communications" Working Party*

- radio-car-call service;
- amateur stations (procedure for issuing licences to foreign radio amateurs).

CHAPITRE X

ASSOCIATION EUROPÉENNE DE LIBRE-ÉCHANGE

A. CHRONOLOGIE

4 janvier: Signature de la Convention de l'A.E.L.E.

12 janvier: Réunion à Paris des Ministres des pays de l'A.E.L.E. Les réunions se poursuivent pendant plusieurs jours.

12–13 janvier: La Conférence économique spéciale de Paris adopte des résolutions portant la création d'un Groupe d'aide au développement, d'un Comité des Questions commerciales composé de 21 membres, et d'un Groupe de quatre membres, chargés de faire rapport sur la réorganisation de l'O.E.C.E.

14 janvier: Les Ministres de vingt gouvernements décident de donner effet à ces résolutions.

18 février: La décision d'installer à Genève le siège de l'A.E.L.E. est publiée.

11-12 mars: Les Ministres des pays de l'A.E.L.E. se réunissent à Vienne. Ils annoncent que leurs gouvernements sont prêts à discuter l'application, dès le premier juillet, aux Six et à d'autres pays, conformément aux principes du G.A.T.T., des réductions de tarifs qu'ils doivent effectuer à cette date, dans la mesure où les Six acceptent de faire des concessions sur une base de réciprocité.

29-30 mars: Réunion à Paris du Comité des Questions commerciales (Comité des 21).

3 mai: Entrée en vigueur de la Convention de l'A.E.L.E. et dépôt des instruments de ratification auprès du Gouvernement suédois, lors d'une cérémonie célébrée à Stockholm.

11 mai: Première réunion à Genève du Conseil de l'A.E.L.E. Les pays membres sont représentés par les chefs de leurs délégations permanentes auprès de l'A.E.L.E.

16 mai-4 juin: Seizième session, à Genève, du G.A.T.T. (Accord général sur les Tarifs douaniers et le Commerce). *Début de la discussion sur l'A.E.L.E.*

19-20 mai: Réunion à Lisbonne du Conseil des Ministres de l'A.E.L.E.

9-10 juin: Réunion à Paris du Comité des Questions commerciales (Comité des 21). Création d'un Groupe pour l'étude des difficultés que posent les aménagements de tarif par les Six et les Sept.

1 juillet: Les pays de l'A.E.L.E. procèdent à la première réduction de droits de 20% entre eux, et relèvent leurs contingents. Les tarifs à l'intérieur du Marché Commun des Six sont encore abaissés de 10%, ce qui aboutit à une réduction globale de 20%.

21 juillet: Les Ministres des pays de l'A.E.L.E. tiennent à Paris une réunion officieuse.

22-23 juillet: Conférence des Ministres, à Paris, sur la réorganisation de l'O.E.C.E. M. T. Kristensen est nommé Secrétaire Général de l'O.E.C.E. pour remplacer M. René Sergent, et il est désigné pour occuper les fonctions de Secrétaire Général de la future organisation qui portera le nom d'Organisation de Coopération et de Développement économiques.

1 septembre: M. F. E. Figgures *occupe le poste de Secrétaire Général de l'A.E.L.E.*

1 septembre: Ouverture de la Conférence tarifaire du G.A.T.T. à Genève. La première partie de cette conférence est principalement consacrée à une nouvelle négociation des droits „consolidés" avec les six pays de la C.E.E.

CHAPTER X

EUROPEAN FREE TRADE ASSOCIATION

A. DIARY OF EVENTS

4 January: E.F.T.A. Convention signed.

12 January: Ministers from E.F.T.A. countries meet in Paris; further meetings are held on following days.

12-13 January: Special Economic Conference in Paris adopts Resolutions providing for a Development Assistance Group, a 21-member Trade Committee, and a Group of Four to report on the Reorganisation of the Organisation for European Economic Co-operation.

14 January: Ministers from Twenty Governments decide to give effect to these Resolutions.

18 February: Decision to establish the E.F.T.A. Secretariat in Geneva is announced.

11-12 March: Ministers from the E.F.T.A. countries meet in Vienna. They declare their Governments' readiness to "discuss extending on 1st July to the Six and to other countries in accordance with the principles of the G.A.T.T. the tariff cuts they are due to make by that date, to the extent that the Six are prepared to act on a reciprocal basis".

29-30 March: Meeting of the 21-member Trade Committee in Paris.

3 May: The E.F.T.A. Convention enters into force when the Instruments of Ratification are deposited with the Swedish Government at a ceremony in Stockholm.

11 May: The E.F.T.A. Council meets in Geneva for the first time; Member countries are represented by the Heads of their Permanent Delegations to E.F.T.A.

16 May-4 June: 16th Session of the G.A.T.T. (General Agreement on Tariffs and Trade) is held in Geneva. *The examination of the E.F.T.A. is begun.*

19-20 May: The E.F.T.A. Ministerial Council meets in Lisbon.

9-10 June: Meeting of 21-member Trade Committee in Paris. A Study Group is set up to review difficulties arising from tariff adjustments by the Seven and the Six.

1 July: E.F.T.A. countries make first 20% tariff reduction among themselves and increase quotas. Tariffs within the Common Market of the Six are reduced by a further 10%, making a total reduction of 20%.

21 July: Ministers from E.F.T.A. countries hold informal meeting in Paris.

22-23 July: Ministerial Conference in Paris on the reorganisation of the O.E.E.C. Mr. T. KRISTENSEN is appointed Secretary-General of the O.E.E.C. in succession to M. René SERGENT, and Secretary-General Designate of the future Organisation, to be known as the Organisation for Economic Co-operation and Development.

1 September: Mr. F. E. FIGGURES *takes up his appointment as Secretary-General of E.F.T.A.*

1 September: G.A.T.T. Tariff Conference opens in Geneva. The first phase is mainly concerned with re-negotiations of "bound" rates of duties with the six Member States of the E.E.C.

29 septembre: L'Assemblée consultative du Conseil de l'Europe réunie à Strasbourg, adopte une recommandation sur les relations économiques européennes, qui envisage la conclusion d'un Accord d'association entre l'A.E.L.E., la C.E.E. et les autres pays membres du Conseil de l'Europe.

11-12 octobre: Deuxième réunion ministérielle du Conseil de l'A.E.L.E. à Berne. Les Ministres font le point des mesures prises pour donner suite à la création de l'Association, d'après un rapport d'activité du Secrétaire Général. Ils envisagent également la modification du calendrier des réductions tarifaires prévues par la Convention de Stockholm, des négociations tarifaires au Comité des Questions commerciales et au G.A.T.T. et la création d'un Comité consultatif.

31 octobre-19 novembre: Dix-septième session, à Genève, des Parties Contractantes au G.A.T.T. Les Parties Contractantes prennent officiellement acte des dispositions de la Convention de Stockholm et des déclarations faites par les représentants des pays membres de l'A.E.L.E. A savoir que leurs gouvernements sont fermement décidés à créer dans les délais stipulés par la Convention une Zone de libre-échange au sens de l'article XXIV du G.A.T.T. Les Parties Contractantes considèrent qu'il reste à résoudre certains problèmes d'ordre juridique et pratique, dont la discussion sera plus fructueuse si elle a lieu à la lumière des constatations tirées de la mise en œuvre de la Convention.

12 décembre: Les Ministres des pays de l'A.E.L.E. procèdent, à Paris, à un échange de vues, sur la création de l'Organisation de Coopération et de Développement économiques, et sur d'autres questions.

13-14 décembre: Réunis à Paris, les Ministres de vingt pays approuvent la Convention portant création de l'Organisation de Coopération et de Développement économiques. La Convention, qui entrera en vigueur en septembre 1961, prévoit la participation à part entière du Canada et des États-Unis.

15 décembre: Une délégation finlandaise, dirigée par M. Olavi Munkki, rencontre, au siège du Secrétariat, les membres du Conseil de l'A.E.L.E.

21 décembre: Vingt-sixième réunion du Conseil de l'A.E.L.E. depuis sa création, coïncidant avec l'entrée en vigueur de la Convention de Stockholm, le 3 mai 1960.

B. DÉCISIONS FORMELLES DU CONSEIL DE L'A.E.L.E. EN 1960

DÉCISION NO. 1: RÈGLEMENT INTÉRIEUR DU CONSEIL [1]

*Décision prise par le Conseil à sa première réunion, le 11 mai 1960, conformément aux dispositions de l'Article 34*a) *de la Convention* (*Dispositions administratives de l'Association*).

Le Règlement intérieur fixe les modalités de convocation du Conseil, de désignation du Président, de vote, *etc.* Il constitue également un code général de procédure pour les instances de l'Association, dans la mesure où les décisions qui en portent création ne leur imposent pas un règlement intérieur spécial. . . . .

DÉCISION NO. 2: AMENDEMENTS AUX APPENDICES DE L'ANNEXE B [1]

Décision prise par le Conseil à sa première réunion, le 11 mai 1960, en vertu des pouvoirs que lui confère le paragraphe 5 de l'Article 4 de la Convention (*Régime tarifaire de la Zone*). Voir également *la Décision no. 22.*

---

[1] *Voir* Décision no. 21.

29 September: Consultative Assembly of the Council of Europe, meeting in Strasbourg, adopts a Recommendation on European Economic Relations, which envisages an Association Agreement between the E.E.C., and E.F.T.A., and the other Member States of the Council of Europe.

11-12 October: The second Ministerial meeting of the E.F.T.A. Council is held in Berne. Ministers review progress made with the establishment of the Association on the basis of a Progress Report prepared by the Secretary-General; they also consider a modification of the time-table for tariff reductions laid down in the Stockholm Convention, tariff negotiations in the Committee on Trade Problems and in the G.A.T.T. and the establishment of a Consultative Committee.

31 October-19 November: 17th Session of the Contracting Parties to the G.A.T.T. takes place in Geneva. *The Contracting Parties formally take note of the provisions of the Stockholm Convention, as well as the statements made by representatives of the Member Governments of E.F.T.A., to the effect that their Governments were firmly determined to establish within the time-limit provided for in the Convention, a Free Trade Area in the sense of Article XXIV of the G.A.T.T.*; it is held that there remain some legal and practical issues which would be more fruitfully discussed in the light of experience of the operation of the Convention.

12 December: Ministers from E.F.T.A. countries hold an informal meeting in Paris to discuss the establishment of the Organisation for Economic Co-operation and Development, and other questions.

13-14 December: The draft Convention setting up the Organisation for Economic Co-operation and Development is approved by the Ministers representing the Twenty Governments, at a meeting in Paris. The Convention, which is likely to come into force in September 1961, provides for full membership on the part of Canada and the United States.

15 December: A Finnish Delegation, led by Mr. Olavi MUNKKI, has a meeting at the Secretariat with the members of the E.F.T.A. Council.

21 December: The E.F.T.A. Council holds its 26th meeting since it came into being with the entry into force on 3rd May of the Stockholm Convention.

B. FORMAL DECISIONS OF THE E.F.T.A. COUNCIL DURING 1960

DECISION NO. 1: RULES OF PROCEDURE OF THE COUNCIL [1]

Taken at the first meeting of the Council, 11th May, 1960, in accordance with the requirements of Article 34 a) *of the Convention (Administrative arrangements of the Association).*

The rules of procedure regulate the calling of Council meetings, the chairmanship, voting, *etc.* These rules also serve as a general guide to the procedure of subordinate bodies of the Association to the extent that specific rules of procedure are not made for them in the decisions setting them up. . . . .

DECISION NO. 2: AMENDMENT OF THE SCHEDULES TO ANNEX B [1]

Taken at the first meeting of the Council, 11th May, 1960, under the powers conveyed by paragraph 5 of Article 4 of the Convention (Area tariff treatment). See also *Decision No. 22.*

[1] Note: See Decision 21.

Le Conseil a apporté dc nombreux amendements de détail aux quatre appendices de l'Annexe B à la Convention, qui contiennent les règles applicables aux processus de production, la liste des matières de base et les formules-types à utiliser pour demander le bénéfice des réductions de tarif de l'A.E.L.E. Plusieurs amendements ont pour objet de préciser les définitions et explications de détail; d'autres se bornent à ajouter de nouvelles positions aux listes existances, afin de faciliter l'application à un nombre plus grand de produits de taux de droits réduits. . . . .
. . . .

DÉCISION NO. 3: AMENDEMENTS A L'ANNEXE D[1]

Décision prise par le Conseil à sa première réunion, le 11 mai 1960, en vertu des pouvoirs que lui confère le paragraphe 1 de l'Article 21 (Produits agricoles).

Cette décision amende deux définitions de la liste des produits agricoles, à l'Annexe D de la Convention, afin de les faire concorder avec les définitions correspondantes des listes relatives aux processus de production, amendées par la Décision No 2. . . . .

DÉCISION NO. 4: PREUVE DE L'ORIGINE DES MARCHANDISES RÉEXPORTÉES ET DES PIÈCES DE RECHANGE D'ÉQUIPEMENT MÉCANIQUE

Décision prise par le Conseil à sa quatrième réunion, le 2 juin 1960, en vertu des pouvoirs discrétionnaires généraux que lui confère le paragraphe 4 de l'Article 32 de la Convention (Attributions du Conseil). Voir aussi *les Décisions nos. 25 et 27.*

Le Conseil a fixé des règles provisoires pour répondre aux besoins des exportateurs dans deux cas où les procédures et les formules que prescrit l'Annexe B pour la preuve d'origine ne seraient pas entièrement adaptées aux circonstances particulières de la transaction. Le premier cas est celui des marchandises produites dans un État membre et réexportées en transit à travers un deuxième à destination d'un troisième État membre. Les règles provisoires relatives à cette catégorie de transactions sont maintenant annulées et remplacées par la Décision no 27 du 7 décembre 1960. Le deuxième cas est celui des pièces de rechange fournies par les fabricants de certains équipements mécaniques et pour lesquelles la production d'une preuve d'origine distincte entraînerait dans la pratique des difficultés considérables pour les exportateurs.

DÉCISION NO. 5: DROITS DE BASE DU PORTUGAL

Décision prise par le Conseil à sa cinquième réunion, le 16 juin 1960, en vertu des dispositions du paragraphe 8 de l'Annexe A à la Convention (Droits de base).

Les droits de base, sur lesquels doivent être calculées les réductions tarifaires de l'A.E.L.E., sont en général, par définition, les droits appliqués par les États membres au 1er janvier 1960 (paragraphe 3 de l'Article 3 de la Convention). Le 1er janvier 1960, le Gouvernement du Portugal a promulgué un tarif revisé, mais, la loi portugaise imposant un délai d'application, les droits du nouveau tarif n'ont été en fait appliqués qu'à partir du 6 janvier 1960. Le Conseil a réglé le cas en décidant formellement que les taux de droits du nouveau tarif, qui diffèrent de ceux du tarif antérieur, devront être considérés comme droits de base pour le Portugal.

---

[1] *Voir* Décision no. 21.

The Council made a large number of detailed amendments to the four Schedules to Annex B of the Convention, which set out the process rules, the basic materials list and the standard forms used in claiming the benefit of the E.F.T.A. tariff reductions. Many of these amendments were made to clarify detailed definitions and explanations, while other amendments consisted of the addition of new items to the list so as to increase the opportunities for goods to qualify for the reduced rates of duty. ....

....

DECISION NO. 3: AMENDMENT OF ANNEX D [1]

Taken at the first meeting of the Council on 11th May, 1960, under the powers conveyed by paragraph 1 of Article 21 (Agricultural goods).

This Decision amended two of the definitions in the list of agricultural goods in Annex D to the Convention so as to bring them into line with the corresponding definitions in the process lists amended by Decision No. 2. ....

DECISION NO. 4: EVIDENCE OF ORIGIN FOR RE-EXPORTED GOODS AND SPARE PARTS FOR ENGINEERING GOODS

Taken at the fourth meeting of the Council on 2nd June, 1960, under the general powers of decision conveyed by paragraph 4 of Article 32 of the Convention (defining the responsibilities of the Council). See also *Decisions Nos 25 and 27.*

The Council introduced interim arrangements to meet the needs of traders in two cases where the procedures and forms for the certification of the origin of goods prescribed in Annex B to the Convention were not entirely appropriate to the circumstances of the trade. The first of these cases concerned goods made in one Member State and re-exported via a second Member State to a third; the interim arrangements covering this class of transaction are now to be superseded by the permanent arrangements introduced by Decision No. 27 taken on 7th December, 1960. The second case concerned the certification of the origin of spare parts supplied by manufacturers of certain engineering goods, were the separate proof of the origin of each spare part could involve traders in considerable practical difficulties.

DECISION NO. 5: PORTUGUESE BASIC DUTIES

Taken at the fifth meeting of the Council on 16th June, 1960, under paragraph 8 of Annex A to the Convention (Basic Duties).

In general the basic duties, on the basis of which the E.F.T.A. tariff reductions are to be calculated, are defined as the duties *applied* by Member States on 1st January, 1960 (paragraph 3 of Article 3 of the Convention). The Portuguese Government introduced a revised tariff on 1st January, 1960, but it was not appreciated at that time that, by reason of a *vacatio legis* required by Portuguese law, the duties set out in the revised tariff could not in fact be *applied* until 6th January, 1960. The Council therefore rectified the position by formally deciding that the rates of duty in the new tariff which differed from those in the previous tariff should be taken as the Portuguese basic duties.

---

[1] **Note: see Decision 21.**

DÉCISION NO. 6: SYSTÈME COMPTABLE POUR LA SÉPARATION DES MATIÈRES

Décision prise par le Conseil à sa sixième réunion, le 22 juin 1960, en vertu des dispositions du paragraphe 2, règle 5, de l'Annexe B à la Convention.

La règle 5 de l'Annexe a trait à la méthode à employer pour déterminer l'origine des marchandises faites de matières dont certaines proviennent de la Zone et d'autres non, et qui ne peuvent matériellement être séparées physiquement. Cette règle prévoit le recours à un système comptable pour pallier l'impossibilité de séparation matérielle, et la Décision no 6 établit à cet effet un système comptable mis au point par les experts douaniers. Ce système sera particulièrement utile aux fabricants de produits chimiques, *etc.*, qui éprouveraient autrement de grandes difficultés pour prouver que tel lot déterminé de produits contient des matières en provenance de l'A.E.L.E., alors même qu'ils pourraient faire cette preuve pour une certaine proportion de leur production totale.

DÉCISION NO. 7: ORIGINE DES MATIÈRES STOCKÉES AVANT LE 1ER JUILLET 1960

Décision prise par le Conseil à sa sixième réunion, le 22 juin 1960, en vertu des pouvoirs discrétionnaires généraux que lui confère le paragraphe 4 de l'Article 32 de la Convention.

Cette décision répond aux exigences d'une situation provisoire, qui s'est présentée immédiatement après la mise en vigueur des premières réductions tarifaires et des règles d'origine. Pour bénéficier des reductions tarifaires que prévoit la règle dite „des 50 pour cent", le producteur doit prouver que la valeur des matières ne provenant pas de l'A.E.L.E. n'est pas supérieure à la moitié de celle des marchandises exportées, et, à cet effet, il doit pouvoir prouver l'origine des matières provenant de l'A.E.L.E. Mais le producteur ne pouvait faire la preuve de l'origine pour les matières stockées, avant l'entrée en vigueur du système des attestations d'origine et il n'aurait donc pu bénéficier des réductions tarifaires, tant qu'il ne se serait pas procuré des matières dont l'origine fût certifiée, pour les incorporer à ses produits. Il a donc été décidé que, dans le cas des marchandises faites de matières stockées par le fabricant au cours des douze derniers mois, ces matières seraient considerées, sauf preuve du contraire, comme provenant de l'A.E.L.E., afin de permettre l'application à ces marchandises de la règle dite „des 50 pour cent" dès la date des premières réductions tarifaires.

DÉCISION NO 8: CRÉATION D'UNE COMMISSION DOUANIÈRE [1]

Décision prise par le Conseil à sa septième réunion, le 29 juin 1960, en vertu des pouvoirs qui lui sont conférés par les dispositions du paragraphe 3 de l'Article 32 (Le Conseil et ses instances).

Au cours des négociations de Stockholm et dans la période qui a conduit à la mise en vigueur de la Convention, il existait un groupe officieux d'experts douaniers venus des divers États membres et dont le Conseil a jugé devoir mettre à profit de façon permanente l'expérience et la science. C'est pourquoi le Conseil a constitué officiellement ce groupe en institution spécialisée de l'Association, lui donnant le titre de Commission douanière. Aux termes de son mandat, la Commission a pour attributions de veiller à l'application pratique des dispositions de la Convention qui relèvent particulièrement de l'Administration des douanes, et notamment à l'application du système des attestations d'origine. Elle a également pour mission d'assurer la collaboration entre les administrations douanières des États membres. Bon nombre des décisions du Conseil s'inspirent de propositions de la Commission douanière.

[1] *Voir* Décision no. 21.

DECISION NO. 6: SEGREGATION BY ACCOUNTING METHODS

Taken by the Council at its sixth meeting on 22nd June, 1960, by virtue of the provisions in paragraph 2 of Rule 5 in Annex B to the Convention.

Rule 5 in Annex B concerns the method of determining the origin of goods made of materials, some of which are of E.F.T.A. origin and some not, which cannot for practical reasons be physically segregated. It was foreseen in this Rule that an accounting method might be used as a practical alternative to physical segregation, and this Decision introduced such an accounting method which had been worked out by Customs experts. This accounting method is of particular value to manufacturers of chemical products and the like, who would otherwise have found it difficult to show that any particular batch of their product contained E.F.T.A. materials, even though they could show with certainty that a certain proportion of their total output did.

DECISION NO. 7: ORIGIN OF MATERIALS TAKEN INTO STOCK BEFORE 1ST JULY, 1960

Taken by the Council at its sixth meeting on 22nd June, 1960, under the general powers of decision conveyed by paragraph 4 of Article 32 of the Convention.

This Decision was designed to meet a transitional situation which arose in the period immediately after the first tariff reductions took effect and the origin rules first began to apply. In order to claim the benefit of the tariff reductions under the "fifty per cent" origin rule, the producer has to show that not more than half the value of the goods exported consists of materials originating outside E.F.T.A. and to do this he must be able to prove the origin of the materials originating inside E.F.T.A. But the producer could not do this for all the materials he had taken into stock before the system for certifying the origin of the materials came into operation, and he would therefore have been prevented from claiming the benefits of the tariff cuts until he had time to obtain certified materials and incorporate them in his products. It was therefore decided that, where goods were made from materials taken into stock by the manufacturer during the preceding twelve months, these materials would be regarded as of E.F.T.A. origin unless there were evidence to the contrary, thus enabling the goods to qualify under the "fifty per cent" rule from the date of the first tariff cuts.

DECISION NO. 8: ESTABLISHMENT OF A CUSTOMS COMMITTEE [1]

Taken at the seventh meeting of the Council on 29th June, 1960, under the powers conveyed by paragraph 3 of Article 32 (on the Council and its subordinate organs).

During the Stockholm negotiations and the preparatory period leading to the coming into force of the Convention, an informal group of customs experts from the Member States existed whose experience and knowledge the Council considered likely to be of continuing value. The Council therefore formally established this group as one of the specialised institutions of the Association under the title of Customs Committee. Its terms of reference require the Committee, in effect, to look after the practical working of those provisions of the Convention which come particularly within the sphere of customs administration, expecially the operation of the origin system, and to promote co-operation between the customs administrations of the Member States. A large proportion of the Decisions taken by the Council has been based on proposals made to it by the Customs Committee.

[1] Note: See Decision 21.

DÉCISION NO. 9: RÈGLEMENT FINANCIER

Décision prise par le Conseil à sa huitième réunion, le 6 juillet 1960, conformément aux dispositions de l'alinéa c) *de l'Article 34 de la Convention (Dispositions administratives de l'Association)*

L'adoption du règlement financier a constitué une étape essentielle de l'organisation financière de l'Association. Ce règlement s'applique aux prévisions annuelles de dépenses et au budget de l'Association, à la gestion de ses fonds et de ses avoirs, au contrôle interne de sa comptabilité et à la vérification extérieure des comptes.

DÉCISION NO. 10: CRÉATION D'UNE COMMISSION DU BUDGET [1]

Décision prise par le Conseil à sa neuvième réunion, le 13 juillet 1960, conformément aux pouvoirs qui lui sont conférés par les dispositions du paragraphe 3 de l'Article 32 de la Convention (Le Conseil et ses instances).

Pour donner suite à l'institution des modalités financières de gestion de l'Association le Conseil a créé une Commission du budget qui a pour mandat de le conseiller sur les questions financières (notamment sur le budget annuel), ainsi que de s'acquitter d'autres tâches qui lui sont attribuées par le Règlement financier.

DÉCISION NO. 11: STATUT DU PERSONNEL DU SECRÉTARIAT [1]

Décision prise par le Conseil à sa dixième réunion, le 20 juillet 1960, conformément aux dispositions de l'alinéa b) *de l'Article 34 de la Convention (Dispositions administratives de l'Association).*

Le Statut du personnel est un des éléments essentiels de la constitution du Secrétariat de l'A.E.L.E. à laquelle était tenu le Conseil par les dispositions de l'Article 34. Le Statut du personnel concerne les obligations et la conduite des fonctionnaires du Secrétariat, leur recrutement et leurs contrats, leur traitement et les indemnités qui leur reviennent, la caisse de prévoyance, le régime des assurances maladie et l'indemnisation pour les accidents subis au service de l'A.E.L.E., les frais de déplacement et de déménagement, l'horaire de travail, les congés et la discipline.

DÉCISION NO. 12: BUDGET

Décision prise par le Conseil à sa onzième réunion, le 27 juillet 1960, en vertu des dispositions de l'alinéa c) *de l'Article 34 de la Convention (Dispositions administratives de l'Association).*

Le Conseil a approuvé le projet de budget établi par le Secrétariat et la Commission du budget, et il a arrêté le premier budget provisoire de l'Association. . . . .
(Un budget revisé a été établi par le Conseil dans sa Décision No. 1 de 1961.)

DÉCISION NO. 13: BARÈME DES CONTRIBUTIONS

Décision prise par le Conseil à sa onzième réunion, le 27 juillet 1960, conformément aux dispositions du paragraphe c) *de l'Article 34 de la Convention.*

A propos du budget et conformément aux dispositions de l'Article 34, le Conseil a décidé que les contributions des États membres aux dépenses de l'Association devaient être fonction de leur produit national brut, calculé au prix coûtant des facteurs, conformément aux mêmes principes que ceux de l'O.E.C.E., sous réserve qu'aucun État membre ne soit appéle à verser une contribution supérieure à 30% des dépenses totales.

---

[1] *Voir* Décision no. 21.

DECISION NO. 9: FINANCIAL REGULATIONS

Taken at the eigth meeting of the Council on 6th July, 1960, in accordance with sub-paragraph c) *of Article 34 of the Convention (Administrative arrangements of the Association).*

The adoption of the Financial Regulations was an essential step in establishing the financial arrangements necessary for the operation of the Association. These Regulations cover the annual estimates and budget of the Association, the custody of funds and assets, internal control and supervision.

DECISION NO. 10: ESTABLISHMENT OF A BUDGET COMMITTEE [1]

Taken at the ninth meeting of the Council on 13th July, 1960, under the powers conveyed by paragraph 3 of Article 32 of the Convention (on the Council and its subordinate organs).

Also in furtherance of the establishment of the financial arrangements necessary for the operation of the Association, the Council set up a Budget Committee to advise it on financial questions (especially the annual budget) and to carry out other tasks allotted to it in the Financial Regulations.

DECISION NO. 11: STAFF REGULATIONS OF THE SECRETARIAT [1]

Taken at the tenth meeting of the Council on 20th July, 1690, in accordance with sub-paragraph b) *of Article 34 of the Convention (on the Administrative arrangements of the Association).*

The Staff Regulations were an essential step in the establishment of the E.F.T.A. Secretariat, which Article 34 required the Council to set up. The Staff Regulations deal with the obligations and conduct of Staff Members of the Secretariat, their recruitment and appointment, their salaries and related allowances, the provident fund, sickness scheme and compensation arrangements, travel and removal expenses, hours of work, leave and discipline.

DECISION NO. 12: ESTABLISHMENT OF THE BUDGET

Taken at the eleventh meeting of the Council on 27th July, 1960, under the provisions of sub-paragraph c) *of Article 34 of the Convention (Administrative arrangements of the Association).*

The Council approved the estimates which had been prepared by the Secretariat and the Budget Committee and established the first, provisional Budget of the Association. . . . .
(A revised Budget was established by Decision No. 1 of 1961).

DECISION NO. 13: DETERMINATION OF THE SCALE OF CONTRIBUTIONS

Taken at the eleventh meeting of the Council on 27th July, 1960, under the provisions of sub-paragraph c) *of Article 34 of the Convention.*

In connection with the establishment of the Budget and as required by Article 34, the Council decided that the contributions of Member States to the expenses of the Association should be determined by reference to their gross national product at factor cost, according to the same principles as those followed by the O.E.C.C., subject to the proviso that no Member State should contribute more than 30 per cent of the total.

[1] Note: See Decision 21.

DÉCISION NO. 14: CONTRIBUTIONS AU BUDGET

Décision prise par le Conseil à sa onzième réunion, le 27 juillet 1960, en vertu des dispositions de l'alinéa c) *de l'Article 34 de la Convention (Dispositions administratives de l'Association).*

Donnant suite à sa Décision no 13, le Conseil a arrêté la contribution en pourcentage des États membres au budget de 1960-1961, ainsi que le montant effectif de la contribution de chaque État membre au budget établi par la Décision no 12 (ces montants ont été augmentés par le Conseil, dans sa Décision No 2 de 1961).

DÉCISION NO. 15: CATÉGORIES DE FONCTIONNAIRES

Décision prise par la Conseil à sa onzième réunion, le 27 juillet 1960, conformément à l'Article 12 du Protocole sur la capacité juridique, les privilèges et immunités de l'Association, que l'Association a été appelée à établir pour donner suite aux dispositions du paragraphe 1 de l'Article 35 de la Convention.

Le Conseil était tenu, par l'Article 12 du Protocole, de préciser les catégories de fonctionnaires de l'Association auxquelles s'appliquaient certaines dispositions du Protocole.

DÉCISION NO. 16: PREUVE D'ORIGINE DES EXPÉDITIONS DE VALEUR MINIME

Décision prise par le Conseil à sa onzième réunion, le 27 juillet 1960, en vertu des pouvoirs généraux qui lui sont conférés par les dispositions du paragraphe 4 de l'Article 32 (Attributions du Conseil).

Afin de faciliter l'application des avantages procurés par les réductions de tarif de l'A.E.L.E. aux marchandises, comme celles importées à titre d'effets personnels dans les bagages des voyageurs, ou aux marchandises expédiées en très petite quantité, le Conseil a décidé que, sous réserve de certaines conditions, il devrait être dérogé aux formalités d'attestation d'origine prescrites par la Convention, si la valeur des marchandises considérées ne dépassait pas certains chiffres prescrits dans le cas de chaque État membre (2.000 shillings autrichiens, 500 couronnes danoises, 500 couronnes norvégiennes, 2.500 escudos portugais, 400 couronnes suédoises, 350 francs suisses ou 25 livres sterling).

DÉCISION NO. 17: AMENDEMENT À L'APPENDICE III DE L'ANNEXE B [1]

Décision prise par le Conseil à sa onzième réunion, le 27 juillet 1960, en vertu des pouvoirs qui lui sont conférés par les dispositions du paragraphe 5 de l'Article 4 de la Convention (Régime tarifaire de la zone).

Le Conseil a ajouté un nouvel article (carbonate anhydre neutre de potassium) à la liste des matières de base qu'il n'y pas lieu de compter dans le calcul des 50% de la valeur d'un produit, qui ne doivent pas être dépassés pour que ce produit bénéficie des réductions de l'A.E.L.E.

DÉCISION NO. 18: CRÉATION D'UNE COMMISSION D'EXPERTS COMMERCIAUX

Décision prise par le Conseil à sa treizième réunion, le 8 septembre 1960, en vertu des pouvoirs qui lui sont conférés par les dispositions du paragraphe 3 de l'Article 32 de la Convention.

La troisième instance créée par le Conseil pour l'aider dans ses travaux a été une Commission d'experts commerciaux, analogue à maints égards à la Commission douanière. Cette commission, comme la Commission douanière, succède à un groupe officieux d'experts qui a joué un rôle dans les négociations de Stockholm et dans la préparation de la mise en vigueur de la Convention. Comme la Commission douanière, cette commission s'occupe de questions techniques liées à la mise en œuvre de la Convention, mais dans le domaine commercial et non plus dans celui de l'administration douanière. . . . .

[1] *Voir* Décision no. 21.

DECISION NO. 14: DETERMINATION OF CONTRIBUTIONS TO THE BUDGET

Taken at the eleventh meeting of the Council on 27th July, 1960, under sub-paragraph c) *of Article 34 of the Convention.*

In the light of Decision No. 13, the Council determined the actual percentage contributions to be made by Member States in 1960–61, and the actual amounts each should contribute to the Budget established by Decision No. 12. (These amounts were increased by Decision No. 2 of 1961).

DECISION NO. 15: SPECIFICATION OF CATEGORIES OF OFFICIALS

Taken at the eleventh meeting of the Council on 27th July, 1960, in accordance with Article 12 of the Protocol on the legal capacity, privileges and immunities of the Association which the Association had to establish in pursuance of paragraph 1 of Article 35 of the Convention.

The Council was required by Article 12 of the Protocol to specify the categories of officials of the Association to whom certain provisions of the Protocol should apply.

DECISION NO. 16: EVIDENCE OF ORIGIN FOR CONSIGNMENTS OF SMALL VALUE

Taken at the eleventh meeting of the Council on 27th July, 1960, by virtue of the general powers conveyed by paragraph 4 of Article 32 (on the responsibilities of the Council).

To facilitate the extenion of the benefits of the E.F.T.A. tariff reductions to goods such as those imported in passengers' baggage for personal use, or goods consigned in very small amounts, the Council made provision that subject to certain conditions the requirements about the certification of origin prescribed in the Convention should be dispensed with if the value of the goods did not exceed the figures specified for each Member State (2,000 Austrian Schillings, 500 Danish Crowns, 500 Norwegian Crowns, 2,500 Portuguese Escudos, 400 Swedish Crowns, 350 Swiss Francs or £ 25 Sterling).

DECISION NO. 17: AMENDMENTS OF SCHEDULE III TO ANNEX B [1]

Taken at the eleventh meeting of the Council on 27th July, 1960, under the powers conveyed by paragraph 5 of Article 4 of the Convention (on Area tariff treatment).

The Council added a further item (anhydrous neutral potassium carbonate) to the list of basic materials which are not counted in calculating whether more than fifty per cent of the value of a product claiming the benefits of the E.F.T.A. tariff reductions consists of materials imported from outside the Association.

DECISION NO. 18: ESTABLISHMENT OF A COMMITTEE OF TRADE EXPERTS

Taken at the thirteenth meeting of the Council on 8th September, 1960, under powers conveyed by paragraph 3 of Article 32 of the Convention.

The third subordinate institution established by the Council to assist it in its work was a Committee of Trade Experts analogous in many respects to the Customs Committee. This new Committee, like the Customs Committee, grew out of an informal group of experts who had played a part in the Stockholm negotiations and in the preparatory work preceding the coming into force of the Convention; again, like the Customs Committee, it is concerned with technical questions arising from the operation of the Convention, only in the trade sphere rather than in the sphere of customs administration. . . . .

[1] Note: See Decision 21.

DÉCISION NO. 19: APPLICATION DES RÉDUCTIONS À CERTAINS PRODUITS EN MATIÈRE PLASTIQUE [1]

Décision prise par le Conseil à sa seizième réunion, le 4 octobre 1960, en vertu des pouvoirs qui lui sont conférés par le paragraphe 5 de l'Article 4 de la Convention (Régime tarifaire de la zone).

Le Conseil a amendé l'Appendice I à l'Annexe B de la Convention, en vue d'y introduire des dispositions spéciales permettant d'appliquer à certains produits en matière plastique les réductions de tarif de l'A.E.L.E. lorsque ces produits contiennent, mélangées, des matières provenant de la Zone et des matières provenant de l'extérieur dans une proportion impossible à déterminer pour chaque article isolé, quand bien même on connaît cette proportion pour un lot d'articles.

DÉCISION NO. 20: DISPOSITIONS SPÉCIALES APPLICABLES À LA COMPTABILISATION ANALYTIQUE DES RÉSINES ARTIFICIELLES

Décision prise par le Conseil à sa seizième réunion, le 4 octobre 1960, en vertu des amendements apportés à la Convention par la Décision no. 19.

Cette décision a énoncé les arrangements de détails prévus dans la Décision no. 19, et précisé les produits en matière plastique visés et les modalités à appliquer. Les méthodes adoptées pour permettre à ces produits de bénéficier des réductions de tarif de l'A.E.L.E. sont à maints égards des méthodes comptables analogues à celles stipulées par la Décision no. 6.

DÉCISION NO. 21: AMENDEMENT DES DÉCISIONS

Décision prise par le Conseil à sa seizième réunion, le 4 octobre 1960, conformément aux dispositions de l'alinéa b) *de l'Article 34 de la Convention (Dispositions administratives de l'Association).*

Donnant suite à la nomination de M. FIGGURES au poste de Secrétaire Général, pour succéder à M. LINDH qui portait le titre de Secrétaire exécutif, le Conseil a modifié ses décisions antérieures de façon à remplacer par „Secrétaire Général" les mots „Secrétaire exécutif" dans ses décisions. Les décisions en cause sont ici marquées d'un astérisque[1]).

DÉCISION NO. 22: AMENDEMENT DE L'APPENDICE I DE L'ANNEXE B

Décision prise par le Conseil à sa vingt-et-unième réunion, le 17 novembre 1960, en vertu des dispositions du paragraphe 5 de l'Article 4 de la Convention (Régime tarifaire de la zone).

Donnant suite à une proposition de la Commission d'experts commerciaux, le Conseil a modifié de nouveau la liste des procédés de fabrication de l'Appendice I de l'Annexe B, à propos de la définition des confiseries de sucre. Cet amendement avait pour objet d'harmoniser davantage cette définition avec celle de l'Annexe D (Liste des produits agricoles) et de la préciser.

DÉCISION NO. 23: AMENDEMENT DE L'ANNEXE D

Décision prise par le Conseil à sa vingt-et-unième réunion, le 17 novembre 1960, en vertu des dispositions du paragraphe 1 de l'Article 21 de la Convention (Produits agricoles).

Le Conseil a légèrement modifié la définition des confiseries de sucre, dans la liste des produits agricoles, afin de préciser cette définition.

DÉCISION NO. 24: RISTOURNE

Décision prise par le Conseil à sa vingt-deuxième réunion, le 23 novembre 1960, en application des dispositions du paragraphe 3 de l'Article 7 de la Convention (Ristourne des droits de douane).

Les règles de la Convention concernant la ristourne des droits de dou-

[1] *Voir* Décision no. 21..

DECISION NO. 19: QUALIFYING PROCESSES FOR CERTAIN PLASTIC PRODUCTS [1]

Taken at the sixteenth meeting of the Council on 4th October, 1960, under the powers conveyed by paragraph 5 of Article 4 of the Convention (Area tariff treatment).

The Council amended Schedule I to Annex B to the Convention to provide for special arrangements to be made to enable certain plastic products to qualify for the benefits of E.F.T.A. tariff reductions, in cases where the plastic products contain mixtures of E.F.T.A. and non-E.F.T.A. materials in proportions which cannot be determined for any individual article even though the proportions may be known for a batch of articles.

DECISION NO. 20: SPECIAL ARRANGEMENTS FOR THE ACCOUNTING MIXING OF ARTIFICIAL RESINS

Taken at the sixteenth meeting of the Council of 4th October, 1960, by virtue of the amendments made to the Convention by Decision No. 19.

This Decision laid down the detailed arrangements provided for in Decision No. 19, specifying the plastic products in question and the procedures to be followed. The methods adopted to enable these products to qualify for the benefits of the E.F.T.A. tariff reductions were accounting methods in many ways analogous to those introduced by Decision No. 6.

DECISION NO. 21: CONSEQUENTIAL AMENDMENT OF PREVIOUS DECISIONS

Taken at the sixteenth meeting of the Council on 4th October, 1960, in accordance with sub-paragraph b) *of Article 34 of the Convention (Administrative arrangements of the Secretariat).*

Following the appointment of Mr. FIGGURES as Secretary-General in succession to Mr. LINDH, who bore the title of Executive Secretary, the Council amended its previous Decisions wherever the words "Executive Secretay" occurred (these Decisions have been marked with an asterisk[1]).

DECISION NO. 22: AMENDMENT OF SCHEDULE I TO ANNEX B

Taken at the twenty-first meeting of the Council on 17th November, 1960, by virtue of paragraph 5 of Article 4 of the Convention (Area tariff treatment).

Acting on a proposal by the Committee of Trade Experts, the Council made a further amendment to the process list in Schedule I to Annex B in respect of the definition of sugar confectionery, to bring it more closely into line with the definition in Annex D (the list of agricultural products) and to clarify it.

DECISION NO. 23: AMENDMENT OF ANNEX D

Taken at the twenty-first meeting of the Council on 17th November, 1960, by virtue of paragraph 1 of Article 2 of the Convention (Agricultural goods).

The Council made a slight clarifying amendment to the definition of sugar confectionery in the list of agricultural goods.

DECISION NO. 24: DRAWBACK

Taken at the twenty-second meeting of the Council on 23rd November, 1960, as required under paragraph 3 of Article 7 of the Convention (Drawback).

The rules in the Convention on Drawback cover the period from 1st

[1] **Note: See Decision 21.**

ane sont applicables à partir du 1er janvier 1970, époque à laquelle des États membres auront supprimé entre eux les droits de douane. Le Conseil devait, avant la fin de 1960, arrêter les dispositions à appliquer durant la période de transition qui commencera le 1er janvier 1962. Donnant suite à une proposition de la Commission d'experts commerciaux, le Conseil a décidé que, pendant cette période de transition, le fait que certaines marchandises avaient bénéficié des dispositions applicables à la ristourne ne devait pas les empêcher *a priori* de bénéficier des réductions de tarif de l'A.E.L.E. dans la mesure où les tarifs étaient réduits de moins de moitié. Le Conseil a donné pour instructions à la Commission d'experts commerciaux de proposer, avant le 1er janvier 1962, les règles à appliquer après la réduction de moitié des tarifs douaniers, et avant le 1er janvier 1970.

DÉCISION NO. 25: AMENDEMENT A LA RÈGLE 8 DE L'ANNEXE B

Décision prise par le Conseil à sa vingt-troisième réunion, le 30 novembre 1960, en vertu des pouvoirs conférés au Conseil par les dispositions du paragraphe 5 de l'Article 4 de la Convention (Régime tarifaire de la zone).

Par sa Décision n° 4, le Conseil a pris des dispositions provisoirement applicables à la modification de la procédure et des formalités requises pour la détermination de l'origine des marchandises en fonction de certains besoins. Par la décision No. 25, le Conseil a amendé la règle 8 de l'Annexe B qui énonce la procédure à suivre, de façon à permettre l'application d'une procédure variable et l'exécution de formalités différentes selon les catégories de marchandises ou de transactions, et sans qu'il y ait besoin de modifier formellement la Convention dans chaque cas. ......

....

DÉCISION NO 26: DROITS DE BASE NORVÉGIENS

Décision prise par le Conseil à sa vingt-troisième réunion, le 30 novembre 1960, en vertu des dispositions du paragraphe 8 de l'Annexe A de la Convention (Droits de base).

Cette décision redressait une erreur faite dans l'établissement du droit pour certaines catégories de soupes. Cette erreur s'était produite au moment d'adapter une position isolée du tarif norvégien à la Nomenclature de Bruxelles. A compter du 1er janvier 1961, les droits sur toutes les catégories de soupes importées en Norvège seront les mêmes, soit 2,80 couronnes norvégiennes par kilo (2,24 couronnes s'il s'agit de soupes provenant de pays de l'A.E.L.E.).

DÉCISION NO 27: PREUVE D'ORIGINE DES MARCHANDISES RÉEXPORTÉES

Décision prise par le Conseil à sa vingt-quatrième réunion, le 7 décembre 1960, en vertu des dipositions du paragraphe 6 de la Règle 8 de l'Annexe B à la Convention.

Le Conseil s'est prévalu des dispositions de la Décision no. 25, qui lui permettait de modifier les procédures et les formalités à suivre pour déterminer l'origine des produits fabriqués dans un État membre, exportés à destination d'un second État membre et réexportés à destination d'un troisième. Ces nouvelles dispositions, qui auront effet jusqu'à la fin de 1962,...

.....faciliteront la tâche des réexportateurs et des administrations douanières qui devront fournir ou contrôler les preuves documentaires nécessaires pour que les marchandises en question bénéficient des réductions de tarif prévues par la Convention de l'A.E.L.E.

January, 1970, when import duties will have been eliminated as between the Member States. The Council was required, before the end of 1960, to decide on the arrangements which should be applied during the transitional period beginning 1st January, 1962. Acting on a proposal by the Committee of Trade Experts, the Council decided that during its transitional period the fact that some goods had benefited from drawback should not disqualify them from enjoying the benefits of E.F.T.A. tariff reductions, so long as the tariffs had been reduced by less than half. The Council instructed the Committee of Trade Experts to make proposals before 1st July, 1962, as to the rules to be applied after tariffs have been halved and before 1st January, 1970.

DECISION NO. 25: AMENDMENT OF RULE 8 OF ANNEX B

Taken at the twenty-third meeting of the Council on 30th November, 1960, under the powers conveyed by paragraph 5 of Article 4 of the Convention (Area tariff treatment).

In Decision No. 4, the Council made provisional arrangements for variations of the procedures and forms required for the determination of the origin of goods to meet cerain specific needs. In Decision No. 25 the Council amended Rule 8 of Annex B, which sets out the procedures, adding a paragraph (number 6) to enable it to vary the procedures and forms in respect of particular categories of goods or classes of transactions, without needing formally to amend the Convention each time it did so...

. . . .

DECISION NO. 26: NORWEGIAN BASIC DUTIES

Taken at the twenty-third meeting of the Council on 30th November, 1960, by virtue of the provisions of paragraph 8 of Annex A to the Convention (Basic Duties).

This Decision rectified an error in the fixing of the rate of duty for certain kinds of soup, which occurred in the process of adapting a residual heading in the Norwegian tariff to the Brussels Nomenclature basis. The rate of duty on all kinds of soup imported into Norway will, as from 1st January, 1961, be the same—2.80 Norwegian Crowns per kilogram (2.24 Crowns for soups of E.F.T.A. origin).

DECISION NO. 27: EVIDENCE OF ORIGIN FOR RE-EXPORTED GOODS

Taken at the twenty-fourth meeting of the Council on 7th December, 1960, under paragraph 6 of Rule 8 of Annex B to the Convention.

The Council made use of the enabling provision established by Decision No. 25 to vary the procedures and form to be used in determining the origin of goods made in one Member State, exported to a second Member State and re-exported to a third. These new arrangements, which will operate until the end of 1962, ... will facilitate the work of traders in re-exported goods and of customs administrations in providing and handling the documentary evidence necessary to enable these goods to enjoy the benefits of the E.F.T.A. tariff reductions.

DÉCISION NO 28: ÉMOLUMENTS DU SECRÉTAIRE GÉNÉRAL ET DU SECRÉTAIRE GÉNÉRAL ADJOINT

Décision prise par le Conseil, à sa vingt-sixième réunion, le 21 décembre 1960, en vertu des dispositions du paragraphe b) *de l'Article 34 de la Convention.*

Cette décision fixe, formellement, les émoluments du Secrétaire Général et ceux de son adjoint; elle était nécessaire pour que les prévisions de dépenses revisées puissent être approuvées et établi le Budget revisé pour 1960–1961.

C. L'A.E.L.E. DANS LE COMMERCE MONDIAL

1. L'A.E.L.E. DANS LE COMMERCE MONDIAL, JANVIER–JUIN 1960

Moyennes mensuelles 1.000 dollars U.S.

Zone d'origine ou de destination / Pays déclarant	Ensemble des pays de l'A.E.L.E.	Monde	Zones sélectionnées		
			G.A.T.T.	O.E.C.E.	C.E.E.
IMPORTATIONS c.a.f.[1] effectuées par:					
Autriche	14.006	112.664	94.693	78.823	63.194
Danemark	53.988	148.882	136.171	114.079	58.486
Norvège	47.447	122.779	113.289	88.266	38.547
Portugal	7.740	39.355	29.152	23.207	14.834
Suède	56.619	236.799	211.332	156.190	96.361
Suisse	20.313	176.477	164.622	127.726	105.231
Royaume-Uni . .	106.118	1.057.208	884.070	313.235	159.235
Ensemble des pays de l'A.E.L.E. . . .	*306.231*	*1.894.164*	*1.633.329*	*901.526*	*535.888*
EXPORTATIONS f.o.b.[2] effectuées par:					
Autriche	10.937	89.696	70.425	58.297	44.922
Danemark	50.315	118.636	107.542	86.773	34.566
Norvège	31.278	73.710	65.698	51.581	18.528
Portugal	4.423	23.553	15.062	9.781	4.879
Suède	70.023	204.254	179.025	138.527	64.167
Suisse	22.848	146.063	122.830	87.532	60.077
Royaume-Uni . .	93.841	881 464	728.322	273.156	134.370
Ensemble des pays de l'A.E.L.E. . . .	*283.665*	*1.537.376*	*1.288.904*	*705.647*	*361.409*

Source: Bulletins statisques de l'O.E.C.E., Série A.

[1] c.a.f. = coût, assurance, fret. [2] f.o.b. = free on board.

DECISION NO. 28: EMOLUMENTS OF THE SECRETARY-GENERAL AND OF THE DEPUTY SECRETARY-GENERAL

Taken at the twenty-sixth meeting of the Council on 21 December, 1960, in accordance with sub-paragraph b) *of Article 34 of the Convention.*

This Decision formally established the emoluments of the Secretary-General and his Deputy, preparatory to the approval of the revised estimates and establishments of the revised Budget for 1960–61.

C. E.F.T.A. POSITION IN WORLD TRADE

1. E.F.T.A. POSITION IN WORLD TRADE JAN.-JUNE 1960

Monthly averages Thousand U.S. dollars

Reporting Country \ Area of origin or destination	E.F.T.A. countries combined	World	Selected areas		
			G.A.T.T. Area	O.E.E.C. countries combined	E.E.C. countries combined
IMPORTS c.i.f.[1] into:					
Austria	14,006	112,664	94,693	78,823	63,194
Denmark	53,988	148,882	136,171	114,079	58,486
Norway	47,447	122,779	113,289	88,266	38,547
Portugal	7,740	39,355	29,152	23,207	14,834
Sweden	56,619	236,799	211,332	156,190	96,361
Switzerland	20,313	176,477	164,622	127,726	105,231
United Kingdom	106,118	1,057,208	884,070	313,235	159,235
E.F.T.A. Countries combined	*306,231*	*1,894,164*	*1,633,329*	*901,526*	*535,888*
EXPORTS f.o.b.[2] from:					
Austria	10,937	89,696	70,425	58,297	44,922
Denmark	50,315	118,636	107,542	86,773	34,566
Norway	31,278	73,710	65,698	51,581	18,528
Portugal	4,423	23,553	15,062	9,781	4,879
Sweden	70,023	203,254	179,025	138,527	64,167
Switzerland	22,848	146,063	122,830	87,532	60,077
United Kingdom	93,841	881,464	728,322	273,156	134,370
E.F.T.A. Countries combined	*283,665*	*1,537,376*	*1,288,904*	*705,647*	*361,409*

Source: O.E.E.C. Statistical Bulletin, Series A.

[1] c.i.f. = cost, insurance, freight [2] f.o.b. = free on board.

2. L'A.E.L.E. DANS LE COMMERCE MONDIAL, JUILLET-SEPTEMBRE 1960

Moyennes mensuelles 1.000 dollars U.S.

Zone d'origine ou de destination / Pays déclarant	Monde	Zones sélectionnées			
		Ensemble des pays de l'A.E.L.E.	C.E.E.	O.E.C.E.	G.A.T.T.
IMPORTATIONS c.a.f.[1] effectuées par:					
Autriche	117.773	14.113	66.004	81.538	98.579
Danemark	139.968	48.411	55.311	104.817	129.976
Norvège	115.483	38.991	42.534	82.726	106.862
Portugal	44.678	8.422	17.649	27.008	33.661
Suède	220.129	51.236	88.803	141.925	197.497
Suisse	187.589	20.577	117.678	140.171	176.145
Royaume-Uni . .	1.044.267	110.590	146.716	302.560	872.997
Ensemble des pays de l'A.E.L.E. . . .	*1.869.887*	*292.340*	*534.695*	*880.745*	*1.615.717*
EXPORTATIONS f.o.b.[2] effectuées par:					
Autriche	95.201	11.492	49.011	62.867	76.222
Danemark	117.118	51.948	31.661	85.336	107.700
Norvège	67.815	29.426	17.941	48.578	61.525
Portugal	27.412	5.644	6.207	12.239	17.715
Suède	207.445	74.679	67.162	146.461	180.142
Suisse	153.546	28.990	61.804	90.955	129.944
Royaume-Uni . .	794.313	81.599	120.488	244.021	655.593
Ensemble des pays de l'A.E.L.E. . . .	*1.462.850*	*283.778*	*305.263*	*690.457*	*1.228.541*

Source: Bulletins statistiques de l'O.E.C.E., Série A.

[1] c.s f. = coût, assurance, fret. [2] f.o.b. = free on board.

2. E.F.T.A. POSITION IN WORLD TRADE, JULY-SEPTEMBER 1960

Monthly averages — Thousand U.S. dollars

Reporting Country \ Area of origin or destination	World	Selected areas			
		E.F.T.A. countries combined	E.E.C. countries combined	O.E.E.C. countries combined	G.A.T.T. Area
IMPORTS c.i.f.[1] into:					
Austria	117,773	14,113	66,004	81,538	98,579
Denmark	139,968	48,411	55,311	104,817	129,976
Norway	115,483	38,991	42,534	82,726	106,862
Portugal	44,678	8,422	17,649	27,008	33,661
Sweden	220,129	51,236	88,803	141,925	197,497
Switzerland	187,589	20,577	117,678	140,171	176,145
United Kingdom	1,044,267	110,590	146,716	302,560	872,997
E.F.T.A. Countries combined	*1,869,887*	*292,340*	*534,695*	*880,745*	*1,615,717*
EXPORTS f.o.b.[2] from:					
Austria	95,201	11,492	49,011	62,867	76,222
Denmark	117,118	51,948	31,661	85,336	107,700
Norway	67,815	29,426	17,941	48,578	61,525
Portugal	27,412	5,644	6,207	12,239	17,715
Sweden	207,445	74,679	67,162	146,461	180,142
Switzerland	153,546	28,990	61,804	90,955	129,944
United Kingdom	794,313	81,599	120,488	244,021	655,593
E.F.T.A. Countries combined	*1,462,850*	*283,778*	*305,263*	*690,457*	*1,228,541*

Source: O.E.E.C. Statistical Bulletin, Series A.

[1] c.i.f. = cost, insurance, freight [2] f.o.b. = free on board.

D. MEMBRES DU CONSEIL

(Le Royaume-Uni préside depuis le 1er janvier 1961)

	Autriche	*Danemark*	*Norvège*	*Portugal*
Ministres:	Dr B. KREISKY (Affaires étrangères) Dr F. BOCK (Commerce et Reconstruction)	M. J. O. KRAG (Affaires étrangères)	M. A. SKAUG (Commerce)	M. J. G. CORREA DE OLIVEIRA (Commerce)
Chefs de Délégations:	M. E. TREU	M. N. V. SKAK-NIELSEN	M. S. C. SOMMERFELT	M. R. T. GUERRA
Adjoints:	M. M. SCHEICH	M. T. JANTZEN	M. A. SKARSTEIN	M. C. R. LOURENÇO

	Royaume-Uni	*Suède*	*Suisse*
Ministres:	M. R. MAUDLING (Board of Trade) M. E. HEATH (Lord Privy Seal)	M. G. LANGE (Commerce)	M. M. PETITPIERRE (Affaires étrangères) M. F. T. WAHLEN (Économie publique)
Chefs de Délégations:	Sir Edgar COHEN	M. N. T. MONTAN	M. O. LONG
Adjoints:	M. G. H. BAKER	M. B. FRIEDMAN	M. F. WALTHARD

E. LE SECRÉTARIAT DE L'A.E.L.E.

Secrétaire Général: M. F. E. FIGGURES.
Adjoint: M. K. HAMMARSKJOELD.
Chefs des Départements:
Affaires générales et juridiques: M. CH. MÜLLER.
Affaires commerciales: M. E. BASTRUP-BIRK (adjoint).
Information et presse: M. P. A. LADAME.
Affaires économiques: M. B. LARSEN.
Comptabilité: M. C. J. PYKE.
Administration: M. I. ETIENNE.

Toutes les demandes de renseignements doivent être adressées au Département de l'Information. :
32, chemin des Colombettes, Genève.
Téléphone: 34 90 00.
Télex: 22660 Genève
Télégrammes: EFTASEC Genève.

D. MEMBERS OF THE COUNCIL

(U. K. in the Chair since 1st january, 1961)

	Austria	*Denmark*	*Norway*	*Portugal*
Ministers:	Mr. B. KREISKY (Foreign Affairs) Mr. F. BOCK (Commerce and Reconstruction)	Mr. J. O. KRAG (Foreign Affairs)	Mr. A. SKAUG (Commerce)	Mr. J. G. CORREA DE OLIVEIRA (Commerce)
Heads of Delegations:	Mr. E. TREU	Mr. N. V. SKAK-NIELSEN	Mr. S. C. SOMMERFELT	Mr. R. T. GUERRA
Deputies:	Mr. M. SCHEICH	Mr. T. JANTZEN	Mr. A. SKAR-STEIN	Mr. C. R. LOURENÇO

	Sweden	*Switzerland*	*United Kingdom*
Ministers:	Mr. G. LANGE (Commerce)	Mr. M. PETITPIERRE (Foreign Affairs) Mr. F. T. WAHLEN (National Economy)	Mr. R. MAUDLING (Board of Trade) Mr. E. HEATH (Lord Privy Seal)
Heads of Delegations:	Mr. N. T. MONTAN	Mr. O. LONG	Sir Edgar COHEN
Deputies:	Mr. B. FRIEDMAN	Mr. F. WALTHARD	Mr. G. H. BAKER

E. E.F.T.A. DIRECTORY

Secretariat

Secretary-General: Mr. F. E. FIGGURES.
Deputy: Mr. K. HAMMARSKJÖLD.
Heads of Department:
General and Legal: Mr. CH. MÜLLER.
Trade Policy: Mr. E. BASTRUP-BIRK (Deputy) .
Information: Mr. P. A. LADAME.
Economic: Mr. B. LARSEN
Finance Officer: Mr. C. J. PYKE.
Administrative Officer: Mr. I. ETIENNE.

Press enquiries should be addressed to The Information Department:
32, chemin des Colombettes, Geneva.
Telephone: 34 90 00
Telex: 22660 GENEVA
Telegrams: EFTASEC GENEVA

SECTION BIBLIOGRAPHIQUE

BIBLIOGRAPHICAL SECTION

I. LIVRES ET BROCHURES SUR L'INTÉGRATION EUROPÉENNE

I. BOOKS AND PAMPHLETS ON EUROPEAN INTEGRATION

Comptes rendus par: Book-reviews by: B. BURTON, J. L. F. VAN ESSEN, LAZAR FOCSANEANU, M. VAN GELDEREN, T. A. M. ALTING VON GEUSAU, W. HORSFALL CARTER, J. KOREVAAR, B. LANDHEER, M. M. PURI, A. H. ROBERTSON, BERNHARD SCHLOH, H. WIEBRINGHAUS.

A. L'INTÉGRATION EUROPÉENNE EN GÉNÉRAL

A. EUROPEAN INTEGRATION IN GENERAL

ALLEN (H. C.), The Anglo-American predicament. London, (Macmillan & Co Ltd.), 1960. xiv, 241 pp.

"The Anglo-American predicament", which is sub-titled "The British Commonwealth, the United States and European unity", pleads eloquently for the cause of Atlantic Union and argues against a purely European union. The author is a Briton but he addresses his book "equally to the British and the American peoples". It was written at the end of 1959, but most of what it says is highly relevant to the debate taking place in the Western World in 1961 on what should be the nature and composition of the European Common Market.

In his first chapter, Professor ALLEN examines the two special features, of the international position of the United Kingdom: "first, the extent, dispersion and complexity of her Empire, which she is now in the process of transforming into a Commonwealth of associated but free and independent nation-States; and second, the degree of her dependence on international trade, with manifold and distant parts of the world, for her very life" (p. 3).

The author goes on in succeeding chapters to sketch in further background to the "Dilemma of Britain". In the concluding paragraphs of his chapter on "Britain and the United States," he states his arguments against Britain entering a purely European union:

... The United Kingdom can hardly even allow herself to envisage in the future any international policy which might result in a clash with the United States: she has no option, indeed, as she has already discovered, but to concert all her major policies with her great transatlantic neighbour... How then can she ever consent to enter a European union in which her independence of action would be lost along with her national sovereignty? The risk to her democratic institutions, the possible commitment to a European "third force" alienated from the United States, which might result, would spell total disaster for her. It would threaten her bonds not merely with America, but with the Commonwealth and the whole world as well; this would be so because the Commonwealth in such circumstances would have little option but to follow America and also because the range and scale of American sea power is so great that all Britain's communications with the outside world would be imperilled. Thus any rift, produced by the policies of a European union of which she was a member, between Britain and the United States would no doubt be less emotionally agonizing for her than a mere breach with the Commonwealth, but it would be potentially infinitely more calamitous. When the United Kingdom held back from the Common Market, clearly involving as it did, ultimate and absolute political commitments, she was not merely giving vent to a reactionary insularity and isolationism, but was showing a profound, if instinctive, understanding of her fundamental interests (pp. 102-3).

What then is the answer for Britain? "Must she remain indefinitely frozen in immobility"? "Must she sit in paralysed inaction while a new political giant is created on her very doorstep in Europe?"

"The answer", says Professor ALLEN, "is that they (the people of Britain) must turn their eyes once more outwards. ...But they must not look to the Commonwealth alone. If all else were to fail Britain might strive to strengthen her exclusive bonds with those parts of the Commonwealth which desired such a development, but in the first place she must set her sights much higher than that: nothing else should content her but the institutional cohesion of all three of her essential circles of association, Europe, the Commonwealth and also the United States" (pp. 115–6). And he adds further: "To enter the Common Market, or even a United States of all Europe, has too many political dangers and disadvantages for her: to stay out may have almost as many. Closer bonds with Europe are not enough: even closer bonds with the Commonwealth or the United States are not a complete answer. There is for Britain no fully satisfactory alternative to Atlantic Union" (p. 120).

Part II of the book is adressed especially to Americans and called "The challenge to America". It examines the stake of the United States in Atlantic Union. "By creating a new body politic she will solve, in a sense automatically, the almost insoluble problem of leading a group of national States, for all will participate in the process of policy making" (p. 153). "The gigantic strength of Atlantic Union will, of course, be supremely valuable in the cold war with Russia: it is perhaps the strongest argument for bringing it into existence" (p. 155). Moreover, Professor ALLEN argues, the advantages of such a Union would not be material ones only: "The power for self-government, the influence for democracy, which a great free constitutional Union, of more than 400 million souls and unprecedented resources and economic strength, would exert in the world would be nothing less than enormous. It would be a strong and practical lever for the accomplishment of America's, and the West's, purpose – to ensure that government of the people, by the people, and for the people shall in the fulness of time come to all the peoples of the earth (pp. 199–200).

So, in the view of the author, America as well as Britain has much to gain from an Atlantic Union. But is American public opinion ready to "buy" the idea? Professor ALLEN recognises there are difficulties here: "If in fact we were to ask the very large majority of Americans today whether they were prepared to accept an Atlantic Union their answer would almost unquestionably be in the negative. The long history of America's actual geographical isolation from the other hemisphere, her persistent tradition of isolationism in international affairs, her deep sense of political "apartness" from the old world, and her real feeling of new world superiority to the moral decadence, corruption and inequity of Europe still make the idea of a real and permanent re-integration of the United States with Western Europe initially repugnant to American sensibilities" (pp. 141–2).

But the author is optimistic about future possibilities: "The time is ripe for Americans to look again with clear eyes at their international situation and their relations with their allies and their enemies. If, as a result, with due and proper public preparation and education, the issue of Atlantic Union were in the fullness of time put fairly before the American people, their response might well, I believe, astonish mankind in its receptiveness and even enthusiasm" (p. 208).

A debatable conclusion, surely? Perhaps the emphasis should be placed on the phrase "in the fullness of time". At present one cannot help wondering whether the actual title of Professor ALLEN's book does not anticipate too much. Certainly there is a "British predicament": the British are now, belatedly, only too well aware of the dilemma confronting them. But are there as yet many Americans who feel that this predicament is also theirs? The author calls his book "a tract for the times" – perhaps, so far as American public opinion is concerned, this tract has come both too late and too early for its times. Too late because the wartime spirit of Anglo-American comradeship has now almost entirely evaporated: too early because present-day Americans will need a lot of convincing before they agree to American participation in an Atlantic Union.

B.B.

BIRKE (WOLFGANG), European elections by direct suffrage. Leyden, (Sythoff), 1961. 124 pp. (European Aspects (Series C, no. 5)).

The ultimate goal of the Movement for European integration is political – the creation of a supranational federation based upon generally accepted democratic practices. To that end an adequately representative and competent parliament, ienjoying the confidence of the peoples concerned and cementing the integration, s imperative and, of course, inevitable. But so far, in spite of constant efforts, no agreement has been possible on a uniform electoral system which would make the

European Parliament a reality. Dr. BIRKE, in the present work (which was done under one of the fellowships of the Council of Europe), suggests a way out. He advocates the adoption of D'HONDT's list system of proportional representiaton in large constituencies together with the possibility of a choice between the candidates within the list. Professor LEIBHOLZ – who was largely responsible for the legal recognition of political parties in the German Basic Law and is an ardent protagonist of proportional representation – naturally, in his preface to the book, finds the author's conclusions "logical" and concurs that this system alone suits the future European structure of government.

Having defined a direct election ("An election is direct or *unmittelbar* in the sense of article 38 of the German Basic Law if the seats are attributed automatically after the act of voting without the insertion of an act of will of a third person") and maintaining that "a list system fulfils the requirements of a direct election", the author examines in clear, concise terms the pros and cons of election for European Parliament by people directly. He finds "a uniform electoral system is a prerequisite" for such an election and feels, quite rightly, that "it is necessary to do this now, even if direct elections seem not yet practicable". And to this end – evolving a uniform electoral system – the rest of the study is devoted. The difficulties posed by elections among fifteen Member States of the Council of Europe accustomed to voting under as many electoral systems (the problems of distribution of seats between parties and candidates, prevention of splinter parties, the selection and presentation of candidates, the privileges of political parties, *etc.*) are examined in detail and substantiated with an excellent handling of the available data. Finally, while discussing the purposes of election in general (creation of a representative, competent parliament which enjoys full confidence of the electorate; personal tie between deputy and voter; opportunity for the elector to express his will, and so on), the realisation of these purposes by various electoral systems (such as Majority system, Bonus system, Mixed system and the two systems of proportional representation) in the election of a European Parliament are critically examined and certain suggestions made.

Dr. BIRKE has written indeed a commendable book; it is cogently reasoned, judiciously documented, lucid, to the point and informative. Of course some of his observations are debatable – definition of "direct" election, purpose of European elections – and the solution he suggests may not be accepted by all concerned. In fact, a considerable reluctance to adopt a party list system is bound to exist among the peoples with different backgrounds and political traditions. But his arguments and the presentation of his case are stimulating enough to deserve a careful consideration, and *could* form a basis for agreement. The great merit of the book, however, lies in the fact that it contains reliable material for a further study by the scholar and, at the same time, has enough to interest and instruct the layman. M.M.P.

BRUGMANS (HENRI), L'Europe prend le large. Tome II. Liège, (Georges Thone), 1961. 367 pp. (Recherches européennes. Collection du Collège d'Europe (Bruges)).

This volume follows the work entitled "Origines de la Civilisation européenne" while both, together with a third volume, will form a "Histoire générale de l'Europe". As historiography has improved its techniques of research, it has become increasingly difficult to create a general image and yet be loyal to details. Judging as a "European reader" and not as a historian, it seems to the reviewer that Professor BRUGMANS has admirably succeeded in his task and has ranked himself with the historians whose works are also of interest to the outsider. He paints a sensitive and colourful canvas of the unfolding of Europe, which he depicts as a gradual process moving through the various sectors of life and segments of society, resulting in growing complexity rather than in any clearcut development as was the favoured image of the preceding generation.

It is as Salvador de MADARIAGA states in his Preface: "L'Europe est un état d'âme. Lisez, lisez encore, lisez toujours, et vous accumulerez des "faits" et encore des "faits". Mais vous n'y trouverez l'Europe que si vous l'y apportez vous-même. N'en concluez pas qu'elle ne s'y trouve pas déjà. Bien sûr, elle s'y trouve. Le dessein est là, l'unité est là, et surtout la communauté de destin est là. Mais afin de les faire ressortir de la masse des faits, de la cohue des êtres, de l'enchevêtrement des courants, il faut que l'oeil qui regarde soit déjà européen".

Perhaps Europe is a state of consciousness more than anything else, and as such it can hardly be regarded as collective but more as a constant process of changes in awareness, which are set off by external factors as well as by an inner development that follows a certain natural pattern. Europe has distinguished itself from other parts of the world by its greater dynamism, and this greater dynamism – call it "Faustian" if you like – makes the pattern of Europe so amazingly intricate, consisting of this inner logic as well as of the continued impact of changing external factors, moving from the influence of Mohammedanism and Judaism to the contact with countless other cultures.

It has been often the custom to depict the Middle Ages as non-dynamic, but Professor Brugmans, as others have done, shows convincingly the error of this thesis, though one occasionally wonders whether he does not somewhat underrate the dualism of the Middle Ages, particularly in his interpretation of the Gothic as a sort of balanced mastery over life. If one de-traditionalizes the conceptions about the Middle Ages, it seems as if their inner tensions which somehow prepared the later unfolding of the European mind become somewhat submerged in its more classical attributes and its social innovations in monastic orders and in the emerging cities.

If the Middle Ages become a more balanced period than was assumed in the past, the further history of Europe becomes so much more due to external factors, while there is nevertheless also the necessary growth and increasing maturity of the European mind itself.

Professor Brugmans combines the various facets in a masterly fashion, though he omits what one might call the "ominous" in this process of preparing for a more complete mastery over the natural and social environment. The gain was in some respects a loss, as the dimensions of the Middle Ages were not again reached by later periods which overcame the severe psychic cleavage of the Middle Ages by seeking rational control rather than outlets for emotional anxiety.

Nevertheless, Professor Brugmans' "gradualism" is quite convincing when he demonstrates the emergence of a certain equilibrium with the Moslems during the Crusades and when he shows the first appearance of representative organs in some of the monastic orders. He is also convincing when he shows that the complexity of the European structure did not run in a straight line towards a more egalitarian order, but that the egalitarian order grew as a correction of a hierarchical structure and as a correction, brought about by certain social groups which gave their aims a more general appeal. The patterns of Europe were hardly ever universal, but always rather specific, local and only in some respects predominantly national as there was the constant interplay between feudal and civic organisation, between State and Church, while economic expansion was carried by a number of different groups and partially determined, sometimes adversedly by the strength of their organisational forms.

It is the great merit of the author that while European integration is now viewed largely piecemeal and by specific mental approaches, like from the viewpoint of economics or law, Professor Brugmans presents it with its universal attributes which are the very essence of Europe and whence the inspiration for European unity must come if it is to develop sufficient reality. Professor Brugmans as one of the pioneers of the unity of contemporary Europe tries to build it upon the solid foundation of its own past that does not call for purely formal solutions of a set pattern, but rather for living forms that grow out of the continuity of the European mind as well as of the impact which it undergoes from the rest of the world. The experience which is essential to this process can be gained only from Europe's history and from a "depth-analysis" of its ascendancy as well as from its present need to live with other civilisations to which it may give a perspective on the universal values to which Europe has always shown such great loyalty, even if they operated against its own more immediate interests.

The continuity of Europe is not conceivable without the "thinking European" who cannot be lost in a mass-society, unless we close our eyes to the precarious position of Europe in the world. The history of Europe is the only realistic basis for European thinking, and under this perspective the reviewer was fascinated by professor Brugmans' work which he undoubtedly aimed not only at the historian, but at those who would like to learn about the reality of things rather than about their appearance.

B.L.

COLLÈGE D'EUROPE, Sciences humaines et intégration européenne. Préface de Robert Schuman. Leyden, (A. W. Sijthoff), 1960. 423 pp.

In this volume the professional European academicians take the floor and present a number of analyses which were evolved within the framework of the College of Europe at Bruges. The studies are largely analytical as one cannot attribute an ideological function to the College of Europe, even though it favours European integration, but not at the cost of scientific veracity. Apparently, no conflict between the two has occurred, and general philosophy as well as specific analyses result in non-controversial studies. In fact, one of the puzzling things about European integration is that nobody is against it, but so few are whole-heartedly for it, at least not to the extent of thinking about it or having particular ideas about it.

It remains in the realm of what PLATO called the "necessary causes", though it does provide an intellectual challenge, notably to the jurists and the economists, but not a general one. An appeal to the imagination is still lacking, though this would be most essential. Among the many sciences which come to the fore in this volume, one cannot help feeling that the established professions, like the ones just mentioned, deal with real problems while the sociological contributions remain vague and confused.

When Mr JANNE states that a sociology of Europe is only possible if Europe is regarded as a sociological fact, one is inclined to ask whether this does not put the horse behind the cart. In addition, one would like a definition, and if culture consists of an interactional process between a social group and its environment, the result is obviously always unique, and it would be more to the point to ask in how far Europe constitutes a social group. As a social group can be more or less integrated, a sociology of Europe would tend to investigate what the present social structure of Europe consists of and what changes are likely to occur as a result of integration via governmental activities. Or more essential still: what effect does the creation of intergovernmental organs have on the social structure of Europe.

This would have been a very noteworthy contribution to the analysis of Europe which could supplement the more goal-directed investigations of the lawyer and the economist.

The analysis of Mr. JANNE, however, gives only some theoretical abstractions which belong to a specific type of sociological theory without ever getting near the realities of social life.

A similar vagueness prevails in the contribution of Leo MOULIN: *Que vaut la réflexion du sociologue ,,engagé"*? After this somewhat irritating title, one does not profit much by reading passages like the following :,,Le sociologue méditant en tant que sociologue sur les problèmes de l'intégration européenne devrait en étudier aussi l'adversaire le plus redoutable et le plus subtil: l'U.R.S.S., la nature exacte du totalitarisme soviétique, les infiltrations communistes en Occident, l'efficacité réelle et le coût humain des méthodes de planification centralisatrice, le colonialisme russe, si justement dénoncé par LÉNINE et qui a survécu au cataclysme d'octobre 1917, d'une façon générale, la portée et la signification de l'effort pharaonique que les grands empires des steppes font en ce moment" (p. 100).

Mr. MOULIN predicts that the integration of Europe will result in an affluent, classless society. Such a prediction which isolates Europe from the rest of the world and ignores the whole problem of fitting Europe into world-society, can hardly have much value. Its author would have to make acceptable first that there is no great probability of increasing pressures on Europe, and on the West in general. This he entirely fails to do while scientific observation would lead to the realisation that these outside pressures have continuously taken place so that it is not convincing to analyse Europe as a separate entity. In the quoted passage the author indicates this himself, but he omits to apply his own warning, while sociology certainly is not the science to isolate social phenomena. This would make it fail in its most realistic objective, *viz.* to supplement and integrate legal and economic thinking.

It is interesting to observe that, though the volume deals with various disciplines, the greatest clarity is reached by the economic analyses. This is perhaps indicative of the fact that integration is largely an economic matter and its goals are most clearcut from the economic viewpoint, *viz.* the larger market as a means to high production and high consumption, though this may involve structural difficulties in regard to agriculture as has become already noticeable.

A very lucid exposé is given by Professor TINBERGEN on the impact of the E.E.C. on third countries. Of considerable interest is also the article by Professor BOMBACH on *Economic growth and stability in a United Europe*, though it deals more with the highly developed economy in general than with specific aspects of Europe. Particularly noteworthy are the author's remarks about "creeping inflation" as a concomitant of economic growth: "Representing one point of view are a group of economists who believe that a certain degree of inflation is actually desirable, to provide the necessary stimulus for economic growth in a free economy. They believe that the choice is either monetary stability or economic growth. Diametrically opposed to them are those who hold the point of view that creeping inflation must inevitably turn into galloping inflation, which will, through a breakdown of the economy, mean an end to growth....". "Between these two extreme standpoints there exists a not inconsiderable group of economists who, recognizing that creeping inflation is basically evil and not a necessary precursor of economic growth, are nevertheless prepared to accept it as the lesser evil when compared to the possibility of direct controls over prices and wages, or to applying pressures on the labour market by means of restrictive monetary and fiscal measures." (pp. 246–247).

The author believes that one of the great problems will be to keep investments at a sufficiently high level and not to yield to the demand to adjust real wages to labour productivity as this would tend to weaken the competitive power of the European economy. In order to keep the economy elastic, it is also essential to channel expansion in the right direction in order to avoid saturation in certain sectors. A normal economy can never be wholly stable, nor should it be overly dynamic as, in the long run, demand cannot be increased *ad infinitum*, but must correspond to the exigencies of a normal and well-balanced life by which material goods are means to an end.

Other economic contributions deal with *Nécessité et dynamisme de l'intégration institutionnelle* (Rolf WAGENFÜHR); *La clef du système monétaire et du développement économique mondial; Le crédit international* (Maurice MASOIN); *Statistique et intégration européenne* (Jean PETRE).

The third section of the book deals with ,,L'Approche juridique" in four different articles. They deal with the symbiotic aspects of legal growth in the fields of public and private law. The following topics are dealt with *Le juriste regarde l'intégration Européenne* (Ignaz SEIDL-HOHENVELDERN); *Perspectives pour un droit européen* (Alphonse de VREESE); *La défense des droits de l'homme en Europe* (Héribert) GOLSONG); *Reciprocal acceptance of the acts of sister states in federations* (Robert L. MORLAN).

Other sections of the volume consists of: "Données de base" (I); "Théorie politique" (II); "Les institutions" (V); "L'Europe occidentale et le monde" (VI).

"Sciences humaines et intégration européenne" is an impressive record of the intellectual activity of the Europe College at Bruges, though one misses a total assessment of integration upon a philosophical or sociological basis, and more particularly of its rôle in regard to the rest of the world which is not getting enough attention and which leaves many unanswered questions which are only dealt with from a European viewpoint. European integration is the response to a global situation which is still very much in flux, and these dynamic aspects do not come sufficiently into focus. Power is the key-word to contemporary world-society; economic prosperity the key-word to western Europe. Between the two there is perhaps not the positive correlation that is often so readily assumed. B.L.

DEHOUSSE, (FERNAND), L'Europe et le monde; Recueil d'études, de rapports et de discours 1945–1960. Paris, 1960. 618 pp.

,,Fernand DEHOUSSE: vingt-cinq ans au service du droit des gens à l'Université et dans la vie internationale," c'était l'occasion de donner au public ce grand volume qui contient la plupart des articles, rapports, conférences et débats de M. DEHOUSSE pendant la période indiquée.

La tâche dont le Comité organisateur s'est acquittée, était, pour employer ses propres mots, de ,,réunir des textes qui s'échelonnent au long de quinze années du siècle le plus chargé d'histoire; les classer selon la pensée qui les anime et le but qui les ordonne; choisir enfin ceux qui, par leur nature, leur argumentation ou leur portée, paraissaient dégager avec le plus de bonheur le sens d'une oeuvre immense, qui est aussi le sens d'une vie."

Dans le chapitre sur les Nations Unies l'auteur s'occupe du rôle, que les petits pays peuvent jouer sur la scène internationale, il parle du Conseil économique et social de l'O.N.U. et des Droits de l'Homme. En Belgique il était actif pour l'inscription des droits économiques et sociaux de l'homme dans la Constitution. De même les questions de la liaison Escaut-Rhin se trouvent dans ce livre, ainsi qu'un débat au Senat sur la politique sociale africaine de la Belgique.

Exception faite des chapitres mentionnés tout le volume est consacré à des problèmes européens.

M. DEHOUSSE, professeur de droit international à l'Université de Liège, Associé de l'Institut de Droit International, compte parmi les grands Européens.

Sénateur de Belgique, membre de l'Assemblée Consultative du Conseil de l'Europe et son Président de 1956 à 1959, membre de l'Assemblée Parlementaire Européenne, il a servi la cause de l'Europe unie dans chaque Institution. Il s'est déclaré partisan resolu de l'Europe des Six, ,,le moyen le plus organique et le plus solide" (p. 446), mais s'est beaucoup soucié de l'union étroite entre l'ensemble des pays européens, comme ses activités pendant sa présidence à Strasbourg l'ont montré.

Lire les chapitres intitulés ,,le Conseil de l'Europe", ,,la C.E.C.A.", le Marché Commun et l'Euratom", c'est, pour le lecteur, vraiment récapituler l'histoire de l'organisation des pays européens. DEHOUSSE a toujours poussé l'évolution, par exemple par des Rapports sur la réorganisation des Institutions européennes auxquelles il a voulu attribuer plus des compétences, notamment à l'Assemblée Consultative; mais les États ne l'ont pas suivi.

Le livre contient aussi les chapitres ,,De la C.E.D. aux Accords de Paris", ,,L'Assemblée *ad hoc* et la Communauté politique européenne", et ,,La Sarre". Les deux premiers nous montrent que les grands et véritables projets d'intégration ont été mis en échec. DEHOUSSE avait pris une attitude ,,entièrement positive" envers le C.E.D. et dans l'Assemblée *ad hoc* il a été le rapporteur et donc le constructeur de la Constitution de la Communité (politique) européenne. Il s'était montré prêt à abandonner cette partie de la souveraineté nationale sans le sacrifice de laquelle l'unification politique de l'Europe – son but – ne pourra pas être atteint.

En 1955 DEHOUSSE a été Président de la Commission européenne pour le referendum en Sarre en se préoccupant de l'honnêteté du referendum. Sa conférence faite sur le sujet en privé en Belgique, merite la lecture.

Comme membre de l'Assemblée Parlementaire Européenne, DEHOUSSE a élaboré le rapport sur le projet d'élection de l'Assemblée au suffrage universel direct adopté par l'Assemblée en mai 1960. C'est une des idées qu'il a traité avec force déjà dans l'Assemblée *ad hoc* et il a toujours poursuivi cette idée. L'unification économique sans une unification politique reste une chose imparfaite et pour une Assemblée Parlementaire sans suffrage universel direct, il en est de même.

Ce livre est une véritable pièce d'histoire européenne et honore l'auteur comme les personnes qui se sont donné pour tâche de réunir ces textes. B.S.

DÜRRENMATT (PETER), Europa will leben. Bern, (Verlag Hallwag), 1960. 198 pp.

The Swiss have their own outlook on European matters, and some of their authors, like DÜRRENMATT, can be thoughtfull as well as thought-provoking. The title "Europa will leben" expresses a reality rather neatly, and one has every reason to accept the point that the Europeans want to live, though one might be inclined to add "if the others let them". Those others, according to the author, are the Communists, and the "new" nations who represent a definite human and political type while in Europe the conservative revolution has been definitely victorious. This rôle fits Europe historically, and it is perhaps true that the manifestations, which went with Marxism, progressism and techno-scientism, have lost their appeal in Europe.

Europe is no longer interested in political philosophy, in materialistic thinking and in the worship of science: this is no lack of a will to live, but it is a will for a balanced life that finds its measure in itself. As the finding of balance is also imperative for the world as a whole, Europe still has a universal mission, more than America or Russia. This might be deduced from the situation in Asia and Africa, where the response to the Europeans is often positive.

Wisdom and balance could become the key-words of Europe if it can live down the last remnants of rationalism, progressism and scientism, but they still have a vigorous life particularly among the "reactionaries" as well as among the "Jacobins".

The author regards the vitality of banality as the basis for a new start. Something to operate with that gets us beyond the eternal conflicts of idealism and realism, spiritualism and the revolt of indifference. If we know that we want to live, the next question becomes "How?" DÜRRENMATT stressest hat the European wants unity, not integration.

"Diese Möglichkeiten eines Programms einer europäischen Politik sind ein Programm des Werdens, der Zukunftserwartung, auf der Grundlage von vier massgebenden aussenpolitischen Realitäten: der neuen Machtstellung und des ständigen drohenden Pochens der Sowjetführer auf diese Position, der raschen Emanzipation Afrikas, verbunden mit der zunehmenden Gefahr der Revolutionierung, und des möglichen Engagements Amerikas durch die Vorgänge im Fernen Osten. Mit anderen Worten, die Situation zwischen 1945 und 1955, in der sich Europa einfach auf die amerikanische Hilfe verlassen konnte, ist überholt. Das Zeitalter der Weltpolitik had Europa zwar abgewertet, gibt ihm aber nun in anderer Weise eine neue Stellung zurück.

Die Zukunft Europas, seine politische Verantwortung vor der Geschichte sind durch jene vier aussenpolitischen Realitäten umschrieben. Vordringlich ist deshalb nicht eine alle europäischen Staaten auf der Grundlage juristischer Gleichheit zum Überstaat konzipierten Verfassung, sondern die variable Assoziierung von Staaten und Staatengruppen, wobei deren Völker das Vertrauen in ihre eigene politische Kraft zurückgewinnen müssen" (pp. 59–60).

The author sees a conflict between legal and centralised thinking and between pragmatic-federative ideas. "Eine Einigung Europas kann in dieser Sicht deshalb nicht heissen, bestimmte geschlossene Gebiete der Staatstätigkeit den einzelnen entziehen zu wollen und durch eine übergeordnete Behörde besorgen zu lassen. "Einigung" im föderativ-pragmatischen Sinne heisst, durch indirekte freiheitlich wirkende Massnahmen die Voraussetzungen zu beeinflussen, unter denen sich das Zusammenspiel zunehmend freier abwickeln kann. In diese indirekte Beeinflussung sind dann aber alle Gebiete der Politik einzubeziehen, nicht nur die wirtschafts- und sozialpolitischen" (p. 65).

Mr. DÜRRENMATT has written an interesting and valuable study, and one could only agree with him that European unity requires its own social forms which should not be seen too much in analogy to those of the nineteenth century. B.L.

HOFFMAN, (STANLEY) (Edited by), Contemporary theory in international relations. New York, (Prentice-Hall, Inc.), 1960. 293 pp.

In the words of the author, "this book is a plea for theory understood as a set of interrelated questions capable of guiding research both of the empirical and of the normative variety".

It comprises a series of selected readings on various aspects of contemporary theory in international relations and a number of commentaries by Professor HOFFMANN himself which discuss the subject-matter of these readings and outline his own views on the study of international relations. "Hence the somewhat unorthodox result: a book of selected readings whose editor criticizes rather harshly the selections he has made".

Part I presents the case for an autonomous discipline and discusses problems of scope, method and purpose. Part II takes a searching look at some contemporary theories of international relations. Professor MORGENTHAU's "realist" theory of power politics is subjected to a critical appraisal, as are the contemporary philosophies of history. Even though these latter "avoid many of the shortcomings of realism", in Professor HOFFMANN's view, they also have their drawbacks. "Here a teleological interpretation which discourages further research and twists the facts into a predetermined pattern is substituted for careful and systematic explanation" (p. 38). The author also gives his reasons for his dissatisfaction with Mr. Morton KAPLAN's "systems theory" and with some current attempts at organizing the discipline around a central "unifying concept" (Professor George LISKA's equilibrium theory and Professor SNYDER's decision-making approach).

In Part III (Suggestions for the Study of International Relations), Professor HOFFMAN agrees that "Nevertheless, the need for conceptualization and theory remains" and offers "some suggestions for a far more modest and slow way of proceeding toward theory". These are based on postulates "which are certainly as debatable as those I have discussed. But there is one difference: I do not claim that it is possible to squeeze the whole camel of international relations through the eye of one needle" (p. 171).

The author suggests two directions ot research – one making use of the "historical sociology" approach and the other attempting to build "Relevant Utopias."

"It (Historical Sociology) is a general approach based on the following ideas. The search for timeless propositions, and the deductive method, are, at present, disappointing. We must proceed inductively; before we reach any conclusions about general trends manifest throughout history, we should resort to systematic historical research, not in order to turn our discipline into history, but in order to accomplish the tasks to be suggested here in general terms" (p. 174).

The first of these tasks would be the description of historical systems of international relations. The second stage would be the comparison of historical systems.

"Finally, we could proceed to comparisons between domestic political systems and international ones, and between types of domestic and international systems" (p. 175).

This reviewer finds it very difficult to find fault with the author's general approach and conclusions since he (the reviewer) has had his main academic training in the field of history. The "historical sociology" approach would certainly appear to him to be the most useful one for would-be theorists to adopt.

Professor HOFFMANN goes on to argue that "in addition to such systematic research, there is a need for a different kind of task". We need a political philosophy of world affairs.

"Our first problem is the clarification of values we would like to see promoted in the world ... Second, we must relate these values to the world as it is, far more closely than we usually do. A total separation of "empirical science" and "moral philosophy" would be disastrous. ... We must try to build relevant Utopias. By spelling out our views on the purposes, the prerequisities, the possibilities and the procedure of an ideal international order, we would accomplish a triple task. We would meet the requirement of clarifying our personal value positions. We would avoid the piece-meal engineering approach of policy scientism. We would avoid the twin escapisms of "realism", which gloomily assumes the inevitability of the customary, and of "idealism", which postulates an easy road to world progress" (pp. 187–9).

Again, this reviewer finds it hard to dissent. B.B.

JENKS (WILFRED C.), International immunities. London, (Stevens & Sons Ltd.), 1961. 171 pp.

In this book, Dr. Wilfred JENKS reviews the legal provisions and administrative practices regarding immunities for international organisations; he gives a comprehensive account of the relevant provisions in the basic treaties, in the Headquarters' Agreements and in the various Agreements on Privileges and Immunities relating to the United Nations itself, the Specialised Agencies and regional organisations in all parts of the world. Part I of the book summarises developments since the War and discussed the general principles involved; Part II deals with immunities of the organisations themselves; Part III with immunities of persons, that is to say of delegates attending their meetings, of the judges of the International Court and of other international tribunals, of international armed forces and of international officials; Part IV relates to present tendencies and future prospects, wisely recognising that "the trend of contemporary legal development is towards the elimination or limitation of all types of immunity".

The recent extension and present scope of the problem is brought out in the Introduction: "there are now at all times substantial numbers of persons involved in New York, Geneva, The Hague, Washington, London, Paris, Rome, Vienna, Brussels, Luxembourg, Strasbourg, Moscow, Montreal, Santiago, Buenos Aires, Rio de Janeiro, Mexico City, Lima, Tokyo, Manila, New Delhi, Bangkok, Beirut, Cairo-Alexandria, and Addis Abeba, and smaller but significant numbers at other duty stations and on temporary missions throughout the world" (p. xxxv).

Particularly valuable is Dr. JENKS' exposé of the basic principle underlying international immunities: "It is not concerned with the status, dignity or privileges of individuals, but with the elements of functional independence necessary to free international institutions from national control and to enable them to discharge their responsibilities impartially on behalf of all their Members" (p. 17). This same point is further developed in the chapter about international officials, which should help to dispel the popular illusion that international officials seek some special status for their own benefit, whereas in fact the true purpose of immunities is to enable international organisations to act in true independence, in the interests of of the Governments by which they are created. Recent events in the Congo should suffice to illustrate the need for the independence of international officials from the control of any one national government. The same point is well developed in one of the concluding chapters on "The Institutional Function of International Immunities" where Dr. JENKS writes: "The basic function of international immunities is to bridle the sovereignty of States in their treatment of international organisations..... It represents, indeed, an indispensable guarantee to each Member State that the organisation will not become, by means of pressure and constraint which are not fully apparent and over which there is therefore no possibility of control, an instrument of the policy of other States directed against its own policy and interests, but will serve legally the common interest as determined by the recognised constitutional processes of the organisation" (p. 166).

Readers of the European Yearbook will be particularly interested in Dr. JENKS' treatment of the immunities of European organisations, which is to be found alongside that of the United Nations' Family though, somewhat naturally, on a less extended scale. The "Agreement on the Status of Western European Union, National Representatives and International Staffs" signed at Paris on May 11th, 1955, is mentioned, but might have been discussed rather more fully, since it reflects a recent restrictive tendency towards the status of international officials, particularly in matters of taxation. It provides, in fact, in its Article 21 that "officials of the Organisation ... shall be subject to taxation by the Organisation, for its own benefit, on the emoluments paid to them in their capacity as officials to such extent and in accordance with such procedure as the Council may decide". The same tendency is also expressed in the Protocols on the Privileges and Immunities of the Economic Community and Euratom, which Dr. JENKS discusses at pp. 123 and 124. He draws attention to the curious arrangement in N.A.T.O. whereby its officials are in principle granted exemption from taxation, but any Member State may conclude an arrangement with the Council whereby such Member State will employ and assign to N.A.T.O. all of its nationals who are to serve on the international staff and pay their salaries and emoluments from its own funds at a scale fixed by itself and subject to such taxation as it may impose. Dr. JENKS observes very justly "the N.A.T.O. arrangement is clearly inconsistent with the whole concept of an international service as generally understood".

Another point which might be mentioned is that the General Agreement on Privileges and Immunities of the Council of Europe and its three Protocols, all remain unratified by the host country, with the result that the immunities granted to the Council, to delegates and to its officials, are still based on the administrative action rather than legal obligation. In the chapter on "International Judicial Immunities," Dr. JENKS draws attention to the fact that a further Supplementary Protocol to the General Agreement on Privileges and Immunities of the Council of Europe is necessary in respect of the European Court of Human Rights (p. 98); it is encouraging to know that such an instrument is now under negotiation. It is, however, curious that the Treaties setting up the European Communities which, as is well known, have gone further than other instruments in curbing national sovereignty, nevertheless do not grant complete jurisdictional immunity even to their most senior officials (p. 114), although this is normally accorded to the Secretaries-General of international organisations on the traditional model.

Dr. JENKS is to be congratulated on having produced such a comprehensive survey of the law and practice relating to international immunities, in the development of which he has himself played a prominent part, and the legal advisers of international organisations and the legal departments of the Foreign Ministries will find this a most useful and authoritative work when dealing with such problems in future.

A.H.R.

NUTTING (The Rt. Hon. ANTHONY), Europe will not wait. A warning and a way out. London, (Hollis & Carter), 1960. 122 pp.

This book is a Conservative censure of the British Labour Government's abject failure to grab the opportunity of moral as well as physical leadership of post-war Europe and an account of Conservative attempts to make amends for the lost chance. The author has been a Minister in the Conservative Governments in Britain from 1951 to 1956 and was directly concerned with European affairs during that period.

He argues that a devastated, depleted, bankrupt and morally disintegrated Europe which counted so heavily on Britain to lead in post-war recovery, was an ideal field for her to assume the responsibility of both coming closer to, and forging the bonds of unity in, Europe. But an unsympathetic, unimaginative and stubborn Labour Government – "The Attlee Cabinet of 1945 contained nobody who understood, still less who sympathised with, the way Europe felt" – not only let an admirable opportunity go by, but also, by act or implication, positively hindered the attempts of the enthusiasts (which, of course, included a strong core of far-sighted Conservatives) of European integration. "Labour", declares Mr. NUTTING reproachfully, "preferred insularity to internationalism". After exposing the "wickedness" and down-right incompetence of Labour in a breezy narrative which also touches upon the origin of MARSHALL Aid, The Hague Conference, Council of Europe, SCHUMAN Plan *etc.*, Mr. NUTTING turns to the rôle of his own Party and leadership in the European Movement. But, unfortunately, there too he does not find much to be proud of. He tells us how and to what extent it was incumbent upon him personally to push his equally reluctant own Party leaders nearer to Europe. In mild reprobation and tones of a disillusioned follower, he explains how the European Defence Community plan so brilliantly and appropriately conceived by CHURCHILL never even saw the light of day because of the intransigence of the federalists, British reluctance to accept supranationalism and disgraceful "sabotage" by the French who are not very keen that Britain should come in. Still, the Conservatives, and he personally, did much to repair the damage done by Labour to Britain's prestige and remove European suspicion and antipathy, as is evidenced by the emergence of the Western European Union on the ruins of the E.D.C. and by the creation of the Outer Seven after the collapse of Free Trade Area proposals. He concludes by scornfully dismissing the popular argument that Britain's Commonwealth responsibilities prevent her from joining any European club, and ardently arguing in favour of building up a comprehensive economic community embracing the whole of the Western world which would automatically out-date "restricted" concepts like those of the E.C.S.C., Common Market, *etc.*

It is perhaps too much to expect objectivity from a politician in the treatment of a complex, delicate and very much an emotional problem. Still, the author could have spared his readers sweeping and acrimonious generalisations, pointless polemics and blatantly biased presuppositions, particularly when his own "solutions" are not much different, let alone better, from those of his political opponents. M.M.P.

STADLER (K. R.), Adult education and European co-operation. Leyden, (Sythoff), 1960. 91 pp. (European Aspects. A collection of studies relating to European integration. Series A: Culture, No. 2).

The "European Aspects Series" brings many interesting and valuable specific studies of which the present one is a good example. Adult education in Europe shows a rather differentiated pattern, and there is a vast distance between the Latin and Germanic countries. In the Latin countries adult education has no roots in the historical and social development of the people, due perhaps to a different value-system and more conservative ideas about education.

After having given some impression about the state of adult education in general, the author deals with the rôle which is played in it by international relations and, more particularly with European affairs. The results are as follows:

Proportion of work devoted to international questions

All or much	23
Some	48
Little or very little	34
	105 (institutions analysed).

The author lists considerable activity in Germany, Austria, England, the Scandinavian countries and Holland, and gives a detailed survey of the techniques used in the various countries. England favours courses stretching over several years while the Continent shows no marked pattern.

The study favours the establishment of the function of an adult education officer at the Council of Europe as much can be done to create more interest in European unity and to approach it more effectively by adult education.

"We know from experience that the most effective way of introducing European problems to a general audience is by starting from the national vocational, or social situation of that audience; hence the most suitable tutor or speaker is a national of that country, and his training cannot be conducted *in vacuo* but must be based on conditions existing there. We also know that there is a place for the international speaker, and it may even be desirable, as is sometimes suggested, to compile a panel of those, stating where and when they are available, the languages they speak, *etc.*; but the principle need is for national speakers. To conduct special seminars or conferences for these, help them to work out the approach best suited to their conditions, enable them through travel abroad to experience the reality of European co-operation, arouse their desire to produce their own texts and illustrations, and keep in touch with them in any way possible – this would seem the most important and the most urgent task facing us today".

The booklet contains a good deal of useful information, but it presents it rather loosely. B.L.

B. L'INTÉGRATION ÉCONOMIQUE

B. ECONOMIC INTEGRATION

ALEKSEEV (D. M.) [i] MIKHAILOV (A. P.), Evropeiskoe ob'edinenie uglia i stali. Moskva, 1960. 284 pp.

This book acquaints us with a Soviet view on the European Coal and Steel Community. The co-authorship should be understood in this way that Mr. MIKHAILOV has written the two chapters that give a more general historical introduction (*The after-war tendency of the ruling powers' in the West for the formation of a military and political block and economic unification* and *The plans for a European "national' Coal and Steel Community*). Mr. ALEKSEEV deals with the existing Coal and Stee' Community, whereby he also pays attention to the other two Communities.

We need not, in this review, go into the history of the Community nor into the economic aspects of the matter which are known to most of us. What interests us, and what most Western readers should like to learn from this book, is to what conclusions on the European Communities Soviet social scientists come, guided by their Marxist principles.

On this point our authors leave little to doubt. When seen as a huge cartel the European Coal and Steel Community seems to fit well into the Marxist view on the Western economy: it is only a new stage in the accumulation of capital and the formation of monopolies, while at the same time antagonism between the monopolies, between countries and classes grow stronger. So this particular form of integration will *e.g.* sharpen the differences in income between the Communities and third countries and between Europe and Asia.

Behind the European Communities the authors see the purpose to form economic and military blocks under U.S. influence.

In his conclusion Mr. ALEKSEEV states that within the Community production has indeed been raised, but that this has been almost exclusively to the benefit of Western Germany. The Community has, on the other hand, failed to keep a check on Western Germany and to prevent her from attaining dominant position in Europe.

Equally unsuccesful was the endeavour to diminish, by a new form of cartel, the existing antagonisms: the differences between the countries of the Community as well as the opposition to third countries do not vanish, but are increasing: the formation of blocks, the division of Germany and the contradictions in Europe being consolidated.

The raising of the standard of living and the concern for employment cannot be but verbiage, for capitalist economy has never had this as a serious point on its program. Not mentioning the hard-pressed labor market in Western Europe today, he reminds us of the closing down of the marginal mines in Belgium, and states that elsewhere the raising of employment in coal and steel has been accompanied by a fall in other branches of industry. Finally it is said that the treaties on the Common Market and Euratom have caused new obstacles for the solution of the essential problems of European politics and economy: the formation of a system of security for Europe as a whole, and the extension of commerce between the West and the East.

Of the considerable amount of literature on this subject a great deal seems to plead for the concept of supranationality and for integration by way of the Communities. Here we have a passionate pleading of the opposite case. J.K.

BEEVER, (R. COLIN), European unity and the Trade Union Movements, Leyden, (A. W. Sythoff), 1960. 304 pp. (European Aspects: Series D, no. 2).

The Rome Treaties (establishing the European Economic Community and the EURATOM) of 1957 and their ratification by national legislatures of the Member countries were proof of the desire for European unity. The pressure exerted by the various groups within, and outside, the signatory countries produced that climate in which such an event could take place. And trade unions, already experienced in taking concerted action on matters of common interest, constituted the largest and the most leading pressure group. The reasons of the trade union initiative in, and support of, European unity and the impact of past as well as future European integration on the trade union movements and *vice versa* form the basis of this study.

The book starts with a discussion of the structure, mutual inter-relations and attitude towards integration of the three major international trade union movements, namely, the International Confederation of Free Trade Unions (I.C.F.T.U.), the World Federation of Trade Unions (W.F.T.U.) and the International Federation of Christian Trade Unions (I.F.C.T.U.). It is pointed out that the international trade union movements are divided along religious and political lines and are likely to remain so in the foreseeable future. This discussion is followed up by an examination of the structure, achievements and trade union representation in the European Coal and Steel Community. It is concluded that the earlier doubts and suspicions of the trade unions about the Community having been dispelled, the unions are now quite satisfied with their relations with it. Then comes an analysis of the Rome Treaties *vis-à-vis* the trade unions, the conclusion of which is that although the trade unions have been somewhat critical of the treaties, it is premature yet to envisage how exactly these treaties work out and what sort of relations would be established between the parties concerned. At any rate for the time being the trade unions are pleased that the treaties are at last in operation. Part IV of the book is devoted to a description of the national trade union viewpoints of those of the "Six "and the "Seven" Member countries, on the ground that these viewpoints are as important as those of the international trade unions. And finally, the conclusions of the study indicate the lines along which international trade union policy and structure might develop. It is pointed out that at present the international trade union movement lack an adequate – "European outlook" – "However much attention the unions pay to their international co-ordinating machinery, they will not succeed in creating a fully European outlook among trade unionists at humbler levels unless they can make them feel directly implicated". And this problem, in the opinion of Mr. BEEVER, can be approached from two psychological angles: *a*) a campaign for European solidarity through the American type of "Union Label" method should be sponsored by the trade unions; and *b*) they should pay their dues by the purchase of specially issued European Trade Union stamps. This of course should be supplemented by an extension of educational and publication services of the trade unions.

Mr. BEEVER has indeed brought together new factual and useful material concerning the rôle of the trade union organisations in the integration process, but has not completely succeeded in organising it in an impressive manner. As a result the presentation of his case is not wholly convincing, nor does he offer any clear answer to such obvious questions as: why different national centres of the trade union movements should have responded differently to the same or similar economic stimuli; how do the political changes in Member countries affect these movements *vis-à-vis* integration; and how far, if at all, the trade union movements become political rather than ecxlusively industrial under the stresses of European unity. On the whole, however, Mr. BEEVER has written a useful and welcome book on a problem which is bound to become increasingly important as the years go by and European horizons shrink to home skies. M.M.P.

FEDERAL (THE) BAR ASSOCIATION, WASHINGTON, D.C.: Proceedings of the 1960 Institute on Legal Aspects of the European Community. Washington, 1960. 218 pp.

During two and a half days in February 1960, the Federal Bar Association arranged for a "short law course on the European Community" of which the proceedings are now available. They reflect the ever growing interest of the U.S. towards Europe. This interest is not only motivated politically, but also the economic interest has increased considerably. There has been a "dramatic upswing in American direct investment in Western Europe from 1950 on" (STEIN). The American attitude may have found one expression in the following remark of Earl W. KINTNER, the Chairman of the Federal Trade Commission: "To lose these markets (*i.e.* the European Common Market) or to see a decline in them because of these new unions of nations is a critical question tied to the economy and vitality of the United States of Ameıica" (p. 15).

The basic objectives of the Institute have been to give to the American lawyer *a*) a broad view of the Community, *b*) an appreciation of some of the day-to-day problems which a lawyer has to face in representing a client who proposes doing business in the Community, and *c*) a perspective on the Community and its day-to-day operation both from the American and the European point of view (Henry T. KING, Jr., Chairman of the Institute).

The work of the Institute might be grouped into three large parts: in the first part, named legal-political framework, Professor Eric STEIN (Ann Arbor) who is well-known for his interest in European problems presents a lucid conference: An American lawyer views the Community. He offers the American reader a survey on the institutions and functions of the Common Market and discusses what its establishment will mean to the U.S. The political aim of the Community is stressed by the member of the E.E.C.-Commission, REY. GAUDET, Director General of the Legal Department of the High Authority (E.C.S.C.) since 1952 and therefore equipped with a long experience, gives a systematic outline of the legal systems of the European Community. He discusses the creation and execution of the Community law and its relations to the national legal orders. The special legal order of the Euratom is presented by VOGELAAR, a Director General of the Joint Legal Service of the three Communities.

In the second part, "technical problems" are presented. Some American lawyers and bankers deal with the operation of American enterprise in the Common Market, with fiscal and financial problems as well as how U.S. government agencies can help the American businessman.

In a more specialized third part, which subject was chosen by the organizers of the Institute from the many topics which would deserve a broader attention, the Restrictive Business Practices are dealt with. Here we find papers of VERLOREN VAN THEMAAT and Fernand SPAAK on the problem of competition in the Common Market and the European Coal and Steel Community respectively. American lawyers treat questions which are really important for the American doing business abroad. We may mention the article on the application of the U.S. antitrust laws to the European Community in which the author, Van CISE, starts his presentation with these lines: "Whither he (*i.e.* the American businessman) goes, our antitrust laws go; and where he lodges, these laws also lodge". There are also papers on Patents and on Trademarks in the European Community.

All these papers show the real interest of the U.S. in the European Community. To America the Community is "almost a new Eastern frontier" (Mark S. MASSEL, Editorial Note to the Proceedings) and Europe should be grateful that the Federal Bar Association has made a beginning to spread to the American lawyer substantial knowledge on the European Community.

We might add here that at the end of last year, Eric STEIN and Thomas L. NICHOLSON have edited two large volumes on *American enterprise in the European Common Market, A legal profile* which provide the American lawyer with both the general views and the necessary details. B.S.

GAY (FRANÇOIS) et WAGRET, (PAUL), Le Benelux. Paris, (Presses universitaires de France), 1960. („Que sais je?" no. 870).

This pocket book written by two French scholars is really an encyclopedia of the socio-economic conditions in Belgium, the Netherlands and Luxemburg, and a most valuable *vade mecum* for everyone who wishes to learn the basic facts about the Benelux Economic Union, its problems and perspectives. Its value has been enhanced by short references to the economic and geographical history of the three partner-countries in each of its three main chapters: utilisation of the soil, sea-ports and transports, and industry in the Benelux. Comparing the fertility of the soil in Belgium and the Netherlands the authors find in the whole the same proportions in more and less cultivable grounds, but they foresee a slight disproportion when the Dutch will have achieved their draining projects (in the former Zuider-zee, the Delta works and the Lauwerszee plan). The agricultural areas in both countries do not differ much in extent: in the Netherlands 61% and in Belgium 58% of the soil, but Belgium produces the double amount of wheat (800,000 tons) as compared with the production in the Netherlands, this country buying half of its need on the world grain market. On the other hand the Dutch export of horticultural and cattle products – the latter owing to the lower grain price – is much higher and comprises nearly 2/3 of its total agricultural exports. However, in the agricultural section Belgium and the Netherlands tend to become more competitive than they were at the time Benelux started. The same can be said of the industrial section where the Netherlands achieved remarkable progress since the end of World War II. As for the agriculture problems, the final success of the Economic Union is likely to depend on the realisation of the harmonisation plans in Benelux contexts, or, better still, of the project-MANSHOLT providing for a "green pool" in the Europe of the Six.

The authors deal at length with the equipment of both countries as to their sea-ports and fluvial- and road transportation. Here they are optimistic as to an ultimate solution of the existing difficulties which they ascribe to a lack of collaboration on the side of the Netherlands. The ports of Rotterdam and Antwerp could be made complementary and would with the ports of Amsterdam, Bremen and Hamburg become an asset of incomparable value for the future of Western Europe.

The chapter on the industries in Benelux contains many details of interest for a comparison of the industrial strength of the three countries involved. They form a genuine industrial region and are of vital importance in the bigger context of the Common Market. The problems of the future are above all connected with the demographic problem and the realisation of regional planification. The difficulties implied are evident. The authors dwell at length on the changed situation in Belgium and the shift of industrial and manpower from Wallonia towards Flanders. They compare herewith the development in the Netherlands where the centralisation in the Western regions (Randstad Holland) is now giving inducement to a reorganisation of the industrial settlements.

In making up the balance of Benelux, the authors are of the opinion that now, 13 years since the coming into force of the Customs Union, (since 1958: Economic Union), real progress has been made, and that Benelux, this "laboratory for the Common Market" may be helpful to show the way for the Europe of the Six to follow.

J.L.F.v.E.

HAESELE (KURT WERNER), Europas letzter Weg, Montan Union und E.W.G.. Frankfurt am Main, (Knapp), 1958. 352 pp.

Analysing the emergence of European greatness and power, and its present eclipse by the two non-European giants in world politics, the United States and the Soviet Union, Mr. HAESELE makes a passionate case for a close spiritual, cultural and economic supranational union which would lead to the recovery of a viable Europe and retrieve her lost prestige, contributing at the same time to the maintenance of world peace. This seems to him to be the only choice – the last chance – before Europe today. The alternative to this would be a perpetually divided Europe inevitably contributing to the growing chasm between the American and the Russian blocs, a constant trouble-spot and a serious menace to peace in the world.

Europe was great because, the author maintains, it was European, it was one. Its power and prestige were the result of the Greek "spiritual culture" (Geisteskultur) that penetrated Europe via Rome; the imperial idea born out of the Roman Imperium with its strong "centralized" organisation which conquered the tribal culture and attitude of the time; and the spread of Christianity. To these might be added the pride in Hellenic heritage; the existence of feudalism; the expression of common cultural forms such as the Gothic, Romanesque *etc.*; and the development of the scholastic, philosophical tradition. In these factors and forces lies the origin of European "unity". This "unity" was further emphasised as Europe began to come into contact with the rest of the world through the Crusades; through the exploration and expansion of trade routes and relations; and in Europe's two major contributions, *viz.*, developing a colonial system and building an image of "mono-culture" in these colonies. This "unity," however, was superficial and indeed generated forces of dissension and disintegration: different and often mutually antagonistic religious interpretations; the growth of science and the sceptical, scientific mind; while the rise of nationalism and national States rendered this "unity" hollow and weak. Internationally, when economic competition became submerged in the scramble for political power and expansion, and, with this, a full-fledged colonial and imperial system was born, European "unity" suffered another vicious blow. The two world wars further weakened Europe. Russia and the United States riding the high tide of economic development have surpassed European supremacy and now Europe lies completely at the mercy of the two power blocs. To meet this challenge, Europe has to develop some kind of "creative power" for unification.

The author then deals with the history of the various steps taken in this direction. He competently covers the well-known ground: the origin, development and strengthening of the movement of European integration; its various manifestations like the E.C.S.C., O.E.E.C., EURATOM, the Common Market; the obstacles and difficulties in the way of the European unity; and the steps taken to meet those obstacles. On the whole Mr. HAESELE is satisfied with these trends and is quite hopeful that the economic dynamics and superior military power of the United States and the Soviet Union would compel the European States to discard the utopian ideal of absolute national sovereignty. It is only a united central Europe with its 160 million people and its powerful industry and economic potential that can respectably co-exist at par with U.S.A. and U.S.S.R., and ensure world peace.

In spite of much that is well-known, enough that is provocative and controversial (for instance the analysis of European imperialism rendered in terms of free-trade versus international trade; the law of comparative costs contributing to the development of "mono-culture", *ect.*), Mr. HAESELE has written an interesting and a competent book.

M.M.P.

KARTELBEPALINGEN (De) in het E.E.G.-verdrag. Praeadviezen van Prof. Mr. M. Bos en Mr. B. BAARDMAN, uitgegeven door de Vereeniging „Handelsrecht". Zwolle, 1960.
(The interpretation of the economic competition-rules in the Articles 85–90 of the Common Market Treaty).

Many studies have already been written on the treaty provisions dealing with free economic competition in the Common Market. Usually these are referred to as the anti-trust clauses in the European Economic Community. The first difficulties with their application originated in the existence of different systems of anti-trust rules in the Member States of the E.E.C. In Germany *e.g.* "Kartells" are probibited by law, but exemptions can at any time be made; in the Netherlands there exists a general control on contracts concerning economic competition which are permitted unless prohibited by decree. The principal difficulty, however, resulted from the European Commission as provided for in Article 87 of the E.E.C.–Treaty. It is one thing to declare any trust prohibited as being in contravention with the free competition-rule in the Common Market, but another to know which contracts between enterprises in fact encroach upon the "spirit" of the Common Market so long as the directives with regard to the exemptions, the permitted competition contracts, are still lacking.

The Netherland association called "Commercial Law" has invited Dr. Maarten Bos, professor of international law at the University of Utrecht, and Dr. B. BAARDMAN, economic legal adviser, to expose before its annual meeting the two opposite interpretations of the aforesaid Treaty provisions 85–90. Their exposés have now been published. They present valuable arguments pro and con. The main line of arguing of Prof. Bos is the different way of interpreting so-called institutional treaties as compared with the usual type of treaty-contracts.

Without going so far as to support an unrestricted interpretation and declaring the Rome Treaty "self executing," Prof. Bos nevertheless considers the prohibition of trusts as the leading principle now in force in the E.E.C. and any national law system that does not conform with this starting point as inadmissible. Dr BAARDMAN, on the contrary, departs from the intrinsic meaning and tendency of the Common Market in order to arrive at the conclusion that everything depends on the forthcoming rules of the European Commission. He defends the point of view that the national Governments are still free to apply the anti-trust clauses each in their own way, provided they do not contraverse the aims and purposes of the Common Market. The Articles 85 and 86 are, in his opinion, not self executing as is evident by the insertion of Article 87, by the autonomous powers provisionally given to the national authorities according to Article 88, and by the reference in this section of the Treaty to special kinds of permitted economic competition practices. Prof. Bos' résumé of the various doctrines of treaty interpretation will be of special interest for the international lawyer. He outlines the danger of departing unilaterally from multilateral obligations by interpretations that infringe the clear wording of a treaty provision. Especially here where we are dealing with a treaty of the institutional kind and with its judicial interpretation belonging to a special international court of justice. On the other hand, Dr. BAARDMAN makes it clear to what complications a treaty-law may lead when it contains mere principles and aims, so long as the practical application is still vague, and especially in this domain of every-day life where harmonisation, let alone unification of "the law of economic competition" is bound to raise manyfold questions.

Finally, the authors illustrate their divergent views with their opposition, resp. defense of the much disputed Dutch law of December 4th, 1957, giving execution to Article 87 of the E.E.C.-Treaty. J.L.F.v.E.

MARCHÉ COMMUN. Institutions Communes. Deuxième congrès de l'Association des universitaires d'Europe. Paris, 1960. 369 pp.

Le volume, de 369 pages, contient les travaux du deuxième congrès de l'Association des universitaires d'Europe, réuni à Bruxelles en avril 1958. Une division tripartite a été adoptée pour la présentation de la matière: Allocutions (20 pages), Communications (200 pages) et Débats (149 pages). La deuxième et la troisième partie sont subdivisées chacune en trois sous-parties traitant respectivement des aspects économiques, juridiques et culturels du problème.

A l'intérieur de ce cadre général il est malaisé de découvrir un plan méthodique dans le choix des sujets traités.

Des seize communications économiques, six sont relatives à des problèmes intéressant spécialement certains pays: Espagne (Miguel CRUZ-HERNANDEZ), Grèce (Antone DAMAS KENIDÈS), Italie (Franco FERRAROTTI, Ugo PAPI et Angelo SABATINI) et Autriche (Wilhelm WEBER). Deux communications sont consacrées aux relations entre le Marché Commun et la zone de libre-échange (André MARCHAL et José-Miguel de AZAOLO), deux aux problèmes monétaires et du change (Harry C. JOHNSON et Alfred KRUSE), trois à l'analyse du caractère et des fondements économiques du Marché Commun (Carlo FERRI, Alexander NIKURADSE, ADOLF WEBER) et les trois restantes à des sujets divers, tels que la liberté d'établissement (Germain BRULLIARD), les rapports entre le Marché Commun et le Mouvement européen (Daniel VILLEY) et les obstacles psychologiques à l'intégration européenne (Miguel CRUZ-HERNANDEZ). Cette dernière question forme également l'objet d'une communication culturelle (Francis WARNE).

La sous-partie juridique ne comprend que deux communications, l'une concernant les incidences du Marché Commun sur le droit privé des États membres (Leontin CONSTANTINESCO), l'autre relative aux institutions politiques européennes (Louis SELA-SAMPIL).

Sur les neuf communications culturelles, deux s'occupent des aspects psychologiques de la C.E.E. (Philippe LERSCH et Francis WARNE), une de ses aspects moraux (Pierre de HOLSTEIN), une de ses aspects sociaux (Georges GORIELY), une de ses aspects scientifiques et techniques (Alexander NIKURADSE), deux des problèmes d'enseignement (Giacomo CIVES et Yves GRAFF), une du travaillisme britannique (Campbell BALFOUR) et une des généralités (Teodore LOPEZ CUESTA DE EGOCHEAGA).

L'intérêt actuel qui s'attache aux contributions est inégal. A trois ans de leur rédaction et compte tenu de l'évolution qui s'est produite depuis, les idées exposées dans une partie des communications sont devenues des vérités évidentes et indiscutées. D'autres contributions conservent toute leur valeur d'actualité par l'analyse pénétrante et les critiques pertinentes qu'elles apportent au Traité de Rome. Il en est ainsi, par exemple, de la remarquable et importante étude de professeur Daniel VILLEY sur *Le Marché Commun dans l'optique européenne*. M. VILLEY voit dans le Traité de Rome un document compliqué, manquant de clarté et de courage et se résumant, au fond, à un calendrier étiré. Faute de dispositions constitutionnelles suffisantes, ce Traité n'est qu'une impasse. Il devra être dépassé par la fédéralisation politique de l'Europe des Six. De son côté, le professeur Leontin CONSTANTINESCO estime que la suppression des barrières économiques ne suffit pas pour réaliser l'unité de marché. Celle-ci suppose, en outre, l'unification juridique qui pourra être réalisée soit par l'unification des lois de conflit, soit par voie de législation communautaire directe. Dans une étude consacrée aux *Problèmes monétaires dans une zone de libre-échange*, le professeur Harry G. JOHNSON aboutit à la conclusion que la stabilité économique générale des États participant à un système de libre échange ne peut être assurée que par voie de consultations régulières et la pratique de taux de change fluctuants.

En ce qui concerne les discussions qui se sont déroulées à Bruxelles, leur intérêt consiste notamment dans le fait qu'elles ont permis de mieux définir les positions des adeptes du libéralisme et de l'interventionnisme dirigiste dans le cadre du Marché Commun. L.F.

LES PROBLÈMES JURIDIQUES ET ÉCONOMIQUES DU MARCHE COMMUN. Colloque des Facultés de Droit. Paris, (Librairie Techniques), 1960.

Ce livre, publiant les travaux du Colloque national annuel des Facultés de Droit et des Sciences Économiques françaises tenu à Lille du 21 au 24 mai 1959, contient une collection des discours prononcés à l'occassion du Colloque, ensuite révisés et mis au point par les rapporteurs. Les contributions sont publiés dans l'ordre du programme du Colloque.

La plupart des contributions ne se borne pas aux problèmes du "Marché Commun".

Le professeur George VEDEL donne une aperçu du Traité instituant la C.E.E.A. (l'Euratom), examinant d'abord les grandes lignes du Traité et étudiant ensuite trois chapitres spéciaux: le problème des utilisations militaires, la propriété des matières fissiles spéciales et l'approvisionnement.

D'autres auteurs devaient nécessairement aborder autant des questions de la C.E.C.A. et de l'Euratom que des questions de la C.E.E., en tant que problèmes communs aux trois Communautés. Parmi eux, le Professeur Paul REUTER nous présente – dans sa contribution: *Les Communautés européennes et techniques d'unification* – une analyse excellente concernant les méthodes d'unification, appliquées aux Communautés européennes; examinant successivement: les rapports d'intimité sociale dans lesquels se trouvent les six États membres, la portée de l'unification entreprise et la voie par laquelle on entend poursuivre cette unification.

Deux auteurs s'occupent spécialement des questions institutionnelles des trois Communautés.

Maurice LAGRANGE – avocat général à la Cour de Justice des Communautés européennes – examine le rôle de cette Cour. Après avoir donné une analyse approfondie de la jurisprudence de la Cour de la C.E.C.A., il souligne spécialement qu'elle joue le rôle d'une Cour fédérale, appliquant un droit interne de la Communauté, désireuse de maintenir l'équilibre institutionnel établi par le Traité sans porter atteinte aux responsabilités des autres institutions de la Communauté.

Le professeur J. de SOTO traite *Le problème de l'exécutif dans les Communautés européennes.* Sans préciser ce qu'il entend par ,,exécutif'' dans les Communautés, l'auteur énumère les dispositions des Traités relatives aux Conseils des Ministres, à la Haute Autorité de la C.E.C.A. et aux Commissions de la C.E.E. et de la C.E.E.A. (structure, composition, fonctionnement, compétence). Dans la dernière partie de son exposé, il discute le contrôle de l'autorité exécutif. Le problème du contrôle politique de l'exécutif – problème central des trois Communautés – est passé presque sous silence.

Le professeur Georges LEVASSEUR examine le problème des sanctions dans les Traités, étroitement lié avec les questions institutionnelles des Communautés.

La dernière contribution qui s'occupe expressément des trois Communautés – écrit par le professeur Maxime CHRÉTIEN – concerne les problèmes fiscaux des trois Communautés. La deuxième partie de cet étude contient une aperçu intéressante des problèmes de l'exonération des impôts nationaux et la création d'impôts supranationaux au profit des Communautés elles-mêmes et de ses fonctionnaires.

Les autres exposés, inclus dans le livre, traitent plus spécialement les problèmes du Marché Commun *stricto sensu* (CE.E.). Le professeur René SAVATIER nous expose d'une manière fort intéressante l'évolution du droit international privé sous l'influence de la Communauté Économique Européenne, dans ses trois matières: la nationalité, la condition des étrangers et les conflicts de lois.

Le professeur André MARCHAL compare le Marché Commun avec la zone de libre-échange comme procédant chacune d'une doctrine économique différente (l'internationalisme et le cosmopolitisme). Il méconnaît trop, à notre avis, les facteurs politiques qui sont à la base du controverse entre les protagonistes du Marché Commun et ceux de la zone de libre-échange.

Les problèmes de l'association des pays africains au Marché Commun prennent une large place dans le colloque.

Robert LEMAIGNEN nous procure du point de vue de la Commission de la C.E.E. sur l'association des pays d'outre mer à la Communauté; le professeur François LUCHAIRE examine les ,,grands'' problèmes juridiques et politiques en ce qui concerne l'association des pays africains au Marché Commun, tandis que M. VIGNES étudie les rapports économiques entre le continent européen et le continent africain.

Restent à mentionner: une contribution du Commissaire de la C.E.E., Robert MARJOLIN, sur les réalisations et problèmes du Marché Commun, un exposé par Jacques RIBAS et Pierre WATHELET – fonctionnaires à la Commission de la C.E.E. – sur les problèmes sociaux dans la C.E.E., une étude excellente de la propriété industrielle et le Marché Commun par le professeur Henri DESBOIS, et un examen assez incomplet des conflits de lois en matière de contrats dans la C.E.E. par le professeur Henri BATIFFOL.

Une publication, ainsi conçue, comporte certaines désavantages. C'est plutôt une série d'études indépendantes que le résultat d'un ,,colloque''.

En outre, la valeur scientifique des contributions varie considérablement.

De toute évidence – comme l'écrit Gérard DEHOVE dans l'introduction – ,,ces contributions n'ont nullement la prétention d'épuiser la question''. ... ,,Il s'agit de poser des problèmes, bien plus que de prétendre les résoudre, d'avancer des interprétations, sinon même des hypothèses, plutôt que d'apporter des solutions et d'affirmer des vérités''.

Les contributions, qui posent des problèmes comme résultat des recherches approfondies, sont celles des contributeurs REUTER, SAVATIER, DESBOIS et LAGRANGE.

T.A.M.A.v.G.

LES RECOURS en annulation et en cas de carence dans le droit de la C.E.C.A. à la lumière de la jurisprudence de la Cour de Justice des Communautés. Chronique de politique étrangère, Volume XIII, Numéro 3, mai 1960.

Aux termes de l'article 31 du Traité instituant la Communauté Européenne du Charbon et de l'Acier, il appartient à la Cour d'assurer le respect du droit dans l'interprétation et l'application du présent Traité et des règlements d'exécution. Elle a pour mission d'excercer un contrôle juridique de la bonne exécution de certaines compétences réglementaires ou autres lui conférées de la Haute Autorité, du Conseil et de l'Assemblée.

Ces dispositions font immédiatement ressortir la fonction spéciale de la Cour des Communautés Européennes et sa place dans l'ordre juridique international. Il ne s'agit pas du règlement de certains conflits juridiques internationaux. La tâche de la Cour se borne à l'exercice d'un contrôle sur l'action ou la carence d'un autre organisme qui fait partie de la même organisation internationale que la Cour elle-même. Le champ d'activité de la Cour est limité aux réglementations adoptées par les Parties Contractantes, réglementations qui appartiennent au domaine du droit administratif et visent un objectif économique.

Toutefois, aucune disposition du Traité instituant la C.E.C.A. n'indique expressément les règles de droit à observer par le juge et les autres organismes appelés à interpréter et à appliquer le Traité. Le juge doit dès lors s'efforcer de dégager les principes généraux de droit applicables aux cas lui présentés. Cette conception se confond avec celle de l'avocat-général LAGRANGE déclarant à propos de l'interprétation de la nation du détournement de pouvoir, ,,que l'appel aux droits nationaux s'impose." ,,La notion du détournement de pouvoir n'a évidemment pas été inventée par les auteurs du Traité et pour essayer de se former une opinion sur ce qui doit être le détournement de pouvoir dans l'application du Traité ... il faut d'abord savoir ce qui en est dans le droit respectif de nos six pays."[1]

Cette conception semble avoir inspiré le paragraphe 2 de l'article 215 du Traité instituant la Communauté Européenne Économique disant qu'en matière de responsabilité non contractuelle, la Communauté doit réparer, ,,conformément aux principes généraux communs aux droits des États membres," des dommages.

Dans sa jurisprudence la Cour a progressivement mis au point les principes généraux de droit qu'elle a formulés et définis compte tenu des dispositions du Traité. Par cette oeuvre créatrice et par son interprétation des dispositions parfois imprécises du Traité la Cour contribue à la constitution d'un droit européen uniforme. C'est donc à bon droit que VALENTINE a fait observer à propos de l'affaire Assider: "it appears to follow from this that because the terms of Art. 33 must apply equally to all the countries of the Community an appeal alleging détournement de pouvoir evidenced by *illogicità manifesta* or *manifesta ingiustizia* must be open even to plaintifs governed by a municipal law that does not recognize these grounds. A new body of unified European law, that is the sum total of national laws, may thus tend to be developed".[2]

Les auteurs de l'étude en cause se sont proposés de faire une synthèse au 30 juin 1959 de la jurisprudence la plus importante existant au sujet des articles 33 et 35 du Traité instituant la Communauté Européenne du Charbon et de l'Acier. Ils ont très bien réussi dans cette tâche difficile. Dès les premières phrases du Chapitre I le lecteur est au vif du sujet et se trouve introduit dans le labyrinthe de la jurisprudence où les auteurs lui tendent leur fil d'Ariane par l'analyse des principes fondamentaux et une présentation claire et précise des différents éléments de la matière examinée.

L'appréciation de la jurisprudence citée révèle un examen approfondi de la ligne maîtresse que la Cour a suivie dans bien des cas. La question délicate du détournement de pouvoir, étant un des quatre voies de recours en annulation contre les décisions et recommandations de la Haute Autorité est analysée systématiquement. Les auteurs attirent l'attention sur les arrêts dans lesquels la Cour s'est ralliée à la conception classique du détournement de pouvoir, adoptée dans de nombreux arrêts par le Conseil d'État en France, selon laquelle il y a détournement de pouvoir lorsqu'il peut être reproché à une autorité administrative ,,d'avoir usé de ses pouvoirs dans un but autre que celui en vue duquel ils lui ont été conférés, conception que la Cour a appliquée d'une façon souple, tout en la précisant progressivement".

Il est intéressant, en particulier, de mentionner la conception de la Cour au sujet

[1] Dans les affaires l'Associazione Industrie Siderurgiche Italiane et l'Industrie Siderurgiche Associate (3-54 et 4-54) contre Haute Autorité.

[2] D. G. VALENTINE dans Symbolae VERZIJL "The competence of the Court of Justice of the European Coal and Steel Community."

de la deuxième phrase du paragraphe 1 de l'article 33. Bien que l'examen de la Cour ne puisse porter sur l'appréciation de la situation découlant des faits ou circonstances économiques au vu de laquelle sont intervenues les décisions ou recommandations de la Haute Autorité, la Cour a toujours dérogé en fait à ce principe. Dans la rédaction de ses arrêts la Cour a pu éviter l'impression qu'elle se soit livrée à un examen sur le fond des circonstances économiques en cause, qui est en principe réservé à la compétence exclusive de la Haute Autorité. Mais en fait la Cour ne s'est jamais déclarée incompétente pour apprécier une situation économique et c'est ainsi que dans l'affaire 2–56 elle a réaffirmé sa position en rejetant expressément la demande préjudicielle concernant la compétence de vérification de la Cour en cette matière, posée par la Haute Autorité.[1]

La compétence de contrôle de la Cour est définie dans de nombreux articles du Traité. Une jurisprudence existe non seulement en ce qui concerne les articles 33 et 35, mais aussi par bien d'autres tels que les articles 37, 40, 53, 65 et 70.

En raison de la corrélation entre les articles 33 et 35, il est logique de soumettre également à une analyse la jurisprudence relative à l'article 35.

L'annexe I donne une ,,économie du recours en annulation et du recours en cas de carence", ainsi qu'un aperçu des autres voies de recours; l'annexe 2 donne, en revanche, un tableau systématique des recours introduits devant la Cour de Justice de la C.E.C.A. depuis son entrée en fonctions.

En se tenant autant que possible à l'écart de toute doctrine, les auteurs ont apporté une contribution de valeur à un exposé clair et critique de l'évolution du droit communautaire de la C.E.C.A. Dans l'avant-propos, les auteurs qualifient modestement leur oeuvre de ,,premier essai de synthèse". A la lecture de leur étude on se rend compte que cet essai n'a rien de provisoire mais constitue au contraire une synthèse pleinement réussie.

M.v.G.

STEIN (ERIC) and THOMAS L. NICHOLSON, American enterprise in the European Common Market: A legal profile. Ann Arbor, (The University of Michigan Law School), 1960. 2 vol. XXIV, 510; XXIX, 932 pp.

Fort pertinemment, la grande revue américaine ,,U.S. News" a écrit tout récemment ,,Dans le monde d'aujourd'hui il existe un géant endormi qui commence à donner les premiers signes de son réveil ...". En commentant longuement ce propos, le quotidien français ,,Combat" devait préciser, quelque temps après: ,,Ce ,,géant" dont parle ainsi la revue ,,U.S. News," particulièrement proche des milieux gouvernementaux et du monde des affaires, c'est l'Europe occidentale et, plus particulièrement celle du Marché Commun ... Il n'y a pas si longtemps que cette même Europe était ... le parent pauvre, un continent condamné à s'entretuer dans des guerres inutiles, ou à s'américaniser ... Aujourd'hui ce sont les Américains qui ... ont peur d'être isolés ... C'est donc au tout de l'Amérique, en cette fin du XXe siècle de découvrir à son tour l'Europe ...".

L'intérêt grandissant des États-Unis pour l'Europe dont parlent les deux publications qui viennent d'être citées se manifeste non seulement sur le plan politique, mais aussi et surtout dans le secteur économique et commercial. Pour justifier cette affirmation, il suffit de jeter un bref coup d'oeil sur l'évolution des investissements directs effectués par les Américains dans les pays étrangers: pour l'Europe occidentale, ces investissements étaient de 1.700 milliards de dollars environ en 1950 et de près de 4.800 milliards en 1959; 2/3 de ces sommes ont été investis dans les seuls pays du Marché Commun; toutefois, la part que ces six pays prennent dans les investissements américains croît même plus rapidement que celle réservée aux autres parties de l'Europe occidentale et même du monde entier.

C'est cette même constatation économico-politique qui fournit à l'ouvrage qu'il s'agit d'analyser ici son véritable *back-ground* et sa réelle raison d'être. Plus que son titre ne le laisse deviner, il s'adresse, en effet, aux hommes d'affaires américains et leurs conseillers juridiques ou avocats en contact avec l'Europe; il leur donne toutes les informations portant sur les institutions et le droit du Marché Commun, et nécessaires à la représentation et à la sauvegarde de leurs intérêts juridiques, commerciaux et économiques dans la sphère des Communautés européennes à Six, et même au-delà, puisque certaines parties de l'ouvrage traitent longuement aussi de la ,,Zone de libre-échange."

Les deux volumes de l'ouvrage sont le résultat d'un travail collectif accompli,

---

[1]) *Voir également* art. 66, par. 5, alinéa 2, 3ème phrase.

dans le cadre des études de droit international et comparé organisées au sein de la "Law School" de l'Université du Michigan, par un groupe de spécialistes composé d'Américains (en majorité) et d'Européens, et au sein duquel les juristes sont plus nombreux (9) que les économistes (2). Dans ses travaux, le Groupe a été dirigé par le professeur E. STEIN, et il ressort de la préface qu'il a été, au cours de l'élaboration de l'ouvrage, en contact avec les milieux européens intéressés et notamment avec de nombreuses personnalités compétentes parmi lesquelles on rélève les noms de Paul REUTER, Michel GAUDET, Theodor VOGELAAR, Robert KRAWIELICKI, BRUYAS, Jean REY, Eugen ULMER, *etc*....

Le premier volume comprend une préface et sept chapitres dont le premier sert d'introduction générale et est intitulé *L'intégration européenne vue par un juriste américain*. Les autres chapitres sont consacrés à une analyse des ,,nouvelles institutions" des Communautés européennes; à une étude sur ,,l'établissement de l'union douanière" parmi les six pays des Communautés et face aux autres pays dont notamment ceux de la E.F.T.A.; à un exposé quelque peu posthume de ,,la réglementation du contrôle des changes en France"; aux problèmes de la ,,propriété industrielle" dans le cadre du Marché commun; au ,,droit du travail" et à la ,,sécurité sociale" dans les six pays de la ,,petite Europe," et à une ,,vue d'ensemble" des ,,nouvelles voies de recours" offertes aux ,,entreprises" des Communautés européennes à Six.

Le deuxième volume comprend les chapitres VIII à XII de l'ouvrage, ainsi, qu'en annexe, le texte officiel de la Convention établissant l'E.F.T.A. et des appendices à cet instrument. Les cinq chapitres traitent de l',,Organisation commerciale" dans le cadre de l'Europe des Six; de ,,l'importance de traités (internationaux (traités de commerce et Traité établissant la C.E.E.)) pour l'établissement de sociétés" commerciales ou industrielles; de ,,la protection de la concurrence" selon les normes juridiques des Communautés européennes à Six et de leurs États membres; des différents systèmes d',,imposition" s'appliquant dans ces pays, dans l'organisation de l'Europe des Six, et dans le cadre des rapports commerciaux avec d'autres pays et notamment avec les États-Unis; et, enfin, de la question de ,,l'association des pays et territoires d'outre-mer".

Les auteurs de l'ouvrage déclarant que celui-ci est principalement destiné à apporter une aide pratique aux avocats américains et autres conseillers d'hommes d'affaires des États-Unis, qui, en raison de l'expansion des activités commerciales et économiques de leurs clients, se voient, pour la première fois, confrontés avec les problèmes posés par le commerce avec et dans le Marché commun; mais, malgré cela, l'utilité de ce travail ne se limite pas aux seuls Américains; celui-ci présente, sans aucun doute, également un grand intérêt pour toute personne désireuse de se renseigner tant sur l'ensemble des règles constituant le nouveau cadre juridique du Marché Commun, que sur les normes régissant, dans ce domaine, notamment l'organisation commerciale, les relations industrielles ou de travail, la propriété industrielle, la concurrence et le régime des contributions. A ce titre, il présente un apport important à la science du Droit comparé et il est à espérer qu'il sera consulté non seulement par des spécialistes, chercheurs et étudiants américains de Droit commercial comparé, mais aussi par leurs collègues d'autres continents.

Par ailleurs, certaines considérations générales des différents auteurs sur des aspects politiques du Marché Commun méritent d'être soulignées. Elles se rapportent, entre autres, à la solution, qualifiée de plus logique, de remplacer les trois Communautés par une seule, à l'improbabilité d'une tentative d'unification brutale, de la part des organes communautaires, à l'égard des législations nationales des États membres, aux chances plus grandes d'un effort d'intégration politique comme résultat d'une action nationale plutôt que de celle entreprise par des institutions communautaires, et, enfin, aux constatations ou citations suivantes: ,,... il suffira de quelques années pour démontrer si la Communauté Économique Européenne, avec son marché commun, deviendra réellement une des plus importantes entreprises du XXe siècle..."; ,,... si l'integration économique amène l'intégration politique, la face de l'Europe continentale subira un changement profond qui aura des répercussions dans le monde entier ...".

Toutefois, ces observations ne doivent pas amener à penser que l'ouvrage de STEIN et de NICHOLSON est une oeuvre politique. Au contraire. Malgré la justesse (prouvée d'ailleurs par des événements récents) de certaines réflexions concernant l'avenir des Communautés européennes à Six se touchant, en particulier, à la politique agricole de plusieurs États membres et aux perspectives d'intégration politique, l'ouvrage est consacré essentiellement à un exposé réaliste des institutions, des normes et d'autres données pratiques caractérisant le Marché Commun tel qu'il se présente aux juristes et hommes d'affaires américains. C'est aussi en raison de cette dernière circonstance qu'il s'abstient de traiter, par exemple, complètement ou partiellement, de la politique agricole, des transports, du rôle des entreprises nationalisées et du contrôle des prix. Il n'en reste pas moins que l'ouvrage est d'une très grande utilité pour tous ceux qui s'intéresssent aux multiples problèmes posés par l'Europe des Six, que ce soient des spécialistes américains du droit constitutionnel ou international dont l'attention est ainsi attirée à nouveau sur un nouveau genre de fédéralisme et d'organisation „supranationale" qui „rompe l'intégrité des systèmes juridiques nationaux", ou des hommes d'affaires de l'autre côté de l'Atlantique qui y trouveront, entre autres, des informations extrêmement précises (avec les références complètes aux textes législatifs et réglementaires en vigueur) sur les possibilités et conditions d'importation dans les six pays, sur les modalités d'établissement dans le cadre de la C.E.E. et même sur des questions de détail, telles que celle, par exemple, de savoir quel pays du Marché Commun (le Luxembourg!) offre les plus grands avantages pour l'établissement d'une société américaine d'investissement.

L'utilisation pratique de l'ouvrage serait facilitée si une nouvelle édition comportait un indexe alphabétique. H.W.

C. CONSEIL DE L'EUROPE

C. COUNCIL OF EUROPE

BRULEY (EDOUARD) and E. H. DANCE, A history of Europe? Preface by W. N. MEDLICOTT. Leyden, (Sythoff), 1960. 82 pp. (European aspects. A collection of studies relating to European integration. Series A: Culture No. 3).

This little book is a survey of six annual Conferences of the Council of Europe, dealing with the study of bias in history textbooks. These conferences examined nearly half of the 2.000 history textbooks of Europe, and they aimed not only at finding specific slants and errors, but also the roots of bias itself. Bias is often unconscious, and this makes it difficult to distinguish bias from error.

Nevertheless, the findings of the Conferences are worthwhile and illuminating. Its task was not a novel one, as already as early as 1889 the World Congress for Peace launched an attack on "drum – and – trumpet" history. After the first World War there was a more intensive attempt to infuse history teaching with a spirit of peace, and particularly the work of the Norden Associations in Scandinavia is worthy of note. In France as well as other countries, efforts were made to free history teaching from jingoism, while the hopes were raised high by proposals of the International Committee for Intellectual Co-operation of the League of Nations.

The end of World War II brought activities of the Brunswick group in Germany, of teachers organizations, of UNESCO and of the Council of Europe. The six Conferences of the latter organization dealt with: The European idea in the teaching of history; the Middle Ages; the Sixteenth Century; the Seventeenth and Eighteenth Centuries; the period of 1789–1871; the period of 1870–1950.

The Conferences resulted in a number of concrete proposals in regard to the substance of teaching as well as in regard to terminology. It was found that there are few misrepresentations of actual facts, but that presentation and choice often indicate a certain bias, either national or religious, particularly in regard to the non-Western European countries as well as to other parts of the world. The rôle of Turkey is often shown purely in regard to Western Europe while also Scandinavia is not given its proper European function. The same holds true for Russia and Poland which are not dealt with as such, but only insofar as they affect Western Europe. B.L.

DUCLOS (PIERRE), Le Conseil de l'Europe. Paris, 1960. 127 pp. (Collection „Que sais-je?").

Le but de ce petit livre est d'informer l'„Européen d'aujourd'hui" sur une institution existant déjà depuis 12 années, pour permettre au lecteur de se former un jugement plus pratique que théorique sur le Conseil de l'Europe et sa signification effective. L'auteur, qui en 1958 a publié un ouvrage sur „la réforme du Conseil de l'Europe" est bien parvenu à ce but.

Il traite l'essentiel de sa tâche dans trois parties: l'acte générateur, la vie institutionelle et l'activité du Conseil.

Pour l'évolution historique qui a mené à la création du Conseil de l'Europe, il se réfère à la littérature existante. Par contre il décrit les problèmes de 1949: créer une Assemblée européenne, munie d'une compétence étendue, englobant pouvoir législatif et constituant, combinée alors avec une abrogation partielle de la souveraineté des États, ou bien instituer une Assemblée des représentants gouvernementaux sans porter atteinte à la souveraineté nationale. Nous savons le résultat: un Comité des Ministres dont les décisions presque toujours exigent l'unanimité, et une Assemblée purement consultative. Le tournant a été pris dans le Statut de 1949 et depuis lors presque tous les projets de réforme ont été refusés.

On peut ici citer le discours d'adieu de M. DEHOUSSE comme Président de l'Assemblée Consultative (1959). Sur le rôle du Comité des Ministres il déplorait que ,,à la verité, l'erreur commise l'a été par le Statut, qui a voulu mélanger, sans se rendre compte qu'ils sont incompatibles, l'élément diplomatique et l'élément parlementaire" (L'Europe et le Monde, p. 166).

Dans la partie qui traite la vie institutionnelle, DUCLOS présente les objectifs (but, moyens et compétences), les associés, les deux organes du Conseil de l'Europe et leur relations entr'eux et, enfin, le Secrétariat Général. Son opinion sur le caractère du Secrétaire Général qui a largement étendu son rôle statutaire surtout après le ,,défonctionnarisation" de ce poste, c. à d. après qu'on ait nommé une personnalité politique, et non plus un fonctionnaire administratif à cette place, nous semble particulièrement intéressante. Tandis que le Statut lui confère seulement les compétences d',,assistance", DUCLOS écrit du Secrétaire Général: ,,Nous inclinons donc à penser qu'il est dans la position requise pour jouer le rôle de chef de voûte, capable de ramener à l'unité, à l'efficacité, la dispersion des activités du Conseil" (p. 81).

Enfin l'auteur examine les diverses activités du Conseil. Il souligne le rôle actif de l'Assemblée; elle a discuté les problèmes communs à tous les pays européens, de politique étrangère, économique, sociale et culturelle. Dans ses résolutions et recommendations l'Assemblée a tenté de pousser l'évolution européenne même sans autant tenir compte de l'attitude retardatrice du Comité des Ministres. Dans certains domaines des conventions ont abouti qui lient les États-signataires. La Convention européenne des Droits de l'Homme en est la plus significatrice.

L'Assemblée n'a pas réussi dans ses divers projets d'augmenter ses compétences et les tentatives communautaires d'intégration ont été prises en dehors du Conseil de l'Europe. Mais il reste, comme DUCLOS l'affirme justement, le seul cadre organique d'une conférence générale permanente des pays européens. Être le forum des peuples européens et promouvoir l'évolution européenne pour atteindre une ,,union plus étroite" (Article premier du Statut), sont les contributions que le Conseil de l'Europe peut fournir. B.S.

HAAS (ERNST B.), Concensus formation in the Council of Europe. London, (Stevens); Berkeley and Los Angeles, (University of California Press), 1960. 70 pp.

This booklet in the University of California series in Political Science is an exposition of the rôle of the Council of Europe in the process of European integration: the integration is measured in terms of the extent to which international parliamentary groups (equivalent to political parties in national legislatures) have emerged and the degree of coherence that has developed in them.

Professor HAAS first of all defines the scope of his argument by analysing the "slippery concept" of concencus, which according to him, "means agreement on a clearly stated program of action endorsed by a clear majority of members" of, at least, a quasi-parliamentary assembly. In the creation of that agreement the existence of a "catalyst" – the political parties – is crucial. Accordingly, he proceeds to evaluate the work of the Consultative Assembly of the Council of Europe from 1949 to 1959 from this angle. While doing so he discusses the development of transitional, "transnational" political groups – the Socialist, the Liberal and the Christian-Democratic – in the Assembly. The voting practice of the Assembly; the roll-call votes cast on the basis of national or party loyalties (which brings out the deviations from unanimity of national delegations according to the political or economic nature of the issues involved); and the record of the three above-mentioned political groups and the "regional political sub-groups" (such as the Members of the Common Market, the W.E.U. and the Nordic Council) in these votes, are examined at great length and substantiated with the aid of a wealth of statistical data. The discussion concludes with the explanation of the failure to develop a concensus strong enough to be called "a federating impulse".

The discussion seems to be based upon the rather erroneous premise that the future "United States of Europe" would be a close-knit federation like America, India or

Canada. Since that is the yard-stick with which the author appears to measure the degree of concensus as well as integration, it is almost pedantic to maintain that this particular institution has not acquired enough of it. M.M.P.

Robertson (A. H.), The Council of Europe. Its structure, functions and achievements. With a foreword by Guy Mollet. Second edition. Published under the auspices of The London Institute of World Affairs. London, (Steven & Sons Limited), 1961. 288 pp.

As the first edition of this work was reviewed in the European Yearbook (Vol. 11), reference will be made only to those sections which were not contained in the previous edition. Those sections occur in the following chapters: The political work of the Council (sub-sections 3 and 4); Economic Questions (sub-sections 4, 5 and 6); Human Rights (sub-sections 4 and 5); Legal Questions (the entire chapter); Administrative Questions and Municipal Affairs (the entire chapter); External Relations (sub-section 6) and the final chapter on Achievements and Prospects.

Since the appearance of the first edition in 1956, there has been a consolidation as well as a certain extension of the functions of the Council of Europe.

The Council gradually became the meeting place between the representatives of the Six and those of the other European countries while it also became the practice that a number of European organisations presented reports to the Assembly on their activities. Thus the Assembly acquired a kind of right of review of the work of other European organisations, thereby exercising the function of the most general political framework of Europe. This tendency received further impetus from the general debate on foreign policy which was initiated in 1953.

"There is, indeed, much to be said for the view that in the face of the welter of European organisations which exist or are in various stages of development, it is necessary to have one institution which maintains a view of the whole ensemble and, as far as possible, co-ordinates – if not controls – them all. It would have functions in some way analogous to that of the United Nations in relation to the Specialized Agencies. If endowed, as is the Council of Europe, with a parliamentary organ, it would respond to the need sometimes expressed for parliamentary supervision of the "international executives," since international agencies now carry out executive functions of increasing importance without being subject – as are the national executives – to the democratic control of the various parliaments; hence arises the fear of the new "international technocracy" which would be assuaged if there were a European Assembly empowered to supervise the activities of the technocrats" (p. 100).

In the other sections mentioned above Dr. Robertson reviews the more recent activities of the Council of Europe in these various fields. Particularly the conventions concluded are dealt with in some detail while also the attention is drawn to the work of the European Committee on Crime Problems. The general conclusions of this very competent survey and analysis of the activities of the Council of Europe deserve to be quoted:

"1. that the Council of Europe has a good record as an instrument of European co-operation in the social, cultural and legal fields, but that this is insufficient to achieve the aim of "greater unity between its Members" which was conferred on it by the Statute;

2. that the Assembly has done valuable work on political and economic subjects, but for one reason or another the Committee of Ministers has not been able to seize the opportunities thus afforded to it;

3. that the main driving force towards European integration has now shifted to the three Six Power Communitees for coal and steel, atomic energy and the common market;

4. that the Council of Europe could still perform a most valuable rôle as the framework in which to bring together, and harmonise the development of, the Six and the other countries of free Europe. If this were to happen, however, a greater degree of political determination would be necessary" (p. 255).

It seems evident that it might be developments outside Europe which would give a renewed impetus to European integration, perhaps in the direction indicated by Dr. Robertson.

B.L.

ROBERTSON (A. H.), The law of international institutions in Europe. Being an account of some recent developments in the field of international law. Manchester, (Manchester University Press); U.S.A.: (Oceana Publications Inc.), 1961. 140 pp.

Dr. ROBERTSON has become one of the well-known publicists on European integration, particularly from the legal and institutional angle. His works distinguish themselves by clarity of concept as well as of style, while Dr. ROBERTSON also firmly believes in the progress of European integration.

The present booklet consists of the text of five lectures, delivered at the University of Manchester under the auspices of Melland Schill Memorial Fund, and introduced with a short note by Professor B. A. WORTLEY.

The lectures deal with "different expressions of the European idea", a survey of the European institutions; with the Assembly of the Council of Europe; with Human Rights and the Commission and Court of Human Rights while the texts of a number of the European Conventions are given as appendices.

As the various works of Dr. ROBERTSON have been reviewed in this Yearbook, the present review will only deal with some of the more recent facets, as seen by the author, and more particularly in regard to the Council of Europe.

The author describes the evolution of the European Assemblies and sees a clear development towards party-blocs in those organs. The factor of the continuity or change of national delegations is analysed according to its impact, while the author also describes a gradual growth in the power of the Consultative Assembly of the Council of Europe and of increased contact with the Committee of Ministers.

A further development which the author deems of importance is the creation by the Assembly of new organs of European co-operation, not only among its own Members, but among other people who hitherto had no constitutional connection with the Council of Europe. Two of those developments have occurred.

The first one is the European Conference of Local Authorities, which goes back to an initiative of 1955 of the Assembly and was convened for the first time in 1957. The Committee of Ministers agreed in 1960 that this Conference should meet every two years. It has adopted a draft Charter which describes its goal as follows:

"Its primary aim is to keep the European institutions informed of the views of the local authorities on measures which are likely to have repercussions on local authorities or to involve the responsibility of local authorities towards the population and towards the Governments".

This growth of European unity on the level of local government is undoubtedly of importance. A more vertical structure is represented by the European Conference on Wines and Spirits which held its first session in 1960. It brought together over eighty representations of the trade organisations, national officials and members of Parliament, at the suggestion of the Assembly's Committee on Agriculture.

Dr. ROBERTSON does not mention how this Conference is co-ordinated with the Brussels Organisation and describes it in terms of the activities of the Assembly. Nevertheless the author is far from satisfied: "-----it must be frankly recognised that the powers of the Assembly are teneous in the extreme". It is however a comforting thought that the example of the Council of Europe in establishing a parliamentary assembly has been copied in six others cases in the last ten years.

Considerable impetus is expected from the direct election of the European Assemblies, and it is to be hoped that the author is not overly optimistic in his great expectations.

B.L.

D. QUESTIONS DE POLITIQUE ET DE DÉFENSE

D. POLITICAL AND DEFENCE QUESTIONS

BAILEY (SYDNEY, D.), The General Assembly of the United Nations. Published under the auspices of the Carnegie Endowment for International Peace. London, (Stevens).

Millions of words have been written about the United Nations, the main organisation in New York and, of course, its Specialised Agencies – not to speak of the idea itself. But there was room for a full-length study of the General Assembly and its day-to-day workings. The Carnegie Endowment, which sponsored Mr Field HAVILAND's book on the political rôle of the Assembly (and two early studies now out of print) has been well inspired in selecting Sydney BAILEY, an English Quaker, to produce this detailed procedural survey. Mr BAILEY, author of a number of books on democratic principles and practice, made his name as Executive Secretary of the Hansard Society.

The various chapters, each of which is adorned by an astonishingly appropriate quotation from William PENN, cover the General Debate (for which, incidentally, there is no provision in the Rules of Procedure); the establishment of the Agenda; the actual operations of debate, the procedure of voting *etc.* by which decisions are reached; the system of election of members of the principal and subsidiary organs; and, for good measure, we have, too, an analysis or case-study of the question of Tibet. The author concludes with a cautious peep into the future: he makes the point that "as the Assembly increases in size, it will become even more important than it was in the past to use to the best advantage the other principal organs of the U.N.". In other words, the Assembly has passed its meridian: we have already seen this happen. Finally, there are 27 tables together with several Appendices supplying documentation on the wisdom of Special Committees reporting on the Assembly.

Based primarily on the official records (it is not for nothing that Mr BAILEY was until recently Director of the Quaker United Nations programme) this factual exegesis is well-constructed and interestingly written. A special need of praise is due to Mr BAILEY for the opening "general" chapter which, in cool and sober language, places the U.N., and particularly the Assembly, in its contemporary setting. Such public debate of international issues as it provides was, undoubtedly, inevitable in the world of today – and, in the author's judgment, it is not wholly harmfull: but, of course, it is no substitute for negotiation. There are elements here of what Mr Dean RUSK has called "parliamentary diplomacy", but the Assembly is emphatically not a parliament. And to say that it is "truly the town meeting of to-morrow's world", which was Senator VANDENBERG's aphorism, verges on sheer guff; it begs far too many questions. W.C.H.

EBSWORTH (RAYMOND), Restoring democracy in Germany. London, (Stevens), 1961. 222 pp.

Democratisation of the German people, after victory in the World War (the Americans had a better word for it – "re-orientation") was a declared Allied objective. The Potsdam Agreement supplied the specific mandate: restoration of local self-government as soon as possible; the holding of local elections; the licensing of democratic political parties and, in the absence of a central German Government (while the Occupation Statute ruled), introduction of the "elective principle" at state and provincial levels. Mr Raymond EBSWORTH, who played an active part in the British version of this process – as a member of the Administrative and Local Government Section of the Control Commission – has given us a lucid and sensible account of this basic preliminary to the Basic Law that governs West Germany today.

Whatever mistakes in detail were made, the British re-educators had the right idea. As Robert BIRLEY, the Educational Advisor to the British Military Governor, remarks in his Foreword, mere directives would have been useless. The primary task was to find Germans willing to accept political responsibility and to give them support and encouragement: which meant in practice, particularly at first, operating by personal contacts and demonstrating, above all, an understanding of the German mind, friendliness and "a good deal of humility".

The author describes in his first chapter the process of denazification, at the lower levels, (since the "big fish" were being dealt with at Nuremberg) – which, somewhat unfortunately, was entrusted to a sub-division of the Public Safety Department and thus too frequently took on the character of a police operation. There were, however, from the outset, a sufficient supply of genuine liberals and underground resisters, with a preponderance of Social Democrats, to provide at least a nucleus of "good Germans." (As early as 1946 British officials were in fact withdrawn from the denazification task, though they retained a shadowy *droit de contrôle* until the Occupation Statute was introduced on 21st September, 1949). No difficulty was experienced in re-constituting political parties, though they were on the whole sternly limited to four: Social Democrats, Communists, Christian-Democrats and Free Democrats (or Liberal Democrats): the lesson of the evil consequences of a multiplicity of small splinter parties (such as had characterised the Weimar *régime*) had been well learned. The temporary guardians of Germany's political well-being were careful, moreover, to ensure that the process of re-building the parties should be "from the bottom upwards" *i.e.* they were licensed initially in the *Kreis* (county). Among the "also ran" the only grouping of any significance was the B.H.E. (*Block der Heimatvertriebenen und Entrechten*), formed in 1949.

As regards an electoral system, not unnaturally the British favoured the system they knew of single-candidate constituencies and majority vote, and they were determined likewise to steer their German wards away from the undiluted P.R. system which had been so firmly anchored in pre-Hitler Germany. But they had the sense to institute an advisory Committee of Germans who, in fact, opted for a system combining features from both traditions – and, as soon as they had the power, the Germans cut away superfluous British trimmings. And this compromise system is what rules in West Germany today.

Mr Ebsworth makes no secret of the fact that in matters of local government, though admirable training was supplied through local government schools or centres, the idea of local officials being subordinate to elected bodies did not take hold, and, as for doing away with the authoritarian traditions and habits of the civil service, the educators had to admit failure. Thus the relevant segment of the Basic Law was specifically required "to pay due regard to the traditional principles of the service".

The work of the Education Branch, on the other hand, in the author's view, registered considerable success *e.g.* adult education centres, "*die Brücken*", – and, of course, Wilton Park, the Foreign Office Conference Centre; but far too little was achieved in the way of independence from State, *Land*, or province authorities of university teachers. They have remained "officials". Finally, efforts to suppress, or at least reform, the traditional student corporations were in vain.

Mr Ebsworth gives frank expression to his colleagues' dismay at the destruction of much of the good work they had done as a result of the new Government policy after 1948 – and the introduction of professional diplomats who made a fetish of non-intervention, he cites specifically as a feature of this policy the forcing of re-armament on the Federal Republic before it was psychologically prepared. Albeit, his final conclusion is that, whatever was to come after, the base established by the "liberators" was a sound one.

W.H.C.

II. BIBLIOGRAPHIE SÉLECTIVE DES PÉRIODIQUES ET BROCHURES 1960

II. SELECTIVE BIBLIOGRAPHY OF PERIODICAL AND PAMPHLET MATERIAL 1960

A. L'INTÉGRATION EUROPÉENNE EN GÉNÉRAL

A. EUROPEAN INTEGRATION IN GENERAL

ARMENGAUD (A.), Les Européens contre l'Europe? Politique étrangère, XXV, no. 2, 1960, p. 122–151.

AUFBAU (Der) einer Europa-Universität: Modell für Europa (aus dem Bericht von Staatssekretär a.D. Hugo GEIGER, München, an das Europäische Parlament). Europa (Bad Reichenhall), no. 8, août 1960, p. 49–52.

BELOFF (M.), Kulturelle Aufgaben der Einigung Europas: TOYNBEE will eine „lingua franca". Europa (Bad Reichenhall), no. 126, juin 1960, p. 48–50.

BERG (FRITZ), Possibilités et limites de l'intégration européenne. Revue des questions allemandes, XV, no. 6, 1960, p. 627–641.

BOS (A.), Enkele Europese organisaties en instellingen. Ars aequi, IX, no. 4–5, janvier-février 1960, p. 67–82.

BRUGMANS (HENDRIK), Betrachtungen eines Historikers zur europäischen Integration. Dokumente, Zeitschrift für übernationale Zusammenarbeit, XVI, no. 5, octobre 1960, p. 329–344.

CAPOTORTI (FRANCESCO), Sulla interpretazione uniforme dei trattati europei. Rivista di diritto internazionale, XLIII, no. 1, 1960, p. 3–25.

CORNIDES (W.), Europas neue Kleider? Europa-Archiv, no. 17, 5 septembre 1960, p. 533–538.

DAUSSIN (A.), Ein europäischer öffentlicher Dienst. Europa-Archiv, XV, no. 21, 5 novembre 1960, p. 655–662.

DEHOUSSE (F.), La rationalisation des institutions européennes autres que celles des Six. Courrier socialiste européen, no. 4, janvier 1960, p. 2–6.

DESJACQUES (PIERRE), L'Europe, l'état, la région. Vers une politique régionale communautaire. Sciences humaines et intégration européenne. Collège d'Europe, 1960, p. 310–323.

DIEGUEZ (M. DE), L'Europe et l'avenir. Esprit, no. 7–8, juillet-août 1960, p. 1254–1277.

ERVEN (L.), Les idées européennes du généal de GAULLE. Revue de la politique internationale, XI, no. 256, 5 décembre 1960, p. 11-13.

FEDERSPIEL (P.), How to end the deadlock in Europe. European-Atlantic Review, X, no. 2, automne 1960, p. 13–14.

FISCHER (J.), Auf dem Weg zum Europa der Hochschulen. Forschung und Wirtschaft, Partner im Fortschriftt, no. 4, 1960, p. 43–49.

FONTAINE (ANDRÉ), De GAULLE und Europa. Dokumente, Zeitschrift für übernationale Zusammenarbeit, XVI, no. 5, octobre 1960, p. 325–328.

KERN (E.), Der Europäische Dienst und das Europäische Dienstrecht (fin.). Europäische Wirtschaft, no. 17, septembre 1960, p. 471–473.

KHAN (MIR MUSTAFA ALI), Schemes for Western European integration – likely effects on the under-developed regions. Pakistan Horizon, XIII, no. 1, 1960, p. 65–77.

LINGUA europaea. Die Friedens-Warte, LV, no. 4, 1960, p. 353–358.

MARCHAL (A.), De quelques faux dogmes en matière d'organisation européenne. Revue économique, XI, no. 5, septembre 1960, p. 673–704.
MONNET (J.), Die Erziehung der künftigen europäischen Bürger. Europäische Erziehung, no. 2, avril 1960, p. 23–25.
SCHÄTZEL (W.), Wege zur Einigung Europas. Die Friedens-Warte, LV, no. 3, 1960, 0. 201–219.
SCHEPEL (J.), Europees recht. Economisch-Statistische Berichten, no. 2257, 19 octobre 1960, p. 1014.
SCHEPEL (J.), Oprichting Nederlandse vereniging voor Europees recht. Advocatenblad, XL no. 9, 15 novembre 1960, p. 396–398.
SCHNORR (GERHARD), Die Rechtseinheit Europas. Neue juristische Wochenschrift, XIII, no. 17, 22 avril 1960, p. 745–749.
SEGUILLON (Y.), Les instituts et l'université européenne. Bulletin du Centre européen de la culture, no. 2, octobre 1960, p. 5–11.
SEIDL-HOHENVELDERN (IGNAZ), Le juriste regarde l'intégration européenne. Sciences humaines et intégration européenne. Collège d'Europe, 1960, p. 177–186.
SIDJANSKI (D.), L'université européenne: de la résolution de Genève au projet des Communautés. Bulletin du Centre européen de la culture, no. 2, octobre 1960, p. 12–24.
SIMMONDS (K. R.), La Gran Bretagna e le Comunità europee: Una fase nuova. Diritto internazionale, XIV, no. 1, 1960, I, p. 3–18.
TRAUTMANN (W.), De GAULLES europäische Initiative. Der Volkswirt, no. 32, 6 août 1960, p. 1735–1736.
TRAUTMANN (W.), Was wird aus den Europaplänen de GAULLES? Zwischenbilanz europäischer Sondierungen. Der Volkswirt, no. 40, 1 octobre 1960, p. 2236–2238.
VECCHIO (GIORGIO DEL), L'ideale cosmopolitico e il problema dell'unificazione europea. Discorso pronunciato all' Istituto di studi europei in Roma il 23 marzo 1957. Roma, 1960. 16 pp.
VREESE (ALPHONSE DE), Perspectives pour un droit européen. Sciences humaines et intégration européenne. Collège d'Europe, 1960, p. 187–203.
WIESE (L. VON), What is European culture? The British Journal of Sociology, XI, no. 1, mars 1960, p. 1–9.
WIGNY (P.), L'Europe communautaire est une Europe „objective." Communes d'Europe, no. 12, décembre 1960, p. 5–6.

B. L'INTÉGRATION ÉCONOMIQUE EN GÉNÉRAL ET O.E.C.E.

B. ECONOMIC INTEGRATION IN GENERAL AND O.E.E.C.

ACCORD (L'), monétaire européen et la convertibilité des monnaies. Banque, no. 170, août 1960, p. 510–513.
ANDREADIS (S. G.), La Grèce: une économie européenne propice aux investissements. Revue de la Société belge d'études et d'expansion, no. 191, mai-juin-juillet 1960, p. 413–416.
ANSWERING Mr MAUDLING (Luncheon address British Chamber of Commerce for Switzerland). The Statist, CLXXI, no. 4277, 27 février 1960, p. 322–323.
AU Comité des „21", les Sept reconnaissent le Marché commun (conc.: réunion des „21" (pays membres de l'O.E.C.E. + U.S., Canada et Commission C.E.E.), Paris, 9-10.6.60). L'Économie, no. 734, 16 juin 1961, p. 6–7.
BACHMANN (H.), Der westeuropäische Integrationsprozess an der Jahreswende 1959–60. Aussenwirtschaft, no. 1–2, mars-juin 1960, p. 1–27.
BASYN (JACQUES), L'assurance de l'organisation de l'Europe. Bulletin des assurances, XL, no. 167, novembre-décembre 1960, p. 729–744.

BECHTOLDT (H.), Finnland sucht Anschluss an die E.F.T.A. Aussenpolitik, no. 7, juillet 1960, p. 444–451.

BERG (F)., Möglichkeiten und Grenzen der wirtschaftlichen Integration Europas. Europa-Archiv ,XV, no. 21, 5 novembre 1960, p. 647–654.

BESCHE (H. DE), Europäische Handelsprobleme in schwedischer Sicht. Aussenpolitik, XI, no. 2, février 1960, p. 80–84.

BIBLIOGRAPHIE zum europäischen Flüchtlings- u. Zwangswanderungsproblem. – BIBLIOGRAPHY relating to the problem of refugees and forced migrations in Europe. – BIBLIOGRAPHIE au sujet du problème des réfugiés et des migrations forcées en Europe. 1958–1959. Intégration, VII, no. 1, janvier-février 1960, p. 31–50.

CANADÀ (Il) ed i raggruppamenti economici europei. Relazioni internazionali, no. 3, 16 janvier 1960, p. 65.

CHABAN-DELMAS (J.), Perspectives eurafricaines. Communautés et continents, no. 5, janvier-mars 1960, p. 22–26.

COMMUNITIES (The other). Other continents are showing an interest in the ideas for international economic groups that are being tried out in Europe. (Latin America E.F.T.A.). The Economist, CXCVII, no. 6117, novembre 19, 1960, p. 758–759.

CONFERENCE (The) of the European Free Trade Association (E.F.T.A.), [Lisbonne, 19 mai 1960]. Portugal, an informative Review, IV, no. 3, mai-juin 1960, p. 161–169.

CUSTOMS UNION (An All-European) the accepted solution? (Fritz BERG), Swiss Bankers' Association, Interlaken, 10.9.60). The Statist, CLXXII, no. 4306, 17 septembre 1960, p. 395–396.

DE la coopération économique européenne à la coopération économique atlantique: la réforme de l'O.E.C.E. Bilans politiques, économiques et sociaux hebdomadaires, no. 723, 7 avril 1960, Problèmes d'actualité.

DIEBOLD (W.). Jr., The changed economic position of Western Europe: Some implications for United States policy and international organization. International Organization, XIV, no. 1, hiver 1960, p. 1–19.

DIETERLEN (P.), Le Traité de Rome et le problème monétaire. Banque, no. 173, novembre 1960, p. 693–697.

DURAND, Vers un code des transports européens? [Texte en allemand et français]. Bulletin des transports internationaux par chemins de fer, LXVIII, no. 9, septembre 1960, p. 202–203.

EUROFIMA: trois années d'activité. Les perspectives d'avenir. Bulletin de l'Union internationale des chemins de fer, no. 2, février 1960, p. 29–33.

EXPLORATION (Atlantic). The DILLON conference did not reconcile the Six and the Seven, but it may have started something new and important. The Economist, CXCIV, no. 6074, 23 janvier 1960, p. 286–287.

FEIDT (J.), Le Fonds social européenn doit être un facteur de progrès. Courrier socialiste européen, no. 4, janvier 1960, p. 13–17.

FINNISS (G.), C. CROON & L. HEYDT, Wege zur Vereinheitlichung des europäischen Markenrechts. Gewerblicher Rechtsschutz und Urheberrecht, Auslands- und Internationaler Teil, no. 7, juillet 1960, p. 337–356.

FISHER (D.), Ireland in Europe. Advantages of joining the E.F.T.A. The Statist, CLXXI, no. 4280, 19 mars 1960, Special Section, Republic of Ireland, p. 15–17.

FORMENTINI (P.), La Banca Europea per gli Investimenti (Conférence Institut belge de finances publiques, 26.11.59). Bancaria, no. 4,, avril 1960, p. 399–404.

FRAENKEL (H.), Der Einbau der Sechs in das G.A.T.T. Die E.W.G.-Zollrunde. Europa (Bad Reichenhall), no. 131, novembre 1960, p. 32–33.

FRANKS (O.), Grossbritannien vor neuen wirtschaftspolitischen Aufgaben. Europa-Archiv, no. 13–14, 5–20 juillet 1960, p. 416–424.

FREE TRADE ASSOCIATION (The European): The Stockholm plan; Move towards Europe; Government's "basic mistake"; Question of preferences; Factor of American investment; Dangers of division. Journal of the Parliaments of the Commonwealth, XLI, no. 1, janvier 1960, p. 13–17.

GRANDE-BRETAGNE (La) et l'Europe: le point de vue de M. EDWARD HEATH, Ministre britannique, chargé des affaires européennes (Échos de Grande-Bretagne, no. 109. 29.9.60). La Documentation française, Articles et documents, no. 0.1008, 11 octobre 1960, Faits et opinions, p. 3–5.

GRANDE-BRETAGNE (La) et l'Europe (MAX BELOFF, Oxford, "Times," 15.12.59). La Documentation française, Chroniques étrangères, Grande-Bretagne, no. 329, 5 janvier 1960, p. 17–18.

GROEBEN (H. VON DER), Problèmes de la politique européenne de concurrence. Bulletin de la C.E.E., no. 3, mars-avril 1960, p. 5–10.

HALFMANN (E. A.), Ausblick auf eine neue Energiestruktur in Europa. Eine kritische Stellungnahme zu dem gleichnamigen Bericht der Beratenden Energiekommission der O.E.E.C. Der Volkswirt, Suppl. au no. 21, 21 mai 1960, p. 24–26.

HASSELBACH (W. VON), Was wird aus den Agrarpreisen? Wachsende Kosten infolge steigender Löhne. – Problematische Brüsseler Marktordnungspläne. Der Volkswirt, no. 25, 18 juin 1960, p. 1200–1202.

HAY (A.), L'Accord monétaire européen a une année d'existence. Revue économique et sociale, no. 2, avril 1960, p. 91–103.

HONIG (FREDERICK), The European Free Trade Association and restrictive trade practices. The Law Journal, LX, no. 4956, 11 novembre 1960, p. 727–728.

HUMMLER (A.), Die Beurteilung des Warenursprungs in der E.F.T.A. Aussenwirtschaft, no. 1–2, mars-juin 1960, p. 64–75.

IVEROTH (A.), Europe's new trading association: in quest of free commerce (papers from the Committee for Economic Development Conference). P.E.P., XXVI, no. 440, 14 mars 1960, p. 94–102.

JACOBSSON (P)., Les monnaies européennes et l'économie mondiale. Revue d'économie politique, no. 6, novembre-décembre 1960, p. 11–24.

KOUWENHOVEN (A.), De Conventie tot oprichting van de Europese Vrijhandelsassociatie. Economisch-Statistische Berichten, XLV, no. 2227, 2228, 23 mars 1960, p. 346–348, 371–374.

KRAFT (H.), Die Europäische Sozialcharta. Dokument des sozialen Fortschritts? Zeitschrift für Sozialreform, no. 5, mai 1960, p. 285–288.

KREININ (M. E.), The "Outer-Seven" and European integration. The American Economic Review, LI, no. 3, juin 1960, p. 370–385.

KROFT (W. C.) & H. L. KLAASSEN, Enkele economische beschouwingen betreffende het staalproject Europoort. Economisch-Statistische Berichten, no. 2220. 3 février 1960, p. 92–106.

LANDHEER (BART), Contemporary social change in Europe. World Affairs, CXXIII, no. 1, printemps 1960, p. 6–8.

LANGUÉTIN (P.), L'Association européenne de Libre-Échange. 1. Les caractéristiques de la Convention de Stockholm. 2. L'A.E.L.E. et l'intégration économique européenne. 3. L'A.E.L.E. et le commerce mondial. Revue économique et sociale, no. 1, janvier 1960, p. 5–20.

LAYTON (CH.), A super-bank for Europe? The Banker, CX, no. 415, septembre 1960, p. 589–592.

LEÇONS (Les) d'un échec: La réglementation sur les transports. Revue du Marché commun, no. 23, mars 1960, p. 85–88.

LEWINSOHN (R.), Majestic-Konferenz: Wende oder Leerlauf? DILLON hat sich in Paris durchgesetzt. – Vielfalt der Organisationen wird unübersehbar. Der Volkswirt, no. 4, 23 janvier 1960, p. 141–142.

MAUDLING (R.), The future of European economic integration (Speech, Swiss Institute of International Studies and the Zürich Economic Society). Board of Trade Journal, CLXXVIII, no. 3283, 19 février 1960, p. 379.

NYSEN (A.), „A travail égal, salaire égal" dans la communauté européenne. Labor, no. 4, 1960, p. 180–183.

PAUES (W.), Skandinavische Überlegungen zur „Kleinen Freihandelszone". Europa-Archiv, XV, no. 1–2, 5–20 janvier 1960, p. 37–40.

POPOVIC (N.), La réorganisation de l'O.E.C.E. – Après la Conférence des Ministres en janvier. Revue de la politique internationale, no. 236, 1 février 1960, p. 15–17.

POURBAIX (H.), Vers une systématisation des concepts de „l'entreprise," de la „propriété commerciale" et du „fonds de commerce" dans les cadres de la communauté européenne? (à suivre). Annales de droit et de sciences politiques. XX, no. 1, 1960, p. 21–58.

PROJET de convention portant exécution des articles **55** et 56 du Traité instituant l'Union économique Benelux. [Textes français et néerlandais.] Nouvelles Benelux, no. 3, mai-juin 1960, p. 25–27.

RAUCHFUSS (A.), Erdöl in den assoziierten Gebieten. (à suivre). Europäische Wirtschaft, no. 4, 31 juillet et no. 18, 30 septembre 1960, p. 406–408, 495–497.

RÉSOLUTIONS adoptées par la conférence économique occidentale des Treize. La Documentation française, Articles et documents, no. 0 902, 26 janvier 1960, Textes du jour.

RUDOLPH (H.), Auf dem Wege zum Europäischen Business-Management. Ausbildung und Entwicklung von Führungskräften in der Wirtschaft – ein internationales Problem. Europäische Wirtschaft, no. 14, 31 juillet 1960, p. 403–405.

RÜHLE VON LILIENSTERN (H.), Das europäische Produktivitätsprogramm 1960 (conc.: Agence européenne de productivité). Der Volkswirt, no. 23, 4 juin 1960, p. 1077–1078.

SALIN (EDGAR), FRIEDRICH LIST, – Kern-Europa und die Freihandelszone. Zwei Reden zur europäischen Politik. Tübingen (Mohr) 1960, 53 pp.

SALOMONSON (F.), Europese kanttekeningen bij de Benelux-ontwerpen. Advocatenblad, XL, no. 1, 15 janvier 1960, p. 7–14.

SANDERS (P)., Vers une société anonyme européenne? (Discours, Institut des Hautes Études économiques, Rotterdam, 22.10.59). Le Droit européen, no. 16, janvier 1960, p. 9–23.

SCHAFFNER (H.), Die Schweiz und der europäische Regionalismus. Aussenpolitik, XI, no. 2, février 1960, p. 84–91.

SCHUYT (W. J.), L'Angleterre et l'organisation de l'Europe .Revue politique et parlementaire, no. 698, janvier 1960, p. 8–15, et no. 699, février 1960, p. 123–131.

TENNFJORD (F.), Element i europeisk social-politik. Europarådets social politiska verksamhet. Sociala Meddelanden, no. 2, 1960, p. 155–171.

TEUNISSEN (P. J.), Naar een Europees sociaal handvest. Ars aequi, IX, no. 4–5, janvier-février 1960, p. 131–139.

TICHMANN (K.), Spaniens Anschluss an Europa braucht viel Zeit. Aussenpolitik, no. 1, janvier 1960, p. 58–61.

TOMASELLI (MARIO PIETRO), La Suisse et l'Association de Libre-Échange. Revue de droit international, XXXVIII, no. 1, janvier-mars 1960, p. 51–53.

TRADE cannot wait for integration. The Statist, CLXXI, no. 4275, 13 février 1960, p. 249–250.

TRIFFIN (R.), Intégration économique et politique monétaire. Revue d'économie politique, no. 6, novembre-décembre 1960, p. 58–81.

TWO-WAY TRADE with the Seven (à suivre): 1. KOLLBERG (P. B.), Good prospects of Anglo-Swedisch Expansion. 2. RIBU (E.), Favourable outlook for further Anglo-Norwegian development. 3. FAESSLER (R.), Trade relations between the United Kingdom and Switzerland. Board of Trade Journal, CLXXIX, no. 3314, 3316, 3318, 23 septembre, 7, 21 octobre 1960, p. 677, 679, 682, 793–798, 953–956.

TWO-WAY TRADE with the Seven (fin): 4. REGO (L. L.), Portugal's increasing industrialization. 5. HJORTH NIELSEN (H.), Increasing trade with Denmark. Board of Trade Journal, CLXXIX, no. 3320, 3322, 4 et 18 novembre 1960, p. 1097–1101, 1197–1200.

U.K. TRADE with E.F.T.A. Countries (suite et fin). 2. Portugal. 3. Swiss Imports. 4. Norway's Expanding Market. 5. Austria. 6. An Expanding Danish Market. Board of Trade Journal, CLXXVIII, no. 3301, 24 juin 1960, p. 1340–1351; CLXXIX, no. 3303, 3304, 3305, 3307, 8, 15, 22 juillet, 5 août 1960, p. 61–64, 113–116, 191–194, 289–292.

UDINK (B.), Les perspectives du marché européen des transports. Revue de la navigation intérieure et rhénane, no. 22, 25 décembre 1960, p. 881–887.

UNIFICATION (L') monétaire de l'Europe. Une conférence de M. PIERRE WERNER, Ministre d'État du Grand-Duché de Luxembourg (Strasbourg, Chambre de Commerce et d'Industrie du Bas-Rhin). La Documentation française, Articles et documents, no. 0.1031 8 décembre 1960, Faits et opinions, p. 1–6.

VERNON (R.), Die Vereinigten Staaten und die europäischen Handelsblöcke: Der künftige Weg. Europa-Archiv, no. 17, 5 septembre 1960, p. 539–550.

WAS erwartet die Uhrenindustrie von der E.F.T.A.? Der Schweizerische Metall-Arbeiter, no. 20, 19 mai 1960, p. 1–2.

WERNER (PIERRE), Les finances et les monnaies européennes au service de l'integration économique et de la solidarité continentale. Bulletin de documentation, XVI, no. 15, 30 novembre 1960, p. 3–10.

WHAT chances for O.E.C.D., Prospects for its playing new roles. The Statist, CLXXII, no. 4300, 6 août 1960, p. 190–191.

WILLEMETZ (L.), Die Harmonisierung der Gesetzgebung. Über die Notwendigkeit einer einheitlichen Regelung der Konflikte zwischen den Gesetzgebungen btr. Handelsgesellschaft. Zeitschrift für europäische Integration, no. 6–7, juin-juillet 1960, p. 24–29.

WILLEMETZ (L.), Une société de type européen. Revue du Marché commun, no. 21, janvier, 1960, p. 38–40.

WOCKENFOTH (K.), Die Ursprungsregelung in der Kleinen Europäischen Freihandelszone. Aussenwirtschaftsdienst des Betriebs-Beraters, VI, no. 2, 29 février 1960, p. 38.

C. CONSEIL DE L'EUROPE

C. COUNCIL OF EUROPE

ADAM (H. T.), L'action du Conseil de l'Europe dans le domaine de la propriété intellectuelle. Études sur la propriété industrielle, littéraire, artistique, Paris, 1960, p. 195–205.

COMPTE-RENDU des manifestations organisées au siège social de la Société belge d'études et d'expansion du 7 au 23 janvier 1960, à l'occasion du Xe anniversaire de la création du Conseil de l'Europe. Conférence de presse par P. LEVY. Allocution de L. BENVENUTI. Exposé: l'Europe et les pays sous-développés, par CH. PINEAU. Introduction et conclusions par F. DEHOUSSE. Revue de la Société belge d'études et d'expansion, no. 189, janvier-février 1960, p. 43–80.

GOLSONG (H.), Minderheitenrechte im Rahmen des Europarats. Europa-Archiv, XV, no. 3, 5 février 1960, p. 85–92.

PROBLEMA (Il) dell'Europa all'Assemblea di Strasburgo. Relazioni internazionali, no. 41, 8 octobre 1960, p. 1305.

RAAD van Europa: Europees sociaal handvest. De Onderneming, no. 3, 6 février 1960, p. 96–98.

SCHLOH (B.), Ein Bericht des Europarates über die nationalen Minderheiten. Jahrbuch für internationales Recht, no. 1, juillet 1960, p. 77–83.

SOLF (H.), Strasbourg erwartet die Eidgenossen: Tuchfühlung mit Europa. Europa (Bad Reichenhall), no. 10, Octobre 1960, p. 9–11.

STARACE (V.), In tema di costituzione delle commissione dell'Assamblea consultiva del Consiglio d'Europa. Rivista di diritto internationale, XLIII, no. 4, 1960, p. 660–679.

STARACE (VINCENZO), La vacanza dell'ufficio di presidente dell'Assamblea consultiva del Consiglio d'Europa. Rivista di diritto internazionale, XLIII, no. 2, 1960, p. 314–320.

STRASBOURG: Accord pour coopérer avec les U.S.A. Le XXe siècle fédéraliste, no. 33, 12 février 1960, p. 12.

VRIES (C. W. DE), Uit de geschiedenis van de Raad van Europa (Historia interna van 19 juli 1948 tot 28 januari 1949). [Avec des documents]. Rechtsgeleerd Magazijn Themis, no. 4, 1960, p. 364–400.

D. COMMUNAUTÉS EUROPÉENNES

D. EUROPEAN COMMUNITIES

AGRICOLTURA (L') nei paesi della Comunità Economica Europea. Il Risparmio, no. 8, août 1960, p. 1322–1353.

AGRICULTURE and Europe. The Economist, CXCVI, no. 6101, 30 juillet 1960, p. 466.

AMORE (G. DELL'), La politica monetaria della Comunità economica europea (Convegno del Movimento europea, 21.3.60). Mondo economico, no. 15, 9 avril 1960, p. 23–28.

ANGEHRN (O.), Anpassung der Absatzwege und Absatzmethoden im Zeichen von E.W.G. und E.F.T.A. Aussenwirtschaft, no. 1–2, mars-juin 1960, p. 76–88.

ANTILLEN (De) en de E.E.G. (conc.: association C.E.E. – Antilles néerlandaises). De Nederlandse Industrie, no. 11, 1 juin 1960, p. 350–351.

ARVISENET (H. D'), Les questions écrites et orales dans le droit parlementaire des Communautés européennes. Le Droit européen, no. 23, octobre 1960, p. 311–314.

AUSTRUY (J.), La réglementation des ententes et les pouvoirs compensateurs dans le Marché commun. Revue économique, XI, no. 5, septembre 1960, p. 770–802.

BACHMANN (H.), Brückenschlag E.W.G., E.F.T.A. durch eine gegenseitige Zollsenkung? Aussenwirtschaft, no. 3, septembre 1960, p. 1–10. – Kritische Stimmen zum Vorschlag eines Brückenschlages E.W.G.-E.F.T.A. (P. BAFFI, W. HALLSTEIN, R. MEIMBERG), p. 11–19.

BÄRMANN (J.), Les communautés européennes et le rapprochement des droits. Revue internationale de droit comparé, XII, no. 1, janvier mars 1960, p. 9–60.

BAIL (Th.), Modifications de la législation douanière allemande dans le cadre de la C.E.E. Europa in Handel und Wirtschaft, no. 4-5, avril-mai 1960, p. 19–26.

BAUDHUIN (F.), La Belgique devant le Marché commun: honnêtes médecins et faux prophètes (Synthèse de la conférence faite à la tribune de la Société belge d'études et d'expansion). Revue de la Société belge d'études et d'expansion, no. 191, mai-juin-juillet 1960, p. 394–399.

BESSELING (R. P.), Beschouwingen over de rechtsmiddelen ten dienste van particulieren krachtens het verdrag der Europese Economische Gemeenschap. Nederlands Juristenblad, no. 39, 12 novembre 1960, p. 851–855.

BEUTLER (W.), Die Europäische Wirtschaftsgemeinschaft: Keimzelle der Integration. Europa (Bad Reichenhall), no. 121, janvier 1960, p. 78–81.

BLACK (H. D.), L'Australie et la Communauté économique européenne. Occident, III, no. 2, février 1960 (numéro spécial), p. 46–56. Ed. angl. p. 46–56.

BOYER (M.), Les points litigieux entre la C.E.E. et le G.A.T.T. Revue du Marché commun, no. 26, juin 1960, p. 237–248.

BRUNNER (H.), Die wirtschaftlichen und technischen Voraussetzungen einer Zollunion zwischen E.W.G. und E.F.T.A. Wirtschaftsdienst, no. 10, octobre 1960, p. 555–558.

BYE (M.), Les problèmes posés par la Communauté européenne du charbon et de l'acier. Revue économique, XI, no. 6, novembre 1960, p. 833–865.

CALAN (P. DE), L'industrie cotonnière dans le Marché commun. Le point de vue de l'industrie française. Les Problèmes de l'Europe, no. 7, 1er trim. 1960, p. 50–59.

CASONI (G.), L'industrie cotonnière et le Marché commun. Les Problèmes de l'Europe, no. 7, 1er trim. 1960. p. 60–65.

CASSESE (ANTONIO), Le relazioni internazionali della Comunità economica europea. La Comunità internazionale, XV, no. 3, juillet 1960, p. 471–486.

CHABROWSKI (S.), Das griechische Assoziierungsmodell. Die Entscheidung über einen Vertrag der E.W.G. mit Griechenland wird dringend. Der Volkswirt, no. 20, 14 mai 1960, p. 919–921.

COMMERCE (Le) des pays du Marché commun en 1959. Bulletin du Conseil national du patronat français, no. 197, juin 1960, p. 16–20.

COMMERCE (Le) extérieur de la Belgique en 1959. Réorientation probable en fonction du Marché commun. Revue du Marché commun, no. 26, juin 1960, p. 217–225.

COORDINATION (La) des politiques énergétiques des pays de la Communauté économique européenne (Rapport LAPIE, „Revue française de l'énergie", déc. 1959). Problèmes économiques, no. 640, 5 avril 1960, p. 1–9.

CORSON (H.), L'établissement de la liste G. Revue du Marché commun, no. 24, avril 1960, p. 136–142.

CRAEN (G.), De Gemeenschappelijke Markt in het groeiproces van de economische integratie. Rechtskundig Weekblad, XXIV, no. 6, 9 octobre 1960, p. 257–276.

CRÉATION (La) des grands axes fluviaux du Marché commun, objet des recommandations de la Commission Économique Européenne aux gouvernements des États membres. Revue de la navigation intérieure et rhénane, no. 13, 10 juillet 1960, p. 492–496.

CURÉ (P.), La notion d'entreprise dans le traité du Marché commun. Le Droit européen, no. 23, octobre 1960, p. 341–349.

DELIVANIS (D. J), La Grèce face à la Communauté européenne. Revue économique, XI, no 5, septembre 1960, p 739–763.

DELVAUX (A.), Investissements étrangers et Marché commun (conc.: surtout investissements américains). Revue du Marché commun., no. 25, mai 1960, p. 183–194.

DELVAUX (A.), Les entreprises belges face au Marché commun. Annales de sciences économiques appliquées, no. 1, mars 1960, p. 59–77.

DEPAS (G.), Petites et moyennes entreprises – Belgique – Marché commun. Europa in Handel und Wirtschaft, no. 6, juin 1960, franç. et all. p. 22–26.

DIDIER (H.), Les investissements dans les pays d'outre-mer associés à la Communauté économique européenne. Communautés et continents, no. 8, octobre-décembre 1960, p. 9–19.

DIVISION in Europe. Part 1. 1959: A year of division. Part 2. Towards an accomodation. P.E.P., XXVI, no. 442, juin 1960, p. 139–202.

DRIEL (M. J. M. VAN), De verbindendheid van de arresten van het Hof van Justitie van de Europese Gemeenschappen. Ars aequi, IX, no. 4–5, janvier-février 1960, p. 95–98.

DROIT (Le) d'établissement dans le Marché commun (Conclusions du Conseil économique et social). Économie contemporaine, no. 144, 26 janvier 1960, p. 16–20.

DUMON (F.), La formation de la règle de droit dans les Communautés européennes. Revue internationale de droit comparé, no. 1, janvier-mars 1960, p. 75–107.

DURÉE (La) effective du travail dans la Communauté européenne. L'Economie, no. 740, 28 juillet 1960, p. 15–16.

DURET (J.), U.S.A. et crise du Marché commun. Cahiers internationaux, no. 110, février 1960, p. 17–30.

ENERGY in the Communities, Policies and oil prices. The Economist, CXCVI, no. 6103, 6104, 13 et 20 août 1960, p. 659–660, 741–742.

ERDMANN (E.) JR., La politique sociale de la Communauté économique européenne. Europa in Handel und Wirtschaft, no. 3, mars 1960, p. 16–20, All.: p. 16–20.

EURATOM-Enttäuschungen. Der Volkswirt, no. 7, 13 février 1960, p. 262.

E.W.G.-GESAMTPLAN (Ein) für den Ausbau der Verkehrswege. Strom und See, no. 7–8, juillet-août 1960, p. 236–241.

FEROLDI (FR.), Caratteristiche dell'economia italiana e regole di concorrenza nel quadro della C.E.E. Rivista internazionale di scienze sociali, XXXI, no. 1, janvier-février 1960, p. 29–39.

FLAMME (E. M.), The nuclear energy industry and the Common Market. Informations internationales du Marché commun, no. 1, avril 1960, p. 7–12.

FONZO (FR. DE), Protezionismo e Mercato comune europeo. Rivista di politica economica, no. 5, mai 1960, p. 963–991.

FRISCH (A.), Nationalegoismen und mangelndes Interesse als Hemmung. Um Euratom wird es zu still. Europa (Bad Reichenhall), no. 131, novembre 1960, p. 6–9.

FUSIONEN (Schwerindustrielle) für den Euromarkt? Wirtschaftsdienst, no. 6, juin 1960, p. 303–306. Ed. angl. p. 3–6.

FUTURE (La) politique laitière commune de la C.E.E. (Exposé de M. R. GABORIAUD, Confér. des producteurs de lait des pays européens, Tours). L'Agriculture dans le monde, IX, no. 3, juillet 1960, p. 12–16.

GAMPERT (A.), Le cuir dans le Marché commun. Revue du Marché commun, no. 21, janvier 1960, p. 22–25.

GARAND (A.), L'Outre-mer français et la Communauté économique européenne (conc.: libre circulation des marchandises, politique agricole, investissements publics et privés). Politique étrangère, XXV, no. 1, 1960, p. 33–51.

GERBERS (O. D.), Publikatieplicht ten aanzien van vervoersvoorwaarden en vrachtprijzen in de E.G.K.S.- en E.E.G.-verdragen? (conc.: art. 70 § 3 concernant prix du fret et conditions de transport). Economisch-Statistische Berichten, no. 2262, 23 novembre 1960, p. 1122–1125.

GIBRAT (R. P.), La mission d'Euratom. Europa Nucléaire, no. 3, mai-juin 1960, p. 9–14. Ital.; p. 15–16, All. p. 16–17, Angl.: p. 17–18.

GIRONELLA (E.), Spanien und der Gemeinsame Markt (suite et fin). Europa-Brücke, mai 1960, p. 24–29.

GORI (PAOLO), Sui poteri d'investigazione dell'Alta Autorità della C.E.C.A. Rivista di diritto internazionale, XLIII, no. 4, 1960, p. 630–647.

GOZARD (G.), L'élaboration de la politique agricole de la Communauté économique européenne. Revue politique et parlementaire, no. 698, janvier 1960, p. 22–29, et no. 699, février 1960, p. 150–162.

GREILING, Chemiewirtschaft integrationsfreudig. Europäische Wirtschaft, no. 12, 30 juin 1960, p. 273–275.

GREILING, Einkaufsgemeinschaften der Textilindustrie. Anpassung an schärferen Wettbewerb im Gemeinsamen Markt. Europäische Wirtschaft, no. 18, 30 septembre 1960, p. 491–493.

GROEBEN (H. VON DER), Probleme der europäischen Wettbewerbspolitik. Mitteilungsblatt, no. 7, juillet 1960, p. 313–315.

HABERKORN (KURT), Behandlung von Konzernunternehmen nach Art. 65 des Montanunionvertrages. Neue juristische Wochenschrift, XIII, no. 3, 15 janvier 1960, p. 86–87.

HALFF (M.), Déséquilibre dans les mesures d'accélération du Traité de Rome. Politique étrangère, XXV, no. 3, 1960, p. 265–274.

HALLSTEIN (W.), Der gemeinsame Agrarmarkt ist das grösste Problem der E.W.G.: Das Abschiednehmen vom Alt-Gewohnten. Europa (Bad Reichenhall) no. 10, octobre 1960, p. 31–33.

HALLSTEIN (W.), Die Dynamik des Gemeinsamen Marktes: es gibt kein zurück. Europa (Bad Reichenhall), no. 121, janvier 1960, p. 39–42.

HALLSTEIN (W.), La Communauté économique européenne: Son rôle, ses responsabilités, son rayonnement dans le monde. Revue du Marché commun, no. 23, mars 1960, p. 95–100.

HALLSTEIN (W.), Les échanges de vues sur la politique européenne et le Marché commun. Revue du Marché commun., no. 29, octobre 1960, p. 322–324.

HARMONISIERUNG (Zolltechnische) zwischen E.W.G. und E.F.T.A. Wirtschaftsdienst, no. 10, octobre 1960, p. 543–549.

HAUNSCHILD (H. H.), Le Marché commun de l'énergie nucléaire. Europa in Handel und Wirtschaft, no. 9, septembre 1960, p. 11–20, All. p. 11–20.

HAVER (K.), Warum Gemeinschaftsverkauf an der Ruhr? Der Volkswirt, Suppl. au no. 21, 21 mai 1960, p. 32–35.

HEFFELE (H.), Die Reifenindustrie im Gemeinsamen Markt. Europäische Wirtschaft, no. 5, 15 mars 1960, p. 83–86.

HELDRICH (ANDREAS), Art. 215 Abs. II des Vertrages über die Europäische Wirtschaftsgemeinschaft – Ein Irrweg zu europäischer Rechtseinheit. Juristenzeitung, XV, no. 22, 18 novembre 1960, p. 681–685.

HELLMANN (H.), Erster Schritt zur E.W.G.-Wettbewerbspolitik. Rechtsgrundlage für eine Bestandsaufnahme von Kartellen. Der Volkswirt, no. 46, 12 novembre 1960, p. 2504–2506.

HEMELRIJCK (W. VAN), Het reglement van het Hof van Justitie der Europese Gemeenschappen. Rechtskundig Weekblad, XXIII, no. 30, 27 mars 1960, p. 1438–1442.

HEMMER (C.), Die Automobilindustrie in der Europäischen Wirtschaftsgemeinschaft. Europäische Wirtschaft, no. 6, 31 mars 1960, p. 106–111.

HEMMER (C.), Die chemische Industrie und der Gemeinsame Markt. Europäische Wirtschaft, no. 12, 30 juin 1960, p. 258–263.

HEMMER (C.), Die Elektroindustrie in der Europäischen Wirtschaftsgemeinschaft. Europäische Wirtschaft, no. 22, 30 novembre, 1960, p. 566–569.

HIRSCH (É), L'Énergie nucléaire et l'Europe. Revue économique, XI, no. 6, novembre 1960, p. 866–881.

HISSENHOVEN (A. VAN), Le problème démographique italien. Revue du Marché commun., no. 28, septembre 1960, p. 297–303.

HOLLANDER (P. DEN) & K. K. VERVELDE, E.E.G.-beleid in de graansector. Economische-Statistische Berichten, no. 2219, 17 janvier 1960, p. 79–82.

HOLMES (F. W.), La Nouvelle-Zélande et la Communauté économique européenne. Occident, III, no. 2, février 1960 (numéro spécial), p. 38–45. Ed. angl.: p. 38–45.

HOUSSIAUX (J.), Probleme einer Anti-Trust-Politik für die E.W.G. Europa-Brücke, no. 9, septembre 1960, p. 11–13.

INVESTISSEMENTS (Les) américains dans les pays du Marché commun. Revue du Marché commun, no. 24, avril 1960, p. 131.

JANSSEN VAN RAAY (J. L.), Een beslissing van het Bundesgerichtshof over E.G.K.S.-recht. Nederlands Juristenblad, no. 21, 21 mai 1960, p. 437–446.

JELDEN (H.), Findet Marokko den Weg zur E.W.G.? Die Volksrepublik China kommt ins Geschäft. Der Volkswirt, no. 39, 24 septembre 1960, p. 2183–2184.

KITZINGER (U. W.), Europe: the Six and the Seven. International Organization, XIV, no. 1, hiver 1960, p. 20–36.

1. KNESCHAUREK (FR.), Die schweizerische Maschinenindustrie. 2. RENFER (TH.), Die schweizerische Uhrenindustrie. 3. BOSSHARDT (A.), Die schweizerische Textilwirtschaft. 4. ROOST (O.), Die schweizerische Lebensmittelindustrie. 5. BERNHARD (H.), Die schweizerische Papierindustrie. [Alle] im Zeichen von E.W.G. und E.F.T.A. Aussenwirtschaft, no. 1–2, mars-juin 1960, p. 105–166.

KONZENTRATION der Europa-Exekutiven. Der Volkswirt, no. 23, 4 juin 1960, p. 1065–1066.

KOPF, (H.), Der europäische Distrikt, Eine Untersuchung zur Frage des Sitzes der europäischen Institutionen. Europa-Archiv, XV, no. 5, 5 mars 1960, p. 167–176.

LADAS (St. P.), Der gewerbliche Rechtsschutz im Gemeinsamen Markt aus amerikanischer Sicht. Gewerblicher Rechtsschutz und Urheberrecht, Auslands- und internationaler Teil, no. 8–11, août-novembre 1960, p. 389–400, 485–494, 551–557.

LALOIRE (M.), L'assistance technique aux petites et moyennes entreprises dans les pays de la Communauté. Revue du Marché commun, no. 28, septembre 1960, p. 304–312.

LANDBOUWMAATREGELEN van de E.E.G. kunnen de Gemeenschap ernstig nadeel berokkenen (conc. répercussions de la politique agricole sur l'ensemble de la Communauté). De Nederlandse Industrie, no. 1, 1 janvier 1960, p. 8–9.

LAPIE (P. O.), L'Énergie atomique et la coordination européenne de l'énergie. Revue politique et parlementaire, LX, no. 702, mai 1960, p. 441–446.

LAPIE (PIERRE-OLIVIER), Les institutions du Marché commun. Revue du Marché commun, no. 30, novembre 1960, p. 376–379.

LASSALLE (C.), Les relations entre le Parlement européen et les Conseils de Ministres des Communautés. Le Droit européen, no. 16, janvier 1960, p. 1–8.

LAUNAY (J. DE), L'adhésion de la Grèce et de la Turquie au Marché commun. Le développement de l'Europe méridionale. Revue de la Société belge d'études et d'expansion, no. 188, novembre-décembre 1959, p. 816–825.

LEE (J. J. VAN DER), The European Common Market and Africa. The World Today, XVI, no. 9, septembre 1960, p. 370–376.

LEGENDRE (P.), L'immigration agricole et les dispositions du Traité de Rome concernant la liberté de circulation, d'emploi et d'établissement. Droit social, no. 3, mars 1960, p. 161–173.

LEGENDRE (P.), The European common market and agricultural migration in France. Migration News, no. 1, janvier-février 1960. p. 12–19.

LEMPERIERE (J.), Structure et évolution des exportations des pays du Marché commun et de la Grande-Bretagne depuis 1951. Études et conjoncture, no. 5, mai 1960, p. 420–454.

LITERATUURLIJST. Bepalingen op sociaal gebied genoemd in het E.E.G.-Verdrag. Samengesteld door de Documentatiedienst P.T.T., Documentatie personeelszaken Hoogovens en de Documentatie de Baak, Centraal sociaal werkgevers-verbond. 's-Gravenhage 1960, 37 pp. [Polycopié].

LONDRA favorevole a un accordo tra C.E.E. ed E.F.T.A. Relazioni internazionali, no. 24, 11 juin 1960, p. 779.

LOUSTEAU (K.), Pour une politique agricole commune des partis socialistes des six pays du Marché commun. La Revue socialiste, no. 129, janvier 1960, p. 17—44.

LÜBKES (FR.), I problemi del credito agrario nella Comunità economica europea. Bancaria, no. 5, mai 1960, p. 537–543.

MALGRAIN (Y.), L'agriculture française devant le Marché commun européen. Revue économique, XI, no. 6, novembre 1960, p. 937–954.

MALLET (J.), Le Marché commun entre dans sa troisième année. Économie et humanisme, no. 123, janvier-février 1960, p. 31–41.

MANDY (P. L.) & G. GHELLINCK, La structure de la dimension des entreprises dans les pays du Marché commun. Revue économique, XI, no. 3, mai 1960, p. 395–413.

MANSHOLT (S. L.), Im Widerstreit der Interessen (Interview conc. agriculture). Zeitschrift für europäische Integration, no. 5, mai 1960, p. 4–7.

MANSHOLT (S. L.), Landbouwprijzen in E.E.G. moeten naar elkaar toe groeien (conc. nivellement des prix agricoles). Ons Platteland, no. 773, 29 avril 1960, p. 3–4.

MARCHÉ (Le) de la banane. Les possibilités offertes par l'Europe des Six. L'Économie, no. 715, 28 janvier 1960, p. 17–19.

MARIE (A.), La législation française concernant les prix imposés et ses répercussions dans le cadre du Marché commun. Le Droit européen, no. 19, avril 1960, p. 140–152.

MARJOLIN (R.), La politique conjoncturelle dans la Communauté économique européenne. Courrier socialiste européen. no. 10, septembre 1960, p. 2–4.

MASOIN (M.), L'harmonisation des politiques monétaires au sein du Marché commun. Revue du Marché commun, no. 28, septembre 1960, p. 283–289.

MENAIS (G. P.), Le Marché commun des capitaux est-il réalisable? Banque, no. 167, mai 1960, p. 281–284.

MIGLIAZZA (ALESSANDRO), Su alcuni caratteri della Corte di giustizia delle Comunità europee. Rivista di diritto internazionale, XLIII, no. 2, 1960, p. 229–256.

MIRABELLA (G.), L'unification monétaire de la Communauté économique européenne. Revue économique, XI, no. 6, novembre 1960, p. 913–936.

MONACO (R.), Comparaison et rapprochement des législations dans le Marché commun européen. (à suivre). Revue internationale de droit comparé, no. 1, janvier-mars 1960, p. 61–74.

MONTGOMERY (A.), Le prospettive di integrazione fra C.E.E. ed E.F.T.A. da un punto di vista scandinavo. Bancaria, no. 8, août 1960, p. 851–864.

MORGENSTERN (W.), Der Agrarplan der europäischen Wirtschaftsgemeinschaft 1959. Europa-Brücke, juillet-août 1960, p. 13–18.

NANES (A. S.) & R. EFRON, The European Community and the United States: evolving relations. The Review of Politics, XXII, no. 2, avril 1960, p. 175–186.

NEBOLSINE (G.), The "Right of Defense" in the control of restrictive practices under the European Community treaties. The American Journal of Comparative Law, VIII, no. 4, automne 1959, p. 433–462.

NOTES juridiques sur l'application du traité C.E.E. Revue du Marché commun, no. 33, février 1961, p. 80.

NYDEGGER (A.), Die Handelsströme innerhalb der E.W.G. und der E.F.T.A. Aussenwirtschaft, no. 1–2, mars-juin 1960, p. 28–44.

OUDEMANS (G.), CH. KOOIJ & J. WOLTERBEEK, Droits de propriété industrielle et règles de concurrence dans le Traité de Rome. La Propriété industrielle, no. 2, février 1960, p. 28–32.

PELLA (G.), Latin America and its future relations with E.E.C. What Europe can do to help Latin America. The Statist, CLXXII, no. 4308, 1 octobre 1960, Survey of Chile, p. 15–19.

PERTINAX, Notre infrastructure se développe-t-elle au rythme des pays du Marché commun? (à suivre). Revue du Conseil économique wallon, no. 45, juillet-août 1960, p. 1–15.

PEYREFITTE (A.), Quel est l'avenir de l'association de l'outre-mer au Marché commun? Politique étrangère, XXV, no. 4, 1960, p. 393–407.

PINDER (J. M. H.), La Grande-Bretagne à l'égard du Marché commun. Revue économique, XI, no. 6, novembre 1960, p. 955–971.

PLAISANT (R.), La C.E.E. et les projets de règlements relatifs au règles de concurrence. Revue du Marché commun, no. 30, novembre 1960, p. 369–371.

PROBLÈMES (Les) de la Communauté européenne pour le charbon et l'acier vus par les Allemands. Europa in Handel und Wirtschaft, no. 8, août 1960, p. 17–21, All.: p. 17–21.

REBOUD (L.), Influence des fiscalités sur les mouvements de capitaux dans le cadre du Marché commun. Revue de science financière, LII, no. 2, avril-juin 1960, p. 314–340.

RECOURS (Les) en annulation et en cas de carence dans le droit de la C.E.C.A., à la lumière de la jurisprudence de la Cour de Justice des Communautés. Chronique de politique étrangère, XIII, no. 3, mai 1960, p. 287–398.

REY (J.), Die Europäische Wirtschaftsgemeinschaft und ihre Beziehungen zu Drittländern. Europa-Archiv. no. 13–14, 5–20 juillet 1960, p. 433–441.

REYNAUD (R.), Réflexions sur un traité: Communauté européenne du charbon et de l'acier. Revue de l'Action populaire, no. 135, février 1960, p. 147–166.

RICHARDSON (B. T.), Le Canada et la Communauté économique européenne. Occident, III, no. 2, février 1960 (numéro spécial), p. 31–37. Ed. angl.: p. 31–37.

RIEBEN (H.), La Suisse et la Communauté européenne. Revue économique, XI, no. 5, septembre 1960, p. 705–738.

ROBERTSON (H. M.), L'Afrique du Sud et la Communauté économique européenne. Occident, III, no. 2, février 1960 (numéro spécial), p. 24–30. Ed. angl.: p. 24–30.

ROUKOUNAS (I. E.), Remarques sur la compétence du Tribunal des Communautés européennes. [En grec]. Journal de jurisprudence hellénique et étrangère, XVIII, janvier-mars 1960, p. 1–23.

SAILLY (J. DE), La Grande-Bretagne et le Marché commun. La Revue des deux mondes, no. 10, 15 mai 1960, p. 219–232.

SAINT-GALY, Une marque européenne dans le cadre du Marché commun est-elle opportune? Revue du Marché commun, no. 23, mars 1960, p. 114–120.
SAUVAGE (A.), Quelle orientation donner à la production agricole de la Communauté économique européenne? Perspectives, no. 717, 10 septembre 1960, Études et articles, p. 1–8.
SAVOUILLAN (CH.), L'harmonisation des salaires et des conditions de travail dans les industries de la C.E.C.A. Droit social, no. 9–10, septembre-octobre 1960, p. 472–486.
SCHEEL (W.), Der direkte Draht zur E.W.G. (Interview). Europa (Bad Reichenhall), no. 8, août 1960, p. 28–30.
SCHEEL (W.), Neue Beziehungen der E.W.G.-Gruppe zu Afrika. Aussenpolitik, no. 6, juin 1960, p. 379–387.
SCHEEL (W.), *etc.*, Was wollen die Engländer? Europa (Bad Reichenhall), no. 8, août 1960, p. 12–14.
SCHLACHTER (ERNEST), Nouveaux aspects de la liberté d'établissement dans le Traité de Rome. Revue du Marché commun, no. 30, novembre 1960, p. 392–396.
SCHLEBITZ (W.), Abschöpfungen anstelle von Zöllen als agrarpolitisches Instrument? Europäische Wirtschaft, no. 17, 15 septembre 1960, p. 463–465.
SCHLEBITZ (W.), Die gemeinsame Agrarpolitik in der Beschleunigung. Europa in Handel und Wirtschaft, no. 7, juillet 1960, p. 18–25. Franç.: p. 18–25.
SCHMITZ (H.), Vorschriften und Normen in der Sicht der europäischen Integration. Zusammenarbeit der Normeninstitute in E.W.G. und E.F.T.A. Europäische Wirtschaft, no. 22, 30 novembre 1960, p. 572–575.
SEIDL-HOHENVELDERN (IGNAZ), Kartellbekämpfung im Gemeinsamen Markt und das Völkerrecht. Aussenwirtschaftsdienst des Betriebs-Beraters, VI, no. 9, 30 septembre 1960, p. 225–233.
SERENI (ANGELO PIERO), Le imprese comuni dell'Euratom. Rivista di diritto internazionale, XLIII, no. 2, 1960, p. 203–228.
SICKLE (J. V. VAN), Il Mercato comune e l'esperienza degli Stati Uniti (conc.: différences entre les économies régionales des pays des Six et celles de l'Amérique). Il Politico, no. 1, mars 1960, p. 52–62.
SITUATION (La) sociale dans les pays d'outre-mer associés à la Communauté économique européenne. Marchés tropicaux et méditerranéens, no 763, 25 juin 1960, p. 1435–1436.
"SIX" (The) and "the Seven" in Europe. The Three Banks Review, no. 45, mars 1960, p. 14–26.
SOLUSTRI (A.), La crisi carbonifera della C.E.C.A. e i programmi di riadattamento per i lavoratori. Rivista di politica economica, no. 5, mai 1960, p. 992–1012.
SOPER (T. P.), Les pays sous-développés en Afrique et en Asie et la Communauté économique européenne. Occident, III, no. 2, février 1960 (numéro spécial), p. 14–23. Ed. angl. p. 14–23.
SPERDUTI (G.), L'organizzazione e le funzioni di governo della Comunità Europea del Carbone e dell'Acciaio (suite). La Comunità internazionale, XV, no. 1, janvier 1960, p. 3–20.
SPIERENBURG (D. P.), Eine einzige Exekutive (Interview). Europa (Bad Reichenhall), no. 8, août 1960, p. 2–4.
SPINDLER (VON), Communauté économique européeenne – Convertibilité et zone de marché libre (suite). Europa in Handel und Wirtschaft, no. 3, mars 1960, p. 7–16, All. p. 7–16.
STEIN (ERIC) & PETER HAY, Legal remedies of enterprises in the European Economic Community. The American Journal of Comparative Law, IX, no. 3, été 1960, p. 375–424.

SU un progetto svizzero di zona preferenziale europea C.E E -E.F.T.A. Bancaria, no. 8, août 1960, p. 888–894.

THOMÄ (K. E.), Le droit de communication dans la Communauté économique européenne. Revue du Marché commun, no. 29, octobre 1960, p. 345–356.

U.S.A. – INVESTITIONEN (Erhöhte) in E.W.G. und E.F.T.A. Europäische Wirtschaft, no. 12, 30 juin 1960, p. 286–287.

VERDROSS (A.), Österreich, die europäische Wirtschaftsintegration und das Völkerrecht. Europa-Archiv, no. 13–14, 5–20 juillet 1960, p. 442–448.

VITTA (E.), Considerazioni sulla natura giuridica delle comunità sovranazionali. Rassegna di diritto pubblico, no. 1, janvier-mars 1960, p. 97–122.

VONDELING (A.), Un programma agricolo socialista per i paesi della C.E.E. Iniziativa Europea, no. 17, mai 1960, p. 11–14.

WANGENHEIM (H. U. VON) Mühsame Koordination der Energiepolitik. Der Volkswirt, no. 49, 3 décembre 1960, p. 2630–2632.

WEGER (H.), Abbau der Zölle in E.W.G. und E.F.T.A. Zollsenkungen werden Handelswege verlagern. Europäische Wirtschaft, no. 22, 30 novembre 1960, p. 578–581.

WELTER (N.), Agrarpolitik in der Europäischen Wirtschaftsgemeinschaft. Europa-Archiv, XV, no. 1–2, 5–20 janvier 1960, p. 25–36.

WESER (M.), Les conflits de juridictions dans le cadre du Marché commun. Difficultés et remèdes. (suite). Revue critique de droit international privé, XLIX, no. 1, 2, 3, janvier-septembre 1960, p. 21–41, 151–172, 313–333.

WIGNY (P.), Ein schnelleres Tempo: Presto statt Adagio. Europa (Bad Reichenhall), no. 121, janvier 1960, p. 16–17.

WILLMANN (JOACHIM), Die Teilintegration als Etappe auf dem Weg zu einer weltweiten Zusammenarbeit [à propos de: W. DIEBOLD. The Schuman Plan. A study in economic co-operation. 1950–1959, New York 1959]. Europa-Archiv, XV, no. 1–2, 5–20 janvier 1960, p. 41–48.

WILLMANN (JOACHIM), The European Economic Community. Its meaning for Europe and the world. India Quarterly, XVI, no. 2, avril-juin 1960, p. 120–138.

WIRNER (H.), S. LORENZ & W. SCHUBERT, Die zuckerwirtschaftliche Integration in der E.W.G. Europäische Wirtschaft, no. 8, 30 avril 1960, p. 177–179, et no. 10, 31 mai 1960, p. 221–223.

WOHLFARTH (E.), Von der Befugnis der Organe der Europäischen Wirtschaftsgemeinschaft zur Rechtsetzung. Jahrbuch für internationales Recht, IX, no. 1, juillet 1960, p. 12–32.

WOLNEY (R.), Die französische Elektroindustrie und der Gemeinsame Markt. Europäische Wirtschaft, no. 22, 30 novembre 1960, p. 581–584.

WOLTERS (A.), Les recours en annulation devant la Cour de Justice des Communautés européennes. Revue de droit international et de droit comparé, XXXVII, no. 3, 1960, p. 165–184.

ZEIDLER (J. K.), Drohende Agrar-Autarkie in Europa. Bedenken der Aussenwirtschaft gegen den Mansholt-Plan der Brüsseler Kommission. Der Volkswirt, no. 22, 28 mai 1960, p. 1029–1031.

ZOTSCHEW (T.), West-europäische Marktzusammenschlüsse und die West-Ost-Wirtschaftsbeziehungen. Ost-Europa Wirtschaft, no. 1, mai 1960, p. 70–82.

E. DROITS DE L'HOMME

E. HUMAN RIGHTS

BALLADORE PALLIERI (GIORGIO), Il regolamento della Corte dei diritti dell'uomo. Diritto internazionale, XIV, no. 2, 1960, I, p. 126–135.
COHEN JEHORAM (H.), Enige preliminaire vragen betreffende de Europese Conventie voor de Rechten van de Mens. Ars aequi, IX, no. 4–5, janvier-février 1960, p. 117–126.
GOLSONG (HERIBERT), Der Europäische Gerichtshof für Menschenrecht. Juristenzeitung, no. 7, 1 avril 1960, p. 193–198.
GOLSONG (HERIBERT), La défense des droits de l'homme en Europe. Sciences humaines et intégration européenne. Collège d'Europe, 1960, p. 204–213.
KOCK (MARCK DE), A. BAYART & ALBERT NYSSENS, Het Europees Verdrag van de Rechten van de Mens, is dit een voldoende bescherming? Rechtskundig Weekblad, XXIII, no. 25, 21 février 1960, p. 1194–1219.
MOSLER (HERMANN), Organisation und Verfahren des Europäischen Gerichtshofes für Menschenrechte. Zeitschrift für ausländisches öffentliches Recht und Völkerrecht, XX, no. 3–4, août 1960, p. 415–449.
RHIJN (K. H. VAN), Jurisprudentie betreffende de ontvankelijkheid van individuele klachten in de Europese Conventie voor de Rechten van de Mens. Ars aequi, IX, no. 4–5, janvier-février 1960, p. 126–131.
ROBERTSON (A. H.), The European Court of Human Rights. The American Journal of Comparative Law, IX, no. 1, hiver 1960, p. 1–28.
SCHINDLER (DIETRICH), Die Europäische Kommission und der Europäische Gerichtshof für Menschenrecht. Schweizerische Juristen-Zeitung – Revue suisse de jurisprudence, LVI, no. 9, mai 1960, p. 133–135.
ÜBERSICHT über die Ratifikationen, Erklärungen und Vorbehalte zur Konvention zum Schutze der Menschenrechte und Grundfreiheiten vom 4. November 1950. Zeitschrift für ausländisches öffentliches Recht und Völkerrecht, XX, no. 3–4, août 1960, p. 633–635.
VERDROSS (ALFRED), Einige Hauptbestimmungen der Geschäftsordnung des Europäischen Gerichtshofes für Menschenrechte. Österreichische Zeitschrift für öffentliches Recht, X, no. 3–4, 1960, p. 475–479.
WEIL (GORDON), Decisions on inadmissible application by the European Commission of Human Rights. The American Journal of International Law, LIV, no. 4, octobre 1960, p. 874–881.
WOLF (JULES), L'affaire LAWLESS devant la Cour européenne des Droits de l'Homme. Journal des tribunaux, LXXV, no. 4299, 11 décembre 1960, p. 735–737.
ZAAK (De eerste) voor het Europese Hof voor de Rechten van de Mens. Nederlands Juristenblad, no. 21, 21 mai 1960, p. 448–450.

F. QUESTIONS DE POLITIQUE ET DE DÉFENSE

F. POLITICAL AND DEFENCE QUESTIONS

ASSEMBLEA (L') europea: un'intervista di Fernand DEHOUSSE: Relazioni internazionali, no. 1, 2 janvier 1960, p. 19–20.
ASSEMBLÉE (L') de l'Union de l'Europe Occidentale seul organe parlementaire européen habilité à s'enquérir de la capacité défensive de l'Europe. Bilans politiques, économiques et sociaux hebdomadaires, no. 731, 2 juin 1960, p. F1–F3.
BERGH (G. VAN DEN), Rechtstreekse verkiezingen voor het Europese parlement. Nederlands Juristenblad, no. 11, 12 mars 1960, p. 217–223.

CONVENZIONE per l'Assemblea parlamentare europea. Rivista di studi politici internazionali, XXVII, no. 3, juillet-septembre 1960, p. 471–476.

DE l'Europe des Communautés à l'Europe politique. Revue de l'Action populaire, no. 143, décembre 1960, p. 1217–1231.

DEHOUSSE (F.), Des élections européennes en 1962? Communes d'Europe, no. 5, mars 1960, p. 10–11.

DELMAS (C.), L'Europe et l'Atlantique. Revue de défense nationale, janvier 1960, p. 50–66.

E.F.B.-KONGRESS vom 29.–31. Januar 1960 in Strassburg; Allgemeine politische Resolution. Der Föderalist, no. 39, mars 1960, p. 3–17.

GAMBLE (Europe's nuclear). Attempts to avoid a chaos of nuclear weapons in Europe bring alive the unsolved problems of Europe's political life. The Economist, CXCIV, no. 6079, 27 février 1956. p. 786–788.

HAAS (ERNST B.) & PETER H. MERKL, Parliamentarians against ministers: the case of Western European Union. International Organization, XIV, no. 1, hiver 1960, p. 37–59.

HEYDTE (F. A. VON DER), Atlantische und europäische Gemeinschafft: Beziehungen, Spannungen, Aufgaben. Politische Studien, XI, no. 117, janvier 1960, p. 5–16.

KAPFERER (C.), 1960: Integration Europas und Koexistenz. Wirtschaftsdienst, no. 1, janvier 1960, p. 3–4. Ed. angl.: p. 3–4.

LASSALLE (C.), A propos de l'élection des membres de l'Assemblée parlementaire européenne au suffrage universel direct. Le Droit européen, no. 21 juin-juillet 1960, p. 227–233.

MASON (HENRY L.), The Assembly of the Western European Union and European defense. Internationale Spectator, XIV, no. 19, 8 novembre 1960, p. 450–476.

MATTERN (K. H.), Rechtsgrundlagen und Praxis des Europäischen Parlaments. Europa-Archiv. no. 13–14, 5–20 juillet 1960, p. 449–458.

MEYER (JAN DE), Les élections directes européennes et la question du régime électoral uniforme. Sciences humaines et intégration européenne. Collège d'Europe, 1960, p. 302–309.

MEYERS (F.), L'évolution de l'administration depuis la guerre dans les pays de l'Union de l'Europe Occidentale (U.E.O.). Revue internationale des sciences administratives, XXVI, no. 2, 1960, p. 122–134.

MULLEY (FREDERICK W.), Eine europäische strategische Abschreckungsmacht. Die Verteidigung Westeuropas unter den Bedingungen des atomaren Gleichgewichts. Europa-Archiv, XV, no. 6, 20 mars 1960, p. 193–202.

PARTIS (Les) socialistes de la Communauté économique européenne approuvent le principe des élections européennes (4e Conférence des partis socialistes des pays de la C.E.E. – Strasbourg, 7–8. 5.60). Courrier socialiste européen, no. 7, mai 1960.

PETOT (JEAN), Des Communautés européennes à la fédération. Revue générale de droit international public, LXIV, no. 2, avril-juin 1960, p. 335–367.

RÉSOLUTIONS du VIIIième congrès du Mouvement fédéraliste européen. Europa, Organe de l'Union européenne des fédéralistes, XXVII, no. 2, février 1960, p. 3.

SNOY ET D'OPPUERS (J.), Towards a European solution. Lloyds Bank Review, no. 57, juillet 1960, p. 1–17.

Liste récapitulative des articles[1] *parus dans les volumes I–VIII (incl.)*

COMMISSION CENTRALE POUR LA NAVIGATION DU RHIN

(Volume II)

UNION DOUANIÈRE BENELUX

(Volume II)

UNION ÉCONOMIQUE BENELUX

(Volume VIII)

ORGANISATION DU TRAITÉ DE BRUXELLES ET UNION EUROPÉENNE OCCIDENTALE

(Volume II)

UNION DE L'EUROPE OCCIDENTALE

(Volume IV)

(Volume V)

[1] Les organisations sont arrangées selon les dates de leur création; une organisation ayant changé de nom (en romain), les noms nouveaux sont imprimés in italique.

Recapitulatory List of Articles[1] *published in vols I–VIII (incl.)*

CENTRAL COMMISSION FOR THE NAVIGATION OF THE RHINE

BENELUX CUSTOMS UNION

BENELUX ECONOMIC UNION

BRUSSELS TREATY ORGANISATION AND WESTERN EUROPEAN UNION

WESTERN EUROPEAN UNION

[1] Organisations are listed in chronological order according to their establishment; where an organisation has changed its original name (in roman), its subsequent names are given in italics.

(Union de l'Europe occidentale, *suite*)

ORGANISATION EUROPÉENNE DE COOPÉRATION ÉCONOMIQUE

ORGANISATION FOR EUROPEAN ECONOMIC CO-OPERATION

COUNCIL OF EUROPE

(Volume I)

(Volume II)

(Volume III)

(Volume IV)

(Volume V)

(Volume VI)

(Volume VII)

COMMUNAUTÉS EUROPÉENNES

—— A. COMMUNAUTÉ EUROPÉENNE DU CHARBON ET DE L'ACIER

—— B. COMMUNAUTÉ ÉCONOMIQUE EUROPÉENNE

(Volume VII)

(Volume VIII)

—— C. COMMUNAUTÉ EUROPÉENNE DE L'ÉNERGIE ATOMIQUE (EURATOM)

(Volume IV)

CONSEIL NORDIQUE

(Volume II)

CONFÉRENCE EUROPÉENNE DES MINISTRES DES TRANSPORTS

(Volume III)

PACTE BALKANIQUE

(Volume II)

—— B. EUROPEAN ECONOMIC COMMUNITY

—— C. EUROPEAN ATOMIC ENERGY COMMUNITY (EURATOM)

NORDIC COUNCIL

EUROPEAN CONFERENCE OF MINISTERS OF TRANSPORT

BALKAN PACT

CONFÉRENCE EUROPÉENNE DES POSTES ET TÉLÉCOMMUNICATIONS

(Volume III)

CONFÉRENCE DES ADMINISTRATIONS EUROPÉENNES DES POSTES ET DES TÉLÉCOMMUNICATIONS

(Volume VII)

ASSOCIATION EUROPÉENNE DE LIBRE-ÉCHANGE

(Volume VIII)

GÉNÉRALITÉS

(Volume I)

EUROPEAN CONFERENCE OF POSTS AND TELECOMMUNICATIONS

EUROPEAN CONFERENCE OF POSTAL AND TELECOMMUNICATIONS ADMINISTRATIONS

EUROPEAN FREE TRADE ASSOCIATION

MISCELLANEOUS

(Généralités, *suite*)

(Volume V)

(Volume VI)

(Généralités, *suite*)

Liste récapitulative des documents officiels, conventions, accords, etc. parus dans les volumes I–VIII (incl.)

COMMISSION CENTRALE POUR LA NAVIGATION DU RHIN

(Volume II)

(Volume III)

(Volume IV)

(Volume VIII)

UNION DOUANIÈRE BENELUX

(Volume II)

Recapitulatory List of Official Documents Conventions, Agreements, etc. published in vols I–VIII (incl.)

CENTRAL COMMISSION FOR THE NAVIGATION OF THE RHINE

(Volume VIII)

BENELUX CUSTOMS UNION

(Volume II)

(Benelux Customs Union, *cont'd*)

BENELUX ECONOMIC UNION

BRUSSELS TREATY ORGANISATION

BRUSSELS TREATY ORGANISATION AND WESTERN EUROPEAN UNION

(Organisation du Traité de Bruxelles et Union européenne occidentale, *suite*)

UNION DE L'EUROPE OCCIDENTALE

(Volume III)

(Volume IV)

(Volume V)

WESTERN EUROPEAN UNION

(Volume III)

(Volume IV)

(Volume V)

(Union de l'Europe occidentale, *suite*)

ORGANISATION EUROPÉENNE DE COOPÉRATION ÉCONOMIQUE

(Western European Union, *cont'd*)

(Volume VI)

(Volume VII)

ORGANISATION FOR EUROPEAN ECONOMIC CO-OPERATION

(Volume I)

(Volume II)

(Volume III)

(Volume V)

(Organisation européenne de coopération économique, *suite*)

(Volume VI)

(Volume VII)

(Volume VIII)

CONSEIL DE L'EUROPE

(Volume I)

(Organisation for European Economic Co-operation, *cont'd*)

COUNCIL OF EUROPE

(Volume I)

(Conseil de l'Europe, *suite*)

(Council of Europe, *cont'd*)

(Volume II)

(Volume III)

(Volume IV)

(Volume V)

(Volume VI)

(Volume VII)

(Conseil de l'Europe, *suite*)

(Council of Europe, *cont'd*)

(Volume VIII)

COMMISSION INTERNATIONALE DE L'ÉTAT CIVIL

CONSEIL DE COOPÉRATION DOUANIÈRE

INTERNATIONAL COMMISSION ON CIVIL STATUS

CUSTOMS CO-OPERATION COUNCIL

ORGANISATION EUROPÉENNE ET MÉDITERRANÉENNE POUR LA PROTECTION DES PLANTES

(Volume II)

COMMUNAUTÉS EUROPÉENNES

(Volume V)

(Volume VII)

(Volume VIII)

—— A. COMMUNAUTÉ EUROPÉENNE DU CHARBON ET DE L'ACIER

(Volume I)

(Volume II)

(Volume III)

EUROPEAN AND MEDITERRANEAN PLANT PROTECTION ORGANISATION

(Volume II)

EUROPEAN COMMUNITIES

(Volume V)

(Volume VIII)

—— A. EUROPEAN COAL AND STEEL COMMUNITY

(Volume I)

(Volume II)

(Volume III)

(Communauté européenne du charbon et de l'acier, *suite*)

—— B. EUROPEAN ECONOMIC COMMUNITY

(Volume IV)

(Volume V)

—— C. COMMUNAUTÉ EUROPÉENNE DE L'ÉNERGIE ATOMIQUE (EURATOM)

C. EUROPEAN ATOMIC ENERGY COMMUNITY (EURATOM)

(Conférence européenne des Ministres des transports, *suite*)

ORGANISATION EUROPÉENNE POUR LA RECHERCE NUCLÉAIRE (C.E.R.N.)

(Organisation européenne pour la recherche nucléaire (C.E.R.N.), *suite*)

CONFÉRENCE EUROPÉENNE SUR L'ORGANISATION DES MARCHÉS AGRICOLES

CONFÉRENCE DE COORDINATION DES TRANSPORTS AÉRIENS EUROPÉENS

COMMISSION EUROPÉENNE DE L'AVIATION CIVILE

(European Organization for Nuclear Research (C.E.R.N.), *cont'd*)

EUROPEAN CONFERENCE ON THE ORGANISATION OF AGRICULTURAL MARKETS

CONFERENCE ON THE COORDINATION OF AIR TRANSPORT IN EUROPE

EUROPEAN CIVIL AVIATION CONFERENCE

(Commission européenne de l'aviation civile, *suite*)

(Volume VII)

PACTE BALKANIQUE

(Volume II)

CONFÉRENCE EUROPÉENNE DES POSTES ET TÉLÉCOMMUNICATIONS

(Volume VI)

CONFÉRENCE DES ADMINISTRATIONS EUROPÉENNES DES POSTES ET DES TÉLÉCOMMUNICATIONS

(Volume VII)

(European Civil Aviation Conference, *cont'd*)

(Volume VII)

BALKAN PACT

(Volume II)

EUROPEAN CONFERENCE OF POSTS AND TELECOMMUNICATIONS

(Volume VI)

EUROPEAN CONFERENCE OF POSTAL AND TELECOMMUNICATIONS ADMINISTRATIONS

(Volume VII)

CONFERENCE EUROPÉENNE DES ADMINISTRATIONS DES POSTES ET DES TÉLÉCOMMUNICATIONS

(Volume VIII)

ASSOCIATION EUROPÉENNE DE LIBRE-ÉCHANGE

(Volume VII)

(Volume VIII)

(Volume VIII)

EUROPEAN FREE TRADE ASSOCIATION

(Volume VII)

(Volume VIII)

TABLE DES NOMS[1] / LIST OF NAMES[1]

[1] Les noms d'auteurs sont marqués d'un astérisque * / Names of authors are indicated by an asterisk *.

INDEX ALPHABÉTIQUE

GENERAL INDEX

www.ingramcontent.com/pod-product-compliance
Ingram Content Group UK Ltd.
Pitfield, Milton Keynes, MK11 3LW, UK
UKHW020652210926
15297UKWH00010B/155
* 9 7 8 9 4 0 1 5 2 8 8 7 0 *